AMERICAN HISTORIC **I N N S**
INCORPORATED

Certificate

redeemable for

One Free Night
at a Bed & Breakfast
or Country Inn

Advance reservations required.
See "How to Make a Reservation."

Compliments of
American Historic Inns, Inc. and
participating Bed & Breakfasts
and Country Inns.

This certificate entitles the bearer to one free night
at nearly 1,500 Bed & Breakfasts
and Country Inns when the
bearer buys the first night at the regular rate.
See back for requirements.

W9-CJD-127

VOID IF DETACHED FROM BOOK OR ALTERED

AMERICAN HISTORIC INNS
INCORPORATED

Free night is provided by participating inn.

Please fax redeemed certificate to (949) 481-3796 or mail to:

American Historic Inns, Inc.

PO Box 669, Dana Point, CA 92629-0669

Inns with most redeemed certificates will be featured on iLoveinns.com as one of "America's Favorite Inns."

_____

Name of Guest

_____

Guest Home Address

_____

Guest City/State/Zip

_____

Guest Home Phone

_____

Guest Email Address

_____

Name of Bed & Breakfast/Inn

_____

Signature of Innkeeper

Certificate is good for one (1) free consecutive night when you purchase the first night at the regular rate. Offer not valid at all times. Contact inn in advance for availability, rates, reservations, meal plans, cancellation policies and other requirements. If book is purchased at the inn, certificate is valid only for a future visit. Offer valid only at participating inns featured in this Bed & Breakfast Guide or online at iLovelnns.com with the FN-Free Night icon. Not valid during holidays. Minimum 2-night stay. Certificate is for no more than two people and no more than one room. Other restrictions may apply. Bed tax, sales tax and gratuities not included. American Historic Inns, Inc. is not responsible for any changes in individual inn operation or policy. By use of this certificate, consumer agrees to release American Historic Inns, Inc. from any liability in connection with their travel to and stay at any participating Inn. This certificate may not be reproduced and cannot be used in conjunction with any other promotional offers. Certificate must be redeemed at participating inn by December 31, 2012. Void where prohibited.

Certificate Expires December 31, 2012

IF BOOK IS PURCHASED AT THE INN, CERTIFICATE IS VALID ONLY FOR FUTURE VISIT

Media Comments

"…lighthouses, schoolhouses, stage coach stops, llama ranches … There's lots to choose from and it should keep B&B fans happy for years." – Cathy Stapells, Toronto Sun

"Anytime you can get superb accommodations AND a free night, well that's got to be great, and it is … I've used this book before, and I must tell you, it's super … The news, information and facts in this book are all fascinating." – On the Road With John Clayton, KKGO, Los Angeles radio

"…helps you find the very best hideaways (many of the book's listings appear in the National Register of Historic Places.)" – Country Living

"I love your book!" – Lydia Moss, Travel Editor, McCall's

"Delightful, succinct, detailed and well-organized. Easy to follow style…"
– Don Wudke, Los Angeles Times

"Deborah Sakach's Bed & Breakfasts and Country Inns *continues to be the premier Bed & Breakfast guide for travelers and tourists throughout the United States."* – Midwest Book Review

"One of the better promotions we've seen." – Baton Rouge Advocate

"…thoughtfully organized and look-ups are hassle-free…well-researched and accurate…put together by people who know the field. There is no other publication available that covers this particular segment of the bed & breakfast industry – a segment that has been gaining popularity among travelers by leaps and bounds. The information included is valuable and well thought out." – Morgan Directory Reviews

"Readers will find this book easy to use and handy to have. An excellent, well-organized and comprehensive reference for inngoers and innkeepers alike."
– Inn Review, Kankakee, Ill.

"This guide has become the favorite choice of travelers and specializes only in professionally operated inns and B&Bs rather than homestays (lodging in spare bedrooms)." – Laguna Magazine

"This is the best bed and breakfast book out. It outshines them all!"
– Maggie Balitas, Rodale Book Clubs

As I began to look through the book, my heart beat faster as I envisioned what a good time our readers could have visiting some of these very special historic bed and breakfast properties." – Ann Crawford, Military Living

"This is a great book. It makes you want to card everything." – KBRT Los Angeles radio talk show

"All our lines were tied up! We received calls from every one of our 40 stations (while discussing your book.)" – Business Radio Network

"For a delightful change of scenery, visit one of these historical inns. (Excerpts from Bed & Breakfasts and Country Inns *follow.) A certificate for one free consecutive night (minimum two nights stay) can be found in the book."* – Shirley Howard, Good Housekeeping

"iLoveInns.com boasts independently written reviews, elegant design, and direct links to inns' URLs." – Yahoo! Internet Magazine referring to iLoveInns.com, winner of their 2002 Best B&B Site.

Recognition for InnTouch, the iLoveInns.com iPhone app

2009 Sunset Magazine, Featured iPhone travel app; 2009 Travel & Leisure, "Best iPhone Apps for Travelers"; 2009 Apple "Staff Favorite" for InnTouch

Comments From Innkeepers

"The guests we receive from the Buy-One-Night-Get-One-Night-Free program are some of the most wonderful people. Most are first time inngoers and after their first taste of the inn experience they vow that this is the only way to travel." – Innkeeper, Mass.

"Guests that were staying here last night swear by your guide. They use it all the time. Please send us information about being in your guide." – Innkeeper, Port Angeles, Wash.

"The people are so nice! Please keep up the great program!"
– K. C, The Avon Manor B&B Inn, Avon-By-the-Sea, N.J.

"I have redeemed several certificates which have led to new loyal customers who, in turn, referred our inn to new guests!" - Manchester Inn Bed & Breakfast, Ocean Grove, N.J.

"We get many good leads from you throughout the year. Anything that we can do to support, we'll be glad to. Thanks for a great publication."
– A Grand Inn-Sunset Hill House, Sugar Hill, N.H.

"We want to tell you how much we love your book. We have it out for guests to use. They love it! Each featured inn stands out so well. Thank you for the privilege of being in your book."
– Fairhaven Inn, Bath, Maine

"We've had guests return two or three times after discovering us through your book. They have turned into wonderful guests and friends." – Port Townsend, Wash.

"I wanted to let you know that I have been getting quite a few bookings from your guide with the certificates."
– Quill Haven Country Inn, Somerset, Pa.

"The response to your book has been terrific and the guests equally terrific! Many are already returning. Thanks for all your hard work." – Rockport, Mass.

"We love your book and we also use it. Just went to New Orleans and had a great trip."
– Gettysburg, Pa.

"Outstanding! We were offering a variety of inn guide books, but yours was the only one guests bought."
– White Oak Inn, Danville, Ohio

"This has been one of the best B&B programs we have done and the guests have been delightful. Thanks!" – Eastern Shore, Md.

"We are grateful that so many of our old friends and new guests have found us through your book. We always recommend your publications to guests who wish to explore other fine country inns of New England."
– Innkeeper, Vt.

"Of all the associations I am a member of you are the most out front and progressive of them all. I guess this is why I have been a member since 1995ish.....this is my 21st year! Bravo to you!!!!" The Lockhart Bed and Breakfast Inn

"Wow! I say it again. You guys are great! BY FAR the most effective and helpful of all the organizations. THANKS!!!!" Nancy Henderson, Sunset Hill House

"You do more for your member inns than any others by far. Your creative programs to promote the inns are awesome!" Ruth McLaughlin, Blair Hill Inn at Moosehead Lake

Comments About
Bed & Breakfasts and Country Inns

"I purchased 8 of these books in January and have already used them up. I am ordering 8 more. I've had great experiences. This year I've been to California, Philadelphia and San Antonio and by ordering so many books enjoyed getting free night at each place. The inns were fabulous." – D. Valentine, Houston, Texas

"Our office went crazy over this book. The quality of the inns and the quality of the book is phenomenal! Send us 52 books." – M.B., Westport, Conn.

"Every time we look at this book we remember our honeymoon! Every time we make another reservation with the free night certificate we relive our honeymoon! We were married in May and visited three fabulous inns that week, in Cape May, Philadelphia and one near Longwood Gardens. They all served phenomenal food and were beautifully decorated. We went back in the summer we loved it so much. It's like our honeymoon again everytime we use this book. You get such a real feel of America's little towns this way." – S. Piniak, N.J.

"The 300 women who attended my 'Better Cents' seminar went wild for the free-night book. I brought my copy and showed them the value of the free-night program. They all wanted to get involved. Thank you so much for offering such a great value."
– R.R., Making Cents Seminars, Texas

"Thank you for offering this special! It allowed us to get away even on a tight budget."
– D.L., Pittsburgh, Pa.

"I'm ordering three new books. We've never stayed in one we didn't like that was in your book!"
– M.R., Canton, Ohio

"This made our vacation a lot more reasonable. We got the best room in a beautiful top-drawer inn for half the price." – L.A., Irvine, Calif.

"I used your book and free night offer and took my 17-year-old daughter. It was our first B&B visit ever and we loved it. (We acted like friends instead of parent vs. teenager for the first time in a long time.) It was wonderful!" – B.F., Clinton, N.J.

"Thanks! Do we love your B&B offer! You betcha! The luxury of getting a two-day vacation for the cost of one is Christmas in July for sure. Keep up the good work."
– R.R., Grapevine, Texas.

"What a great idea for gifts. I'm ordering five to use as birthday, housewarming and thank-you gifts." – J.R., Laguna Niguel, Calif.

"The best thing since ice cream – and I love ice cream!" – M.C., Cape May, N.J.

"I keep giving your books away as gifts and then don't have any for myself. Please send me three more copies." – D.T., Ridgewood, N.J.

"Out of 25 products we presented to our fund raising committee your book was No. 1 and it generated the most excitement." – H.U., Detroit, Mich.

ෑඥෑඥෑඥෑඥෑඥෑඥෑඥ

To my friends Alice Jensen and Linda White, who are always ready and willing to take the Roads Best Traveled with me to America's beautiful and historic little inns around the country.

ෑඥෑඥෑඥෑඥඥෑඥෑඥ

American Historic Inns™

Bed & Breakfasts

a n d C o u n t r y I n n s

by Deborah Edwards Sakach

Published by

AMERICAN
HISTORIC
INNS
INCORPORATED

PO Box 669
Dana Point
California
92629-0669
www.iLoveInns.com

Bed & Breakfasts and Country Inns

AUTHOR:
Deborah Sakach

COVER DESIGN:
David Sakach

COVER PHOTO EDITING:
David Sakach

PRODUCTION MANAGER:
Jamee Danihels

BOOK LAYOUT:
Jamee Danihels

SENIOR EDITOR
Shirley Swagerty

ASSISTANT EDITORS:
Jamee Danihels

DATABASE ASSISTANTS:
Jamee Danihels

CARTOGRAPHY:
Maurice Phillips

PROOFREADING:
Jamee Danihels

For the up-to-the-minute information on participating properties, please visit iLoveInns.com or the iPhone free application "InnTouch"
Participating inns are designated by the "FN" - Free Night icon.

Publisher's Cataloging in Publication Data
Sakach, Deborah Edwards
American Historic Inns, Inc.
Bed & Breakfasts and Country Inns

1. Bed & Breakfast Accommodations - United States, Directories, Guide Books.
2. Travel - Bed & Breakfast Inns, Directories, Guide Books.
3. Bed & Breakfast Accommodations - Historic Inns, Directories, Guide Books.
4. Hotel Accommodations - Bed & Breakfast Inns, Directories, Guide Books.
5. Hotel Accommodations - United States, Directories, Guide Books.
I. Title. II Author. III Bed & Breakfast, Bed & Breakfasts and Country Inns.

American Historic Inns is a trademark of American Historic Inns, Inc.
ISBN: **9781888050080**
Softcover
Printed in the United States of America.
10 9 8 7 6 5 4 3 2 1

Table Of Contents

How To Make A Reservation

1 Call

The FREE Night offer **requires advance reservations** and is subject to availability.*

To use the Free Night Certificate call the inn of your choice in advance of your stay and identify yourself as holding a Certificate from American Historic Inns, Inc. and iLoveinns.com.

2 Confirm

Verify availabilty, rates and the inn's acceptance of the Free Night Certificate for your requested dates. Make a written note of the name of the reservationist and confirmation code.

This offer is subject to availability. All holidays are excluded as well as certain local event dates. A consecutive two-night minimum is required.

Ask about cancellation policies as some inns may require at least a two-week notice in order to refund your deposit. (Also, please note some locales require bed tax be collected, even on free nights.) Find out what meals are included in the rates. A few properties particiapting in this program do not offer a free breakfast.

3 Check-in

Don't forget to take this book with the Free Night Certificate with you.

The FREE Night is given to you as a gift directly from the innkeeper in the hope that you or your friends will return and share your discovery with others. The inns are not reimbursed by American Historic Inns, Inc.

IMPORTANT NOTE

*"Subject to availability" and "anytime based on availability": each innkeeper interprets availability for their own property. Just as airlines may set aside a number of seats for discounted fares, so small inns in our program may use different formulas to manage the number of rooms and the times available for the Buy-One-Night-Get-One-Night-Free program. You must call the innkeeper to see if any of their vacant rooms are available for the free night. While innkeepers have proven to be extremely generous with the program, each reservation must be made by first stating that you wish to use the Free Night Certificate toward your two-night stay. When innkeepers foresee a full house during peak times, they might not be able to accept this certificate. Our innkeepers welcome your reservation and are looking forward to your visit.

How To Use This Book

You hold in your hands a delightful selection of America's best bed & breakfasts and country inns. The innkeeper of each property has generously agreed to participate in our FREE night program.

Most knowledgeable innkeepers enjoy sharing regional attractions, local folklore, history, and pointing out favorite restaurants and other special features of their areas. They are a tremendous resource, treat them kindly and you will be well rewarded.

Accommodations

You'll find bed & breakfasts and country inns in converted schoolhouses, churches, lighthouses, 18th-century farmhouses, Queen Anne Victorians, adobe lodges, plantations and more.

Many are listed in the National Register of Historic Places and have preserved the stories and memorabilia from their participation in historical events such as the Revolutionary or Civil Wars.

The majority of inns included in this book were built in the 18th, 19th and early 20th centuries. We have stated the date each building was constructed at the beginning of each description.

A Variety of Inns

A **Country Inn** generally serves both breakfast and dinner and may have a restaurant associated with it. Many have been in operation for years; some, since the 18th century as you will note in our "Inns of Interest" section. Although primarily found on the East Coast, a few country inns are in other regions of the nation. Always check as to what meals are provided.

A **Bed & Breakfast** facility's primary focus is lodging. It can have from three to 20 rooms or more. The innkeepers usually live on the premises. Breakfast is the only meal served and can be a full-course, gourmet breakfast or a simple buffet. Many B&B owners pride themselves on their culinary skills.

As with country inns, many B&Bs specialize in providing historic, romantic or gracious atmospheres with amenities such as canopied beds, fireplaces, hot tubs, whirlpools, afternoon tea in the library and scenic views.

Some give great attention to recapturing a specific historic period, such as the Victorian or Colonial eras. Many display antiques and other furnishings from family collections.

Area Codes

Although we have made every effort to update area codes throughout the book, new ones pop up from time to time. For up-to-the-minute phone numbers, please check our Web site at iLoveInns.com.

Baths

Most bed & breakfasts and country inns provide a private bath for each guest room. We have included the number of rooms and the number of private baths in each facility.

Beds

K, **Q**, **D**, **T**, indicates King, Queen, Double or Twin beds available at the inn.

Meals

Continental breakfast: Coffee, juice, toast or pastry.

Continental-plus breakfast: A continental breakfast plus a variety of breads, cheeses and fruit.

Country breakfast: Includes all the traditional fixings of home-cooked country fare.

Full breakfast: Coffee, juice, breads, fruit and an entree.

Full gourmet breakfast: May be an elegant four-course candlelight offering or especially creative cuisine.

Teas: Usually served in the late afternoon with cookies, crackers or other in-between-meal offerings.

Vegetarian breakfast: Vegetarian fare.

Meal Plans

AP: American Plan. All three meals may be included in the price of the room. Check to see if the rate quoted is for two people or per person.

MAP: Modified American Plan. Breakfast and dinner may be included in the price of the room.

EP: European Plan. No meals are included. We have listed only a few historic hotels that operate on an European Plan.

Always find out what meals, if any, are included in the rates. Not every establishment participating in this program provides breakfast, although most do. Inns offering the second night free may or may not include a complimentary lunch or dinner with the second night. Occasionally an innkeeper has indicated MAP and AP when she or he actually means that both programs are available and you must specify which program you are interested in.

Please do not assume meals are included in the rates featured in the book.

Rates

Rates are usually listed in ranges, i.e., $65-175. The LOWEST rate is almost always available during off-peak periods and may apply only to the least expensive room. Rates are subject to change and are not guaranteed. Always confirm the rates when making reservations. Rates for Canadian listings usually are listed in Canadian dollars. Rates are quoted for double occupancy for two people. Rates for this program are calculated from regular rates and not from seasonal promotional offers.

Breakfast and other meals MAY or MAY NOT be included in the rates and may not be included in the discount.

Smoking

The majority of country inns and B&Bs in historic buildings prohibit smoking; therefore, if you are a smoker we advise you to call and specifically check with each nn to see if and how they accommodate smokers.

Rooms

Under some listings, you will note that suites are available. We typically assume that suites include a private bath and a separate living room. If the inn contains suites that have more than one bedroom, it will indicate as such.

Additionally, under some listings, you will note a reference to cottages. A cottage may be a rustic cabin tucked in the woods, a seaside cottage or a private apartment-style accommodation.

Fireplaces

When fireplaces are mentioned in the listing they may be in guest rooms or in common areas. The fireplace could be either a gas or wood-burning fireplace. If it mentions that the inn contains a fireplace in room, please keep in mind that not every room may have a fireplace. A few inns have fireplaces that are non-working because of city lodging requirements. Please verify this if you are looking forward to an intimate, fireside chat in your room.

State maps

The state maps have been designed to help travelers find an inn's location quickly and easily. Each city shown on the maps contains one or more inns.

As you browse through the guide, you will notice coordinates next to each city name, i.e. C3. The coordinates designate the location of inns on the state map.

Media coverage

Some inns have provided us with copies of magazine or newspaper articles written by travel writers about their establishments, and we have indicated that in the listing. Articles written about the inns may be available either from the source as a reprint, through libraries or from the inn itself. Some inns have also been featured by local radio and TV stations.

Comments from guests

Over the years, we have collected reams of guest comments about thousands of inns. Our files are filled with these documented comments. At the end of some descriptions, we have included a guest comment received about that inn.

Guest reviews are now a popular feature on iLoveInns.com. You can easily "write a review" by looking up any inn you have visited and click on "write a review". Up to 85% of travelers are said to consider other guests experiences before making their lodging choices. Innkeepers appreciate the ways their guests express the unique aspects of their bed and breakfast stays. Guest comments give them a spring in their step. Please read reviews on iLoveInns.com by going to the city of your choice and click on the "read reviews." You can also write a review on the iPhone application, "InnTouch" created by the iLoveInns.com staff.

Minimum stays

Many inns require a two-night minimum stay on weekends. A three-night stay often is required during holiday periods.

Cancellations

Cancellation policies are individual for each bed & breakfast. It is not unusual to see 7 to 14 day cancellation periods or more. Please verify the inn's policy when making your reservation.

What if the inn is full?

Ask the innkeeper for recommendations. They may know of an inn that has opened recently or one nearby.

Call the local Chamber of Commerce in the town you hope to visit as an additional resource. Please let us know of any new discoveries you make.

We want to hear from you!

If you wish to participate in evaluating your inn experiences, use the **Inn Evaluation Form** in the back of this book. You might want to make copies of this form prior to departing on your journey. You can also email us at comments@iloveinns.com with your questions and comments.

We hope you will enjoy this book so much that you will want to keep an extra copy or two on hand to offer to friends. Many readers have called to purchase our "Buy-One-Night-Get-One-Night-Free" certificate book for hostess gifts, birthday presents, or for seasonal celebrations. It's a great way to introduce your friends to America's enchanting country inns and bed & breakfasts.

Visit us online at iLoveInns.com!

Would you like more information about the inns listed in this book? For color photos, links to the inns' Web sites and more, search our Web site at **iLoveInns.com**. You'll find reviews of inns throughout the United States and Canada and you can also post your own review. We think you'll agree with Yahoo! Internet Magazine who named iLoveInns.com "Best B&B Site."

Have Fun with iloveInns iPhone B&B Application

Add some excitement to any road trip you take this year by downloading the free "InnTouch" bed and breakfast application to your iPhone. (If you have another smart phone, please note that iLoveInns.com is mobile compatible.) The "innTouch" application is available free at the iPhone App Store. When traveling use the "Nearby" feature and it will pull your GPS coordinates and you'll see all the nearby inns within 60 miles of your location. You will be surprised at the inns you discover and may want to make a spontaneous visit. That's what *Travel & Leisure* noted when they chose their list of "best travel applications on the iPhone" and included InnTouch.

Because the phone is an all-in-one device, you can call the inn for reservations with one touch, not dialing each digit of the phone number. You can see the inn's address on a map, get directions, save the address in your contact list, as well as e-mail or visit the inn's Web site with single-click actions. You can read descriptions, see photos, videos and guest reviews. There are more than 6,000 inns on the iPhone application, including the 1500 that honor the Buy-

One-Night-Get-the-Second Night Free certificate.

Make an online review at iLoveInns.com and be entered into contest for daily prizes

You may never have considered writing an online review but it's really very easy. Simply log on to iLoveInns.com and look up the inn you visited though the easy city or name search. Then click on the "Review this Inn" link and enter your thoughts.

Innkeepers want you to enjoy your stay and return home refreshed and relaxed. While you are there they want to know if there is anything they can do to meet your expectations for a wonderful getaway so be sure to let them know during your stay. If you think of something afterwards, send an email or a short note.

If you remember inns from past stays that were pleasant and for which you still hold a fond memory, be sure to make a comment about them on iLoveInns.com. We have always counted on our readers to tell us about their experiences. Our more than two and a half million Bed and Breakfast books have included review forms for this purpose. You can find this form at the back of the book . We also highly encourage you to make online reviews. Watch for our frequent rewards (such as a GPS, free books, gift certificates, etc.) to guests who complete the online review at iLoveInns.com.

How to Read an Inn Listing

Anytown ① **G6**

An American Historic Inn

② 123 S Main St
Anytown, MA 98765-4321
(123)555-1212 (800)555-1212 Fax:(123)555-1234
Internet: www.iLoveInns.com
E-mail: comments@iLoveInns.com

③ **Circa 1897.** Every inch of this breathtaking inn offers something special. The interior is decorated to the hilt with lovely furnishings, plants, beautiful rugs and warm, inviting tones. Rooms include four-poster and canopy beds combined with the modern amenities such as fireplaces, wet bars and stocked refrigerators. Enjoy a complimentary full breakfast at the inn's gourmet restaurant. The chef offers everything from a light breakfast of fresh fruit, cereal and a bagel to heartier treats such as pecan peach pancakes and Belgium waffles served with fresh fruit and crisp bacon.

④

⑤ Innkeeper(s): Michael & Marissa Chaco. $125-195. 13 rooms with PB, 4 with FP, 1 suite and 1 conference room. ⑧ Breakfast and afternoon tea included in rates. ⑨ Types of meals: Full bkfst, country bkfst, veg bkfst, early coffee/tea, picnic lunch, gourmet lunch and room service. ⑩ Beds: KQDT. ⑪ Phone, air conditioning, turndown service, ceiling fan, TV and VCR in room. Fax, copier and bicycles on premises. Handicap access. Antiques, fishing, parks, shopping, theater and watersports nearby.

⑫ Location: One-half mile from Route 1A.

⑬ Publicity: *Beaufort, Southern Living, Country Inns, Carolina Style, US Air, Town & Country.*

⑭ "A dream come true!"

⑮ **Certificate may be used:** December, January and February, Sunday through Wednesday night only. Good only for four rooms which have a rate of $175.

① **Map coordinates**
Easily locate an inn on the state map using these coordinates.

② **Inn address**
Mailing or street address and all phone numbers for the inn. May also include the inn's Web site and email address.

③ **Description of inn**
Descriptions of inns are written by experienced travel writers based on visits to inns, interviews and information collected from inns.

④ **Drawing of inn**
Many listings include artistic renderings.

⑤ **Innkeepers**
The name of the innkeeper(s).

⑥ **Rates**
Rates are quoted for double occupancy. The rate range includes off-season rates and is subject to change.

⑦ **Rooms**
Number and types of rooms available.
PB=Private Bath   FP=Fireplace
HT=Hot Tub   WP=Whirlpool

⑧ **Included Meals**
Types of meals included in the rates.

⑨ **Available meals**
This section lists the types of meals that the inn offers. These meals may or may not be included in the rates.

⑩ **Beds**
King, Queen, Double, Twin

⑪ **Amenities and activities**
Information included here describes amenities or services available at the inn. If handicap access is available, it will be noted here. Nearby activities also are included.

⑫ **Location**
Type of area where inn is located.

⑬ **Publicity**
Newspapers, magazines and other publications which have featured articles about the inn.

⑭ **Guest comments**
Comments about the inn from guests.

⑮ **Certificate dates**
Indicates when inn has agreed to honor the Buy-One-Night-Get-One-Night-Free Certificate™. Always verify availability of discount with innkeeper.

Alabama

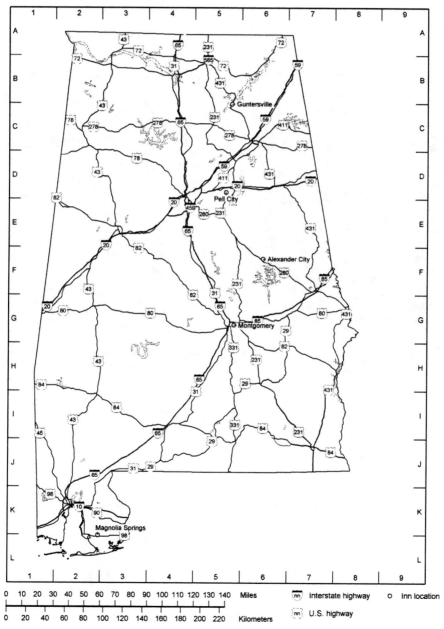

0 10 20 30 40 50 60 70 80 90 100 110 120 130 140 Miles

0 20 40 60 80 100 120 140 160 180 200 220 Kilometers

nn Interstate highway   o Inn location

nn U.S. highway

Magnolia Springs
L2

Magnolia Springs

14469 Oak St
Magnolia Springs, AL 36555
(251)965-7321 (800)965-7321
Internet: www.magnoliasprings.com
E-mail: info@magnoliasprings.com

Circa 1897. A canopy of ancient oak trees line the streets leading to the Magnolia Springs bed & breakfast. Softly framed by more oaks, and in springtime, pink azaleas, the National Register inn with its dormers and spacious wraparound porch offers an inviting welcome. Warm hospitality enfolds guests in the Great Room with its pine walls and ceilings and heart pine floors, as well as the greeting from the innkeeper. Curly pine woodwork is found throughout the home, which was originally an area hotel. Guest rooms are appointed with a variety of carefully chosen antiques. Breakfast favorites often include pecan-topped French toast, bacon, grits, fresh fruit with cream dressing and blueberry muffins. Guests may also request a special breakfast to accommodate dietary needs. The innkeepers will recommend some memorable adventures, or simply stroll to Magnolia River and enjoy the area.

Innkeeper(s): David Worthington & Eric. $139-219. 5 rooms, 4 with PB, 1 two-bedroom suite. Breakfast, afternoon tea and snacks/refreshments included in rates. Types of meals: Full gourmet bkfst and early coffee/tea. Beds: KQT. Data port, cable TV, reading lamp, ceiling fan, telephone, turn-down service, desk, hair dryer, bath amenities, wireless Internet access and iron/ironing board in room. Central air. VCR, DVD, fax, copier, gift shop and high-speed wireless Internet on premises. Amusement parks, antiquing, art galleries, beach, bicycling, canoeing/kayaking, fishing, golf, hiking, horseback riding, live theater, museums, parks, shopping, water sports, Weeks Bay National eastuary reserve and Bon Secour National refuge area nearby.

Publicity: *Southern Living, Coastal Living, Southern Breeze, Mobile Bay Monthly, Romantic Destinations, Travel America, Atlanta Journal Constitution, Memphis Commercial Appeal, Birmingham News, Pensacola News Journal, Mobile Press Register, Montgomery Advertiser., HGTV-Bob Vila's Restore America, Alabama Public Television, Fox 10 Mobile.*

Certificate may be used: September-February, Sunday-Thursday. Subject to availability. Excludes holidays and special events.

Montgomery
G5

Red Bluff Cottage B&B

551 Clay Street
Montgomery, AL 36104
(334)264-0056 (888)551-2529 Fax:(334)263-3054
Internet: www.redbluffcottage.com
E-mail: info@redbluffcottage.com

Circa 1987. "Heavenly beds! The most comfortable accommodations on our whole trip!" is one of numerous comments from guests who have discovered Red Bluff Cottage B&B. Filled with

warmth, comfort and an abundance of thoughtful touches that guarantee a delightful night's sleep, the inn overlooks the Alabama River Plain in historic Cottage Hill, near the heart of Montgomery, Alabama's downtown business district. Many favorite tourist attractions are within walking distance. Yet, what sets the spacious cottage apart is genuine Southern charm and a welcoming atmosphere. Relax in clean, comfortable and cozy

rooms or unwind in the peaceful gazebo on the lush grounds. After a peaceful night's rest, enjoy an amazing home-cooked breakfast. Two of Bonnie's recipes are featured in the Alabama Tourism Department's brochure, "100 Dishes to Eat in Alabama Before You Die." Guests are within walking distance of Biscuits Baseball at Riverwalk Stadium, Civil Rights Memorial, Davis Theatre, First White House of the Confederacy, Hank Williams Museum, Montgomery Performing Arts Center, Old Alabama Town, Riverfront Amphitheater and State Archives and Capitol.

Innkeeper(s): Barry & Bonnie Ponstein. $110-155. 4 rooms with PB, 1 with WP, 1 two-bedroom suite. Breakfast included in rates. Types of meals: Full gourmet bkfst, early coffee/tea, afternoon tea and snacks/refreshments. Beds: KQT. Clock radio, telephone, turn-down service, desk, some with hot tub/spa, hair dryer, bathrobes, bath amenities, wireless Internet access, iron/ironing board, telephones and data ports in room. Central air. TV, VCR, fax, copier, laundry facility, fresh flowers and candy throughout the house, coffee, tea, cold drinks and snacks conveniently located near guest rooms and TV/VCR located in library with lots of books and video tapes on premises. Antiquing, art galleries, canoeing/kayaking, fishing, golf, live theater, museums, parks, shopping, sporting events, tennis, Jubilee CityFest Weekend Stages, The Montgomery Conference Center, The Montgomery Zoo & Mann Wildlife Museum, The Montgomery Museum of Fine Arts, The Junior League Annual Holiday Market, The Rosa Parks Museum & Library, The Alabama Dance Theatre, The Alabama Junior Miss Pageant, Lagoon Park Softball, Maxwell AFB, Hyundai Motor Manufacturing Alabama, The Alabama Shakespeare Festival Theatre, Prattville's Robert Trent Jones Golf Trail (15 minutes), Capitol Hill, The Bass Pro Shop and The LPGA Golf tournament nearby.

Location: City. Located in downtown Montgomery, AL.

"This was our first time to a bed & breakfast and I dare say it won't be our last after this wonderful experience."

Certificate may be used: Monday-Thursday only.

Pell City
D5

Treasure Island Bed & Breakfast

Treasure Island
Pell City, AL 35054
(205)525-5172
Internet: www.treasureislandbedandbreakfast.com
E-mail: info@treasureislandbedandbreakfast.com

Treasure awaits at this contemporary inn on the shores of the Coosa River overlooking Logan Martin Lake. Play pool in the game room, watch the big screen plasma TV in the great room or work out on the Universal gym. Snacks and beverages are always available. Guest bedrooms offer thoughtful amenities that include bathrobes and hair dryers. Laundry, ironing, phone and computer access are provided upon request. Savor a hearty, Plantation Breakfast with waterfront views in the dining room. Enjoy a complimentary sunset pontoon boat river cruise in the evening.

Innkeeper(s): Earl and Lillie Hardy. $100-175. 4 rooms with PB, 1 suite. Breakfast and snacks/refreshments included in rates. Types of meals: Full bkfst. Beds: KQ. Reading lamp, ceiling fan, clock radio, turn-down service, some with hot tub/spa, some with fireplace, hair dryer, bathrobes, wireless Internet access and wireless Internet hook-up in room. Central air. TV, VCR, DVD, fax, copier, swimming, library, parlor games, telephone and laundry facility on premises. Amusement parks, antiquing, art galleries, beach, fishing, golf, hiking, live theater, museums, parks, shopping, water sports, wineries and complimentary pontoon cruise on the river (with two-night stay) nearby.

Location: Waterfront. On the shores of the Coosa River at Lake Logan Martin.

Certificate may be used: November-March, Monday, Tuesday or Wednesday. Subject to availability.

Alaska

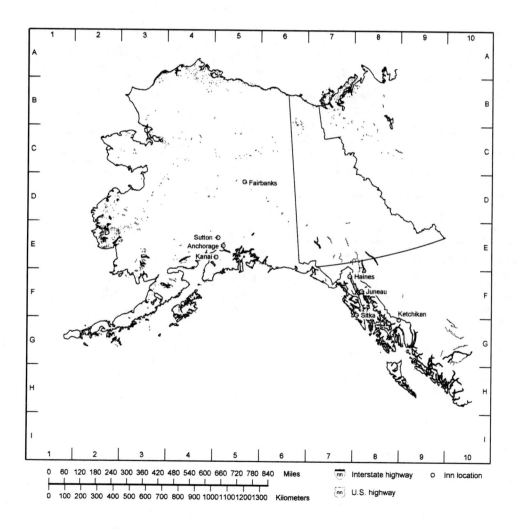

0 60 120 180 240 300 360 420 480 540 600 660 720 780 840 Miles

0 100 200 300 400 500 600 700 800 900 1000 1100 1200 1300 Kilometers

(nn) Interstate highway   O Inn location

(nn) U.S. highway

Anchorage
E5

Alaska House of Jade Bed & Breakfast

3800 Delwood Place
Anchorage, AK 99504
(907)337-3400 (866)337-3410 Fax:(907)333-2329
Internet: www.alaskahouseofjade.com
E-mail: alaskahouseofjade@ak.net

Built specifically with comfort in mind, this custom tri-level
home provides gracious hospitality. The innkeepers are fluent
in many languages and welcome world travelers. Relax in the
living room or on a spacious balcony and sitting area. Spacious
suites feature robes, jetted tubs, showers and an intercom system. Bountiful hot gourmet breakfasts and evening desserts are
always raved about. The Museum of Natural History and Fine
Arts and the Alaska Native Heritage Center are nearby. Visit the
Saturday Market for local products to bring home. Ask about
day trip activities.

Innkeeper(s): Yves & Dee Memoune. $75-189. 5 rooms, 2 with FP, 4 with
WP, 5 total suites, including 1 two-bedroom suite. Breakfast and
snacks/refreshments included in rates. Types of meals: Full gourmet bkfst.
Beds: KQDT. Cable TV, reading lamp, ceiling fan, clock radio, telephone,
desk, hair dryer, wireless Internet access, iron/ironing board, Intercom
between rooms and Jetted tubs (three suites) in room. VCR, fax, copier, bicycles, parlor games, fireplace and laundry facility on premises. Limited handicap access. Amusement parks, antiquing, art galleries, bicycling,
canoeing/kayaking, cross-country skiing, downhill skiing, fishing, golf, hiking,
horseback riding, live theater, museums, parks, shopping, sporting events,
tennis, water sports, Native cultural center, Day cruises, Whale watching,
Glacier cruises, Botanical gardens, Kenai Fjords and Fishing nearby.

Location: City, mountains. Near Cook Inlet.

Certificate may be used: September, October, April & May. 4 months or last
minute, subject to availability.

Fairbanks
D5

7 Gables Inn & Suites

4312 Birch Ln
Fairbanks, AK 99709
(907)479-0751 Fax:(907)479-2229
Internet: www.7gablesinn.com
E-mail: gables7@alaska.net

Circa 1982. There are actually 14 gables on this modern
Tudor-style inn, which is located a short walk from the
University of Alaska and the Chena River. Inside the foyer, a
seven-foot waterfall is an amazing welcome. A two-story, flower-
filled solarium and a meeting room are wonderful gathering
places. Seasonally enjoy the magnificent aurora borealis or a
white world of snowflakes and dog mushing, and then relax in
a steaming in-room Jacuzzi tub. In summertime the midnight
sun allows canoe trips down the river for a progressive dinner
from restaurant to deck to dock. The innkeepers received the
city's Golden Heart Award for exceptional hospitality.

Innkeeper(s): Paul & Leicha Welton. $50-200. 30 rooms, 25 with PB, 25
with WP, 15 suites, 4 cottages. Breakfast and snacks/refreshments included
in rates. Types of meals: Full gourmet bkfst. Beds: KQDT. Cable TV, VCR,
DVD, reading lamp, clock radio, telephone, desk, hot tub/spa, wireless
Internet, most with Jacuzzi tubs, some suites with fireplaces and all suites
have full private kitchens in room. Fax, copier, bicycles, library, parlor
games, fireplace, laundry facility and wireless internet on premises.
Antiquing, bicycling, cross-country skiing, downhill skiing, fishing, golf, hiking, museums, parks and shopping nearby.

Location: City.

Certificate may be used: Oct. 1-April 30.

Haines
F7

The Summer Inn Bed & Breakfast

117 Second Avenue
Haines, AK 99827
(907)766-2970 Fax:(906)766-2970
Internet: www.summerinnbnb.com
E-mail: innkeeper@summerinnbnb.com

Circa 1912. This historic farmhouse has an infamous beginning, it was built by a member of a gang of claimjumpers who
operated during the Gold Rush. The home affords stunning

mountain and water
views. The home is com-
fortably furnished, and
one guest bathroom
includes a clawfoot tub
original to the home.
Breakfasts include fresh
fruit and entrees such as
sourdough pancakes with ham. The area offers many activities,
including museums and a historic walking tour, skiing, snowshoeing, ice fishing, hiking, fishing and much more.

Innkeeper(s): Jenty Fowler & Mary Ellen Summer. $80-120. 5 rooms.
Breakfast and afternoon tea included in rates. Types of meals: Full bkfst, early
coffee/tea and snacks/refreshments. Beds: DT. Reading lamp and alarm clocks
in room. Fax, library, telephone and BBQ on premises. Art galleries, beach,
bicycling, canoeing/kayaking, cross-country skiing, fishing, golf, hiking, live
theater, museums, parks, shopping, tennis, water sports and birding nearby.

Location: Ocean community. Coastal town.

Publicity: *American History (April 2000) and Historic Sears Mail Order
Houses Roebucks.*

Certificate may be used: Dec. 1-March 31, subject to availability.

Juneau
F8

Pearson's Pond Luxury Inn & Adventure Spa

4541 Sawa Cir
Juneau, AK 99801-8723
(907)789-3772 (888)658-6328
Internet: www.pearsonspond.com
E-mail: book@pearsonspond.com

Circa 1990. Cruise glaciers, view bears and whales, climb the
ice, mush dogs, go fishing, or take a chance at gold-panning
while staying at this award-winning luxury resort. Enchanted
master-planned gardens, lined with wild Alaska blueberry bushes
and dotted with hot tubs and gazebos, give you an immediate
feeling of serenity. Exquisitely appointed accommodations make
you feel so pampered and comfortable that you won't ever want
to leave. Every room has a fireplace, kitchenette, sitting area, flat
panel TV, water or forest views, and much more. Near to everything, yet seeming a world apart, this is the perfect place for an
Alaska adventure vacation, wedding, or romantic interlude.

Innkeeper(s): Maryann Ray, Rachael Ray & Rick Nelson. $219-799. 7 rooms
with PB, 5 with FP, 5 with HT, 2 with WP, 1 cottage. Breakfast, hors d'oeuvres, wine and Self serve breakfast in winter included in rates. Types of
meals: Full bkfst, veg bkfst, early coffee/tea, picnic lunch, afternoon tea,
snacks/refreshments, room service, Expanded continental breakfast with hot
entree in summer and self-serve anytime. Self-serve expanded continental
breakfast in fall/winter/spring. Beds: KQDT. Modem hook-up, data port, cable
TV, VCR, DVD, reading lamp, stereo, refrigerator, snack bar, clock radio, telephone, coffeemaker, turn-down service, desk, most with hot tub/spa, voice

mail, fireplace, hair dryer, bathrobes, bath amenities, wireless Internet access, iron/ironing board, Canopy beds, sitting areas, kitchenettes, most rooms with water view, some rooms with rainfall showers & whirlpool tubs and some rooms with cathedral ceiling & skylight in room. Fax, copier, spa, sauna, bicycles, library, parlor games, laundry facility, gift shop, Waterfall, Kayaks, Paddle Boat, Row Boat, Bikes, Campfire, BBQs, Fishing Equipment, Dock, Fitness Center, Massage room, Wedding gazebos, Trails, Award-winning gardens and nature trails on premises. Limited handicap access. Antiquing, art galleries, beach, bicycling, canoeing/kayaking, cross-country skiing, downhill skiing, fishing, golf, hiking, horseback riding, live theater, museums, parks, shopping, tennis, water sports, wineries, Mendenhall Glacier, Glacier Bay National Park, bear & whale viewing, hiking, ziplining, plane & helicopter flight-seeing, Mt. Roberts Tramway, Glacier Gardens Rainforest Adventure. Glacier cruises, Glacier trekking and dog mushing, rafting and jet skiing & much more! nearby.

Location: Waterfront. On private lake, in forest, next to mountains & glacier.

Publicity: *AAA Four Diamond, Fodor's Choice, Frommer's Exceptional, MSN.com (#4 in the World Most Romantic Hotel Destination), Forbes (Among World's Best Wellness Spas), Top 10 Most Romantic Destinations, Top 100 Most romantic wedding destinations, 1,000 Places to See Before You Die, Most Perfect Stay, Juneau's Best B&B, top rated in most popular Alaska guides, National Geographic, Pacific Northwest, Sunset, The Knot, Sherman's Travel, Forbes, Destination Alaska, Modern Bride, Alaska Bride and Groom, Perfect Stay and Best B&B of Alaska, North American Inns (named a Best Rooms of North America), Frommers and Fodors, Healing Spas and Retreats, Healing Lifestyles, Country Discovery, Atlantic Monthly, Country Inns, Good Housekeeping, LA Times Exotic Weddings, CBS "Eye on the Bay," Discovery network Travel Feature Big Skies and Glaciers, KING TV in Seattle, WA (featured the inn on Alaska Vacations), Fine Living Network, numerous articles and travel blogs. and Innkeeper has been interviewed on several local radio stations.*

Certificate may be used: October-April.

Kenai E5

Blonde Bear Bed and Breakfast

47004 Emery Street
Kenai, AK 99611
(907)776-8957 (888)776-8956
Internet: www.blondebear.com
E-mail: info@blondebear.com

Recently built on 21 acres with lawns, rock gardens, perennials and natural forest, this two-story ranch exudes Alaskan Sourdough Hospitality. Blonde Bear Bed and Breakfast is open year round in Kenai, Alaska. Sip homemade wine and locally made treats by the outdoor bonfire. A canoe and a barbecue grill are available to use. Stay in one of the comfortable guest bedrooms with a rustic Alaskan country decor. The Blonde Bear Den features robes, an amenities basket, entertainment center and a private bath with a soaker tub. Wake up to a hearty breakfast before beginning the day's scenic adventures.

Innkeeper(s): George and Tina Showalter. Call for rates. 6 rooms, 2 with PB, 2 suites. Breakfast, hors d'oeuvres and wine included in rates. Types of meals: Full gourmet bkfst, early coffee/tea, lunch, picnic lunch and snacks/refreshments. Beds: QT. Data port, TV, VCR, DVD, reading lamp, stereo, refrigerator, clock radio, telephone, desk, hair dryer, bathrobes, bath amenities, wireless Internet access and iron/ironing board in room. Fax, copier, parlor games and laundry facility on premises. Limited handicap access. Art galleries, beach, bicycling, canoeing/kayaking, cross-country skiing, fishing, golf, hiking, horseback riding, museums, parks, shopping, sporting events, tennis, water sports, flyout fishing, hunting, bear viewing, sightseeing guides, recreation facility includes swimming pool, racketball courts, workout gym and rock wall nearby.

Location: Country, ocean community.

Publicity: *Entrepreneur Magazine (March 2007).*

Certificate may be used: Anytime, November-March, subject to availability.

Ketchikan F8

Black Bear Inn

5528 North Tongass Highway
Ketchikan, AK 99901
(907)225-4343 Fax:(907)225-4353
Internet: www.stayinalaska.com
E-mail: blackbearalaska@aol.com

Circa 2005. Designed for relaxed privacy with an elegant décor and an assortment of upscale amenities, this premier island retreat boasts a park-like one-acre setting. It is bordered by spruce and cedar trees accented by eagles, ravens and seagulls. Black Bear Inn is the perfect Alaskan B&B getaway or vacation rental in Ketchikan. Enjoy multi-level wraparound decks, a covered outdoor hot tub, fire pit and barbecue at the water's edge. Gather to watch a movie in the fireside living room. Local artists are featured throughout the inn. Accommodations with stunning views of the Tongass Narrows include guest rooms in the main house, a luxury apartment and a 2-bedroom cabin. Customize each stay with a driver and catered meals. Use of the kitchen and laundry room is provided.

Innkeeper(s): Nicole & James Church. $100-300. 6 rooms with PB, 5 with FP, 1 guest house, 1 cabin, 1 conference room. Breakfast, afternoon tea, snacks/refreshments, hors d'oeuvres, wine, soft drinks and first beer and glass of wine included in rates. Types of meals: Cont plus, veg bkfst, early coffee/tea, picnic lunch and full meals packages available for groups of 4 or more. Beds: KQDT. Modem hook-up, cable TV, VCR, DVD, reading lamp, stereo, refrigerator, ceiling fan, clock radio, telephone, coffeemaker, hot tub/spa, hair dryer, bathrobes, bath amenities, wireless Internet access and iron/ironing board in room. Fax, copier, spa, library, parlor games, fireplace and laundry facility on premises. Limited handicap access. Art galleries, beach, bicycling, canoeing/kayaking, fishing, hiking, museums, parks, shopping, water sports, Black Bear watching, float plane trips and zipp lines nearby.

Location: Waterfront.

Certificate may be used: Anytime, October-April, Subject to availability.

Sitka
F8

Alaska Ocean View Bed & Breakfast Inn

1101 Edgecumbe Dr
Sitka, AK 99835-7122
(907)747-8310 (888)811-6870 Fax:(907)747-3440
Internet: www.sitka-alaska-lodging.com
E-mail: info@sitka-alaska-lodging.com

Circa 1986. Alaska Ocean View Bed & Breakfast Inn is a
red-cedar executive home is located in a quiet neighborhood
one block from the seashore and the Tongass National Forest
in Sitka. Witness spectacular sunsets over stunning Sitka
Sound and on clear days view majestic Mt. Edgecumbe, an
extinct volcano located offshore on Kruzoff Island. Binoculars
are kept handy for guests who take a special interest in looking for whales and eagles. Guest bedrooms are named after
popular local wildflowers. Explore the scenic area after a
hearty breakfast.

Innkeeper(s): Carole & Bill Denkinger. $129-249. 3 rooms with PB, 2 with
FP, 1 conference room. Breakfast, afternoon tea and snacks/refreshments
included in rates. Types of meals: Full gourmet bkfst, veg bkfst, early
coffee/tea, hors d'oeuvres and room service. Beds: KQT. Data port, cable TV,
VCR, DVD, reading lamp, stereo, refrigerator, ceiling fan, snack bar, clock
radio, telephone, coffeemaker, turn-down service, desk, hot tub/spa, most
with fireplace, hair dryer, bathrobes, bath amenities, wireless Internet access,
iron/ironing board, one room with ocean view balcony, two furnished with
table and chairs on patio, HEPA Air cleaners, wine glasses, wine opener, can
opener, coffee creamers, cappuccinos, teas, etc. and picnic supplies in room.
Fax, copier, spa, library, pet boarding, parlor games, gift shop, water garden
fish pond with waterfall area set with table, chairs and stone checkerboard
and covered shuttle bus/taxi waiting area on premises. Limited handicap
access. Antiquing, art galleries, beach, bicycling, canoeing/kayaking, fishing,
golf, hiking, museums, parks, shopping, Whale watching, Wildlife viewing,
Underwater discovery tours, Fly fishing, Ocean salmon & halibut fishing, Bird
watching, Glaciers, Totem poles, Chamber music concerts, Crab feeds,
Russian and Tlingit Indian folk dance, Heli skiing, Hang gliding, Kruzoff
Island, Wilderness Hot Springs and Baranof Island nearby.

Location: Mountains, ocean community. One block from Tongass National
Forest.

Publicity: *Ladies Home Journal, Washington Post, Sunday New York Times
and Alaska Airlines in flight magazine.*

Certificate may be used: Sunday-Wednesday, October-March, Sunday-
Wednesday, April-May 7. Space subject to availability. Anytime at the last
minute.

Sutton
E5

Matanuska Lodge

34301 West Glenn Hwy
Sutton, AK 99674
(907)746-0378
Internet: www.matanuskalodge.com
E-mail: nuska1@mac.com

Circa 2006. Lavish luxury and traditional comfort are offered
at Matanuska Lodge, a newly built log home sitting on two
acres in Sutton, Alaska. This romantic getaway, surrounded by
wildflowers, is open all year-round and boasts views of the
Saddlenotch Mountains and Matanuska Glacier. It is a short
walk to enjoy the activities of 100 Mile Lake. The gathering
area has games and a big screen TV with DVDs. Appetizers,
snacks and beverages are provided. Sit in the English garden, at
the picnic table or the fire pit. Stay in a guest bedroom with a
whirlpool tub and deck access. One room also features a fireplace. Radiant heated floors and blackout shades are among
the pampering amenities. Savor a bountiful breakfast with a
continental flair. Dinner is available upon request.

Innkeeper(s): Brenda Goldberg. $200-400. 4 rooms with PB, 1 with FP, 4
with WP. Breakfast, snacks/refreshments and hors d'oeuvres included in
rates. Types of meals: Full gourmet bkfst, early coffee/tea and Dinner as well
as lunch can be arranged on a one to one basis. There will be an additional
fee for this special service. Picnic lunches may also be provided if there is a
need. Beds: K. Reading lamp, ceiling fan, clock radio, telephone, turn-down
service, hot tub/spa, some with fireplace, hair dryer, bathrobes, bath amenities, wireless Internet access, Beautiful bed covers & Accessories, Arm chairs,
Rocking chairs, In-floor heating, Deck access for viewing and sitting in room.
Central air. TV, VCR, DVD, fax, copier, spa, library, parlor games and Big
screen TV available in gathering area on premises. Bicycling, canoeing/kayak-
ing, cross-country skiing, fishing, hiking, horseback riding, parks, shopping
and water sports nearby.

Location: Mountains.

Certificate may be used: Anytime, subject to availability.

Arizona

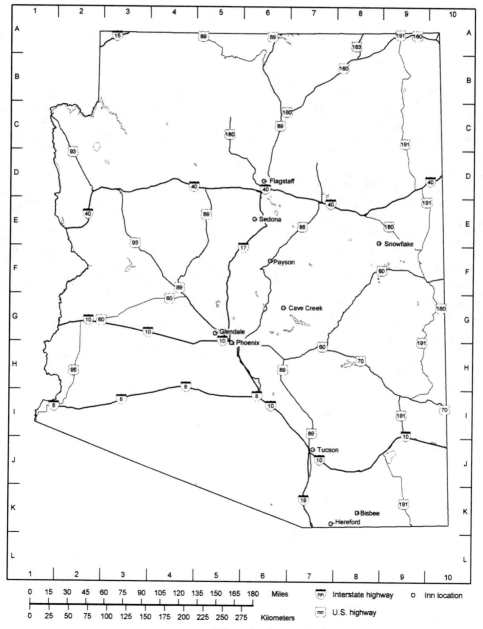

		Miles
0 15 30 45 60 75 90 105 120 135 150 165 180		
0 25 50 75 100 125 150 175 200 225 250 275		Kilometers

Interstate highway   o   Inn location

U.S. highway

Cave Creek   G7

Full Circle Ranch

40205 N. 26th Street
Cave Creek, AZ 85331
(623) 742-0390 Fax:(623)742-0392
Internet: www.fullcircleranchaz.com
E-mail: info@fullcircleranchaz.com

Circa 1995. Secluded amid the scenic valley area of the
Sonoran Desert surrounded by mountains, enjoy this oasis of
peaceful comfort and stunning beauty. Conveniently located
close enough to Phoenix Sky Harbor Airport and the art galleries, shopping and dining of Scottsdale, this eco-friendly ranch
is away from the bustle of city life. Equestrians appreciate the
traveling horse accommodations and nearby trails. Relax by the
beehive fireplace and waterfalls or in the shade of the ramada;
swim in the pool and soak in the heated whirlpool spa.
Featuring Southwest décor, stay in an inviting guest room in the
main house or in an air-conditioned casita with fireplace, spa
tub, kitchenette and patio. Breakfast is not to be missed and the
recipes are always requested. Concierge services arrange on-site
massages and Reiki, bull-riding events, jeep tours, golf tee times,
hot air balloon and horseback rides, among other activities.

Innkeeper(s): Sherrie Sheldon. $140-235. 5 rooms with PB, 2 with FP, 2
with HT, 1 conference room. Breakfast and snacks/refreshments included in
rates. Types of meals: Full gourmet bkfst. Beds: KQT. Cable TV, refrigerator,
ceiling fan, clock radio, coffeemaker, desk, hair dryer, bath amenities and
wireless Internet access in room. Central air. Fax, copier, spa, swimming, stable, library, fireplace, laundry facility and traveling horse accommodations on
premises. Limited handicap access. Antiquing, art galleries, bicycling, golf,
hiking, horseback riding, museums, parks and shopping nearby.

Location: Country, mountains. Sonoran Desert.

Certificate may be used: Anytime, subject to availability.

Flagstaff   D6

Starlight Pines Bed & Breakfast

3380 E Lockett Rd
Flagstaff, AZ 86004-4039
(928)527-1912 (800)752-1912
Internet: www.starlightpinesbb.com
E-mail: romance@starlightpinesbb.com

Circa 1996. Tall pine trees and nearby mountains create a peaceful ambiance at this Victorian-styled home. Relax on the wraparound porch with a swing or curl up with a book in front of the
fireplace in the parlor. Guest bedrooms include amenities such as
a fireplace and/or antique clawfoot tub. Country antiques are
placed on oak-plank floors and luxurious spreads top the beds.
Bathrobes and bubble baths are found in the private baths. The
innkeepers pamper with fresh flowers, gourmet breakfasts, enjoyable conversation and friendly pet Shih Tzus, Mooshu and Taz.

Innkeeper(s): Richard Svends'en & Michael. $159-189. 4 rooms with PB,
1 with FP, 1 suite. Breakfast included in rates. Types of meals: Full gourmet
bkfst, veg bkfst, early coffee/tea, Refreshments and Special occasions
receive a complementary bottle of wine! Must ask for it when reserving.
Beds: KQD. Modem hook-up, data port, DVD, reading lamp, CD player,
refrigerator, desk, some with fireplace, hair dryer, bathrobes, bath amenities, wireless Internet access and iron/ironing board in room. Fax, copier,
parlor games, telephone, 70' x 12' wraparound porch with swing and Guest
refrigerator with complimentary bottled water on premises. Antiquing, art
galleries, bicycling, cross-country skiing, downhill skiing, fishing, golf, hiking, horseback riding, live theater, museums, parks, shopping, sporting
events and tennis nearby.

Location: Mountains.

Certificate may be used: November-May. Sunday-Friday, Anytime, Last
Minute-Based on Availability.

Hereford   K7

Casa De San Pedro

8933 S Yell Ln
Hereford, AZ 85615-9250
(520)366-1300 (888)257-2050 Fax:(520)366-0701
Internet: www.bedandbirds.com
E-mail: info@bedandbirds.com

Circa 1996. Built around a courtyard and fountain, this
Territorial hacienda-style bed & breakfast inn is furnished with
hand-carved wood furnishings and accent tiles from Mexico. Its
care for the environment as well as its location on ten acres of
high prairie grassland adjacent to the San Pedro River and
Riparian Reserve create a world-class hideaway for naturalists
and ecotourism. Relax by the fire in the Great Room, or
research birds on the computer. Romantic guest bedrooms offer
quiet privacy and the warm hospitality includes quality
concierge services. Experience the made-to-satisfy breakfast
that will include old favorites and wonderful new recipes.
Special dietary needs are easily accommodated.

Innkeeper(s): Karl Schmitt and Patrick Dome. $169. 10 rooms with PB, 6
with FP, 1 conference room. Breakfast, afternoon tea, snacks/refreshments,
Full served breakfast each morning featuring fresh seasonal fruit, fresh baked
muffins/scones and egg entre' with optional meats. Vegetarian and special
diets supported included in rates. Types of meals: Full gourmet bkfst, veg
bkfst and early coffee/tea. Beds: KD. Modem hook-up, reading lamp, CD
player, ceiling fan, clock radio, telephone, desk, hot tub/spa, most with fireplace, hair dryer, bath amenities, wireless Internet access, iron/ironing board
and Wi-Fi in room. Central air. TV, VCR, DVD, fax, copier, spa, swimming,
library, parlor games, laundry facility, gift shop, Ramada for bird watching,
Gas grills for your BBQ, Butterfly garden, Xeriscape low water use landscaping and Native habitat for wildlife on premises. Handicap access. Antiquing,
art galleries, bicycling, fishing, golf, hiking, live theater, museums, parks,
shopping, tennis, wineries, Ramsey Canyon, Miller Canyon, Ash Canyon,
Tombstone, Bisbee, Coronado National Monument, Kartchner Caverns,
Garden Canyon and Some of the best birdwatching in the nation nearby.

Location: Country, mountains, waterfront. San Pedro River and Riparian
Reserve.

Publicity: *AZ Tourist News, Minneapolis Herald Tribune, Arizona Highways
and Rated the Best Breakfasts in the Southwest by Arrington's Inn Traveler*
magazine.

Certificate may be used: Anytime, Last Minute-Based on Availability except
holidays, Feb.15-May 15, Aug.1-8 or Dec. 2 and Jan. 1.

Payson   F6

Verde River Rock House
Bed and Breakfast

602 W. Eleanor Drive
Payson, AZ 85541
(928)472-4304 Fax:(480)444-0235
Internet: verderiverrockhouse.com
E-mail: verderiverbnb@aol.com

Circa 1949. Feel mesmerized by the picturesque views of
Payson Rim Country from this secluded hilltop setting along
the banks of the East Verde River in Tonto National Forest. The
inn is poised to offer comfort and charm amid casual elegance.
Sit on a glider or hammock on the creekside deck and gather
for evening appetizers and beverages. Relax in the four-person
Canadian cedar sauna then soak in the Jacuzzi hot tub/spa.

Massage and spa services can be arranged. Stay in a private suite with a den, fireplace and extensive Blue-Ray DVD library. Linger over a gourmet breakfast. Fishing gear and a gas barbecue grill are available as well as kitchen usage. Rent bikes, ATVs and paddle boats right at the inn.

Innkeeper(s): Steve and Maggie Evans. $185-245. Call inn for details. The Basic Daily Weekend Rate of $225 (based on double occupancy) is inclusive of fresh Belgium chocolate dipped strawberries upon arrival (in season), Evening Hors d`Oeuvres / Appetizers with Beverage (wine and beer or non-alcoholic selections) & Full Breakfast in the morning – additionally there are complimentary snacks and beverages provided – Call us for details of our weekday and special "no host" rates included in rates. Types of meals: Full gourmet bkfst, early coffee/tea, gourmet lunch, picnic lunch, snacks/refreshments, wine, gourmet dinner, Evening Hors d`Oeuvres, We also offer a full menu of dinner entrees (call or visit our website for details); wine tastings, belgium chocolate strawberries and "to die for desserts" All meals are served on one of the Riverside Decks (weather permitting) or in the Dining Room (at guest's preference). Specialty meals to meet dietary restrictions are available – just ask, we strive to please. and. Beds: Q. Data port, cable TV, VCR, DVD, reading lamp, stereo, refrigerator, ceiling fan, snack bar, clock radio, telephone, coffeemaker, turn-down service, desk, hot tub/spa, voice mail, fireplace, hair dryer, bathrobes, bath amenities, wireless Internet access, iron/ironing board, Infrared Sauna, Paddleboat, A T V Rental, Gourmet Dining available on premises, Full wine Cellar, Scotch Tastings, Gourmet Cooking Lessons available from profession chef and On-site massages and facials available in room. Central air. Fax, copier, spa, sauna, bicycles, library, parlor games, laundry facility and We can arrange for our guests to play golf at the exclusive private - Rim Golf Club - at a special rate on premises. Antiquing, art galleries, bicycling, canoeing/kayaking, cross-country skiing, fishing, golf, hiking, horseback riding, museums, parks, shopping, tennis, water sports, Tonto Natural Bridge, Fossil Creek Hot Springs. We are also able to afford our guests the opportunity to play golf at the Exclusive Rim Golf Club (Rated the No. 1 residential golf course in the Southwest three years in a row in Golfweek magazine's list of "America's Best Residential Golf Courses," and No. 1 in Arizona, The Rim Golf Club's par-71 championship course is the highlight of the community and the collaboration of the legendary design team of Tom Weiskopf and Jay Morrish. Antiquing, art galleries, bicycling, hiking, fishing, golf, tennis, casino, adventure tours, ATV trail riding, horseback riding, llama & goat ranch nearby and within 3 miles of Tonto Natural Bridge (Arizona's 3rd most visited attraction and only a scenic two hour drive to Meteor Crater nearby.

Location: Country, mountains, waterfront. surrounded by Tonto National Forest.

Certificate may be used: December-March, Monday-Thursday, excluding holidays, rack rates apply, cannot be used in conjunction with any other discounts, subject to availability.

Phoenix   F5

Maricopa Manor Bed & Breakfast Inn

15 W Pasadena Ave
Phoenix, AZ 85013
(602)264-9200 (800)292-6403 Fax:(602)264-9204
Internet: www.maricopamanor.com
E-mail: res@maricopamanor.com

Circa 1928. Secluded amid palm trees on an acre of land, this Spanish-style house features four graceful columns in the entry hall, an elegant living room with a marble mantel and a music room. Completely refurbished suites are very spacious and distinctively furnished with style and good taste. Relax on the private patio or around the pool while enjoying the soothing sound of falling water from the many fountains.

Innkeeper(s): Scott and Joan Eveland. $129-239. 7 rooms, 4 with FP, 4 with WP, 7 total suites, including 2 two-bedroom suites, 1 conference room. Breakfast and snacks/refreshments included in rates. Types of meals: Cont plus and Breakfast delivered to suite. Beds: KQ. Modem hook-up, data port, cable TV, VCR, DVD, reading lamp, stereo, refrigerator, ceiling fan, clock radio, telephone, coffeemaker, desk, most with hot tub/spa, most with fireplace, hair dryer, bathrobes, bath amenities, wireless Internet access, iron/ironing board and Digital cable with HBO in room. Central air. Fax, copier, spa, swimming, library, parlor games and off-street parking on premises. Handicap access. Amusement parks, antiquing, art galleries, bicycling, golf, hiking, horseback riding, live theater, museums, parks,

shopping, sporting events, tennis, water sports and restaurants nearby.

Location: City.

Publicity: *Arizona Business Journal, Country Inns, AAA Westways, San Francisco Chronicle, Focus, Sombrero, NY Times, USA Weekend Magazine, AZ Republic YES Magazine and FOX 15 "Sonoran Living"*

"I've stayed 200+ nights at B&Bs around the world, yet have never before experienced the warmth and sincere friendliness of Maricopa Manor."

Certificate may be used: Anytime, subject to availability.

Sedona   E6

Lodge at Sedona-A Luxury Bed and Breakfast Inn

125 Kallof Place
Sedona, AZ 86336-5566
(800) 619-4467 (800) 619-4467 Fax:(928)204-2128
Internet: www.lodgeatsedona.com
E-mail: info@lodgeatsedona.com

Circa 1959. Elegantly casual, this newly renovated mission-style B&B sits on three secluded acres with expansive red rock views, mature juniper, sculpture gardens, fountains and a private labyrinth. Enjoy Sunset Snacks in the Fireplace Lounge, Celebration Porch or outdoor terrace. Artfully decorated king suites feature romantic fireplaces, spa tubs, sitting areas, private  decks and entrances. Linger over a five-course breakfast. Massage therapy is available. Exclusive receptions, weddings and executive meetings are accommodated. The lodge offers health club privileges, including access to two swimming pools. The Grand Canyon is a two-hour day trip, and the area includes hiking trails, Jeep tours and hot air balloons.

Innkeeper(s): Innkeeper. $115-349. 15 rooms, 14 with PB, 13 with FP, 2 with HT, 8 with WP, 9 suites, 2 conference rooms. Breakfast, Sunday brunch, afternoon tea, snacks/refreshments, hors d'oeuvres and Special catering available at Lodge at Sedona. Call 800-619-4467 included in rates. Types of meals: Full gourmet bkfst, veg bkfst, early coffee/tea, gourmet lunch, dinner, room service and Dinners and Special Events Can be catered. Call 800 619 4467 for Details. Beds: KQ. Cable TV, DVD, reading lamp, CD player, refrigerator, ceiling fan, snack bar, clock radio, turn-down service, desk, most with hot tub/spa, fireplace, hair dryer, bathrobes, bath amenities, wireless Internet access and iron/ironing board in room. Central air. VCR, fax, copier, spa, swimming, stable, library, parlor games, telephone, gift shop, Large private decks on all King suites, Celebration Terrace for Outdoor Dining and Free Wireless Internet throughout Lodge Fitness center and pool privileges on premises. Handicap access. Antiquing, art galleries, bicycling, canoeing/kayaking, cross-country skiing, downhill skiing, fishing, golf, hiking, horseback riding, live theater, museums, parks, shopping, tennis, water sports, wineries, Jeep tours, Cycling, Hot air ballooning, Biplane Rides, Casino, Camping, Adventure tours, Wine tours, Horseback tours and Oak Creek Fishing nearby.

Location: City, country, mountains. Sedona Red Rock Country.

Publicity: *Real Simple Magazine, Forbes.com, Arizona Republic, Sedona, Red Rock News, San Francisco Examiner, Country Register, New York Post, Bon Appetit, Mountain Living, Sunset Magazine, AZ News, AZ Travel, Arizona Getaways,Road & Travel, North American Inns, KPNX Channel 10 Phoenix and Sedona the Movie...Coming Soon..*

"What a wonderful hideaway you have! Everything about your inn was and is fantastic! The friendly service made me feel as if I was home. More importantly, the food made me wish that was my home!"

Certificate may be used: Anytime, subject to availability. Holidays excluded.

Snowflake   E8

Osmer D. Heritage Inn

161 North Main
Snowflake, AZ 85937
(928)536-3322 (866)486-5937 Fax:(928)536-4834
Internet: www.heritage-inn.net
E-mail: heritageinn@live.com

Circa 1890. A loving heritage surrounds this restored inn boasting two-story brick buildings. The decor is Victorian, and the antique furnishings can be purchased. Visit the adjacent antique shop to find more treasures. For solitude or socializing, ample common rooms include the parlor with DVD, library and reception room. Gas-log stoves highlight guest bedrooms and a honeymoon suite. Several rooms feature romantic spa tubs for two. Linger over a hearty gourmet breakfast in the dining room. French or cowboy steak-dinner parties can be arranged. After a day of touring historic pioneer homes, relax in the large hot tub.

Innkeeper(s): Craig and JoAnne Guderian. Call for rates. 14 rooms. Breakfast and snacks/refreshments included in rates. Types of meals: Full gourmet bkfst, early coffee/tea, gourmet lunch, gourmet dinner, We are flexible with our menu, just let us know in advance your dietary requirements. We also offer evening meals as long as we are given advance notice. We will cater to large groups up to 100 as long as the banquet room is rented. We also offer group lunches and brunches and meals. Restaurant on premises. Beds: KQ. Cable TV, VCR, DVD, reading lamp, clock radio, telephone, desk, hair dryer, bathrobes, bath amenities, wireless Internet access, iron/ironing board, Fireplace, Jacuzzi spa for eight people and exercise equipment in room. Air conditioning. Fax, copier, spa, library, parlor games, fireplace, laundry facility, antique shop next door and gift shop on premises. Handicap access. Antiquing, art galleries, bicycling, canoeing/kayaking, cross-country skiing, downhill skiing, fishing, golf, hiking, horseback riding, live theater, museums, parks, shopping, tennis, Tours of historic pioneer homes & cabins, National parks, Three Indian Reservation day trips, Casinos on Indian land, Off-road vehicles, Star gazing, Birding, Birdwatching, Nature Reserves, Petrified Forest and Painted Desert nearby.

Location: Country.
Publicity: *Arizona Highways.*

Certificate may be used: Sunday-Thursday.

Tucson   J7

Casa Tierra Adobe B&B Inn

11155 W Calle Pima
Tucson, AZ 85743-9462
(520)578-3058 (866)254-0006 Fax:(520)578-8445
Internet: www.casatierratucson.com
E-mail: info@casatierratucson.com

Circa 1988. The Sonoran Desert surrounds this secluded, adobe retreat. The mountain views and brilliant sunsets are spectacular. The interior arched courtyard, vaulted brick ceilings and Mexican furnishings create a wonderful Southwestern atmosphere. Each guest room has a private entrance and patios that overlook the desert landscape. The rooms open up to the courtyard. Freshly ground coffee and specialty teas accompany the full vegetarian breakfast. Old Tucson, the Desert Museum and a Saguaro National Park are nearby. The inn also provides a relaxing hot tub and telescope.

Innkeeper(s): Dave Malmquist. $135-325. 4 rooms with PB, 1 suite. Breakfast and snacks/refreshments included in rates. Types of meals: Full gourmet bkfst, veg bkfst and early coffee/tea. Beds: Q. Data port, reading lamp, refrigerator, ceiling fan, snack bar, clock radio and telephone in room. Air conditioning. TV, VCR, fax, spa, telescope and guest computer with high-speed Internet connection on premises. Bicycling, golf, hiking and horseback riding nearby.

Location: Country.

Publicity: *Arizona Daily Star, Smart Money Magazine, Washington Post, Phoenix Magazine and Scottsdale Tribune.*

Certificate may be used: April 15-June 15, Aug. 15-Nov. 15.

Arkansas

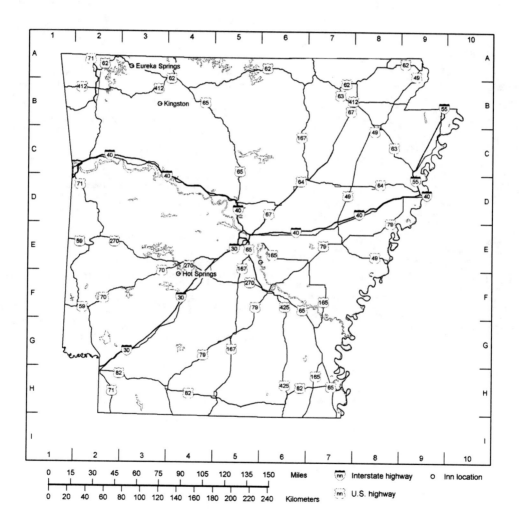

0 15 30 45 60 75 90 105 120 135 150 Miles

0 20 40 60 80 100 120 140 160 180 200 220 240 Kilometers

(nn) Interstate highway   o Inn location

(nn) U.S. highway

Eureka Springs A3

Cliff Cottage Inn - Luxury B&B Suites & Historic Cottages

Heart of Historic Downtown
Eureka Springs, AR 72632
(479)253-7409
Internet: www.cliffcottage.com
E-mail: cliffcottage@sbcglobal.net

Circa 1880. The Cliff Cottage Inn is the only B&B in the heart of Historic Downtown with an elf who delivers full-gourmet breakfasts to each suite and puts a complimentary bottle of Champagne or white wine in the fridge. Comprised

of three houses in a row, the inn is just steps to the shops and restaurants of Main Street in Eureka Springs, Arkansas. An 1880 Eastlake Victorian, Sears' first kit home, is a State and National Landmark. It features suites with private front porches and decks tucked into the three-story high rock bluff. The Place Next Door is a Victorian replica boasting two upstairs suites with balconies. The Artist's Cottage is a renovated 1910 Craftsman. Two elegant suites include pure-air whirlpool tubs, a porch and a deck.

Innkeeper(s): Sandra CH Smith . $189-230. 8 rooms with PB, 4 with FP, 2 with HT, 6 with WP, 6 suites, 2 cottages, 5 guest houses, 1 conference room. Breakfast, snacks/refreshments, wine, The two stand-alone Cottages have fully-equipped kitchens/rate does not include breakfast and Gourmet hot breakfast is delivered to all suites except From Nov. 1 to March 1 when a Continental Plus breakfast is included in the discounted winter rates. Full gourmet breakfasts delivered to suites March 1 to Oct. 31 included in rates. Types of meals: Full gourmet bkfst, veg bkfst, early coffee/tea, room service, All suites/cottages have coffeemakers with large selection of imported teas, coffee, hot chocolate, chai, granola/dry cereals and cookie samplers and complimentary bottle of Champagne or white wine chilled in your fridge. Beds: KQ. Modem hook-up, cable TV, VCR, reading lamp, stereo, refrigerator, ceiling fan, snack bar, clock radio, coffeemaker, desk, hot tub/spa, voice mail, most with fireplace, hair dryer, bathrobes, bath amenities, wireless Internet access, iron/ironing board, Full-gourmet delivered breakfasts to suites, suites have two-person Jacuzzi and Cottages have private outdoor hot tubs. Off-street parking (a real premium downtown!) for all our guests in room. Central air. Spa, library, parlor games, telephone, Complimentary champagne or white wine, In-room beverage bars with complimentary coffee, Imported teas, Hot chocolate, Chai, Sodas and Concierge service on premises. Amusement parks, antiquing, art galleries, beach, canoeing/kayaking, fishing, golf, hiking, horseback riding, live theater, museums, parks, shopping, tennis, water sports, Great Passion Play (six-minute drive), discount golf, canoe excursions, guided fishing expeditions, horseback trips and carriage rides nearby.

Location: Country, mountains. Historic Downtown, 17 steps up from Main St.

Publicity: *Arkansas Democrat Gazette, Country Inns, Modern Bride, Southern Living, Southern Bride, Sandra was guest chef on a CBS-TV cooking show, Romantic Destinations Magazine (One of the Top Six Most Romantic Inns of the South), Southern Bride and American Bed & Breakfast Association (highest rating as well as an Award for Excellence).*

Certificate may be used: Monday to Thursday stays only no holidays/festival events, Queen Jacuzzi Suite, Subject to availability. Not valid with other coupons or promotions. Call for other Last-Minute specials based on projected availability.

The Heartstone Inn & Cottages

35 King's Highway
Eureka Springs, AR 72632-3534
(479)253-8916 (800)494-4921
Internet: www.heartstoneinn.com
E-mail: info@heartstoneinn.com

Circa 1903. A white picket fence leads to this spacious Victorian inn and its pink and cobalt blue wraparound porch filled with potted geraniums and Boston ferns. Located on the Eureka Springs historic loop, The Heartstone Inn & Cottages offers English country antiques, private entrances and pretty linens. Private Jacuzzis, refrigerators and VCRs are available in some guest bedrooms. Pamper yourself in the massage therapy studio. Walk to shops, restau-

rants and galleries or hop on the trolley to enjoy all the pleasures of the town. Golf privileges at a private club are extended to guests. The New York Times praised the inn's cuisine as the "Best Breakfast in the Ozarks."

Innkeeper(s): Rick & Cheri Rojek. $99-169. 11 rooms with PB, 4 with FP, 6 suites, 2 cottages, 1 conference room. Breakfast and snacks/refreshments included in rates. Types of meals: Full gourmet bkfst. Beds: KQ. Cable TV, VCR, DVD, reading lamp, refrigerator, ceiling fan, clock radio, coffeemaker, desk, some with hot tub/spa, some with fireplace, hair dryer, bathrobes, bath amenities, wireless Internet access, iron/ironing board and whirlpool tub in room. Air conditioning. Fax, copier, spa, library, parlor games, telephone, gift shop, massage therapy and gift shop on premises. Limited handicap access. Amusement parks, antiquing, art galleries, bicycling, canoeing/kayaking, fishing, golf, hiking, horseback riding, live theater, parks, shopping, restaurants and opera nearby.

Location: City, mountains.

Publicity: *Innsider, Arkansas Times, New York Times, Arkansas Gazette, Southern Living, Country Home, Country Inns and USA Today.*

"Extraordinary! Best breakfasts anywhere!"

Certificate may be used: Sunday-Wednesday, January & February, Based on Availability.

Hot Springs F4

Lookout Point Lakeside Inn

104 Lookout Circle
Hot Springs, AR 71913
(501)525-6155 (866)525-6155 Fax:(501)525-5850
Internet: www.lookoutpointinn.com
E-mail: innkeeper@lookoutpointinn.com

Circa 2002. Feel rejuvenated in the tranquil setting of this newly built Arts and Crafts inn sitting on 1 1/2 spectacular acres in the Ouachita Mountains overlooking a serene bay. Nap in a hammock, stroll by a stream and waterfall on garden paths or walk the labyrinth. Gather for afternoon refreshments with dessert, fruit and wine. Luxurious guest bedrooms boast views of Lake Hamilton and include an assortment of amenities to assist business travelers. Stay in a romantic room with a whirlpool tub, fireplace, private terrace or deck. Savor a hearty breakfast with homemade breads and delicious entrees made with fresh herbs grown on-site. Hike the many trails of Lake Catherine State Park or explore Hot Springs National Park. Fish on nearby DeGray Lake.

Innkeeper(s): Ray & Kristie Rosset, Tricia Bradley. $125-300. 10 rooms with PB, 7 with FP, 8 with WP, 1 conference room. Breakfast, snacks/refreshments and wine included in rates. Types of meals: Full gourmet bkfst, veg bkfst, early coffee/tea and picnic lunch. Beds: KQT. Modem hook-up, data port, cable TV, VCR, DVD, reading lamp, stereo, ceiling fan, clock radio, telephone, desk, most with hot tub/spa, voice mail, most with fireplace, hair dryer, bathrobes, bath amenities, wireless Internet access, iron/ironing board, Lake view and Desk in room. Central air. Fax, copier, swimming, library, parlor games, gift shop, snack bar, refrigerator, microwave, coffeemaker, canoe, labyrinth, hammock, waterfalls and gardens on premises. Handicap access. Amusement parks, antiquing, art galleries, bicycling, canoeing/kayaking, fishing, golf, hiking, horseback riding, live theater, museums, parks, shopping, tennis, water sports, Music Festivals, Documentary Film Festival and Garvan Woodland Gardens nearby.

Location: Waterfront.

Publicity: *Southern Living (August 2005), Arrington's Inn Traveler magazine ("Top ten B&B/Inns for Rest & Relaxation in North America" - summer 2004), Active Years magazine ("One of the three top B&B/Inns in Arkansas" - May 2004), Arrington's Bed & Breakfast Journal (May 2004), Past Careers Profile, Good Morning and Arkansas (December 2005).*

Certificate may be used: Dec. 1-Jan. 31, Sunday-Thursday, except Dec. 25-Jan. 2.

Kingston   B3

Fool's Cove Ranch B&B

360 Madison 2729
Kingston, AR 72742-2729
(479)665-2986 (866)665-2986 Fax:(479)665-2986
E-mail: foolscoveranch@aol.com

Circa 1979. Situated in the Ozark's Boston Mountain range, this 6000 sq. ft. farmhouse, part of a family farm, offers 130

acres of meadows and forests. Guests may angle for bass or catfish in one of several ponds on the property. Favorite gathering spots are the roomy parlor with large screen TV and the outside deck with a great view of the mountains. Area attractions include the Buffalo National River with canoeing and elk watching, several fine fishing areas and great sightseeing opportunites. The inn is fairly close to Branson, Missouri and Eureka Springs, Arkansas.

Innkeeper(s): Mary Jo & Bill Sullivan. $65-110. 4 rooms, 2 with PB, 1 with WP. Breakfast included in rates. Types of meals: Full bkfst, early coffee/tea and snacks/refreshments. Beds: QD. Reading lamp, ceiling fan, clock radio and wireless Internet access in room. Air conditioning. TV, VCR, DVD, fax, copier, spa, library, pet boarding, parlor games, telephone, fireplace, laundry facility, bird watching, hiking and fishing on premises. Handicap access. Amusement parks, antiquing, canoeing/kayaking, fishing, hiking, horseback riding, live theater, parks, shopping, sporting events and water sports nearby.

Location: Country.

Certificate may be used: May 15 to Dec. 15, Anytime, subject to availability.

California

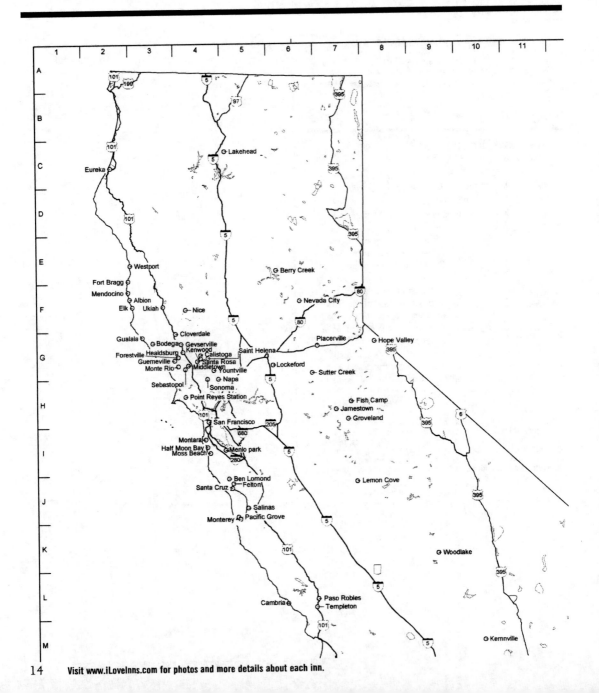

Visit www.iLoveInns.com for photos and more details about each inn.

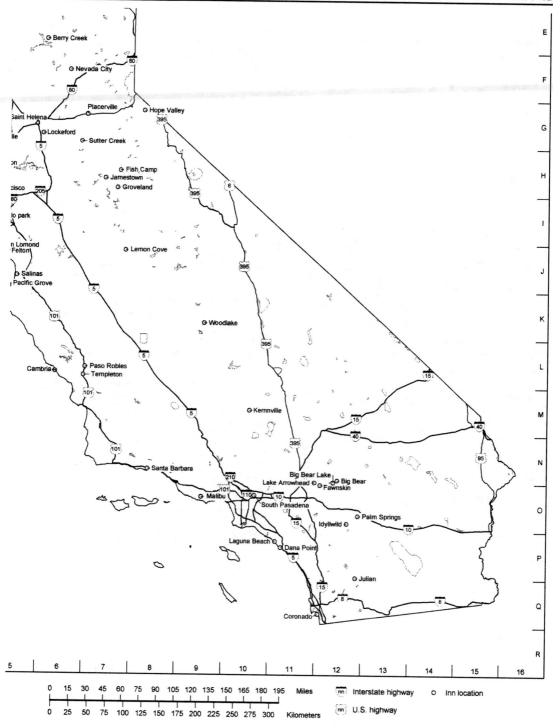

E
F
G
H
I
J
K
L
M
N
O
P
Q
R

G Berry Creek

G Nevada City

80

80

Saint Helena
Placerville
G Hope Valley
395

Lockeford

5 Sutter Creek

G Fish Camp
G Jamestown
G Groveland

395

6

cisco
205
80

lo park
5

n Lomond
Felton

Salinas
Pacific Grove
5

101

G Lemon Cove

395

G Woodlake

395

101

Paso Robles
Templeton
Cambria

101

5

G Kernnville

395

15

5

15

40
95

Santa Barbara

210
101

110
10

Malibu

South Pasadena

15

Idyllwild G

Lake Arrowhead G G Big Bear
Big Bear Lake G Fawnskin

G Palm Springs

10

Laguna Beach G
G Dana Point
5

15
G Julian

8
8

Coronado

5   6   7   8   9   10   11   12   13   14   15   16

0   15   30   45   60   75   90   105 120 135 150 165 180 195   Miles

0   25   50   75   100 125 150 175 200 225 250 275 300   Kilometers

nn   Interstate highway   o   Inn location

nn   U.S. highway

Albion   F2

Fensalden Inn

33810 Navarro Ridge Rd
Albion, CA 95410-0099
(707) 937-4042 (800) 959-3850
Internet: www.fensalden.com
E-mail: inn@fensalden.com

Circa 1860. Originally a stagecoach station, Fensalden looks
out over the Pacific Ocean as it has for more than 100 years.

The Tavern Room has wit-
nessed many a rowdy scene,
and if you look closely you
can see bullet holes in the
original redwood ceiling.
The inn provides 20 acres
for walks, whale-watching,
viewing deer and bicycling.

Relax with wine and hors d'oeuvres in the evening.

Innkeeper(s): Lyn Hamby. $139-253. 8 rooms with PB, 8 with FP, 2 suites,
1 cottage, 2 conference rooms. Breakfast, hors d'oeuvres, wine, Full three
course breakfast each morning and with champagne on Sundays - evening
wine and hors d'oeuvres at 5pm daily - complimentary wine in room upon
arrival included in rates. Types of meals: Full bkfst. Beds: KQ. Reading lamp,
CD player, refrigerator, ceiling fan, clock radio, coffeemaker, fireplace, hair
dryer, bathrobes, wireless Internet access, iron/ironing board and bungalow
has Jacuzzi bathtub in room. Fax, copier, parlor games and telephone on
premises. Handicap access. Antiquing, art galleries, beach, bicycling, canoe-
ing/kayaking, fishing, golf, hiking, horseback riding, live theater, parks, shopping, tennis and wineries nearby.

Location: Country.

Publicity: *Sunset, Focus, Peninsula, Country Inns, Steppin' Out, LA Times,
Vine Times* and 1950s B movie *The Haunting of Hill House.*

"Closest feeling to heaven on Earth."

Certificate may be used: Anytime, November-April, subject to availability in
selected rooms, excluding holidays and special events.

Ben Lomond   J5

Fairview Manor

245 Fairview Ave
Ben Lomond, CA 95005-9347
(831)336-3355
Internet: www.fairviewmanor.com
E-mail: FairviewBandB@comcast.net

Circa 1924. The Santa Cruz Mountains serve as a backdrop at
this private and restful getaway. The inn is surrounded by nearly three acres of park-like wooded gardens. The Redwood
County inn offers comfort and relaxation. The deck off the
Great Room overlooks the San Lorenzo River. Built in the early
1920s, the décor reflects that era. Each of the cozy guest bedrooms boasts a private bath and delightful garden view. Enjoy a
full country breakfast and afternoon snacks. The inn is an
excellent place for family get-togethers as well as small meetings
and outdoor weddings. Beaches, thousands of acres of state
parks and many wineries are nearby.

Innkeeper(s): Gael Glasson Abayon/Jack Hazelton. $149-159. 5 rooms with
PB, 1 conference room. Breakfast, snacks/refreshments, hors d'oeuvres,
wine, Raves for our new Breakfast Menu that could include German Apple
Pancakes, Eggs Benedict, Citrus Slices in ginger or Blueberry Panckes and
just to name a few included in rates. Types of meals: For a nominal charge
and we can assist with picnic lunches and such. Beds: KQT. Reading lamp,
snack bar, desk, some with fireplace, hair dryer, bath amenities, iron/ironing

board and sitting area in room. Parlor games, refrigerator, complimentary
drinks, large deck and acreage on premises. Amusement parks, antiquing, art
galleries, beach, fishing, golf, hiking, museums, parks, shopping, water
sports, wineries, Santa Cruz Beach Boardwalk, Ano Nuevo State Park, Big
Basin State Park and Roaring Camp Railroad nearby.

Location: Country, mountains.

Certificate may be used: Sunday-Thursday.

Big Bear   N12

Gold Mountain Manor Historic B&B

1117 Anita
Big Bear, CA 92314
(909)585-6997 (800)509-2604 Fax:(909)585-0327
Internet: www.goldmountainmanor.com
E-mail: info@goldmountainmanor.com

Circa 1928. This spectacular log mansion was once a hideaway
for the rich and famous. Ten fireplaces provide a roaring fire in
each room in fall and winter. The Presidential Suite offers a
massive rock fireplace embedded with fossils and quartz, facing

the two-person Jacuzzi rock tub and
four-poster bed. In the Clark Gable
room is the fireplace Gable and
Carole Lombard enjoyed on their
honeymoon. Gourmet country
breakfasts and afternoon hors d'oeuvres are served. In addition to the
guest rooms, there are home rentals.

Innkeeper(s): Cathy Weil. $129-259. 7
rooms with PB, 7 with FP, 3 suites, 1 conference room. Afternoon tea and
snacks/refreshments included in rates. Types of meals: Full gourmet bkfst and
early coffee/tea. Beds: Q. Reading lamp, CD player, ceiling fan, clock radio,
desk, some with hot tub/spa, fireplace, hair dryer, bathrobes, bath amenities,
wireless Internet access, Suites have a Jacuzzi and 2 rooms with DVD
Players in room. DVD, fax, spa, library, parlor games, telephone, pool table,
kayaks and wireless Internet on premises. Cross-country skiing, downhill skiing, fishing, parks, water sports, hiking/forest and mountain biking nearby.

Location: Mountains. Forest at end of street.

Publicity: *Best Places to Kiss, Fifty Most Romantic Places* and *Kenny G holiday album cover.*

"A majestic experience! In this magnificent house, history comes alive!"

Certificate may be used: Monday-Thursday, within March 24-Dec.13, no holidays, anytime subject to availability.

Big Bear Lake   N12

Eagle's Nest B&B

41675 Big Bear Blvd, Box 1003
Big Bear Lake, CA 92315
(909)866-6465 (888)866-6465 Fax:(909)866-6025
Internet: www.eaglesnestlodgebigbear.com
E-mail: stay@eaglesnestlodgebigbear.com

Circa 1983. Poised amid the tall pines of the San Bernardino
Mountains in Big Bear Lake, California, Eagle's Nest Bed and
Breakfast Lodge and Cottage Suites offers four seasons of relaxing comfort and hospitality. Accommodations in the Ponderosa-
style log lodge include guest rooms with gas or electric fireplaces. Gather for a hearty breakfast in the dining area each
morning. The secluded log cabin cottage suites boast river rock
fireplaces, microwaves, mini-refrigerators and other amenities
for a pleasing stay. This B&B is conveniently located near the
lake, shops, restaurants and local ski resorts. Take day trips to
the many Southern California attractions.

Innkeeper(s): Mark & Vicki Tebo. $110-130. 5 rooms with PB, 3 with FP. Breakfast and snacks/refreshments included in rates. Types of meals: Country bkfst. Beds: Q. Cable TV, reading lamp, ceiling fan, clock radio and fireplace in room. VCR, fax, parlor games, telephone and fireplace on premises. Antiquing, bicycling, canoeing/kayaking, cross-country skiing, downhill skiing, fishing, golf, hiking, horseback riding, live theater, parks, shopping, water sports, mountain biking, rock climbing and movie theatres nearby.

Location: Mountains.

"Each breakfast was delicious and beautiful. A lot of thought and care is obvious in everything you do."

Certificate may be used: Anytime except holidays and weekends from Dec. 15-April 15, subject to availability.

Knickerbocker Mansion Country Inn

869 Knickerbocker Rd
Big Bear Lake, CA 92315
(909)878-9190 (877)423-1180 Fax:(909)878-4248
Internet: www.knickerbockermansion.com
E-mail: knickmail@knickerbockermansion.com

Circa 1920. Knickerbocker Mansion Country Inn sits on more than two acres overlooking Big Bear Lake and the forest. This historic California B&B has four buildings with accommodations in the three-story main house and converted carriage house. Gather by the rock fireplace in the living room of the historic log main lodge, nap in a hammock, play croquet or hike the scenic area. The back yard borders the San Bernardino National Forest and the wraparound deck offers spectacular tree-top views. Stay in a guest room or luxury suite with a fireplace and spa tub. Savor a two-course breakfast in the dining room or on the back patio. Bistro at the Mansion opens for dining on Friday and Saturday nights with comfort food creations by Chef Thomas.

Innkeeper(s): Stanley Miller & Thomas Bicanic. $110-280. 12 rooms with PB, 2 with FP, 2 with WP, 2 total suites, including 1 two-bedroom suite, 1 conference room. Breakfast included in rates. Types of meals: Full gourmet bkfst, veg bkfst, early coffee/tea, picnic lunch, snacks/refreshments, wine and gourmet dinner. Restaurant on premises. Beds: KQ. Modem hook-up, data port, cable TV, VCR, DVD, reading lamp, stereo, refrigerator, ceiling fan, clock radio, telephone, coffeemaker, desk, some with hot tub/spa, voice mail, some with fireplace, hair dryer, bathrobes, bath amenities, wireless Internet access and iron/ironing board in room. Fax, copier, library, parlor games and gift shop on premises. Handicap access. Antiquing, art galleries, bicycling, canoeing/kayaking, cross-country skiing, downhill skiing, fishing, golf, hiking, horseback riding, live theater, museums, parks, shopping, tennis and water sports nearby.

Location: Mountains. Winter Ski Resort.

Publicity: *Los Angeles Magazine, Yellow Brick Road, San Bernardino Sun and Daily Press.*

"Best breakfast I ever had in a setting of rustic elegance, a quiet atmosphere and personal attention from the innkeepers. The moment you arrive you will realize the Knickerbocker is a very special place."

Certificate may be used: Sunday-Thursday, non-holiday, subject to availability and prior booking.

Bodega   G3

Sonoma Coast Villa Inn & Spa

16702 Coast Highway One
Bodega, CA 94922
(707)876-9818 (888)404-2255 Fax:(707)876-9856
Internet: www.scvilla.com
E-mail: reservations@scvilla.com

Circa 1976. Experience a taste of the Mediterranean and Old World Tuscany after a drive past the ocean, vineyards and rural countryside through the cypress tree-lined, 200-foot drive to this amazing terra cotta stucco villa. Secluded and luxurious, this red-tile roofed B&B resort offers 60 acres of pleasurable serenity. Choose a standard country or deluxe villa room with a private deck or courtyard, fireplace and double-size jetted tub. Classic junior suites also are available. A nine-hole putting green prepares the golfer for a game nearby. Play billiards, ping pong or read a book in the Tower Library. Swim in the pool, or relax in the courtyard spa.

Innkeeper(s): Johannes Zachbauer. $175-365. 18 rooms with PB, 18 with FP, 2 conference rooms. Breakfast and snacks/refreshments included in rates. Types of meals: Country bkfst, wine, gourmet dinner and room service. Restaurant on premises. Beds: KQT. Cable TV, VCR, reading lamp, CD player, refrigerator, clock radio, telephone, coffeemaker, desk, most with hot tub/spa, voice mail, fireplace, hair dryer, bathrobes, bath amenities and iron/ironing board in room. Fax, spa, swimming, library, pet boarding, parlor games, gift shop, nine-hole putting green, courtyard spa and pool table & horseback riding on property on premises. Handicap access. Antiquing, art galleries, beach, bicycling, canoeing/kayaking, fishing, golf, hiking, horseback riding, parks, shopping, water sports and wineries nearby.

Location: Country. Located on 60 acres of rolling hills and pasture land just 5 miles from the Pacific Ocean.

Publicity: *Diablo Magazine, San Jose Magazine, San Francisco Magazine, Allure Magazine, Sky West Magazine, Inns & Retreats Magazine, The Business Journal, New York Times, Sunset, John Travolta, Sylvester Stalone, Senator Tip O'Neil and Robert Duval and Rebecca DeMornay have been our guests.*

Certificate may be used: Sunday-Thursday (Junior Suite $245)offer cannot be combined with any other offers or discounts.

Calistoga   G4

Brannan Cottage Inn

109 Wapoo Ave
Calistoga, CA 94515-1136
(707) 942-4200 Fax:(707)942-2507
Internet: www.brannancottageinn.com
E-mail: brannancottageinn@sbcglobal.net

Circa 1860. This Greek Revival cottage was built as a guest house for the old Calistoga Hot Springs Resort. Behind a white picket fence towers the original palm tree planted by Sam Brannan and noted by Robert Louis Stevenson in his "Silverado Squatters." Five graceful arches, an intricate gingerbread gableboard, and unusual scalloped ridge cresting make this a charming holiday house. Six spacious guest  rooms feature down comforters; three have four-poster beds. Guests enjoy a full breakfast and evening wine and cheese.

Innkeeper(s): Doug & Judy Cook. $160-280. 6 rooms with PB, 5 with FP, 2 suites, 1 conference room. Breakfast, Guest local winery tastings with hors d'oeuvres provided on Fridays (5:30 to 7 pm) and check Web site for schedule included in rates. Types of meals: Full gourmet bkfst, veg bkfst, early coffee/tea and Above breakfast choices offered to guests. Picnic lunches prepared by request at additional cost. Can provide catered dinners to guests at extra cost. Beds: QDT. Cable TV, reading lamp, refrigerator, ceiling fan, clock radio, hair dryer, bath amenities, wireless Internet access, iron/ironing board, Free WI-FI and Mini suites (only) with TV. Hot tub/spa at nearby (3 blocks) resort in room. Air conditioning. DVD, fax, copier, library, parlor games, telephone, fireplace, gift shop and Office equipment (by prior arrangement) on premises. Limited handicap access. Amusement parks, antiquing, art galleries, beach, bicycling, fishing, golf, hiking, horseback riding, live theater, museums, parks, shopping, tennis, wineries, Wineries, The Petrified Forest, The Old Faithful Geyser of California, Access to pool & geothermal mineral springs jacuzzi tubs at the Golden Haven Hot Springs (3 blocks away) and Tennis and handball and basketball courts(1 block away) nearby.

Location: Country. Wine country, Napa Valley.

Publicity: *Food Network ("Tasting Napa").*

Certificate may be used: Anytime, November-March on weekdays, subject to availability.

Chelsea Garden Inn

1443 2nd St
Calistoga, CA 94515-1419
(707)942-0948 (800)942-1515 Fax:(707)942-5102
Internet: www.chelseagardeninn.com
E-mail: innkeeper@chelseagardeninn.com

Circa 1940. Located in the heart of Napa Valley, this delightfully different California-style inn features two-room suites with fireplaces and private entrances. The romantic ground-level Palm Suite has a large sitting room with fireplace, additional Queen bed and library. The adjoining Lavender Suite is perfect for couples traveling together. Named for its view of the mountains, the second-floor Palisades Suite boasts a four-poster bed and a small balcony overlooking the pool. A full gourmet breakfast is served in the dining room or garden with fresh-brewed coffee from a local roastery. Enjoy afternoon hors d'oeuvres. Explore the extensive gardens with grapevines, flowers, fruit and nut trees. Swim in the pool (seasonal) or relax by the fire in the social room. Visit local shops, wineries, museums, spas, art galleries and restaurants just two blocks away.

Innkeeper(s): Dave and Susan DeVries. $160-275. 5 rooms with PB, 5 with FP, 3 suites, 1 cottage, 1 conference room. Breakfast and hors d'oeuvres included in rates. Types of meals: Full gourmet bkfst, veg bkfst, early coffee/tea and snacks/refreshments. Beds: KQDT. Modem hook-up, cable TV, VCR, DVD, reading lamp, stereo, refrigerator, ceiling fan, clock radio, coffeemaker, desk, fireplace, hair dryer, bathrobes, bath amenities, wireless Internet access, iron/ironing board, Central heating, Microwave and Video library in room. Central air. Fax, copier, swimming, library, parlor games, telephone, laundry facility, Guest computer, Complimentary Wi-Fi, Social room with vaulted ceiling, Gardens, Office telephone with free local calls, Wine tasting coupons and Concierge service on premises. Limited handicap access. Amusement parks, antiquing, art galleries, bicycling, canoeing/kayaking, fishing, golf, hiking, horseback riding, live theater, museums, parks, shopping, tennis, water sports, wineries, mud baths, massage, ballooning, glider rides and natural wonders and historical sites nearby.

Location: Country. Small town in the Wine Country.

Publicity: *Sunset Magazine, Access Press and The Best Places to Kiss in Northern California.*

Certificate may be used: November-April, Monday-Wednesday. Valid only on rooms at $225 or more.

Coronado

Cherokee Lodge

964 D Avenue
Coronado, CA 92118
(619)437-1967 Fax:(619)437-1012
Internet: www.cherokeelodge.com
E-mail: info@cherokeelodge.com

Experience the delights of Coronado Island while staying at this bed and breakfast located just one block from downtown and four blocks from the beach. Named after the Cherokee roses that framed the property in the late 1800s, it is steeped in history. There are common areas to relax in and one offers a computer to use as well as wireless high-speed Internet. Enjoy comfortable, smoke-free accommodations with a choice of twelve guest bedrooms that feature VCRs and refrigerators. A washer and dryer are available. A continental breakfast is provided daily. Walk to nearby bistros and restaurants.

Innkeeper(s): Phyllis. Call for rates. 12 rooms with PB. Free continental breakfast at a local diner included in rates. Types of meals: Cont and Breakfast vouchers are provided for a free continental breakfast at a local diner. Coffee and tea are in each room. Beds: KQDT. Modem hook-up, data port, cable TV, VCR, reading lamp, refrigerator, ceiling fan, clock radio, telephone, coffeemaker, desk, hair dryer, bath amenities, wireless Internet access, iron/ironing board, Free telephone calls within the United States & most countries, Regular & decaf coffee and tea in all rooms in room. Air conditioning. Fax, copier, laundry facility and future handicap room on premises. Limited handicap access. Amusement parks, antiquing, art galleries, beach, bicycling, canoeing/kayaking, fishing, golf, hiking, horseback riding, live theater, museums, parks, shopping, sporting events, tennis, water sports, wineries, sailing and kite surfing among locally available water sports nearby.

Location: City, ocean community.

Certificate may be used: October-May, anytime subject to availability, no holidays.

Dana Point

Blue Lantern Inn

34343 Street of the Blue Lantern
Dana Point, CA 92629
(949)661-1304 (800)950-1236 Fax:(949)496-1483
Internet: www.bluelanterninn.com
E-mail: bluelanterninn@foursisters.com

Circa 1990. Blue Lantern Inn is situated high on a blufftop overlooking a stunning coastline and the blue waters of Dana Point harbor with its pleasure craft, fishing boats and the tall ship, Pilgrim. Each guest bedroom of  this four-diamond inn features both a fireplace and a whirlpool tub and many offer private sun decks. Afternoon tea, evening turndown service and bicycles are just a few of the amenities available. In the evening, wine and hors d'oeuvres are served. Shops, restaurants and beaches are nearby, and popular Laguna Beach, California is just a few miles to the north. Blue Lantern is one of the Four Sisters Inns.

Innkeeper(s): Lin McMahon. $175-600. 29 rooms with PB, 29 with FP, 2 conference rooms. Breakfast, afternoon tea, snacks/refreshments, hors d'oeuvres and wine included in rates. Types of meals: Full gourmet bkfst. Beds: KQ. Modem hook-up, data port, cable TV, VCR, reading lamp, stereo, refrigerator, ceiling fan, snack bar, clock radio, telephone, coffeemaker, turn-down service, desk, hot tub/spa, voice mail, fireplace, hair dryer, bathrobes, bath amenities, iron/ironing board, signature breakfast, afternoon wine and hors d'oeuvres, morning newspaper delivery, complimentary sodas and home-baked cookies in room. Central air. Bicycles, library, parlor games, gift shop, complimentary parking and gym on premises. Handicap access. Amusement parks, antiquing, art galleries, beach, bicycling, canoeing/kayaking, fishing, golf, hiking, horseback riding, live theater, museums, parks, shopping, water sports, beach and Dana Point Harbor nearby.

Location: Ocean community, waterfront.

Certificate may be used: Sunday–Thursday, December-February, based on promotional discount availability and excludes special event periods, holidays and certain room types. First night must be at full rack rate to receive second night free.

Elk   F3

Greenwood Pier Inn

5926 S Highway 1
Elk, CA 95432
(707)877-9997 (800)807-3423 Fax:(707)877-1802
Internet: www.greenwoodpierinn.com
E-mail: gwpier@mcn.org

Feel immersed in the expansive views of the Mendocino Coast and the Pacific Ocean while staying at Greenwood Pier Inn in Elk, California. The grounds are accented with colorful gardens and include a hot tub on a cliff for a relaxing soak. Walk along the wide sandy beach of the nearby state park. Schedule in advance an in-room therapeutic or herbal facial massage. Stay in a guest room or suite in the main house or multi-level accommodations in a redwood cabin or converted high rise water tower. Amenities may include a two-person Jacuzzi, private deck, water view and kitchenette. Some rooms are designated pet friendly. A continental breakfast is delivered to each room every morning. Browse the garden shop and country store and linger over a meal in the Greenwood Pier Café.

$150-350. 15 rooms with PB. Beds: KQ. CD player, refrigerator, coffeemaker, fireplace, bath amenities, Great ocean views, Private decks and Microwaves available in several rooms in room. TV, telephone, Hot tub on deck and In-house wedding coordinator on premises.

Publicity: *Arts & Entertainment Magazine, Coastal Living, USAir Magazine, Weekends for Two in Northern California and Country Inns Bed & Breakfast.*

Certificate may be used: Nov. 1-March 30, Sunday-Thursday, no holidays, subject to availability.

Eureka   C2

Carter House Inns

301 L St
Eureka, CA 95501
(707)444-8062 (800)404-1390 Fax:(707)444-8067
Internet: www.carterhouse.com
E-mail: reserve@carterhouse.com

Circa 1884. Superior hospitality is offered in these Victorian inns that grace the historic district. Perched alongside Humboldt Bay, blissfully relax amid appealing views. Carter House Inns in Eureka, California boasts luxurious guest rooms and suites that feature fireplaces, antique furnishings and spas. Begin each morning with a highly acclaimed breakfast. Renowned for regional, seasonal cuisine, many ingredients are grown in the garden or bought from local purveyors. Restaurant 301 boasts a coveted international Wine Spectator Grand

Award, maintaining in its cellars an extensive collection of the world's finest vintages.

Innkeeper(s): Audrey Archibald - mgr. $155-615. 32 rooms with PB, 11 with FP, 7 with HT, 6 with WP, 9 total suites, including 2 two-bedroom suites, 2 cottages, 1 conference room. Breakfast, afternoon tea, hors d'oeuvres and wine included in rates. Types of meals: Full gourmet bkfst, early coffee/tea, snacks/refreshments, gourmet dinner and room service. Restaurant on premises. Beds: KQDT. Cable TV, VCR, DVD, reading lamp, stereo, refrigerator, snack bar, clock radio, telephone, turn-down service, desk, some with hot tub/spa, voice mail, some with fireplace, hair dryer, bathrobes, bath amenities, wireless Internet access and iron/ironing board in room. Fax, copier, spa, bedtime tea & cookies and wine & hors d'oeuvres before dinner available on premises. Handicap access. Antiquing, fishing, live theater, parks, shopping, sporting events, water sports and beaches nearby.

Location: Ocean community, waterfront.

Publicity: *Sunset, U.S. News & World Report, Country Home, Country Living, Bon Appetit, San Francisco Focus, Northwest Palate, Gourmet, Art Culinare, San Francisco Chronicle, Wine Spectator, New York Times Magazine and Organic Gardening.*

Certificate may be used: Anytime, November-April, subject to availability.

Ships Inn Bed and Breakfast

821 D St
Eureka, CA 95501-1711
(707)443-7583 (877)443-7583 Fax:(707)443-6215
Internet: www.shipsinn.net
E-mail: genie@shipsinn.net

Circa 1887. Built by a master ship builder for a sea captain in 1882, this Victorian bed and breakfast is accented with a nautical décor. It is located just blocks from the quaint Old Town and the new Boardwalk. Relax, read or play games in the Fireside Room with a writing deck and soft music playing in the background. On the first Saturday evening of each month an Arts Alive! reception is held for a local artist or photographer and the artwork hangs in the gallery all month. Each guest bedroom features a private bath, TV, VCR and robes. Stay in the spacious Captain's Quarters, the fantasy Rose Garden Room or the Mission Room with DSL modem. Savor breakfast served in the dining room with general seating or provided in-room.

Innkeeper(s): Genie Wood. $130-175. 3 rooms with PB, 2 suites. Breakfast included in rates. Types of meals: Full bkfst, veg bkfst and early coffee/tea. Beds: KQ. Modem hook-up, data port, cable TV, VCR, reading lamp, refrigerator, ceiling fan, clock radio, telephone, coffeemaker, turn-down service, desk, fireplace, hair dryer, bathrobes, bath amenities, iron/ironing board, turndown service with ice water and chocolates each evening and down comforters in room. Fax, copier, library, parlor games and featured work by a different artist or photographer each month on premises. Antiquing, art galleries, beach, bicycling, canoeing/kayaking, fishing, golf, hiking, live theater, museums, parks, shopping and wineries nearby.

Location: City, waterfront. The Victorian Seaport.

Certificate may be used: Sept. 15-Dec.15, excluding holidays, Jan. 5-Feb.10, Must mention this promotion up front.

Fawnskin   N12

Inn At Fawnskin

880 Canyon Rd
Fawnskin, CA 92333
(909)866-3200 (888)329-6754 Fax:(909)878-2249
Internet: www.fawnskininn.com
E-mail: innatfawnskin@charter.net

Circa 1976. Listen to the quiet at this contemporary log home on an acre with scores of pine trees. The inn is located across the street from the North Shore of Big Bear Lake. It has four guest bedrooms and is decorated in elegant country style with antiques and reproductions. The large master suite has a rock fireplace, a sitting area and a private balcony that overlooks the lake. Guests are free to use the living room (with its large rock fireplace), TV/VCR/DVD and dining room. A country breakfast is served on china in the dining room. The meal includes such delicacies as fresh peaches, a brie and ham omelette with maple-smoked bacon, fresh-squeezed orange juice and freshly-ground coffee. The inn is minutes from boating, fishing, biking trails, ski areas, shops and restaurants. Guests enjoy moonlight walks by the lake and skies filled with stars. Guests who listen carefully may be rewarded by hearing innkeeper Nancy, who once sang at the White House, singing as she creates a perfect atmosphere for guests to relax and unwind.

Innkeeper(s): Nancy & Bill Hazewinkel. $135-285. 5 rooms with PB, 4 with FP, 3 suites, 6 cabins. Breakfast included in rates. Types of meals: Full gourmet bkfst, veg bkfst, early coffee/tea, snacks/refreshments, hors d'oeuvres and wine. Beds: KQ. Cable TV, VCR, DVD, reading lamp, CD player, refrigerator, ceiling fan, clock radio, desk, hot tub/spa and fireplace in room. Fax, copier, spa, parlor games and gift shop on premises. Limited handicap access. Antiquing, art galleries, bicycling, canoeing/kayaking, cross-country skiing, downhill skiing, fishing, golf, hiking, horseback riding, live theater, museums, parks, shopping and water sports nearby.

Location: Mountains.

Publicity: *LA Times, Inland Empire magazine and Valley Messenger.*

Certificate may be used: Sunday-Thursday, non-holiday.

Forestville   G4

Case Ranch Inn B&B

7446 Poplar Dr.
Forestville, CA 95436
(707)887-8711 (877)887-8711 Fax:(707)887-8607
Internet: www.caseranchinn.com
E-mail: diana@caseranchinn.com

Circa 1894. Enjoy a peaceful respite in the Russian River Valley (quietly secluded between Healdsburg and Guerneville) and surrounding wine country at this Sonoma County Historic Landmark. The inn offers personalized service and warm hospitality in an intimate setting. Relax by the fireplace in the large parlor or on the wicker-filled wraparound porch. Beverages are available any time at the self-serve bar in the dining room. Stay in one of the guest suites in the Victorian main house or in the private luxury cottage with upscale amenities that are sure to pamper and please. Breakfasts are made with natural and organic ingredients. Dietary needs are easily accommodated. Stroll the pleasant two-acre setting with a deck, gazebo, pond and fountain bordered by flower gardens.

Innkeeper(s): Diana Van Ry & Allan Tilton. $180-240. 4 rooms, 1 with FP, 1 with HT, 4 suites, 1 cottage. Breakfast and snacks/refreshments included in rates. Types of meals: Full gourmet bkfst and early coffee/tea. Beds: Q. Modem hook-up, cable TV, VCR, DVD, reading lamp, CD player, refrigerator, ceiling fan, clock radio, telephone, coffeemaker, some with hot tub/spa, hair dryer, bathrobes, bath amenities, wireless Internet access, iron/ironing board, high-speed digital cable in all rooms and complimentary sherry available in room. Central air. Fax, spa, parlor games, fireplace and Electric Vehicle (EV) charging station on site for guests' use on premises. Limited handicap access. Antiquing, art galleries, beach, bicycling, canoeing/kayaking, fishing, golf, hiking, horseback riding, live theater, museums, parks, shopping, tennis, wineries, Sonoma Coast and Armstrong Woods Redwood Preserve nearby.

Location: Country, mountains.

Publicity: *Www.gonomad.com and S.F. Chronicle "Follow the Reader"*

Certificate may be used: November-March, Sunday-Thursday.

Fort Bragg   E2

Country Inn

632 N Main St
Fort Bragg, CA 95437-3220
(707)964-3737 (800)831-5327 Fax:(707)964-0289
Internet: www.beourguests.com
E-mail: cntryinn@mcn.org

Circa 1893. The Union Lumber Company once owned this two-story townhouse built of native redwood. It features rooms with slanted and peaked ceilings, and several rooms have fireplaces. Camellia trees, flower boxes, and a picket fence accent the landscaping, while two blocks away a railroad carries visitors on excursions through the redwoods.

Innkeeper(s): Cynthia & Bruce Knauss. $55-145. 8 rooms with PB, 2 with FP. Breakfast and wine included in rates. Types of meals: Full gourmet bkfst, early coffee/tea and room service. Beds: KQ. Clock radio, some with fireplace, hair dryer, bath amenities, wireless Internet access and iron/ironing board in room. Spa, parlor games and telephone on premises. Handicap access. Antiquing, art galleries, beach, bicycling, canoeing/kayaking, fishing, golf, hiking, horseback riding, live theater, museums, parks, shopping, tennis, water sports, wineries, Botanical Gardens and Skunk Train nearby.

Location: Country, ocean community.

Certificate may be used: Anytime subject to availability, Sunday-Thursday.

Glass Beach B&B

726 N Main St
Fort Bragg, CA 95437-3017
(707)964-6774
Internet: www.glassbeachinn.com
E-mail: glassbeachinn@hotmail.com

Circa 1920. Each of the guest rooms at this Craftsman-style home is decorated in a different theme and named to reflect the decor. The Malaysian and Oriental Jade rooms reflect Asian artistry, while the Forget-Me-Not and Victorian Rose rooms are bright, feminine rooms with walls decked in floral prints. Antiques are found throughout the home and the back cottage, which includes three of the inn's nine guest rooms. The inn also offers a hot tub for guest use. Breakfasts are served in the inn's dining room, but guests are free to take a tray and enjoy the meal in the privacy of their own room.

Innkeeper(s): Nancy Cardenas/RichardFowler. $60-195. 9 rooms with PB, 4 with FP, 1 suite, 1 cottage. Breakfast and snacks/refreshments included in rates. Types of meals: Country bkfst, afternoon tea and room service. Beds: Q. Cable TV, VCR, reading lamp, refrigerator, clock radio, hot tub/spa and fireplace in room. Spa, parlor games and telephone on premises. Handicap access. Antiquing, art galleries, beach, bicycling, canoeing/kayaking, fishing, golf, hiking, horseback riding, live theater, museums, parks, shopping, water sports, wineries and scuba diving nearby.

Location: City, ocean community.

Certificate may be used: Jan. 5-June 4, Oct. 1-Dec. 31, Sunday-Thursday. Most holidays excluded.

Geyserville   G4

Hope-Merrill House

21253 Geyserville Ave.
Geyserville, CA 95441-9637
(707) 857-3356 (800) 825-4233 Fax:(707)857-4673
Internet: www.hope-inns.com
E-mail: moreinfo@hope-inns.com

Circa 1870. The Hope-Merrill House is a classic example of

the Eastlake Stick style that was so popular during Victorian times. Built entirely from redwood, the house features original wainscoting and silk-screened wallcoverings. A swimming pool, vineyard and gazebo are favorite spots for guests to relax. The Hope-Bosworth House, on the same street, was built in 1904 in the Queen Anne style by an early Geyserville pioneer who lived in the home until the 1960s. The front picket fence is covered with roses. Period details include oak woodwork, sliding doors, polished fir floors and antique light fixtures.

Innkeeper(s): Cosette & Ron Scheiber. $149-289. 8 rooms with PB, 4 with FP, 2 with WP, 1 suite. Breakfast included in rates. Types of meals: Full gourmet bkfst, veg bkfst, early coffee/tea, picnic lunch, wine and Gluten free. Beds: Q. Reading lamp, ceiling fan, desk, some with fireplace, hair dryer and wireless Internet access in room. Air conditioning. Fax, copier, telephone, coffee, tea and hot chocolate available 24 hours a day on premises. Antiquing, parks, shopping, water sports, wineries and redwoods nearby.

Location: Country. Wine country.

Publicity: *New York Times, San Francisco Chronicle, San Diego Union, Country Homes, Sunset, Sacramento Union, Los Angeles Times and Bay Area Back Roads.*

Certificate may be used: From Dec. 1-March 31 anyday, Monday-Thursday April 1-Nov. 30.

Groveland   H7

Hotel Charlotte

18736 Main Street
Groveland, CA 95321
(209)962-6455 Fax:(209)962-6254
Internet: www.HotelCharlotte.com
E-mail: HotelCharlotte@aol.com

Circa 1921. Gracing one acre in the Sierra Nevada Mountains of California, the Hotel Charlotte is on the way to Yosemite near Stanislaus National Forest. Find entertainment in the game room or relax on the balcony overlooking the gold rush town of Groveland. Beverages are usually available at any time. Listed in the National Register, this bed and breakfast hotel provides comfortable and convenient accommodations. Air-conditioned guest bedrooms feature new, soundproof windows and a variety of sleeping arrangements. Several rooms boast a clawfoot tub, one room with a spa tub. Enjoy a buffet breakfast in the morning. Café Charlotte, the onsite full-service restaurant and bar, offers good food and spirits.

Innkeeper(s): Lynn & Victor. $99-199. 10 rooms with PB, 1 with FP, 1 with WP, 2 two-bedroom suites, 7 guest houses. Breakfast, Daily pancake and scrambled eggs & sausage buffet breakfast included in rates. Types of meals: Country bkfst, veg bkfst, Sun. brunch, early coffee/tea, picnic lunch, wine, dinner, On-site restaurant popular with locals is open 7 days a week from 11:30 to 3:30 for lunch and and from 5:30 to Close for dinner. Special needs from dietary restrictions to picnic baskets to go can be accommodated. Restaurant on premises. Beds: QDT. Modem hook-up, data port, cable TV, reading lamp, refrigerator, telephone, hair dryer, bath amenities, wireless Internet access, All rooms have Wi-Fi Access, DISH television & telephones, Some rooms have microwave, refrigerator & VCR; Hair driers, Alarm clocks and irons available from the front desk in room. Central air. DVD, fax, copier, library, parlor games, laundry facility, Shared balcony, Ice machine for guests, Almost anytime beverage service (coffee, tea and iced tea) on premises. Limited handicap access. Antiquing, art galleries, beach, bicycling, canoeing/kayaking, cross-country skiing, fishing, golf, hiking, horseback riding, live theater, museums, parks, shopping, tennis, water sports, wineries, Whitewater river rafting, Yosemite National Park & Hetch Hetchy Reservoir, Stanislaus National Forest, Mono Lake, Gold Country and Gold Panning, Foothills Wineries and Wine Tasting, Casino and Hunting nearby.

Location: Country, mountains. Yosemite.

Publicity: *Www.tripadvisor.com rates us as number one in Groveland for both our hotel and restaurant.*

Certificate may be used: Nov. 2-April 2, Sunday-Thursday, all holidays excluded.

The Groveland Hotel at Yosemite National Park

18767 Main St.
Groveland, CA 95321-0289
(209) 962-4000 (800) 273-3314 Fax:(209)962-6674
Internet: www.groveland.com
E-mail: guestservices@groveland.com

Circa 1849. Located 23 miles from Yosemite National Park, the 1992 restoration features both an 1849 adobe building with 18-inch-thick walls constructed during the Gold Rush and a 1914 building erected to house workers for the Hetch Hetchy Dam. Both feature two-story balconies. There is a Victorian parlor, a gourmet restaurant and a Western saloon. Guest  rooms feature European antiques, down comforters, some feather beds, in-room coffee, phones with data ports, and hair dryers. The feeling is one of casual elegance.

Innkeeper(s): Peggy & Grover Mosley. $145-285. 17 rooms with PB, 3 with FP, 3 with WP, 3 suites, 1 conference room. Breakfast and Full Breakfast included in rates. Types of meals: Country bkfst, veg bkfst, early coffee/tea, picnic lunch, wine, gourmet dinner, room service and Cellar Door Restaurant features gourmet California cuisine. . Restaurant on premises. Beds: KQT. Modem hook-up, data port, cable TV, reading lamp, CD player, ceiling fan, clock radio, telephone, coffeemaker, desk, some with hot tub/spa, voice mail, some with fireplace, hair dryer, bathrobes, bath amenities, wireless Internet access, iron/ironing board, Our in-room coffee features fresh beans with grinders, all rooms have period antiques, feather beds with down comforters and 600-thread count luxury linens and Our bath robes are plush and comfortable in room. Central air. VCR, fax, copier, parlor games, gift shop, Spa services, Special in-room extras for additional fees and Handicap access to some rooms on premises. Handicap access. Antiquing, art galleries, bicycling, canoeing/kayaking, cross-country skiing, downhill skiing, fishing, golf, hiking, horseback riding, live theater, museums, parks, shopping, tennis, water sports, wineries, Live Summer Entertainment through the Yosemite Courtyard Cabaret (open air theater), Jazz & blues, Country music, Big band, Popular music, Tributes to famous stars, Historical dramas (Open weekends from May through September), Yosemite National Park (23 miles), Tuolumne River world class White Water Rafting, Caverns to explore, Spelunking, Gold panning, Historic towns to explore, Art gallery, Mountain Sage Coffee House and The Iron Door Saloon: the oldest continuously operating Saloon in California (right next door) featuring live music nearby.

Location: Country, mountains.

Publicity: *Sonora Union Democrat, Los Angeles Times, Penninsula, Sunset (February 2001-West's Best Inns), Stockton Record, Country Inns Magazine (Top 10 Inns in U.S.), Men's Journal Magazine, 25 Best Hideaways, Associated Press, Huell Howser's California's Gold "Roads Go Through" (Episode #9002), Peter Greenburg for The Today Show's Halloweens Scariest Inns (October 2008) and Wine Spectator Award of Excellence for our wine list.*

Certificate may be used: Oct. 15-April 15, Sunday-Thursday, excluding holidays.

Gualala   G4

Breakers Inn

39300 Old Highway 1
Gualala, CA 93445
(707)884-3200
Internet: www.breakersinn.com
E-mail: info@breakersinn.com

Breathtaking views of the water are seen from these accommodations that are poised on a bluff overlooking the Gualala River and the Pacific Ocean. The location is great for a visit to

Sonoma and the Mendocino Coast in scenic Northern California. Elegantly furnished and custom designed with a European flair, there is radiant floor heat, artwork and private decks. Stay in a delightful guest room that boasts a regional theme and features a whirlpool spa, fireplace, DVD player, wet bar, microwave and a refrigerator. Start each day with a continental breakfast in the lobby before embarking on the day's adventures. Peruse the local menus available to help choose a restaurant for dinner.

Innkeeper(s): Rick & Sue Callahan. Call for rates. 28 rooms with PB, 27 with FP, 25 with WP, 4 suites. Breakfast, afternoon tea and snacks/refreshments included in rates. Types of meals: Cont plus and early coffee/tea. Beds: KQ. Modem hook-up, cable TV, VCR, DVD, reading lamp, refrigerator, clock radio, telephone, coffeemaker, desk, voice mail, fireplace, hair dryer, bath amenities, wireless Internet access, Large decks, radiant floor heating, fine furnishings and artwork, wet bars and irons and ironing boards in room. Fax, copier, spa and sauna on premises. Handicap access. Art galleries, beach, bicycling, canoeing/kayaking, fishing, golf, hiking, horseback riding, live theater, parks, shopping, water sports and wineries nearby.

Certificate may be used: Nov. 15-Feb. 28, Sunday-Thursday, holiday weeks excluded.

Guerneville   G3

Fern Grove Cottages

16650 Highway 116
Guerneville, CA 95446-9678
(707)869-8105 (888)243-2674
Internet: www.ferngrove.com
E-mail: innkeepers@ferngrove.com

Clustered in a village-like atmosphere and surrounded by redwoods, these craftsman cottages have romantic fireplaces, private entrances, and are individually decorated. The cottages were built in the 1920s and served as little vacation houses for San Francisco families visiting the Russian River. Some units have a kitchen or wet bar, some have double whirlpool tubs and other cottages are suitable for families. Guests enjoy use of the swimming pool. The cottages are just a few blocks from shops and restaurants, as well as a swimming beach on the river. Visit a nearby redwood state reserve or the Russian River Valley wineries for wine tasting and tours.

Innkeeper(s): Mike & Margaret Kennett. $89-259. 20 cottages with PB, 14 with FP, 1 conference room. Breakfast included in rates. Types of meals: Cont plus and Wines By The Fireside during winter months: on non-event Saturdays. Beds: KQ. Cable TV, VCR, DVD, reading lamp, CD player, refrigerator, clock radio, coffeemaker, some with fireplace, hair dryer and wireless Internet access in room. Swimming, telephone, guest barbeque and picnic/eating area on premises. Limited handicap access. Antiquing, art galleries, beach, bicycling, canoeing/kayaking, fishing, golf, hiking, horseback riding, live theater, museums, parks, shopping, tennis, water sports, wineries, Armstrong Redwood State Reserve, Ocean beaches and Surfing nearby.

Location: River and vineyards.

Certificate may be used: Anytime, November-March, event and holidays excluded, subject to availability.

Half Moon Bay   I4

Landis Shores Oceanfront Inn

211 Mirada Rd
Half Moon Bay, CA 94019
(650)726-6642 Fax:(650)726-6644
Internet: www.landisshores.com
E-mail: luxury@landisshores.com

Circa 1999. Luxuriate in pampered pleasure at this

Contemporary Mediterranean bed & breakfast inn overlooking Miramar Beach. Guest bedrooms boast impressive extras that include binoculars, private balconies, fireplaces, robes, radiant heated floors, a generous assortment of personal grooming amenities and mini-refrigerators with bottled water. Marble or granite bathrooms feature whirlpools and separate showers except for the ADA San Francisco Bay room, with a large limestone shower. Enjoy in-room entertainment centers and business services. Choose a movie selection from the library. Savor a gourmet breakfast in the dining room at a table for two or on a tray delivered to the door. The restaurant has a sommelier and an award-winning wine list. Exercise in the fully equipped fitness center or jog along the coastline trail. Guest services can arrange horseback riding or bike rentals.

Innkeeper(s): Ken & Ellen Landis. $295-345. 8 rooms with PB, 8 with FP, 1 conference room. Breakfast, hors d'oeuvres and wine included in rates. Types of meals: Full gourmet bkfst and early coffee/tea. Beds: KQ. Modem hook-up, data port, cable TV, VCR, reading lamp, CD player, refrigerator, clock radio, telephone, coffeemaker, turn-down service, desk, hot tub/spa, voice mail, fireplace, private balconies, wireless Internet access and radiant heated floors in room. Fax, copier, library, parlor games, fitness center, movie library and award-winning wine list on premises. Handicap access. Antiquing, art galleries, beach, bicycling, canoeing/kayaking, fishing, golf, hiking, horseback riding, live theater, parks, shopping, tennis, water sports, wineries, tide pools, redwoods and birdwatching nearby.

Location: Ocean community, waterfront. Beach access.

Publicity: *Half Moon Bay Review, Arrington's Bed & Breakfast Journal, Inn Traveler and KGO Radio (Dining Around with Gene Burns).*

Certificate may be used: Sunday-Thursday, except holidays.

Old Thyme Inn

779 Main Street
Half Moon Bay, CA 94019-1924
(650)726-1616 (800)720-4277 Fax:(650)726-6394
Internet: www.oldthymeinn.com
E-mail: innkeeper@oldthymeinn.com

Circa 1898. Spend enchanted nights in this "Princess Anne" Victorian inn located on the historic Main Street of Old Town, Half Moon Bay. Its lush, aromatic English flower and herb gar-

den with a bubbling fountain provides a perfect backdrop for casual conversations or romantic tete-a-tetes. Just 28 miles from San Francisco and less than one hour from San Jose and the Silicon Valley, the inn is within walking distance of a crescent-shaped beach, art galleries, shops and fine dining. Furnished in antiques and adorned with the innkeeper's art collection, it offers seven freshly decorated guest rooms, each with a queen bed and hypoallergenic featherbed and down comforter. Two rooms have both Jacuzzis and fireplaces. Savor the inn's tantalizing full breakfast before a day of relaxing or sightseeing.

Innkeeper(s): Rick & Kathy Ellis. $149-329. 7 rooms with PB, 3 with FP, 3 with WP. Breakfast, snacks/refreshments and wine included in rates. Types of meals: Full gourmet bkfst, veg bkfst, early coffee/tea and hors d'oeuvres. Beds: Q. Cable TV, VCR, reading lamp, clock radio, some with hot tub/spa, some with fireplace, hair dryer, bathrobes, bath amenities, wireless Internet access and iron/ironing board in room. Fax, parlor games, telephone and gift shop on premises. Antiquing, art galleries, beach, bicycling, canoeing/kayaking, fishing, golf, hiking, horseback riding, live theater, parks, shopping, water sports and wineries nearby.

Location: Ocean community.

Publicity: *California Weekends, Los Angeles, San Mateo Times, San Jose Mercury News, Herb Companion and San Francisco Examiner.*

Healdsburg G4

Camellia Inn

211 North St
Healdsburg, CA 95448-4251
(707)433-8182 (800)727-8182 Fax:(707)433-8130
Internet: www.camelliainn.com
E-mail: info@camelliainn.com

Circa 1869. Just two blocks from the tree-shaded town plaza, this Italianate Victorian townhouse elegantly graces a half-acre of award-winning grounds. Architectural details include ceiling medallions, ornate mahogany and Palladian windows. Gather in the double parlor with twin marble fireplaces and antiques. Spacious guest bedrooms feature inlaid hardwood floors with Oriental rugs and chandeliers. Many feature whirlpool tubs for two, gas-log fireplaces, canopy beds, sitting areas and private entrances. The Memento can be used as a family suite with an adjoining room. Savor a hearty breakfast buffet fireside in the main dining room. Relax in the swimming pool, and enjoy the more than 50 varieties of camellias.

Innkeeper(s): Lucy Lewand. $139-299. 9 rooms with PB, 4 with FP, 1 two-bedroom suite, 1 conference room. Breakfast and wine included in rates. Types of meals: Full bkfst. Beds: KQD. Modem hook-up, reading lamp, CD player, desk, some with hot tub/spa, most with fireplace, bath amenities and wireless Internet access in room. Air conditioning. TV, VCR, DVD, fax, swimming, parlor games, telephone and gift shop on premises. Limited handicap access. Antiquing, art galleries, beach, bicycling, canoeing/kayaking, fishing, golf, hiking, horseback riding, live theater, museums, parks, shopping, water sports and wineries nearby.

Location: City. Town surrounded by vineyards.

Publicity: *Sunset, Travel & Leisure, New York Times, San Fernando Valley Daily News, San Diego Union, Sacramento Bee, Healdsburg Tribune, Washington Post, Cooking Light and Food & Travel.*

"A bit of paradise for city folks."

Certificate may be used: Sunday-Thursday, November-April, Weekends, Holiday Periods and Special Events are excluded.

Haydon Street Inn

321 Haydon St
Healdsburg, CA 95448-4411
(707)433-5228 (800)528-3703 Fax:(707) 433-6637
Internet: www.haydon.com
E-mail: innkeeper@haydon.com

Circa 1912. Gracing the heart of wine country in Sonoma County, Haydon Street Inn Bed and Breakfast is located in a secluded, tree-shaded neighborhood in small-town Healdsburg, California. Sit on a rocker or swing on the curving front porch of this Queen Anne Victorian or relax in the award-winning gardens with a waterfall. The parlors are accented by antiques. Gather for afternoon refreshments and in the early evening wine and appetizers are served.

Delightful accommodations are found in the 1912 Main House and two-story Victorian Cottage. Savor a wonderful and creative three-course breakfast. Special dietary requests can be prepared with advance notice. There is much to see and do in this pic-

turesque and historic area of Northern California.

Innkeeper(s): John Harasty and Keren Colsten. $190-425. 8 rooms with PB, 4 with FP, 1 with HT, 3 with WP, 1 suite. Breakfast, snacks/refreshments and wine included in rates. Types of meals: Full gourmet bkfst, early coffee/tea and Wine hour every evening from 6 - 7 PM with local wines and delicious hors d'ouevres. Beds: KQT. Reading lamp, ceiling fan, clock radio, desk, some with hot tub/spa, some with fireplace, hair dryer, bathrobes, bath amenities, wireless Internet access, Iron and ironing board available upon request in room. Central air. TV, VCR, fax, parlor games, telephone and Complimentary wireless Internet access on premises. Antiquing, beach, bicycling, canoeing/kayaking, fishing, golf, hiking, horseback riding, live theater, parks, shopping, water sports, wineries, hot air ballooning, wine tours and walking tours nearby.

Location: City. Sonoma Wine Country.

Publicity: *Los Angeles and San Francisco.*

"Adjectives like class, warmth, beauty, thoughtfulness with the right amount of privacy, attention to details relating to comfort, all come to mind. Thank you for the care and elegance."

Certificate may be used: Dec. 15-Apr. 1, King Rooms Only, Sunday-Thursday.

Healdsburg Inn on The Plaza

112 Matheson St.
Healdsburg, CA 95448-4108
(707)433-6991 (800)431-8663 Fax:(707)433-9513
Internet: www.healdsburginn.com
E-mail: Healdsburginn@foursisters.com

Circa 1900. Located in a former Wells Fargo building, the Healdsburg Inn on the Plaza is a renovated brick gingerbread overlooking the plaza in historic downtown Healdsburg, California. Ornate bay windows, embossed wood paneling and broad, paneled stairs present a welcome entrance. Relax by a fireplace and the halls are filled with sunlight from

vaulted, glass skylights. A solarium is the setting for breakfast and evening wine and hors d'oeuvres. A large covered balcony extends along the entire rear of the building. Shops on the premises sell gifts, toys, quilts and fabric as well as an antique shop and art gallery to browse through. The surrounding area is full of things to do, including vineyards and wine-tasting rooms.

Innkeeper(s): Wanda & Kristen. $295-395. 10 rooms with PB, 9 with FP, 1 conference room. Breakfast and snacks/refreshments included in rates. Types of meals: Full gourmet bkfst and early coffee/tea. Beds: KQT. Cable TV, VCR, reading lamp, refrigerator, ceiling fan and telephone in room. Air conditioning. TV, fax, copier, parlor games, fireplace and wine tasting on premises. Antiquing, fishing, parks, shopping, water sports, wineries, balloon, canoe and historic walking tour nearby.

Location: Small town.

Publicity: *Healdsburg Tribune, Los Angeles Daily News, New York Times and San Francisco Chronical Travel Section.*

"The first-thing-in-the-morning juice and coffee was much appreciated."

Certificate may be used: Sunday–Thursday, December-February, based on promotional discount availability and excludes special event periods, holidays and certain room types. First night must be at full rack rate to receive second night free.

Hope Valley   G8

Sorensen's Resort

14255 Hwy 88
Hope Valley, CA 96120
(530)694-2203 (800)423-9949
Internet: www.sorensensresort.com
E-mail: info@sorensensresort.com

Circa 1876. Where Danish sheepherders settled in this 7,000-foot-high mountain valley, the Sorensen family built a cluster of fishing cabins. Thus began a century-old tradition of valley hospitality. The focal point of Sorensen's is a "stave" cabin — a

reproduction of a 13th-century Nordic house. Now developed as a Nordic ski resort, a portion of the Mormon-Emigrant Trail and Pony Express Route pass near the inn's 165 acres. In the summer, river rafting, fishing, pony express re-rides and llama treks are popular Sierra pastimes. Lake Tahoe lies 20 miles to the north. Breakfast is included in the rates for bed & breakfast units only. All other cabins are equipped with kitchens.

Innkeeper(s): John & Patty Brissenden. $115-425. 33 rooms, 31 with PB, 23 with FP, 28 cottages, 2 conference rooms. Types of meals: Full bkfst, early coffee/tea, lunch, picnic lunch, snacks/refreshments and gourmet dinner. Restaurant on premises. Beds: QD. Reading lamp and refrigerator in room. Copier, sauna, library, parlor games, telephone, fireplace, e-mail hook-up, complimentary wine, tea and cocoa on premises. Handicap access. Antiquing, cross-country skiing, downhill skiing, fishing, parks and water sports nearby.

Location: Mountains.

Publicity: *Sunset, San Francisco Chronicle, Los Angeles Times, Motorland, Outside, New York Times* and *Travel & Leisure.*

"In one night's stay, I felt more comfortable, relaxed, and welcome than any vacation my 47 years have allowed. Thank you for the happiness you have given my children."

Certificate may be used: Monday-Thursday, non-holiday, excluding February, July, August and October.

Idyllwild   O12

Strawberry Creek Inn Bed & Breakfast

26370 Highway 243
Idyllwild, CA 92549-1818
(951)659-3202 (800)262-8969 Fax:(951)659-4707
Internet: www.strawberrycreekinn.com
E-mail: innkeeper@strawberrycreekinn.com

Circa 1941. Each of the rooms at this country inn is individually decorated with its own theme. Six of the guest rooms include fireplaces. Skylights, window seats and mini refrigerators are a few of the other items guests might find in their room. The innkeepers also offer a private cottage with a whirlpool tub, river rock fireplace, fully equipped kitchen, a bedroom, living area and two bathrooms. The full breakfasts are served in the glassed-in porch where

guests can enjoy Idyllwild's scenery. The one-acre grounds include outdoor decks and hammocks.

Innkeeper(s): Rodney Williams & Ian Scott. $119-249. 10 rooms with PB, 7 with FP, 1 with HT, 1 two-bedroom suite, 1 cottage, 1 cabin. Breakfast and snacks/refreshments included in rates. Types of meals: Country bkfst, Hors d'oeuvres (Fridays/Saturdays), Organic full gourmet breakfast, Fresh-ground organic fair-trade coffee and Organic black/white/green/herbal teas. Beds: KQ. Cable TV, VCR, DVD, reading lamp, stereo, refrigerator, clock radio, telephone, coffeemaker, desk, some with hot tub/spa, most with fireplace, wireless Internet access, Aveda bath amenities and Luxurious double-layer robes in room. Air conditioning. Library, parlor games and gift shop on premises. Limited handicap access. Antiquing, art galleries, bicycling, cross-country skiing, fishing, hiking, horseback riding, live theater, museums, parks, shopping, wineries, Bird-watching, Shopping (outlet), Casinos and Farmers Market nearby.

Location: Country, mountains. San Bernardino National Forest.

Publicity: *Sunset Magazine, Black Enterprise, The San Diegan, Quick Escapes San Diego, Great Towns of Southern California, Best Places to Kiss Southern California, Karen Brown's Charming Inns & Itineraries, American Profile Magazine, North County Times* and *Press-Enterprise.*

Certificate may be used: Sunday-Thursday, excludes Independence, Memorial and Labor Day, Wednesday and Thursday of Thanksgiving and last two weeks of Decemeber.

Jamestown   H7

1859 Historic National Hotel, A Country Inn

18183 Main St,
Jamestown, CA 95327-0502
(209)984-3446 (800)894-3446 Fax:(209)984-5620
Internet: www.national-hotel.com
E-mail: info@national-hotel.com

Circa 1859. Located between Yosemite National Park and Lake Tahoe, in Gold Country, this is one of the 10 oldest continuously operating hotels in the state. The inn maintains its original redwood bar where thousands of dollars in gold dust were once spent. Original furnishings, Gold Rush period antiques, brass beds, lace curtains and regal comforters grace the guest bedrooms. A soaking room is an additional amenity, though all rooms include private baths. Enjoy a daily bountiful buffet breakfast. Arrange for romantic dining at the on-site gourmet restaurant, considered to be one of the finest in the Mother Lode. Order a favorite liquor or espresso from the saloon, or try the area's wine tasting. Favorite diversions include gold panning, live theatre and antiquing, golf and shopping.

Innkeeper(s): Stephen Willey. $140-175. 9 rooms with PB, 1 conference room. Breakfast and Buffet breakfast in dining room for hotel guests included in rates. Types of meals: Country bkfst, Sun. brunch, early coffee/tea, gourmet lunch, picnic lunch, snacks/refreshments, hors d'oeuvres, wine, gourmet dinner, room service, Banquets, meetings, seminars, weddings and receptions. Restaurant on premises. Beds: QT. Modem hook-up, cable TV, DVD, reading lamp, ceiling fan, clock radio, telephone, coffeemaker, desk, hair dryer, bathrobes, bath amenities, wireless Internet access, iron/ironing board, Antique furnishings, Old fashioned claw-footed tub for two soaking room, Pull-chain toilets, Memory foam mattress pads and Alarm clocks in room. Central air. VCR, fax, copier, spa, library, pet boarding, parlor games, highly-acclaimed restaurant with patio dining, original Gold Rush saloon, espresso bar and soaking room for house guests on premises. Antiquing, art galleries, bicycling, canoeing/kayaking, cross-country skiing, downhill skiing, fishing, golf, hiking, horseback riding, live theater, museums, parks, shopping, tennis, water sports, wineries, gold panning, antiquing, shopping, multiple golf courses, Historic Steam Railroad State Park, Columbia Gold Rush State Park, Big Trees State Park, watersports of all types - kayaking, canoeing, rafting, sailing, etc., hiking, fishing and horseback riding nearby.

Location: Country, mountains. Yosemite National Park, Sonora.

Publicity: *Bon Appetit, California Magazine, Focus, San Francisco Magazine, Gourmet, Sunset, San Francisco Chronicle, Modesto Bee, Sacramento Bee, San Jose Mercury, The Union Democrat, Razor Magazine, Fabulous Foods.com, Via Magazine, Stockton Record, San Francisco Downtown*

Magazine, NBC, Channel 13, PBS, *Bound For Glory, Back to the Future-3, Redemption of the Ghost, Little House on the Prairie and Gambler #2.*
Certificate may be used: (24 hour)Last minute availability only, no weekends.

The Victorian Gold Bed and Breakfast

10382 Willow St
Jamestown, CA 95327-9761
(209)984-3429 (888)551-1852 Fax:(209)984-4929
Internet: www.victoriangoldbb.com
E-mail: innkeeper@victoriangoldbb.com

Circa 1890. Enjoy Gold Country at this Victorian, which was home to Albert and Amelia Hoyt, publishers of the Mother Lode Magnet. In the 1890s, the home served as a boarding house. Today, it offers eight guest rooms with lacy curtains, fresh flowers, clawfoot tubs, marble showers and robes. A full breakfast is served each morning along with The Palm's special blend of coffee. The inn is located two-and-a-half hours from San Francisco and about an hour from Yosemite Valley, and it is within walking distance of Main Street, boutiques, galleries, restaurants and Railtown State Park.

Innkeeper(s): Ken & Anita Spencer. $110-185. 8 rooms with PB. Breakfast included in rates. Types of meals: Full gourmet bkfst and early coffee/tea. Beds: KQD. Cable TV, DVD, reading lamp, refrigerator, ceiling fan, clock radio, hair dryer, bathrobes, bath amenities, wireless Internet access and iron/ironing board in room. Central air. Fax and copier on premises. Limited handicap access. Antiquing, cross-country skiing, fishing, golf, hiking, live theater, museums, parks, shopping, water sports, wineries, Railtown State Park and Yosemite and Calaveras Big Trees nearby.

Location: Mountains. California gold country.

Publicity: *Avalon Bay News, San Jose Mercury News, Sacramento Bee, Modesto Bee, San Francisco Chronicle, Sonora Union Democrat, Central Valley Chronicles on KVIE TV and Central Sierra Bank 1999 calendar.*

"The simple elegance of our room and ambiance of the Palm in general was a balm for our souls."

Certificate may be used: Anytime, November-March, subject to availability.

Julian   P12

Butterfield B&B

2284 Sunset Dr
Julian, CA 92036
(760)765-2179 (800)379-4262 Fax:(760)765-1229
Internet: butterfieldbandb.com
E-mail: info@butterfieldbandb.com

Circa 1935. On an ivy-covered hillside surrounded by oaks and pines, the Butterfield is a peaceful haven of hospitality and country comfort. Overlooking the countryside, several of the charming guest bedrooms feature fireplaces and fluffy featherbeds. A delicious gourmet breakfast is served in the gazebo during summer or by a warm fire in cooler months. The parlor is a delightful place to enjoy hot beverages and afternoon treats. Whether it is scheduling an in-room massage, or making dinner reservations, the innkeepers are always happy to oblige.

Innkeeper(s): Ed & Dawn Glass. $135-185. 5 rooms with PB, 3 with FP, 1 cottage. Breakfast and snacks/refreshments included in rates. Types of meals: Full gourmet bkfst, veg bkfst and early coffee/tea. Beds: KQD. Cable TV, VCR, DVD, reading lamp, stereo, refrigerator, ceiling fan, clock radio, coffeemaker, most with fireplace, hair dryer, bathrobes, bath amenities, wireless Internet access and iron/ironing board in room. Air conditioning. Fax, copier, library, parlor games and telephone on premises. Limited handicap access. Antiquing, art galleries, canoeing/kayaking, fishing, golf, hiking, horseback riding, live theater, museums, parks, shopping and wineries nearby.

Location: Mountains.

Publicity: *South Coast and Travel Agent.*

Certificate may be used: Jan. 7-Aug. 31, Sunday-Thursday, last minute based on projected availability.

Orchard Hill Country Inn

2502 Washington Street
Julian, CA 92036-0425
(760)765-1700 (800)716-7242
Internet: www.orchardhill.com
E-mail: information@orchardhill.com

Circa 1992. Reminiscent of America's great national park lodges, this award-winning inn is cradled in the heart of the Julian Historic Mining District. Enjoy the hilltop vistas and warm hospitality. A mountain spring, colorful native gardens and hiking trails lead to abandoned mines. The inn features a guest-only dining room, bar and on-site masseuse. The conference room is available

for weddings and retreats. Air-conditioned cottage rooms with porches offer comfort and abundant amenities that include fireplace, whirlpool tub, wet bar, refrigerator coffee maker and phone with modem. The area is renowned for birding, star gazing, hiking and nearby desert wildflower preserves. Relax and be refreshed in the romantic setting.

Innkeeper(s): Pat & Darrell Straube. $195-450. 22 rooms with PB, 12 with FP, 1 conference room. Breakfast and hors d'oeuvres included in rates. Types of meals: Country bkfst, early coffee/tea, picnic lunch, wine and gourmet dinner. Beds: KQ. Cable TV, VCR, reading lamp, CD player, refrigerator, ceiling fan, clock radio, telephone, coffeemaker, turn-down service, desk, some with hot tub/spa, voice mail, some with fireplace, hair dryer, bathrobes, bath amenities, wireless Internet access and iron/ironing board in room. Air conditioning. Fax, copier, library, parlor games and gift shop on premises. Handicap access. Antiquing, art galleries, bicycling, fishing, hiking, horseback riding, live theater, parks, shopping, wineries, music/art festivals, horse trails and bird watching nearby.

Location: Mountains. Northeast San Diego County.

Publicity: *San Diego Union Tribune, Los Angeles Times, Orange County Register, Orange Coast, San Francisco Chronicle, San Bernardino Sun, Oceanside Blade-Citizen and "Top Six Lodges in the West" Sunset Magazine.*

"The quality of the rooms, service and food were beyond our expectations."

Certificate may be used: Cottage Rooms only. Sunday-Thursday. The purchase of two, four-course dinners are required. Not valid during holidays. Reservations taken no more than two weeks from the arrival date.

Kenwood   G4

Birmingham Bed and Breakfast

8790 Sonoma Hwy
Kenwood, CA 95452
(707)833-6996 (800)819-1388 Fax:(707)833-6398
Internet: www.birminghambb.com
E-mail: info@birminghambb.com

Circa 1915. Set amongst vineyards, this two-acre Prairie-style country estate with breathtaking views was given historic designation by Sonoma County. A fireplace, library and game table are located in the Victorian breakfast parlor. The sitting parlor offers a reading nook and small visitors center. Romantic guest bedrooms and suites feature four-poster and sleigh beds. The spacious Red Room boasts a soaking tub with shower and a private balcony overlooking the pond and hazelnut trees. Fresh produce from the orchard and garden provides ingredients for seasonal breakfast recipes like artichoke cheese frittata, scones and poached pears. Relax on the wraparound porch facing mountain vistas.

Innkeeper(s): Nancy & Jerry Fischman. $160-295. 5 rooms, 4 with PB, 1 two-bedroom suite, 1 cottage, 1 conference room. Breakfast and afternoon tea included in rates. Types of meals: Full gourmet bkfst, veg bkfst and early coffee/tea. Beds: KQT. Reading lamp, desk, some with fireplace, hair dryer, bath amenities, wireless Internet access, iron/ironing board, clock and toiletries in room. Central air. Fax, copier, library and parlor games on premises. Antiquing, art galleries, beach, bicycling, golf, hiking, horseback riding, museums, parks, shopping and wineries nearby.

Location: Country, mountains. Vineyards.

Publicity: *Travel Holiday.*

Certificate may be used: November-March, anytime subject to availability.

Kernville   M10

Kern River Inn B&B

119 Kern River Dr
Kernville, CA 93238
(760)376-6750 (800)986-4382
Internet: www.kernriverinn.com
E-mail: kernriverinn@gmail.com

Circa 1991. Kern River Inn overlooks the river in Kernville, California amid the Southern Sierra Nevada Mountains. Relaxing and comfortable, this B&B has an inviting front porch and fireside gathering room for pleasant conversation. Stay in a delightful guest room with picturesque water and mountain views, a wood-burning fireplace or spa shower. The first-floor

Piute Room is wheelchair accessible and meets ADA requirements. Savor a bountiful breakfast that may include the inn's renowned waffles, egg and cheese dishes or stuffed French toast; then explore

the Kern River Valley and Lake Isabella. Whitewater rafting and fly fishing are popular outdoor sports. The local area offers many seasonal annual events and year-round activities. Ask about inn specials available.

Innkeeper(s): Virginia McLaughlin. $135-175. 5 rooms with PB, 3 with FP. Breakfast, afternoon tea and snacks/refreshments included in rates. Types of meals: Full bkfst, early coffee/tea, picnic lunch and Birder breakfasts. Beds: KQ. Cable TV, VCR, reading lamp, refrigerator, ceiling fan, clock radio, desk, hair dryer, bath amenities and wireless Internet access in room. Central air. Copier, library, telephone, fireplace and gift shop on premises. Handicap access. Antiquing, art galleries, bicycling, canoeing/kayaking, cross-country skiing, downhill skiing, fishing, golf, hiking, horseback riding, museums, parks, shopping, water sports, Whitewater rafting, Windsurfing and Birdwatching nearby.

Location: Country, mountains, waterfront.

Publicity: *Westways, Los Angeles Times, Bakersfield Californian, Kern Valley Sun and Valley News.*

"For us, your place is the greatest. So romantic."

Certificate may be used: Anytime, subject to availability.

Lemon Cove   J7

Plantation B&B

33038 Sierra Drive (hwy 198)
Lemon Cove, CA 93244-1700
(559) 597-2555 Fax:(559)597-2551
Internet: www.theplantation.net
E-mail: relax@plantationbnb.com

Circa 1908. The history of orange production is deeply entwined in the roots of California, and this home is located on

what once was an orange plantation. The original 1908 house burned in the 1960s, but the current home was built on its foundation. In keeping with the home's plantation past, the innkeepers decorated the bed and breakfast with a "Gone With the Wind" theme. The comfortable, country guest rooms sport names such as the Scarlett

O'Hara, the Belle Watling, and of course, the Rhett Butler. A hot tub is located in the orchard, and there also is a heated swimming pool.

Innkeeper(s): Scott & Marie Munger. $149-239. 8 rooms with PB, 2 with WP, 1 with FP, 3 suites. Breakfast and snacks/refreshments included in rates. Types of meals: Full gourmet bkfst and early coffee/tea. Beds: KQDT. Cable TV, VCR, reading lamp, ceiling fan and hot tub/spa in room. Air conditioning. Fax, spa, swimming, parlor games, telephone and fireplace on premises. Antiquing, cross-country skiing, fishing, golf, parks, shopping, sporting events and water sports nearby.

Location: Country, mountains.

Publicity: *Exeter Sun, Kaweah Commonwealth, Los Angeles Times, Fresno Bee, Visalia Delta Times, Westways Magazine and Sunset Magazine.*

"Scarlett O'Hara would be proud to live on this lovely plantation."

Certificate may be used: Sept. 7-May 15, subject to availability.

Malibu   09

Malibu Country Inn

6506 Westward Beach Rd
Malibu, CA 90265-4147
(310) 457-9622 (877) 386-6787 Fax:(310)457-1349
Internet: www.malibucountryinn.com/
E-mail: ivyamaral@malibucountryinn.com

Circa 1947. Poised on a beachside bluff overlooking the famed beaches of Malibu, California, this Cape-Cod style country inn sits on the ocean side of Pacific Coast Highway. Walk along Zuma Beach, or swim in the heated pool. Guest rooms are airy with a mixture of country furnishings and floral prints, and offer mountain or garden views. An assortment of generous amenities include refrigerators, coffee makers, fireplaces, Jacuzzis, private patios, skylights and a basket with snacks. Daily continental fare is served in the poolside breakfast room. The many attractions of Los Angeles are nearby. Visit popular amusement parks, take a movie studio tour, see the historic La Brea Tar Pits or learn how to surf.

Innkeeper(s): Ivy Amaral, General Manager. $130-320. 16 rooms with PB, 1 with FP, 5 suites. Types of meals: Lunch, dinner and room service. Restaurant on premises. Beds: KQD. Data port, cable TV, reading lamp, refrigerator, ceiling fan, clock radio, telephone, coffeemaker, voice mail, hair dryer, bath amenities, wireless Internet access, iron/ironing board, coffeemaker in room, air conditioning in suites, private patio in most and 40"-42" LCD TV in room. Fax, copier, spa, swimming, fireplace, Pool, Garden, Fire Pit and

Restaurant on premises. Handicap access. Fishing, parks, shopping, sporting events and water sports nearby.

Location: Mountains, ocean community. Nestled in the beachside bluffs of Malibu, across from world-famous Zuma Beach.

Publicity: *Victoria.*

"We make the Malibu Country Inn part of our vacation plan every year."

Certificate may be used: Subject to availability, not valid July and August.

Mendocino F2

Alegria Oceanfront Inn & Cottages

44781 Main St
Mendocino, CA 95460
(707)937-5150 (800)780-7905 Fax:(707)937-5151
Internet: www.oceanfrontmagic.com
E-mail: inn@oceanfrontmagic.com

Circa 1861. Sitting in the historic village on a bluff overlooking an ocean cove, this inn lightens the sprits just as the name Alegria means when translated. The main house was built in 1861 as a saltbox and recently renovated. Stay in one of the guest bedrooms or a private cottage. They all feature generous amenities and some include wood-burning stoves. The second-floor Pacific Suite boasts a microwave and wet bar sink. The ocean view dining room is the perfect spot for an incredible breakfast that is made with organically grown produce when possible. The ever-changing perennial garden includes antique roses and a relaxing hot tub. Take the trail 200 footsteps from the garden's edge down to Big River Beach.

Innkeeper(s): Eric and Elaine Wing Hillesland. $159-299. 10 rooms with PB, 1 suite, 4 cottages. Breakfast included in rates. Types of meals: Full gourmet bkfst, veg bkfst and early coffee/tea. Beds: KQ. Cable TV, VCR, reading lamp, refrigerator, ceiling fan, clock radio, coffeemaker, fireplace, private decks, panoramic ocean views, some with wood burning stoves, microwave and wet bar sink in room. Fax, copier, spa, telephone and gift shop on premises. Art galleries, beach, bicycling, canoeing/kayaking, fishing, golf, hiking, horseback riding, live theater, museums, parks, shopping, tennis, wineries, used book store, Big River Beach, Big River Estuary, Headlands State Park, Montgomery Woods, Jackson State Demonstration Forest, Van Damme State Park & Beach, Russian Gulch State Park & Beach, Caspar State Beach, Mendocino Coast Botanical Gardens, Glass Beach and MacKerricher State Park & Beach nearby.

Location: Ocean community, waterfront. Wine country.

Publicity: *Country Inns Magazine and Horticulture Magazine.*

Certificate may be used: November-February, Sunday-Thursday, excluding holidays, subject to availability.

Brewery Gulch Inn

9401 North Highway One
Mendocino, CA 95460-9767
(707)937-4752 (800)578-4454 Fax:(707)937-1279
Internet: www.brewerygulchinn.com
E-mail: guestservices@brewerygulchinn.com

Circa 2001. Brewery Gulch Inn is located on three acres with coastal spruce, mature pine and redwood trees, hundreds of rhododendrons and many native plants in Mendocino, California. This extraordinary inn features ancient virgin redwood timbers eco-salvaged from Big River. Guest rooms, eight with private decks, are furnished to provide the ultimate in comfort. Each room has a fireplace, quality Sferra Italian linens, a cozy seating area with leather club chairs, a desk, excellent lighting and an ocean view framed by trees. Additional amenities include LCD flat screen TVs with cable and DVD, iHome clock radios, complimentary local and domestic long distance

service and Wi-fi high-speed Internet. Indulge in an outstanding cooked-to-order breakfast each morning. The evening wine hour features bountiful hors d'oeuvres and carefully chosen wines from Mendocino County wineries.

Innkeeper(s): Jo Ann Stickle, GM. $210-465. 11 rooms, 10 with PB, 10 with FP, 2 with HT, 2 with WP, 1 two-bedroom suite. Breakfast, snacks/refreshments, hors d'oeuvres, wine, Full and cooked to order breakfast; evening wine hour includes light dinner buffet included in rates. Types of meals: Full gourmet bkfst, veg bkfst, early coffee/tea, gourmet lunch, picnic lunch and room service. Beds: KQT. Modem hook-up, data port, cable TV, DVD, reading lamp, stereo, clock radio, telephone, turn-down service, desk, some with hot tub/spa, voice mail, fireplace, hair dryer, bathrobes, bath amenities, wireless Internet access, iron/ironing board, Decks/balconies in most rooms and iPod docks in room. Fax, copier, library, parlor games and gift shop on premises. Handicap access. Antiquing, art galleries, beach, bicycling, canoeing/kayaking, fishing, golf, hiking, horseback riding, live theater, museums, parks, shopping, tennis, water sports, wineries, Skunk steam engine train, historical village, botanical gardens and whale watching nearby.

Location: Ocean community.

Publicity: *Food & Wine, Sunset Magazine, San Francisco Chronicle, Appellation, NY Times, Gourmet, Wine Enthusiast, Coastal Living, Robb Report, Travel & Leisure, Conde Nast; Examiner.com, Best of California, KGO, Travel & Leisure, Diablo Magazine 12 Great Gateways and Food & Wine.*

Certificate may be used: November-April, Sunday-Thursday, subject to availability, except during holidays or local special events.

Headlands Inn

10453 Howard Street
Mendocino, CA 95460
(707)937-4431 (800)354-4431 Fax:(707)937-0421
Internet: www.headlandsinn.com
E-mail: innkeeper@headlandsinn.com

Circa 1868. A historic setting by the sea in the village of Mendocino complements this New England Victorian Salt Box. The quaintness of the past combines with amenities of the present. Meet new friends sharing afternoon tea and cookies in the

parlor. Almost all of the romantic guest bedrooms feature fireplaces, comfortable feather beds with down comforters, fresh flowers and bedside chocolates. Some have whitewater ocean views. A cottage provides more spacious privacy. Indulge in a full breakfast delivered to the room with homemade treats and creative entrees. The front porch is also an ideal spot for ocean views. Lawn seating gives ample opportunity to enjoy the year-round English garden. Many unique shops and fine restaurants are within walking distance.

Innkeeper(s): Denise & Mitch. $99-249. 7 rooms with PB, 6 with FP, 1 suite, 1 cottage. Breakfast, afternoon tea and snacks/refreshments included in rates. Types of meals: Full gourmet bkfst and veg bkfst. Beds: KQ. Reading lamp, clock radio, desk, fireplace, hair dryer, bathrobes, wireless Internet access, ocean views, feather beds, hair dryers, robes, cottage has cable TV/VCR, refrigerator & microwave and daily morning newspaper delivered in room. DVD, fax, copier, parlor games and telephone on premises. Limited handicap access. Antiquing, art galleries, beach, bicycling, canoeing/kayaking, fishing, golf, hiking, horseback riding, live theater, museums, parks, shopping, tennis and wineries nearby.

Location: Ocean community. Mendocino Village.

Publicity: *"Best Places to Kiss" Romantic Travel Guide and "Best Places to Stay" Travel Guide.*

"If a Nobel Prize were given for breakfasts, you would win hands down. A singularly joyous experience!!"

Certificate may be used: November-March, Monday-Thursday, excluding holiday periods, Strauss, Cottage or Barry rooms only.

MacCallum House Inn

45020 Albion St
Mendocino, CA 95460
(707)937-0289 (800)609-0492
Internet: www.maccallumhouse.com
E-mail: innkeeper@maccallumhouse.com

Circa 1882. Choose from a variety of accommodations with ocean views and upscale amenities at this Mendocino inn on the coast of northern California. Winner of the iLoveInns.com Top 10 Romantic Inns of 2009, MacCallum House was built in 1882 and includes a renowned restaurant situated in the sun porch, library and dining rooms of this vintage Victorian. The menus showcase regional organic products and a gourmet breakfast is included in your room fee. Surrounding the main house, cottages feature wood stoves and decks, some with private hot tubs. The original barn was restored and boasts river stone fireplaces in each guest bedroom. Properties also include the MacCallum Suites, a luxury mansion on two hilltop acres and the Mendocino Village Inn, an historic three-story 1882 mansion. Massage and Spa services are available, as well as limousine tours of Anderson Valley wine country.

Innkeeper(s): Herman Seidell Sarah Mitchell. $149-399. 30 rooms with PB, 20 with FP, 9 with HT, 16 with WP, 13 suites, 7 cottages, 1 conference room. Breakfast and Daily "Food and Wine" Credits included in rates. Types of meals: Full gourmet bkfst, veg bkfst, Sun. brunch, early coffee/tea, gourmet lunch, picnic lunch, afternoon tea, snacks/refreshments, hors d'oeuvres, wine, gourmet dinner, Executive Chef Alan Kantor showcases regional North Coast wines, seafood and meats and produce with an emphasis on organics and quality purveyors. We change our menus seasonally. Restaurant on premises. Beds: KQDT. Modem hook-up, data port, cable TV, DVD, reading lamp, refrigerator, snack bar, clock radio, telephone, coffeemaker, turn-down service, voice mail, hair dryer, bathrobes, bath amenities, wireless Internet access, iron/ironing board, 24-hour Internet access and Mini Bar in room. Fax, copier, spa, bicycles, library, pet boarding, child care, parlor games, fireplace, gift shop and Renowned restaurant on premises on premises. Handicap access. Antiquing, art galleries, beach, bicycling, canoeing/kayaking, fishing, golf, hiking, horseback riding, live theater, museums, parks, shopping, tennis, wineries and Whale Watching nearby.

Location: Ocean community.

Publicity: *New York Times, Sunset Magazine, San Francisco Chronicle, Vogue, Savor Wine Country, Santa Rosa Press Democrat, San Francisco Magazine, Wine Spectator, Chocolatier, Wine X, Wine Enthusiast, Coastal Living and California Visitors Review.*

Certificate may be used: November-April, Sunday-Thursday, non holiday.

Sea Gull Inn

44960 Albion St
Mendocino, CA 95460
(707)937-5204 (888)937-5204
Internet: www.seagullbb.com
E-mail: seagull@mcn.org

Circa 1883. Shaded by a giant holly tree, this house built in 1878 was one of the area's first bed & breakfast inns. Relax on the front porch or in the lush private garden. Stay in a spacious upstairs or first-floor guest bedroom or a private cottage with antiques, fresh flowers and original artworks. A variety of amenities are offered from sitting areas to ocean views. A light breakfast is delivered to the room at a prearranged time and a morning newspaper is available upon request. Walk to the village shops and art galleries. Visit the Mendocino Art Center or the botanical coastal gardens. Tour Anderson Wine Valley and take the Skunk Train at Fort Bragg through the mountains and redwoods.

Innkeeper(s): Jim and Ayla Douglas. $65-198. 9 rooms with PB, 1 with FP, 1 cottage. Breakfast included in rates. Types of meals: Cont plus. Beds: KQD. Reading lamp, some with fireplace, hair dryer, bath amenities and wireless

Internet access in room. Fax, parlor games and telephone on premises. Limited handicap access. Antiquing, art galleries, beach, bicycling, canoeing/kayaking, fishing, golf, hiking, horseback riding, live theater, museums, parks, shopping, tennis, water sports, wineries, Scuba diving, Whale watching, Mendocino Coast Botanical Gardens, Great area for road & off-road bicycling and motorcycling nearby.

Location: Ocean community.

Certificate may be used: November 1-March 31.

The Inn at Schoolhouse Creek

7051 N Hwy 1
Mendocino, CA 95460
(707)937-5525 (800)731-5525 Fax:(707)937-2012
Internet: www.schoolhousecreek.com
E-mail: innkeeper@schoolhousecreek.com

Circa 1860. The Inn at School House Creek offers private cottages and rooms on its eight acres of rose gardens, forests and meadows. (The inn's gardens have been featured in several magazines.) Many cottages include views of the ocean and all have a fireplace. The inn offers a quiet getaway, while still being close to all of the fun in Mendocino just two miles away. Private beach access to Buckhorn Cove allows guests to enjoy whale watching, sea lions and the crashing waves of the Pacific. Organize your day to include a picnic lunch (available by advance notice) to enjoy at a secluded waterfall in the redwoods. Then take a sunset soak in the inn's ocean view hot tub. The next morning's breakfast may include a hot apple crisp with whipped cream, eggs, fruit and a variety of freshly baked muffins and breads, jams and juices.

Innkeeper(s): Steven Musser & Maureen Gilbert. $130-399. 19 rooms with PB, 19 with FP, 4 with HT, 6 with WP, 1 total suite, including 2 two-bed-room suites, 12 cottages, 2 conference rooms. Breakfast, afternoon tea, snacks/refreshments, hors d'oeuvres and wine included in rates. Types of meals: Full bkfst, veg bkfst, early coffee/tea, picnic lunch and Lunch by request. Beds: KQD. Modem hook-up, cable TV, VCR, DVD, reading lamp, CD player, refrigerator, clock radio, telephone, coffeemaker, some with hot tub/spa, voice mail, fireplace, hair dryer, bathrobes, bath amenities, wireless Internet access, iron/ironing board, Microwave and Refrigerator in room. Fax, spa, sauna, library, parlor games, gift shop, Evening wine and hors d'oeuvres, Ocean view, Hot tub and Sauna on premises. Handicap access. Antiquing, art galleries, beach, bicycling, canoeing/kayaking, fishing, golf, hiking, horseback riding, live theater, parks, shopping, tennis, water sports and wineries nearby.

Location: Country, ocean community.

Publicity: *"Eye on the Bay"*

Certificate may be used: Nov. 1-Feb. 28, Sunday-Thursday, holidays and local festivals excluded.

Menlo Park /5

Adella Villa B&B

Po Box 7112
Menlo Park, CA 94026
(650)321-5195
Internet: www.adellavilla.com
E-mail: adellavilla@gmail.com

Circa 1923. This Italian villa is located in an area of one-acre estates five minutes from Stanford University. One guest room features a whirlpool tub; four guest rooms have showers. The

music room boasts a 1920 mahogany Steinway grand piano. There is a seasonal swimming pool set amid manicured gardens.

Innkeeper(s): Tricia Young. $119-159. 4 rooms with PB, 1 guest house. Breakfast, afternoon tea and snacks/refreshments included in rates. Types of meals: Full gourmet bkfst, early coffee/tea and wine. Beds: KQ. Cable TV, DVD, reading lamp, stereo, clock radio, telephone, desk, hair dryer, bathrobes, wireless Internet access and iron/ironing board in room. Central air. Fax, copier, swimming, library, fireplace and laundry facility on premises. Amusement parks, antiquing, art galleries, beach, bicycling, golf, live theater, museums, parks, shopping, sporting events, tennis and wineries nearby.

Location: City. Palo Alto California.

Publicity: *L.A. Times- Reader's Choice.*

"This place is as wonderful, gracious and beautiful as the people who own it!"

Certificate may be used: Anytime, subject to availability; not valid on holiday weekends, Valentine's day, Thanksgiving or Christmas week.

Middletown   G4

Backyard Garden Oasis B&B

24019 Hilderbrand Dr
Middletown, CA 95461-1760
(707)987-0505
Internet: www.backyardgardenoasis.com
E-mail: greta@backyardgardenoasis.com

Circa 1997. Be renewed by the blend of simple elegance and rustic ambiance in the Collayomi Valley of North Calistoga over Mt. St. Helens. Stay in one of the individual cottages that feature air conditioning, skylight, gas fireplaces, a refrigerator and coffeemaker and access to the video collection. The private redwood decks overlook the Manzanita grove, pond and waterfall. One cottage is wheelchair accessible. Gather in the dining room of the main house for a hearty country breakfast that begins with fresh-squeezed orange juice. Schedule a massage with a certified therapist then soak under the stars in the hot tub. Harbin Hot Springs is ten minutes away and it is a two-hour drive to San Francisco or Sacramento. Take a wine tasting tour of nearby Lake County wineries.

Innkeeper(s): Greta Zeit. $139-159. 3 cottages with PB, 3 with FP, 1 suite. Breakfast included in rates. Types of meals: Cont plus and early coffee/tea. Beds: KQT. Modem hook-up, data port, cable TV, VCR, reading lamp, stereo, refrigerator, ceiling fan, telephone, coffeemaker, turn-down service, desk, some with hot tub/spa, fireplace, hair dryer, bathrobes, bath amenities, wireless Internet access and iron/ironing board in room. Air conditioning. Fax, spa, creek and pond on property on premises. Limited handicap access. Antiquing, bicycling, canoeing/kayaking, fishing, golf, hiking, horseback riding, museums, parks, tennis, water sports and wineries nearby.

Location: Country, mountains.

Certificate may be used: Monday-Thursday, excluding holidays.

Montara   I4

The Goose & Turrets B&B

835 George St.
Montara, CA 94037-0937
(650) 728-5451 Fax:(650)728-0141
Internet: www.gooseandturretsbandb.com
E-mail: goosenturretsbnb@gmail.com

Circa 1908. Now a haven focusing on comfort and hospitality, this classic bed & breakfast once served as Montara's first post office, the town hall, and a country club for Spanish-American War veterans. Large living and dining room areas are filled with art and collectibles. Sleep

soundly in one of the tranquil guest bedrooms then linger over a leisurely four-course breakfast. Stimulating conversation comes easily during afternoon tea. There are plenty of quiet spots including a swing and a hammock, to enjoy the fountains, orchard, rose, herb and vegetable gardens.

Innkeeper(s): Raymond & Emily Hoche-Mong. $145-190. 5 rooms with PB, 3 with FP. Breakfast and afternoon tea included in rates. Types of meals: Full gourmet bkfst and veg bkfst. Beds: KQDT. Reading lamp, clock radio, desk, some with fireplace, hair dryer, bath amenities, wireless Internet access and iron/ironing board in room. Fax, library, parlor games, telephone, bocce ball court and piano on premises. Antiquing, art galleries, beach, bicycling, canoeing/kayaking, fishing, golf, hiking, horseback riding, live theater, parks, shopping, water sports, wineries, nature reserves, whale watching, aero sightseeing and birding nearby.

Location: Seaside village.

Publicity: *San Diego Union, Tri-Valley, Los Angeles Times, Pilot Getaways, AOPA Magazine, San Jose Mercury News, Half Moon Bay Review, Peninsula Times Tribune, San Mateo Times, Contra Costa Times, The Wall Street Journal, Home & Garden Channel "If Walls Could Talk", Ramblin' with Ramsey and LA Times Travel.*

"You have truly made an art of breakfast and tea-time conversation. We will be back."

Certificate may be used: Monday-Thursday September-May. Major holidays excluded.

Monterey   J5

The Jabberwock

598 Laine St
Monterey, CA 93940-1312
(831)372-4777 (888)428-7253 Fax:(831)655-2946
Internet: www.jabberwockinn.com
E-mail: innkeeper@jabberwockinn.com

Circa 1911. Set in a half-acre of gardens, this Craftsman-style inn provides a fabulous view of Monterey Bay with its famous barking seals. When you're ready to settle in for the evening, you'll find huge Victorian beds complete with lace-edged sheets and goose-down comforters. Three rooms include Jacuzzi tubs. In the late afternoon, hors d'oeuvres and aperitifs are served on an enclosed sun porch. After dinner, guests are

tucked into bed with homemade chocolate chip cookies and milk. To help guests avoid long lines, the innkeepers have tickets available for the popular and nearby Monterey Bay Aquarium.

Innkeeper(s): Dawn Perez & John Hickey. $169-299. 7 rooms with PB, 4 with FP, 3 with HT. Breakfast, afternoon tea, snacks/refreshments, hors d'oeuvres and wine included in rates. Types of meals: Full gourmet bkfst, veg bkfst, early coffee/tea, picnic lunch and Evening Wine. Beds: KQ. Reading lamp, clock radio, some with hot tub/spa, hair dryer, bathrobes, wireless Internet access and three with Jacuzzi for two in room. Fax, copier, spa, library, parlor games, telephone, fireplace, Bocce ball court, Beautiful water falls & gardens and Private parking lot on premises. Antiquing, art galleries, beach, bicycling, canoeing/kayaking, fishing, golf, hiking, horseback riding, live theater, museums, parks, shopping, tennis, water sports, wineries, restaurants, Cannery Row, Carmel shopping and Monterey Bay Aquarium nearby.

Location: City, ocean community, waterfront. 8 blocks to Monterey Bay Aquarium.

Publicity: *Sunset, Travel & Leisure, Sacramento Bee, San Francisco Examiner, Los Angeles Times, Country Inns, San Francisco Chronicle, Diablo and Elmer Dill's KABC-Los Angeles TV.*

"Words are not enough to describe the ease and tranquility of the atmosphere of the home, rooms, owners and staff at the Jabberwock."

Certificate may be used: Sunday-Thursday, Nov. 1-April 30, excluding holidays. Subject to availability.

Moss Beach 14

Seal Cove Inn

221 Cypress Ave
Moss Beach, CA 94038
(650)728-4114 (800)995-9987 Fax:(650)728-4116
Internet: www.sealcoveinn.com
E-mail: sealcoveinn@foursisters.com

Circa 1991. Considered a European sanctuary on the California coast, Seal Cove Inn in Moss Beach is a serene hideaway with a border of cypress trees and a wildflower meadow. The inn overlooks acres of a county park and the Pacific Ocean beyond. Stroll the tree-lined trail along the waterfront bluffs. Gorgeous guest bedrooms are delightful, spacious retreats with a fireplace, towel warmer and private balcony or terrace. Hospitality is in abundance at a Four Sisters Inn with afternoon tea and appetizers, home-baked cookies and a signature breakfast as well as their renowned adoptable teddy bears. Located just 24 miles south of San Francisco, the surrounding area offers many activities from wine tasting to whale watching. Horseback riding is available on Half Moon Bay and two golf courses are nearby.

Innkeeper(s): Dana Kelley. $235-350. 10 rooms with PB, 2 with WP. Breakfast, afternoon tea and hors d'oeuvres included in rates. Types of meals: Full bkfst, veg bkfst, early coffee/tea and snacks/refreshments. Beds: K. Cable TV, VCR, DVD, reading lamp, CD player, clock radio, telephone, turn-down service, desk, some with hot tub/spa, fireplace, hair dryer, bathrobes, bath amenities, wireless Internet access and iron/ironing board in room. Central air. Fax, bicycles and library on premises. Handicap access. Antiquing, art galleries, beach, bicycling, canoeing/kayaking, fishing, golf, hiking, horseback riding, museums, parks, shopping, tennis, water sports and wineries nearby.

Location: Ocean community. Half Moon Bay.

Certificate may be used: Sunday-Thursday, December-February, based on promotional discount availability and excludes special event periods, holidays and certain room types. First night must be at full rack rate to receive second night free.

Napa H4

Blackbird Inn

1755 First St
Napa, CA 94559
(707)226-2450 (888)567-9811
Internet: www.blackbirdinnnapa.com
E-mail: blackbirdinn@foursisters.com

Circa 2001. Blackbird Inn in Napa, California is a meticulously restored hideaway, built with Greene and Greene-type architecture. It is within an easy walk to town and the surrounding area is picturesque and inviting. The stone pillared porch, leaded glass and blackbird vines are a welcome setting for the wonderful atmosphere found inside. True to the Craftsman-style furnishings and decor, the period lighting accents the subdued colors and warm ambiance. Double-paned windows offer quiet views of the garden fountain. Many of the guest bedrooms feature private decks, spa tubs and fireplaces. Wine and hors d'oeuvres are served in the afternoon.

Innkeeper(s): Edward Hansen. $185-285. 8 rooms with PB, 6 with FP. Breakfast, afternoon tea, snacks/refreshments, hors d'oeuvres and wine included in rates. Types of meals: Full bkfst and early coffee/tea. Beds: KQ. Data port, cable TV, VCR, reading lamp, stereo, clock radio, telephone, turn-down service, hot tub/spa, jetted spa tub and/or private deck and some with fireplace in room. Air conditioning. DVD, fax, parlor games, fireplace, full signature breakfast, afternoon wine and hors d'oeuvres, morning

newspaper delivery, evening turndown service, complimentary sodas and home-baked cookies on premises. Handicap access. Antiquing, art galleries, bicycling, golf, hiking, live theater, museums, parks, shopping, wineries and wine tasting nearby.

Location: City. Downtown Historic Napa.

Certificate may be used: Sunday–Thursday, December-February, based on promotional discount availability and excludes special event periods, holidays and certain room types. First night must be at full rack rate to receive second night free.

Candlelight Inn, a Napa Valley Bed & Breakfast

1045 Easum Drive
Napa, CA 94558-5524
(707) 257-3717 (800) 624-0395 Fax:(707) 257-3762
Internet: www.candlelightinn.com
E-mail: mail@candlelightinn.com

Circa 1929. Located on a park-like acre with gardens, this elegant English Tudor-style house is situated beneath redwood groves and towering trees that shade the banks of Napa Creek. Six rooms feature a marble fireplace and two-person marble Jacuzzi inside the room. The Candlelight Suite offers cathedral ceilings, stained-glass windows and a private sauna. The inn's breakfast room has French doors and windows overlooking the garden. Breakfast is served by candlelight.

Innkeeper(s): Sam Neft. $239-359. 10 rooms with PB, 6 with FP, 6 with WP, 1 cottage. Breakfast and snacks/refreshments included in rates. Types of meals: Full gourmet bkfst, early coffee/tea and wine. Beds: KQ. Modem hookup, cable TV, reading lamp, clock radio, telephone, most with hot tub/spa, voice mail, most with fireplace, hair dryer, bathrobes, bath amenities, wireless Internet access and iron/ironing board in room. Air conditioning. DVD, fax, copier, swimming, parlor games and gift shop on premises. Limited handicap access. Amusement parks, antiquing, art galleries, bicycling, canoeing/kayaking, golf, hiking, horseback riding, live theater, museums, parks, shopping, wineries, hot air ballooning and spas nearby.

Location: Wine country.

Publicity: *Wine Country This Week and CNN.com.*

"We still haven't stopped talking about the great food, wonderful accommodations and gracious hospitality."

Certificate may be used: December-February, Sunday-Thursday, holiday periods excluded, subject to availability.

Hennessey House-Napa's 1889 Queen Anne Victorian B&B

1727 Main St
Napa, CA 94559-1844
(707)226-3774 Fax:(707)226-2975
Internet: www.hennesseyhouse.com
E-mail: inn@hennesseyhouse.com

Circa 1889. Colorful gardens greet you at this gracious Victorian. It was once home to Dr. Edwin Hennessey, a Napa County physician and former mayor. Pristinely renovated, the  inn features stained-glass windows and a curving wraparound porch. A handsome hand-painted, stamped-tin ceiling graces the dining room. The inn's romantic rooms are furnished in antiques. Some offer fireplaces, feather beds and spa tubs. The bathrooms all feature marble floors and antique brass fixtures. There is a sauna and a garden fountain. The innkeepers serve gourmet breakfasts with specialties such as blueberry-stuffed French toast and Eggs Florentine. Tea and cookies are offered at 3 p.m. Later in the evening, wine and cheese is served. Walk to inviting restaurants, shops and theaters. Nearby are the world-famous Napa Valley wineries. The innkeepers will be happy to make recommendations or reservations for wineries, the area's spas and mud baths, hot air balloons, the Wine Train, horseback riding, cycling and hiking.

Innkeeper(s): Kevin Walsh & Lorri Walsh. $139-325. 10 rooms with PB, 7 with FP, 4 with WP. Breakfast and Evening Wine and Cheese Service included in rates. Types of meals: Full bkfst and Evening Wine and Cheese Service. Beds: KQT. Modern hook-up, data port, reading lamp, ceiling fan, clock radio, telephone, voice mail, hair dryer, bath amenities, wireless Internet access, iron/ironing board, Some with Cable TV and CD players in room. Air conditioning. TV, DVD, fax, sauna, parlor games, fireplace, High Speed Wireless Internet Access and Sauna on premises. Antiquing, shopping, Restaurants, Shops, Napa Opera House, Oxbow Public Market and Wine Train nearby.

Location: Napa Valley Wine Country.

Publicity: *Kevin and Lorri Walsh featured on the Napavalley.com and WineCountry.com WineCountry Personality, Favorite Recipes from Northern California Inns - Crowley's Creations, Mary Claire Magazine, Napa Valley Marketplace Magazine, Napa County Landmarks Holiday Candlelight Tour, New York Times, "Beautiful Bedrooms - Design Inspirations from the Worlds Leading Inns and Hotels," a book by Tina Skinner, Arrington's Inn Traveler "2004 Book of Lists" and NBC11 News.*

"A great place to relax in Napa!"

Certificate may be used: Nov. 27-March 8, Sunday-Thursday only, Dec. 26-Jan. 2 excluded; holidays and weekends excluded.

The Beazley House Bed & Breakfast Inn

1910 1st Street
Napa, CA 94559-2351
(707)257-1649 (800)559-1649 Fax:707-257-1518
Internet: www.beazleyhouse.com
E-mail: innkeeper@beazleyhouse.com

Circa 1902. Nestled in green lawns and gardens, this graceful shingled mansion is frosted with white trim on its bays and balustrades. Stained-glass windows and polished-wood floors set the atmosphere in the parlor.
There are five rooms in the main house, and the carriage house features five more, all with fireplaces and whirlpool tubs. The venerable Beazley House was Napa's first bed & breakfast inn.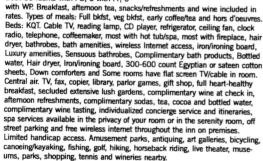

Innkeeper(s): Jim & Carol Beazley. $99-339. 11 rooms with PB, 6 with FP, 5 with WP. Breakfast, afternoon tea, snacks/refreshments and wine included in rates. Types of meals: Full bkfst, veg bkfst, early coffee/tea and hors d'oeuvres. Beds: KQT. Cable TV, reading lamp, CD player, refrigerator, ceiling fan, clock radio, telephone, coffeemaker, most with hot tub/spa, most with fireplace, hair dryer, bathrobes, bath amenities, wireless Internet access, iron/ironing board, Luxury amenities, Sensuous bathrobes, Complimentary bath products, Bottled water, Hair dryer, Iron/ironing board, 300-600 count Egyptian or sateen cotton sheets, Down comforters and Some rooms have flat screen TV/cable in room. Central air. TV, fax, copier, library, parlor games, gift shop, full heart-healthy breakfast, secluded extensive lush gardens, complimentary wine at check in, afternoon refreshments, complimentary sodas, tea, cocoa and bottled water, complimentary wine tasting, individualized concierge service and itineraries, spa services available in the privacy of your room or in the serenity room, off street parking and free wireless internet throughout the inn on premises. Limited handicap access. Amusement parks, antiquing, art galleries, bicycling, canoeing/kayaking, fishing, golf, hiking, horseback riding, live theater, museums, parks, shopping, tennis and wineries nearby.

Location: City. Napa Valley Wine Country.

Publicity: *Los Angeles Times, USA Today, Sacramento Bee, Yellow Brick Road, Emerge, Bay Area Backroads, Wine Spectator 25th Anniversary Edition, HGTV's Dream Drives, San Francisco Chronicle and North Bay Biz.*

"There's a sense of peace & tranquility that hovers over this house, sprinkling magical dream dust & kindness."

Certificate may be used: November-March, Sunday-Thursday, excludes holidays, subject to availability.

The McClelland-Priest Bed & Breakfast Inn

569 Randolph Street
Napa, CA 94559
(707)224-6875 (800)290-6881 Fax:(707)224-6782
Internet: www.mcclellandpriest.com

Circa 1879. Experience the stately elegance and Victorian splendor of this 1879 historic landmark. Pass through the grand foyer to the formal parlor for an early evening reception with hors d'oeuvres and Napa Valley wines amid European antiques, handcrafted plaster ceilings and authentically ornate chandeliers. Innkeeper/owner Celeste offers concierge services that will assist with local attractions, reservations and travel planning. Take a self-guided, complimentary wine-tasting tour. The onsite Sole Spa and Fitness Center features a variety of treatments and exercise options. Guest suites reflect the luxurious ambiance of a famed writer, composer or artist and boast fireplaces, large soaking tubs or Jacuzzis. The Firenze Suite also includes an outdoor garden terrace. Special packages are available.

Innkeeper(s): Celeste. $189-289. 5 rooms with PB, 4 with FP, 5 with HT. Breakfast, snacks/refreshments, hors d'oeuvres and wine included in rates. Beds: KQ. CD player, clock radio, most with hot tub/spa, fireplace, hair dryer, bath amenities, wireless Internet access and iron/ironing board in room. Central air. TV, parlor games, telephone, Private gym on premises, Complimentary travel/tour planning, Maps and Wine tasting passes to many of the famed Napa Valley Wineries. on premises. Antiquing, art galleries, bicycling, golf, hiking, parks, shopping, tennis, Walking trails, Winery tours, Fine dining, Balloon flights, Wine train and Picnics nearby.

Location: Napa Valley.

Publicity: *Napa Valley Register and North Bay Biz.*

Certificate may be used: November 24-February. Block out dates December 24-27, December 29-January 2 and January 7-16, no weekends.

Nevada City   F6

Emma Nevada House

528 E Broad St
Nevada City, CA 95959-2213
(530)265-4415 (800)916-3662 Fax:(530)265-4416
Internet: www.emmanevadahouse.com
E-mail: mail@emmanevadahouse.com

Circa 1856. The childhood home of 19th-century opera star Emma Nevada now serves as an attractive Queen Anne Victorian inn. English roses line the white picket fence in front, and the forest-like back garden has a small stream with benches. The Empress' Chamber is the most romantic room with ivory linens atop a French antique bed, a bay window and a massive French armoire. Some rooms have whirlpool baths and TV. Guests  enjoy relaxing in the hexagonal sunroom and on the inn's wrap-around porches. Empire Mine State Historic Park is nearby.

Innkeeper(s): Susan & Andrew Howard. $149-249. 6 rooms with PB, 2 with FP, 2 with WP, 1 two-bedroom suite. Breakfast and afternoon tea included in rates. Types of meals: Full gourmet bkfst, early coffee/tea and snacks/refreshments. Beds: KQ. Modern hook-up, cable TV, VCR, DVD, reading lamp, CD player, ceiling fan, clock radio, desk, some with fireplace, hair dryer, bathrobes, bath amenities, wireless Internet access, iron/ironing board, clawfoot bathtubs and Jacuzzi tubs in room. Central air. Fax, parlor games, telephone and gift shop on premises. Antiquing, art galleries, bicycling, canoeing/kayaking, cross-country skiing, downhill skiing, fishing, golf, hiking, horseback riding, live theater, museums, parks, shopping, tennis, water sports and wineries nearby.

Location: City, country, mountains. Town in foothills.

Publicity: *Country Inns, Gold Rush Scene, Sacramento Focus, The Union, Los Angeles Times, San Jose Mercury News, Sacramento Bee and Karen Browns.*

"A delightful experience: such airiness and hospitality in the midst of so much history. We were fascinated by the detail and the faithfulness of the restoration. This house is a quiet solace for city-weary travelers. There's a grace here."

Certificate may be used: Jan. 2 to April 30, Monday-Thursday, no holidays.

Nice   F4

Featherbed Railroad Company B&B

2870 Lakeshore Blvd
Nice, CA 95464
(707)274-8378 (800)966-6322
Internet: www.featherbedrailroad.com
E-mail: room@featherbedrailroad.com

Circa 1988. On the shores of Clear Lake in Northern California, Featherbed Railroad Company Bed & Breakfast Resort spans five park-like acres. Luxuriously refurbished railroad cabooses provide unusual yet inviting accommodations. Each one is individually furnished and decorated around a theme with its own feather bed and upscale amenities. Most feature Jacuzzi tubs for two. Swim in the pool or explore the scenic area on a tanden bike. This lakefront resort also boasts a private dock and boat launch.

Innkeeper(s): Tony & Peggy Barthel. $99-190. 9 rooms with PB, 7 with HT, 1 conference room. Breakfast and snacks/refreshments included in rates. Types of meals: Full bkfst. Beds: Q. Cable TV, VCR, reading lamp, refrigerator, ceiling fan, clock radio, coffeemaker, most with hot tub/spa, hair dryer, bath amenities and wireless Internet access in room. Central air. Fax, copier, spa, swimming, bicycles, library, parlor games, fireplace, gift shop, Swimming pool, Boat launch, Pier/Dock, Ping Pong, Basketball hoop and Lakeshore access on premises. Antiquing, art galleries, beach, bicycling, canoeing/kayaking, fishing, golf, hiking, horseback riding, live theater, museums, parks, shopping, water sports and wineries nearby.

Location: Country, mountains, waterfront.

Publicity: *Santa Rosa Press Democrat, Fairfield Daily Republic, London Times, Travel & Leisure., Eye on the Bay and Bay Area Back Roads.*

Certificate may be used: Sunday-Thursday, Oct. 15-April 15.

Pacific Grove   J5

Centrella Inn

612 Central Ave
Pacific Grove, CA 93950-2611
(831)372-3372 (800)233-3372 Fax:(831)372-2036
Internet: www.centrellainn.com
E-mail: reserve@centrellainn.com

Circa 1889. Pacific Grove was founded as a Methodist resort in 1875, and this home, built just after the town's incorporation, was billed by a local newspaper as, "the largest, most commodious and pleasantly located boarding house in the Grove." Many a guest is still sure to agree. The rooms are well-appointed in a comfortable, Victorian style. Six guest rooms

include fireplaces. The Garden Room has a private entrance, fireplace, wet bar, Jacuzzi tub and a canopy bed topped with designer linens. Freshly baked croissants or pastries and made-to-order waffles are common fare at the inn's continental buffet breakfast. The inn is within walking distance of the Monterey Bay Aquarium, the beach and many Pacific Grove shops.

Innkeeper(s): Honey Green. $109-289. 26 rooms, 21 with PB, 6 with FP, 1 with WP, 5 suites, 5 cottages. Breakfast and snacks/refreshments included in rates. Types of meals: Full bkfst, veg bkfst and hors d'oeuvres. Beds: KQT. Reading lamp, telephone, hair dryer, bath amenities, wireless Internet access, iron/ironing board, Cottages have amenities that include Fireplace, TV/VCR, Sofa bed, CD player and Mini fridge in room. VCR, fax, copier, fireplace and TVs upon request on premises. Antiquing, art galleries, beach, bicycling, canoeing/kayaking, fishing, golf, horseback riding, museums, parks, shopping, water sports and wineries nearby.

Location: City, ocean community.

Publicity: *Country Inns, New York Times and San Francisco Examiner.*

"I was ecstatic at the charm that the Centrella has been offering travelers for years and hopefully hundreds of years to come. The bed—perfect! I am forever enthralled by the old beauty and will remember this forever!"

Certificate may be used: Sunday-Thursday, November-February, excluding holidays and special events, subject to availability.

Gosby House Inn

643 Lighthouse Ave
Pacific Grove, CA 93950-2643
(831)375-1287 (800)527-8828 Fax:(831)655-9621
Internet: www.gosbyhouseinn.com
E-mail: gosbyhouseinn@foursisters.com

Circa 1887. Built as an upscale Victorian inn for those visiting the old Methodist retreat in Pacific Grove, California, this sunny yellow mansion features an abundance of gables, turrets and bays. During renovation the innkeeper slept in all the guest bedrooms to determine just what antiques were needed and how the beds should be situated. Many of the romantic rooms include fireplaces and offer canopy beds. The Carriage House rooms include fireplaces, decks and spa tubs. Savor a delicious breakfast before visiting nearby attractions. The Monterey Bay Aquarium and Carmel are nearby. Historic Gosby House Inn, which has been open for more than a century, is in the National Register and is one of the Four Sisters Inns.

$185-300. 22 rooms with PB, 11 with FP. Breakfast, afternoon tea, snacks/refreshments, hors d'oeuvres and wine included in rates. Types of meals: Full gourmet bkfst and early coffee/tea. Beds: KQD. Stereo, clock radio, telephone, turn-down service, some with hot tub/spa, hair dryer, bath amenities, iron/ironing board, signature breakfast and afternoon wine and hors d'oeuvres, evening turndown service, morning newspaper delivery, bicycles to borrow and home-baked cookies in room. TV, fax, copier, bicycles, parlor games and fireplace on premises. Handicap access. Antiquing, art galleries, beach, bicycling, canoeing/kayaking, golf, hiking, live theater, museums, parks, shopping, tennis, wineries and Monterey Bay Aquarium nearby.

Location: Ocean community.

Publicity: *San Francisco Chronicle, Oregonian, Los Angeles Times and Travel & Leisure.*

Certificate may be used: Sunday–Thursday, December-February, based on promotional discount availability and excludes special event periods, holidays and certain room types. First night must be at full rack rate to receive second night free.

Green Gables Inn

301 Ocean Avenue
Pacific Grove, CA 93950
(831)375-2095 (800)722-1774 Fax:(831)375-5437
Internet: www.greengablesinnpg.com
E-mail: greengablesinn@foursisters.com

Circa 1888. Green Gables Inn, a half-timbered Queen Anne Victorian in Pacific Grove, California, appears as a fantasy of gables overlooking spectacular Monterey Bay. The parlor has stained-glass panels framing the fireplace and bay windows looking out to the sea. A favorite focal point is an antique carousel horse. Most of the guest rooms have panoramic views of the ocean, fireplaces, gleaming woodwork, soft quilts and teddy bears, and four rooms have spa tubs. After a bountiful breakfast borrow a bike from the inn and ride along cross the paved oceanfront cycling path across the street. Green Gables Inn is one of the Four Sisters Inns.

Innkeeper(s): Honey Spence. $140-300. 11 rooms, 7 with PB, 6 with FP, 5 suites. Breakfast, afternoon tea, snacks/refreshments, hors d'oeuvres and wine included in rates. Types of meals: Full gourmet bkfst and early coffee/tea. Beds: KQD. Cable TV, VCR, reading lamp, stereo, ceiling fan, snack bar, clock radio, telephone, turn-down service, desk, some with hot tub/spa, voice mail, hair dryer, bath amenities and iron/ironing board in room. Fax, copier, bicycles, library, parlor games, fireplace, signature breakfast, afternoon wine and hors d'oeuvres, evening turndown service, morning newspaper delivery, home-baked cookies and bicycles to borrow on premises. Handicap access. Antiquing, art galleries, beach, bicycling, canoeing/kayaking, fishing, golf, hiking, horseback riding, live theater, museums, parks, shopping, tennis, water sports, wineries and aquarium nearby.

Location: Ocean community, waterfront.

Publicity: *Travel & Leisure and Country Living.*

Certificate may be used: Sunday–Thursday, December-February, based on promotional discount availability and excludes special event periods, holidays and certain room types. First night must be at full rack rate to receive second night free.

Inn at Seventeen Mile Drive

213 Seventeen Mile Dr
Pacific Grove, CA 93950-2400
(831)642-9514 (800)526-5666 Fax:(831)642-9546
Internet: www.innat17.com
E-mail: innkeeper@innat17.com

Circa 1925. The only challenging part of a visit to this 1920s craftsman-style house is figuring out where the deep blue sea ends and clear skies begin. Located in the heart of the Monterey Peninsula, this two-story, three-building inn offers sea or garden views from the main house, while you will find rustic ambiance, surrounded by oak and redwood trees, in the cottage and redwood chalet rooms. Relax in the spa beneath the tall trees in the gardens, which are often visited by deer and monarch butterflies, or enjoy a glass of champagne while observing Koi in the fountain ponds. Or, spend time in the wood-paneled dining, sitting and reading rooms while enjoying complimentary hors d'oeuvres and planning a day full of activities.

Innkeeper(s): Jas Barbe'. $145-290. 14 rooms with PB, 2 with FP, 1 cottage. Breakfast, snacks/refreshments, hors d'oeuvres, wine, Special occassion catering is available for weddings, reunions and and meetings included in rates. Types of meals: Full gourmet bkfst, veg bkfst and Our chef and dining style served breakfast is considered to be the best on the Monterey Peninsula. Beds: KQ. Data port, cable TV, reading lamp, clock radio, telephone, some with fireplace, hair dryer, bathrobes, bath amenities and wireless

Internet access and iron/ironing board in room. Central air. VCR, fax, copier, spa, library and parlor games on premises. Handicap access. Antiquing, art galleries, beach, bicycling, canoeing/kayaking, fishing, golf, hiking, live theater, museums, parks, shopping, sporting events, tennis, water sports, wineries, Monterey Bay Aquarium, The Monarch Butterfly Sanctuary, Pebble Beach Golfing, Big Sur and and 17 Mile Drive nearby.

Location: City, ocean community. Close to golf course.

Certificate may be used: Nov. 1 to March 31, Sunday-Thursday, except holidays, special events.

Martine Inn

255 Ocean View Blvd
Pacific Grove, CA 93950
(831)373-3388 (800)852-5588 Fax:(831)373-3896
Internet: www.martineinn.com
E-mail: don@martineinn.com

Circa 1899. This turn-of-the-century oceanfront manor sits atop a jagged cliff overlooking the coastline of Monterey Bay, just steps away from the water's edge. Bedrooms are furnished with antiques, and each room contains a fresh rose. Thirteen rooms also boast fireplaces. Some of the museum-quality antiques were exhibited in the 1893 Chicago World's Fair. Other bedroom sets include furniture that belonged to Edith Head, and there is an 1860 Chippendale Revival four-poster bed with a canopy and side curtains.

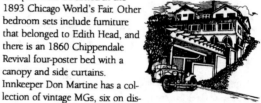

Innkeeper Don Martine has a collection of vintage MGs, six on display for guests. Twilight wine and hors d'oeuvres are served, and chocolates accompany evening turndown service. The inn is a beautiful spot for romantic getaways and weddings.

Innkeeper(s): Don Martine. $169-450. 25 rooms with PB, 13 with FP, 2 total suites, including 1 two-bedroom suite, 6 conference rooms. Breakfast, snacks/refreshments, hors d'oeuvres and wine included in rates. Types of meals: Full gourmet bkfst and early coffee/tea. Beds: KQDT. Reading lamp, refrigerator, clock radio, telephone, turn-down service, desk, most with fireplace, hair dryer, bathrobes, bath amenities, wireless Internet access, Fresh Flowers and Refrigerator in room. TV, fax, copier, library, parlor games, gift shop, Evening wine, DSL Internet, Billiard table, MG car display, Piano, Wi-Fi, Landscaped courtyards, Fish pond and Meeting rooms on premises. Handicap access. Antiquing, art galleries, beach, bicycling, canoeing/kayaking, fishing, golf, hiking, horseback riding, live theater, museums, parks, shopping, sporting events, tennis, water sports, wineries, Monterey Bay Aquarium, Cannery Row, 17-Mile Drive and Fishermans Wharf nearby.

Location: Ocean community, waterfront.

Publicity: *Sunday Oregonian, Bon Appetit, Vacations APAC, Fresno Bee, San Francisco Magazine, Santa Barbara News-Press, Victory Lane and North American Classic MG Magazine.*

"Wonderful, can't wait to return."

Certificate may be used: Anytime, November-February, subject to availability. Not on Valentine's and between Christmas and New Year's.

Palm Springs   012

Sakura, Japanese B&B Inn

1677 N Via Miraleste at Vista Chino
Palm Springs, CA 92262
(760)327-0705 Fax:(760)327-6847
Internet: www.sakurabedandbreakfast.com
E-mail: george@sakurabedandbreakfast.com

Circa 1945. An authentic Japanese experience awaits guests of this private home, distinctively decorated with Japanese artwork and antique kimonos. Guests are encouraged to leave their shoes at the door, grab kimonos and slippers and discover what real relaxation is all about. Futon beds, and in-room refrigerators and microwaves are provided. Guests may choose either American or Japanese breakfasts, and Japanese or vegetarian dinners also are available. The Palm Springs area is home to more than 100 golf courses and hosts annual world-class golf and tennis charity events. A favorite place for celebrity watching, the area also is the Western polo capital and offers the famous 9,000-foot aerial tram ride that climbs through several temperature zones. There are cycling trails, theater, horseback riding in the canyons and fine dining, skiing and antiquing. During the summer months, the innkeepers conduct tours in Japan.

Innkeeper(s): George Cebra. $75-125. 3 rooms, 2 with PB, 1 suite. Breakfast included in rates. Types of meals: Full bkfst, early coffee/tea, picnic lunch, afternoon tea and dinner. Beds: QDT. TV, VCR, refrigerator and clock radio in room. Central air. Swimming, Jacuzzi, outdoor barbeque and Japanese Gardens on premises. Amusement parks, antiquing, cross-country skiing, fishing, live theater, parks and shopping nearby.

Location: City, mountains. California desert.

Certificate may be used: Anytime, Sunday-Thursday.

Placerville   G7

Albert Shafsky House Bed & Breakfast

2942 Coloma St
Placerville, CA 95667
(530)642-2776 (877)BNBINNS Fax:(503)642-2109
Internet: www.shafsky.com
E-mail: stay@shafsky.com

Circa 1902. Gold Country hospitality is offered at this Queen Anne Victorian Bed and Breakfast located just a stroll to the historic district and the shops of Old Hangtown. Enjoy a welcome snack and refreshments in the elegant living room. Pleasantly decorated guest bedrooms are furnished with antiques and offer individually controlled heat and air conditioning as well as feather beds and goosedown comforters during winter. The two-room Lighthouse Suite also boasts a sitting room for a private breakfast. Arrangements can be made for special occasions, or a personalized bouquet of flowers.

Innkeeper(s): Rita Timewell and Stephanie Carlson. $135-185. 3 rooms with PB. Breakfast, snacks/refreshments and wine included in rates. Types of meals: Full gourmet bkfst, veg bkfst, early coffee/tea and hors d'oeuvres. Beds: KQ. Reading lamp, CD player, ceiling fan, clock radio, turn-down service, desk, hair dryer, bathrobes, bath amenities, wireless Internet access and iron/ironing board in room. Air conditioning. TV, VCR, fax, copier, library, parlor games, telephone, fireplace, gift shop, satellite TV, video library, games and guest refrigerator on premises. Limited handicap access. Antiquing, art galleries, canoeing/kayaking, cross-country skiing, downhill skiing, fishing, golf, hiking, horseback riding, live theater, museums, parks, shopping, tennis, water sports, wineries, Apple Hill, Sutter's Mill, Gold Bug Mine, Gold Discovery Park and whitewater rafting nearby.

Location: City, country, mountains. Located a short stroll from historic Placerville, aka Old Hangtown.

Publicity: Mountain Democrat, San Francisco Chronicle, San Jose Mercury News, The El Dorado Guide, KCRA, Taste of California (Travel Channel), KNCI and KAHI.

Certificate may be used: Sunday-Thursday, subject to availability.

Point Reyes Station   H4

The Black Heron Inn

51 Cypress Road
Point Reyes Station, CA 94956
(415)663-8846 (415)-663-1894OFFICE
Internet: www.blackheroninn.com
E-mail: susan@blackthorneinn.com

Centrally located for the perfect Northern California getaway, enjoy sweeping vistas of Tomales Bay and the stunning Inverness Ridge next to Point Reyes National Seashore. Step out the front door to explore the more than 70,000 acres of protected land. Limantour Beach is nearby and sea kayaking, biking, hiking and horseback riding are popular activities. San Francisco and Napa are about a one-hour drive. Stay in a guest room with a great view, spacious deck, private entrance, sitting area, robes and furnished marble wet bars; or relax in the two-story Grand View Suite with an upstairs loft and three-sided, glass-enclosed tower lounge. Breakfast foods, beverages and supplies are provided in-room upon arrival with everything needed to fully enjoy a morning meal.

Innkeeper(s): Bill & Susan Wigert. Call for rates. Call inn for details.

Certificate may be used: Anytime, November-March, subject to availability.

Saint Helena   G5

Ink House

1575 S. Saint Helena Hwy
Saint Helena, CA 94574-9775
(866)963-3890 (866)963-3890 Fax:707-9630739
Internet: www.inkhouse.com
E-mail: inkhousebb@aol.com

Circa 1884. Theron H. Ink, owner of thousands of acres in Marin, Napa and Sonoma counties, was an investor in livestock, wineries and mining. He built his Italianate Victorian with a glass-walled observatory on top, and from this room, visitors can enjoy 360-degree views of the Napa Valley and surrounding vineyards. Listed in the National Register, the Ink House is an elegant, spacious retreat of a time gone by.

Innkeeper(s): Kevin Outcalt. $159-299. 7 rooms, 5 with PB. Breakfast, hors d'oeuvres and wine included in rates. Types of meals: Full gourmet bkfst and veg bkfst. Beds: Q. Reading lamp, clock radio and hair dryer in room. Air conditioning. TV, bicycles, library, parlor games, telephone, fireplace, pool table, observatory, picnic table, historic barn, gardens and horseshoes on premises. Antiquing, art galleries, bicycling, golf, horseback riding, shopping, wineries, spas, horseback riding and hot air balloon rides nearby.

Location: Country, mountains. Wine country.

Publicity: Newsweek, Time, Forbes, Los Angeles Times, Wine Spectator., CBS and The Price is Right.

"Your hospitality made us feel so much at home. This is a place and a time we will long remember."

Certificate may be used: Weekdays (Sunday-Thursday night) All year. Weekend (Friday-Saturday night) from November 25-April 15.

Salinas   *J5*

Chateau Coralini Retreat & Spa

100 River Rd
Salinas, CA 93908
(831)455-2100 Fax:(831)455-2154
Internet: www.chateaucoralini.com
E-mail: info@chateaucoralini.com

Circa 1891. This historic Queen Anne Victorian mansion, in the National Register, was once the center of a large farming estate. Recently restored and refurbished, it offers guest parlors, a wine cellar dining room, and 10 guest room, furnished in fine European antiques and with luxurious marble and stone bathrooms. Amenities include flat screen TVs, fireplaces, and European cotton linens with feather down comforters. There are two acres of beautiful gardens that include a gazebo and a separate spa. The inn is located along the River Road wine trail.

Innkeeper(s): Samuel & Linda Persall. $225-550. 9 rooms with PB, 7 with FP, 6 with WP, 1 conference room. Breakfast, snacks/refreshments and A welcome fruit and cheese amenity and fresh baked cookies at bedtime are also included for each guest during their stay at the Chateau included in rates. Types of meals: Full gourmet bkfst, veg bkfst, early coffee/tea, wine, gourmet dinner, room service, Chateau Coralini is a full service Retreat and Spa. Included are a welcome cheese and fruit amenity on arrival, fresh baked cookies at bedtime and and a full gourmet breakfast served in the elegant dining room each morning. Additional meal services are provided on request. Wine Pairing Dinners are featured. . Beds: KQ. Modem hook-up, data port, cable TV, telephone, coffeemaker, turn-down service, desk, most with hot tub/spa, most with fireplace, hair dryer, bathrobes, bath amenities, wireless Internet access, iron/ironing board, All of our Luxury Suites feature plush Euro pillow top mattress, fine linens, elegant bedcrowns, antique furnishings, spacious bathrooms with air masseur tubs/shower combos or large shower environments, aromatic L'Occitane amenities, and more. Guests receive a welcome cheese & fruit platter on arrival, turn down service with fresh baked cookies and milk and and a gourmet breakfast each morning served in the Versailles Dining Room in room. Air conditioning. DVD, fax, copier, spa, bicycles, library, parlor games, laundry facility, Elegant parlors filled with antiques and art, a rustic wine cellar event space, beautiful French Country gourmet kitchen, two acres of beautifully landscaped gardens, serene gazebo with comfortable lounge chairs , surrounded by angelic fountains, outdoor BBQ kitchen and terrace, Full service day spa offering hair salon services, massage, facials, body scrubs and wraps, manicures and pedicures and and more on premises. Handicap access. Antiquing, art galleries, beach, bicycling, canoeing/kayaking, fishing, golf, hiking, horseback riding, live theater, museums, parks, shopping, sporting events, tennis, water sports, wineries, Monterey Peninsula is home to a variety of activities to please every style of tourist. From golfing at Pebble Beach and surrounding golf courses, home to the US Open & AT&T golf events, to Mazda Laguna Seca Raceway to enjoy the US Grand Prix & Historic Automobile Races and more, to Cannery Row for shopping, dining, biking, fishing, whale watching, kayaking and a visit to the Aquarium, to the Steinbeck Museum in Salinas, Carmel-by-the-Sea offering galleries and boutiques and fine dining, and of course just moments from the Chateau and fine wine tasting throughout the River Road Wine Trail and various Monterey vineyards nearby.

Location: Country, ocean community. Wine Country Destination, Monterey Peninsula.

Certificate may be used: Anytime, subject to availability; holidays or event weekends may be excluded.

Vision Quest Safari Bed & Breakfast

400 River Rd
Salinas, CA 93908-9627
(831)455-1901 (800)228-7382 Fax:(831)455-1902
Internet: www.visionquestranch.com
E-mail: reservations@wildthingsinc.com

Circa 2001. Exotic and domestic birds and animals reside at this 51-acre ranch in Salinas, California that also includes the unique Vision Quest Safari Bed & Breakfast. Stay in an animal-themed canvas-walled African bungalow that is complete with bathroom facilities, a refrigerator and coffee maker. A continental breakfast is delivered to the tent daily, sometimes by a pachyderm patrol. Browse the collection of educational animal videos to watch on a VCR. There may be an opportunity to join the facility trainers on an evening walk with the ranch animals. Located in Monterey County, the attractions and sites of Carmel, Pebble Beach and Monterey are a short drive.

Innkeeper(s): Heather Greaux & Christy Ingram. $195-225. 4 cabins, 4 suites, 1 conference room. Breakfast included in rates. Types of meals: Cont, early coffee/tea and gourmet dinner. Beds: KQD. TV, VCR, reading lamp, refrigerator, clock radio, coffeemaker, hair dryer, bath amenities and iron/ironing board in room. Fax, copier, stable, pet boarding, telephone and gift shop on premises. Limited handicap access. Antiquing, art galleries, beach, bicycling, canoeing/kayaking, fishing, golf, hiking, horseback riding, live theater, museums, parks, shopping, tennis, water sports, wineries, Some of the more adventurous choose to add a full-contact animal tour to their stay. Wild Things offers a Pachyderm Package – which is a full contact elephant tour, a VIP Package – which is a full contact tour with an elephant, bear, and a small exotic cat and and the Walk With the Animals Package – which is an all day tour were guests tailor their day to what animals they would like to spend time with nearby.

Location: Country. Monterey Bay.

Certificate may be used: Sunday-Thursday, subject to availability.

San Francisco   *H4*

Petite Auberge

863 Bush St
San Francisco, CA 94108-3312
(415)928-6000 (800)365-3004 Fax:(415)673-7214
Internet: www.petiteaubergesf.com
E-mail: petiteauberge@jdvhospitality.com

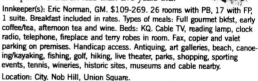

Circa 1917. An ornate baroque design with curved bay windows highlight this five-story hotel that has now been transformed into a French country inn. This Joie de Vivre property boasts antiques, fresh flowers and country accessories. Most guest bedrooms feature working fireplaces. Take a short walk to the Powell Street cable car. In the evenings, wine and cheese, sherry, tea, coffee and cake are served. There is an extra fee for an additional guest in room, except for children less than five years old.

Innkeeper(s): Eric Norman, GM. $109-269. 26 rooms with PB, 17 with FP, 1 suite. Breakfast included in rates. Types of meals: Full gourmet bkfst, early coffee/tea, afternoon tea and wine. Beds: KQ. Cable TV, reading lamp, clock radio, telephone, fireplace and terry robes in room. Fax, copier and valet parking on premises. Handicap access. Antiquing, art galleries, beach, canoeing/kayaking, fishing, golf, hiking, live theater, parks, shopping, sporting events, tennis, wineries, historic sites, museums and cable nearby.

Location: City. Nob Hill, Union Square.

Publicity: *Travel & Leisure, Oregonian, Los Angeles Times, Brides, Conde Nast Traveler Top 75 in US and 2005 Gold List.*

"Breakfast was great, and even better in bed!"

Certificate may be used: November-February, Sunday-Thursday, excluding holidays and special events.

The Inn San Francisco

943 South Van Ness Ave
San Francisco, CA 94110-2613
(415)641-0188 (800)359-0913 Fax:(415)641-1701
Internet: www.innsf.com
E-mail: innkeeper@innsf.com

Circa 1872. Built on one of San Francisco's earliest "Mansion Rows," this 21-room Italianate Victorian is located near the civic and convention centers, close to Mission Dolores. Antiques, marble fireplaces and Oriental rugs decorate the opulent grand double parlors. Most rooms have featherbeds, Victorian wallcoverings and desks, while deluxe rooms offer private spas, fireplaces or bay windows. There is a rooftop deck with a 360-degree view of San Francisco. Complimentary beverages are always available. The inn is close to the opera, symphony, theaters, Mission Dolores, gift and jewelry centers and antique shopping.

Innkeeper(s): Marty Neely & Connie Wu. $120-335. 21 rooms, 19 with PB, 3 with FP, 3 suites, 1 cottage. Breakfast included in rates. Types of meals: Full bkfst and afternoon tea. Beds: QD. TV, reading lamp, refrigerator, clock radio, telephone, desk, hot tub/spa, one suite with redwood hot tub, flowers and truffles in room. Fax, fireplace, garden, rooftop view sundeck and parlor on premises.

Location: City.

Publicity: *Innsider, Sunset Magazine, San Francisco Chronicle and American Airlines Magazine.*

"Breakfast; marvelous. The best B&B we've visited. We were made to feel like family."

Certificate may be used: Monday-Thursday, subject to availability, holidays excluded. Check with innkeeper for weekend night availability.

White Swan Inn

845 Bush St
San Francisco, CA 94108-3300
(415)775-1755 (800)999-9570 Fax:(415)775-5717
Internet: www.whiteswaninnsf.com
E-mail: whiteswan@jdvhospitality.com

Circa 1915. This four-story inn is near Union Square and the Powell Street cable car. Beveled-glass doors open to a reception area with granite floors and English artwork. Bay windows and a rear deck contribute to the feeling of an English garden inn. The guest rooms are decorated with bold English wallpapers and prints. All rooms have fireplaces. Turndown service and complimentary newspapers are included, and in the evenings wine, sherry, tea, coffee, cake and hors d'oeuvres are served. There is a $20 fee for an additional guest in room, except for children less than 5 years old.

Innkeeper(s): Eric Norman & Pam Wright. $139-309. 26 rooms with PB, 26 with FP, 3 suites, 1 conference room. Breakfast and afternoon tea included in rates. Types of meals: Full gourmet bkfst, early coffee/tea, snacks/refreshments and wine. Beds: KQT. Data port, cable TV, reading lamp, refrigerator, clock radio, telephone, coffeemaker, turn-down service, desk, fireplace, terry robes, newspaper and complimentary beverages in room. Fax, copier, library, parlor games and wireless Internet on premises. Antiquing, art galleries, beach, canoeing/kayaking, fishing, golf, hiking, live theater, museums, parks, shopping, sporting events, tennis and wineries nearby.

Location: City. Nob Hill, Union Square.

Publicity: *Travel & Leisure, Victoria and Wine Spectator.*

"Wonderfully accommodating. Absolutely perfect."

Certificate may be used: December and January, Sunday-Thursday, excluding holidays and special events.

Santa Barbara   N8

A White Jasmine Inn

1327 Bath St
Santa Barbara, CA 93101-3630
(805)966-0589
Internet: www.whitejasmineinnsantabarbara.com
E-mail: stay@whitejasmineinnsantabarbara.com

Circa 1885. A Craftsman Bungalow, Victorian Cottage and an Artisan Cottage comprise A White Jasmine Inn, located in the theatre and arts district of Santa Barbara, California. Accommodations include guest rooms and elegant suites with antiques and rich wood trim. Some rooms also have

fireplaces, mini refrigerators or whirlpools tubs. Each cottage has private gardens, but everyone is welcome in the main house common areas that include the parlor and secluded garden hot tub. Homemade breakfasts in a basket are delivered to each room. It's a three-block walk to restaurants, shops and the shuttle to the beach.

Innkeeper(s): Marlies Marburg and John Cicekli. $154-309. 12 rooms with PB, 12 with FP, 2 with HT, 8 with WP, 4 suites, 3 cottages. Breakfast, afternoon tea, snacks/refreshments, hors d'oeuvres, wine and Various treats included in rates. Types of meals: Full gourmet bkfst, veg bkfst, early coffee/tea, In-room, full and hot breakfast is standard. This may be taken in various other areas. Continental breakfast also available. Beds: KQ. Modem hook-up, data port, cable TV, VCR, DVD, reading lamp, stereo, refrigerator, ceiling fan, clock radio, telephone, coffeemaker, desk, hot tub/spa, fireplace, hair dryer, bathrobes, bath amenities, wireless Internet access, iron/ironing board, Microwave, Kitchenette, Steamshower, Flat panel TV, Coffee and Tea in room. Air conditioning. Fax, copier, spa, parlor games, gift shop, Steamshower, Gardens, In-room, Full, hot breakfast which may be taken elsewhere, Gift shop, In-room massages and Fax service on premises. Antiquing, art galleries, beach, bicycling, canoeing/kayaking, fishing, golf, hiking, horseback riding, live theater, museums, parks, shopping, sporting events, tennis, water sports, wineries and Large array of sundry acivites in near proximity nearby.

Location: City, mountains, ocean community. Downtown, proximity to beach, and near wineries.

Publicity: *Houston Post, Los Angeles Times and Pasadena Choice.*

"Only gracious service is offered at the Glenborough Inn."

Certificate may be used: Sunday-Thursday, November-December and January-May, valid on rooms priced at $209 or higher. Excludes holiday weeks.

Cheshire Cat Inn & Spa

36 W Valerio St
Santa Barbara, CA 93101-2524
(805)569-1610 Fax:(805)682-1876
Internet: www.cheshirecat.com
E-mail: cheshire@cheshirecat.com

Circa 1894. This elegant inn features three Queen Anne Victorians, a Coach House and three cottages surrounded by fountains, gazebos and lush flower gardens. The guest bedrooms and suites are furnished with English antiques, Laura Ashley fabrics and wallpapers or oak floors, pine furniture and down comforters. Some boast fireplaces, Jacuzzi tubs, private balconies, VCRs and refrigerators. Wedgewood china set in the formal dining room or brick patio enhances a delicious breakfast. Local wine and hors d'oeuvres are served in the evening. Spa facilities offer massage and body treatments.

Innkeeper(s): Connie and Bharti. $143-399. 17 rooms with PB, 3 with FP, 3 with HT, 4 total suites, including 3 two-bedroom suites, 3 cottages, 1 conference room. Breakfast, hors d'oeuvres and wine included in rates. Types of meals: Cont plus, early coffee/tea and room service. Beds: KQT. Cable TV, VCR, reading lamp, refrigerator, ceiling fan, clock radio, telephone, some with hot tub/spa, some with fireplace, hair dryer, bathrobes, wireless Internet access and iron/ironing board in room. Air conditioning. Fax, copier, spa and spa facilities on premises. Antiquing, art galleries, beach, bicycling, canoeing/kayaking, fishing, golf, hiking, horseback riding, live theater, museums, parks, shopping, sporting events, tennis, water sports and wineries nearby.

Location: City.

Publicity: Two on the Town, KABC, Los Angeles Times, Santa Barbara, American In Flight and Elmer Dills Recommends.

"Romantic and quaint."

Certificate may be used: Anytime, subject to availability.

Old Yacht Club Inn

431 Corona Del Mar
Santa Barbara, CA 93103-3601
(805)962-1277 (800)676-1676 Fax:(805)962-3989
Internet: www.oldyachtclubinn.com
E-mail: info@oldyachtclubinn.com

Circa 1912. One block from famous East Beach, this California Craftsman house was the home of the Santa Barbara Yacht Club during the Roaring '20s. It was opened as Santa Barbara's first B&B and has become renowned for its gourmet food and superb hospitality. The Old Yacht Club Inn features an evening social hour. Inviting guest bedrooms boast fresh flowers and a decanter of sherry. Wake up to start the day with a gourmet breakfast.

Innkeeper(s): Eilene Bruce. $119-459. 12 rooms with PB, 2 with FP, 5 with WP, 2 two-bedroom and 1 three-bedroom suites, 1 cottage. Snacks/refreshments, Full breakfast, afternoon wine social and free parking and bike rentals included in rates. Types of meals: Full bkfst and Early Coffee/Tea/Hot Chocolate. Beds: KQT. Cable TV, reading lamp, ceiling fan, clock radio, telephone, some with hot tub/spa, hair dryer, wireless Internet access, iron/ironing board, Complimentary use of bicycles and beach chairs and beach towels. Sherry in all rooms in room. Fax, copier, bicycles, parlor games, fireplace, gift shop, Sherry, bicycles, helmets and locks, beach chairs and beach towels on premises. Antiquing, art galleries, beach, bicycling, canoeing/kayaking, fishing, golf, hiking, horseback riding, live theater, museums, parks, shopping, sporting events, tennis, water sports, wineries, Natural Habitat Zoo, Farmer's Market, Stearn's Wharf, Santa Barbara Marina, craft shows, Mission Santa Barbara, Botanical Gardens, Lotus Land, whale watching, sunset cruises and and surfing nearby.

Location: Ocean community. Santa Barbara.

Publicity: Los Angeles, Valley, Bon Appetit, Gourmet, Arrington's Bed and Breakfast Journal and Travel Channel with Chuck Henry.

"One of Santa Barbara's better-kept culinary secrets."

Certificate may be used: Anytime, subject to availability.

The Country House

1323 De La Vina St
Santa Barbara, CA 93101-3120
(805) 962-0058 (800) 727-0876
Internet: www.countryhousesantabarbara.com
E-mail: innkeeper@uphamhotel.com

Circa 1898. Gracing Santa Ynez wine country in a picturesque Santa Barbara, California neighborhood, this classic Victorian features a steep front gable and Colonial diamond-paned bay windows. A veranda and balcony invite relaxation. Gather for afternoon wine and appetizers and indulge in homemade cookies in the evening. Romantic, upscale accom-

modations boast modern conveniences amid well-placed antique furnishings. Stay in a spacious guest room or the Penthouse Suite with a living room, fireplace, whirlpool tub, waterfall shower and private terrace. After breakfast, take a short walk to the theater district or browse through local shops. Several packages are available with a variety of activities included. Hop on the electric shuttle to savor the urban wine trail to sample the harvest from local vintners. Save time to take a day trip to tour the stunning Hearst Castle.

Innkeeper(s): Jan Martin Winn. $200-475. 8 rooms with PB, 5 with FP, 5 with WP. Breakfast, snacks/refreshments and wine included in rates. Types of meals: Full bkfst and early coffee/tea. Beds: KQ. Data port, cable TV, reading lamp, ceiling fan, clock radio, telephone, hair dryer, bath amenities, wireless Internet access, iron/ironing board and Jacuzzi tub (five rooms) in room. Fax and fireplace on premises. Antiquing, art galleries, beach, bicycling, canoeing/kayaking, fishing, golf, hiking, horseback riding, live theater, museums, parks, shopping, tennis, water sports and wineries nearby.

Location: City, mountains, ocean community.

Publicity: Www.prlog.org/11660150-fall-food-and-wine-favorites-at-three-top-california-inns.html.

"We have stayed at a number of B&Bs, but this is the best. We especially liked the wonderful breakfasts on the porch overlooking the garden."

Certificate may be used: Sunday-Thursday, subject to availability. Not valid July and August. No holidays.

The Upham Hotel

1404 De La Vina St
Santa Barbara, CA 93101-3027
(805)962-0058 (800)727-0876 Fax:(805)963-2825
Internet: www.uphamhotel.com
E-mail: innkeeper@uphamhotel.com

Circa 1871. Antiques and period furnishings decorate each of the inn's guest rooms and suites. The inn is the oldest continuously operating hostelry in Southern California. Situated on an acre of gardens in the center of downtown, it's within easy walking distance of restaurants, shops, art galleries and museums. The staff is happy to assist guests in discovering Santa Barbara's varied attractions. Garden cottage units feature porches or secluded patios and several have gas fireplaces.

Innkeeper(s): Jan Martin Winn. $220-475. 58 rooms with PB, 8 with FP, 5 with WP, 4 total suites, including 1 two-bedroom suite, 3 cottages, 3 conference rooms. Breakfast, snacks/refreshments and wine included in rates. Types of meals: Cont plus and early coffee/tea. Beds: KQD. Cable TV, VCR, DVD, reading lamp, ceiling fan, clock radio, telephone, desk, hair dryer, bathrobes, bath amenities, wireless Internet access, iron/ironing board and master suite has hot tub/spa in room. Fax, copier, library and fireplace on premises. Antiquing, art galleries, beach, bicycling, canoeing/kayaking, fishing, golf, hiking, horseback riding, live theater, museums, parks, shopping, tennis and wineries nearby.

Location: City, mountains, ocean community.

Publicity: Los Angeles Times, Santa Barbara, Westways, Santa Barbara News-Press and Avenues.

"Your hotel is truly a charm. Between the cozy gardens and the exquisitely comfortable appointments, The Upham is charm itself."

Certificate may be used: Sunday-Thursday, subject to availability.

Cliff Crest Bed & Breakfast Inn

407 Cliff St
Santa Cruz, CA 95060-5009
(831)427-2609 (831)252-1057 Fax:(831)427-2710
Internet: www.cliffcrestinn.com
E-mail: Innkpr@CliffCrestInn.com

Circa 1887. Warmth, friendliness and comfort characterize this elegantly restored Queen Anne Victorian home. An octagonal solarium, tall stained-glass windows, and a belvedere overlook Monterey Bay and the Santa Cruz Mountains. The mood is airy and romantic. The spacious gardens were designed by John McLaren, landscape architect for Golden Gate Park. Antiques and fresh flowers fill the rooms, once home to William Jeter, lieutenant governor of California.

Innkeeper(s): Constantin Gehriger, Adriana Gehriger Gil. $95-245. 6 rooms with PB, 2 with FP, 1 with HT, 1 four-bedroom suite, 1 guest house. Breakfast, Healthy full gourmet breakfast and everything made from scratch included in rates. Types of meals: Full gourmet bkfst, early coffee/tea, Lunches, dinners and and special events are provided to order. Just ask us!. Beds: KQ. Cable TV, DVD, reading lamp, clock radio, telephone, desk, hair dryer, bathrobes, bath amenities, wireless Internet access and iron/ironing board in room. Fax, copier, spa, parlor games, fireplace, Beautiful backyard with ocean view, designed by John MacLaren and the architect of Golden Gate Park in San Francisco on premises. Handicap access. Amusement parks, antiquing, art galleries, beach, bicycling, canoeing/kayaking, fishing, golf, hiking, horseback riding, live theater, museums, parks, shopping, sporting events, tennis, water sports, wineries, Walk to Main Beach, Municipal Wharf and downtown Santa Cruz nearby.

Location: Waterfront.

Publicity: *The New York Times, Sunset Magazine, San Francisco Chronicle Magazine and many guidebooks, Sudden Impact and the 1983 Dirty Harry movie with Clint Eastwood was filmed here.*

"Delightful place, excellent food and comfortable bed."
Certificate may be used: Sunday-Thursday, subject to availability.

Pleasure Point Inn

23665 E Cliff Dr
Santa Cruz, CA 95062-5543
(831)475-4657
Internet: www.pleasurepointinn.com
E-mail: inquiries@pleasurepointinn.com

Circa 2001. Located in front of the popular Pleasure Point Surfing Beach, this oceanfront estate was completely remodeled recently. The modern Mediterranean-style architecture and design has an upscale appearance. Guest bedrooms all feature gas fireplaces, custom furniture, private patios and entrances. Some offer heated floor tiles and Jacuzzi tubs. Enjoy the sights and sounds of the sea from the large roof top deck overlooking Monterey Bay. Chaise lounges encourage soaking up the sun by day. A heater gas lamp placed near the outdoor dining tables provides warmth for cool evenings. Gaze at the stars while relaxing in the big hot tub. Capitola Village, only two miles away, offers shopping, dining, a sandy beach and nightly entertainment. Cruises can be arranged at the local yacht harbor.

Innkeeper(s): Tara. $225-295. 4 rooms with PB, 4 with FP. Breakfast and snacks/refreshments included in rates. Types of meals: Cont plus. Beds: KQ. Cable TV, VCR, DVD, reading lamp, refrigerator, ceiling fan, telephone, coffeemaker, desk, fireplace, hair dryer, bathrobes, bath amenities, wireless Internet access, iron/ironing board, Fireplace, some rooms with Jacuzzi tubs,

WiFi and iPod docks in room. Fax, spa, bicycles and library on premises. Limited handicap access. Amusement parks, antiquing, art galleries, beach, bicycling, canoeing/kayaking, golf, hiking, horseback riding, live theater, museums, parks, shopping, sporting events and wineries nearby.

Location: Ocean community, waterfront.

Publicity: *Www.pleasurepointinn.com/media.html.*

Certificate may be used: Sunday-Wednesday from Jan. 10-March 31.

The Darling House
A B&B Inn By The Sea

314 W Cliff Dr
Santa Cruz, CA 95060-6145
(831) 458-1958 Fax:(831)458-0320
Internet: www.darlinghouse.com
E-mail: info@darlinghouse.com

Circa 1911. Overlook the Monterey Bay while staying in lavish accommodations in Santa Cruz, California. Relax amid the peaceful elegance of this ocean-side inn with beveled glass, Tiffany lamps, open hearths and warm hearts. Verandas on the first and second floors are inviting sitting areas. Stay in a guest room that features a fireplace, antique furnishings, fresh flowers, an ice bucket, wine glasses, turndown service and other pampering amenities. Gather for a hearty breakfast then take an easy stroll to Lighthouse Point, Steamer Lane, Cowell's Beach and the Boardwalk. Ask about special packages that can include gourmet wine dinners and house concerts.

Innkeeper(s): Denise Darling. $195-225. 6 rooms. Breakfast included in rates. Types of meals: Cont plus. Beds: KQDT. Modem hook-up, VCR, turndown service, desk, message service, clothes press, reservation service and TV on request in room. Fax, copier, library, parlor games, telephone and fireplace on premises. Limited handicap access. Amusement parks, antiquing, art galleries, beach, bicycling, canoeing/kayaking, fishing, golf, hiking, live theater, museums, parks, shopping, sporting events, tennis, water sports, wineries, Narrow Gauge Railway, aquarium, ocean research, Shakespeare Festival in July and August, Begonia Festival, Cabrillo Music Festival, Jazz Festival, PGA Tournaments and international ocean sport contests nearby.

Location: City, country, ocean community. Redwoods, UCSC.

Publicity: *Modern Maturity, Pacific, New York Times, LA Times, Sacramento Bee Fresno, San Francisco Chronicle, Oakland Tribune, Santa Cruz Sentinel, Bay Guardian, San Jose Mercury News and Thrill (ABC made-for-TV movie).*

"So pretty, so sorry to leave."
Certificate may be used: November-April, Sunday-Thursday, holidays excluded.

West Cliff Inn

174 West Cliff Drive
Santa Cruz, CA 95060
(831)457-2200 (800)979-0910 Fax:(831)457-2221
Internet: www.westcliffinn.com
E-mail: westcliffinn@foursisters.com

Circa 1877. Boasting seaside serenity in Santa Cruz, California, West Cliff Inn sits on a bluff across from the beach. Originally built in 1877 as a private home, this renovated and stately three-story Victorian Italianate has become a Four Sisters Inn. The coastal décor is inviting with a clean and fresh ambiance. Feel the ocean breeze while relaxing on the wraparound porch. Gather for afternoon wine and appetizers. Stay in a guest bedroom with a marble tile bathroom, fireplace and jetted spa tub. A second-story room boasts a private outdoor hot tub and the two top-floor suites include sitting areas. Breakfast is a satisfying way to begin each day's adventures. Explore the local surfing museum or hit the waves and hang ten. Stroll along the famous beach boardwalk. Seasonal packages are offered.

$195-400. 9 rooms with PB, 9 with FP. Breakfast, afternoon tea, snacks/refreshments, wine and Afternoon wine and Hors d'oeuvres included in rates. Types of meals: Full gourmet bkfst and hors d'oeuvres. Modem hook-up, data port, cable TV, DVD, reading lamp, stereo, clock radio, telephone, turn-down service, desk, most with hot tub/spa, voice mail, fireplace, hair dryer, bathrobes, bath amenities, wireless Internet access and iron/ironing board in room. Central air. Fax, bicycles and library on premises. Handicap access. Antiquing, art galleries, beach, bicycling, canoeing/kayaking, fishing, golf, hiking, live theater, museums, parks, shopping, water sports and wineries nearby.

Location: Ocean community, waterfront.

Certificate may be used: Sunday-Thursday, December-February, based on promotional discount availability and excludes special event periods, holidays and certain room types. First night must be at full rack rate to receive second night free.

Santa Rosa G4

Melitta Station Inn

5850 Melitta Rd
Santa Rosa, CA 95409-5641
(707)538-7712 (800)504-3099 Fax:(707)538-7565
Internet: www.melittastationinn.com
E-mail: info@melittastationinn.com

Circa 1885. Originally built as a stagecoach stop, this inn was the focus for the little town of Melitta. Still located down a country lane with walk-in access to a state park, the station has been charmingly renovated.
Oiled-wood floors, a rough-beam cathedral ceiling and French doors opening to a balcony are features of the sitting room. Upon arrival, enjoy English tea and homemade scones. Three inviting guest bedrooms feature antique clawfoot tubs. Linger

over a hearty country breakfast in the great room. Wineries and vineyards stretch from the inn to the town of Sonoma. Basalt stone, quarried from nearby hills, was sent by rail to San Francisco where it was used to pave the cobblestone streets.

Innkeeper(s): Jackie & Tim Thresh. $149-219. 6 rooms with PB, 1 two-bedroom suite, 1 conference room. Breakfast, afternoon tea, snacks/refreshments, Full gourmet 3-course cooked breakfast and complimentary water and sodas included in rates. Types of meals: Full gourmet bkfst, veg bkfst, early coffee/tea and Complimentary water/sodas. Beds: KQT. Cable TV, reading lamp, ceiling fan, hair dryer, bathrobes, bath amenities and wireless Internet access in room. Central air. Fax, copier, spa, parlor games, telephone, fireplace, gift shop, Spa/massage services in dedicated area, Relaxation space, 40-jet luxury hot-tub in sun-room, Meeting space for up to 14 (requires overnight room rental), King suite with disabled access & private patio, Public patio and Deck area on premises. Limited handicap access. Antiquing, beach, bicycling, canoeing/kayaking, fishing, golf, hiking, horseback riding, live theater, museums, parks, tennis, wineries, Safari West Animal Kingdom, Pacific Coast Air Museum, Luther Burbank Home and Gardens, Charles Schulz Museum and Ice Skating Rink nearby.

Location: Country. Wine country.

Publicity: *Delta Airlines Inflight magazine, Amaze Green magazine, San Joaquin Magazine, Santa Clara Weekly and Journalist John Clayton (copyright KNX 1070 NEWSRADIO)* .

Certificate may be used: Monday-Thursday, November-April, excludes holidays.

Sebastopol G4

Vine Hill Inn

3949 Vine Hill Rd
Sebastopol, CA 95472
(707)823-8832 Fax:(707)824-1045
Internet: www.vine-hill-inn.com
E-mail: innkeeper@vine-hill-inn.com

Circa 1897. Situated between picturesque apple orchards and vineyards, this Victorian farmhouse is an eclectic country-style bed & breakfast. An intimate ambiance is imparted, with gathering places to play games or converse. Spacious guest bedrooms boast antiques, Egyptian towels and bathrobes. Choose between a clawfoot tub or Jacuzzi. Relax on private decks or porches with gorgeous views. Savor a satisfying breakfast that may include fresh fruit, chicken sausage, frittata and beverages. A swimming pool provides added enjoyment.

Innkeeper(s): Kathy Deichmann. $160-200. 4 rooms with PB, 2 with WP. Breakfast included in rates. Types of meals: Full gourmet bkfst. Beds: Q. Reading lamp, hair dryer, bath amenities and wireless Internet access in room. Central air. Fax, copier, swimming, library, parlor games, telephone and fireplace on premises. Antiquing, art galleries, beach, bicycling, canoeing/kayaking, fishing, golf, hiking, horseback riding, live theater, parks, shopping and wineries nearby.

Location: Country.

Certificate may be used: Anytime, Sunday-Thursday, subject to availability.

Sonoma H4

Inn at Sonoma

630 Broadway
Sonoma, CA 95476
(707)939-1340 (888)568-9818 Fax:(707)939-8834
Internet: www.innatsonoma.com
E-mail: innatsonoma@foursisters.com

Circa 2002. Located within walking distance to the historic Sonoma Plaza, this delightful new inn is sure to please. Inn at Sonoma reflects a casual California décor. The well-furnished guest bedrooms feature fireplaces and some offer private balconies. Start the day with a sumptuous breakfast then grab a bicycle to explore the local area. Hors d'oeuvres and afternoon wine are a welcome respite, and the rooftop Jacuzzi is a soothing relaxer. Take time to tour the nearby wineries of Somona and Napa Valley in the wine country of Northern California.

Innkeeper(s): Rachel Retterer. $205-300. 19 rooms with PB, 19 with FP. Breakfast, snacks/refreshments and Afternoon wine included in rates. Types of meals: Full bkfst, early coffee/tea and Afternoon wine. Beds: KQ. Data port, cable TV, DVD, reading lamp, stereo, clock radio, telephone, coffeemaker, turn-down service, desk, voice mail, hair dryer, bathrobes, bath amenities, iron/ironing board, DVD player, fireplace, private decks and terry robes in room. Air conditioning. Fax, spa, bicycles, library, parlor games, fireplace, signature breakfast, afternoon wine and hors d'oeuvres, evening turndown, morning newspaper delivery, home-baked cookies and bicycles to borrow on premises. Handicap access. Antiquing, art galleries, bicycling, canoeing/kayaking, golf, hiking, live theater, museums, parks, shopping, tennis and wineries nearby.

Location: City, country. Wine country.

Publicity: *Sunset, Coastal Living and Travel and Leisure.*

Certificate may be used: Sunday–Thursday, December-February, based on promotional discount availability and excludes special event periods, holidays and certain room types. First night must be at full rack rate to receive second night free.

South Pasadena — O10

Bissell House

201 Orange Grove Ave
South Pasadena, CA 91030-1613
(626)441-3535 Fax:(626)441-3671
Internet: www.bissellhouse.com
E-mail: info@bissellhouse.com

Circa 1887. Adorning famous Orange Grove Avenue on historic Millionaire's Row, this restored three-story Victorian mansion is a cultural landmark that offers an elegant ambiance and inviting hospitality. Spacious guest bedrooms feature antique furnishings, tasteful décor and modern conveniences that include DSL. Linger over a scrumptious full breakfast in the formal dining room served with crystal glassware, vintage silver and fresh flowers. Apricot bread pudding, egg strata, ginger scones, crème brulee and lemon soufflé French toast are some of the popular specialties. Swim in the pool surrounded by lush foliage or relax in the gorgeous English garden. Visit nearby Old Town Pasadena with a small-town atmosphere and big-city entertainment, boutiques, and upscale restaurants.

Innkeeper(s): Janet Hoyman . $155-350. 7 rooms with PB, 1 with WP. Breakfast, afternoon tea, snacks/refreshments and wine included in rates. Types of meals: Full gourmet bkfst, veg bkfst, early coffee/tea and 24 hour tea table with afternoon dessert. Beds: KQT. Data port, cable TV, reading lamp, clock radio, desk, some with hot tub/spa, hair dryer, bathrobes, bath amenities, wireless Internet access, iron/ironing board, Hypoallergenic duvets, Featherbeds, Luxury linens, Comfy robes, DSL, Hi Speed Internet Wi-Fi, Premium Cable channels in most rooms and some dvd players in room. Central air. VCR, DVD, fax, swimming, library, parlor games, fireplace and gift shop on premises. Antiquing, art galleries, golf, hiking, horseback riding, live theater, museums, parks, shopping, sporting events, tennis, wineries and Old Town Pasadena nearby.

Location: City.

Publicity: "9 on the Town" and voted #5 top romantic getaway along with the Ritz Carlton Spa.

Certificate may be used: Last minute availability, excludes weekends and Dec. 15-Jan. 15.

Sutter Creek — G6

Grey Gables B&B Inn

161 Hanford St
Sutter Creek, CA 95685-1687
(209)267-1039 (800)473-9422
Internet: www.greygables.com
E-mail: reservations@greygables.com

Circa 1897. The innkeepers of this Victorian home offer poetic accommodations both in the delightful decor and by the names of their guest rooms. The Keats, Bronte and Tennyson rooms afford garden views, while the Byron and Browning rooms

include clawfoot tubs. The Victorian Suite, which encompasses the top floor, affords views of the garden, as well as a historic churchyard. All of the guest rooms boast fireplaces. Stroll down brick pathways through the terraced garden or relax in the parlor. A proper English tea is served with cakes and scones. Hors d'oeuvres and libations are served in the evenings.

Innkeeper(s): Roger & Susan Garlick. $153-236. 8 rooms with PB, 8 with FP.

Breakfast, afternoon tea, hors d'oeuvres and wine included in rates. Types of meals: Full gourmet bkfst, veg bkfst and early coffee/tea. Beds: KQT. Modern hook-up, reading lamp, ceiling fan, clock radio, fireplace, hair dryer, bath amenities and free wireless high speed Internet access in room. Central air. Fax, copier, parlor games and telephone on premises. Handicap access. Antiquing, art galleries, cross-country skiing, downhill skiing, fishing, golf, horseback riding, live theater, museums, parks, shopping, water sports, wineries, Taste, Sutter Creek Palace, Caffe Via d'Oro and Susam's Place nearby.

Location: City, mountains. Gold Country.

Certificate may be used: Sunday-Thursday, excludes all holidays, some black-out dates.

The Hanford House B&B Inn

61 Hanford St Hwy 49
Sutter Creek, CA 95685
(209)267-0747 Fax:(209)267-1825
Internet: www.hanfordhouse.com
E-mail: info@hanfordhouse.com

Circa 1929. Hanford House is located on the quiet main street of Sutter Creek, a Gold Rush town. The ivy-covered brick inn features spacious, romantic guest rooms; eight have a fireplace. The Gold Country Escape includes a Jacuzzi tub, canopy bed, sitting area and a private deck. Guests can enjoy breakfast in their room or in the inn's cheerful breakfast room. Guests can relax in the front of a fire in the Hanford Room, which doubles as facilities for conferences, retreats, weddings and social events. Wineries, antique shops and historic sites are nearby.

Innkeeper(s): Robert and Athena Gordon. $99-2279. 13 rooms, 10 with PB, 11 with FP, 5 with HT, 3 with WP, 5 suites, 1 conference room. Types of meals: Full gourmet bkfst, early coffee/tea, afternoon tea, hors d'oeuvres and wine. Cable TV, DVD, reading lamp, CD player, refrigerator, ceiling fan, clock radio, telephone, desk, some with fireplace, hair dryer, bathrobes, wireless Internet access and iron/ironing board in room. Central air. Fax, copier, library, parlor games and complimentary wireless Internet access on premises. Handicap access. Antiquing, fishing, golf, live theater, water sports, skiing, Gold Rush historic sites and 25 wineries nearby.

Publicity: Best Places to Kiss and 50 Best Inns in Wine Country.

Certificate may be used: Jan. 1-Dec. 31; Sunday-Thursday, excluding holidays, first night at peak weekend holiday rates. Second-floor suites are excluded from the program.

Templeton — L6

Carriage Vineyards Bed and Breakfast

4337 S. El Pomar Road
Templeton, CA 93465
(805)227-6807 (800)617-7911 Fax:(805)226-9969
Internet: www.carriagevineyards.com
E-mail: Stay@CarriageVineyards.com

Circa 1995. Named after the owners' horse-drawn carriage collection, this 100-acre ranch is tucked away in the country of the Central Coast. Enjoy vineyards, orchards, pastures, gardens and a creek. Hike the hillsides to be immersed in the peaceful scenery of the area. Tastefully decorated guest bedrooms are furnished with well-placed antiques. The Victoria Room is a second-story master suite featuring an oversize shower and Jacuzzi tub for two. Savor a hot gourmet breakfast served daily. Overnight horse facilities are available.

Innkeeper(s): Leigh Anne Farley. $140-230. 4 rooms with PB. Breakfast included in rates. Types of meals: Full gourmet bkfst, veg bkfst, early coffee/tea, afternoon tea and snacks/refreshments. Beds: KQDT. Reading lamp, clock radio, coffeemaker, desk, hot tub/spa, hair dryer, bathrobes, wireless Internet access and iron/ironing board in room. Central air. TV, DVD, fax, spa, stable, telephone, fireplace, laundry facility, gift shop, Carriage rides and vineyard tours - Grape Ed 101 on premises. Antiquing, art galleries, beach, bicycling, fishing, golf, hiking, live theater, museums, parks, sporting events, water sports and wineries nearby.

Location: Country.

Certificate may be used: Sunday-Thursday excludes holidays and the months of, May and October. No other discounts, Please make reservations online.

Ukiah   F3

Vichy Hot Springs Resort & Inn

2605 Vichy Springs Rd
Ukiah, CA 95482-3507
(707)462-9515 Fax:(707)462-9516
Internet: www.vichysprings.com
E-mail: vichy@vichysprings.com

Circa 1854. This famous spa, now a California State Historical Landmark (#980), once attracted guests Jack London, Mark Twain, Robert Louis Stevenson, Ulysses Grant and Teddy Roosevelt. Eighteen rooms and eight cottages comprise the property. Some of the cottages are historic and some are new. The 1860s naturally warm and carbonated mineral baths remain unchanged. A hot soaking pool and historic Olympic-size pool await your arrival. A magical waterfall is a 30-minute walk along a year-round stream.

Innkeeper(s): Gilbert & Marjorie Ashoff. $195-390. 26 rooms with PB, 8 with FP, 1 suite, 8 cottages, 3 conference rooms. Breakfast and Sunday brunch included in rates. Types of meals: Country bkfst. Beds: QT. Modem hook-up, data port, reading lamp, CD player, refrigerator, clock radio, telephone, coffeemaker, desk, voice mail, some with fireplace, hair dryer, bath amenities, wireless Internet access, iron/ironing board and Wi-Fi high speed in room. Air conditioning. Fax, copier, spa, swimming, naturally sparkling mineral baths, massages, facials, walking, hiking, 700 acres of private park to explore, hot pool and Olympic size pool on premises. Handicap access. Antiquing, beach, bicycling, canoeing/kayaking, fishing, golf, hiking, live theater, museums, parks, shopping, tennis, water sports, wineries, redwood parks, lakes, rivers, Sun House Museum and Montgomery Woods tallest trees in the world nearby.

Location: Country, mountains. 700 acres on property.

Publicity: *Sunset, Sacramento Bee, San Jose Mercury News, Gulliver (Japan), Oregonian, Contra Costa Times, New York Times, San Francisco Chronicle, San Francisco Examiner, Adventure West, Gulliver (Italy), Bay Area Back Roads, Huell Hauser California Gold, PBS, California Farm Bureau and Too numerous to mention.*

Certificate may be used: Sunday-Thursday; April-September, Sunday-Friday; October-March, excludes holidays.

Westport   E3

Howard Creek Ranch

40501 N Hwy One
Westport, CA 95488
(707)964-6725 Fax:(707)964-1603
Internet: www.howardcreekranch.com
E-mail: Please Call 707-964-6725

Circa 1871. First settled as a land grant of thousands of acres, Howard Creek Ranch in Westport, California is now a 60-acre farm with sweeping views of the Pacific Ocean, sandy beaches and rolling mountains. A 75-foot bridge spans a creek that flows past barns and outbuildings to the beach 200 yards away. The farmhouse is surrounded by green lawns, an award-winning flower garden, and grazing cows, horses and llama. This rustic rural location offers antiques, a

hot tub, sauna and heated pool. A traditional ranch breakfast is served each morning.

Innkeeper(s): Charles & Sally Grigg. $75-198. 12 rooms, 11 with PB, 5 with FP, 2 suites, 3 cabins. Breakfast included in rates. Types of meals: Country bkfst and early coffee/tea. Beds: KQD. TV, VCR, reading lamp, refrigerator, ceiling fan, coffeemaker, desk, some with hot tub/spa and some with fireplace in room. Fax, copier, spa, sauna, library, parlor games, telephone, farm animals, hiking trails, beach-combing, whale watching (in season), birdwatching, surfing, exploring tide pools and creek running through ranch on premises. Antiquing, art galleries, beach, bicycling, canoeing/kayaking, fishing, golf, hiking, horseback riding, live theater, museums, parks, shopping, water sports, wineries, horseback riding on the beach, state parks, surfing and surf fishing, wildlife observation (fox, bobcat, mountain lion, deer), sealife observation (starfish, sea lions, whales and pelicans) nearby.

Location: Mountains, ocean community.

Publicity: *San Francisco Magazine, San Francisco Chronicle, California Country Vacations, Forbes Magazine, Sunset Magazine, Diablo, FYI, Vacations (Americas Best Romantic Inns issue) , PBS American Heartland and KETH Channel 54.*

"This is one of the most romantic places on the planet."

Certificate may be used: Oct. 15-May 15, Sunday-Thursday, excluding holiday periods.

Woodlake   K9

Wicky-Up Ranch B&B

22702 Avenue 344
Woodlake, CA 93286
(559)564-8898 Fax:(559)564-3981
Internet: www.wickyup.com
E-mail: innkeeper@wickyup.com

Circa 1902. Surrounded by 20 acres of organic orange groves, this turn-of-the-century Craftsman-style home was built by President Warren Harding's family. Now five generations strong, the historical integrity has been preserved. Treasures that include heirlooms, antiques, Oriental rugs and fine arts are cherished and shared. Experience a slower pace of living while here, whether staying in one of the beautifully appointed guest bedrooms or the private country cottage. French toast naranjo, Mexican souffle, omelettes and pancakes are some of the hearty breakfast specialties served. Relax on the wraparound veranda or the Sunset Deck. A stroll through the many gardens with fountains and cooing doves imparts a peaceful tranquility.

Innkeeper(s): Monica R. & Jack Pizura. $90-150. 3 rooms, 2 with PB, 1 two-bedroom suite, 1 cottage, 1 conference room. Breakfast included in rates. Types of meals: Full gourmet bkfst, veg bkfst and afternoon tea. Beds: QDT. Cable TV, VCR, reading lamp, stereo, refrigerator, ceiling fan, clock radio, telephone, turn-down service, desk, fireplace, fluffy bathrobes, bath and shower soaps from Bath & Body Works and hair dryer in room. Central air. Fax, copier, library and parlor games on premises. Limited handicap access. Antiquing, bicycling, cross-country skiing, fishing, golf, hiking, horseback riding, live theater, parks, shopping and water sports nearby.

Location: Country, mountains.

Publicity: *Fresno Bee, Visalia Times, Delta, San Francisco Chronicle and CA Heartland.*

Certificate may be used: November-March, Sunday-Thursday except holidays.

Yountville   G4

Lavender

2020 Webber Ave
Yountville, CA 94599
(707) 944-1388 (800) 522-4140 Fax:(707)944-1579
Internet: www.lavendernapa.com
E-mail: lavender@foursisters.com

Circa 1999. Stroll through lavender and flower gardens or relax on the veranda of this French farmhouse located in California's Napa Valley wine country. Privacy and elegant country comfort are the order of the day in guest bedrooms decorated in bold natural colors. Each cottage boasts a private entrance, patio and two-person bathtubs. The farm breakfast is an all-you-can-eat buffet with a variety of courses sure to please the most discriminating palate. Gather for afternoon teatime with wine, cheese, crackers and baked goods. Walk through the small town of Yountville with vintage 1870 shopping center, cafes and historic residential homes. Check out a bicycle and explore the area. Take the Wine Train tour and visit nearby Calistoga.

Innkeeper(s): Gina Massolo. $225-325. 8 rooms with PB, 8 with FP, 3 with HT, 3 with WP, 6 cottages. Breakfast, hors d'oeuvres and wine included in rates. Types of meals: Full bkfst and early coffee/tea. Beds: K. Modem hook-up, data port, cable TV, DVD, reading lamp, stereo, refrigerator, clock radio, telephone, turn-down service, desk, some with hot tub/spa, voice mail, hair dryer, bathrobes, bath amenities, wireless Internet access and iron/ironing board in room. Air conditioning. Fax, copier, bicycles, fireplace and Pool and hot tub privileges at neighboring sister-inn Maison Fleurie on premises. Handicap access. Antiquing, art galleries, bicycling, fishing, golf, hiking, horseback riding, live theater, museums, parks, shopping, tennis and wineries nearby.

Location: Wine country.

Certificate may be used: Sunday–Thursday, December-February, based on promotional discount availability and excludes special event periods, holidays and certain room types. First night must be at full rack rate to receive second night free.

Maison Fleurie

6529 Yount St
Yountville, CA 94599-1278
(707)944-2056 (800)788-0369 Fax:(707)944-9342
Internet: www.maisonfleurienapa.com
E-mail: maisonfleurie@foursisters.com

Circa 1894. Vines cover the two-foot thick brick walls of the Bakery, Carriage House and the Main House of this French country inn. One of the Four Sisters Inns, it is reminiscent of a bucolic setting in Provence. Guest bedrooms are decorated in a warm, romantic style, some with vineyard and garden views. Accommodations in the Old Bakery have fireplaces. After a satisfying breakfast go for a swim in the pool and soak in the outdoor hot tub. Bicycles are available for wandering the surrounding countryside. In the evenings, wine and hors d'oeuvres are served. Yountville, just north of Napa, California, offers close access to the multitude of wineries and vineyards in the valley.

Innkeeper(s): Gina Massolo. $235-300. 13 rooms with PB, 7 with FP, 7 with WP. Breakfast, afternoon tea and wine included in rates. Types of meals: Full gourmet bkfst. Beds: KQD. Cable TV, DVD, clock radio, telephone, turn-down service, most with hot tub/spa, hair dryer, bathrobes, bath amenities, wireless Internet access, iron/ironing board, Terry robes and Newspaper delivery to room in room. Air conditioning. Fax, bicycles, fireplace, outdoor pool and hot tub on premises. Handicap access. Antiquing and wineries nearby.

Location: Country. Napa Valley.

"Peaceful surroundings, friendly staff."

Certificate may be used: Sunday–Thursday, December-February, based on promotional discount availability and excludes special event periods, holidays and certain room types. First night must be at full rack rate to receive second night free.

Colorado

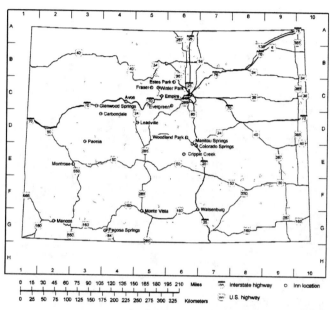

0 15 30 45 60 75 90 105 120 135 150 165 180 195 210 Miles
0 25 50 75 100 125 150 175 200 225 250 275 300 325 Kilometers

Avon   C4

West Beaver Creek Lodge

220 W Beaver Creek Blvd
Avon, CO 81620
(970)949-9073 (888)795-1061
Internet: wbclodge.com
E-mail: info@wbclodge.com

Circa 1996. Feel rejuvenated by the personalized service and award-winning accommodations at the newly built West Beaver Creek Lodge in picturesque Vail Valley in Avon, Colorado. Relax on the patio or deck with complimentary snacks and beverages or soak in the hot tub. Watch a movie in the lounge area, read in the loft, play a game of pool or sit by the fire in the Great Room. Contemporary Western-style décor and furnishings accent the guest bedrooms and suites. Indulge in a healthy, hearty breakfast each morning. Concierge services, laundry facilities, ski equipment storage and discount lift tickets are available. A shuttle to Beaver Creek or Vail leaves just outside the front door every 20 minutes.

Innkeeper(s): Bob and Terry Borg. $99-129. 9 rooms with PB. Breakfast and snacks/refreshments included in rates. Types of meals: Full bkfst and All-day coffee/tea/cocoa. Beds: KT. Cable TV, DVD, reading lamp, refrigerator, clock radio, coffeemaker, hair dryer, bathrobes, bath amenities, wireless Internet access and iron/ironing board in room. VCR, fax, copier, library, parlor games, telephone, fireplace and laundry facility on premises. Antiquing, art galleries, bicycling, canoeing/kayaking, cross-country skiing, downhill skiing, fishing, golf, hiking, horseback riding, live theater, museums, parks, shopping, tennis and wineries nearby.

Location: Mountains. 2 Blocks from Riverfront Express Gondola.

Certificate may be used: April-June and Oct.1-Dec.15, subject to availability.

Carbondale   D3

Ambiance Inn

66 N 2nd St
Carbondale, CO 81623-2102
(970)963-3597 (800)350-1515 Fax:(970)963-1360
Internet: www.ambianceinn.com
E-mail: ambiancein@aol.com

Located in the gorgeous Crystal Valley between Aspen and Glenwood Springs, this contemporary chalet-style home offers all-season accommodations for a wonderful getaway. Relax with one of the books or magazines in the second-floor New Orleans Library, or plan the next day?s activities using the convenient desk. Themed guest bedrooms include sitting areas and soft robes. The Aspen Suite features a ski lodge décor with knotty pine paneling and snowshoes hung on the walls. It is the perfect size for two couples or a large family traveling together. In the morning, savor a lavish breakfast at the oak table in the dining room before exploring the scenic area.

Innkeeper(s): Norma & Robert Morris. Call for rates. 5 rooms. Breakfast included in rates. Types of meals: Full gourmet bkfst, veg bkfst, early coffee/tea and gourmet lunch. Beds: Q. Modem hook-up, reading lamp, refrigerator, ceiling fan, clock radio, telephone, coffeemaker, desk, hot tub/spa, some with fireplace, hair dryer, bathrobes, bath amenities and iron/ironing board in room. Air conditioning. Amusement parks, antiquing, art galleries, bicycling, canoeing/kayaking, cross-country skiing, downhill skiing, fishing, golf, hiking, horseback riding, live theater, museums, parks, shopping, sporting events, tennis, water sports and wineries nearby.

Location: Mountains.

Certificate may be used: Excludes holidays, Christmas week and peak summer weekends.

Colorado Springs   E6

Black Forest B&B Lodge & Cabins

11170 Black Forest Rd
Colorado Springs, CO 80908-3986
(719)495-4208 (800)809-9901 Fax:(719)495-0688
Internet: www.blackforestbb.com
E-mail: blackforestbb@msn.com

Circa 1984. Surrounded by the scenic beauty of the Pikes Peak region of Colorado, Black Forest Bed and Breakfast Lodge and Cabins in Colorado Springs sits at the highest point east of the Rocky Mountains. Ponderosa Pines, golden Aspens and

fragrant meadows highlight the 20 scenic acres that boast panoramic views. The rustic mountain setting includes a log pavil-

ion and cabins. Stay in a guest bedroom or suite with a stocked kitchen or kitchenette, fireplace, and whirlpool tub. Select a movie to watch from the video collection. A breakfast tray is delivered to the room each morning. There is an abundance of outdoor activities to enjoy in the area.

Innkeeper(s): Susan Redden. $75-350. 7 rooms with PB, 4 with FP, 1 with WP, 2 two-bedroom, 1 three-bedroom and 1 four-bedroom suites, 1 guest house, 2 cabins, 2 conference rooms. Breakfast and snacks/refreshments included in rates. Types of meals: Cont plus, early coffee/tea, All rooms have full kitchens or kitchenettes and are stocked with coffees, teas, cocoas, cereal, oatmeal, microwave popcorn, milk, juice and etc. Beds: KQDT. Modem hook-up, data port, cable TV, VCR, reading lamp, CD player, refrigerator, ceiling fan, snack bar, clock radio, telephone, coffeemaker, desk, most with fireplace, hair dryer, bathrobes, bath amenities, wireless Internet access and iron/ironing board in room. Fax, copier, library, parlor games, laundry facility and gift shop on premises. Limited handicap access. Antiquing, art galleries, bicycling, canoeing/kayaking, cross-country skiing, fishing, golf, hiking, horseback riding, live theater, museums, parks, shopping, sporting events, tennis, water sports, wineries, Focus on the Family, Olympic Training Center, Pikes Peak, Garden of the Gods and World Prayer Center nearby.

Location: Country, mountains.

Certificate may be used: Accepts Weekends, Anytime, subject to availability, Anytime, Last Minute-Based on Availability.

Holden House-1902 Bed & Breakfast Inn

1102 W Pikes Peak Avenue
Colorado Springs, CO 80904-4347
(719) 471-3980 (888) 565-3980 Fax:(719) 471-4740
Internet: www.HoldenHouse.com
E-mail: mail@HoldenHouse.com

Circa 1902. Built by the widow of a prosperous rancher and businessman, this Victorian inn has rooms named after the Colorado towns in which the Holden's owned mining interests.

The main house, adjacent carriage house and Victorian house next door include the Cripple Creek, Aspen, Silverton, Goldfield and Independence suites. The inn's suites boast fireplaces and oversized tubs for two.

Guests can relax in the living room with fireplace, front parlor, veranda with mountain views or garden with gazebo and fountains. There are friendly cats in residence.

Innkeeper(s): Sallie & Welling Clark. $145-160. 5 rooms, 5 with FP, 5 suites. Breakfast, snacks/refreshments, hors d'oeuvres and wine included in rates. Types of meals: Full gourmet bkfst, veg bkfst, early coffee/tea, afternoon tea and Breakfast ensuite for additional $15 charge. Beds: Q. Modem hook-up, data port, cable TV, DVD, reading lamp, CD player, refrigerator, ceiling fan, clock radio, telephone, turn-down service, desk, fireplace, hair dryer, bathrobes, bath amenities, wireless Internet access, iron/ironing board and tubs for two in room. Central air. VCR, fax, copier, library, parlor games and gift shop on premises. Handicap access. Antiquing, art galleries, bicycling, fishing, golf, hiking, horseback riding, live theater, museums, parks, shopping, sporting events, tennis, wineries, historic sites, rock climbing and whitewater rafting nearby.

Location: City, mountains. Central to downtown & Historic District.

Publicity: *Denver Post, Victorian Homes, Pikes Peak Journal, Glamour, Country Inns, Vacations, Rocky Mountain News, Cats, Rocky Mountain Motorist, Colorado Springs Business Journal, Colorado Springs Gazette, Colorado Homes and Lifestyles, Home & Away, Country Register, Home Magazine, Rocky Mountain Resorts, Colorado Homes and Lifestyles, KKTV 11, KRDO Radio/TV, KOAA 5/30, FOX News, KVOR Radio, KKLI Radio and 1460 KKCS.*

Certificate may be used: Oct. 15-April 30, Sunday-Thursday, excludes holidays.

Old Town GuestHouse

115 S 26th St
Colorado Springs, CO 80904
(719)632-9194 (888)375-4210 Fax:(719)632-9026
Internet: www.oldtown-guesthouse.com
E-mail: luxury@oldtown-guesthouse.com

Circa 1997. Serving as the gateway to Old Colorado City, this recently built urban inn is surrounded by galleries, boutiques and restaurants. The three-story brick Federal-style design is in keeping with the 1859 period architecture of the historic area. Enjoy the breathtaking views of Pike's Peak and Garden of the Gods. It is entirely handicap accessible, soundproof, has an elevator, sprinklers and a security system, and boasts a four-diamond rating. International videoconferencing is available with WIFI 802.11 wireless fidelity hot spot. Play pool or work out on equipment in the game room and plan to join the innkeepers for a daily social hour. Elegant guest bedrooms are named after flowers and offer luxurious comfort with fireplaces, steam showers or hot tubs on private porches. Linger over breakfast in the indoor/outdoor fireside dining room.

Innkeeper(s): Shirley & Don Wick. $99-215. 8 rooms with PB, 5 with FP, 4 with HT, 1 two-bedroom suite, 1 conference room. Breakfast and snacks/refreshments included in rates. Types of meals: Full bkfst, early coffee/tea, Evening Reception w/Wine, Beer, Sodas and Snacks. Beds: KQT. Cable TV, VCR, DVD, reading lamp, CD player, refrigerator, ceiling fan, clock radio, telephone, coffeemaker, turn-down service, desk, most with hot tub/spa, voice mail, most with fireplace, hair dryer, bathrobes, bath amenities, wireless Internet access, iron/ironing board, Steam showers, Private outside hot tubs, Views of Pikes Peak & Garden of the Gods, Private balconies and Butler's pantry in room. Central air. Fax, copier, spa, library, parlor games, gift shop, Exercise Equipment and Pool table on premises. Handicap access. Amusement parks, art galleries, bicycling, cross-country skiing, fishing, golf, hiking, horseback riding, live theater, museums, parks, shopping, sporting events, tennis, Gold mine, Cave of the Winds, Cliff dwellings, Olympic Training Center, Broadmoor Hotel, Carriage rides, Library, Historic district, History Center, Simpich Museum and Antique shops nearby.

Location: City.

Publicity: *Colorado Springs Gazette, Colorado Springs Business Journal, Sunset Magazine, Colorado Springs Independent, Westside Pioneer, NBC, CBS, ABC, Cable, KRXP, KCMI and KVOR.*

Certificate may be used: Last minute subject to availability, not valid Fridays.

Cripple Creek   E6

Whispering Pines Bed and Breakfast

127 Stratton Circle
Cripple Creek, CO 80813
(719)689-2316
Internet: www.whisperingpinesbandb.net
E-mail: info@whisperingpinesbandb.net

A newly built, Whispering Pines Bed and Breakfast sits on ten acres in the Rocky Mountains, one mile from the historic gold mining town of Cripple Creek, Colorado. Incredible views of several ranges including the Sangre de Cristo Mountains surround the Victorian-style B&B that boasts natural rock outcroppings, large pine trees and wildflowers. Soak up the sun and the beauty while relaxing on the huge outdoor covered deck with two wicker swings. Game and pool tables are in the recreation room and the community room has a microwave, refrigerator and satellite TV. Beverages are available anytime. Feel pampered in a guest bedroom with a two-person hydrotherapy air tub, some with underwater lights; or stay in a romantic suite with a fireplace. A three-course breakfast welcomes hearty appetites.

Innkeeper(s): Peggy and Ed Schillerberg. Call for rates. Call inn for details. Breakfast, 24 hour coffee and hot chocolate and tea included in rates. Types of meals: Full gourmet bkfst, early coffee/tea, afternoon tea and room service. Beds: KQ. TV, VCR, stereo, refrigerator, ceiling fan, telephone, coffeemaker, desk, hot tub/spa, some with fireplace, hair dryer, bathrobes, bath amenities, wireless Internet access, iron/ironing board, private baths, hydrotherapy air tubs and satellite TV in all rooms in room. Fax, spa, library, parlor games, Recreation room with pool table and dart board on premises. Antiquing, art galleries, bicycling, canoeing/kayaking, cross-country skiing, downhill skiing, fishing, golf, hiking, horseback riding, live theater, museums, parks, shopping, wineries, Historic Cripple Creek gold mine tours, Ghost walks, Gaming, Pikes Peak Cog Railway, Royal Gorge Park/bridge, Florissant Fossil Bed National Monument and fossil quarry, Cave of the Winds, Seven Falls, Cliff Dwellings, Garden of the Gods, Horseback riding, Air Force Academy, Whitewater rafting, Shelf and Phantom Canyon Roads, Visit the historic neighboring gold mining town of Victor and Many more interesting sites to see nearby.

Location: Country, mountains.

Certificate may be used: Anytime, subject to availability except for July-August and holidays.

Empire   C5

Mad Creek B&B

167 Park Avenue
Empire, CO 80438-0404
(303) 569-2003
Internet: www.madcreekbnb.net
E-mail: madmadam@aol.com

Circa 1881. There is just the right combination of Victorian décor with lace, flowers, antiques and gingerbread trim on the façade of this mountain town cottage. The home-away-from-home atmosphere is inviting and the Eastlake furnishings are comfortable. Relax in front of the rock fireplace while watching a movie, peruse the library filled with local lore or plan an adventure with local maps and guide books. Empire was once a mining town, conveniently located within 20 to 60 minutes of at least six major ski areas.

Innkeeper(s): Myrna Payne. $85-105. 3 rooms with PB. Breakfast, afternoon tea, snacks/refreshments and Full breakfast at your choice of time. We cater to special needs included in rates. Types of meals: Full bkfst and early coffee/tea. Beds: KQDT. Cable TV, VCR, DVD, reading lamp, CD player, ceiling fan, clock radio, hair dryer, bathrobes, bath amenities, wireless Internet access, toiletries and down comforters in room. Spa, parlor games, telephone, fireplace and outdoor hot tub and gazebo where breakfast is served when weather permits among the beautiful wildflower gardens on premises. Antiquing, cross-country skiing, downhill skiing, fishing, horseback riding, parks, shopping, tennis, water sports, gambling, white water rafting and zipline and canoeing nearby.

Location: Mountains. Rivers.

Certificate may be used: Oct. 15-Nov. 20, Sunday-Thursday; April 16-May 20, Sunday-Thursday.

The Peck House

83 Sunny Ave.
Empire, CO 80438-0428
(303)569-9870 Fax:(303)569-2743
Internet: www.thepeckhouse.com
E-mail: thepeckhouse@yahoo.com

Circa 1862. Built as a residence for gold mine owner James Peck, this is the oldest hotel still in operation in Colorado. Many pieces of original furniture brought here by ox cart remain in the inn, including a red antique fainting couch and walnut headboards. Rooms such as the Conservatory provide magnificent views of the eastern slope of the Rockies, and a panoramic view of Empire Valley can be seen from the old front porch.

Innkeeper(s): Gary & Sally St. Clair. $75-135. 11 rooms, 9 with PB, 1 suite. Breakfast included in rates. Types of meals: Cont, hors d'oeuvres, wine and gourmet dinner. Restaurant on premises. Beds: QDT. Reading lamp and bath amenities in room. Fax, spa, library, parlor games, telephone, fireplace and gift shop on premises. Antiquing, art galleries, bicycling, cross-country skiing, downhill skiing, fishing, hiking, horseback riding, museums, parks, shopping, Gold Panning and Rafting nearby.

Location: Country, mountains.

Publicity: *American West, Rocky Mountain News, Denver Post and Colorado Homes.*

Certificate may be used: January-May and October-November, Sunday-Thursday, subject to availability.

Evergreen   C6

Bears Inn B&B

27425 Spruce Lane
Evergreen, CO 80439
(303)670-1205 (800)863-1205 Fax:(303)670-8542
Internet: www.bearsinn.com
E-mail: booknow@bearsinn.com

Circa 1924. Enjoy stunning mountain views and a tradition of hospitality at this historic lodge in Evergreen, Colorado. Bears Inn Bed & Breakfast is open year-round. The comfortable rustic interior boasts exposed logs and hardwood floors. Relax by the inviting, large stone fireplace in the Great Room. Guest bedrooms are decorated and furnished to reflect a theme. Antiques and clawfoot tubs add a nostalgic elegance. Linger over a gourmet candlelight breakfast each morning. Soak up the scenery on the spacious deck with a gas log campfire or in the outdoor hot tub. Biking, hiking, fishing, ice skating, and cross-country skiing are some of the myriad of local activities available. Wedding parties, as well as corporate, association and religious retreats are always welcome. Visit Denver just 35 miles away.

Innkeeper(s): Vicki Bock. $145-220. 11 rooms with PB, 1 suite, 1 cabin, 1 conference room. Breakfast and snacks/refreshments included in rates. Types of meals: Full gourmet bkfst, veg bkfst and afternoon tea. Beds: KQ. Modem hook-up, data port, cable TV, VCR, reading lamp, clock radio, telephone, hair dryer, bathrobes and wireless Internet access in room. Fax, copier, spa, library, parlor games and fireplace on premises. Amusement parks, antiquing, art galleries, bicycling, canoeing/kayaking, cross-country skiing, downhill skiing, fishing, golf, hiking, horseback riding, live theater, museums, parks, shopping, sporting events, tennis, water sports and wineries nearby.

Location: Mountains.

Certificate may be used: October-April, Sunday-Thursday.

Highland Haven Creekside Inn

4395 Independence Trail
Evergreen, CO 80439
(303)674-3577 (800)459-2406 Fax:(303)674-9088
Internet: www.highlandhaven.com
E-mail: info@highlandhaven.com

Circa 1884. Feel rejuvenated at this classic Colorado style inn situated just 30 miles west of Denver in the foothills of the Rocky Mountains. Winner of the iLoveInns.com Top 10 Romantic Inns of 2009, Highland Haven Creekside Inn borders Bear Creek and is accented with blue spruce and columbine. Guest bedrooms, suites and cottages feature a casual elegance, mountain ambiance and intimate balance of romance and professionalism. Select from accommodations with a private entrance, whirlpool tub, fireplace, walk-out balcony or secluded deck. A hearty breakfast is served in the historic Dailey Cabin, a restored log structure from 1884. Nearby Evergreen Lake offers boating or winter ice skating. Visit Creekside Cellars, the local winery or Tall Grass, the day spa. Browse through art galleries, museums and eclectic shops in nearby downtown.

Innkeeper(s): Blake & Roxy. $155-550. 17 rooms, 18 with PB, 10 with FP, 3 with HT, 4 with WP, 7 two-bedroom suites, 5 cottages, 2 conference rooms. Breakfast included in rates. Types of meals: Full bkfst and Friday night Port Night. Beds: KQD. Modem hook-up, cable TV, VCR, DVD, reading lamp, stereo, refrigerator, ceiling fan, clock radio, telephone, coffeemaker, desk, voice mail, most with fireplace, hair dryer, bathrobes, bath amenities, wireless Internet access and iron/ironing board in room. Air conditioning. Fax, copier and spa on premises. Antiquing, art galleries, bicycling, cross-country skiing, downhill skiing, fishing, golf, hiking, horseback riding, museums, parks, shopping, sporting events, tennis, water sports, wineries, Evergreen Lake and Bear Creek nearby.

Location: Mountains, waterfront. Picturesque foothills just 30 minutes west of Denver.

Publicity: *Best of the High Country (2008), Mountain Living (January 2008), "Top 10 Romantic Cottages" in Sunset Magazine (February 2007) and Voted "Best Small Inn" by Mountain Living (January 2007).*

Certificate may be used: January-May 19, Sunday-Thursday only in rooms $290 and above in price.

Fraser   C5

Wild Horse Inn Bed and Breakfast

PO Box 609
Fraser, CO 80442
(970)726-0456 Fax:(970)726-9678
Internet: www.wildhorseinn.com
E-mail: info@wildhorseinn.com

Circa 1994. Surrounded by majestic mountains, this inn was built from handhewn 400-year-old Engleman pine logs, moss-covered rock and huge picture windows. Sitting among acres of meadows and trees on a ridge above Fraser Valley, the casual lodge atmosphere exudes a rustic flair with superb hospitality and gracious service. Plan the next day's activities by the massive stone fireplace. Read a book from the library. Munch on a treat from the bottomless cookie jar. Each spacious guest bedroom features a private balcony, cozy robes and a whirlpool bath. Taste buds are teased and tempted with locally roasted coffee, blackberry scones, orange muffins or brioche. Ham crisps with baked eggs and mushrooms, Mexican Frittata or Lemon Souffle Crepes are additional breakfast favorites served in the dining room. Schedule a massage, soak in the hot tub or lounge on a sun deck.

Innkeeper(s): Judy A. Stanfill. $165-245. 10 rooms with PB, 3 cabins. Breakfast, afternoon tea and snacks/refreshments included in rates. Types of meals: Full gourmet bkfst, veg bkfst, early coffee/tea, picnic lunch and room service. Beds: KQT. Modem hook-up, data port, TV, VCR, reading lamp, clock radio, telephone, robes and slippers, private balconies and jetted tubs in room. Fax, spa, sauna, library, parlor games, fireplace, gift shop, massage services, fitness equipment, movie library and winter-season soups on premises. Antiquing, art galleries, bicycling, canoeing/kayaking, cross-country skiing, downhill skiing, fishing, golf, hiking, horseback riding, museums, parks, shopping, water sports, Rocky Mountain National Park, rafting, mountain biking, hot air ballooning, snowmobiling, dog sled rides and ice skating nearby.

Location: Mountains.

Publicity: *Quick Escapes and Travel & Leisure.*

Certificate may be used: April, May, October-Nov. 15.

Manitou Springs   E6

1892 Victoria's Keep Bed & Breakfast

202 Ruxton Ave
Manitou Springs, CO 80829
(719)685-5354 (800)905-5337 Fax:(719)685-5913
Internet: www.victoriaskeep.com
E-mail: info@victoriaskeep.com

Circa 1892. A stream passes by the wraparound front porch of this Queen Anne Victorian. Stained glass windows and a turret complete the picture. The home is furnished in period antiques, and there are coordinated wallpapers. Most rooms have a fireplace of its own as well as Queen beds. Most have whirlpool tubs for two and feather beds. Gourmet breakfast is served in the morning

Innkeeper(s): Jay Rohrer and Karen Cullen. $80-185. 6 rooms with PB, 5 with FP, 4 suites. Breakfast, afternoon tea and snacks/refreshments included in rates. Types of meals: Full gourmet bkfst, veg bkfst and early coffee/tea.

Beds: Q. Reading lamp, CD player, refrigerator, clock radio, fireplace and Jacuzzi tub in room. Air conditioning. TV, VCR, library, parlor games and telephone on premises. Antiquing, art galleries, bicycling, canoeing/kayaking, fishing, golf, hiking, horseback riding, live theater, museums, parks, shopping, sporting events, tennis, wineries, United States Olympic Training Center, Garden of the Gods, The Pikes Peak Cog Railway, Cave of the Winds, The Cliff Dwellings, Seven Falls and Cheyenne Mountain Zoo nearby.

Location: Mountains. Base of Pikes Peak.

Certificate may be used: November-April, Sunday-Thursday, except special events and holidays.

Avenue Hotel, A Victorian B&B

711 Manitou Ave
Manitou Springs, CO 80829-1809
(719) 685-1277 (800) 294-1277
Internet: www.AvenueHotelBandB.com
E-mail: info@avenuehotelbandb.com

Circa 1886. Sitting on a hillside with a terraced back garden and scenic views of Pikes Peak, this historic Queen Anne Victorian has been recently renovated to offer the utmost of modern comfort and vintage style. A
parlor and fireside living
room grace either side of
the three-story turned
staircase which leads to
spacious guest rooms and
two-room suites. Many
include an antique claw-

foot tub and shower. Private accommodations in the two-level Carriage House feature fully equipped kitchens and are ideal for longer visits, business travel or romantic getaways. The secluded garden-level bungalow is ideal for families. Hosts Gwenn and Randy generously provide thoughtful amenities that make each stay a pampering delight. A hot beverage area with muffins and fresh cookies, and a snack station with a refrigerator stocked with bottled water enhance the relaxed setting. Savor a hearty breakfast in the dining room and feel satisfied until dinner time. Explore the picturesque area then soak in the hot tub on the patio. Spa services can be scheduled in advance.

Innkeeper(s): Gwenn David. $95-145. 9 rooms, 7 with PB, 3 with FP, 3 total suites, including 2 two-bedroom suites, 2 cottages. Breakfast, snacks/refreshments and wine included in rates. Types of meals: Full bkfst, veg bkfst, early coffee/tea and hors d'oeuvres. Beds: KQDT. Cable TV, DVD, reading lamp, refrigerator, ceiling fan, snack bar, clock radio, turn-down service, desk, some with hot tub/spa, most with fireplace, hair dryer, bathrobes, bath amenities, wireless Internet access and iron/ironing board in room. Air conditioning. VCR, fax, copier, spa, library, parlor games, telephone, gift shop, wide selection of movies, snacks, melt in your mouth homemade cookies and wonderful relaxing onsite massages on premises. Antiquing, art galleries, bicycling, fishing, golf, hiking, horseback riding, live theater, museums, parks, shopping, sporting events, tennis, Garden of the Gods, Pikes Peak, Pikes Peak Cograilway, Cave of the Winds, Manitou Cliff Dwelinngs, Barr trail and Manitou Incline nearby.

Location: City, mountains. Pikes Peak.

Publicity: Camille's Magic.

Certificate may be used: Nov.1 to April 30, Sunday-Thursday, excluding holidays and special events.

Montrose   E3

Uncompahgre Bed and Breakfast

21049 Uncompahgre Rd.
Montrose, CO 81401
(970)240-4000 (800)318-8127 Fax:(970)249-6546
Internet: www.uncbb.com
E-mail: uncompahgre_bnb@yahoo.com

Open year-round so guests enjoy the scenic area during every season, the inn is centrally located in southwest Colorado between the San Juan mountain range and the Grand Mesa. This historic property was remodeled into a spacious, white mansion with themed guest rooms on the main floor. The huge fireside gathering room of The Uncompahgre Bed & Breakfast does double duty as a dining room and living room as well as boasting a hardwood dance floor. Feel pampered and stay in the Romantic French Country Jacuzzi Room with electric log fireplace. The French Provincial Room is handicap accessible. Linger over breakfast then explore the picturesque region surrounding Montrose with many attractions available. Black Canyon of the Gunnison State Park is nearby.

Innkeeper(s): Barbara & Don Helm. $70-120. 7 rooms with PB, 1 with FP, 1 with WP. Breakfast, afternoon tea and hors d'oeuvres included in rates. Types of meals: Full gourmet bkfst, veg bkfst and early coffee/tea. Beds: KQT. Data port, cable TV, VCR, DVD, reading lamp, CD player, refrigerator, ceiling fan, clock radio, coffeemaker, desk, hot tub/spa, some with fireplace, hair dryer, bathrobes and iron/ironing board in room. Fax, copier, library, parlor games, telephone and laundry facility on premises. Handicap access. Antiquing, beach, cross-country skiing, downhill skiing, fishing, golf, hiking, horseback riding, live theater, parks, shopping, tennis, wineries and elk and deer hunting in season nearby.

Location: Country. Black Canyon of the Gunnison National Park.

Publicity: Montrose Daily Press, Denver Post and Public Television.

Certificate may be used: Last Minute, subject to availability.

Pagosa Springs   G4

Canyon Crest Lodge

201A Yeoman Dr
Pagosa Springs, CO 81147
(970)731-3773 Fax:(970)731-5502
Internet: www.canyoncrestpagosa.com
E-mail: canyoncrest@pagosa.net

Circa 1998. Sitting on 40 acres of tall pine trees and mountainous rocky terrain with magnificent views of Pagosa Peak, Valley and the Great Divide, this English Country House is a traditional rock structure with 18-inch thick walls. Gather by the large fireplace in the lounge and enjoy the relaxing ambiance. Guest suites are named after famous castles, and can be accessed from the private upper deck. Each suite includes a comfortable sitting area with a TV and a walk-in closet with robes and slippers. Breakfast is served in the dining room and can be taken to the dining deck or back to the room. Other meals can be arranged in advance. Soak in the hot tub overlooking the gorgeous scenery.

Innkeeper(s): Valerie Green. $100-200. 6 rooms, 1 with FP, 6 suites, 1 conference room. Types of meals: Country bkfst, veg bkfst, early coffee/tea, picnic lunch, afternoon tea, gourmet dinner and room service. Beds: KQ. Modern hook-up, data port, TV, VCR, reading lamp, stereo, refrigerator, snack bar, clock radio, telephone, turn-down service, hot tub/spa and voice mail in room. Fax, copier, spa, sauna, bicycles, library, parlor games, fireplace and laundry facility on premises. Handicap access. Antiquing, art galleries, bicycling, canoeing/kayaking, cross-country skiing, downhill skiing, fishing, golf, hiking, horseback riding, live theater, museums, parks, shopping, sporting events, tennis, water sports and wineries nearby.

Location: Mountains.

Certificate may be used: Anytime excluding national holidays and subject to projected availability.

Paonia   D3

The Bross Hotel B&B

312 Onarga Ave.
Paonia, CO 81428
(970) 527-6776 Fax:(970)527-7737
Internet: www.paonia-inn.com
E-mail: brosshotel@paonia.com

Circa 1906. This turn-of-the-century western hotel was restored to its original splendor with a front porch and balcony while being updated with late-century amenities in the mid-1990s. Wood floors and trim, dormer windows and exposed brick walls all add to the Victorian decor. For pleasure, relax in the sitting area or library/TV/game room. A conference room and communications center is perfect for business. Guest bedrooms feature antiques and handmade quilts. Some rooms can be adjoined into suites. Breakfast is an adventure in seasonal culinary delights that cover the antique back bar in the dining room. Visit Black Canyon of the Gunnison National Park, Grand Mesa, West Elk and Ragged Wilderness areas and Fort Uncompaghre-a Living History Museum.

Innkeeper(s): Linda Lentz. $125-138. 10 rooms with PB, 1 conference room. Breakfast included in rates. Types of meals: Full gourmet bkfst, veg bkfst and early coffee/tea. Beds: D. Reading lamp, ceiling fan, telephone, desk, voice mail, bath amenities and wireless Internet access in room. TV, VCR, DVD, fax, copier, spa, library, child care, parlor games, gift shop and Breakfast dining area on premises. Antiquing, art galleries, bicycling, canoeing/kayaking, cross-country skiing, fishing, golf, hiking, horseback riding, live theater, museums, parks, shopping, water sports, wineries, Dinosaur dig, Black Canyon of the Gunnison National Park, Award-winning local produce of cherries, peaches and apricots. Wineries nearby.

Location: Mountains. Vineyards, Orchards, Black Canyon.

Publicity: Denver Post, Grand Junction Sentinel, 52-80 Magazine (the Denver City Magazine, September 2004), Nexus ("brown palace of the town," September-October 2003) and Gourmet (July 2004).

Certificate may be used: Anytime, at the last minute.

Winter Park   C5

Winter Park Chateau

405 Lions Gate Drive
Winter Park, CO 80482
(970)726-2884 Fax:(877)581-2536
Internet: www.winterparkchateau.com
E-mail: wpchateau@aol.com

Circa 1998. An upscale B&B Inn located in the heart of downtown Winter Park, Colorado, this newly built bed and breakfast inn offers modern style with a Victorian flair. All rooms have beautiful views, are large, bright, and stylish. Each features free wireless internet, flat screen high definition television, designer furnishings and a bathroom with shower and jetted tub. Some also feature private balconies and gas fireplaces. A spacious social and entertaining area offers games, books, movies, travel maps and local tourist media. An inviting outdoor hot tub is on the 2nd floor deck. The property offers a romantic getaway as well as an ideal place for multi-family gatherings, group vacations, business retreats, and can accommodate special events of parties of 50 or more. It is adjacent to Main Street, and two miles from the Winter Park/Mary Jane Ski Resort. You can walk to numerous restaurants, the local cinema, Hideaway Park, and evening entertainment. Fishing, the bicycle path and golf are closeby and Amtrak services the town (WP. The station is five minutes from the property with free shuttle service. There are four world class golf courses and the Rocky Mountain National Park a short drive away. Winter Park Chateau is the only upscale bed and breakfast in downtown Winter Park.

Innkeeper(s): Greg and Laura Lewis. $125-225. 8 rooms with PB, 2 with FP, 1 conference room. Breakfast, snacks/refreshments, hors d'oeuvres and wine included in rates. Types of meals: Full gourmet bkfst, veg bkfst and early coffee/tea. Beds: KQT. Cable TV, reading lamp, clock radio, desk, hair dryer, bathrobes, wireless Internet access and iron/ironing board in room. Copier, spa, library, telephone and fireplace on premises. Handicap access. Art galleries, cross-country skiing, downhill skiing, fishing, golf, hiking, horseback riding, live theater, museums, parks, shopping, tennis and wineries nearby.

Location: Mountains. Ski Resort.

Certificate may be used: Sunday-Wednesday check-ins, excluding holidays and special events.

Woodland Park   D6

Pikes Peak Paradise

236 Pinecrest Road
Woodland Park, CO 80863
(719)687-6656 (800)728-8282 Fax:(719)687-6335
Internet: www.pikespeakparadise.com
E-mail: info@pikespeakparadise.com

Circa 1988. Pikes Peak Paradise in Woodland Park, Colorado is a three-story Georgian Colonial with stately white columns rising unexpectedly from the wooded hills 25 minutes west of

Colorado Springs. All rooms of this B&B have incredible 9000-foot secluded views of Pikes Peak and 1 million acres of Pikes National Forest. Modern, updated suites feature luxurious bed sheets, down pillows, comforters, duvets, Egyptian cotton towels, and Soybu Robes. Amenities include in-room private hot tubs or Jacuzzis, fireplaces, decks, WIFI, HDTV, DVD players and DVDs. Savor a gourmet breakfast each morning, snacks and soft drinks throughout the day, four hours of complimentary wine and dessert in the evening.

Innkeeper(s): Ron Pijut & Michael Zacharias. $180-240. 5 rooms, 1 with FP, 3 with HT, 1 with WP, 5 suites. Breakfast, afternoon tea, snacks/refreshments and wine included in rates. Types of meals: Full gourmet bkfst, early coffee/tea, room service and Beverages and snacks are provided throughout the day plus dessert and 4 hours of wine in the evening. Beds: KQ. TV, DVD, reading lamp, stereo, ceiling fan, clock radio, desk, hot tub/spa, hair dryer, bathrobes, bath amenities, wireless Internet access, iron/ironing board, Deluxe Suites have a Hot Tub or Jacuzzi tub inside suite and Separate from private bath in room. VCR, fax, spa, parlor games, telephone and gift shop on premises. Amusement parks, antiquing, bicycling, cross-country skiing, fishing, golf, hiking, horseback riding, live theater, parks, shopping, sporting events, water sports, Cripple Creek Gambling, Cog Railway up Pikes Peak, Manitou Cliff Dwellings, Cave of the Winds, White Water rafting, Royal Gorge, Colorado Wolf & Wildlife Center, Eleven Mile Reservoir, Rampart Range Reservoir, Mueller State Park and Garden of the Gods nearby.

Location: Mountains. Colorado Springs.

Publicity: Rocky Mountain News, Denver Post, Arlington's B&B Journal List, ZDF.de cam (December and 2007).

Certificate may be used: Nov. 1-April 30, Sunday-Thursday (excluding holidays).

Connecticut

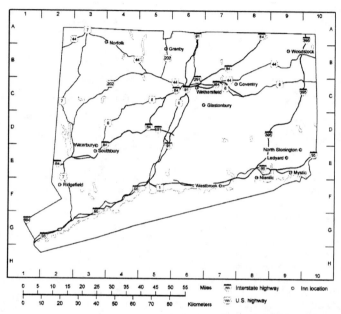

Coventry   C7

The Daniel Rust House

2011 Main St
Coventry, CT 06238-2034
(860)742-0032
Internet: www.TheDanielRustHouse.com
E-mail: drhbnb@charter.net

Circa 1731. Prepare for a remarkable journey back in time at
this former 18th-century tavern. Original wide-board floors,
fireplaces and raised paneled walls reflect that era. Romantic
canopy beds and Jacuzzi tubs
boast added comfort to the
guest bedrooms. A secret closet may have harbored runaway
slaves during the Underground
Railroad. Spacious privacy is
offered in the cottage.
Conferences and small wed-
dings are accommodated easily. Local universities, Caprilands
Herb Farm and Nathan Hale Homestead all are nearby.

Innkeeper(s): Germaine Salvatore & Cathy Mitchell. $120-185. 3 rooms with
PB, 2 with FP, 1 with WP, 1 cottage. Breakfast included in rates. Types of
meals: Country bkfst and early coffee/tea. Beds: KQDT. TV, DVD, reading
lamp, refrigerator, ceiling fan, clock radio, turn-down service, some with hot
tub/spa, most with fireplace, hair dryer, bathrobes, bath amenities, wireless
Internet access and iron/ironing board in room. Air conditioning. Parlor games
and telephone on premises. Handicap access. Antiquing, art galleries, beach,
bicycling, canoeing/kayaking, cross-country skiing, fishing, golf, hiking, live
theater, museums, parks, shopping, sporting events, water sports, wineries
and casinos nearby.

Location: Country.

Publicity: *Journal Inquirer, Willimantic Chronicle, The Hartford Courant,
WFSB and WRCH.*

"We were delighted then, to find such a jewel in the Bird-In-Hand."
Certificate may be used: Jan. 3-April 1, Sunday-Thursday.

Glastonbury   C6

Connecticut River Valley Inn

2195 Main Street
Glastonbury, CT 06033
(860)633-7374 Fax:(860)633-0776
Internet: www.ctrivervalleyinn.com/
E-mail: frontdesk@CtRiverValleyInn.com

Circa 1740. Considered an inn for all seasons, Connecticut
River Valley Inn is situated in the midst of the pastoral and picturesque yet progressive town of Glastonbury, Connecticut.

Innkeepers Patricia and Wayne are restoring the inn with a vision to blend the historic past with the style and conveniences of today. Business and leisure travelers alike will feel pampered and relaxed amid the pleasant surroundings. A quiet stroll along the Connecticut River is a must for any romantic getaway and casual or fine dining restaurants are nearby.

Innkeeper(s): Patricia & Wayne Brubaker. $185-250. 4 rooms with PB, 4 with FP, 1 two-bedroom suite, 1 conference room. Breakfast, afternoon tea, snacks/refreshments, hors d'oeuvres, wine, Afternoon Tea, Wine and Snacks and hors d'oeuvres vary from day to day included in rates. Types of meals: Country bkfst, veg bkfst, early coffee/tea and picnic lunch. Beds: K. Cable TV, VCR, reading lamp, snack bar, clock radio, telephone, coffeemaker, desk, fireplace, hair dryer, bathrobes, bath amenities, wireless Internet access, iron/ironing board, balconies, steam showers in each room coming soon, California King beds in each room, LCD Hi-Def TV and in room. Central air. DVD, fax, copier and library on premises. Antiquing, beach, bicycling, canoeing/kayaking, cross-country skiing, fishing, golf, hiking, horseback riding, live theater, museums, parks, shopping, sporting events, tennis, water sports, wineries, bird watching, Casinos and nearby.

Location: City, country.

Certificate may be used: Sunday-Thursday, subject to availability or call.

Granby   B5

The Dutch Iris Inn B&B

239 Salmon Brook Street
Granby, CT 06035
(860)844-0262 (877)280-0743
Internet: www.dutchirisinn.com
E-mail: info@dutchirisinn.com

Circa 1812. For many years this historic Colonial was used as a summer home. Some of the inn's antiques were the original furnishings, including a Louis XIV couch, Chickering grand piano, fainting couch, four-poster bed and marble-top dresser. Relax in the keeping room by a roaring fire, where the previous owners did the cooking. Several guest bedrooms feature working fireplaces. A customized breakfast menu is savored by candlelight and classical music. Half of the three acres feature perennial and bulb gardens, as well as wild blackberries and blueberries. Sip a cold beverage in a rocking chair on the side porch.

Innkeeper(s): Nancy & William Ross. $110-180. 6 rooms with PB, 3 with FP, 2 with WP. Breakfast and snacks/refreshments included in rates. Types of meals: Full bkfst. Beds: KQD. Cable TV, VCR, reading lamp, clock radio, desk, most with fireplace, hair dryer, bath amenities, wireless Internet access and iron/ironing board in room. Central air. Fax and parlor games on premises. Amusement parks, antiquing, art galleries, beach, bicycling, canoeing/kayaking, cross-country skiing, downhill skiing, fishing, golf, hiking, horseback riding, live theater, museums, parks, shopping, tennis, water sports, wineries, private schools: Westminster, Ethel Walker, Avon Olf Farm, Suffield Academy, Loomis Chaffee and Miss Porter's nearby.

Location: Country.

Certificate may be used: Anytime, Sunday-Thursday, except on holidays.

Ledyard   E9

Stonecroft Country Inn

515 Pumpkin Hill Road
Ledyard, CT 06339
(860)572-0771 (800)772-0774 Fax:(860) 572-9161
Internet: www.stonecroft.com
E-mail: info@stonecroft.com

Circa 1807. Perfect for a romantic getaway or a tranquil retreat, this 1807 sea captain's estate exudes a quiet country elegance and smoke-free environment. The Main House, a sunny Georgian Colonial, and the Grange, a recently converted post

and beam barn with granite fieldstone foundation, are both listed in The National Register of Historic Places. Choose to stay in a guest bedroom or luxury suite with a fireplace, two-person whirlpool bath, towel warmer and separate shower. The Great Room, Red Room and Snuggery offer gathering and reading spots in the Main House. Breakfast and dinner are served in the Grange's ground floor dining room or through the French doors on the outdoor stone terrace overlooking the landscaped grounds with a water garden and grapevine-shaded pergola. Ask about special packages.

Innkeeper(s): Jason Crandall. $99-275. 10 rooms with PB, 9 with FP, 6 with HT, 6 with WP, 2 suites. Breakfast included in rates. Types of meals: Full gourmet bkfst, veg bkfst, Sun. brunch, early coffee/tea, snacks/refreshments, wine, gourmet dinner and room service. Restaurant on premises. Beds: KQ. Cable TV, DVD, reading lamp, CD player, clock radio, telephone, coffeemaker, desk, most with hot tub/spa, voice mail, most with fireplace, hair dryer, bathrobes, bath amenities, wireless Internet access, iron/ironing board, In the Grange, wide screen HD TVs with DVD, Gas Fireplaces and Heated Towl Racks and Free Wireless Internet in room. Central air. Fax, copier, library, parlor games, On-site dining room serving seasonal gourmet cuisine for dinner Wednesday through Saturday and Sunday Brunch and country breakfast for inn guests each morning on premises. Handicap access. Antiquing, art galleries, beach, bicycling, canoeing/kayaking, fishing, golf, hiking, horseback riding, live theater, museums, parks, shopping, tennis, water sports, wineries, Foxwoods & Mohegan Sun Casinos, Mystic Seaport & Aquarium and Newport and RI nearby.

Location: Country. 5 miles from the Casinos & Mystic.

Publicity: 30 Strategic Retreats New York Magazine, Passport to New England, New England Inns & Resorts, Select Registry and Bed & Breakfast of Mystic Coast & Country.

Certificate may be used: November-March, Sunday-Thursday. Not available on holidays. Based on room availability.

Mystic   E9

The Whaler's Inn

20 E Main St
Mystic, CT 06355-2646
(860)536-1506 (800)243-2588 Fax:(860)572-1250
Internet: www.whalersinnmystic.com
E-mail: sales@whalersinnmystic.com

Circa 1901. This classical revival-style inn is built on the historical site of the Hoxie House, the Clinton House and the U.S. Hotel. Just as these famous 19th-century inns offered, the Whaler's Inn has the same charm and convenience for today's visitor to Mystic. Once a booming ship-building center, the town's connection to the sea is ongoing, and the sailing schooners still pass beneath the Bascule Drawbridge in the center of town. More than 75 shops and restaurants are within walking distance.

Innkeeper(s): Richard Prisby. $79-259. 49 rooms with PB, 8 with FP, 8 with WP, 1 conference room. Types of meals: Cont plus, gourmet lunch and gourmet dinner. Restaurant on premises. Beds: KQD. Modem hook-up, cable TV, VCR, reading lamp, clock radio, telephone, coffeemaker, desk, voice mail, some with fireplace, hair dryer, bath amenities, wireless Internet access, iron/ironing board, cable TV, telephone, voice mail, data port, alarm clock, air conditioning, eight luxury rooms with water views, Jacuzzi tubs and fireplaces in room. Central air. Fax, copier, bicycles, Fitness Center, Hospitality Room and Business Center on premises. Handicap access. Antiquing, art galleries, beach, bicycling, canoeing/kayaking, fishing, golf, hiking, live theater, museums, parks, shopping, water sports, wineries, walk to Mystic Seaport and harbor & schooner cruises nearby.

Location: City, country, ocean community, waterfront. Historic Downtown Mystic.

Certificate may be used: Nov.28-April 30, excluding holidays.

Niantic F8

Inn at Harbor Hill Marina

60 Grand St
Niantic, CT 06357
(860)739-0331 Fax:(860)691-3078
Internet: www.innharborhill.com
E-mail: info@innharborhill.com

Circa 1890. Arise each morning to panoramic views of the Niantic River harbor at this traditional, late-19th-century inn. Travel by boat or car to neighboring cities and enjoy the finest culture New England has to offer. This three-story, harbor-front inn offers rooms filled with antiques and seaside décor. Some have balconies and fireplaces. Experience true adventure at sea on a chartered fishing trip, or spend the day in town shopping or relaxing on the beach, all within walking distance. During the summer, guests can listen to outdoor concerts in the park while overlooking Long Island Sound. Whatever the day has in store, guests can start each morning the right way with a fresh, continental breakfast on the wraparound porch overlooking the marina and gardens.

Innkeeper(s): Sue & Dave Labrie. $135-325. 9 rooms, 15 with PB, 12 with FP, 1 suite, 2 conference rooms. Breakfast, afternoon tea and snacks/refreshments included in rates. Types of meals: Cont plus, early coffee/tea and wine. Beds: KQDT. Cable TV, reading lamp, CD player, ceiling fan, clock radio, desk, most with fireplace, hair dryer, bath amenities, wireless Internet access, iron/ironing board, 'Main Inn' suite, balcony rooms and corner rooms and Captain Clark House rooms with fireplaces in room. Central air. Fax, copier, parlor games, telephone, gift shop, Complimentary beach passes, coolers, chairs, umbrella and and beach towels on premises. Antiquing, art galleries, beach, bicycling, canoeing/kayaking, fishing, golf, hiking, live theater, museums, parks, shopping, sporting events, water sports, wineries, Mohegan Sun Casino, Foxwoods Casino, Mystic Seaport, Mystic Aquarium and Outlet shopping nearby.

Location: Ocean community, waterfront. One to two miles away from beaches.

Publicity: *Mystic Coast & Country Travel Industry Association, TWICE (2009, 2005) awarded the Golden Pineapple Award in Excellence in Tourism Service and Hospitality. Selected 2009-2010 "Best of New England" "Editors' Pick" -Yankee Magazine Travel Guide to New England Chosen one of "Ten Top New England Inns" by TravelChannel.com "Location, Location and Location - makes all the difference" ~ Connecticut Magazine.*

Certificate may be used: Nov. 1-March 31, Sunday-Thursday, not valid on holidays.

Norfolk B4

Blackberry River Inn

538 Greenwoods Road W
Norfolk, CT 06058
(860)542-5100 Fax:(860)542-1763
Internet: www.blackberryriverinn.com
E-mail: jangel7257@gmail.com

Circa 1763. In the National Register, the Colonial buildings that comprise the inn are situated on 27 acres. A library with cherry paneling, three parlors and a breakfast room are offered for guests' relaxation. Guest rooms are elegantly furnished with antiques. Guests can choose from rooms in the main house with a fireplace or suites with a fireplace or Jacuzzi. The Cottage includes a fireplace and Jacuzzi. A full country breakfast is included.

Innkeeper(s): Jeanneth. $155-289. 15 rooms, 14 with PB, 2 two-bedroom suites, 1 cottage, 1 conference room. Breakfast and afternoon tea included in rates. Types of meals: Full bkfst. Beds: KQT. Cable TV, VCR, ceiling fan, clock radio, some with fireplace, hair dryer, bath amenities and iron/ironing board in room. Air conditioning. DVD, fax, copier, swimming, library, telephone, Hiking, Fishing and Wireless access in the Main House on premises.

Antiquing, canoeing/kayaking, cross-country skiing, downhill skiing, fishing, golf, hiking, horseback riding, shopping, wineries, sleigh rides, hay rides, auto racing and music festivals nearby.

Location: Country.

Certificate may be used: May-November only, Sunday-Thursday, subject to availability.

Mountain View Inn

67 Litchfield Road, Rt 272
Norfolk, CT 06058
(860)542-6991 (866)792-7812
Internet: www.mvinn.com
E-mail: innkeepers@mvinn.com

Circa 1900. Sitting on more than three scenic hillside acres in Norfolk, Connecticut, this Gilded Age Victorian bed and breakfast offers the New England tradition of gracious hospitality and treasured privacy. Listen to classical music with a glass of sherry in the main parlor or sit by the fire in the great room. Relax in the elegance and comfort of a spacious guest bedroom with antique furnishings or stay in the two-bedroom guest house with  fireplace, kitchen and dining area. A farm-fresh breakfast is served fireside or on the sunny garden porch. Browse through the vintage boutique, admire the work in the art gallery and ask about Mountain View Photography. The quiet country surroundings in the foothills of the Berkshire Mountains and the warm ambiance inspire creativity.

Innkeeper(s): Dean & Jean Marie Johnson. $100-400. 7 rooms with PB, 1 guest house. Breakfast and Afternoon Sherry and Evening Port included in rates. Types of meals: Full gourmet bkfst, early coffee/tea, Breakfast in Bed Available, Afternoon Sherry and Evening Port. Beds: KQDT. Reading lamp, hair dryer, bathrobes, wireless Internet access, WiFi throughout the Inn and Room 4 has a private "Sleeping Porch in room. Air conditioning. TV, fax, parlor games, telephone, gift shop, "The Gilded Peacock", A whimsical Vintage Boutique located on the Main floor, WiFi throughout the Inn, 4 Fireplaces, Large Victorian Courtyard and Great Room - Perfect for business meetings and conferences on premises. Antiquing, canoeing/kayaking, cross-country skiing, downhill skiing, fishing, hiking, horseback riding, parks, shopping, wineries, Private Lake located less than 2 miles away - (first come first serve for Lake Passes), we are the closest inn (walking distance) to the Yale Chamber Music Festival and Horse Drawn Carriage Rides available by appointment and subject to availiblity nearby.

Location: Country.

Publicity: *Hartford Courant, Litchfield County Times and Gourmet.*

"Newly decorated with delightful results - B&B Travelers Review."

Certificate may be used: September, November-April, excluding holidays and holiday weekends, subject to availability.

North Stonington E9

Inn at Lower Farm

119 Mystic Rd
North Stonington, CT 06359
(860) 535-9075 (866) 535-9075
Internet: www.lowerfarm.com
E-mail: info@lowerfarm.com

Circa 1740. Fully restored, this 1740 center-chimney Georgian Colonial boasts six working fireplaces. The bed and breakfast is located on more than four acres of lawns, gardens and cattail marshes. Enjoy the scenic surroundings while relaxing in the hammock or on the comfortable outdoor furniture scattered throughout the property. Swing on the porch swing and breathe in the fresh country air. Well-appointed guest bedrooms feature queen-size beds, en-suite private baths and bright sitting areas with recliner chairs. Three rooms have fireplaces and a fourth includes a whirlpool tub. Wake up to a full country breakfast served by candlelight in front of the original open hearth and beehive oven. In the afternoon gather for tea and homemade cookies.

Innkeeper(s): Mary & Jon Wilska. $100-180. 4 rooms with PB, 3 with FP, 1 with WP, 1 two-bedroom suite, 1 conference room. Breakfast, afternoon tea and snacks/refreshments included in rates. Types of meals: Full gourmet bkfst, veg bkfst and early coffee/tea. Beds: Q. Reading lamp, stereo, clock radio, desk, most with fireplace, hair dryer, bath amenities, wireless Internet access, Recliner Queen Anne chairs, individual wall-mounted reading lamps, Make-up mirror and Wireless Internet in room. Central air. TV, VCR, fax, copier, library, parlor games, telephone, hammock, porch swing and outdoor sitting areas on premises. Antiquing, art galleries, beach, bicycling, canoeing/kayaking, fishing, golf, hiking, horseback riding, live theater, museums, parks, shopping, sporting events, tennis, water sports, wineries, Foxwood and Mohegan Sun Casinos, birdwatching, foliage tour, cider mill and apple and berry picking nearby.

Location: Country.

Publicity: *Yankee magazine Editors Choice Award (2008).*

Certificate may be used: November-May, Sunday-Thursday.

Norwalk   B4

Silvermine Tavern

194 Perry Ave
Norwalk, CT 06850-1123
(203)847-4558 (888)693-9967 Fax:(203)847-9171
Internet: www.silverminetavern.com
E-mail: SilvermineTavernInn@gmail.com

Circa 1790. The Silvermine consists of the Old Mill, the Country Store, the Coach House and the Tavern itself. Primitive paintings and furnishings, as well as family heirlooms, decorate the inn. Guest rooms and dining rooms overlook the Old Mill, the waterfall and swans gliding across the millpond. Some guest rooms offer items such as canopy bed or private decks. In the summer, guests can dine al fresco and gaze at the mill pond.

Innkeeper(s): Frank Whitman. Call for rates. 11 rooms, 10 with PB, 1 suite. Breakfast included in rates. Types of meals: Cont, lunch and dinner. Restaurant on premises. Beds: QDT. Reading lamp, clock radio, desk, Some with canopied beds, American country antiques, Bathrooms equipped with comfortable old-time fixtures including some clawfoot tubs, Hooked rugs, Candlewick spreads, Antique beds, Historic prints, Jar of cracked corn to feed the always-hungry ducks and A happy-massager in room. Air conditioning. VCR, fax, copier, parlor games, telephone and fireplace on premises. Antiquing, fishing, parks and shopping nearby.

Location: Residential area.

Certificate may be used: No Friday nights, no September or October. No holidays.

Ridgefield   F2

West Lane Inn

22 West Ln
Ridgefield, CT 06877-4914
(203)438-7323 Fax:(203)438-7325
Internet: www.westlaneinn.com
E-mail: west_lane_inn@sbcglobal.net

Circa 1849. Listed in the National Register, this 1849 Victorian mansion combines the ambiance of a country inn with the convenience of a boutique hotel. An enormous front porch is filled with black wrought iron chairs and tables overlooking a manicured lawn on two acres. A polished oak staircase rises to a third-floor landing and lounge. Chandeliers, wall sconces and floral wallpapers accent the intimate atmosphere. Elegant, oversized guest bedrooms feature individual climate control, four-poster beds and upscale amenities like heated towel racks, voice mail, wireless DSL and refrigerators. Two include fireplaces and a kitchenette. Wake up and enjoy a morning meal in the Breakfast Room before experiencing one of New England's finest towns with a variety of boutiques, museums, antique shops and restaurants.

Innkeeper(s): Maureen Mayer & Deborah Prieger. $185-450. 18 rooms with PB, 2 with FP, 1 suite, 1 conference room. Breakfast included in rates. Types of meals: Cont plus, room service and Bernard's restaurant is next door serving lunch and dinner. Restaurant on premises. Beds: KQ. Cable TV, VCR, reading lamp, refrigerator, ceiling fan, clock radio, telephone, desk, voice mail, some with fireplace, hair dryer, bath amenities, wireless Internet access, iron/ironing board, free wireless DSL, full private baths, heated towel racks and satellite TV in room. Air conditioning. DVD, fax and copier on premises. Antiquing, cross-country skiing, golf, hiking, live theater, museums, parks, shopping, tennis, wineries, Award-winning restaurants, Boutiques and Movies nearby.

Location: City. New England town.

"Thank you for the hospitality you showed us. The rooms are comfortable and quiet. I haven't slept this soundly in weeks."

Certificate may be used: All year, subject to availability, for standard rooms only, not valid Friday, Saturday and holidays.

Southbury   E3

Cornucopia At Oldfield

782 Main St North
Southbury, CT 06488-1898
(203)267-6772 Fax:(203)267-6773
Internet: cornucopiabnb.com
E-mail: innkeeper@cornucopiabnb.com

Circa 1818. Cornucopia at Oldfield is surrounded by acres of rolling lawns and gardens that are bordered by huge sugar and Norway maples and the original stone walls. Experience country elegance in a relaxed setting at this stately Georgia Federal home in the historic district. The fireside public rooms include the Keeping Room for watching a DVD, video or playing games. The front parlor offers a more reserved, quiet ambiance. A desk and a library of books, magazines and CDs are on the second floor. Inviting guest bedrooms feature fleece robes and all the modern amenities. Stay in a room with a clawfoot tub, fireplace or balcony. A full hot breakfast is served daily. In summertime, sit by the lily pond, relax in the shady gazebo or nap in a hammock or take a refreshing dip in the swimming pool. In winter, curl up with a book or play a game by our fireplace.

Innkeeper(s): Christine & Ed Edelson. $160-275. 6 rooms, 5 with PB, 4 with FP, 1 with WP, 1 two-bedroom suite, 2 conference rooms. Breakfast, snacks/refreshments and wine included in rates. Types of meals: Full gourmet bkfst, veg bkfst, early coffee/tea, picnic lunch and afternoon tea. Beds: KQT. Cable TV, DVD, reading lamp, CD player, ceiling fan, turn-down service, most with fireplace, hair dryer, bathrobes, bath amenities and wireless Internet access in room. Central air. VCR, fax, swimming, library, parlor games and telephone on premises. Amusement parks, antiquing, art galleries, canoeing/kayaking, cross-country skiing, downhill skiing, fishing, golf, hiking, horseback riding, live theater, museums, parks, shopping, tennis, water sports and wineries nearby.

Location: Country.

Certificate may be used: Sunday-Thursday, Jan. 1-May 30, subject to availability, no holidays.

Westbrook   E7

Angels' Watch Inn

902 Boston Post Rd
Westbrook, CT 06498-1848
(860)399-8846 Fax:(860)399-2571
Internet: www.angelswatchinn.com
E-mail: info@angelswatchinn.com

Circa 1830. Appreciate the comfortable elegance and tranquil ambiance of this stately 1830 Federal bed and breakfast that is situated on one acre of peaceful grounds in a quaint New England village along the Connecticut River Valley Shoreline. Romantic guest bedrooms are private retreats with canopy beds, fireplaces, stocked refrigerators, strawberries dipped in chocolate, fresh fruit and snack baskets, whirlpools or two-person clawfoot soaking tubs. Maintaining a fine reputation of impeccable standards, the inn caters to the whole person. After breakfast choose from an incredible assortment of spa services that include massage therapy, yoga, intuitive guidance, as well as mind, body and spirit wellness. Go horseback riding then take a sunset cruise. Ask about elopement/small wedding packages and midweek or off-season specials.

Innkeeper(s): Bill , Peggy and Diane. $115-195. 4 rooms, 5 with PB, 5 with FP, 4 with HT. Breakfast, afternoon tea, snacks/refreshments and wine included in rates. Types of meals: Full gourmet bkfst, veg bkfst, early coffee/tea, picnic lunch and dinner. Beds: KQT. Cable TV, DVD, reading lamp, stereo, refrigerator, ceiling fan, snack bar, clock radio, desk, hot tub/spa, fireplace, hair dryer, bathrobes, bath amenities, wireless Internet access, iron/ironing board, Complimentary beverages, bottled water, soda & a choice of beer and white wine or sparkling cider in room. Air conditioning. Fax, copier, spa, parlor games, telephone, laundry facility and Wireless Internet access for laptops on premises. Limited handicap access. Antiquing, art galleries, beach, bicycling, canoeing/kayaking, cross-country skiing, fishing, golf, hiking, live theater, museums, parks, shopping, sporting events, water sports and wineries nearby.

Location: Ocean community.

Publicity: *The Hartford Courant, New Haven Register, Main Street News, Pictorial and ABC affiliate Positively Connecticut.*

Certificate may be used: Sunday-Thursday year-round, holidays and special events excluded. Full season rates, double occupancy only.

Captain Stannard House

138 South Main Street
Westbrook, CT 06498-1904
(860)399-4634
Internet: www.stannardhouse.com
E-mail: info@stannardhouse.com

Circa 1872. Abundant in history, space and charm, Captain Stannard House is a sea captain's manor located on the Connecticut shore in quaint Westbrook. Experience this all-season home away from home for a romantic winter getaway, spring renewal, autumnal adventure or summer love at the

beach. Stay in a delightfully furnished guest bedroom with individual climate control, desk and sitting area. Anticipate a satisfying candlelit breakfast in the warm and inviting dining room. Linger with morning coffee or an evening glass of wine by the fire in the great room or on the huge south porch overlooking landscaped grounds. Add a piece to the ongoing jigsaw puzzle in the Captain's Room. Visit the nearby casinos, go to the theater and take a wine-tasting tour of Chamard Vineyard. Ask about specials and packages.

Innkeeper(s): Jim & Mary Brewster. $150-220. 9 rooms with PB. Breakfast and snacks/refreshments included in rates. Types of meals: Full gourmet bkfst, early coffee/tea, Early Riser Station w/seasonal fresh fruit, yogurt selection, homemade granola, cereal variety, nutritional bars, homemade baked goods, juice, coffee, decaf, tea and hot chocolate and the best coffee in town. Beds: QDT. Cable TV, reading lamp, clock radio, desk, hair dryer, bathrobes, bath amenities, wireless Internet access, iron/ironing board, Desks, Sitting areas and Snack basket w/Perrier water in room. Air conditioning. TV, VCR, DVD, fax, copier, bicycles, library, parlor games, telephone, fireplace, Regulation pool table, Game rooms for chess, checkers, cards, board games, On-going jig-saw puzzle table, Guest refrigerator, Stocked mini-fridge, Multi CD player w/CD music selection, Great room with fieldstone fireplace, PC room with lap top, scanner, copier, fax, Complimentary WiFi throughout Inn and 80' South porch on premises. Limited handicap access. Antiquing, art galleries, beach, bicycling, canoeing/kayaking, fishing, golf, hiking, live theater, museums, parks, shopping, water sports, wineries, Factory outlets, Birdwatching, Casinos, Sleigh & Carriage rides, Premium shopping outlets, Boat cruises, Mystic Aquarium, Mystic Seaport, Essex Steam Train and Riverboat nearby.

Location: Ocean community. Old Saybrook, Clinton, Essex.

Publicity: *New York Daily News, New York Times, Hartford Courant, Main Street News, River & Shore Magazine, elan Magazine, ABC and NBC.*

Certificate may be used: Anytime November-May, subject to availability.

Westbrook Inn B&B

976 Boston Post Rd
Westbrook, CT 06498-1852
(860) 399-4777 (800) 342-3162 Fax:(860) 399-8023
Internet: www.westbrookinn.com
E-mail: info@westbrookinn.com

Circa 1876. A wraparound porch and flower gardens offer a gracious welcome to this elegant Victorian inn. The innkeeper, an expert in restoring old houses and antiques, has filled the B&B with fine Victorian period furnishings, handsome paintings and wall coverings. Well-appointed guest bedrooms and a spacious two-bedroom cottage provide comfortable accommodations. Some guest rooms include a fireplace, four-poster canopy bed or balcony. A full breakfast features homemade baked goods that accompany a variety of delicious main entrees. Complimentary beverages are available throughout the day. Enjoy bike rides and walks to the beach. Nearby factory outlets and casinos are other popular activities.

Innkeeper(s): Glenn & Chris Monroe. $180. 14 rooms with PB, 8 with FP, 3 with WP, 3 total suites, including 1 two-bedroom suite, 1 cottage, 1 conference room. Breakfast, afternoon tea, snacks/refreshments and Coffee & tea is always available included in rates. Types of meals: Full gourmet bkfst, veg bkfst, early coffee/tea, Complimentary Wine & Cheese every Saturday night and homemade cookies & cream sherry daily. Beds: KQT. Data port, cable TV, DVD, reading lamp, refrigerator, clock radio, telephone, coffeemaker, desk, most with fireplace, hair dryer, bathrobes, bath amenities, wireless Internet access, iron/ironing board, All guest rooms offer luxurious beds with triple-sheeted linens, period antiques, some w/Sani-Jet Jaccuzzis, suites with sitting areas, balconies, working gas fireplaces, porcelain heated bathroom floors, monogrammed robes and some rooms with full kitchen or kitchettes in room. Central air. Fax, copier, spa, bicycles, library, parlor games, gift shop, picturesque gardens, gazebo, bistro-style patio, historic front porch, two-person hammock and cottage with full kitchen on premises. Limited handicap access. Antiquing, art galleries, beach, bicycling, canoeing/kayaking, fishing, golf, hiking, horseback riding, live theater, museums, parks, shopping, sporting events, tennis, water sports, wineries, Boat cruises, boutique shops, dinner train, Goodspeed Opera House, Ivoryton Playhouse theater, casinos, outlet malls, quaint downtown, movie theaters, historic home tours and sailing excursions & much more! A link to additional area attractions can be found at the Inns website nearby.

Location: Ocean community. Historic Shoreline Village.

Publicity: *Harbor News, New Haven Register, Middletown Press, Pictorial Newspaper, Arrington's B&B Journal "Best Inn with Nearby Attraction," voted "Most Elegant", "Best Weekend Getaway", NBC, Comcast Cable and Positively Connecticut.*

Certificate may be used: Nov. 1-April 30. Sunday-Thursday, select rooms. Not valid on holidays or special events. Can not be combined with other discounts or packages.

Wethersfield   C6

Chester Bulkley House B&B

184 Main St
Wethersfield, CT 06109-2340
(860) 563-4236 Fax:(860)257-8266
Internet: www.chesterbulkleyhouse.com
E-mail: chesterbulkley@aol.com

Circa 1830. Offering the best of both worlds, this renovated Greek Revival structure is ideally located in the historic village of Old Weathersfield with its quaint sites, museums and shops, yet the inn also boasts a 10-minute drive to downtown Hartford with ballet, Broadway shows, opera and the symphony. Hand-carved woodwork, wide pine floors, working fireplaces and period pieces enhance the comfortable ambiance. Cut flowers, pillow chocolates and other thoughtful treats ensure a pleasant and gracious stay for business or leisure.

Innkeeper(s): Tom Aufiero. $105-165. 5 rooms, 3 with PB, 1 suite. Breakfast and afternoon tea included in rates. Types of meals: Full gourmet bkfst, veg bkfst and early coffee/tea. Beds: KQDT. Ceiling fan, clock radio, hair dryer, bath amenities and iron/ironing board in room. Air conditioning. TV, fax, library, telephone and fireplace on premises. Antiquing, downhill skiing, fishing, live theater, parks, shopping and sporting events nearby.

Location: Village.

Certificate may be used: January-August, Sunday to Thursday.

Woodstock   B9

B&B at Taylor's Corner

880 Route 171
Woodstock, CT 06281
(860)974-0490 (888)974-0490
Internet: www.taylorsbb.com
E-mail: reservations@taylorsbb.com

Traditional lodging and hearthside cooking is part of the historic yet romantic ambiance of this restored 18th-century central-chimney Colonial and attached Connecticut cottage, listed in the National Register. It boasts two beehive ovens, eight fireplaces, original wide-floor boards, moldings, gunstock beams, mantels and stair rails. Relax by the fireside in the keeping room, parlor or in an Adirondack chair on the patio. Spacious guest bedrooms are furnished with antiques and reproductions. Besides a daily breakfast in the dining room, light snacks and beverages are available. Ask about getaway specials. Popular Old Sturbridge Village is 15 miles away.

Innkeeper(s): Brenda Van Damme. $125-145. 3 rooms with PB, 3 with FP. Breakfast and snacks/refreshments included in rates. Types of meals: Full bkfst, veg bkfst, early coffee/tea and Gluten-free breakfast available upon request. Beds: QT. Reading lamp, clock radio, fireplace, hair dryer, bath amenities, wireless Internet access and iron/ironing board in room. Air conditioning. TV, DVD, fax, copier, library, parlor games, XBox and movie library on premises. Antiquing, bicycling, cross-country skiing, fish-

ing, hiking, parks, shopping, sporting events and wineries nearby.

Certificate may be used: November-April, subject to availability.

Elias Child House B&B

50 Perrin Rd
Woodstock, CT 06281
(860)974-9836 (877)974-9836 Fax:(860)974-1541
Internet: www.eliaschildhouse.com
E-mail: afelice@earthlink.net

Circa 1700. Nine fireplaces warm this heritage three-story colonial home, referred to as "the mansion house" by early settlers. There are two historic cooking hearths, including a beehive oven. Original floors, twelve-over-twelve windows and paneling remain. A bountiful breakfast is served fireside in the dining room and a screened porch and a patio provide nesting spots for reading and relaxing. The inn's grounds are spacious and offer a pool and hammocks. Woodland walks on the 47 acres and antiquing are popular activities.

Innkeeper(s): Anthony Felice, Jr. & MaryBeth Gorke-Felice. $125-150. 3 rooms with PB, 3 with FP, 1 suite. Breakfast included in rates. Types of meals: Country bkfst and early coffee/tea. Beds: QDT. Reading lamp, clock radio, turn-down service, bathrobes, suite has two fireplaces, sitting room and two baths (one with a clawfoot tub) in room. Air conditioning. TV, VCR, DVD, fax, copier, swimming, bicycles, library, parlor games, telephone, fireplace, hearth-cooking demonstrations, cross-country skiing and snowshoeing on premises. Antiquing, bicycling, canoeing/kayaking, fishing, golf, hiking, museums, parks, shopping and wineries nearby.

Location: Country.

Publicity: *Time Out New York, Best Fares Magazine, Distinction, Wine Gazette, Car & Driver Magazine, Worcester Telegram and Gazette.*

"Comfortable rooms and delightful country ambiance."

Certificate may be used: Anytime, subject to availability.

Delaware

Milford H3

The Towers B&B

101 NW Front St
Milford, DE 19963-1022
(302)422-3814
Internet: www.mispillion.com

Circa 1783. Once a simple colonial house, this ornate Steamboat Gothic fantasy features every imaginable Victorian architectural detail, all added in 1891. This winner of the iLoveInns.com Top 10 Romantic Inns of 2009 has 10 distinct styles of gingerbread as well as towers, turrets, gables, porches and bays. Inside, chestnut and cherry woodwork, window seats and stained-glass windows are complemented with American and French antiques. The back garden boasts a sunroom and swimming pool. Ask for the splendid Tower Room or Rapunzel Suite.

Innkeeper(s): Daniel & Rhonda Bond. $110-160. 4 rooms with PB, 1 two-bedroom suite. Breakfast and Full gourmet breakfast. Please advise innkeeper of any dietary restrictions. Complimentary sherry available in Music Room included in rates. Types of meals: Full bkfst and veg bkfst. Beds: QD. Reading lamp, ceiling fan, clock radio, hair dryer, bathrobes, bath amenities and wireless Internet access in room. Air conditioning. TV, DVD, telephone, fireplace, gift shop and Wi-Fi on premises. Antiquing, art galleries, beach, bicycling, canoeing/kayaking, fishing, live theater, museums, parks, shopping, water sports, wineries, Near Atlantic Ocean beaches, Cape Henlopen, Rehoboth, Dewey and Bethany nearby.

Location: City, ocean community. Atlantic Ocean beaches within 25 miles.

Publicity: *Washington Post, Baltimore Sun, Washingtonian, Mid-Atlantic Country and Inn Traveler.*

"I felt as if I were inside a beautiful Victorian Christmas card, surrounded by all the things Christmas should be."

Certificate may be used: Any night of the week throughout the year, except NASCAR Race weekends and holidays.

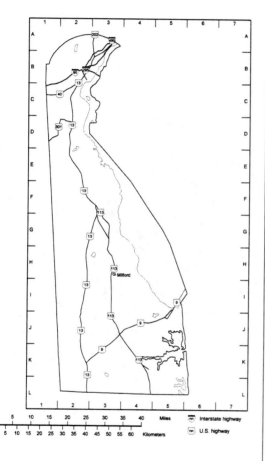

0 5 10 15 20 25 30 35 40 Miles
0 5 10 15 20 25 30 35 40 45 50 55 60 Kilometers

Interstate highway
U.S. highway

Florida

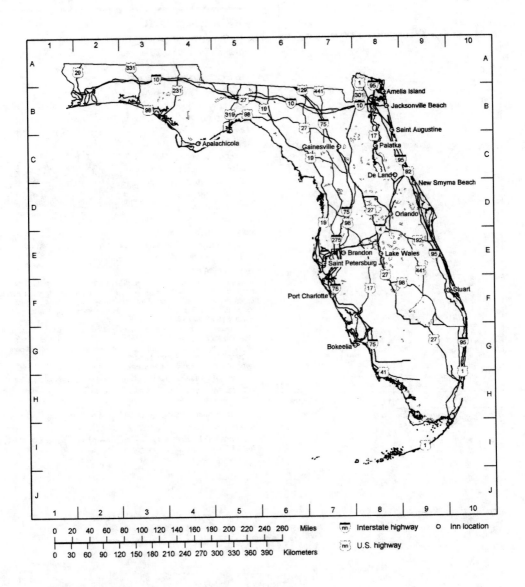

Amelia Island   B8

Hoyt House Bed & Breakfast Inn

804 Atlantic Ave
Amelia Island, FL 32034-3629
(904)277-4300 (800)432-2085 Fax:(904)277-4305
Internet: www.hoythouse.com
E-mail: innkeeperhoythouse@gmail.com

Circa 1905. A centerpiece of the historic district, this 1905
Queen Anne Victorian mansion blends warm hospitality and
delightful comforts with the grace of a bygone era. Feel the ocean
breeze from a swing or rockers on broad porches while sipping
lemonade or iced tea. Relax in our heated pool and hot tub.
Elegant guest bedrooms feature a private bath, some include a
whirlpool tub. Enjoy a chef's breakfast, afternoon refreshments
and evening wine. Bike to the sea to take in the island sunshine,
birds and dolphins. Beach gear is provided. Explore fascinating
shops and dine in excellent restaurants all within an easy stroll.
Innkeeper(s): Myrta & Deborah. $175-395. 10 rooms with PB, 3 with WP, 2
cabins, 1 conference room. Breakfast, snacks/refreshments and Gourmet
Breakfast made to order for a amazing & relaxing dining experience.
Complimentary Cocktail Hour and full liquor license to fill any libations request
in the Amelia English Pub included in rates. Types of meals: Full gourmet
bkfst, early coffee/tea, gourmet lunch, picnic lunch, afternoon tea, hors d'oeuvres, wine, gourmet dinner, room service and Gourmet Lunches and Dinner
available at special request for an additional charge. Full services meals on
Private Yacht available. Special events always welcome. Beds: KQ. Cable TV,
DVD, reading lamp, ceiling fan, clock radio, telephone, some with hot tub/spa,
some with fireplace, hair dryer, bathrobes, bath amenities, wireless Internet
access and iron/ironing board in room. Central air. Fax, copier, spa, swimming,
bicycles, library, parlor games, gift shop and Full Service Bar & Lounge on
premises. Handicap access. Antiquing, art galleries, beach, bicycling, canoe-
ing/kayaking, fishing, golf, hiking, horseback riding, live theater, museums,
parks, shopping, sporting events, tennis and water sports nearby.
Location: City, ocean community. Historic district of Fernandina, within walking distance of shops, dining, museums and galleries.
Publicity: The Washington Times, PBS, Southern Living, Intimate
Destinations and Jacksonville Times-Union.
Certificate may be used: Anytime, subject to availability, excluding holidays
and special events.

Apalachicola   C4

Coombs House Inn

80 6th St
Apalachicola, FL 32320
(850)653-9199 (888)244-8320 Fax:(850)653-2785
Internet: www.coombshouseinn.com
E-mail: info@coombshouseinn.com

Circa 1905. Located in the antebellum fishing village of
Apalachicola on Florida's unspoiled Gulf Coast, this exquisitely
restored historic inn consists of three stately mansions. A member of Select Registry, it is known for its grace and elegance with
fine antiques, oil paintings and oriental carpets. There are seventeen original fireplaces, gleaming wood paneling and hardwood
floors. Lavish guest suites are equipped with modern amenities
including private baths, sumptuous bedding, and plush robes.
Savor a delicious breakfast each morning. Spacious Camellia
Gardens and a gazebo are ideal for weddings, while broad wraparound verandas with comfortable wicker chairs are a perfect
setting for afternoon teas or wine tastings. Complimentary pro-
visions include bicycles for touring the historic district as well as
beach chairs and umbrellas for enjoying the pristine beaches of
nearby St. George Island.

Innkeeper(s): Estella & Destinee. $109-269. 23 rooms with PB, 7 with WP,
3 suites, 3 guest houses, 1 conference room. Breakfast, afternoon tea,
snacks/refreshments, wine and Weekend wine and cheese
receptions 6-7 PM included in rates. Types of meals: Full bkfst, veg bkfst and
early coffee/tea. Beds: KQDT. Modem hook-up, data port, cable TV, reading
lamp, refrigerator, ceiling fan, clock radio, telephone, coffeemaker, desk, some
with hot tub/spa, hair dryer, bathrobes, bath amenities, wireless Internet
access and iron/ironing board in room. Central air. Fax, copier, bicycles, parlor
games, fireplace, gift shop, Complimentary beach chairs, Umbrellas and
Towels on premises. Handicap access. Antiquing, art galleries, beach, bicycling, canoeing/kayaking, fishing, golf, hiking, horseback riding, live theater,
museums, parks, shopping, tennis, water sports and Sailing nearby.
Location: City, ocean community. Historic District.
Publicity: Southern Living, Florida Design, Country Inns Magazine, NY
Times, CNN and Travel & Leisure Magazine.
Certificate may be used: Sunday-Thursday.

Bokeelia   G7

Bokeelia Tarpon Inn

8241 Main St
Bokeelia, FL 33922-1550
(239)283-8961 (866)TARPON2 Fax:(239)283-8215
Internet: www.tarponinn.com
E-mail: Info@tarponinn.com

Circa 1914. Originally known as the 1914 Poe Johnson home,
this historic waterfront bed and breakfast is located on the Gulf
Coast?s Pine Island. Restored to offer a relaxed pace, it especially caters to fisherfolk. Deepwater fishing is accessible from the
private dock and boat ramp. Tackle, rods and equipment can be
requested. The Knot Room is filled with fishing resources, memorabilia and a library. Enjoy twilight-time refreshments by the
fireplace in the living room. The screened-in second-story porch
features sweeping views of Charlotte Harbor and Gasparilla
Island. Guest bedrooms are all named for local islands in the
Pine Island Sound. An expanded tropical breakfast is sure to
please. Golf carts, kayaks, and bikes are available to explore the
area. A wine cellar and cigar humidor add to the amenities.
Innkeeper(s): Cynthia Welch. $159-325. 5 rooms with PB. Breakfast,
snacks/refreshments, hors d'oeuvres and wine included in rates. Types of
meals: Cont plus, picnic lunch and room service. Beds: Q. Modem hook-up,
reading lamp, ceiling fan, clock radio, telephone, hair dryer, bathrobes, bath
amenities, wireless Internet access and iron/ironing board in room. Air conditioning. Fax, copier, bicycles, parlor games, fireplace, laundry facility, gift
shop, Kayaks, Golf carts and Charter boat on premises. Handicap access. Art
galleries, beach, bicycling, canoeing/kayaking, fishing, golf, museums, parks,
shopping and tennis nearby.
Location: Waterfront.
Certificate may be used: June 30-Dec. 1.

Brandon   E7

Behind The Fence B&B Inn

1400 Viola Dr
Brandon, FL 33511-7327
(813)685-8201
Internet: www.behindthefencebb.com

Circa 1976. Warm and welcoming, this Colonial salt box replica
features New England antiques and Amish country furniture to
provide a realistic view of life as it once was with simple needs
and sacred values. Experience the historically accurate ambiance
and folklore at this quiet retreat from today's stressful schedules.
The oak-shaded property features accommodations in the main
house or in the Caretakers Cabin with two porches. One faces
the in-ground swimming pool and the other overlooks the

private wooded setting. Gather for a continental-plus breakfast each morning with homemade Amish sweet rolls, fresh fruit, cereal, toast, coffee, tea and orange juice. Brandon, Florida is within five minutes of downtown Tampa and Ybor City.

Innkeeper(s): Larry & Carolyn R. Yoss. $79-95. 5 rooms, 3 with PB, 1 suite, 1 cottage, 1 conference room. Breakfast and afternoon tea included in rates. Types of meals: Cont plus, early coffee/tea and snacks/refreshments. Beds: QDT. Cable TV, VCR, reading lamp, refrigerator, clock radio and desk in room. Air conditioning. Swimming, telephone and fireplace on premises. Amusement parks, antiquing, canoeing/kayaking, fishing, horseback riding, parks, shopping, sporting events and water sports nearby.

Location: Subdivision to County Park.

Publicity: Brandon News, Travel Host, Country Living, Country Home and Florida Secrets.

"One of the best kept secrets in all of Tampa! Thanks again!"

Certificate may be used: Anytime, subject to availability.

De Land   C8

Deland Country Inn

228 W Howry Ave
De Land, FL 32720-5424
(386) 736-4244 (866) 403-8009
Internet: www.delandcountryinn.com
E-mail: info@delandcountryinn.com

Circa 1883. British owned, this historic Victorian home has been family-run for more than two decades. Gracing an acre in DeLand, Florida, this traditional B&B features an antique guest house that is handmade and hand-painted as well as a separate cottage that is air conditioned and fully equipped. Pets are usually welcome with advance preparation. The guest rooms include a refrigerator, coffee/tea facility, evening turndown service and some rooms have a microwave or one can be provided upon request. Gather for a pot of tea in the parlor, and read the morning newspaper on the front porch rocker or swing. Savor a customized hot English Breakfast made to please with menu selections. Skydiving is a popular activitiy in this area or visit the Naval Air Museum. Explore nearby Blue Spring and DeLeon Spring State Parks, offering boat tours, canoes, kayaks, fishing and trails.

Innkeeper(s): Mark Sutton. $69-149. 5 rooms with PB, 1 cottage. Breakfast, snacks/refreshments and Breakfast is served from: 7 - 9:00 included in rates. Types of meals: Full gourmet bkfst and early coffee/tea. Beds: KQT. Cable TV, reading lamp, refrigerator, ceiling fan, clock radio, coffeemaker, turn-down service, hair dryer, bath amenities and wireless Internet access in room. Central air. VCR, DVD, library, parlor games, telephone and fireplace on premises. Limited handicap access. Antiquing, art galleries, beach, bicycling, canoeing/kayaking, fishing, golf, hiking, horseback riding, live theater, museums, parks, shopping, sporting events, tennis, water sports and wineries nearby.

Location: City.

Certificate may be used: Anytime, subject to availability. Not valid February, March or Special Events such as Bike Week, Daytona 500, Pepsi 400 etc.

Gainesville   C7

Camellia Rose Inn

205 S. E. 7th Street
Gainesville, FL 32601
(352)395-7673 Fax:(352)378-8030
Internet: www.camelliaroseinn.com
E-mail: info@camelliaroseinn.com

Circa 1903. Recently renovated, Camellia Rose Inn offers modern technology and pleasing amenities wrapped in a warm and cozy ambiance that reflects its Queen Anne-era beginning in historic Gainesville, Florida. Relax on the wraparound porch with a beverage or snack. More than forty different varieties of camellias, azaleas, crape myrtle, oak and red bud trees adorn the grounds. Stay in one of the spacious guest bedrooms with freshly pressed bed linens. Most feature a fireplace and spa shower. The Anticipation master suite boasts a corner bubble tub while Southern Charm has a clawfoot. On the second floor, Stardust includes a private balcony overlooking the gardens. A detached cottage offers even more privacy. Wake up and indulge in a delicious three-course breakfast in the dining room.

Innkeeper(s): Tom & Patricia McCants. $125-250. 7 rooms, 6 with PB, 1 cottage. Breakfast, snacks/refreshments, hors d'oeuvres and wine included in rates. Types of meals: Full bkfst, early coffee/tea, Fresh baked cookies and Evening happy hour. Beds: KQT. Cable TV, VCR, DVD, reading lamp, ceiling fan, snack bar, clock radio, turn-down service, desk, most with fireplace, hair dryer, bathrobes, bath amenities, wireless Internet access, iron/ironing board, Spa showers in all rooms except Master Suite that has a two person bubble tub with a rain shower, the cottage has a two-person Jacuzzi tub and as well as a traditional tub/shower in room. Central air. Fax, bicycles and library on premises. Handicap access. Antiquing, art galleries, bicycling, canoeing/kayaking, fishing, golf, hiking, horseback riding, live theater, museums, parks, shopping, sporting events, water sports and Shands Teaching Hospital nearby.

Location: City.

Certificate may be used: June-August, anytime subject to availability.

Magnolia Plantation Cottages and Gardens

309 SE 7th Street
Gainesville, FL 32601-6831
(352)375-6653 Fax:(352)338-0303
Internet: www.magnoliabnb.com
E-mail: info@magnoliabnb.com

Circa 1885. This restored French Second Empire Victorian is in the National Register. Magnolia trees surround the house. Five guest rooms are filled with family heirlooms. All bathrooms feature clawfoot tubs and candles. There are also private historic cottages available with Jacuzzis. Guests may enjoy the gardens, reflecting pond with waterfalls and gazebo. Bicycles are also available. Evening wine and snacks are included. The inn is two miles from the University of Florida.

Innkeeper(s): Joe & Cindy Montalto. $135-335. 5 rooms with PB, 5 with FP, 5 with WP, 7 cottages, 6 guest houses. Breakfast and afternoon tea included in rates. Types of meals: Full bkfst. Beds: Q. Cable TV, VCR, DVD, reading lamp, CD player, ceiling fan, clock radio, coffeemaker, desk, most with hot tub/spa, most with fireplace, hair dryer, bathrobes, wireless Internet access, iron/ironing board, cottages have Jacuzzi, fireplace, full kitchen and private garden in room. Air conditioning. Fax, bicycles, library, telephone and cocktail hour on premises. Antiquing, live theater, parks, shopping and sporting events nearby.

Location: City.

Publicity: Florida Living Magazine and Inn Country USA.

"This has been a charming, once-in-a-lifetime experience."

Certificate may be used: Sunday-Thursday, all year or anytime, last minute.

Jacksonville Beach
B8

Fig Tree Inn

185 4th Ave S
Jacksonville Beach, FL 32250
(904)246-8855 (877)217-9830
Internet: www.figtreeinn.com
E-mail: egghouse@comcast.net

Circa 1915. Whether staying here for a romantic getaway or to cheer for a favorite football team, this cedar shake bed & breakfast inn with Victorian accents offers an inviting and relaxing atmosphere. Sip a cool beverage in a rocker or swing on the acclaimed front porch. Games, books and magazines as well as an extensive video library are in the parlor. Wireless high-speed Internet service is available. Stay warm by the fire on cool nights. Themed guest bedrooms feature a handmade willow and canopy bed, Jacuzzi and clawfoot tub. The backyard's namesake produces enough fruit to make fig walnut pancakes, fig jelly and preserves served on scones. A light meal is served weekdays, a full breakfast is enjoyed on weekends. The kitchen can be used at any time. Walk to the beach, only half a block away.

Innkeeper(s): Dawn & Kevin Eggleston. $85-195. 6 rooms with PB, 1 with WP, 2 conference rooms. Breakfast, snacks/refreshments and wine included in rates. Types of meals: Full bkfst and Full breakfast on weekends and self serve continental on weekdays. Access to the main kitchen all day. Beds: KQT. Modem hook-up, cable TV, VCR, DVD, reading lamp, stereo, refrigerator, ceiling fan, snack bar, clock radio, telephone, coffeemaker, desk, hot tub/spa, hair dryer, bathrobes, bath amenities, wireless Internet access and iron/ironing board in room. Central air. Fax, copier, spa, bicycles, library, parlor games, fireplace, laundry facility, Movie and Book library on premises. Limited handicap access. Amusement parks, antiquing, art galleries, beach, bicycling, canoeing/kayaking, fishing, golf, hiking, live theater, museums, parks, shopping, sporting events, tennis, water sports, wineries, Beautiful beach just 1/2 block away, cruise ships, NFL Jacksonville Jaguars, college football, over 30 local golf courses and The Players Championship nearby.

Location: Ocean community.

Certificate may be used: Anytime, subject to availability; Special events and holidays excluded. Must mention certificate at time of requesting reservation.

Lake Wales
E8

Chalet Suzanne Country Inn & Restaurant

3800 Chalet Suzanne Dr
Lake Wales, FL 33859-7763
(863)676-6011 (800)433-6011 Fax:(863)676-1814
Internet: www.chaletsuzanne.com
E-mail: info@chaletsuzanne.com

Circa 1924. Situated on 70 acres adjacent to Lake Suzanne, this country inn's architecture includes gabled roofs, balconies, spires and steeples. The superb restaurant has a glowing reputation and offers a six-course candlelight dinner. Places of interest on the property include the Swiss Room, Wine Dungeon, Gift Boutique, Autograph Garden, Museum, Ceramic Salon, Airstrip and the Soup Cannery. The inn has been transformed into a village of cottages and miniature chateaux, one connected to the other seemingly with no particular order.

Innkeeper(s): Eric & Dee Hinshaw. $129-189. 26 rooms with PB. Breakfast included in rates. Types of meals: Full bkfst, lunch and Call for days and times of gourmet dinner. Beds: KDT. Cable TV, reading lamp, clock radio and telephone in room. Air conditioning. TV, VCR, fax, copier, swimming, library, parlor games and spa services on premises. Handicap access. Amusement parks, antiquing, fishing, golf, live theater, parks, shopping, sporting events, tennis and water sports nearby.

Location: Waterfront. Rural-lakefront.

Publicity: *National Geographic Traveler, Southern Living, Country Inns, Uncle Ben's 1992 award and Country Inn Cooking.*

"I now know why everyone always says, 'Wow!' when they come up from dinner. Please don't change a thing."

Certificate may be used: Anytime, subject to availability, Excludes weekends and holidays.

New Smyrna Beach
D9

Night Swan Intracoastal B&B

512 S Riverside Dr
New Smyrna Beach, FL 32168-7345
(386)423-4940 (800)465-4261 Fax:(386)427-2814
Internet: www.nightswan.com
E-mail: info@nightswan.com

Circa 1906. From the 140-foot dock at this waterside bed & breakfast, guests can gaze at stars, watch as ships pass or per-

haps catch site of dolphins. The turn-of-the-century home is decorated with period furnishings, including an antique baby grand piano, which guests are invited to use. Several guest rooms afford views of the Indian River, which is part of the Atlantic Intracoastal Waterway. Seven rooms include a large whirlpool tub. The innkeepers have created several special packages, featuring catered gourmet dinners, boat tours or romantic baskets with chocolate, wine and flowers.

Innkeeper(s): Martha & Chuck Nighswonger. $110-200. 15 rooms with PB, 1 with FP, 3 total suites, including 2 two-bedroom suites, 1 cottage, 1 conference room. Breakfast and snacks/refreshments included in rates. Types of meals: Full bkfst and early coffee/tea. Beds: KQ. Modem hook-up, cable TV, VCR, DVD, reading lamp, refrigerator, ceiling fan, clock radio, telephone, desk, hair dryer, wireless Internet access, iron/ironing board and seven whirlpool tubs in room. Air conditioning. Fax, library, fireplace and laundry facility on premises. Handicap access. Antiquing, art galleries, beach, bicycling, canoeing/kayaking, fishing, golf, horseback riding, live theater, museums, parks, shopping, tennis and water sports nearby.

Location: Waterfront.

Publicity: *Ft. Lauderdale Sun Sentinel and Florida Living.*

Certificate may be used: Sunday-Thursday, subject to availability.

Orlando
D8

The Courtyard at Lake Lucerne

211 N Lucerne Circle E
Orlando, FL 32801-3721
(407)648-5188 (800)444-5289 Fax:(407)246-1368
Internet: www.orlandohistoricinn.com
E-mail: orlandohistoricinn@hotmail.com

Circa 1883. This award-winning inn, precisely restored with attention to historical detail, consists of four different architectural styles. The Norment-Parry House is Orlando's oldest home. The Wellborn, an Art-Deco Modern Building, offers one-bedroom suites with kitchenettes. The I.W. Phillips is an antebellum-style manor where breakfast is served in a large reception room with a wide veranda overlooking the courtyard fountains and lush gardens. The Grand Victorian Dr. Phillips House is listed in the National Register of Historic Places. For an enchanting treat, ask for the Turret Room.

Innkeeper(s): David Messina. $99-225. 30 rooms with PB, 3 with FP, 8 with WP, 15 suites, 4 guest houses, 3 conference rooms. Breakfast included in rates. Types of meals: Cont plus. Beds: KQDT. Cable TV, reading lamp, CD player, refrigerator, clock radio, telephone, coffeemaker, turn-down service, desk, some with hot tub/spa, voice mail, some with fireplace, hair dryer, bathrobes, bath amenities, wireless Internet access and iron/ironing board in room. Central air. Copier on premises. Amusement parks, antiquing, art galleries, beach, fishing, golf, horseback riding, live theater, museums, parks, shopping, sporting events and water sports nearby.

Location: City.

Publicity: *Florida Historic Homes, Miami Herald, Southern Living and Country Victorian.*

"Best-kept secret in Orlando."

Certificate may be used: Anytime except New Year's Eve/Valentines weekend.

Port Charlotte   F7

Tropical Paradise

19227 Moore Haven Court
Port Charlotte, FL 33948
(941)626-8940 Fax:941-624-4533
Internet: www.tropicalparadisebb.com
E-mail: tropicalparadisebb@msn.com

Gracing the southwest waterfront on Charlotte County's Bluewater Trails, this quiet haven boasts a wall mural and furnishings that evoke the ambiance of a private tropical island. Take a relaxing swim in the screened-in, heated pool or lounge on the lanai near a waterfall into a fish pond accented with water lilies. Stay in a sound-insulated guest room or The Island Suite which features a whirlpool tub and private poolside exit. Savor breakfast each morning then go fishing from the grounds or by boat with access to the harbor and the Gulf of Mexico. Kayaking and canoeing are popular activities on the creeks with coves.

Innkeeper(s): Joanne & Clift McMahon. Call for rates. 2 rooms with PB, 1 with WP. Beds: KQ. TV, fax, copier, swimming, telephone, heated pool, kayaking, canoeing and deep water boat access and free docking for guests on premises. Handicap access.

Certificate may be used: Anytime, subject to availability.

Saint Augustine   B8

Casa de Solana, B&B Inn

21 Aviles St
Saint Augustine, FL 32084-4441
(904) 824-3555 (877) 824-3555 Fax:(904)824-3316
Internet: www.casadesolana.com
E-mail: casadsolana@gmail.com

Circa 1763. Poised inside a private walled courtyard surrounded by tropical gardens in the historic district of St. Augustine Antigua, Florida, this bed and breakfast inn is an easy walk along brick-paved streets to all the sites and attractions of America's oldest city. Casa de Solana B&B Inn has been recently renovated to be an oasis of comfort. Sit on the second-floor balcony with

horse-drawn carriages passing below. Gather for beverages and appetizers at the inn's evening social. Antique-filled guest bedrooms and suites feature pleasing amenities. Many of the romantic rooms include a fireplace, whirlpool tub, writing desk and refrigerator. Two homemade hot entrees, just-baked pastries, fresh fruit and special blend coffees accent a satisfying breakfast. There are facilities for small group functions and weddings.

Innkeeper(s): Jeff/Jamie/Lynne/Luis. $129-259. 10 rooms with PB, 7 with FP, 7 with WP. Breakfast, afternoon tea, snacks/refreshments, hors d'oeuvres and wine included in rates. Types of meals: Full gourmet bkfst, room service, Social hour 4:30-5:30 PM, daily with wine and snacks. Rotating Breakfast Menu Cinnamon raisin soufflé Cheese soufflé Crème Brulee or traditional French toast Ham and cheese quiche served croissant Spinach quiche served with croissant and bacon Cheesy eggs and sausage or bacon Apple Harvest or blueberry pancakes Vegan/Vegatarian Breakfast Options Vegan Southwestern Quinoa Burro. Vegan Blueberry-Banana Walnut Pancakes. Potato Patties and Morning Star Sausage Pumpkin Muffins A healthy good morning start!! Vegan Scrambled Tofu. **We request that you notify us at least two days prior to arrival. Beds: KQD. Cable TV, reading lamp, refrigerator, ceiling fan, clock radio, desk, most with hot tub/spa, most with fireplace, hair dryer, wireless Internet access, iron/ironing board and Most with private porches or balconies in room. Central air. Fax, copier, bicycles, Private parking available and Free Wi-Fi on premises. Limited handicap access. Amusement parks, antiquing, art galleries, beach, bicycling, canoeing/kayaking, fishing, golf, hiking, horseback riding, live theater, museums, parks, shopping, sporting events, tennis, water sports, wineries, Horse-drawn carriage rides, Trolley tours, Ghost tours, Bay cruises, Historic sites in the Nation's Oldest City, Year-round festivals & events, Concerts and First Friday Art Walks nearby.

Location: City, ocean community, waterfront.

Publicity: *Times Union, House Beautiful, Palm Beach Post, Innsider, North Florida Living, Jacksonville Today and PM Magazine.*

Certificate may be used: Sunday-Thursday, June 1-Nov. 15, subject to availability.

Casablanca Inn on The Bay

24 Avenida Menedez
Saint Augustine, FL 32084
(904)829-0928 (800)826-2626 Fax:904-826-1892
Internet: www.casablancainn.com
E-mail: innkeeper@casablancainn.com

Circa 1914. Casablanca Inn on The Bay is a lovingly restored Mediterranean revival bed and breakfast inn gracing the premium bayfront location of historic St. Augustine, Florida. Listed in the National Register, elegant suites and rooms boast panoramic Matanzas Bay views, whirlpools, rainfall showers, private porches and sundecks, antiques, decorative fireplaces, luxurious bedding and large flat screen TVs. Secret Garden rooms are pet friendly. Be pampered with a two-course gourmet breakfast. View the historic Fort Castillo de San Marcos from the sprawling verandas, watch the horse and carriage tours, or sink into a hammock while the tropical palms sway in the breeze. The Tini Martini Bar is surrounded by colorful art, intimate porch seating, tables under the stars and exotic concoctions or a complimentary glass of wine or beer.

$99-349. 23 rooms with PB, 11 with FP, 17 with HT, 17 with WP, 10 suites. Breakfast, afternoon tea, snacks/refreshments and Your stay includes a two-course gourmet sit-down breakfast served daily from 8:15 to 10:00 AM in the breakfast dining room and on the grand front verandas included in rates. Types of meals: Full gourmet bkfst and early coffee/tea. Beds: KQ. Modem hook-up, data port, cable TV, DVD, reading lamp, ceiling fan, clock radio, telephone, desk, most with hot tub/spa, hair dryer, bathrobes, bath amenities, iron/ironing board and Please visit Web site for room rates and detailed room/suite descriptions and photos in room. Central air. Fax and fireplace on premises. Limited handicap access. Antiquing, art galleries, beach, bicycling, canoeing/kayaking, fishing, golf, hiking, horseback riding, live theater, museums, parks, shopping, sporting events, tennis, water sports, wineries, boating, World Golf Village and Jacksonville Jaguars (NFL) nearby.

Location: City, ocean community, waterfront. Historic District of nation's oldest city.

Publicity: *Atlanta Journal* and featured on St. Augustine Ghost tour.

Certificate may be used: June-November, Sunday-Thursday.

Castle Garden B&B

15 Shenandoah St
Saint Augustine, FL 32084-2817
(904)829-3839
Internet: www.castlegarden.com
E-mail: castlegarden@bellsouth.net

Circa 1860. This newly-restored Moorish Revival-style inn was the carriage house to Warden Castle. Among the seven guest rooms are three bridal rooms with in-room Jacuzzi tubs and sunken bedrooms with cathedral ceilings. The innkeepers offer packages including carriage rides, picnic lunches, gift baskets and other enticing possibilities. Guests enjoy a homemade full, country breakfast each morning.

Innkeeper(s): Bruce & Brian Kloeckner. $99-229. 7 rooms with PB, 3 suites. Breakfast included in rates. Types of meals: Full bkfst, early coffee/tea and picnic lunch. Beds: KQT. TV and ceiling fan in room. Air conditioning. Telephone and common sitting room with cable on premises. Antiquing, fishing, golf, live theater, shopping, tennis, water sports and ballooning nearby.

Location: City.

Certificate may be used: Sunday-Thursday. Other times if available.

Centennial House

26 Cordova St
Saint Augustine, FL 32084-3627
(904)810-2218 (800)611-2880 Fax:(904)810-1930
Internet: www.centennialhouse.com
E-mail: innkeeper@centennialhouse.com

Circa 1899. In the heart of the historic district on the horse-drawn carriage route, this meticulously restored home maintains 19th century aesthetics with generous modern amenities. Relax in the garden courtyard and enjoy the landscaped grounds of this premier inn. Impressive suites and guest bedrooms are sound insulated and offer almost every luxury imaginable for leisure or business. The inn is handicap accessible. Savor a complete gourmet breakfast each morning. Special dietary requests are met with gracious hospitality. It is an easy stroll to a wide variety of local sites and attractions.

Innkeeper(s): Lou & Beverlee Stines. $135-265. 8 rooms with PB, 3 with FP. Breakfast included in rates. Types of meals: Full gourmet bkfst and early coffee/tea. Beds: KQ. Data port, cable TV, VCR, reading lamp, ceiling fan, clock radio, telephone, desk, most with hot tub/spa, some with fireplace, hair dryer, bathrobes, bath amenities, wireless Internet access, iron/ironing board, down pillows, Egyptian cotton towels, video library, complimentary soft drinks, early morning coffee/tea, 19th-century aesthetics and soundproof insulation in room. Central air. Fax, copier, parlor games and video library on premises. Handicap access. Amusement parks, antiquing, art galleries, beach, bicycling, canoeing/kayaking, fishing, golf, hiking, horseback riding, live theater, museums, parks, shopping, sporting events, tennis, water sports and wineries nearby.

Location: City, ocean community.

Certificate may be used: May-October, Sunday-Thursday, excluding holidays, subject to availability.

St. Francis Inn

279 Saint George St
Saint Augustine, FL 32084-5031
(904)824-6068 (800)824-6062 Fax:(904)810-5525
Internet: www.stfrancisinn.com
E-mail: info@stfrancisinn.com

Circa 1791. St. Francis Inn reflects the rich culture and heritage of St. Augustine, America's oldest city. Gracious and inviting, it boasts a tranquil garden courtyard and pleasing amenities. This Florida bed and breakfast is centrally located amid a quiet setting in the historic district. Bikes are provided to easily explore the surrounding area. Take a relaxing swim in the pool and later, gather for evening socials with homemade desserts. Stay in a delightful guest room or suite infused with a perfect blend of romance, old world charm and modern comforts. Each accommodation provides unique amenities and many include a fireplace, balcony, kitchenette and whirlpool, clawfoot or Jacuzzi tub. Wake up refreshed and savor a satisfying gourmet breakfast before visiting the local attractions. Ask about specials and packages available.

Innkeeper(s): Joe Finnegan. $129-279. 17 rooms with PB, 8 with HT, 11 with WP, 4 suites, 1 cottage, 1 conference room. Breakfast, snacks/refreshments and hors d'oeuvres included in rates. Types of meals: Full gourmet bkfst, Daily evening social, evening desserts. Bloody Marys and Mimosas with breakfast on weekends and holidays. Inn-baked cookies, apples and coffee and other beverages all day. Complimentary sherry in every room. Picnic Baskets also are available. Beds: KQDT. Cable TV, VCR, DVD, reading lamp, CD player, refrigerator, ceiling fan, clock radio, telephone, desk, some with hot tub/spa, voice mail, most with fireplace, wireless Internet access, iron/ironing board, Fresh flowers and Complimentary Sherry greet you in your room in room. Central air. Fax, copier, swimming, bicycles, parlor games, gift shop, Free parking, Fri/Sat/Holiday complimentary local evening transportation, Facilities to spend a day on St. Augustine Beach, Free & discount attractions admissions and Local health club access on premises. Limited handicap access. Antiquing, art galleries, beach, bicycling, canoeing/kayaking, fishing, golf, hiking, horseback riding, live theater, museums, parks, shopping, sporting events, tennis, water sports, wineries, Horse-drawn carriage rides, Trolley tours, Bay cruises, Many superb restaurants, Historic sites, Reenactments, Ghost tours, Festivals, Art fairs and Musical performances nearby.

Location: City. Historic Old City.

Publicity: *Orlando Sentinel, Palm Beach Post* and *New York Times.*

"We have stayed at many nice hotels but nothing like this. We are really enjoying it."

Certificate may be used: May 1 to Feb.10, Sunday-Thursday, excluding holiday periods.

Saint Petersburg E7

Beach Drive Inn

532 Beach Drive NE
Saint Petersburg, FL 33701
(727)822-2244 Fax:(813)354-4702
Internet: www.beachdriveinn.com
E-mail: roland@beachdriveinn.com

Circa 1910. Gracing the downtown waterfront district of St. Petersburg, Florida, Beach Drive Inn Bed & Breakfast is just across from Tampa Bay. Built in 1910 in the Key West style, this historic home was nationally designated The Vinoy House. Surrounded by palm trees and other lush plants, the setting is truly tropical. Stay in one of the delightful guest bedrooms or a spacious suite with a whirlpool, entertainment center and attached private sunroom with kitchenette. A made-to-order breakfast is served daily. Walk to Bayside Beach and the many popular local attractions and cultural sites.

Innkeeper(s): Roland Martino. $129-275. 6 rooms with PB, 2 suites. Breakfast and snacks/refreshments included in rates. Types of meals: Full gourmet bkfst, hors d'oeuvres and wine. Beds: KQ. Modem hook-up, cable TV, VCR, reading lamp, CD player, refrigerator, ceiling fan, clock radio, telephone, desk, some with hot tub/spa, voice mail, hair dryer, bathrobes, bath amenities, wireless Internet access and iron/ironing board in room. Central air. DVD, fax, copier, bicycles, parlor games, fireplace, laundry facility, VHS movies, Cable TV, Free Wireless Wi-Fi, Parking, Complementary Bicycles and Beer and Wine License on premises. Antiquing, art galleries, beach, bicycling, fishing, golf, live theater, museums, parks, shopping, sporting events, water sports, wineries, Live Music, Restaurants, The Pier, Tropicana Field, Baseball, Vinoy Park, Straub Park and Carriage rides nearby.

Location: City, waterfront.

Publicity: *Our Bed and Breakfast turns 100 years old this year and was designated a historical landmark by The Colonial Dames., Psychic Kids: Children of the Paranormal Season 3 and Episode 2 "The Lost Girl"*

Certificate may be used: June-September, last minute subject to availability.

La Veranda Bed & Breakfast

111 5th Ave. N
Saint Petersburg, FL 33701
(727)224-1057 (800)484-8423X8417 Fax:(727)827-1431
Internet: www.laverandabb.com
E-mail: info@laverandabb.com

Circa 1910. Featuring Old World charm in an urban setting, this classic Key West-style mansion is only two blocks from the waterfront. Antiques, Oriental rugs and artwork accent the gracious elegance. Lounge by the fire in the living room or on one of the large wicker-filled wraparound verandas overlooking lush tropical gardens. Romantic one- and two-bedroom suites boast private entrances, as well as indoor and outdoor sitting areas. A gourmet breakfast with Starbucks coffee is served on settings of china, silver and crystal. Corporate services are available with assorted business amenities.

Innkeeper(s): Nancy Mayer. $89-299. 5 suites. Breakfast included in rates. Types of meals: Full gourmet bkfst, veg bkfst, early coffee/tea and snacks/refreshments. Beds: KQT. Cable TV, VCR, reading lamp, CD player, refrigerator, ceiling fan, snack bar, clock radio, telephone, turn-down service, desk and fireplace in room. Air conditioning. Fax, copier, bicycles, library, fireplace and laundry facility on premises. Limited handicap access. Amusement parks, antiquing, art galleries, beach, bicycling, canoeing/kayaking, fishing, golf, hiking, live theater, museums, parks, shopping, sporting events, water sports and wineries nearby.

Location: City.

Publicity: *NY Daily Times and Interstate 75.*

Certificate may be used: Anytime, Last Minute-Based on Availability. Must mention coupon prior to making reservation.

Larelle House Bed & Breakfast

237 6th Avenue NE
Saint Petersburg, FL 33701-2603
(727) 490-3575
Internet: www.larellehouse.com
E-mail: info@larellehouse.com

Circa 1908. Surrounded by a wrought-iron fence, the lushly landscaped grounds of this 1908 three-story Queen Anne Victorian feature a four-tiered, fountain on a brick courtyard. Relax on the spacious wicker-filled front veranda or two back porches with tropical breezes. An in-ground hot tub in the backyard garden sits under a gazebo with Corinthian columns and flowering bougainvillea. Home-made snacks and refreshments and a guest refrigerator are available any time in the din-

ing room. Browse the video and DVD library in the sunroom. Evening wine and cheese are offered in the fireside parlor. Guest bedrooms feature an assortment of pleasing amenities and some boast a bay window, clawfoot tub and pedestal sink. Turndown service includes handmade chocolates and port or sherry. After breakfast take a scenic bike ride.

Innkeeper(s): Ellen & Larry Nist. $139-209. 4 rooms with PB. Breakfast, snacks/refreshments included in rates. Types of meals: Full gourmet bkfst. Beds: KQD. Cable TV, DVD, reading lamp, CD player, ceiling fan, clock radio, turn-down service, desk, hair dryer, bathrobes, bath amenities, wireless Internet access and iron/ironing board in room. Central air. VCR, fax, copier, spa, bicycles, library, parlor games, telephone, fireplace, HDTV/DVD in common area Sun Room, beautiful in-ground hot tub in back yard garden, refreshments and home made snacks available 24/7, guest refrigerator in dining room, wireless Internet access throughout house and free phone calls on premises. Amusement parks, antiquing, art galleries, beach, bicycling, fishing, golf, live theater, museums, parks, shopping, sporting events, tennis, water sports, wineries, The Pier, BayWalk, regular weekend events in the numerous waterfront parks, air shows and fireworks from our unique widow's walk for a perfect view nearby.

Location: City.

Publicity: *Superior Small Lodging Association's Highest Honor - The Donal A. Dermody White Glove Award (WGA).*

Certificate may be used: June-October, Sunday-Thursday, subject to availability when presented at time of reservation, excludes holidays and special events.

Stuart   F10

Inn Shepard's Park Bed and Breakfast

601 SW. Ocean Blvd.
Stuart, FL 34994
(772)781-4244
Internet: www.innshepard.com
E-mail: marilyn@innshepard.com

Circa 1924. Gracing the heart of The River Front Village, this quaint and intimate Key West style home is an easy walk to the shops, restaurants and entertainment of historic downtown. Nap in the hammock surrounded by a garden oasis or relax on the wraparound porch. Socialize in the sunroom or in the main parlor area. Browse the video library. Themed guest bedrooms are air-conditioned and boast an assortment of white or natural wicker accents, an antique mahogany four-poster bed, oak furnishings and an iron bed. Enjoy views of Shepard's Park and Frazier Creek. A breakfast buffet is served on the covered front porch. Take an early-morning bike ride. The waterfront is only 400 feet away. Beach chairs, coolers and a single or double kayak are available.

Innkeeper(s): Marilyn Miller. $85-200. 4 rooms, 2 with PB. Breakfast, afternoon tea and snacks/refreshments included in rates. Types of meals: Cont plus and early coffee/tea. Beds: QD. Cable TV, VCR, DVD, ceiling fan, snack bar, hair dryer, bathrobes, bath amenities, wireless Internet access and iron/ironing board in room. Central air. Copier, spa, bicycles, library, telephone and fireplace on premises. Antiquing, art galleries, beach, bicycling, canoeing/kayaking, fishing, golf, hiking, horseback riding, live theater, museums, parks, shopping, sporting events, tennis and water sports nearby.

Location: Ocean community, waterfront.

Certificate may be used: June-September, weekdays excluding holidays.

Georgia

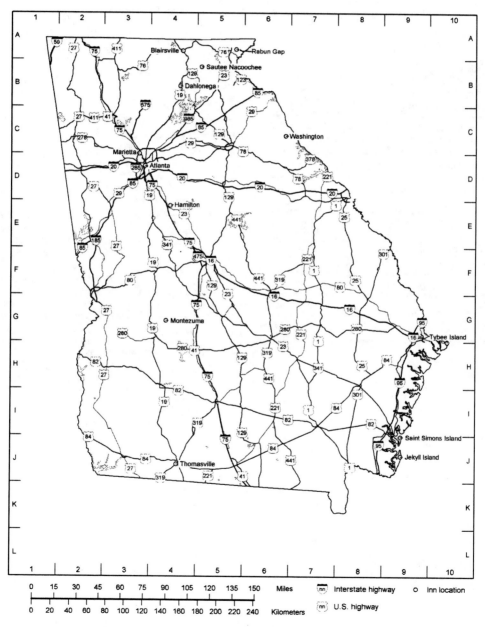

Blairsville
Rabun Gap
Sautee Nacoochee
Dahlonega
Washington
Marietta
Atlanta
Hamilton
Montezuma
Tybee Island
Saint Simons Island
Jekyll Island
Thomasville

| 0 | 15 | 30 | 45 | 60 | 75 | 90 | 105 | 120 | 135 | 150 | Miles |

| 0 | 20 | 40 | 60 | 80 | 100 | 120 | 140 | 160 | 180 | 200 | 220 | 240 | Kilometers |

nn Interstate highway   o Inn location

nn U.S. highway

Atlanta   D3

King-Keith House B&B

889 Edgewood Ave NE
Atlanta, GA 30307
(404)688-7330 (800)728-3879
Internet: www.kingkeith.com
E-mail: kingkeith@mindspring.com

Circa 1890. The 1890 King-Keith House Bed and Breakfast is
listed in the National Register and boasts twelve-foot ceilings and
carved fireplaces. One of Atlanta's most photographed houses,

this Queen Anne Victorian sits
among live oaks and prominent
homes in the restored neighborhood of Inman Park in Georgia.
Play the baby grand piano in one
of the elegant public rooms and
stroll through private gardens.
Enjoy complimentary snacks and
beverages. Romantic guest rooms offer a variety of pleasing amenities, gorgeous antiques and some feature clawfoot tubs. The
Downstairs Suite includes a Jacuzzi tub, living room and private
entrance off the front porch. The spacious Cottage is a honeymoon favorite with a double Jacuzzi. Linger over a gourmet breakfast served with generous southern hospitality at this Atlanta inn.

Innkeeper(s): Jan & Windell Keith. $90-200. 4 rooms with PB, 1 suite, 1
cottage. Breakfast included in rates. Types of meals: Full bkfst and early cof-
fee/tea. Beds: KQDT. Cable TV, reading lamp, refrigerator, ceiling fan, snack
bar, clock radio, telephone, desk, hair dryer and cottage with Jacuzzi and
fireplace in room. Air conditioning. Parlor games on premises. Antiquing, golf,
live theater, parks, shopping, sporting events, tennis and restaurants nearby.

Location: City. Downtown.

Publicity: *Southern Living, Victorian Homes (cover), Collector Inspector
and HGTV.*

Certificate may be used: Good only Sunday, Monday, Tuesday, Wednesday
and Thursday.

Dahlonega   B4

Lily Creek Lodge

2608 Auraria Rd
Dahlonega, GA 30533
(706)864-6848 (888)844-2694
Internet: www.lilycreeklodge.com
E-mail: lilycreeklodge@windstream.net

Circa 1984. Seven forested acres surround Lily Creek Lodge,
and guests will enjoy grounds that offer gardens, a secluded
hot tub, a swimming pool with a waterfall and a treehouse
where breakfasts can be served. There is a common area
indoors with a large stone fireplace, or guests can relax on the
deck or in the pavilion out by the pool. A gazebo and swing
also are romantic items guests will discover on the lush
grounds. Each room has been decorated with a special theme
in mind, from the Montana Suite with its oak log bed to the
Geisha Suite with its Asian appointments. On arrival, guests are
greeted with a selection of port, wine and homemade cookies
or other treat. Dahlonega is rich in history, and it is in this historic town that gold was first discovered in the United States.
Guests can look for antiques, pan for gold or enjoy the many
outdoor activities.

Innkeeper(s): Don & Sharon Bacek. $115-225. 13 rooms with PB, 1 with
FP, 1 with WP, 7 suites, 1 conference room. Breakfast, snacks/refreshments
and wine included in rates. Types of meals: Full gourmet bkfst, veg bkfst, picnic lunch and Vegetarian by advance request. Beds: KQ. TV, VCR, DVD, reading lamp, desk, some with hot tub/spa, some with fireplace, bath amenities,
wireless Internet access, Some with kitchens, MP3 players, Ceiling fans,
Coffeemakers, Bathrobes, Microwave, Satellite, Clocks, Iron & ironing board
and hairdryers available on request in room. Central air. Fax, copier, spa,
swimming, bicycles, library, parlor games, telephone, gift shop, Bocci court,
Treehouse, Gazebo, Walking trails, Hammock, Fire pit, Gardens, Swing and
Bicycles can be delivered on premises. Antiquing, art galleries, bicycling,
canoeing/kayaking, fishing, golf, hiking, horseback riding, live theater, muse-
ums, parks, shopping, water sports, wineries, Arts, Crafts, Waterfalls,
Festivals, Apple orchards, Vineyards & tasting rooms, Zoo, Kangaroo
Conservation Center, Cabbage Patch dolls, Musical venues, State parks,
Appalachian Trail, Amicalola Falls and Spas nearby.

Location: Country, mountains.

Publicity: *New York Times, Nashville Tennessean, Montgomery Alabama
Advertiser, Walking Magazine, Dahlonega Nugget, Atlanta Journal
Constitution, Piedmont Review, Blue Ridge Country Magazine, Huntsville
Alabama Times and PBS Chattanooga - Southern Accents.*

Certificate may be used: Sunday-Thursday, subject to availability, from Jan. 1
to April 30, excluding holidays and special events.

Marietta   D3

Stanley House

236 Church St NE
Marietta, GA 30060-1604
(770)426-1881 Fax:(770)426-6821
Internet: www.thestanleyhouse.com
E-mail: info@thestanleyhouse.com

Circa 1897. Stanley House mansion reflects the elegance and
grace of the Victorian era. This historic 1897 three-story luxury
inn is located just off Antebellum Marietta Square only 20 miles
from downtown Atlanta. Experience the romantic ambiance and
enjoy gracious hospitality. Meet new friends over afternoon
treats. Delightful guest bedrooms are named after popular cities
in Georgia and feature a variety of pleasing amenities. Stay in a
room with a clawfoot tub, vaulted ceiling, ornamental fireplace,
four-poster bed or wicker furnishings. Savor a gourmet southern-style breakfast in the formal dining room.

Innkeeper(s): Cathy & Lloyd Kilday. Call for rates. 5 rooms with PB. Breakfast
and snacks/refreshments included in rates. Types of meals: Full gourmet
bkfst, early coffee/tea and afternoon tea. Beds: KQT. Cable TV, ceiling fan,
wireless Internet access and iron/ironing board in room. Central air. VCR, fax,
copier and fireplace on premises. Limited handicap access. Antiquing, art
galleries, bicycling, golf, hiking, live theater, museums, parks, shopping and
sporting events nearby.

Location: City. Small town in suburban Atlanta.

Certificate may be used: Anytime, subject to availability.

Rabun Gap   A5

Sylvan Falls Mill

156 Taylors Chapel Rd
Rabun Gap, GA 30568
(706)746-7138
Internet: www.sylvanfallsmill.com
E-mail: linda3010@windstream.net

Circa 1840. The Sylvan Falls Mill Site has been the location of
a working gristmill for more than 150 years. The mill was constructed in 1840 from wormy chestnutwood. The original
waterwheel was replaced in 1950 by a steel waterwheel from
Tennessee. The mill is still powered by the waterfall that cas-
cades over one side of the property that overlooks picturesque

Wolffork Valley. The property has been a home since then, offering four unique guest rooms with private baths. Refreshments are served at check-in and a full, gourmet breakfast is served in the morning.

Outdoor activities are the highlight of the inn. Guests will delight in hiking the Bartram Trail or rafting down the Chattooga River.

Innkeeper(s): Michael & Linda Johnson. $115-145. 4 rooms with PB, 1 with FP. Breakfast, snacks/refreshments and wine included in rates. Types of meals: Full gourmet bkfst, veg bkfst, early coffee/tea, afternoon tea, Gourmet gift baskets in rooms, Cakes for special occasions and Homemade candies. Beds: QD. Reading lamp, refrigerator, ceiling fan, desk, some with fireplace, wireless Internet access, Luxury linens & deluxe bedding, Private decks, Fireplace and Coffee service in room. Air conditioning. Library, pet boarding, parlor games, telephone, gift shop, informal gardens, gas grill for cookouts and 100-foot waterfall on premises. Limited handicap access. Antiquing, art galleries, bicycling, canoeing/kayaking, downhill skiing, fishing, golf, hiking, horseback riding, live theater, parks, shopping, water sports, wineries, Nature hiking, Viewing foliage, Birding, Whitewater rafting, Craft and Herbal seminars nearby.

Location: Mountains, waterfront.

Publicity: Country Inns, Mountain Review, The Atlanta Journal-Constitution, Old Mill News, Savannah Morning News, Coastal Senior, Southern Living, Food Network - Good Eats and WNEG - weekend getaway.

Certificate may be used: Anytime, subject to availability.

Saint Simons Island   J9

Village Inn and Pub

500 Mallery St
Saint Simons Island, GA 31522
(912)634-6056 (888)635-6111 Fax:(912)634-1464
Internet: www.villageinnandpub.com
E-mail: kristy@villageinnandpub.com

Circa 1930. Between the parks and oceanfront village, this award-winning island B&B inn sits under ancient live oaks. Restored and carefully expanded, the 1930 beach cottage houses the reception, sitting and breakfast areas as well as the Village Pub, a solid mahogany olde English bar and original stone fireplace. Standard and deluxe guest bedrooms are named after historical people with local significance and feature upscale amenities, soothing color palettes, crown molding and custom-built armoires that hold large TVs. Most rooms include a balcony with a view of the pool and flower-filled courtyard or the neighborhood. A generous continental breakfast is available on the sun porch.

Innkeeper(s): Kristy Murphy. $99-220. 28 rooms with PB. Breakfast included in rates. Types of meals: Cont plus, wine and Pub on property. Beds: KQD. Data port, cable TV, reading lamp, ceiling fan, clock radio, telephone, desk, voice mail, hair dryer, bathrobes, bath amenities, wireless Internet access and iron/ironing board in room. Central air. Fax, copier, swimming and fireplace on premises. Limited handicap access. Antiquing, art galleries, beach, bicycling, canoeing/kayaking, fishing, golf, hiking, horseback riding, live theater, museums, parks, shopping, tennis and water sports nearby.

Location: Ocean community.

Certificate may be used: August-February, Sunday-Thursday, based on availability.

Sautee Nacoochee   B5

The Stovall House

1526 Hwy 255 N
Sautee Nacoochee, GA 30571
(706)878-3355
Internet: www.stovallhouse.com
E-mail: stovallhouse@hemc.net

Circa 1837. This house, built by Moses Harshaw and restored in 1983 by Ham Schwartz, has received two state awards for its restoration. The handsome farmhouse has an extensive wraparound porch providing vistas of 26 acres of cow pastures and mountains. High ceilings, polished walnut woodwork and decorative stenciling provide a pleasant backdrop for the inn's collection of antiques. Victorian bathroom fixtures include pull-chain toilets and pedestal sinks. The inn has its own restaurant.

Innkeeper(s): Ham Schwartz. $98-113. 5 rooms with PB. Breakfast included in rates. Types of meals: Cont. Beds: KQDT. Ceiling fan and clock radio in room. Air conditioning. Library, parlor games, telephone and fireplace on premises. Amusement parks, antiquing, art galleries, bicycling, canoeing/kayaking, fishing, golf, hiking, horseback riding, live theater, museums, parks, shopping, water sports and wineries nearby.

Location: Mountains.

Publicity: Atlanta Journal and GPTV - Historic Inns of Georgia.

"Great to be home again. Very nostalgic and hospitable."

Certificate may be used: Anytime subject to availability.

Tybee Island   G9

Tybee Island Inn

24 Van Horne Ave
Tybee Island, GA 31328-9780
(912)786-9255 (866)892-4667 Fax:(912)786-5772
Internet: www.tybeeislandinn.com
E-mail: info@tybeeislandinn.com

Circa 1902. Visit Savannah then experience the Southern beach town of Tybee Island. Just 20 minutes from historic Savannah and a five-minute walk from the Atlantic Ocean, Tybee Island Inn offers whimsical seashore themed guest bedrooms, all with updated private baths and cable TV. Other amenities may include jetted or oversized tubs for two, skylights, a private deck or a porch. Several rooms have optional sleeping arrangements with two beds. Step through the trellis entrance into the delightful garden graced with a canopy of magnificent live oaks. Enjoy a full breakfast in the dining

room or the garden gazebo. After a day at the ocean or touring and shopping, relax in the hot tub.

Innkeeper(s): Cathy & Lloyd Kilday. $99-249. 7 rooms, 5 with PB, 1 with WP. Breakfast and snacks/refreshments included in rates. Types of meals: Full bkfst. Beds: Q. Cable TV, reading lamp, CD player, ceiling fan, clock radio, telephone, hair dryer, iron/ironing board, some rooms have two beds, most rooms have large tubs for two and private deck or porch in room.

Central air. Fax, copier, spa, library, fireplace and A beautiful shaded semi-tropical garden on premises. Antiquing, art galleries, beach, bicycling, canoeing/kayaking, fishing, golf, hiking, live theater, parks, water sports and Tybee Island Lighthouse nearby.

Location: Ocean community. Savannah (15 miles).

Publicity: *Cooking with Paula, (Paula Deen and March 2006).*

Certificate may be used: Sunday-Thursday, subject to availability, excludes weekends and holidays.

Washington   C6

Washington Plantation

15 Lexington Avenue
Washington, GA 30673
(706)678-2006 (877)405-9956 Fax:(706)678-3454
Internet: www.washingtonplantation.com
E-mail: info@washingtonplantation.com

Circa 1828. Period antiques and reproductions furnish this restored 1828 Greek Revival plantation home. Enjoy the seven acres of natural beauty with rose gardens, fountains, a waterfall, stream and koi pond. Scattered seating with tables are shaded by magnolia, oak, dogwood, pecan, hickory, elm and crape myrtle. Relax on a porch rocker or wicker chair. Large, bright guest bedrooms feature lavish draperies, Oriental rugs, brass and crystal chandeliers and fireplaces. Generous upscale amenities pamper and please. Early risers partake of juice and goodies before a full-service Southern breakfast is provided daily. Lunch and dinner can be ordered in advance for an extra charge.

Innkeeper(s): Tom and Barbara Chase. $162-232. 5 rooms with PB, 5 with FP, 1 with WP. Breakfast, snacks/refreshments and wine included in rates. Types of meals: Full gourmet bkfst, veg bkfst, early coffee/tea, picnic lunch, hors d'oeuvres and gourmet dinner. Beds: KQ. Cable TV, VCR, DVD, reading lamp, stereo, clock radio, telephone, coffeemaker, turn-down service, desk, some with hot tub/spa, fireplace, hair dryer, bathrobes, bath amenities, wireless Internet access and iron/ironing board in room. Central air. Fax, copier, library and parlor games on premises. Antiquing, art galleries, bicycling, fishing, golf, hiking, horseback riding, live theater, museums, parks, shopping, sporting events, tennis, water sports, Augusta National Golf Club (one hour) and University of Georgia football stadium (40 miles) nearby.

Location: Country. Historic District.

Publicity: *Washington Tour of Homes, Southern Distinction Magazine, Southern Living Magazine (March and 2006).*

Certificate may be used: June-August anytime, September-May Sunday-Thursday except April 1-10.

Hawaii

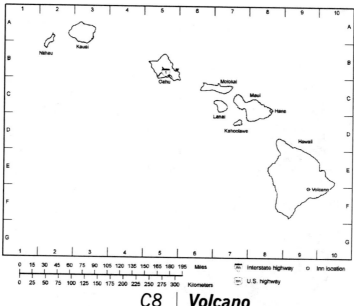

Hana   C8

Hana Maui Botanical Gardens B&B

470 Ulaino Road
Hana, HI 96713
(808) 248-7725
Internet: ecoclub.com/hanamaui
E-mail: JoLoyce@aol.com

Circa 1976. This Hawaiian country farm features a ranch house and duplex with two studio apartments set on 27 acres that include a public botanical garden, fruit trees and flowers. The Flower and Marine studio have a private bath, kitchen, lanai and carport. Also offered is Volcano Heart Chalet near Volcano National Park on the Big Island. The chalet features two keyed rooms, each decorated in an individual theme, private half baths, a shared shower and a shared kitchenette and sitting room with a gas fireplace.

Innkeeper(s): JoLoyce Kaia. $100-125. 3 rooms, 2 suites, 1 cottage. Coffee, tea, box juice and pastry snack usually muffins included in rates. Types of meals: Cont. Beds: QT. Reading lamp, refrigerator, coffeemaker, full gas appliance kitchen and car port and lanai in room. Parlor games, telephone, no alcohol, no smoking, free access to 10-acre botanical gardens and fruit picking in season on premises. Art galleries, canoeing/kayaking, hiking, horseback riding, museums, parks, shopping and swimming nearby.

Location: Country. Public Botanical garden.

Certificate may be used: Anytime, subject to availability. Reservations may be made only one month in advance to qualify for one night free.

Volcano   E9

A'Alani Volcano Heart Hawaii

11th St
Volcano, HI 96785
(808)248-7725 Fax:(808)248-7725
Internet: ecoclub.com/hanamaui
E-mail: joloyce@aol.com

Circa 1987. This comfortable cedar home can be your base for visiting one of Hawaii's most fascinating landscapes. The entrance to Volcano National Park is just two miles away from this inn, which is nestled in a natural setting of tree ferns and ohia trees. The park features hiking trails around Kilauea volcano crater and through landscape that changes from forest to arid to tropical. The Volcano Art Center, volcano exhibit and observatory are a must for everyone and provide great insight into the Hawaiian culture.

Innkeeper(s): Jo Loyce Kaia. $100-125. 3 rooms. Types of meals: Cont. Beds: QT. Reading lamp, no alcohol and no smoking in room. VCR, telephone, fireplace, laundry facility and sitting room with gas fireplace on premises. Antiquing, art galleries, beach, golf, hiking, horseback riding, museums, parks, shopping, Volcano National Park, Orchid Nursery and Winery nearby.

Location: Mountains. Near Volcano National Park.

Certificate may be used: Reservations may be made only one month in advance to qualify for one free night.

Idaho

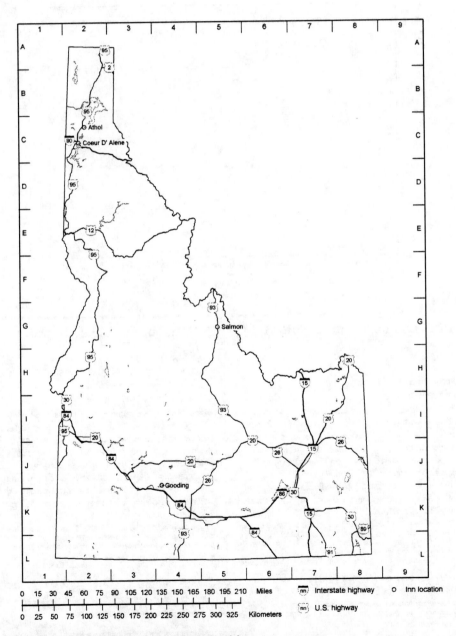

Athol

C2

Cedar Mountain Farm

25249 N Hatch Rd
Athol, ID 83801-8683
(208)683-0572 (866)683-0572
Internet: www.cedarmountainfarm.com
E-mail: info@cedarmountainfarm.com

Circa 1998. Expect down-home peaceful hospitality at Cedar Mountain Farm in Athol, the heart of Northern Idaho. This working family farm spans 440 acres of field, creek, mountains and forest; perfect for vacations, reunions, retreats, seminars and weddings. Enjoy hiking, biking, sledding, cross-country skiing or snowshoeing. Fish in Sage Creek, watch for birds and wildlife and pet the farm animals. The library invites relaxation and the game closet is well-stocked. Stay in a guest suite or log cabin with kitchen and laundry facilities. The Forest Suite boasts an electric fireplace, and the Bunkhouse offers more space and privacy. Wheelchair-accessible Granny's Woods features a jetted tub, two-headed walk-in shower and can be adjoined with Spring, both located in one wing of the main cabin. Savor a hearty breakfast served family style.

Innkeeper(s): Al and Daryl Kyle. $115-150. 4 rooms with PB, 1 with FP, 1 with WP, 3 two-bedroom suites, 2 cabins, 1 conference room. Breakfast and snacks/refreshments included in rates. Types of meals: Country bkfst, veg bkfst and early coffee/tea. Beds: KQDT. Modem hook-up, reading lamp, ceiling fan, hair dryer and bath amenities in room. TV, VCR, DVD, fax, copier, library, parlor games, laundry facility, desk, refrigerator, kitchen privileges, laundry privileges, snacks, telephone, iron/ironing board and microwave on premises. Limited handicap access. Amusement parks, antiquing, art galleries, beach, bicycling, canoeing/kayaking, cross-country skiing, downhill skiing, fishing, golf, hiking, horseback riding, live theater, museums, parks, shopping, tennis, water sports and wineries nearby.

Location: Country, mountains.

Publicity: *Horizon Air Magazine (June 2006 and AgraTourism).*

Certificate may be used: Sunday-Thursday during October, November, Early December, January, February, March and April. Not valid with any other special. Good for 2 days only.

Coeur D'Alene

C2

The Roosevelt Inn

105 E Wallace Ave
Coeur D'Alene, ID 83814-2947
(208)765-5200 (800)290-3358 Fax:(208)664-4142
Internet: www.therooseveltinn.com
E-mail: info@therooseveltinn.com

Circa 1905. Elegant yet comfortable, this grand four-story red brick Coeur d' Alene bed and breakfast was named for President Roosevelt and is the town's oldest schoolhouse. Relax in the front or back parlor and play a game or read a book. Listed in the National Register, The Roosevelt Inn offers elegant yet comfortable guest suites and rooms that boast a nostalgic ambiance. The Bell Tower Suite and the Honeymoon Suite are popular favorites. Breakfast is always such a delight that the inn sells a cookbook that includes the often-requested recipes. Lake Coeur d' Alene provides a variety of fun activities and the area features the world's longest floating boardwalk and Tubb's Hill Nature Park. Shops and restaurants are within a five-minute stroll from the inn. The natural surroundings offer mountain biking, boating, skiing and hiking.

Innkeeper(s): John & Tina Hough. $89-319. 15 rooms, 12 with PB, 3 with

FP, 6 total suites, including 4 two-bedroom suites, 2 conference rooms. Breakfast, afternoon tea and snacks/refreshments included in rates. Types of meals: Full gourmet bkfst, veg bkfst, early coffee/tea, Murder Mystery Dinners and Special party dinners for groups. Beds: KQ. Reading lamp, CD player, clock radio, turn-down service, hair dryer, bath amenities, wireless Internet access and iron/ironing board in room. Central air. TV, VCR, DVD, fax, copier, spa, swimming, sauna, library, pet boarding, parlor games, telephone, fireplace, gift shop and Rose greeting in room on premises. Handicap access. Amusement parks, antiquing, art galleries, beach, bicycling, canoeing/kayaking, cross-country skiing, downhill skiing, fishing, golf, hiking, horseback riding, live theater, museums, parks, shopping, sporting events, tennis, water sports, wineries, Lake Cruises, boating, para sailing, Catamaran Cruises and exercise room & pool at 24 hour fitness center free to all Roosevelt Guests nearby.

Location: City, mountains.

Publicity: *Spokesman Review, Coeur d'Alene Press, KSPS in Spokane, Washington, KETH San Jose and California.*

Certificate may be used: September-May, Sunday-Thursday.

Gooding

J4

Gooding Hotel Bed & Breakfast

112 Main St
Gooding, ID 83330-1102
(208)934-4374 (888)260-6656
Internet: www.goodinghotelbandb.com

Circa 1906. An early Gooding settler, William B. Kelly, built this historic hotel, which is the oldest building in town. Each of the guest rooms is named in honor of someone significant in the history of Gooding or the hotel. A buffet breakfast is served every morning in the William Kelly Room. The area offers many activities, from golfing and fishing to exploring ice caves or visiting wineries and museums.

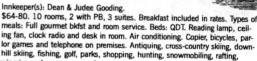

Innkeeper(s): Dean & Judee Gooding. $64-80. 10 rooms, 2 with PB, 3 suites. Breakfast included in rates. Types of meals: Full gourmet bkfst and room service. Beds: QDT. Reading lamp, ceiling fan, clock radio and desk in room. Air conditioning. Copier, bicycles, parlor games and telephone on premises. Antiquing, cross-country skiing, downhill skiing, fishing, golf, parks, shopping, hunting, snowmobiling, rafting, wineries and museums nearby.

Location: Small town.

Certificate may be used: Labor Day through April 1, upon availability.

Salmon   G5

Greyhouse Inn B&B

1115 Hwy 93 South
Salmon, ID 83467
(208)756-3968 (800)348-8097
Internet: www.greyhouseinn.com
E-mail: greyhouse@greyhouseinn.com

Circa 1894. The scenery at Greyhouse is nothing short of wondrous. In the winter, when mountains are capped in white and the evergreens are shrouded in snow, this Victorian appears as a safe haven from the chilly weather. In the summer, the rocky peaks are a contrast to the whimsical house, which looks like something out of an Old West town. The historic home is known  around town as the old maternity hospital, but there is nothing medicinal about it now. The rooms are Victorian in style with antique furnishings. The parlor features deep red walls and floral overstuffed sofas and a dressmaker's model garbed in a brown Victorian gown. Outdoor enthusiasts will find no shortage of activities, from facing the rapids in nearby Salmon River to fishing to horseback riding. The town of Salmon is just 12 miles away.

Innkeeper(s): David & Sharon Osgood. $89-124. 7 rooms with PB. Breakfast included in rates. Types of meals: Country bkfst, veg bkfst, early coffee/tea, picnic lunch and dinner. Beds: KQDT. TV, VCR, reading lamp, refrigerator, ceiling fan, clock radio, coffeemaker, desk and bathrobes in room. Bicycles, library, parlor games, telephone, gift shop, carriage house and two log cabin rooms on premises. Antiquing, art galleries, bicycling, canoeing/kayaking, cross-country skiing, downhill skiing, fishing, golf, hiking, horseback riding, live theater, museums, parks, shopping, tennis, water sports, We now offer whitewater rafting and float trips with Kookaburra Rafting www.raft4fun.com, hot springs and mountain biking nearby.

Location: Mountains.

Publicity: *Idaho Statesman Newspaper, PBS and Travel Channel.*

"To come around the corner and find the Greyhouse, as we did, restores my faith! Such a miracle. We had a magical evening here, and we plan to return to stay for a few days. Thanks so much for your kindness and hospitality. We love Idaho!"

Certificate may be used: Anytime, subject to availability.

Illinois

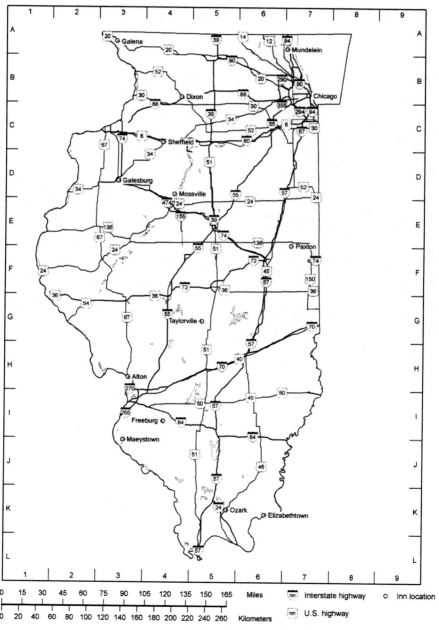

0 15 30 45 60 75 90 105 120 135 150 165 Miles

0 20 40 60 80 100 120 140 160 180 200 220 240 260 Kilometers

nn Interstate highway   o Inn location

nn U.S. highway

Alton H3

Beall Mansion, An Elegant B&B

407 E. 12th St.
Alton, IL 62002-7230
(618)474-9100 (866)843-2325
Internet: www.beallmansion.com
E-mail: bepampered@beallmansion.com

Circa 1903. An eclectic blend of Neoclassic, Georgian and Greek Revival styles, the mansion was designed as a wedding gift by world renown architect, Lucas Pfeiffenberger. Original woodwork, eleven and a half-foot ceilings, leaded-glass windows, pocket doors, crystal chandeliers and imported marble and bronze statuary reflect the era's opulence. Elegantly appointed guest bedrooms are unique in size and decor. Each includes a private bath with shower and clawfoot tub or whirlpool for two, imported marble floor and chandelier. Voted "Illinois Best Bed & Breakfast" by Illinois Magazine's Readers Poll.

Innkeeper(s): Jim & Sandy Belote. $119-358. 5 rooms with PB, 2 with FP, 4 with WP, 1 suite, 2 conference rooms. Plans are available with your choice of self-serve continental breakfast or gourmet breakfast in bed (or the formal dining room). All stays include our famous 24 hour "all you can eat" chocolate buffet included in rates. Types of meals: Full gourmet bkfst, veg bkfst, early coffee/tea, snacks/refreshments, room service and 24 Hour "All You Can Eat" Chocolate Buffet. Beds: KQD. Cable TV, VCR, DVD, reading lamp, CD player, ceiling fan, clock radio, telephone, turn-down service, desk, most with hot tub/spa, voice mail, some with fireplace, hair dryer, bathrobes, bath amenities, wireless Internet access, iron/ironing board, Luxury bath amenities including the B&B's homemade lavender bath salts, telephone with free local calling and voice mail in room. Central air. Fax, copier, library, parlor games, gift shop, complimentary 24 hour "all you can eat" chocolate buffet, verandah, hammock, badminton, horseshoes and croquet on premises. Amusement parks, antiquing, art galleries, bicycling, canoeing/kayaking, fishing, golf, hiking, horseback riding, live theater, museums, parks, shopping, sporting events, tennis, water sports, wineries, Meeting of the Great Rivers National Scenic Byway, Lewis & Clark Interpretive Center and Trailsite Number 1 and boat rental nearby.

Location: City. St. Louis, MO Metropolitan Area.

Publicity: *Illinois Magazine, Illinois Now, St. Louis Bride, St. Louis Magazine, AAA Midwest Motorist, AAA Home & Away, BBW Magazine, The Daily Journal, St. Louis Post Dispatch, Pequot Press, NorthShore Magazine, The Telegraph, Edwardsville Intelligencer, DeForest Times, Show Me St. Louis, News 4 St. Louis, TLC's "While You Were Out", WBGZ, KWMU and Silence of the Yams (a made for TV spoof of Silence of the Lambs).*

Certificate may be used: Sunday-Thursday night stays for the standard everyday rack rate. Not available with any other certificate, discount or coupon. Blackout dates apply, subject to availability. Not valid if booked through a third party. Restrictions apply.

Chicago B7

China Doll Guest House

738 West Schubert Avenue
Chicago, IL 60614
(773)525-4967 (866)361-1819 Fax:(773)525-3929
Internet: www.chinadollguesthouse.com
E-mail: chinadollchicago@yahoo.com

Circa 1895. Everything needed is included for a wonderful visit to the Windy City. Stay in a self-contained, one-bedroom garden apartment with exposed brick walls. It is complete with an entertainment system, fireplace, private Jacuzzi, sauna and a fully stocked island kitchen with customized breakfast foods per advance request. A larger accommodation of one to two bedrooms with up to six rooms is available on the second-floor, and features a private deck in addition to all the same amenities. Both apartments have an office with computers, high-speed Internet and other equipment. A laundry room facility is the only shared amenity. Chinese-Mandarin and English are spoken.

Innkeeper(s): Jim & Yanan Haring. $135-415. 6 two-bedroom and 1 three-bedroom suites. Breakfast, afternoon tea and snacks/refreshments included in rates. Types of meals: Cont plus. Beds: QDT. Modem hook-up, data port, cable TV, VCR, DVD, reading lamp, stereo, refrigerator, ceiling fan, clock radio, telephone, coffeemaker, desk, voice mail, most with fireplace, hair dryer, bathrobes, bath amenities, wireless Internet access, iron/ironing board, Complete in-unit office, computer, multi-function printer, fax, copier, steam rooms, high end kitchens and complete private homes with private entrances in room. Central air. Fax, copier, spa, library, laundry facility, sauna, conference room with projector and air conditioning on premises. Antiquing, art galleries, beach, bicycling, cross-country skiing, fishing, golf, hiking, live theater, museums, parks, shopping, sporting events, tennis and water sports nearby.

Location: City.

Certificate may be used: Anytime, November-April, subject to availability, except holiday periods.

Hansen House Mansion, The Centennial Houses of Lincoln Park

164 W. Eugenie St.
Chicago, IL 60614
(773)871-6020 Fax:(773)871-0412
Internet: CentennialHouses.net
E-mail: HansenMansion@aol.com

Circa 1886. This elegant urban inn boasts a perfect downtown location a few blocks or less from many city attractions and the lake. All public transportation is within 1/2 to 2 blocks. Hansen House Mansion, a Historically Significant Building in Chicago, Illinois, has retained all its original Victorian detail, even Giannini and Hilgart stained glass. The carefully selected 19th century furnishings reflect the home's original charms, and the 21st century conveniences such as central air conditioning, high-speed Internet, WiFi and free local calls all provide complete comfort. Select a single deluxe room with private bath, a suite with private deck, or the entire inn, all with use of the living room, dining room and fully-equipped kitchen. Plan a special event with the renowned chef or architectural docent.

Innkeeper(s): Frances Ramer & Quincy Stringham. Call for rates. 4 rooms, 2 with PB, 1 two-bedroom suite. Types of meals: Veg bkfst, early coffee/tea, gourmet lunch, snacks/refreshments, hors d'oeuvres, dinner, 24-hour Continental breakfast is included with every stay. You may book our chef for a custom Saturday brunch and or the head of a local cooking school for other meals or private classes. Beds: QT. Modem hook-up, data port, TV, VCR, DVD, reading lamp, stereo, refrigerator, ceiling fan, clock radio, telephone, coffeemaker, turn-down service, desk, hair dryer, bathrobes, bath amenities, wireless Internet access and iron/ironing board in room. Central air. Fax, copier, library, child care, parlor games, fireplace and gift shop on premises. Antiquing, art galleries, beach, bicycling, canoeing/kayaking, cross-country skiing, fishing, golf, hiking, horseback riding, live theater, museums, parks, shopping, sporting events, tennis, water sports, The free zoo and botanical gardens, Music venues, Restaurants, Cafes, Day Spas and Comedy clubs including Second City nearby.

Location: City.

Certificate may be used: Reservations accepted no more than two weeks in advance and must be mentioned at the time of the request.

Dixon   B4

Crawford House Inn

204 E Third St
Dixon, IL 61021
(815)288-3351
Internet: www.crawfordhouseinn.com
E-mail: crawfordinn@grics.net

Circa 1854. In 1854, Joseph Crawford, who counted Abraham
Lincoln among his friends, built this Italianate Victorian house
that bears his name. Now a B&B, Crawford House offers a
glimpse into small-town
America. Guest bedrooms feature feather beds. Breakfasts
are served with white linens,
china and stemware in the
dining room. Gourmet breakfasts include juice, coffee, an
egg entree, fresh baked goods

and seasonal fruits. The streets of Dixon are lined with colorful
flower beds. The area is popular for cycling and scenic country
trails offer opportunities for walking, horseback riding and
cross-country skiing. Visit the Ronald Reagan boyhood home,
John Deere Historical Site or local antique stores. Rock River is
two blocks away for boating, fishing and canoeing.

Innkeeper(s): Lyn Miliano. $85-135. 4 rooms, 1 with PB. Breakfast included
in rates. Types of meals: Full gourmet bkfst. Beds: KQ. Cable TV, VCR, reading lamp, ceiling fan, clock radio, hair dryer, bathrobes, wireless Internet
access and iron/ironing board in room. Air conditioning. Library, parlor games
and fireplace on premises. Antiquing, bicycling, canoeing/kayaking, fishing,
golf, hiking, horseback riding, live theater, museums, parks, shopping, tennis
and water sports nearby.

Location: Small town.

Certificate may be used: Anytime, subject to availability.

Galena   A3

Aaron's Cottages and Goldmoor Inn

9001 W. Sand Hill Rd
Galena, IL 61036-9341
(815)777-3925 (800)255-3925 Fax:(815)777-3993
Internet: www.goldmoor.com
E-mail: goldmoor@galenalink.com

Circa 1966. Luxurious cottages, suites and contemporary log
cabins on a bluff overlooking the Mississippi River are poised in
a delightful country setting. Aaron's Cottages and Goldmoor
Inn boast the perfect location and ambiance for romance. Just
six miles south of Galena, Illinois, all accommodations include
fireplaces, double whirlpool tubs, entertainment systems, galley
kitchens with microwaves, coffeemakers and mini-fridges
stocked with complimentary non-alcoholic beverages. An elegant gourmet breakfast is available each morning by free room
service or in the dining area. Goldmoor Spa offers body treatments by certified therapists.

Innkeeper(s): Patricia Smith. $155-335. 17 rooms with PB, 17 with FP, 17
with HT, 17 with WP, 12 suites, 3 cottages, 2 cabins, 1 conference room.
Breakfast and snacks/refreshments included in rates. Types of meals: Full
gourmet bkfst. Beds: K. Modem hook-up, cable TV, VCR, DVD, reading lamp,
stereo, refrigerator, ceiling fan, clock radio, telephone, coffeemaker, voice
mail, fireplace, hair dryer, bathrobes, bath amenities, wireless Internet
access, iron/ironing board, DSS satellite and Wireless Internet in room.
Central air. Fax, copier, Complimentary beverages, Terry robes, Hair dryers,

Iron and Ironing board on premises. Limited handicap access. Antiquing,
cross-country skiing, downhill skiing, golf, horseback riding, live theater,
museums, shopping and wineries nearby.

Location: Country.

Publicity: *Chicago Tribune, Chicago Magazine, Redbook Magazine (Nov
2004) and Midwest Living.*

Certificate may be used: Sunday-Thursday, subject to availability, minimum 2
nights, no other discounts apply.

Cloran Mansion

1237 Franklin St
Galena, IL 61036-1309
(815)777-0583 (866)234-0583 Fax:(815)777-0580
Internet: www.cloranmansion.com
E-mail: innkeeper@cloranmansion.com

Circa 1880. 2009 Winner - Travelers' Choice for Romance.
Historic Galena, Illinois serves as the perfect backdrop for this
1880 red brick Italianate Victorian mansion. The half-acre manicured lawn and gardens feature a romantic gazebo, pond and a
firepit. Books, magazines, board games and a movie and CD
collection are available in the Library. Spacious guest bedrooms
and suites include a fireplace, whirlpool tub, candles, entertainment center, and a mini-refrigerator with complimentary beverages. Antonio's Cottage is pet and child-friendly as well as
handicap accessible. Cloran Mansion serves a family-style six-
course country breakfast in the dining room on fine china and
crystal. For the ultimate pampering, schedule a massage with
an onsite therapist.

Innkeeper(s): Carmine and Cheryl Farruggia. $99-225. 6 rooms, 5 with FP,
5 with WP, 6 total suites, including 2 two-bedroom suites, 1 cottage.
Breakfast, Early morning coffee and tea and hot chocolate included in
rates. Types of meals: Full bkfst, veg bkfst, picnic lunch, snacks/refresh-
ments and gourmet dinner. Beds: KQ. Cable TV, VCR, DVD, reading lamp,
stereo, refrigerator, ceiling fan, clock radio, coffeemaker, turn-down service,
hot tub/spa, fireplace, hair dryer, bathrobes, bath amenities, wireless
Internet access, iron/ironing board and Double Whirlpool/Jacuzzi in room.
Central air. Fax, copier, sauna, bicycles, library, parlor games, telephone,
pet friendly, gazebo, pond, gardens, fire pit, on-site parking and motorcycle
garage parking on premises. Handicap access. Antiquing, art galleries,
bicycling, canoeing/kayaking, cross-country skiing, downhill skiing, fishing,
golf, hiking, horseback riding, live theater, museums, parks, shopping and
wineries nearby.

Location: City.

Certificate may be used: Sunday-Thursday.

Farmers' Guest House

334 Spring St
Galena, IL 61036-2128
(815)777-3456 (888)459-1847 Fax:(815)777-3202
Internet: www.farmersguesthouse.com
E-mail: farmersgh@galenalink.net

Circa 1867. This two-story brick Italianate building was built
as a bakery and served as a store and hotel, as well. Rows of
arched, multi-paned windows add charm to the exterior. The
rooms are decorated with antiques, lace curtains and floral
wallpapers. The accommodations include seven rooms with
queen-size beds, one room with a double bed, and two, two-
room king Master Suites. There's a bar, featured in the movie
"Field of Dreams." A hot tub is offered in the backyard. The
inn also has a cabin in the woods available for rent.

Innkeeper(s): Kathie, Jess Farlow. $124-250. 9 rooms with PB, 5 with FP, 3
with WP, 3 suites, 1 cottage, 1 cabin. Breakfast, snacks/refreshments and
wine included in rates. Types of meals: Full bkfst, veg bkfst and early
coffee/tea. Beds: KQD. Cable TV, DVD, reading lamp, stereo, coffeemaker,
some with hot tub/spa, hair dryer, bathrobes and wireless Internet access in
room. Central air. Fax, copier, spa, library, parlor games, telephone, fireplace,

gift shop, hot tub and evening wine and cheese hour on premises. Limited handicap access. Antiquing, art galleries, bicycling, canoeing/kayaking, cross-country skiing, downhill skiing, golf, hiking, horseback riding, live theater, museums, parks, shopping, wineries and hot air ballooning nearby.

Location: City.

Publicity: *Better Homes & Gardens, Country Discoveries, Comforts at Home, Country Extra and Field of Dreams.*

"Neat old place, fantastic breakfasts."

Certificate may be used: All year, must be Sunday-Monday, Monday-Tuesday, Tuesday-Wednesday or Wednesday-Thursday nights. Based on availability.

The Steamboat House Bed and Breakfast

605 S. Prospect
Galena, IL 61036
(815)777-2317 Fax:(815)776-0712
Internet: www.thesteamboathouse.com
E-mail: glenchar@thesteamboathouse.com

Circa 1855. Truly elegant as well as historic, this brick Gothic Revival, pre-Civil War mansion was built for a renowned Mississippi River steamboat captain. The inn exudes luxury while imparting a welcome, friendly ambiance. Main-floor parlors include a library and billiards room. A central parlor on the second floor offers early-morning Gevalia coffee and tea. Enjoy midweek afternoon treats or wine and cheese on the weekends. Each guest bedroom features a fireplace, heirloom furniture, vintage photographs and original artwork. The formal dining room is set with antique china, crystal and silver for a breakfast that is sure to please. Relax on the front porch overlooking roses.

Innkeeper(s): Glen and Char Carlson. $105-160. 5 rooms with PB, 5 with FP, 1 suite. Breakfast and Wine time included in rates. Types of meals: Full gourmet bkfst, early coffee/tea, snacks/refreshments and wine. Beds: QDT. Cable TV, VCR, DVD, reading lamp, CD player, clock radio, fireplace, hair dryer, wireless Internet access, iron/ironing board, Heirloom antique furnishings, Flat screen LCD TVs, DVD players (video library), Early morning coffee and late night hot beverages outside room in room. Central air. Library, parlor games, telephone, gift shop, Billiard room, Original parlors, Gazebo, Large covered front porch and LCD TVs on premises. Antiquing, art galleries, bicycling, canoeing/kayaking, cross-country skiing, downhill skiing, fishing, golf, hiking, horseback riding, live theater, museums, parks, shopping, sporting events, tennis, water sports, wineries, Historic district, Trolley tours, Ghost tours, Historic attractions and Riverboat cruises nearby.

Location: City. Near downtown Galena.

Publicity: *Country Magazine, Illinois Now Magazine, America's Best Bed & Breakfast Recipes, Chicago Tribune, Daily Herald (northwest Illinois suburbs) and ABC and WGN TV in 2007.*

Certificate may be used: November-February, Monday/Tuesday, Tuesday/Wednesday, Wednesday/Thursday. Bess or Amanda Room, subject to availability.

Maeystown   J3

Corner George Inn

1101 Main
Maeystown, IL 62256
(618)458-6660 (800)458-6020
Internet: www.cornergeorgeinn.com
E-mail: cornrgeo@htc.net

Circa 1884. This inn is located in a restored hotel listed in the National Register of Historic Places. The inn originally served as both a hotel and saloon, but eventually served as a general store. Rooms in the inn are named after prominent local citizens and include Victorian appointments and antiques. The

Summer Kitchen, a rustic cottage, once served as a smoke house, bakery and kitchen for the hotel's earliest owners. The cottage features original limestone walls and exposed beams. Another suite is also available in an 1859 rock house, and it includes two bedrooms. Breakfasts include entrees such as baked Victorian French toast, fresh fruit and homemade muffins or coffeecake.

Innkeeper(s): David & Marcia Braswell. $89-169. 7 rooms with PB, 3 suites, 1 cottage, 1 conference room. Breakfast included in rates. Types of meals: Full bkfst. Beds: QD. Reading lamp and fresh flowers in room. Central air. Library, parlor games, telephone, Gift shop, Sweet Shoppe, Christmas and Antique shops on premises. Limited handicap access. Antiquing, fishing, golf, hiking, live theater, wineries, Fults Hill Prairie Nature Preserve, Fort de Chartres Historic Site, Fort Kaskaskia Historic Site, Acorns Golf Course and Annbriar Golf Course nearby.

Location: Country.

Publicity: *Midwest Living, Midwest Motorist, St. Louis Magazine, St. Louis Post-Dispatch, Belleville News Democrat, Show Me St. Louis and KWMU-FM 90.1.*

Certificate may be used: Anytime, Wednesday-Saturday, subject to availability.

Mossville   D4

Old Church House Inn

1416 E Mossville Rd.
Mossville, IL 61552
(309)579-2300
Internet: www.oldchurchhouseinn.com
E-mail: oldchurchhouseinn@frontier.com

Circa 1869. Take sanctuary at this lovingly restored 1869 brick Colonial country church situated on Peoria's north side. The inn offers warm hospitality and comfortable elegance. Relax by a wood-burning fire with afternoon tea or sit on a bench among colorful garden blooms. Each guest bedroom features pampering amenities and distinctive details that may include an antique carved bedstead, handmade quilts and lacy curtains. Chocolates are a pleasant treat with turndown service in the evening.

Innkeeper(s): Dean & Holly Ramseyer. $139-179. 1 two-bedroom suite. Breakfast included in rates. Types of meals: Cont plus, veg bkfst, early coffee/tea, picnic lunch, afternoon tea, room service and Gourmet Continental Plus Breakfast. Beds: Q. TV, DVD, reading lamp, CD player, refrigerator, clock radio, telephone, coffeemaker, turn-down service, desk, hair dryer, bathrobes, bath amenities, wireless Internet access and iron/ironing board in room. Central air. Fax, copier, library, parlor games and fireplace on premises. Antiquing, art galleries, bicycling, cross-country skiing, fishing, golf, hiking, live theater, museums, parks, shopping, sporting events, tennis, water sports, wineries, Bike trail and Riverfront nearby.

Location: Country. Village.

Publicity: *Chillicothe Bulletin, Peoria Journal Star, The Chicago Tribune, Country Inns Magazine, McCalls Needlework & Craft Magazine. and WEEK TV Peoria & Bloomington.*

"Your hospitality, thoughtfulness, the cleanliness, beauty, I should just say everything was the best."

Certificate may be used: Monday-Thursday all year or anytime with reservations within 48 hours of requested date.

Mundelein   *A7*

Round-Robin Inn

231 Maple Ave
Mundelein, IL 60060
(847)566-7664 (800)301-7664 Fax:(847)566-4021
Internet: www.RoundRobinInn.com
E-mail: RndRobin@aol.com

Escape from the big city at this peaceful bed & breakfast, located just 38 miles from Chicago. Guests can relax on the porch swing or take a stroll into town and browse for antiques. Candlelight decorates the welcoming interior. Each guest room has a different theme. The Stars & Stripes Forever room honors President Lincoln and includes Civil War decorations. Other rooms include canopy, four-poster or brass beds. The suites can accommodate more than two guests, for an additional charge. Breakfasts include items such as quiche, banana bread and fresh fruit. As guests enjoy the morning meal, innkeeper Laura Loffredo serenades guests with piano music. Museums, gardens, the Long Grove Historical Village and Six Flags are among the area's attractions.

Innkeeper(s): Laura Loffredo. Call for rates. 7 rooms with PB.

Certificate may be used: Anytime, November-March, Subject to availability.

Ozark   *K5*

The Irish Inn

600 Soloman Lane
Ozark, IL 62972
(618) 695-3355 (618) 695-5683 Fax:(618) 695-LOVE
Internet: irishinn.tripod.com/
E-mail: irishinn@lycos.com

Circa 1997. Experience a taste of Europe in Southern Illinois' wine country near the Tunnel Hill State Bicycle Trail, springs, falls, Lake Glendale, the Ohio River, and other beautiful nature areas. Stay in a stone and log chalet that stays comfortably cool in summer and invitingly warm in winter with blazing log fires and fireplaces in each bedroom. Enjoy the company of the Belfast-born innkeeper and a hearty full Irish breakfast that is sure to please. There is no extra charge for the blarney, storytelling, and good luck. Plan a celebration here or elope to romantic settings in the Shawnee National Forest. This acclaimed inn has been noted as one of the 100 must-see places in eight states surrounding Missouri.

Innkeeper(s): Brian & Lynn McCreery. $131-199. 3 rooms, 2 with PB, 3 with FP, 1 with WP, 2 total suites, including 1 two-bedroom suite. Breakfast, snacks/refreshments, Full Irish Breakfast, Known For Exceptional Food and Cover Inn of "Illinois Bed & Breakfast Cookbook included in rates. Types of meals: Afternoon tea, gourmet dinner, room service and America's Best Full Irish Breakfast. Beds: KDT. TV, DVD, reading lamp, CD player, refrigerator, ceiling fan, clock radio, some with hot tub/spa, fireplace, hair dryer, bath amenities, wireless Internet access and iron/ironing board in room. Central air. Spa, library, pet boarding, parlor games, Fishing In Our Lake, Nature Hikes and Ghost & Paranormal Tours on premises. Limited handicap access. Antiquing, beach, bicycling, canoeing/kayaking, fishing, golf, hiking, horseback riding, live theater, museums, parks, shopping, water sports, wineries, American Revolution, Ancient Spanish Fort, Cherokee Culture & Festivals, Civil War, Deer Festival, French & British Colonial, Ghost & Paranormal Sites, Historical Sites, Military Reenactments, Museums, Native American Sites, Shawnee Adventure Guides, Shawnee National Forest, Shopping, Local Crafts, Minor League Baseball, Colleges & Universities and Tunnel Hill State Bicycle Trail nearby.

Location: Country. Shawnee National Forest, Waterfront, Wilderness Area.

Publicity: *This feature by Linda Rush in the Southern Illinoisan entitled "Charm of the Irish" discusses The Irish Inn winning the award for being the "Most International B&B in North America" for 2011. This feature on "Luxury B&Bs" by Adam Testa was published in Life & Style magazine, and features The Irish Inn, along with three other choice Midwestern properties. The Illinois Amtrak 2011 Bed & Breakfast Guide features The Irish Inn on its cover. The B&B has been an Amtrak rail partner for a decade. "100 Must-See Sites" in the eight states surrounding Missouri (St. Louis Magazine). The Irish Inn was the only B&B mentioned on the Illinois page in this traveler's take-out section. The photograph featured on this site was also selected as the cover photo for the "Illinois Bed & Breakfast Cookbook." This compendium of recipes and vignettes about Illinois' best B&Bs, boutique hotels, and inns is a regional favorite. Two books on area tourism to include The Irish Inn are "Sandstone Warrior," the definitive guide to boulder climbing, as well as a guide to the wineries of Southern Illinois published by Lusk Creek Publishing. The ghost stories by Lynn Moore McCreery appear in Flo Austin Dunning's book, "Walk These Haunted Hills." The Irish Inn is often featured in footage depicting wilderness, architectural gems, travel pieces, and adventure outings. Brian Marshall McCreery has a charming Anglo/Irish accent reporters just love, who welcomes interviews on tourism in Southernmost Illinois and his ancient Celtic genealogy. A DNA project proves him to be a direct descendant of the Dark Ages King considered progenitor of the Irish race, Niall of the Nine Hostages., Innkeeper Lynn Moore McCreery has been featured on radio shows discussing genealogy, hauntings, and the history of Southernmost Illinois. She is a direct descendant of area pioneer families and of a Virginia Burgess who was named in the first Jamestowne census. Last Halloween she was on a syndicated radio show about haunted inns and ghost tours, featuring B&B owners from New Orleans, Montana, Maine, and Southernmost Illinois. Brian McCreery has been known to play "Danny Boy" (also known as "Londonderry Aire") on the clarinet. His mother was from Derry, too., "How The West Was Won" featured a scene at Cave in Rock. "U.S. Marshalls" filmed the plane crash scene in Southern Pope County. "Superman" has his home town in Metropolis, Illinois and and The Irish Inn sponsors "The Superman Festival" in June.*

Certificate may be used: January and August.

Paxton   *E7*

TimberCreek Bed & Breakfast

1559 E. State Route 9
Paxton, IL 60957
(217) 379-2589
Internet: www.timbercreekbb.com
E-mail: info@timbercreekbb.com

Circa 2003. In a secluded meadow on 25 acres with trees and a stream, this newly built country retreat is the perfect place to relax in an upscale setting. The English Cottage décor compliments the hardwood, brick and tile floors, knotty alder beams and white pickled wood ceilings. Play board games or read in the Gathering Room. The Kitchen is stocked with beverages and an evening snack is offered. Stay in a handicap-accessible first-floor suite with a canopy bed and black marble fireplace. The romantic Rose Garden Suite is a honeymoon favorite with a Jacuzzi, two-person shower and 14-foot fireplace. A rustic Americana cabin is also available. Savor a hearty morning meal in the Breakfast Room. Two stone patios feature wrought iron tables and chairs and the porch boasts wood rockers.

Innkeeper(s): Connie Bahler. $99-199. 6 rooms, 3 with FP, 1 with WP, 6 suites, 1 cabin, 1 conference room. Breakfast included in rates. Types of meals: Country bkfst, veg bkfst, afternoon tea and room service. Beds: KQ. Reading lamp, clock radio, hot tub/spa, some with fireplace and wireless Internet access in room. Central air. TV, VCR, DVD, fax, copier and telephone on premises. Antiquing, fishing, golf, hiking, parks, shopping and wineries nearby.

Location: Country.

Certificate may be used: Anytime, subject to availability.

Sheffield C4

Chestnut Street Inn

301 E Chestnut St
Sheffield, IL 61361
(815)454-2419 (800)537-1304
Internet: www.chestnut-inn.com
E-mail: monikaandjeff@chestnut-inn.com

Circa 1854. This inn is an award winning bed and breakfast featuring gourmet Mediterranean cuisine using locally grown foods. The four elegantly appointed guests suites offer signature toiletries, satellite TV, a VCR/DVD with more than 1000 titles

and snacksand beverages. The innkeeper serves a full hot breakfas. This inn is near antiquing, shopping, hiking and biking and fishing. Nearby are also several

historical sites, theater, golf, wineries and more. Experience big city dining in a small town atmosphere.

Innkeeper(s): Monika & Jeff Sudakov. $109-179. 4 rooms with PB, 1 with FP, 2 total suites, including 1 two-bedroom suite, 1 conference room. Breakfast and snacks/refreshments included in rates. Types of meals: Full gourmet bkfst, veg bkfst, early coffee/tea, gourmet lunch, afternoon tea, hors d'oeuvres, wine, gourmet dinner, 4-Course Fixed Price Menu served daily by reservation only and Beer and Wine license on premises. Restaurant on premises. Beds: KQDT. Cable TV, VCR, DVD, reading lamp, CD player, snack bar, clock radio, telephone, desk, some with fireplace, hair dryer, bathrobes, bath amenities, wireless Internet access, iron/ironing board and Full Gourmet 4-Course Dinner Available by Reservation Only in room. Central air. Copier, library, parlor games, laundry facility, gift shop, Complimentary non-alcoholic beverages & snacks available at all times and Video/DVD library of over 1000 selections on premises. Antiquing, bicycling, canoeing/kayaking, fishing, golf, hiking, horseback riding, live theater, museums, parks, shopping, tennis, wineries, Bishop Hill, Goods Furniture, Hornbaker Gardens, Tanner's Orchard, Festival 56, Starved Rock, Geocaching and Letterboxing nearby.

Location: Country. Village.

Publicity: *The Illinois Review, Illinois Country Living, Inn Traveler Magazine, Star Courier, Bureau County Republican, Paula Sands Live, www.therecipeboxshow.com, QC Times, Gluten Free Frenzy, Recipelion.com., Paula Sands Live! KWQC and WZOE.*

"Without a doubt, the best B&B I've ever been to."
Certificate may be used: Anytime, subject to availability.

Taylorville G5

Market Street Inn

220 E Market St
Taylorville, IL 62568-2212
(217) 824-7220 (800) 500-1466
Internet: www.marketstreetinn.com
E-mail: innkeeper@marketstreetinn.com

Circa 1892. Carefully and lovingly renovated, this vintage 1892 Queen Anne Victorian home and Carriage House in Taylorville is perfectly located in central Illinois, in the heart of historic Lincolnland. The common area with a kitchenette is on the third floor. Most of the well-appointed guest bedrooms feature double whirlpool tubs and some have fireplaces. Stay in one of the two romantic suites in the Carriage House with pampering amenities. Wake up each day to enjoy a satisfying fireside breakfast. There are many local attractions and activities to enjoy and plan to take a day trip to St. Louis, Missouri, 93 miles away.

Innkeeper(s): Myrna Hauser. $145-235. 10 rooms with PB, 7 with FP, 8 with WP, 2 suites, 1 cottage, 1 conference room. Breakfast, wine, complimentary social hour 4 to 6 pm, wine and fruit & cheese included in rates. Types of meals: Country bkfst, veg bkfst, early coffee/tea, There are restaurants nearby and within walking distance. Beds: KQ. Cable TV, VCR, DVD, reading lamp, CD player, ceiling fan, clock radio, telephone, desk, most with hot tub/spa, most with fireplace, hair dryer, bathrobes, bath amenities, wireless Internet access and iron/ironing board in room. Central air. Fax, copier, bicycles, parlor games, laundry facility, Great porch for sitting, sipping, socializing or just being quiet on, Fax send & receive and Social hour on premises. Handicap access. Antiquing, bicycling, fishing, golf, hiking, museums, parks, tennis, Open mike entertainment, Periodic live entertainment, Wine tasting every Saturday, Festivals and Events (see events section on Web site) nearby.

Location: City.

Certificate may be used: Anytime, subject to availability.

Indiana

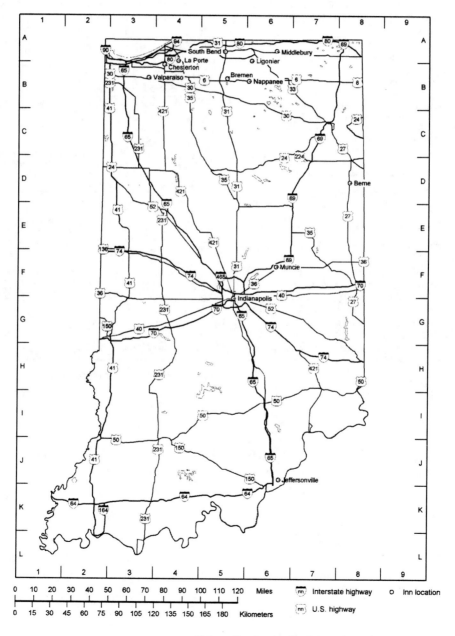

Miles: 0 10 20 30 40 50 60 70 80 90 100 110 120

Kilometers: 0 15 30 45 60 75 90 105 120 135 150 165 180

⬚ Interstate highway   o   Inn location

⬚ U.S. highway

Berne   D8

Historic Schug House Inn

706 W Main St
Berne, IN 46711-1328
(260)589-2303
E-mail: schughouseinn@comcast.net

Circa 1907. This Queen Anne home was built in 1907 by
Emanuel Wanner. It was constructed for the Schug family,
who occupied the home for 25 years, and whom the innkeepers chose the name of their inn. Victorian features decorate
the home, including inlaid floors, pocket doors and a wraparound porch. Guest rooms boast walnut, cherry and oak furnishings. Fruit, cheeses and pastries are served on antique
china each morning in the dining room. Horse-drawn carriages from the nearby Old Order Amish community often
pass on the street outside.

Innkeeper(s): John Minch. $50-60. 9 rooms with PB, 1 conference room.
Breakfast included in rates. Types of meals: Cont. Beds: KQDT. TV, telephone
and Free WiFi on premises.

Certificate may be used: Jan. 2-Dec. 20, except July 20-27 and Aug. 23-30.

Bremen   B5

Scottish Bed and Breakfast

2180 Miami Trail
Bremen, IN 46506
(574)220-6672
Internet: www.scottishbb.com
E-mail: info@scottishbb.com

Circa 1999. Close to the Amish region, this year-round bed
and breakfast sits on two park-like acres in the country.
Practice golf on the putting green. Stay in a comfortable
guest bedroom or suite with a Jacuzzi tub, TV and DVD player. The King Suite boasts a private entrance to the indoor
swimming pool. Start the day with a hot continental-plus
breakfast and enjoy evening refreshments. An assortment of
pleasing packages is offered from theater to romance or create a customized getaway.

Innkeeper(s): Homer & Brenda Miller. $99-169. 4 rooms with PB, 2 with FP,
1 with WP, 1 two-bedroom suite, 1 cottage, 1 guest house, 1 conference
room. Breakfast and snacks/refreshments included in rates. Types of meals:
Full gourmet bkfst, veg bkfst, early coffee/tea, picnic lunch, afternoon tea,
Homemade Soup and Sandwich Dinner extra cost and advance reservation
only. Beds: KQ. Data port, cable TV, DVD, stereo, refrigerator, ceiling fan,
snack bar, clock radio, desk, some with hot tub/spa, some with fireplace, hair
dryer, bathrobes, bath amenities, wireless Internet access, iron/ironing board,
King/Queen select comfort number beds, Bottled water and Snacks in all guestrooms in room. Central air. Copier, swimming, bicycles, pet boarding, parlor
games, telephone, gift shop, Two garden areas, one with two-tier pond, one
with patio furniture for relaxing outside, "Doggie Hotel" indoor/outdoor kennel, Indoor heated pool and Game room on premises. Limited handicap
access. Antiquing, art galleries, beach, bicycling, canoeing/kayaking, cross-
country skiing, downhill skiing, fishing, golf, hiking, horseback riding, live
theater, museums, parks, shopping, sporting events, tennis, water sports,
wineries, Potato Creek State Park, Amish Acres, Blueberry Festival, Zoo,
College Football Hall of Fame, Studebaker Museum, Shipshewana Flea
Market and Rent a Pontoon Boat for the day nearby.

Location: Country.

Publicity: South Bend Tribune, Bremen Enquirer, IN Michiana, Business
Weekly, Tails Pet Magazine featured article on welcoming pets to B&B.,
Brenda, the Innkeeper and was in the movie "Rudy"

Certificate may be used: November-April, Sunday-Thursday, subject to availability. Excluding Holidays.

Chesterton   B4

The Gray Goose

350 Indian Boundary Rd
Chesterton, IN 46304-1511
(219)926-5781 (800)521-5127 Fax:(219)926-4845
Internet: www.graygooseinn.com
E-mail: graygoose350@gmail.com

Circa 1939. Situated on 100 wooded acres, just under one
hour from Chicago, this English country inn overlooks a private lake. Guests can see Canadian geese and ducks on the

lake and surrounding
area. Rooms are decorat-
ed in 18th-century
English, Shaker and
French-country styles.
Some of the rooms fea-
ture fireplaces, Jacuzzi
and poster beds. Complimentary snacks, soft drinks, coffee
and tea are available throughout the day. Strains of Mozart or
Handel add to the ambiance.

Innkeeper(s): Tim Wilk. $110-195. 8 rooms with PB, 3 with FP, 3 suites,
1 conference room. Breakfast, afternoon tea and snacks/refreshments
included in rates. Types of meals: Full gourmet bkfst, veg bkfst and early
coffee/tea. Beds: KQ. Modem hook-up, data port, TV, VCR, reading lamp,
ceiling fan, clock radio, telephone, turn-down service, desk, hot tub/spa,
fireplace and one room with fireplace and Jacuzzi in room. Central air.
Fax, copier, library, parlor games, gift shop, snack/service bar, large
screened gazebo and gift shop on premises. Antiquing, art galleries,
beach, bicycling, cross-country skiing, downhill skiing, fishing, golf, hiking,
horseback riding, live theater, museums, parks, shopping, sporting events,
tennis, water sports and wineries nearby.

Location: Waterfront.

Publicity: Innsider, Post-Tribune, Glamour, Country Inns, Midwest Living,
Indianapolis Star, Indianapolis Woman and Arrington's Inn Traveler.

"Extremely gracious! A repeat stay for us because it is such a wonderful place to stay."

Certificate may be used: November to April.

Indianapolis   G5

The Old Northside Bed & Breakfast

1340 North Alabama St.
Indianapolis, IN 46202
(317)635-9123 (800)635-9127 Fax:(317)635-9243
Internet: www.oldnorthsideinn.com
E-mail: garyh@hofmeister.com

Circa 1885. This Romanesque Revival mansion is fashioned
out of bricks, and the grounds are enclosed by a wrought-iron
fence. Border gardens and an English side garden complete
the look. Rooms are decorated with a theme in mind. The
Literary Room, which includes a fireplace and Jacuzzi tub, is
decorated to honor Indiana authors. Another room honors
the Hollywood's golden years. The home has many modern
conveniences, yet still retains original maple floors and hand-
carved, mahogany woodwork. Full breakfasts are served in
the formal dining room or on the patio. Guests can walk to
many city attractions.

Innkeeper(s): Gary Hofmeister. $135-215. 7 rooms with PB, 5 with FP, 7
with WP, 1 suite. Breakfast, afternoon tea and snacks/refreshments included
in rates. Types of meals: Full bkfst. Beds: KQ. Cable TV, VCR, clock radio,
telephone, desk and hot tub/spa in room. Central air. Fireplace on premises.

Antiquing, art galleries, bicycling, live theater, museums, parks, shopping and sporting events nearby.

Location: City.

Certificate may be used: August, September, October, November, Sunday-Friday.

Jeffersonville   J6

Market Street Inn

330 West Market Street
Jeffersonville, IN 47130
(812)285-1877 (888)284-1877 Fax:(812)218-0926
Internet: www.innonmarket.com
E-mail: info@innonmarket.com

Circa 1881. One block from the Ohio River, Market Street Inn is a stately, three-story Second Empire mansion built in 1881 and recently restored in downtown Jeffersonville, Indiana. Sit on the front porch or relax on the third-floor deck by the fountain and outdoor fireplace. Guest bedrooms feature fireplaces and each suite also includes a double Jacuzzi tub, separate shower, two sinks, bidet and wet bar. Savor a magnificent breakfast made by a professional chef and served in one of the two dining rooms. Browse through the antique and gift shop for treasures to take home.

Innkeeper(s): Carol & Steve Stenbro. $79-199. 7 rooms with PB, 7 with FP, 6 with WP, 3 suites, 1 conference room. Breakfast and snacks/refreshments included in rates. Types of meals: Full gourmet bkfst, veg bkfst, early coffee/tea, lunch, picnic lunch, afternoon tea and gourmet dinner. Beds: KQT. Modem hook-up, data port, cable TV, VCR, DVD, reading lamp, CD player, ceiling fan, clock radio, telephone, desk, most with hot tub/spa, fireplace, bathrobes, wireless Internet access, Suites have Double Jacuzzis, Separate showers, Two sinks, Bidet and Wet bar in room. Central air. Fax, copier, library and parlor games on premises. Handicap access. Amusement parks, antiquing, art galleries, bicycling, canoeing/kayaking, downhill skiing, fishing, golf, hiking, horseback riding, live theater, museums, parks, shopping, sporting events, tennis, water sports, wineries, Antiques, Candy Museum and Fossil Beds nearby.

Location: City. Near Louisville, KY.

Certificate may be used: Anytime except during Thunder, Derby and holidays.

La Porte   B4

Arbor Hill Inn

263 W Johnson Rd
La Porte, IN 46350-2026
(219)362-9200 Fax:219-362-9200
Internet: www.arborhillinn.com
E-mail: info@arborhillinn.com

Circa 1910. Built with classic Greek Revival architecture, this premiere bed and breakfast is furnished in an upscale designer décor. The back of the grounds sits on the third hole green of Beacon Hills Golf Course. Accommodations in the main inn or in the guest house include guest bedrooms and suites with an assortment of amenities. Choose a room with single or double whirlpool tub, fireplace, oversized shower or private balcony. Browse the video library. A bountiful breakfast is served daily at a pre-arranged time. Evening dining can be scheduled with advance notice. Special events, meetings and retreats are welcome and business support services are provided. Ask about available packages.

Innkeeper(s): Laura Kobat & Kris Demoret. $79-259. 12 rooms with PB, 9 with FP, 9 with WP, 9 suites, 1 conference room. Breakfast, A full hot breakfast, fresh baked cookies every evening and some packages include special snacks and dinners included in rates. Types of meals: Full bkfst, veg bkfst, early coffee/tea, lunch, hors d'oeuvres, dinner, room service, Lunches and

dinners and catered affairs served with 48-hour notice (menus can be viewed online). Beds: KQ. Modem hook-up, data port, cable TV, VCR, reading lamp, refrigerator, ceiling fan, clock radio, telephone, coffeemaker, desk, most with hot tub/spa, voice mail, most with fireplace, hair dryer, bath amenities, wireless Internet access and iron/ironing board in room. Central air. Fax, copier, parlor games, gift shop, Gas grill, Kitchenette and Massages on premises. Handicap access. Antiquing, art galleries, beach, bicycling, canoeing/kayaking, cross-country skiing, fishing, golf, hiking, horseback riding, live theater, museums, parks, shopping, sporting events, tennis, water sports, wineries, Lake Michigan, Dunes National Lakeshore, Lighthouse Place Premium Outlet, Notre Dame, Apple & blueberry orchards, Pumpkin farms, Corn mazes, Christmas trees and Micro-brewery tours nearby.

Location: Country. Lake Michigan.

Publicity: *2010 Landmark Award.*

Certificate may be used: Midweek only (Sunday-Thursday) Not available holiday and specialty days. No packages or discounts apply.

Ligonier   B6

Solomon Mier Manor Bed Breakfast

508 South Cavin Street
Ligonier, IN 46767-1802
(260)894-3668
Internet: www.smmanor.com
E-mail: stay@smmanor.com

Circa 1899. This turn-of-the-century Queen Anne-Italianate manor boasts hand-painted ceilings, intricate woodwork and stained-glass windows. The ornate carved staircase is especially appealing with its staircase library. Antiques fill the guest rooms and common areas. The home is eligible to be on the National Register and originally was home to Solomon Mier, one of the area's first Jewish residents who came to the Ligonier area in search of religious tolerance and word of the railroad to come. Guests will find many areas of interest, such as the Shipshewana Flea Market & Auction and the on-site antique shop.

Innkeeper(s): Amanda Moser. $79-129. 4 rooms with PB, 4 with FP, 1 total suite, including 2 two-bedroom suites. Breakfast, afternoon tea and snacks/refreshments included in rates. Types of meals: Full gourmet bkfst, veg bkfst and early coffee/tea. Beds: KQ. Cable TV, VCR, DVD, reading lamp, refrigerator, ceiling fan, coffeemaker, desk, hair dryer, bath amenities, wireless Internet access, iron/ironing board and Snacks in the evening in room. Air conditioning. Bicycles, library, parlor games, telephone, fireplace and gift shop on premises. Antiquing, art galleries, beach, bicycling, canoeing/kayaking, downhill skiing, fishing, golf, hiking, live theater, museums, parks, shopping, sporting events, tennis, water sports, Shipshewana Flea Market, Chain of Lakes State Park and Zoo nearby.

Location: City. Amish Country.

Publicity: *Kendallville News Sun, Ligonier Advanced Leader and Goshen News.*

"Complete and beautiful experience."

Certificate may be used: Anytime, November-March, subject to availability; October - Monday through Thursday, subject to availability.

Middlebury   A6

Country Victorian Bed & Breakfast

435 S Main St
Middlebury, IN 46540
(574)825-2568 (800)262-7829 Fax:(574)822-9465
Internet: www.countryvictorian.com
E-mail: stay@countryvictorian.com

Circa 1894. Built in 1894, Country Victorian Bed & Breakfast in Middlebury, Indiana has been recently renovated to provide country comfort while remaining true to its original Victorian splendor. Located in the heart of Amish country, sit on the front porch and watch the buggies go by. Relax inside by the fire with a good book. Guest bedrooms and a guest suite are furnished with antiques. Some feature whirlpools and one has a clawfoot soaking tub. Wake up each morning to enjoy a different breakfast menu that starts with the signature Country Victorian Breakfast Blend Coffee. Ask about special getaway packages available.

Innkeeper(s): Lori & Arnie Schumacher. $89-159. 5 rooms with PB, 1 with FP, 1 with WP. Breakfast and hors d'oeuvres included in rates. Types of meals: Full bkfst, veg bkfst and early coffee/tea. Beds: KQDT. Cable TV, DVD, reading lamp, CD player, ceiling fan, clock radio, turn-down service, some with hot tub/spa, some with fireplace, hair dryer, bathrobes, bath amenities, wireless Internet access and iron/ironing board in room. Central air. Fax, copier, library, parlor games and telephone on premises. Limited handicap access. Antiquing, art galleries, bicycling, canoeing/kayaking, cross-country skiing, fishing, golf, hiking, horseback riding, live theater, museums, parks, shopping, sporting events, water sports, Shipshewana Flea Market (May-Oct) and American Countryside Farmers Market (Mar-Dec) nearby.

Location: Country.

Certificate may be used: December-April, Sunday-Thursday.

Nappanee   B6

Homespun Country Inn

302 N Main St
Nappanee, IN 46550
(574)773-2034 (800)311-2996 Fax:(574)773-3456
Internet: www.homespuninn.com
E-mail: homespun@kcaccess.com

Circa 1902. Windows of stained and leaded glass create colorful prisms at this Queen Anne Victorian inn built in 1902. Quarter-sawn oak highlights the entry and first-floor common rooms. Comfortable antiques and family heirlooms accent the inn. Two parlors offer areas to read, do a jigsaw puzzle or watch satellite TV or a movie. Each guest bedroom displays photos of the home's original occupants. Early risers enjoying a cup of coffee or tea might see a passing horse and buggy while sitting on the porch swing. Breakfast is served in the dining room. Ask about the assortment of special packages and how to add a Homespun Memory Gift Bag to a reservation.

Innkeeper(s): Dianne & Dennis Debelak. $89. 5 rooms with PB. Breakfast and snacks/refreshments included in rates. Types of meals: Full bkfst and early coffee/tea. Beds: QDT. Cable TV, VCR, reading lamp, ceiling fan, snack bar, clock radio, wireless Internet access, iron/ironing board and night lights in room. Central air. Fax, copier, parlor games, telephone and fireplace on premises. Antiquing, golf, live theater, parks, shopping, sporting events and tennis nearby.

Location: Amish heritage.

Publicity: *The Elkhart Truth.*

"We have been telling all our friends about how wonderful your establishment is."

Certificate may be used: Any day January-April. Discount based on regular room rates. No other discount applies.

South Bend   A5

Oliver Inn

630 W Washington St
South Bend, IN 46601-1444
(574)232-4545 (888)697-4466 Fax:(574)288-9788
Internet: www.oliverinn.com
E-mail: oliver@michiana.org

Circa 1886. This stately Queen Anne Victorian sits amid 30 towering maples and was once home to Josephine Oliver Ford, daughter of James Oliver, of chilled plow fame. Located in South Bend's historic district, this inn offers a comfortable library and nine inviting guest rooms, some with built-in fireplaces or double Jacuzzis. The inn is within walking distance of

downtown and is next door to the Tippecanoe Restaurant in the Studebaker Mansion.

Innkeeper(s): Tom & Alice Erlandson. $95-329. 10 rooms, 8 with PB, 6 with FP, 4 with WP, 4 total suites, including 2 two-bedroom suites, 1 guest house, 1 conference room. Breakfast and snacks/refreshments included in rates. Types of meals: Full gourmet bkfst, veg bkfst, early coffee/tea and Adjacent to Tippecanoe Place Restaurant. Beds: KQ. Modem hook-up, data port, cable TV, DVD, reading lamp, CD player, ceiling fan, clock radio, telephone, turn-down service, desk, some with fireplace, hair dryer, bathrobes, bath amenities, wireless Internet access, iron/ironing board and several with double whirlpool tubs in room. Central air. Fax, library, parlor games, gift shop and baby grand with computer disk system on premises. Limited handicap access. Antiquing, art galleries, beach, bicycling, canoeing/kayaking, cross-country skiing, fishing, golf, hiking, live theater, museums, parks, shopping, sporting events, tennis, water sports, wineries, fine dining, Amish country and Notre Dame nearby.

Location: City. Lake Michigan (35 miles), Chicago (90 miles).

Certificate may be used: January-December, Sunday-Thursday.

Valparaiso

Inn at Aberdeen

3158 South SR 2
Valparaiso, IN 46385
(219)465-3753 (866)761-3753 Fax:(219)465-9227
Internet: www.innataberdeen.com
E-mail: inn@innataberdeen.com

Circa 1856. An old stone wall borders this inn, once a dairy farm, horse farm and then hunting lodge. Recently renovated and expanded, this Victorian farmhouse is on more than an acre. An elegant getaway, there's a solarium, library, dining room and parlor for relaxing. The inn offers traditional Queen Anne furnishings in the guest rooms. The Timberlake Suites include fireplaces, two-person Jacuzzi tubs and balconies. The Aberdeen Suite includes a living room and fireplace, while the Alloway Suite offers a living room, kitchenette and a balcony. A conference center on the property is popular for executive meetings and special events, and there is a picturesque gazebo overlooking the inn's beautifully landscaped lawns and English gardens. Golf packages and mystery weekends have received enthusiastic response from guests. There is a golf course, spa and microbrewery adjacent to the inn.

Innkeeper(s): Bill Simon, Val & Chris Urello, Audrey Slingsby, Mandy Wiley, John & Lyn Johnson. $102-198. 11 rooms, 10 with FP, 11 with HT, 11 with WP, 11 suites, 1 conference room. Breakfast, snacks/refreshments, Evening dessert, Flavia Coffee Bar, Hot tea, Cocoa, Snacks and Beverages included in rates. Types of meals: Full gourmet bkfst, early coffee/tea, The inn's chef for special functions - dinners, luncheons, showers, weddings, wine tasting dinners, mystery dinners and etc. Beds: KQ. Modem hook-up, cable TV, VCR, DVD, reading lamp, refrigerator, ceiling fan, snack bar, clock radio, telephone, desk, hot tub/spa, hair dryer, bathrobes, bath amenities, wireless Internet access, iron/ironing board and Balcony or Patio in room. Central air. Fax, copier, swimming, tennis, library, parlor games, fireplace, gift shop, Flavia Coffee Bar, Evening dessert, Unlimited snacks & beverages, Toll-free local calls, Gazebo, Outdoor pool and Golf within Aberdeen on premises. Handicap access. Amusement parks, antiquing, art galleries, beach, bicycling, cross-country skiing, downhill skiing, fishing, golf, hiking, horseback riding, live theater, museums, parks, shopping, sporting events, tennis, water sports and wineries nearby.

Location: Rural.

Publicity: *Midwest Living, Chicago Magazine, Chicago Tribune, Country Inns, Indiana Business Magazine ("Best Retreat Site")* and *WLS - ABC TV's 190-North Show* .

"Every time we have the good fortune to spend an evening here, it is like a perfect fairy tale, transforming us into King and Queen."

Certificate may be used: Anytime, subject to availability.

Songbird Prairie B&B

174 N 600 W
Valparaiso, IN 46385-9233
(219)759-4274 (877)766-4273 Fax:646-304-7635
Internet: www.songbirdprairie.com
E-mail: Barbara@songbirdprairie.com

Circa 2000. Recently built in the stately, red-brick Federal style, Songbird Prairie Bed and Breakfast in Valparaiso, Indiana spans six acres with landscaped lawns, woodland areas and lush wetlands. Walk paths through prairie grass and wild rose. Ethan Allen furnishings accent the B&B with a colonial country ambiance. Songbird-themed guest bedrooms and suites feature luxurious European linens, robes and towels, fireplaces and whirlpool tubs. Savor a three-course hot breakfast presented with flowers and creative garnishes in the sunroom overlooking serenading songbirds. Ask about special packages available. Downtown Chicago is just one hour away for a fun trip to the city.

Innkeeper(s): Barbara and Efrain Rivera . $179-249. 5 rooms with PB, 5 with FP, 5 with WP, 1 conference room. Breakfast, snacks/refreshments and Three Course Hot Breakfast served in the sunroom where songbirds serenade and entertain included in rates. Types of meals: Full gourmet bkfst, veg bkfst, early coffee/tea and Non-alcoholic premises. Beds: KQ. VCR, DVD, reading lamp, CD player, ceiling fan, snack bar, clock radio, turn-down service, fireplace, hair dryer, bathrobes, bath amenities, wireless Internet access, iron/ironing board, Flat screen TV and DirecTV in room. Central air. Fax, copier, parlor games and gift shop on premises. Amusement parks, antiquing, art galleries, beach, fishing, golf, hiking, horseback riding, live theater, parks, shopping, sporting events, water sports, wineries and National Dunes Lakeshore: Taltree Arboretum nearby.

Location: Country.

Publicity: *2006 nominee for Hotel of the Year, 2003 Sunflower Award from Innsidescoop, 2004 Hotel of the Year PCCVC, 2005 Chosen 1 of 25 Best Undiscovered Inns of America, 2005 Travel Smart one of 24 Best, September/Oct Midwest Living-Out and About Chicago, May June 2011 Midwest Living- "30 Favorite Bed and Breakfasts", 20 Perfect Summer Getaways Travel & Leisure Magazine May 2008, One of Midwest Living's 30 Favorite B&Bs May/June 2011 and May/ June issue One of Midwest Living's 30 Favorite B&Bs 2011 R.O.S.E. Award for recognition of service excellence Hotel of the Year.*

Certificate may be used: November–March, Monday-Thursday no holidays or special events subject to availability. Valid only for Warbler Suite.

Iowa

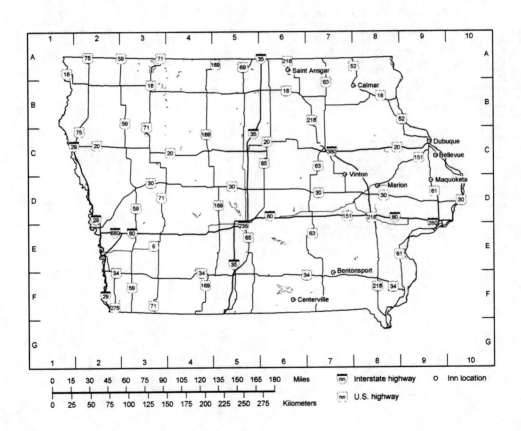

Visit www.iLoveInns.com for photos and more details about each inn.

Bellevue   C9

Mont Rest

300 Spring St
Bellevue, IA 52031-1125
(563)872-4220 (877)872-4220 Fax:(563)872-5094
Internet: www.montrest.com
E-mail: innkeeper@montrest.com

Circa 1893. Built with an unusual mix of architectural designs, the 1893 mansion was labeled Gothic Steamboat Revival and underwent an extensive restoration in 1997. Inside the inn a splendid Victorian atmosphere is enhanced by vintage woodwork, chandeliers and antique furnishings. The welcome begins with homemade cookies. In the early evening mingle at the hors d'oeuvres party. Enjoy parlor games or sing to the 1905 player grand piano. The guest kitchen provides complimentary beverages. Luxurious guest bedrooms and suites feature fresh flowers, chocolates, robes, heated towel bars and many include fireplaces and Jacuzzis. Arrange for an in-room therapeutic massage or reflexology. Stay in one of the Moon River Cabins on the banks of the Mississippi.

Innkeeper(s): Naomi. $149-199. 12 rooms with PB, 10 with FP, 9 with WP, 4 cabins, 2 conference rooms. Breakfast, snacks/refreshments and Complimentary non-alcoholic beverages are available in main floor kitchen included in rates. Types of meals: Full gourmet bkfst, veg bkfst, early coffee/tea, picnic lunch, afternoon tea, hors d'oeuvres, gourmet dinner and room service. Beds: KQ. Modem hook-up, cable TV, VCR, ceiling fan, clock radio, telephone, turn-down service, desk, hair dryer, bathrobes, bath amenities, wireless Internet access, Heated towel bars, Egyptian cotton towels, Turtle Wear robes, Fresh flowers, Imported chocolates and Most rooms with Jacuzzis in room. Central air. DVD, fax, copier, spa, bicycles, library, child care, parlor games, fireplace, gift shop, Concierge service, In-room therapeutic massages and reflexology on premises. Limited handicap access. Antiquing, art galleries, bicycling, canoeing/kayaking, cross-country skiing, downhill skiing, fishing, golf, hiking, horseback riding, live theater, museums, parks, shopping, sporting events, tennis, water sports, wineries, Floating gambling facilities and Ski resorts nearby.

Publicity: *Quad City Times, The Register, Mature Outlook and Ladies Home Journal.*

Certificate may be used: Anytime subject to availability.

Bentonsport   F8

Mason House Inn and Caboose Cottage of Bentonsport

21982 Hawk Dr
Bentonsport, IA 52565
(319)592-3133 (800)592-3133
Internet: www.masonhouseinn.com
E-mail: stay@masonhouseinn.com

Circa 1846. A Murphy-style copper bathtub folds down out of the wall at this unusual inn built by Mormon craftsmen who stayed in Bentonsport for three years on their trek to Utah. More than half of the furniture is original to the home, including a nine-foot walnut headboard and a nine-foot mirror. The Caboose Cottage, a self-contained apartment within a real railroad caboose, is the newest lodging addition. It features a kitchen, dining area and Queen bed. This is the oldest operating pre-Civil War steam-

boat inn in Iowa. Guests can imagine the days when steamboats made their way up and down the Des Moines River, while taking in the scenery. A full breakfast is served in the main house dining room, but if guests crave a mid-day snack, each room is equipped with its own stocked cookie jar.

Innkeeper(s): Chuck & Joy Hanson. $64-105. 9 rooms with PB, 1 two-bedroom suite, 1 cottage. Breakfast included in rates. Types of meals: Country bkfst and early coffee/tea. Beds: KQDT. Data port, reading lamp, ceiling fan, wireless Internet access and filled cookie jar in room. Air conditioning. TV, VCR, DVD, fax, parlor games, telephone, fireplace and Free wireless Internet access on premises. Handicap access. Antiquing, bicycling, canoeing/kayaking, fishing, golf, hiking, horseback riding, parks, shopping, wineries, Rose Garden, Historic Church and Native American artifact museum nearby.

Location: Country, waterfront. Rural by river.

Publicity: *Des Moines Register, Decatur Herald & Review, AAA Home & Away, Country Magazine, Veteran's View, Iowa Public Television, Today Show, KWWL Halloween Special 2010, KYOU Community Spotlight July 2011 and Coast to Coast AM with George Noory.*

"The attention to detail was fantastic, food was wonderful and the setting was fascinating."

Certificate may be used: Anytime, subject to availability.

Calmar   B8

Calmar Guesthouse Bed & Breakfast

103 W North St
Calmar, IA 52132-7605
(563)562-3851
Internet: www.travelassist.com/reg/ia102s.html
E-mail: calmarguesthouse@gmail.com

Circa 1890. This beautifully restored Victorian home was built by John B. Kay, a lawyer and poet. Stained-glass windows, carved moldings, an oak and walnut staircase and gleaming woodwork highlight the gracious interior. A grandfather clock ticks in the living room. In the foyer, a friendship yellow rose is incorporated into the stained-glass window pane. Breakfast is served in the formal dining room. The Laura Ingalls Wilder Museum is nearby in Burr Oak. The Bily Brothers Clock Museum, Smallest Church, Luther College, Niagara Cave, Lake Meyer and Norwegian Museum are located nearby.

Innkeeper(s): Lucille Kruse. $59-65. 5 rooms, 1 with PB. Breakfast included in rates. Types of meals: Full bkfst. Beds: Q. Cable TV, VCR, DVD, reading lamp, refrigerator, ceiling fan, clock radio, telephone, coffeemaker, desk, bathrobes, iron/ironing board and clock in room. Air conditioning. Bicycles, library, parlor games and laundry facility on premises. Antiquing, bicycling, canoeing/kayaking, cross-country skiing, fishing, golf, hiking, horseback riding, live theater, museums, parks, shopping, sporting events and water sports nearby.

Location: City.

Publicity: *Iowa Farmer Today, Calmar Courier, Minneapolis Star-Tribune, Home and Away, The Iowan and Alive at five on KWWL.*

"What a delight it was to stay here. No one could have made our stay more welcome or enjoyable."

Certificate may be used: Monday-Thursday, April-October only.

Centerville   F6

One of A Kind

314 W State St
Centerville, IA 52544
(641)437-4540 Fax:(641)437-4540
Internet: www.oneofakindbedandbreakfast.com
E-mail: jjstuff@iowatelecom.net

Circa 1867. This large, three-story brick home with mansard
roof and tall bays is the second oldest house in town. The
innkeeper has filled the inn with "One of a Kind" craft and decorative items for sale, created on the premises or by local artisans.
There is also a tea room, popular for its chicken soup and homemade croissant sandwiches, so of course you can expect a
yummy breakfast, as well. Guest quarters are decorated with
antiques and reproductions spiced with a variety of collectibles.
The largest fish hatchery in the world is a short drive away at
Lake Rathbun, but there is plenty to do within walking distance.
Innkeeper(s): Jack & Joyce Stufflebeem. $50-80. 5 rooms, 3 with PB.
Breakfast and snacks/refreshments included in rates. Types of meals: Full
bkfst, early coffee/tea, lunch, picnic lunch, afternoon tea and gourmet dinner.
Beds: QDT. Cable TV, reading lamp, ceiling fan and turn-down service in
room. Air conditioning. VCR, fax, copier, parlor games, telephone and tea
room on premises. Antiquing, fishing, golf, live theater, parks, shopping,
sporting events, tennis and water sports nearby.

Location: Small town.

Certificate may be used: Anytime, subject to availability.

Dubuque   C9

The Hancock House

1105 Grove Ter
Dubuque, IA 52001-4644
(563)557-8989 Fax:(563)583-0813
Internet: www.TheHancockHouse.com
E-mail: chuckdbq@mchsi.com

Circa 1891. Victorian splendor can be found at The Hancock
House, one of Dubuque's most striking examples of Queen

Anne architecture. Rooms feature period furnishings and
offer views of the Mississippi
River states of Iowa, Illinois
and Wisconsin. The Hancock
House, listed in the National
Register, boasts several unique
features, including a fireplace
judged blue-ribbon best at the
1893 World's Fair in Chicago.
Guests can enjoy the porch swings, wicker furniture and spectacular views from the wraparound front porch.
Innkeeper(s): Chuck & Susan Huntley. $80-175. 9 rooms with PB, 3 with FP,
4 with WP, 4 suites. Breakfast and snacks/refreshments included in rates.
Types of meals: Full bkfst, veg bkfst and early coffee/tea. Beds: Q. Data port,
cable TV, reading lamp, clock radio, desk, bath amenities, wireless Internet
access, iron/ironing board and feather mattress in room. Air conditioning. Fax,
copier, parlor games, telephone, fireplace, gift shop and gift shop on premises. Antiquing, art galleries, bicycling, canoeing/kayaking, cross-country skiing,
downhill skiing, fishing, golf, hiking, horseback riding, live theater, museums,
parks, shopping, sporting events, tennis, water sports, wineries and riverboat
casino nearby.

Location: City.

Publicity: *Victorian Sampler (Cover).*

Certificate may be used: Sunday-Thursday, excluding holidays.

The Mandolin Inn

199 Loras Blvd
Dubuque, IA 52001-4857
(563)556-0069 (800)524-7996
Internet: www.mandolininn.com
E-mail: innkeeper@mandolininn.com

Circa 1908. This handicapped-accessible three-story brick
Edwardian with Queen Anne wraparound veranda boasts a
mosaic-tiled porch floor. Inside are inlaid mahogany and

rosewood floors, bay windows
and a turret that starts in the
parlor and ascends to the second-floor Holly Marie Room,
decorated in a wedding motif.
This room features a seven-
piece Rosewood bedroom
suite and a crystal chandelier.
A gourmet breakfast is served
in the dining room with a fan-
tasy forest mural from the turn of the century. There is an
herb garden outside the kitchen. Located just 12 blocks
away, is the fabulous National Mississippi River Museum and
Aquarium. The inn can equally accommodate both business
and pleasure travel.
Innkeeper(s): Amy Boynton. $85-150. 8 rooms, 6 with PB, 1 with FP, 1
two-bedroom suite, 2 conference rooms. Breakfast included in rates. Types of
meals: Full gourmet bkfst and early coffee/tea. Beds: KQT. Cable TV, VCR,
reading lamp, clock radio, desk, some with fireplace, bathrobes and wireless
Internet access in room. Central air. DVD, fax, parlor games, high speed wireless, gourmet breakfast and central air on premises. Handicap access.
Antiquing, art galleries, bicycling, cross-country skiing, downhill skiing, fishing, golf, hiking, horseback riding, live theater, museums, parks, shopping,
sporting events, tennis, water sports and wineries nearby.

Location: City.

Publicity: *USA Today's "10 Best" Places to Stay, Arrington's BNB Journal,
2006 Summer Inn Traveler magazine, Iowan Magazine, Dubuque, Des
Moines and Chicago newspapers, Emerging Horizons (Accessible Travel
News) Magazine, Lakehom Magazine, Japanese TELPAL F, a Japanese Travel
Show, local FOX TV, local television Promo for Cinderella (Cinderella reading
her story in the parlour of the Mandolin Inn) and This American Life segment on NPR.*

*"From the moment we entered the Mandolin, we felt at home. I know
we'll be back."*

Certificate may be used: Sunday-Thursday, no holidays.

Maquoketa   D9

Squiers Manor B&B

418 W Pleasant St
Maquoketa, IA 52060-2847
(563)652-6961 Fax:(563)652-5995
Internet: www.squiersmanor.com
E-mail: innkeeper@squiersmanor.com

Circa 1882. Innkeepers Virl and Kathy Banowetz are ace
antique dealers, who along with owning one of the Midwest's
largest antique shops, have refurbished this elegant, Queen
Anne Victorian. The inn is furnished with period antiques that
are beyond compare. Guest rooms boast museum-quality
pieces such as a Victorian brass bed with lace curtain wings
and inlaid mother-of-pearl or an antique mahogany bed with
carved birds and flowers. Six guest rooms include whirlpool
tubs, and one includes a unique Swiss shower. The innkeepers

restored the home's original woodwork, shuttered-windows, fireplaces, gas and electric chandeliers and stained- and engraved-glass windows back to their former glory. They also recently renovated the mansion's attic ballroom into two luxurious suites. The Loft, which is made up of three levels, features pine and wicker furnishings, a sitting room and gas-burning wood stove. On the second level, there is a large Jacuzzi, on the third, an antique queen-size bed. The huge Ballroom Suite boasts 24-foot ceilings, oak and pine antiques, gas-burning wood stove and a Jacuzzi snuggled beside a dormer window. Suite guests enjoy breakfast delivered to their rooms. Other guests feast on an array of mouth-watering treats, such as home-baked breads, seafood quiche and fresh fruits. Evening desserts are served by candlelight.

Innkeeper(s): Virl & Kathy Banowetz. $80-195. 8 rooms with PB, 3 suites. Breakfast included in rates. Types of meals: Full gourmet bkfst. Beds: KQT. Antiquing, cross-country skiing, downhill skiing, fishing, parks, shopping and water sports nearby.

Publicity: *Des Moines Register Datebook and Daily Herald.*

"We couldn't have asked for a more perfect place to spend our honeymoon. The service was excellent and so was the food! It was an exciting experience that we will never forget!"

Certificate may be used: Anytime based on projected availability, not valid in October, Valentines week or holidays.

Marion D8

Victorian Lace Bed & Breakfast

300 E Main St
Marion, IA 52302-9343
(319) 377-5138 (888) 377-5138 Fax:319 3773560
Internet: www.victorian-lace-iowa.com
E-mail: viclacebb@aol.com

Circa 1900. Enjoy this peaceful and romantic Victorian refuge that is perfect for a weekend getaway or a memorable wedding event. Jim Condit, the innkeeper, is also a reverend who performs many ceremonies each year. Stay in the inviting Summer Kitchen or Cottage or the third-floor Holiday Suite with four rooms, including one that is hidden. Both accommodations feature stocked refrigerators with beer, wine, soda, cheese, chocolates and evening dessert. After breakfast, grab a pair of binoculars and a bike to explore the surrounding area. In the afternoon, relax on the terrace with a good book and take a refreshing swim in the heated in-ground pool.

Innkeeper(s): Jim & Renee Condit. Call for rates. 2 rooms, 2 with WP, 2 suites, 1 cottage. Breakfast, afternoon tea, snacks/refreshments, hors d'oeuvres and wine included in rates. Types of meals: Full gourmet bkfst, veg bkfst, early coffee/tea and room service. Beds: Q. Modem hook-up, data port, cable TV, VCR, DVD, reading lamp, stereo, refrigerator, ceiling fan, clock radio, telephone, coffeemaker, turn-down service, desk, hot tub/spa, hair dryer, bathrobes, bath amenities, wireless Internet access, iron/ironing board, heated swimming pool, weddings, stocked refrigerator full of free beer,wine,soda pop,cheese, and chocolates. antiques, oddities, binoclers for a great view. old books, movies, hidden room, record player w/45,36 and &78s old ones to enjoy in room. Central air. Copier, spa, swimming, bicycles and WHIRLPOOL IN ROOM JACUZZI 2 SEATERS AND A HEATED SWIMMING POOL on premises. Amusement parks, antiquing, art galleries, beach, bicycling, canoeing/kayaking, cross-country skiing, downhill skiing, fishing, golf, hiking, horseback riding, live theater, museums, parks, shopping, sporting events, tennis, water sports and wineries nearby.

Location: City.

Certificate may be used: Sunday-Thursday only.

Saint Ansgar A6

Blue Belle Inn B&B

PO Box 205, 513 W 4th St
Saint Ansgar, IA 50472-0205
(641)713-3113 (877)713-3113
Internet: www.bluebelleinn.com
E-mail: innkeeper@bluebelleinn.com

Circa 1896. This home was purchased from a Knoxville, Tenn., mail-order house. It's difficult to believe that stunning features, such as a tin ceiling, stained-glass windows, intricate woodwork and pocket doors could have come via the mail, but these original items are still here for guests to admire. Rooms are

named after books special to the innkeeper. Four of the rooms include a whirlpool tub for two, and the Never Neverland room has a clawfoot tub. Other rooms offer a skylight, fireplace or perhaps a white iron bed. During the Christmas season, every room has its own decorated tree. The innkeeper hosts a variety of themed luncheons, dinners and events, such as the April in Paris cooking workshop, Mother's Day brunches, the "Some Enchanted Evening" dinner, Murder Mysteries, Ladies nights, Writer's Retreats, quilting seminars and horse-drawn sleigh rides.

Innkeeper(s): Sherrie Hansen. $45-375. 11 rooms, 8 with PB, 2 with FP, 3 with WP, 5 total suites, including 2 two-bedroom suites and 1 three-bedroom suite, 1 cottage, 1 guest house, 2 conference rooms. Breakfast and snacks/refreshments included in rates. Types of meals: Full gourmet bkfst, veg bkfst, early coffee/tea, gourmet lunch, afternoon tea, gourmet dinner, room service and Visit our main website for a quaterly schedule of events and menus with weekly specials. Restaurant on premises. Beds: KQDT. Cable TV, VCR, reading lamp, stereo, refrigerator, clock radio, coffeemaker, desk, most with hot tub/spa, some with fireplace, bathrobes, bath amenities, wireless Internet access, iron/ironing board, Handicap accessibility and Jacuzzis for two in room. Central air. Fax, copier, library, parlor games, telephone, laundry facility, handicap unit with ramp & roll-in shower, kitchenette with refrigerator and microwave, wireless Internet access, piano, movies, popcorn and complimentary snacks on premises. Handicap access. Antiquing, bicycling, canoeing/kayaking, cross-country skiing, fishing, golf, hiking, live theater, museums, parks, shopping, water sports, wineries, hunting, Music Man Square, Hormel Spam museum and Clear Lake nearby.

Location: Country. Small town.

Publicity: *Minneapolis Star Tribune, Post-Bulletin, Midwest Living, Country, AAA Home & Away, Des Moines Register, Country Home, Iowan Magazine, American Patchwork and Quilting, New York Times, HGTV Restore America, KTTC - Rochester and MN.*

Certificate may be used: Nov. 1-April 30, Monday-Thursday nights only, holidays excluded, Dec. 26-31 excluded, subject to availability.

Kansas

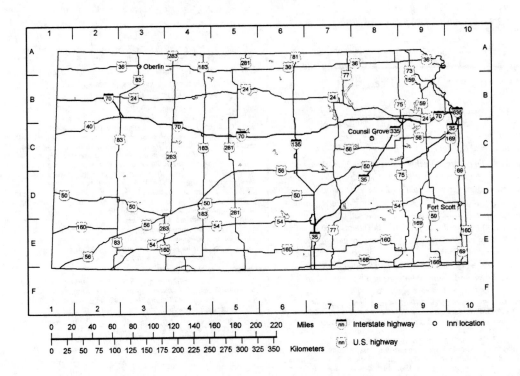

| | Miles | | | | | | | | | | |
0 20 40 60 80 100 120 140 160 180 200 220 Miles

0 25 50 75 100 125 150 175 200 225 250 275 300 325 350 Kilometers

Interstate highway O Inn location

U.S. highway

Council Grove   C8

The Cottage House Hotel

25 N Neosho St
Council Grove, KS 66846-1633
(620)767-6828 (800)727-7903 Fax:(620)767-6414
Internet: www.cottagehousehotel.com
E-mail: cotthouse@tctelco.net

Circa 1898. The inn is located in Council Grove, the rendezvous point on the Santa Fe Trail. The building grew from a
boarding house to an elegant home before it became the
hotel of a local banker. The home's original section dates to
1872, and the home was built in stages until 1898. Listed in
the National Register of Historic Places, the inn has been
completely renovated and is a beautiful example of Victorian
architecture in a prairie town. There is a honeymoon cottage
on the premises, as well.

Innkeeper(s): Dawn Hershberger. $75-175. 26 rooms with PB, 2 cottages, 2
conference rooms. Breakfast included in rates. Types of meals: Cont plus.
Beds: KQD. Data port, cable TV, VCR, reading lamp, refrigerator, ceiling fan,
clock radio, telephone, coffeemaker, desk, hot tub/spa, wireless Internet
access and whirlpool tubs in room. Air conditioning. Fax, copier, spa, sauna,
library and parlor games on premises. Handicap access. Antiquing, fishing,
golf, hiking, horseback riding, museums, parks, shopping, sporting events,
tennis, water sports and riverwalk nearby.

Location: City.

Publicity: Manhattan Mercury, Gazette, Globe & Mail, Kansas City Star,
Wichita Eagle, Midwest Living and Kansas Magazine.

"A walk back into Kansas history; preserved charm and friendliness."
Certificate may be used: November-March, Sunday-Thursday, subject to
availability.

Fort Scott   D9

Lyons' Twin Mansions B&B, Spa, Corporate Center

742 & 750 S National Ave
Fort Scott, KS 66701-1319
(620)223-3644 (800)784-8378
Internet: www.LyonsTwinMansions.com
E-mail: FallinLove@LyonsTwinMansions.com

Circa 1876. For a business trip, vacation or romantic getaway,
this landmark Victorian mansion is a luxurious choice. This
gracious home has parlors to gather and Paradise, a full service
spa. Extreme Media TV, 42" Plasma in one, 50" flat screen in
another. All guest rooms have full cable with movie channels.
Spacious guest bedrooms offer king-size beds, refined comfort
and modern technology with refreshment centers and high-
speed Internet. The baths feature oversized jetted whirlpools
that are made to look like antique clawfoot tubs. Enjoy a hearty
breakfast in the grand dining room, unless a breakfast basket
delivered to the door is preferred. The grounds are showcased
by a gazebo, fish ponds, picnic areas and an enclosed starlit hot
tub. Ask about the creative specialty packages offered such as
mystery, private dining and couples and ladies spa packages.

Innkeeper(s): Pat & Larry Lyons and Nate Lyons. $109-159. 8 rooms, 7 with
PB, 3 with FP, 4 with WP, 1 two-bedroom suite, 1 cottage, 1 guest house, 3
conference rooms. Breakfast and snacks/refreshments included in rates.
Types of meals: Full gourmet bkfst, veg bkfst, picnic lunch, hors d'oeuvres,
wine, gourmet dinner and room service. Beds: KQ. Modem hook-up, cable
TV, VCR, DVD, reading lamp, stereo, refrigerator, ceiling fan, snack bar, clock
radio, telephone, coffeemaker, turn-down service, desk, most with hot

tub/spa, some with fireplace, hair dryer, bathrobes, bath amenities, wireless
Internet access, iron/ironing board, Three with two-person whirlpool and one
with two-person therapeutic massage with built in ChromoTherapy in room.
Central air. Fax, copier, spa, library, parlor games, laundry facility, High-speed
Internet, Outdoor Grill and Picnic area on premises. Antiquing, art galleries,
canoeing/kayaking, fishing, golf, hiking, horseback riding, live theater, museums, parks, shopping, sporting events, tennis, Olympic-size swimming pool,
(open Memorial Day thru Labor Day), city park with playgrounds, community
center, tennis, baseball, archery and movie theater nearby.

Publicity: Midwest Living, Victorian Homes, Kansas Magazine, AAA
Midwest Traveler, Travel Kansas Magazine, Fort Scott Tribune and Topeka
Capitol Journal.

Certificate may be used: Accepts weekends, Anytime, last minute-based
on availability.

Oberlin   A3

The Landmark Inn at The Historic Bank of Oberlin

189 S Penn
Oberlin, KS 67749
(785)475-2340 (888)639-0003
Internet: www.landmarkinn.com
E-mail: info@landmarkinn.com

In 1886, this inn served as the Bank of Oberlin, one of the
town's most impressive architectural sites. The bank lasted
only a few years, though, and went through a number of
uses, from county courthouse to the telephone company.
Today, it serves as both inn and a historic landmark, a
reminder of the past with rooms decorated Victorian style
with antiques. One room includes a fireplace; another has a
whirlpool tub. In addition to the inviting rooms, there is a
restaurant serving dinner specialties such as buttermilk pecan
chicken and roasted beef with simmered mushrooms. The inn
is listed in the National Register.

Innkeeper(s): Gary Anderson. Call for rates. 7 suites. Breakfast included in
rates. Types of meals: Full gourmet bkfst, early coffee/tea, gourmet lunch,
afternoon tea, snacks/refreshments, gourmet dinner and room service.
Restaurant on premises. Beds: QD. Cable TV, VCR, reading lamp, ceiling fan,
clock radio, telephone, desk, bathrobes and wireless Internet access in room.
Central air. Sauna, library, parlor games, fireplace and gift shop on premises.
Limited handicap access. Antiquing, bicycling, golf, hiking, museums, parks,
shopping and tennis nearby.

Location: Small town/country.

Publicity: Kansas Magazine, Dining out in Kansas, Wichita Eagle-Beacon,
Salina Journal, Hays Daily News, Denver Post, Midwest Living, Front Cover
Kansas Magazine Fall 2009, Hog Tails Harley Davidson Magazine,, KSN TV-
Wichita, KS, High Plains Public TV, Kansas Public TV Taste of Kansas and
Vintage Exercise room equipment featured in movie "Cinderella Man"

Certificate may be used: January-April, Sunday-Thursday, subject to availability.

Kentucky

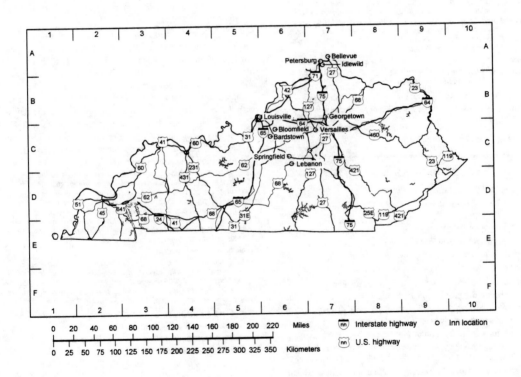

Bardstown   C6

Red Rose Inn

209 E Stephen Foster Ave
Bardstown, KY 40004-1513
(502)349-3003 Fax:(502)349-7322
Internet: www.redroseinnbardstown.com
E-mail: redroseinn@bardstown.com

Circa 1820. This late Victorian style home in the National
Register, is located in the historic district a block and a half
from Courthouse Square. Some of the rooms offer fireplaces, all
have cable TV and VCRs. (The inn's fireplaces were made by
Alexander Moore, the master craftsman of "My Old Kentucky
Home.") Full gourmet country breakfasts are served, often on
the outdoor terrace in view of the gardens, Koi pond and fountain. Smoking is not permitted.

Innkeeper(s): Audrey A. Simek. $99-139. 4 rooms with PB, 4 with FP, 1 con-
ference room. Breakfast and snacks/refreshments included in rates. Types of
meals: Full gourmet bkfst and early coffee/tea. Beds: KQT. Modem hook-up,
data port, cable TV, VCR, reading lamp, CD player, ceiling fan, clock radio,
telephone, desk and fireplace in room. Central air. Fax, copier, parlor games,
fireplace, hot tub/spa and gift shop on premises. Limited handicap access.
Antiquing, art galleries, golf, hiking, horseback riding, live theater, museums,
parks, shopping, tennis, distilleries and Civil War Monastery nearby.

Location: Historic town.

Publicity: *Kentucky's Best B&B 2001.*

"The food was delicious, our room very attractive and cozy."

Certificate may be used: November-April, Sunday-Thursday. April-November,
Monday-Thursday. Kentucky Derby, Bourbon Festival and holidays excluded.

Bellevue   A7

Christopher's B&B

604 Poplar St
Bellevue, KY 41073
(859)491-9354 (888)585-7085
Internet: www.christophersbb.com
E-mail: christophers@insightbb.com

Circa 1889. The former home of Bellevue Christian Church,
this unique inn sits in one of the area's three historic districts.
The spacious building was transformed into a delightful residence and B&B featuring the original hardwood floors and
stained-glass windows. Tastefully decorated and furnished in a
Victorian style, the gracious guest bedrooms and suite feature
Jacuzzi tubs and VCRs.

Innkeeper(s): Brenda Guidugli. $125-189. 3 rooms with PB, 3 with WP, 1
suite. Breakfast and snacks/refreshments included in rates. Beds: KQ.
Modem hook-up, cable TV, VCR, DVD, reading lamp, CD player, refrigerator,
ceiling fan, snack bar, clock radio, telephone, coffeemaker, desk, hair dryer,
bathrobes, bath amenities, wireless Internet access, iron/ironing board,
Jacuzzi, ironing board, iron, hair dryer and DVD/VHS movies in room. Central
air. Fax, copier, parlor games, fireplace, gift shop, continental plus breakfast
(weekdays only); full breakfast (weekends) and single/double Jacuzzi tubs on
premises. Limited handicap access. Amusement parks, antiquing, art galleries, fishing, golf, hiking, live theater, museums, parks, shopping, sporting
events, water sports, wineries, Newport Aquarium, Newport on the Levee,
Millennium Peace Bell, Riverbend outdoor concerts, Bengals Paul Brown
Stadium, Cincinnati Reds Great American Ball Park, National Underground
Railroad Freedom Center, Creation Museum, Cincinnati Zoo, Cincinnati
Museum Center, Paramount King's Island, BB Riverboats dinner/lunch cruises
and Restaurants with a river view nearby.

Location: City, in Taylor's Daughters Historic District, Near Ohio River.

Publicity: *Midwest Living, The Cincinnati Enquirer, The Kentucky Post,
Kentucky Monthly, Arts Across Kentucky, AAA Home Away, City Beat,
Kentucky Living, Cleveland Magazine, Kentucky Enquirer, Places To Go,*

Channel 12 Local News and *Arrington's Bed and Breakfast Journal 2003
& 2004 Book of Lists* (voted "One of the Top 15 B&Bs/Inns for Best
Design and Decor").

Certificate may be used: Sunday-Friday only, toward a two-night stay in JR
Jacuzzi Room, subject to availability. Excludes room and sales tax. During
week: Continental plus breakfast, Weekends: full breakfast early coffee/tea.

Bloomfield   C6

Springhill Plantation B&B

3205 Springfield Rd
Bloomfield, KY 40008
(502)252-9463 Fax:502-252-9463
Internet: www.springhillwinery.com
E-mail: wineshop@springhillwinery.com

Circa 1857. Poised on five acres of rolling hills and vineyards
in the Bardstown area of central Kentucky in Bloomfield,
Springhill Plantation Bed & Breakfast is a stately, historic antebellum mansion boasting Federal and Victorian architecture
with Greek and Egyptian influences. Relax on the patio or take
a complimentary wine-tasting tour. Visit the gift store featuring
the inn's award-winning wines and locally made arts, crafts and
food products. Themed guest suites are named after types of
wines and accented with fresh flowers seasonally. Early risers
appreciate coffee and tea available outside each room in the
morning before enjoying a hearty country breakfast. The surrounding Bluegrass region offers popular activities from horse
racing to the Bourbon Trail.

Innkeeper(s): Eddie and Carolyn ODaniel. $115-152. 6 rooms, 4 with PB.
Breakfast, Complimentary wine tasting in the gift shop and Coffee & tea
served outside suite each morning included in rates. Beds: KQ. Reading lamp,
stereo, refrigerator, ceiling fan, clock radio and bath amenities in room. Central
air. TV, VCR, DVD, fax, parlor games, telephone, fireplace, gift shop, Ironing
board, Hair dryer and Trundle bed upon request on premises. Amusement
parks, antiquing, art galleries, bicycling, fishing, golf, hiking, live theater,
museums, parks, shopping, sporting events, water sports, wineries, Racehorse
tracks, Bourbon distilleries, Railway museum and Gethsemani Abby nearby.

Location: Country.

Certificate may be used: November-March, Monday-Thursday.

Lebanon   C6

Myrtledene B&B

370 N Spalding Ave
Lebanon, KY 40033-1557
(270)692-2223 (800)391-1721
Internet: www.myrtledene.com
E-mail: myrtledene@windstream.net

Circa 1833. Once a Confederate general's headquarters at one
point during the Civil War, this pink brick inn, located at a
bend in the road, has greeted visitors entering Lebanon for
more than 150 years. When General John Hunt Morgan
returned in 1863 to destroy the town, the white flag hoisted to
signal a truce was flown at Myrtledene. A country breakfast
usually features ham and biscuits as well as the innkeepers'

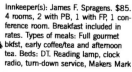

specialty, peaches and cream
French toast.

Innkeeper(s): James F. Spragens. $85.
4 rooms, 2 with PB, 1 with FP, 1 conference room. Breakfast included in
rates. Types of meals: Full gourmet
bkfst, early coffee/tea and afternoon
tea. Beds: DT. Reading lamp, clock
radio, turn-down service, Makers Mark

bourbon and bourbon chocolates in room. Air conditioning. VCR, library, parlor games, telephone and fireplace on premises. Antiquing, fishing, live theater, parks, shopping and water sports nearby.

Location: City.

Publicity: *Lebanon Enterprise, Louisville Courier-Journal, Lebanon/Marion County Kentucky and Sunnyside.*

"Our night in the Cabbage Rose Room was an experience of another time, another culture. Your skill in preparing and presenting breakfast was equally elegant! We'll be back!"

Certificate may be used: Sunday–Thursday, year-round.

Louisville B6

1853 Inn at Woodhaven

401 South Hubbard Lane
Louisville, KY 40207-4074
(502)895-1011 (888)895-1011 Fax:(502)896-0449
Internet: www.innatwoodhaven.com
E-mail: woodhavenb@aol.com

Circa 1853. This Gothic Revival, painted in a cheerful shade of yellow, is still much the same as it was in the 1850s, when it served as the home on a prominent local farm. The rooms still feature the outstanding carved woodwork, crisscross window designs, winding staircases, decorative mantels and hardwood floors. Guest quarters are tastefully appointed with antiques, suitable for their 12-foot, nine-inch tall ceilings.

Complimentary coffee and tea stations are provided in each room. There are several common areas in the Main House and Carriage House, and guests also take advantage of the inn's porches. Rose Cottage is octagon shaped and features a 25-foot vaulted ceiling, a king bed, fireplace, sitting area, double whirlpool, steam shower and wraparound porch. The National Register home is close to all of Louisville's attractions.

Innkeeper(s): Marsha Burton. $95-225. 8 rooms with PB, 3 with FP, 6 suites, 1 cottage. Breakfast included in rates. Types of meals: Full gourmet bkfst. Beds: KQ. Cable TV, reading lamp, stereo, ceiling fan, clock radio, telephone, desk, coffee, tea, hot chocolate facility, six with double whirlpool and four with steam shower in room. Air conditioning. Fax, copier, library, parlor games, fireplace and wireless Internet on premises. Handicap access. Amusement parks, antiquing, golf, live theater, parks, shopping, sporting events, tennis and water sports nearby.

Location: City.

Publicity: *Courier Journal, New York Times, WAVE and WHAS.*

Certificate may be used: Sunday-Thursday, January-March.

Petersburg A7

First Farm Inn

2510 Stevens Rd
Petersburg, KY 41080
(859) 586-0199
Internet: www.firstfarminn.com
E-mail: info@firstfarminn.com

Circa 1870. Elegantly updated, this 1870s farm house and historic wooden barn with tobacco rails are located just outside Cincinnati and surrounded by 21 acres of rolling hills, ponds stocked with bass, centuries-old maple trees, gardens and horses. Situated above the Ohio River, where Kentucky joins Ohio and Indiana, city sites and country pleasures are equally accessible. Spend two hours learning about horses and riding one of the friendly equines. Lessons begin with grooming, working in the arena, then graduating to a trail ride around the farm, along

the pond and through the woods. Schedule a massage with a licensed therapist in a spacious guest bedroom furnished with antique oak heirlooms. Indulge in a bountiful homemade breakfast of fresh fruit, assorted breads and an entree served family style around the big dining room table. Sit by the fire or play the grand piano. Relax in the outdoor hot tub; swing or rock on the veranda.

Innkeeper(s): Jen Warner & Dana Kisor. $90-162. 2 rooms with PB, 1 with FP. Breakfast and Full healthy balanced all-you-can eat breakfast included in rates. Types of meals: Full gourmet bkfst, veg bkfst, early coffee/tea, Swiss Rosti, FFI Pasta Carbonara, Multi-grain pancakes, Latkes, Quiches, Carmel-walnut French toast and more conventional breakfasts. Beds: QT. Data port, TV, VCR, DVD, reading lamp, stereo, refrigerator, ceiling fan, clock radio, telephone, desk, some with fireplace, hair dryer, bathrobes, bath amenities, wireless Internet access and iron/ironing board in room. Central air. Fax, copier, spa, stable, library, pet boarding, parlor games, gift shop, Horseback riding lessons, Porch swing, Porch rockers, Tire swing, Hammock, Cats, Dogs, Horses, Grand piano, Fishing pond and Hiking on premises. Limited handicap access. Amusement parks, antiquing, art galleries, canoeing/kayaking, downhill skiing, fishing, golf, hiking, horseback riding, live theater, museums, parks, shopping, sporting events, tennis, water sports, wineries, Perfect North ski slopes, Cincinnati Zoo, Newport Aquarium, shopping, Galerie of Chocolate outlet, Gap Outlet, Quilt shops, Big Bone Lick State Park (mammoth and mastodon bones found here in 1740s), 1830s vintage Rabbit Hash General Store, Historic Burlingotn shops, Cabin Arts Quilt Shop, Creation Museum, Behringer-Crawford Museum, Freedom Center, Center for Holocaust & Humanity Education, BB Riverboats (dinner and sightseeing cruises), James A. Ramage Civil War Museum, Railway Exposition Museum, Vent Haven Museum, Cathedral Basilica of the Assumption (replica of Notre Dame in Paris), Mainstrasse Village, Rabbit Hash General Store, World Peace Bell, Footlighters Community Theater, Stained Glass Theater, Ensemble Theater, Northern Kentucky Symphony, Cincinnati Pops, Turfway Park Thoroughbred Racing, Florence Speedway, Florence Freedom, Shadowbox Cabaret, Southgate House, Kentucky Haus Craft Gallery and nearby.

Location: Country. Country, near downtown Cincinnati.

Publicity: *Kentucky Monthly, Cincinnati Monthly, Chicago Herald, Columbus Parent, Kentucky Post, Cincinnati Enquirer, Louisville Courier-Journal, Indianapolis Monthly, City Beat, The Downtowner, The Community Recorders, Arrington's Inn Traveler named "Best for Rest and Relaxation" New Holland Tractor Magazine feature, Kentucky Educational Television program "Kentucky Life" April 2010; Channel 12 One Tank Trip, Channel 6 Travel specials, NPR Brainbrew, WBOB Travel Trips in Cincinnati, N. Kentucky Chamber Small Business Success finalist (2001, 2002, 2003, 2004 and 2005).*

Certificate may be used: Monday-Tuesday, December-March, last minute subject to availability.

Springfield C6

1851 Historic Maple Hill Manor B&B

2941 Perryville Rd (US 150 EAST)
Springfield, KY 40069-9611
(859) 336-3075 (800) 886-7546
Internet: www.maplehillmanor.com
E-mail: maplehillmanorbb@aol.com

Circa 1851. In a tranquil country setting on 14 acres, this Greek Revival mansion with Italianate detail is considered a Kentucky Landmark home and is listed in the National Register of Historic Places. Numerous architectural features include 14-foot ceilings, nine-foot windows, 10-foot doorways and a grand cherry spiral staircase. Guest bedrooms provide spacious serenity, and some boast fireplaces and or Jacuzzis.

Enjoy a full country breakfast, and then take a peaceful stroll through flower gardens and the fruit orchard, or relax on a patio swing or porch rocker. The local area has a rich abundance of attractions including Bardstown, Shaker Village, Bourbon, historic Civil War areas and Lincoln Trails. Lexington and Louisville are within an hour's drive.

Innkeeper(s): Todd Allen & Tyler Horton. $119-189. 7 rooms with PB, 4 with FP, 2 with WP, 4 suites, 1 conference room. Breakfast, afternoon tea and snacks/refreshments included in rates. Types of meals: Full gourmet bkfst, veg bkfst, early coffee/tea, lunch, gourmet dinner and 24-hour beverages. Beds: QDT. Modem hook-up, cable TV, VCR, DVD, reading lamp, CD player, ceiling fan, snack bar, clock radio, telephone, coffeemaker, turn-down service, desk, some with hot tub/spa, most with fireplace, hair dryer, bathrobes, bath amenities, wireless Internet access, iron/ironing board, Two with Jacuzzi tubs for two, Four with fireplace, Luxury linens, Turkish Towels, Alpaca-made Teddy Bears, Antique furnishings, Roll-away beds available, Satellite TV/VCR/DVD/CD player(includes movies/music) and Each Guest Room has a private bath in room. Central air. Fax, copier, library, parlor games, laundry facility, gift shop, orchard, grape vineyard, nature walking paths, flower gardens, fountains, patio, Gazebo, snack bar, complimentary homemade evening desserts, 24-hour beverage service, alpaca and llama farm, Fiber Studio & Farm Store and Murder Mystery Events on premises. Limited handicap access. Antiquing, art galleries, bicycling, canoeing/kayaking, fishing, golf, hiking, horseback riding, live theater, museums, parks, shopping, sporting events, tennis, water sports, wineries, My Old Kentucky Home & Golf Course State Park, Stephen Foster Musical, Kentucky Dinner Train, Historic Bardstown, Bernheim Forest, Kentucky Railway Museum, Civil War Museums, Lincoln Homestead State Park & Golf Course, Maywood Golf Course, Abbey of Gethsemani, Lincoln National Museum & Birthplace, Kentucky Bourbon Distilleries, Bourbon Heritage Center, Maker's Mark Bourbon Distillery, Heaven Hill Bourbon Distillery, Jim Beam Bourbon Distillery, Oscar Getz Museum of Whiskey History, Nettie Jarvis Antiques, Kentucky Wine Trail, Antique Shopping, U-Pick Farms, Horse Stables, Shaker Village at Pleasant Hill, Old Fort Harrod State Park, Willisburg Lake, Perryville Civil War Battlefield, Constitution Square, Big Red Stables, Taylorsville Lake, Green River Lake, Herrington Lake, Mt. Zion Covered Bridge, St. Catherine Motherhouse, Washington County Courthouse, Keeneland, Around the Town Carriage Rides, Basilica of St. Joseph, Old Talbott Tavern, Springhill Winery, Rolling Hills Vineyard, Chateau Du Viex Corbeau Winery, Amish/Mennonite Shops, Wickland, Wildlife/Natural History Museum, Lincoln Boyhood Home, Abraham Lincoln Museum, Lebanon Civil War Par, Loretto Motherhouse, Pioneer Playhouse Outdoor Dinner Theater, Ragged Edge Community Theater, Norton Centre for the Arts, Centre College, Campbellsville University and Central Kentucky Agritourism Association nearby.

Location: Country. Rural.

Publicity: *Southern Living, Danville's Advocate-Messenger, Springfield Sun, Cincinnati's Eastside Weekend and Enquirer, Louisville Courier Journal, Lexington Herald-Leader, Arts Across Kentucky, Kentucky Monthly, Arrington's Inn Traveler Magazine - "Best Breakfast in the Southeast" (2005), #1 in the U.S. as the B&B with the "Most Historic Charm" (2003 & 2004), "Kentucky's Best B&B" - Kentucky Monthly Magazine for 2004, "Best of the South" in 2009, TOP 10 Innkeepers in the U.S 2010-2011., Kentucky Educational Television feature on "Kentucky Life" Series., Springfield, Bardstown, Kentucky Farm Bureau Ag Report, Voted "Best Breakfast in the Southeast" for 2005 and 2006 by Arrington's B&B Journal, Voted #1 in the US as the B&B with the "most Historical Charm" and voted as "One of Kentucky's Finest B&Bs"*

"Thank you again for your friendly and comfortable hospitality."
Certificate may be used: April-October, Sunday-Thursday, Anytime November-March, subject to availability.

Versailles C7

Montgomery Inn Bed & Breakfast
270 Montgomery Ave
Versailles, KY 40383
(859)251-4103 Fax:(859)251-4104
Internet: www.montgomeryinnbnb.com
E-mail: innkeeper@montgomeryinnbnb.com

Circa 1911. Located in the horse capital of the world, Montgomery Inn Bed & Breakfast is a restored 1911 Victorian in the Kentucky Bluegrass region of Versailles. This family-operated inn offers concierge service and many upscale amenities with Southern hospitality. Munch on fresh-baked cookies in the Library upon check-in, swing on the wraparound porch or nap in the double hammock. Snacks, beverages, and access to a microwave and refrigerator are in the Media Room. Play the antique baby grand piano in the front parlor. Stay in a guest bedroom or spa suite with a two-person whirlpool tub, cotton sateen sheets, oversized Egyptian cotton towels and terry robes. A hearty gourmet breakfast is served in the GardenSide Dining Room. Dinner is available by reservation.

Innkeeper(s): Pam Matthews. $119-179. 10 rooms, 8 with FP, 10 with HT, 10 with WP, 10 total suites, including 2 two-bedroom suites, 1 conference room. Breakfast and snacks/refreshments included in rates. Types of meals: Full gourmet bkfst, early coffee/tea, gourmet lunch, picnic lunch, afternoon tea, hors d'oeuvres, wine and gourmet dinner. Beds: KQ. Cable TV, VCR, DVD, reading lamp, stereo, refrigerator, snack bar, clock radio, telephone, desk, hot tub/spa, hair dryer, bathrobes, bath amenities, wireless Internet access, iron/ironing board, 600-count sheets, Egyptian cotton towels, Wine & beverage set-ups, Periodicals and DVD movies in room. Central air. Fax, copier, library, parlor games, fireplace, laundry facility, gift shop and Complimentary snacks & beverages on premises. Antiquing, art galleries, bicycling, canoeing/kayaking, fishing, hiking, horseback riding, live theater, museums, parks, shopping, sporting events, tennis, wineries, Bourbon Distilleries, Candy factory, Keeneland Horse Racing, Kentucky Horse Park, Red Mile Harness Racing, Shaker Village, Berea Art & Craft Colony, Mammoth National Park, Diamond Caves and Kentucky River nearby.

Location: Village.

Certificate may be used: Not valid during Equestrian Events, subject to availability.

Louisiana

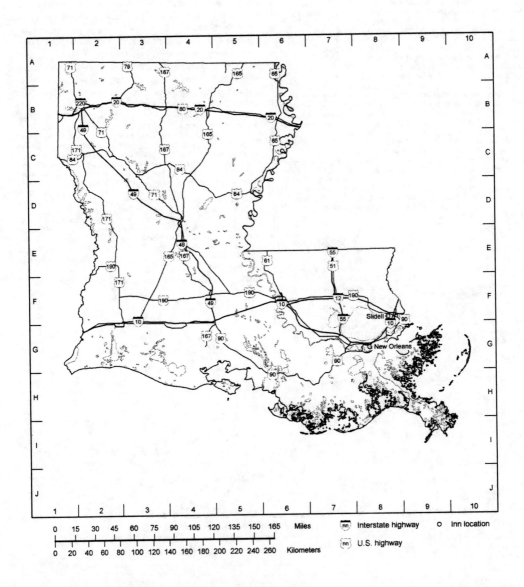

New Orleans
C3

Avenue Inn Bed & Breakfast

4125 St. Charles Avenue
New Orleans, LA 70115
(504)269-2640 (800)490-8542 Fax:(504)269-2641
Internet: www.avenueinnbb.com
E-mail: info@avenueinnbb.com

Circa 1891. Set among timeless oaks on famous St. Charles
Street is this 1891 Thomas Sully mansion. The inn has high ceilings and hardwood floors, and its 17 guest rooms are furnished
with period pieces. Come during Mardi Gras and you can sit on
the big front porch and watch the 18 Mardi Gras parades that
come down St. Charles Avenue. The French Quarter, Central
Business District, Convention Center as well as Tulane and
Loyola Universities are all within 1 3/4 miles. Antique shops,
restaurants and night spots are within walking distance.

Innkeeper(s): Joe & Bebe Rabhan. $89-399. 17 rooms with PB, 5 with FP.
Breakfast included in rates. Types of meals: Cont. Beds: KQD. Modem hook-
up, data port, cable TV, reading lamp, ceiling fan, clock radio, telephone,
desk and voice mail in room. Central air. VCR, fax, copier, library, parlor
games and fireplace on premises. Limited handicap access. Amusement
parks, antiquing, art galleries, bicycling, canoeing/kayaking, fishing, golf, live
theater, museums, parks, shopping, restaurants, cultural events, sightseeing
and day spa nearby.

Location: City.

Certificate may be used: Subject to availability, excludes holidays and
special events.

Fairchild House

1518 Prytania Street
New Orleans, LA 70130-4416
(504)524-0154 (800)256-8096 Fax:(504)568-0063
Internet: www.fairchildhouse.com
E-mail: info@fairchildhouse.com

Circa 1841. Situated in the oak-lined Lower Garden District of
New Orleans, this Greek Revival home was built by architect
L.H. Pilie. The house and its guest houses maintain a Victorian
ambiance with elegantly appointed guest rooms. Wine and
cheese are served upon guests' arrival. The bed & breakfast,
which is on the Mardi Gras parade route, is 17 blocks from the
French Quarter and 12 blocks from the convention center.
Streetcars are just one block away, as are many local attractions,
including paddleboat cruises, Canal Place and Riverwalk shopping, an aquarium, zoo, the St. Charles Avenue mansions and
Tulane and Loyola universities.

Innkeeper(s): Rita Olmo & Beatriz Aprigliano-Ziegler. $65-145. 5 rooms, 9
with PB, 1 suite. Breakfast included in rates. Types of meals: Cont plus.
Beds: KQD. Cable TV, refrigerator, clock radio, coffeemaker, desk and wireless
Internet access in room. Air conditioning. Fax, copier and telephone on
premises. Antiquing, art galleries, bicycling, golf, museums, parks, shopping,
Restaurants, Audubon Zoo, French Quarter and Walking Tours nearby.

Location: City.

"Accommodations were great; staff was great ... Hope to see y'all soon!"
Certificate may be used: June 1-Aug. 31. Please call during other seasons.

HH Whitney House on the Historic Esplanade

1923 Esplanade Avenue
New Orleans, LA 70116-1706
(504)948-9448 (800)924-9448
Internet: www.hhwhitneyhouse.com
E-mail: stay@hhwhitneyhouse.com

Circa 1865. The Civil War had barely ended when builders
broke ground on this elegant Italianate mansion. More than a
century later, much of its original charm has been maintained.
The intricate molding and plasterwork are of the highest quality. Common rooms with Victorian furnishings and appointments complement the architecture. Distinctive antiques
include an early 20th-century player piano. A decorative fireplace is featured in each guest bedroom. The Bride's Room,
with a lace-draped canopy bed, makes a spacious two- or three-
bedroom suite when combined with the Solarium or Groom's
rooms. The romantic Honeymoon Suite in the former servants'
quarters offers total privacy. Located in the Esplanade Ridge
historic district, the French Quarter is just a half-mile walk.

Innkeeper(s): Glen Miller/Randy Saizan. $75-259. 5 rooms, 3 with PB, 5
with FP. Breakfast and snacks/refreshments included in rates. Types of meals:
Full bkfst. Beds: Q. Cable TV, DVD, reading lamp, CD player, ceiling fan,
clock radio, hair dryer, bathrobes, bath amenities, wireless Internet access,
iron/ironing board, Flat-panel hi-def TV with DVD player and Room safe in
room. Central air. VCR, fax, spa, swimming, bicycles, parlor games, fireplace
and laundry facility on premises. Amusement parks, antiquing, art galleries,
bicycling, canoeing/kayaking, fishing, golf, horseback riding, live theater,
museums, parks, shopping, sporting events, tennis, French Quarter and fairgrounds nearby.

Location: City. Near French Quarter, Lakefront.

Certificate may be used: Last minute bookings, subject to availability.

Magnolia Mansion

2127 Prytania Street
New Orleans, LA 70130
(504)412-9500 Fax:(504)412-9502
Internet: www.magnoliamansion.com
E-mail: reserve@magnoliamansion.com

Circa 1857. Experience a high standard of opulence at this
upscale, adults-only, non-smoking bed & breakfast. It is the
perfect romantic getaway, quiet and peaceful weekend retreat,
or a wonderful place to celebrate an anniversary, birthday,
honeymoon or other special occasion. The Mansion is centrally located in what is considered to be "The Gateway To The
Garden District." It is just one block from St. Charles Ave.
streetcar on the Mardi Gras Parade Route and within minutes
of the French Quarter. Relax with friends or read a good book
on the wraparound veranda overlooking the enchanting courtyard surrounded by massive 150-year-old oak trees. Wake
each morning from a great night's sleep in a luxurious
themed guest bedroom to enjoy a continental breakfast in the
formal dining room. Visit the area's major attractions, including the Superdome; enjoy fine dining and ride on a
Mississippi River Paddlewheel.

Innkeeper(s): Hollie Vest. $119-399. 9 rooms with PB, 5 with FP, 2 with HT,
2 conference rooms. Continental Plus breakfast included in rates. Types of
meals: Cont plus, veg bkfst, early coffee/tea, snacks/refreshments, Hot
Breakfast Sandwiches are available upon requests and Complimentary Hot
Tea & Snack Bars available 24 hrs. . Beds: KQT. Modem hook-up, cable TV,
VCR, DVD, reading lamp, refrigerator, ceiling fan, snack bar, clock radio, telephone, desk, hair dryer, bathrobes, bath amenities, wireless Internet access,
iron/ironing board, Makeup mirrors, Valet/Clothes, Some rooms have desks

w/data ports as well and Black-out curtains in room. Central air. Fax, library, FREE local calls, Concierge service, Video/DVD/Book Library, WI-FI and Data Ports on premises. Amusement parks, antiquing, art galleries, beach, bicycling, canoeing/kayaking, fishing, golf, hiking, horseback riding, live theater, museums, parks, shopping, sporting events, tennis, water sports, wineries, Walking Tours, Bus Tours, Horse & Carriage Rides/Tours, St. Charles Street Car, Mardi Gras Parade Route & Restaurants, Deli's/Markets, French Quarter, Superdome, Convention Center and Riverwalk nearby.

Location: City. French Quarter.

Publicity: *American Airlines, American Way Inflight Magazine, Times Picayune, Off Beat Publications, Weddings With Style, Chris Rose Times Picayune Columnist, Live on Internet Talk Show and New Orleans Bride on Cox Cable.*

Certificate may be used: Sunday-Thursday, blackout dates and restrictions apply.

Sully Mansion - Garden District

2631 Prytania St
New Orleans, LA 70130-5944
(504)891-0457 (800)364-2414 Fax:(504)269-0793
Internet: www.sullymansion.com
E-mail: reservations@sullymansion.com

Circa 1890. This handsome Queen Anne Victorian, designed by its namesake, Thomas Sully, maintains many original features common to the period. A wide veranda, stained glass, heart-of-pine floors and a grand staircase are among the notable items. Rooms are decorated in a comfortable mix of antiques and more modern pieces. Sully Mansion is the only inn located in the heart of New Orleans' Garden District.

Innkeeper(s): Nancy & Guy Fournier. $89-200. 8 rooms with PB, 6 with FP. Breakfast and snacks/refreshments included in rates. Types of meals: Cont plus. Beds: KQDT. Cable TV, DVD, reading lamp, stereo, refrigerator, clock radio, telephone, desk, voice mail, bath amenities, wireless Internet access, iron/ironing board, guest refrigerator and "sully's satchel" home away from home medicine chest available to all guests in room. Air conditioning. Fax, copier, library, fireplace and Beautiful wraparound porch allows guests to savor the unique Garden District environment on premises. Amusement parks, antiquing, art galleries, bicycling, fishing, golf, horseback riding, live theater, museums, parks, shopping, sporting events, tennis, wineries, French Quarter, Audobon Zoo, Warehouse district and antique stores of Magazine Street nearby.

Location: City.

Publicity: *Houston Chronicle, Travel & Leisure, New Orleans Times Picayune, Los Angeles Times, Travel & Holiday, San Francisco Chronicle Richmond Times Dispatch and Independent film "Seizure" shot at the inn.*

"I truly enjoyed my stay at Sully Mansion—the room was wonderful, the pastries memorable."

Certificate may be used: Sunday-Wednesday excluding special events (New Years Eve, Sugar Bowl, Mardi Gras, Jazz Fest and Halloween). Not valid during Tulane graduation.

Terrell House

1441 Magazine St.
New Orleans, LA 70130
(504)247-0560 (866)261-9687 Fax:(504)247-0565
Internet: www.terrellhouse.com
E-mail: lobrien@terrellhouse.com

Circa 1858. Gracing the Lower Garden District in an historic area near the French Quarter, Terrell House is a grand three-story Italianate stucco-over-brick antebellum mansion in New Orleans, Louisiana. Relax in elegance and comfort on a porch, in the den or double parlors with period English and American antiques. Air-conditioned guest bedrooms with generous upscale amenities in the main house and the adjacent carriage house look out or open onto the courtyard with lush gardens, fountains and shaded sitting areas. The carriage house is furnished with locally handcrafted cypress furniture. Linger over a satisfying breakfast that reflects warm southern hospitality before exploring the popular sites of the city.

Innkeeper(s): Ed and Linda O'Brien. $125-250. 8 rooms with PB, 1 two-bedroom suite. Breakfast included in rates. Types of meals: Full bkfst, early coffee/tea, snacks/refreshments and hors d'oeuvres. Beds: KQT. Cable TV, reading lamp, ceiling fan, clock radio, coffeemaker, fireplace, hair dryer, bathrobes, bath amenities, wireless Internet access and iron/ironing board in room. Central air. DVD, fax, copier, bicycles, library and telephone on premises. Amusement parks, antiquing, art galleries, bicycling, fishing, golf, live theater, museums, parks, shopping, sporting events, Zoo, St Charles Streetcar, Convention Center and Riverwalk nearby.

Location: City. Near historic French Quarter.

Certificate may be used: July 5-September and December-January, subject to availability.

Maine

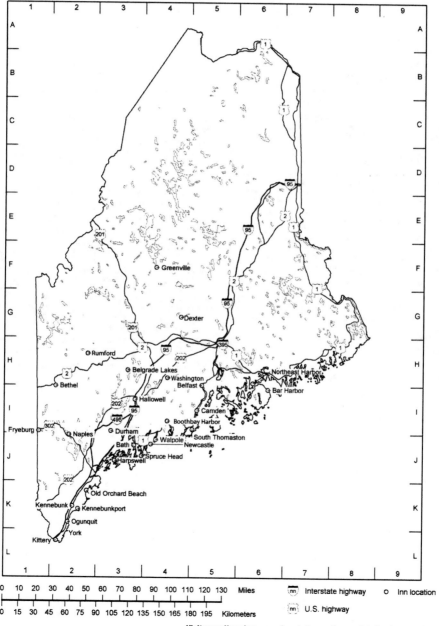

| 1 | 2 | 3 | 4 | 5 | 6 | 7 | 8 | 9 |

A
B
C
D
E
F
G
H
I
J
K
L

201

95

2

201

Greenville

Dexter

Rumford
2
95
202
395
2
95

Belgrade Lakes
Washington
Belfast
Bethel
2

Hallowell
202
95

Camden
495
Boothbay Harbor

Fryeburg
302
Naples
Durham
Bath
1
Walpole
South Thomaston
Newcastle
Harpswell
Spruce Head

Northeast Harbor

Bar Harbor

1

202
Old Orchard Beach

Kennebunk
Kennebunkport
Ogunquit
York
Kittery

| 1 | 2 | 3 | 4 | 5 | 6 | 7 | 8 | 9 |

0 10 20 30 40 50 60 70 80 90 100 110 120 130   Miles

0 15 30 45 60 75 90 105 120 135 150 165 180 195   Kilometers

(nn) Interstate highway   O Inn location

(nn) U.S. highway

Bar Harbor
I6

Primrose Inn-Historic Bar Harbor Bed and Breakfast

73 Mount Desert Street
Bar Harbor, ME 04609-1327
(207)288-4031 (877)TIME4BH Fax:(207)2888241
Internet: www.primroseinn.com
E-mail: relax@primroseinn.com

Circa 1878. Primrose Inn-Historic Bar Harbor Bed and
Breakfast in Maine is a romantic 1878 Victorian B&B perfectly
located a short stroll from Main Street and only a mile from
Acadia National Park. The inn features 15 spacious guest
rooms, all with private bathrooms, luxurious linens, select
antiques and period reproductions, air conditioning and flat-
panel TV/DVD. Many rooms feature gas fireplaces, spa tubs
and private porches. Enjoy a hearty full breakfast each morning
and gather for conversation during the popular Afternoon Tea
with fresh baked goods.

Innkeeper(s): Catherine and Jeff Shaw. $99-249. 15 rooms with PB, 6 with
FP, 5 with WP. Breakfast, afternoon tea and snacks/refreshments included in
rates. Types of meals: Full gourmet bkfst, early coffee/tea and Guests enjoy a
hearty full breakfast each morning with a choice of hot entrees served fireside
in the dining room or the outdoor wraparound front porch. Afternoon Tea features an assortment of freshly baked treats from the Primrose Inn's kitchen.
Guest refreshments at no additional charge "24/7." Beds: KQ. Cable TV,
DVD, CD player, ceiling fan, telephone, some with hot tub/spa, some with
fireplace, hair dryer, bathrobes, bath amenities, wireless Internet access,
iron/ironing board and Daily newspaper delivered to each room in room.
Central air. Fax, copier, library, parlor games, gift shop and Guest refreshments at no additional charge on premises. Antiquing, art galleries, beach,
bicycling, canoeing/kayaking, fishing, golf, hiking, horseback riding, live theater, museums, parks, shopping, tennis, water sports, wineries, Acadia
National Park, Whale Watching and Kayaking nearby.

Location: Mountains, ocean community, waterfront. Island.

Certificate may be used: May 21-27 and Oct. 18-30.

Bath
J3

Inn At Bath

969 Washington St
Bath, ME 04530-2650
(207)443-4294 Fax:(207)443-4295
Internet: www.innatbath.com
E-mail: innkeeper@innatbath.com

Circa 1835. Located in the heart of Bath's Historic District,
this Greek Revival home is surrounded by fabulous gardens.
Well-appointed, spacious guest bedrooms are furnished with
antiques. Some feature two-person Jacuzzis, wood-burning fireplaces, sofas, writing desks and private entrances. Breakfast
includes buttermilk blueberry pancakes, green chili egg puff,
pecan waffles with fresh fruit, homemade granola and organic
yogurt. Walk to the Kennebec River, the Chocolate Church Arts
Center or local shops, galleries and restaurants. Visit the Maine
Maritime Museum. Innkeeper Elizabeth will assist with arrang-
ing guided fishing trips; spotting bald eagles, ospreys and seals;
taking a lighthouse tour; finding the perfect lobster roll on a
dock or booking a sailing excursion.

Innkeeper(s): Elizabeth Knowlton. $150-190. 8 rooms with PB, 4 with FP, 1
suite. Breakfast included in rates. Types of meals: Full bkfst, veg bkfst and
early coffee/tea. Beds: KQDT. Cable TV, VCR, reading lamp, clock radio, telephone, some with hot tub/spa, some with fireplace, hair dryer, bath amenities, wireless Internet access, iron/ironing board, Fax and Computer available

for guests at no charge in room. Air conditioning. Fax, copier, bicycles and
parlor games on premises. Handicap access. Antiquing, art galleries, beach,
bicycling, canoeing/kayaking, cross-country skiing, fishing, golf, hiking, horseback riding, live theater, museums, parks, shopping, sporting events, tennis,
water sports, Some winters, great snow for Cross Country Skiing and
Downhill Skiing (about 2 hour drive) nearby.

Location: Coastal town.

Publicity: *House Beautiful.*

Certificate may be used: Nov. 1-May 15, Sunday-Thursday, excludes holiday
weeks and school weekends and graduations.

Belfast
H5

The Jeweled Turret Inn

40 Pearl St
Belfast, ME 04915-1907
(207)338-2304 (800)696-2304
Internet: www.jeweledturret.com
E-mail: info@jeweledturret.com

Circa 1898. This grand Victorian is named for the staircase
that winds up the turret, lighted by stained- and leaded-glass
panels and jewel-like embellishments. It was built for attorney
James Harriman. Dark pine beams adorn the ceiling of the den,
and the fireplace is constructed of bark and rocks from every
state in the Union. Elegant antiques furnish the guest rooms.
Guests can relax in one of the inn's four parlors, which are furnished with period antiques, wallpapers, lace and boast fireplaces. Some rooms have a ceiling fan and whirlpool tub or
fireplace. The verandas feature wicker and iron bistro sets and
views of the historic district. The inn is within walking distance
of the town and its shops, restaurants and the harbor.

Innkeeper(s): Cathy & Carl Heffentrager. $125-165. 7 rooms with PB, 1 with
FP, 1 with WP. Breakfast and afternoon tea included in rates. Types of meals:
Full gourmet bkfst, early coffee/tea, Crakers and cheese and sherry served
during social hour 5:30-6:30 pm. Beds: QDT. Reading lamp, ceiling fan,
clock radio, some with fireplace, bath amenities and one with whirlpool tub
in room. TV, parlor games and telephone on premises. Antiquing, art galleries, beach, bicycling, canoeing/kayaking, cross-country skiing, downhill skiing, fishing, golf, hiking, horseback riding, live theater, museums, parks,
shopping, tennis, water sports and wineries nearby.

Location: Small historic coastal town.

Publicity: *News Herald, Republican Journal, Waterville Sentinel, Los Angeles
Times, Country Living, Victorian Homes and The Saturday Evening Post.*

*"The ambiance was so romantic that we felt like we were on our
honeymoon."*

Certificate may be used: April, May and November, holidays excluded.

Belgrade Lakes
H3

Wings Hill Inn

PO Box 386
Belgrade Lakes, ME 04918-0386
(207)495-2400 (866)495-2400
Internet: wingshillinn.com
E-mail: innkeeper@wingshillinn.com

Circa 1800. Enjoy an ideal romantic getaway at this year-round
post and beam farmhouse in a picturesque lakefront village.
Relaxation comes easy by the fireplace in the Great Room or
the extensive screened wraparound porch overlooking the lake.
Savor afternoon tea with pastries. The guest bedrooms feature a
comfortable elegance. Start each day with a satisfying gourmet
breakfast. Intimate candlelit dining is available Thursday
through Sunday evenings. Hiking, fishing, boating, golf and

cross-country skiing are just outside the front door. Other popular New England sites and activities are an easy drive away.

Innkeeper(s): Christopher & Tracey Anderson. $115-195. 6 rooms with PB, 1 with WP. Breakfast and afternoon tea included in rates. Types of meals: Full bkfst and early coffee/tea. Beds: KQ. TV, VCR, reading lamp, ceiling fan, clock radio, hair dryer and iron/ironing board in room. Air conditioning. Library, parlor games, fireplace and gift shop on premises. Handicap access. Antiquing, cross-country skiing, downhill skiing, fishing, golf, hiking, shopping, sporting events and water sports nearby.

Certificate may be used: November-April, excluding holidays and special events.

Boothbay Harbor   14

Harbour Towne Inn on The Waterfront

71 Townsend Ave
Boothbay Harbor, ME 04538-1158
(207) 633-4300 (800) 722-4240
Internet: www.harbourtowneinn.com
E-mail: info@harbourtowneinn.com

Circa 1840. This Victorian inn's well-known trademark boasts that it is "the Finest B&B on the Waterfront." The inn's 12 air-conditioned rooms offer outside decks, and the Penthouse has an outstanding view of the har-

bor from its private deck. Breakfast is served in the inn's Sunroom, and guests also may relax in the parlor, which has a miniature antique library and a beautiful antique fireplace. A conference area is available for meetings. The inn's meticulous grounds include flower gardens and well-kept shrubs and trees. A wonderful new addition is a dock and float for sunning, sketches/painting, reading or hopping aboard a canoe, kayak or small boat. It's a pleasant five-minute walk to the village and its art galleries, restaurants, shops and boat trips. Special off-season packages are available. Ft. William Henry and the Fisherman's Memorial are nearby.

Innkeeper(s): Stefanie McElman and Patricia Richardson. $99-399. 8 rooms with PB, 1 two-bedroom suite. Breakfast and afternoon tea included in rates. Types of meals: Full gourmet bkfst, early coffee/tea, picnic lunch, snacks/refreshments and wine. Beds: KQ. Cable TV, VCR, reading lamp, CD player, refrigerator, ceiling fan, telephone, desk, hair dryer, bath amenities, wireless Internet access, iron/ironing board, free WiFi, satellite TV, most rooms with refrigerators, microwave ovens and free off street parking. Walking distance to downtown shops, restaurants and boats and galleries in room. Air conditioning. DVD, fax, copier, fireplace, most rooms have outside decks and we also have a waterfront dock and float on premises. Limited handicap access. Antiquing, art galleries, beach, bicycling, canoeing/kayaking, cross-country skiing, fishing, golf, hiking, horseback riding, live theater, museums, parks, shopping, sporting events, tennis, water sports, wineries, boating and trips to lighthouses nearby.

Location: Ocean community. Boothbay Harbor, Coastal Village, Oceanfront.

Certificate may be used: May-October, Sunday-Thursday, no holidays or special events, subject to availability.

Camden   15

Blue Harbor House, A Village Inn

67 Elm St
Camden, ME 04843-1904
(207)236-3196 (800)248-3196 Fax:(207)236-6523
Internet: www.blueharborhouse.com
E-mail: info@blueharborhouse.com

Circa 1810. Blue Harbor House is a classic village inn on the coast of Maine. This Camden bed and breakfast is comfortably elegant yet refreshingly casual. Historic charms blend well with

modern comforts. Relax in the parlor or on a front-porch rocker. Stroll to the picturesque harbor, dine on lobster and seafood chowder in the wonderful local restaurants, browse the art galleries and shop in the boutiques.

Inviting guest rooms or suites boast four-poster beds with soft linens, fireplaces, Jacuzzi tubs, robes and WiFi. Begin each day with a delicious breakfast offer-ing popular specialties that may include hazlenut waffles, blue-

berry pancakes with maple syrup and blueberry butter or porta-bella mushroom and gruyere omelet with Irish soda bread. Go on a windjammer cruise or take a day trip to Acadia National Park. Ask about special packages available.

Innkeeper(s): Annette and Terry Hazzard. $95-185. 11 rooms with PB, 3 with FP, 1 with HT, 4 total suites, including 2 two-bedroom suites, 1 conference room. Breakfast and afternoon tea included in rates. Types of meals: Full gourmet bkfst, early coffee/tea and wine. Beds: KQDT. Cable TV, VCR, reading lamp, refrigerator, clock radio, telephone, desk, hair dryer, bathrobes, bath amenities, wireless Internet access and iron/ironing board in room. Air conditioning. Fax, copier, library and parlor games on premises. Antiquing, art galleries, beach, bicycling, canoeing/kayaking, cross-country skiing, downhill skiing, fishing, golf, live theater, parks, shopping and water sports nearby.

Location: Ocean community. Coastal village.

Publicity: *Dallas Morning News, Discerning Traveler and Country Living.*

"I don't know when I've enjoyed my stay in a country inn more."

Certificate may be used: Anytime, November-March, subject to availability.

Captain Swift Inn

72 Elm St
Camden, ME 04843-1907
(207)236-8113 (800)251-0865 Fax:(207)230-0464
Internet: www.swiftinn.com
E-mail: swiftinn@roadrunner.com

Circa 1810. This inviting Federal-style home remains much as it did in the 19th century, including the original 12-over-12 windows and a beehive oven. The home's historic flavor has been diligently preserved and the original five fireplaces, handsome wide pine floors, restored moldings and exposed beams

add to the warm and cozy interi-or. Air-conditioned guest bed-rooms feature warm quilts on comfortable beds and private baths. On the first floor a guest bedroom is entirely handicapped accessible. A full and hearty breakfast is offered daily and includes specialties such as Blueberry French Toast or Sausage and Brie Casserole. Situated in Camden, the Captain Swift Inn is centrally located on the Mid-Coast of Maine to easily explore all that this scenic state has to offer.

Innkeeper(s): Norm & Linda Henthorn. $99-245. 8 rooms with PB, 4 with FP, 2 with WP, 2 suites. Breakfast and snacks/refreshments included in rates. Types of meals: Full bkfst, veg bkfst and early coffee/tea. Beds: KQT. Cable TV, reading lamp, refrigerator, ceiling fan, clock radio, coffeemaker, some with fireplace, hair dryer, wireless Internet access, 2 new suites featuring loft, fire-places, whirlpool tubs and King-size beds in room. Air conditioning. Fax and library on premises. Handicap access. Antiquing, art galleries, beach, bicy-cling, canoeing/kayaking, cross-country skiing, downhill skiing, fishing, golf, hiking, horseback riding, live theater, museums, parks, shopping, water sports, wineries, schooner and windjammer cruises, lighthouses and compli-mentary gym passes nearby.

Location: Maine Seaport.

Certificate may be used: Anytime, November-April, subject to availability.

Hartstone Inn

41 Elm St
Camden, ME 04843-1910
(207)236-4259 (800)788-4823 Fax:(207)236-9575
Internet: www.hartstoneinn.com
E-mail: info@hartstoneinn.com

Circa 1835. This historic home was transformed into a Victorian at the turn-of-the-century with the addition of large bay windows and a mansard roof. The inn is located in the heart of the village of Camden and is within walking distance of the harbor. Romantic guest rooms offer amenities such as fireplaces, lace canopy beds, designer linens, fresh robes, candlelight, flowers and chocolate truffles. The innkeepers careers were in luxury hotels and Michael was awarded Caribbean Chef of the Year. He prepares the inn's gourmet breakfasts which may include Maine Lobster and Asparagus Quiche or perhaps, Atlantic Smoked Salmon Benedict. Dinners are also available and all meals are presented elegantly on fine china and crystal.

Innkeeper(s): Mary Jo & Michael Salmon. $105-280. 21 rooms with PB, 12 with FP, 10 with WP, 11 total suites, including 1 two-bedroom suite, 2 guest houses, 1 conference room. Breakfast and afternoon tea included in rates. Types of meals: Full gourmet bkfst, veg bkfst, early coffee/tea, picnic lunch, wine and gourmet dinner. Restaurant on premises. Beds: KQT. Cable TV, DVD, reading lamp, clock radio, telephone, coffeemaker, desk, bathrobes, bath amenities, wireless Internet access and two with Cable TV in room. Air conditioning. Fax, copier, spa, library, pet boarding, parlor games, fireplace and gift shop on premises. Antiquing, art galleries, beach, bicycling, canoeing/kayaking, cross-country skiing, downhill skiing, fishing, golf, hiking, horseback riding, live theater, museums, parks, shopping, tennis, water sports, wineries, Furniture Maker, Lighthouses and Schooner rides nearby.

Location: Ocean community. Village.

Publicity: Gourmet, Discerning Traveler, Shape Magazine, Boston Globe, Rachael Ray, New England Travel, Yankee, Down East, Boston Travel Magazine, Travel & Leisure, Food & Wine, Maine Explorers Guide, Fodors, Maine 207 and PBS.

"When can I move in?"

Certificate may be used: November-June 15, excluding holidays.

Lord Camden Inn

24 Main Street
Camden, ME 04843
(207)236-4325 (800)336-4325 Fax:(207)236-7141
Internet: www.lordcamdeninn.com
E-mail: info@lordcamdeninn.com

Circa 1893. Lord Camden Inn, a fine luxury boutique inn, has been extensively renovated to offer pampering new amenities while retaining its classic, richly elegant heritage. Adorning the coastal village of Camden, Maine, it boasts award-winning hospitality and comfort. Work out in the Fitness Room and schedule in-room spa services. An assortment of lavish guest bedrooms and suites offer modern-day comfort and a warm and inviting ambiance. Sleep in a Suite Dreams Bed by a gas fireplace and private balcony overlooking the Megunticook River or Camden Harbor and Penobscot Bay. Some rooms are ADA accessible, child and pet friendly. Linger over a breakfast buffet before embarking on the scenic sites and historic attractions of the area. This B&B is a popular choice for intimate weddings and romantic or family getaways.

Innkeeper(s): Megan Stilwell. $99-299. 36 rooms with PB, 11 with FP, 2 with WP, 7 suites, 1 conference room. Breakfast and snacks/refreshments included in rates. Types of meals: Full bkfst, early coffee/tea and wine. Beds: KQD. Cable TV, DVD, CD player, refrigerator, clock radio, telephone, coffeemaker, desk, voice mail, some with fireplace, hair dryer, bath amenities, wireless Internet access and iron/ironing board in room. Air conditioning. Fax,

copier and Complimentary buffet breakfast on premises. Handicap access. Antiquing, art galleries, beach, bicycling, canoeing/kayaking, cross-country skiing, downhill skiing, fishing, golf, hiking, museums, parks, shopping, tennis, water sports, wineries and Schooner & Kayak Trips nearby.

Location: Ocean community.

Publicity: Portland Magazine, Downeast Magazine and New York Times.

Certificate may be used: Nov.1-June 15.

Dexter G4

Brewster Inn of Dexter, Maine

37 Zion's Hill Rd
Dexter, ME 04930-1122
(207)924-3130 Fax:(207)924-9768
Internet: www.brewsterinn.com
E-mail: innkeeper@brewsterinn.com

Circa 1860. Formerly the mansion home of State Governor Owen Brewster who was portrayed in the award-winning movie, "The Aviator," this B&B continues to exude a classic elegance. Located on two acres in the Highlands with an ornamental pond as well as rose and perennial gardens, the historic Brewster Inn of Dexter, Maine is listed in the National Register. Air-conditioned guest rooms and suites are distinctive and some feature a whirlpool tub and/or gas fireplace. Linger over a continental-plus buffet breakfast with a daily hot dish before walking to local shops or Wassookeag Lake. Bangor and the scenic Moosehead Lake and Mount Katahdin region are less than an hour's drive. Enjoy Camden, Bar Harbor, Freeport or Portland within two-hours. Relax on one of the covered porches.

Innkeeper(s): Mark and Judith Stephens. $69-149. 9 rooms with PB, 2 with FP, 2 with WP, 1 two-bedroom suite. Breakfast included in rates. Types of meals: Full bkfst, veg bkfst, early coffee/tea, wine, dinner, Gluten free, Vegetarian, nut free and lactose free. Beds: KQDT. Cable TV, DVD, reading lamp, ceiling fan, clock radio, desk, some with fireplace, hair dryer, bathrobes, bath amenities, wireless Internet access and iron/ironing board in room. Air conditioning. VCR, fax, copier, bicycles, library, parlor games, telephone, laundry facility and gift shop on premises. Handicap access. Antiquing, beach, bicycling, canoeing/kayaking, cross-country skiing, downhill skiing, fishing, golf, hiking, horseback riding, live theater, museums, parks, shopping, water sports, Moose watching. Whitewater rafting, Snowmobiling, Snowshoeing, Public beach, Birdwatching and Dog sledding nearby.

Location: Country, mountains. Small town.

Publicity: Bangor Daily News, People, Places & Plants, Portland Press Herald, Sunday Maine, Telegram, Portland magazine, HGTV "If Walls Could Talk" and Governor and Senator Owen Brewster who was the owner of the property was portrayed in "The Aviator"

Certificate may be used: Anytime, subject to availability, excludes holidays.

Durham I3

Royalsborough Inn at the Bagley House

1290 Royalsborough Rd
Durham, ME 04222-5225
(207)353-6372 (800)765-1772 Fax:(207)353-5878
Internet: www.royalsboroughinn.com
E-mail: royalsboro@suscom-maine.net

Circa 1772. Royalsborough Inn at the Bagley House is surrounded by six acres of fields and woods. This Durham, Maine bed and breakfast boasts a peaceful country setting, yet near enough to easily shop the popular outlets stores of downtown Freeport. Relax in the fireside living room with adjoining library in the main house or sit by the wood-burning stove in the common room of the carriage house which also features spacious suites with gas log fireplaces. The main house guest rooms include electric log stoves. Antiques and crafted furnishings are accented by hand-sewn quilts and pleasurable amenities that include robes, spring water and chocolates for pampering accommodations. Savor a multi-course gourmet breakfast and schedule an afternoon massage/spa treatment. Take a drive along the rocky shoreline of mid-coast Maine and explore the area museums and lighthouses.

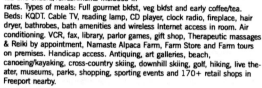

Innkeeper(s): Marianne and Jim Roberts. $135-175. 7 rooms with PB, 7 with FP, 1 conference room. Breakfast, afternoon tea and snacks/refreshments included in rates. Types of meals: Full gourmet bkfst, veg bkfst and early coffee/tea. Beds: KQDT. Cable TV, reading lamp, CD player, clock radio, fireplace, hair dryer, bathrobes, bath amenities and wireless Internet access in room. Air conditioning. VCR, fax, library, parlor games, gift shop, Therapeutic massages & Reiki by appointment, Namaste Alpaca Farm, Farm Store and Farm tours on premises. Handicap access. Antiquing, art galleries, beach, canoeing/kayaking, cross-country skiing, downhill skiing, golf, hiking, live theater, museums, parks, shopping, sporting events and 170+ retail shops in Freeport nearby.

Location: Country.

"I had the good fortune to stumble on the Bagley House. The rooms are well-appointed and the innkeepers are charming."

Certificate may be used: November-June, Sunday-Thursday.

Greenville   F4

Greenville Inn

40 Norris Street
Greenville, ME 04441-1194
(207)695-2206 (888)695-6000
Internet: www.greenvilleinn.com
E-mail: innkeeper@greenvilleinn.com

Circa 1885. Lumber baron William Shaw built this inn, which sits on a hill overlooking Moosehead Lake and the Squaw Mountains. The inn includes many unique features. Ten years

were needed to complete the embellishments on the cherry and mahogany paneling, which is found throughout the inn. A spruce tree is painted on one of the leaded-glass windows on the stairway landing. The inn's six fireplaces are adorned with carved mantels, English tiles and mosaics. The inn's dining room is ideal for a romantic dinner. Fresh, seasonal ingredients fill the ever-changing menu, and the dining room also offers a variety of wine choices.

Innkeeper(s): Terry & Jeff Johannemann. $100-450. 14 rooms with PB, 6 with FP, 1 with WP, 4 two-bedroom suites, 6 cottages, 2 conference rooms. Breakfast included in rates. Types of meals: Country bkfst, veg bkfst, early coffee/tea, picnic lunch, wine and gourmet dinner. Restaurant on premises. Beds: KQD. Cable TV, VCR, DVD, reading lamp, stereo, refrigerator, ceiling fan, coffeemaker, desk, some with hot tub/spa, some with fireplace, hair dryer, bathrobes, bath amenities, wireless Internet access, iron/ironing board, Private en-suite bathrooms,exclusive toiletries,seasonal packages & tours available, private entrances, private sitting rooms, gourmet breakfast and private breakfast tables in room. Air conditioning. Copier, spa, library, parlor games, telephone, gift shop, Hearty buffet breakfast, private breakfast tables, fine dining restaurant, full service bar, extensive wine cellar, wrap-around veranda, private porches, two historic sitting rooms and pantry with coffee maker on premises. Limited handicap access. Antiquing, art galleries, beach, bicycling, canoeing/kayaking, cross-country skiing, downhill skiing, fishing, golf, hiking, horseback riding, live theater, museums, parks, shopping, tennis,

water sports, snowmobiling, leaf peeping, whitewater rafting, moose safaris, mountain climbing, sea plane rides, ice fishing, dog sledding, snowshoeing and waterfall tours nearby.

Location: Country, mountains. On top of mountain, overlooking lake, town and mountains. Walking distance to town.

Publicity: *USA Today June 2011 recommended "Anniversary Getaway" Yankee Magazine (2008), One of the five "Best of New England B&Bs" (2007 and 2008), Arrington's Book of Lists (2006), Travel & Leisure, Travel Holiday, Conde Nast-Johansens Recommended Hotels, Inns & Resorts, The Washington Post, Down East Magazine, Portland Press Herald, The Providence Sunday Journal, The Boston Sunday Globe, Morning Sentinel, Aero Zambia Magazine, Gray's Sporting Journal, A Sports Afield Guide, Charleston's Free Time, National Geographic Guide to America's Hidden Corners, Maine Times, Portland Monthly, Bangor Daily News, Channel 2, NBC/Bangor and Channel 5, ABC/Bangor and voted "New England - Best Places to Stay"*

"The fanciest place in town. It is indeed a splendid place."

Certificate may be used: Nov. 1-April 30.

Pleasant Street Inn

26 Pleasant St
Greenville, ME 04441
(207)695-3400 Fax:(207)695-2004
Internet: www.pleasantstreetinn.com
E-mail: innkeeper@pleasantstinn.com

Circa 1889. Situated at the gateway to the Great North Woods, this grand Queen Anne Victorian is a historic gem with rare Tiger Oak woodwork in the foyer, staircase and main parlor. The eclectic décor includes original artwork and antiques. Gather in the entertainment parlor, or in the fourth floor Tower Room with panoramic views of the mountains, village and lake. Romantic and elegant guest bedrooms provide restful retreats. Several rooms may be adjoined as suites. Early risers can visit the Butler's Pantry for a hot beverage before a hearty breakfast served by the fireplace in the dining room or on the huge wraparound porch. Open year-round, it is a short walk to the pubs, shops and restored steamship Katahdin. The East Cove of Moosehead Lake is only half a block away.

Innkeeper(s): Mary and Jim Bobletz. $90-160. 6 rooms, 4 with PB, 2 two-bedroom suites. Breakfast and snacks/refreshments included in rates. Types of meals: Country bkfst and dinner. Beds: QT. Reading lamp, CD player, clock radio, fireplace, hair dryer, bath amenities and wireless Internet access in room. TV, VCR, DVD, fax, parlor games, telephone and Wireless computer hook up on premises. Antiquing, beach, bicycling, canoeing/kayaking, cross-country skiing, downhill skiing, fishing, golf, hiking, horseback riding, museums, parks, shopping, tennis, water sports, moose safaris, snowmobiling, dogsledding, scenic floatplane ridesWater Sports,Snowmobiling,Leaf Peeping,Whitewater Rafting,Moose Safaris,Mountain Climbing,Sea Plane Rides, Ice Fishing,Dog Sledding ,Snowshoeing and nearby.

Location: Country, mountains.

Publicity: *Boston Globe and Port City Life Magazine.*

Certificate may be used: November-May 15, excluding holidays.

Hallowell   I3

Maple Hill Farm B&B Inn

11 Inn Road
Hallowell, ME 04347
(207)622-2708 (800)622-2708 Fax:(207)622-0655
Internet: www.MapleBB.com
E-mail: stay@MapleBB.com

Circa 1906. See much of Maine from Maple Hill Farm Bed & Breakfast Inn and Conference Center in the four-season location of Hallowell, near Augusta. This award-winning, eco-friendly B&B spans 130 acres of wildflower fields, pastures, woods, a

pond and more than 800 neighboring acres of public land. Ask for a trail map to hike, walk, run, snowshoe or cross-country ski. Relax on a hammock or chair in the shade of a maple tree or on the front porch. Sit by the fire in the living room, sip a locally brewed beer in the full-service bar and use the well-equipped guest kitchen. This renovated Victorian house boasts guest rooms that may include a double whirlpool tub, fireplace and secluded deck. A custom country breakfast uses fresh eggs from the farm. Maple Hill is a certified environmental leader with comprehensive renewable energy systems and daily green practices.

Innkeeper(s): Scott Cowger & Vince Hannan. $90-205. 8 rooms with PB, 5 with FP, 4 with WP, 3 conference rooms. Breakfast and afternoon tea included in rates. Types of meals: Country bkfst, early coffee/tea, snacks/refreshments, wine and Full custom catering on request. Beds: KQD. Modem hook-up, cable TV, VCR, DVD, reading lamp, CD player, clock radio, telephone, desk, some with hot tub/spa, voice mail, most with fireplace, hair dryer, bath amenities, wireless Internet access, iron/ironing board, three with private decks and four with large whirlpool tubs in room. Air conditioning. Fax, copier, library, parlor games, gift shop, Common guest kitchen with Refrigerator, Microwave, Sink, Plates, Silverware, Glasses, Anytime Coffee, Tea, Cocoa and Home-baked goodies on premises. Handicap access. Antiquing, art galleries, bicycling, canoeing/kayaking, cross-country skiing, fishing, golf, hiking, live theater, museums, parks, shopping, water sports, State Capitol building and Maine State Museum nearby.

Location: Country. Spacious country farm.

Publicity: *An Explorer's Guide to Maine, The Forecaster, Portland Press Herald, Kennebec Journal, Maine Times, Travel and Leisure "Special Hotels" issue as one of 30 Great U.S. Inns, Editor's Pick in the 2002 & 2003 Yankee Magazine Travel Guide to New England and See web site for link to numerous recent articles.*

"You add many thoughtful touches to your service that set your B&B apart from others, and really make a difference. Best of Maine, hands down!" — Maine Times"

Certificate may be used: May-October, Sunday-Wednesday. November-April, anytime, but not both Friday and Saturday. Discount is off rack rates. Please inquire.

Harpswell   J3

Harpswell Inn

108 Lookout Point Rd
Harpswell, ME 04079
(207)833-5509 (207)800-8435509 Fax:(207)833-2437
Internet: www.harpswellinn.com
E-mail: reservations@harpswellinn.com

Circa 1761. Originally the cookhouse of the shipyard, Harpswell Inn was built in 1761 as a three-story Colonial at Lookout Point on a knoll overlooking the cove in Harpswell, Maine. Now completely renovated, this inn is furnished with antiques and offers pleasant surroundings on more than two acres with oak-shaded lawns. Watch the sunsets over Middle Bay from the front porch. Play pool in the Billiards Room or do a jigsaw puzzle in the Great Room. The Middle Bay Room is perfect for special events and meetings. Stay in a gracious guest bedroom or suite that may include a gas fireplace, private ocean-view deck, Jacuzzi or clawfoot tub and skylights. Start each day with Chef Moseley's famous breakfast in the dining room.

Innkeeper(s): Anne and Richard Moseley. $110-249. 12 rooms, 10 with PB, 5 with FP, 2 with WP, 3 suites, 4 cottages, 1 conference room. Breakfast included in rates. Types of meals: Full bkfst and Evening meals for overnight function room guests. Beds: KQT. Ceiling fan, telephone, some with fireplace, hair dryer, wireless Internet access, iron/ironing board, Water views and 6 pri-

vate decks in room. Air conditioning. TV, fax, copier, New function room, Wireless Internet access, Picnic tables and Kayaks on premises. Antiquing, art galleries, beach, bicycling, canoeing/kayaking, cross-country skiing, fishing, golf, hiking, live theater, museums, parks, shopping, sporting events, tennis, water sports, Swimming and Tennis nearby.

Location: Ocean community, waterfront.

"A gracious, luxurious home in a most wonderful setting."

Certificate may be used: mid-October though mid-May, subject to availability and discount must be mentioned when making the actual reservation.

Kennebunk   K2

Lake Brook Bed & Breakfast

57 Western Ave, Lower Village
Kennebunk, ME 04043
(207)590-4275
Internet: www.lakebrookbb.com
E-mail: carolyn@lakebrookbb.com

Circa 1900. This pleasant old farmhouse is situated on a tidal brook. Comfortable rockers offer an inviting rest on the wraparound porch where you can enjoy the inn's flower gardens that trail down to the marsh and brook. Gourmet breakfasts are served. Walk to Kennebunkport's Dock Square and lower village to visit fine galleries, shops and restaurants.

Innkeeper(s): Carolyn A. McAdams. $95-150. 3 rooms with PB, 1 suite. Breakfast included in rates. Types of meals: Full gourmet bkfst. Beds: QD. Reading lamp, ceiling fan, clock radio and kitchen in suite available July and August only in room. Air conditioning. Telephone on premises. Antiquing, cross-country skiing, fishing, golf, live theater, parks, shopping, tennis, water sports and historical seaport nearby.

Location: Country village.

"Truly wonderful atmosphere."

Certificate may be used: Anytime, subject to availability, phone reservations only. 207-590-4275.

The Kennebunk Inn

45 Main St
Kennebunk, ME 04043-1888
(207)985-3351 Fax:(207)985-8865
Internet: www.thekennebunkinn.com
E-mail: info@thekennebunkinn.com

Circa 1799. Built in 1799 and serving guests since the 1920s, this historic inn offers full-service hospitality. Feel welcomed in the Phineas Cole Parlour. Guest bedrooms are named after presidents and their first ladies. Two pet-friendly rooms and three family suites are available. For a special treat, make dinner reservations at Academe, the inn's fine dining restaurant. Chef-owners, Brian and Shanna both graduates of the Culinary Institute of America, will tantalize and delight with creativity and execution. Lunch and dinner pub fare is available in The Tavern. The Baitler Board Room is perfect for special events. Free beach passes are provided.

Innkeeper(s): Brian & Shanna O'Hea. $85-120. 22 rooms with PB, 1 with FP, 3 suites, 1 conference room. Types of meals: Early coffee/tea. Restaurant on premises. Beds: KQDT. Cable TV, VCR, reading lamp, clock radio, telephone and desk in room. Air conditioning. Fax, copier, library, pet boarding, fireplace and online access on premises. Handicap access. Amusement parks, antiquing, cross-country skiing, fishing, golf, live theater, parks, shopping, sporting events, tennis and water sports nearby.

Publicity: *Down East Magazine.*

Certificate may be used: Weekdays only June and September, Oct. 15-May 15. Excludes all holidays, subject to availability.

Kennebunkport   K2

1802 House

15 Locke Street
Kennebunkport, ME 04046-1646
(207)967-5632 (800)932-5632
Internet: www.1802inn.com
E-mail: info@1802inn.com

Circa 1802. The rolling fairways of Cape Arundel Golf Course, old shade trees and secluded gardens create the perfect setting for this historic 19th-century farmhouse. Located along the gentle shores of the Kennebunk River, the inn is accentuated by personal service and attention to detail. Romantic guest bedrooms offer four-poster canopy beds, two-person whirlpool tubs and fireplaces. The luxurious three-room Sebago Suite tucked into a private wing is a favorite choice. Homemade specialties and regional delights are part of a gourmet breakfast served in the sunlit dining room. Popular Dock Square is within walking distance for browsing in boutiques and art galleries. Golf packages are available.

Innkeeper(s): Linda and Jay. $146-376. 6 rooms with PB, 5 with FP, 4 with WP, 1 three-bedroom suite. Breakfast and snacks/refreshments included in rates. Types of meals: Full gourmet bkfst, veg bkfst, early coffee/tea, afternoon tea, GoBag breakfasts for guests with early commitments, In-room gourmet fruit & cheese platters, Hand-dipped chocolate-covered strawberries and Holiday treats. Beds: Q. Cable TV, VCR, reading lamp, CD player, clock radio, most with hot tub/spa, most with fireplace, hair dryer, bathrobes, bath amenities, wireless Internet access, Whirlpool tub (most), fireplaces (most), bottled water, gourmet chocolates and luxury bath amenities in room. Air conditioning. Fax, parlor games, telephone and gift shop on premises. Limited handicap access. Antiquing, art galleries, beach, bicycling, canoeing/kayaking, cross-country skiing, fishing, golf, hiking, horseback riding, live theater, museums, parks, shopping, tennis, water sports, wineries, Summer theater, Schooner trips, Lighthouse & harbor tours, Horse & carriage rides, Horse-drawn sleigh rides, Whale watches, Lobster cruises, Historic village tours and Nature preserves nearby.

Location: Ocean community. On the Cape Arundel Golf Course.

Publicity: *Down East Magazine, Golf Digest and Modern Bride.*

Certificate may be used: Sunday-Thursday, November and January-March-April-May.

Kittery   L2

Enchanted Nights B&B

29 Wentworth St
Kittery, ME 03904-1720
(207)439-1489
Internet: www.enchantednights.org

Circa 1890. The innkeepers bill this unique inn as a "Victorian fantasy for the romantic at heart." Each of the guest rooms is unique, from the spacious rooms with double whirlpool tubs and fireplaces to the cozy turret room. A whimsical combination of country French and Victorian decor permeates the interior. Wrought-iron beds and hand-painted furnishings add to the ambiance. Breakfasts, often with a vegetarian theme, are served with gourmet coffee in the morning room on antique floral china.

Innkeeper(s): Nancy Bogenberger & Peter

Lamandia. $52-300. 8 rooms, 6 with PB, 4 with FP, 2 conference rooms. Breakfast included in rates. Types of meals: Full gourmet bkfst, veg bkfst and early coffee/tea. Beds: KQDT. Cable TV, VCR, reading lamp, refrigerator, ceiling fan, clock radio, microwave, five have whirlpools and four have fireplaces in room. Air conditioning. Telephone and refrigerator on premises. Handicap access. Antiquing, art galleries, beach, bicycling, canoeing/kayaking, golf, hiking, horseback riding, live theater, museums, parks, shopping, sporting events, tennis, water sports, wineries, outlet shopping, historic homes, whale watching and harbor cruises nearby.

Location: City, ocean community.

"The atmosphere was great. Your breakfast was elegant. The breakfast room made us feel we had gone back in time. All in all it was a very enjoyable stay."

Certificate may be used: Nov. 1-April 30, Sunday-Thursday. No holidays.

Naples   J2

Augustus Bove House

11 Sebago Rd
Naples, ME 04055
(207)693-6365 (888)806-6249
Internet: www.naplesmaine.com
E-mail: augbovehouse@roadrunner.com

Circa 1820. A long front lawn nestles up against the stone foundation and veranda of this house, once known as the Hotel Naples, one of the area's summer hotels in the 1800s. In the 1920s, the inn was host to a number of prominent guests, including Enrico Caruso, Joseph P. Kennedy and Howard Hughes. The guest rooms are decorated in a Colonial style and modestly furnished with antiques. Many rooms provide a view of Long Lake. A fancy country breakfast is provided.

Innkeeper(s): David & Arlene Stetson. $99-250. 10 rooms with PB, 3 suites. Breakfast and afternoon tea included in rates. Types of meals: Full bkfst and early coffee/tea. Beds: KQT. Cable TV, VCR, DVD, reading lamp, CD player, refrigerator, clock radio, telephone, coffeemaker, turn-down service, hair dryer, bathrobes, bath amenities, wireless Internet access and iron/ironing board in room. Central air. Fax, copier, spa, library, fireplace and canoe and kayak on premises. Limited handicap access. Antiquing, beach, bicycling, canoeing/kayaking, cross-country skiing, downhill skiing, fishing, golf, hiking, horseback riding, live theater, parks, shopping, water sports, wineries and boat rentals at 5 marinas nearby.

Location: Waterfront.

Publicity: *Brighton Times, Yankee Magazine and Quality Travel Value Award.*

"Beautiful place, rooms, and people."

Certificate may be used: Sunday-Thursday, must mention certificate before making reservation.

Newcastle   J4

Tipsy Butler B&B

11 High St
Newcastle, ME 04553
(207)563-3394
Internet: www.thetipsybutler.com
E-mail: innkeeper@thetipsybutler.com

Circa 1845. Sprawled on two acres of lawns with gardens bordering the Greek Revival house, this bed and breakfast is open year-round in a delightful coastal village. Sit on one of the two-story covered front porches. Relax with a good book or try your hand at croquet. Spacious, air-conditioned guest bedrooms on all three floors boast views of the twin villages of Damariscotta and Newcastle. Stay in a room with a King-size fourpost bed, floor to ceiling windows or clawfoot tub. Savor the fragrance of hot coffee and a home-cooked breakfast every morning. Begin with a pastry and fresh fruit then linger over a main course of cream cheese-stuffed French toast with wild Maine blueberry sauce, breakfast pizza, cheddar and potato bake, southern pecan pancakes or garden vegetable frittata with a meat entrée and beverages. Special dietary needs are accommodated.

Innkeeper(s): Sarah Davison-Jenkins. $130-205. 4 rooms with PB. Breakfast and afternoon tea included in rates. Types of meals: Full gourmet bkfst, veg bkfst, early coffee/tea and snacks/refreshments. Beds: KQ. TV, VCR, DVD, reading lamp, CD player, clock radio, turn-down service, some with fireplace, hair dryer, bathrobes, bath amenities, wireless Internet access, iron/ironing board, Satellite TV with XM radio stations & HBO, room with a clawfoot tub, room with a fourpost Bed and room that can sleep up to 5 people in room. Air conditioning. Fax, copier, library, parlor games, telephone, Croquet and Bocce on premises. Limited handicap access. Antiquing, art galleries, beach, bicycling, canoeing/kayaking, cross-country skiing, downhill skiing, fishing, golf, hiking, horseback riding, live theater, museums, parks, shopping, tennis, water sports and Lighthouse nearby.

Location: Country, ocean community. Coastal Village.

Publicity: *Fodor's (Highly Recommended Star)* .

Certificate may be used: Nov. 1-April 30, last minute, excluding holiday weekends.

Ogunquit K2

Yardarm Village Inn

406 Shore Road
Ogunquit, ME 03907-0773
(207)646-7006 (888)927-3276
Internet: www.yardarmvillageinn.com
E-mail: yardarm@maine.rr.com

Circa 1892. In the quiet part of town, just south of the entrance to Perkins Cove, this three-story classic New England inn offers a delightful selection of accommodations. The large veranda is the perfect spot for relaxing on a white wicker rocker. Comfortable guest bedrooms and two-room suites are furnished and decorated in a Colonial-country style. Start the day with homemade blueberry muffins, fruit and beverages. Take an afternoon or evening charter on the Inn's private sailboat past the three-mile beach or along the rocky coast. The on-site wine and cheese shop is well-stocked to satisfy the most discriminating palate.

Innkeeper(s): Scott & Beverlee Drury. $135-165. 10 rooms with PB, 4 suites. Breakfast included in rates. Types of meals: Continental breakfast, beer; wine and cheese shop. Beds: KQT. Cable TV, reading lamp, refrigerator, clock radio, hair dryer, bath amenities and wireless Internet access in room. Air conditioning. Fax, copier, library, parlor games, telephone, fireplace, gift shop, private sailboat charters, wine and cheese shop, hand-painted blueberry dinnerware made in Maine, computer with Internet access, free wireless access and gift shop on premises. Amusement parks, antiquing, art galleries, beach, bicycling, canoeing/kayaking, fishing, golf, hiking, horseback riding, live theater, museums, parks, shopping, tennis, water sports, deep sea fishing, whale watching, boat charters and Marginal way walking trail nearby.

Location: Ocean community. Adjacent to Perkins Cove.

Certificate may be used: May, June, Sept. 17-30 and October 1-5 and 9-20, Sunday-Thursday, excluding holidays. Anytime, at the last minute. Not to be combined with any other special promotions.

Old Orchard Beach K2

Atlantic Birches Inn

20 Portland Ave Rt 98
Old Orchard Beach, ME 04064-2212
(207)934-5295 (888)934-5295 Fax:(207)934-3781
Internet: www.atlanticbirches.com
E-mail: info@AtlanticBirches.com

Circa 1903. The front porch of this Shingle-style Victorian and

1920s bungalow are shaded by white birch trees. The houses are a place for relaxation and enjoyment, uncluttered, simple havens filled with comfortable furnishings. The guest rooms are decorated with antiques and pastel wallcoverings. Maine's coast offers an endless amount of activities, from boating to whale watching. It is a five-minute walk to the beach and the pier.

Innkeeper(s): Ray & Heidi Deleo. $101-216. 10 rooms with PB, 3 two-bedroom suites. Breakfast included in rates. Types of meals: Cont plus and early coffee/tea. Beds: KQDT. Modern hook-up, data port, cable TV, VCR, DVD, reading lamp, refrigerator, ceiling fan, clock radio, telephone, desk, hair dryer, bathrobes, bath amenities, wireless Internet access, iron/ironing board, Pool towels and Beach chairs in room. Air conditioning. Fax, copier, swimming, library, parlor games, badminton, basketball, horseshoes, volleyball, pool towels and pool lounge chairs on premises. Limited handicap access. Amusement parks, antiquing, art galleries, beach, bicycling, canoeing/kayaking, cross-country skiing, downhill skiing, fishing, golf, hiking, horseback riding, live theater, museums, parks, shopping, sporting events, tennis, water sports, wineries, Water parks, Whale-watching tours, Deep sea fishing, Hot air ballooning, Fireworks, Lighthouses, Movie theaters, Outlets, Cemetery tours, Farm stands, Tree farms, Elk farm, Walking trails and Garden tours nearby.

Location: Ocean community.

Publicity: *Down East Magazine - Feb 2004.*

"Your home and family are just delightful! What a treat to stay in such a warm & loving home."

Certificate may be used: Nov.1-May 15, no holidays.

Rumford H2

The Perennial Inn

141 Jed Martin Road
Rumford, ME 04276
(207)369-0309 Fax:(207)369-8016
Internet: Perennialinn.com
E-mail: info@perennialinn.com

Circa 1884. Encompassing 42 acres of scenic beauty in the Blue Mountains, this historic 1884 Victorian farmhouse is surrounded by grassy fields, ponds, streams and pine forests. The renovated New England home with a wraparound porch and huge red barn offers secluded comfort and convenient access to Route 2. Read a book from the library in the cheery parlor or watch a DVD by the fieldstone fireplace in the Gathering Room. Play pool on a maple table in the billiard parlor. Genuine hospitality is extended with thoughtful details to pamper and please. Romantic guest bedrooms and a two-room suite feature wide pine floors, high ceilings, sunny windows and sitting areas with family heirlooms and fine furnishings. A hearty country breakfast is served in the dining room. Soak in the hot tub under the stars.

Innkeeper(s): Jenna & Darlene Ginsberg. $85-175. 7 rooms, 4 with PB, 1 two-bedroom suite. Breakfast, afternoon tea, snacks/refreshments and wine included in rates. Types of meals: Country bkfst and early coffee/tea. Beds: QT. Cable TV, VCR, reading lamp, clock radio and desk in room. Air conditioning. DVD, fax, copier, spa, library, pet boarding, parlor games, telephone and fireplace on premises. Limited handicap access. Amusement parks, antiquing, art galleries, bicycling, canoeing/kayaking, cross-country skiing, downhill skiing, fishing, golf, hiking, horseback riding, live theater, parks, shopping and water sports nearby.

Location: Country, mountains.

Certificate may be used: Sunday-Thursday, May-June and September-Dec. 15.

South Thomaston I5

Weskeag Inn B&B at the Water

14 Elm St.
South Thomaston, ME 04858-0213
(207)596-6676 (800)596-5576
Internet: www.weskeag.com
E-mail: innkeeper@weskeag.com

Circa 1830. The backyard of this three-story house stretches to the edge of Weskeag River and Ballyhac Cove. Fifty yards from the house, there's reversing white-water rapids, created by the 10-foot tide that narrows into the estuary. Guests often sit by the water's edge to watch the birds and the lobster fishermen. Sea kayakers can launch at the inn and explore the nearby coves and then paddle on to the ocean. The inn's furnishings include a mixture of comfortable antiques. Featherbed eggs are a house specialty.

Innkeeper(s): Gray Smith and Hazel Giberson. $95-150. 8 rooms, 6 with PB, 1 two-bedroom suite. Breakfast included in rates. Types of meals: Full bkfst and early coffee/tea. Beds: QD. Cable TV, reading lamp, ceiling fan, bathrobes, bath amenities, wireless Internet access, Use of ironing board, Iron, Hair dryer and Telephone in room. VCR, library, telephone and Space in kitchen refrigerator available upon request on premises. Antiquing, art galleries, beach, canoeing/kayaking, cross-country skiing, downhill skiing, fishing, golf, live theater, museums, parks, shopping and wineries nearby.

Location: Ocean community, waterfront. Tidal saltwater inlet.

Certificate may be used: Oct. 16 through June 14.

Walpole I4

Brannon-Bunker Inn

349 S St Rt 129
Walpole, ME 04573
(207)563-5941 (800)563-9225
Internet: www.brannonbunkerinn.com
E-mail: brbnkinn@lincoln.midcoast.com

Circa 1820. This Cape-style house has been a home to many generations of Maine residents, one of whom was captain of a ship that sailed to the Arctic. During the '20s, the barn served as a dance hall. Later, it was converted into comfortable guest rooms. Victorian and American antiques are featured, and there are collections of WWI military memorabilia.

Innkeeper(s): Joe & Jeanne Hovance. $90-100. 7 rooms, 5 with PB, 1 suite. Breakfast included in rates. Types of meals: Cont plus. Beds: QDT. TV, reading lamp, clock radio and desk in room. VCR, library, child care, parlor games, telephone and fireplace on premises. Handicap access. Antiquing, art galleries, beach, bicycling, canoeing/kayaking, fishing, golf, hiking, horseback riding, museums, parks, shopping, tennis and water sports nearby.

Location: Country, Damariscotta river.

Publicity: *Times-Beacon Newspaper*.

"Wonderful beds, your gracious hospitality and the very best muffins anywhere made our stay a memorable one."

Certificate may be used: September-June, except holiday weekends, subject to availability.

Washington H4

Blueberry Fields Bed and Breakfast

673 Razorville Road
Washington, ME 04574
(207)446-2407
Internet: www.blueberryfieldsbandb.com
E-mail: blueberryfieldsbandb@gmail.com

Circa 2010. Poised on more than 100 acres along the Central Coast of Maine in the town of Washington, the post and beam inn and rustic cottage sit on the edge of ten acres of well-maintained and cultivated blueberry fields and a large sugar maple grove. A small brook passes through the land and there is a small marsh on the eastern part where wild animals reside. Hike, cross country, snowshoe or ski the wooded trails. Stay in the Eustis Suite with a whirlpool tub, sitting area and private entrance or a pleasant guest room with private access to the outdoors. Debbie, an experienced professional baker, enjoys serving a hearty breakfast and afternoon treats made from delicious New England recipes. The two-bedroom cottage features a wood-burning stove and screened-in porch. It is a short walk from the main house and food is not inclusive.

Innkeeper(s): Debbie & Cyd Zeigler. $79-150. 5 rooms with PB, 1 with WP, 1 cottage. Breakfast, afternoon tea, soups and homemade rolls when pre-ordered. $10.00 room upgrade included in rates. Types of meals: Full bkfst, early coffee/tea and snacks/refreshments. Beds: KQT. Cable TV, DVD, reading lamp, ceiling fan, clock radio, desk, wireless Internet access and iron/ironing board in room. Air conditioning. Library, parlor games, woodstove, table tennis, refrigerator and dvds to borrow on premises. Antiquing, art galleries, beach, canoeing/kayaking, cross-country skiing, downhill skiing, fishing, golf, hiking, museums, shopping and wineries nearby.

Location: Country.

Certificate may be used: September-June, subject to availability.

Maryland

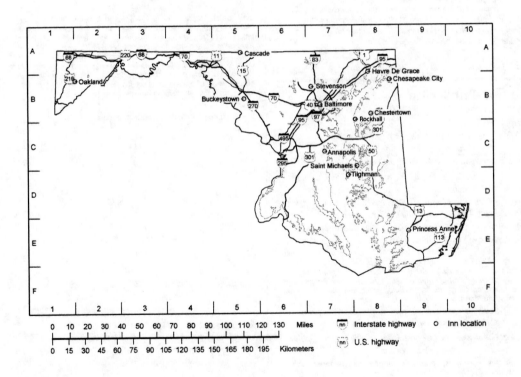

Annapolis   C7

Annapolitan Bed & Breakfast

1313 West Street
Annapolis, MD 21401
(410)990-1234 (866)990-2330 Fax:(410)990-1660
Internet: theannapolitan.com
E-mail: annapolitanbandb@yahoo.com

Circa 1862. Centrally located near the waterfront and the historic downtown Annapolis area of Maryland, Annapolitan Bed & Breakfast is an elegant place to stay at any time of the year. Relax on the wicker furnishings that grace the veranda, a wraparound porch. Catch a top name music act at Rams Head Tavern and enjoy one of the numerous restaurants in our town or watch a DVD on the widescreen TV in the president's Parlor. Select a spacious, air-conditioned guest bedroom or suite for restful nights. Full hot 3 course breakfast in the formal dining room or the veranda. Tour the monuments and museums of Washington, DC and the scenic sites of Baltimore, Maryland.

Innkeeper(s): Joetta and John Holt. $75-220. 15 rooms, 12 with PB, 4 with WP, 3 total suites, including 2 two-bedroom suites. Breakfast, afternoon tea and snacks/refreshments included in rates. Types of meals: Full bkfst, veg bkfst and early coffee/tea. Beds: KQD. Cable TV, refrigerator, ceiling fan, snack bar, clock radio, turn-down service, some with hot tub/spa, hair dryer, bathrobes, bath amenities, wireless Internet access and iron/ironing board in room. Central air. VCR, DVD, copier and fireplace on premises. Limited handicap access. Antiquing, art galleries, beach, bicycling, canoeing/kayaking, fishing, golf, hiking, live theater, museums, parks, shopping, sporting events, tennis, water sports, croquet, water polo, soccer and nearby.

Location: City. 1313 West St., Annapolis MD 21401.

Certificate may be used: June 14-Aug. 14 and Oct. 30-Feb. 30, Sunday-Thursday.

Gibson's Lodgings

110 Prince George St
Annapolis, MD 21401-1704
(410) 268-5555 (877) 330-0057
Internet: www.gibsonslodgings.com
E-mail: gibsonslodgings@starpower.net

Circa 1774. This Georgian house in the heart of the Annapolis Historic District was built on the site of the Old Courthouse, circa 1680. Two historic houses make up the inn, and there was a new house built in 1988. All the rooms, old and new, are furnished with antiques. Only a few yards away is the City Dock Harbor and within two blocks is the Naval Academy visitor's gate.

Innkeeper(s): Meredith Lauer & Peggy Summers. $99-259. 21 rooms, 17 with PB, 6 total suites, including 2 two-bedroom suites, 1 conference room. Breakfast included in rates. Types of meals: Cont plus. Beds: KQT. Cable TV, clock radio, telephone, hair dryer, bath amenities and wireless Internet access in room. Central air. Free parking on premises. Handicap access. Antiquing, art galleries, beach, bicycling, canoeing/kayaking, fishing, golf, live theater, museums, parks, shopping, sporting events and water sports nearby.

Location: City.

Publicity: *Mid-Atlantic Country and New York.*

"We had a delightful stay! We enjoyed the proximity to the waterfront, the fun atmosphere and the friendly people."

Certificate may be used: Anytime, subject to availability, Sunday-Thursday.

Baltimore   B7

1840s Carrollton Inn

50 Albemarle Street
Baltimore, MD 21202
(410)385-1840 Fax:(410)385-9080
Internet: www.1840scarrolltoninn.com
E-mail: info@1840scarrolltoninn.com

Circa 2007. Stay at historic 1840s Carrollton Inn for a romantic getaway or an executive retreat. Interconnected row homes surrounding a brick courtyard feature antiques and decorator furnishings. This boutique B&B graces the center of Heritage Walk in Baltimore, Maryland and is perfectly suited for relaxation or activity. Walk to Inner Harbor, Little Italy and experience the local nightlife. Lavish comfort is found in guest rooms and suites with whirlpools, fireplaces with marble and oak mantles, fresh flowers, robes, handcrafted Kingsdown mattresses and other upscale amenities to meet most every need. Linger over a gourmet breakfast before exploring the surrounding area or taking care of business. Ask about specials and packages available.

Innkeeper(s): Tim Kline. $175-375. 13 rooms with PB, 13 with FP, 13 with WP, 4 two-bedroom suites, 1 conference room. Breakfast included in rates. Types of meals: Full gourmet bkfst. Beds: KQ. Modem hook-up, cable TV, reading lamp, refrigerator, clock radio, telephone, desk, hot tub/spa, voice mail, fireplace, hair dryer, bathrobes, bath amenities, wireless Internet access and iron/ironing board in room. Central air. Fax, copier and gift shop on premises. Handicap access. Antiquing, art galleries, live theater, museums, parks, shopping, sporting events, Inner Harbor, Bars & Pubs of Fells Point, Canton, Harbor East, Little Italy, Fine dining and National Aquarium nearby.

Location: City.

Certificate may be used: Sunday-Thursday.

Hopkins Inn

3404 St Paul St
Baltimore, MD 21218
(410)235-8600 (800)537-8483 Fax:(410)235-7051
Internet: www.hopkinsinnbaltimore.com
E-mail: info@hopkinsinnbaltimore.com

Circa 1920. Major renovations have turned this inn with Spanish Revival architecture into uptown elegance. Victorian decor and antique furnishings reside with original artwork in tasteful luxury. A meeting room and a conference room are available for business or pleasure. The inviting guest bedrooms have a cozy ambiance. Start the day with a continental breakfast. Centrally located across from Johns Hopkins University on renown Homewood Campus, it is close to all the attractions this area has to offer.

$89-159. 26 rooms, 15 with PB, 11 suites, 2 conference rooms. Breakfast and afternoon tea included in rates. Types of meals: Cont plus and early coffee/tea. Beds: QDT. Modem hook-up, cable TV, reading lamp, clock radio, telephone and desk in room. Air conditioning. Fax, copier, parlor games, complimentary continental breakfast, afternoon cookies and tea served daily, garage parking available at $8 per day and front desk open 6 AM-10 PM daily on premises. Antiquing, art galleries, bicycling, golf, hiking, museums, parks, shopping, sporting events, Baltimore Inner Harbor, Union Memorial Hospital, Baltimore Museum of Art, Camden Yards, PSI Net Stadium and Convention Center nearby.

Location: City. Uptown location adjacent to Johns Hopkins University.

Certificate may be used: Monday-Thursday, for further available dates please contact innkeeper.

Buckeystown   B5

The Inn at Buckeystown

3521 Buckeystown Pike
Buckeystown, MD 21717
(301)874-5755 (800)272-1190 Fax:(301)874-1842
Internet: www.innatbuckeystown.com
E-mail: info@innatbuckeystown.com

Circa 1897. Gables, bay windows and a wraparound porch are features of this grand Victorian mansion located on two-and-a-half acres of lawns and gardens (and an ancient cemetery). The inn features a polished staircase, antiques and elegantly decorated guest rooms. Ask for the Victoriana Suite, which boasts a working fireplace and oak decor. A gourmet dinner is served with advance reservation. High tea and monthly murder mysteries are also offered. The inn also hosts weddings, rehearsals and retreats. The village of Buckeystown is in the National Register.

Innkeeper(s): Janet Wells. $125-200. 7 rooms, 5 with PB. Breakfast included in rates. Types of meals: Full gourmet bkfst, veg bkfst, early coffee/tea and Fine dining restaurant on premises. Beds: QD. Cable TV, reading lamp, refrigerator and desk in room. Air conditioning. TV, VCR, fax, parlor games, telephone, fireplace and tea room on premises. Limited handicap access. Antiquing, art galleries, bicycling, canoeing/kayaking, downhill skiing, fishing, golf, hiking, live theater, museums, parks, shopping, sporting events and wineries nearby.

Location: Country.

Publicity: *Mid-Atlantic, Innsider, The Washingtonian, Washington Post, Baltimore Sun,Frederick Magazine (Voted #1 B&B 2003, 2004, 2005), Weekend Wonder, Great Getaway by Baltimore and Washingtonian Magazine, The Afternoon Tea Society and many Red Hat Societies (DC Metro's #1 Tea Room), Channel 9 and Travel Channel.*

"This was one of the best bed and breakfast experiences we have ever had."

Certificate may be used: Sunday-Thursday, subject to availability, except holidays.

Chesapeake City   B8

Blue Max

300 Bohemia Ave.
Chesapeake City, MD 21915-1244
(410)885-2781 (877)725-8362 Fax:(410)885-2809
Internet: www.bluemaxinn.com
E-mail: innkeeper@bluemaxinn.com

Circa 1854. Known as "the house with generous porches," this is one of the town's largest residences, built with Georgian architecture by the owner of the sawmill. This elegant inn has working fireplaces and a parlor with a grand player piano. Elaborate upscale amenities in the romantic suites and guest bedrooms include robes, flowers, chocolates and luxurious linens. Whirlpool tubs, a private balcony and second-floor verandas are also featured. Mouth-watering dishes like peaches and kiwi with amaretto cream sauce, apple crisp pancakes and country bacon, and eggs Benedict souffle are enjoyed in the fireside dining room or in the solarium overlooking gardens and a fish pond. A waterfall and gazebo highlight lush landscaping.

Innkeeper(s): Christine Mullen. $90-300. 9 rooms with PB, 2 suites. Breakfast, afternoon tea and snacks/refreshments included in rates. Types of meals: Full gourmet bkfst, early coffee/tea and picnic lunch. Beds: KQ. Modem hook-up, data port, cable TV, VCR, DVD, reading lamp, CD player, refrigerator, ceiling fan, snack bar, clock radio, telephone, desk, most with hot tub/spa, most with fireplace, hair dryer, bathrobes, bath amenities, wireless Internet access, iron/ironing board, Jacuzzi for two, fireplace and private balcony in the honeymoon suite in room. Central air. Fax, copier, bicycles, library, parlor games and gift shop on premises. Handicap access. Antiquing, art galleries, beach, bicycling, canoeing/kayaking, fishing, golf, hiking, horseback riding, museums, parks, shopping, sporting events, tennis, water sports, wineries and Boating on the C&D canal nearby.

Location: Waterfront.

Certificate may be used: November-April weekday/weekend. May-September weekdays only (Monday-Thursday). Subject to availability and not valid holidays or special events.

Chestertown   B8

Great Oak Manor

10568 Cliff Rd
Chestertown, MD 21620-4115
(410)778-5943 (800)504-3098 Fax:(410)810-2517
Internet: www.greatoak.com
E-mail: innkeeper@greatoak.com

Circa 1938. This elegant Georgian mansion anchors vast lawns at the end of a long driveway. Situated directly on the Chesapeake Bay, it is a serene and picturesque country estate. A library with fireplace, den and formal parlors are available to guests. With its grand circular stairway, bayside gazebo, private beach and nearby marina, the Manor is a remarkable setting for events such as weddings and reunions. Chestertown is eight miles away.

Innkeeper(s): Cassandra and John Fedas. $149-315. 12 rooms with PB, 5 with FP, 3 suites, 2 conference rooms. Breakfast and snacks/refreshments included in rates. Types of meals: Full gourmet bkfst, veg bkfst, early coffee/tea and hors d'oeuvres. Beds: KQ. Modem hook-up, TV, VCR, DVD, reading lamp, stereo, ceiling fan, clock radio, telephone, turn-down service, desk, most with fireplace, hair dryer, bathrobes, bath amenities, wireless Internet access and iron/ironing board in room. Central air. Fax, copier, swimming, bicycles, library, parlor games, Two computer-ready rooms, Private beach, In-door endless pool, Day/evening cruises and Access to Chester River Yacht & Country Club 18-hole golf course on premises. Handicap access. Antiquing, art galleries, beach, bicycling, canoeing/kayaking, fishing, golf, hiking, horseback riding, live theater, museums, parks, shopping, tennis, water sports, wineries, Historic Chestertown, Md., Chesapeake Bay and Hunting nearby.

Location: Country, waterfront.

Publicity: *Southern Living, Philadelphia, Diversions, Road Best Traveled, Washingtonian, Country Inns, New Choices, Chesapeake Life, Time Magazine., Today Show with Peter Greenberg and July 2005.*

"The charming setting, professional service and personal warmth we experienced at Great Oak will long be a pleasant memory. Thanks for everything!"

Certificate may be used: Nov. 1-March 31, Sunday-Thursday, Gold rooms only.

The Inn at Mitchell House

8796 Maryland Pkwy
Chestertown, MD 21620-4209
(410)778-6500
Internet: www.innatmitchellhouse.com
E-mail: innkeeper@innatmitchellhouse.com

Circa 1743. This pristine 18th-century manor house sits as a jewel on 12 acres overlooking Stoneybrook Pond. The guest rooms and the inn's several parlors are preserved and appointed in an authentic Colonial mood, heightened by handsome polished wide-board floors. Eastern Neck Island National Wildlife Refuge, Rock Hall, Chesapeake Farms, St. Michaels, Annapolis and nearby Chestertown are all delightful to explore. The Inn at Mitchell House is a popular setting for romantic weddings and small corporate meetings.

Innkeeper(s): Tracy & Jim Stone. $109-239. 6 rooms, 5 with PB, 4 with FP, 1 cottage. Breakfast, snacks/refreshments and wine included in rates. Types of meals: Full gourmet bkfst, veg bkfst and early coffee/tea. Beds: KQ. Cable TV, VCR, DVD, reading lamp, refrigerator, clock radio, turn-down service, desk, most with fireplace, hair dryer, bath amenities, wireless Internet access and iron/ironing board in room. Air conditioning. Library, parlor games and telephone on premises. Antiquing, art galleries, beach, bicycling, canoeing/kayaking, fishing, golf, hiking, live theater, museums, parks, shopping, sporting events, tennis, water sports and private beach nearby.

Location: Country.

Publicity: *Washingtonian, New York Magazine, Glamour, Philadelphia Inquirer, Baltimore Sun, Kent County News, Ten Best Inns in the Country, New York Times, Washington Post and National Geographic Traveler.*

Certificate may be used: Sunday-Thursday, excluding holidays.

Havre De Grace   A8

Vandiver Inn, Kent & Murphy Homes

301 S Union Ave
Havre De Grace, MD 21078-3201
(410)939-5200 (800)245-1655 Fax:(410)939-5202
Internet: www.vandiverinn.com
E-mail: vandiverinn@comcast.net

Circa 1886. Three acres surround this three-story historic Victorian mansion. A chandelier lights the entrance. Some of the rooms offer gas fireplaces and clawfoot tubs, and all are furnished with Victorian antiques. For instance, a king-size Victorian bed, original to the house, is one of the features of the Millard E. Tydings Room, also offering a decorative fireplace and sitting area. The innkeeper creates gourmet breakfasts with freshly baked scones or muffins. Spend some time in the garden where a summer gazebo is supported by 12 cedar tree trunks.

Innkeeper(s): John and Susan Muldoon. $109-159. 19 rooms with PB, 4 with FP. Breakfast included in rates. Types of meals: Full gourmet bkfst, veg bkfst, early coffee/tea, picnic lunch and dinner. Beds: KQDT. Data port, cable TV, reading lamp, clock radio, telephone and desk in room. Central air. Fax, parlor games, fireplace, laundry facility and indoor and outdoor conference rooms on premises. Limited handicap access. Antiquing, beach, canoeing/kayaking, downhill skiing, golf, horseback riding, museums, shopping and wineries nearby.

Certificate may be used: Sunday-Thursday, September-April. Not valid on holidays and other blackout dates.

Princess Anne   E9

The Alexander House Booklovers B&B

30535 Linden Ave
Princess Anne, MD 21853
(410)651-5195
Internet: BookloversBnB.com
E-mail: alexanderbooklover@verizon.net

Circa 1885. Cradled between Chesapeake Bay and the beach, this Queen Anne Victorian graces the historic district with an inviting, wicker-furnished wraparound front porch and a veranda with a flower garden shaded by a large magnolia tree. The bed and breakfast is filled with literary memorabilia and portraits that honor writers and their books. Sit by the fire in the Mark Twain Reading Parlor. Each guest bedroom realistically reflects a famous author. Select the 1920s jazzy Harlem Renaissance of the Langston Hughes Room or the romantic Jane Austen Room with a clawfoot tub and ambiance of Regency England. The Robert Louis Stevenson Room offers 19th-century high-seas adventure. Linger over a gourmet breakfast in the French Café Colette where afternoon tea and evening liqueur are also served. A stocked refrigerator and microwave is available for guest use.

Innkeeper(s): Elizabeth and Peter Alexander. $85-140. 3 rooms with PB. Breakfast, afternoon tea, snacks/refreshments and Evening liqueurs and teas served (complimentary) included in rates. Types of meals: Full gourmet bkfst, veg bkfst and early coffee/tea. Beds: QD. Modem hook-up, reading lamp, stereo, desk, some with fireplace, hair dryer, wireless Internet access and iron/ironing board in room. Central air. Library, parlor games, telephone, gift shop, Internet access, Refrigerator, Microwave (in cafe), Bike rack, Iron & board available by request and Wi-Fi available June 2009 on premises. Antiquing, art galleries, beach, bicycling, canoeing/kayaking, fishing, golf, hiking, live theater, museums, parks, shopping, sporting events, tennis, water sports, Wild ponies of Assateague/Chincoteague, Smith and Tangier Islands, Boat eco tours, Salisbury Zoo, Ocean City (35 minutes). Three local golf courses, Salon

Location: Country. Historic district near Chesapeake Bay.

Publicity: *Budget Travel Magazine, The Washington Post, Salisbury Daily Times, Chesapeake Life Magazine, Today Show NBC (February 2004), WBOC TV local CBS affiliate Travels with Charley and Peter Greenberg travel show (2009).*

Certificate may be used: Any day, December and January.

Rock Hall B7

Inn at Osprey Point

20786 Rock Hall Ave.
Rock Hall, MD 21661
(410) 639-2194
Internet: www.ospreypoint.com
E-mail: innkeeper@ospreypoint.com

Circa 1993. Spread over 30 acres on the Eastern Shore, this inn and restaurant are open year-round with a marina accessible during boat season. A casual and friendly ambiance accents modern luxury and colonial sophistication. Swim in the pool, play volleyball, pitch horseshoes and take a nature walk. Picnic areas and bicycles are available to use. Accommodations include guest suites and rooms in the main inn and annex with contemporary amenities and classic style. Some rooms boast a balcony, porch, fireplace or whirlpool tub. A generous continental breakfast is provided daily. Savor fine dining on Chef Abbey's creations in the restaurant. Ask about special packages and events happening in Rock Hall, Maryland.

Innkeeper(s): Terry Nelson. $80-280. 15 rooms, 13 with PB, 1 with FP, 1 with WP, 1 two-bedroom suite. Breakfast included in rates. Beds: KQT. Cable TV, clock radio, some with fireplace, hair dryer, bathrobes, bath amenities, wireless Internet access, In some rooms: coffee maker, desk, ironing board/iron upon request and bottled water in room. Central air. Fax, copier, swimming, bicycles, library, parlor games, telephone, laundry facility, Kayaks, yard games, volleyball, restaurant, ice machine, weekend bar and grill at the pool and on premises. Antiquing, beach, bicycling, canoeing/kayaking, fishing, golf, horseback riding, museums, parks, shopping, wineries, Sailing charters and bird watching nearby.

Location: Waterfront.

Certificate may be used: Anytime, November-March, subject to availability. Cannot be combined with any other offers or discounts. Night free is least expensive.

Saint Michaels C8

Hambleton Inn

202 Cherry St
Saint Michaels, MD 21663
(410)745-3350 (866)745-3350 Fax:(410)745-5709
Internet: www.hambletoninn.com
E-mail: innkeeper@hambletoninn.com

Relax at year-round accommodations on the harbor overlooking the Miles River and the Chesapeake Bay in scenic St. Michaels, Maryland. Gracious amenities hallmark this elegant and historic shipbuilder's home in the popular Eastern Shore area. Walk to local galleries, boutiques, antique shops and meander across the Honeymoon Bridge to the Maritime Museum. Hop on a bike to explore nearby towns of Tilghman Island, Easton and Oxford. Sit on one of the two porches with fabulous views. Stay in a spacious air-conditioned guest room or suite with modern conveniences and wake up to savor a gourmet breakfast. Gather for sherry and port wine in the evening amid the distinctive character and ambiance of this wonderful inn. Weddings and special events are memorable experiences in this picturesque and hospitable setting.

Innkeeper(s): Sherry Manning. $245-265. 5 rooms with PB. Beds: KQ.

Certificate may be used: October 15-March 15, Last minute, subject to availability.

Parsonage Inn

210 N Talbot St
Saint Michaels, MD 21663-2102
(410)745-8383
Internet: www.parsonage-inn.com
E-mail: parsinn@atlanticbb.net

Circa 1883. A striking Victorian steeple rises next to the wide bay of this brick residence, once the home of Henry Clay Dodson, state senator, pharmacist and brickyard owner. The house features brick detail in a variety of patterns and inlays, perhaps a design statement for brick customers. Porches are decorated with filigree and spindled columns. Waverly linens, late Victorian furnishings, fireplaces and decks add to the creature comforts. Six bikes await guests who wish to ride to Tilghman Island or to the ferry that goes to Oxford. Gourmet breakfast is served in the dining room.

Innkeeper(s): Char & Bill Wilhelm. $100-195. 8 rooms with PB, 3 with FP. Breakfast and afternoon tea included in rates. Types of meals: Full bkfst. Beds: KQD. Reading lamp, ceiling fan, clock radio, bath amenities, two with TV and three with fireplace in room. Central air. TV, bicycles, parlor games, telephone, fireplace, swimming pool and hot tub privileges nearby on premises. Handicap access. Antiquing, art galleries, canoeing/kayaking, fishing, golf, shopping, Chesapeake Bay Maritime Museum and Pickering Creek Audubon Center nearby.

Location: City. Main St of Historic Town.

Publicity: *Philadelphia Inquirer Sunday Travel, Wilmington and Delaware News Journal.*

"Striking, extensively renovated."

Certificate may be used: Sunday-Thursday, Nov.1-May 1.

Stevenson   B7

Gramercy Mansion

1400 Greenspring Valley Rd
Stevenson, MD 21153-0119
(410)486-2405 Fax:(410)486-1765
Internet: www.gramercymansion.com
E-mail: info@gramercymansion.com

Circa 1902. Dreams come true at this English Tudor mansion and gardens that crown 45 acres of woodlands. A superb grand staircase, high ceilings, artwork, antiques and Oriental carpets exude historic elegance. Retire to handsome guest suites decorated with lavish comfort and style. Comparable to a master suite, they feature wood-burning fireplaces and whirlpool tubs. Wake up to birds singing and the aroma of a multi-course gourmet  breakfast. Dine by the fire in the dining room or at a private table on the flower-filled porch by the Olympic-size swimming pool. The terraced lower garden, "Our Special Place," overlooking historic Greenspring Valley is long remembered. Downtown Baltimore is a 20-minute drive.

Innkeeper(s): Anne Pomykala & Cristin Kline. $150-375. 11 rooms with PB, 7 with FP, 9 with WP, 2 two-bedroom suites, 7 conference rooms. Breakfast, snacks/refreshments, All-inclusive package available including dinner with wine at nearby restaurant and inquire for details included in rates. Types of meals: Full gourmet bkfst, veg bkfst, early coffee/tea, In-room dinner basket available by special order and Wine dinners hosted once a month (dates listed at www.gramercymansion.com). Beds: KQDT. Modem hook-up, data port, cable TV, VCR, DVD, reading lamp, refrigerator, ceiling fan, snack bar, clock radio, telephone, coffeemaker, turn-down service, desk, most with hot tub/spa, voice mail, most with fireplace, hair dryer, bathrobes, bath amenities, wireless Internet access, iron/ironing board, Fresh flowers, Microwave and Complimentary drinks in room. Central air. Fax, copier, swimming, tennis, library, parlor games, laundry facility, gift shop, Piano, Gardens, Trails, Terrace and Organic farm on premises. Handicap access. Antiquing, art galleries, bicycling, canoeing/kayaking, fishing, golf, hiking, horseback riding, live theater, museums, parks, shopping, sporting events, tennis, wineries, Baltimore's Inner Harbor, Little Italy, Fells Point, Mt. Washington and Greenspring Station nearby.

Location: Country. Greenspring Valley, 15 minutes from Baltimore.

Publicity: *Washington Post, Baltimore Sun, Country Folk Art, Vegetarian Times, Mid-Atlantic Country Magazine, Baltimore Magazine, Owings Mills Times, Jeffersonian, HGTV, Fox 45 and WBAL.*

"The hospitality, atmosphere, food, etc. were top-notch."
Certificate may be used: Monday-Thursday.

Massachusetts

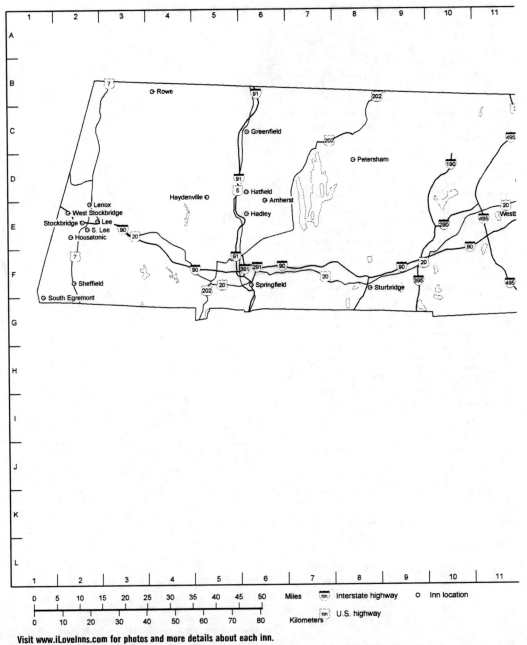

0 5 10 15 20 25 30 35 40 45 50   Miles
0   10   20   30   40   50   60   70   80   Kilometers

Interstate highway
U.S. highway
Inn location

Visit www.iLoveInns.com for photos and more details about each inn.

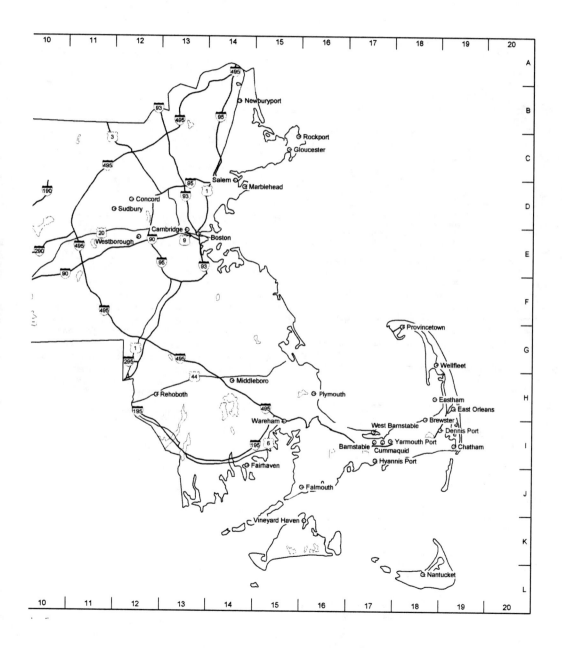

Amherst   D6

Allen House Victorian Inn

599 Main St
Amherst, MA 01002-2409
(413)253-5000
Internet: www.allenhouse.com
E-mail: allenhouse@webtv.net

Circa 1886. This stick-style Queen Anne is much like a Victorian museum with guest rooms that feature period reproduction wallpapers, pedestal sinks, carved golden oak and brass beds, painted wooden floors and plenty of antiques. Among its many other treasures include Eastlake fireplace mantels. Unforgettable breakfasts include specialties such as eggs Benedict or French toast stuffed with rich cream cheese. Afternoon tea is a treat, and the inn offers plenty of examples of poetry from Emily Dickinson, whose home is just across the street from the inn.

Innkeeper(s): Alan & Ann Zieminski. $75-195. 7 rooms with PB. Breakfast, afternoon tea and snacks/refreshments included in rates. Types of meals: Full bkfst and early coffee/tea. Beds: QDT. Modem hook-up, reading lamp, ceiling fan, clock radio, telephone, coffeemaker, desk, wireless Internet access, Down comforters & pillows, Free Local & Long distance calls, Free use of laptops, Free use of Fax and Copier in room. Air conditioning. Fax, copier, library, parlor games and fireplace on premises. Amusement parks, antiquing, cross-country skiing, downhill skiing, fishing, golf, live theater, parks, shopping, sporting events, tennis and water sports nearby.

Location: Mountains. Small college town.

Publicity: *New York Times, Boston Magazine, Bon Appetit, Yankee Travel and Victorian Homes.*

"Our room and adjoining bath were spotlessly clean, charming, and quiet, with good lighting. Our meals were delicious and appetizing, and the casual, family-like atmosphere encouraged discussions among the guests."

Certificate may be used: Jan. 1-April 1, Sunday-Thursday.

Barnstable   I17

Lamb and Lion Inn

2504 Main Street (Rt. 6A)
Barnstable, MA 02630-0511
(508)362-6823 (800)909-6923 Fax:(508) 362-0227
Internet: www.lambandlion.com
E-mail: info@lambandlion.com

Circa 1740. This rambling collection of Cape-style buildings sits on four acres overlooking the Old King's highway. Newly decorated, the inn offers a feeling of casual elegance. The Innkeeper's Pride is a romantic suite with sunken tub, fireplace, kitchenette and a deck overlooking a garden and woods. The Barn-stable is one of the original buildings and now offers three sleeping areas, a living and dining area and French doors to a private patio. A large central courtyard houses a generous sized heated pool and hot tub spa.

Innkeeper(s): Ali & Tom. $165-250. 10 rooms with PB, 8 with FP, 2 with HT, 2 with WP, 6 total suites, including 1 two-bedroom suite and 1 three-bedroom suite, 1 cottage, 1 guest house, 1 cabin, 1 conference room. Breakfast included in rates. Types of meals: Cont plus, early coffee/tea, picnic lunch, Our breakfast is far from "continental" and every day is a surprise. Beds: KQ. Cable TV, VCR, DVD, reading lamp, refrigerator, clock radio, telephone, some with hot tub/spa, most with fireplace, hair dryer, bath amenities, wireless Internet access and iron/ironing board in room. Air conditioning. Fax, copier, spa, swimming, library, parlor games, gift shop, Solar-heated pool in central courtyard, Outdoor hot tub spa, "rolling" outdoor wood-burning fireplace and "Famous" self-guided driving tours on premises. Antiquing, art galleries, beach, bicycling, canoeing/kayaking, cross-country skiing, fishing, golf, hiking, horseback riding, live theater, museums, parks, shopping, sporting events, tennis, water sports, wineries and Whale watching (1 mile) nearby.

Location: Ocean community.

Publicity: *"Best Mid-Cape Inn/B&B ~ 2007", Cape Cod Life Magazine. Cape Cod Journal's "EDITOR'S CHOICE ~ 2005" and Arrington's Bed & Breakfast Journal "One of the Top 15 Best Overall Inns in America"*

Certificate may be used: Oct. 31-May 18, Sunday-Friday, excluding holidays.

Boston   E13

Clarendon Square Inn

198 W. Brookline Street
Boston, MA 02118-1280
(617)536-2229
Internet: www.clarendonsquare.com
E-mail: stay@clarendonsquare.com

Circa 1860. Business travelers and discriminating tourists to Boston will appreciate the impeccable service at this luxuriously renovated Boston townhouse bed and breakfast in the South End. The side street location allows easy access to all that Boston offers, without the noise of the city intruding. Each elegantly furnished room, many with original local artwork, provides a spacious seating/working area as well as a private bathroom, complete with plush robes and high-end toiletries. There is a satellite flat screen TV, wireless Internet access and a docking station for your iPod and CD/DVD player in addition to new pillow-top mattresses. A special treat is the city view available from the hot tub on the roof deck. Each morning enjoy a variety of appetizing and substantial continental breakfasts.

Innkeeper(s): Stephen Gross. $155-455. 3 rooms with PB. Breakfast included in rates. Types of meals: Expanded continental breakfast. Beds: Q. Modem hook-up, cable TV, DVD, ceiling fan, clock radio, telephone, voice mail, hair dryer, bathrobes, bath amenities, wireless Internet access, iron/ironing board, 600 TC Egyptian cotton sheets,down pillows and duvet, Eco-friendly luxury cotton towels, iPod dock,LCD TV and DVD and Aveda bath amenities in room. Central air. Fax, copier, spa, library, fireplace, laundry facility, roof deck with hot tub, outdoor breakfast patio, swimming and tennis just steps away and on premises. Antiquing, art galleries, beach, bicycling, live theater, museums, parks, shopping, sporting events, tennis and water sports nearby.

Location: City.

Publicity: *Condé Nast Traveler Travel and Leisure Everyday with Rachael Ray and 2008 New York Times London Sunday Times Chicago Tribune Miami Herold Interiors Magazine.*

Certificate may be used: Sunday-Thursday, November-March for last minute availability in Deluxe Queen or Luxury Suites.

College Club

44 Commonwealth Ave
Boston, MA 02116
(617) 536-9510 Fax:(617)247-8537
Internet: www.thecollegeclubofboston.com
E-mail: accommodations@thecollegeclubofboston.com

Circa 1800. Established in 1890, the oldest women's college club in America was formed in the heart of historic Back Bay in

Boston, Massachusetts. Open year-round, College Club offers accommodations and hosts events in a classic Victorian Brownstone. Snacks and tea are available throughout the day. Period antiques, reproductions and artwork accent the inviting guest bedrooms. Some boast decorative fireplaces and private baths. A complimentary continental breakfast buffet is provided daily in the dining room. The Drawing Room and the Members Room are elegant venues for weddings, concerts, business meetings or other special events. Onsite catering is available. The bed and breakfast is one block from the Public Garden, Newberry Street and Boylston Street, near Beacon Hill. Take a walking tour of the city and be immersed in a rich heritage.

Innkeeper(s): Edith Toth, General Manager. $129-275. 11 rooms, 6 with PB, 2 conference rooms. Breakfast, afternoon tea and snacks/refreshments included in rates. Types of meals: Cont and early coffee/tea. Beds: KT. Modem hook-up, reading lamp, CD player, clock radio, telephone, desk, voice mail, hair dryer, bath amenities, wireless Internet access, Free wi-fi and free local and US long distance calls. Bathrobes available on request in room. Air conditioning. TV, fax, copier, library, Complimentary afternoon sweets and coffee/tea available anytime on premises. Antiquing, art galleries, beach, golf, live theater, museums, parks, shopping, sporting events, tennis and water sports nearby.

Location: City.

Certificate may be used: Anytime, November-March via telephone/email reservations only.

Brewster   H18

Old Sea Pines Inn

2553 Main St.
Brewster, MA 02631-1959
(508)896-6114 Fax:(508)632-0084

Internet: www.oldseapinesinn.com
E-mail: info@oldseapinesinn.com

Circa 1900. Formerly the Sea Pines School of Charm and Personality for Young Women, this turn-of-the-century mansion sits on three-and-one-half acres of trees and lawns. Recently renovated, the inn displays elegant wallpapers and a grand sweeping stairway. On Sunday
evenings, mid June
through mid
September, enjoy a
dinner show in con-
junction with Cape

Cod Repertory Theatre. Beaches and bike paths are nearby, as are village shops and restaurants.

Innkeeper(s): Michele & Stephen Rowan. $85-165. 24 rooms, 16 with PB, 3 with FP, 2 suites, 2 conference rooms. Breakfast included in rates. Types of meals: Full bkfst, early coffee/tea, afternoon tea, snacks/refresh-ments and room service. Beds: QDT. Cable TV and reading lamp in room. Air conditioning. TV, telephone and fireplace on premises. Handicap access. Antiquing, fishing, live theater, shopping, water sports and dinner theatre in summer nearby.

Publicity: *New York Times, Cape Cod Oracle, For Women First, Home Office, Entrepreneur, Boston Magazine, Redbook, Travel & Leisure and Better Homes & Gardens-British Edition.*

"The loving care applied by Steve, Michele and staff is deeply appreciated."

Certificate may be used: Sunday-Thursday April 1-June 15 and Sept. 15-Dec. 1.

Cambridge   D13

A Bed & Breakfast In Cambridge

1657 Cambridge St
Cambridge, MA 02138-4316
(617)868-7082 (800)795-7122 Fax:(617)876-8991
Internet: www.cambridgebnb.com
E-mail: doaneperry@yahoo.com

Circa 1897. Located minutes from Harvard Square, this colonial revival house reflects the rich ambiance of the Cambridge historical district. Surround yourself in the finest New England culture, located walking distance from the house. Visit museums, theaters and fine restaurants. Rest under the voluminous trees in the park across the street, or hop on the Red Line for an excursion to Boston. After an active day of sight seeing, return to the warmth of turn-of-the-century antique decor at this three-story home away from home. Enjoy a savory breakfast featuring such delights as home-baked, sesame-orange spice bread and cranberry brody, and spend the afternoon relaxing in an overstuffed chair or Grandmother's cane rockers with some tea or sherry.

Innkeeper(s): Doane Perry. $95-160. 3 rooms. Breakfast and afternoon tea included in rates. Types of meals: Full gourmet bkfst, veg bkfst and early cof-fee/tea. Beds: KQT. Cable TV, reading lamp, clock radio, telephone, turn-down service, desk and voice mail in room. Air conditioning. Fax, copier and library on premises. Antiquing, art galleries, beach, bicycling, canoeing/kayaking, cross-country skiing, live theater, museums, parks, shop-ping, sporting events, tennis and water sports nearby.

Location: City.

Certificate may be used: Jan. 7-Feb. 11, Feb. 23-March 4, Dec. 8-18, based on Availability.

Chatham   I19

Chatham Old Harbor Inn

22 Old Harbor Rd
Chatham, MA 02633-2315
(508)945-4434 (800)942-4434 Fax:(508)945-7665
Internet: www.chathamoldharborinn.com
E-mail: info@chathamoldharborinn.com

Circa 1932. This pristine New England bed & breakfast was once the home of "Doc" Keene, a popular physician in the area. A meticulous renovation has created an elegant, beautifully appointed inn offering antique furnishings, designer linens and lavish amenities in an English country decor. A buffet breakfast, featuring Judy's homemade muffins, is served in the sunroom or on the deck. The beaches, boutiques and galleries are a walk away and there is an old grist mill, the Chatham Lighthouse and a railroad museum. Band concerts are offered Friday nights in the
summer at Kate
Gould Park.

Innkeeper(s): Judy & Ray Braz. $149-329. 8 rooms with PB, 2 with FP, 1 with WP, 1 suite, 1 con-ference room. Breakfast, afternoon tea and snacks/refreshments included in rates. Types of meals: Full bkfst, veg bkfst and early coffee/tea. Beds: KQT. Cable TV, VCR, DVD, reading lamp, CD player, refrigerator, ceiling fan, clock radio, desk, some with hot tub/spa, some with fireplace, hair dryer, bathrobes, bath amenities, wireless Internet access, iron/ironing board, Jacuzzi in suite, Most rooms have refrigerators, All rooms have combination TV/VCR units and some have TV/VCR/DVD in room. Air conditioning. Fax, copier, parlor games, telephone, gift shop, Sand chairs, Beach umbrellas, Beach towels Fitness room, Coffee & tea service is complimentary from 7:30 AM until 7:30 PM, Bottled water & soft drinks are always complimentary, Tape & disc library of over 280 pieces is complimentary and Concierge service from 9 AM until 9 PM on premises. Antiquing, art galleries, beach, bicycling, canoeing/kayaking, fishing, golf, hiking, live theater, museums, parks, shopping, sporting events, tennis, water sports, wineries, Art festivals, Concerts, Cape Cod League Baseball, Nature walks, Guided Audubon excursions, Whale watches and Seal tours nearby.

Location: Ocean community. Seaside Village/National Seashore.

Publicity: *Boston Globe, Honeymoon, Cape Cod Life, Boston, Cape Cod Travel Guide, Country Inns, Cape Cod Dreams and Off Shore.*

Certificate may be used: Nov. 1-April 30, Sunday-Thursday.

Chatham Wayside Inn

512 Main St
Chatham, MA 02633-2239
(508) 945-5550 (800) 391-5734 Fax:(508) 945-3407
Internet: www.waysideinn.com
E-mail: info@waysideinn.com

Circa 1860. For well over a century, guests have been staying at this historic inn, which served originally as a stagecoach stop. The inn's Main Street address offers an ideal location for enjoying the Cape Cod village of Chatham. The individually appointed guest rooms are designed in a romantic mix of Colonial and English country styles. A dozen rooms include a fireplace. Canopy and four-poster beds, as well as whirlpool tubs, are some of the romantic offerings. There is a veranda lined with wicker chairs, and the inn also offers an outdoor heated swimming pool. The inn has a full-service restaurant, and the menu is filled with traditional New England fare, including fresh local seafood.

Innkeeper(s): Shane Coughlin - General Manager   Jennifer Kellie - Innkeeper. $120-475. 56 rooms with PB, 5 with FP, 5 with WP. Complimentary continental breakfast is served during the off-season included in rates. Types of meals: Full bkfst, lunch and dinner. Restaurant on premises. Beds: KQ. Cable TV, DVD, reading lamp, CD player, clock radio, telephone, voice mail, hair dryer, bath amenities, wireless Internet access and iron/ironing board in room. Central air. Fax, copier, swimming and fireplace on premises. Handicap access. Antiquing, fishing, golf, live theater, parks, shopping, tennis and beaches nearby.

Location: Ocean community.

Certificate may be used: February-April, November-December, Sunday-Wednesday, excludes holidays.

Concord   D12

Hawthorne Inn

462 Lexington Rd
Concord, MA 01742-3729
(978)369-5610 Fax:(978)287-4949
Internet: www.concordmass.com
E-mail: inn@concordmass.com

Circa 1870. Share the joy of history, literature, poetry and artwork at this intimate New England bed & breakfast. For 25 years, the inn's ambiance has imparted the spirit of writers and philosophers such as the Alcotts, Emerson, Hawthorne and Thoreau, who once owned and walked the grounds. Antique furnishings, weavings, hardwood floors, a welcoming fireplace and stained-glass windows all exude a wonderful warmth and gentility. Enjoy afternoon tea on a rustic garden bench in the shade of aged trees and colorful plants. The area offers woods to explore, rivers to canoe, a quaint village with museums, infamous Sleepy Hollow Cemetery, and untold treasures.

Innkeeper(s): Marilyn Mudry & Gregory Burch. $125-315. 7 rooms with PB, 1 with FP, 1 conference room. Breakfast, afternoon tea and Ask about our Special platters with complimentary wine up-grades included in rates. Types of meals: Full bkfst, early coffee/tea, snacks/refreshments, wine and Ask about the Romantic wine package upgrade. Beds: QD. Modem hook-up, data port, DVD, reading lamp, CD player, clock radio, telephone, desk, voice mail, some with fireplace, hair dryer, bathrobes, bath amenities, wireless Internet access and iron/ironing board in room. Air conditioning. Fax, library and parlor games on premises. Antiquing, art galleries, bicycling, canoeing/kayaking, cross-country skiing, fishing, hiking, live theater, museums, parks, shopping, tennis, Homes of Hawthorne, the Alcotts (Little Women), Emerson and Henry Thoreau, Close to Walden Pond, Great Meadows Wildlife refuge, Old North Bridge of the famed "shot heard 'round the world," Public tennis courts, Swimming in historic Walden Pond, Boat rentals on the Concord River, Boston (19 miles) and Cambridge (12 miles) nearby.

Location: Historic Village.

Publicity: *Forbes Magazine, Yankee, New York Times, Los Angeles Times, Boston Globe, Le Monde(France), Early American Life, Evening, National Geographic Traveler, Nono (Japan), guidebook publications such as Select Registry, Karen Brown Guides and Elegant Small Hotels, Norm Abrams of This Old House filmed a special public service safety film and South Korean Public TV - 2008 film highlighting its history and decor.*

"*Surely there couldn't be a better or more valuable location for a comfortable, old-fashioned country inn.*"

Certificate may be used: January-March, Sunday-Thursday (premium rooms only).

Dennis Port   I19

Joy House Inc., B&B

181 Depot Street
Dennis Port, MA 02639
(508)760-3663 (877)569-4687 Fax:(508)760-6618
Internet: www.joyhousecapecod.com
E-mail: sales@joyhousecapecod.com

Circa 1730. Remodeled for comfort and privacy, this Pre-Revolutionary War, Antique Colonial house is an ideal place to be pampered and served with joy. An old sea captain's home with wide pumpkin pine floors, the foyer gives access to a large common room and fireside sitting area. Listen to classical music or watch cable TV. Attractive guest bedrooms offer a restful stay. Sleep on a four-poster bed under a skylight in the romantic Lighthouse Suite with a decorative fireplace. Wake up to Chef Barbara's breakfast in the dining room. Splendidly landscaped gardens are resplendent with hollies, hydrangeas, roses, rhododendrons and cherry trees.

Innkeeper(s): Barbara and Peter Bach. $110-170. 3 rooms with PB, 2 with FP, 1 two-bedroom suite. Breakfast and snacks/refreshments included in rates. Types of meals: Cont plus and early coffee/tea. Beds: KQD. Modem hook-up, cable TV, VCR, DVD, stereo, refrigerator, snack bar, clock radio, telephone, fireplace, Direct TV and daily newspaper in room. Air conditioning. Fax, copier, spa, library, parlor games and WIFI Internet access on premises. Limited handicap access. Antiquing, art galleries, beach, bicycling, canoeing/kayaking, fishing, golf, hiking, live theater, museums, parks, shopping, tennis, water sports and wineries nearby.

Location: Ocean community.

Certificate may be used: April-June, subject to availability.

East Orleans   H19

Ship's Knees Inn

186 Beach Rd
East Orleans, MA 02643
(508)255-1312 (888)744-7756 Fax:(508)240-1351
Internet: www.shipskneesinn.com
E-mail: info@shipskneesinn.com

Circa 1820. This 180-year-old restored sea captain's home is a
three-minute walk to the ocean. Rooms are decorated in a nautical style with antiques. Several rooms feature authentic ship's
knees, hand-painted trunks, old clipper ship models and four-
poster beds. Some
rooms boast ocean
views, and the
Master Suite has a
working fireplace.
The inn offers swim-
ming and tennis
facilities on the grounds. About three miles away, the innkeepers also offer three rooms, a bedroom efficiency apartment and
two heated cottages on the Town Cove. Head into town, or
spend the day basking in the beauty of Nauset Beach with its
picturesque sand dunes.

Innkeeper(s): Pete & Denise Butcher. $90-325. 18 rooms, 14 with PB, 2
with FP, 2 suites. Breakfast included in rates. Types of meals: Cont plus.
Beds: KQDT. Cable TV, reading lamp, refrigerator, clock radio, some with fireplace, hair dryer, bath amenities, wireless Internet access and iron/ironing
board in room. Air conditioning. Fax, copier, swimming, library, parlor games
and our courtyard garden patio includes a gas fire pit on premises. Antiquing,
art galleries, beach, bicycling, canoeing/kayaking, fishing, golf, hiking, live
theater, museums, parks, shopping, tennis, water sports, wineries, Cape Cod
National Seashore guided beachwalks, swimming-ocean, bay & fresh water
lakes, whale & seal watching cruises, boating, bird watching and
gourmet/fine dining nearby.

Location: Ocean community.

Publicity: Cape Cod Travel Guide, Cape Cod Life Magazine, Cape Cod View
Magazine, Yankee Magazine and Florida Senior Traveler Magazine.

"Warm, homey and very friendly atmosphere. Very impressed with
the beamed ceilings."

Certificate may be used: Nov. 1-March 31.

The Nauset House Inn

143 Beach Rd, PO Box 774
East Orleans, MA 02643
(508)255-2195 (800)771-5508
Internet: www.nausethouseinn.com
E-mail: info@nausethouseinn.com

Circa 1810. Located a 1/2 mile from Nauset Beach, this inn
is a renovated farmhouse set on three acres, which include
an old apple orchard. A Victorian conservatory was purchased from a
Connecticut estate and
reassembled here, then
filled with wicker fur-
nishings, Cape flowers
and stained glass. Hand-
stenciling, handmade
quilts, antiques and more bouquets of flowers decorate the
rooms. The breakfast room features a fireplace, brick floor
and beamed ceiling. Breakfast includes treats such as ginger

pancakes or waffles with fresh strawberries. Wine and cranberry juice are served in the evenings.

Innkeeper(s): Diane Johnson, John & Cindy Vessella. $80-185. 14 rooms, 8
with PB, 1 cottage. Breakfast, snacks/refreshments, hors d'oeuvres and wine
included in rates. Types of meals: Full bkfst, early coffee/tea and afternoon
tea. Beds: KQDT. Reading lamp, some with fireplace and terry robes for
shared bath guests in room. Parlor games and telephone on premises.
Antiquing, art galleries, beach, bicycling, canoeing/kayaking, fishing, golf, hiking, horseback riding, live theater, museums, parks, shopping, sporting
events, tennis and water sports nearby.

Location: Ocean community.

Publicity: Country Living, Glamour, West Hartford News and Travel & Leisure.

"The inn provided a quiet, serene, comforting atmosphere."

Certificate may be used: Sunday-Thursday, excludes July-September and
Holidays.

The Parsonage Inn

202 Main St.
East Orleans, MA 02643
(508)255-8217 (888)422-8217 Fax:(508)255-8216
Internet: www.parsonageinn.com
E-mail: innkeeper@parsonageinn.com

Circa 1770. Originally a parsonage, this Cape-style home is
now a romantic inn nestled in the village of East Orleans and
only a mile and a half from Nauset Beach. Rooms are decorated
with antiques, quilts, Laura
Ashley fabrics and stenciling,
and they include the original
pine floors and low ceilings.
Cooked breakfasts are served
either in the dining room or
on the brick patio. The
innkeepers keep a selection of menus from local restaurants on
hand and in the summer season serve appetizers and refreshments each evening while guest peruse their dining choices.
The Parsonage is the perfect location to enjoy nature, with the
national seashore, Nickerson State Park and whale-watching
opportunities available to guests.

Innkeeper(s): Ian & Elizabeth Browne. $100-195. 8 rooms with PB.
Breakfast included in rates. Types of meals: Full bkfst. Beds: QT. Cable TV,
reading lamp, clock radio, coffeemaker, wireless Internet access, iron/ironing
board, all with private en-suite bathrooms, one has a kitchen, all rooms have
queen bed, two also have a twin bed and some with refrigerator in room. Air
conditioning. Fax, parlor games, telephone, fireplace, telephone, refrigerator
and grand piano on premises. Antiquing, art galleries, beach, bicycling,
canoeing/kayaking, fishing, golf, hiking, horseback riding, live theater, museums, parks, shopping, tennis, National Sea Shore, Nauset Beach, Skaket
Beach and Flax Pond nearby.

Publicity: Conde Nast Traveler and Bon Appetit.

"Your hospitality was as wonderful as your home. Your home was as
beautiful as Cape Cod. Thank you!"

Certificate may be used: Anytime, November-April, except holidays, subject
to availability.

Eastham   H18

Inn at the Oaks

3085 State Highway
Eastham, MA 02642
(508) 255-1886 (877) 255-1886 Fax:(508)240-0345
Internet: www.InnAtTheOaks.com
E-mail: reservations@InnAtTheOaks.com

Circa 1870. Originally an 1870 sea captain's home, this Queen
Anne Victorian listed in the National Register, graces the Eastham

Center Historic District in Massachusetts. Inn at the Oaks offers family-friendly amenities and packages. Children enjoy the out-

door playground and Little Acorns Play Room inside. Play pool, chess, checkers, games, puzzles and use the computer with Internet access in the Billiard Room. Relax on a porch rocker or hammock and read by the fire in the parlor.

Select a Suite, Getaway Room or Traditional Room. Some include a fireplace, porch or clawfoot tub. The Carriage House offers two pet-friendly rooms. Savor a country breakfast with specialty entrees in the Gathering Room or on the porch. The signature dish is Abelskivers, Danish pancakes. Spa services feature a two-person hot tub and massage therapy.

$120-300. 13 rooms with PB, 2 with FP, 4 suites, 1 conference room. Breakfast and snacks/refreshments included in rates. Types of meals: Cont, early coffee/tea and Afternoon Cookies. Beds: KQT. Cable TV, ceiling fan, some with fireplace, hair dryer, bath amenities and wireless Internet access in room. Central air. Fax, copier, parlor games and telephone on premises. Antiquing, art galleries, beach, bicycling, canoeing/kayaking, fishing, golf, hiking, horseback riding, live theater, museums, parks, shopping, sporting events, tennis, water sports, wineries, Whale watching, Cape Cod National Seashore and Summer Childrens' Theatre nearby.

Location: Ocean community.

"A delightful experience—Max Nichols, Oklahoma City Journal Record."

Certificate may be used: Anytime September-June, Sunday-Thursday only. July and August subject to availability.

Fairhaven I14

Baggins End Guest House

2 West Street
Fairhaven, MA 02719
(508)326-2567 Fax:(508)992-5608
Internet: www.bagginsendguesthouse.com
E-mail: info@bagginsendguesthouse.com

Relaxing and comfortable waterfront accommodations are accented by the beautiful setting. Sit on the stone patio deck or dock and enjoy the 180 degree view of the working harbor. Baggins End Guest House offers spacious yet intimate guest rooms and a continental breakfast to linger over while watching the swans go by. This Fairhaven, Massachusetts bed and breakfast is also for weddings and tented events. Take a harbor tour, or visit the New Bedford Whaling Museum. Ferry boats go to Martha's Vineyard and Nantucket. Wi-fi is available for exploring the world from indoors.

Innkeeper(s): Diane Tomassetti. Call for rates. 2 rooms, 1 conference room. Breakfast and wine included in rates. Types of meals: Cont plus, veg bkfst and early coffee/tea. Beds: Q. Reading lamp, CD player, bathrobes, wireless Internet access and iron/ironing board in room. TV, DVD, copier and telephone on premises. Antiquing, art galleries, beach, bicycling, canoeing/kayaking, fishing, golf, hiking, live theater, museums, parks, shopping, water sports and wineries nearby.

Certificate may be used: November-January, Monday-Thursday.

Falmouth J16

The Beach Rose Inn

17 Chase Road
Falmouth, MA 02540
(508)540-5706 (800)498-5706 Fax:(508)540-4880
Internet: www.thebeachroseinn.com
E-mail: innkeepers@thebeachroseinn.com

Circa 1863. Gracing the historic district in a peaceful village setting, this meticulously restored inn is listed in the National Register. The Main Inn, Carriage House and a Housekeeping Cottage offer tastefully decorated accommodations. Antique furnishings mingle well with period reproductions, cheery quilts and fine linens. Some guest bedrooms feature a variety of amenities that may include a whirlpool, fireplace, canopy bed, refrigerator, robes and private entrance. A well-presented breakfast is served in the gathering room or on the sun porch. After a day of exploring Cape Cod, sit and chat in the fireside sitting room.

Innkeeper(s): Sheryll & Douglas Reichwein. $135-250. 8 rooms with PB, 2 with FP, 1 with WP, 2 total suites, including 1 two-bedroom suite, 1 cottage. Breakfast and snacks/refreshments included in rates. Types of meals: Full gourmet bkfst, veg bkfst, Sun. brunch, early coffee/tea, hors d'oeuvres and wine. Beds: KQT. Cable TV, VCR, DVD, reading lamp, CD player, refrigerator, ceiling fan, clock radio, some with hot tub/spa, hair dryer, bathrobes, bath amenities, wireless Internet access and iron/ironing board in room. Air conditioning. Fax, copier, spa, telephone and fireplace on premises. Limited handicap access. Antiquing, art galleries, beach, bicycling, canoeing/kayaking, fishing, golf, hiking, horseback riding, live theater, museums, parks, shopping, water sports and Martha's Vineyard nearby.

Location: Country, ocean community. Cape Cod.

Certificate may be used: Sunday-Thursday anytime; Weekends April- 15-May 22 and Oct. 14-Jan. 2, Subject to availability, excluding holidays.

Greenfield C6

The Brandt House

29 Highland Ave
Greenfield, MA 01301-3605
(413)774-3329 (800)235-3329 Fax:(413)772-2908
Internet: www.brandthouse.com
E-mail: info@brandthouse.com

Circa 1890. Three-and-a-half-acre lawns surround this impressive three-story Colonial Revival house, situated hilltop. The library and poolroom are popular for lounging, but the favorite

gathering areas are the sunroom and the covered north porch. Ask for the aqua and white room with the fireplace, but all the rooms are pleasing. A full breakfast often includes homemade scones and is sometimes available on the slate patio in view of the expansive lawns and beautiful gardens.

A full-time staff provides for guest needs. There is a clay tennis court and nature trails, and in winter, lighted ice skating at a nearby pond. Historic Deerfield and Yankee Candle Company are within five minutes.

Innkeeper(s): Full time staff. $105-359. 9 rooms, 7 with PB, 2 with FP, 1 suite, 1 conference room. Breakfast included in rates. Types of meals: Full bkfst and early coffee/tea. Beds: KQT. Cable TV, reading lamp, refrigerator, ceiling fan, clock radio, telephone, desk, hot tub/spa, two with fireplace and microwave in room. Air conditioning. VCR, fax, copier, tennis, library, parlor games and fireplace on premises. Antiquing, cross-country skiing, downhill skiing, fishing, live theater, parks, shopping, sporting events, water sports, Old Deerfield and Lunt Silver nearby.

Location: Country, mountains.

Certificate may be used: Sunday-Thursday only.

Hadley   E6

Ivory Creek Bed and Breakfast Inn

31 Chmura Rd
Hadley, MA 01035-9727
(413)587-3115 (866)331-3115 Fax:(413)587-9751
Internet: www.ivorycreek.com
E-mail: pachaderm@aol.com

Circa 1996. Situated waterside on 24 wooded acres of the Mount Holyoke Range, this rambling bed and breakfast boasts a wraparound front porch, decks and balconies for ample opportunities to enjoy the surrounding scenic beauty. Each spacious guest bedroom features a fireplace, Oriental carpets and Continental furnishings. On the first floor a handicapped accessible room has an oversized bath and private deck. A multi-course breakfast served in the fireside dining room or plant-filled sun porch is sure to please. The Metacomet Monadnock Trail crosses the top of the 24-acre grounds for hiking. Mountain bikes and gear are available. Skinner State Park is an easy ride. After the day's adventures enjoy a soak in the hot tub.

Innkeeper(s): Tod & Judith Loebel. $135-250. 6 rooms with PB, 6 with FP, 1 two-bedroom suite, 2 conference rooms. Breakfast, Sunday brunch, snacks/refreshments, Butler's Pantry with complimentary cold beverages, hot tea or coffee, microwave popcorn and granola bars included in rates. Types of meals: Full gourmet bkfst, veg bkfst, early coffee/tea and picnic lunch. Beds: KQT. Modem hook-up, data port, cable TV, reading lamp, ceiling fan, snack bar, clock radio, telephone, turn-down service, desk, fireplace, hair dryer, bath amenities, wireless Internet access, iron/ironing board, all unique, some with decks and balconies in room. Central air. TV, VCR, DVD, fax, copier, spa, library, parlor games, laundry facility, gift shop, hiking trails, mountain bike trails and picnic areas on premises. Handicap access. Amusement parks, antiquing, art galleries, bicycling, canoeing/kayaking, cross-country skiing, fishing, golf, hiking, horseback riding, live theater, museums, parks, shopping, sporting events, water sports, Basketball Hall of Fame, Eric Carle Museum, Yankee Candle Factory, National Yiddish Bookstore and Historic Old Deerfield Village nearby.

Location: Country. Located on the side of the Mount Holyoke Range and bordering Skinner State Park.

Publicity: *Daily Hampshire Gazette (the premier home on the Historic Amherst House Tour 2005).*

Certificate may be used: December-March, Sunday-Thursday excluding holidays (Christmas, New Year's, Valentine's), Anytime, Last Minute-Based on Availability, Free room upgrade based on availability at check in.

Hatfield   D6

Old Mill on The Falls Inn

87 School Street
Hatfield, MA 01038
(413)247-3301
Internet: www.theoldmillonthefallsinn.com
E-mail: tjmapleheights@aol.com

Spanning one acre, this historic grist mill was built in 1880 as a mill and was restored in 2006 and converted to a B&B with a banquet facility. Old Mill Bed and Breakfast sits on Mill River with landscaped grounds, flower gardens and a koi pond. Located in Hatfield, Massachusetts it is just five miles from downtown Northampton. Guest bedrooms feature antiques, fine art and modern amenities. Some include whirlpool tubs. A

handicap-accessible room and a pet-friendly room are available. Breakfast is served in the dining room or on the deck that overlooks the waterfalls.

Innkeeper(s): Ted Jarrett . Call for rates. 9 rooms with PB, 2 with WP, 1 conference room. Breakfast included in rates. Types of meals: Full bkfst, early coffee/tea, picnic lunch, High Tea most Sundays, Full banquet room for event catering with on-site chef and Special catered dinners or brunches for groups of 12 or more. Beds: KQT. Data port, cable TV, reading lamp, clock radio, some with fireplace, hair dryer, bathrobes, bath amenities, wireless Internet access, iron/ironing board, Water views from every room, Several rooms over the falls with fantasic water views and sounds of the falls to fall asleep to in room. Central air. A fully handicapped accessible room and a Pet friendly room on premises. Handicap access. Amusement parks, antiquing, art galleries, bicycling, canoeing/kayaking, cross-country skiing, downhill skiing, fishing, golf, hiking, museums, parks, shopping, sporting events, wineries, Northampton and MA center (4 miles) nearby.

Location: Country, waterfront.

Certificate may be used: Anytime, November-March, subject to availability. Not valid Thanksgiving week or Christmas week.

Haydenville   D5

Penrose Victorian Inn

133 Main Street
Haydenville, MA 01060
(413)268-3014 (888)268-7711 Fax:(413)268-9232
Internet: www.penroseinn.com
E-mail: zimmer@penroseinn.com

Circa 1820. Experience Victorian elegance at this distinctive Queen Anne that sits on two resplendent acres across from the river. Recently renovated, the inn's antique furnishings and period decor offer a warm hospitality. Common rooms include the music room and parlor. Most of the well-appointed guest bedrooms feature fireplaces. Savor Penrose French toast with fresh seasonal fruit, juice and hot beverages by candlelight. Stroll the perennial and rose gardens with fountain, relax on the porch or go for a swim. Explore Emily Dickens House, Old Deerfield and Calvin Coolidge House, each less than 10 miles away.

Innkeeper(s): Nancy & Dick Zimmer. $125-165. 3 rooms with PB. Breakfast included in rates. Types of meals: Full gourmet bkfst and veg bkfst. Beds: Q. Data port, reading lamp, clock radio, telephone, turn-down service and fireplace in room. Air conditioning. TV, VCR, fax, copier, swimming, library, fireplace and laundry facility on premises. Amusement parks, antiquing, art galleries, bicycling, canoeing/kayaking, cross-country skiing, fishing, golf, hiking, horseback riding, live theater, museums, parks, shopping, sporting events, tennis and water sports nearby.

Location: City. Historic District.

Publicity: *Arrington's Bed and Breakfast Journal (voted "Best in the North" and "Best Near a College or University") and Christmas special with Mark Twain House.*

Certificate may be used: Nov. 30-May 1.

Hyannis Port   I17

The Simmons Homestead Inn

288 Scudder Ave
Hyannis Port, MA 02647
(508)778-4999 (800)637-1649 Fax:(508)790-1342
Internet: www.simmonshomesteadinn.com
E-mail: simmonshomestead@aol.com

Circa 1805. The only bed and breakfast in Hyannis Port, Massachusetts, The Simmons Homestead Inn is a relaxing and pleasant place for a getaway or vacation. Sit on a porch and sip wine during the social hour. On cooler evenings, gather in the fireside common room. Bikes are available for exploring Cape

Cod, and beach chairs and towels are provided too. Take a nap in a backyard hammock. A billiard room offers more entertainment. Animal-themed guest rooms and a two-bedroom family suite feature optional air conditioning and some rooms boast canopy or brass beds. Breakfast is a fresh and filling way to start each day. Ask about the inn's pet-friendly policy.

Innkeeper(s): Bill Putman. $120-320. 14 rooms with PB, 2 with FP, 2 suites. Breakfast included in rates. Types of meals: Full bkfst and early coffee/tea. Beds: KQT. Reading lamp, ceiling fan, clock radio and desk in room. VCR, fax, copier, bicycles, library, pet boarding, child care, parlor games, telephone, fireplace, billiard room and modern hook-up on premises. Antiquing, fishing, golf, live theater, parks, shopping, tennis and water sports nearby.

Location: Ocean community. Cape Cod.

Publicity: *Bon Appetit, Cape Code Life and Yankee.*

"I want to say that part of what makes Cape Cod special for us is the inn. It embodies much of what is wonderful at the Cape. By Sunday, I was completely rested, relaxed, renewed and restored."

Certificate may be used: Anytime, November-May except holiday weekends, subject to availability. June-October, Sunday-Thursday only, subject to availability.

Lee   E2

1800 Devonfield Inn, an English Country Estate

85 Stockbridge Rd
Lee, MA 01238-9308
(413)243-3298 (800)664-0880 Fax:(413)243-1360
Internet: www.devonfield.com
E-mail: innkeeper@devonfield.com

Circa 1800. 2009 Winner - Travelers' Choice for Romance. Devonfield is a gracious English-Style country house built in the late 1800s. Overlooking a pastoral meadow shaded by graceful birch trees with the rolling tapestry of the Berkshire Hills beyond, the B&B sits on 29 acres. In the main house, a

fireside living room is complete with grand piano, library and stereo. Relax in the television room and on the porch. A guest pantry is always stocked with coffee, tea, hot chocolate, popcorn and fresh-baked cookies. Browse through the movie library. Many spacious guest bedrooms have wood-burning fireplaces; some boast Jacuzzis and terry robes. All rooms have complimentary cognac, locally hand-made chocolates and bottled water. A hearty country breakfast proudly features foods locally grown and/or prepared. A tennis court and heated swimming pool offers pleasant onsite activities.

Innkeeper(s): Ronnie & Bruce Singer. $160-375. 10 rooms with PB, 4 with FP, 4 suites, 1 cottage. Breakfast, snacks/refreshments, Fully stocked guest pantry with coffee, tea, hot chocolate, popcorn and fresh baked cookies. The pantry also has a full-size refrigerator for guest use for special snacks or refreshments. All rooms have complimentary cognac and locally and hand-made chocolates as well as bottled water. included in rates. Types of meals: Full gourmet bkfst, early coffee/tea, afternoon tea and A fireside (fall and winter) candlelit gourmet breakfast is served on fine china accompanied by clas-

sical music. Breakfast includes a bountiful buffet followed by a specially selected hot entree served table-side each day. Beds: KQ. Modern hook-up, cable TV, VCR, DVD, reading lamp, CD player, refrigerator, clock radio, telephone, coffeemaker, hair dryer, bathrobes, bath amenities, wireless Internet access and iron/ironing board in room. Central air. Fax, copier, swimming, bicycles, tennis, library, child care, parlor games, fireplace, gift shop, Flower-filled gardens, Tennis court and Heated pool on premises. Limited handicap access. Antiquing, art galleries, bicycling, canoeing/kayaking, cross-country skiing, downhill skiing, fishing, golf, hiking, horseback riding, live theater, museums, parks, shopping, tennis, wineries, Tanglewood, The Norman Rockwell Museum, Jacobs Pillow, Shakespeare & Company, Horseback riding, Ballooning, Downhill & cross-country skiing, Greenock Golf Club, Hiking, Biking, Archery, Fishing and Kayaking nearby.

Location: Country, mountains.

Publicity: *Discerning Traveler, New York Magazine, Karen Brown's Guides, Pamela Lanier, Berkshire Living and Berkshire Eagle.*

"A special thank you for your warm and kind hospitality. We feel as though this is our home away from home."

Certificate may be used: Nov. 15-May 15, Rooms 6 and 7 only, Sunday-Thursday.

Lenox   E2

Birchwood Inn

7 Hubbard St, Box 2020
Lenox, MA 01240-4604
(413)637-2600 (800)524-1646 Fax:(413)637-4604
Internet: www.birchwood-inn.com
E-mail: innkeeper@birchwood-inn.com

Circa 1767. Experience comfortable country elegance at this Colonial Revival mansion that has welcomed friends since 1767. The inn's antiques, collectibles, quilts, canopy beds and

nine fireplaces create an idyllic getaway. The inn is renowned for sumptuous breakfasts and afternoon tea and was voted "Best Breakfast in New England." Enjoy Berkshire breezes and fireflies on the porch in summer, spring blossoms in stone-fenced gardens, vibrant fall foliage, and the welcome warmth of the firesides in winter. The oldest home in Lenox, it is a short walk from its tranquil hilltop setting to the village's restaurants, galleries and shops.

Innkeeper(s): Ellen Gutman Chenaux. $180-345. 11 rooms with PB, 6 with FP, 4 total suites, including 1 two-bedroom suite, 2 conference rooms. Breakfast and afternoon tea included in rates. Types of meals: Full gourmet bkfst, early coffee/tea, snacks/refreshments and Midnight snack. Beds: KQT. Cable TV, reading lamp, ceiling fan, clock radio, telephone, desk, most with fireplace, hair dryer, bathrobes, bath amenities, wireless Internet access and Free wireless Internet access in room. Air conditioning. VCR, DVD, fax, copier, library, parlor games, gift shop and Free wireless Internet access on premises. Limited handicap access. Antiquing, art galleries, beach, bicycling, canoeing/kayaking, cross-country skiing, downhill skiing, fishing, golf, hiking, horseback riding, live theater, museums, parks, shopping, tennis, water sports, wineries, Tanglewood, music and theater festivals and the Norman Rockwell Museum nearby.

Location: Mountains. Village.

Publicity: *Country Inns, Country Living, New York Magazine, Montreal Gazette, Gourmet Magazine and The Discerning Traveler.*

"Thank you for memories that we will cherish forever."

Certificate may be used: Monday-Thursday, Jan. 5-April 15, holidays excluded.

Walker House

64 Walker St
Lenox, MA 01240-2718
(413)637-1271 (800)235-3098 Fax:(413)637-2387
Internet: www.walkerhouse.com
E-mail: walkerhouse.inn@verizon.net

Circa 1804. This beautiful Federal-style house sits in the center of the village on three acres of graceful woods and restored gardens. Guest rooms have fireplaces and private baths. Each is named for a favorite composer such as Beethoven, Mozart or Handel. The innkeepers'
musical backgrounds include
associations with the San
Francisco Opera, the New York
City Opera, and the Los
Angeles Philharmonic. Walker
House concerts are scheduled
from time to time. The innkeepers offer film and opera screenings nightly on a twelve-foot screen. With prior approval, some pets may be allowed.

Innkeeper(s): Peggy & Richard Houdek. $90-220. 8 rooms with PB, 5 with FP, 1 conference room. Breakfast and afternoon tea included in rates. Types of meals: Cont plus, veg bkfst and early coffee/tea. Beds: QDT. Reading lamp, clock radio and desk in room. Air conditioning. TV, VCR, DVD, fax, copier, library, parlor games, telephone, fireplace, theatre with Internet access and 100-inch screen on premises. Limited handicap access. Antiquing, art galleries, bicycling, cross-country skiing, downhill skiing, fishing, golf, hiking, horseback riding, live theater, museums, parks, shopping, water sports and music nearby.

Location: In small village.

Publicity: *Boston Globe, PBS, Los Angeles Times, New York Times* and *Dog Fancy.*

"We had a grand time staying with fellow music and opera lovers! Breakfasts were lovely."

Certificate may be used: Nov. 1-April 30, Sunday-Thursday, excluding holiday periods.

Marblehead   D14

Harborside House B&B

23 Gregory Street
Marblehead, MA 01945
(781)631-1032
Internet: www.harborsidehouse.com
E-mail: stay@harborsidehouse.com

Circa 1850. Enjoy the Colonial charm of this home, which overlooks Marblehead Harbor on Boston's historic North Shore. Rooms are decorated with antiques and period wallpaper. A third-story sundeck offers excellent views. A generous continental breakfast of home-baked breads, muffins and fresh fruit is served each morning in the well-decorated dining room or on the open porch. The village of Marblehead provides many shops and restaurants. Boston and Logan airport are 30 minutes away.

Innkeeper(s): Susan Livingston. $90-1125. 2 rooms. Breakfast, afternoon tea and snacks/refreshments included in rates. Types of meals: Cont plus, veg bkfst, early coffee/tea and Homemade cookies. Beds: DT. Modem hook-up, cable TV, VCR, reading lamp, CD player, clock radio, desk, hair dryer, bathrobes, bath amenities, wireless Internet access, iron/ironing board, toiletries, Harbor Sweets candy and fresh flowers in room. Bicycles, library, telephone and fireplace on premises. Antiquing, art galleries, beach, bicycling, canoeing/kayaking, fishing, museums, parks, shopping, water sports, historical house tour and museum nearby.

Location: Waterfront. Historic harbor.

Publicity: *Marblehead Reporter.*

"Harborside Inn is restful, charming, with a beautiful view of the water. I wish we didn't have to leave."

Certificate may be used: January-April, Sunday-Saturday.

Middleboro   H14

On Cranberry Pond B&B

43 Fuller St
Middleboro, MA 02346-1706
(508)946-0768 Fax:(508)947-8221
Internet: www.oncranberrypond.com
E-mail: OnCranberryPond@Gmail.com

Circa 1989. Nestled in the historic "cranberry capital of the world," this 8,000 square-foot modern farmhouse rests on a working cranberry bog. There are two miles of trails to meander, and during berry picking season guests can watch as buckets of the fruit are collected. Rooms are comfortable and well appointed. The Master Suite includes a whirlpool bath for two. A 93-foot deck overlooks the cranberry bog. Innkeeper Jeannine LaBossiere creates gourmet breakfasts and yummy homemade snacks at night. Honeymoons and anniversaries are popular here. There is a spacious conference room with plenty of business amenities. Borrow a fishing rod or one of the innkeeper's mountain bikes for an afternoon's adventure you will long remember. Plymouth, Mass. is nearby and whale watching is a popular activity.

Innkeeper(s): Jeannine LaBossiere- Krushas, Ken Krushas and son Tim. $95-180. 6 rooms, 4 with PB, 2 suites, 2 conference rooms. Breakfast and snacks/refreshments included in rates. Types of meals: Full gourmet bkfst, veg bkfst, early coffee/tea and lunch. Beds: Q. Modem hook-up, data port, cable TV, VCR, reading lamp, CD player, ceiling fan, clock radio, telephone, coffeemaker, turn-down service, desk and hot tub in room. Air conditioning. Fax, copier, bicycles and library on premises. Antiquing, art galleries, beach, bicycling, fishing, golf, live theater, museums, parks, shopping, tennis and wineries nearby.

Location: Oversized Cape.

"Your dedication to making your guests comfortable is above and beyond. You are tops in your field."

Certificate may be used: Anytime subject to availability.

Nantucket   L18

Brass Lantern

11 N Water St
Nantucket, MA 02554-3521
(508)228-4064 (800)377-6609 Fax:(508)325-0928
Internet: www.brasslanternnantucket.com
E-mail: info@brasslanternnantucket.com

Circa 1838. Ideally located in the residential historic district of town, the Main Inn is a Greek Revival home with a newer Garden Wing that blends harmoniously. Both sections were renovated recently. The Main Inn offers Old World ambiance enhanced by the traditional elegance of antiques, Oriental rugs, chair rail and wainscoting. The Garden Wing features a more contemporary Nantucket-style decor. Guest bedrooms and suites pamper with Egyptian cotton sheets, fluffy pillows and soft robes. Enjoy a tempting continental breakfast in the sunny dining room or on teak furniture in the garden. Walk down the cobblestone street to the ferry, harbor and other amazing sites and activities in the local area. Rent a bike or take a shuttle bus to explore Sconset and Surfside.

Innkeeper(s): Michelle and Sharon. $125-500. 17 rooms, 15 with PB, 1 two-bedroom suite. Breakfast included in rates. Types of meals: Cont plus. Beds: KQDT. Cable TV, DVD, reading lamp, refrigerator, clock radio, telephone, voice mail, hair dryer, bathrobes, bath amenities, wireless Internet access, iron/ironing board, Spa robes and Pet amenities in pet-friendly rooms in room. Air conditioning. Fax, copier, library, child care, parlor games, fireplace and Pet friendly on premises. Antiquing, art galleries, beach, bicycling, canoeing/kayaking, fishing, golf, hiking, live theater, museums, parks, shopping, tennis, water sports, wineries and The Nantucket Whaling Museum (on Yahoo list of "10 places to see before you die") nearby.

Location: Ocean community. The Brass Lantern is ideally located in the residential Historic District in Nantucket Town, an easy walk from Steamship Wharf and the shops and restaurants of Main Street.

Publicity: Boston Globe and PlumTV-Nantucket.

Certificate may be used: April-June 15, Sunday-Thursday; Sept.15-Nov. 15, Sunday-Thursday; Last minute subject to availability.

Cliff Lodge Bed & Breakfast

9 Cliff Rd
Nantucket, MA 02554-3639
(508)228-9480
Internet: www.clifflodgenantucket.com
E-mail: info@clifflodgenantucket.com

Circa 1771. Poised on a hill on Nantucket Island, off the coast of Massachusetts, Cliff Lodge Bed & Breakfast boasts spectacular ocean views. Be revived by the warm and inviting ambiance, casual elegance and thoughtful attention to detail. Original artwork by local artists adorns the walls. Gather for afternoon tea and refreshments. Stay in a spacious guest room or suite; many include a fireplace. A generous breakfast buffet can be enjoyed on Nantucket patterned Wedgwood china in the dining room, garden patio or fireside living room. Gracing the Old Historic District, this B&B is just a short walk from the ferry. Soak up the sun and sea breeze at the beach; browse the shops and dine in the restaurants of famous cobblestoned Main Street. Specials and packages may be available.

Innkeeper(s): Sally Beck. $145-320. 12 rooms with PB, 5 with FP, 2 suites. Breakfast, afternoon tea, snacks/refreshments and wine included in rates. Types of meals: Cont, hors d'oeuvres, room service, A bountiful continental breakfast prepared by the pastry chef is served each morning, featuring her famous homemade granola and scones, another pastry, cereals, fruit, juices, gourmet coffee and tea. In the afternoon and homemade treats are served and Cliff Lodge is the only inn on Nantucket to offer regularly scheduled afternoon teas. Beds: KT. Cable TV, reading lamp, clock radio, hair dryer, bathrobes, bath amenities, wireless Internet access and iron/ironing board in room. Air conditioning. Library, parlor games, telephone and fireplace on premises. Antiquing, art galleries, beach, bicycling, canoeing/kayaking, fishing, golf, hiking, live theater, museums, shopping, tennis, water sports, wineries, Located inn the heart of Nantucket's historic district, Shops, Beaches and Restaurants in town are short walk away nearby.

Location: City. Boston, Martha's Vineyard.

Certificate may be used: Oct. 15-May 15, excluding Christmas Stroll and Daffodil weekend, subject to availability.

House of The Seven Gables

32 Cliff Rd
Nantucket, MA 02554-3644
(508)228-4706
Internet: www.houseofthesevengables.com
E-mail: walton@nantucket.net

Circa 1880. Originally the annex of the Sea Cliff Inn, one of the island's oldest hotels, this three-story Queen Anne Victorian inn offers 10 guest rooms. Beaches, bike rentals, museums, restaurants, shops and tennis courts are all found

nearby. The guest rooms are furnished with king or queen beds and period antiques. Breakfast is served each morning in the guest rooms and often include homemade coffee cake, muffins or Portuguese rolls.

Innkeeper(s): Sue Walton. $100-300. 10 rooms, 8 with PB. Breakfast included in rates. Types of meals: Cont. Beds: KQ. Telephone, fireplace and bird watching on premises. Antiquing, fishing, live theater, shopping and water sports nearby.

Location: The Old Historic District.

"You have a beautiful home and one that makes everyone feel relaxed and at home."

Certificate may be used: Anytime, Sunday-Thursday.

Martin House Inn

61 Centre Street
Nantucket, MA 02554
(508)228-0678 Fax:(508)325-4798
Internet: www.martinhouseinn.net
E-mail: info@martinhouseinn.net

Circa 1803. Take the ferry from Martha's Vineyard, Hyannis or Harwich to begin an island holiday on Nantucket at Martin House Inn in Massachusetts. Open year round, this Greek Revival mariner's mansion is a comfortable, refreshing blend of old-world flair and new-world luxury. Relax on the wicker-filled veranda or sit by the fire in the living room. Afternoon tea and treats are served daily. The inn is accented by a revolving collection of original paintings from local artists. Inviting guest rooms and a suite boast canopy and four-poster beds; some include fireplaces. Indulge in a bountiful continental breakfast that features homemade granola, cereals, fruit, scones and other creations made by the pastry chef. Walk to the beach or browse the galleries, museums and shops along the famous cobblestone Main Street.

Innkeeper(s): Skye Schuyler. $95-395. 13 rooms, 9 with PB, 5 with FP, 1 suite. Breakfast, afternoon tea, snacks/refreshments, hors d'oeuvres and wine included in rates. Types of meals: Cont, A bountiful continental breakfast prepared by pastry chef is served each morning, featuring her famous homemade granola and scones, another pastry, cereals, fruit, juices, gourmet coffee and tea. In the afternoon and homemade treats are served and the only inn on Nantucket to offer regularly scheduled afternoon teas. Beds: QDT. Reading lamp, clock radio, desk, hair dryer, bathrobes, bath amenities, wireless Internet access and iron/ironing board in room. Air conditioning. TV, library, parlor games, telephone and fireplace on premises. Antiquing, art galleries, beach, canoeing/kayaking, fishing, hiking, live theater, museums, parks, shopping, tennis, water sports and wineries nearby.

Location: City. Boston, Martha's Vineyard.

Publicity: Cape Cod Life.

"A wonderful weekend filled with warm hospitality. We enjoyed it all."

Certificate may be used: Oct. 15-May 15, excluding Christmas Stroll and Daffodil weekend, subject to availability.

Petersham   D8

Clamber Hill Inn & Restaurant

111 N Main St
Petersham, MA 01366-9501
(978)724-8800 (888)374-0007 Fax:(978)724-8829
Internet: www.clamberhill.com
E-mail: relax@clamberhill.com

Circa 1927. Sitting in the midst of 33 peaceful and secluded wooded acres this statuesque 1927 European country estate is just minutes from Quabbin Reservoir. The local forests, known for their dramatic seasonal color changes, draw many leaf peepers to the inn. Furnished with antiques and Oriental carpets, guest bedrooms are inviting retreats. Stay in a suite with a sitting room and fireplace. Breakfast is a gourmet delight with fresh fruit, homemade cinnamon rolls, muffins, waffles with strawberries, peach-filled French toast and wild blueberry pancakes. High tea is available by arrangement. A full-service restaurant serves dinner Friday, Saturday and Sunday. Stroll through the colorful gardens and bird watch. Visit the Fisher Museum just three miles away at the 3,000-acre Harvard Forest.

Innkeeper(s): Mark & Deni Ellis. $165-235. 5 rooms with PB, 4 with FP, 2 total suites, including 1 two-bedroom suite, 2 conference rooms. Breakfast and snacks/refreshments included in rates. Types of meals: Full gourmet bkfst, veg bkfst, early coffee/tea, afternoon tea, wine and Please visit Web site for full details on dining services . Restaurant on premises. Beds: QT. Reading lamp, CD player, clock radio, coffeemaker, desk, most with fireplace, hair dryer, bath amenities, wireless Internet access, iron/ironing board, Amenities tray, Complimentary brandy and Information on the surrounding area in room. Air conditioning. Fax, copier, library, parlor games, telephone, laundry facility, Parlor, Terraces, Gardens and Restaurant on premises. Antiquing, art galleries, beach, bicycling, canoeing/kayaking, cross-country skiing, downhill skiing, fishing, golf, hiking, live theater, museums, parks, shopping, water sports and wineries nearby.

Location: Country. Central Massachusetts.

Publicity: *Yankee Travel Magazine Editor's Choice for Central Massachusetts (April 2005), Boston Globe (December 2006), Worcester Living (January 2007) and Restaurant featured on Fox 25 August 2006.*

Certificate may be used: Nov. 1-March 31, excluding holidays and Valentine's Day.

Winterwood at Petersham

19 N Main St
Petersham, MA 01366
(978)724-8885
Internet: www.winterwoodinn.net
E-mail: winterwoodatpetersham@verizon.net

Circa 1842. The town of Petersham is often referred to as a museum of Greek Revival architecture. One of the grand houses facing the common is Winterwood. It boasts fireplaces in almost every room. Private dining is available for groups of up to 70 people. The inn is listed in the National Register.

Innkeeper(s): Jean & Robert Day. $149-199. 6 rooms with PB, 5 with FP, 1 with WP, 1 two-bedroom suite. Breakfast included in rates. Types of meals: Cont plus. Beds: QDT. Reading lamp, ceiling fan, clock radio, most with fireplace and bath amenities in room. Air conditioning. TV, VCR, DVD, fax, copier, library, parlor games and telephone on premises. Antiquing, art galleries, bicycling, canoeing/kayaking, cross-country skiing, downhill skiing, fishing, golf, hiking, horseback riding, live theater, museums, shopping and wineries nearby.

Location: Country. Town Common.

Publicity: *Boston Globe, Yankee Magazine, Athol Daily News, Greenfield Recorder, The Gardner News and The Fitchburg Sentinel.*

"Between your physical facilities and Jean's cooking, our return to normal has been made even more difficult. Your hospitality was just a fantastic extra to our total experience."

Certificate may be used: Sunday-Thursday, Not valid in October or any holiday.

Plymouth   H16

A White Swan Bed and Breakfast

146 Manomet Point Road
Plymouth, MA 02360
(508)224-3759
Internet: www.whiteswan.com
E-mail: relax@whiteswan.com

Built as a farmhouse in 1796, A White Swan Bed and Breakfast has been offering a New England ambiance of warmth and hospitality for more than a century in historic Plymouth, Massachusetts. It is named after the 100-plus onsite swans that glide along the ocean's edge. Relax on the front porch, in the garden or in the living room with a snack. Browse through the video collection for a movie to watch. Some of the guest bedrooms and suites feature clawfoot tubs and on the uppermost level they boast their own entry and deck. Depending on the day of the week enjoy a served breakfast or a buffet. Bike beside the Cape Cod Canal, take the ferry to Martha's Vineyard or Nantucket Island and plan a day trip to Boston.

Innkeeper(s): Christine Cox. Call for rates. Call inn for details. Breakfast, afternoon tea and Other meals available on advance requests included in rates. Types of meals: Full bkfst, early coffee/tea, snacks/refreshments and Occasional dinners served with advance reservation. Beds: KQDT. Cable TV, VCR, DVD, reading lamp, refrigerator, ceiling fan, telephone, desk, hair dryer, bath amenities, wireless Internet access, iron/ironing board, specific rooms have ceiling fans and DVD players and phone is in common area in room. Air conditioning. Bicycles, parlor games, fireplace and Guests are welcome to use the outdoor grill on premises. Antiquing, art galleries, beach, bicycling, canoeing/kayaking, cross-country skiing, fishing, golf, hiking, horseback riding, live theater, museums, parks, shopping, tennis, water sports, wineries and Whale watching nearby.

Location: Ocean community. Close to Cape Cod.

Publicity: *Patriot Ledger article on Holiday House Tour sponsored by Pilgrim Hall Museum 2007.*

Certificate may be used: March-May, Monday-Friday, subject to availability.

Provincetown   G18

Gabriel's at the Ashbrooke Inn

102 Bradford St
Provincetown, MA 02657
(508)487-3232
Internet: www.gabriels.com
E-mail: gabrielsma@aol.com

Circa 1830. Experience Gabriel's heavenly setting and cozy hospitality that have been enjoyed by many since 1979. Restored homes are graced with sky-lit common areas to gather in as a group or an individual. Each guest bedroom and suite is distinguished by the name and character of a famous personality. Most feature fireplaces, many boast Jacuzzi tubs and some include kitchenettes, skylights, sleeping lofts and semi-private porches. Modern amenities include high-speed Internet access and computers, voice mail, VCRs and a video library. Savor a full breakfast each morning. Lounge on a sun deck with afternoon wine and cheese. After a work out in the exercise gym, relax in the sauna or steam room. Soak in one of the two soothing outdoor hot tubs. Conveniently located in the heart of quaint Provincetown, the beach is only one block away.

Innkeeper(s): Elizabeth and Elizabeth Brooke. $125-350. 14 rooms with PB, 13 with FP, 10 with WP, 2 suites, 1 conference room. Breakfast, afternoon tea and snacks/refreshments included in rates. Types of meals: Full bkfst and veg bkfst. Beds: KQD. Cable TV, VCR, DVD, reading lamp, stereo, refrigerator, ceiling fan, snack bar, clock radio, coffeemaker, desk, hot tub/spa, fireplace, hair dryer, bathrobes, bath amenities, wireless Internet access and iron/ironing board in room. Air conditioning. Fax, copier, sauna, library, child care, parlor games, telephone and e-mail on premises. Limited handicap access. Antiquing, art galleries, beach, bicycling, canoeing/kayaking, cross-country skiing, fishing, golf, hiking, live theater, museums, parks, shopping, tennis, water sports, wineries and whale watching nearby.

Location: Ocean community.

Certificate may be used: Nov. 1 to April 1 except weekends and holidays.

Rehoboth   H12

Gilbert's B&B

30 Spring St
Rehoboth, MA 02769-2408
(508)252-6416
Internet: www.gilbertsbb.com
E-mail: jg@gilbertsbb.com

Circa 1835. This country farmhouse sits on 17 acres of woodland that includes an award-winning tree farm. Cross-country skiing and hiking are found right outside the door. If they choose to, guests can even help with the farm chores, caring for horses and gardening. Three antique-filled bedrooms share a second-floor sitting room and bathroom. There are two first-floor rooms with a working fireplace and private bath. The nearby town of Rehoboth is 360 years old.

Innkeeper(s): Jeanne Gilbert & Donald Beardsworth. $79-99. 5 rooms, 2 with PB, 1 conference room. Breakfast, afternoon tea and snacks/refreshments included in rates. Types of meals: Full bkfst, afternoon tea and snacks/refreshments. Beds: KQDT. Reading lamp, desk and two with fireplace in room. VCR, DVD, fax, copier, swimming, stable, library, telephone, fireplace and horse boarding only on premises. Antiquing, cross-country skiing, fishing, live theater, parks, shopping, sporting events and water sports nearby.

Location: Country.

Publicity: *Attleboro Sun Chronicle, Country, Somerset Spectator, Country Gazette and Pawtucket Times.*

"This place has become my second home. Thank you for the family atmosphere of relaxation, fun, spontaneity and natural surroundings."

Certificate may be used: Sunday-Thursday, Dec.1-April, subject to availability.

Rockport   C15

Emerson Inn By The Sea

One Cathedral Avenue
Rockport, MA 01966
(978)546-6321 (800)964-5550 Fax:(978)546-7043
Internet: www.emersoninnbythesea.com
E-mail: info@emersoninnbythesea.com

Circa 1846. This Greek Revival inn's namesake, Ralph Waldo Emerson, once called the place, "thy proper summer home." As it is the oldest continuously operated inn on Cape Ann,

decades of travelers agree with his sentiment. The guest rooms are comfortable, yet tastefully furnished, and some boast ocean views. The grounds include a heated swimming pool as well as landscaped gardens. Breakfast is included in the rates. Guests also can enjoy dinner at The Grand Cafe, the inn's award winning restaurant.

Innkeeper(s): Bruce & Michele Coates. $99-379. 36 rooms with PB, 2 with FP, 2 two-bedroom suites, 2 cottages, 3 conference rooms. Breakfast and afternoon tea included in rates. Types of meals: Full gourmet bkfst, early coffee/tea, snacks/refreshments, wine and gourmet dinner. Restaurant on premises. Beds: KQDT. Modem hook-up, data port, cable TV, refrigerator, clock radio, telephone, desk, hair dryer, bath amenities, wireless Internet access, iron/ironing board, fireplace, 11 with spa tubs and wireless Internet access in room. Air conditioning. TV, VCR, fax, copier, swimming, sauna, parlor games and gift shop on premises. Limited handicap access. Antiquing, art galleries, beach, bicycling, canoeing/kayaking, fishing, golf, hiking, horseback riding, live theater, museums, shopping and wineries nearby.

Location: Ocean community, waterfront.

Publicity: *Yankee Magazine Travel Guide to New England "Must-See" Destination, Arrington's Inn Traveler, The Discerning Traveler, Karen Brown's Guide to New England and TV 40 Springfield.*

"We were very impressed with every aspect of the Emerson Inn."

Certificate may be used: November-April, May and October, Sunday-Thursday only, subject to availability.

Linden Tree Inn

26 King St
Rockport, MA 01966-1444
(978)546-2494 (800)865-2122 Fax:(978)546-3297
Internet: www.lindentreeinn.com
E-mail: ltree@shore.net

Circa 1870. The breakfasts at this Victorian-style inn keep guests coming back year after year. Guests feast on home-baked treats such as scones, coffee cakes or Sunday favorites, French toast bread pudding, asparagus frittatas and spinach quiche. Each of the bedchambers features individual decor, and the innkeepers offer a formal living room and sun room for relaxation. The cupola affords a view of Mill Pond and Sandy Bay.

Innkeeper(s): Tobey and John Shepherd. $105-162. 16 rooms with PB, 1 two-bedroom suite. Breakfast, afternoon tea and Full breakfast served buffet style included in rates. Types of meals: Full bkfst, early coffee/tea, Breakfast served buffet style and afternoon tea available throught day and evening. Beds: KQT. Reading lamp, clock radio, wireless Internet access, Some with cable TV, Some with CD player and Some with ceiling fans in room. Air conditioning. TV, VCR, DVD, fax, copier, parlor games, telephone, fireplace, Carriage house has semi-efficiency kitchen and DVD player in living room on premises. Amusement parks, antiquing, art galleries, beach, bicycling, canoeing/kayaking, fishing, golf, hiking, live theater, museums, parks, shopping, tennis, water sports and wineries nearby.

Location: Ocean community.

Publicity: *Boston Globe and Boston Magazine.*

"Great coffee! Love that apple walnut bread. Thank you for making this home."

Certificate may be used: Anytime, November-March, subject to availability.

Sally Webster Inn

34 Mount Pleasant St
Rockport, MA 01966-1713
(978) 546-9251
Internet: www.sallywebster.com
E-mail: sallywebsterinn@hotmail.com

Circa 1832. William Choate left this pre-Civil War home to be divided by his nine children. Sally Choate Webster, the ninth child, was to receive several first-floor rooms and the attic chamber, but ended up owning the entire home. The innkeepers have filled the gracious home with antiques and period reproductions, which complement the original pumpkin pine floors, antique door moldings and six fireplaces. Shops, restaurants, the beach and the rocky coast are all within

three blocks of the inn. Whale watching, kayaking, antique shops, music festivals, island tours and museums are among the myriad of nearby attractions. In addition to these, Salem is just 15 miles away, and Boston is a 35-mile drive.

Innkeeper(s): Suzan & Dean. $105-150. 8 rooms with PB, 2 with FP, 1 suite. Breakfast included in rates. Types of meals: Full bkfst, early coffee/tea, We offer refrigeration services, cold teas and water, Keurig Machine for Coffee, Hot Tea and and Hot Cocoas. Beds: KQDT. Cable TV, reading lamp, clock radio, some with fireplace, hair dryer, bath amenities, wireless Internet access and iron/ironing board in room. Air conditioning. DVD, parlor games, We offer Concierge Service for reservations, travel to Commuter Rail and Bicycle and Kayak Rentals on premises. Antiquing, art galleries, beach, bicycling, canoeing/kayaking, fishing, golf, hiking, horseback riding, live theater, museums, parks, shopping, sporting events, water sports, Many scenic walks from the Inn, Walk to Harbor, Shops, Galleries and Dining nearby.

Location: Ocean community.

Publicity: WNBP and AM1450.

"All that a bed and breakfast should be."

Certificate may be used: Sunday-Friday, Nov. 15-March, excluding holidays.

Seven South Street Inn

7 South Street
Rockport, MA 01966-1799
(978)546-6708 (888)284-2730
Internet: www.sevensouthstreetinn.com
E-mail: theinn@sevensouth.net

Circa 1766. Relax in the friendly and gracious atmosphere of this family-owned inn, open year-round. The 1766 Colonial with antiques and reproductions was recently renovated to provide a warm haven of peace and privacy. Gather in the fireside living room, library or sitting room to watch a movie, play games or chat. An outdoor deck is surrounded by colorful, well-kept gardens. Guest bedrooms, a two-room suite and an efficiency suite are inviting accommodations for vacations or extended stays. Enjoy fine linens, towels and robes. Two gourmet breakfast seatings are offered each morning for well-presented, elegant dining that tastes as great as it looks. Swim in the seasonal pool, or ride a bike to explore the scenic area. Make whale watching reservations and visit the local Circles Day Spa.

Innkeeper(s): Debbie & Nick Benn. $79-179. 8 rooms with PB, 1 two-bedroom suite. Breakfast and snacks/refreshments included in rates. Types of meals: Full gourmet bkfst, veg bkfst and early coffee/tea. Beds: QDT. Data port, cable TV, VCR, DVD, reading lamp, stereo, refrigerator, clock radio, telephone, desk, hair dryer, bathrobes, bath amenities, wireless Internet access and iron/ironing board in room. Air conditioning. Swimming, bicycles, library, parlor games and laundry facility on premises. Antiquing, art galleries, beach, bicycling, canoeing/kayaking, cross-country skiing, fishing, golf, hiking, horseback riding, live theater, museums, parks, shopping, tennis, water sports and Whale Watching nearby.

Location: Ocean community.

Certificate may be used: Oct. 1 through May 20, subject to availability.

The Inn on Cove Hill

37 Mount Pleasant St
Rockport, MA 01966-1727
(978)546-2701 (888)546-2701 Fax:(978)546-1095
Internet: www.innoncovehill.com
E-mail: Betsy25@verizon.net

Circa 1771. Pirate gold found at Gully Point paid for this Georgian Federal-style house. A white picket fence and granite walkway welcome guests. Inside, an exquisitely crafted spiral staircase, random-width, pumpkin-pine floors and hand-forged hinges display the original artisan's handiwork. Furnishings include family heirlooms, four-poster canopy beds, and paint-

ings by area artists. Muffin Du Jour is baked fresh each day by Betsy. Take a train to Boston or walk nearby and enjoy whale watching, fishing the local waters, or simply exploring the antique shops and village streets.

Innkeeper(s): Betsy Eck. $145-170. 6 rooms with PB, 1 two-bedroom suite. Breakfast included in rates. Types of meals: Cont plus and early coffee/tea. Beds: QDT. Cable TV and reading lamp in room. Central air. TV, library, parlor games, telephone and fireplace on premises. Antiquing, art galleries, beach, bicycling, canoeing/kayaking, fishing, golf, hiking, horseback riding, live theater, museums, parks, shopping, tennis, water sports, wineries, state park, castle and train to Boston nearby.

Location: Ocean community.

Certificate may be used: Anytime, November-April, subject to availability.

Rowe B4

Maple House Bed & Breakfast

51 Middletown Hill Rd
Rowe, MA 01367-9702
(413)339-0107
Internet: www.maplehousebb.com
E-mail: info@maplehousebb.com

Circa 1784. Sitting on a hilltop in the Berkshires, this 200-year-old Colonial homestead farm is also known as The House on the Hill with a View of Yesteryear. Twenty scenic acres provide an assortment of activities. Hike, cross-country ski, nap on a hammock or feed the animals. Relax in the solarium by the brick fireplace. Recently renovated guest bedrooms and a suite feature the original hand-hewn beams and knotty pine flooring with antique furnishings and colorful quilts. Savor a hearty, home-grown and homemade breakfast with choices of baked goods, fruited pancakes, Maple House Granola, fresh egg dishes and much more. Lunch and dinner are available by request for groups of 8 or more. Walk or bike to Rowe Town Forest and play tennis, volleyball or basketball. Swim, fish or canoe at Pelham Lake Park.

Innkeeper(s): Rebecca & Michael Bradley. $60-100. 5 rooms, 3 with PB, 1 suite, 2 conference rooms. Breakfast, afternoon tea and snacks/refreshments included in rates. Types of meals: Country bkfst, veg bkfst, early coffee/tea, gourmet lunch, picnic lunch and gourmet dinner. Beds: KQDT. Modem hook-up, reading lamp, clock radio, desk and window fan in room. TV, swimming, bicycles, tennis, library, child care, parlor games, telephone, fireplace, petting farm, snow shoes, hiking and cross-country skiing on premises. Antiquing, art galleries, beach, bicycling, canoeing/kayaking, cross-country skiing, downhill skiing, fishing, hiking, horseback riding, live theater, museums, parks, shopping, tennis and wineries nearby.

Location: Country, mountains.

Publicity: The Sunday Republican, West County News, Rowe Goal Post and Shelburne Falls Business Association.

Certificate may be used: Sunday-Thursday.

Salem D14

The Salem Inn

7 Summer St
Salem, MA 01970-3315
(978)741-0680 (800)446-2995 Fax:(978)744-8924
Internet: www.saleminnma.com
E-mail: reservations@saleminnma.com

Circa 1834. Located in the heart of one of America's oldest cities, the inn's 41 individually decorated guest rooms feature an array of amenities such as antiques, Jacuzzi baths, fireplaces and canopy beds. Comfortable and spacious one-bedroom family suites with kitchenettes are available. A complimentary continental breakfast is offered. Nearby are fine restaurants, shops, museums, Pickering Wharf and whale watching boats for cruises.

Innkeeper(s): Jennifer MacAllister. $119-350. 40 rooms with PB, 18 with FP, 11 suites. Breakfast included in rates. Types of meals: Cont plus. Beds: KQT. Cable TV, reading lamp, refrigerator, clock radio, telephone, coffeemaker, desk, some with hot tub/spa, most with fireplace, hair dryer, wireless Internet access and iron/ironing board in room. Air conditioning. Fax on premises. Antiquing, art galleries, beach, bicycling, canoeing/kayaking, fishing, live theater, museums, parks, shopping, sporting events and water sports nearby.

Location: City.

Publicity: *New York Times, Boston Sunday Globe and Country Living Magazine.*

Certificate may be used: Anytime, at the last minute based on projected availability. Excludes October and May-September weekends.

Sheffield   F2

Staveleigh House

59 Main St
Sheffield, MA 01257-9555
(413)229-2129 (800)980-2129 Fax:(413)229-3234
Internet: www.staveleigh.com
E-mail: innkeeper@staveleigh.com

Circa 1821. The Reverend Bradford, minister of Old Parish Congregational Church, the oldest church in the Berkshires, built this home for his family. Afternoon tea is served and the inn is especially favored for its splendid breakfast and gracious hospitality. Located next to the town green, the house is in a historic district in the midst of several fine antique shops. It is also near Tanglewood, skiing and all Berkshire attractions.

Innkeeper(s): Ali A. Winston. $145-189. 7 rooms, 5 with PB. Breakfast and afternoon tea included in rates. Types of meals: Full bkfst and early coffee/tea. Beds: KQDT. Reading lamp, ceiling fan, clock radio, turn-down service and desk in room. Air conditioning. Telephone, fireplace, Terrycloth bath robes and Chickens on premises. Handicap access. Antiquing, cross-country skiing, downhill skiing, fishing, live theater, parks, shopping, water sports and art galleries nearby.

Location: Village, historic district.

Publicity: *Los Angeles Times, Boston Globe and House and Garden Magazine.*

"The hospitality at Staveleigh House is deeper and more thoughtful than any you will find elsewhere. — House & Gardens Magazine"

Certificate may be used: Sunday-Thursday, November-March, exclude holidays.

South Lee   E2

Historic Merrell Inn

1565 Pleasant St, Rt 102
South Lee, MA 01260
(413)243-1794 (800)243-1794
Internet: www.merrell-inn.com
E-mail: info@merrell-inn.com

Circa 1794. This elegant stagecoach inn was carefully preserved under supervision of the Society for the Preservation of New England Antiquities. Architectural drawings of Merrell Inn have been preserved by the Library of Congress. Eight fireplaces in the inn include two with original beehive and warming ovens. An antique circular birdcage bar serves as a check-in desk. Comfortable rooms feature canopy and four-poster beds with Hepplewhite and Sheraton-

style antiques. The Riverview Suite is tucked on the back wing of the building and has a private porch which overlooks the Housatonic River.

Innkeeper(s): George Crockett. $100-295. 8 rooms, 10 with PB, 4 with FP. Breakfast included in rates. Types of meals: Full bkfst. Beds: KQT. Cable TV, reading lamp, stereo, clock radio, telephone, desk, some with fireplace, bathrobes, bath amenities, wireless Internet access, some with fireplaces and all have wireless web access in room. Air conditioning. Fax, parlor games, Refrigerator, Iron & Ironing board and Screened-in gazebo on premises. Limited handicap access. Antiquing, art galleries, bicycling, canoeing/kayaking, cross-country skiing, downhill skiing, fishing, golf, hiking, horseback riding, live theater, museums, parks, shopping, tennis, wineries, Tanglewood Music Festival, Norman Rockwell Museum, Jacob's Pillow Modern Dance Festival and Berkshire Theater Festival nearby.

Location: Country, waterfront.

Publicity: *Americana, Country Living, New York Times, Boston Globe, Country Accents, Travel Holiday and USA Today.*

"We couldn't have chosen a more delightful place to stay in the Berkshires. Everything was wonderful. We especially loved the grounds and the gazebo by the river."

Certificate may be used: November-April, Except Holiday Weekends.

Springfield   F6

Lathrop House Bed and Breakfast

188 Sumner Avenue
Springfield, MA 01108
(413)736-6414 Fax:(413)736-6414
Internet: www.lathrophousebandb.com
E-mail: dmh@dianamarahenry.com

Circa 1899. Located in the midst of the historic residential district of Forest Park Heights, this 1899 Victorian was known as "The Mansion House." The recently restored Lathrop House Bed and Breakfast features original carved mantels, wood paneling, stained glass and a formal staircase. Swing on a columned porch overlooking the wide lawn. Relax on the veranda, smell the scent of the rose garden or picnic under the shade trees in the back yard. Elegant guest bedrooms with high-ceilings and king beds are accented with contemporary art, in-room libraries, wireless Internet access, designer bathrooms with showers and clawfoot tubs. A generous continental breakfast is provided and available at any time.

Innkeeper(s): Diana Henry. $100-175. 3 rooms, 1 two-bedroom suite. Breakfast, afternoon tea, snacks/refreshments, Guests are welcome to use our dining room for takeout or brought from home meals and and to barbecue and picnic in our back yard! included in rates. Types of meals: Cont plus and early coffee/tea. Beds: KQDT. Cable TV, VCR, reading lamp, CD player, refrigerator, ceiling fan, snack bar, clock radio, coffeemaker, turn-down service, desk, hair dryer, wireless Internet access and iron/ironing board in room. Air conditioning. DVD, fax, copier, library, parlor games, laundry facility, gift shop and Wireless Internet access on premises. Amusement parks, antiquing, art galleries, beach, bicycling, canoeing/kayaking, fishing, golf, hiking, horseback riding, live theater, museums, parks, shopping, tennis, water sports, wineries, Basketball Hall of Fame, Big E (New England Regional Fair in September), Six Flags New England, Eric Carle Museum of Picture Book Art, National Yiddish Book Center, Yankee Candle Factory and river rides nearby.

Location: City. Historic residential district, Forest Park Heights.

Publicity: *The Springfield Republican, The Jewish Ledger, The Northampton Gazette and Peminder Publications.*

Certificate may be used: Anytime, Last Minute-Based on Availability.

Sudbury D11

Inn on The Horse Farm

277 Old Sudbury Road
Sudbury, MA 01776
(978)443-7400 (800)272-2426
Internet: www.InnOnTheHorseFarm.com
E-mail: joanbeers@aol.com

Circa 1880. Secluded on nine wooded acres with a horse farm, this 1880 Queen Anne Victorian offers the ultimate in privacy and romance. This inn is the perfect retreat to celebrate birthdays, anniversaries or other special occasions. The three-room Tanah Suite with a canopy bed, two-person Jacuzzi and fireplace is a honeymoon favorite. A stay in the two-room Orlandra Suite featuring a draped four-poster bed, two-person Jacuzzi and huge balcony is also a popular pleaser. A complete breakfast is made at a flexible time to suit every taste with delicious entrees and accompaniments. Enjoy the meal in the Ye Old Worlde Café, on the veranda under the pergola or in-room. Lunch or dinner can be arranged with advance reservation. Tours are gladly given of the original four-story barn with post and beam ceiling and huge cupola.

Innkeeper(s): Joan & Rick Beers. $129-319. 3 rooms with PB, 1 with FP, 2 with WP, 1 cottage. Breakfast included in rates. Types of meals: Full gourmet bkfst, veg bkfst, early coffee/tea, You can reserve Lunch, Dinner and Brunch or Afternoon tea and cookies with 48 hours notice. You can invite up to 50 family/friends for a special occasion. Beds: KQDT. Cable TV, VCR, reading lamp, stereo, refrigerator, ceiling fan, clock radio, telephone, coffeemaker, desk, some with hot tub/spa, some with fireplace, hair dryer, bathrobes, bath amenities, wireless Internet access and iron/ironing board in room. Central air. Spa, stable, library, parlor games, There is a walking trail that goes all around our nine acres. It winds around the horse pastures, the pond with ducks and gees and across the stream and through the woods on premises. Amusement parks, antiquing, art galleries, beach, bicycling, canoeing/kayaking, cross-country skiing, downhill skiing, fishing, golf, hiking, horseback riding, live theater, museums, parks, shopping, sporting events, tennis, water sports, wineries, Garden In The Woods is just ten minutes away. Historic Concord Massachusetts is just fifteen minutes away, birthplace of America, Walden Pond and Little Women etc nearby.

Location: Country.

Certificate may be used: Anytime, subject to availability.

Vineyard Haven K16

Hanover House at Twin Oaks

28 Edgartown Rd
Vineyard Haven, MA 02568
(508)693-1066 (800)339-1066 Fax:(508)696-6099
Internet: www.twinoaksinn.net
E-mail: innkeeper@twinoaksinn.net

Circa 1906. When visiting Martha's Vineyard, Twin Oaks offers two pleasurable places to choose from that are within walking distance to the beach, ferry or downtown shops. Stay at the award-winning Clark House, a classic bed & breakfast or the Hanover House, an elegant three-diamond country inn just next door. Gather on one of the porches, the large backyard or private brick patio and gazebo. Complimentary bikes and high-speed Internet access are available on a first come first serve basis. Each of the comfortable guest bedrooms offer Internet access. Join the "breakfast party" for a bountiful continental-plus morning meal.

Innkeeper(s): Steve and Judy Perlman. $99-285. 15 rooms. Breakfast and snacks/refreshments included in rates. Types of meals: Cont plus. Beds: KQD.

Cable TV, reading lamp, refrigerator, ceiling fan and two with fireplace in room. Air conditioning. VCR, DVD, fax, copier, bicycles, parlor games, telephone, gift shop, Bikes are on a first come first served basis and some rooms have DVD or VCR on premises. Antiquing, art galleries, beach, bicycling, canoeing/kayaking, fishing, golf, hiking, horseback riding, live theater, museums, parks, shopping, tennis, water sports and wineries nearby.

Location: Ocean community.

Publicity: *New York Times.*

Certificate may be used: Post Columbus Day through the Thursday prior to Memorial Day. Subject to availability. Cannot combine with any other discount or program.

Wareham I15

Mulberry B&B

257 High St
Wareham, MA 02571-1407
(508)295-0684 (866)295-0684
Internet: www.virtualcities.com/ons/ma/z/maza801.htm
E-mail: mulberry257@comcast.net

Circa 1847. This former blacksmith's house is in the historic district of town and has been featured on the local garden club house tour. Frances, a former school teacher, has decorated the  guest rooms in a country style with antiques. A deck, shaded by a tall mulberry tree, looks out to the back garden. There are two resident cats on the premises.

Innkeeper(s): Frances Murphy. $60-100. 3 rooms. Breakfast included in rates. Types of meals: Full bkfst and afternoon tea. Beds: KDT. TV, reading lamp, clock radio and turn-down service in room. Air conditioning. VCR, parlor games and telephone on premises. Antiquing, cross-country skiing, fishing, live theater, parks, shopping, sporting events, water sports and whale watching nearby.

Location: Atlantic Ocean.

Publicity: *Brockton Enterprise and Wareham Courier.*

"Our room was pleasant and I loved the cranberry satin sheets."

Certificate may be used: Sunday-Thursday, Sept. 15-May 15, Anytime, Last Minute-Based on Availability, no holidays.

Wellfleet G18

The Inn at Duck Creeke

70 Main St, PO Box 364
Wellfleet, MA 02667-0364
(508)349-9333
Internet: www.innatduckcreeke.com
E-mail: info@innatduckcreeke.com

Circa 1815. The five-acre site of this sea captain's house features both a salt-water marsh and a duck pond. The Saltworks house and the main house are appointed in an old-fashioned style with antiques, and the rooms are comfortable and cozy. Some have views of the nearby salt marsh or the pond. The inn is favored for its two restaurants; Sweet Seasons and the Tavern Room. The latter is popular for its jazz performances.

Innkeeper(s): Bob Morrill & Judy Pihl. $95-160. 25 rooms, 18 with PB. Breakfast included in rates. Types of meals: Cont and dinner. Restaurant on premises. Beds: QDT. Reading lamp, ceiling fan, Eight rooms with air conditioning and the others with ceiling or

oscillating fans in room. Fax, parlor games, telephone and fireplace on premises. Antiquing, art galleries, beach, canoeing/kayaking, fishing, golf, hiking, live theater, parks, shopping, tennis, water sports, wineries, National Seashore, Audubon Sanctuary, Bike trails, Marconi site, Whale watching, Wellfleet Historical Museum and Drive-In theater nearby.

Location: Ocean community. Close to harbor.

Publicity: *Italian Vogue, Travel & Leisure, Cape Cod Life, Providence Journal, New York Times, Provincetown, Conde Nast Traveler, British Vogue and Bon a Parte (Denmark).*

"Duck Creeke will always be our favorite stay!"

Certificate may be used: May 1-June 15, Sunday-Thursday.

Yarmouth Port   117

One Centre Street Inn

1 Center St
Yarmouth Port, MA 02675-1342
(508)362-9951 (866)362-9951
Internet: www.onecentrestreetinn.com
E-mail: sales@onecentrestreetinn.com

Circa 1824. Originally a church parsonage, this Greek Revival-style inn is listed in the National Register. Located one mile from Cape Cod Bay, the classic elegance enhances the comfort and amenities offered, including luxurious linens, robes, flat screen TV, in-room WiFi, CD players and refrigerators. After a restful night's sleep, indulge in a gourmet breakfast featur-

ing hot coffee, specialty teas, fresh baked muffins and seasonal fresh fruit served with entrees such as Lemon Ricotta Pancakes, One Centre Street Inn Eggs Benedict or Oven Baked Stuffed French Toast, served on the screened porch or in the sun-filled dining room. A short drive away is the Cape Playhouse, Cape Cod Melody Tent, whale watching tours, golf courses, deep sea fishing, and ferries to Nantucket or Martha's Vineyard. Take day trips to Provincetown, Chatham, and the National Seashore beaches as well as Boston, Plymouth and Newport Rhode Island.

Innkeeper(s): Mary Singleton. $135-250. 5 rooms, 4 with PB, 1 with FP, 1 suite. Breakfast included in rates. Types of meals: Full gourmet bkfst, early coffee/tea, afternoon tea and snacks/refreshments. Beds: KQDT. Cable TV, VCR, CD player, refrigerator, clock radio, some with fireplace, hair dryer, bath amenities, wireless Internet access, iron/ironing board and CD Clock Radio in room. Air conditioning. Library, parlor games, telephone, gift shop and WiFi on premises. Antiquing, art galleries, beach, bicycling, canoeing/kayaking, fishing, golf, hiking, horseback riding, live theater, museums, parks, shopping, tennis, water sports and wineries nearby.

Location: Waterfront. Cape Cod, historic village.

Certificate may be used: Sept. 1-May 31, subject to availability.

Michigan

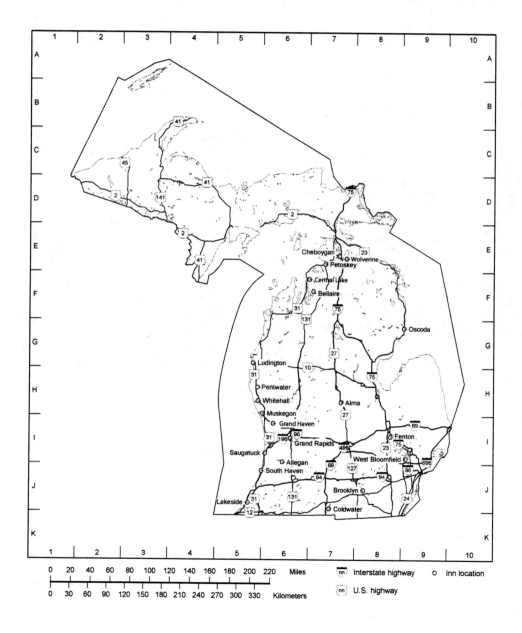

0   20   40   60   80   100   120   140   160   180   200   220   Miles

0   30   60   90   120   150   180   210   240   270   300   330   Kilometers

Interstate highway   o   Inn location
U.S. highway

Allegan 16

Castle In The Country Bed and Breakfast

340 M 40 S
Allegan, MI 49010-9609
(269)673-8054 (888)673-8054
Internet: www.castleinthecountry.com
E-mail: info@castleinthecountry.com

Circa 1906. Reflecting its nickname and castle-like appearance, a three-story turret and wide wraparound porch accent this 1906 Queen Anne Victorian adoring five acres of scenic countryside. Gather in one of the several common rooms or sitting areas. A Guest Refreshment Center has a coffee pot and refrigerator. Romantic guest bedrooms and a suite feature fresh flowers, candles, terry robes, handmade bath products, a video library and VCR. Several rooms include whirlpool tubs, fireplaces and CD players. Breakfast is specially prepared and served on fine china and vintage crystal. Innkeepers Herb and Ruth enjoy providing personalized service that ensures a pleasant stay. Ask for an Adventure Map, a helpful tool to enjoy local activities and sites. Many special packages are regularly offered.

Innkeeper(s): Herb & Ruth Boven. $135-245. 10 rooms, 5 with PB, 8 with FP, 7 with WP, 1 two-bedroom suite, 5 conference rooms. Breakfast included in rates. Types of meals: Full gourmet bkfst, veg bkfst, early coffee/tea, picnic lunch, afternoon tea, snacks/refreshments, wine, dinner and room service. Beds: KQT. Modem hook-up, data port, cable TV, VCR, DVD, reading lamp, stereo, refrigerator, ceiling fan, snack bar, clock radio, turn-down service, desk, hot tub/spa, fireplace, bathrobes, bath amenities, wireless Internet access, Antiques, High-quality linens & fabrics, Two-person whirlpool tubs plus separate shower, Some two-person tiled showers, Full gourmet breakfast served daily, with package served in-room, Robes, DVD/VHS library, CD library, On-site spa area for side by side couple's massage and Complimentary toiletries in room. Central air. Fax, copier, spa, library, parlor games, telephone, gift shop, 65 wooded acres with groomed trails, private lake and ponds, gardens, firepit, wraparound porch, patio, decks, gazebo, screened porch w/dock at private lake and snowshoes bicycles available on premises. Limited handicap access. Antiquing, art galleries, beach, bicycling, canoeing/kayaking, cross-country skiing, downhill skiing, fishing, golf, hiking, horseback riding, live theater, museums, parks, shopping, sporting events, tennis, water sports and wineries nearby.

Location: Country, waterfront.

Publicity: *Arrington's B&B Journal Book of Lists 2002, on the cover of Arrington's B&B Journal 2000, Voted "Most Perfect Stay" 2005 and Voted "Most Romantic Hideaway in North America" 2006.*

Certificate may be used: Sunday-Thursday, Nov. 1-May 31 (excluding holidays).

Alma H7

Saravilla

633 N State St
Alma, MI 48801-1640
(989)463-4078
Internet: www.saravilla.com
E-mail: Ljdarrow@saravilla.com

Circa 1894. This 11,000-square-foot Dutch Colonial home with its Queen Anne influences was built as a magnificent wedding gift for lumber baron Ammi W. Wright's only surviving child, Sara. Wright spared no expense building this mansion for his daughter, and the innkeepers have spared nothing in restoring the home to its former prominence. The foyer and dining room boast imported English oak woodwork. The foyer's hand-painted canvas wallcoverings and the ballroom's embossed wallpaper come from France. The home still features original leaded-glass windows, built-in bookcases, window seats

and light fixtures. In 1993, the innkeepers added a sunroom with a hot tub that overlooks a formal garden. The full, formal breakfast includes such treats as homemade granola, freshly made coffeecakes, breads, muffins and a mix of entrees.

Innkeeper(s): Linda and Jon Darrow. $99-169. 7 rooms with PB, 3 with FP, 2 with WP, 2 conference rooms. Breakfast and snacks/refreshments included in rates. Types of meals: Full bkfst, early coffee/tea and room service. Beds: KQT. Cable TV, VCR, DVD, reading lamp, ceiling fan, clock radio, telephone, desk, some with hot tub/spa, some with fireplace, hair dryer, bathrobes, bath amenities, wireless Internet access, iron/ironing board and Two rooms with whirlpool tubs in room. Air conditioning. Fax, spa, library, parlor games and complimentary beverages and snacks available on premises. Antiquing, bicycling, canoeing/kayaking, cross-country skiing, fishing, golf, live theater, sporting events, tennis and Soaring Eagle Casino nearby.

Location: City.

Publicity: *Midwest Living, Michigan Living, Morning Sun, Saginaw News, Sault Sunday., WCMU-TV, WCFX and WCZY.*

"I suggest we stay longer next time. We are looking forward to that visit."

Certificate may be used: Sunday-Thursday from Jan. 2 to Dec. 30, excluding holidays.

Bellaire F7

Grand Victorian Bed & Breakfast Inn

402 North Bridge Street
Bellaire, MI 49615-9591
(231)533-6111 (877)438-6111
Internet: www.grandvictorian.com
E-mail: innkeeper@grandvictorian.com

Circa 1895. Featured in Country Inns and Midwest Living magazines, this Queen Anne Victorian mansion boasts three original fireplaces, hand-carved mantels, intricate fretwork and numerous architectural details.

Relax with a glass of wine before the fire in the formal front parlor, or listen to music while playing cards and games in the back parlor. Guest bedrooms offer an eclectic mix of antique furnishings including Victorian Revival, Eastlake and French Provincial.

Soak in an 1890s clawfoot tub, or enjoy the park view from a private balcony. Be pampered with an incredible stay in one of the country's most remarkable and unique inns. The gazebo is a perfect spot to while away the day, or take advantage of the area's many nearby activities.

Innkeeper(s): Ken & Linda Fedraw. $95-195. 6 rooms with PB, 4 with FP, 2 with WP. Breakfast and snacks/refreshments included in rates. Types of meals: Full gourmet bkfst. Beds: KQ. Cable TV, VCR, reading lamp, refrigerator, ceiling fan, clock radio, most with fireplace and wireless Internet access in room. Central air. DVD, fax, copier, bicycles, parlor games, telephone and gift shop on premises. Antiquing, art galleries, beach, bicycling, canoeing/kayaking, cross-country skiing, downhill skiing, fishing, golf, hiking, horseback riding, shopping, tennis, water sports, wineries, fine dining, restaurants and touring nearby.

Location: City. Northwest Lower Michigan.

Publicity: *Detroit Free Press "Victorian Winter Getaway" highlighted with large picture and article (Dec 2007), Pictured on over 30 million Post Cereal boxes in 2006, The cover of Midwest Living, Country Inns, Traverse Magazine of northern Michigan, pictured on millions of Nabisco Cracker/Cookie Boxes, Arrington's B&B Journal Book of Lists Award—Most Elegant (2003/2005), Featured for 3 minute interview on 9&10 News of Cadillac and Michigan.*

"We certainly enjoyed our visit to the Grand Victorian. It has been our pleasure to stay in B&Bs in several countries, but never one more beautiful and almost never with such genial hosts."

Certificate may be used: November 15-May 31.

Brooklyn J8

Dewey Lake Manor

11811 Laird Rd
Brooklyn, MI 49230-9035
(517)467-7122 Fax:517 467 2356
Internet: www.deweylakemanor.com
E-mail: deweylk@frontiernet.net

Circa 1868. This Italianate house overlooks Dewey Lake and is situated on 18 acres in the Irish Hills. The house is furnished in a country Victorian style with antiques. An enclosed porch is a favorite spot to relax and take in the views of the lake while having breakfast. Favorite pastimes include lakeside bonfires in the summertime and ice skating or cross-country skiing in the winter. Canoe and paddleboats are available to guests.

Innkeeper(s): Barb & Joe Phillips. $89-139. 5 rooms with PB, 5 with FP, 1 with WP, 1 conference room. Breakfast, snacks/refreshments and Certain specials have meals included included in rates. Types of meals: Country bkfst, early coffee/tea, picnic lunch and Can cater lunch & dinner for groups. Beds: Q. Cable TV, VCR, DVD, reading lamp, CD player, refrigerator, ceiling fan, snack bar, clock radio, telephone, coffeemaker, desk, some with hot tub/spa, hair dryer, bathrobes, bath amenities, iron/ironing board, one with Jacuzzi, five with VCR and one with VCR/DVD in room. Central air. Fax, copier, swimming, parlor games, fireplace, gift shop, VCR in sitting room and baby grand piano in parlor on premises. Antiquing, canoeing/kayaking, cross-country skiing, fishing, golf, hiking, horseback riding, live theater, parks, shopping, sporting events, water sports, wineries, Botanical Gardens, car shows at MIS and Civil War Reenactments nearby.

Location: Country, waterfront. Country.

Publicity: *Ann Arbor News, Jackson Citizen Patriot and Toledo Blade.*

"I came back and brought my friends. It was wonderful."

Certificate may be used: November-April, subject to availability, special events excluded.

Central Lake F6

Bridgewalk B&B

2287 S Main, PO Box 399
Central Lake, MI 49622-0399
(231)544-8122
Internet: www.bridgewalkbandb.com
E-mail: bridgewalkbb@earthlink.net

Circa 1895. Secluded on a wooded acre, this three-story Victorian is accessible by crossing a foot bridge over a stream. Guest rooms are simply decorated with Victorian touches, floral prints and fresh flowers. The Garden Suite includes a clawfoot tub. Much of the home's Victorian elements have been restored, including pocket doors and the polished woodwork. Breakfasts begin with such items as a cold fruit soup, freshly baked muffins or scones accompanied with homemade jams and butters. A main dish, perhaps apple-sausage blossoms, tops off the meal.

Innkeeper(s): Janet & Tom Meteer. $100-135. 5 rooms with PB, 1 suite. Breakfast included in rates. Types of meals: Full bkfst and early coffee/tea. Beds: KQT. Reading lamp and ceiling fan in room. Parlor games, telephone and fireplace on premises. Antiquing, cross-country skiing, downhill skiing, fishing, parks, shopping, golf and gourmet restaurants nearby.

Location: Village.

Certificate may be used: Sunday-Thursday, can also check Last Minute-Based on Availability.

Grand Haven I6

Boyden House Bed & Breakfast

301 South Fifth Street
Grand Haven, MI 49417-1413
(616)846-3538
Internet: www.boydenhouse.com
E-mail: boydenhouse@gmail.com

Circa 1874. A lavish garden surrounds this nineteenth century Victorian/Queen Anne-style home, filled with elegant, cozy, eclectic rooms. Some guest bedrooms feature Jacuzzi tubs and fireplaces. Hardwood floors, massive pocket doors and handcrafted wood details offer a nostalgic journey upon the first step over the threshold of this bed and breakfast in Grand Haven, Michigan. It is an easy walk from Boyden House to shops, restaurants, cafes and the beach. Enjoy a stroll on the boardwalk along the Grand River, ending with a sunset at the lighthouse pier.

Innkeeper(s): Gail Kowalski. $125-280. 7 rooms, 2 with FP, 2 with WP, 7 suites. Breakfast included in rates. Types of meals: Full gourmet bkfst, veg bkfst, snacks/refreshments, room service, Extra food services include dinner, lunch and snack baskets, wine and champagne and special dessert. . Beds: KQD. Cable TV, DVD, refrigerator, ceiling fan, clock radio, some with hot tub/spa, some with fireplace, hair dryer, bath amenities, wireless Internet access, iron/ironing board, Individual temperature control, Feather beds, Private balconies on two rooms, Private baths for every room, Outside Balconies in 3 Rooms and Wi-Fi available throughout property in room. Central air. Library, Guest lounge with books, CDs, Board games, Fireplace & cozy seating, Expansive porches & abundant landscaping, Guest kitchen with snacks & refreshments and Common area for guests on premises. Limited handicap access. Amusement parks, antiquing, art galleries, beach, bicycling, canoeing/kayaking, cross-country skiing, downhill skiing, fishing, golf, hiking, horseback riding, live theater, museums, parks, shopping, sporting events, tennis, water sports, wineries and Please check Web site for a listing of "Things to do" along with the Grand Haven Visitors Bureau nearby.

Location: City. Walking distance to downtown, restaurants, shopping boardwalk and beaches.

Certificate may be used: Anytime, November-April, subject to availability.

Khardomah Lodge

1365 Lake Ave
Grand Haven, MI 49417
(616)842-2990 (800)530-9898
Internet: www.khardomahlodge.com
E-mail: info@khardomahlodge.com

Circa 1873. A favorite place for family gatherings, the inn's natural wooded surroundings and flower gardens instill an overall sense of well-being. Built in the late 1800s and sitting amongst other historic homes, the lodge's cottage-style decor and antiques create a delightful nostalgia. The great room fireplace is an instant socializer. Choose to stay in the lodge suites or guest bedrooms. A hot tub is the highlight of the hot tub suite. Create memorable meals in the fully-equipped kitchen and gas grill. A catering service also can be arranged. Relax by the fireplace, read a book from the library, watch a video or play a game.

$75-200. 18 rooms, 3 with PB, 2 with FP, 1 with HT, 1 with WP, 2 two-bedroom suites, 1 conference room. Complimentary coffee and tea furnished included in rates. Types of meals: Cont, early coffee/tea, Breakfast basket is offered off-season by arrangement outside your door. Offered in main lodge and suites, individual stays and cost added if stay has been discounted. Many special baskets can be arranged. Beds: QDT. Cable TV, VCR, DVD, reading lamp, stereo, refrigerator, ceiling fan, clock radio, telephone, coffeemaker, desk, some with hot tub/spa, some with fireplace, hair dryer, bathrobes, bath amenities, wireless Internet access, iron/ironing board, Private suites are spacious & have separate entries, Modern amenities, Full kitchens and Great scenery in room. Air conditioning. Spa, library, parlor games, laundry facility, gift shop, In-season coin laundry available and Free on-site parking on premises. Limited handicap access. Amusement parks, antiquing, art galleries, beach, bicycling, canoeing/kayaking, cross-country skiing, fishing, golf, hiking, horseback riding, live theater, museums, parks, shopping, tennis, water sports, wineries, Boutique shopping, Bookstores, Great dining options, Martini bar & musical fountain plays nightly in-season, Free weekly outdoor concerts, Sailing, Fishing, Bike rental and paths nearby.

Location: Lake Michigan shoreline.

Publicity: *Hunts Guide, Michigan Meetings and Events, Off the Beaten Bath travel guides, State Historic Travel Guide, Michigan Vacation and Cottage Guide, Grand Rapids Press, Booth Newspapers, 125th birthday feature on Michigan Live TV , WGHN and CMU Public Radio.*

Certificate may be used: November-May, weekdays, suites only, no holidays.

Grand Rapids   I6

Prairieside Suites Luxury B&B

3180 Washington Ave SW
Grand Rapids, MI 49418
(616)538-9442 Fax:(616) 538-9440
Internet: www.prairieside.com
E-mail: cheri@prairieside.com

Circa 1920. 2009 Winner - Travelers' Choice for Romance. Stay at this luxury bed and breakfast in Grandville, Michigan. Spacious guest suites feature pampering details that include heated towel bars, heated toilet seats and tile floors, Jacuzzis, Fireplace, coffee makers, refrigerators, microwaves, CD players and VCRs. Special amenities are offered for business travelers in three suites that boast executive business centers. The European Shower Experience in three of the private baths has body massaging sprays, and has hand held shower heads. Evening snacks are available. full breakfast in the dining room or a deluxe continental breakfast packed in the refrigerator in your room plus cookies and baked goods. Swim in the heated outdoor pool with a waterfall, relax in the pergola's double slider, or wander the perennial gardens accented by a fountain. Special arrangements and personal services are gladly taken care of at Prairieside Suites.

Innkeeper(s): Cheri & Paul Antozak. $179-259. 5 rooms with PB, 5 with FP, 5 with WP, 1 two-bedroom suite, 1 conference room. Breakfast, afternoon tea, snacks/refreshments, Cookies, homemade cocoa & Micro Popcorn for a Snack! In-Room Coffee Makers & Tea Service and Soda is waiting in your refrigerator upon arrival! included in rates. Types of meals: Full bkfst, veg bkfst, early coffee/tea, Breakfast- At Prairieside Suites, we serve a full hot candle light breakfast in our dining room every morning 30 OR you can order "Room Service" and we'll deliver a full hot breakfast to your room K. Modern hook-up, data port, cable TV, VCR, reading lamp, CD player, refrigerator, ceiling fan, clock radio, telephone, coffeemaker, desk, hair dryer, bathrobes, bath amenities, wireless Internet access, iron/ironing board, Jacuzzi tubs, Heated towel bars, Heated toilet seats, TV/VCR/movie library, Refrigerator, Microwave, Coffee pots and Warm cozy robes in room. Central air. Fax, copier, swimming, library, fireplace, gift shop, Video Library of more than 300 titles, music library of 160+ CDs, Make your stay extra special and check out our "Room Service" tab on our website on premises. Antiquing, art galleries, beach, golf, museums, parks, shopping, tennis, wineries, Gourmet/Fine Dining, Lake, Rivertown Crossings Mall & movie theater (2 minutes), Frederick Meijer Gardens, Grand Lady Riverboat, Van Andel Arena & Museum, John Ball Park Zoo, 20+ Restaurants within 5 minutes, pool, Lake Michigan, Kent Trails system, Millenium Park, Bike Trails, Devos Theater, Performing Theater, Picnic area and downtown Grand Rapids nearby.

Publicity: *Arrington's Inn Traveler Magazine, (Fall/Winter 2006), Voted "Best of the Great Lakes" (2008-2009), Voted "Best in The Midwest" (2007 - 2008 & 2009-2010) and Arrington's 2006 Book of List Voted 3rd "Best Overall Bed & Breakfast" in North America.*

Certificate may be used: Anytime for any suite if booked the day you are arriving. Or for advance reservations anytime Monday-Thursday during November-May (excludes holidays).

Lakeside   J5

Lakeside Inn

15251 Lakeshore Rd
Lakeside, MI 49116-9712
(269)469-0600 Fax:(269)469-1914
Internet: www.lakesideinns.com
E-mail: reservationslk@lakesideinns.com

Circa 1890. Totally renovated in 1995, the Lakeside Inn features original wood pillars and rustic stone fireplaces in the lobby and ballroom. The inn overlooks Lake Michigan located just across the street, and was featured in a USA Today article "Ten Great Places to Sit on the Porch" because of its 100-foot-long veranda. Each individually decorated room combines the special ambiance of comfortable antique furnishings with modern amenities like TVs, air conditioning and private baths. Many of the rooms are on the lake side, and some offer Jacuzzi tubs. Besides board games or cards for indoor recreation, the inn offers an exercise room and dry sauna. Cycling, horseback riding, swimming, antique shops, art galleries and a state park are nearby.

Innkeeper(s): Connie Williams. $75-175. 31 rooms with PB, 1 suite, 1 conference room. Beds: KQDT. TV, reading lamp, clock radio and some with Jacuzzi in room. Air conditioning. Fax, copier, swimming, sauna, bicycles, parlor games, telephone, fireplace and seasonal cafe open for breakfast on premises. Handicap access. Antiquing, art galleries, bicycling, cross-country skiing, fishing, golf, parks, shopping and swimming nearby.

Publicity: *Chicago Tribune, USA Today, Midwest Living, Chicago Magazine, Washington Post and Lake Magazine.*

Certificate may be used: Nov.1 through the Wednesday before Memorial Day Weekend.

Ludington   G5

The Inn at Ludington

701 E Ludington Ave
Ludington, MI 49431-2224
(231)845-7055 (800)845-9170
Internet: www.inn-ludington.com
E-mail: innkeeper@inn-ludington.com

Circa 1890. Experience an informal elegance at this Victorian bed and breakfast in the Great Lakes region near Lake Michigan beach that offers a fine blend of the past and the present. Built in 1890, it has been locally awarded for retaining its historical integrity during replicate restoration. Lounge by one of the four fireplaces and savor afternoon refreshments. Choose from one of the six ethnically-themed guest bedrooms. Early risers can enjoy fresh coffee, cereal, yogurt and nut bread. A personally tailored meal is offered at an agreed-upon, pre-determined time. Ask about seasonal getaway or family packages, special events and murder mystery weekends.

Innkeeper(s): Kathy & Ola Kvalvaag. $90-225. 7 rooms, 1 with PB, 2 with FP, 1 with HT, 3 suites. Breakfast included in rates. Types of meals: Full bkfst and early coffee/tea. Beds: KQD. Modern hook-up, cable TV, VCR, DVD, reading lamp, ceiling fan, clock radio, desk, some with hot tub/spa, some with fireplace, hair dryer, bath amenities, wireless Internet access and iron/ironing board in room. Air conditioning. Fax, copier, spa, library, parlor games, telephone, laundry facility, gift shop, Free high speed Internet access, One family style apartment (see Web site for details and pictures) and Lovely English Gardens perfect for a wedding on premises. Antiquing, beach, bicycling, canoeing/kayaking, cross-country skiing, fishing, golf, hiking, horseback riding, parks, shopping, tennis and water sports nearby.

Location: Walk in town to beach.

Publicity: *Ludington Daily News, Detroit Free Press, Chicago Tribune, Country Accents and Michigan Living.*

"Loved the room and everything else about the house."

Certificate may be used: November-April, anytime; May, June, September, October, Sunday-Thursday as available at last minute.

Muskegon   H6

Port City Victorian Inn

1259 Lakeshore Dr
Muskegon, MI 49441-1659
(231)759-0205 (800)274-3574
Internet: www.portcityinn.com
E-mail: pcvicinn@comcast.net

Circa 1877. Old world elegance characterizes this Queen Anne Victorian mansion gracing the bluff of Muskegon Lake. The front parlor boasts curved leaded-glass windows with views of the harbor. A paneled grand entryway is accented by the carved posts and spindles of an oak staircase leading up to a TV room and rooftop balcony overlooking the state park. Luxurious honeymoon suites boasts two-person whirlpool baths, and romantic guest bedrooms include desks, modems, refrigerators and ice buckets. Early risers sip morning coffee while reading the local newspaper. A hot breakfast can be delivered to the room, enjoyed in the formal dining room or served in the 14-window sunroom. Ask about special packages available.

Innkeeper(s): Barbara Schossau & Fred Schossau. $125-225. 5 rooms with PB, 2 with FP, 1 with HT, 3 with WP, 3 suites. Breakfast and wine included in rates. Types of meals: Country bkfst, early coffee/tea, snacks/refreshments and room service. Beds: Q. Modern hook-up, data port, cable TV, VCR, DVD, reading lamp, stereo, refrigerator, ceiling fan, snack bar, clock radio, telephone, coffeemaker, turn-down service, desk, some with hot tub/spa, some with fireplace, hair dryer, bathrobes, bath amenities, wireless Internet access, iron/ironing board, double whirlpool tubs, 2-person Jacuzzi, fireplace, hair dryers, robes, lake views and individual remote control air conditioning in room. Central air. Fax, copier, bicycles and parlor games on premises. Amusement parks, antiquing, art galleries, beach, bicycling, canoeing/kayaking, cross-country skiing, fishing, golf, hiking, horseback riding, live theater, museums, parks, shopping, sporting events, tennis, water sports, Lake Michigan, Muskegon Lake and Port City Princess cruise ship Cross Lake Ferry nearby.

Location: City, waterfront. Grand Rapids.

Publicity: *Muskegon Chronicle, Detroit Free Press, Arrington's Bed & Breakfast Journal and Arrington's Bed & Breakfast Journal's award "Best In The Midwest."*

"The inn offers only comfort, good food and total peace of mind."

Certificate may be used: October-May 29, anytime.

Oscoda   G9

Huron House Bed & Breakfast

3124 N US-23
Oscoda, MI 48750
(989)739-9255 Fax:(989)739-0195
Internet: www.huronhouse.com
E-mail: huron@huronhouse.com

From this romantic setting you can enjoy strolls along the beach, sunrise over the lake, or a soak in a private hot tub. The waterside inn offers warmly decorated guest rooms with antiques, handsome beds, wallpapers, and a variety of amenities including decks, fireplaces and Jacuzzi tubs. Breakfast is brought to your room in the morning. Plan a drive, cycling excursion or hiking trip on the scenic 22-mile River Road National Scenic Byway along the AuSable River.

Innkeeper(s): Denny & Martie Lorenz,Bev McLaughlin, Rosalyn Covert & Joy Vito. $175-205. 14 rooms with PB, 13 with FP, 6 with HT, 8 with WP, 1 conference room. Breakfast included in rates. Types of meals: Cont plus. Beds: K. Cable TV, VCR, DVD, CD player, refrigerator, ceiling fan, clock radio, coffeemaker, hot tub/spa, fireplace, hair dryer, bath amenities, wireless Internet access, Lake Huron views, Fireplaces, King-size feather beds and Private decks in room. Air conditioning. Spa, swimming, Private outdoor hot tubs, Private decks, Miles of walking beach and Gardens on premises. Antiquing, beach, canoeing/kayaking, cross-country skiing, fishing, golf, hiking, horseback riding, parks, shopping and water sports nearby.

Location: Waterfront.

Publicity: *Midwest Living.*

Certificate may be used: Sunday-Thursday, November, December 1-23, January-April.

Pentwater   H6

Hexagon House Bed & Breakfast

760 6th St
Pentwater, MI 49449-9504
(231)869-4102 Fax:(231)869-9941
Internet: www.hexagonhouse.com
E-mail: innkeepers@hexagonhouse.com

Circa 1870. Open year round, The Hexagon House Bed and Breakfast in the quaint village of Pentwater, Michigan is the perfect location for a vacation. Lake Michigan and Silver Lake sand dunes are nearby. This historic, hexagonal-designed home boasts Victorian decor and is surrounded by perennial gardens with sandstone footpaths on three acres. Relax by the fire in the parlor. Stay in the first-floor Cottage Rose Suite with a Jacuzzi and a private porch area. Wraparound porches on both levels provide ample space for outdoor relaxation. Gourmet breakfasts are served outside as weather permits. Hiking and cross-country trails are minutes away.

Innkeeper(s): Amy & Tom Hamel. $119-234. 5 rooms with PB, 2 with FP, 1 suite. Breakfast, snacks/refreshments, hors d'oeuvres and wine included in rates. Types of meals: Full gourmet bkfst, veg bkfst, early coffee/tea, picnic lunch and prior arrangements can be made for dinner at the inn (at an additional charge) or reservations can be made for you at local restaurants. Beds: KQ. TV, VCR, DVD, reading lamp, stereo, refrigerator, ceiling fan, snack bar, clock radio, telephone, hair dryer, bath amenities, wireless Internet access and iron/ironing board in room. Central air. Fax, bicycles, library, parlor games, fireplace, wraparound porches, other meals available upon request, 3 acres, bird watching library and DVD collection on premises. Limited handicap access. Amusement parks, antiquing, art galleries, beach, bicycling, canoeing/kayaking, cross-country skiing, fishing, golf, hiking, horseback riding, museums, parks, shopping, tennis, water sports and wineries nearby.

Location: Country. Near Lake Michigan.

Publicity: *The Ludington Daily News, The Chicago Herald Newspaper,*

Midwest Living Magazine, Weekend Magazine, Grand Rapids Magazine, Lifestyles Magazine, The Healing Garden Magazine, West Michigan Tourist Guide and The Shoreline Guide Magazine.

Certificate may be used: April, Subject to availability.

Petoskey E7

BayView Terrace Inn

1549 Glendale Ave.
Petoskey, MI 49770
(231)347-2410 (800)530-9898
Internet: www.theterraceinn.com
E-mail: info@theterraceinn.com

Circa 1911. Poised in the picturesque Victorian village of Bay View, Petoskey, the 1911 Terrace Inn is located just 45 minutes south of Mackinac Island near sandy Lake Michigan beaches in scenic Northwest Michigan. This year-round bed and breakfast inn is a National Historic Landmark. Feel refreshed by the warm and friendly service perfectly blended with privacy. Sit in a rocker on the wide veranda or relax by the fire in the lobby. Accommodations include themed guest bedrooms, from cottage style to deluxe rooms with fireplaces to whirlpool suites. After a hearty continental breakfast play croquet, then visit the nearby sophisticated downtown area for recreational and cultural activities. The inn's restaurant with owner and chef Mo Rave, offers in-season dinners.

Innkeeper(s): Mo and Patty Rave. $69-169. 37 rooms with PB, 7 with FP, 6 with WP, 6 suites, 1 conference room. Breakfast, All stays include an Expanded Continental Breakfast. On-sight restaurant offers lunch and dinner in season, and dinner weekends off season. See web site for dinner packages and specials and Special Event Calendar included in rates. Types of meals: Cont plus, early coffee/tea, lunch, afternoon tea, hors d'oeuvres, wine, gourmet dinner and Inn offers open dining in the summer months (June-August). Dinner is served Tuesday-Saturday 5PM-9PM and lunch Tues-Sat 12PM-3PM. Currently open Thurs/Fri/Sat through October then weekend until March for dinner. Reservations. Restaurant on premises. Beds: KQT. Cable TV, reading lamp, clock radio, hair dryer, bath amenities, wireless Internet access, All rooms have private bath and wireless access, clock radio and breakfast, suites have more amenities like electric fireplace, microwaves, whirlpool tubs. Cottage rooms are most original and cozy and suites more spacious in room. Air conditioning. VCR, fax, library, parlor games, telephone, fireplace, gift shop, Private beach access, Liquor license & restaurant, Horse & carriage rides January/February Saturday nights, Porch & veranda, Great views, Wireless access and Soda machine/ice cream parlor open in summer on premises. Antiquing, art galleries, beach, bicycling, canoeing/kayaking, cross-country skiing, downhill skiing, fishing, golf, hiking, horseback riding, live theater, museums, parks, shopping, tennis, water sports, wineries, Indoor waterpark at Boyne year-round, Winter park with outdoor ice skating & warming lodge with fireplace (1/2 mile), Beach and Wheelway nearby.

Location: City. Lake Michigan Resort town, Northwest Michigan.

Publicity: MidWest Living, Haunted Travels of Michigan, Booth News articles on dog sledding and ghost hunting weekends, local news for gingerbread contest for charity and other fundraising events, publicity for our historic marker,, Fox News, Michigan Live, Channel 8, destination Michigan CMU public radio, Central Michigan University Radio, Interlochen Public Radio, WJML, Fox News, WHRN Chicago, Lite 96.3, Destination Michigan PBS special, and book on haunted inns in Michigan.

Certificate may be used: Weekdays year-round. Standard Rooms. Upgrade if available on Deluxe Room and Suites Only.

Hidden Garden Cottages & Suites

247 Butler St
Saugatuck, MI 49453
(269)857-8109 (888)857-8109
Internet: www.hiddengardencottages.com
E-mail: Indakott@AOL.com

Circa 1879. Perfect for a secluded bed breakfast experience, these elegantly furnished cottages are designed for two. Tucked away in the downtown area, the quiet location is convenient to all of the local shopping, dining and attractions. Each luxurious cottage features a gorgeous canopy or four-poster bed, down comforter and exquisite bed linens. Relax in the romantic seating area by the fireplace with color cable TV, VCR, CD stereo system and a phone. The luxurious bathroom has a whirlpool for two, plush robes and complete bath amenities. A mini-kitchen includes a refrigerator, icemaker and microwave oven. Overlook the intimate courtyard garden and fountains from a private porch that completes the tranquil setting. A continental breakfast is offered each morning. Take a boat cruise on Lake Michigan, play golf or ride the dunes.

Innkeeper(s): Daniel Indurante & Gary Kott. $135-225. 4 rooms with PB, 4 with FP, 4 with WP. Breakfast and snacks/refreshments included in rates. Types of meals: Cont plus. Beds: Q. Cable TV, VCR, DVD, reading lamp, stereo, refrigerator, ceiling fan, snack bar, clock radio, telephone, coffeemaker, desk, hot tub/spa, voice mail, fireplace, hair dryer, bathrobes, bath amenities, wireless Internet access and iron/ironing board in room. Central air. Fax, copier, parlor games and Movie library on premises. Limited handicap access. Antiquing, art galleries, beach, bicycling, canoeing/kayaking, cross-country skiing, fishing, golf, hiking, horseback riding, live theater, museums, parks, shopping, sporting events, tennis, water sports and wineries nearby.

Location: City.

Publicity: Travel Holiday Magazine (September 1998).

Certificate may be used: Sunday-Thursday, November-May.

Kingsley House

626 W Main St
Saugatuck, MI 49408-9442
(269)561-6425 (866)561-6425
Internet: www.kingsleyhouse.com
E-mail: romanticgetaways@kingsleyhouse.com

Circa 1886. Experience the elegance of this Victorian Queen Anne mansion located near the resort towns of Saugatuck, Holland and South Haven. Restored and opened as a bed and breakfast, this relaxing retreat specializes in thoughtful hospitality and generous amenities. Sip lemonade on the wraparound front porch. Savor afternoon tea by the fire in the parlor.

Indulge in a treat from the dining room cookie jar. Tastefully appointed and well-decorated guest bedrooms feature an assortment of pleasing comforts. Stay in the Jonathan Room with a two-person Hydromassage tub and gas log fireplace. The Northern Spy is a popular honeymoon suite on the entire third floor, with a double whirlpool tub, fireplace and sitting area in the turret. Royal Doulton china, heirloom silver and vintage linens accent a plentiful gourmet breakfast. Bikes are provided for an easy ride to Hutchins Lake or the winery. Drive to the nearby beaches of Lake Michigan.

Innkeeper(s): Dave Drees. $69-249. 8 rooms with PB, 8 with FP, 4 with WP, 4 suites. Breakfast, afternoon tea and snacks/refreshments included in rates. Types of meals: Full gourmet bkfst, veg bkfst, early coffee/tea, picnic lunch and gourmet dinner. Beds: KQ. Cable TV, VCR, DVD, reading lamp, stereo, refrigerator, ceiling fan, clock radio, desk, most with hot tub/spa, fireplace, hair dryer, bathrobes, bath amenities, wireless Internet access and iron/ironing board in room. Central air. Fax, copier, bicycles, library, parlor games, telephone, gift shop, Large video library, Complimentary coffee/tea/sodas, Hammock, Porch swing, Croquet, Afternoon treats/refreshments and Cross country skis on premises. Limited handicap access. Amusement parks, antiquing, art galleries, beach, bicycling, canoeing/kayaking, cross-country skiing, downhill skiing, fishing, golf, hiking, horseback riding, live theater, museums, parks, shopping, sporting events, tennis, water sports, wineries and wintertime activities nearby.

Location: Small town.

Publicity: *Time Magazine, Forbes Magazine, The New York Times, Grand Rapids Press, Saugatuck Local Observer, Country, Glamour, Country Victorian Decorating, Innsider, National Geographic Traveler, Holland Sentinel's and WJR (Detroit) Travel Show.*

"It was truly enjoyable. You have a lovely home and a gracious way of entertaining."

Certificate may be used: November-April, Sunday-Thursday, excluding holidays.

The Beachway Resort & Hotel

106 Perryman
Saugatuck, MI 49453
(269)857-3331
Internet: www.beachwayresort.com
E-mail: info@beachwayresort.com

Circa 1900. Overlooking the Kalamazoo River, The Beachway Resort & Hotel is a relaxing destination in Saugatuck, Michigan. Lake Michigan's award-winning Oval Beach is popular nearby. Swim in the large, heated pool and relax on a sundeck. Browse through the movie and game library for inside entertainment. Accommodations offer something for everyone from romantic waterfront suites that may include a balcony, fireplace and Jacuzzi, to family-friendly cottages or more economic B&B-style guest rooms. Start each day with coffee, fruit and donuts before exploring the area attractions and seasonal festivals.

$60-550. 40 rooms with PB, 2 with FP, 2 with WP, 10 total suites, including 2 two-bedroom suites and 2 four-bedroom suites, 4 cottages, 3 guest houses. Types of meals: Early coffee/tea and snacks/refreshments. Beds: KQDT. Cable TV, VCR, DVD, refrigerator, ceiling fan, telephone, coffeemaker, desk, some with hot tub/spa, voice mail, some with fireplace, hair dryer, wireless Internet access and iron/ironing board in room. Central air. Fax, copier, swimming, library, child care and parlor games on premises. Handicap access. Antiquing, art galleries, beach, bicycling, canoeing/kayaking, cross-country skiing, downhill skiing, fishing, golf, hiking, horseback riding, live theater, museums, parks, shopping, tennis, water sports and wineries nearby.

Location: Overlooking the Kalmazoo.

Certificate may be used: May, September-October, Sunday-Thursday, no holidays. Closed November-April.

Twin Oaks Inn

PO Box 818, 227 Griffith St
Saugatuck, MI 49453-0818
(269)857-1600 (800)788-6188 Fax:(269)857-7446
Internet: www.twinoaksinn.com
E-mail: twinoaks@sirus.com

Circa 1860. This large Queen Anne Victorian inn was a boarding house for lumbermen at the turn of the century. Now an old-English-style inn, it offers a variety of lodging choices, including a room with its own Jacuzzi. There are many diversions at Twin Oaks,  including a collection of video-taped movies numbering more than 700. Guests may borrow bicycles or play horseshoes on the inn's grounds.

Innkeeper(s): Willa Lemken. $110-150. 6 rooms with PB, 1 conference room. Types of meals: Full bkfst, early coffee/tea and snacks/refreshments. Beds: KQ. Cable TV, VCR, reading lamp, stereo, clock radio, desk and hot tub/spa in room. Air conditioning. Parlor games, telephone and fireplace on premises. Antiquing, cross-country skiing, fishing, live theater, parks, shopping and water sports nearby.

Location: Downtown small village.

Certificate may be used: Nov. 1-April 30, Sunday through Thursday.

South Haven   J5

Martha's Vineyard Bed and Breakfast

473 Blue Star Hwy
South Haven, MI 49090
(269)637-9373 Fax:(269)639-8214
Internet: www.marthasvy.com
E-mail: adamson@marthasvy.com

Circa 1852. In a park-like setting of more than four acres, this 1852 Federal style estate offers a quiet respite for all of its guests. Stroll the beautifully landscaped gardens or private vineyard, sit by the pond or one of its waterfalls, or stroll along the golf course. You will be pampered by its luxurious accommodations and the hosts extravagant hospitality. Each guest bedroom boasts a fireplace, steeped with charm and your comfort in mind, guest bathrobes provided. A four-course breakfast with antique china, silver settings, and cloth napkins may include the inns signature caramel apple pancakes. Indulge in special packages designed as personally requested. Choose golf, massage or an assortment of getaway amenities. Lou and Ginger look forward to having you as their guests.

Innkeeper(s): Lou & Ginger Adamson. $99-205. 11 rooms with PB, 11 with FP, 7 with WP, 1 guest house. Breakfast, afternoon tea and snacks/refreshments included in rates. Types of meals: Full bkfst, veg bkfst, early coffee/tea, picnic lunch and room service. Beds: Q. Cable TV, DVD, reading lamp, CD player, ceiling fan, clock radio, coffeemaker, most with hot tub/spa, fireplace, hair dryer, bathrobes, bath amenities, wireless Internet access, iron/ironing board, Bathrobes, Sun porches, Verandah, Guest refrigerator & microwave available, Games and DVD library in room. Central air. Fax, copier, swimming, parlor games, telephone and gift shop on premises. Limited handicap access. Antiquing, art galleries, beach, bicycling, canoeing/kayaking, cross-country skiing, downhill skiing, fishing, golf, hiking, horseback riding, live theater, museums, parks, shopping, tennis, water sports and wineries nearby.

Location: Country, waterfront. Lakeside resort town.

Publicity: *Inn Traveler Magazine - Award for "Most Romantic Hideaway" in North America for four consecutive years, MidWest Living Magazine and Martha Stewart Radio.*

Certificate may be used: Sunday-Thursday during months of November-April.

West Bloomfield I9

The Wren's Nest Bed & Breakfast

7405 West Maple Rd.
West Bloomfield, MI 48322
(248)624-6874
Internet: www.thewrensnestbb.com
E-mail: thewrensnestbb@sbcglobal.net

Circa 1840. Stay at this delightful farmhouse adjacent to a woodland in a country setting. It is surrounded by professionally landscaped grounds that are accented by numerous birdhouses created by the innkeeper,
a plethora of perennial
and annual flower beds
and a heritage vegetable
garden with more than
60 varieties of heirloom
tomatoes. Watch TV by
the fire or play piano in the living room. Relax on one of the two sun porches. Feel at home in one of the comfortable guest bedrooms. Start each morning with a full-course breakfast made from scratch with fresh ingredients and no preservatives. Personal dietary needs are accommodated with advance notice. This historic bed and breakfast is available for special events, adult or children's tea gatherings and other parties.

Innkeeper(s): Irene Scheel. $95-115. 6 rooms, 3 with PB, 1 guest house, 1 conference room. Breakfast, afternoon tea and snacks/refreshments included in rates. Types of meals: Full gourmet bkfst, veg bkfst and room service. Beds: KQDT. Modem hook-up, data port, cable TV, VCR, reading lamp, stereo, refrigerator, ceiling fan, snack bar, clock radio, telephone, coffeemaker, turn-down service, desk, voice mail and fireplace in room. Central air. Fax, copier, library, laundry facility, heirloom vegetables in the summer and pygmy goats on premises. Limited handicap access. Antiquing, art galleries, beach, bicycling, cross-country skiing, downhill skiing, fishing, golf, hiking, horseback riding, live theater, museums, parks, shopping, sporting events, tennis, water sports, theatres and malls nearby.

Location: City, country.

Publicity: *Detroit News, The West Bloomfield Eccentric, Midwest Living, Japanese Free Press and WDIV 4 Detroit.*

Certificate may be used: Anytime.

Whitehall H5

Cocoa Cottage Bed and Breakfast

223 S. Mears Avenue
Whitehall, MI 49461
(231) 893-0674 (800) 204-7596
Internet: www.cocoacottage.com
E-mail: innkeeper@cocoacottage.com

Circa 1912. Historically restored, this authentic 1912 Arts and Crafts bungalow is accented with period furniture, pottery, wallpaper and copper work. Several common areas, including an intimate fireplace room, sunny screened-in porch and lush gardens with a pergola and patio, offer peaceful surroundings that enhance relaxation and conversation. Reflecting the inn's delicious theme, each tempting guest bedroom is named after chocolates. Lavish amenities will pamper and please. Soak in the large whirlpool bath in the Ghirardelli Room. Pillow-topped mattresses invite sleep on a brass bed in the Godiva or on the Cadbury's white wrought iron. Evening port, handmade confections and turndown service are thoughtful touches. Indulge in a bountiful, award-winning breakfast that may feature Cottage eggs, Lemon-ricotta pancakes, stuffed French toast and other popular favorites. Bikes are available to explore the scenic area.

Innkeeper(s): Larry Robertson & Lisa Tallarico. $119-179. 4 rooms with PB, 1 with HT, 1 with WP. Breakfast, hors d'oeuvres and wine included in rates. Types of meals: Full gourmet bkfst, veg bkfst, early coffee/tea, gourmet lunch, picnic lunch, afternoon tea and gourmet dinner. Beds: KQ. Modem hook-up, data port, cable TV, DVD, reading lamp, CD player, ceiling fan, clock radio, turn-down service, desk, hair dryer, bathrobes, bath amenities, wireless Internet access, iron/ironing board, Free WiFi, DVD Player, Wine Cheese and Chocolate reception at check-in and in room. Central air. VCR, fax, copier, library, parlor games, telephone, fireplace and gift shop on premises. Limited handicap access. Amusement parks, antiquing, art galleries, beach, bicycling, canoeing/kayaking, cross-country skiing, downhill skiing, fishing, golf, hiking, horseback riding, live theater, museums, parks, shopping, tennis, water sports and wineries nearby.

Location: City, waterfront. 2 blocks from downtown.

Publicity: *White Lake Beacon, Muskegon Chronicle, Travel 50 and Beyond, Midwest Living, Arrington's Inn Traveler Magazine (rated #5 in National category, Best Breakfasts), Grand Rapids Press, Kalamazoo Gazette, Flint Journal, Jackson Patriot and Wood-TV NBC Channel 8.*

Certificate may be used: January-May 25, anytime. May 25-Oct. 31, Sunday-Thursday only. Nov. 1-Dec. 31, anytime. Subject to availability. Can not be combined with other promotions or 3rd party gift certificates.

White Swan Inn

303 S Mears Ave
Whitehall, MI 49461-1323
(231)894-5169 (888)948-7926
Internet: www.whiteswaninn.com
E-mail: info@whiteswaninn.com

Circa 1884. Maple trees shade this sturdy Queen Anne home, a block from White Lake. A screened porch filled with white wicker and an upstairs coffee room are leisurely retreats. Parquet floors in the dining room, antique furnishings and chandeliers add to the comfortable decor. Chicken and broccoli quiche is a favorite breakfast recipe. Cross the street for summer theater or walk to shops and restaurants nearby.

Innkeeper(s): Cathy & Ron Russell. $109-179. 4 rooms with PB, 2 with FP, 1 with WP. Breakfast and snacks/refreshments included in rates. Types of meals: Full bkfst, veg bkfst, early coffee/tea and Dinner upon request. Beds: KQDT. Cable TV, DVD, reading lamp, ceiling fan, clock radio, desk, some with fireplace, hair dryer, bathrobes, bath amenities, wireless Internet access and one suite with whirlpool tub in room. Air conditioning. Fax, copier, parlor games, telephone, gift shop, beverage center, secure bicycle storage and screened porch on premises. Amusement parks, antiquing, art galleries, beach, bicycling, canoeing/kayaking, cross-country skiing, fishing, golf, hiking, horseback riding, live theater, museums, parks, shopping, sporting events, tennis, water sports, wineries, Luge run, Dune rides, Seasonal festivals and Scenic and Sunset Cruises nearby.

Location: Small resort town.

Publicity: *White Lake Beacon, Muskegon Chronicle, Michigan Travel Ideas, Bed, Breakfast and Bike Midwest, Book of Lists, Arrington's B&B Journal, Cookbook-Great Lakes, Great Breakfasts, Cookbook-Celebrate Breakfast, WKAR TV ("Best of Bed & Breakfast"), Cookbook-Inn Time for Breakfast and Voted by inngoers-Best in the Midwest 2003.*

"What a great place to gather with old friends and relive past fun times and create new ones."

Certificate may be used: May 25-Oct. 25, Sunday-Thursday and Oct. 26-May 24 anytime.

Wolverine   *E7*

Silent Sport Lodge

8300 Trout Lily Trail
Wolverine, MI 49799
(231) 525-6166
Internet: www.silentsportlodge.com
E-mail: info@silentsportlodge.com

Circa 1997. Experience peaceful tranquility amid this 30-acre
north woods setting on the Sturgeon River, a Blue Ribbon trout
stream in Wolverine, Michigan. Nap in a hammock, relax in a
swing or sit on the waterfront deck. Ponds connect to a stream
with waterfalls by the bonfire pit. Stroll through the gardens,
ski or snowshoe the grounds and soak in the outdoor hot tub.
The wilderness log lodge is a green facility with sustainable
practices. Stay in a pleasantly themed, spacious guest room or
the separate River Cabin. The River Room boasts a private balcony and The Cedar Room includes a two-person whirlpool
tub and fireplace. Hearty breakfasts include signature recipes
made with local, seasonal and organic ingredients. The area has
many attractions from elk viewing to casinos. Be sure to visit
Mackinac Island. Custom romance packages are available.

Innkeeper(s): John & Rhonda Smit. $110-125. 4 rooms with PB, 1 with
FP, 1 with WP, 1 cabin. Breakfast and Other meals included in specialty
package pricing included in rates. Types of meals: Full bkfst, veg bkfst and
Other meals included in specialty packages. Beds: QT. Reading lamp,
refrigerator, ceiling fan, clock radio, turn-down service, some with hot
tub/spa, some with fireplace, hair dryer, bathrobes, bath amenities, wireless Internet access and iron/ironing board in room. Central air. TV, VCR,
fax, copier, spa, library, parlor games, gift shop, bonfire pit, hammocks,
garden pond and trails on premises. Amusement parks, antiquing, art galleries, beach, bicycling, canoeing/kayaking, cross-country skiing, downhill
skiing, fishing, golf, hiking, horseback riding, museums, parks, shopping,
tennis, water sports and wineries nearby.

Location: Country, waterfront. Woodland setting on the River.

Certificate may be used: Anytime, subject to availability.

Minnesota

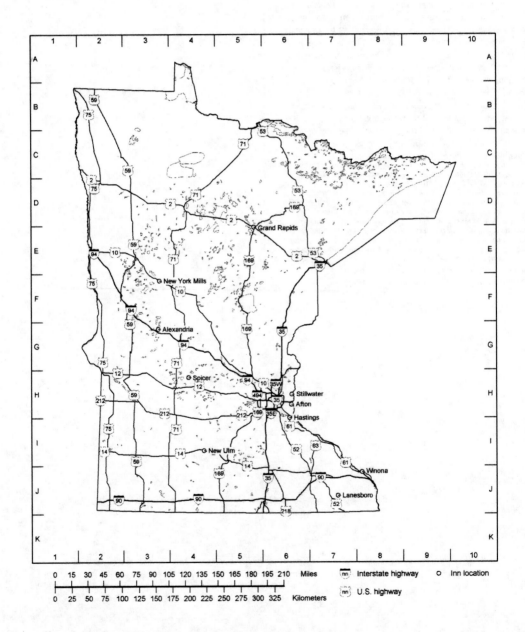

Afton
H6

The Historic Afton House Inn

3291 S. St. Croix Trail
Afton, MN 55001
(651)436-8883 Fax:(651)436-6859
Internet: www.aftonhouseinn.com
E-mail: reservations@aftonhouseinn.com

Circa 1867. Located on two acres of waterfront on the St. Croix River, this historic inn reflects an old New England-style architecture. Guest rooms offer Jacuzzi tubs, fireplaces, waterfront balconies and are decorated with American country antiques. A restaurant on the premises provides candlelight dining in the Wheel Room. Ask for Bananas Foster, a house specialty, or any flaming dessert. Or you might prefer to dine in the Catfish Saloon & Cafe, which has a more casual menu. Champagne Brunch  cruises are offered on the Grand Duchess May-October. Three charter vessels are available for private cruises for weddings, birthdays, anniversaries, corporate getaways or for groups of 10-350. Visit the inn's web site for online availability.

Innkeeper(s): Gordy & Kathy Jarvis. $79-285. 25 rooms with PB, 19 with FP, 3 total suites, including 2 two-bedroom suites, 2 conference rooms. Continental plus breakfast included in rates. Types of meals: Cont plus, Sun. brunch, early coffee/tea, lunch, wine, gourmet dinner and room service. Restaurant on premises. Beds: KQ. Modem hook-up, data port, cable TV, VCR, ceiling fan, clock radio, telephone, desk, most with hot tub/spa, hair dryer, bath amenities and wireless Internet access in room. Central air. Fax, copier, spa and gift shop on premises. Handicap access. Antiquing, art galleries, beach, bicycling, canoeing/kayaking, cross-country skiing, downhill skiing, fishing, golf, hiking, horseback riding, live theater, museums, parks, shopping, tennis, water sports and wineries nearby.

Location: Country, waterfront.

Publicity: *St. Paul Pioneer Press, Woodbury Bulletin, Hudson Star Observer and Stillwater Gazette.*

Certificate may be used: Anytime, Sunday-Thursday and available weekends on last minute availability.

Grand Rapids
E5

Morning Glory Bed and Breakfast

726 NW 2nd Ave
Grand Rapids, MN 55744
(218)326-3978 (866)926-3978
Internet: www.morningglorybandb.com
E-mail: mgbb1@qwestoffice.net

Circa 1960. The many activities of downtown are just a few blocks away from this comfortable two-story brick bed and breakfast. Relax by the wood-burning fireplace in the living room that also has a piano, library, game area and terrace door leading to a private patio with a garden fountain. Cookies and beverages are always available. On the weekends wine and appetizers are also served. Each air-conditioned guest suite features a sitting room. The romantic Champagne and Roses Suite includes a two-person whirlpool and two-sided gas fireplace. In the cheery breakfast room, full breakfast fare is offered weekdays and a three-course meal is served on weekends. Play championship golf, bike the Mesabi Trail or take a drive through the Chippewa National Forest on the Edge of the Wilderness Scenic Byway.

Innkeeper(s): Karen and Ron Herbig. $100-125. 4 rooms, 3 with FP, 1 with WP, 4 total suites, including 1 two-bedroom suite. Breakfast, snacks/refreshments and Wine/cheese on Friday and Saturday from 5-6pm included in rates. Types of meals: Full gourmet bkfst, veg bkfst and early coffee/tea. Beds: KQT. Cable TV, VCR, DVD, reading lamp, CD player, ceiling fan, clock radio, telephone, desk, some with fireplace, hair dryer and wireless Internet access in room. Central air. Library, parlor games and Wireless Internet on premises. Antiquing, art galleries, beach, bicycling, canoeing/kayaking, cross-country skiing, fishing, golf, hiking, live theater, museums, parks, shopping, tennis, water sports and Dog sled rides nearby.

Location: City.

Certificate may be used: Sunday-Thursday, November-April.

Hastings
H6

Classic Rosewood - A Thorwood Property

620 Ramsey Street
Hastings, MN 55033-1137
(651)437-3297 Fax:(651)437-4129
Internet: www.classicrosewood.com
E-mail: pam@classicrosewood.com

Circa 1880. This Queen Anne Victorian has several verandas and porches. Grained cherry woodwork and fireplaces add elegance to the inn. All but two of the 15 rooms have fireplaces. In the Mississippi Under the Stars Room, a skylight shines down on the teak whirlpool tub. This 900-square-foot suite features tapestries, paisleys and a copper soaking tub as well as a round shower. The innkeepers serve a formal, five-course afternoon tea on Wednesday and Sundays, which guests can enjoy with a prior reservation.

Innkeeper(s): Dick & Pam Thorsen. $97-277. 8 rooms with PB, 7 with FP, 7 with WP, 3 total suites, including 1 two-bedroom suite, 3 conference rooms. Breakfast and snacks/refreshments included in rates. Types of meals: Full gourmet bkfst, veg bkfst, early coffee/tea, gourmet dinner and room service. Beds: QDT. Modem hook-up, data port, reading lamp, refrigerator, snack bar, telephone, desk, most with hot tub/spa, most with fireplace, hair dryer, bath amenities, wireless Internet access and iron/ironing board in room. Central air. Fax, copier, spa, library, parlor games, laundry facility and gift shop on premises. Limited handicap access. Antiquing, art galleries, beach, bicycling, canoeing/kayaking, cross-country skiing, downhill skiing, fishing, golf, hiking, horseback riding, live theater, museums, parks, shopping, sporting events, tennis, water sports and wineries nearby.

Location: City. Small rivertown.

Publicity: *Minneapolis-St. Paul Magazine, Minnesota Monthly, Midwest Living, Glamour, National Geographic Traveler, Jason Davis Show, Channel 5, Channel 11, public television, several local cable shows, KSTP Talk Radio, MPR (Minnesota Public Radio) and Hometown Boy Makes Good (HBO movie).*

Certificate may be used: Nov. 1-Sept. 30, Sunday-Friday except holidays. Valid in 177, 247, 277 rooms only.

Lanesboro
J7

Stone Mill Suites

100 Beacon Street East
Lanesboro, MN 55949
(507)467-8663 (866)897-8663
Internet: www.stonemillsuites.com
E-mail: stonemillsuites@hotmail.com

Circa 1885. Combining a historical heritage with modern conveniences, this nineteenth-century stone building was built using limestone quarried from the area's surrounding bluffs. The original clay ceilings and stair railings accent the decor. Themed suites and guest bedrooms reflect local history and its undeniable charm. Relaxing amenities feature a fireplace, whirlpool tub, microwave and refrigerator. Children are welcome, ask about family packages. A generous continental breakfast may include English muffins, bakery items from Lanesboro Pastries, cereal, fruit, beverages and French toast topped with strawberries, blueberries and whipped cream. A variety of museums and the Laura Ingalls Wilder Site are all within a 30-minute drive.

Innkeeper(s): Dorothy Amanda (Mandy) Smith. $80-180. 10 rooms with PB, 4 with FP, 5 with WP, 7 suites. Breakfast included in rates. Types of meals: Cont plus and early coffee/tea. Beds: KQDT. Modem hook-up, data port, cable TV, VCR, reading lamp, refrigerator, ceiling fan, clock radio, telephone, coffeemaker, desk, some with hot tub/spa, hair dryer, wireless Internet access, iron/ironing board, Mini micro-fridge and Coffeemaker in room. Air conditioning. Fax and parlor games on premises. Handicap access. Antiquing, art galleries, bicycling, canoeing/kayaking, cross-country skiing, fishing, golf, hiking, live theater, museums, parks, shopping and wineries nearby.

Location: Historic Bluff Country.

Publicity: *MN Monthly, Midwest Getaway, Wisconsin State Journal, Minneapolis Star Tribune, Yahoo / Forbes Traveler: America's Prettiest Towns and Mother Earth News: "Great Places You've (Maybe) Never Heard Of"*

Certificate may be used: Anytime, Sunday-Thursday, Anytime, subject to availability, Anytime, Last Minute-Based on Availability. One certificate per customer per year.

New Ulm   I4

Deutsche Strasse (German Street) B&B

404 South German Street
New Ulm, MN 56073
(507) 354-2005 (866) 226-9856
Internet: www.deutschestrasse.com
E-mail: info@deutschestrasse.com

Circa 1884. Overlooking the Minnesota River Valley, this stately 1884 home located in the historic district blends Craftsman or Arts and Crafts architecture with a Victorian flair. Common rooms offer a variety of relaxing settings. Play games in the formal dining room, watch the fish in the huge aquarium, sit by the candlelit fireplace in the living room, or play the piano in the Welcome Room. Guest bedrooms exude Old World charm and are furnished with antiques and decorative accents. Breakfast is served on fine crystal and china in the All-Season Sun Porch. Accompanied by the inn's special blend coffee, signature dishes may include homemade granola, German sautéed apples with cinnamon-swirl French toast and Deutsche Strasse Potato Hash.

Innkeeper(s): Gary and Ramona Sonnenberg. $109-189. 5 rooms with PB, 4 with FP, 1 with HT, 1 with WP, 1 suite, 1 conference room. Breakfast and wine included in rates. Types of meals: Full gourmet bkfst, veg bkfst, early coffee/tea, Breakfast menus will be modified to accommodate special dietary restrictions - advance notice and please. Catered Dinners available upon arrangement. Beds: KQ. Reading lamp, telephone, most with fireplace, bathrobes, bath amenities, wireless Internet access, iron/ironing board, Filtered drinking water, DVD & CD players available upon request, Iron and ironing board available upon request in room. Air conditioning. TV, spa, library, parlor games, gift shop, Baby Grand Piano, Porch swing, Lawn swing in garden, Complimentary wine, Snack, DVD Player available and Television in family room on premises. Limited handicap access. Antiquing, art galleries, beach, bicycling, cross-country skiing, fishing, golf, hiking, museums, parks, shopping, sporting events, tennis, wineries, Morgan Creek Vineyards tours and events, Schell's Brewery tours, Historic home tours: John Lind Home & Wanda Gag Home, Minnesota Music Hall of Fame, Glockenspiel, Putting Green Environmental Adventure Park, Frisbee golf and Minnesota River Valley National Scenic Byway nearby.

Publicity: *"New In Town" featured the Deutsche Strasse sign as Renée Zellweger first entered New Ulm.*

Certificate may be used: Sunday-Thursday anytime, weekends Dec. 15-April 15, excludes festivals and holidays.

New York Mills   F3

Whistle Stop Inn B&B

107 Nowell E
New York Mills, MN 56567-9704
(218)385-2223 (800)328-6315
Internet: www.whistlestopbedandbreakfast.com
E-mail: whistlestopbandb@aol.com

Circa 1903. A choo-choo theme permeates the atmosphere at this signature Victorian home. Antiques and railroad memorabilia decorate guest rooms with names such as Great Northern  or Burlington Northern. The Northern Pacific room includes a bath with a clawfoot tub. For something unusual, try a night in the beautifully restored 19th-century Pullman dining car. It is paneled in mahogany and features floral carpeting as well as a double whirlpool, TV, VCR, refrigerator and fireplace. A caboose offers a queen-size Murphy bed, whirlpool, TV, VCR and refrigerator. A second Pullman car with the same amenities has just been added and it features a gas-burning fireplace.

Innkeeper(s): Roger & Jann Lee. $80-150. 5 rooms with PB. Breakfast included in rates. Types of meals: Full bkfst and early coffee/tea. Beds: QD. Cable TV, VCR, DVD, reading lamp, refrigerator, ceiling fan, clock radio, telephone, coffeemaker, desk, hot tub/spa, fireplace, hair dryer, bathrobes, wireless Internet access and microwave in room. Air conditioning. Spa and sauna on premises. Handicap access. Antiquing, cross-country skiing, fishing, golf, parks, shopping, tennis, snowmobiling trails and cultural center nearby.

Publicity: *USA Weekend, Minneapolis Tribune, Fargo Forum, ABC-Fargo, WDAY, Fargo, Channel 14 and Fergus Falls.*

Certificate may be used: Sunday-Thursday, November-April, excluding holidays.

Spicer   H4

Spicer Castle Inn

11600 Indian Beach Rd
Spicer, MN 56288-9694
(320)796-5870 (800)821-6675 Fax:(320)796-4076
Internet: www.spicercastle.com
E-mail: spicercastle@spicercastle.com

Circa 1895. On the scenic shores of Green Lake, this Tudor castle with English Country decor is listed in the National and State Registers of Historic Places. Air conditioned suites and guest bedrooms feature a variety of delightful amenities. Choose Amy's Room, boasting a clawfoot tub and balcony overlooking gardens, woods and a lagoon. Stay in the masculine Mason's or romantic Eunice's Room each with a double whirlpool tub. John's Cottage also offers a refrigerator, microwave and coffeemaker. A lumberjack built Raymond's Cabin with rustic logs and a stone fireplace chimney. Hospitality includes full breakfast and afternoon tea. A Murder Mystery Dinner, Belle Dinner Cruise, and holiday festivities are some of the special events to ask about.

Innkeeper(s): Mary Swanson. $94-165. 18 rooms, 7 with PB, 10 with FP, 12 with WP, 2 suites, 1 cottage, 1 cabin, 3 conference rooms. Breakfast and afternoon tea included in rates. Types of meals: Full gourmet bkfst, veg bkfst, Sun. brunch, early coffee/tea, gourmet lunch, picnic lunch, snacks/refreshments, hors d'oeuvres, gourmet dinner and room service. Restaurant on premises. Beds: KQT. Reading lamp, refrigerator, ceiling fan, clock radio, coffeemaker, desk, most with hot tub/spa, most with fireplace, bath amenities, wireless Internet access, 10 guest rooms have microwaves and Two guest rooms with private balconies in room. Air conditioning. Fax, copier, swimming, library, parlor games, telephone and Wireless Internet Access on premises. Amusement parks, antiquing, art galleries, beach, bicycling, canoeing/kayaking, cross-country skiing, fishing, golf, hiking, live theater, museums, parks, shopping, tennis, water sports, wineries, Mr. B's Chocolatier Shoppe and Bison Ranch nearby.

Location: Country, waterfront. Located on the shores of beautiful Green Lake.

Publicity: *Minneapolis Star & Tribune, St. Cloud Times, West Central Tribune, WCCO and 102.5.*

"What a wonderfully hospitable place!"

Certificate may be used: November-June, not valid on Friday and Saturday.

Stillwater   H6

Aurora Staples Inn

303 N 4th St
Stillwater, MN 55082
(651)351-1187 (800)580-3092 Fax:(651)351-9061
Internet: www.aurorastaplesinn.com
E-mail: info@aurorastaplesinn.com

Circa 1892. This historic Queen Anne Victorian Inn was built in the 1890s for Isaac Staple's daughter, Aurora. Her husband, Adolphus Hospes, was a Civil War veteran and survivor of the famous first Minnesota charge at Gettysburg. The inn is elegantly decorated to reflect the Victorian era with five guest rooms offering a variety of amenities such as double whirlpool tubs, private baths and fireplaces. The Carriage House is also open as a guest room. A full breakfast is served, as well as wine and hors d'oeuvres during check-in. Enjoy our formal gardens or walk through the scenic St. Croix Valley.

Innkeeper(s): Cathy & Jerry Helmberger. $119-249. 5 rooms with PB, 5 with FP, 5 with HT, 5 with WP, 2 suites, 1 cottage. Breakfast included in rates. Types of meals: Full bkfst. Beds: KQD. Air conditioning. TV, VCR, fax, copier, library, parlor games, fireplace, gift shop, parlor and dining room on premises. Antiquing, art galleries, beach, bicycling, canoeing/kayaking, cross-country skiing, downhill skiing, fishing, golf, hiking, horseback riding, live theater, museums, parks, shopping, tennis, water sports, wineries, train rides and trolley rides nearby.

Location: Stillwater.

Certificate may be used: Anytime, based on projected availability, carriage house not part of program.

Rivertown Inn

306 Olive St W
Stillwater, MN 55082-4932
(651) 430-2955 Fax:(651)430-2206
Internet: www.rivertowninn.com
E-mail: rivertown@rivertowninn.com

Circa 1882. Rivertown Inn is a lovingly restored lumber baron mansion with European-style elegance located three blocks above historic downtown. Delightful gardens, trickling fountains, winding paths with intimate benches and ornate wrought iron gates instill a warm welcome. The largest bed and breakfast in Stillwater, Minnesota, it offers bedchambers and suites, including two grand suites located in the separate carriage house. All accommodations feature a private bath with a whirlpool tub, gas fireplace and a themed décor that pays respect to and is named after a famous romantic poet or literary figure of the 19th century. Indulge in a chef-prepared four-course gourmet breakfast every morning and in the evening, gather for light hors d'oeuvres and fine wines. Bi-monthly wine tastings, food and wine events, and monthly cooking classes are held in the gourmet kitchen.

Innkeeper(s): Marty Rem. $195-395. 9 rooms with PB, 9 with FP, 9 with WP, 5 suites. A sumptuous three-course breakfast prepared by inn's chef, Snacks/Refreshments and Social hour each day between 5 & 6 PM with complimentary wine & Hors D'oeuvres included in rates. Types of meals: Full gourmet bkfst, veg bkfst, early coffee/tea, picnic lunch, snacks/refreshments, hors d'oeuvres and wine. Beds: KQD. Reading lamp, stereo, clock radio, desk, hot tub/spa, hair dryer, bathrobes, bath amenities, wireless Internet access, iron/ironing board, Double whirlpool tubs, Gas fireplaces, Luxury bathrobes, Goose down pillows & comforters, Bose radio sound system, Climate control air conditioning with individual remote, Molton Brown spa-quality bath amenities. Social Hour each day between 5 & 6 PM, with Complimentary Wine and Hors D'oeuvres, Coffee and Tea Service on each floor by 7:30 AM each Morning. A gourmet chef prepares a 3 course breakfast and Sundays include champagne!! in room. Air conditioning. Fax, copier, spa, parlor games, telephone, fireplace, gift shop, Complimentary bottled water, Coffee, Tea, Soft drinks & ice, Nightly social hour with complimentary hors d'oeuvres & wine, Champagne & fine wines available for purchase and In-house massages available with our massage therapist on premises. Limited handicap access. Antiquing, art galleries, beach, bicycling, canoeing/kayaking, cross-country skiing, downhill skiing, fishing, golf, hiking, horseback riding, museums, parks, shopping, sporting events, tennis, water sports, wineries, Complimentary health club passes are provided to guests for River Valley Athletic Club. We also have picnic baskets available for purchase, along with dining, kayaking, snowshoeing, bicycling and photography & garden tour packages nearby.

Location: Historic downtown Stillwater.

Publicity: *Country Magazine, Minneapolis Star Tribune, Pioneer Press, Minnesota Monthly,* Voted one of the *"Top 10 Most Romantic Inn's"* by iLoveInns.com (2007, featured in Midwest Living Magazine's December 2010 issue and Voted "Best Antiques" 2011 by LanierBB.com.

Certificate may be used: Sunday-Thursday, holidays excluded. Not valid for Agatha Christie or Oscar Wilde Suite.

Winona   J8

Alexander Mansion Historic Bed & Breakfast

274 East Broadway St
Winona, MN 55987
(507)474-4224
Internet: www.alexandermansionbb.com

Circa 1886. Indulge in a pampering stay at this renovated, historic Victorian that graces a scenic bluff in the Mississippi River town of Winona, Minnesota. Distinctive surroundings include inviting gardens with benches and statuaries. Wicker furnishings adorn the veranda. Gather for wine and cheese socials, peruse the book collection in the cherry wood library or relax in the balcony music room. Feel pampered by the gracious amenities, European-quality linens and period antiques. Spacious guest suites feature soaking tubs and fireplaces. Early risers savor hot beverages in the breakfast room. Linger over a hearty four-course gourmet breakfast made with fresh local ingredients accented by Watkins spices in the formal candlelit dining room or dine alfresco. Browse the gift shop for J.R. Watkins Natural Apothecary personal products and other items to take home as souvenirs.

Innkeeper(s): Richard, GM. $149-229. 4 rooms with PB, 2 with FP, 2 suites. Breakfast, snacks/refreshments and wine included in rates. Types of meals: Full gourmet bkfst, veg bkfst and early coffee/tea. Beds: KQDT. Reading lamp, stereo, ceiling fan, clock radio, turn-down service, hair dryer, bathrobes, bath amenities, wireless Internet access and iron/ironing board in room. Air conditioning. TV, DVD, fax, copier, bicycles, library, parlor games, telephone, fireplace and gift shop on premises. Antiquing, art galleries, beach, bicycling, canoeing/kayaking, cross-country skiing, fishing, golf, hiking, horseback riding, live theater, museums, parks, shopping, sporting events, tennis and water sports nearby.

Location: City. Mississippi River Road.

Certificate may be used: November-March, Sunday-Thursday.

Mississippi

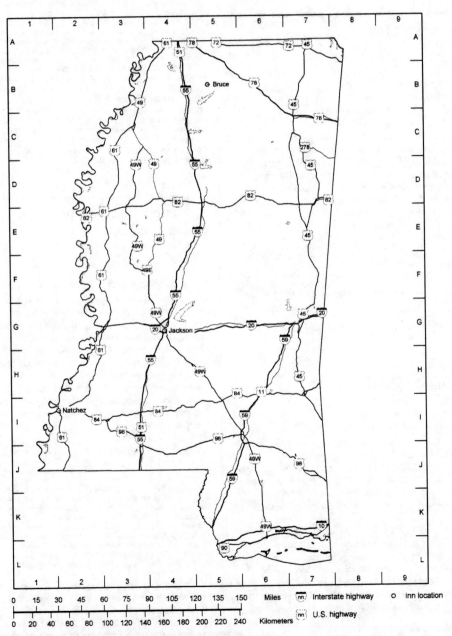

	Miles
0 15 30 45 60 75 90 105 120 135 150	
0 20 40 60 80 100 120 140 160 180 200 220 240	Kilometers

inn Interstate highway   ○ Inn location

inn U.S. highway

Bruce   B5

Cart Barn Inn

74 CR 259
Bruce, MS 38915
(662)983-7829
Internet: www.cartbarninn.com
E-mail: innkeeper@cartbarninn.com

Circa 2007. Totally renovated inside with an eclectic luxury, Cart Barn Inn originally housed the electric carts for the onsite Yoda Creek Golf Course. This delightful B&B is located just outside the small town of Bruce, Mississippi. Relax in the fenced courtyard or porch with swings and a view. Take the boardwalk to the gazebo and swim in the pool. There is also a barbecue grill and fire pit on the grounds. Soft drinks, ice and snacks are available near the hall of bookcases with books and magazines to read. Each guest room and suite is handicap accessible and features a microwave, refrigerator, LCD TV, desk, chair, climate control and Wi-Fi. Coffee is in the lobby and a hearty southern breakfast is served daily.

Innkeeper(s): Paul & Kay Tyler. $129-189. 10 rooms with PB, 4 two-bedroom suites. Breakfast included in rates. Types of meals: Country bkfst, early coffee/tea, picnic lunch, snacks/refreshments and dinner. Beds: KQ. Data port, cable TV, VCR, DVD, reading lamp, refrigerator, snack bar, clock radio, telephone, desk, hair dryer, bath amenities, wireless Internet access, iron/ironing board, fridge,microwave,full southern breakfast,back porch w/table &chairs, swings,grills,gazebo,courtyard,on golf course,RV parking and Ipod ports in room. Central air. Swimming, library, parlor games, laundry facility, gift shop, golf, walking track and on premises. Handicap access. Amusement parks, antiquing, art galleries, beach, bicycling, fishing, golf, hiking, horseback riding, live theater, museums, parks, shopping, sporting events, tennis, water sports, Elvis Presley birthplace, Buffalo Park, Car museum (38 miles), Vaught Hemmingway Stadium,Ole Miss and Ford Center nearby.

Location: Country. Golf Course, live theatre,horsback Riding.

Certificate may be used: January-February, excluding valentines special.

Jackson   G4

Fairview Inn & Sophia's Restaurant

734 Fairview Street
Jackson, MS 39202-1624
(601) 948-3429 (888) 948-1908 Fax:(601)948-1203
Internet: www.fairviewinn.com
E-mail: fairview@fairviewinn.com

Circa 1908. Built in 1908, the Fairview Inn is a small luxury hotel with a four-diamond AAA rating. This historic Colonial Revival mansion is one of the few architecturally designed homes of that period remaining, which exudes the rich history of Jackson, Mississippi. The Inn boasts eighteen luxurious guest rooms, Sophia's Restaurant serving lunch, dinner,

and Sunday brunch, nomiSpa for relaxation, a game room, private guest lounge, 24-hour guest kitchen and a gift shop. An oasis for leisure and business travelers alike, the Inn provides a tranquil setting with more than an acre of grounds featuring pristine gardens, outdoor decks and a gazebo. The Fairview Inn offers the charm, ambiance, and hospitality of a bed and breakfast with the service and amenities of a small luxury hotel. Come see why the Fairview Inn is Jackson's best kept secret.

Innkeeper(s): Tamar and Peter Sharp . $139-314. 18 rooms with PB, 9 with FP, 13 with WP, 13 total suites, including 1 two-bedroom suite, 7 conference rooms. Breakfast and snacks/refreshments included in rates. Types of meals: Full bkfst, Sun. brunch, early coffee/tea, lunch, wine, gourmet dinner and room service. Restaurant on premises. Beds: KQ. Cable TV, reading lamp, ceiling fan, snack bar, clock radio, telephone, coffeemaker, turn-down service, desk, voice mail, hair dryer, bathrobes, bath amenities, wireless Internet access and iron/ironing board in room. Central air. VCR, fax, copier, spa, library, parlor games, fireplace, gift shop, Voice mail, Data ports, Complimentary health club facilities close by, On-site restaurant and Full service day spa on premises. Handicap access. Antiquing, art galleries, bicycling, fishing, golf, live theater, museums, parks, shopping, sporting events, tennis and water sports nearby.

Location: City.

Publicity: *Country Inns, Travel & Leisure, Southern Living, "Most Outstanding Inn North America 2003" by Conde Nast Johansen and VIP Jackson Wedding Edition.*

"Fairview Inn is southern hospitality at its best — Travel and Leisure."

Certificate may be used: Jan. 1 to Dec. 31, except for Thanksgiving and Christmas Day.

Missouri

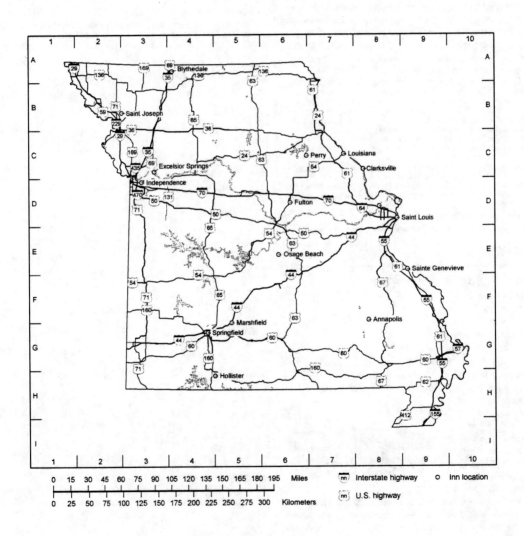

Clarksville   C8

Cedarcrest Manor at Overlook Farm

901 S Highway 79
Clarksville, MO 63336
(573)242-3310 Fax:(573)242-3433
Internet: www.overlookfarmmo.com
E-mail: chip@overlookfarmmo.com

Circa 1842. Luxurious accommodations await your arrival at
Overlook Farm and offer you an incomparable experience of
country living. Cedarcrest Manor is set in a cluster of towering
cedars and tucked away just up the hill from The Station
Restaurant. Built in 1842 by Captain Benjamin Clifford, a
prominent riverboat captain, Cedarcrest began its life as a plantation home, and quickly became the archetype for a number
of houses built in the Mississippi River Valley. It was acquired
and renovated in 2005 by Nathalie Pettus, and today, its neoclassic interior, heated Romanesque pool, and stunning views
of the Mississippi offer peace, quiet and a restful place to relax
and recharge. Rich with amenities, this enchanting Missouri
inn is adorned with antiques and features a fireplace in every
room. You can also book a room at Rackheath House, as both
properties are part of Overlook Farm. Check-in for each of the
inns is located at The Station Restaurant.

Innkeeper(s): Nathalie Pettus. $125-225. 6 rooms with PB, 6 with FP.
Breakfast and Continental breakfast will be served in the dining room at
8:30am included in rates. Types of meals: Full gourmet bkfst, gourmet lunch,
picnic lunch, hors d'oeuvres, gourmet dinner and The Station at Overlook
Farm. Restaurant on premises. Beds: Q. Cable TV, VCR, DVD, reading lamp,
stereo, refrigerator, ceiling fan, clock radio, telephone, coffeemaker, fireplace,
bathrobes, bath amenities, wireless Internet access and iron/ironing board in
room. Central air. Fax, swimming, bicycles and gift shop on premises.
Antiquing, bicycling, canoeing/kayaking, fishing, golf, hiking, museums,
parks, shopping and water sports nearby.

Location: Country.

Certificate may be used: Anytime, subject to availability.

Rackheath House at Overlook Farm

901 S Highway 79
Clarksville, MO 63336
(573)242-9677 Fax:(573)242-3455
Internet: www.overlookfarmmo.com
E-mail: chip@overlookfarmmo.com

Circa 1860. Rackheath House is perched atop the hills of the
Mississippi River Valley, and situated just a short walk from the
Overlook Farm – one of the highest spots along the river. Built
in 1860 and restored in 2006 by Nathalie Pettus, this Greek
revival-style manor features sprawling grounds, a spacious
veranda, and a romantic, flourishing garden filled with walking
paths. Its accessible, state-of-the art kitchen and elegant dining
room provide guests with the ideal place to uncork a bottle of
wine – or enjoy a fresh, seasonally inspired meal, prepared
exclusively by The Station's award-winning chef, Timothy
Grandinetti. Prepare to lose yourself in rich country warmth,
enchanting amenities, and strikingly serene landscapes at
Rackheath or at its sister property Cedarcrest Manor. Each of
the two inns offer quiet corners and cozy spots to relax, enjoy a
lively conversation, or get lost in a good book. Oversized
Jacuzzi tubs and plush, comfy bathrobes are a feature in every
room, offering the utmost in relaxation. In-suite coffee makers
provide instant access to your morning pick-me-up. Check-in

for each of the inns is located at The Station Restaurant.

Innkeeper(s): Nathalie Pettus. $125-225. 3 rooms with PB. Breakfast and
Continental Breakfast will be served at 8:30am in the dining room included in
rates. Types of meals: Full gourmet bkfst, gourmet lunch, picnic lunch, hors
d'oeuvres, wine, gourmet dinner and The Station at Overlook Farm.
Restaurant on premises. Beds: Q. Cable TV, VCR, reading lamp, stereo, refrigerator, ceiling fan, clock radio, telephone, coffeemaker, hot tub/spa,
bathrobes, bath amenities, wireless Internet access, iron/ironing board,
Heated towel bars and double jaccuzi bath tubs in room. Central air. DVD,
fax, spa, swimming, bicycles and gift shop on premises. Handicap access.
Amusement parks, antiquing, art galleries, bicycling, canoeing/kayaking, fishing, golf, hiking, museums, parks, shopping, sporting events, water sports
and Enjoy kayaking down the Mississippi with a Certified ACA Instructer 2
hour tours and 4 hour tours nearby.

Location: Country.

Certificate may be used: Anytime, subject to availability.

Excelsior Springs   C3

The Inn on Crescent Lake

1261 Saint Louis Ave
Excelsior Springs, MO 64024-2938
(816) 630-6745 (866) 630LAKE
Internet: www.crescentlake.com
E-mail: info@crescentlake.com

Circa 1915. Located on 22 acres of lush grounds with woodland
and bucolic ponds, this three-story, Georgian-style house is just a
half-hour drive from downtown Kansas City and the airport.
Spacious suites and guest rooms all have private baths, and
guests can choose to have either a whirlpool or clawfoot tub.
Enjoy a delicious hot breakfast in the sun-filled solarium. Relax
in the outdoor hot tub after a refreshing dip in the pool. Try the
paddle boats, or borrow a fishing rod and take out the bass boat.

Innkeeper(s): Beverly Delugeau. $120-250. 10 rooms with PB, 3 with FP, 1
with HT, 6 with WP, 3 suites, 1 cottage. Breakfast included in rates. Types of
meals: Country bkfst, veg bkfst and wine. Beds: KQT. Cable TV, DVD, reading
lamp, stereo, ceiling fan, clock radio, some with hot tub/spa, some with fireplace, hair dryer, bath amenities, wireless Internet access and iron/ironing
board in room. Central air. Spa, swimming, parlor games, telephone, gift
shop, Fishing, Paddleboats, Rowboat and Gas firepit on premises. Handicap
access. Amusement parks, antiquing, art galleries, fishing, golf, hiking, live
theater, museums, parks and shopping nearby.

Location: Country.

Certificate may be used: November-April, Sunday-Thursday, higher rates prevail.

Fulton   D6

Loganberry Inn

310 W Seventh St
Fulton, MO 65251-2608
(573)642-9229 (888)866-6661
Internet: www.loganberryinn.com
E-mail: info@loganberryinn.com

Circa 1899. Adorning the historic district, this 1899 grand
Victorian is an award-winning inn on one acre surrounded by
extensive gardens accented by a gazebo. The English country
décor also boasts some well-placed French antiques. All of the
pampering guest bedrooms feature fireplaces and entertainment
centers. The Garden Room includes a spa tub. A Corporate
Cottage is perfect for business travelers. Complimentary
refreshments are provided and a celebrity chef creates bountiful
breakfasts served on fine china and crystal in the elegant dining
room. A sample menu might offer cinnamon pears with raspberry coulis, crab and roasted artichoke quiche, banana pecan

waffles, maple pepper bacon as well as an extensive assortment of coffees, teas and juices. Hike or bike the easily accessible Katy Trail. Special packages are available.

Innkeeper(s): Carl & Cathy McGeorge. $89-189. 6 rooms with PB, 6 with FP. Breakfast and snacks/refreshments included in rates. Types of meals: Full gourmet bkfst, veg bkfst, early coffee/tea, picnic lunch and afternoon tea. Beds: KQ. Modem hook-up, data port, cable TV, VCR, DVD, reading lamp, stereo, refrigerator, ceiling fan, snack bar, clock radio, telephone, coffeemaker, desk, hot tub/spa, voice mail, fireplace, hair dryer, bathrobes, bath amenities, wireless Internet access and iron/ironing board in room. Central air. Fax, copier, spa, bicycles, library, laundry facility and gift shop on premises. Antiquing, art galleries, bicycling, fishing, golf, hiking, horseback riding, live theater, museums, parks, shopping, sporting events, tennis, wineries, Katy Trail, National Churchill Museum, Auto World Antique Auto Museum and Biking nearby.

Location: City.

Publicity: *Missouri Life, Show Me Missouri, Show me Romance, Ozark Days, Off the Beaten Path and Pepper & Friends.*

"Thank you for sharing your lovely home and gracious hospitality with us."

Certificate may be used: Sunday-Thursday, no holidays.

Hollister H4

Cameron's Crag

738 Acacia Club Road
Hollister, MO 65672
(417) 334-4720 (800) 933-8529 Fax:(417)335-8134
Internet: www.camerons-crag.com
E-mail: stay@camerons-crag.com

Circa 1986. Sitting high on a bluff, this contemporary bed and breakfast overlooks Lake Taneycomo and the Branson, Missouri skyline. Cameron's Crag offers breathtaking panoramic views of spectacular Ozark scenery, warm hospitality and spacious accommodations. Stay in a guest suite that includes a separate entrance, entertainment center with movie library and private deck area with hot tub. Suites in the detached guest house also offer full kitchens and deluxe whirlpool tubs for two. Innkeeper Glen serves delicious breakfasts using the traditionally southern, local cuisine that blends the influence of early German, French, English and Scandinavian settlers.

Innkeeper(s): Glen Cameron and Janet Miller. $125-165. 4 rooms, 4 with HT, 2 with WP, 4 suites. Breakfast included in rates. Types of meals: Full bkfst and Attempt to accommodate dietary restrictions whenever possible. Beds: K. Cable TV, VCR, DVD, reading lamp, CD player, refrigerator, ceiling fan, clock radio, coffeemaker, hot tub/spa, hair dryer, bathrobes, bath amenities, wireless Internet access, iron/ironing board, Microwave, Coffee service and Wi-Fi in some suites in room. Central air. Fax, copier and library on premises. Amusement parks, antiquing, beach, bicycling, canoeing/kayaking, fishing, golf, hiking, horseback riding, live theater, museums, parks, shopping, sporting events, tennis, water sports, wineries, Trout hatchery, Lake cruises, Civil War battlefield and Water and fire show on the lakefront nearby.

Publicity: *Recognized as an "Affordable Romance Destination" by iLoveInns (Feb 2009), Picked by travel editors as one of the best Bed & Breakfasts in USA for fall foliage viewing (Fall 2008), Missouri Life Magazine (Aug 2007) and Arrington Inn Traveler's 2006 Official Book of Lists - #9 B&B/Country Inn throughout North America in category of "Best Kept Secret".*

Certificate may be used: April-December, Sunday-Thursday, January-March any day; Holidays excluded.

Independence D3

Serendipity B&B

116 S Pleasant St
Independence, MO 64050
(816)833-4719 (800)203-4299
Internet: www.serendipitybedandbreakfast.com
E-mail: Please call the inn

Circa 1887. This three-story brick home offers guests the ultimate Victorian experience. Antique furnishings and period appointments create an authentic period ambiance. Victorian children's books and toys, antique pictures, china figurines and a  collection of antique colored glassware add to the home's charm. Stereoscopes and music box tunes are other special touches. A full breakfast is served by candlelight in the formal dining room. Outside gardens include arbors, Victorian gazing balls, birdhouses, birdbaths, a hammock, swing and fountain. If time and weather permit, guests may request a ride in an antique car and tour of the house.

Innkeeper(s): Susan & Doug Walter. $95. 5 rooms with PB. Types of meals: Full bkfst. Beds: KQT. Air conditioning. TV, VCR, fax and copier on premises. Amusement parks, antiquing, fishing, golf, live theater, parks, shopping, sporting events, tennis, water sports, historic sites and casinos nearby.

Location: City.

"It was so special to spend time with you and to share your lovely home."

Certificate may be used: Sunday-Thursday, excluding holidays and local festivals.

Marshfield G5

The Dickey House B&B

331 S Clay St
Marshfield, MO 65706-2114
(417)468-3000 Fax:(417)859-5478
Internet: www.dickeyhouse.com
E-mail: info@dickeyhouse.com

Circa 1908. This Greek Revival mansion is framed by ancient oak trees and boasts eight massive two-story Ionic columns. Burled woodwork, beveled glass and polished hardwood floors accentuate the gracious rooms. Interior columns soar in the parlor, creating a suitably elegant setting for the innkeeper's outstanding collection of antiques. A queen-size canopy bed, fireplace and sunporch are featured in the Heritage Room. Some rooms offer amenities such as Jacuzzi tubs and a fireplace. All rooms include cable TV and a VCR. The innkeepers also offer a sun room with a hot tub.

Innkeeper(s): Larry & Michaelene Stevens. $89-169. 3 rooms with PB, 4 suites. Breakfast included in rates. Types of meals: Full gourmet bkfst, veg bkfst, early coffee/tea, snacks/refreshments and Friday and Saturday evening dinners by advance reservations only. Limited seating. Beds: KQD. Cable TV, VCR, reading lamp, CD player, refrigerator, ceiling fan, clock radio, telephone, coffeemaker, most with fireplace, hair dryer, bathrobes, bath amenities, wireless Internet access,

iron/ironing board, All four suites feature double Jacuzzis, Fireplaces, TV/VCR, microwave, coffee maker and full bath with shower in room. Central air. Handicap access.

Location: City. Small town.

Certificate may be used: Jan. 10 to April 30, Sunday-Thursday, excluding Valentines Day.

Osage Beach   E6

Inn at Harbour Ridge

6334 Red Barn Road
Osage Beach, MO 65065
(573)302-0411 (877)744-6020
Internet: www.harbourridgeinn.com
E-mail: info@harbourridgeinn.com

Circa 1999. Romantic and inviting, the Inn at Harbour Ridge Bed and Breakfast boasts a contemporary setting with modern and French décor. Poised on a ridge overlooking Lake of the Ozarks in Central Missouri, there are almost two well-landscaped acres with oak trees, goldfish ponds and an herb garden. A gazebo near the waterfall is the perfect place for a wedding. Osage Beach is conveniently located between Kansas City and St. Louis. Select a delightful guest bedroom that may feature a fireplace, whirlpool, private deck or a patio with a hot tub. An early-morning coffee tray is delivered to each room. Indulge in an incredible breakfast in the solarium dining room. Swim in the cove or sun on the dock. Special requests are granted with pleasure.

Innkeeper(s): Sue Westenhaver. $104-199. 5 rooms with PB, 5 with FP, 3 with HT, 3 with WP, 1 cottage. Breakfast and snacks/refreshments included in rates. Types of meals: Full gourmet bkfst and early coffee/tea. Beds: KQ. Cable TV, VCR, DVD, reading lamp, stereo, refrigerator, ceiling fan, snack bar, clock radio, telephone, turn-down service, most with hot tub/spa, fireplace, hair dryer, bathrobes, bath amenities, wireless Internet access, iron/ironing board, Complimentary Wi-Fi, Movie & music library, Private decks or patios and Early morning coffee trays delivered to guestroom door before a full gourmet breakfast is served in room. Central air. Copier, spa, swimming, library, parlor games, gift shop, Paddleboat, Goldfish ponds, Gazebo, Swim platform, Dock on Lake and 24-hour concierge services on premises. Handicap access. Antiquing, art galleries, beach, bicycling, fishing, golf, hiking, horseback riding, museums, parks, shopping, tennis, water sports, wineries, Party Cove, Mennonite community, Osage Beach Premium Outlets, Two state parks and Lake of the Ozarks water activities nearby.

Location: City. Central Missouri, located halfway between Kansas City and St. Louis, MO.

Publicity: *The Missouri Life Magazine (2/06) and Lake Sun Reader's Choice Award (9/06)* .

Certificate may be used: November-March, Monday-Thursday excluding holidays, anytime at the last minute.

Perry   C6

Kennedy's Red Barn Inn

22748 Joanna Dr
Perry, MO 63462
(573)565-0111 (573)567-4155 Fax:(573)567-4068
Internet: www.redbarninn.com
E-mail: redbarn@redbarninn.com

Circa 1898. Country living is at its best at this old Missouri red barn that has been restored as a delightful home on Mark Twain Lake. Beamed ceilings, an antique staircase, rustic wood floors and lots of room inside and out instill a relaxing ambiance. The main floor includes a gift shop, sitting room, library and dining room where a hearty breakfast is served. Guest bedrooms feature quilt-covered brass beds, lace curtains,

antiques and wicker. A red heart whirlpool tub with bath products enhances a romantic setting. After a workout in the exercise room, an outdoor aroma-scented hot tub feels great.

Innkeeper(s): Jack & Rebecca Kennedy. $60-90. 3 rooms, 1 with PB. Breakfast and snacks/refreshments included in rates. Types of meals: Country bkfst, early coffee/tea and afternoon tea. Beds: KQDT. Ceiling fan, clock radio and desk in room. Central air. TV, VCR, fax, copier, spa, bicycles, library, telephone, fireplace, laundry facility and gift shop on premises. Amusement parks, antiquing, art galleries, beach, bicycling, canoeing/kayaking, fishing, golf, hiking, horseback riding, live theater, museums, parks, shopping, tennis and water sports nearby.

Location: Country. Mark Twain Lake.

Publicity: *Courier Post and Lake Gazette.*

Certificate may be used: November-January, anytime.

Saint Joseph   B2

Museum Hill Bed & Breakfast

1102 Felix St
Saint Joseph, MO 64501-2816
(816)387-9663
Internet: www.museumhill.com
E-mail: museumhillbandb@yahoo.com

Circa 1880. Poised on a hill in the historic district overlooking downtown St. Joseph, Missouri, this three-story Italianate red brick mansion was built in 1880 and has been fully restored. Museum Hill Bed & Breakfast features an elegant Great Room with an antique upright piano and inviting sitting areas. Relax with a glass of wine on the wraparound porch with a swing and a grand view of the city. Guest bedrooms boast luxury linens and one room includes a whirlpool tub. Lunch won't be needed after a complete gourmet signature breakfast service. A well-stocked guest kitchen adds to the pampering touches provided. Package deals and getaway specials are offered. The central location is perfect for visiting popular spots in several neighboring states.

Innkeeper(s): John and Beth Courter. $120-160. 4 rooms with PB, 1 with WP, 1 conference room. Breakfast, snacks/refreshments and wine included in rates. Types of meals: Full gourmet bkfst, picnic lunch, hors d'oeuvres and gourmet dinner. Beds: QD. Modem hook-up, cable TV, reading lamp, clock radio, desk, hair dryer, bath amenities, wireless Internet access, Living air purifiers, Soft water, 2" memory foam bed toppers, Extra pillow, 1000-count sheets and Direct Satellite TV in all rooms in room. Central air. VCR, DVD, library, parlor games, telephone, gift shop, Full-size ironing board & iron, Fully stocked guest kitchen, Refrigerator, Microwave and Coffeepot on premises. Antiquing, art galleries, beach, bicycling, canoeing/kayaking, cross-country skiing, downhill skiing, fishing, golf, hiking, live theater, museums, parks, shopping, sporting events, tennis, water sports, wineries and Historical walking tours nearby.

Location: Historic Downtown.

Publicity: *This Old House Magazine (October 2002), "Save This Old House", Missouri Life Magazine (February 2008 "Hot of the Griddle" section). and HGTV's "If Walls Could Talk"* .

Certificate may be used: Good for Empire Rose or Emma's Rose Garden Rooms. Anytime, Monday-Thursday, based on availability. Excludes Trails West and Valentines weekend.

Saint Louis   D8

Lehmann House B&B

10 Benton Place
Saint Louis, MO 63104-2411
(314)422-1483 Fax:(314)621-5449
Internet: www.lehmannhouse.com
E-mail: lehmann.house@sbcglobal.net

Circa 1893. This National Register manor's most prominent resident, former U.S. Solicitor General Frederick Lehmann, hosted Presidents Taft, Theodore Roosevelt and Coolidge at this gracious home. Several key turn-of-the-century literary figures also visited the Lehmann family. The inn's formal dining room, complete with oak paneling and a fireplace, is a stunning place to enjoy the formal breakfasts. Antiques and gracious furnishings dot the well-appointed guest rooms. The home is located in St. Louis' oldest historic district, Lafayette Square.

Innkeeper(s): Marie Davies. $109-139. 5 rooms, 3 with PB, 3 with FP. Breakfast included in rates. Types of meals: Full bkfst, veg bkfst and early coffee/tea. Beds: KQD. Reading lamp, refrigerator, ceiling fan, clock radio, desk, most with fireplace, hair dryer, bathrobes, bath amenities and iron/ironing board in room. Central air. Swimming, tennis, library, parlor games and telephone on premises. Amusement parks, antiquing, art galleries, bicycling, golf, live theater, museums, parks, shopping, sporting events, tennis, museums, zoos and botanical gardens nearby.

Location: City.

Publicity: *St. Louis Post Dispatch and KTVI-St. Louis.*

"Wonderful mansion with great future ahead. Thanks for the wonderful hospitality."

Certificate may be used: Nov. 1-March 1, Sunday-Thursday only, holidays and special events excluded. Anytime, Last Minute-Based on Availability.

Sainte Genevieve   E9

Inn St. Gemme Beauvais

78 N Main St
Sainte Genevieve, MO 63670-1336
(573) 883-5744 (800) 818-5744 Fax:(573)880-1953
Internet: www.stgem.com
E-mail: stgemme@brick.net

Circa 1848. This three-story, Federal-style inn is an impressive site on Ste. Genevieve's Main Street. The town is one of the oldest west of the Mississippi River, and the St. Gemme Beauvais is the oldest operating Missouri bed & breakfast. The rooms are nicely appointed in period style, but there are modern amenities here, too. The Jacuzzi tubs in some guest rooms are one relaxing example. There is an outdoor hot tub, as well. The romantic carriage house includes a king-size bed, double Jacuzzi tub and a fireplace. Guests are pampered with all sorts of cuisine, including full breakfasts served at individual candle-lit tables with a choice of eight entrees. Later, tea, drinks, hors d'oeuvres and refreshments are also served.

Innkeeper(s): Janet Joggerst. $89-179. 9 rooms, 5 with FP, 1 with WP, 9 suites, 1 cottage. Breakfast, afternoon tea, snacks/refreshments and wine included in rates. Types of meals: Full gourmet bkfst and veg bkfst. Restaurant on premises. Beds: KQ. Cable TV, VCR, reading lamp, ceiling fan, clock radio and wireless Internet access in room. Air conditioning. Library, parlor games, telephone and fireplace on premises. Antiquing, golf, parks, shopping and historic area nearby.

Location: Historic town 60 miles south of St. Louis.

Certificate may be used: Sunday-Thursday, Nov. 1-April 30.

Springfield   G4

Virginia Rose B&B

317 E Glenwood St
Springfield, MO 65807-3543
(417)883-0693 (800)345-1412

Circa 1906. Three generations of the Botts family lived in this home before it was sold to the current innkeepers, Virginia and Jackie Buck. The grounds still include the rustic red barn. Comfortable, country rooms are named after Buck family members and feature beds covered with quilts. The innkeepers

also offer a two-bedroom suite, the Rambling Rose, which is decorated in a sportsman theme in honor of the nearby Bass Pro. Hearty breakfasts are served in the dining room, and the innkeepers will provide low-fat fare on request.

Innkeeper(s): Jackie & Virginia Buck. $70-120. 4 rooms, 2 with PB, 1 suite. Breakfast included in rates. Types of meals: Full bkfst, early coffee/tea, picnic lunch and snacks/refreshments. Beds: KQT. Reading lamp, clock radio, telephone and turn-down service in room. Air conditioning. VCR, fax and parlor games on premises. Amusement parks, antiquing, fishing, live theater, parks, shopping, sporting events and water sports nearby.

Location: City.

Publicity: *Auctions & Antiques, Springfield Business Journal, Today's Women Journal and Springfield News-leader.*

"The accommodations are wonderful and the hospitality couldn't be warmer."

Certificate may be used: Sunday-Thursday, Jan. 7-Dec. 13, subject to availability and excluding holidays.

Walnut Street Inn

900 E Walnut St
Springfield, MO 65806-2603
(417)864-6346 (800)593-6346 Fax:(417)864-6184
Internet: www.walnutstreetinn.com
E-mail: stay@walnutstreetinn.com

Circa 1894. This three-story Queen Anne gabled house has cast-iron Corinthian columns and a veranda. Polished wood floors and antiques are featured throughout. Upstairs you'll find the gathering room with a fireplace. Ask for the McCann guest room with two bay windows, or one of the five rooms with a double Jacuzzi tub. A full breakfast is served, including items such as strawberry-filled French toast.

Innkeeper(s): Gary & Paula Blankenship. $89-169. 12 rooms with PB, 10 with FP, 5 with WP, 2 suites. Breakfast and Homemade cookies in your room every day! included in rates. Types of meals: Full gourmet bkfst, veg bkfst, early coffee/tea, snacks/refreshments, wine, room service and Special meals for dietary restrictions or special needs. Beds: KQ. Modem hook-up, data port, cable TV, VCR, DVD, reading lamp, stereo, refrigerator, ceiling fan, clock radio, telephone, coffeemaker, turn-down service, desk, hair dryer, bath amenities, wireless Internet access, iron/ironing board, beverage bars, health club access and wake-up calls in room. Central air. Fax, copier, parlor games, fireplace, gift shop and the best porch swing setting in the state! on premises. Handicap access. Amusement parks, antiquing, art galleries, canoeing/kayaking, fishing, golf, hiking, live theater, museums, parks, shopping, sporting events, tennis, Bass Pro Shop, Wonders of Wildlife Museum, 20+ Art Galleries, Springfield Cardinals (St. Louis Cardinals AA team), Springfield Expo Center, restaurants, shopping and entertainment within walking distance nearby.

Location: City.

Publicity: *Southern Living, Women's World, Midwest Living, Victoria, Country Inns, Innsider, Glamour, Midwest Motorist, Missouri, Saint Louis Post, Kansas City Star, USA Today and 417 Magazine.*

"Rest assured your establishment's qualities are unmatched and through your commitment to excellence you have won a life-long client."

Certificate may be used: Sunday-Thursday, excluding holidays and certain dates.

Montana

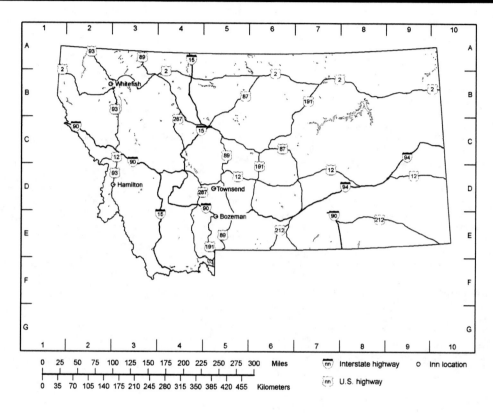

1	2	3	4	5	6	7	8	9	10

0 25 50 75 100 125 150 175 200 225 250 275 300   Miles

0 35 70 105 140 175 210 245 280 315 350 385 420 455   Kilometers

[nn] Interstate highway   o   Inn location

[nn] U.S. highway

Hamilton   *D3*

Deer Crossing B&B

396 Hayes Creek Rd
Hamilton, MT 59840-9744
(406)363-2232 (800)763-2232
Internet: www.deercrossingmontana.com
E-mail: info@deercrossingmontana.com

Circa 1980. This Western-style ranch bed & breakfast is located on 25 acres of woods and pastures. One suite includes a double Jacuzzi tub and another has a private balcony. In addition to the suites and guest rooms, travelers also can opt to stay in the bunkhouse, a historic homestead building with a wood-burning stove. A new creekside log cabin includes a covered porch, fireplace and full kitchen especially appealing to families with small children or long-term guests who want to regroup while enjoying a scenic setting. The area offers many activities, including horseback riding, hiking, fly fishing and historic sites.

Innkeeper(s): Stu & Linda Dobbins. $75-149. 5 rooms, 4 with PB, 2 suites, 2 cabins. Breakfast and snacks/refreshments included in rates. Types of meals: Full bkfst and early coffee/tea. Beds: KQDT. Cable TV, reading lamp, stereo, refrigerator, clock radio, coffeemaker, desk, hair dryer, bathrobes and bath amenities in room. VCR, fax, copier, stable, library, parlor games, telephone, fireplace, Satellite dish, Fireplace and WiFi on premises. Antiquing, bicycling, canoeing/kayaking, cross-country skiing, downhill skiing, fishing, golf, hiking, horseback riding, parks, shopping and water sports nearby.

Location: Mountains. Ranch, 50 miles south of Missoula.

Publicity: *Country Magazine and Montana Handbook.*

"It is so nice to be back after three years and from 5,000 miles away!"
Certificate may be used: Oct. 1-May 1.

Townsend

D5

Canyon Ferry Mansion Inn

7408 US Highway 287 Mile Post 74
Townsend, MT 59644-9669
(406)266-3599 (877)WEDSPA1 Fax:(406)266-4003
Internet: www.canyonferrymansion.com
E-mail: sandy@canyonferrymansion.com

Circa 1914. Open all year-round, Canyon Ferry Mansion is a lake-view bed and breakfast resort on six acres between Elk Horn and Big Belt Mountain. This historic Montana inn in Townsend, 33 minutes from Helena and halfway between Yellowstone and Glacier National Parks, boasts a panoramic view of Mt. Baldy and overlooks the lake. Take the hiking trail from Missouri Wildlife Refuge to where the Missouri River flows into Canyon Ferry Lake, then soak in the Jacuzzi or sit in the sauna. Luxurious accommodations and a casual sports lodge setting combine with warm hospitality and generous amenities to offer a pleasantly memorable stay. Fireside snacks and refreshments at the library table as well as bedside candies and sherry are provided. Weddings, retreats and reunions are popular here.

Innkeeper(s): Sandy Rose - Wedding Hostess. $100-295. 9 rooms, 2 with PB, 1 with FP, 2 with WP, 1 two-bedroom and 1 three-bedroom suites, 1 guest house, 2 cabins, 4 conference rooms. Breakfast, afternoon tea, snacks/refreshments, Bedside Candies, Library Table Snacks, Bedtime Sherry and Spa Waters included in rates. Types of meals: Country bkfst, early coffee/tea, lunch, picnic lunch, hors d'oeuvres, wine, gourmet dinner, room service, Vegetarian & other dietary needs met when ordered ahead. Designer wedding cakes, BBQ's & Hayrides, Murder Mystery Dinners & Luncheons by appointment for private groups, Gourmet and Western & Country catering for weddings & events. Beds: KQDT. Data port, cable TV, VCR, reading lamp, refrigerator, ceiling fan, snack bar, clock radio, hot tub/spa, hair dryer, bathrobes, bath amenities, wireless Internet access and iron/ironing board in room. Air conditioning. Fax, copier, spa, sauna, library, parlor games, fireplace, gift shop, Full Service Day Spa, Spa events, Sauna and Suntan on premises. Limited handicap access. Antiquing, art galleries, fishing, golf, hiking, horseback riding, museums, parks, shopping, sporting events, water sports, Boat Rental, Shooting Club, Golf & Carts, Swim Club, Marina, Boat Rentals, Ghost Town, EZ River Rafting Rentals, Picnics Packed, Sapphire Hunting, Glass Blowing Studio, World's Fastest Ice Sailing Lake, Ice Fishing, Tournaments, Rodeo and Fall Fest nearby.

Location: Country, mountains, waterfront. Canyon Ferry Lake at Missouri River Confluence.

Publicity: *The Helena Independent Record, The Bozeman Chronicle, FEDOR'S Travel Guide, Elegible for the National Historic Record, Montana NRA Bed n Breakfast of the Year (2006), Associated Press & Reuters (2008 - Double Proxy Military Weddings), CBS Bridal Show, NBC Historic Highway 12, Local Helena Capital Coffee Talk and Alleged to be Montana's most paranormal friendly haunt.*

Certificate may be used: Monday-Thursday, subject to availability, holidays excluded. Regular room rates apply, good for Romance rooms only. Not valid with any other discounts.

Whitefish

B2

Good Medicine Lodge

537 Wisconsin Ave
Whitefish, MT 59937-2127
(406)862-5488 (800)860-5488 Fax:(406)862-5489
Internet: www.goodmedicinelodge.com
E-mail: info@goodmedicinelodge.com

Circa 1976. Fashioned from square cedar logs, this modern Montana-style lodge bed and breakfast boasts a Western décor with comfortable furnishings and textiles reminiscent of Native American themes. Relax by the fire in one of the common areas. Guest bedrooms feature natural cedar walls and ceilings with exposed cedar beams. Two rooms have a fireplace. A European-style breakfast buffet includes homemade baked goods and granola, cereals, yogurt, a specialty entrée, fresh fruit, brewed coffee and juices. The bed and breakfast is located in a mountain setting near Glacier Park, golf courses, cross country and alpine skiing, water sports, fishing and Big Mountain Resort.

Innkeeper(s): Betsy & Woody Cox. $110-265. 9 rooms, 6 with PB, 2 with FP, 2 with WP, 3 total suites, including 2 two-bedroom suites, 1 conference room. Breakfast, hors d'oeuvres and A full breakfast is complimentary to all guests included in rates. Types of meals: Full gourmet bkfst and room service. Beds: KQT. Data port, reading lamp, CD player, refrigerator, ceiling fan, clock radio, telephone, desk, some with hot tub/spa, voice mail, some with fireplace, hair dryer, bathrobes, bath amenities, wireless Internet access and iron/ironing board in room. Central air. TV, VCR, DVD, fax, copier, spa, library, parlor games, laundry facility, gift shop, TV/Library Room with big screen TV and Gas Firepit on premises. Handicap access. Amusement parks, antiquing, art galleries, beach, bicycling, canoeing/kayaking, cross-country skiing, downhill skiing, fishing, golf, hiking, horseback riding, live theater, museums, parks, shopping, sporting events, tennis and water sports nearby.

Location: City, mountains. Mountains near Glacier National Park and Big Mountain Ski Resort.

Publicity: *USA Today ("Great Places," Sept. 2006); United Airlines - Hemispheres 2006 and Travel Channel ("Wide Open Spaces: Montana & Wyoming").*

Certificate may be used: Oct. 1-April 30.

Nebraska

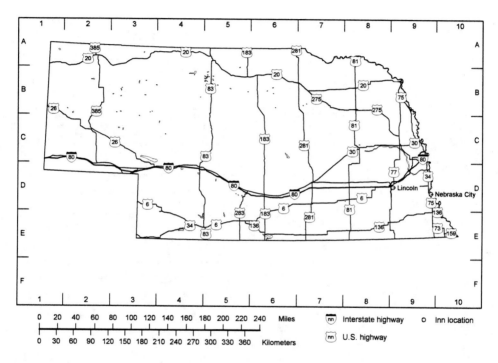

			Miles
nn	Interstate highway	o	Inn location
nn	U.S. highway		

Lincoln   D9

The Atwood House B&B

740 S 17th St
Lincoln, NE 68508-3799
(402)438-4567 (800)884-6554 Fax:(402)477-8314
Internet: www.atwoodhouse.com
E-mail: larry@atwoodhouse.com

Circa 1894. Located two blocks from the state capitol, this 7,500-square-foot mansion, in the Neoclassical Georgian Revival style, features four massive columns. Interior columns are repeated throughout such as on the dressing room vanity, on the staircase and on the parlor fireplace. Classically appointed, the parlor and entranceway set an elegant yet inviting tone. Guest suites are large and feature spacious sitting rooms, fireplaces, massive bedsteads and Oriental carpets. The 800-square-foot bridal suite consists of three rooms, and it includes a fireplace, a carved walnut bed and a large whirlpool tub set off by columns. Breakfast is served on bone china with Waterford crystal and sterling flatware.

Innkeeper(s): Ruth & Larry Stoll. $85-199. 4 rooms, 2 with FP, 4 suites, 1 cottage, 1 conference room. Breakfast and snacks/refreshments included in rates. Types of meals: Full gourmet bkfst, veg bkfst and early coffee/tea.

Beds: K. Modern hook-up, cable TV, VCR, DVD, reading lamp, stereo, refrigerator, ceiling fan, clock radio, telephone, coffeemaker, turn-down service, desk, hot tub/spa, most with fireplace, hair dryer, bathrobes, bath amenities, wireless Internet access, iron/ironing board and three with two-person whirlpool in room. Central air. Fax, copier and library on premises. Antiquing, bicycling, cross-country skiing, fishing, golf, horseback riding, live theater, parks, shopping, sporting events, tennis and water sports nearby.

Location: City.

Publicity: *Lincoln Journal Star, Midwest Living*, Channel 8 local (ABC), Channel 10/11 local (CBS), KLIN and AM1400.

"Such a delightful B&B! It is such a nice change in my travels."

Certificate may be used: Jan. 2 to April 30, Monday-Thursday for the Atwood or Carriage House suite.

Nevada

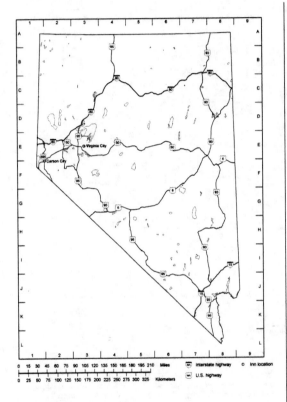

Miles
0 15 30 45 60 75 90 105 120 135 150 165 180 195 210
Kilometers
0 25 50 75 100 125 150 175 200 225 250 275 300 325

Interstate highway   • Inn location
U.S. highway

Carson City   F2

Bliss Bungalow

408 West Robinson Street
Carson City, NV 89703-3865
(775)883-6129
Internet: www.blissbungalow.com
E-mail: reservations@blissbungalow.com

Circa 1914. Surrounded by mature maple and cottonwood trees, this fully restored Arts and Crafts home in the historic district of Carson City, Nevada has original fir floors and pine molding with leaded glass windows. Sit on the inviting front porch, read in a sitting room or watch a movie in the TV/office area. All rooms have large custom Turkish-type rugs with vibrant colors and designs. Each guest room features a bed with pillow-top mattress, refrigerator, handmade soaps and other thoughtful amenities. Bliss Bungalow offers a self-serve, 24-hour continental breakfast available in the kitchen with hot and cold beverages, cereal, toast and snacks. Perfect for the discerning traveler and business person, WIFI is throughout the B&B.

Innkeeper(s): Joyce Harrington. $88-145. 5 rooms with PB. Breakfast included in rates. Types of meals: Cont, snacks/refreshments and Self-serve. Beds: Q. Cable TV, reading lamp, refrigerator, hair dryer, wireless Internet access and iron/ironing board in room. Air conditioning. Fireplace and Breakfast snacks and beverages available all hours on premises. Handicap access. Antiquing, cross-country skiing, downhill skiing, fishing, golf, museums, parks, water sports, gambling and historical tours nearby.

Location: City. Carson City Historic District.

"A Hearst Castle with air conditioning, pillowtop mattresses and instant hot water."

Certificate may be used: November-June, last minute, subject to availability. holidays excluded.

Virginia City   E3

B Street House Bed and Breakfast

58 North B Street
Virginia City, NV 89440
(775) 847-7231
Internet: www.BStreetHouse.com
E-mail: innkeepers@BStreetHouse.com

Circa 1875. Set on an idyllic small town street in the Old West town of Virginia City, the B Street House is a Victorian home with comforts and amenities galore. Recently renovated in 2007, the home is the only B&B in Virginia City with a listing in the National Register of Historic Places. Spring and summer guests will enjoy a beautiful garden with butterflies and quail, and in colder weather the parlor and library are great places to relax out of the cold. The inn's guest rooms all feature private baths, satellite TV and high speed internet, and many have huge windows with picturesque views. The inn's location allows guests to experience all of the sights, sounds and outdoor activities of Reno, Lake Tahoe and Carson City.

Innkeeper(s): Chris and Carolyn. $99-139. 3 rooms with PB. Breakfast, afternoon tea and Full gourmet breakfast; snacks and fresh fruit available 24/7 included in rates. Beds: Q. Cable TV, DVD, reading lamp, refrigerator, ceiling fan, clock radio, hair dryer, bath amenities, wireless Internet access and Fresh seasonal flowers from our garden; Swiss chocolates in room. Air conditioning. Library, parlor games and telephone on premises. Antiquing, art galleries, beach, bicycling, canoeing/kayaking, fishing, golf, hiking, horseback riding, live theater, museums, parks, shopping, water sports, wineries and mine tours; cemetery tours; nearby.

Location: Country. Reno; Carson City.

Certificate may be used: May-October, subject to availability.

New Hampshire

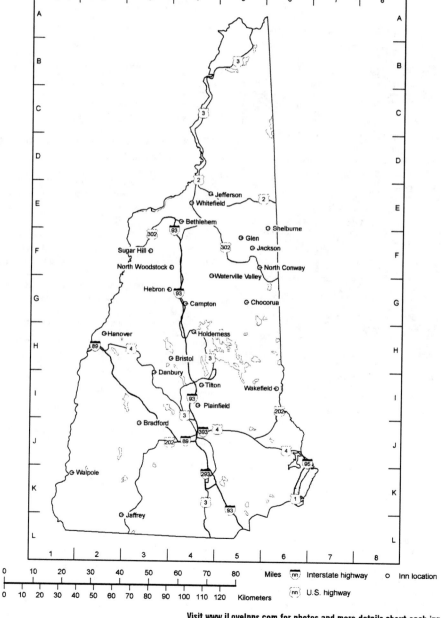

0 10 20 30 40 50 60 70 80   Miles
0 10 20 30 40 50 60 70 80 90 100 110 120 Kilometers

(nn) Interstate highway   o Inn location

(nn) U.S. highway

Bethlehem E4

Adair Country Inn and Restaurant

80 Guider Lane
Bethlehem, NH 03574
(603)444-2600 (888)444-2600 Fax:(603)444-4823
Internet: www.adairinn.com
E-mail: innkeeper@adairinn.com

Circa 1927. Representing all that a New England country inn is hoped to be, enjoy relaxation and tranquility on more than 200 picturesque acres with mountain views and perennial gardens. This four-diamond-rated inn was originally a wedding gift

from Frank Hogan to his daughter, Dorothy Adair Hogan. Dorothy hosted many famed guests here, including presidential candidates, Supreme Court justices and actors. Just-baked popovers start the morning fare, followed by fresh fruit, yogurt and specialty dishes such as pumpkin pancakes with Vermont bacon. Homemade cakes and cookies are served during the complimentary afternoon tea service. Flavorful food, made with only the freshest ingredients and artfully presented, is a point of pride at Adair. The intimate dining room with fireplace and wonderful views of gardens, both front and back, is filled with enticing aromas morning and night. Make reservation at Adair's gourmet restaurant for a dinner to remember.

Innkeeper(s): Ilja and Brad Chapman. $195-375. 9 rooms with PB, 7 with FP, 1 with WP, 1 suite. Breakfast, afternoon tea and snacks/refreshments included in rates. Types of meals: Full gourmet bkfst, veg bkfst, Sun. brunch, early coffee/tea, picnic lunch, hors d'oeuvres, wine, gourmet dinner and Fine New England Style Cuisine. Restaurant on premises. Beds: KQ. Reading lamp, stereo, snack bar, clock radio, turn-down service, desk, hair dryer, bathrobes, bath amenities, wireless Internet access, iron/ironing board, All rooms have beautifull views of the mountains, gardens and surroundings. No television or phones in the room. Large comfortable entertainment room offering TV, DVD and Games and billiard in room. Air conditioning. TV, VCR, fax, copier, tennis, library, parlor games, telephone, fireplace, gift shop and Pool table on premises. Antiquing, bicycling, canoeing/kayaking, cross-country skiing, downhill skiing, fishing, golf, hiking, horseback riding, live theater, museums, parks, shopping, tennis, On-site hiking, Snowshoeing, Tennis and Outdoor games nearby.

Location: Country, mountains.

Publicity: Travel & Leisure, Yankee Connecticut Magazine, New England Travel, Gourmet, Cosmopolitan, New Hampshire Magazine, USA Today, Men's Journal and HGTV "If Walls Could Talk"

"What can we say, we expected a lot — and got much more."

Certificate may be used: Anytime, subject to availability, Not valid during holidays or foliage season.

Bristol H4

A Newfound Bed & Breakfast

94 Mandi Lane
Bristol, NH 03222
(603)986-0745 (877)444-3442 Fax:(603)744-9548
Internet: anewfoundbnb.com
E-mail: sondra@anewfoundbnb.com

Circa 1985. This pristine inn offers mountainside views of Newfound Lake and Cardigan Mountain. Room choices include some with fireplaces, flat screen TVs, and large baths. All are supplied with fine linens and Turkish towels. Acres of woodland surround the property with an abundance of trails and a small brook. The inn's grounds offer vegetable gardens, a frog pond and even a handsome chicken coop from which fresh eggs are gathered for breakfast dishes which are finely crafted each morning. The lake provides boating and swimming in summer and in winter there are snowmobile trails right from the property. A huge fireplace in the common room invites relaxing in the evening after daytime excursions.

Innkeeper(s): Sondra J. Keene. $199-250. 4 rooms with PB, 4 with FP, 1 with HT, 1 with WP, 1 two-bedroom suite, 1 conference room. Breakfast, snacks/refreshments, hors d'oeuvres and Will accommodate diet restrictions upon request included in rates. Types of meals: Full bkfst, early coffee/tea, picnic lunch and Outdoor gas grill and kitchen available to guests any time after breakfast. Will accommodate diet restrictions upon request. Beds: KQT. Cable TV, DVD, reading lamp, CD player, refrigerator, ceiling fan, clock radio, some with hot tub/spa, fireplace, hair dryer, bathrobes, bath amenities, wireless Internet access and iron/ironing board in room. Fax, copier, library, parlor games, telephone, laundry facility, gift shop, 24-hr coffee/tea station, horseshoe pit, tether ball, outdoor fire pit, hiking, snowshoeing and snowmobile trail access. Trailer parking on premises. Limited handicap access. Amusement parks, antiquing, art galleries, beach, bicycling, canoeing/kayaking, cross-country skiing, downhill skiing, fishing, golf, hiking, horseback riding, live theater, museums, parks, shopping, sporting events, tennis, water sports, wineries, Free boat ramp, snow mobile trails and ice fishing nearby.

Location: Mountains. Newfound Lake.

Certificate may be used: Sunday-Thursday.

Pleasant View Bed and Breakfast

22 Hemp Hill Road
Bristol, NH 03222
(603)744-5547 (888)909-2700 Fax:(603)744-9757
Internet: www.pleasantviewbedandbreakfast.com
E-mail: theinnwench@metrocast.net

Circa 1832. Gracing the heart of the state's Lakes Region on a scenic rural road, this bed and breakfast was built as a farmhouse prior to 1832 for a local blacksmith with land extending to the shores of Newfound Lake. Relax in country elegance in the great room or on the patio. Play games or read a book from the library by a warm fire. Comfortable guest bedrooms include turndown service. After a satisfying breakfast take a bike ride to enjoy the surrounding beauty.

Innkeeper(s): Heidi Milbrand. $110-150. 6 rooms with PB, 1 cottage. Breakfast, afternoon tea and snacks/refreshments included in rates. Types of meals: Country bkfst, early coffee/tea and picnic lunch. Beds: KQD. TV, reading lamp, clock radio, turn-down service, desk, hair dryer, bath amenities, wireless Internet access and iron/ironing board in room. Fax, copier, swimming, library, parlor games and fireplace on premises. Antiquing, art galleries, beach, bicycling, canoeing/kayaking, cross-country skiing, downhill skiing, fishing, golf, hiking, horseback riding, live theater, museums, parks, shopping, sporting events, water sports, wineries, Mt Cardigan, Wellington State Park, Profile Falls and Sculptured Rocks Natural Area nearby.

Location: Country, mountains.

Certificate may be used: Anytime, Sunday-Thursday, not applicable for cottage, Anytime, Last Minute-Based on Availability.

The Henry Whipple House Bed & Breakfast

75 Summer Street
Bristol, NH 03222
(603)744-6157 Fax:(603)744-6569
Internet: www.thewhipplehouse.com
E-mail: info@thewhipplehouse.com

Circa 1904. Centrally located in scenic New England, this Queen Anne is a grand example of a typical Victorian-era home. Stained-glass windows, oak woodwork, chandeliers and hardwood floors all add to the historic charm. Bedchambers in the main house and two carriage house suites are furnished with antiques, candles, personal spa amenities and plush towels. Several rooms feature bronze-engraved fireplaces. Locally grown produce and high-quality meats from Edwards of Surrey, Virginia are used to make a gourmet breakfast of homemade scones or baked goods, eggs Benedict, potato cakes with warm apple sauce, asparagus frittata, crispy bacon and gruyere omelets, tipsy orange French toast and apple pecan pancakes. Enjoy the year-round beauty and activities available nearby.

Innkeeper(s): Sandra Heaney. $110-190. 8 rooms with PB, 2 with FP, 2 suites. Breakfast included in rates. Types of meals: Full gourmet bkfst, veg bkfst and early coffee/tea. Beds: KQDT. Modem hook-up, cable TV, VCR, reading lamp, stereo, refrigerator, ceiling fan, clock radio, telephone, coffeemaker, desk, some with fireplace, hair dryer, bath amenities, wireless Internet access and iron/ironing board in room. Air conditioning. Fax, copier, library, parlor games and gift shop on premises. Amusement parks, antiquing, art galleries, beach, bicycling, canoeing/kayaking, cross-country skiing, downhill skiing, fishing, golf, hiking, horseback riding, live theater, museums, parks, shopping, tennis and water sports nearby.

Location: Country, mountains. Newfound Lake.

Certificate may be used: Anytime, subject to availability.

Campton   G4

Mountain-Fare Inn

Mad River Rd, PO Box 553
Campton, NH 03223
(603)726-4283 Fax:(603)726-8188
Internet: www.mountainfareinn.com
E-mail: info@mountainfareinn.com

Circa 1830. Located in the White Mountains between Franconia Notch and Squam Lake, this white farmhouse is surrounded by flower gardens in the summer and unparalleled foliage in the fall. Mountain-Fare is an early 19th-century village inn in an ideal spot from which to enjoy New Hampshire's many offerings. Each season brings with it different activities, from skiing to biking and hiking or simply taking in the beautiful scenery. 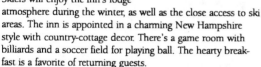 Skiers will enjoy the inn's lodge atmosphere during the winter, as well as the close access to ski areas. The inn is appointed in a charming New Hampshire style with country-cottage decor. There's a game room with billiards and a soccer field for playing ball. The hearty breakfast is a favorite of returning guests.

Innkeeper(s): Susan & Nick Preston. $85-145. 10 rooms with PB. Breakfast and afternoon tea included in rates. Types of meals: Full bkfst. Beds: QDT. Reading lamp and clock radio in room. TV, VCR, sauna, telephone, fireplace, game room with billiards and soccer field on premises. Antiquing, cross-country skiing, downhill skiing, fishing, hiking, live theater, parks, sporting events and water sports nearby.

Location: Mountains. New Hampshire White Mountains.

Publicity: *Ski, Skiing and Snow Country.*

"Thank you for your unusually caring attitude toward your guests."

Certificate may be used: Sunday-Thursday, excluding Dec. 15-Jan. 2 and Sept. 15-Oct. 20.

Chocorua   G5

Brass Heart Inn

88 Philbrick Neighborhood Road
Chocorua, NH 03817
(603)323-7766 (800)833-9509 Fax:(603)323-8769
Internet: www.thebrassheartinn.com
E-mail: info@thebrassheartinn.com

Circa 1778. The main building of Harte's, home to a prosperous farm family for over 150 years, is Federal style. It became a guest house in the 1890s. An old apple orchard and sugar house remain, and there's a kitchen garden. A rocky brook still winds through the rolling fields, and in the adjacent woods, there's a natural swimming hole. Guest rooms are furnished in antiques and replicas.

Innkeeper(s): DJ and Sheena Harte. $80-260. 17 rooms, 6 with PB, 1 with FP, 6 suites, 5 cottages, 1 conference room. Breakfast included in rates. Types of meals: Country bkfst, veg bkfst and early coffee/tea. Restaurant on premises. Beds: KQDT. Reading lamp, refrigerator, clock radio, coffeemaker, turn-down service, some with fireplace, hair dryer and iron/ironing board in room. TV, fax, copier, library, parlor games, telephone and gift shop on premises. Limited handicap access. Antiquing, art galleries, beach, bicycling, canoeing/kayaking, cross-country skiing, downhill skiing, fishing, golf, hiking, horseback riding, live theater, museums, parks, shopping, tennis and water sports nearby.

Location: Country.

Publicity: *Esquire, Boston Globe, Seattle Times, Los Angeles Times, WRCH, WPKQ and WMagic.*

"Delicious food, delightful humor!"

Certificate may be used: Anytime, subject to availability.

Riverbend Inn Bed & Breakfast

273 Chocorua Mountain Highway
Chocorua, NH 03817-0288
(603)323-7440 (800)628-6944 Fax:(603)323-7554
Internet: www.riverbendinn.com
E-mail: info@riverbendinn.com

Circa 1968. Sitting on 15 scenic acres, this secluded country estate is conveniently located between the White Mountains and Lakes Region. Recently renovated, a luxurious decor is accented by antique furnishings. Enjoy afternoon drinks by the fire. Air conditioned bedrooms feature cotton linens, mahogany beds, terry robes and cable TV. One room boasts a private deck and entrance. Breakfast is a multi-course delight that may include favorites like  fresh fruit compote and maple yogurt with roasted granola or grapefruit sections with rum-raisin sauce, cinnamon plum cake or cranberry-bran muffins, eggs florentine or Creme Brulee French Toast. Wander through the gorgeous gardens, meadows and be refreshed by the Chocorua River that runs through the grounds. Relax on the deck or in a hammock.

Innkeeper(s): Craig Cox, Jerry Weiss. $100-250. 10 rooms, 6 with PB. Breakfast and snacks/refreshments included in rates. Types of meals: Full gourmet bkfst. Beds: KQD. Cable TV, reading lamp, hair dryer, bathrobes, bath amenities, wireless Internet access, luxurious all-cotton bed linens and massage available in room. Air conditioning. Fax, copier, library, parlor games, telephone, fireplace, gift shop, hammocks, yoga/meditation room and massage available on premises. Antiquing, art galleries, beach, bicycling, canoeing/kayaking, cross-country skiing, downhill skiing, fishing, golf, hiking, horseback riding, live theater, museums, parks, shopping, water sports, sled dog races and scenic train rides nearby.

Location: Country, mountains, waterfront. Babbling brook frontage.

Publicity: *Best Breakfast in New England 2006 Inn Traveler magazine, Best Romantic B&B 2005 New Hampshire Magazine, Best Interior Design and Decor Inn Traveler Magazine, Boston Globe, Washington Post, New Hampshire Magazine, New Hampshire Union Leader and Yankee Magazine.*

"We can't wait to see all four seasons here. Thank you for all the extra touches."

Certificate may be used: November-May, subject to availability, or anytime at the last minute.

Glen F5

Bernerhof Inn

342 US Route 302
Glen, NH 03838-0240
(603)383-4200 (877)389-4852 Fax:603-)452-0016
Internet: www.BernerhofInn.com
E-mail: Stay@BernerhofInn.com

Circa 1880. Built in the late 19th century for travelers passing through Crawford Notch, this historic Victorian Inn was named by the Zumsteins, its proprietors. They were known for providing fine accommodations, musi-
cal enjoyment and outstanding
food. Today's innkeepers contin-
ue this hospitable commitment
offering country gourmet breakfasts in the dining room and
savory spirits in the Black Bear
Pub. Elegantly decorated guest
bedrooms are non-smoking, some feature brass beds, antiques, stained glass, spa tub Jacuzzis and fireplaces. Each guest has access to a complimentary iPad, as well as iMacs on all three floors. Located in the foothills of the White Mountains, a variety of outdoor activities and fine dining are easily accessible.

Innkeeper(s): Melissa Leonard and Leonard Magliocca. $98-228. 12 rooms with PB, 12 with FP, 7 with HT, 2 two-bedroom suites. Breakfast included in rates. Types of meals: Country bkfst, veg bkfst, early coffee/tea, afternoon tea, Full country breakfast, restaurant and pub on premises. Restaurant on premises. Beds: KQT. Data port, cable TV, DVD, reading lamp, stereo, ceiling fan, clock radio, most with hot tub/spa, fireplace, hair dryer, bath amenities, wireless Internet access, iron/ironing board, Wi-Fi hookup. IPOD docking sta-
tions, IPAD available for guests. Eco Friendly Bed and Breakfast, Apple Computers and printers for guest use, coffee, tea available all day and English Pub for guest in room. Central air. VCR, fax, copier, spa, sauna, library, parlor games, telephone, IPADS, IPODS, Pub with soft drinks, wine and beer on premises. Handicap access. Amusement parks, antiquing, art galleries, bicycling, canoeing/kayaking, cross-country skiing, downhill skiing, fishing, golf, hiking, horseback riding, live theater, parks, shopping, water sports, In middle of the White Mountains at base of Mount Washington, Rivers nearby, over 200 outlets and retail shops and 1 1/2 to 2 major air-
ports and 2 1/2 hours from Boston nearby.

Location: Country, mountains.

Publicity: *Yankee Magazine, Boston Globe, Bon Appetit, Good Housekeeping, Skiing, Gault Millau, Country New England Inns and Weekends for Two in New England: 50 Romantic Getaways Inn Spots & Special Places in New England.*

"When people want to treat themselves, this is where they come."

Certificate may be used: Nov. 1-June 15; Sunday-Thursday, non-holiday week, Anytime, Last Minute-Based on Availability.

Hanover H2

The Trumbull House Bed & Breakfast

40 Etna Road
Hanover, NH 03755
(603)643-2370 (800)651-5141 Fax:(603)643-0079
Internet: www.trumbullhouse.com
E-mail: Trumbull.House@gmail.com

Circa 1919. This handsome two-story farmhouse was built by Walter Trumbull using treasures he gathered from old Dartmouth College buildings and fraternity houses. Presiding over 16 acres with stands of maple and a meandering brook, the inn offers a cozy refuge for all, including cross-country skiers and Dartmouth College alumni and parents. The parlor features comfortable Country English chairs and sofas.

Innkeeper(s): Hillary Pridgen. $150-315. 6 rooms with PB, 1 with FP, 2 with WP, 1 two-bedroom suite, 1 cottage. Breakfast and A sumptuous breakfast served whenever you wish included in rates. Types of meals: Full gourmet bkfst, early coffee/tea and Tea or coffee throughout the day. Beds: KQT. Modem hook-up, data port, cable TV, VCR, DVD, reading lamp, stereo, clock radio, telephone, coffeemaker, desk, hair dryer, bath amenities, wireless Internet access, iron/ironing board, Luxury feather pillows, Down comforters and Thick towels in room. Air conditioning. Fax, copier, swimming, library, parlor games, fireplace, Swimming pond, Business center and Hiking trails linking to Appalachian Trail on premises. Antiquing, art galleries, bicycling, canoeing/kayaking, cross-country skiing, downhill skiing, fishing, golf, hiking, horseback riding, live theater, museums, parks, shopping, sporting events, tennis, water sports, River Valley Club (health club available to guests at a nominal charge), Lebanon Opera House, Northern Stage and Hopkins Center of Performing Arts nearby.

Location: Country, mountains. Rural setting 4 miles from Dartmouth College.

Publicity: *Boston Magazine, Dartmouth Alumni, VPR Classical, Boston Globe and Upper Valley News.*

"From the beautiful setting outdoors through every elegant and thoughtful detail indoors, including your exquisite sunlit breakfast, we were in heaven!"

Certificate may be used: November-March.

Hebron G3

Coppertoppe Inn & Retreat Center

8 Range Road
Hebron, NH 03241
(603)744-3636 (866)846-3636 Fax:603-744-5036
Internet: www.coppertoppe.com
E-mail: info@coppertoppe.com

Circa 1999. Poised on 15 acres at the top of Tenney Mountain Ridge in the foothills of the White Mountains, Coppertoppe Inn & Retreat Center overlooks Newfound Lake. The modern setting is in the timeless New England town of Hebron, New Hampshire. Can host up to 150 people for weddings. Feel pampered and appreciated at this intimate and secluded luxury retreat. Beverages and snacks are available all day. Common areas include the living room, library and fitness area. Guest bedrooms and a suite are named after colorful gemstones and boast balconies, large whirlpool tubs and two-person European-style showers. Make a reservation for an in-room spa service. Breakfast is served family-style or as a buffet in the elegant dining room with balcony access.

Innkeeper(s): Sheila Oranch/Bill Powers. $125-275. 4 rooms with PB, 1 with FP, 2 with WP, 2 two-bedroom suites, 2 conference rooms. Breakfast, after-
noon tea, snacks/refreshments, wine, Meal plans including lunch and dinner may be arranged at reasonable cost. Kitchen and charcoal grill are available

for guests. Kosher and vegetarian and vegan menus available. Allergy avoidance is a specialty and special requests will be accommodated if possible included in rates. Types of meals: Full gourmet bkfst, veg bkfst, Sun. brunch, early coffee/tea, gourmet lunch, picnic lunch, hors d'oeuvres, gourmet dinner, room service, Gourmet coffee, espresso, cappuccino, tea variety, fresh fruits, fresh baked goods. We customize food service for each guest. Gourmet chefs are available in the area, if you want to plan a dinner party. We use organic or local foods whenever possible. You pick it or catch it and we'll make it. Allergy avoidance is a specialty here. Beds: KQDT. Modem hook-up, data port, cable TV, VCR, DVD, reading lamp, stereo, refrigerator, ceiling fan, snack bar, clock radio, telephone, turn-down service, desk, some with hot tub/spa, some with fireplace, hair dryer, bath amenities, wireless Internet access, iron/ironing board, Towel warmers, Robes, Slippers, Office supplies, Flowers or live plants, Choice of fiber, feather or memory foam pillows, Binoculars, Nature guides, Restaurant menus, Books, Magazines, Games, Puzzles and Playing cards in room. Air conditioning. Fax, copier, spa, library, pet boarding, child care, parlor games, laundry facility, gift shop, Yard & indoor toys, Pool shoes, Sunscreen, Insect repellent, Picnic area, Charcoal grill & supplies, Large pond with wildlife, Perennial/herb garden, 15 acres of field & woods to explore, Dirt road for exercise walks, Slopes for sliding, Pond for ice skating, Room for badminton, croquet, frisbee or catch, Crib, High chair, Stools & toddler dish sets available and Gated stairways on premises. Limited handicap access. Amusement parks, antiquing, art galleries, beach, bicycling, canoeing/kayaking, cross-country skiing, downhill skiing, fishing, golf, hiking, horseback riding, live theater, museums, parks, shopping, sporting events, tennis, water sports, wineries, Natural Science Center, mineral and gemstone mines open to the public, glacial caves and features, swimming holes, Audubon centers, guided adventures, dinner cruises, dinner train rides, cooking classes, open mic nights, jazz and folk festivals, marathon, triathlon, motorcycle rally, NASCAR, county fairs, holiday light park in December, brew pubs, D-Acres conservation farm and school, animal farms open to the public with pony rides, pick-your-own farms, cooking classes, quilting retreats, children's camps, family camps and much more nearby.

Location: Country, mountains. Lakes Region of New Hampshire.

Certificate may be used: June-September, Sunday-Thursday; October-May; all subject to availability.

Jackson F5

Inn at Ellis River

17 Harriman Road
Jackson, NH 03846
(603)383-9339 (800)233-8309 Fax:(603)383-4142
Internet: www.InnAtEllisRiver.com
E-mail: stay@InnAtEllisRiver.com

Circa 1893. Imagine a romantic getaway or relaxing vacation at an award-winning New England bed and breakfast, then make that vision a reality by visiting Inn at Ellis River in Jackson, New Hampshire. Surrounded by the White Mountains, the inn has a trout stream flowing by and nearby hiking trails. Enjoy the intimate ambiance while soaking in the atrium-enclosed hot tub looking out  on the river or reading in the sunny sitting room. Gather for afternoon refreshments in the game room and pub, sit in the sauna or swim in the seasonal outdoor heated pool. Period furnishings along with traditional and modern amenities are featured in the guest bedrooms and separate cottage. Many rooms boast two-person Jacuzzis and/or balconies. Most include gas or woodburning fireplaces. Savor a gourmet country breakfast made with local and regional foods.

Innkeeper(s): Frank Baker & Lyn Norris-Baker. $119-299. 21 rooms with PB, 17 with FP, 9 with WP, 1 suite, 1 cottage, 1 conference room. Breakfast and snacks/refreshments included in rates. Types of meals: Full gourmet bkfst, veg bkfst, early coffee/tea, gourmet lunch, picnic lunch, wine and cheese. Beds: KQD. Cable TV, reading lamp, CD player, clock radio, telephone, some with hot tub/spa, most with fireplace, hair dryer, bath amenities, wireless Internet access, iron/ironing board, Many rooms with DVD, VCR and Some

with balconies or patios in room. Central air. VCR, DVD, fax, copier, spa, swimming, sauna, library, parlor games, gift shop and dinner with advance reservations on premises. Limited handicap access. Amusement parks, antiquing, art galleries, bicycling, canoeing/kayaking, cross-country skiing, downhill skiing, fishing, golf, hiking, horseback riding, live theater, parks, shopping, sporting events, tennis, water sports, Mt. Washington Auto Road, Cog Railway and waterfalls nearby.

Location: Mountains. River frontage.

Publicity: *Yankee Magazine (2007), The Boston Globe (2007), New Hampshire Magazine (2006), The Rutland Herald (2006), Arrington's Inn Traveler (2005) and Inn Traveler's "Best of" Lists (2003 through 2006).*

"We have stayed at many B&Bs all over the world and are in agreement that the beauty and hospitality of Ellis River House is that of a world-class bed & breakfast."

Certificate may be used: Midweek, Sunday-Thursday; January, March, April, May, June and November (non-holiday periods).

Jefferson E4

Applebrook B&B

110 Meadows Road / Rt 115A
Jefferson, NH 03583-0178
(603)586-7713 (800)545-6504
Internet: www.applebrook.com
E-mail: info@applebrook.com

Circa 1797. Panoramic views surround this large Victorian farmhouse nestled in the middle of New Hampshire's White Mountains. Guests can awake to the smell of freshly baked muffins made with locally picked berries. A comfortable, fire-lit sitting room boasts stained glass, a goldfish pool and a beautiful view of Mt. Washington. The romantic Nellie's Nook, includes a king-size bed and a balcony  with views of the mountains and a two-person spa. Test your golfing skills at the nearby 18-hole championship course, or spend the day antique hunting. A trout stream and spring-fed rock pool are nearby. Wintertime guests can ice skate or race through the powder at nearby ski resorts or by way of snowmobile, finish off the day with a moonlight toboggan ride. After a full day, guests can enjoy a soak in the hot tub under the stars, where they might see shooting stars or the Northern Lights.

Innkeeper(s): Joy & Tom McCorkhill. $95-215. 9 rooms with PB, 2 with HT, 2 two-bedroom and 1 three-bedroom suites. Breakfast and snacks/refreshments included in rates. Types of meals: Country bkfst, veg bkfst and Dinner available for groups over 10 people. Beds: KQDT. Reading lamp, clock radio, telephone, some with hot tub/spa, wireless Internet access, Two suites have LCD TVs, Hot tub rooms have air conditioners in summer and All rooms have ceiling fans in room. TV, VCR, DVD, copier, library, parlor games, fireplace, gift shop, Outdoor kid's play equipment, Nature trails, Outdoor fire pit, Common room has a wood stove and Common TV room on premises. Amusement parks, antiquing, bicycling, canoeing/kayaking, cross-country skiing, downhill skiing, fishing, golf, hiking, live theater, parks, shopping, water sports, Santa's Village, Six Gun City and Story Land nearby.

Location: Mountains.

Publicity: *Coos County Democrat and Berlin Reporter.*

"We came for a night and stayed for a week."

Certificate may be used: January-May and Oct. 15-Dec. 15, Sunday-Thursday.

North Conway   F5

1785 Inn & Restaurant

3582 White Mountain Hwy
North Conway, NH 03860-1785
(603)356-9025 (800)421-1785
Internet: www.the1785inn.com
E-mail: the1785inn@aol.com

Circa 1785. The main section of this center-chimney house was
built by Captain Elijah Dinsmore of the New Hampshire
Rangers. He was granted the land for service in the American
Revolution. Original hand-hewn
beams, corner posts, fireplaces,
and a brick oven are still visible
and operating. The inn is located
at the historical marker popular-
ized by the White Mountain
School of Art in the 19th century.

Innkeeper(s): Becky & Charlie Mallar.
$69-219. 17 rooms, 12 with PB, 1 suite, 3 conference rooms. Breakfast
included in rates. Types of meals: Country bkfst, veg bkfst, early coffee/tea,
afternoon tea, snacks/refreshments, hors d'oeuvres, wine, gourmet dinner and
room service. Restaurant on premises. Beds: KQDT. Cable TV, VCR, reading
lamp, refrigerator, ceiling fan, snack bar, clock radio, coffeemaker, turn-down
service and bath amenities in room. Air conditioning. DVD, fax, copier, swimming, bicycles, library, parlor games, telephone, fireplace, cross-country skiing, nature trails and gardens on premises. Limited handicap access.
Amusement parks, antiquing, art galleries, beach, bicycling, canoeing/kayak-
ing, cross-country skiing, downhill skiing, fishing, golf, hiking, horseback riding, live theater, museums, parks, shopping, tennis, water sports, walking,
gardens, nature trails, rock climbing and ice climbing nearby.
Location: Country, mountains. Famous view of Mt. Washington.
Publicity: *Yankee, Country, Bon Appetit, Travel & Leisure, Ski, Travel
Holiday, Connecticut Magazine, Better Homes & Gardens, New Hampshire
Magazine, Boston Globe, Montreal Gazette, Manchester Union Leader, The
Wedding Story and I Dine.*

*"Occasionally in our lifetime is a moment so unexpectedly perfect
that we use it as our measure for our unforgettable moments. We just
had such an experience at The 1785 Inn."*

Certificate may be used: Anytime, non-holiday, November-June, subject to
availability.

Cabernet Inn

3552 White Mountain Highway
North Conway, NH 03860
(603)356-4704 (800)866-4704
Internet: www.cabernetinn.com
E-mail: info@cabernetinn.com

Circa 1842. The Cabernet Inn is a vintage bed and breakfast in
North Conway, New Hampshire secluded amid towering pines
in the heart of White Mountain National Forest. Enjoy a short
stroll to see an incredible view of Mt. Washington. This romantic New England inn caters to couples who will enjoy an intimate getaway in a completely refurbished 1842 country cottage. Experience the warm and elegant setting that boasts modern conveniences and pampering amenities. Select a delightful
guest room that includes a double Jacuzzi and a fireplace. Savor
a hearty country breakfast that is made to order and served in
the dining room or al fresco when weather permits. Choose the
chef's special of the day or an entrée from the extensive menu.
Special packages are available.
Innkeeper(s): Bruce & Jessica Zarenko. $99-239. 11 rooms with PB, 7 with
FP, 5 with HT, 1 suite. Breakfast, afternoon tea and snacks/refreshments

included in rates. Types of meals: Full gourmet bkfst, veg bkfst, early
coffee/tea, Full cook to order gourmet breakfast and Afternoon refreshments
and snacks. Beds: KQ. Reading lamp, ceiling fan, clock radio, telephone,
most with hot tub/spa, hair dryer, bath amenities, wireless Internet access,
iron/ironing board and antiques in room. Air conditioning. TV, VCR, DVD, fax,
library, parlor games, fireplace, gift shop, Wet bar, Iron, ironing board, refrigerator, player piano and snowshoes on premises. Handicap access.
Amusement parks, antiquing, art galleries, bicycling, canoeing/kayaking,
cross-country skiing, downhill skiing, fishing, golf, hiking, horseback riding,
live theater, museums, parks, shopping, tennis, wineries, Railroad,
Snowshoeing, Dog sledding, Snowmobiling, Ice climbing, Ice skating and
Sleigh rides nearby.
Location: Mountains. Mt. Washington Valley.
Certificate may be used: November-June, Sunday-Thursday, subject to
availability.

Old Red Inn & Cottages

2406 White Mountain Highway
North Conway, NH 03860-0467
(603)356-2642 (800)338-1356 Fax:(603)356-6626
Internet: www.oldredinn.com
E-mail: oldredinn@roadrunner.com

Circa 1810. Guests can opt to stay in an early 19th-century
home or in one of a collection of cottages at this country inn.
The rooms are decorated with handmade quilts and stenciling
dots the walls. Several rooms include four-poster or canopy
beds. Two-bedroom cottages feature a screened porch. A
hearty, country meal accompanied by freshly baked breads,
muffins and homemade preserves starts off the day. The inn is
near many of the town's shops, restaurants and outlets.
Innkeeper(s): Susan & Richard LeFave. $79-198. 15 rooms with PB, 13
with FP, 1 two-bedroom suite, 10 cottages, 10 cabins. Breakfast included in
rates. Types of meals: Full bkfst and early coffee/tea. Beds: KQDT. Cable TV,
reading lamp, refrigerator, clock radio, coffeemaker, most with fireplace, hair
dryer, bath amenities and wireless Internet access in room. Air conditioning.
Fax, copier, swimming, parlor games and telephone on premises. Amusement
parks, antiquing, bicycling, canoeing/kayaking, cross-country skiing, downhill
skiing, fishing, golf, hiking, horseback riding, live theater, museums, parks,
shopping, sporting events, tennis, water sports and wineries nearby.
Location: Country, mountains.
Certificate may be used: Jan. 2-June 1, Sunday-Thursday, (inn rooms only),
non-holiday or vacation weeks.

Plainfield   I4

Home Hill Country Inn

703 River Road
Plainfield, NH 03781
(603)675-6165 Fax:(603)675-5220
Internet: www.homehillinn.com
E-mail: inquiries@homehillinn.com

Circa 1818. Home Hill Inn provides a romantic retreat with
attentive service and inventive cuisine on 25 secluded acres in
Plainfield, New York. Experience the many activities from snowshoes to croquet, a putting green and clay tennis court. The fitness room is the perfect way to stay in shape anytime. Catch
some sun on lounges by the in-ground swimming pool or take
a bike ride with a trail map and explore the scenic area. The
inn offers breathtaking views of the Connecticut River, hills and
valleys. Stay in a fireside guest room or suite in the main
house, the Carriage House with a private terrace, or in the Pool
House cottage. Accommodations boast Frette towels and robes,
tile and marble baths and specialty personal products. Savor a
country breakfast that is made using local bounty.
Innkeeper(s): Paula Snow. $80-250. 12 rooms with PB, 6 with FP, 1 two-

bedroom suite, 1 cottage, 2 conference rooms. Breakfast included in rates. Types of meals: Country bkfst, veg bkfst, Sun. brunch, early coffee/tea, picnic lunch, wine and gourmet dinner. Restaurant on premises. Beds: KQ. Reading lamp, stereo, clock radio, telephone, desk, voice mail, hair dryer, bathrobes, bath amenities, wireless Internet access and iron/ironing board in room. Central air. TV, VCR, fax, copier, swimming, stable, bicycles, tennis, library, parlor games, fireplace, laundry facility and gift shop on premises. Handicap access. Antiquing, art galleries, bicycling, canoeing/kayaking, cross-country skiing, downhill skiing, fishing, golf, hiking, horseback riding, live theater, museums, parks, shopping, sporting events, tennis, water sports, Saint Gaudens National historic site, Covered bridges and Fly fishing nearby.

Location: Country, waterfront.

Publicity: *Rated Best of New Hampshire (2008) and Karen Brown Guides .*

Certificate may be used: January-June, anytime subject to availability.

Sugar Hill
F3

A Grand Inn-Sunset Hill House

231 Sunset Hill Rd
Sugar Hill, NH 03586
(603) 823-5522 (800) 786-4455 Fax:(603)823-5523
Internet: www.sunsethillhouse.com
E-mail: innkeeper@sunsethillhouse.com

Circa 1882. This Second Empire luxury inn has views of five mountain ranges. Three parlors, all with cozy fireplaces, are favorite gathering spots. Afternoon tea is served here. The inn's lush grounds offer many opportunities for recreation or relaxing, and guests often enjoy special events here, such as the Fields of Lupine Festival. The Cannon Mountain Ski Area and Franconia Notch State Park are nearby, and there is 30 kilometers of cross-country ski trails at the inn. Be sure to inquire about golf and ski packages. In the fall, a Thanksgiving package allows guests to help decorate the inn for the holidays as well as enjoy Thanksgiving dinner together. NH Magazine just named Sunset Hill House — A Grand Inn the "Very Best in NH for a Spectacular Meal."

Innkeeper(s): Lon, Nancy, Mary Pearl, Adeline, Yani, and Tad Henderson. $99-499. 28 rooms with PB, 10 with FP, 12 with WP, 2 two-bedroom suites, 3 conference rooms. Breakfast and afternoon tea included in rates. Types of meals: Full gourmet bkfst, veg bkfst, early coffee/tea, lunch, picnic lunch, snacks/refreshments, hors d'oeuvres, wine, gourmet dinner, room service, Award winning fine dining restaurant, Chaine Des Rotisseurs property, Wine spectator award and casual tavern. Restaurant on premises. Beds: KQDT. Modern hook-up, data port, cable TV, reading lamp, ceiling fan, clock radio, telephone, coffeemaker, desk, some with fireplace, hair dryer, bath amenities, wireless Internet access, iron/ironing board, coffeemaker and wifi access in room. Air conditioning. Fax, copier, swimming, library, pet boarding, child care, parlor games, laundry facility, gift shop, irons available at desk, 24/7 coffee in public areas, golf course with discounted golf privileges for guests of Sunset Hill House, heated mountainside swimming pool, decks with incredible mountain views, full computer center with high speed Internet available for guest use and babysitting available on premises. Handicap access. Amusement parks, antiquing, art galleries, beach, bicycling, canoeing/kayaking, cross-country skiing, downhill skiing, fishing, golf, hiking, horseback riding, live theater, museums, parks, shopping, tennis, water sports, Franconia Notch State Park, Appalachian Trail, rock climbing, day hikes, waterfalls, Flume Gorge, the Basin, Mt. Washington, Cog Railway and Clarks Trading Post nearby.

Location: Country, mountains.

Publicity: *Yankee Travel Guide, Courier, Caledonia Record, Boston Globe, Portsmouth Herald, Manchester Union Leader, Journal Enquirer, Sunday Telegraph, Boston Herald, New Hampshire Magazine, GeoSaison, National Geographic, Traveller, Small Meeting Marketplace, BBW Magazine, Ski Magazine, Peoples Places and Plants Magazine, Korean Times, Deutsche Rundfunk, WMUR and Iron Bride.*

"I have visited numerous inns and innkeepers in my 10 years as a travel writer, but have to admit that few have impressed me as much as yours and you did."

Certificate may be used: Not valid weekends Sept. 15-Oct. 15.

Tilton
14

The Tilton Inn and Onions Pub & Restaurant

255 Main St
Tilton, NH 03276-5113
(603) 286-7774 Fax:(603)286-8340
Internet: www.thetiltoninn.com
E-mail: tiltoninn@metrocast.net

Circa 1875. Originally known as the Tilton Inn, this country retreat was built for the many visitors who came to the scenic village to enjoy the Winnipesaukee River, including Thomas Edison and Henry Ford. It is centrally located in Lakes Region amidst the White Mountains. Recent renovations have restored its historical integrity as well as its tradition. The second-floor Sanbornton Bridge Library welcomes relaxation and the book-lined walls are full of local information and knowledge to delve into and absorb. Each guest bedroom is named and decorated to reflect a locally prominent person or well-known influence. A continental breakfast is served daily. Fine dining is offered at The Olive Branch Restaurant and Tavern.

Innkeeper(s): Marge. $79-139. 11 rooms with PB, 1 two-bedroom suite. Coffee and muffin included in rate. Discounted Sunday Brunch for all guests. Winter rates can be all inclusive included in rates. Types of meals: Full gourmet bkfst, Sun. brunch, early coffee/tea, gourmet lunch, picnic lunch, wine, gourmet dinner and room service. Restaurant on premises. Beds: KQDT. Cable TV, VCR, DVD, reading lamp, ceiling fan, clock radio, desk, bath amenities and wireless Internet access in room. Central air. Fax, copier, library, parlor games, telephone, fireplace, laundry facility and Onions Pub and Restaurant on premises. Handicap access. Antiquing, art galleries, beach, bicycling, canoeing/kayaking, cross-country skiing, downhill skiing, fishing, golf, hiking, horseback riding, live theater, museums, parks, shopping, sporting events, water sports and wineries nearby.

Location: Country, mountains, waterfront.

Publicity: *Weir's Times, Concord Monitor, Laconia Daily Sun, WMVR Ch 9 and Mix 94.1.*

Certificate may be used: Sunday-Thursday, subject to availability. Some blackout dates may apply.

Wakefield
16

Wakefield Inn, LLC

2723 Wakefield Rd
Wakefield, NH 03872-4374
(603)522-8272 (800)245-0841 Fax:(603)218-6714
Internet: www.wakefieldinn.com
E-mail: info@wakefieldinn.com

Circa 1804. Early travelers pulled up to the front door of the Wakefield Inn by stagecoach, and while they disembarked, their luggage was handed up to the second floor. It was brought in through the door, which is still visible over the porch roof. A spiral staircase, ruffled curtains, wallpapers and a wraparound porch all create the romantic ambiance of days gone by. In the living room, an original three-sided fireplace casts a warm glow on guests as it did more than 190 years ago.

Innkeeper(s): Janel Martin. $79-189. 6 rooms with PB, 1 with FP. Breakfast, snacks/refreshments and wine included in rates. Types of meals: Full gourmet bkfst, veg bkfst, early coffee/tea, picnic lunch, gourmet dinner and room ser-

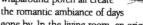

vice. Restaurant on premises. Beds: KQT. Reading lamp, ceiling fan, clock radio, some with fireplace, hair dryer, bathrobes, bath amenities and wireless Internet access in room. Air conditioning. TV, VCR, DVD, library, parlor games, telephone, gift shop and Cooking Classes on premises. Antiquing, art galleries, bicycling, canoeing/kayaking, cross-country skiing, downhill skiing, fishing, golf, hiking, horseback riding, parks, shopping, water sports and Historic Museums nearby.

Location: Country.

Publicity: *Foster's Daily Democrat, ToDo New Hampshire, New Hampshire Magazine and WASR 1420.*

"Comfortable accommodations, excellent food and exquisite decor highlighted by your quilts."

Certificate may be used: Anytime, November-May, June-October Sunday-Thursday, Subject to availability, excludes all holidays and holiday weekends.

Walpole   K1

Inn at Valley Farms B&B and Cottages

633 Wentworth Road
Walpole, NH 03608
(603)756-2855 (877)327-2855 Fax:(603)756-2865
Internet: www.innatvalleyfarms.com
E-mail: info@innatvalleyfarms.com

Circa 1774. Experience New England hospitality at this elegantly restored 1774 Colonial home surrounded by 105 acres of certified organic farmland and bordered by a 500-acre orchard in a picturesque town. Use one of the field guides in the library to identify the many species of the diverse habitats on the farm. Relax by the fire or chat in the plant-filled sunroom. The terraced gardens are seen from the comfortable living room. Award-winning handmade Burdick chocolates and fresh flowers are placed bedside in the large guest bedrooms and Garden Suite with antique furnishings. A multi-course breakfast features recipes using fresh eggs and produce grown onsite. Each cottage includes a private entrance, fully equipped kitchen with stocked refrigerator, two-person shower and mini-library. Each morning a basket of baked goods is delivered to the doorstep. Hike nearby Mt. Monadnock.

Innkeeper(s): Jacqueline Caserta. $175-299. 3 rooms with PB, 2 cottages, 1 guest house, 1 conference room. Breakfast and snacks/refreshments included in rates. Types of meals: Full gourmet bkfst, veg bkfst and early coffee/tea. Beds: KQT. Modem hook-up, cable TV, reading lamp, clock radio, telephone, desk, voice mail, fresh flowers in-season, world-renowned Burdick chocolates at bedside and bathrobes in room. Air conditioning. TV, VCR, fax, copier, library, parlor games, fireplace, picnic table, charcoal grills, pick-your-own organic produce from our gardens and collect your own fresh eggs on premises. Limited handicap access. Antiquing, art galleries, beach, bicycling, canoeing/kayaking, cross-country skiing, fishing, golf, hiking, live theater, museums, parks, shopping, sporting events, tennis and water sports nearby.

Location: Country. 105 acres of rolling farmland and woodland, yet conveniently located to numerous activities.

Publicity: *Yankee Magazine's 2001 Travel Guide to New England.*

Certificate may be used: Sunday-Thursday except holidays or fall foliage season, Anytime, Last Minute-Based on Availability.

Waterville Valley   I4

Snowy Owl Inn

41 Village Rd
Waterville Valley, NH 03215
(603)236-8383 (800)766-9969 Fax:(603)236-4890
Internet: www.snowyowlinn.com
E-mail: snowy@snowyowlinn.com

Circa 1974. Snowy Owl Inn is poised in the center of Waterville Valley and the White Mountain National Forest in New Hampshire. This four-season New England country inn is perfect for family getaways, corporate retreats and romantic destination weddings. Enjoy the many recreational activities and resort amenities that include a fitness center, men's and women's saunas, brook-side lawn and shuttle to ski areas. Swim in the indoor and outdoor pools and soak in one of the Jacuzzis. Some of the air-conditioned guest rooms and suites at this traditional natural wood lodge feature fireplaces, wet bars, Jacuzzi tubs and fully equipped kitchens. Handicapped accessible and pet-friendly rooms are also available. Start each day with a continental breakfast and gather for the afternoon wine and cheese social.

Innkeeper(s): Steve Hodges. $99-265. 82 rooms with PB, 1 with FP, 40 with HT, 1 two-bedroom suite, 2 conference rooms. Breakfast included in rates. Types of meals: Full gourmet bkfst, veg bkfst, picnic lunch, snacks/refreshments and wine. Restaurant on premises. Beds: KQDT. Cable TV, reading lamp, refrigerator, clock radio, telephone, most with hot tub/spa, voice mail, some with fireplace, hair dryer, bath amenities and wireless Internet access in room. Air conditioning. VCR, DVD, fax, copier, spa, swimming, sauna, bicycles, tennis, library, parlor games, laundry facility, gift shop, Indoor pool and Outdoor pool on premises. Handicap access. Amusement parks, antiquing, beach, bicycling, canoeing/kayaking, cross-country skiing, downhill skiing, fishing, golf, hiking, horseback riding, live theater, parks, shopping, sporting events, tennis and water sports nearby.

Location: Mountains.

Certificate may be used: Sunday-Thursday, subject to availability, non-holiday only.

New Jersey

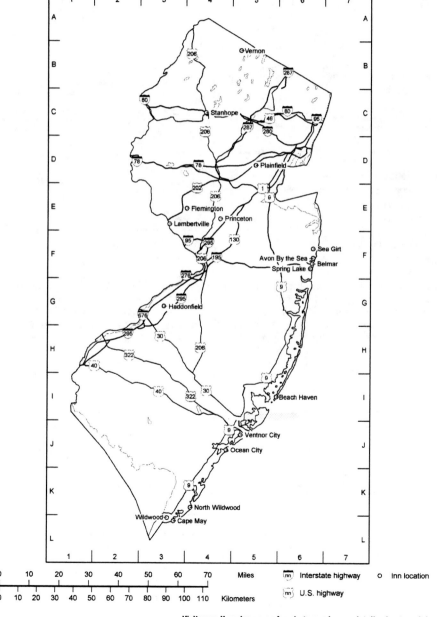

Vernon

206

287

80

Stanhope

287

46

80

95

206

280

78

78

Plainfield

202

206

1

9

Flemington

Princeton

Lambertville

95

295

130

206

195

276

9

295

Haddonfield

676

295

30

206

40

322

40

322

30

9

Beach Haven

9

Ventnor City

Ocean City

9

North Wildwood

Wildwood

Cape May

| 0 | 10 | 20 | 30 | 40 | 50 | 60 | 70 | Miles |

| 0 | 10 | 20 | 30 | 40 | 50 | 60 | 70 | 80 | 90 | 100 | 110 | Kilometers |

(nn) Interstate highway   o Inn location

(nn) U.S. highway

Avon By The Sea   F6

The Avon Manor B&B
& Cottage Rentals

109 Sylvania Ave
Avon By The Sea, NJ 07717-1338
(732)776-7770
Internet: www.avonmanor.com
E-mail: gregmav@aol.com

The Avon Manor was built as a private summer residence in
the Colonial Revival style. The handsome facade is graced by a
100-foot wraparound veranda.

Light, airy bedrooms are decorated with antiques, wicker
and period pieces. Guests
breakfast in a sunny dining
room or on the veranda.

Innkeeper(s): Greg Dietrich. Call for
rates. Call inn for details. Breakfast and afternoon tea included in rates.
Types of meals: Full bkfst. Beds: KQT. TV and reading lamp in room. Air conditioning. Child care and fireplace on premises. Amusement parks, antiquing,
fishing, live theater, shopping, sporting events and water sports nearby.

Location: Ocean community. Spring Lake.

Certificate may be used: Oct. 1-May 10, not valid holidays or special events.

Beach Haven   I6

Williams Cottage Inn

506 South Atlantic Avenue
Beach Haven, NJ 08008
(609)492-7272 Fax:(609)492-7112
Internet: www.williamscottageinn.com
E-mail: innkeeper@williamscottageinn.com

Circa 1886. Gracing the south end of Long Beach Island in the
seaside New Jersey town of Beach Haven, Williams Cottage Inn
was built in 1886. The inn has been meticulously restored and
is listed in the National Historic Register. Relax in the grand
entry parlor and enjoy refreshments in the large library or on
the veranda. Themed guest bedrooms boast a designer décor
with opulent furnishings and generous amenities. Select a room
with a fireplace and either a multi-jet shower, whirlpool or
soaking tub and L'Occitane toiletries. Start each day with a
gourmet breakfast served in the formal dining room.
Complimentary beach passes are provided as well as use of
towels, chairs, umbrellas, bikes and tennis rackets.

Innkeeper(s): Bette & Merle VanLiere. $195-425. 8 rooms with PB, 2 with
FP, 1 with WP, 1 two-bedroom suite, 1 conference room. Breakfast and
snacks/refreshments included in rates. Types of meals: Full bkfst, veg bkfst
and early coffee/tea. Beds: KQD. Cable TV, DVD, reading lamp, CD player,
telephone, voice mail, hair dryer, bathrobes, bath amenities and wireless
Internet access in room. Central air. Fax, copier, bicycles, library, parlor
games, fireplace, gift shop, Wireless Internet access, Gourmet breakfast and
Afternoon refreshments on premises. Handicap access. Amusement parks,
antiquing, art galleries, beach, bicycling, fishing, golf, live theater, museums,
shopping, tennis and water sports nearby.

Location: Ocean community.

Certificate may be used: Oct. 15-May 15, Sunday-Friday.

Belmar   F6

The Inn at The Shore Bed & Breakfast

301 4th Ave
Belmar, NJ 07719-2104
(732)681-3762 Fax:(732)280-1914
Internet: www.theinnattheshore.com
E-mail: tomvolker@optonline.net

Circa 1880. This child friendly country Victorian actually is
near two different shores. Both the ocean and Silver Lake are
within easy walking distance of the inn. From the inn's wraparound porch, guests can view swans on the lake. The innkeepers decorated their Victorian home in period style. The inn's
patio is set up for barbecues.

Innkeeper(s): Rosemary & Tom Volker. $145-295. 10 rooms, 4 with PB, 4
with FP, 1 conference room. Breakfast, afternoon tea and snacks/refreshments
included in rates. Types of meals: Full gourmet bkfst. Beds: KQDT. Modem
hook-up, data port, cable TV, VCR, reading lamp, CD player, ceiling fan, clock
radio, telephone, voice mail, fireplace, modem, whirlpool tubs, fireplaces and
guest pantry in room. Central air. Fax, copier, bicycles, library, parlor games,
aquarium, patio with gas grill, guest pantry with refrigerator and microwave on
premises. Amusement parks, antiquing, art galleries, beach, bicycling, canoe-
ing/kayaking, fishing, golf, hiking, horseback riding, live theater, museums,
parks, shopping, sporting events, tennis and water sports nearby.

Location: Ocean community.

"You both have created a warm, cozy and comfortable refuge for us
weary travelers."

Certificate may be used: Anytime, subject to availability, except weekends in
June, July and August.

Cape May   L3

Albert Stevens Inn

127 Myrtle Ave
Cape May, NJ 08204-1237
(609)884-4717 (800)890-2287 Fax:(609)884-8320
Internet: www.albertstevensinn.com
E-mail: albertstevensinn@hotmail.com

Circa 1898. Dr. Albert Stevens built this Queen Anne Free
Classic house for his home and office. Carved woodwork and
Victorian antiques enhance the delightful architectural details.
The floating staircase and tower lead to spacious air-conditioned
guest bedrooms. Enjoy a complete breakfast as well as afternoon
tea and refreshments. Relax in the comfortably heated sunroom,
or on the inviting veranda. Free on-site parking is convenient for
shopping, restaurants and the beach a short walk away. Bicycles,
beach towels and chairs are gladly provided.

Innkeeper(s): Jim & Lenanne Labrusciano. $100-265. 10 rooms with PB, 2
with FP, 1 with WP, 3 total suites, including 2 two-bedroom suites. Breakfast,
afternoon tea and wine included in rates. Types of meals: Full bkfst and early
coffee/tea. Beds: KQD. Cable TV, VCR, DVD, reading lamp, refrigerator, ceiling fan, clock radio, telephone, some with fireplace, hair dryer, bathrobes,
bath amenities, wireless Internet access, iron/ironing board and Ipod alarm
clocks in room. Air conditioning. Fax, copier, bicycles, parlor games and Free
on-site parking on premises. Amusement parks, antiquing, art galleries,
beach, bicycling, canoeing/kayaking, fishing, golf, hiking, horseback riding,
live theater, museums, parks, shopping, sporting events, tennis, water sports,
wineries and bird watching nearby.

Location: City, ocean community.

Publicity: The Jersey Shore, Mid-Atlantic Country, Atlantic City Press, Cape
May Star and Wave, The Herald, Washington Post, The New York Times,
Philadelphia Inquirer and NBC News.

Certificate may be used: Oct.30-April 26, Sunday-Thursday, except weeks
that contain a holiday (based on season high rate).

Bedford Inn

805 Stockton Ave
Cape May, NJ 08204-2446
(609)884-4158 (866)215-9507 Fax:(609)884-6320
Internet: www.bedfordinn.com
E-mail: info@bedfordinn.com

Circa 1883. The Bedford, decked in gingerbread trim with verandas on both of its two stories, has welcomed guests since its creation in the 19th century. Electrified gaslights, period wallcoverings and rich, Victorian furnishings create an air of nostalgia. The inn is close to many of Cape May's shops and restaurants, as well as the beach, which is just half a block away. Guests are pampered with breakfasts of quiche, gourmet egg dishes, French toast and freshly baked breads.

Innkeeper(s): Archie & Stephanie Kirk. $120-265. 10 rooms with PB, 3 total suites, including 1 two-bedroom suite. Breakfast and afternoon tea included in rates. Types of meals: Full bkfst and early coffee/tea. Beds: KQT. Cable TV, VCR, DVD, reading lamp, ceiling fan, clock radio, some with fireplace, hair dryer, bath amenities, wireless Internet access and iron/ironing board in room. Air conditioning. Fax, copier, library, parlor games, telephone, gift shop, Refrigerator, Free limited driveway parking, Hot beverage service 24/7, Wireless Internet access, Small collection of VHS tapes and DVDs at no charge on premises. Amusement parks, antiquing, art galleries, beach, bicycling, canoeing/kayaking, fishing, golf, hiking, horseback riding, live theater, museums, parks, shopping, tennis, water sports, wineries, house tours, trolley tours, restaurants and beach nearby.

Location: Ocean community.

Certificate may be used: October-June, Sunday-Thursday, excluding holidays, based on availability.

Fairthorne B&B

111 Ocean St
Cape May, NJ 08204-2319
(609)884-8791 (800)438-8742 Fax:(609)898-6129
Internet: www.fairthorne.com
E-mail: fairthornebnb@aol.com

Circa 1892. Antiques abound in this three-story Colonial Revival. Lace curtains and a light color scheme complete the charming decor. There is a new, yet historic addition to the B&B. The innkeepers now offer guest quarters (with fireplaces) in The Fairthorne Cottage, a restored 1880s building adjacent to the inn. The signature breakfasts include special daily entrees along with an assortment of home-baked breads and muffins. A light afternoon tea also is served with refreshments. The proximity to the beach will be much appreciated by guests, and the innkeepers offer the use of beach towels, bicycles and sand chairs. The nearby historic district is full of fun shops and restaurants.

Innkeeper(s): Diane & Ed Hutchinson. $145-280. 10 rooms with PB, 9 with FP, 6 with WP. Breakfast, afternoon tea, snacks/refreshments and hors d'oeuvres included in rates. Types of meals: Full bkfst and early coffee/tea. Beds: KQ. Cable TV, DVD, reading lamp, CD player, refrigerator, ceiling fan, snack bar, clock radio, most with fireplace, hair dryer, bathrobes, bath amenities, wireless Internet access and iron/ironing board in room. Central air. Fax, bicycles, telephone and gift shop on premises. Amusement parks, antiquing, art galleries, beach, bicycling, canoeing/kayaking, fishing, golf, horseback riding, live theater, museums, parks, shopping, tennis, water sports, wineries and historic lighthouse & Victorian architectural tours nearby.

Location: City. In historic district.

Publicity: *New Jersey Countryside, The Discerning Traveler, Arrington's, NJ*

Golf, Westchester Magazine and South Jersey Magazine.

"I feel as if I have come to stay with a dear old friend who has spared no expense to provide me with all that my heart can desire! ... I will savor the memory of your hospitality for years to come. Thanks so much."

Certificate may be used: Nov. 1-May 31, Sunday-Thursday, except holidays.

Gingerbread House

28 Gurney St
Cape May, NJ 08204
(609)884-0211
Internet: gingerbreadinn.com
E-mail: info@gingerbreadinn.com

Circa 1869. The Gingerbread is one of eight original Stockton Row Cottages, summer retreats built for families from Philadelphia and Virginia. It is a half-block from the ocean and breezes waft over the wicker-filled porch. The inn is listed in the National Register. It has been meticulously restored and decorated with period antiques and a fine collection of paintings. The inn's woodwork is especially notable, guests enter through handmade teak double doors.

Innkeeper(s): Fred & Joan Echevarria. $110-330. 6 rooms, 3 with PB, 1 suite. Breakfast and Coffee/Tea & innkeepers choice of snacks available throughout the day included in rates. Types of meals: Full bkfst and afternoon tea. Beds: QD. Cable TV, ceiling fan, bath amenities and wireless Internet access in room. Central air. Fax, parlor games, telephone and fireplace on premises. Antiquing, bicycling, canoeing/kayaking, fishing, golf, hiking, live theater, parks, shopping, tennis, water sports, birding and Victorian homes nearby.

Location: Ocean community.

Publicity: *Philadelphia Inquirer, New Jrsey Monthly and Atlantic City Press Newspaper.*

"The elegance, charm and authenticity of historic Cape May, but more than that, it appeals to us as 'home.'"

Certificate may be used: Oct.1-May 25, Monday-Thursday.

John Wesley Inn & Carriage House

30 Guerney Ave
Cape May, NJ 08204
(609)884-1012 (800)616-5122
Internet: www.johnwesleyinn.com
E-mail: info@johnwesleyinn.com

Circa 1869. Just one-half block from the beach, this American classic features Carpenter Gothic architecture and adorns the serene primary Historic District. The inn has undergone meticulous Victorian restorations with extensive attention paid to details. Sip afternoon tea on a veranda rocker while watching a horse and carriage go by. Gather by the fire in the family parlor or in the spacious third-floor sun parlor. Delightful guest bedrooms offer a variety of choices. The Stockton room features a private front porch. Share lively conversation over a bountiful homemade breakfast in the dining room.

Innkeeper(s): Bonnie & Lance Pontin. $150-325. 6 rooms with PB, 6 with FP, 1 with WP, 2 suites, 2 cottages. Breakfast, afternoon tea, snacks/refreshments, Iced peach and/or raspberry tea freshly brewed daily all summer long, hot Earl Grey and/or the flavor of your choice, piping hot all winter and cookies baked daily included in rates. Types of meals: Full gourmet bkfst, early coffee/tea, Belgium waffles with whipped cream and fresh strawberries, specialty of the house and served every Sunday. Beds: KQ. Cable TV, DVD, reading lamp, stereo, ceiling fan, clock radio, desk, fireplace, hair dryer, bathrobes, bath amenities, wireless Internet access, iron/ironing board, LCD TV/DVD, Ipod docking stations and Personal safes in all rooms in room. Air conditioning. TV, VCR, fax, parlor games, telephone, Beach chairs, Towels, Coolers, Beautiful Sun Room with wet bar, ice maker & refrigerator, Wireless Internet, Historic District, Onsite parking and 1/2 block to the beach on premises. Amusement parks, antiquing, art galleries, beach, bicycling, canoeing/kayaking, fishing, golf, hiking, live theater, parks, shopping, tennis, water sports, wineries, Whale/dolphin watching and Birding nearby.

Location: City, ocean community.

Certificate may be used: November through April, midweek only.

Linda Lee Bed & Breakfast

725 Columbia Ave
Cape May, NJ 08204-2305
(609)884-1240 Fax:(609)884-6762
Internet: thelindalee.com
E-mail: LindaLeeCapeMay@aol.com

Circa 1872. Built in Carpenter Gothic style, this recently renovated cottage still reflects its origins. Located in the National Historic Landmark District, it is appropriately furnished in authentic Victorian decor. Comfortable guest bedrooms offer quiet relaxation; some feature fireplaces. A complete breakfast is served in the dining room on fine china and sterling silver settings at nine every morning. Don't miss afternoon tea at 5 p.m. with finger sandwiches and sweets. It is an easy walk to the beach in this waterfront community, and towels and chairs are provided for use. Free on-site parking is available, as is a bike rack to secure a personal or rented bike.

Innkeeper(s): Julie & Matt Scassero. $100-205. 5 rooms with PB, 3 with FP. Breakfast and afternoon tea included in rates. Types of meals: Full gourmet bkfst, early coffee/tea and wine. Beds: KQ. Cable TV, DVD, reading lamp, ceiling fan, clock radio, some with fireplace, hair dryer, bathrobes, bath amenities and iron/ironing board in room. Air conditioning. Fax, bicycles, parlor games, telephone and gift shop on premises. Amusement parks, antiquing, art galleries, beach, bicycling, canoeing/kayaking, fishing, golf, horseback riding, live theater, museums, parks, shopping, tennis, water sports and wineries nearby.

Location: Ocean community.

Certificate may be used: October-June, Sunday-Thursday, excluding holidays, based on availability.

Rhythm of The Sea

1123 W. Beach Ave
Cape May, NJ 08204-2628
(609)884-7788
Internet: www.rhythmofthesea.com
E-mail: stay@rhythmofthesea.com

Circa 1915. The apt name of this oceanfront inn describes the soothing sounds of the sea that lull many a happy guest into a restful night's sleep. Watching sunsets, strolling the beach, bird watching and whale

watching are popular activities. Many of the features of a Craftsman home are incorporated in this seaside inn, such as light-filled spacious rooms, adjoining dining and living areas and gleaming natural wood floors. Mission oak furnishings compliment the inn's architecture. For guests seeking an especially private stay, ask for the three-room suite and arrange for a private dinner prepared by the innkeeper Wolfgang Wendt, a European trained chef. Full breakfasts are provided each morning. Guests are given complimentary beach towels and chairs. There is free parking and complimentary use of bicycles.

Innkeeper(s): Robyn & Wolfgang Wendt. $225-399. 9 rooms, 7 with PB, 2 with FP, 1 suite. Breakfast and snacks/refreshments included in rates. Types of meals: Full bkfst and dinner. Beds: Q. Reading lamp and clock radio in room. Air conditioning. VCR, bicycles, telephone and fireplace on premises. Amusement parks, antiquing, fishing, live theater, shopping and water sports nearby.

Location: Ocean community.

Publicity: Atlantic City Press, New Jersey Monthly and POV.

"Your home is lovely, the atmosphere is soothing."

Certificate may be used: November-April, Sunday-Thursday, not valid on holidays or with any other promotional offer. Based on regular rack rate.

The Abbey Bed & Breakfast

34 Guerney St.
Cape May, NJ 08204
(609)884-4506 (866)884-8800 Fax:(609)884-2379
Internet: www.abbeybedandbreakfast.com
E-mail: theabbey1@verizon.net

Circa 1869. This historic inn consists of two buildings, one a Gothic Revival villa with a 60-foot tower, Gothic arched windows and shaded verandas. Furnishings include floor-to-ceiling

mirrors, ornate gas chandeliers, marble-topped dressers and beds of carved walnut, wrought iron and brass. The cottage adjacent to the villa is a classic Second Empire-style cottage with a mansard roof. A full breakfast is served in the dining room in spring and fall and on the veranda in the summer. Late afternoon refreshments and tea are served each day at 5 p.m. The beautiful inn is featured in the town's Grand Christmas Tour, and public tours and tea are offered three times a week in season.

Innkeeper(s): Colleen. $95-205. 7 rooms with PB. Breakfast and afternoon tea included in rates. Types of meals: Full bkfst and early coffee/tea. Beds: KQD. Reading lamp, refrigerator, ceiling fan, some with air conditioning and antiques in room. Parlor games, beach passes, beach chairs, on- and off-site parking and house telephone for local and long distance toll calls on premises. Antiquing, art galleries, beach, bicycling, canoeing/kayaking, fishing, golf, hiking, horseback riding, live theater, museums, parks, shopping, tennis, wineries, birding, free zoo, nature center, nature walks and Cape May Point State Park nearby.

Location: Ocean community. National Historic District.

Publicity: Richmond Times-Dispatch, New York Times, Glamour, Philadelphia Inquirer, National Geographic Traveler, Smithsonian and Victorian Homes Magazine.

"Staying with you folks really makes the difference between a 'nice' vacation and a great one!"

Certificate may be used: Midweek, Sunday or Monday-Thursday. April, May, June, October, except for Victorian Week.

The Carroll Villa B&B

19 Jackson St
Cape May, NJ 08204-1417
(609)884-9619 (877)275-8452 Fax:(609)884-0264
Internet: www.carrollvilla.com
E-mail: manager@carrollvilla.com

Circa 1882. This Victorian hotel is located one-half block from the ocean on the oldest street in the historic district of Cape May. Breakfast at the Villa is a memorable event, featuring dishes acclaimed by the New York Times and Frommer's. Homemade fruit breads, Italian omelets and Crab Eggs Benedict are a few specialties. Meals are served in the Mad Batter Restaurant on a European veranda, a secluded garden terrace or in the sky-lit Victorian dining room. The restaurant serves breakfast, lunch, dinner and cocktails daily. The decor of this inn is decidedly Victorian with period antiques and wallpapers.

Innkeeper(s): Mark Kulkowitz & Pamela Ann Huber. $110-299. 21 rooms with PB, 2 conference rooms. Breakfast included in rates. Types of meals: Full bkfst, lunch and dinner. Beds: QD. Data port, cable TV, VCR, ceiling fan, clock radio, telephone, voice mail, hair dryer, bath amenities, wireless Internet access and iron/ironing board in room. Air conditioning. Fax, copier and fireplace on premises. Amusement parks, antiquing, fishing, live theater, parks and shopping nearby.

Location: City.

Publicity: *Atlantic City Press, Asbury Press, Frommer's, New York Times and Washington Post.*

"Mr. Kulkowitz is a superb host. He strives to accommodate the diverse needs of guests."

Certificate may be used: Sept. 19-May 19, Sunday-Thursday, no holidays, weekends or Christmas week.

The Henry Sawyer Inn

722 Columbia Ave
Cape May, NJ 08204-2332
(609)884-5667 (800)449-5667 Fax:(609)884-9406
Internet: www.henrysawyerinn.com
E-mail: henrysawyerinn@verizon.net

Circa 1877. This fully restored, three-story peach Victorian home boasts a gingerbread embellished veranda, brick-colored shutters and brown trim. Inside, the parlor features Victorian antiques, a marble fireplace, polished wood floors, an Oriental rug, formal wallcoverings, a crystal chandelier and fresh flowers. Guest rooms have been decorated with careful attention to a romantic and fresh Victorian theme, as well. One room includes a whirlpool tub, one includes a private porch, and another a fireplace.

Innkeeper(s): Mary & Barbara Morris. $120-295. 5 rooms with PB, 1 with FP, 2 suites. Breakfast and afternoon tea included in rates. Types of meals: Full bkfst and early coffee/tea. Beds: KQT. Cable TV, reading lamp, ceiling fan, clock radio, small refrigerator and one with whirlpool or private porch in room. Air conditioning. VCR, fax, telephone, fireplace and parking on premises. Antiquing, fishing, golf, live theater, parks, shopping, tennis, water sports, carriage and Victorian trolley nearby.

Location: City, ocean community.

Certificate may be used: November-April, subject to availability, Anytime, Last Minute-Based on Availability.

The Queen Victoria

102 Ocean St
Cape May, NJ 08204-2320
(609)884-8702
Internet: www.queenvictoria.com
E-mail: reservations@queenvictoria.com

Circa 1881. 2009 Winner - Travelers' Choice for Romance. This nationally acclaimed inn, a block from the ocean and shops in the historic district, is comprised of two beautiful Victorian homes, restored and furnished with antiques. "Victorian Homes" magazine featured 23 color photographs of The Queen Victoria, because of its décor and luxurious amenities. Guest rooms offer handmade quilts, antiques, air conditioning, mini-refrigerators and all have private baths. Luxury suites and many rooms have a whirlpool tub and some with handsome fireplace. Afternoon tea is enjoyed while rocking on the porch in summer or before a warm fireplace in winter. Breakfast is hearty buffet style and the inn has its own cookbook. The innkeepers keep a fleet of complimentary bicycles available for guests and there are beach chairs and beach towels as well. The inn is open all year with special Christmas festivities and winter packages.

Innkeeper(s): Doug & Anna Marie McMain. $120-510. 34 rooms with PB, 6 with FP, 14 with WP, 6 suites, 2 cottages. Breakfast, afternoon tea and snacks/refreshments included in rates. Types of meals: Full bkfst and early coffee/tea. Beds: KQ. Cable TV, DVD, reading lamp, refrigerator, ceiling fan, clock radio, turn-down service, some with hot tub/spa, some with fireplace, hair dryer, bathrobes, bath amenities, wireless Internet access, iron/ironing board, Some with phones, Pantry with beverages and snacks in room. Air conditioning. Bicycles, parlor games, telephone, gift shop, Beach Chairs, Beach towels and Bicycles on premises. Amusement parks, antiquing, art galleries, beach, bicycling, canoeing/kayaking, fishing, golf, hiking, live theater, museums, parks, shopping, tennis, water sports, wineries, Historic tours and Lighthouse nearby.

Location: Waterfront.

Publicity: *Philadelphia Magazine and Baltimore Magazine.*

Certificate may be used: Monday-Thursday, November-March, except holidays, Christmas week and special events.

Flemington   E3

Main Street Manor Bed and Breakfast

194 Main Street
Flemington, NJ 08822
(908)782-4928 Fax:(908)782-7229
Internet: www.mainstreetmanor.com
E-mail: innkeeper@mainstreetmanor.com

Circa 1901. Located in the quaint village of Flemington, this bed and breakfast has been welcoming guests for 13 years. Elegantly restored, the Queen Anne Victorian adorns the historic district. Sip lemonade on the front porch, converse by the fire in the formal front parlor or catch up on reading in the intimate side parlor. Visit local wineries, dine in great restaurants and explore the many shops. All guest bedrooms feature private baths; one room boasts a balcony and another has a clawfoot tub. Each morning a delicious gourmet breakfast is served in the block-paneled dining room. Feel spoiled in the delightful setting so filled with comfort it will be hard to leave.

Innkeeper(s): Donna & Ken Arold & resident Retriever, Quincy. $145-215. 5 rooms with PB, 1 with FP, 1 with HT, 1 conference room. Breakfast, afternoon tea, snacks/refreshments and wine included in rates. Types of meals: Full gourmet bkfst, veg bkfst, Sun. brunch, early coffee/tea, gourmet lunch, picnic lunch, hors d'oeuvres, gourmet dinner, room service, All food is prepared on premisis and no preservatives of any kind are used. Fresh-baked goods are always offered for guests to enjoy. Full gourmet breakfasts include fresh and seasonal fruit and ingredients from our local organic farm. The Inn's herb garden helps to supply the fresh herbs which are incorporated into all meals prepared at Main Street Manor. Beds: Q. Modem hook-up, cable TV, VCR, DVD, reading lamp, stereo, refrigerator, ceiling fan, snack bar, clock radio, coffeemaker, desk, some with fireplace, hair dryer, bath amenities, wireless Internet access and iron/ironing board in room. Central air. Fax, copier, library, parlor games, gift shop, Afternoon tea with home-baked treats, Fresh seasonal fruit, Complimentary wine & cordials in evening, 24-hour coffee & tea, Bottomless cookie jar, DVD library and Private off-street on-site parking on premises. Antiquing, art galleries, bicycling, canoeing/kayaking, fishing, golf, hiking, horseback riding, live theater, museums, parks, shopping, water sports, wineries, Walking Tour of Historic Downtown, Botanical Gardens - both formal international and informal Wildflower Gardens, Delaware river tubing, Rafting and Personalized itineraries planned by innkeepers for guests at their request nearby.

Location: Country. Historic District.

Publicity: *AM NY - 'A Weekend In Hunterdon County' Press Review, Garden State Town & Country Living Magazine (Winter 2007/08) and WOR Radio (May 2008).*

Certificate may be used: July, August, February and March, Monday through Thursday excluding certain rooms, holidays and special event dates, based on availabilty.

Lambertville   E3

Chimney Hill Estate Inn

207 Goat Hill Rd
Lambertville, NJ 08530
(609)397-1516 (800)211-4667 Fax:(609)397-9353
Internet: www.chimneyhillinn.com
E-mail: frontdesk@chimneyhillinn.com

Circa 1820. Chimney Hill, in the hills above the riverside town of Lambertville, is a grand display of stonework, designed with both Federal and Greek Revival-style architecture. The inn's sunroom is particularly appealing, with its stone walls, fireplaces and French windows looking out to eight acres of gardens and fields. Most of the guest rooms in the estate farmhouse include fireplaces, and some  have canopied beds. The Ol' Barn has four suites with fireplaces, Jacuzzis, steam rooms, guest pantries, spiral staircases and loft bedrooms. The innkeepers offer adventure, romance and special interest packages for their guests, and the inn is also popular for corporate retreats. There are plenty of seasonal activities nearby, from kayaking to skiing. New Hope is the neighboring town and offers many charming restaurants and shops, as well.

Innkeeper(s): Terry & Richard Anderson. $169-409. 11 rooms, 9 with PB, 10 with FP, 5 with WP, 4 total suites, including 1 two-bedroom suite, 1 guest house, 2 conference rooms. Breakfast and snacks/refreshments included in rates. Types of meals: Country bkfst, early coffee/tea, Wine and Cheese - Friday and Saturday evenings and Breakfast in Bed upon request. Beds: KQ. Modem hook-up, data port, cable TV, DVD, reading lamp, refrigerator, ceiling fan, snack bar, clock radio, telephone, coffeemaker, desk, most with fireplace, hair dryer, bathrobes, bath amenities, wireless Internet access, iron/ironing board and Jacuzzi in room. Air conditioning. VCR, fax, copier, parlor games, gift shop, Alpaca farm and Lovely garden areas on premises. Limited handicap access. Antiquing, art galleries, bicycling, canoeing/kayaking, fishing, golf, hiking, horseback riding, live theater, museums, parks, shopping, sporting events, tennis, water sports, wineries, Golden Nugget Flea Market, Peddlers Village, Michner Museum, Ivyland Railroad, New Hope, Frenchtown, Washington Crossing Park, River Country and Doylestown nearby.

Location: Country. Bucks County, PA.

Publicity: *New Jersey Monthly (November-December 2008 Feature), Cover Inn of Country Inns, Colonial Homes Magazine, Country Roads Magazine,*

NY Times, NJ Magazine, Best Places to Kiss, New Jersey Network, New Jersey Tourism Commercial (2006-2007) and Nassau Broadcasting: 94.5 Hawk Radio-WPST.

"We would be hard pressed to find a more perfect setting to begin our married life together."

Certificate may be used: Jan. 3-Dec. 20, Monday-Thursday. No holidays, no October dates.

Ocean City   J4

Inn The Gardens Bed & Breakfast

48 Wesley Rd
Ocean City, NJ 08226-4462
(609)399-0800
Internet: www.innthegardens.com
E-mail: innthegardens@aol.com

Circa 1923. Adorning the quiet, residential Gardens neighborhood on the New Jersey Shore, this relaxing bed and breakfast is only eight miles from Atlantic City. Enjoy the ocean breeze while sitting on a porch with a beverage or on the backyard patio surrounded by gardens. Complimentary beach tags are also provided. Comfortable guest bedrooms feature refrigerators and the Daybreak Room boasts a private balcony. Indulge in an extensive continental breakfast each morning. A computer is available to check e-mail. Ask about specials and packages offered.

Innkeeper(s): Jennifer Torres. $139-189. 7 rooms with PB. Breakfast included in rates. Types of meals: Scrumptious Continental Plus buffet served between 8-10 AM. Beds: KQDT. Cable TV, VCR, DVD, reading lamp, refrigerator, ceiling fan, clock radio, hair dryer, wireless Internet access, iron/ironing board and Porch/balcony in room. Air conditioning. Library, parlor games, telephone, laundry facility and beach tags available at no charge on premises. Amusement parks, antiquing, art galleries, beach, bicycling, canoeing/kayaking, fishing, golf, hiking, museums, parks, shopping, water sports, wineries, Atlantic City with concerts, sports events, trade shows and casinos (8 miles) nearby.

Location: Ocean community.

Certificate may be used: October-May, excluding holidays.

Plainfield   D5

The Pillars of Plainfield Bed and Breakfast Inn

922 Central Ave
Plainfield, NJ 07060
(908)753-0922 (888)PIL-LARS
Internet: www.pillars2.com
E-mail: info@pillars2.com

Circa 1870. Victorian and Georgian influences are mingled in the design of this grand historic mansion, which boasts majestic columns and a wraparound porch. An acre of well-manicured grounds and gardens surrounds the home, which is located in Plainfield's Van Wyck Historic District. Guest rooms and suites are appointed with traditional furnishings, and each room has its own special decor. The romantic Van Wyck Brooks Suite includes a fireplace and a canopy bed topped with a down quilt. A wicker table and chairs are tucked into the bay window alcove of the Clementine Yates room. Another spacious room includes a full kitchen. Business travelers will appreciate the private in-room phones with voice mail and wi-fi. Swedish home cooking highlights the morning meal, which is accompanied by freshly ground coffee. Plainfield, the first inland settlement in New Jersey, offers many historic attractions, including the Drake House Museum.

Innkeeper(s): Nancy Fiske and Lamont Blowe. $125-190. 7 rooms with PB, 2 with FP. Snacks/refreshments and Full Gourmet Breakfast included in rates. Types of meals: Full bkfst, veg bkfst and early coffee/tea. Beds: QT. Modem hook-up, data port, cable TV, VCR, reading lamp, ceiling fan, clock radio, telephone, coffeemaker, turn-down service, desk, voice mail and fireplace in room. Air conditioning. Fax, copier, library, parlor games and laundry facility on premises. Amusement parks, antiquing, art galleries, beach, golf, hiking, live theater, museums, parks, shopping, sporting events and tennis nearby.

Location: City.

Certificate may be used: Last minute bookings, booked within one week of arrival date.

Princeton   E4

Inn at Glencairn

3301 Lawrenceville Road
Princeton, NJ 08540
(609)497-1737 Fax:(609)497-0390
Internet: www.innatglencairn.com
E-mail: innkeeper@innatglencairn.com

Circa 1736. Situated on three park-like acres on a hill in Princeton, New Jersey, this renovated 1736 Georgian manor house is just three miles from downtown. The original smokehouse and stable, both made of stone and a three-story red frame barn are some of the outbuildings at Inn at Glencairn. This bed and breakfast blends the historic setting and traditional décor of antique furnishings with a touch of modern and updated amenities. Relax with refreshments in the parlor or great room by the huge working fireplace under a beamed ceiling with oriental rugs accenting the random-width pine floors. Luxurious guest bedrooms and a two-room suite feature Frette robes and featherbeds with Egyptian cotton linens. Savor a gourmet breakfast that is made with fresh ingredients from local orchards and organic farms.

Innkeeper(s): Bob Riggs. $195-235. 5 rooms with PB, 1 two-bedroom suite. Breakfast, snacks/refreshments and wine included in rates. Types of meals: Full gourmet bkfst, veg bkfst, early coffee/tea and We serve our guests a full gourmet breakfast daily made with fresh ingredients from local farms and orchards. Beverages are available throughout the day and afternoon refreshments are served during the 3:00-5:00 check-in period. Beds: QDT. Modem hook-up, data port, cable TV, reading lamp, hair dryer, bathrobes, bath amenities, wireless Internet access, luxurious beds that include featherbeds, Egyptian cotton linens and down comforters, renovated en-suite baths that feature fluffy cotton towels and Frette bathrobes in room. Central air. Fax, library, parlor games, telephone, fireplace, large gathering spaces include a nearly 500 square foot Great Room with a beamed ceiling and a twelve foot wide original cooking fireplace, fine antiques, a revolving art collection and oriental carpets over original random width pine floors on premises. Limited handicap access. Amusement parks, antiquing, art galleries, bicycling, canoeing/kayaking, cross-country skiing, fishing, golf, hiking, horseback riding, live theater, museums, parks, shopping, sporting events, tennis and wineries nearby.

Location: Country.

Publicity: New Jersey Monthly, New Jersey Countryside, Princeton Magazine, Trenton Times, Lawrence Ledger, Town Topics and US1.

Certificate may be used: Anytime, Last Minute-Based on Availability, reservation must be made via telephone.

Sea Girt   F6

Beacon House

100 & 104 Beacon Blvd
Sea Girt, NJ 08750-1609
(732)449-5835 (866)255-0005 Fax:732-282-0974
Internet: www.beaconhouseinn.com
E-mail: beaconhouse@aol.com

Circa 1879. Built in classic Victorian style, this recently renovated inn has been a relaxing getaway for more than a century. Splendidly furnished parlors with fireplaces, crystal chandeliers and oak floors are pleasurable places to while away time. The two main houses, a cottage and a carriage house offer the best in casual elegance. Encounter wicker, brass and chintz in the sunny guest bedrooms. Some boast oceanview balconies, fireplaces and Jacuzzi tubs. Morning is a celebration when a memorable gourmet breakfast is served in the candle-lit dining room. Enjoy the colorful landscape from a rocker on one of the wraparound porches, lounge by the swimming pool, or take a bike ride to the popular boardwalk in this quaint seaside community.

Innkeeper(s): Candace Kadimik. $89-365. 18 rooms with PB, 7 with FP, 2 with WP, 2 two-bedroom suites, 3 cottages, 1 conference room. Breakfast included in rates. Types of meals: Full gourmet bkfst, veg bkfst, early coffee/tea and snacks/refreshments. Beds: KQDT. Cable TV, reading lamp, ceiling fan, clock radio, some with hot tub/spa, most with fireplace, hair dryer, bath amenities and wireless Internet access in room. Central air. VCR, DVD, fax, copier, swimming, bicycles, library, parlor games, telephone, gift shop and Pool on premises. Limited handicap access. Amusement parks, antiquing, art galleries, beach, bicycling, canoeing/kayaking, fishing, golf, hiking, horseback riding, live theater, museums, parks, shopping, tennis and water sports nearby.

Location: Waterfront.

Publicity: The Coast Star, The Asbury Park Press and Vacations On The Fly.

Certificate may be used: October-April, subject to availability and excluding holiday weekends.

Spring Lake   F6

Spring Lake Inn

104 Salem Ave
Spring Lake, NJ 07762-1040
(732)449-2010 Fax:(732)449-4020
Internet: www.springlakeinn.com
E-mail: springlakeinn@aol.com

Circa 1888. Only a block from the beach, this historic Victorian inn boasts an informal seaside atmosphere. Relax on the 80-foot, rocker-lined porch or fireside in the parlor. Well-decorated guest bedrooms and suites offer a variety of peaceful settings including the Turret, surrounded by four windows, and the Tower View suite with sleigh bed and ocean views. Enjoy a leisurely breakfast served in the spacious dining room featuring a 12-foot ceiling. Walk to the town center, with more than 60 shops to explore.

Innkeeper(s): Barbara & Andy Seaman. $99-499. 16 rooms with PB, 8 with FP, 2 suites, 2 conference rooms. Breakfast and snacks/refreshments included in rates. Types of meals: Full gourmet bkfst, Sun. brunch, early coffee/tea and afternoon tea. Beds: QD. Modem hook-up, cable TV, VCR, reading lamp, stereo, refrigerator, ceiling fan, snack bar, clock radio, desk, fireplace, wireless Internet access, beach chairs, beach badges, beach towels and ocean views in room. Air conditioning. Fax, copier, swimming, library, parlor games, telephone and gift shop on premises. Limited handicap access. Amusement parks, antiquing, art galleries, beach, bicycling, canoeing/kayaking, fishing, golf, hiking, horseback riding, live theater, museums, parks, shopping, sporting events, tennis, water sports and wineries nearby.

Location: Ocean community. Two blocks from the lake and one block from the ocean. The town center is within walking distance.

Publicity: *Asbury Press, Westchester Magazine and NJ 12.*

Certificate may be used: Oct. 1 to May 15, subject to availability.

White Lilac Inn

414 Central Ave
Spring Lake, NJ 07762-1020
(732)449-0211 (866)449-0211
Internet: www.whitelilac.com
E-mail: mari@whitelilac.com

Circa 1880. The White Lilac looks like a sweeping Southern home with wide wraparound private and semi-private porches decorating its three stories.
The first story veranda is lined with wicker rockers and baskets of flowering plants hang from the ceiling, creating an ideal spot for relaxation. Inside, the Victorian decor contains period furnishings, antiques, double whirlpool tubs, fireplaces, air conditioning in every room and queen beds. Breakfast is served fireside on intimate tables for two in the Garaden Room and on the enclosed porch. The ocean is less than five blocks from the inn.

Innkeeper(s): Mari Kennelly. $139-359. 10 rooms with PB, 10 with FP, 5 with WP, 1 two-bedroom suite. Breakfast, snacks/refreshments, Tea and soda and guest refrigerator always accessible to guests included in rates. Types of meals: Full bkfst, early coffee/tea and Victorian Treasure has the option of a full breakfast delivered to their sitting room. Beds: QT. Cable TV, VCR, reading lamp, refrigerator, ceiling fan, clock radio, desk, fireplace, hair dryer, bathrobes, bath amenities, wireless Internet access, iron/ironing board, Double whirlpool tubs in 5 rooms, Private porches and with private entrance in room. Central air. Bicycles, library, parlor games, telephone and gift shop on premises. Amusement parks, antiquing, art galleries, beach, bicycling, canoeing/kayaking, fishing, golf, hiking, horseback riding, live theater, museums, parks, shopping, sporting events, tennis, water sports, wineries, Parasailing, jet skining, River cruises and deep sea fishing (seasonal) nearby.

Location: Ocean community.

Publicity: *The Star-Ledger, Asbury Park Press, Coast Star, Philadelphia Inquirer, Best Romantic Inns and The Breeze (New Jersey station).*

Certificate may be used: Sunday-Thursday, September-May; subject to availability, holidays excluded.

Stanhope   C4

Whistling Swan Inn

110 Main St
Stanhope, NJ 07874-2632
(973)347-6369 (888)507-2337 Fax:(973)347-6379
Internet: www.whistlingswaninn.com
E-mail: wswan@att.net

Circa 1905. This Queen Anne Victorian has a limestone wraparound veranda and a tall, steep-roofed turret.
Family antiques fill the rooms and highlight the polished ornate woodwork, pocket doors and winding staircase. It is a little more than a mile from Waterloo Village and the International Trade Center.

Innkeeper(s): Liz Armstrong. $119-259. 9 rooms with PB, 3 with FP, 3 with WP. Breakfast and snacks/refreshments included in rates. Types of meals: Full bkfst. Beds: KQ. Data port, cable TV, VCR, DVD, reading lamp, CD player, ceiling fan, clock radio, telephone, desk, hair dryer, bath amenities, wireless Internet access and iron/ironing board in room. Central air. Fax, copier, bicycles, parlor games, fireplace, gift shop, Video library, Hospitality bar with complimentary beverages, snacks and homemade cookies on premises. Antiquing, art galleries, bicycling, canoeing/kayaking, cross-country skiing, fishing, golf, hiking, horseback riding, live theater, museums, parks, shopping, sporting events, water sports and wineries nearby.

Location: Country, mountains. Rural village.

Publicity: *Sunday Herald, New York Times, New Jersey Monthly, Mid-Atlantic Country, Star Ledger, Daily Record, Philadelphia, Country and Chicago Sun Times.*

"Thank you for your outstanding hospitality. We had a delightful time while we were with you and will not hesitate to recommend the inn to our listening audience, friends and anyone else who will listen! — Joel H. Klein, Travel Editor, WOAI AM."

Certificate may be used: Sunday-Thursday nights, not valid in August-October or holidays. Not Available for suites.

Ventnor City   J5

Carisbrooke Inn

105 S Little Rock Ave
Ventnor City, NJ 08406-2840
(609)822-6392 Fax:(609)822-9710
Internet: www.carisbrookeinn.com
E-mail: info@carisbrookeinn.com

Circa 1918. Relaxation is easy at this enticing seaside bed & breakfast just a few steps away from the world-famous boardwalk and only one mile from Atlantic City. Delight in the ocean view from the front deck or the tranquility of the back patio. Afternoon refreshments are enjoyed in the sunny Main Parlor, or by the warmth of a winter fire. Pleasant guest bedrooms feature comfortable amenities and the romantic accents of plants, fresh flowers and lacy curtains. The innkeepers offer a huge breakfast that may include homemade waffles and fresh berries, banana pecan pancakes, Italian frittata with fresh herbs and cheese, Quiche Lorraine and French toast, accompanied by fruit and just-baked muffins and breads. Beach towels and tags are provided for fun in the sun at the shore.

Innkeeper(s): John Battista. $85-360. 9 rooms with PB. Breakfast, snacks/refreshments, hors d'oeuvres and wine included in rates. Types of meals: Full gourmet bkfst, veg bkfst and early coffee/tea. Beds: KQT. Cable TV, VCR, DVD, reading lamp, CD player, ceiling fan, clock radio, desk, some with hot tub/spa, some with fireplace, hair dryer, bath amenities, wireless Internet access and iron/ironing board in room. Central air. Fax, copier, library, parlor games, telephone, Complimentary wine and snacks in main parlor, Beach tags, Towels, Chairs and Umbrellas (in season) on premises. Amusement parks, antiquing, art galleries, beach, bicycling, canoeing/kayaking, fishing, golf, horseback riding, live theater, museums, parks, shopping, sporting events, tennis, water sports, wineries, Casinos, Shopping, Dining and Clubs nearby.

Location: City, ocean community.

Publicity: *Voted Best on the Shore in Philadelphia Magazine.*

"You have a beautiful, elegant inn. My stay here was absolutely wonderful."

Certificate may be used: Nov. 1-April 30, Sunday-Thursday. All major holidays excluded. Other black out days may apply, subject to availability.

Vernon   B5

Alpine Haus B&B

217 State Rt 94
Vernon, NJ 07462
(973)209-7080 (877)527-6854 Fax:(973)209-7090
Internet: www.alpinehausbb.com
E-mail: alpinehs@warwick.net

Circa 1885. A private hideaway in the mountains, this former farmhouse is more than 100 years old. The renovated Federal-style inn with Victorian accents offers comfortable guest bedrooms named after mountain flowers with a decor reflecting that theme. Antiques also highlight the inn. The adjacent Carriage House has two suites with four-poster beds, stone fireplace and Jacuzzi. A generous country breakfast is enjoyed in the dining room or a continental breakfast on the second-story covered porch with majestic views. The family room and formal sitting room with fireplace are wonderful gathering places for games or conversation. Located next to Mountain Creek Ski and Water Park.

Innkeeper(s): Jack & Allison Smith. $110-225. 10 rooms with PB, 3 with FP, 2 suites, 1 conference room. Breakfast included in rates. Types of meals: Country bkfst, veg bkfst, early coffee/tea and snacks/refreshments. Beds: QDT. Modern hook-up, data port, cable TV, VCR, reading lamp, refrigerator, clock radio, telephone, coffeemaker, desk, some with hot tub/spa, voice mail, hair dryer, wireless Internet access, Internet access and two suites with fireplace and Jacuzzi in room. Central air. Fax, copier, parlor games and fireplace on premises. Handicap access. Antiquing, art galleries, bicycling, canoeing/kayaking, cross-country skiing, downhill skiing, fishing, golf, hiking, horseback riding, live theater, museums, parks, shopping, water sports and wineries nearby.

Location: Country, mountains.

Certificate may be used: Anytime, except Friday-Saturday for the periods Dec. 15-March 15 and June 15-Sept. 7 not valid holiday periods.

New Mexico

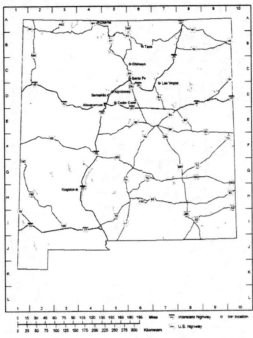

Albuquerque   D5

Bottger Mansion of Old Town

110 San Felipe St., NW
Albuquerque, NM 87104
(505)243-3639 (800)758-3639
Internet: www.bottger.com
E-mail: info@bottger.com

Gracing the historic district of Old Town Albuquerque, Bottger
Mansion of Old Town B&B is a Victorian delight listed in the
National Register. Sitting amid the vibrant southwestern culture
and distinct architecture of New Mexico, this elegant B&B
focuses on comfort and convenience while offering gracious
hospitality. Enjoy the inn's sig-
nature chocolate chip cookies
and other afternoon treats in the
parlor or relax in the courtyard
shaded by massive ancient
Chinese elms. Accommodations
boast pleasing color schemes
and furnishings and vary from

an intimate sun porch room to a two-bedroom suite with living
area. Indulge in a gourmet breakfast before taking a day trip to
Santa Fe, the lava tubes, Salinas National Monument, the
Turquoise Trail, or Bopsque del Apache National Wildlife
Refuge. Special packages are available.

Innkeeper(s): Steve & Kathy Hiatt. $104-179. 7 rooms with PB, 1 with WP,
1 two-bedroom suite. Breakfast and snacks/refreshments included in rates.
Types of meals: Full gourmet bkfst, veg bkfst and early coffee/tea. Beds: KQT.
Modem hook-up, cable TV, VCR, reading lamp, ceiling fan, clock radio, telephone, desk, some with hot tub/spa, hair dryer, bathrobes, bath amenities,
wireless Internet access and iron/ironing board in room. Air conditioning. Fax,
copier, library, parlor games and fireplace on premises. Antiquing, art galleries, cross-country skiing, downhill skiing, fishing, golf, hiking, horseback
riding, live theater, museums, parks, shopping, sporting events, tennis and
wineries nearby.

Location: City.

Publicity: PBS Public Television.

Certificate may be used: Week of International Balloon Fiesta is excluded,
anytime subject to availability.

The Mauger

701 Roma Ave NW
Albuquerque, NM 87102-2038
(505) 242-8755 (800) 719-9189 Fax:(505)842-8835
Internet: www.maugerbb.com
E-mail: maugerbb@aol.com

Circa 1897. Now an elegantly restored Victorian, this former boarding house is listed in the National Register. Guest bedrooms offer amenities that
include satellite television,
refrigerators, a basket with
snacks, voice mail and
European down comforters
on the beds. The inn is located four blocks from the convention center/business district and Historic Route 66.

Old Town is less than one mile away. There are many interesting museums to visit locally, featuring topics from Native
American culture to the atomic age.

Innkeeper(s): Tammy Walden. $89-209. 10 rooms, 8 with PB, 1 suite, 2
guest houses, 1 conference room. Breakfast, snacks/refreshments and wine
included in rates. Types of meals: Full bkfst, veg bkfst, early coffee/tea and
Breakfast to-go for early departures. Beds: KQDT. Cable TV, reading lamp,
refrigerator, ceiling fan, clock radio, telephone, coffeemaker, voice mail, hair
dryer, bath amenities, wireless Internet access and iron/ironing board in
room. Air conditioning. DVD, fax and Off-street parking on premises.
Amusement parks, antiquing, art galleries, cross-country skiing, horseback
riding, live theater, museums, parks, shopping, sporting events, wineries,
Albuquerque Bio Park, Zoo, Old Town, Rio Grande Nature Center, Convention
Center and Health Club nearby.

Location: City. Downtown Albuquerque.

Publicity: *Albuquerque Journal, Phoenix Home and Garden, Albuquerque
Monthly, National Geographic Traveler, New Mexico Business Week, Golf
Digest, Washington Post and Duke City Shootout Movie "Easy Pickins"* (2007).

*"Because of your hospitality, kindness and warmth, we will always
compare the quality of our experience by the W.E. Mauger Estate."*

Certificate may be used: Nov. 15-March 1, except Thanksgiving and
Christmas, Sunday-Thursday. Friday and Saturday subject to availability,
Anytime, subject to availability.

Algodones   D5

Hacienda Vargas

PO Box 307
Algodones, NM 87001-0307
(505)867-9115 (800)261-0006 Fax:(505)867-0640
Internet: www.haciendavargas.com
E-mail: stay@haciendavargas.com

Circa 1840. Nestled among the cottonwoods and mesas of the
middle Rio Grande Valley, between Albuquerque and Santa Fe,
Hacienda Vargas has seen two centuries of Old West history. It
once served as a trading post for Native Americans as well as a
19th-century stagecoach stop between Santa Fe and Las

Cruces. The grounds contain an
adobe chapel, courtyard and gardens. The main house features five
kiva fireplaces, Southwest antiques,
Spanish tile, a library and suites with
private Jacuzzis.

Innkeeper(s): Cynthia & Richard Spence.
$79-149. 7 rooms with PB, 6 with FP, 4
suites. Breakfast included in rates. Types of

meals: Full bkfst. Beds: QT. Reading lamp, ceiling fan, clock radio, desk and
suites have spa in room. Air conditioning. Parlor games, telephone and fireplace on premises. Antiquing, downhill skiing, fishing, live theater, shopping,
sporting events, Golf MECCA and car racing nearby.

Location: Valley.

Publicity: *Albuquerque Journal (Country Inns), Vogue and San Francisco
Chronicle.*

"This is the best! Breakfast was the best we've ever had!"

Certificate may be used: Sunday-Thursday except holidays or Balloon Fiesta.

Cedar Crest   D5

Elaine's, A B&B

72 Snowline Rd
Cedar Crest, NM 87008-0444
(505)281-2467 (800)821-3092 Fax:(505)281-1384
Internet: www.elainesbnb.com
E-mail: elaine@elainesbnb.com

Circa 1979. Ideally located on the historic Turquoise Trail
adjacent to the Cibola National Forest, this three-story log
home is situated on four acres of evergreens in the forests of
the Sandia Peaks. Over one hundred
varieties of birds, including three types
of hummingbirds, visit the property.
Enchanting mountain views from one
of the three balconies are unforgettable. Furnished with European country antiques, several of the guest bedrooms feature private fireplaces and
Jacuzzis. Start the day off right with a
substantial breakfast of favorite comfort
foods. Visit the historic sites, shops

and galleries in Albuquerque and Santa Fe, only minutes
away from this secluded inn.

Innkeeper(s): Elaine O'Neil. $89-139. 5 rooms, 2 with FP, 5 suites.
Breakfast included in rates. Types of meals: Full gourmet bkfst, veg bkfst,
early coffee/tea and snacks/refreshments. Beds: KQ. Reading lamp, ceiling
fan, most with hot tub/spa, most with fireplace and European country
antiques in room. Air conditioning. TV, VCR, DVD, fax, copier, spa, library,
parlor games, telephone, over 100 varieties of birds, views of the mountains,
three balconies, flagstone patios and garden on premises. Amusement parks,
antiquing, art galleries, bicycling, cross-country skiing, downhill skiing, golf,
hiking, horseback riding, museums, parks, shopping and wineries nearby.

Location: Mountains. Four acres of evergreens in the forests of the Sandia Peaks.

Publicity: *Fodor's, L.A. Times, Albuquerque Journal, New Mexico Magazine,
Fort Worth Star-Telegram, Washington Post, Pittsburgh-Gazette and St.
Petersburg Times.*

"Fabulous! Mystical in the spring snow!"

Certificate may be used: Jan. 15-April 15, excluding holidays.

Chama   A4

Parlor Car Bed & Breakfast

311 Terrace Ave
Chama, NM 87520
(575) 756-1946 Fax:(575)756-1057
Internet: www.parlorcar.com/

Circa 1924. Reflecting the distinctive luxury of historic parlor
cars, this is the perfect getaway destination to experience the
Spirit of the West in the Northern New Mexico Rocky
Mountains. Pan for gold, go fossil hunting, take a walking tour,
chow down on a chuck wagon dinner and listen to a cowboy
poetry reading. Relax in a common room accented with origi-

nal artwork, oriental rugs and antiques, or enjoy the outside sitting areas that invite bird watching. Delightful guest rooms are named after men who gained notoriety through their involvement in the railroad era. The Chama Valley offers horseback riding, hiking, water sports and hunting.

Innkeeper(s): Bonsall and Wendy Johnson. $79-159. 3 rooms with PB, 1 with WP. Breakfast, snacks/refreshments and bedtime treats included in rates. Types of meals: Full bkfst, vegetarian breakfast on request and bedtime treats. Beds: Q. Cable TV, VCR, DVD, reading lamp, desk, bath amenities, WiFi available, Bath robes in Harvey room, hair dryer available on request, ironing on request, ceiling fan in Pullman room, no fireplace, no hot tub, whirl pool tub in Pullman room and alarm clock in each room in room. Library and parlor games on premises. Bicycling, canoeing/kayaking, cross-country skiing, fishing, hiking, horseback riding, museums, parks, shopping, water sports and historic railroad nearby.

Location: Mountains. 10 miles to Lake Heron, 15 miles to El Vado Lake.

Certificate may be used: Anytime, subject to availability.

Chimayo C6

Casa Escondida Bed & Breakfast
64 County Road 0100
Chimayo, NM 87522
(505)351-4805 (800)643-7201
Internet: www.casaescondida.com
E-mail: info@casaescondida.com

Circa 1970. Secluded on six acres in an historic mountain village, this Adobe-style inn features Spanish Colonial architecture. Tongue and groove ceilings, heavy beams known as vigas, French doors, wood, brick and Saltillo tile floors all add to the warm ambiance. The air is scented with the fragrance of pinon wood from kiva fireplaces. A library offers quiet entertainment. Inviting guest bedrooms include bathrobes to relax in. Some rooms boast gorgeous views, oversized tubs, fireplaces, private access to a deck or patio, and can be made into an adjoining suite. Enjoy a leisurely gourmet breakfast in the sunny dining room, or alfresco. Surrounded by trees, an outside hot tub is the perfect spot to relax.

Innkeeper(s): Belinda Bowling. $105-165. 8 rooms with PB, 3 with FP, 1 suite. Breakfast and snacks/refreshments included in rates. Types of meals: Full bkfst and coffee/teas and snacks 24/7. Beds: QT. Reading lamp, ceiling fan, some with fireplace, hair dryer, bathrobes, wireless Internet access, kitchenette, wood-burning stove, oversized tub, private deck, private patio, hair dryer upon request, iron/ironing board upon request and alarm clock upon request in room. Air conditioning. Fax, copier, spa, library, parlor games, telephone, guest phone, laptop hook-up, wireless Internet access, outdoor hot tub, unlimited free local calls and free parking on premises. Limited handicap access. Art galleries, bicycling, canoeing/kayaking, cross-country skiing, downhill skiing, fishing, golf, hiking, horseback riding, live theater, museums, parks, shopping, wineries, hot air ballooning, ancient ruins, Indian pueblos, rafting, bird watching, Southwest cooking classes, casinos, concerts, Cumbre & Toltec Scenic Railroad, Lensic Performing Arts Center, Santa Fe Southern Railway, Santa Fe Horse Park, Santa Fe Farmers Market, Santa Fe Community College Planetarium, laundry facilities and dry cleaning services nearby.

Location: Country, mountains.

Certificate may be used: May-October, Sunday-Thursday, Any day November-April. Excluding holiday periods and special events all year. Anytime, Last Minute-Based on Availability.

Kingston H3

The Black Range Lodge
119 Main Street
Kingston, NM 88042
(575) 895-5652 (800) 676-5622
Internet: www.blackrangelodge.com
E-mail: cat@blackrangelodge.com

Circa 1884. Ivy covers the three-story high vigas (log-beamed ceilings) and stone walls of this old hotel, a remnant of the bustling days when silver was discovered nearby and the town mushroomed to 7,000 people. Now only a few dozen citizens populate the hamlet, tucked in a mountain valley of the Gila National Forest. Cavalry soldiers are said to have headquartered here while protecting miners from the Indians. Hosts Catherine and Mike pursue movie script writing careers. Furnishings from the '40s fill the guest rooms on the second floor. There is a room with pool table and free video games. Pets and children are welcome.

Innkeeper(s): Catherine Wanek. $79-149. 15 rooms, 7 with PB, 4 two-bedroom suites, 1 cottage, 2 guest houses, 2 conference rooms. Breakfast included in rates. Types of meals: Full bkfst, veg bkfst, early coffee/tea and snacks/refreshments. Beds: KQDT. Clock radio, desk, bathrobes and wireless Internet access in room. TV, VCR, DVD, fax, copier, spa, library, parlor games, telephone, Free game room, Wi-fi Internet and Kitchen facilities on premises. Handicap access. Antiquing, art galleries, bicycling, fishing, golf, hiking, horseback riding, museums, shopping and Wilderness activities nearby.

Location: Country, mountains. Near National Forest.

Publicity: New Mexico Magazine, National Geographic Traveler, AAA Magazine, Albuquerque Journal, El Paso Times, Santa Fe Reporter, Las Cruces Sun-News, Albuquerque Tribune. and The Travel Channel - Amazing Vacation Homes and New Mexico's Visitors (as in ghosts).

"We all had a splendiferous time and can't wait to return."

Certificate may be used: Anytime, except holidays, subject to availability.

Las Vegas D7

Plaza Hotel
230 Plaza
Las Vegas, NM 87701
(505)425-3591 (800)328-1882 Fax:(505)425-9659
Internet: www.plazahotel-nm.com
E-mail: lodging@plazahotel-nm.com

Circa 1882. This brick Italianate Victorian hotel, once frequented by the likes of Doc Holliday, Big Nose Kate and members of the James Gang, was renovated in 1982. A stencil pattern found in the dining room inspired the selection of Victorian wallpaper borders in the guest rooms, decorated with period furnishings. Guests also have access to a business center and T-1 internet.

Innkeeper(s): William L Slick (Anne is GM). $71-152. 71 rooms with PB, 1 conference room. Breakfast included in rates. Types of meals: Full bkfst, Sun. brunch, lunch, wine, dinner, room service and afternoon teas Third Sunday March June Sept Dec. Restaurant on premises. Beds: KQD. Cable TV, reading lamp, refrigerator, clock radio, telephone, coffeemaker, desk, hair dryer, wireless Internet access and iron/ironing board in room. Air conditioning. Fax, copier, laundry facility, gift shop and Pet friendly on premises. Handicap access. Antiquing, art galleries, cross-country skiing, fishing, golf, hiking, museums, parks, shopping, water sports, wineries and hot springs nearby.

Location: City.

Certificate may be used: January 2 to March 15 - subject to availability.

Santa Fe   C6

Alexander's Inn

529 E Palace Ave
Santa Fe, NM 87501-2200
(505)986-1431 (888)321-5123 Fax:(505)982-8572
Internet: www.alexanders-inn.com
E-mail: alexinn@osogrande.com

Circa 1903. Alexander's Inn offers the distinctive southwestern flavor of a Santa Fe hotel with great value and a memorable experience in New Mexico. This inn recently changed from a bed & breakfast to more of a private vacation rental with

upscale services. Traditional casitas provide a relaxing oasis and the welcome warmth of a kiva fireplace after a great day of skiing.

New Mexican furnishings and décor, full kitchens and patios are perfect for family vacations or romantic holidays. Comfort and convenience is found in the heavenly beds, fine linens, down comforters, feather pillows, daily maid service and luxuriously soft robes. A basket filled with homemade cookies, fresh fruit, coffee & teas, wine, chips & salsa is provided upon arrival. Packages, facials, various massages and rose petal baths are available at the inn's Absolute Nirvana Spa.

Innkeeper(s): Carolyn Lee. $170-240. 4 cottages, 4 with FP. Welcome basket of fruit, coffee, wine, chips, salsa, homemade cookies. Each unit stocked with locally roasted organic coffee, teas, sweeteners and creamer included in rates. Beds: KQ. Cable TV, VCR, DVD, reading lamp, CD player, refrigerator, ceiling fan, clock radio, telephone, coffeemaker, desk, hot tub/spa, voice mail, fireplace, hair dryer, bathrobes, bath amenities, wireless Internet access, iron/ironing board and Absolute Nirvana Spa in room. Air conditioning. Fax, library, child care, parlor games and laundry facility on premises. Antiquing, art galleries, bicycling, cross-country skiing, downhill skiing, fishing, golf, hiking, horseback riding, live theater, museums, parks, shopping, tennis, water sports, wineries, museums and Pueblos nearby.

Location: City.

Publicity: New Mexican, Glamour, Southwest Art and San Diego Union Tribune.

"Thanks to the kindness and thoughtfulness of the staff, our three days in Santa Fe were magical."

Certificate may be used: Nov. 1-Feb. 28, Sunday-Thursday, no holidays.

El Paradero

220 W Manhattan Ave
Santa Fe, NM 87501-2622
(505)988-1177 (866)558-0918 Fax:(505)988-3577
Internet: www.elparadero.com
E-mail: info@elparadero.com

Circa 1820. This was originally a two-bedroom Spanish farmhouse that doubled in size to a Territorial style in 1860, was remodeled as a Victorian in 1912 and became a Pueblo Revival in 1920. All styles are present and provide a walk through many years of history. Located in historic downtown Santa Fe, the inn is within easy walking distance to the Plaza and Canyon Road.

Innkeeper(s): Sue Jett. $110-200. 15 rooms, 13 with PB, 7 with FP, 2 suites, 1 conference room. Breakfast and afternoon

tea included in rates. Types of meals: Full gourmet bkfst and early coffee/tea. Beds: QT. TV, reading lamp, clock radio, telephone, voice mail, some with fireplace, hair dryer, bath amenities, wireless Internet access, suite has cable TV and refrigerator in room. Air conditioning. Art galleries, bicycling, cross-country skiing, downhill skiing, fishing, golf, hiking, live theater, museums, parks, shopping, pueblos, opera and mountains nearby.

Location: City.

Publicity: Denver Post, Innsider, Country Inns, Outside, Sunset, New York Times, Los Angeles Times, Travel & Leisure, America West and Travel & Holiday.

"I'd like to LIVE here."

Certificate may be used: Nov. 1-March 31, excluding weekends and holidays (Nov. 24-28, Dec. 20-31).

Hacienda Nicholas

320 East Marcy Street
Santa Fe, NM 87501
(505)992-8385 (888)284-3170 Fax:(505)982-8572
Internet: www.haciendanicholas.com
E-mail: info@haciendanicholas.com

Circa 1930. Tranquility surrounds Hacienda Nicholas, a historic Santa Fe B&B inn that boasts eco-friendly lodging in New Mexico. Experience the extreme comfort and modern conveniences with a minimal environmental impact. Thick Adobe walls and an interior courtyard provide a quiet, peaceful retreat. Guest rooms feature upscale amenities for total relaxation and pampering. Linger over an organic breakfast that includes vegetarian options. Indulge in homemade treats served at teatime and gather for the fireside wine and cheese hour. The inn's luxurious Absolute Nirvana Spa in the back garden offers Asian spa rituals, rose petal baths and a selection of massages and facials. Ask about special packages available. Fitness privileges are offered at the El Gaucho Health Club.

Innkeeper(s): Anna Tenaglia. $100-249. 7 rooms with PB, 3 with FP, 3 suites, 1 conference room. Breakfast and afternoon tea included in rates. Types of meals: Full gourmet bkfst, veg bkfst, early coffee/tea, snacks/refreshments, hors d'oeuvres, wine, Local dishes featured at breakfast and during happy hour, utilizing natural and organic ingredients in all cooking and baking, bottomless plates of cookies and pastries available all afternoon and nightly wine & appetizer hour in front of the roaring fire or outside on the garden patio. Beds: KQ. Cable TV, reading lamp, clock radio, telephone, voice mail, some with fireplace, hair dryer, bathrobes, bath amenities, wireless Internet access and iron/ironing board in room. Central air. Fax, child care, parlor games, Wine & cheese 5-7 nightly and Absolute Nirvana Spa on premises. Handicap access. Antiquing, art galleries, bicycling, canoeing/kayaking, cross-country skiing, downhill skiing, fishing, golf, hiking, horseback riding, live theater, museums, parks, shopping, sporting events, tennis, water sports and wineries nearby.

Location: City.

Publicity: Travel Holiday.

Certificate may be used: Nov. 1-Feb. 28, Sunday-Thursday, no holidays.

The Madeleine (formerly The Preston House)

106 Faithway St
Santa Fe, NM 87501
(505)982-3465 (888)877-7622 Fax:(505)982-8572
Internet: www.madeleineinn.com
E-mail: info@madeleineinn.com

Circa 1886. Gracing a quiet neighborhood in Santa Fe, New Mexico, this historic and romantic bed and breakfast combines Asian and Victorian décor. Guests are invited for complimentary tea, wine and cheese at Hacienda Nicholas, just across the street. Each delightful guest bedroom is a warm and inviting retreat that features generous upscale amenities

to please and pamper both business and leisure travelers. After a satisfying breakfast indulge the senses at the Madeleine's Absolute Nirvana Spa, Tea Room and Gardens. Select a therapeutic massage or treatment from the spa menu. Schedule a facial, bathe in a sea of rose petals and be sure to visit the blissful gardens and the tea room for delectable treats. Ask about special packages.

Innkeeper(s): Carolyn Lee. $110-210. 7 rooms with PB, 4 with FP, 2 cottages. Breakfast, afternoon tea and nightly wine & appetizer hour included in rates. Types of meals: Full gourmet bkfst, early coffee/tea, hors d'oeuvres and wine. Beds: KQ. Data port, cable TV, reading lamp, CD player, refrigerator, ceiling fan, clock radio, telephone, coffeemaker, desk, voice mail, some with fireplace, hair dryer, bathrobes, bath amenities, wireless Internet access and iron/ironing board in room. Air conditioning. Fax, copier, spa, parlor games, gift shop and New Absolute Nirvana Spa selected by Conde Nast Traveler as "One of the Hottest New Spas in the World on premises. Antiquing, cross-country skiing, downhill skiing, fishing, live theater, parks and shopping nearby.

Location: City, mountains.

Publicity: Country Inns, Bliss Magazine, New Mexican and Local Flavor .

"We were extremely pleased — glad we found you. We shall return."

Certificate may be used: Nov. 1-Feb. 28, Sunday-Thursday, no holidays.

Taos   B6

Adobe & Pines Inn

4107 State Road 68
Taos, NM 87557
(575)751-0947 (800)723-8267 Fax:(575)758-8423
Internet: www.adobepines.com
E-mail: mail@adobepines.com

Circa 1832. Two country acres create the setting for this classic 1832 Spanish adobe hacienda with its original architectural details and Southwest eclectic décor and furnishings. Old Taos charm has been transformed into a romantic and luxurious bed and breakfast. Relax on bent apple furniture by the fountain in the back courtyard with an afternoon snack or on secluded patios. Guest bedrooms and suites
offer privacy and
rejuvenation.
Entertainment cen-
ters accent the

ambiance with music and many rooms feature fireplaces and oversized Jacuzzis. Stay in Puerta Rosa with a dry cedar sauna and Roman-style soaking tub. Savor the morning with a satisfying gourmet breakfast. Schedule an in-room massage or available spa service. Ask about special packages.

Innkeeper(s): Katherine and Louis Costabel. $98-225. 8 rooms with PB, 8 with FP, 4 with WP, 3 total suites, including 1 two-bedroom suite, 3 cottages. Breakfast included in rates. Types of meals: Full gourmet bkfst, veg bkfst and early coffee/tea. Beds: Q. Cable TV, VCR, DVD, reading lamp, CD player, refrigerator, clock radio, coffeemaker, most with hot tub/spa, fireplace, hair dryer, bathrobes, bath amenities and iron/ironing board in room. Fax, copier, library, pet boarding, parlor games, telephone, laundry facility, outdoor fire ring, country gardens, hammock and alpacas on premises. Antiquing, art galleries, bicycling, canoeing/kayaking, cross-country skiing, downhill skiing, fishing, golf, hiking, horseback riding, live theater, museums, parks, shopping, tennis, wineries, hot air ballooning and llama trekking nearby.

Location: Country, mountains. High desert.

Publicity: Yellow Brick Road, Denver Post, Los Angeles Times, San Francisco

Examiner, New York Times, Weekends for Two in the Southwest, Lonely Planet, New Mexico for Dummies and HGTV.

"The Adobe & Pines Inn warms your soul and your senses with traditional New Mexican decor, hospitality and comfort."

Certificate may be used: Anytime, Sunday-Thursday, not valid Christmas week.

Adobe and Stars B&B Inn

PO Box 2285
Taos, NM 87571
(575)776-2776 (800)211-7076 Fax:(575)776-2872
Internet: www.TaosAdobe.com
E-mail: jsalathiel@yahoo.com

Circa 1996. Sangre de Christo Mountains provide breathtaking views while staying at the Adobe and Stars Bed and Breakfast Inn located in Taos, New Mexico. It's a few minutes from either the historic Taos Plaza or the Taos Ski Valley slopes. The guest room decor complements the Southwestern adobe exterior. Kiva fireplaces, wood beam ceilings, hand-carved furnishings and artwork complete the look. Radiant heat floors, terra cotta tiles and a Jacuzzi tub or double shower are pleasant amenities. Several rooms boast a mountain or mesa view. Hearty country breakfasts include a changing daily entrée and homemade baked goods, fruit, juice and coffee served in the dining room or on the patio. Soak in the hot tub under a starry sky after rafting down the Rio Grande. Bike or hike in the national forest or ski local slopes. Shops, galleries and restaurants are nearby.

Innkeeper(s): Judy Salathiel. $95-205. 8 rooms with PB, 8 with FP, 5 with WP. Breakfast and snacks/refreshments included in rates. Types of meals: Full bkfst. Beds: KQ. Reading lamp, ceiling fan and telephone in room. VCR, fax, copier, library and fireplace on premises. Bicycling, cross-country skiing, downhill skiing, fishing, golf, hiking, horseback riding, museums, wineries, River rafting, Ballooning, Llama trekking and National Forest nearby.

Location: Mountains.

Certificate may be used: April 15-May 15; Nov. 3-21, subject to availabilty.

Indian Hills Inn

233 Paseo Del Pueblo Sur
Taos, NM 87571-4011
(575) 758-4293 (800) 444-2346 Fax:(575)758-1702
Internet: www.newmex.com/indianhillsinn
E-mail: IndianHills@newmex.com

Circa 1910. More than one acre of trees and lawns surround this traditional Southwest Pueblo-designed inn. It is just two blocks south of Taos Plaza in the historic district with galleries, museums, shops and restaurants. Enjoy the convenient location, best value, great service and friendly hospitality. Tour guides provide local travel info as well as for the mountain areas of North Central New Mexico. Relax in the courtyard by the Horno grill/firepit or swim in the fenced, solar-heated seasonal pool. The guest service area features vintage wooden hand-carved pieces. A vending and ice machine is in the lobby. Many of the inviting guest rooms boast gas log fireplaces and walls accented by Mary Silverwood matted prints. Some rooms are designated to allow pets and/or smoking. Start each day with a generous continental breakfast. Ask about discounted ski packages and other specials.

Innkeeper(s): John Slenes. $69-139. 55 rooms with PB, 30 with FP, 1 conference room. Breakfast and Continental breakfast included with all lodging except extremely low cost monthly rentals included in rates. Types of meals: Cont, Modest continental breakfast usually includes eggs, yogurt, bread, oatmeal, teas, coffee and and cocoa. Full grocery store across street.

Numerous eating and dining places within a couple blocks. Beds: KQ. Cable TV, telephone, desk, voice mail, some with fireplace, bath amenities, wireless Internet access, All rooms individual HVAC, single King rooms all include gas log fireplace and most rooms face over an acre of grass and tall trees in room. Air conditioning. Fax, swimming, laundry facility, gift shop, Guest BBQ in central courtyard, Generous free guest parking, seasonal (summer) solar heated swimming pool. On property: flower shop (Enchanted Florist), winter ski shop (Adventure Ski Shops) and summer white water rafting shop (Los Rios River Runners), yoga and massage studio (Santosha Yoga), SOMOS - Society of the Muse of the Southwest. Local bus stop (Chili Line) about 100 feet North. Ski shuttle (winters) stops at hotel. Smith's Grocery, Liquor and Deli store and gas station across the street on premises. Handicap access. Antiquing, art galleries, bicycling, canoeing/kayaking, cross-country skiing, downhill skiing, fishing, golf, hiking, horseback riding, live theater, museums, parks, shopping, tennis, wineries, Walking distance to all downtown sights - historic Taos Plaza, 70 art galleries, 100 shops, 6 museums. About 2 miles from World Heritage site, Taos Pueblo and their Taos Mountain Casino. Downhill skiing at Taos Ski Valley, Sipapu, Angel Fire and and Red River. Kit Carson National Forest and trails just a few miles distant. Viet Nam Veterans Memorial state park in Angel Fire is a must see nearby.

Location: City, mountains. Historic Taos Plaza district.

Certificate may be used: Monday-Thursday except Dec. 26-Jan. 1. Available some weekends, call.

The Historic Taos Inn

125 Paseo Del Pueblo Norte
Taos, NM 87571-5901
(575) 758-2233 (800) 826-7466 Fax:(575)758-5776
Internet: www.taosinn.com
E-mail: taosinn@newmex.com

Circa 1936. Voted by National Geographic Traveler as one of "America's 54 Great Inns", The Taos Inn is a historic landmark with sections dating back to the 1600s. The inn's authentic adobe pueblo architecture enhances the inviting wood-burning fireplaces (kivas), vigas and wrought iron accents. Handsomely decorated rooms include reflections of the area's exotic tri-cultural heritage of Spanish, Anglo and Indian in the hand-loomed Guatamalan Indian bedspreads, antique armoires and Taos furniture. The Doc Martin's well reviewed restaurant includes the legendary Adobe Bar. Ancient Taos Pueblo and the historic taos Plaza are nearby.

Innkeeper(s): Douglas Smith & Carolyn Haddock. $75-250. 44 rooms with PB, 3 with FP, 3 suites. Types of meals: Full gourmet bkfst, veg bkfst, early coffee/tea, gourmet lunch, snacks/refreshments and gourmet dinner. Restaurant on premises. Beds: KQDT. Cable TV, clock radio, telephone and voice mail in room. Air conditioning. VCR, fax, copier, fireplace, greenhouse, Jacuzzi, full bar (legendary margaritas) with live music seven nights per week and free wireless Internet on premises. Handicap access. Art galleries, bicycling, canoeing/kayaking, cross-country skiing, downhill skiing, fishing, golf, hiking, live theater, museums, parks, shopping and wineries nearby.

Location: Country, mountains.

Publicity: *Travel & Leisure, Gourmet, Bon Appetit, National Geographic Traveler, New York Times, Los Angeles Times, New Mexico Magazine, Inside Oustide Magazine and Wine Spectator Award - 18 years in a row.*

"It is charming, warm, friendly and authentic in decor with a real sense of history."

Certificate may be used: All year, Sunday-Thursday, subject to availability. Holiday period exclusions apply. Call for availablity and reservations.

Touchstone Inn, Spa & Gallery

110 Mabel Dodge Ln
Taos, NM 87571
(575) 779-1174
Internet: www.touchstoneinn.com
E-mail: touchstoneinn@gmail.com

Circa 1800. Touchstone Inn is a quiet, historic adobe estate secluded among tall trees at the edge of Taos Pueblo lands. The grounds have an unobstructed view of Taos Mountain. USA Today calls it "the place to stay in Taos." The inn, connected to a spa and a gallery, features cozy rooms with fireplaces, luxurious textiles, intimate patios and exquisite tiled baths (four of which have Jacuzzi tubs). The inn offers full gourmet vegetarian and continental breakfasts. The spa offers massages, yoga and art classes, facials and therapeutic baths and wraps. Guests enjoy the outdoor hot tub with choice vistas of Taos Mountain. Taos Ski valley is 18 miles to the north.

Innkeeper(s): Brad and Amber Gordon. $145-350. 9 rooms with PB, 3 with FP, 4 with WP, 1 suite, 1 conference room. Breakfast and snacks/refreshments included in rates. Types of meals: Full gourmet bkfst, We have vegetarian breakfasts available upon request. If you book a large party like a birthday bash, girls weekend away and or reunions then we can cater for you. Call us to ask our classically trained Chef for details. 575-779-8712. Beds: KQDT. Cable TV, VCR, DVD, reading lamp, stereo, refrigerator, ceiling fan, clock radio, coffeemaker, most with fireplace, hair dryer, bathrobes, bath amenities, Four rooms with Jacuzzi tubs and most rooms have small refrigerators and microwaves. The Inn has wi-fi available in the common areas and it works better in some rooms than in others in room. Sauna, library, telephone, Spa services available, piano, labyrinth and wireless internet access throughout building on premises. Antiquing, art galleries, bicycling, canoeing/kayaking, cross-country skiing, downhill skiing, fishing, golf, hiking, horseback riding, live theater, museums, parks, shopping, tennis, water sports, wineries and Opera nearby.

Location: City, mountains. Santa Fe, New Mexico.

Publicity: *USA Today, Bride's Magazine, Modern Bride, Mountain Living, Getaways, Mentioned in "Winter in Taos" by Mabel Dodge Luhan and subject of the book "Taos a Memory" by Miriam Hapgood Dewitt.*

Certificate may be used: Monday-Wednesday, November-April excluding holidays and fiestas. Subject to availability. Free night does not include breakfast. Not valid on Groups and Destination Spa Packages.

New York

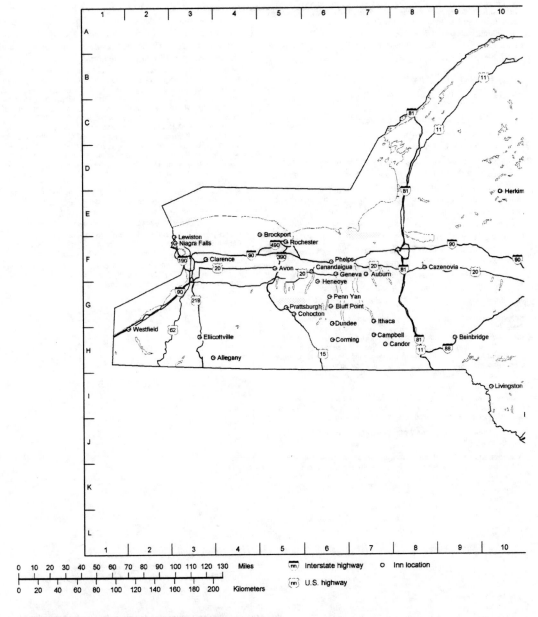

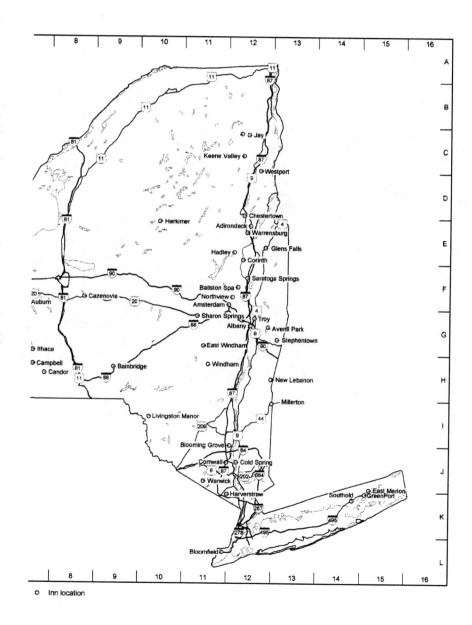

8 9 10 11 12 13 14 15 16

A
B
C
D
E
F
G
H
I
J
K
L

Jay
Keene Valley
Westport
Chestertown
Herkimer
Adirondack
Warrensburg
Hadley
Glens Falls
Corinth
Saratoga Springs
Ballston Spa
Northview
Amsterdam
Sharon Springs
Troy
Albany
Averill Park
Stephentown
East Windham
Windham
New Lebanon
Millerton
Livingston Manor
Blooming Grove
Cornwall
Cold Spring
Warwick
Harverstraw
Southold
East Marion
GreenPort
Bloomfield
Cazenovia
Auburn
Ithaca
Campbell
Candor
Bainbridge

○   Inn location

Adirondack   D12

Adirondack Pines Bed & Breakfast & Vacation Cabin's

1257 Valentine Road
Adirondack, NY 12808
(518)494-5249
Internet: www.adirondackpines.com
E-mail: stay@adirondackpines.com

Circa 1837. Surrounded by year-round scenic beauty, there is much to experience while staying at this historic 1837 Country Farmhouse, just two minutes from Schroon Lake's beach and boat launch. Relax in the living room with cable TV. Antiques and handmade quilts accent the pleasant décor of the air-conditioned guest bedrooms. The Master Suite boasts wide plank flooring, a refrigerator, gas stove and a two-person Jacuzzi tub. The spacious Balsam Room offers a Queen and a twin bed. A small room with a twin bed accommodates a fourth person. Linger over a candlelit country breakfast in the dining room by the wood stove. A private, newly renovated three-bedroom house with a gas fireplace is also available. Soak up nature while strolling the 100 acres of grounds. Ski nearby Gore Mountain or hike Pharaoh Mountain for breathtaking views.

Innkeeper(s): Dan & Nancy Lindsley-Freebern. $65-150. 3 rooms, 2 with PB, 1 with FP, 2 guest houses. Breakfast and snacks/refreshments included in rates. Types of meals: Country bkfst. Beds: KQDT. Cable TV, VCR, refrigerator, clock radio, coffeemaker, most with hot tub/spa, most with fireplace, hair dryer, wireless Internet access, iron/ironing board, two-person Jacuzzi tub and gas freestanding fireplace in room. Air conditioning. Fax, copier, parlor games and telephone on premises. Amusement parks, antiquing, art galleries, beach, bicycling, canoeing/kayaking, cross-country skiing, downhill skiing, fishing, golf, hiking, horseback riding, museums, shopping, tennis, water sports and wineries nearby.

Location: Country, mountains.

Certificate may be used: Sunday-Thursday, subject to availability.

Albany   G12

Pine Haven B&B

531 Western Ave
Albany, NY 12203-1721
(518)482-1574
Internet: www.pinehavenbedandbreakfast.com

This turn-of-the-century Victorian is located in Pine Hills, an Albany historic district. In keeping with this history, the innkeepers have tried to preserve the home's 19th-century charm. The rooms offer old-fashioned comfort with Victorian influences. The Capitol Building and other historic sites are nearby.

Innkeeper(s): Janice Tricarico. Call for rates. Call inn for details. Breakfast included in rates. Types of meals: Cont plus and early coffee/tea. Beds: QDT. Cable TV, reading lamp, clock radio, telephone and desk in room. Air conditioning. Parlor games, fireplace and free off-street parking on premises. Antiquing, cross-country skiing, live theater, parks, shopping and sporting events nearby.

Location: City.

Certificate may be used: Year-round, anytime, subject to availability.

Allegany   H3

Gallets House B&B

1759 Four Mile Rd
Allegany, NY 14706-9724
(716) 373-7493 Fax:(716)806-0384
Internet: www.galletshouse.com
E-mail: info@galletshouse.com

Circa 1896. Built by the innkeeper's great uncle Joseph Gallets, who was an oil producer, lumberman and farmer, this historic Victorian home features a third-floor museum with original family photos and heirlooms to browse through. Relax by the fireplaces in the parlor and common room. Enjoy refreshments on the 100-foot porch. Elegant air-conditioned guest bedrooms feature private baths and robes. Two rooms boast whirlpool tubs. Perfect for families and pets, the Carriage House Apartment has three bedrooms, two baths and a full kitchen. Fruits, homemade breads and biscuits are a prelude to sumptuous hot entrees and Joan's memorable French toast or apple cinnamon pancakes for breakfast in the formal dining room. The B&B is near ski resorts, Allegany State Park, St. Bonaventure University, golf courses and a main snowmobile trail. Ask about romance packages and monthly murder mysteries.

Innkeeper(s): Joan & Gary Boser & Cheri Stady. $79-140. 6 rooms with PB, 2 with FP, 2 with WP, 2 two-bedroom and 1 three-bedroom suites, 1 cottage, 3 guest houses, 1 conference room. Breakfast and snacks/refreshments included in rates. Types of meals: Full gourmet bkfst, veg bkfst, early coffee/tea, afternoon tea and Murder mystery dinner package. Beds: KQDT. Modem hook-up, data port, cable TV, VCR, DVD, reading lamp, CD player, ceiling fan, clock radio, telephone, coffeemaker, desk, some with hot tub/spa, hair dryer, bathrobes, bath amenities, wireless Internet access, iron/ironing board, two with whirlpool tub and wireless Internet connection in room. Air conditioning. Fax, copier, spa, parlor games, fireplace, laundry facility, gift shop and outdoor hot tub on premises. Limited handicap access. Antiquing, art galleries, bicycling, canoeing/kayaking, cross-country skiing, fishing, golf, hiking, horseback riding, live theater, museums, parks, shopping, sporting events, Allegany State Park, Seneca Allegany casino, Golfing, Skiing at Holiday Valley or HoliMont ski areas, Rock City Park and Pfeiffer Nature Center nearby.

Location: Country, mountains.

Publicity: Refresh and Refuel— Stay two nights Sunday to Thursday get the third night 1/2 off and Plus receive a $25 gas card.

Certificate may be used: Anytime, subject to availability.

Amsterdam   F12

Amsterdam Castle

49 Florida Avenue
Amsterdam, NY 12010
(518) 843-5201
Internet: www.amsterdamcastle.com
E-mail: events@amsterdamcastle.com

Circa 1894. Amsterdam Castle is truly a castle on a hill surrounded by two acres of grounds. Built by the state of New York in 1894 as an armory and now listed in the National Register, this red brick Victorian-Romanesque is accented by ivy climbing its walls and turrets. Living, reception and ballrooms are perfect for a variety of events. Relax in the Billiard Room or on the terrace. Recently renovated, the castle offers modern technology and spacious accommodations. Stay in a guest bedroom or suite with a fireplace and a clawfoot tub. Amsterdam is located just 30 miles from Albany, the state capital. Visit the scenic Mohawk Valley, Saratoga Springs and Fort Ticonderoga.

New York City is three hours away.

Innkeeper(s): Susan and Manfred Phemister. $175-225. 2 suites, 1 conference room. Breakfast included in rates. Types of meals: Full bkfst and 4 restaurants in walking distance for dinner. Beds: KQDT. Modern hook-up, cable TV, VCR, DVD, reading lamp, CD player, ceiling fan, coffeemaker, desk, hair dryer, bathrobes, bath amenities, wireless Internet access, iron/ironing board and mini-fridge and microwave available in billiard room in room. Air conditioning. Parlor games, fireplace, Billiard room and 10 and 000 sq ft. gymnasium on premise - shoot hoops or pool! on premises. Handicap access. Bicycling, fishing, golf, Erie Canalway (2 mins), Saratoga Springs, Cooperstown and Albany (all 30 minutes). Robert Trent Jones golf course. Delightful neighborhood Italian restaurants nearby.

Location: City, country.

Certificate may be used: January-April.

Halcyon Farm Bed & Breakfast

157 Lang Road
Amsterdam, NY 12010
(518)842-7718 (800)470-2170
E-mail: june@halcyonfarm.com

Circa 1800. Situated in historic Mill Point along the Schoharie River, this Federal brick home is surrounded by a peaceful country setting with 300 acres of spacious lawns, blooming perennials, hay fields, woods and the Blue Bank cliff. A living room and adjoining library boasts relaxed seating by the fire. Peach trees shade the private entrance to spacious guest bedrooms that include gas fireplaces. Full gourmet breakfasts may be a selection of the following: basil and vegetable strata, fresh-picked red raspberries and cream, portobello mushrooms with fresh sliced tomatoes and herbed scrambled eggs, homemade sage sausage, crispy parmesan potatoes, buttery currant scones, John's famous cornbread and June's renowned buttermilk blueberry pancakes. Fall is a wonderful time for hiking the cliff and old stagecoach trail behind the farm.

Innkeeper(s): June & John Leonard. $100-160. 5 rooms with PB, 5 with FP, 1 with WP. Breakfast and snacks/refreshments included in rates. Types of meals: Full gourmet bkfst, early coffee/tea and afternoon tea. Beds: KQT. Modern hook-up, TV, DVD, reading lamp, clock radio, desk, fireplace, hair dryer, bath amenities, wireless Internet access, iron/ironing board and Flatscreen TV with DVD player in all rooms in room. Air conditioning. Fax, copier, library, parlor games, telephone, Guest refrigerator, Piano, Aerobed for extra person, Free national calling on host phone and High speed Wireless Internet access on premises. Antiquing, cross-country skiing, fishing, golf, hiking, horseback riding and tennis nearby.

Location: Country. On Schoharie River. Five miles from Mohawk River.

Certificate may be used: Jan. 1 to March 31, Sunday-Thursday.

Auburn   H3

10 Fitch

10 Fitch Avenue
Auburn, NY 13021
(315)255-0934 Fax:(315)255-1660
Internet: www.10Fitch.com
E-mail: innkeeper@10Fitch.com

Circa 1920. 2009 Winner - Travelers' Choice for Romance. For a truly luxurious setting in the Finger Lakes region, stay at 10 Fitch, an elegant Colonial mansion built in 1920 and fully restored. A spacious yet intimate ambiance reflects upscale boutique accommodations at this bed and breakfast. Sitting rooms include the library, formal living room and sunroom. Guest bedrooms are professionally decorated with designer fabrics, original artwork, silk window treatments, Anichini sheeting, custom bedding, marble rain showers and Jacuzzi

tubs. There are five fireplaces. A delicious breakfast is flexible, perfect for sleeping in on a romantic getaway or for early risers on business. Relax in the gardens, some created by a Cornell landscaper. Visit the shops and historic sites of nearby Skaneateles, New York.

Innkeeper(s): Cheryl Barber. $200-330. 3 rooms, 3 with FP, 1 with WP, 3 suites. Breakfast and snacks/refreshments included in rates. Types of meals: Full bkfst, veg bkfst, early coffee/tea, picnic lunch, hors d'oeuvres, Breakfast in suite, romantic in-suite picnic dinner for two and picnic lunch basket. Beds: KQT. Cable TV, DVD, reading lamp, refrigerator, snack bar, clock radio, turn-down service, desk, fireplace, hair dryer, bathrobes, bath amenities, wireless Internet access, iron/ironing board, iPod docking stations, iPods with romantic music playlists, Turn down service with chocolate and Spa robes in room. Air conditioning. Fax, copier, library, parlor games, telephone, gift shop, Concierge, 24 hr hot/cold beverages and Endless homemade chocolate chip cookie jar on premises. Antiquing, art galleries, canoeing/kayaking, cross-country skiing, downhill skiing, fishing, golf, hiking, horseback riding, live theater, museums, parks, shopping, sporting events, tennis, water sports, wineries, Lake village of Skaneateles with an array of boutiques & shops, the Historic William Seward House (2 blocks), Harriet Tubman's House, Willard Memorial Chapel, Mackenzie Childs shop and Fort Hill Cemetery nearby.

Location: City. Finger Lakes, Skaneateles, Cayuga Wine Trail.

Publicity: *April 2010 Prize Package on Wheel Of Fortune February 2010 YNN News Rochester- Getaway Guy: Romantic Getaway February 2011 Prize Package on Wheel Of Fortune April 2011 Prize Package on Wheel Of Fortune.*

Certificate may be used: September-May, except holiday/special event weekends and weekends in September and October, Subject to availability, not valid with any other gift card, certificate, promo or offer.

Averill Park   G12

La Perla at the Gregory House, Country Inn & Restaurant

Rt 43 PO Box 401
Averill Park, NY 12018-0401
(518)674-3774 Fax:(518)674-8916
Internet: www.gregoryhouse.com
E-mail: innkeeper@gregoryhouse.com

Circa 1830. Stockbroker Elias Gregory built what is now the restaurant, as his Colonial home in the 1800s. The newer B&B inn, just twelve years old, blends well with the original house to retain the ambiance of its Victorian heritage. Gather by the dramatic fireplace in the common room which boasts vaulted ceilings, comfy furniture and a big-screen TV. The decor of each well-appointed guest bedroom is inviting. Award-winning La Perla offers Italian continental cuisine and is personally run by innkeeper Alfonso. This rural country town is surrounded by the Adirondacks, Berkshires, Hudson River, Saratoga and Albany with a variety of historic and scenic attractions.

Innkeeper(s): Anna Maria & Alfonso Acampora. $100-125. 12 rooms with PB, 1 conference room. Breakfast included in rates. Types of meals: Cont. Restaurant on premises. Beds: QDT. TV, reading lamp, clock radio, telephone and desk in room. Air conditioning. VCR, fax, copier and fireplace on premises. Amusement parks, antiquing, cross-country skiing, downhill skiing, fishing, live theater, parks, shopping, sporting events and water sports nearby.

Location: Village.

Publicity: *Hudson Valley, Albany Times Union, Schenectady Gazette, Courier and Sunday Record.*

"We experienced privacy and quiet, lovely surroundings indoors and out, excellent service and as much friendliness as we were comfortable with, but no more."

Certificate may be used: November-April, Sunday-Thursday.

Avon
F5

White Oak Bed and Breakfast

277 Genesee Street
Avon, NY 14414
(585)226-6735
Internet: whiteoakbandb.com
E-mail: avon-bnb@frontiernet.net

Circa 1860. Built as a summer home in the 1860s, this distinctive Second Empire Victorian with a mansard roof and wraparound porch has been recently renovated to retain its original charm and traditional decor. A private den/parlor with TV/VCR and board games is a convenient gathering place. Well-placed period furnishings accent the guest bedrooms and spacious Pine Suite. Enjoy the expansive view from the dining room while savoring home-baked breads, fresh fruit, and perhaps a broccoli cheddar omelette with home fries and bacon for breakfast. The one acre of gardens, with flowers for every season, include private sitting areas to chat. Visit nearby Genesee Country Village, a living history village or take day trips to explore the scenic Finger Lakes Region.

Innkeeper(s): Barbara Herman. $105-125. 3 rooms with PB. Breakfast and snacks/refreshments included in rates. Types of meals: Country bkfst, veg bkfst, early coffee/tea and picnic lunch. Beds: QD. Reading lamp, turn-down service, desk and wireless Internet access in room. Air conditioning. TV, VCR, DVD, library, parlor games, telephone, laundry facility and gift shop on premises. Antiquing, art galleries, bicycling, canoeing/kayaking, fishing, golf, hiking, horseback riding, live theater, museums, parks, shopping and wineries nearby.
Location: Country. Close to N.Y. S.Letchworth Park, Rochester, Geneseo.
Certificate may be used: Nov. 1-April 30, subject to availability.

Bainbridge
H9

Berry Hill Gardens B&B

242 Ward Loomis Rd.
Bainbridge, NY 13733
(607)967-8745 (800)497-8745 Fax:(607)967-2227
Internet: www.berryhillgardens.com
E-mail: info@berryhillgardens.com

Circa 1820. Located off the beaten path on a secluded lane, this country bed and breakfast graces the heart of Central New York. Two different B&B experiences are offered on 300 acres of

gardens, lakes, ponds, woods and meadows. Berry Hill Gardens Inn is situated on a hilltop overlooking miles of rural beauty; the Buckthorn Lodge is poised in a sunny glen deep in the woods. Find comfortable antiques, fireplaces and all-natural luxury linens. Delicious breakfasts are served in a friendly, healthy informal atmosphere. Conveniently centered between Bainbridge, Afton and Oxford, the scenic Leatherstocking Region features museums, sporting facilities, artisans and fascinating history.

Innkeeper(s): Jean Fowler. $115-190. 8 rooms with PB, 3 with FP, 1 guest house. Breakfast and snacks/refreshments included in rates. Types of meals: Country bkfst and early coffee/tea. Beds: KQDT. Reading lamp, ceiling fan, clock radio, desk, hair dryer, bathrobes, bath amenities, wireless Internet access and iron/ironing board in room. TV, VCR, DVD, fax, copier, swimming, library, parlor games, telephone, fireplace, Guest kitchen with refrigerator, microwave, sink & dishes provided in general area, Picnic area, Gas grill & Full

kitchen and all amenities provided at lodge on premises. Antiquing, art galleries, bicycling, canoeing/kayaking, cross-country skiing, downhill skiing, fishing, golf, hiking, horseback riding, live theater, museums, parks, shopping, sporting events, tennis, water sports, wineries and Downhill Skiing is Available at Greek Peak about 45 minutes away. Cross county skiing onsite nearby.
Location: Country.
Publicity: *Country Living Gardener Magazine (August 2001), Binghamton Press and Sun, People and Places and Plants Magazine (Autumn 2006).*

"The house is just wonderful and our rooms were exceptionally comfortable."

Certificate may be used: Jan. 2-April 30, anytime. May 1-Dec. 20, Sunday through Thursday only. Holidays and special events excluded.

Ballston Spa
F12

Medbery Inn & Spa

48 Front Street
Ballston Spa, NY 12020
(518)-885-SPAS7727
Internet: www.medberyinnandspa.com
E-mail: relax@medberyinnandspa.com

Circa 1878. Indulge in the rejuvenating effects of this feng shui boutique hotel and historic destination spa with relaxing

accommodations, natural mineral waters and a full-service spa menu. Luxuriously furnished for the casual and business traveler, choose a candlelit deluxe guest bedroom, or mini-suite with whirlpool tub, body shower and fireplace. Enjoy the complete line from Stonewall Kitchens and refreshing L?Erbolario fragrances. Savor a dazzling breakfast served daily in the Sans Souci Room. Getaway and spa packages are available. A coordinator will provide assistance in planning and catering special events.

Innkeeper(s): Dolores & Jim Taisey. $125-299. 10 rooms with PB, 3 with FP, 3 with WP, 3 suites, 1 conference room. Breakfast included in rates. Types of meals: Full bkfst and early coffee/tea. Beds: Q. Data port, cable TV, VCR, DVD, reading lamp, CD player, refrigerator, clock radio, telephone, coffeemaker, desk, some with hot tub/spa, some with fireplace, hair dryer, bathrobes, bath amenities, wireless Internet access and iron/ironing board in room. Central air. Spa, parlor games and gift shop on premises. Handicap access. Amusement parks, antiquing, art galleries, beach, bicycling, canoeing/kayaking, cross-country skiing, downhill skiing, fishing, golf, hiking, horseback riding, live theater, museums, parks, shopping, sporting events, tennis, water sports, wineries, Saratoga Horse Racing and Saratoga Gaming and Racino nearby.
Location: Village (Historic District).
Publicity: *Country Folk Art Magazine.*
Certificate may be used: Sunday-Thursday, January-April.

Bloomfield
L11

Abner Adams House Bed and Breakfast

2 Howard Ave.
Bloomfield, NY 14469
(585) 657-4681 (888) 657-4682
Internet: www.abneradamshouse.com
E-mail: innkeeper@abneradamshouse.com

Circa 1810. Three scenic acres surround historic Abner Adams House Bed and Breakfast in Bloomfield. This upstate New York B&B sits in the Finger Lakes region near Canandaigua and Rochester, amid the wine trails. Take a nap in the hammock under a shade tree, sit on a rocker on the screened porch or walk along wooded trails with inviting benches. Comfortable furniture, books, games and movies are enjoyed in the Keeping Room with original beehive oven. The dining room features a guest amenity cabinet with utensils, microwave, snacks and refrigerator stocked with beverages. Select a guest room with amenities that may include a fireplace, sitting area, balcony overlooking the gardens and a balneotherapy or champagne massage clawfoot tub for two. Indulge in a hearty country breakfast each morning.

Innkeeper(s): Bob and Lynda Dobberstein. $159-179. 3 rooms with PB, 3 with FP, 2 with WP, 1 two-bedroom suite. Breakfast and snacks/refreshments included in rates. Types of meals: Country bkfst, veg bkfst, early coffee/tea, Lactose free and gluten free and vegetarian available upon request. Beds: KQDT. Cable TV, VCR, DVD, reading lamp, stereo, refrigerator, ceiling fan, clock radio, turn-down service, desk, fireplace, hair dryer, bathrobes, bath amenities, wireless Internet access, iron/ironing board, Amenity cabinet with complimentary beverages and snacks in room. Central air. Fax, copier and parlor games on premises. Antiquing, art galleries, beach, bicycling, canoeing/kayaking, cross-country skiing, downhill skiing, fishing, golf, hiking, horseback riding, live theater, museums, parks, shopping, sporting events, water sports, wineries, Alpaca Farm and Erie Canal nearby.

Location: City, country.

Certificate may be used: Anytime, November-April, subject to availability, excludes holidays.

Blooming Grove   J12

The Dominion House
50 Old Dominion Road
Blooming Grove, NY 10914
(845)496-1826 Fax:(845)496-3492
Internet: www.thedominionhouse.com
E-mail: kathy@thedominionhouse.com

Circa 1880. At the end of a country lane in the scenic Hudson Valley, this Victorian Farmhouse has been adorning four-and-a-half acres since 1880. Original marble mantels, ornate cornice work, wide-plank floors, large pocket doors and eleven-foot ceilings with plaster medallions reflect a well-maintained elegance. The library offers a large book selection or relax by the fire in the oak den. Play a game of pool on the slate-top table and listen to music in the parlor. Large guest bedrooms and a private Honeymoon Cottage are furnished with antiques. A hearty breakfast is served in the dining room with specialty dishes that may include caramel sticky buns, featherlight scones, stuffed croissants, peach French toast and sausage. Swim in the inground pool, play horseshoes or relax on the wraparound porch.

Innkeeper(s): Kathy & Joe Spear. $125-199. 4 rooms, 1 with PB, 1 cottage. Breakfast and snacks/refreshments included in rates. Types of meals: Country bkfst and early coffee/tea. Beds: QT. Modem hook-up, cable TV, reading lamp, clock radio, telephone and robes in room. Air conditioning. Fax, copier, spa, swimming, library, parlor games, fireplace, slate-top pool table, horseshoes, guest refrigerator and complimentary snacks and drinks on premises. Antiquing, art galleries, canoeing/kayaking, cross-country skiing, downhill skiing, fishing, golf, hiking, live theater, museums, parks, shopping and wineries nearby.

Location: Country.

Certificate may be used: Sunday-Thursday, November-April, subject to availability. Excludes holidays.

Brockport   E5

The Victorian B&B
320 S Main St
Brockport, NY 14420-2253
(585)637-7519 Fax:(585)637-7519
Internet: www.victorianbandb.com
E-mail: sk320@aol.com

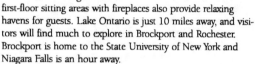

Circa 1889. Within walking distance of the historic Erie Canal, this Queen Anne Victorian inn is located on Brockport's Main Street. Visitors select from five second-floor guest rooms, all with phones, private baths and TVs. Victorian furnishings are found throughout the inn. A favorite spot is the solarium, with its three walls of windows and fireplace, perfect for curling up with a book or magazine. Two first-floor sitting areas with fireplaces also provide relaxing havens for guests. Lake Ontario is just 10 miles away, and visitors will find much to explore in Brockport and Rochester. Brockport is home to the State University of New York and Niagara Falls is an hour away.

Innkeeper(s): Sharon Kehoe. $79-150. 5 rooms with PB. Breakfast and afternoon tea included in rates. Types of meals: Country bkfst, veg bkfst and early coffee/tea. Beds: KQT. Cable TV, reading lamp, clock radio, telephone, desk, hair dryer, bath amenities, wireless Internet access and flower arrangements and/or gift baskets by special arrangement in room. Central air. VCR, fax, library, parlor games, fireplace, iron/ironing board and free off-road parking on premises. Amusement parks, antiquing, art galleries, beach, bicycling, canoeing/kayaking, cross-country skiing, downhill skiing, fishing, golf, hiking, horseback riding, live theater, museums, parks, shopping, sporting events, tennis, water sports, wineries, farmers market and movie theater nearby.

Location: Village, Erie Canal.

Certificate may be used: Oct. 1 to April 30, no holidays and special events.

Canandaigua   F6

1792 Filigree Inn
5406 Bristol Valley Rd.(RT.64S.)
Canandaigua, NY 14424
(585)229-5460 (888)560-7614 Fax:(585)229-4487
Internet: www.filigreeinn.com
E-mail: filigree@filigreeinn.com

Circa 1792. Escape to 1792 Filigree Inn, a four-season country retreat in the Finger Lakes wine country region of New York. Relax on 180 breathtaking acres in Bristol Hills of Canandaigua. Renovated guest suites boast air-conditioned comfort, feather beds, whirlpool tubs, fully equipped kitchens, entertainment centers and a private deck. Each refrigerator is stocked with breakfast foods to enjoy when desired. Ski and snowboard at local Bristol Mountain Resort or try cross-county trails at the nearby Cumming Nature Center. Weddings are popular at this bed and breakfast amid a gorgeous setting and a peaceful ambiance. Ask about special promotions and packages available.

Innkeeper(s): Don & Connie Simmons. $100-180. 8 rooms with PB, 8 with FP, 8 with WP, 4 two-bedroom suites. Breakfast and snacks/refreshments included in rates. Types of meals: Full bkfst. Beds: KQ. Modem hook-up, cable TV, VCR, reading lamp, stereo, refrigerator, snack bar, clock radio, telephone, coffeemaker, fireplace, hair dryer, bath amenities, iron/ironing board, Full kitchens, private decks, dining areas and Jacuzzi tubs in room. Central air. Fax, copier, Hiking trails and snowmobile trails on premises. Limited handicap access. Amusement parks, antiquing, art galleries, beach, bicycling, canoeing/kayaking, cross-country skiing, downhill skiing, fishing, golf, hiking, horseback riding, live theater, museums, parks, shopping, tennis, water sports, wineries, Wine and Culinary Center nearby.

Location: Country, mountains.

Certificate may be used: Sunday-Thursday only, subject to availability.

1840 Inn on the Main

176 N. Main Street
Canandaigua, NY 14424
(585)394-0139 (877)659-1643
Internet: www.innonthemain.com
E-mail: questions@innonthemain.com

Circa 1840. Gracing one acre in the scenic Finger Lakes region of Upstate New York in the historic district of Canandaigua, 1840 Inn on the Main is a renovated Victorian known as The Alfred Morris Gifford House. Relax on period furnishings in the foyer or antique wicker on the porch. Indulge in fresh baked goods and hot coffee or tea in the parlor. The upstairs sitting area features a nonalcoholic beverage bar with a guest refrigerator. Select an inviting guest bedroom with a Jacuzzi, clawfoot or soaking tub and/or a fireplace. The two-bedroom suite boasts a full kitchen, a DVD/VCR and CD player. Savor a delicious breakfast in the fireside dining room. Explore the local wineries, swim in Canandaigua Lake and browse through quaint shops. Ask about available specials.

Innkeeper(s): Jaynee and Guy Straw. $145-210. 4 rooms with PB, 3 with FP, 2 with WP, 1 two-bedroom suite. Breakfast and snacks/refreshments included in rates. Types of meals: Full gourmet bkfst, early coffee/tea and Early/late continental breakfast available upon request. Beds: KQT. Cable TV, DVD, reading lamp, CD player, ceiling fan, clock radio, turn-down service, some with hot tub/spa, most with fireplace, hair dryer, bath amenities, wireless Internet access and Turn down service available upon request in room. Central air. Fax, copier, parlor games, telephone, Non-alcoholic beverage bar available in guest area outside rooms with shared refrigerator, Coffee, Tea, Fresh baked goods available throughout the late afternoon and evening in dining room on premises. Amusement parks, antiquing, art galleries, beach, bicycling, canoeing/kayaking, cross-country skiing, downhill skiing, fishing, golf, hiking, horseback riding, live theater, museums, parks, shopping, tennis, water sports and wineries nearby.

Location: City. Historic District, 1/2 hr. from Rochester.

Certificate may be used: November-April, Sunday-Thursday, subject to availability. Fridays and Saturdays last minute within 2 days before stay, subject to availability. Holidays and holiday weekends excluded.

Bed & Breakfast at Oliver Phelps

252 N Main St
Canandaigua, NY 14424-1220
(585)396-1650 (800)926-1830
Internet: www.oliverphelps.com
E-mail: oliverphelpsbb@aol.com

Circa 1812. Century-old chestnut trees frame this historic Federal-style inn, which has offered elegant accommodations to Finger Lakes visitors since 1986. Gracing Main Street in Canandaigua, New York this B&B features arched entryways, handsome fireplaces and chestnut plank flooring that reflect a time of grace and simplicity. Romantic and spacious guest bedrooms boast poster beds, period antiques and luxurious amenities. Savor a candlelight gourmet breakfast each morning. The surrounding area is filled with attractions for every season and every interest, including winery tours, winter and summer sports, antiquing, shopping, biking and hiking.

Innkeeper(s): Jack & Donna Delehanty. $125-180. 5 rooms with PB, 2 with FP, 1 suite, 1 conference room. Breakfast, afternoon tea and snacks/refreshments included in rates. Types of meals: Full gourmet bkfst, veg bkfst, early

coffee/tea and picnic lunch. Beds: KQD. Cable TV, VCR, DVD, reading lamp, clock radio, turn-down service, desk, hot tub/spa, hair dryer, bathrobes, bath amenities and wireless Internet access in room. Central air. Copier, spa, bicycles, library, parlor games, telephone and fireplace on premises. Amusement parks, antiquing, art galleries, beach, bicycling, canoeing/kayaking, cross-country skiing, downhill skiing, fishing, golf, hiking, horseback riding, live theater, museums, parks, shopping, tennis, water sports and wineries nearby.

Location: City. Sonnenberg Garden, Granger Homestead.

Certificate may be used: Sunday-Thursday, September-May, excludes holidays.

Morgan Samuels B&B Inn

2920 Smith Rd
Canandaigua, NY 14424-9558
(585)394-9232
Internet: www.morgansamuelsinn.com
E-mail: morsambb@aol.com

Circa 1812. A luxurious Victorian estate on 46 acres of peaceful countryside, this inn offers elegance and comfort. Fireplaces, floor to ceiling windows, museum-quality furnishings, stained glass, and wide plank floors are delightful features found in both common and private areas. The guest bedrooms boast French doors leading to balconies that overlook landscaped gardens, fountains and a tennis court, or have a private entrance with an ivy-covered archway. Candlelight and soft music accentuate a lavish gourmet breakfast served in the formal dining room, intimate tea room or glass-enclosed stone porch. Afternoon tea and appetizers are welcome treats.

Innkeeper(s): Brad & Connie Smith. $129-295. 6 rooms with PB, 4 with FP, 3 with WP, 1 suite, 1 conference room. Breakfast and afternoon tea included in rates. Types of meals: Full gourmet bkfst, early coffee/tea, hors d'oeuvres, Gourmet dinner on a pre fixed basis and Afternoon Tea is available upon request. Beds: KQ. Reading lamp, CD player, clock radio, turn-down service, hair dryer, bathrobes, bath amenities, Two rooms have refrigerator and Two rooms have ceiling fans in room. Central air. TV, VCR, DVD, fax, copier, spa, tennis, library, parlor games, telephone, fireplace and gift shop on premises. Antiquing, art galleries, beach, bicycling, canoeing/kayaking, cross-country skiing, downhill skiing, fishing, golf, hiking, horseback riding, live theater, museums, parks, shopping, sporting events, water sports, wineries, Sonnenburg Gardens, Cumming Nature Center, horse racing and Eastman House nearby.

Location: Country.

Certificate may be used: May 1-Nov. 1, Sunday-Thursday only and November -May, anytime.

Candor   H7

The Edge of Thyme, A B&B Inn

6 Main St
Candor, NY 13743-0048
(607)659-5155 (800)722-7365 Fax:(607)659-5155
Internet: www.edgeofthyme.com
E-mail: innthyme@twcny.rr.com

Circa 1840. Originally the summer home of John D. Rockefeller's secretary, this two-story Georgian-style inn offers  gracious accommodations a short drive from Ithaca. The inn sports many interesting features, including an impressive stairway, marble fireplaces, parquet floors, pergola (arbor) and windowed porch with leaded glass. Guests may relax in front of the inn's fireplace, catch up with reading in its library or watch television in the sitting room. An authentic turn-of-the-century full breakfast is served, and guests also may arrange for special high teas.

Innkeeper(s): Prof. Frank & Eva Mae Musgrave. $95-145. 5 rooms, 3 with PB, 2 suites. Breakfast included in rates. Types of meals: Full gourmet bkfst, veg bkfst, early coffee/tea and High Tea by appointment. Beds: KQDT. Reading lamp, ceiling fan, clock radio and desk in room. Air conditioning. TV, VCR, fax, library, child care, parlor games, telephone, fireplace, gift shop and high tea by appointment on premises. Antiquing, art galleries, cross-country skiing, downhill skiing, fishing, golf, hiking, horseback riding, live theater, museums, parks, shopping, sporting events and wineries nearby.

Location: Village.

Publicity: *Historic Inns of the Northeast, 17 newspapers across the US by a freelance writer concentrating on the Finger Lakes, The Ithaca Journal, The Press and Sun Bullitan.*

Certificate may be used: Sunday-Thursday. Not valid in May, excluding specific weekends, Anytime, Last Minute-Based on Availability.

Cazenovia F8

Brae Loch Inn

5 Albany St
Cazenovia, NY 13035-1403
(315)655-3431 Fax:(315)655-4844
Internet: www.braelochinn.com
E-mail: braeloch1@aol.com

Circa 1805. Hunter green awnings accentuate the attractive architecture of the Brae Loch. Since 1946 the inn has been owned and operated by the same family. A Scottish theme is evident throughout, including in the inn's restaurant. Four of the oldest rooms have fireplaces (non-working). Stickley, Harden and antique furniture add to the old-world atmosphere, and many rooms offer canopy beds. Guest rooms are on the second floor above the restaurant.

Innkeeper(s): Jim & Val Barr. $85-155. 12 rooms with PB, 3 with FP, 3 with WP, 1 conference room. Breakfast and You can have a getaway package that includes dinner or brunch included in rates. Types of meals: Cont, Sun. brunch, wine and gourmet dinner. Restaurant on premises. Beds: KQDT. Cable TV, reading lamp, clock radio, telephone, coffeemaker, desk, hair dryer, wireless Internet access, iron/ironing board and All with Tempur-Pedic mattresses in room. Air conditioning. VCR, fax, copier, child care, parlor games, fireplace and gift shop on premises. Antiquing, art galleries, beach, bicycling, cross-country skiing, downhill skiing, fishing, golf, hiking, horseback riding, live theater, museums, parks, shopping, sporting events, tennis, water sports, wineries and swimming just across the street at a public beach nearby.

Location: Small village by lake.

Publicity: *The Globe and Mail, Traveler Magazine and CNY.*

"Everything was just perfect. The Brae Loch and staff make you feel as if you were at home."

Certificate may be used: Sunday-Thursday.

Clarence F3

Asa Ransom House

10529 Main St
Clarence, NY 14031-1684
(716)759-2315 (800)841-2340 Fax:(716)759-2791
Internet: www.asaransom.com
E-mail: innfo@asaransom.com

Circa 1853. Set on spacious lawns, behind a white picket fence, the Asa Ransom House rests on the site of the first grist mill built in Erie County. Silversmith Asa Ransom constructed

an inn and grist mill here in response to the Holland Land Company's offering of free land to anyone who would start and operate a tavern. A specialty of the dining room is "Veal Perrott" and "Pistachio Banana Muffins."

Innkeeper(s): Robert & Abigail Lenz. $120-185. 10 rooms with PB, 9 with FP, 2 with WP, 2 two-bedroom suites, 1 conference room. Breakfast included in rates. Types of meals: Full gourmet bkfst, early coffee/tea, lunch, afternoon tea, snacks/refreshments, wine and dinner. Restaurant on premises. Beds: KQT. Modem hook-up, data port, cable TV, VCR, DVD, reading lamp, stereo, refrigerator, snack bar, clock radio, telephone, coffeemaker, turn-down service, desk, hair dryer, bathrobes, bath amenities, wireless Internet access, iron/ironing board, some with porch or balcony, old-time radio tapes and some with heated towel bars. Cheese & fruit bowl in room upon arrival in room. Air conditioning. Fax, copier, bicycles, library, parlor games, fireplace, gift shop, Herb and flower gardens on premises. Handicap access. Amusement parks, antiquing, art galleries, bicycling, cross-country skiing, golf, hiking, live theater, museums, parks, shopping, tennis and wineries nearby.

Location: Village.

Publicity: *Toronto Star, Buffalo News, Prevention Magazine, Country Living, Country Inns, Buffalo Spree and Inn Country USA.*

"Popular spot keeps getting better."

Certificate may be used: March-June, September-Dec. 15, Sunday-Thursday.

Cold Spring J12

Pig Hill Inn

73 Main St
Cold Spring, NY 10516-3014
(845) 265-9247 Fax:(845)265-9154
Internet: www.pighillinn.com
E-mail: pighillinn@aol.com

Circa 1808. The antiques at this stately three-story inn can be purchased, and they range from Chippendale to chinoiserie style. Rooms feature formal English and Adirondack decor with special touches such as four-poster or brass beds, painted rockers and, of course, pigs. The delicious breakfasts can be shared with guests in the Victorian conservatory dining room or a tri-level garden, or it may be served in the privacy of your room. The inn is about an hour out of New York City, and the train station is only two blocks away.

Innkeeper(s): David Vitanza. $150-250. 9 rooms with PB, 6 with FP, 2 with WP, 1 conference room. Breakfast, afternoon tea and Refreshments or

Afternoon Tea included in rates. Types of meals: Full gourmet bkfst, wine and room service. Beds: KQDT. Modem hook-up, reading lamp, ceiling fan, clock radio, some with hot tub/spa, most with fireplace, hair dryer, bathrobes, bath amenities, wireless Internet access, iron/ironing board and Telephone available in room. Central air. TV, fax, copier, spa, library, parlor games, telephone, gift shop and wireless high-speed Internet on premises. Handicap access. Antiquing, art galleries, beach, bicycling, canoeing/kayaking, cross-country skiing, fishing, golf, hiking, horseback riding, live theater, museums, parks, shopping, sporting events, tennis, water sports, wineries and great restaurants nearby.

Location: Country, mountains. Small Hudson River town.

Publicity: *National Geographic, Woman's Home Journal, Country Inns and Getaways for Gourmets.*

"Some of our fondest memories of New York were at Pig Hill."

Certificate may be used: Monday-Thursday, Nov. 1-April 30, excluding holidays.

Corinth   E12

Agape Farm B&B and Paintball

4839 Rt 9N
Corinth, NY 12822-1704
(518)654-7777 Fax:(518)654-7777
Internet: www.geocities.com/agapefarm
E-mail: agapefarmbnb@adelphia.net

Circa 1870. Amid 33 acres of fields and woods, this Adirondack farmhouse is home to chickens and horses, as well as guests seeking a refreshing getaway. Visitors have their choice of six guest rooms, all with ceiling fans, phones, private baths and views of the tranquil surroundings. The inn's wraparound porch lures many visitors, who often enjoy a glass of icy lemonade. Homemade breads, jams, jellies and muffins are part of the full breakfast served here, and guests are welcome to pick berries or gather a ripe tomato from the garden. A trout-filled stream on the grounds flows to the Hudson River, a mile away.

Innkeeper(s): Fred & Sigrid Koch. $120-150. 3 rooms with PB, 1 conference room. Breakfast and snacks/refreshments included in rates. Types of meals: Full gourmet bkfst, veg bkfst and early coffee/tea. Beds: KQDT. Reading lamp, ceiling fan, clock radio, telephone and desk in room. TV, VCR, fax, swimming, child care, parlor games, laundry facility and downstairs HC room and bath on premises. Handicap access. Amusement parks, antiquing, art galleries, beach, bicycling, canoeing/kayaking, cross-country skiing, downhill skiing, fishing, golf, hiking, horseback riding, museums, parks, shopping, sporting events, tennis and water sports nearby.

Location: Country. Saratoga Region.

"Clean and impeccable, we were treated royally."

Certificate may be used: Sept. 15-June 1, no holidays, premium rooms.

Corning   H6

Rosewood Inn

134 E 1st St
Corning, NY 14830-2711
(607)962-3253
Internet: www.rosewoodinn.com
E-mail: stay@rosewoodinn.com

Circa 1855. Rosewood Inn was originally built as a Greek Revival house. In 1917, the interior and exterior were remodeled in an English Tudor style. Original black walnut and oak woodwork grace the interior, decorated with authentic wallpapers, period draperies and fine antiques. It is within walking distance to historic, restored Market Street and museums.

Innkeeper(s): Stewart & Suzanne Sanders. $99-209. 7 rooms with PB, 2 suites. Breakfast and afternoon tea included in rates. Types of meals: Full bkfst. Beds: QDT. Wireless Internet access, Ground floor suites with Refrigerator, Television, Private entrance; Second Floor Sitting Room with Television, Refrigerator, Hair dryer, Iron/Ironing Board and Board games in room. Air conditioning. TV, parlor games, telephone and fireplace on premises. Antiquing, fishing, hiking, museums and wineries nearby.

Location: City.

Publicity: Syracuse Herald-Journal, New York Times, National Geographic Traveler, Wonderful Hotels and Inns and Innroads.

"Rosewood Inn is food for the soul! You both made us feel like friends instead of guests. We'll be back!"

Certificate may be used: Anytime, November-March, subject to availability. Not honored on holiday weekends.

Cornwall   J12

Cromwell Manor Inn B&B

174 Angola Rd
Cornwall, NY 12518
(845)534-7136
Internet: www.cromwellmanor.com
E-mail: cmi@hvc.rr.com

Circa 1820. Listed in the National Register of Historic Places, this stunning Greek Revival mansion sits on seven lush acres with scenic Hudson Valley views. It is elegantly furnished with period antiques and fine reproductions. The Chimneys Cottage, built in 1764, features romantic bedrooms with a more rustic colonial decor. Awaken to the aroma of a gourmet breakfast served in the country dining room or outside veranda. More than 4,000 acres of hiking trails are steps from the front door. Arrange for a picnic or enjoy a fireside massage. Nap in the hammock, sip wine on the patio next to the classic fountain and watch the sunset from the rear lawn. The farm next door offers unique gifts and treats. Each season has plenty to explore.

Innkeeper(s): Jack. $165-380. 13 rooms, 12 with PB, 7 with FP, 3 total suites, including 1 two-bedroom suite, 1 conference room. Breakfast and afternoon tea included in rates. Types of meals: Full gourmet bkfst, early coffee/tea, picnic lunch, snacks/refreshments and room service. Beds: KQDT. Reading lamp, CD player, snack bar, clock radio, turn-down service, desk, some with hot tub/spa, most with fireplace, hair dryer, bathrobes, wireless Internet access and iron/ironing board in room. Central air. TV, VCR, fax, copier, parlor games, telephone, refrigerator and coffee maker on premises. Limited handicap access. Antiquing, art galleries, bicycling, canoeing/kayaking, cross-country skiing, downhill skiing, fishing, golf, hiking, horseback riding, live theater, museums, parks, shopping, sporting events, tennis, water sports, wineries, Hudson Valley Mansions, Woodbury Common Premium Outlets, Storm King Art Center, Renaissance Festival, West Point sports and mountain biking nearby.

Location: Country, mountains. Hudson River Valley.

Publicity: USA Today, New York Times, Wall Street Journal, Fox, CBS Early Show and Top 10 Inns of NY.

Certificate may be used: Anytime, Sunday-Thursday, subject to availability, holidays excluded.

Dundee   G6

Sunrise Landing B&B

4986 Apple Road Extension
Dundee, NY 14837
(607)243-7548 (866)670-5253
Internet: www.sunriselandingbb.com
E-mail: relax@sunriselandingbb.com

Circa 2004. Poised on a wooded hillside on the west shore of Seneca Lake in Dundee, Sunrise Landing Bed & Breakfast is a perfect upstate New York getaway. A large dock, paddle boat and canoe make it easy to fully enjoy the scenic surroundings. Locally handcrafted furnishings and family heirlooms accent the contemporary architecture of this small country inn. Relax on a deck or patio or sit by the fire in the great room. Stay in one of the spacious guest suites that may feature a private balcony or patio, kitchen or mini-fridge stocked with beverages and snacks. Linger over a satisfying breakfast in the garden-view dining room. This Finger Lakes B&B is located on the wine trail with easy access to many local events and activities.

Innkeeper(s): Robert & Barbara Schiesser. $150-215. 3 rooms, 1 with FP, 3 suites. Full gourmet breakfast and Homemade cookies every afternoon included in rates. Beds: Q. Modem hook-up, data port, cable TV, VCR, DVD, reading lamp, CD player, refrigerator, ceiling fan, snack bar, clock radio, telephone, turn-down service, desk, some with fireplace, hair dryer, bathrobes, bath amenities, wireless Internet access, iron/ironing board, One suite has private entrance & private patio overlooking the lake and another suite has private balcony overlooking the lake in room. Central air. Fax, copier, swimming, bicycles, library and parlor games on premises. Art galleries, beach, bicycling, canoeing/kayaking, cross-country skiing, fishing, golf, hiking, horseback riding, live theater, museums, parks, shopping, tennis, water sports and wineries nearby.

Location: Country, waterfront.

Certificate may be used: March and November, Monday-Thursday in the Rose or Morning Glory Suite.

East Marion   J15

Arbor View House B&B

8900 Main Road
East Marion, NY 11939-0226
(631)477-8440 (800)963-8777
Internet: www.Arborviewhouse.com
E-mail: wjoseph@earthlink.net

Circa 1820. Elegant and romantic in Long Island's North Fork Wine Country, this bed and breakfast was originally built with Federal architecture and was later renovated with Victorian design. Relax with afternoon tea and refreshments or sit by the fireplace with a good book. Luxurious guest bedrooms offer an assortment of pleasing amenities that include bottles of spring water, plush robes, entertainment centers and other comforts. Indulge in the spacious Champagne Suite with a whirlpool bath. An optional private deck can be reserved. The Merlot Room boasts a cast iron tub. A four-course brunch-style breakfast is served by candlelight in the formal dining room or al fresco when weather permits. Walk to the beach, tour a local winery or schedule a massage from an extensive spa services menu.

Innkeeper(s): Veda Daley Joseph & Wilfred Joseph. $195-325. 4 rooms with PB, 2 with WP, 1 suite. Breakfast, Sunday brunch, afternoon tea, snacks/refreshments and hors d'oeuvres included in rates. Types of meals: Full gourmet bkfst, early coffee/tea and picnic lunch. Beds: KQ. Modem hook-up, data port, cable TV, VCR, DVD, reading lamp, stereo, refrigerator, ceiling fan, clock radio, turn-down service, desk, some with hot tub/spa, some with fireplace, hair dryer, bathrobes, bath amenities, wireless Internet access, iron/ironing board, Flat Panel TV and IPod Dock in room. Air conditioning. Fax, copier, library, parlor games, telephone and Wireless Internet on premises. Limited handicap access. Amusement parks, antiquing, art galleries, beach, bicycling, canoeing/kayaking, cross-country skiing, fishing, golf, hiking, horseback riding, live theater, museums, parks, shopping, sporting events, tennis, water sports, wineries and Birding nearby.

Location: Country. Lake.

Publicity: *Voted "Best of the Best" by Hampton's Dan's Paper in 2005.*

Certificate may be used: Anytime, subject to availability, Monday-Thursday December-March, except holidays and local special events.

Quintessentials B&B and Spa

8985 Main Rd
East Marion, NY 11939-1537
(631)477-9400 (800)444-9112
Internet: www.quintessentialsinc.com
E-mail: innkeeper@quintessentialsinc.com

Feel rejuvenated at this historic 1840's Victorian bed and breakfast in a sea captain's mansion with a Widow's Walk. Situated between the villages of Greenport and Orient on North Fork's East End of Long Island, it is an easy walk to the beach. Complimentary passes and towels are provided. Relax with afternoon tea on the wraparound porch. A second-floor office/sitting area features a computer, high-speed Internet access, fax, desk and refrigerator. Choose to stay in a guest bedroom with a fireplace, private sun deck, clawfoot tub or whirlpool bath and wireless Internet access. Each room boasts upscale amenities, fine linens, fresh flowers, monogrammed robes, mineral water and chocolates on pillows. Savor a lavish brunch-style breakfast and the famous afternoon high tea. Stroll the Japanese meditation garden and schedule a massage or European skin treatment at the on-site, full-service day spa.

Innkeeper(s): Sylvia Daley. $249-359. 5 rooms with PB, 2 suites. Breakfast, afternoon tea and snacks/refreshments included in rates. Beds: KQ. Modem hook-up, cable TV, VCR, DVD, reading lamp, CD player, ceiling fan, clock radio, desk, some with hot tub/spa, some with fireplace, bathrobes, wireless Internet access, hand-made slippers, fluffy towels, deluxe down comforter and pillows, aromatherapy bed and bath products, fresh flowers, bottled water and wrapped sweets and chocolates in room. Air conditioning. Gift shop, Office/Sitting area with computer with high speed Internet, fax, desk, refrigerator, complimentary beach passes, towels, concierge and butler service on premises. Antiquing, art galleries, beach, parks, vineyard tours, Mohegan and Foxwoods casinos and outlet shopping nearby.

Location: East end of Long Island.

Certificate may be used: Sunday-Thursday, December-March, Monday-Thursday, April-November excludes holidays and special events.

East Windham   G11

Point Lookout Mountain Inn

The Mohican Trail, Rt 23
East Windham, NY 12439
(518)734-3381 Fax:(518)734-6526
Internet: www.pointlookoutinn.com
E-mail: pointlookoutinn@yahoo.com

Circa 1965. Renown internationally for its panoramic five-state view, this cliffside country inn is a landmark in the Northern Catskill Mountains. Gather to play games in the Great Room, read a book on the balcony or enjoy the peaceful courtyard. Newly redecorated guest bedrooms offer comfort and style while boasting  incredible vistas during sunrise, moonrise or sunset. The first meal of the day is the popular "Raid the Refrigerator" breakfast, conveniently indulged when desired. After a day of visiting local historic sites, hiking, golf or skiing, the hot tub and in-house massage therapy offer total relaxation.

Innkeeper(s): Ron and Laurie Landstrom. $75-175. 14 rooms with PB, 1 conference room. Breakfast included in rates. Types of meals: Full gourmet bkfst, veg bkfst, early coffee/tea, gourmet lunch, picnic lunch, afternoon tea, snacks/refreshments, gourmet dinner and room service. Restaurant on premises. Beds: QDT. Cable TV, reading lamp, ceiling fan and clock radio in room. VCR, fax, copier, spa, library, parlor games, telephone, fireplace and 180 mile view of five states on premises. Handicap access. Amusement parks, antiquing, art galleries, bicycling, canoeing/kayaking, cross-country skiing, downhill skiing, fishing, golf, hiking, horseback riding, live theater, museums, parks, shopping, sporting events, tennis, water sports and wineries nearby.

Location: Country.

Publicity: *Hudson Valley Magazine and Ski Magazine.*

"Just wanted to thank you, once again, for a great time."

Certificate may be used: January-December, Sunday-Thursday, excludes holidays. Subject to availability.

Ellicottville H3

The Jefferson Inn of Ellicottville

3 Jefferson St,
Ellicottville, NY 14731-1566
(716)699-5869 (800)577-8451 Fax:(716)699-5758
Internet: www.thejeffersoninn.com
E-mail: info@thejeffersoninn.com

Circa 1835. The Allegheny Mountains provide a perfect backdrop for this restored Victorian home built by Robert H. Shankland, an influential citizen who owned the local newspaper, along with other enterprises. The home's 100-foot wraparound Greek Revival porch was added in the 1920s and patterned after the summer home of President Woodrow Wilson. A full breakfast is served to B&B guests. (There are two separate efficiency units offered to visitors with children or pets. Breakfast is not included in Efficiency units) The only bed & breakfast within the village, it is located in the center of town where you'll enjoy following the tree-lined streets to restaurants and shops.

Innkeeper(s): Jean Kirsch. $89-229. 7 rooms with PB, 3 with FP, 1 suite. Breakfast and snacks/refreshments included in rates. Types of meals: Full gourmet bkfst and early coffee/tea. Beds: KQT. Modem hook-up, reading lamp, CD player, clock radio, telephone, desk, some with fireplace, hair dryer, bathrobes and wireless Internet access in room. Central air. TV, VCR, DVD, fax, spa, library and parlor games on premises. Handicap access. Antiquing, art galleries, bicycling, canoeing/kayaking, cross-country skiing, downhill skiing, fishing, golf, hiking, horseback riding, museums, parks, shopping, tennis, wineries, Casino, Griffis Sculpture Park, Rock City Park and Amish country nearby.

Location: Village.

Publicity: Arrington's Bed and Breakfast Journal, Book of Lists, Genesse Country Magazine, Buffalo Spree Magazine, Olean Chronicle and Ellicottville News.

"Even though we just met, we are leaving with the feeling we just spent the weekend with good friends."

Certificate may be used: April-June, Sunday to Thursday and November Sunday to Thursday.

Geneva F6

Geneva On The Lake

1001 Lochland Rd, Rt 14S
Geneva, NY 14456
(315)789-7190 (800)343-6382 Fax:(315)789-0322
Internet: www.genevaonthelake.com
E-mail: info@genevaonthelake.com

Circa 1911. This opulent world-class inn is a replica of the Renaissance-era Lancellotti Villa in Frascati, Italy. It is listed in the National Register. Although originally built as a residence, it became a monastery for Capuchin monks. Now it is one of the finest resorts in the U.S. Renovated under the direction of award-winning designer William Schickel, there are 10 two-bedroom suites, some with views of the lake. Here, you may have an experience

as fine as Europe can offer, without leaving the country. Some compare it to the Grand Hotel du Cap-Ferrat on the French Riviera. The inn has been awarded four diamonds from AAA for more than two decades. Breakfast is available daily and on Sunday, brunch is served. Dinner is served each evening, and in the summer lunch is offered on the terrace.

Innkeeper(s): William J. Schickel. $165-795. 29 rooms with PB, 3 with FP, 23 suites, 3 conference rooms. Breakfast included in rates. Types of meals: Cont, gourmet dinner and room service. Restaurant on premises. Beds: KQDT. TV, DVD, CD player, refrigerator, clock radio, telephone, turn-down service and desk in room. Air conditioning. VCR, fax, copier, swimming, bicycles, parlor games, fireplace, sailing, fishing, lawn games and boats on premises. Antiquing, cross-country skiing, downhill skiing, live theater, parks, shopping, sporting events, water sports and wineries nearby.

Location: Waterfront.

Publicity: Travel & Leisure, Bon Appetit, Country Inns, The New York Times, Bride's, Catholic Register, Pittsford-Brighton Post, New York, Glamour, Gourmet, Washingtonian, Toronto Star, Globe & Mail, Rochester Democrat & Chronicle and Cooking Light magazine.

"The food was superb and the service impeccable."

Certificate may be used: Sunday-Thursday, Nov. 1-June 20.

Greenport K15

Stirling House Bed & Breakfast

104 Bay Avenue
Greenport, NY 11944
(631)477-0654 (800)551-0654 Fax:(631)477-2885
Internet: www.stirlinghousebandb.com
E-mail: info@stirlinghousebandb.com

Circa 1880. Located in the heart of the village in the historic district, this water-view bed and breakfast offers old-world southern charm combined with modern luxuries. Attention to detail is given all year round. Unwind on the wraparound porch with changing views of Shelter Island. Explore quaint shops, museums and art galleries, all a few steps from the resort. Richly appointed guest bedrooms are inviting and pampering retreats. Dine on bold, contemporary cuisine at one of the award-winning area restaurants. Discover world-class Long Island Wine Country vineyards on a tasting tour or take to the water on an exclusive lighthouse cruise.

Innkeeper(s): Clayton Sauer. $175-320. 3 rooms with PB, 3 with FP, 1 with WP, 1 total suite, including 2 two-bedroom suites. Breakfast, afternoon tea, snacks/refreshments, wine and The only B&B on the North Fork of Long Island licensed by the State of New York to serve and sell wine. Wine and cheese are now served as alternating weekend snack and on request included in rates. Types of meals: Full gourmet bkfst, early coffee/tea, Homemade special home-baked treats on weekend afternoons and Wine & Cheese Hour announced during stay. Beds: KQ. Modem hook-up, data port, cable TV, VCR, DVD, reading lamp, stereo, refrigerator, ceiling fan, clock radio, some with hot tub/spa, fireplace, hair dryer, bathrobes, bath amenities, wireless Internet access, iron/ironing board, i-Pod docking station and Flat screen cable TV/DVD in room. Air conditioning. Fax, library, parlor games, telephone, Refrigerator, Cable TV, DVD, Outdoor garden & dining area and Front porch with view of water on premises. Antiquing, art galleries, beach, bicycling, canoeing/kayaking, cross-country skiing, fishing, golf, hiking, horseback riding, live theater, museums, parks, shopping, tennis, water sports and wineries nearby.

Location: Country, ocean community, waterfront. Central to seaport town.

Publicity: Coastal Living (September 2007 - chosen as one of the top five waterfront wine destinations in North America), New York Daily News, Wine Enthusiast, Well Wed, Pulse, Edible East End, Vox, News 12 Long Island, Gambling on Gambling and WOR radio.

Certificate may be used: January 1-March 31, Monday through Thursday subject to availability. Cannot be combined with other offers.

Wells House

Right on Main St -National Historic Register District
Greenport, NY 11944
(631)477-0674
Internet: www.thewellshousebnb.com
E-mail: wellshousebnb@aol.com

Circa 1859. Recently renovated with meticulous care for its historic integrity, this Italianate sea captain's home is listed in the National Register and boasts original marble fireplace mantles, wide plank floors and a red mahogany curved banister. Relax beyond the iron gates amid a Victorian ambiance and peacefully secluded grounds with shade trees, flowers, a stone patio and two private covered porches. Sip a beverage or play the piano in the great room. Guest rooms feature a tasteful décor, walk-in closets and plush Turkish towels. Air conditioning and wifi are among the modern amenities. Linger over a European-style breakfast before going to the beach or taking a tour of the local vineyards. Bike rentals are available nearby to explore the town and it is easy to charter a boat or play golf.

Innkeeper(s): Vince Albert . $225-325. 3 rooms, 2 with PB. Breakfast, snacks/refreshments and wine included in rates. Types of meals: Full bkfst and early coffee/tea. Beds: QD. Reading lamp, turn-down service, hair dryer, bathrobes, bath amenities, wireless Internet access and 2 rooms with non-operational fireplaces and one with ceiling fan in room. Central air. Parlor games, telephone, fireplace, outside original stone patio for all day relaxation , breakfast and snacks, central air conditioning, on site parking for each guest room and very private grounds completely surrounded my trees on premises. Antiquing, art galleries, beach, bicycling, canoeing/kayaking, fishing, golf, museums, parks, shopping, water sports, wineries, boating and sailing, yoga and nearby.

Location: Wine country, Home on Historic National Registry.

Publicity: *SUFFOLK TIMES Posted: Thursday, July 01 and 2010 Wells House greets first visitors.*

Certificate may be used: Anytime, subject to availability.

Haverstraw J12

Bricktown Inn

112 Hudson Avenue
Haverstraw, NY 10927
(845)429-8447
Internet: www.bricktowninnbnb.com
E-mail: michelle@bricktowninnbnb.com

Circa 1885. Surrounded by thousands of acres of scenic parkland, Bricktown Inn in Haverstraw, Rockland County, New York, is near the many historic sites and attractions of the Hudson River. Built in 1885, this brick Mansard Colonial home has been recently renovated to offer modern technology while retaining its original heritage. Furnished with antiques and family heirlooms, the Victorian B&B has many common areas to enjoy. The front porch boasts wicker, rockers and a swing. Conversation flows easily in the parlor or the garden room has a movie library and Internet access. Cookies and beverages are available at the hospitality station. Gather for breakfast after a restful sleep in a comfortable guest bedroom. New York City is only 40 minutes away.

Innkeeper(s): Michelle & Joe Natale . $115-165. 4 rooms with PB. Breakfast, snacks/refreshments, Hospitality station with cookies, soda, coffee and tea included in rates. Types of meals: Full bkfst and early coffee/tea. Beds: KQT. Ceiling fan, clock radio, turn-down service, desk, hair dryer, bathrobes, bath amenities and wireless Internet access in room. Central air. TV, VCR, DVD, fax, parlor games, telephone, gift shop, Iron/Ironing board, Garden room with TV, Wireless Internet, Movie library and Swing on front porch on premises. Amusement parks, antiquing, art galleries, bicycling,

canoeing/kayaking, downhill skiing, fishing, golf, hiking, horseback riding, live theater, museums, parks, shopping, wineries and Historical sites nearby.

Location: Country, mountains, waterfront.

Certificate may be used: Anytime, subject to availability. Not valid during West Point graduation week.

Herkimer D12

Bellinger Rose Bed & Breakfast

611 W German St
Herkimer, NY 13350
(315)867-2197 (866)867-2197 Fax:3158672197
Internet: www.bellingerrose.com
E-mail: bellingerrose@hotmail.com

Circa 1865. Originally built in 1865 by the prominent Bellinger family, this recently renovated inn exudes Victorian grace and charm. The exquisite decor and splendid antique furnishings invite pleasantries and relaxation. The common rooms include a formal parlor with a vintage player piano and a sitting room offering modern entertainment such as videos or DVD with surround sound. Both areas provide the warmth and ambiance of wood-burning marble fireplaces. In keeping with the name, a romantic theme of roses adorns the two unique guest bedrooms with spacious sitting areas. A full breakfast is served daily in the elegant dining room. The pampering continues with plush robes, a year-round hot tub, and a chair massage that is included with each night's stay.

Innkeeper(s): Chris and Leon Frost. $129-169. 4 rooms with PB, 3 with FP, 2 with WP. Breakfast included in rates. Types of meals: Full bkfst and snacks/refreshments. Beds: Q. Data port, cable TV, DVD, reading lamp, stereo, refrigerator, clock radio, telephone, turn-down service, hair dryer, bathrobes, bath amenities, wireless Internet access and iron/ironing board in room. Air conditioning. Fax, copier, spa, bicycles, parlor games, fireplace, gift shop and professional massage on premises. Antiquing, art galleries, bicycling, canoeing/kayaking, cross-country skiing, fishing, golf, hiking, live theater, museums, parks, shopping and sporting events nearby.

Location: Village.

Certificate may be used: Sunday-Thursday, excludes July 25-28, subject to availability.

Ithaca G7

2 Cayuga LakeFront Inns-Ithaca's Hotel Alternative

Eastern Shore of Cayuga Lake
Ithaca, NY 14882
(607)533-4804
Internet: www.LakeFrontInn2.com
E-mail: info@LakeFrontInn.com

Circa 1930. In the heart of the Finger Lakes region on the scenic shore of Cayuga Lake, experience the timeless accommodations and casual elegance of this Mediterranean country villa B&B inn. Six acres of woodland, meadow gardens and lakefront beach accent the surroundings that inspire and renew. Five terraced hillside levels include private entrances, fireplaces, rich fabrics, cathedral ceilings and period furnishings. Each one is close to the aromatic Swedish sauna and the 30-jet Jacuzzi hot tub. Healthy yet delicious culinary delights are created each morning and served Tuscany style on one of the larger balconies or in-room when requested. Spend a day tasting the fruit of the vine at one of the local wineries on the popular Cayuga Wine Trail.

Innkeeper(s): Diane Rutherford. $165-275. 4 rooms with PB, 2 with FP. Breakfast, snacks/refreshments and wine included in rates. Types of meals: Full gourmet bkfst, veg bkfst, early coffee/tea, picnic lunch, afternoon tea, dinner and room service. Beds: Q. DVD, stereo, refrigerator, telephone, hot tub/spa, fireplace, hair dryer, bathrobes, bath amenities, wireless Internet access and iron/ironing board in room. Spa, sauna and laundry facility on premises. Antiquing, art galleries, beach, bicycling, canoeing/kayaking, cross-country skiing, fishing, golf, hiking, horseback riding, live theater, museums, parks, shopping, tennis, water sports and wineries nearby.

Location: Waterfront.

Certificate may be used: January-March, Monday-Thursday, excluding the Business of Holiday Celebrations, Anytime, Last Minute-Based on Availability.

Log Country Inn - B&B of Ithaca

PO Box 581
Ithaca, NY 14851
(607)589-4771 (800)274-4771 Fax:(607)589-6151
Internet: www.logtv.com/inn
E-mail: wanda@logtv.com

Circa 1969. As the name indicates, this bed & breakfast is indeed fashioned from logs and rests in a picturesque country setting surrounded by 100 wooded acres. The cozy rooms are rustic with exposed beams and country furnishings. There is also a Jacuzzi, fireplace and sauna. The decor is dotted with a European influence, as is the morning meal. Guests enjoy a full breakfast with blintzes or Russian pancakes. The innkeeper welcomes children and pets.

Innkeeper(s): Wanda Grunberg. $85-250. 9 rooms, 3 with PB, 1 suite. Breakfast included in rates. Types of meals: Full bkfst and Wanda's famous cheese blintzes and Russian pancakes and potato pancakes. Beds: QDT. Cable TV, DVD, reading lamp, telephone, desk and hair dryer in room. Air conditioning. TV, VCR, fax, copier, spa, swimming, sauna, library, fireplace, laundry facility and Double Jacuzzi on premises. Antiquing, bicycling, cross-country skiing, downhill skiing, fishing, hiking, live theater, parks, shopping, sporting events, water sports, wineries, Wine vineyards and Ponds nearby.

Location: On the edge of state forest.

Certificate may be used: Jan. 15-May 1, Sunday-Thursday.

Jay   C12

Book and Blanket B&B

Rt 9N, PO Box 164
Jay, NY 12941-0164
(518)946-8323
Internet: www.bookandblanket.com
E-mail: bookinnjay@aol.com

Circa 1860. This Adirondack bed & breakfast served as the town's post office for many years and also as barracks for state troopers. Thankfully, however, it is now a restful bed & breakfast catering to the literary set. Guest rooms are named for authors and there are books in every nook and cranny of the house. Guests may even take a book home with them. Each of the guest rooms is comfortably furnished. The inn is a short walk from the Jay Village Green and the original site of the Historic Jay covered bridge.

Innkeeper(s): Kathy, Fred, Sam & Zoe the Basset Hound. $80-100. 3 rooms, 1 with PB. Breakfast, afternoon tea and snacks/refreshments included in rates. Types of meals: Full bkfst, veg bkfst and early coffee/tea. Beds: QDT. Reading lamp and clock radio in room. TV, VCR, library, parlor games, telephone, fireplace and whirlpool tub on premises. Antiquing, art galleries, beach, bicycling, canoeing/kayaking, cross-country skiing, downhill skiing, fishing, golf, hiking, parks, sporting events, tennis, water sports and Olympic venues i.e. bobsled, luge, ski jump and ice skating nearby.

Location: Country, mountains, waterfront. Small hamlet.

Certificate may be used: Jan. 15 to June 20, Sunday-Thursday.

Keene Valley   C12

Trail's End Inn

62 Trail's End Way
Keene Valley, NY 12943
(518)576-9860 (800)281-9860 Fax:(518)576-9235
Internet: www.trailsendinn.com
E-mail: innkeeper@trailsendinn.com

This charming mountain inn is in the heart of the Adirondack's High Peaks. Surrounded by woods and adjacent to a small pond, the inn offers spacious guest rooms with antique furnishings and country quilts. All-you-can-eat morning meals in the glassed-in breakfast room not only provide a lovely look at the countryside, but often a close-up view of various bird species. Fresh air and gorgeous views abound, and visitors enjoy invigorating hikes, trout fishing and fine cross-country skiing. Downhill skiers will love the challenge of nearby White Mountain, with the longest vertical drop in the East.

Call for rates. 15 rooms, 8 with PB, 4 with FP, 4 with WP, 2 two-bedroom suites, 3 cottages, 2 conference rooms. Breakfast included in rates. Types of meals: Full bkfst, early coffee/tea, picnic lunch and dinner. Beds: KQDT. Reading lamp, telephone and desk in room. Fax, copier, library, child care, parlor games, fireplace, Guest kitchenette, TV and VCR in living room and Wireless high-speed Internet on premises. Antiquing, cross-country skiing, downhill skiing, fishing, golf, parks, shopping, tennis, water sports, 1980 Olympic headquarters in Lake Placid, rock climbing, ice climbing and major hiking trails nearby.

Location: Mountains.

Publicity: *Outside, Mid-Atlantic and Lake Placid News.*

"Felt like home. What a treasure we found."

Certificate may be used: Jan. 1-June 15 and Oct. 15-Dec. 31; Sunday through Thursday, when available, excluding holiday periods.

Lewiston   F3

Sunny's Roost Bed & Breakfast

421 Plain Street
Lewiston, NY 14092
(716)754-1161
Internet: www.sunnysroost.com
E-mail: sunny@sunnysroost.com

Circa 1900. Formerly a church rectory, Sunny's Roost now nurtures visitors to this area from it's Historic District location. From the inn, guests love to meander the streets and take in the shops, museums and special restaurants. In the summer there are midweek concerts in the park, but often guests just find their way to the back garden and listen amidst the flowers and lawns. Sunny is known for his scones – blueberry, pecan praline and cranberry-orange to name a few.

Innkeeper(s): Sunny and Bob. $110. 4 rooms, 3 with PB. Types of meals: Full bkfst. Beds: KQT. Reading lamp, ceiling fan, clock radio, turn-down service, hair dryer, bathrobes, wireless Internet access and iron/ironing board in room. Air conditioning. TV, VCR, DVD, library, parlor games, telephone, laundry facility, Television with basic cable, DVD and VCR in common room and access to refrigerator and microwave in kitchen on premises. Antiquing, art galleries, bicycling, fishing, golf, hiking, live theater, museums, parks, shopping, sporting events, water sports, wineries, Old Fort Niagara, Our Lady of Fatima Shrine, Shrine to Saint Jude, Niagara Falls, ArtPark and Seneca Niagara Casino nearby.

Location: Village on Niagara River.

Certificate may be used: Anytime, November-March, subject to availability.

Livingston Manor   I10

Guest House

408 Debruce Rd
Livingston Manor, NY 12758
(845)439-4000 Fax:(845)439-3344
Internet: www.theguesthouse.com
E-mail: andrea@theguesthouse.com

Circa 2000. This 40-acre estate near New York City boasts the best private fly fishing on the Willowemoc River. The inn has five guest bedrooms and three private cottages, one is located on the edge of the woods and across a footbridge that spans the river. This cottage has two bedrooms, a living room, an outdoor Jacuzzi, covered porches and even an enclosed dog run at the back. Guests in the main house and the cottages have views of the pond, woods, river and gardens. Breakfast is a sumptuous beginning to an active, or perhaps, a leisurely day. It includes items such as freshly pressed orange or grapefruit juice, eggs, French toast, pancakes, Belgian waffles and blueberry, corn or oat muffins. Near the inn are golf courses, many tennis courts, hiking, riding and biking trails, cross-country skiing, ice skating and a dozen antique stores.

Innkeeper(s): Shaun & Andrea Plunket. $176-245. 6 cottages with PB, 4 with FP, 2 with HT, 2 with WP. Breakfast and "Cocktail hour" with hosts (complimentary) included in rates. Types of meals: Room service. Beds: KQT. Cable TV, VCR, reading lamp, refrigerator, ceiling fan, clock radio, telephone, coffeemaker, desk, hot tub/spa, hair dryer, bathrobes, bath amenities and iron/ironing board in room. Central air. Fax, copier, spa, swimming, tennis, pet boarding, fireplace, laundry facility, Fly fishing and Hiking on property on premises. Limited handicap access. Antiquing, art galleries, bicycling, canoeing/kayaking, cross-country skiing, downhill skiing, fishing, golf, hiking, horseback riding, live theater, museums, parks, shopping, tennis and water sports nearby.

Location: Country, mountains.

Publicity: *Eye Witness News WABC live.*

Certificate may be used: Mid-week all months except July, August and Public Holidays. Subject to availability.

Millerton   I13

Simmons' Way Village Inn

53 Main Street
Millerton, NY 12546
(518) 789-6235 Fax:(518)789-6236
Internet: www.simmonsway.com
E-mail: info@simmonsway.com

Circa 1854. Enjoy warm American hospitality and charm in this 150-year-old Victorian in the Berkshire foothills. Simmons' Way Village Inn is located in the village of Millerton near Lakeville, Conn., and is the birthplace of famed baseball great Eddie Collins. The inn was chosen by American Express/Hertz as the "Quintessential County Inn 1991." Recently, the inn and restaurant were acclaimed by Gannett papers. Its nine guest bedrooms and one suite, some with fireplaces, are each uniquely decorated with antiques. A full breakfast is included in the tariff. Picnic lunches, dinners, banquets and catering can be arranged through the restaurant on premises. The frequently changing menu includes a variety of fare from seasonal game to pasta to vegetarian and international specialties. Outdoor activities abound, including fishing, hiking, tennis, golf, swimming, boating, cross-country skiing, biking and horseback riding. The inn is near the Lime Rock Race center, summer home of the Boston Symphony Orchestra, historic homes and the Culinary Institute of America.

Innkeeper(s): Jay & Martha Reynolds. $199-240. 9 rooms with PB. Breakfast included in rates. Types of meals: Full bkfst, early coffee/tea and dinner. Restaurant on premises. Beds: KQDT. Reading lamp, clock radio, hair dryer, bathrobes, bath amenities and wireless Internet access in room. Central air. TV, VCR, fax, copier, library, parlor games, telephone and fireplace on premises. Antiquing, art galleries, bicycling, canoeing/kayaking, cross-country skiing, downhill skiing, fishing, golf, hiking, horseback riding, live theater, museums, parks, shopping, tennis and wineries nearby.

Location: Village.

Certificate may be used: November-May anytime subject to availability. Except Thanksgiving and Christmas weeks. June-October; midweek only. Except Holiday weeks and graduation weeks.

New Lebanon   H13

Shaker Meadows

14209 State Route 22
New Lebanon, NY 12125
(518)794-9385 Fax:(518)794-9381
Internet: www.shakermeadows.com
E-mail: shakermeadows@surfbest.net

Circa 1795. Bordering the original Shaker settlement in Lebanon Valley at Mount Lebanon, New York, Shaker Meadows Bed & Breakfast spans fifty acres of meadows and woods in the Berkshire Hills. Built in 1795 and boasting recent renovations, the B&B offers rustic charm and modern conveniences. Relax on a porch, in the library or by the lily pond. Saunter along the peaceful, mile-long walking trail. Enjoy access to a private, sandy beach on Queechy Lake with towels and chairs provided. Delightful guest bedrooms in the farmhouse and spacious suites in the creamery have pastoral and mountain views. Savor a complete breakfast in the dining room. Picnic areas are inviting spots for lunch.

Innkeeper(s): Sean and Jean Cowhig. $85-195. 9 rooms, 6 with PB, 3 total suites, including 1 two-bedroom suite, 1 cottage, 1 guest house, 1 conference room. Breakfast. Rates include a full breakfast each morning in the Creamery Dining Room (Weekly Farmhouse rates do not include breakfast as most weekly guests prefer to prepare their own; however and breakfast can be requested for any morning at a rate of $10.00 per adult and $6.00 per child) included in rates. Types of meals: Full bkfst, early coffee/tea, picnic lunch, Lunch or dinner in the dining room will be provided for your family or workshop group of up to 50 people with previous arrangement. Rehearsal dinners, BBQs and tented parties on the 100'x24' outdoor tenting site can be arranged. Beds: KQDT. Cable TV, VCR, reading lamp, refrigerator, clock radio, telephone, coffeemaker, hair dryer, bathrobes, bath amenities and iron/ironing board in room. Air conditioning. Fax, library, parlor games and laundry facility on premises. Antiquing, art galleries, beach, bicycling, canoeing/kayaking, cross-country skiing, downhill skiing, hiking, horseback riding, live theater, museums, parks, shopping, sporting events, tennis, water sports, wineries, Tanglewood, Hancock Shaker Village, Old Chatham Shaker Museum, New Lebanon Theatre Barn, Access to private town beach on Queechy Lake, Towels & beach chairs and Norman Rockwell Museum nearby.

Location: Country. Berkshires.

Certificate may be used: Any Sunday-Thursday night and any weekend last minute (one week ahead).

Penn Yan
G6

Fox Inn

158 Main St
Penn Yan, NY 14527-1201
(800)901-7997
Internet: www.foxinnbandb.com
E-mail: cliforr@aol.com

Circa 1820. Experience the pleasant elegance of a fine, historic home at this Greek Revival Inn. Furnished with Empire antiques, the accommodations include a living room with marble fireplace, sun porch, parlor with billiards table and formal rose gardens. Five guest rooms and one two-bedroom suite each have private baths. The gourmet breakfast provides a selection of nine main entrees. Located near the Windmill Farm Market, the largest farm market in New York, you can spend a casual day shopping or visiting nearby museums or wineries. Or, enjoy more active alternatives such as biking, hiking and picnicking or boating on Keuka Lake.

Innkeeper(s): Cliff & Michele Orr. $109-173. 6 rooms with PB, 1 with FP, 1 suite, 1 conference room. Breakfast included in rates. Types of meals: Full gourmet bkfst and early coffee/tea. Beds: QD. Cable TV, VCR, clock radio, telephone, turn-down service and hot tub/spa in room. Air conditioning. Library, parlor games, fireplace and billiard table on premises. Amusement parks, antiquing, art galleries, beach, bicycling, canoeing/kayaking, cross-country skiing, downhill skiing, fishing, golf, hiking, horseback riding, live theater, museums, parks, shopping, tennis, water sports and wineries nearby.

Publicity: *Inn Times "Top 50 Inns in America Award."*

Certificate may be used: Anytime, December-April, subject to availability.

Phelps
F6

Yorkshire Inn

1135 State Route # 96
Phelps, NY 14532-9549
(315)548-9675
Internet: www.theyorkshireinn.com
E-mail: innkeeper@theyorkshireinn.com

Circa 1796. Built as a two-story farmhouse in 1796, it was converted to a three-story inn in 1819 to service the stagecoach run. Meticulously restored, this Colonial/Federal inn with a country décor sits on two acres with a stream in the backyard. Located halfway between Rochester and Syracuse, it is the perfect place to stay while visiting the Finger Lakes. Gather for conversation in the living room. Decanters of locally made sherry and port are on the sideboard in the dining room for a nightcap. Guest suites are all on the first floor. The Rose Room opens out onto the deck. After a hearty breakfast take a driving tour of the lighthouses along Lake Ontario, fish or go wine tasting at nearby vineyards.

Innkeeper(s): Doug and Kathe Latch. $109-179. 2 rooms with PB, 1 two-bedroom suite. Breakfast and wine included in rates. Types of meals: Full bkfst, veg bkfst and early coffee/tea. Beds: Q. Data port, cable TV, reading lamp, coffeemaker, desk, hair dryer, bathrobes, bath amenities, wireless Internet access, iron/ironing board and iPod stereo/alarm clock in room. Air conditioning. Telephone and laundry facility on premises. Limited handicap access. Antiquing, art galleries, beach, bicycling, canoeing/kayaking, cross-country skiing, fishing, golf, hiking, parks, shopping, sporting events, wineries and snowmobiling nearby.

Location: Country.

Publicity: *Food Network's All American Festivals.*

Certificate may be used: November-March, Sunday-Thursday.

Prattsburgh
G5

Feather Tick 'N Thyme B&B

7661 Tuttle Rd
Prattsburgh, NY 14873-9520
(607)522-4113
Internet: www.bbnyfingerlakes.com
E-mail: info@bbnyfingerlakes.com

Circa 1890. Feel revived and refreshed after a stay in the peaceful valley that surrounds this 1890's Victorian Country bed and breakfast inn. Prattsburgh is situated in the New York Finger Lakes wine country between Keuka Lake and Canandaigua Lake. Soak up the scenic view from the wraparound porch. Stroll among the flower gardens by the creek. Enjoy a restful sleep in an ornate iron bed, a four-poster rice bed or a sleigh bed depending upon the room selected. Breakfast is served family style in the dining room with heirloom recipes accented by the collection of depression glass. Feather Tick 'N Thyme B&B offers special weekend packages for a romantic getaway.

Innkeeper(s): Maureen Kunak. $100-125. 4 rooms, 2 with PB. Breakfast and snacks/refreshments included in rates. Types of meals: Full bkfst, picnic lunch and hors d'oeuvres. Beds: QD. Reading lamp, clock radio, turn-down service, hair dryer, bathrobes, bath amenities, wireless Internet access, Welcome baskets and Feather beds in room. Fax, copier, parlor games, gift shop, Walking trails, Campsite, Game room, Exercise room, Free Wi-Fi, Guest refrigerator, Coffeemaker, Tea and Snacks on premises. Antiquing, bicycling, canoeing/kayaking, downhill skiing, fishing, golf, hiking, live theater, museums, parks, shopping, sporting events, wineries, Hot Air Balloon launch on premises and Watkins Glen nearby.

Location: Country.

Certificate may be used: December-May, Sunday-Thursday, subject to availability.

Rochester
F5

Reen's Bed and Breakfast

44 Magee Avenue
Rochester, NY 14613
(585)458-9306
Internet: www.stayatreens.com
E-mail: reen@stayatreens.com

Circa 1910. Gracing the Maplewood neighborhood in Rochester, New York, Reen's Bed and Breakfast is just three miles from downtown and four miles from Lake Ontario. The list of amenities seems endless at this very comfortable B&B that was built in 1910 in the Edwardian style and boasts leaded and stained-glass windows, hardwood floors and oak woodwork. Relax in the living room or fireside den. Air-conditioned guest bedrooms are named after the children who grew up in this house. Start each day with a hearty breakfast in the dining room, front porch or back patio. Tour the George Eastman House, visit the planetarium or history museum. Ask about special packages available.

Innkeeper(s): Irene Zaremski-Saltrelli. $70-130. 3 rooms. Breakfast included in rates. Types of meals: Full gourmet bkfst and veg bkfst. Beds: QD. Reading lamp, clock radio, desk, hair dryer, bathrobes, wireless Internet access and iron/ironing board in room. TV, DVD, library, parlor games, telephone, fireplace and laundry facility on premises. Amusement parks, antiquing, art galleries, beach, bicycling, canoeing/kayaking, cross-country skiing, downhill skiing, fishing, golf, hiking, horseback riding, live theater, museums, parks, shopping, sporting events, tennis, water sports and wineries nearby.

Location: City.

Certificate may be used: January-February.

The Edward Harris House B&B Inn

35 Argyle Street
Rochester, NY 14607
(585)473-9752 (800)419-1213 Fax:(585)473-9752
Internet: www.edwardharrishouse.com
E-mail: innkeeper@edwardharrishouse.com

Circa 1896. Acclaimed as one of the finest early examples of architect Claude Bragdon's work, this restored Georgian mansion is one of the iLovelnns.com Top 10 romantic Inns for 2009. Its history only enhances the rich warmth, and the immense size reflects a cozy ambiance. Relax in a leather chair in the traditional library. Antiques and collectibles combine well with florals and chintz for a touch of romance. Two guest bedrooms and the Garden Suite boast fireplaces. Four-poster rice beds and hand-painted furniture add to the individual decorating styles. A gourmet candlelight breakfast is served in the formal dining room on crystal and china or on the brick garden patio. Enjoy afternoon tea on the wicker-filled front porch. Walk one block down tree-lined streets to the urban village of Park Avenue. A plethora of historic sites, including The George Eastman House and Strong Museum, are within a one-mile range.

Innkeeper(s): Susan Alvarez. $169-189. 5 rooms with PB, 4 with FP, 3 total suites, including 1 two-bedroom suite, 1 cottage, 1 conference room. Breakfast, afternoon tea, snacks/refreshments and Afternoon tea provided upon request. Please contact the Innkeeper included in rates. Types of meals: Full bkfst, veg bkfst, early coffee/tea, picnic lunch, hors d'oeuvres, room service and Catering can be arranged easily for lunch or dinner. Please call the Inn for more information. Beds: KQT. Modern hook-up, data port, cable TV, VCR, DVD, reading lamp, stereo, refrigerator, ceiling fan, clock radio, telephone, turn-down service, desk, fireplace, hair dryer, bathrobes, bath amenities, wireless Internet access, iron/ironing board, For those late night munchie attacks, each room is provided a complimentary welcome basket of bottled water,'healthy' chips, cookies and chocolates in room. Air conditioning. Fax, copier, library, parlor games, laundry facility, Spanish spoken and A complimentary coffee & tea service area with a guest refrigerator centrally situated on the guest room floor on premises. Limited handicap access. Amusement parks, antiquing, art galleries, beach, bicycling, canoeing/kayaking, cross-country skiing, downhill skiing, fishing, golf, hiking, horseback riding, live theater, museums, parks, shopping, sporting events, tennis, water sports, wineries, Just blocks from area shops, Cafes, Restaurants, The George Eastman House (2.5 blocks), Park Avenue District (1 block), Tennis courts (4 blocks), Rochester Museum and Science Center (5 blocks), Memorial Art Gallery (1 mile), Susan B. Anthony House (2 mi.), Eastman Theater (20 min. walk), GEVA Theater (2.5 mi.) and All major colleges within a 10-15 minute drive of the Inn nearby.

Location: City. Nestled within the Arts/Cultural District of Rochester.

Publicity: 2009 Top 10 Most Romantic Inn for Ilovelnns.com, North American Inns, Rochester Business Journal, The Democrat and Chronicle, The Seaway Trail Magazine, Local & national photographic shoots by photographers such as Kodak and Bausch & Lomb, a frequent locale for commercials and movie shoots and promotional videos.

Certificate may be used: Sunday-Thursday, subject to availability, holiday and special events may be excluded. Anytime, at the last minute. Please call the Inn.

Saratoga Springs F12

Country Life B&B

67 Tabor Road
Saratoga Springs, NY 12834
(518)692-7203
Internet: www.countrylifebb.com
E-mail: stay@countrylifebb.com

Circa 1829. Near the Battenkill River in the Adirondack foothills, this Flat Front farmhouse sits on 118 acres surrounded by rolling hills. Filled with antiques and traditional furnishings, romantic guest bedrooms feature comfortable terry robes, sherry and candy. A free breakfast is a delicious way to begin the day. Relax on three acres of groomed lawn with flower gardens, a two-person hammock and a porch swing. The bridge across an old mill stream leads to woodland trails. Swim in the ponds with two waterfalls and a rock slide.

Innkeeper(s): Wendy & Richard Duvall. $95-185. 4 rooms with PB. Breakfast included in rates. Types of meals: Country bkfst, veg bkfst and early coffee/tea. Beds: KQ. TV, reading lamp, ceiling fan, clock radio, turn-down service, hair dryer, bathrobes, bath amenities, wireless Internet access, iron/ironing board, sherry, candy, extra blankets, pillows and full-length mirror in room. Air conditioning. Fax, copier, swimming, library, child care, parlor games, telephone, fireplace, coffeemaker and high speed Internet access on premises. Limited handicap access. Antiquing, art galleries, beach, bicycling, canoeing/kayaking, cross-country skiing, downhill skiing, fishing, golf, hiking, horseback riding, live theater, museums, parks, shopping, tennis, water sports, Horse racing and Water sports nearby.

Location: Country, mountains. In the Adirondack foothills, near Saratoga Springs.

Publicity: Long Island Newsday, Inn Times, NY Times, Country Extra, Long Island Lifestyles Magazine, Washington County Magazine, Glens Falls Business News, ABC TV-Weekend Report and CBS-TV This Morning.

Certificate may be used: November-May, Sunday-Thursday, holidays excluded, last minute only for weekends, cannot be combined with any other specials or discounts. Anytime, Last Minute-Based on Availability.

Sharon Springs F12

Edgefield

153 Washington Street
Sharon Springs, NY 13459
(518)284-3339
Internet: www.edgefieldbb.com
E-mail: dmwood71@hotmail.com

Circa 1865. This home has seen many changes. It began as a farmhouse, a wing was added in the 1880s, and by the turn of the century, sported an elegant Greek Revival facade. Edgefield is one of a collection of nearby homes used as a family compound for summer vacations. The rooms are decorated with traditional furnishings in a formal English-country style. In the English tradition, afternoon tea is presented with cookies and tea  sandwiches. Sharon Springs includes many historic sites, and the town is listed in the National Register.

Innkeeper(s): Daniel Marshall Wood. $150-250. 5 rooms with PB. Breakfast, afternoon tea, hors d'oeuvres and wine included in rates. Types of meals: Full gourmet bkfst and early coffee/tea. Beds: QT. Reading lamp, ceiling fan, clock radio, turn-down service and desk in room. Air conditioning. Library, fireplace, antique furnishings and veranda on premises. Antiquing, cross-country skiing, golf, hiking, live theater, museums, parks, shopping, water sports, wineries and Glimmerglass Opera nearby.

Location: Village.

Publicity: Conde Nast Traveler (Oct. 2003), Colonial Homes Magazine, Philadelphia Inquirer and Boston Globe.

"Truly what I always imagined the perfect B&B experience to be!"
Certificate may be used: Anytime, subject to availability.

Stephentown G13

Berkshire Mountain House

150 Berkshire Way
Stephentown, NY 12168
(518)733-6923
Internet: www.berkshirebb.com
E-mail: info@berkshirebb.com

Circa 1962. This inn is situated on a hill overlooking 50 acres with wooded trails, a spring-fed pond and meadows. Views look out to the Berkshire Mountains. Guest rooms offer a combination of antique and contemporary furnishings, and all have views. The inn's wide deck invites conversation. A private two-bedroom, two-bath cottage overlooks the pond. Tanglewood, Jacobs Pillow and Shaker Village are close by.

Innkeeper(s): Mona & Lee Berg. $109-650. 12 rooms, 9 with PB, 1 with HT, 3 suites, 1 cottage. Breakfast, afternoon tea and wine included in rates. Types of meals: Full gourmet bkfst, veg bkfst and early coffee/tea. Beds: KQDT. Modem hook-up, cable TV, VCR, reading lamp, CD player, refrigerator, ceiling fan, clock radio, telephone, coffeemaker, some with hot tub/spa, hair dryer, bathrobes, iron/ironing board and makeup mirrors in room. Air conditioning. DVD, fax, copier, swimming, library, child care, parlor games, fireplace and laundry facility on premises. Limited handicap access. Antiquing, art galleries, bicycling, canoeing/kayaking, cross-country skiing, downhill skiing, fishing, golf, hiking, horseback riding, live theater, museums, parks, shopping, tennis, water sports, wineries, Hancock Shaker Village, Tanglewood, Shakespeare and Co. Jacobs Pillow, Norman Rockwell Museum, Clark Art Institute, MassMoca and Berkshire Theater Festival nearby.

Location: Country, mountains.

Certificate may be used: November-May, excluding holiday weeks and weekends (Christmas, New Years etc.).

Troy G12

Olde Judge Mansion B&B

3300 6th Ave
Troy, NY 12180-1206
(518)274-5698
Internet: www.oldejudgemansion.com
E-mail: ojm@nycap.rr.com

Circa 1892. Experience the Victorian splendor of oak woodwork, 12-foot ceilings, pocket doors and embossed tin walls at this Gothic Italianate built in 1892. In the oak archway entry, view the photos displayed of historic Troy. Gather in the formal parlor to converse by the glow of kerosene lamps. An inviting Lazy Boy is perfect for video watching in the TV room. A sunny sitting room features reading materials and a chest stocked with forgotten conveniences. Kitchen privileges and laundry facilities are available. A stained-glass Newel Post Lamp on the ornate staircase leads to the comfortable guest bedrooms which are all on the second floor. Enjoy a casual, self-serve expanded continental breakfast buffet in the dining room. Shoot pool, play traditional feather, baseball or electric darts in the recreation/game room.

Innkeeper(s): Christina A. Urzan. $50-90. 5 rooms, 3 with PB, 1 guest house. Breakfast, afternoon tea, snacks/refreshments, No breakfast is included with Monthly discount plan. It is in the Weekly discount plan and Weekly is 7 days or more included in rates. Types of meals: Full bkfst, veg bkfst, early coffee/tea, Kitchen available for very light cooking and use of Microwave and Refrigerator. Beds: KQDT. Cable TV, VCR, ceiling fan, clock radio, telephone, bathrobes, wireless Internet access, iron/ironing board and broadband hook-up in room. Air conditioning. Fax, parlor games, laundry facility and Jacuzzi in shared bathroom on premises. Amusement parks, antiquing, art galleries, bicycling, canoeing/kayaking, fishing, golf, live theater, museums, parks, shopping, sporting events, tennis and year-round ice skating at Knickerbacker Arena nearby.

Location: City.
Certificate may be used: Anytime, subject to availability.

Warrensburg E12

Country Road Lodge B&B

115 Hickory Hill Rd
Warrensburg, NY 12885-3912
(518)623-2207
Internet: www.countryroadlodge.com
E-mail: mail@countryroadlodge.com

Circa 1929. Originally built for a local businessman as a simple "camp," this bed & breakfast has expanded to offer comfortable accommodations. At the end of a short country road in a secluded setting on the Hudson River, 40 acres of woodlands and fields are surrounded by a state forest preserve. Common rooms boast panoramic views of the river and the Adirondack Mountains. After a restful night's sleep, enjoy homemade bread and muffins in the dining room while selecting from the breakfast menu. Nature walks, bird watching, hiking and cross-country skiing are just out the front door.

Innkeeper(s): Sandi & Steve Parisi. $105-115. 4 rooms with PB. Breakfast included in rates. Types of meals: Country bkfst, veg bkfst and early coffee/tea. Beds: KQT. Reading lamp, ceiling fan, hair dryer and wireless Internet access in room. Air conditioning. Library, parlor games, telephone, Franklin stove in common room, 24-hour hot and cold beverage counter, screened gazebo, Adirondack lawn chairs, perennial gardens, walking and skiing trails and WI-FI throughout on premises. Amusement parks, antiquing, art galleries, beach, bicycling, canoeing/kayaking, cross-country skiing, downhill skiing, fishing, golf, hiking, horseback riding, live theater, museums, parks, shopping, tennis, water sports, whitewater rafting, snowshoeing, scenic drives, lake cruises, Colonial history sites and garage sales nearby.

Location: Country, mountains, waterfront.

Publicity: *North Jersey Herald & News, New York Times, Adirondack Journal and Christian Science Monitor.*

"Homey, casual atmosphere. We really had a wonderful time. You're both wonderful hosts and the Lodge is definitely our kind of B&B! We will always feel very special about this place and will always be back."

Certificate may be used: Sunday-Thursday, excluding July-August, holidays and special events. Not valid with other discount programs.

Glen Lodge B&B

1123 State Route 28
Warrensburg, NY 12885-5606
(518)494-4984 (800)867-2335 Fax:(518)494-7478
Internet: www.TheGlenLodge.com
E-mail: info@TheGlenLodge.com

Feel rejuvenated after a visit to this newly built bed and breakfast that reflects an authentic Adirondack lodge. Relax on one of the large porches or in the quiet sitting room. Furnished entirely with cedar log furniture, watch satellite TV in the Great Room by the stone fireplace. Comfortable guest bedrooms are carpeted and boast private baths. Start each day with classic breakfast favorites such as pancakes, French toast, eggs, bacon, sausage and muffins. Browse through the country store. Situated in the scenic North Country area of upstate New York, activities abound. Ski at nearby Gore and Whiteface Mountains or swim at Lake George. Ask about available packages that include rafting on the Hudson River.

Innkeeper(s): Aimee & Douglas Azaert. Call for rates. Call inn for details. Breakfast included in rates. Types of meals: Country bkfst, veg bkfst and early coffee/tea. Beds: QT. Reading lamp, ceiling fan, clock radio, hair dryer and bath amenities in room. Central air. VCR, sauna, telephone, fireplace and gift shop on premises. Handicap access. Amusement parks, antiquing, art galleries, beach, bicycling, canoeing/kayaking, cross-country skiing, downhill skiing, fishing, golf, hiking, horseback riding, live theater, museums, parks, shopping, tennis, water sports and whitewater rafting nearby.

Location: Mountains.

Publicity: *Arrington's "Best Bed & Breakfast for Sports Enthusiasts" (2004 & 2005)* .

Certificate may be used: October-April, last minute, subject to availability.

Warwick   J11

Warwick Valley Bed & Breakfast

24 Maple Ave
Warwick, NY 10990-1025
(845)987-7255 (888)280-1671 Fax:(845)988-5318
Internet: www.wvbedandbreakfast.com
E-mail: loretta@warwick.net

Circa 1900. This turn-of-the-century Colonial Revival is located in Warwick's historic district among many of the town's other historic gems. The B&B includes five guest rooms decorated with antiques and country furnishings. Breakfasts are a treat with entrees such as eggs Benedict, apple pancakes or a savory potato, cheese and egg bake. Wineries, antique shops and many outdoor activities are nearby, and innkeeper Loretta Breedveld is happy to point guests in the right direction.

Innkeeper(s): Loretta Breedveld. $120-185. 6 rooms with PB. Breakfast included in rates. Types of meals: Full gourmet bkfst and early coffee/tea. Beds: KQT. Cable TV, VCR, DVD, reading lamp, ceiling fan, clock radio, telephone, desk, some with fireplace, hair dryer, wireless Internet access, iron/ironing board, sitting area and high-speed Internet access in room. Central air. Fax, copier and bicycles on premises. Amusement parks, antiquing, cross-country skiing, downhill skiing, fishing, golf, live theater, parks, shopping, sporting events, tennis, water sports and wineries nearby.

Location: Historic village.

Publicity: *Warwick Advertiser.*

Certificate may be used: Anytime, subject to availability, except holidays/holiday weekends. Saturdays not included unless approved by Loretta the owner.

Westport   C12

The Victorian Lady

6447 Main St
Westport, NY 12993
(518)962-2345 (877)829-7128
Internet: www.victorianladybb.com
E-mail: victorianlady@westelcom.com

Circa 1856. This Second Empire home features all the delicate elements of a true "Painted Lady," from the vivid color scheme to the Eastlake porch that graces the exterior. Delicate it's not, however, having stood for more than a century. Its interior is decked in period style with antiques from this more gracious era. Gourmet breakfast is served by candlelight or on the veranda with views of Lake Champlain, a mere 100 yards from the front door. Lovely gardens surround the home.

Innkeeper(s): Wayne. $115-185. 5 rooms, 4 with PB, 1 two-bedroom suite. Breakfast, afternoon tea and snacks/refreshments included in rates. Types of meals: Full gourmet bkfst, early coffee/tea and wine. Beds: KQT. Cable TV, reading lamp, ceiling fan, clock radio, desk and bath amenities in room. Air conditioning. VCR, DVD, fax, copier, library, parlor games, telephone and fireplace on premises. Antiquing, art galleries, beach, bicycling, canoeing/kayak-

ing, cross-country skiing, downhill skiing, fishing, golf, hiking, horseback riding, live theater, museums, parks, shopping, tennis and water sports nearby.

Location: Mountains, waterfront. Historic village.

Publicity: *Victorian Homes Magazine and local PBS.*

Certificate may be used: Anytime, May 29 to Oct. 15, subject to availability.

Windham   H11

Albergo Allegria B&B

#43 Route 296, PO Box 267
Windham, NY 12496-0267
(518)734-5560 Fax:(518)734-5570
Internet: www.albergousa.com
E-mail: mail@albergousa.com

Circa 1892. Two former boarding houses were joined to create this luxurious, Victorian bed & breakfast whose name means "the inn of happiness." Guest quarters, laced with a Victorian theme, are decorated with period wallpapers and antique furnishings. One master suite includes an enormous Jacuzzi tub. There are plenty of relaxing options at Albergo Allegria, including an inviting lounge with a large fireplace and over-stuffed couches. Guests also  can choose from more than 300 videos in the innkeeper's movie collection. Located just a few feet behind the inn are the Carriage House Suites, each of which includes a double whirlpool tub, gas fireplace, king-size bed and cathedral ceilings with skylights. The innkeepers came to the area originally to open a deluxe, gourmet restaurant. Their command of cuisine is evident each morning as guests feast on a variety of home-baked muffins and pastries, gourmet omelettes, waffles and other tempting treats. The inn is a registered historic site.

Innkeeper(s): Marianna and Leslie Leman. $99-269. 21 rooms with PB, 8 with FP, 8 with WP, 9 suites. Breakfast included in rates. Types of meals: Full gourmet bkfst. Beds: KQT. Cable TV, VCR, reading lamp, refrigerator, ceiling fan, clock radio, telephone and desk in room. Air conditioning. Fax, copier, bicycles, parlor games, fireplace, afternoon tea on Saturdays, 24-hour guest pantry with soft drinks and hot beverages and sweets on premises. Handicap access. Amusement parks, antiquing, bicycling, cross-country skiing, downhill skiing, fishing, hiking, parks, shopping, tennis, water sports, bird watching and waterfalls nearby.

Location: Mountains.

Publicity: *Yankee.*

Certificate may be used: Mid-week, Sunday-Thursday, non-holiday.

North Carolina

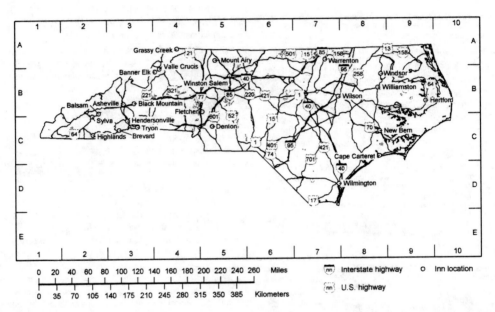

	Miles
0 20 40 60 80 100 120 140 160 180 200 220 240 260	
0 35 70 105 140 175 210 245 280 315 350 385	Kilometers

(nn) Interstate highway   o Inn location
(nn) U.S. highway

Asheville   B3

1847 Blake House Inn Bed & Breakfast

150 Royal Pines Drive
Asheville, NC 28704
(828) 681-5227 (888) 353-5227
Internet: www.blakehouse.com
E-mail: blakehouseinn@gmail.com

Circa 1847. Adorning a quiet residential neighborhood in the
Historic Royal Pines Area of Asheville, North Carolina, the
1847 Blake House Inn Bed & Breakfast features Italianate
architecture with a Gothic Revival influence. The walls are 22-
inch thick granite, and the 12-foot ceilings are ornamental plaster. Surrounded by mature pines and sycamores, this B&B has
been named a Treasures Tree Preserve of Buncombe County.
Enjoy spacious common areas with seating and games. Gather
in the Labrador Landing Pub for conversation by a warm fire.
The second-floor guest bedrooms each include a sitting area
and some feature a clawfoot tub and fireplace. Linger over a
two-course breakfast served in one of the two fireside dining
rooms or on the porch or patio.

Innkeeper(s): Leslie Kimball. $120-160. 5 rooms with PB, 3 with FP, 1

suite. Breakfast included in rates. Types of meals: Full bkfst, veg bkfst, early
coffee/tea and snacks/refreshments. Beds: KQDT. Cable TV, DVD, reading
lamp, refrigerator, ceiling fan, snack bar, telephone, coffeemaker, desk, voice
mail, some with fireplace, hair dryer, bathrobes, bath amenities, wireless
Internet access and iron/ironing board in room. Central air. Child care, parlor
games and gift shop on premises. Limited handicap access. Antiquing, art
galleries, bicycling, canoeing/kayaking, cross-country skiing, fishing, golf, hiking, horseback riding, live theater, museums, parks, shopping, sporting
events, tennis and wineries nearby.

Location: Mountains.

Certificate may be used: January-April, Sunday-Thursday, subject to availability. May not be used on weekends or holidays.

Albemarle Inn

86 Edgemont Rd
Asheville, NC 28801-1544
(828)255-0027 (800)621-7435 Fax:(828)236-3397
Internet: www.albemarleinn.com
E-mail: info@albemarleinn.com

Circa 1907. In the residential
Grove Park area, this AAA four-
diamond elegant Greek Revival
Mansion graces almost an acre
of landscaped grounds. The
inn features an exquisite

carved-oak staircase and period furnishings. Enjoy late afternoon refreshments on the veranda overlooking award-winning English gardens or fireside in the parlor. Spacious guest bedrooms and suites boast fine linens, antique clawfoot tubs and showers, televisions and phones. Some rooms include a whirlpool tub and a fireplace. A sumptuous candlelight breakfast is served at individual tables in the dining room or on the plant-filled sun porch. Gourmet dishes may include poached cinnamon pears, stuffed French toast with orange sauce and sausages. Inspired by the singing birds, composer Bela Bartok wrote his third piano concerto while staying here. The inn is a member of Select Registry.

Innkeeper(s): Cathy & Larry Sklar. $100-370. 11 rooms with PB, 1 with FP, 1 with WP, 2 suites. Breakfast, afternoon tea, snacks/refreshments, hors d'oeuvres and wine included in rates. Types of meals: Full gourmet bkfst and early coffee/tea. Beds: KQDT. Modem hook-up, cable TV, reading lamp, ceiling fan, clock radio, telephone, coffeemaker, turn-down service, hair dryer, bathrobes, bath amenities, wireless Internet access, iron/ironing board and Royal Hideaway has 2-person marble whirlpool tub in room. Air conditioning. Fax, copier, parlor games, fireplace and Veranda on premises. Antiquing, art galleries, bicycling, canoeing/kayaking, downhill skiing, fishing, golf, hiking, horseback riding, live theater, museums, parks, shopping, sporting events, tennis, water sports, wineries, golf, Biltmore Estate and Grove Park Resort and Spa nearby.

Location: City, country, mountains. Residential area.

Publicity: *National Geographic Traveler, Travel Holiday, Charleston Living & Home Design, Arrington's Inn Traveler, Marquee Magazine and WLOS TV (ABC).*

"Most outstanding breakfast I've ever had. We were impressed to say the least!"

Certificate may be used: Sunday-Thursday, Jan. 2-June 30, Aug. 1-Sept. 30, Nov. 1-Dec. 12, except holidays, subject to availability, not to be combined with any other promotions or discounts.

Corner Oak Manor

53 Saint Dunstans Rd
Asheville, NC 28803-2620
(828)253-3525 (888)633-3525
Internet: www.corneroakmanor.com
E-mail: corneroak@aol.com

Circa 1920. Surrounded by oak, maple and pine trees, this English Tudor inn is decorated with many fine oak antiques and handmade items. Innkeeper Karen Spradley has handstitched something special for each room, and the house features handmade items by local artisans. Breakfast delights include entrees such as Blueberry Ricotta Pancakes, Four Cheese and Herb Quiche

and Orange French Toast. When you aren't enjoying local activities, you can sit on the shady deck, relax in the Jacuzzi, play a few songs on the piano or curl up with a good book.

Innkeeper(s): Karen & Andy Spradley. $135-195. 4 rooms with PB, 1 cottage. Breakfast and snacks/refreshments included in rates. Types of meals: Full gourmet bkfst and picnic lunch. Beds: KQ. Reading lamp, ceiling fan, clock radio, some with fireplace, hair dryer, bathrobes, bath amenities, wireless Internet access and one cottage with fireplace in room. Air conditioning. Parlor games and telephone on premises. Antiquing, art galleries, bicycling, fishing, golf, hiking, live theater, museums, parks and shopping nearby.

Location: City. Quiet neighborhood, 1/2 mile from Biltmore Estate.

"Great food, comfortable bed, quiet, restful atmosphere, you provided it all and we enjoyed it all!"

Certificate may be used: Anytime, subject to availability.

Wright Inn & Carriage House

235 Pearson Dr
Asheville, NC 28801-1613
(828)251-0789 (800)552-5724 Fax:(828)251-0929
Internet: www.ashevillebedbreakfastinn.com
E-mail: info@wrightinn.com

Circa 1899. A true landmark that is timeless in the old-fashioned graciousness and modern conveniences offered, this gabled Queen Anne boasts an award-winning restoration and lavish gardens. Gather in the Coleman Parlor and the Drawing Room with period decor, fireplaces and inviting activities. Romantic suites and guest bedrooms feature distinctive designs; several feature fireplaces and high-speed wireless Internet.

The three-bedroom Carriage House is perfect for larger groups or families. Enjoy a gourmet breakfast and a weekend social hour. Relax on the large wraparound porch and gazebo.

Innkeeper(s): Bob & Barbara Gilmore. $105-235. 11 rooms with PB, 4 with FP, 1 with WP, 1 cottage. Breakfast included in rates. Types of meals: Full gourmet bkfst, early coffee/tea and snacks/refreshments. Beds: KQDT. Cable TV, reading lamp, clock radio, telephone, desk, some with fireplace, hair dryer, bathrobes, bath amenities, wireless Internet access and iron/ironing board in room. Central air. Fax, library, parlor games, weekend social hour included in rates, high-speed wireless Internet and cable TV on premises. Hiking, shopping and water sports nearby.

Location: City. Historic Montford District, Biltmore Estate.

Certificate may be used: January-March, Sunday-Thursday, certain rooms eligible-subject to availability. Holidays excluded.

Balsam B2

Balsam Mountain Inn, Inc.

Seven Springs Drive
Balsam, NC 28707
(828)456-9498 (800)224-9498 Fax:(503)212-9855
Internet: www.balsaminn.com
E-mail: relax@balsammountaininn.com

Circa 1905. This inn, just a quarter mile from the famed Blue Ridge Parkway, is surrounded by the majestic Smoky Mountains. The inn was built in the Neoclassical style and overlooks the scenic hamlet of Balsam. The inn is listed in the National Register of Historic Places and is designated a Jackson County Historic Site. It features a mansard roof and wraparound porches with mountain views. A complimentary full breakfast is served daily, and dinner also is available daily.

Innkeeper(s): Kim and Sharon Shailer. $125-175. 50 rooms with PB, 8 suites. Breakfast included in rates. Types of meals: Full bkfst, early coffee/tea, picnic lunch and dinner. Restaurant on premises. Beds: KD. Reading lamp and desk in room. Fax, copier, parlor games, fireplace, hiking trails and wildflower walks on premises. Handicap access. Antiquing, downhill skiing, fishing, parks, shopping, whitewater rafting, hiking and Blue Ridge Pkwy nearby.

Location: Mountains.

"What wonderful memories we have of this beautiful inn."

Certificate may be used: Sunday-Thursday, November-June & September, excluding holiday periods.

Banner Elk   B4

Beech Alpen Inn

700 Beech Mountain Pkwy
Banner Elk, NC 28604-8015
(828)387-2252 Fax:(828)387-2229
Internet: www.beechalpen.com
E-mail: oceanreal@msn.com

Circa 1968. This rustic inn is a Bavarian delight affording
scenic vistas of the Blue Ridge Mountains. The innkeepers offer
accommodations at Top of the Beech, a Swiss-style ski chalet
with views of nearby slopes. The interiors of both properties are
inviting. At the Beech Alpen, several guest rooms have stone
fireplaces or French doors that open onto a balcony. Top of the
Beech's great room is a wonderful place to relax, with a huge
stone fireplace and comfortable furnishings. The Beech Alpen
Restaurant serves a variety of dinner fare.

Innkeeper(s): Steve Raymond. $79-159. 25 rooms with PB, 4 with FP.
Breakfast included in rates. Types of meals: Cont, early coffee/tea and
gourmet dinner. Restaurant on premises. Beds: KQD. Cable TV in room. Fax,
copier, parlor games, telephone and fireplace on premises. Antiquing, cross-
country skiing, downhill skiing, fishing, live theater, parks, shopping and
sporting events nearby.
Location: Mountains.
Certificate may be used: Sunday-Thursday, Jan. 3-Dec. 14.

Black Mountain   B3

Red Rocker Inn

136 N Dougherty St
Black Mountain, NC 28711-3326
(828)669-5991 (888)669-5991
Internet: www.redrockerinn.com
E-mail: info@redrockerinn.com

Circa 1896. Voted as the best B&B in Asheville, Black Mountain
and all of Western North Carolina for the past six years, this
three-story inn sits on one acre of pristinely landscaped grounds.
Located just 14 miles east of Asheville and the famous Biltmore
Estate, discover why the Atlanta Journal named this inn one of
its "Top 12 Favorites in the Southeast." Elegant, air-conditioned
guest bedrooms exude an inviting ambiance. Many feature fireplaces and whirlpool tubs. Each morning sit down to a heaping
Southern breakfast that is sure to satisfy. Stroll through gorgeous
gardens with a view of the mountains or relax in front of a roaring fire. Red rockers line the expansive wraparound porch, a perfect spot to enjoy tea and hand-dipped macaroons. Special dining packages are available year-round which include homemade
specialties and award-winning desserts.

Innkeeper(s): Doug & Jenny Bowman. $95-200. 17 rooms with PB, 4 with
FP, 5 with WP. Breakfast, afternoon tea, snacks/refreshments, Breakfast buffet
complimentary to house guests and available to others at $10.00 each.
Includes egg casseroles, hot baked goods and home made granola and
Southern favorites included in rates. Types of meals: Full bkfst, veg bkfst,
early coffee/tea, wine and dinner. Restaurant on premises. Beds: KQDT.
Reading lamp, ceiling fan, clock radio, desk, hair dryer, bath amenities, wire-
less Internet access and In-room safes in room. Central air. TV, VCR, DVD,
fax, library, parlor games, telephone, fireplace and gift shop on premises.
Antiquing, art galleries, bicycling, cross-country skiing, downhill skiing, fish-
ing, golf, hiking, horseback riding, live theater, museums, parks, shopping,
sporting events, tennis, water sports and wineries nearby.
Location: Mountains. Three blocks from downtown Black Mountain.
Certificate may be used: Feb. 1 to March 15, Sunday-Thursday; Nov. 15 to
Dec. 20, Sunday-Thursday.

Brevard   C3

The Inn at Brevard

315 E Main St
Brevard, NC 28712-3837
(828)884-2105 Fax:(828)885-7996
Internet: www.theinnatbrevard.com
E-mail: brevard@theinnatbrevard.com

Circa 1885. Furnished with 17th and 18th century décor, this
renovated Antebellum mansion is listed in the National
Register. The Inn at Brevard is located in the mountains of
Western North Carolina in Transylvania County, known as the
Land of Waterfalls. Feel refreshed by the relaxed elegance of
this southern B&B with a pond as well as herb and flower gardens. Stay in a guest room or suite in the main house, some
feature fireplaces and ball and claw tubs. Cabin-style rooms are
available in the annex. Breakfast is bountiful, with entrees plat-
ed individually and side dishes served family style. Dinner at
the inn is open to the public. Enjoy the Brevard Music Center
adjoining Pisgah National Forest in the valley of the French
Broad River, easily accessible from Blue Ridge Parkway.

Innkeeper(s): Howard & Faye Yager. $99-225. 15 rooms with PB, 4 with FP, 1
with WP, 2 suites, 3 conference rooms. Breakfast included in rates. Types of
meals: Full gourmet bkfst, veg bkfst, early coffee/tea, gourmet lunch, picnic
lunch, afternoon tea, snacks/refreshments, wine, gourmet dinner, room service
and Special occasion desserts and cakes. Restaurant on premises. Beds: QDT.
Modem hook-up, cable TV, reading lamp, CD player, ceiling fan, snack bar,
clock radio, coffeemaker, desk, hair dryer, bath amenities, wireless Internet
access, iron/ironing board and All rooms are decorated with antiques in room.
Air conditioning. VCR, DVD, fax, copier, library, child care, parlor games, telephone, fireplace, laundry facility, gift shop, Art and Antique gallery on premises.
Limited handicap access. Antiquing, art galleries, bicycling, canoeing/kayaking,
downhill skiing, fishing, golf, hiking, horseback riding, live theater, museums,
parks, shopping, sporting events, tennis and wineries nearby.
Location: Mountains.
Certificate may be used: Jan.1-May 15, Nov. 1-Dec. 30; $165/night Annex,
$175/night Main House, does not include breakfast or tax.

Cape Carteret   C8

Harborlight Guest House

332 Live Oak Drive
Cape Carteret, NC 28584
(252)393-6868 (800)624-VIEW
Internet: www.harborlightnc.com
E-mail: info@harborlightnc.com

Circa 1963. This three-story home rests on a peninsula just
yards from Bogue Sound and the Intracoastal Waterway. In-
room amenities might include a massive whirlpool tub, a clawfoot tub or fireplace, and each of the guest suites feature a
beautiful water view. The décor is done in a modern, coastal
style. Multi-course, gourmet breakfasts begin with fresh juices,
coffee, tea and an appetizer, perhaps a stuffed mushroom. From
there, guests enjoy a fresh fruit dish followed by a creative
entrée. All of which is served in suite or deckside. Museums,
an aquarium, historic sites, Hammocks Beach State Park and
harbor tours are among the attractions. Fort Macon State Park
affords guests an opportunity to view a restored Civil War fort.
Popular beaches and horseback riding are just minutes away.

Innkeeper(s): Leah. $110-300. 7 rooms, 5 with FP, 6 with HT, 7 suites, 1
conference room. Breakfast included in rates. Types of meals: Full gourmet
bkfst, early coffee/tea and picnic lunch. Beds: KQ. Modem hook-up, cable TV,
VCR, DVD, reading lamp, CD player, refrigerator, ceiling fan, snack bar, clock

radio, coffeemaker, turn-down service, most with hot tub/spa, most with fireplace, hair dryer, bathrobes, bath amenities, wireless Internet access, iron/ironing board, complimentary use of robes and slippers for stays of two nights or more, two-person jetted whirlpool tubs and 6 suites with Jacuzzi tub in room. Air conditioning. Fax, copier, library, parlor games, telephone, video library and wireless Internet access on premises. Limited handicap access. Antiquing, art galleries, beach, canoeing/kayaking, fishing, golf, horseback riding, parks, shopping, tennis, water sports and island excursions nearby.

Location: Ocean community, waterfront.

Publicity: *Southern Living, The State Magazine, Carolina Style Magazine, Coastal Living and Cary Magazine.*

Certificate may be used: Nov. 1-Feb. 28, Sunday-Thursday, excluding holidays. Only certain suites available for this special.

Fletcher   C5

Chateau on the Mountain

22 Vineyard Hill Dr.
Fletcher, NC 28732
(828)651-9810 (888)591-6281 Fax:(828)651-9811
Internet: www.ChateauOnTheMountain.com
E-mail: innkeepers@ChateauOnTheMountain.com

Circa 1990. Lush landscaping and incredible views of Mt. Pisgah are enjoyed at this ten-acre bed and breakfast built in the style of a French chateau. Poised atop Hoopers Creek Valley in Fletcher, North Carolina, Chateau on the Mountain is surrounded by meadows and mountains. Hiking trails are accented with native plants and wooded areas. Work out in the exercise room, swim in the outdoor pool and schedule spa services. Gather for refreshments or relax by the fire. Stay in a guest bedroom or suite with a sitting area, two-person steam shower, whirlpool, fireplace and adjoining patio or porch with a private hot tub. Accommodations in the Carriage House welcome pets and children. Savor a hearty country breakfast in the formal dining room.

Innkeeper(s): Lee & Jeanne Yudin. $185-350. 6 rooms with PB, 4 with FP, 6 with WP, 3 total suites, including 1 two-bedroom suite, 1 conference room. Breakfast, wine and Hors d'oeuvres on weekends included in rates. Types of meals: Full gourmet bkfst, veg bkfst, early coffee/tea, picnic lunch, snacks/refreshments, hors d'oeuvres, gourmet dinner, room service and Dinner prepared by a personal chef is available with 24-hour notice. Beds: KQ. Cable TV, VCR, DVD, reading lamp, CD player, refrigerator, ceiling fan, clock radio, telephone, coffeemaker, turn-down service, desk, hot tub/spa, fireplace, hair dryer, bathrobes, bath amenities, wireless Internet access, iron/ironing board, Laundry service with fee, Sound wave radios, Satellite TV including music channels and Wet bars in room. Central air. Fax, copier, spa, swimming, stable, library, parlor games, laundry facility, gift shop, Pool, Hiking trails and Numerous spa treatments on premises. Limited handicap access. Antiquing, art galleries, bicycling, canoeing/kayaking, downhill skiing, fishing, golf, hiking, horseback riding, live theater, museums, parks, shopping, tennis, water sports, wineries, Biltmore Estate, Chimney Rock Park, Kayaking, Pisgah Forest, Dupont Forest, Waterfalls, Fine & casual restaurants, Flower gardens, Downhill skiing, Snow tubing and White water rafting nearby.

Location: Country, mountains.

Publicity: *Pisgah Mountain magazine.*

Certificate may be used: Anytime, subject to availability.

Hertford   B9

1812 on The Perquimans B&B Inn

385 Old Neck Road
Hertford, NC 27944
(252)426-1812

Circa 1812. William and Sarah Fletcher were the first residents of this Federal-style plantation home, and the house is still in the family today. The Fletchers were Quakers and the first

North Carolina residents to offer to pay the way for workers who wished to return to Africa. The farm rests along the banks of the Perquimans River, and the grounds retain many original outbuildings, including a brick dairy, smokehouse and a 19th-century frame barn. In the National Register of Historic Places, the inn is appropriately appointed with antiques highlighting the restored mantels and woodwork. The inn is a lovely, pastoral retreat with bikes and canoeing available.

Innkeeper(s): Peter & Nancy Rascoe. $80-85. 4 rooms. Breakfast included in rates. Types of meals: Cont plus and Full Plantation Breakfast available for $5 per person. Beds: KQD. Fireplace in room. Central air. Bicycles, canoeing/kayaking and riverfront on premises.

Location: Riverfront. 12 miles from Historic Edenton.

Certificate may be used: All year, except for weekends in April, May, September, October and Easter weekend or Christmas Eve or night.

Highlands   C2

Colonial Pines Inn Bed and Breakfast

541 Hickory St
Highlands, NC 28741
(828)526-2060 (866)526-2060
Internet: www.colonialpinesinn.com
E-mail: sleeptight@colonialpinesinn.com

Circa 1937. Secluded on a hillside just half a mile from Highlands' Main Street, this inn offers relaxing porches that boast a mountain view. The parlor is another restful option, offering a TV, fireplace and piano. Rooms, highlighted by knotty pine, are  decorated with an eclectic mix of antiques. The guest pantry is always stocked with refreshments for those who need a little something in the afternoon. For breakfast, freshly baked breads accompany items such as a potato/bacon casserole and baked pears topped with currant sauce. In addition to guest rooms and suites, there are two cottages available, each with a fireplace and kitchen.

Innkeeper(s): Chris & Donna Alley. $95-165. 8 rooms, 5 with PB, 1 with FP, 2 two-bedroom suites, 1 cottage, 1 guest house. Breakfast, afternoon tea and snacks/refreshments included in rates. Types of meals: Full gourmet bkfst, veg bkfst and early coffee/tea. Beds: KQDT. Data port, cable TV, VCR, reading lamp, CD player, refrigerator, ceiling fan, snack bar, telephone, some with fireplace and wireless Internet access in room. DVD, fax and gift shop on premises. Antiquing, art galleries, canoeing/kayaking, downhill skiing, fishing, golf, hiking, horseback riding, live theater, shopping and tennis nearby.

Location: Mountains.

Publicity: *Greenville News, Atlanta Journal, Highlander, Atlanta Constitution and Birmingham News.*

"There was nothing we needed which you did not provide."

Certificate may be used: Mon, Tues, or Wed during May, June, or Sept, excluding holidays. Anytime, Last Minute-Based on Availability.

Inn At Half-Mile Farm

214 Half Mile Dr
Highlands, NC 28741
(828)526-8170 (800)946-6822 Fax:(828)526-2625
Internet: www.halfmilefarm.com
E-mail: stay@halfmilefarm.com

Circa 1870. Spread across 14 scenic acres with fields, forests, streams, two stocked ponds and a six-acre lake, this country inn exudes a casual elegance. Inn at Half-Mile Farm is located in Highlands, North Carolina, at the southern end of the Blue Ridge Mountains near Asheville. Atlanta is a two-hour drive. Enjoy wine and appetizers while relaxing on the landscaped courtyard or patio. Swim in the outdoor pool, go fly fishing or whitewater rafting on Chattooga River. Simple yet luxurious accommodations feature guest bedrooms, suites and cabins with an assortment of amenities that may include a fireplace, jetted tub, deck, fresh flowers and thick robes. Savor a hearty breakfast before exploring the area. Special and packages are usually available.

Innkeeper(s): The Messer Family. $160-550. 23 rooms with PB, 18 with FP, 22 with WP, 3 cabins. Breakfast, snacks/refreshments, hors d'oeuvres and wine included in rates. Types of meals: Full gourmet bkfst, veg bkfst, early coffee/tea and picnic lunch. Beds: KQ. Modem hook-up, data port, cable TV, VCR, DVD, ceiling fan, snack bar, clock radio, telephone, turn-down service, desk, voice mail, most with fireplace, hair dryer, bathrobes, bath amenities, wireless Internet access and iron/ironing board in room. Central air. Fax, copier and swimming on premises. Handicap access. Antiquing, art galleries, bicycling, canoeing/kayaking, downhill skiing, fishing, golf, hiking, horseback riding, live theater, parks, shopping, tennis, water sports, In the heart of the Blue Ridge Mountains, Surrounded by waterfalls, Scenic drives and All that nature has to offer nearby.

Location: Mountains.

Certificate may be used: Sunday-Wednesday; not valid on weekends or during the month of October.

Mount Airy   A5

Sobotta Manor Bed and Breakfast

347 West Pine Street
Mount Airy, NC 27030
(336)786-2777
Internet: www.sobottamanor.com
E-mail: sobottamanor@aol.com

Circa 1932. Feel surrounded by a casual elegance at Sobotta Manor Bed and Breakfast in Mount Airy, North Carolina, just ten miles from the Blue Ridge Parkway. Built in 1932 and recently renovated, this stately Tudor-style mansion offers romantic accommodations in the Yadkin Valley, now known for its vineyards. Gather for the social hour and sip a glass of local wine with appetizers. A variety of newspapers are available to read in the parlor and afternoon treats are also provided. The B&B has a complete concierge service. Enjoy a pleasant night's rest in one of the well-appointed guest bedrooms with upscale amenities. Linger over a lavish three-course gourmet breakfast in the European-inspired dining room overlooking the formal English gardens, in the intimate nook or on an open-air porch.

Innkeeper(s): Thurman and Robin Hester. $139-149. 4 rooms with PB. Breakfast and snacks/refreshments included in rates. Types of meals: Full gourmet bkfst, early coffee/tea, wine and Every day starts off with a leisurely but gourmet three-course breakfast served in the European inspired dining room overlooking the formal gardens. Different dining venues such as the cozy breakfast nook or the open-air porches provide for the option for privacy or for conversation with fellow guests. Beds: KQ. Cable TV, DVD, reading lamp, CD player, ceiling fan, clock radio, telephone, turn-down service, hair dryer, bathrobes, bath amenities and wireless Internet access in room. Central air. Fax, copier, bicycles, library, parlor games, fireplace and laundry facility on premises. Antiquing, art galleries, canoeing/kayaking, fishing, golf, hiking, horseback riding, live theater, museums, parks, shopping, sporting events, wineries, mountain biking, road biking, whitewater paddling, campgrounds, winery tours, Andy Griffith Playhouse, Wally Service Station and Squad Car Tour, concerts and jam sessions including Saturday Morning Jam at the Historic downtown cinema, Blue Ridge Jamboree and Thursday Night Jams, Tom Fry's Pickin on the Creek, Bright Leaf Drive In, Blue Ridge Parkway – Known as "America's Favorite Drive" (15 minutes), Mount Rogers National Recreation Area, Appalachian Mountains, Piedmont Regions, Winston-Salem-Greensboro Area, Mount Rogers National Recreation Area Region, Mabry Mill, Horne Creek Farm, Historic Rockford Village, Stone

Mountain State Park, Pilot Mountain State Park, Hanging Rock State Park and Outdoor Center, Tanglewood State Park, The Historic Town of Salem, The Museum of Early Southern Decorative Arts (MESDA), The Old Salem Toy Museum and Children's Museum, Reynolda House Museum of Art, Levering Orchard, Yadkin Valley Wines Trail, Panos Old North State Winery and Restaurant, Yadkin Valley Balloon Adventures and Korner's Folly nearby.

Location: City, mountains.

Publicity: *Our State Magazine (July 2008), Voted "Top Ten Bed and Breakfast in United States for 2007-2008, North Carolina Public Television Show "Simple Living" as a wedding destination and "The Sugar Creek Gang" (2008 movie by Kalon Media).*

Certificate may be used: December-March, Sunday-Thursday. Holidays and special events excluded.

New Bern   C8

Harmony House Inn

215 Pollock St
New Bern, NC 28560-4942
(252)636-3810 (800)636-3113
Internet: www.harmonyhouseinn.com
E-mail: harmony@cconnect.net

Circa 1850. Long ago, this two-story Greek Revival was sawed in half and the west side moved nine feet to accommodate new hallways, additional rooms and a staircase. A wall was then built to divide the house into two sections. The rooms are decorated with antiques, the innkeeper's collection of handmade crafts and other collectibles. Two of the suites include a heart-shaped Jacuzzi tub. Offshore breezes sway blossoms in the lush garden. Cross the street to an excellent restaurant or take a picnic to the shore.

Innkeeper(s): Ed & Sooki Kirkpatrick. $109-175. 10 rooms with PB, 2 with WP, 3 total suites, including 1 two-bedroom suite, 2 conference rooms. Breakfast, snacks/refreshments and wine included in rates. Types of meals: Full bkfst, veg bkfst and early coffee/tea. Beds: KQT. Modem hook-up, data port, cable TV, reading lamp, ceiling fan, telephone, bath amenities and wireless Internet access in room. Central air. Fax, copier, spa, library, parlor games and gift shop on premises. Limited handicap access. Antiquing, art galleries, beach, bicycling, golf, live theater, museums, parks and shopping nearby.

Location: City.

"We feel nourished even now, six months after our visit to Harmony House."

Certificate may be used: Year-round, Sunday-Thursday. Weekends November-February on a space available basis, excluding holidays and special events.

Sylva   C2

Mountain Brook Cottages

208 Mountain Brook Rd
Sylva, NC 28779-9659
(828)586-4329
Internet: www.mountainbrook.com
E-mail: mcmahon@mountainbrook.com

Circa 1931. Located in the Great Smokies, Mountain Brook in western North Carolina consists of 14 cabins on a hillside amid rhododendron, elm, maple and oak trees. The resort's 200-acre terrain is crisscrossed with brooks and waterfalls, contains a trout-stocked pond and nature trail. Two cabins are constructed with  logs from the property, while nine are made from native stone. They feature fireplaces, full kitchens, porch swings and some have Jacuzzi's.

Innkeeper(s): Gus, Michele, Maqelle McMahon. $100-150. 12 cottages with PB, 12 with FP. Types of meals: Early coffee/tea. Beds: KD. Reading lamp, refrigerator, ceiling fan, clock radio and coffeemaker in room. Spa, sauna, parlor games, fireplace, Game room, Spa/sauna bungalow, Brooks crisscross the property and are tributaries for great fly fishing rivers on premises. Handicap access. Amusement parks, antiquing, art galleries, bicycling, canoeing/kayaking, downhill skiing, fishing, golf, hiking, horseback riding, live theater, parks, shopping, sporting events, tennis, water sports, wineries, casino, Great Smokies National Park, railroad and nature trail nearby.

Location: Mountains. Rural.

Publicity: *Brides Magazine, Today, Charlotte Observer, Tampa Tribune, Bristol Herald Courier and Independent Tribune.*

"The cottage was delightfully cozy, and our privacy was not interrupted even once."

Certificate may be used: Feb. 1 to Oct. 1, Nov. 1 to Dec. 20, holidays excluded.

Tryon   C3

1906 Pine Crest Inn and Restaurant

85 Pine Crest Lane
Tryon, NC 28782-3486
(828)859-9135 (800)633-3001 Fax:(828)859-9136
Internet: pinecrestinn.com
E-mail: iloveinns@pinecrestinn.com

Circa 1906. Once a favorite of F. Scott Fitzgerald, this inn is nestled in the foothills of the Blue Ridge Mountains. Opened in 1917 by famed equestrian Carter Brown, the inn offers guests romantic fireplaces, gourmet dining and wide verandas that offer casual elegance. The Blue Ridge Parkway and the famous Biltmore House are a short drive away. Rooms are available in the Main Lodge and cottages. Original buildings include a 200-year-old log cabin, a woodcutter cottage and a stone cottage. Elegant meals are served in a Colonial tavern setting for full breakfasts and gourmet dinners.

Innkeeper(s): Carl Caudle. $89-299. 35 rooms with PB, 29 with FP, 2 with HT, 16 with WP, 8 total suites, including 2 two-bedroom suites and 1 three-bedroom suite, 10 cottages, 2 cabins, 3 conference rooms. Breakfast, afternoon tea, snacks/refreshments and Complimentary Port & Sherry in the evenings included in rates. Types of meals: Full gourmet bkfst, veg bkfst, Sun. brunch, early coffee/tea, gourmet lunch, picnic lunch, hors d'oeuvres, wine, gourmet dinner and room service. Restaurant on premises. Beds: KQDT. Modem hook-up, data port, cable TV, VCR, DVD, reading lamp, CD player, refrigerator, ceiling fan, clock radio, telephone, coffeemaker, turn-down service, desk, most with hot tub/spa, voice mail, most with fireplace, hair dryer, bathrobes, bath amenities, wireless Internet access and iron/ironing board in room. Central air. Fax, copier, swimming, library, parlor games, laundry facility and gift shop on premises. Handicap access. Antiquing, art galleries, bicycling, canoeing/kayaking, fishing, golf, hiking, horseback riding, live theater, museums, parks, shopping, tennis, water sports, wineries, Local Wineries and Numerous area waterfalls nearby.

Location: City, mountains.

Publicity: *Wine Spectator Best of Award of Excellence 10 consecutive years, Select Registry (15 consecutive years), AAA Four-Diamond 13 consecutive years, Southern Living, Our State magazine (August 2006) and Frommer's Budget Travel (2007).*

Certificate may be used: Anytime subject to availability excluding October, holidays and special events.

Valle Crucis   B4

The Mast Farm Inn

2543 Broadstone Road
Valle Crucis, NC 28691
(828)963-5857 (888)963-5857 Fax:(828) 963-6404
Internet: www.mastfarminn.com
E-mail: stay@mastfarminn.com

Circa 1812. Listed in the National Register of Historic Places,

this 18-acre farmstead includes a main house and ten outbuildings, one of them a log cabin built in 1812. The inn features a wraparound porch with rocking chairs, swings and a view of the mountain valley. Fresh flowers gathered from the garden add fragrance throughout the inn. Rooms are furnished with antiques, quilts and mountain crafts. In addition to the inn rooms, there are seven cottages available, some with kitchens.

Before breakfast is served, early morning coffee can be delivered to your room. Organic home-grown vegetables are featured at dinners, included in a contemporary regional cuisine.

Innkeeper(s): Sandra Deschamps Siano & Danielle Deschamps. $125-450. 15 rooms with PB, 8 with HT, 7 cottages, 2 guest houses. Breakfast included in rates. Types of meals: Full gourmet bkfst, veg bkfst, early coffee/tea, picnic lunch, snacks/refreshments, wine and gourmet dinner. Restaurant on premises. Beds: KQT. Modem hook-up, data port, reading lamp, CD player, refrigerator, ceiling fan, clock radio, telephone, coffeemaker, hot tub/spa, fireplace, bathrobes and the two cottages have a kitchen in room. Central air. DVD, fax, copier, spa, parlor games and gift shop on premises. Handicap access. Amusement parks, antiquing, art galleries, bicycling, canoeing/kayaking, cross-country skiing, downhill skiing, fishing, golf, hiking, horseback riding, live theater, museums, parks, shopping, water sports, River Sports, Blue Ridge Parkway and Grandfather Mountain nearby.

Location: Country, mountains.

Publicity: *Travel & Leisure, Cooking Light, Blue Ridge Country, Southern Living, New York Times, Our State, Carolina Gardener, Charlotte Taste, Appalachian Voice and The North Carolina Motorsport Association.*

"We want to live here!"

Certificate may be used: May and September only.

Warrenton   A7

Ivy Bed & Breakfast

331 North Main Street
Warrenton, NC 27589
(252)257-9300 (800)919-9886
Internet: www.ivybedandbreakfast.com
E-mail: info@ivybedandbreakfast.com

Circa 1903. Open year-round, this Queen Anne Victorian B&B is located near Lake Gaston and Kerr Lake. It is an easy stroll to quaint downtown shops and an old-fashioned drug store and soda fountain. The one-acre grounds include an English-style box garden with sitting area and fountain. Pat's Porch has inviting rockers and wicker chairs. Evening social hour with appetizers and beverages is hosted in Carter Williams Parlour with a vintage grand piano. Named after the ladies who have lived here, guest bedrooms feature heart pine floors, antiques and Waverly window and bed treatments. Stay in a room with a Jacuzzi and canopy bed or a clawfoot tub and brass bed. The Ivy Suite adjoins two rooms with a connecting bathroom. An incredible three-course candlelit breakfast is served in the Nannie Tarwater Dining Room.

Innkeeper(s): Ellen and Jerry Roth. $100-120. 4 rooms, 3 with PB, 1 with WP, 1 two-bedroom suite, 1 conference room. Breakfast and A full 3-course candlelit breakfast of your choosing is served at a time that fits your schedule included in rates. Types of meals: Full gourmet bkfst, veg bkfst and early coffee/tea. Beds: Q. Cable TV, reading lamp, clock radio, telephone, hair dryer, bath amenities, wireless Internet access, Some rooms with DVD player, Ceiling Fans and Tub with Jacuzzi Jets in room. Central air. Fax, copier, library, parlor games, fireplace, laundry facility, gift shop, Guest refrigerator with soft drinks and bottled water, Coffeemaker, Rocking chairs, Iron/ironing board, Washer/dryer and Wireless high speed Internet on premises. Antiquing, beach, bicycling, canoeing/kayaking, fishing, golf, hiking, horseback riding, live theater, parks, shopping, sporting events, water sports and historic homes nearby.

Location: Country.

Publicity: *Charlotte Magazine, Lake Gaston Gazette, Warren Record, Birmingham News, www.associatedcontent.com, The Great Country Inns of America Cookbook and US Local Business Association Best of Warrenton Award.*

Certificate may be used: Anytime, subject to availability.

Williamston   B8

Big Mill Bed & Breakfast

1607 Big Mill Rd
Williamston, NC 27892-8032
(252) 792-8787
Internet: www.bigmill.com
E-mail: info@bigmill.com

Circa 1918. Originally built as a small arts and crafts frame house, the many renovations conceal its true age. The historic farm outbuildings that include the chicken coop, smokehouse, pack house, tobacco barns and potato house, were built from on-site heart pine and cypress trees that were felled and floated down the streams of this 250-acre woodland estate. The Corncrib guest bedroom is in the pack house that originally housed mules. Each of the guest bedrooms feature climate control, stenciled floors, faux-painted walls, hand-decorated tiles on the wet bar and a private entrance. The suite also boasts a stone fireplace and impressive view. The countryside setting includes a three-acre lake with bridges, fruit orchard, vegetable and flower gardens. Eighty-year-old pecan trees planted by Chloe's parents provide nuts for homemade treats as well as shade for the inn.

Innkeeper(s): Chloe Tuttle. $85-145. 4 rooms with PB, 1 with FP, 2 suites, 1 conference room. Breakfast and We offer catered candlelight dinners under the grapevine or in your room included in rates. Types of meals: Full plus, veg bkfst, early coffee/tea, picnic lunch, gourmet dinner and Catered candlelight meals delivered to your room or on your private patio. Picnic lunches for your outings. Beds: QT. Cable TV, VCR, DVD, reading lamp, CD player, refrigerator, ceiling fan, clock radio, telephone, coffeemaker, desk, some with fireplace, hair dryer, bath amenities, wireless Internet access, iron/ironing board, private entrances, individual climate control, wet bars, kitchenettes with sinks, refrigerators, microwave, coffee pot and laundry facilities in room. Central air. Fax, bicycles, parlor games, laundry facility, candlelight dinner in room, lake fishing and off-street parking for any size vehicle on premises. Limited handicap access. Antiquing, bicycling, canoeing/kayaking, fishing, golf, hiking, horseback riding, live theater, parks, sporting events, water sports, horse shows, nature trails, nature preserves, boating access, Roanoke River Refuge, Roanoke River camping platforms, Bob Martin Agriculture Center, catered meals, couples massage, spa services, Turnage Theater and Rocky Hock Dinner Theater nearby.

Location: Country. Carolina countryside.

Publicity: *Washington Post, Daily Reflector, Inn Cuisine, Down East Magazine, Our State Magazine, Inns, the Perfect Place to Stay, NC Bed & Breakfast Cookbook, Best Recipes from American County Inns and Bed & Breakfasts, Her Magazine, WRAL-TV, WITN-TV and Patricia Raskin's Positive Living Radio.*

Certificate may be used: December-February, subject to availability, excluding Valentine's Day, applies to nightly rates only. No other coupons with this offer.

Wilmington   D7

Graystone Inn

100 S 3rd St
Wilmington, NC 28401-4503
(910)763-2000 (888)763-4773 Fax:(910)763-5555
Internet: www.graystoneinn.com
E-mail: contactus@graystoneinn.com

Circa 1906. If you are a connoisseur of inns, you'll be delight-

ed with this stately mansion in the Wilmington Historic District and in the National Register. Recently chosen by American Historic Inns as one of America's Top Ten Romantic Inns, towering columns mark the balconied grand entrance. Its 14,000 square feet of magnificent space includes antique furnishings, art and amenities. A staircase of hand-carved red oak rises three stories. Guests lounge in the music room, drawing room and library. A conference room and sitting area are on the third floor, once a grand ballroom. The elegant guest rooms are often chosen for special occasions, especially the Bellevue, which offers a King bed, sofa and handsome period antiques with a 2-person soaking tub and shower.

Innkeeper(s): Rich & Marcia Moore. $169-359. 9 rooms with PB, 7 with FP, 1 conference room. Breakfast included in rates. Types of meals: Full gourmet bkfst and early coffee/tea. Beds: KQ. Cable TV, reading lamp, ceiling fan, telephone, coffeemaker, turn-down service, desk, some with hot tub/spa, voice mail, hair dryer, bathrobes, bath amenities, wireless Internet access and iron/ironing board in room. Central air. Fax, copier, library, parlor games and fireplace on premises. Antiquing, art galleries, beach, fishing, golf, live theater, museums, parks, shopping, sporting events, tennis and water sports nearby.

Location: City.

Publicity: *Country Inns, Young Indiana Jones, Matlock, Dawsons Creek, One Tree Hill, Rambling Rose, Mary Jane's Last Dance, Cats Eye, The Locket and The Water is Wide.*

Certificate may be used: Nov. 1-March 31, Sunday-Thursday, holidays excluded.

Windsor   C6

The Inn at Gray's Landing

401 S King St
Windsor, NC 27983-6721
(252) 794-2255 (877) 794-3501 Fax:(252)794-2254
Internet: www.grayslanding.com
E-mail: innkeepersgrayslanding@yahoo.com

Circa 1790. Experience classic Southern tradition at this historic Georgian Colonial B&B that is furnished with Victorian period antiques and reproductions. The Inn at Grays Landing Bed & Breakfast is surrounded by cotton, corn and tobacco fields in the historic district of Windsor, North Carolina. This small town sits on the banks of the Cashie River and is a short drive to the Outer Banks. Stroll by the English side garden then sit on the porch and look out on magnolias and crepe myrtles. Stay in a guest room or suite with a canopy, sleigh or brass bed and a spa, steam or rain shower, Jacuzzi or clawfoot tub. After a satisfying breakfast explore the many regional activities. Ask about the special weekend getaway package offered.

Innkeeper(s): Lynette Mallery. $79-139. 5 rooms with PB, 1 with WP, 2 suites, 1 conference room. Breakfast and Sunday brunch included in rates. Types of meals: Full bkfst, veg bkfst, early coffee/tea, wine, Dinners on Thursday and Friday nights by reservation Back Porch bar opens in April 2011 and. Restaurant on premises. Beds: KQDT. Cable TV, reading lamp, CD player, snack bar, clock radio, desk, hair dryer, bathrobes, bath amenities, wireless Internet access and iron/ironing board in room. Central air. DVD, library, telephone, fireplace and gift shop on premises. Handicap access. Antiquing, canoeing/kayaking, fishing, golf, Free pontoon rides on Saturday mornings, by reservation. Fishing, river walk and zoo nearby.

Location: City.

Certificate may be used: Anytime, subject to availability.

North Dakota

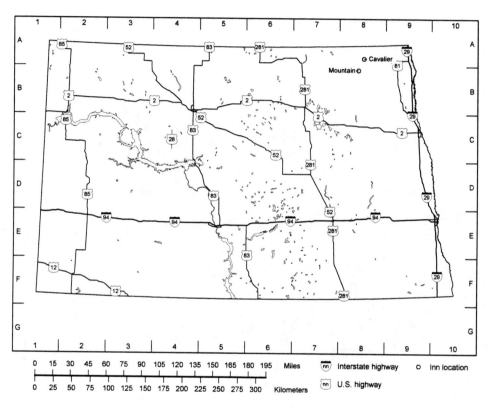

0 15 30 45 60 75 90 105 120 135 150 165 180 195 Miles

0 25 50 75 100 125 150 175 200 225 250 275 300 Kilometers

(nn) Interstate highway   o Inn location

(nn) U.S. highway

Cavalier   A8

The Inn At Cavalier B&B

9417 Hwy 18
Cavalier, ND 58220
(701) 265-8739
Internet: www.ndbba.com/ic.htm
E-mail: geigerbandb@yahoo.com

Circa 1920. Close to both Minnesota and Canada, this North Dakota inn offers gracious hospitality and generous service from Memorial Day to Labor Day. Gracing the heart of Cavalier, it is an easy walk to shops, a theater, gym, restaurants, hiking and nature trails. Savor afternoon tea in the Victorian tea room, relax on all-season porches and read in the library. Stay in a themed guest room or suite with a clawfoot soaking tub. Start each glorious day with in-room coffee or tea followed by a leisurely multi-course breakfast served on fine china in the formal dining room, or enjoyed al fresco. The facilities and setting are perfect for meetings and special events. Ask about nearby recreation sites and local farm tours.

Innkeeper(s): Geraldine Geiger. Call for rates. 3 rooms. Library and claw foot tubs in room.

Location: Country.

Certificate may be used: Labor Day to Memorial Day, Sunday-Thursday.

Ohio

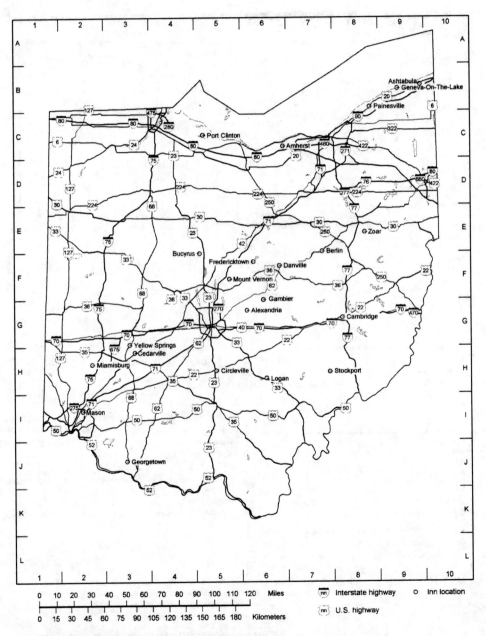

	Miles												
0	10	20	30	40	50	60	70	80	90	100	110	120	Miles

| 0 | 15 | 30 | 45 | 60 | 75 | 90 | 105 | 120 | 135 | 150 | 165 | 180 | Kilometers |

Interstate highway   o Inn location

U.S. highway

Alexandria G6

WillowBrooke Bed 'n Breakfast

4459 Morse Road
Alexandria, OH 43001
(740)924-6161 (800)722-6372
Internet: www.willowbrooke.com
E-mail: wilbrk@aol.com

Circa 1980. There are no worries at this English Tudor Manor House and Guest Cottage located in a secluded 34-acre wooded setting. Furnished in a traditional decor, spacious guest bedrooms and romantic suites offer extensive amenities that pamper and please like feather beds or pillowtop mattresses, candlelight, whirlpool tubs, kitchens and balconies or patios. Families are welcome to stay in the Garden Suite or Guest House. For breakfast, choose from three juices along with French toast and strawberries, scrambled eggs and ham. Enjoy year-round use of the outdoor hot tub, and browse the gift shop for glass oil candles and crystal table accessories.

Innkeeper(s): Sandra Gilson. $115-270. 6 rooms with PB, 3 with FP, 3 suites, 1 cottage, 1 guest house. Breakfast included in rates. Types of meals: Full gourmet bkfst and early coffee/tea. Beds: KQ. Modem hook-up, cable TV, VCR, DVD, reading lamp, stereo, refrigerator, ceiling fan, clock radio, telephone, coffeemaker, turn-down service, desk, most with hot tub/spa, most with fireplace, hair dryer, bathrobes, bath amenities, featherbeds and candlelight in room. Central air. Fax, copier, spa, sauna, parlor games, gift shop, gift shop with Firelight oil candles, crystal table setting accessories and outdoor five-person hydrotherapy hot tub on premises. Limited handicap access. Antiquing, art galleries, beach, bicycling, fishing, golf, hiking, live theater, museums, parks, shopping, sporting events, tennis, wineries, Longaberger Basket Homestead, Heisey Glass Museum and National Trails Raceway nearby.

Location: Country. Located 1/4 mile back into the woods.

Certificate may be used: Monday-Thursday, subject to availability, excludes October.

Ashtabula B9

Gilded Swan B&B

5024 West Ave
Ashtabula, OH 44004
(440)992-1566 (888)345-7926
Internet: www.thegildedswan.com
E-mail: gsinfo@roadrunner.com

Circa 1902. Romantic interludes and memorable moments are easily experienced at this lavish Queen Anne Victorian in a Lake Erie harbor town. Painstakingly restored, the B&B is furnished with cherished family heirlooms and antiques. Comfortable guest bedrooms and suites boast welcoming decor, canopy beds, whirlpool tubs, a fireplace and pillow chocolates. In the elegant dining room, a sumptuous breakfast may include raspberry-stuffed French toast and grilled sausage links. Afternoon snacks are also offered. Centrally located, the inn is within easy access to wine country, Cleveland's museums, Pennsylvania's attractions and Amish country.

Innkeeper(s): Elaine Swanson. $75-105. 4 rooms, 2 with PB, 1 with FP. Breakfast and snacks/refreshments included in rates. Types of meals: Full gourmet bkfst, early coffee/tea, picnic lunch and afternoon tea. Beds: KQT. Cable TV, reading lamp, ceiling fan, clock radio, telephone, coffeemaker, desk, most with hot tub/spa, most with fireplace, hair dryer, bathrobes, bath amenities and wireless Internet access in room. Central air. VCR, spa, library, parlor games and gift shop on premises. Amusement parks, antiquing, beach, bicycling, canoeing/kayaking, fishing, golf, hiking, live theater, museums, parks, shopping, water sports and wineries nearby.

Publicity: *Country Extra Magazine.*

Certificate may be used: Anytime, subject to availability.

Berlin E7

Donna's Premier Lodging B&B

5523 Twp Rd 358 East Street
Berlin, OH 44610
(330)893-3068 (800)320-3338
Internet: www.donnasofberlin.com
E-mail: info@donnasb-b.com

Circa 1991. Staying here for any reason is a pleasure. Come for the perfect romantic getaway, a respite from everyday cares or just because. Every season is a great time to visit. See glistening snow-covered hills and experience the holiday season. Travel country roads in spring and glimpse new life on Amish farms. Catch the many summer festivals with out-of-this-world local foods or take in the awe-inspiring colorful displays of autumn. Accommodations range from gorgeous villas and suites to secluded cedar cabins in the woods with cascading waterfalls, fireplaces and Jacuzzis. Indulge in a full-course breakfast in bed before beginning the day's adventures. Special touches may include a couples' massage, sleigh and carriage rides, gift baskets and much more. Gracious and friendly staff go out of their way to make each visit memorable. Donna's is conveniently located close to gift shops and attractions in Berlin, Ohio.

Innkeeper(s): Donna Marie Schlabach. $99-369. 3 rooms, 17 with PB, 17 with FP, 17 with HT, 17 cabins. Breakfast, Fruit & cookie platter and Sparkling sweet apple cider included in rates. Types of meals: Country bkfst, veg bkfst, picnic lunch and snacks/refreshments. Beds: KQ. Cable TV, VCR, DVD, reading lamp, stereo, refrigerator, ceiling fan, clock radio, telephone, coffeemaker, hot tub/spa, fireplace, hair dryer, bath amenities, iron/ironing board, Steam Sauna, Billiards, Barbecue grills, Kitchenette and Kitchens in room. Central air. Fax, copier, parlor games, gift shop, Landscaped grounds with waterfall/stream/pond combination, Picnic table and Fire ring with furnished wood on premises. Limited handicap access. Antiquing, art galleries, canoeing/kayaking, fishing, golf, hiking, horseback riding, live theater, museums, parks, shopping, tennis, wineries, Carriage, Sleigh & Buggy Rides, Cheese & chocolate factories and Amish country nearby.

Location: Country.

Publicity: *Akron Beacon Journal* - "One of the top B&B's of NE Ohio," *Arrington Publishing* - "Most Romantic Hideaway," *Country Traveler, Amish Heartland, Country Living Magazine, Canton Repository Newspaper* , *Neil Zurker's "One Tank Trips"* - Channel 8, Cleveland, "Kicking it with Kenny" - *Cleveland Fox News* and "Morning Show" - TV 27 Youngstown.

Certificate may be used: November-May, Sunday-Thursday, Honeymoon/Anniversary Villa only.

Hannah's House Bed & Breakfast

5410 County Road 201
Berlin, OH 44610
(330)893-2368 (800)329-9434
Internet: www.hannahshouseretreat.com
E-mail: info@hannahshouseretreat.com

Circa 1997. Spanning five acres with a rock waterfall and spacious patio area, this premier B&B in Holmes County boasts a Victorian style. Guest bedrooms and suites overlook a wooded valley. Select a room with a natural gas fireplace or a stay in a suite on the main floor with a Jacuzzi for two, as well as kitchen, dining and sitting areas and a patio entrance. Hannah's House Bed & Breakfast in Berlin, Ohio provides a hot and hearty breakfast each morning. Ask about specials and packages available. Browse in the local Amish Country Leather Shop for quality items to keep or give as gifts.

Innkeeper(s): Barbara. $90-215. 5 rooms with PB, 1 with FP, 2 with WP, 2 suites. Breakfast and Sparkling Grape Juice included in rates. Types of meals: Full bkfst. Beds: KQ. Cable TV, refrigerator, ceiling fan, clock radio, coffeemaker, desk, some with hot tub/spa, some with fireplace, hair dryer, bath amenities, wireless Internet access and iron/ironing board in room. Central air. Telephone on premises. Antiquing, bicycling, canoeing/kayaking, golf, hiking, horseback riding, museums, shopping, wineries, Cheese & Chocolate Factories, Shopping (Local Crafts) and Amish Country nearby.

Location: Country. Millersburg.

Certificate may be used: November-April, Sunday-Thursday (All rooms must be consecutive nights stay). Not Valid on Holidays or Holiday Weekends; subject to availability.

Bucyrus   E5

HideAway Country Inn

1601 SR 4
Bucyrus, OH 43302
(419)562-3013 (800)570-8233 Fax:(419)562-3003
Internet: www.HideAwayInn.com
E-mail: innkeeper@hideawayinn.com

Circa 1938. Experience a refreshing getaway while staying at this remarkable inn. Because of the inn's outrageous service, even the business traveler will feel rejuvenated after embarking on a rendezvous with nature here. Exquisite guest suites feature private Jacuzzis, fireplaces and amenities that pamper. Savor a leisurely five-course breakfast. Enjoy fine dining in the restaurant, or ask for an intimate picnic to be arranged. A productive conference room instills a personal quiet and inspires the mind.

Innkeeper(s): Debbie Miller, Chef Michael Thompson, Krys Fearing - Guest Services. $79-290. 12 rooms with PB, 7 with FP, 1 with HT, 10 with WP, 10 total suites, including 2 two-bedroom suites, 2 guest houses, 2 conference rooms. Breakfast included in rates. Types of meals: Full gourmet bkfst, veg bkfst, Sun. brunch, early coffee/tea, gourmet lunch, picnic lunch, afternoon tea, snacks/refreshments, hors d'oeuvres, wine, gourmet dinner, room service, Cher to 12 Presidents around the world. Enjoy Breakfast, Lunch or Dinner in the fine dining atmosphere of the on-site restaurant and or choose from the menu and have it delivered to your room in a Picnic Basket. Enjoy wine and spirits in the fully inclusive wine cellar and martini bar. Restaurant on premises. Beds: KQDT. Cable TV, VCR, DVD, reading lamp, stereo, refrigerator, ceiling fan, clock radio, telephone, coffeemaker, turn-down service, desk, voice mail, most with fireplace, hair dryer, bathrobes, bath amenities, wireless Internet access, iron/ironing board, Room Service, Packages in room prior to arrival and Wifi in room. Central air. Fax, copier, spa, library, parlor games, laundry facility, gift shop, Full kitchen, Restaurant, Patio area, Life-size one-of-a-kind checker board, Fountains for relaxation, Full spa service, Satellite TV, 5-course gourmet breakfast, Wireless Internet anywhere on property and bilingual on premises. Handicap access. Amusement parks, antiquing, bicycling, canoeing/kayaking, downhill skiing, fishing, golf, hiking, horseback riding, live theater, museums, parks, shopping, sporting events, tennis, water sports, wineries, Historic Speakeasy visited by Al Capone and Walking trails nearby.

Location: Country.

Publicity: *New York Times, Columbus Dispatch, Ohio Country Journal, Akron Beacon Journal, Cleveland Plain Dealer, Travel & Leisure,MidWest Living, Ohio Proud, Neil Zurcker One Tank-Trips-Cleveland, Akron WKBN, Del's Folks and Del's Feasts Cleveland and Cleveland WKYC.*

Certificate may be used: Sunday-Thursday, excluding holidays and special event dates. Room pricing at rack rate. Not available with any other discounts.

Cambridge   G8

Colonel Taylor Inn Bed & Breakfast

633 Upland Rd
Cambridge, OH 43725
(740) 432-7802
Internet: www.coltaylorinnbb.com
E-mail: coltaylor@coltaylorinnbb.com

Circa 1878. Be pampered by warm country hospitality at this majestic Victorian mansion with a rich historic heritage and modern comforts. The Colonel Taylor Inn Bed & Breakfast,

poised on a hill above Cambridge, Ohio, is open year-round for a perfect vacation, romantic getaway or pleasant business trip. Relax upon arrival with an afternoon snack in one of the two parlors or on one of the three porches. The large deck overlooks enchanted flower gardens. Beverages are always available. Delightful guest bedrooms are on the second floor with working fireplaces and antique furnishings. Most rooms feature four-poster beds and sitting areas by bay windows. The spacious Rose Room also boasts a whirlpool tub. Linger over a five-course breakfast served each morning.

Innkeeper(s): Jim & Patricia Irvin. $135-210. 4 rooms with PB, 4 with FP, 1 two-bedroom suite, 2 conference rooms. Breakfast, afternoon tea and Dinner for two at the Inn for an extra charge by reservation only included in rates. Types of meals: Full gourmet bkfst, veg bkfst, early coffee/tea, picnic lunch, dinner and Dinner for two or twelve by reservation only! $70+tax per couple. Beds: KQ. Cable TV, reading lamp, ceiling fan, clock radio, fireplace, hair dryer, bathrobes, bath amenities, wireless Internet access, iron/ironing board, fireplace, one with bathroom whirlpool tub/fireplace, wireless high speed Internet connection, cable TV in Lilac room and phone available in room. Central air. TV, VCR, library, parlor games, telephone, gift shop, large-screen TV, two parlors, formal dining room, three porches and wireless Internet on premises. Antiquing, art galleries, beach, bicycling, canoeing/kayaking, cross-country skiing, fishing, golf, hiking, horseback riding, live theater, museums, parks, shopping, tennis, water sports, wineries, the wilds, salt fork state park, glass factories, potteries, festivals, concerts, outdoor drama theatre, museums and antique stores nearby.

Location: Small town historic area.

Publicity: *Mid-West Living Magazine, Arrington's Bed & Breakfast Journal, Inn Traveler 4 years of awards, Mid-West Living (Spring 2006), Tea Time Magazine (2009) and voted "Best in the USA" & awarded "The Inn with the most Hospitality" 2003 by inngoers.*

Certificate may be used: Monday-Thursday for all months except May and October.

Cedarville   H3

Hearthstone Inn & Suites

10 S Main St
Cedarville, OH 45314-9760
(937)766-3000 (187)764-46466 Fax:(N/A)
Internet: www.hearthstoneinn.com
E-mail: Please call our toll-free number

Circa 2001. Blending regional themes with small-town hospitality, this country inn hotel with an upscale bed and breakfast ambiance is family-owned and non-smoking. Enjoy old-fashioned friendliness, generous service and impeccable cleanliness. Relax on the wraparound porch or on the leather sofa by the huge Ohio River rock hearth in the Fireplace Lounge with Queen Anne decor. Browse through the historical displays and the cottage gift shop. Pleasant guest bedrooms and Jacuzzi suites feature pampering amenities. Hand-hewn beams beneath the second-floor balcony and mural art accent the Breakfast Commons where a Supreme Selections morning buffet is served. The inn is conveniently located right on the Ohio to Erie Bike Trail.

Innkeeper(s): Stuart & Ruth Zaharek. $109-169. 20 rooms with PB, 2 with HT, 2 suites, 1 conference room. Breakfast included in rates. Types of meals: Cont plus. Beds: KQ. Modem hook-up, data port, cable TV, reading lamp, refrigerator, ceiling fan, clock radio, telephone, coffeemaker, desk, some with hot tub/spa, hair dryer, bath amenities, wireless Internet access and iron/ironing board in room. Air conditioning. VCR, DVD, fax, copier, spa, bicycles, library, fireplace, laundry facility and gift shop on premises. Handicap access. Antiquing, bicycling, canoeing/kayaking, fishing, golf, hiking, live theater, museums, parks, shopping and tennis nearby.

Location: Country.

Publicity: *Cincinnati Enquirer, Ohio Magazine and Fodor's Travel Guides.*

Certificate may be used: November-January, Sunday-Wednesday; April-May, Sunday-Wednesday. Last minute subject to availability (same day, anytime).

Circleville H5

Castle Inn Romantic Retreat B&B

610 S Court St
Circleville, OH 43113
(740)412-2472 Fax:(740)477-2342
Internet: www.castleinn.net
E-mail: thecastleinn@aol.com

Circa 1890. Feel like royalty in this romantic castle retreat built by Samuel Ruggles in the late 1800s. The Castle Inn provides accommodations in Circleville, Central Ohio. Authentic documentation of the castle's history adorns the walls of the grand staircase. Gather in the parlor to relax, read or plan the day. Stay in a delightful guest bedroom on the second floor tower or a third-floor honeymoon suite. Select a room with a gas honeycomb fireplace, canopy bed, entertainment center, double Jacuzzi, heart-shaped jetted tub or marble bath with soaking tub.

Innkeeper(s): Jeannie Shaw. $119-279. 6 rooms with PB, 2 with FP, 3 suites. Beds: Q. Cable TV, VCR, CD player, ceiling fan and clock radio in room. Air conditioning.

Certificate may be used: Anytime, subject to availability.

Danville F6

The White Oak Inn

29683 Walhonding Rd, SR 715
Danville, OH 43014
(740)599-6107 (877)908-5923
Internet: www.whiteoakinn.com
E-mail: info@whiteoakinn.com

Circa 1915. Large oaks and ivy surround the wide front porch of this three-story farmhouse situated on 13 green acres. It is located on the former Indian trail and pioneer road that runs along the Kokosing River, and an Indian mound has been discovered on the property. The inn's woodwork is all original white oak, and guest rooms are furnished in antiques. Visitors often shop for maple syrup, cheese and handicrafts at nearby Amish farms. Three cozy fireplace rooms and two cottages provide the perfect setting for romantic evenings.

Innkeeper(s): Yvonne & Ian Martin. $140-240. 12 rooms with PB, 6 with FP, 3 with WP, 2 cottages, 1 conference room. Breakfast and snacks/refreshments included in rates. Types of meals: Country bkfst, veg bkfst, early coffee/tea, gourmet dinner and Romantic dinner baskets delivered to rooms. Beds: KQDT. Reading lamp, CD player, ceiling fan, clock radio, telephone, coffeemaker, some with hot tub/spa, some with fireplace, hair dryer and wireless Internet access in room. Air conditioning. TV, DVD, library, parlor games, gift shop, guest refrigerator and piano on premises. Limited handicap access. Antiquing, bicycling, canoeing/kayaking, fishing, golf, hiking, horseback riding, parks, shopping, water sports, wineries, Amish area, Longaberger Baskets and Roscoe Village nearby.

Location: Country. Rural.

Publicity: *Ladies Home Journal, Columbus Monthly, Cleveland Plain Dealer, Country, Glamour, Columbus Dispatch, Midwest Living, Ohio Magazine and PBS - Country Inn Cooking.*

"The dinner was just fabulous and we enjoyed playing the antique grand piano."

Certificate may be used: Sunday-Thursday.

Fredericktown F6

Heartland Country Resort

3020 Township Rd 190
Fredericktown, OH 43019
(419)768-9300 (800)230-7030 Fax:(419)768-9133
Internet: www.heartlandcountryresort.com
E-mail: heartbb@bright.net

Circa 1996. Peacefully secluded among shady woodlands and rolling hills, this upscale country resort and relaxing retreat is a sprawling haven on more than one hundred acres. The newly constructed log home offers a private setting and luxurious comfort. The refurbished main farmhouse boasts a screened porch and spacious deck. A pool table, games and puzzles are enjoyed in the recreation room. A video library provides a large selection of movies. Stay in a deluxe guest suite with cathedral ceilings, two-person Jacuzzis, full kitchens or kitchenettes, private entrances and porches. Start the day with a scrumptious breakfast. A variety of wrangling and horseback riding activities are available for everyone, from beginners to the experienced. Explore nearby Amish country, Mohican and Malabar State Parks and Kingwood Garden Center.

Innkeeper(s): Dorene Henschen. $180-240. 4 rooms, 3 with PB, 3 with FP, 3 with WP, 3 total suites, including 1 two-bedroom suite, 3 cabins, 1 conference room. Breakfast, afternoon tea and snacks/refreshments included in rates. Types of meals: Country bkfst, veg bkfst, early coffee/tea, lunch, picnic lunch, dinner and room service. Beds: QT. TV, VCR, DVD, reading lamp, stereo, refrigerator, ceiling fan, snack bar, clock radio, telephone, coffeemaker, desk, hot tub/spa, fireplace, bathrobes, bath amenities and Suites have Jacuzzis in the private baths. in room. Central air. Fax, copier, spa, stable, library, pet boarding, parlor games, laundry facility, gift shop, Pool table, Wrangler activities, Chickens, Horses, Cattle, Golden retrievers, Cats, Screened porch, Lawn games such as badminton, volleyball, croquet & Bocce Ball, Stone fire ring for evening bonfires, Newly renovated Lodge has corner stone fireplace and DirecTV on premises. Antiquing, bicycling, canoeing/kayaking, cross-country skiing, downhill skiing, fishing, golf, hiking, horseback riding, live theater, museums, parks, shopping, wineries, Amish Country, Birding, Mid-Ohio raceway, Mohegan and Malabar Farm State Parks, Kingwood Garden Center, Knox Co. Rails-to-Trails paved 14 mile bike path, Knox Co. Pool and Water Park nearby.

Location: Country.

Publicity: *Columbus Dispatch, Country Extra, One Tank Trips, Getaways, Home and Away, Ohio Magazine, Horse and Rider, Cincinnati Enquirer, Arrington's B&B Journal, Columbus Channel 10 and Cleveland Channel 7.*

"Warm hospitality . . . Beautiful surroundings and pure peace & quiet. What more could one want from a B&B in the country? Thank you for an excellent memory!"

Certificate may be used: Monday-Thursday, November-April, subject to availability.

Gambier F5

Gambier House

107 East Wiggin St
Gambier, OH 43022
(740)427-2668
Internet: www.gambierhouse.com
E-mail: gambierhouse@earthlink.net

Circa 1845. Located across from the main campus of Kenyon College in Knox County, this 1845 Victorian clapboard has been fully restored as a welcome retreat in Gambier, Ohio. Gambier House offers several areas to gather in from the formal fireside parlor to the family room with games to play and movies to watch. Sit in a front porch rocker or in the peaceful weeping cherry courtyard. Guests of this B&B enjoy access to Kenyon Athletic Center. The kitchen features complimentary soda, tea, coffee, snacks and fruit. Three of the inviting guest bedrooms boast fireplaces and the two-story Carriage House Suite includes a small kitchen. The dining room provides an elegant setting for a gourmet breakfast made with local organic produce. Ask about celebratory packages available.

Innkeeper(s): E.J. Heer. $110-155. 6 rooms with PB, 3 with FP, 1 two-bedroom suite. Breakfast and snacks/refreshments included in rates. Types of meals: Full gourmet bkfst, veg bkfst and early coffee/tea. Beds: QDT. Reading lamp, clock radio, some with fireplace, bath amenities, wireless Internet access and Carriage House suite has small kitchen with fridge/toaster/coffeemaker/stove as well as TV/VCR in room. Central air. TV, VCR, library, parlor games, telephone, Complimentary sodas, Cookies, Microwave, Dishes, Easy access to comprehensive athletic facilities and Bike trail on premises. Limited handicap access. Antiquing, bicycling, canoeing/kayaking, cross-country skiing, fishing, golf, hiking, horseback riding, live theater, parks, shopping, sporting events, tennis, water sports, wineries, Amish Country, Mohican State Park, Kokosing Gap Bike Trail, Brown Family Environmental Center and Knox County Fairgrounds nearby.

Location: Country. Adjacent to Kenyon College campus.

Certificate may be used: Jan. 1-31, March 1-15, subject to availability.

Geneva On The Lake B9

Eagle Cliff Inn

5254 Lake Road East
Geneva On The Lake, OH 44041
(440)466-1110 Fax:(440)466-0315
Internet: www.eaglecliffinn.com
E-mail: beachclub5@roadrunner.com

Circa 1880. Catering to adults, this recently renovated 1880 Victorian inn graces one acre of the Strip in the state's first resort village. It is listed in the National Register, noted as significantly reflecting the dominant recreation history of Geneva On The Lake. Enjoy the relaxed atmosphere while sitting on white wicker cushioned chairs and rockers or a porch swing. Elegantly functional guest bedrooms and a suite offer views of the Strip and lake. The cottages are situated privately in the back. Savor a satisfying daily breakfast. Magnificent sunsets are best viewed from the inn's easy beach access. Sip a local wine from famed Ashtabula County while chatting by the fireplace. Visit the nearby Jenny Munger Museum.

Innkeeper(s): LuAnn, Michelle & Peggy. $115-159. 7 rooms, 6 with PB, 2 total suites, including 1 two-bedroom suite, 3 cottages. Breakfast, afternoon tea and snacks/refreshments included in rates. Types of meals: Full bkfst, veg bkfst and early coffee/tea. Beds: KQ. Cable TV, VCR, DVD, reading lamp, stereo, ceiling fan, clock radio, telephone, hair dryer, bath amenities, wireless Internet access and iron/ironing board in room. Air conditioning. Fax, copier,

parlor games, fireplace, laundry facility and parlor & sitting room with fireplace on premises. Amusement parks, antiquing, art galleries, beach, bicycling, canoeing/kayaking, cross-country skiing, fishing, golf, hiking, horseback riding, live theater, museums, parks, shopping, sporting events, tennis, water sports and wineries nearby.

Location: Directly on Geneva-On-the-Lake, Ohio Strip.

Publicity: *"Superior Small Lodging."*

Certificate may be used: mid-May through mid-October, Sunday-Thursday, excludes holidays.

The Lakehouse Inn

5653 Lake Road E
Geneva On The Lake, OH 44041
(440)466-8668 Fax:(440)466-2556
Internet: www.thelakehouseinn.com
E-mail: inquiries@thelakehouseinn.com

Circa 1940. In a quaint lakefront location, this inn offers a variety of accommodations that boast a nautical/country décor. Stay "bed and breakfast style" in standard guest bedrooms or Jacuzzi suites with fireplaces, DVD players, microwaves and refrigerators. Renovated cottages include a living room, fully equipped kitchen, bath and one or two bedrooms. The secluded Beach House features a living and dining area, kitchen, Jacuzzi bath, two-person shower, spacious bedroom and outdoor deck. Enjoy the central air and heat as well as panoramic views of Lake Erie and the Geneva Marina.

Innkeeper(s): Andrea Bushweiler. $120-350. 8 rooms with PB, 4 with FP, 4 with WP, 3 two-bedroom suites, 3 cottages, 1 guest house, 1 conference room. Breakfast included in rates. Types of meals: Full bkfst, veg bkfst, early coffee/tea, snacks/refreshments and wine. Restaurant on premises. Beds: KQT. Cable TV, DVD, CD player, refrigerator, ceiling fan, clock radio, telephone, some with fireplace, hair dryer, bath amenities, wireless Internet access, iron/ironing board and Jacuzzi tub in some rooms in room. Central air. Fax, copier, swimming, parlor games, gift shop, Lakefront winery, Lakefront decks and Casual restaurant on premises. Amusement parks, antiquing, beach, bicycling, canoeing/kayaking, fishing, golf, hiking, museums, parks, shopping, tennis, water sports, wineries, Geneva-on-the-Lake summer resort, historic Ashtabula Harbor and covered bridges nearby.

Location: Waterfront.

Certificate may be used: October-May, Sunday-Friday, subject to availability.

Georgetown J3

Bailey House

112 N Water St
Georgetown, OH 45121-1332
(937)378-3087
Internet: www.baileyhousebandb.com
E-mail: baileyho@frontier.com

Circa 1830. The stately columns of this three-story Greek Revival house once greeted Ulysses S. Grant, a frequent visitor  during his boyhood when he was sent to buy milk from the Bailey's. A story is told that Grant accidentally overheard that the Bailey boy was leaving West Point. Grant immediately ran through the woods to the home of Congressman Thomas Hamer and petitioned an appointment in Bailey's place which he received, thus launching his military career. The inn has double parlors, pegged oak floors and Federal-style fireplace mantels. Antique washstands, chests and beds are found in the large guest rooms.

Innkeeper(s): Nancy Purdy. $65-70. 4 rooms, 1 with PB, 2 with FP. Breakfast included in rates. Types of meals: Full bkfst and early coffee/tea. Beds: QD. Cable TV, reading lamp, clock radio, telephone, desk, hair dryer, bath amenities, wireless Internet access, iron/ironing board, fireplace (two rooms) and desk (one room) in room. Air conditioning. VCR, DVD, library, parlor games, fireplace, herb garden, garden shed, screened porch, rustic cabin and unique train display in recreation area on premises. Antiquing, art galleries, fishing, golf, museums, parks, shopping, tennis, water sports, private tours of U.S. Grant Home, historic sites and John Ruthven Art Gallery nearby.

Location: Country. Historic District town.

Publicity: *If Walls Could Talk* on HGTV (Feb. 2006).

"Thank you for your warm hospitality, from the comfortable house to the delicious breakfast."

Certificate may be used: Anytime, subject to availability.

Logan H6

Inn & Spa At Cedar Falls

21190 State Route 374
Logan, OH 43138
(740)385-7489 (800)653-2557 Fax:(740)385-0820
Internet: innatcedarfalls.com
E-mail: info@innatcedarfalls.com

Circa 1987. This sophisticated inn, complete with traditional rooms along with separate cottages and cabins, was constructed on 75 acres adjacent to Hocking Hills State Parks and one-half mile from the waterfalls. The kitchen and dining rooms are in a 19th-century log house.

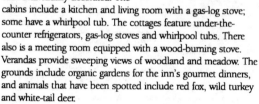

Accommodations in the two-story barn-shaped building are simple and comfortable, each furnished with antiques. There are six fully equipped log cabins and twelve cozy cottages available, each individually decorated. The cabins include a kitchen and living room with a gas-log stove; some have a whirlpool tub. The cottages feature under-the-counter refrigerators, gas-log stoves and whirlpool tubs. There also is a meeting room equipped with a wood-burning stove. Verandas provide sweeping views of woodland and meadow. The grounds include organic gardens for the inn's gourmet dinners, and animals that have been spotted include red fox, wild turkey and white-tail deer.

Innkeeper(s): Ellen Grinsfelder & Terry Lingo. $125-304. 5 cabins, 26 with PB, 19 with FP, 15 with WP, 12 cottages, 1 conference room. Breakfast, snacks/refreshments and Homemade cookies in the room on arrival included in rates. Types of meals: Full gourmet bkfst, veg bkfst, early coffee/tea, gourmet lunch, picnic lunch, wine, gourmet dinner, room service, Picnic lunch, Cheese and fruit trays, Picnic dinner and Brown bag lunch. Restaurant on premises. Beds: KQDT. Reading lamp, CD player, refrigerator, ceiling fan, clock radio, coffeemaker, desk, hair dryer, bathrobes, bath amenities, wireless Internet access, iron/ironing board, whirlpool tub, cabins and cottages with gas-log stoves and ceiling fans in room. Central air. Fax, copier, parlor games, telephone, fireplace, gift shop, WI-FI and Spa on premises. Handicap access. Antiquing, art galleries, beach, bicycling, canoeing/kayaking, cross-country skiing, fishing, golf, hiking, horseback riding, live theater, museums, parks, shopping, sporting events, Mountain bike trails, 25 miles of hiking trails at surrounding Hocking Hills State Park, Year-round park events, Zipline and ATV Riding nearby.

Location: Country. Surrounded on 3 sides by the Hocking Hills State Park.

Publicity: *Country Living, Ohio Magazine, Columbus Dispatch, Country, Post, Channel 4* and Ed Johnson.

"Very peaceful, relaxing and friendly. Couldn't be nicer."

Certificate may be used: Year-round, Sunday-Thursday only, except holidays.

Mason l2

Kirkwood Inn

4027 US Route 42
Mason, OH 45040
(513)398-7277 (800)732-4741
Internet: www.kirkwoodinn.com
E-mail: sandraeves@aol.com

Circa 1973. Gracing six acres, this recently renovated Colonial farmhouse and inn features a Williamsburg décor and cherry furnishings. Kirkwood Inn boasts a rich tradition of excellence steeped in history. Surrounded by the sites and major attractions of Cincinnati and Dayton, its location in Mason, Ohio is convenient. Stay in a pleasant guest bedroom or remodeled suite with a Jacuzzi and fireplace. A breakfast buffet is served daily. Experience the best of both worlds; the private intimacy of personal space yet the ambiance of this historic colonial home while dining. Swim in the outdoor pool, relax on the patios and enjoy the bountiful flower gardens and walking paths. Ask about special packages available.

Innkeeper(s): Sandra and David Eves. $59-189. 48 rooms, 3 with FP, 2 suites, 2 conference rooms. Breakfast included in rates. Types of meals: Early coffee/tea, snacks/refreshments and Full hot breakfast buffet. Beds: KQ. Modem hook-up, data port, cable TV, DVD, reading lamp, refrigerator, clock radio, telephone, coffeemaker, desk, some with fireplace, hair dryer and bath amenities in room. Air conditioning. Fax, swimming and laundry facility on premises. Limited handicap access. Amusement parks, antiquing, art galleries, bicycling, canoeing/kayaking, fishing, golf, hiking, horseback riding, live theater, museums, parks, shopping, sporting events, tennis and wineries nearby.

Location: City, country.

Certificate may be used: Nov. 1-April 1, Sunday-Thursday. Special Rates and Discounted Rates not applicable. Promotion must be mentioned at time of reservation.

Miamisburg H2

English Manor B&B

505 E Linden Ave
Miamisburg, OH 45342-2850
(937)866-2288
Internet: www.englishmanorohio.com
E-mail: englishmanorohio@yahoo.com

Circa 1924. This is a beautiful English Tudor mansion situated on a tree-lined street of Victorian homes. Well-chosen antiques combined with the innkeepers' personal heirlooms added to the inn's polished floors, sparkling leaded-and stained-glass windows and shining silver, make this an elegant retreat. Breakfast is served in the formal dining room. Fine restaurants, a water park, baseball, air force museum and theater are close by, as is The River Corridor bikeway on the banks of the Great Miami River.

Innkeeper(s): Julie & Larry Chmiel. $89-125. 5 rooms, 3 with PB, 1 total suite, including 2 two-bedroom suites, 1 conference room. Breakfast included in rates. Types of meals: Full gourmet bkfst, veg bkfst, early coffee/tea, picnic lunch, afternoon tea and dinner. Beds: KQDT. Modem hook-up, data port, reading lamp, clock radio, telephone, turn-down service, bath amenities, wireless Internet access and iron/ironing board in room. Air conditioning. TV, VCR, DVD, bicycles, library, parlor games and fireplace on premises. Amusement parks, antiquing, art galleries, beach, bicycling, canoeing/kayaking, fishing, golf, hiking, horseback riding, live theater, museums, parks, shopping, sporting events, tennis and water sports nearby.

Location: City.

Certificate may be used: Sunday-Thursday all year, upon availability.

Painesville   B8

Fitzgerald's Irish B&B

47 Mentor Ave
Painesville, OH 44077-3201
(440)639-0845
Internet: www.FitzgeraldBB.com
E-mail: fitzbb@gmail.com

Circa 1937. Warm Irish hospitality is extended at this 1937 French Tudor home situated in the historic district. It was recently restored as a landmark of craftsmanship with its castle-like design, unusual turret, slate roof, ornate staircase, hardwood floors and elaborate 11-foot fireplace. Watch satellite TV in the sitting room, play games and relax by the fire in the large gathering room. Lounge on the sun porch overlooking the park-like grounds and frequent birds. Air-conditioned guest bedrooms include pleasing amenities. Sleep on a four-poster or sleigh bed. The third-floor Bushmills Room features a microwave, refrigerator, VCR, CD player, Jacuzzi tub and Roman shower. Savor a full breakfast on weekends and holidays and a generous continental breakfast during the week. Popular trails and beaches of the Great Lakes region are nearby.

Innkeeper(s): Debra & Tom Fitzgerald. $105-150. 4 rooms with PB. Breakfast included in rates. Types of meals: Full bkfst and early coffee/tea. Beds: Q. TV, VCR, DVD, reading lamp, CD player, ceiling fan, clock radio, telephone, coffeemaker, desk, some with hot tub/spa, hair dryer, bathrobes, bath amenities, wireless Internet access and iron/ironing board in room. Central air. Parlor games and fireplace on premises. Amusement parks, antiquing, art galleries, beach, bicycling, canoeing/kayaking, cross-country skiing, downhill skiing, fishing, golf, hiking, horseback riding, live theater, museums, parks, shopping, sporting events, tennis, water sports and wineries nearby.

Location: City.

Publicity: New Herald, The Cleveland Plain Dealer, Midwest Irish News, Cleveland Magazine, Arrington's 2003, 2004 & 2005 Book of Lists winner of top 15 B&Bs for interior design and decor and WVIZ the Cleveland PBS station.

Certificate may be used: Sunday-Thursday, Nov. 1-April 29, holidays excluded, for the Mayo and Dublin rooms only.

Rider's 1812 Inn

792 Mentor Ave
Painesville, OH 44077-2516
(440)354-8200 Fax:(440)350-9385
Internet: www.ridersinn.com
E-mail: ridersinninfo@yahoo.com

Circa 1812. In the days when this inn and tavern served the frontier Western Reserve, it could provide lodging and meals for more than 100 overnight guests. Restored in 1988, the pub features an original fireplace and wavy window panes. Most of the inn's floors are rare, long-needle pine. A passageway in the cellar is said to have been part of the Underground Railroad. An English-style restaurant is also on the premises. Guest rooms are furnished with antiques. Breakfast in bed is the option of choice.

Innkeeper(s): Elaine Crane & Gary Herman. $90-110. 10 rooms, 9 with PB, 1 suite, 3 conference rooms. Breakfast included in rates. Types of meals: Full bkfst, veg bkfst, Sun. brunch, early coffee/tea, lunch, picnic

lunch, afternoon tea, wine, dinner and room service. Restaurant on premises. Beds: KQDT. Cable TV, reading lamp, ceiling fan, clock radio, telephone, turn-down service, desk, voice mail, bath amenities and wireless Internet access in room. Air conditioning. Fax, copier, library, pet boarding, child care, parlor games, fireplace and laundry facility on premises. Limited handicap access. Antiquing, art galleries, beach, bicycling, canoeing/kayaking, cross-country skiing, downhill skiing, fishing, golf, hiking, horseback riding, live theater, museums, parks, shopping, sporting events, tennis, water sports and wineries nearby.

Location: College town, County Seat.

Publicity: Business Review, News-Herald, Midwest Living, WEWS, Haunted Ohio V and Channel 5.

Certificate may be used: Sunday-Friday, year round, not valid on Saturdays.

Stockport   H7

Stockport Mill

1995 Broadway Avenue
Stockport, OH 43787
(740)559-2822 Fax:(740)559-2236
Internet: www.stockportmill.com
E-mail: mill@stockportmill.com

Stay at this century-old restored grain mill on the Muskingum River for a truly authentic historic experience combined with everything desired for a romantic getaway, business retreat or stress-free change of pace. Each of the four floors offers an assortment of common areas and accommodations. Browse the main lobby, an inviting library and the gift gallery showcasing local craftsman and artists. The Massage Therapy Room was the original grain bin. Themed guest bedrooms are named and decorated as a tribute to the local region and its prominent people. Stay in a luxurious suite with a two-person whirlpool spa and private balcony. Riverview Rooms feature clawfoot tubs, southern views of the river and private terraces. Ask about special packages and scheduling events at the Boathouse Banquet Hall.

Innkeeper(s): Dottie Singer. Call for rates. Call inn for details. Types of meals: Cont, lunch, picnic lunch, snacks/refreshments, hors d'oeuvres, dinner and room service. Restaurant on premises. Beds: KQ. Cable TV, VCR, DVD, reading lamp, ceiling fan, clock radio, telephone, coffeemaker, most with hot tub/spa, some with fireplace, hair dryer, wireless Internet access, iron/ironing board and refrigerator in one suite in room. Air conditioning. Fax, copier, spa, library, parlor games, gift shop, massage therapy by appointment and boat dock on premises. Handicap access. Antiquing, bicycling, canoeing/kayaking, fishing, golf, hiking, live theater, museums, parks, shopping, sporting events, water sports, walk track, boat launching, swimming pool and bowling nearby.

Location: Country, waterfront.

Certificate may be used: Anytime, November-March, subject to availability, suites only (2nd or 3rd floor). Does not include Valentines Day or holidays.

Yellow Springs G3

Arthur Morgan House Bed & Breakfast

120 W Limestone St
Yellow Springs, OH 45387-1803
(937)767-1761
Internet: www.arthurmorganhouse.com
E-mail: susanne@arthurmorganhouse.com

Circa 1921. Just steps from downtown, this modern stucco bed and breakfast was built for a local notable in 1921 and now provides smoke-free, pet-free accommodations. Play games at a table in the living room. Browse through the books and crafts from southern Africa for sale in the small shop. The second-floor sunroom features a reading nook with views of the wooded backyard. Comfortable guest bedrooms on the second and third floors boast oak floors, air conditioning and wireless Internet. Breakfast is made with organically grown ingredients, cage-free eggs and locally roasted coffee. The Little Miami Scenic Bike Path runs through the village that has more than fifty gift shops.

Innkeeper(s): Susanne Oldham. $80-125. 6 rooms with PB. Breakfast included in rates. Types of meals: Full bkfst. Beds: KQT. Reading lamp, clock radio, turn-down service, desk, hair dryer, bathrobes, wireless Internet access and iron/ironing board in room. Air conditioning. Library, parlor games, telephone, DSL, Screened porch, Laptop computer for guests' use, Portable DVD players and Fireplace in living room on premises. Limited handicap access. Antiquing, art galleries, bicycling, canoeing/kayaking, cross-country skiing, hiking, live theater, museums, parks, shopping, tennis, water sports, music and film nearby.

Location: Village.

Certificate may be used: Sunday-Thursday Nights, subject to availability.

Oklahoma

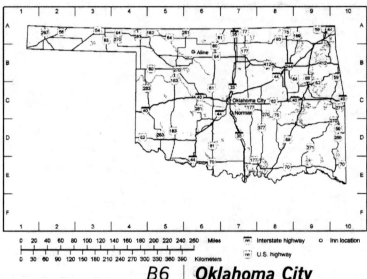

Miles: 0 20 40 60 80 100 120 140 160 180 200 220 240 260

Kilometers: 0 30 60 90 120 150 180 210 240 270 300 330 360 390

- Interstate highway
- U.S. highway
- ○ Inn location

Norman   B6

Montford Inn

322 W Tonhawa St
Norman, OK 73069-7124
(405)321-2200 (800)321-8969 Fax:(405)321-8347
Internet: www.montfordinn.com
E-mail: innkeeper@montfordinn.com

Circa 1994. Although this inn was built just a few years ago, the exterior is reminiscent of a country farmhouse, with its covered front porch lined with rockers. The interior is a mix of styles, from the decidedly Southwestern Chickasaw Rancher room to the romantic Solitude room, which includes a king-size bed canopied in Battenburg lace. Each of the guest rooms has a fireplace. The gourmet breakfasts are arranged and presented artfully, featuring succulent egg dishes, freshly baked breads and fruit smoothies.

Innkeeper(s): William and Ginger Murray, Phyllis and Ron Murray. $99-239. 16 rooms with PB, 16 with FP, 2 with HT, 10 with WP, 6 suites, 6 cottages. Breakfast, snacks/refreshments and wine included in rates. Types of meals: Full gourmet bkfst and early coffee/tea. Beds: KQT. Cable TV, VCR, DVD, reading lamp, ceiling fan, snack bar, clock radio, telephone, coffeemaker, desk, hair dryer, bathrobes, bath amenities, wireless Internet access and iron/ironing board in room. Central air. Fax, copier, library, fireplace and gift shop on premises. Handicap access. Amusement parks, antiquing, art galleries, bicycling, fishing, golf, hiking, horseback riding, live theater, museums, parks, shopping, sporting events, tennis, water sports, Horse racing, Polo, Zoo and Casino nearby.

Location: City.

Certificate may be used: June-Aug. 15.

Oklahoma City   C7

The Grandison Inn at Maney Park

1200 N Shartel Ave
Oklahoma City, OK 73103-2402
(405) 232-8778 (888) 799-4667 Fax:(405)232-5039
Internet: www.grandisoninn.com
E-mail: innkeeper@grandisoninn.com

Circa 1904. This spacious Victorian has been graciously restored and maintains its original mahogany woodwork, stained glass, brass fixtures and a grand staircase. Several rooms include a Jacuzzi, and all have their own unique décor. The Treehouse Hideaway includes a Queen bed that is meant to look like a Hammock and walls that are painted with a blue sky and stars. The Jacuzzi tub rests beneath a skylight. The home is located north of downtown Oklahoma City in a historic neighborhood and is listed in the National Register.

Innkeeper(s): Claudia Wright. $99-199. 8 rooms with PB, 4 with FP, 7 with WP. Breakfast and snacks/refreshments included in rates. Types of meals: Cont plus, early coffee/tea, wine, room service, In-room dinners, Picnic Basket, Cheese and Cracker Tray, Full Breakfast - Weekends Only. Beds: KQD. Cable TV, DVD, reading lamp, stereo, ceiling fan, clock radio, telephone, desk, most with hot tub/spa, some with fireplace, bathrobes, bath amenities, wireless Internet access in room. Iron/Ironing Board and hair dryer - In guest closet, Refrigerator available, Snack Bar and coffeemaker in Butler's Pantry. Central air. Fax, copier, bicycles and gift shop on premises. Handicap access. Antiquing, art galleries, bicycling, golf, live theater, museums, parks, shopping and sporting events nearby.

Publicity: *Daily Oklahoman, Oklahoma Gazette, Discover Oklahoma, Tulsa People Magazine, Travel & Leisure, Country Discoveries Magazine.*

Certificate may be used: Anytime, Sunday-Thursday.

Oregon

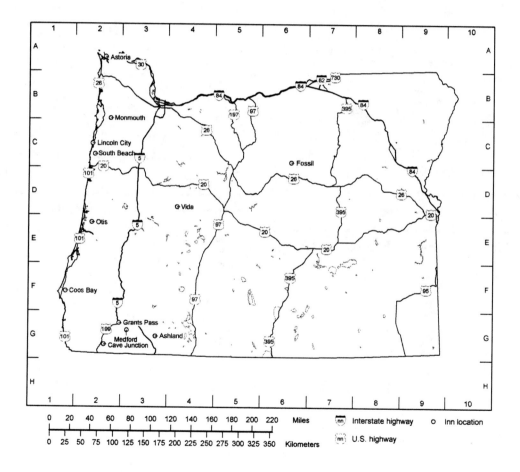

Ashland
G3

Albion Inn

34 Union Street
Ashland, OR 97520-2958
(541) 488-3905 (888) 246-8310
Internet: www.albion-inn.com
E-mail: info@albion-inn.com

Circa 1905. One block off the main street, this inn is an oasis of peace, quiet, and beauty in the historic Hargadine District. This modest farmhouse has grown over the years with architecturally harmonious additions and was transformed into a bed and breakfast in 1990. To better serve theatre-goers to Ashland's world-famous Oregon Shakespeare Festival, guest rooms include private bathrooms and two courtyard suites were added by the rose garden. Watch satellite TV in the downstairs den that also has an extensive collection of games and puzzles. Read the newpaper and magazines or use the guest computer in the living room. Fine art hangs throughout the inn. A delicious, organic breakfast always starts with a fresh fruit smoothie and a fruit parfait, then fresh baked goods. The hot main course alternates between a savory meal one day and a sweeter meal the next. Mention special dietary needs when booking and Cyd will cook you a special meal.

Innkeeper(s): Cyd and Gary Ropp. $99-164. 5 rooms with PB, 1 with FP, 1 conference room. Breakfast, snacks/refreshments, wine, Fresh cookies daily. Cashews, fresh and dried fruit, sweets, sherry and unlimited tea bar included in rates. Beds: KQT. Reading lamp, clock radio, desk, hair dryer, bath amenities and wireless Internet access in room. Central air. TV, VCR, DVD, fax, copier, library, pet boarding, parlor games, telephone, fireplace and Shared guest kitchenette on premises. Limited handicap access.

Location: City.

Certificate may be used: Anytime, November-March, subject to availability.

Astoria
A2

Franklin Street Station Bed & Breakfast

1140 Franklin Ave
Astoria, OR 97103-4132
(503)325-4314 (800)448-1098
Internet: www.astoriaoregonbb.com
E-mail: franklinststationbb@yahoo.com

Circa 1900. Sit out on the balcony and take in views of the Columbia River and beautiful sunsets from this 1900 Victorian-style inn. Ornate craftsmanship and antique furnishings, right down to the clawfoot bathtubs, transport visitors into the past. The six guest rooms are named Starlight Suite, Sweet Tranquility, the Hide-away, the Magestic, Magnolia Retreat and Enchanted Haven. The full breakfast includes dishes like fruit, waffles and sausage. The Flavel House Museum and Heritage Museum within walking distance, and the Astoria Column and Fort Clatsop are a short drive from the inn.

Innkeeper(s): Rebecca Greenway. $60-135. 6 rooms, 5 with PB, 1 with FP, 3 total suites, including 2 two-bedroom suites. Breakfast included in rates. Types of meals: Full bkfst and Coffee. Beds: Q. Cable TV, VCR, DVD, reading lamp, stereo, refrigerator, clock radio, coffeemaker, some with fireplace, hair dryer, wireless Internet access, iron/ironing board, Clawfoot tubs, Balconies with views and Direct TV in room. Copier, library, parlor games and telephone on premises. Antiquing, art galleries, beach, fishing, golf, hiking, horseback riding, live theater, museums, parks, shopping, wineries and swimming nearby.

Publicity: *LA Times*.

Certificate may be used: Oct. 15-Jan. 15, Sunday-Friday.

Cave Junction
G2

The Chateau at the Oregon Caves

20000 Caves Hwy
Cave Junction, OR 97523
(541)592-3400
Internet: www.oregoncaveschateau.com
E-mail: caves@cavenet.com

Featured as one of the Great Lodges of the National Parks, lodging and dining are available at this six-story destination resort from May through late October. There is so much to experience in a setting full of historic ambiance and natural beauty. Enjoy classic American foods and a nostalgic soda fountain atmosphere in Cave's Café, the 1930's-era coffee shop. The Gift Gallery features an assortment of local products from soaps and jams to jewelry and wines as well as artistic works and memorabilia. Relax in the large fourth-floor lobby boasting a huge marble double fireplace. Fresh foods are made daily at the Gallery Deli for on-the-go excursions. Hike through old-growth forests on well-maintained trails in Oregon Caves National Monument. Stay in one of a variety of different guest room and spacious suites. Delicious Northwest cuisine from the Illinois and Rogue Valleys is featured in the Dining Room.

Innkeeper(s): Judy, Marketing. Call for rates. Call inn for details. Reading lamp, clock radio, desk and bath amenities in room. Parlor games, telephone, fireplace and gift shop on premises. Amusement parks, art galleries, bicycling, canoeing/kayaking, cross-country skiing, fishing, golf, hiking, horseback riding, museums, parks, shopping, wineries and Cave Tours Great Cats World Park Kirbyville Museam nearby.

Certificate may be used: May 4-June 30 and Sept. 4-Oct. 14.

Coos Bay
F1

Old Tower House Bed & Brkfst

476 Newmark Ave
Coos Bay, OR 97420-3201
(541)888-6058
Internet: www.oldtowerhouse.com
E-mail: oldtowerhouse@yahoo.com

Fully restored and listed in the National Register, Old Tower House Bed & Breakfast offers a delightful setting to relax and enjoy the Oregon coast. Located just a few yards from the ocean in Coos Bay, there are many beaches to explore as well as other activities and attractions. Visit Shore Acres Park and play on one of the top-rated Bandon Dunes golf courses. Browse through the movie collection in the enclosed sun porch. Stay in a guest bedroom in the main house or enjoy the spacious privacy in Ivy Cottage, the original carriage house and tack room. It features a sitting room, microwave and clawfoot tub. A continental breakfast is provided in the formal dining room of the main house or on the sunny veranda.

Innkeeper(s): Stephanie Kramer. Call for rates. Call inn for details. A gourmet breakfast is offered for an additional $9.50 per person or a Continental Breakfast is included in rates. Types of meals: Full gourmet bkfst. Cable TV, VCR, reading lamp, refrigerator, clock radio, coffeemaker, hair dryer, bathrobes, bath amenities and wireless Internet access in room. DVD, fax, telephone and fireplace on premises. Antiquing, beach, fishing, golf, hiking, horseback riding, museums, parks and shopping nearby.

Location: Waterfront.

Certificate may be used: December-April, Monday-Thursday, except holidays.

Fossil C6

Wilson Ranches Retreat Bed and Breakfast

16555 Butte Creek Rd
Fossil, OR 97830
(541)763-2227 (866)763-2227 Fax:(541)763-2719
Internet: www.wilsonranchesretreat.com
E-mail: npwilson@wilsonranchesretreat.com

Circa 1910. Amidst wide open spaces off a quiet country road in North Central Oregon, the Wilson Ranches Retreat Bed and Breakfast in Fossil is a 9,000-acre working cattle and hay ranch. Scenic and secluded, the retreat was designed for comfort and relief from stress. It sits in Butte Creek Valley in the John Day Basin surrounded by the Cascade Mountain Range. Bird watch from the large deck or relax in the living room Called the "best rest in Wheeler County," western-themed guest bedrooms are on the main floor and upstairs as well as two spacious accommodations in the daylight basement that are perfect for families. Hunger disappears after a hearty cowboy breakfast served on the handcrafted 11-foot knotty pine dining room table. Experience cattle drives, horseback rides, hikes, and four-wheel drive ranch tours.

Innkeeper(s): Phil & Nancy Wilson. $79-149. 6 rooms, 2 with PB, 1 with FP, 1 conference room. Breakfast included in rates. Types of meals: Country bkfst and early coffee/tea. Beds: KQDT. Cable TV, VCR, DVD, reading lamp, CD player, refrigerator, telephone, coffeemaker, desk, some with fireplace, hair dryer, bathrobes, bath amenities, iron/ironing board and Microwave in room. Central air. Fax, copier, stable, parlor games and gift shop on premises. Limited handicap access. Bicycling, canoeing/kayaking, fishing, golf, hiking, horseback riding, live theater, museums, parks, shopping and tennis nearby.

Location: Country. Ranch.

Certificate may be used: January and February, Monday-Thursday.

Grants Pass G2

Weasku Inn

5560 Rogue River Hwy
Grants Pass, OR 97527
(541)471-8000 (800)493-2758 Fax:(541)471-7038
Internet: www.weasku.com
E-mail: kirt@countryhouseinns.com

Circa 1924. Built as a secluded fishing lodge, this historic inn once hosted the likes of President Herbert Hoover, Zane Grey, Walt Disney, Clark Gable and Carole Lombard. It is said that after Lombard's death, Gable spent several weeks here lamenting the loss of his beloved wife. A complete restoration took place in the late 1990s, reviving the inn back to its former glory. The log exterior, surrounded by towering trees and 10 fragrant acres, is a welcoming site. Inside, crackling fires from the inn's rock fireplaces warm the common rooms. Vaulted ceilings and exposed log beams add a cozy, rustic touch to the pristine, airy rooms all decorated in Pacific Northwest style. Many rooms include a whirlpool tub and river rock fireplace, and several offer excellent views of the Rogue River, which runs through the inn's grounds. In addition to the inn rooms, there are riverfront cabins, offering an especially romantic setting. In the evenings, guests are treated to a wine and cheese reception, and in the mornings, a continental breakfast is served. The staff can help plan many activities, including fishing and white-water rafting trips.

Innkeeper(s): Kirt Davis. $150-329. 14 rooms, 17 with PB, 12 with FP, 3 with HT, 3 suites, 1 guest house, 12 cabins, 2 conference rooms. Breakfast, afternoon tea, snacks/refreshments, wine, Afternoon wine and cheese social and fresh coffee and tea available through the day included in rates. Types of meals: Cont plus, early coffee/tea, A selection of local wines and beers and micro brews available for purchase from the front desk. Beds: KQ. Data port, cable TV, VCR, reading lamp, refrigerator, ceiling fan, clock radio, telephone, desk, some with hot tub/spa, voice mail, most with fireplace, hair dryer, bathrobes, bath amenities, wireless Internet access, iron/ironing board and All river cabins have coffeemakers in room in room. Central air. Fax, copier, parlor games, gift shop and Wireless Internet access on premises. Handicap access. Antiquing, art galleries, canoeing/kayaking, fishing, golf, hiking, horseback riding, live theater, museums, parks, shopping, tennis, water sports, wineries, Hellgate Jetboat Excursions, Wild Life Images Animal Rehabilitation Center, Howling Acres Wolf Sanctuary and Whitewater rafting nearby.

Location: Country, waterfront. On the bank of Rogue River.

Publicity: *Travel & Leisure Magazine, New York Magazine, LA Magazine, Sunset, SF Magazine, Affluent Living, Country Living, Western Interiors Magazine, Select Registry, Ashland Magazine, 1000 Places to See Before You Die, Oregon Business Magazine and Best Places to Kiss in the Northwest travel guide.*

Certificate may be used: Anytime, subject to availability.

Lincoln City C2

Brey House

3725 NW Keel Ave
Lincoln City, OR 97367
(541)994-7123 (877)994-7123
Internet: www.breyhouse.com
E-mail: sbrey@wcn.net

Circa 1941. The innkeepers at this three-story, Cape Cod-style house claim that when you stay with them it's like staying with Aunt Shirley and Uncle Milt. Guest rooms include some with ocean views and private entrances, and the Deluxe Suite offers a living room with fireplace, two baths and a kitchen. The Admiral's Room on the third floor has knotty pine walls, a skylight, fireplace and the best view.

Innkeeper(s): Shirley Brey. $90-160. 4 rooms with PB, 3 with FP, 2 suites. Breakfast included in rates. Types of meals: Full gourmet bkfst, early coffee/tea and snacks/refreshments. Beds: KQ. Cable TV, VCR, DVD, reading lamp, refrigerator, ceiling fan, clock radio, desk, hair dryer, bath amenities and wireless Internet access in room. Parlor games, telephone, fireplace and Outdoor Hot Tub/Spa on premises. Antiquing, art galleries, beach, canoeing/kayaking, fishing, golf, hiking, horseback riding, live theater, parks, shopping, tennis, water sports and Indian casino nearby.

Location: City, ocean community.

Certificate may be used: September-June, Sunday-Friday. No Saturdays, no holiday weekends.

Coast Inn B&B

4507 SW Coast Ave
Lincoln City, OR 97367
(541)994-7932 (888)994-7932 Fax:(541)994-7935
Internet: www.oregoncoastinn.com
E-mail: coastinn@oregoncoastinn.com

Circa 1939. A short walk from Siletz Bay with its herd of seals, this 4,000-square-foot house is 300 feet from the beach. A serene decor and mission-style furnishings provide a comfortable area to read a good book from the B&Bs library. Enjoy the sights and sounds of the Pacific from a window-wrapped botanical sunroom and deck. Writing journals are placed in the light and airy guest bedrooms and suites featuring luxury beds with down comforters, plush robes and a small refrigerator stocked with bottled water and fruit drinks. One romantic suite's amenities include a gas fireplace, microwave, flat screen TV with DVD and a vintage bathtub. Healthy gourmet breakfasts with fresh Oregon berries and peaches are served in the dining room, accented with vibrant art quilt designs. Small pets are allowed in one room with prior arrangement.

Innkeeper(s): Rosie Huntemann. $109-198. 4 rooms with PB, 1 with FP, 2 suites. Breakfast and snacks/refreshments included in rates. Types of meals: Full gourmet bkfst, early coffee/tea, gourmet dinner and room service. Beds: Q. Cable TV, refrigerator, one bathtub and some with microwaves in room. TV, VCR, fax, copier, library and Internet access on premises. Antiquing, fishing, golf, live theater, parks, tennis, water sports, Oregon Coast Aquarium, factory outlet shopping, beachcombing, whale watching and lighthouses nearby.

Location: Ocean community.

Publicity: *Oregonian & L C Newsguard.*

Certificate may be used: October-April, Sunday-Friday; May-September, Sunday-Thursday, no holidays.

Medford   G3

Under The Greenwood Tree

3045 Bellinger Ln
Medford, OR 97501-9503
(541)776-0000 Fax:(541)776-0000
Internet: www.greenwoodtree.com
E-mail: utgtree@qwest.net

Circa 1862. Pleasurable luxuries and gracious hospitality are the hallmarks of this romantic country inn. Ten acres of serene, idyllic grounds are accented with hand-hewn, hand-pegged Civil War-era buildings. Professionally decorated guest bedrooms offer amenities such as soft robes, triple sheeting with fine ironed linens, turndown service with chocolate truffles, fresh flowers and other pampering treats that surpass expectations. Rely on famous three-course gourmet country breakfasts made with the freshest ingredients that include herbs, seasonal fruit and vegetables from the garden. Relax on hammocks and lounge chairs amongst flower gardens in the shade of 300-year-old trees before afternoon tea with treats. A furnished porch and deck provides more enjoyment, or explore the pond and honeysuckle/rose gazebo.

Innkeeper(s): Joseph & Barbara Lilley. $115-140. 4 rooms with PB. Breakfast, afternoon tea and snacks/refreshments included in rates. Types of meals: Full gourmet bkfst, veg bkfst and early coffee/tea. Beds: QD. Reading lamp, clock radio, telephone, turn-down service, hair dryer, bathrobes and bath amenities in room. Air conditioning. Fax, copier, bicycles, library and parlor games on premises. Antiquing, art galleries, bicycling, canoeing/kayaking, cross-country skiing, downhill skiing, fishing, golf, hiking, horseback riding, live theater, museums, parks, shopping, sporting events, tennis, water sports and wineries nearby.

Location: Country. Farmland.

Publicity: *Sunset Magazine, Romantic Homes and the barn has been seen in several movies.*

Certificate may be used: October-May based on availability.

Monmouth   B2

Airlie Farm

14810 Airlie Road
Monmouth, OR 97361
(503)838-1500
Internet: www.airliefarm.com
E-mail: airliefarm@aol.com

Circa 1910. Delightfully situated on 226 spectacular, scenic acres in Oregon, this tastefully remodeled 1910 farm home

reminds you of a cozy, comforting, updated visit to Grandma's house with an eye to luxury. Walk through the informal gardens, pick luscious berries, listen to the fountain or watch the koi pond. Check out the new foals or get lucky and help deliver a new foal on this well known and active Quarter Horse Breeding farm. Relax before the fireplace and play the piano amid antiques and paintings. Snuggle into a guest room with a down comforter, private balcony or petite fireplace, slippers, candies, robes, heated towel racks and modern amenities. Savor a full gourmet breakfast on fine china. Willamette Valley boasts over 250 gracious wineries. Monmouth is home to WOU, one of the oldest universities west of the Mississippi. Recreational options are endless, including live theater, concerts, museums and onsite rides and riding lessons.

Innkeeper(s): Nancy and Joe Petterson. $95-120. 5 rooms, 2 with PB, 1 with FP, 1 total suite, including 1 two-bedroom suite, 1 three-bedroom suite and 1 four-bedroom suite, 1 conference room. Breakfast, afternoon tea, snacks/refreshments, wine and Charge for High Tea included in rates. Types of meals: Full gourmet bkfst, veg bkfst, early coffee/tea, lunch, picnic lunch, gourmet dinner and room service. Beds: QDT. Modern hook-up, data port, reading lamp, CD player, snack bar, desk, hair dryer, bathrobes, bath amenities, wireless Internet access, iron/ironing board, The Sitting room has piano, games, coffee maker, refrigerator, Stereo, TV and and fireplace in room. Amusement parks, antiquing, art galleries, bicycling, canoeing/kayaking, fishing, golf, hiking, horseback riding, live theater, museums, parks, shopping, sporting events, water sports and wineries nearby.

Location: Country. 60 miles to Pacific Ocean.

Certificate may be used: Anytime, subject to availability.

Otis   E2

Lake House Bed & Breakfast

2165 NE East Devils Lake Rd
Otis, OR 97368-9612
(541) 996-8938 (888) 996-8938
Internet: www.lakehousebb.com
E-mail: mary@lakehousebb.com

Circa 1910. Conveniently located for a scenic adventure in the Pacific Northwest, this inn sits on Devils Lake in Otis. The private dock offers easy access to the 680 acres of fresh water for swimming, canoeing and kayaking. Amazing views from the deck are especially enjoyed while soaking in the outdoor hot tub. Stay in a spacious room or suite with a private deck and hot tub or the adjacent cottage that features a gas fireplace, kitchen with refrigerator and microwave, living room and porch. Gather in the dining room of the main house for a sumptuous breakfast. Beach lovers will appreciate the short two-mile drive to the Oregon coast, Lincoln City and the many other local attractions.

Innkeeper(s): Mary Sell. $95-150. 3 rooms with PB, 2 with FP, 1 with HT, 1 cottage. Breakfast included in rates. Beds: KQ. Data port, cable TV, VCR, DVD, reading lamp, CD player, refrigerator, ceiling fan, clock radio, coffeemaker, desk, most with fireplace, bathrobes, bath amenities and wireless Internet access in room. Antiquing, art galleries, beach, bicycling, canoeing/kayaking, fishing, golf, hiking, horseback riding, live theater, museums, parks, shopping, water sports and wineries nearby.

Location: Waterfront.

Certificate may be used: September-June, Sunday-Thursday.

Vida   *D4*

McKenzie River Inn

49164 McKenzie Hwy
Vida, OR 97488-9710
(541)822-6260 Fax:(541)same# call 1st
Internet: www.mckenzieriverinn.com
E-mail: innkeeper@mckenzieriverinn.com

Circa 1933. Three acres of lush grounds and river frontage
highlight the McKenzie River Inn B&B and Cabins in Vida,
Oregon. Meander along trails that lead to hammocks, benches
and picnic areas. Stay in a romantic suite or a guest bedroom
on the second floor of the inn with a Jacuzzi tub. Spacious and
private, the cabins offer a variety of accommodations that may
include decks, whirlpool tubs and full kitchens. Breakfast caters
to specialties such as vegetarian and allergy-free diets with delicious and satisfying dishes sure to please everyone. Many
recipes include fresh fruit from the orchard. Ask about guided
fly-fishing and rafting trips or eco-packages.

Innkeeper(s): Ellie de Klerk. $98-185. 6 rooms with PB, 2 with WP, 2
suites, 1 cottage, 2 cabins, 1 conference room. Breakfast and afternoon tea
included in rates. Types of meals: Full gourmet bkfst, veg bkfst, early
coffee/tea, picnic lunch, hors d'oeuvres, wine and Organic juices and fruit
from own orchard. Beds: KQDT. Cable TV, VCR, DVD, reading lamp, stereo,
ceiling fan, clock radio, coffeemaker, some with hot tub/spa, bathrobes, bath
amenities, wireless Internet access, iron/ironing board, Antiques, Panoramic
river view, Central living room with fireplace and Library in room. Air conditioning. Fax, copier, library, pet boarding, telephone, fireplace, gift shop,
Trails, Easy river access with fishing holes, (Guided-)fly fishing, Scenic
floats, Rafting, Eco-tours, Orchard, Fire pit, Outdoor furnace, Picnic areas,
Hammocks and Wildlife view areas on premises. Handicap access.
Antiquing, art galleries, bicycling, canoeing/kayaking, cross-country skiing,
downhill skiing, fishing, golf, hiking, horseback riding, parks, shopping,
sporting events, tennis, water sports, wineries, Hot springs, Guided fly fishing, Rafting, Scenic floats, Eco-tours, Lava beds/fields, Wildlife areas, Bird
watching, Mountain biking, Quilt show, Antique car show, Home & Garden
show, Art show and Wine tasting nearby.

Location: Country, mountains, waterfront.

Publicity: *Portland Tribune (August edition), Channel 6 KEZI Eugene, KBNP
1410 Portland radio and The Money Station.*

Certificate may be used: Nov. 1-May 31.

Pennsylvania

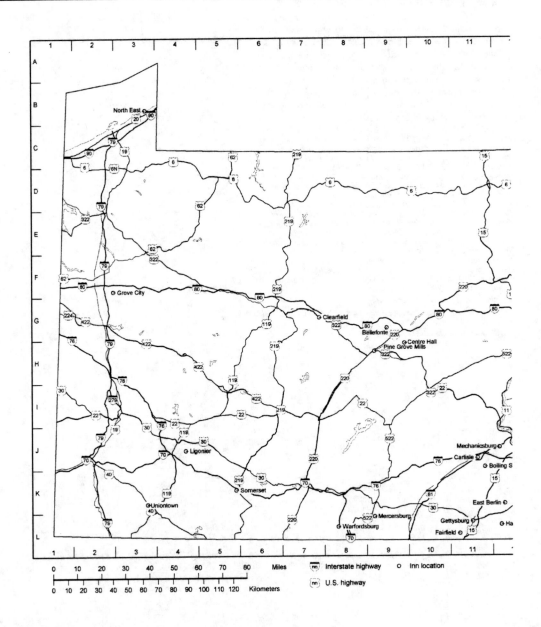

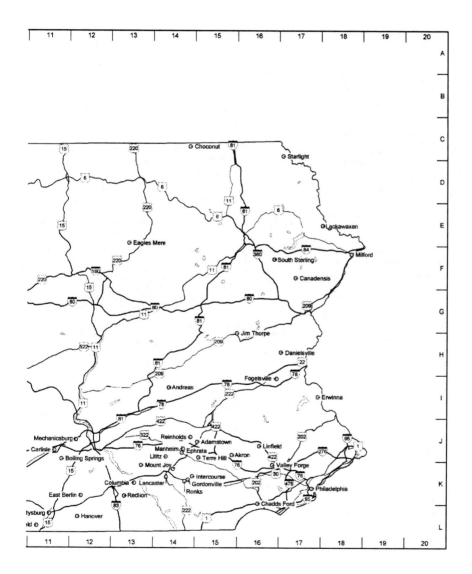

Adamstown J15

Adamstown Inns & Cottages

144 W Main St
Adamstown, PA 19501
(717)484-0800 (800)594-4808
Internet: www.adamstown.com
E-mail: stay@adamstown.com

Circa 1830. This restored Victorian with its 1850s pump organ found in the large parlor and other local antiques, fits right into this community known as one of the antique capitals of America (3,000 antique dealers). Other decorations include family heirlooms, Victorian wallpaper, handmade quilts and lace curtains. For outlet mall fans, Adamstown is 10 miles from Reading, which offers a vast assortment of top-quality merchandise.

Innkeeper(s): Kristin Rathman. $99-219. 6 rooms, 10 with PB, 8 with FP, 8 with WP, 2 total suites, including 1 two-bedroom suite, 3 cottages, 1 cabin. Breakfast, afternoon tea and snacks/refreshments included in rates. Types of meals: Cont plus, early coffee/tea and picnic lunch. Beds: KQD. Cable TV, DVD, reading lamp, CD player, ceiling fan, clock radio, desk, some with hot tub/spa, fireplace, hair dryer, bathrobes, bath amenities, wireless Internet access and iron/ironing board in room. Air conditioning. VCR, copier, spa, library, child care, parlor games, telephone, laundry facility and gift shop on premises. Amusement parks, antiquing, art galleries, bicycling, fishing, golf, hiking, live theater, museums, parks, shopping, sporting events, tennis and wineries nearby.

Location: Lancaster County's Amish Country.

Publicity: *Country Victorian, Lancaster Intelligencer, Reading Eagle, Travel & Leisure, Country Almanac, Lancaster Magazine and Chester County Magazine.*

"Your warm hospitality and lovely home left us with such pleasant memories."

Certificate may be used: Nov. 1-April 15, Sunday-Thursday.

Akron J15

Boxwood Inn Bed & Breakfast

1320 Diamond Street
Akron, PA 17501
(717)859-3466 (800)238-3466 Fax:(717)859-4507
Internet: www.theboxwoodinn.net
E-mail: innkeeper@theboxwoodinn.net

Circa 1768. Bordered by boxwood hedges and evergreens, Boxwood Inn Bed & Breakfast graces three acres of landscaped grounds. The backyard boasts a wooden bridge over a stream surrounded by holly bushes and lilac, weeping willow and magnolia trees. Relax on an Amish rocker on the front porch of this 1768 renovated stone farmhouse in Akron, Pennsylvania near the popular Lancaster County attractions. Elegant, tranquil and hospitable guest bedrooms are available in the main house. Pets and children are welcome in the Carriage House with a wood-burning fireplace, Jacuzzi, refrigerator and balcony. Start each day with a bountiful breakfast. Ask about gift certificates and specials offered.

Innkeeper(s): Betsy & Greg Fitzpatrick. $110-235. 5 rooms, 4 with PB, 1 with FP, 2 with WP, 1 cottage, 1 conference room. Breakfast and snacks/refreshments included in rates. Types of meals: Country bkfst, veg bkfst and early coffee/tea. Beds: KQT. Cable TV, reading lamp, ceiling fan, clock radio, desk, hair dryer, bathrobes and wireless Internet access in room. Central air. VCR, telephone, fireplace, Free WiFi and Dogs allowed in the Carriage House on premises. Amusement parks, antiquing, art galleries, bicy-

cling, golf, hiking, live theater, museums, parks, shopping, sporting events and wineries nearby.

Location: Country.

Certificate may be used: January 1 through February 29.

Andreas I14

The Alexander Benjamin House

818 Lizard Creek Rd
Andreas, PA 18211
(570) 386-3731 (866) 610-5569
Internet: www.alexanderbenjaminhouse.com
E-mail: theabhouse@yahoo.com

Circa 1880. Open year-round, historic Alexander Benjamin House Country Lodging and Breakfast boasts a traditional American Victorian theme. Modern comforts and amenities make each stay enjoyable. Bicycle and ski storage is available and the Appalachian Trail and Blue Mountain Ski Resort are nearby. Hawk Mountain Bird Sanctuary and Lehigh Valley Wine Trail are popular too. Relax in the sitting room or porch, visit the onsite art studio or stroll down to Lizard Creek. An upstairs guest kitchenette includes a refrigerator, microwave, toaster, snacks and beverages. Guest rooms feature flowers and chocolates. Select one with a Jacuzzi for two or a balcony. In-house massage and spa services can be arranged. Savor a hearty and healthy organic home-cooked breakfast each morning. Ask about specials and packages offered.

Innkeeper(s): Mark VanBuskirk & Hilary England. $125-150. 5 rooms with PB, 1 with HT, 1 with WP. Breakfast, afternoon tea, snacks/refreshments, wine is included in certain packages and promotions included in rates. Types of meals: Full gourmet bkfst, veg bkfst, gourmet lunch, picnic lunch, hors d'oeuvres, gourmet dinner, room service, Picnic lunches for at additional cost, wine as part of certain packages and catering available for events. Beds: KQ. Cable TV, reading lamp, refrigerator, ceiling fan, snack bar, clock radio, telephone, coffeemaker, turn-down service, desk, some with hot tub/spa, hair dryer, bath amenities and wireless Internet access in room. Central air. Kitchenette upstairs for guests w/refrigerator, beverages, snacks, microwave, toaster and coffeemaker on premises. Amusement parks, antiquing, art galleries, beach, bicycling, canoeing/kayaking, cross-country skiing, downhill skiing, fishing, golf, hiking, horseback riding, live theater, museums, parks, shopping, sporting events, tennis, water sports and wineries nearby.

Location: Country, mountains. Farmland, Wine Country.

Certificate may be used: Anytime, subject to availability.

Bellefonte G9

The Queen, A Victorian B&B

176 East Linn St.
Bellefonte, PA 16823
(814)355-7946 (888)355-7999
Internet: www.thequeenbnb.com
E-mail: thequeenbnb@psualum.com

Circa 1885. Adorning the historic district, this Queen Anne Victorian bed and breakfast is open year-round. It is ornately decorated with collectibles and memorabilia. Relax on the terraced landscaped grounds with a patio, waterfall and perennial gardens. Experience a taste of the past in the parlor with a Victrola, player piano, and stereoptic viewers. The foyer is accented with a fireplace. After a restful night's sleep in a tastefully appointed guest bedroom linger over a gourmet breakfast in the spacious dining room with vintage glassware and linens. Pastries and fruit accompany Crème Brulee French Toast, Eggs

Benedict, Grecian Omelet or waffles with fresh-picked berries. A refrigerator and microwave are available to use anytime.

Innkeeper(s): Nancy Noll & Curtis Miller. $95-195. 7 rooms, 4 with PB, 3 with FP, 1 suite, 1 guest house. Breakfast, afternoon tea and snacks/refreshments included in rates. Types of meals: Full gourmet bkfst, veg bkfst, early coffee/tea and Flexible breakfast time. Beds: QDT. Cable TV, reading lamp, CD player, ceiling fan, clock radio, telephone, turn-down service, desk, most with fireplace, hair dryer, bathrobes, bath amenities, wireless Internet access and iron/ironing board in room. Central air. VCR, DVD, fax, parlor games, laundry facility, 24-hour availabilty of refrigerator, microwave, hot and cold beverages in central area and Patio dining for breakfast on premises. Amusement parks, antiquing, art galleries, beach, bicycling, canoeing/kayaking, cross-country skiing, downhill skiing, fishing, golf, hiking, horseback riding, live theater, museums, parks, shopping, sporting events, tennis, water sports, wineries, exceptional flyfishing area, glider rides and caves nearby.

Location: Historic District of small community.

Publicity: *Country Victorian Magazine, PA Magazine, America's Most Charming Towns and Villages, InnSpots and numerous newspapers.*

Certificate may be used: not valid for special event weekends including but not limited to football and graduation (PSU).

Boiling Springs   J11

Gelinas Manor Victorian B&B

219 Front Street
Boiling Springs, PA 17007
(717)258-6584 (888)789-9411 Fax:(717)245-9328
Internet: www.gelinasmanor.com
E-mail: Lee@GelinasManor.com

Circa 1869. One of the first homes in the quiet historic village by the lake, this 1869 Victorian is listed in the National Register. Enjoy comfortable accommodations and a satisfying breakfast before embarking on the day's activities. The well-stocked lake and crystal-clear Yellow Breeches Creek are considered some of the country's best trout fishing areas. The nearby Fly Shop features locally tied flies, fishing gear, clothing and gifts as well as offering experienced tips for any interested fisherman. The famous Allenberry Resort and Playhouse is minutes away for fine dining and entertainment in the evening. Visit the sites of Gettysburg within a 30-minute drive, or savor the flavors of Hershey in an hour. The inn is about 1½ hours away from Pennsylvania Dutch Country in Lancaster County.

Innkeeper(s): Lee & Kitty Gelinas. $79-139. 4 rooms, 3 with PB, 1 two-bedroom suite. Breakfast included in rates. Types of meals: Full gourmet bkfst. Beds: QDT. Cable TV, refrigerator, ceiling fan, clock radio, telephone, turn-down service, bathrobes, bath amenities and wireless Internet access in room. Air conditioning. Fax, copier, library and fireplace on premises. Amusement parks, antiquing, art galleries, cross-country skiing, downhill skiing, fishing, golf, hiking, live theater, museums, parks, shopping, sporting events, tennis and Casino nearby.

Location: Historic Village.

Certificate may be used: Accepts Weekends, Anytime, subject to availability; Anytime, last minute - based on availability.

Canadensis   F17

Brookview Manor Inn

RR 2 Box 4534, Route 447
Canadensis, PA 18325
(570) 595-2451 (800) 585-7974 Fax:(570)595-7154
Internet: www.brookviewmanor.com
E-mail: innkeepers@thebrookviewmanor.com

Circa 1901. By the side of the road, hanging from a tall evergreen, is the welcoming sign to this forest retreat on six acres adjoining 250 acres of woodland and hiking trails. The expansive

wraparound porch overlooks a small stream. There are brightly decorated common rooms and eight fireplaces. Ten guest rooms include two with Jacuzzis and two deluxe suites. The carriage house has three additional rooms. One of the inn's dining rooms is surrounded by original stained glass, a romantic location for the inn's special six-course dinners prepared by an award-winning New York chef now on staff.

Innkeeper(s): Gaile & Marty Horowitz. $130-250. 10 rooms with PB, 6 with FP, 2 with WP, 2 two-bedroom suites, 1 conference room. Breakfast included in rates. Types of meals: Full gourmet bkfst, veg bkfst, wine, gourmet dinner, Restaurant on premise,international cusine and Bar and lounge on premise. Restaurant on premises. Beds: KQ. Cable TV, DVD, reading lamp, CD player, ceiling fan, clock radio, turn-down service, most with hot tub/spa, most with fireplace, bathrobes, bath amenities, wireless Internet access, Two rooms with Jacuzzis & fireplaces, Suites have sitting rooms and private porches in room. Air conditioning. VCR, fax, copier, swimming, library, parlor games, telephone, Swing, Wraparound porch overlooking small stream, Gourmet dinner in our restaurant, Bar and lounge, Scheduled murder mystery weekends see our website www.Brookviewmanor.com for dates and on premises. Amusement parks, antiquing, beach, canoeing/kayaking, cross-country skiing, downhill skiing, fishing, golf, hiking, horseback riding, live theater, parks, shopping, tennis, water sports, wineries, Mount Airy Casino (10 minutes), Bushkill Falls, Camelback Waterpark, Camelback Ski Mountain, Skiing, Horseback riding,Skytop, Buck Hill golf club and Delaware Water Gap nearby.

Location: Country, mountains.

Publicity: *Mid-Atlantic Country, Bridal Guide, New York Times and Pocono Record.*

"Thanks for a great wedding weekend. Everything was perfect."

Certificate may be used: Sunday to Thursday, subject to availability, not on holiday or special event weeks.

Carlisle   J11

Carlisle House

148 South Hanover Street
Carlisle, PA 17013
(717) 249-0350 Fax:(717) 249-0458
Internet: www.thecarlislehouse.com
E-mail: info@thecarlislehouse.com

Circa 1826. Located in the downtown Historic District, the inn is within easy walking distance of Dickinson College, the Carlisle Fairgrounds, the Historical Museum and some of the best restaurants and shopping in Pennsylvania. Blending a rich history with modern comforts, excellent standards and high-tech amenities for business or leisure, this elegant bed and breakfast offers a memorable stay. Chat with new acquaintances in the sitting room. Relax on the veranda or downstairs patio. Enjoy 24-hour access to the fully equipped kitchen with complimentary fruits and beverages. Guest bedrooms feature period décor and furnishings. Some include a private entrance, fireplace and Jacuzzi bath. Three suites are available, each with two bedrooms. Savor an international-themed quiche breakfast. Conveniently situated in the heart of the state, Gettysburg battlefields, Hershey's Chocolate World, and Lancaster's Amish Country are some of the many day trips available.

Innkeeper(s): Alan & Mary Duxbury. $129-229. 10 rooms with PB, 3 with WP, 3 two-bedroom suites. Breakfast and snacks/refreshments included in rates. Types of meals: Full gourmet bkfst, veg bkfst and early coffee/tea. Beds: KQDT. Modem hook-up, data port, cable TV, DVD, reading lamp, CD player, refrigerator, clock radio, telephone, coffeemaker, turn-down service, desk, voice mail, hair dryer, bathrobes, bath amenities, wireless Internet access, complimentary juices, soda and bottled water, complimentary domestic long-distance and local calls in room. Air conditioning. Fax, copier, library, parlor games, Fresh fruit, ice, coffee, sitting room with Recliners, TV/DVD and Penn Suite has Washer/Dryer on premises. Amusement parks, antiquing, art galleries, fishing, golf, hiking, live theater, museums, parks, shopping and sporting events nearby.

Location: City. Downtown Historic District.

Publicity: *Washington Post Travel Escapes, The Dickinsonian, Pittsburgh Mt. Lebanon Magazine, Heart of PA Travel Guide, Central PA Business Journal, Cars & Places, Backroads Magazine, The Sentinel "Best Bed and Breakfast 2004 through 1010" in the Carlisle, Shippensburg, Mechanicsburg and Perry County area.*

Certificate may be used: Anytime, Sunday-Thursday.

Pheasant Field B&B

150 Hickorytown Rd
Carlisle, PA 17015-9732
(717)258-0717 (877)258-0717
Internet: www.pheasantfield.com
E-mail: stay@pheasantfield.com

Circa 1800. Located on 10 acres of central Pennsylvania farm-land, this brick, two-story Federal-style farmhouse features wooden shutters and a covered front porch. Rooms include a TV and telephone. An early 19th-century stone barn is on the property, and horse boarding is available. The Appalachian Trail is less than a mile

away. Fly-fishing is popular at Yellow Breeches and Letort Spring. Dickinson College and Carlisle Fairgrounds are other points of interest.

Innkeeper(s): Dee Fegan. $117-219. 8 rooms with PB, 1 with FP, 2 with WP, 1 cottage, 1 conference room. Breakfast and snacks/refreshments includ-ed in rates. Types of meals: Full bkfst and early coffee/tea. Beds: KQT. Cable TV, VCR, DVD, reading lamp, refrigerator, ceiling fan, snack bar, clock radio, telephone, coffeemaker, desk, some with hot tub/spa, some with fireplace, hair dryer, bathrobes, bath amenities, wireless Internet access and iron/iron-ing board in room. Central air. Fax, stable, tennis, library, parlor games, laun-dry facility, gift shop, Labyrinth, Piano, Overnight horse boarding and Pet Friendly on premises. Handicap access. Amusement parks, antiquing, art gal-leries, bicycling, canoeing/kayaking, cross-country skiing, downhill skiing, fishing, golf, hiking, horseback riding, live theater, museums, parks, shop-ping, sporting events, wineries, Army Heritage and Education Center and Appalachian Trail Museum nearby.

Location: Country.

Publicity: *Outdoor Traveler, Harrisburg Magazine, Central PA Magazine and Voted "Simply The Best" B&B by readers of Harrisburg Magazine for 2005 and 2006.*

"You have an outstanding, charming and warm house. I felt for the first time as being home."

Certificate may be used: January and March.

Chadds Ford   K16

Pennsbury Inn

883 Baltimore Pike
Chadds Ford, PA 19317-9305
(610)388-1435 (888)388-1435 Fax:(610)388-1436
Internet: www.pennsburyinn.com
E-mail: info@pennsburyinn.com

Circa 1714. Originally built with Brandywine Blue Granite rub-ble stone and later enlarged, this country farmhouse with hand-molded Flemish Bond brick facade is listed in the National Historic Register. Retaining its colonial heritage with slanted doorways, wooden winder stairs and huge fireplaces, it

boasts modern conveniences that include complimentary wire-less Internet. There are elegant public sitting areas such as the parlor, music room, library with an impressive book collection and breakfast in the garden room. Comfortable guest rooms feature antiques, feather beds and unique architectural details. The eight-acre estate boasts formal gardens with a fish pond and a reflection pool in a serene woodland setting.

Innkeeper(s): Cheryl & Chip Grono. $105-230. 7 rooms, 6 with PB, 5 with FP, 2 suites, 3 conference rooms. Breakfast, afternoon tea and snacks/refresh-ments included in rates. Types of meals: Full gourmet bkfst, veg bkfst, early coffee/tea, gourmet lunch, picnic lunch and hors d'oeuvres. Beds: KQDT. Modem hook-up, data port, cable TV, VCR, DVD, reading lamp, CD player, refrigerator, ceiling fan, clock radio, telephone, coffeemaker, turn-down service, desk, voice mail, hair dryer, bathrobes, bath amenities, wireless Internet access, iron/ironing board, Three with decorative fireplaces & electric firestove inserts and Two rooms have freestanding electric firestoves in room. Central air. Fax, copier, library, child care, parlor games, fireplace, laundry facility, gift shop, Horseshoes, Putting Green, Volleyball and Bocce on premises. Limited handicap access. Antiquing, art galleries, bicycling, canoeing/kayaking, fishing, golf, hiking, horseback riding, live theater, museums, parks, shopping, sporting events, tennis, wineries, Longwood Gardens, Winterthur, Brandywine River Museum, Nemours, Hagley Museum and QVC nearby.

Location: City, country. Between Philadelphia & Wilmington.

Publicity: *NY Times & LA Times Travel sections, Philadelphia Inquirer Business, LI Press-Away for the Weekend, Main Line Times Travel & Leisure Inn of the Month, Numerous QVC spots and Interviewed on local station WKBW - Ralph Colliers Travel Moment.*

Certificate may be used: 7 days per week, January & February, Sunday-Thursday, March, July-August, no holidays. Not valid April, May, June, September, October, November & December. Last Minute any month (less than 24 hours) subject to availability.

Choconut   C14

Addison House B&B

Rural Route 267
Choconut, PA 18818
(570)553-2682
Internet: www.1811addison.com
E-mail: dmclallen@stny.rr.com

Circa 1811. Addison House was built by one of Choconut's earliest settlers, an Irish immigrant who purchased the vast homestead for just under a dollar an acre. The early 19th-cen-tury house is built in Federal style, but its interior includes many Victorian features, from the rich décor to the hand-carved marble fireplaces. A creek rambles through the 260-acre property, and guests will enjoy the secluded, wilderness setting. In the guest rooms, fluffy comforters top antique beds and flo-ral wallcoverings add to the country Victorian ambiance. Breakfasts begin with items such as fresh berries with cream, followed by a rich entrée. The innkeepers are happy to help guests plan their days. The area offers a multitude of outdoor activities, as well as historic sites, antique shops, covered bridges and much more.

Innkeeper(s): Dennis & Gloria McLallen. $75-110. 4 rooms, 1 suite. Breakfast included in rates. Types of meals: Full gourmet bkfst, early coffee/tea and afternoon tea. Beds: D. Turn-down service, ice water and chocolates in room. Central air. TV, VCR, swimming, library, parlor games, telephone, fireplace and afternoon tea and house tour (by appointment) on premises. Antiquing, art galleries, bicycling, canoeing/kayaking, cross-country skiing, fishing, golf, hiking, live theater, museums, parks, shopping, sporting events, wineries and zoo nearby.

Location: Country, mountains. Farm, horses.

Certificate may be used: Anytime, subject to availability.

Danielsville   H17

Filbert Bed & Breakfast

3740 Filbert Drive
Danielsville, PA 18038
(610)428-3300
Internet: filbertbnb.com
E-mail: filbertbnb@aol.com

Circa 1800. Feel refreshed in the quiet country setting of this restored 1800 Queen Anne Victorian on six acres in Danielsville, Pennsylvania. Adorning the foothills of Blue Mountains between Lehigh Valley and the Pocono Mountains, The Filbert Bed & Breakfast is a warm and welcoming B&B open all year. Relax on the 60-foot porch, play games or watch movies in the large sitting room or gather for conversation in the greeting parlor. Air-conditioned guest suites boast hardwood floors and antiques. Savor a bountiful breakfast in the dining room before embarking on the day's adventures. Massage and skin care appointments are available from a certified therapist and licensed cosmetologist.

Innkeeper(s): Kathy Silfies. $100-200. 5 total suites, including 1 two-bedroom suite. Breakfast and snacks/refreshments included in rates. Types of meals: Country bkfst and early coffee/tea. Beds: Q. Cable TV, VCR, DVD, CD player, clock radio, turn-down service, hair dryer, bathrobes, bath amenities, wireless Internet access and iron/ironing board in room. Air conditioning. Copier, parlor games, telephone and laundry facility on premises. Amusement parks, antiquing, art galleries, beach, bicycling, canoeing/kayaking, cross-country skiing, downhill skiing, fishing, golf, hiking, horseback riding, live theater, museums, parks, shopping, sporting events, tennis, water sports and wineries nearby.

Location: Country, mountains. Original farm setting.

Certificate may be used: March-November, subject to availability, Anytime, Last Minute-Based on Availability.

Eagles Mere   E13

Crestmont Inn

Crestmont Dr
Eagles Mere, PA 17731
(570)525-3519 (800)522-8767 Fax:570-525-3534
Internet: www.crestmont-inn.com
E-mail: crestmnt@epix.net

Circa 1914. "The Crestmont Inn is the prime of Nature and Romance. In the heart of the Endless Mountains enjoy an array of outside activities at any time of year including hiking and even cross country skiing. Luxurious rooms furnished with antique furniture, two person whirlpool tubs,private baths and heavenly beds. Dine in the 'Fouquet Room' for a fine dining experience or in the 'Woodlands Pub' near the fireplace for a more casual setting. Room rate includes a full country breakfast and privileges to the Eagles Mere Country Club and the Eagles Mere Lake and Beach.

Innkeeper(s): Elna & Fred Mulford. $110-240. 15 rooms with PB, 2 with FP, 4 with WP, 3 two-bedroom suites. Breakfast and snacks/refreshments included in rates. Types of meals: Country bkfst, early coffee/tea, wine and dinner. Restaurant on premises. Beds: KQDT. Cable TV, DVD, reading lamp, refrigerator, clock radio, telephone, some with fireplace, hair dryer, bathrobes, bath amenities, wireless Internet access and iron/ironing board in room. Central air. Fax, copier, tennis, parlor games and gift shop on premises. Antiquing, art galleries, beach, canoeing/kayaking, cross-country skiing, fishing, golf, hiking, horseback riding, live theater, museums, parks, shopping, tennis, water sports and wineries nearby.

Location: Country, mountains. Endless mountain 2,200 feet.

Certificate may be used: Monday-Thursday, Anytime, subject to availability.

East Berlin   K12

Bechtel Victorian Mansion B&B Inn

400 W King St
East Berlin, PA 17316
(717)259-7760 (800)579-1108
Internet: www.BechtelVictorianMansion.com
E-mail: bechtelvictbb@aol.com

Circa 1897. The town of East Berlin, near Lancaster and 18 miles east of Gettysburg, was settled by Pennsylvania Germans prior to the American Revolution. William Leas, a wealthy banker, built this many-gabled romantic Queen Anne mansion, now listed in the National Register. The inn is furnished with an abundance of museum-quality antiques and collections. Rooms are decorated in country Victorian style with beautiful quilts and comforters, lace, dolls and teddy bears.

Innkeeper(s): Richard & Carol Carlson. $115-175. 6 rooms with PB, 2 suites. Breakfast included in rates. Types of meals: Full bkfst, early coffee/tea and snacks/refreshments. Beds: KQD. Reading lamp and turn-down service in room. Air conditioning. TV, VCR, parlor games, telephone and fireplace on premises. Amusement parks, antiquing, bicycling, downhill skiing, fishing, golf, hiking, live theater, museums, shopping and wineries nearby.

Location: Historic district-German town.

Publicity: *Washington Post and Richmond Times.*

Certificate may be used: December-August.

Ephrata   J14

Historic Smithton Inn

900 W Main St
Ephrata, PA 17522-1328
(717)733-6094
Internet: www.historicsmithtoninn.com
E-mail: smithtoninn@gmail.com

Circa 1763. This colonial inn is located just a quarter mile from the Ephrata Cloister in the heart of Pennsylvania Dutch Country, an area known for the Amish, antiques, rolling hills and farm land, and quaint towns and shops. The innkeepers, Dave and Rebecca Gallagher, have blended historic charm with modern comfort and convenience, to create a casual, homey atmosphere for their guests. Breakfast is always a treat and includes the Smithton's signature granola, homemade yogurt, muffins and breads in addition to a delicious hot entrée that alternates between sweet and savory. Each spacious guest room boasts a working fireplace and is decorated with hand-sewn Amish quilts, antique & hand crafted furniture. Modern conveniences include a flat screen TV with DVD player, clock radio with iPod docking station, and wireless internet access throughout the inn. After a day of taking in all the activities Lancaster County has to offer, guests can be found rocking on the front porch, watching horse and buggies pass by, or relaxing by the fire pit in the back garden, surrounded by flowers, birds and bunnies. Families traveling with young children or with pets can be accommodated in Tailor's Cottage.

Innkeeper(s): Rebecca and Dave Gallagher. $119-179. 7 rooms with PB, 7 with FP, 3 with HT, 2 suites. Breakfast and snacks/refreshments included in rates. Types of meals: Full bkfst and early coffee/tea. Beds: KQT. Reading lamp, refrigerator, clock radio, desk, hair dryer, bathrobes, bath amenities, wireless Internet access and Hand sewn quilts in every guestroom. Full length mirrors and make up mirrors. Snack trays with bottled water in room. Air conditioning. TV, copier, library, parlor games, telephone, fireplace, laundry facility, Access (additional cost) to fitness center 1 block up the road and including indoor pool and full weight / cardio rooms on premises. Amusement parks, antiquing, art galleries, bicycling, canoeing/kayaking, golf, hiking, live theater, museums, parks, shopping, tennis, wineries, farmland, handcrafts and farmers market nearby.

Location: Country. Village.

Publicity: *New York, Country Living, Early American Life, Washington Post, Philadelphia Inquirer. and Channel 2 News.*

"After visiting over 50 inns in four countries, Smithton has to be one of the most romantic, picturesque inns in America. I have never seen its equal!"

Certificate may be used: Year-Round based on availability, Sunday-Thursday.

Erwinna   I17

Golden Pheasant Inn on the Delaware

763 River Rd
Erwinna, PA 18920-9254
(610)294-9595 (800)830-4474 Fax:(610)294-9882
Internet: www.goldenpheasant.com
E-mail: barbara@goldenpheasant.com

Circa 1857. The Golden Pheasant is well established as the location of a wonderful, gourmet restaurant, but it is also home to six charming guest rooms decorated by Barbara Faure. Four-poster canopy beds and antiques decorate the rooms, which offer views of the canal and river. The fieldstone inn was built as a mule-barge stop for travelers heading down the Delaware Canal. The five-acre grounds resemble a French-country estate, and guests can enjoy the lush surroundings in a plant-filled greenhouse dining room. There are two other dining rooms, including an original fieldstone room with exposed beams and stone walls with decorative copper pots hanging here and there. The restaurant's French cuisine, prepared by chef Michel Faure, is outstanding. One might start off with Michel's special pheasant pate, followed by a savory onion soup baked with three cheeses. A mix of greens dressed in vinaigrette cleanses the palate before one samples roast duck in a luxurious raspberry, ginger and rum sauce or perhaps a sirloin steak flamed in cognac.

Innkeeper(s): Barbara & Michel Faure. $95-225. 6 rooms with PB, 4 with FP, 1 suite, 1 cottage, 3 conference rooms. Breakfast included in rates. Types of meals: Cont plus, early coffee/tea, picnic lunch, snacks/refreshments, gourmet dinner and room service. Restaurant on premises. Beds: Q. Reading lamp, CD player, refrigerator, ceiling fan, clock radio, telephone, coffeemaker, desk, hot tub/spa and fireplace in room. Air conditioning. Fax, copier, swimming, library, parlor games and canal path for walking on premises. Limited handicap access. Antiquing, art galleries, bicycling, canoeing/kayaking, cross-country skiing, fishing, golf, hiking, horseback riding, live theater, museums, parks, shopping, tennis, water sports, wineries, historic Doylestown, New Hope and Washington Crossing nearby.

Location: Country.

Publicity: *The Philadelphia Inquirer, New York Times, Philadelphia Magazine, Food Network and Fox.*

"A more stunningly romantic spot is hard to imagine. A taste of France on the banks of the Delaware."

Certificate may be used: Sunday-Thursday, excluding holidays.

Fairfield   L11

The Fairfield Inn 1757

15 West Main Street (Rt. 116 West)
Fairfield, PA 17320
(717)642-5410 Fax:(717)642-5920
Internet: www.thefairfieldinn.com
E-mail: innkeeper@thefairfieldinn.com

Circa 1757. Rich in history, this authentic American treasure has been a continuously operating tavern, restaurant and inn for 180 years and its origins as the Mansion House of the town's founder date back 245 years. Tour the Gettysburg battlefield then retreat to the hospitality and refinement expected from a small luxury hotel yet enjoyed at this inn. Sip a hot beverage by one of the eight fireplaces. Squire Miller's Tavern offers conversation and libations. Renovated guest bedrooms and suites boast air conditioning and cable television. The Mansion House Restaurant serves an imaginative menu of classically prepared and artistically presented dishes. A patio garden is bordered with privacy hedges and filled with flowers. Cooking classes, special dinners and holiday activities are among the many events planned throughout the year.

Innkeeper(s): Joan & Sal Chandon. $99-225. 6 rooms with PB, 2 with FP, 4 with WP, 2 suites, 1 conference room. Breakfast included in rates. Types of meals: Full bkfst, Sun. brunch, lunch, picnic lunch, snacks/refreshments, wine and dinner. Restaurant on premises. Beds: QDT. Cable TV, reading lamp, refrigerator, ceiling fan, clock radio, coffeemaker, turn-down service, desk, some with fireplace, hair dryer, wireless Internet access and iron/ironing board in room. Central air. Fax, parlor games and telephone on premises. Limited handicap access. Antiquing, bicycling, cross-country skiing, downhill skiing, golf, hiking, horseback riding, live theater, museums, parks, shopping, sporting events, tennis, wineries and Gettysburg National Military Park nearby.

Location: Country. Eight miles west of Gettysburg.

Publicity: *Gettysburg Times, Hanover Evening Sun, York Daily Record, Frederick Magazine, Cleveland Magazine, Celebrate Gettysburg Magazine, Travel Channel, Discovery Channel and WABC New York.*

Certificate may be used: Anytime, November-March, subject to availability, may not be combined with any other discounts, vouchers, coupons or gift certificates.

Gettysburg   L11

James Gettys Hotel

27 Chambersburg St
Gettysburg, PA 17325
(717)337-1334 (888)900-5275 Fax:(717)334-2103
Internet: www.jamesgettyshotel.com
E-mail: info@jamesgettyshotel.com

Circa 1803. Listed in the National Register, this newly renovated four-story hotel once served as a tavern through the Battle of Gettysburg and was used as a hospital for soldiers. Outfitted with cranberry colored awnings and a gold painted entrance, the hotel offers a tea room, nature store and gallery on the street level. From the lobby, a polished chestnut staircase leads to the guest quarters. All accommodations are suites with living rooms appointed with home furnishings, and each has its own kitchenette. Breakfasts of home-baked scones and coffee cake are brought to your room.

Innkeeper(s): Stephanie Stephan. $140-250. 12 rooms, 1 with FP, 1 with WP, 12 suites. Breakfast included in rates. Types of meals: Cont. Beds: KQD. Data port, cable TV, reading lamp, refrigerator, clock radio, telephone, coffeemaker, turn-down service, some with hot tub/spa, voice mail, some with fireplace, hair dryer, bath amenities, wireless Internet access and iron/ironing board in room. Central air. VCR, DVD, fax, copier and gift shop on premises.

Handicap access. Amusement parks, antiquing, art galleries, bicycling, cross-country skiing, downhill skiing, fishing, golf, hiking, horseback riding, live theater, museums, parks, shopping, tennis, wineries, Gettysburg National Military Park and Eisenhower National Historic Site nearby.

Location: Small historic town.

Certificate may be used: Monday-Thursday, excluding holidays and special events, Jan. 1-Dec. 30.

Keystone Inn B&B

231 Hanover St
Gettysburg, PA 17325-1913
(717)337-3888
Internet: www.keystoneinnbb.com
E-mail: Keystoneinn@comcast.net

Circa 1913. Furniture maker Clayton Reaser constructed this three-story brick Victorian with a wide-columned porch hugging the north and west sides. Cut stone graces every door and window sill, each with a keystone. A chestnut staircase ascends the full three stories, and the interior is decorated with comfortable furnishings, ruffles and lace.

Innkeeper(s): Michael & Marjorie Day.
$99-169. 7 rooms with PB, 1 with WP, 2 suites. Breakfast and snacks/refreshments included in rates. Types of meals: Full bkfst and early coffee/tea. Beds: KQT. Cable TV, reading lamp, refrigerator, clock radio, desk, hair dryer and wireless Internet access in room. Air conditioning. Library, parlor games and telephone on premises. Antiquing, art galleries, bicycling, cross-country skiing, downhill skiing, golf, hiking, horseback riding, live theater, museums, parks, shopping, sporting events, tennis, wineries, Civil War Battlefield and historic sites nearby.

Location: Small town.

Publicity: *Lancaster Sunday News, York Sunday News, Hanover Sun, Allentown Morning Call, Gettysburg Times, Pennsylvania and Los Angeles Times.*

"We slept like lambs. This home has a warmth that is soothing."
Certificate may be used: November-April, Monday-Thursday.

The Gaslight Inn

33 E Middle St
Gettysburg, PA 17325
(717)337-9100 (800)914-5698 Fax:(717)337-1100
Internet: www.thegaslightinn.com
E-mail: info@thegaslightinn.com

Circa 1872. Gaslights illuminate the brick pathways leading to this 130-year-old Italianate-style, expanded farmhouse. The inn boasts two elegant parlors separated by original pocket doors, a spacious dining room and a first-floor guest room with wheelchair access that opens to a large, brick patio. An open switchback staircase leads to the second- and third-floor guest rooms, all individually decorated in traditional and European furnishings. Some of the rooms feature covered decks, fireplaces, whirlpool tubs and steam showers for two. Guests are invited to enjoy a hearty or heart-healthy breakfast and inn-baked cookies and brownies and refreshments in the afternoon. Winter weekend packages are available and carriage rides, private guides and a variety of activities can be arranged with the help of the innkeepers.

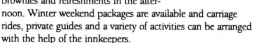

Innkeeper(s): Mike and Becky Hanson. $123-178. 9 rooms with PB, 6 with

FP, 2 with HT. Breakfast and snacks/refreshments included in rates. Types of meals: Full gourmet bkfst and early coffee/tea. Beds: KQ. Cable TV, VCR, reading lamp, ceiling fan, clock radio, telephone, some with hot tub/spa, most with fireplace, wireless Internet access and Spa showers for 2 which with the touch of a button provide a 20 minute steam bath in room. Central air. Fax, spa, library, parlor games and Wireless Internet access throughout the inn on premises. Limited handicap access. Antiquing, art galleries, bicycling, cross-country skiing, downhill skiing, fishing, golf, hiking, horseback riding, live theater, museums, parks, shopping, tennis, water sports, wineries and historic educational tours and lectures nearby.

Location: City. Small town, historic site.

Publicity: *Tyler Texas Times, Hanover Sun, Los Angeles Times, Southern Living and Country Inns.*

Certificate may be used: Dec. 1-March 31, Sunday-Thursday, except New Year's Eve and Valentine's Day.

Gordonville   K14

Osceola Mill House

313 Osceola Mill Rd
Gordonville, PA 17529
(717)768-3758 (800)878-7719
Internet: www.lancaster-inn.com
E-mail: osceolamill@frontiernet.net

Circa 1766. In a quaint historic setting adjacent to a mill and a miller's cottage, this handsome limestone mill house rests on the banks of Pequea Creek. There are deep-set windows and wide pine floors. Guest bedrooms and the keeping room feature working fireplaces that add to the warmth and charm. Breakfast fare may include tasty regional specialties like locally made Pennsylvania Dutch sausage, and Dutch babies- an oven-puffed pancake filled with fresh fruit. Amish neighbors farm the adjacent fields, their horse and buggies enhance the picturesque ambiance.

Innkeeper(s): Patricia & Ron Ernst. $110-190. 5 rooms with PB, 4 with FP, 1 cottage. Breakfast included in rates. Types of meals: Country bkfst, veg bkfst and snacks/refreshments. Beds: Q. Cable TV, VCR, DVD, reading lamp, ceiling fan, clock radio, some with fireplace, hair dryer, wireless Internet access and iron/ironing board in room. Air conditioning. Fax, copier, parlor games and Coffee & Tea is available in Gathering room anytime on premises. Amusement parks, antiquing, art galleries, bicycling, canoeing/kayaking, fishing, golf, hiking, live theater, museums, parks, shopping, sporting events and wineries nearby.

Location: Country. Intercourse, Paradise, Strasburg.

Publicity: *The Journal, Country Living, Washington Times, Gourmet and BBC.*

"We had a thoroughly delightful stay at your inn. Probably the most comfortable overnight stay we've ever had."

Certificate may be used: January-March, Sunday-Thursday, subject to availability, excludes holidays and special events, can not be combined with any other offers, discounts or gift certificates.

Grove City   F2

Snow Goose Inn

112 E Main St
Grove City, PA 16127
(724)458-4644
Internet: www.bbonline.com/pa/snowgoose
E-mail: msgoose1@zoominternet.net

Circa 1895. Snow Goose Inn Bed & Breakfast is cradled amid the rolling hills of Northwestern Pennsylvania, 50 miles from of

Pittsburgh. This Grove City B&B was built for young women attending Grove City College. It was later used as a family home and offices for a local doctor before being transformed into a child-friendly bed and breakfast decorated with antiques and country touches that include stenciling, collectibles and a few signature geese on display. Stay in a comfortable guest room with a private bath and wake up to savor a home-cooked breakfast made with satisfying favorite recipes. Museums, shops, Amish farms, colleges and several state parks are in the vicinity, offering many activities to participate in. Take an easy day trip to Cleveland, Ohio, just 85 miles away.

Innkeeper(s): Orvil & Dorothy McMillen. $75. 4 rooms with PB. Breakfast and snacks/refreshments included in rates. Types of meals: Full gourmet bkfst and early coffee/tea. Beds: QD. Reading lamp, stereo, refrigerator and clock radio in room. Air conditioning. VCR, parlor games, telephone and fireplace on premises. Amusement parks, antiquing, cross-country skiing, downhill skiing, fishing, golf, live theater, parks, shopping, sporting events, tennis and water sports nearby.

Location: City.

Publicity: *Allied News.*

"Your thoughtful touches and homey atmosphere were a balm to our chaotic lives."

Certificate may be used: Anytime, subject to availability.

Hanover   L12

The Beechmont B&B Inn

315 Broadway
Hanover, PA 17331-2505
(717)632-3013 (800)553-7009
Internet: www.thebeechmont.com
E-mail: innkeeper@thebeechmont.com

Circa 1834. Feel welcomed by centuries of charm at this gracious Georgian inn, a witness to the Battle of Hanover, the Civil War's first major battle on free soil. A 130-year-old magnolia tree shades the flagstone patio and wicker furniture invites a lingering rest on the front porch. The romantic Magnolia Suite features a marble fireplace, whirlpool tub and Queen canopy bed. The inn is noted for its sumptuous breakfasts.

Innkeeper(s): Kathryn & Thomas White. $119-169. 7 rooms with PB, 4 with FP, 1 with WP, 3 suites. Breakfast and snacks/refreshments included in rates. Types of meals: Full gourmet bkfst and early coffee/tea. Beds: QD. Cable TV, reading lamp, ceiling fan, clock radio, telephone, desk, voice mail, hair dryer, bathrobes, bath amenities and wireless Internet access in room. Central air. DVD, fax, copier, library and parlor games on premises. Handicap access. Antiquing, bicycling, canoeing/kayaking, cross-country skiing, fishing, golf, hiking, horseback riding, live theater, museums, parks, shopping, sporting events, tennis, water sports and wineries nearby.

Location: City.

Publicity: *Evening Sun and York Daily Record.*

"I had a marvelous time at your charming, lovely inn."

Certificate may be used: Sunday-Thursday, Dec. 1-March 31, excluding holidays.

Intercourse   K14

Carriage Corner

3705 E Newport Rd.
Intercourse, PA 17534-0371
(717)768-3059 (800)209-3059
Internet: www.carriagecornerbandb.com
E-mail: gschuit@comcast.net

Circa 1979. Located in the heart of Amish farmland, this two-story Colonial rests on a pastoral acre. Homemade, country breakfasts are served, often including innkeeper Gordon

Schuit's special recipe for oatmeal pancakes. A five-minute walk will take guests into the village where they'll find Amish buggies traveling down the lanes and more than 100 shops displaying local crafts, pottery, quilts and furniture, as well as art galleries. The innkeepers can arrange for dinners in an Amish home, buggy rides and working Amish farm tours. Longwood Gardens, Hershey's Chocolate World and Gettysburg are also nearby.

Innkeeper(s): Gordon & Gwen Schuit. $68-94. 5 rooms with PB, 1 conference room. Breakfast included in rates. Types of meals: Full bkfst and early coffee/tea. Beds: Q. Cable TV and clock radio in room. Central air. VCR, fax, library, parlor games, telephone and fireplace on premises. Amusement parks, antiquing, art galleries, bicycling, live theater, museums, parks, shopping, wineries, hub of Amish farmland, Amish dinners arranged, buggy rides, working Amish farm tours, Strasburg Steam Railroad, Railroad Museum of PA, "Daniel" at Sight and Sound, festivals and auctions, craft and quilt fairs, farmers' markets and roadside stands, Longwood Gardens, Hershey's Chocolate World and Gettysburg nearby.

Location: Country. Amish farmland.

Certificate may be used: December, January and February, excluding holiday weekends. March-April, November, Sunday-Wednesday, excluding special events.

The Inn & Spa at Intercourse Village

3542 Old Philadelphia Pike, POB 598
Intercourse, PA 17534
(717)768-2626 (800)664-0949
Internet: www.inn-spa.com
E-mail: innkeeper@inn-spa.com

Circa 1909. Located in historic Intercourse, Pennsylvania, near Lancaster this winner of the iLoveInns.com Top 10 Romantic Inns of 2009 caters to couples. Relax on white wicker furniture on the front porch as the Amish pass by in horse-drawn carriages. The Intercourse Village Inn & Spa offers guest rooms in the two-story 1909 Victorian main house. The Homestead Suites are in more modern buildings with gas-burning fireplaces, refrigerators and microwaves. The Summer House Suite stands alone and boasts a heart-shaped whirlpool. A gourmet five-course breakfast is served by candlelight in the formal dining room of the main house on fine English china. Visit the town's craft, quilt and antique shops or tour the candle and pretzel factories. Hershey is only an hour away and Gettysburg an hour and a half.

Innkeeper(s): Ruthann Thomas. $149-399. 9 rooms, 9 with FP, 3 with WP, 9 total suites, including 6 two-bedroom suites. Breakfast included in rates. Types of meals: 5-course Full Breakfast. Beds: KQ. Data port, cable TV, VCR, DVD, CD player, refrigerator, clock radio, telephone, coffeemaker, fireplace, hair dryer, bathrobes, wireless Internet access and New Flat Panel TV's in room.

Central air. Antiquing, art galleries, golf, live theater and shopping nearby.

Location: Country. Historic Amish Village.

Publicity: *Washingtonian, Vogue, National Geographic, Lancaster Sunday News* and ILoveInns.com 2009 Top 10 Romantic Inn.

Certificate may be used: December-August, Tuesday/Wednesday stay only. Must be used for Thomas Jacuzzi suite only (#141). Subject to availability.

Jim Thorpe H15

The Inn at Jim Thorpe

24 Broadway
Jim Thorpe, PA 18229
(570)325-2599 (800)329-2599 Fax:(570)325-9145
Internet: www.innjt.com
E-mail: reservations@innjt.com

Circa 1849. Sit on the grand balcony of this New Orleans-style boutique hotel and overlook the historic district of the scenic village of Jim Thorpe in the Pocono Mountains of Pennsylvania. The Inn at Jim Thorpe is one of the town's landmark treasures and is listed in the National Register. Stay in an air-conditioned guest room or world-class suite with a fireplace and whirlpool tub. The décor reflects the Victorian age and bathrooms boast pedestal sinks and marble floors. Upscale amenities include exercise facilities, spa services, wireless Internet, bike storage and fully equipped meeting rooms. Dine in the on-site Emerald Restaurant and relax over drinks in the authentic Irish Pub. Ask about the variety of packages available. Shops, galleries, train rides, river rafting and hiking/biking trails are nearby.

Innkeeper(s): David Drury. $103-399. 45 rooms, 34 with PB, 5 with FP, 11 with WP, 2 conference rooms. Breakfast included in rates. Types of meals: Cont plus, lunch, dinner and room service. Beds: KQ. Cable TV, DVD, reading lamp, refrigerator, ceiling fan, clock radio, telephone, coffeemaker, most with hot tub/spa, voice mail, some with fireplace, hair dryer, wireless Internet access, iron/ironing board and Free wireless Internet in all rooms in room. Air conditioning. Fax, copier, Suites with whirlpools and fireplaces, Spa services, Authentic Irish pub & restaurant, Exercise room, Bike storage, Cable TV/HBO & phones w/voice mail and Fully-equipped meeting rooms on premises. Handicap access. Antiquing, art galleries, bicycling, canoeing/kayaking, cross-country skiing, downhill skiing, fishing, golf, hiking, horseback riding, museums, parks, shopping and wineries nearby.

Location: Mountains. Historic Downtown.

Publicity: *Philadelphia Inquirer, Pennsylvania Magazine* and *Allentown Morning Call.*

"We had the opportunity to spend a weekend at your lovely inn. Your staff is extremely friendly, helpful, and courteous. I can't remember when we felt so relaxed, we hope to come back again soon."

Certificate may be used: Sunday-Thursday excluding holidays and Christmas week and the month of August. All discounts and promotions based on weekend rack rates.

Lackawaxen E18

Roebling Inn on the Delaware

155 Scenic Dr
Lackawaxen, PA 18435
(570)685-7900 Fax:(570)685-1718
Internet: www.roeblinginn.com
E-mail: info@roeblinginn.com

Circa 1870. Elegant, country accommodations located just two hours from New York City and two and a half from Philadelphia offer the opportunity to relax and enjoy two pristine rivers, the Delaware and the Lackawaxen. Sit on the front porch or at water's edge amid the mountain beauty and forested landscape. Watch for bald eagles and other birds. Air-conditioned guest bedrooms are comfortably furnished with antiques. Some include a fireplace. Start the day with a bountiful breakfast before exploring the picturesque area. Walk across the Roebling Bridge, America's oldest wire cable suspension bridge, view the picture exhibits and visit the small tollhouse museum. Tour the home of Zane Grey, open seasonally and maintained by the National Park Service. Hike at Minisink Battleground Park, site of a Revolutionary War battle or take in area waterfalls with a self-guided driving/hiking tour.

Innkeeper(s): Don & JoAnn Jahn. $99-185. 6 rooms with PB, 3 with FP, 1 cottage, 1 conference room. Breakfast, snacks/refreshments and Full breakfast from 8-10am. Tea & cookie jar available included in rates. Types of meals: Country bkfst, veg bkfst, early coffee/tea and afternoon tea. Beds: QDT. Cable TV, DVD, CD player, ceiling fan, clock radio, most with fireplace, bath amenities, wireless Internet access, alarm clock, free wi-fi, some with fireplace, all private bath, a/c, tv with dvd, free phone calls and free dvd library in room. Air conditioning. Fax, telephone, generous full breakfast with a hot offering daily, cookies jar, tea available, front porch, hammock and sitting room with fireplace on premises. Antiquing, canoeing/kayaking, downhill skiing, fishing, golf, hiking, horseback riding, parks, tennis, water sports, eagle viewing, fishing, drift boat service, white water rafting on the Lackawaxen, tubing/rafting/canoeing on the Delaware and Bethel Woods (30 mins) nearby.

Location: Country, mountains, waterfront.

Publicity: *New York Times, Pennsylvania Magazine, New York Magazine* and *New York Daily News.*

Certificate may be used: Monday-Thursday in April and September.

Lancaster K14

A New Beginning Bed & Breakfast

1400 East King Street
Lancaster, PA 17602
(717) 393-5935
Internet: www.anewbeginningbb.com
E-mail: info@anewbeginningbb.com

Circa 1912. Located in the heart of Pennsylvania Dutch Country in Lancaster, this historic home has been restored with its original chestnut woodwork and updated to offer modern technology like Wifi. Sit in the fireside parlor and play games or watch a movie. Tour the Amish countryside, shop the outlet malls, visit a museum and enjoy Hershey Park. Stay in an inviting air-conditioned guest room or the spacious two-room Country Suite. The Serenity Room boasts a whirlpool tub.

Linger over a hearty breakfast in the formal dining room or on the front porch. It includes homemade granola and cereals, yogurts, breads and pastries that complement gourmet and classic entrees and made-to-order eggs accompanied by locally cured meats. Afternoon tea and treats are provided on weekends and indulge in refreshments each evening before retiring.

Innkeeper(s): Al & Denise Ricci. $90-125. 4 rooms with PB, 1 with WP, 1 two-bedroom suite. Breakfast, afternoon tea and snacks/refreshments included in rates. Types of meals: Full gourmet bkfst, veg bkfst, early coffee/tea and On weekends we have 4:00 pm tea and goodies. We also cater to restricted and gluten free diets. Beds: QDT. Cable TV, ceiling fan, clock radio, hair dryer, bath amenities, wireless Internet access, During the winter months, each room will have an Amish Electric Fireplace. All rooms have private baths with the Serenity Room having a whirlpool bathtub. In the common area of the hallway is a refrigerator (stocked with water & soda), a microwave with glasses and cups and plates all for your use in room. Air conditioning. VCR, copier, library, parlor games, telephone and fireplace on premises. Amusement parks, antiquing, art galleries, bicycling, golf, hiking, horseback riding, live theater, museums, parks, shopping, sporting events, wineries, Lancaster Barnstormers (local baseball team), Long's Park (summer Sunday music) and First Fridays (in the city) nearby.

Location: Country.

Certificate may be used: Jan. 1-April 30.

Hollinger House

2336 Hollinger Rd
Lancaster, PA 17602-4728
(717)464-3050 Fax:(717)464-3053
Internet: www.hollingerhousebnb.com
E-mail: majestic@hollingerhousebnb.com

Circa 1870. Become part of the family while staying at this Lancaster County B&B in the heart of Amish Country with hardwood floors, high ceilings and fireplaces. Hollinger House Bed & Breakfast welcomes children of all ages. Relax on the wraparound veranda. Guest room amenities include bottled water, glycerin soaps and a special blended shampoo. Add romantic touches by requesting an in-room mas-  sage by candlelight, soft music, fresh flowers and a welcome basket with an assortment of local goodies, cocktail napkins, glasses, wine, champagne, bottled juices and more. Enjoy a bountiful hot breakfast each morning. The generous hospitality extends to providing evening desserts. Stroll the grounds or go sightseeing. Drive to nearby Harrisburg, or be in Baltimore in two hours and New York in 2-1/2 hours. It is 60 miles to Philadelphia.

Innkeeper(s): David & Cindy Mott. $125-165. 5 rooms with PB, 5 with FP, 1 conference room. Breakfast and snacks/refreshments included in rates. Types of meals: Country bkfst and early coffee/tea. Beds: KQDT. Cable TV, VCR, DVD, reading lamp, refrigerator, snack bar, clock radio, coffeemaker, turndown service, desk, most with fireplace, hair dryer, bathrobes, bath amenities, wireless Internet access, iron/ironing board, Bottled water, Soaps, Shampoos and Toothpaste in room. Central air. Fax, copier, library, parlor games, telephone, laundry facility, reading material, cable TV, VCR, High speed Internet access and Wireless Internet access on premises. Amusement parks, antiquing, art galleries, bicycling, canoeing/kayaking, cross-country skiing, downhill skiing, fishing, golf, hiking, horseback riding, live theater, museums, parks, shopping, sporting events, tennis, water sports, wineries, Amish attractions, historic sites, outlet shopping, parks, covered bridges, mini golf, tours and quilt shops nearby.

Location: Country. Rural, private setting.

Publicity: *Victoria Magazine, Hallmark Greeting Cards photo shoot, People's Place photo shoot, Eisenhart Wallpaper photo shoot, Lancaster Magazine, WLAN (one of top B&Bs in Lancaster County), Centennial (Novel, too) and by James Michener.*

Certificate may be used: November-April, Sunday-Thursday.

Ligonier   J4

Campbell House B&B

305 E Main St
Ligonier, PA 15658-1417
(724)238-9812 (888)238-9812 Fax:(724)238-9951
Internet: www.campbellhousebnb.com
E-mail: innkeeper@campbellhousebnb.com

Circa 1868. Old-fashioned charm blends with modern confort at this Victorian 1868 city cottage in Ligonier, Pennsylvania. Campbell House Bed and Breakfast is a peaceful retreat with a romantic ambiance. Find complimentary snacks, beverages, videos, wine glasses and ice buckets in the Strawberry Pantry. Relax and let the world go by on the front covered porch. Enjoy the smoke-free environment. Guest bedrooms and suites boast an assortment of pleasing amenities that may include a canopy or sleigh bed and a slipper or clawfoot tub. Start each day with a scrumptious breakfast.

Innkeeper(s): Patti Campbell. $115-190. 6 rooms. Types of meals: Full bkfst, veg bkfst, snacks/refreshments and wine. Cable TV, VCR, DVD, reading lamp, stereo, refrigerator, ceiling fan, snack bar, clock radio, telephone, hair dryer, bathrobes, bath amenities, wireless Internet access and iron/ironing board in room. Central air. Fax, copier, parlor games and gift shop on premises. Amusement parks, antiquing, art galleries, bicycling, canoeing/kayaking, cross-country skiing, downhill skiing, fishing, golf, hiking, live theater, museums, parks, shopping and wineries nearby.

Location: City. Ligonier is an Historical Village.

Certificate may be used: Oct. 31-April 15. This offer not valid with any other discounts or packages. Excludes holidays including Valentines and President's weekends.

Lititz   J14

The Lititz House B&B

301 N Broad St
Lititz, PA 17543
(717)626-5299 (800)464-6764
Internet: www.lititzhouse.com
E-mail: stay@lititzhouse.com

Circa 1904. Experience small-town charm at this 1904 bed and breakfast situated in the heart of downtown in Pennsylvania Dutch Country in Lancaster County. It is mingled with elegant touches for enjoyment and comfort. The first floor has been redecorated with Scandinavian teak, glass and leather furniture on area rugs. Relax in the second-floor sitting room. Air-conditioned guest bedrooms and a two-bedroom suite with private entrances are tasteful and inviting. Let your taste buds rejoice in the elegant gourmet breakfast. Sit on the wraparound front porch rockers, the landscaped decks or the backyard swing amid the flower garden with a fountain.

Innkeeper(s): Heidi & John Lucier. $95-169. 5 rooms with PB, 1 two-bedroom suite. Breakfast, hors d'oeuvres and wine included in rates. Types of meals: Full gourmet bkfst, veg bkfst, early coffee/tea and snacks/refreshments. Beds: QD. Data port, cable TV, VCR, DVD, reading lamp, ceiling fan, clock radio, hair dryer, bath amenities, wireless Internet access, iron/ironing board, extra fluffy towels, ultra soft sheets and back care mattresses in room. Air conditioning. Free WiFi on premises. Amusement parks, antiquing, art galleries, bicycling, fishing, golf, hiking, live theater, museums, parks, shopping, tennis and wineries nearby.

Location: Lancaster County.

Certificate may be used: January-April, subject to availability.

Manheim   *J14*

Rose Manor B&B

124 S Linden St
Manheim, PA 17545-1616
(717)664-4932 (800)666-4932 Fax:(717)664-1611
Internet: www.rosemanor.net
E-mail: inn@rosemanor.net

Circa 1905. A local mill owner built this manor house and it
still maintains original light fixtures, woodwork and cabinetry.
The grounds are decorated with roses and herb gardens. An
herb theme is played out in the guest rooms, which feature
names such as the Parsley, Sage, Rosemary and Thyme rooms.
The fifth room is named the Basil, and its spacious quarters
encompass the third story and feature the roof's angled ceiling.
One room offers a whirlpool and another a fireplace. The decor
is a comfortable English manor style with some antiques. The
inn's location provides close access to many Pennsylvania
Dutch country attractions.

Innkeeper(s): Susan Jenal. $99-140. 5 rooms, 3 with PB, 3 with FP, 2 with
WP. Breakfast included in rates. Types of meals: Full bkfst and picnic lunch.
Beds: QDT. Cable TV, reading lamp, ceiling fan, some with hot tub/spa, some
with fireplace and one with whirlpool in room. Air conditioning. Fax, copier,
library and telephone on premises. Amusement parks, antiquing, fishing, live
theater, parks and shopping nearby.

Location: Small village.

Publicity: *Harrisburg Patriot, Lancaster County Magazine and Central
Pennsylvania Life.*

Certificate may be used: January-June and December subject to availability
excluding holidays, Anytime, Last Minute-Based on Availability.

Mechanicsburg   *J12*

Kanaga House B&B Inn

6940 Carlisle Pike (US Rt 11)
Mechanicsburg, PA 17050
(717)766-8654 (877)9KA-NAGA Fax:(717)697-3908
Internet: www.kanagahouse.com
E-mail: stay@kanagahouse.com

Circa 1775. Stay in this restored 1775 stone house while visiting the area's many tourist attractions such as Gettysburg Civil
War Battlefield, Hershey Chocolate World, Lancaster Dutch
Country or Harrisburg (the state capital). The well-appointed
guest bedrooms offer canopy beds, and one boasts a fireplace.
Tree-studded grounds and a large gazebo are perfect for weddings. The first-floor rooms and catering staff also enhance
business meetings and retreats. Walk the nearby Appalachian
Trail, or fly fish in the Yellow Breeches and Letort Springs.

Innkeeper(s): Mary Jane & Dave Kretzing. $95-165. 7 rooms with PB, 1
with FP, 1 conference room. Breakfast included in rates. Types of meals: Full
bkfst and early coffee/tea. Beds: KD. TV, reading lamp, refrigerator, clock
radio, telephone and desk in room. Air conditioning. VCR, copier, fireplace
and gazebo with table and chairs on premises. Amusement parks, antiquing,
downhill skiing, live theater and shopping nearby.

Location: Rural setting.

Certificate may be used: Oct. 15 to March 31, Sunday-Thursday only,
excluding holidays.

Mercersburg   *L9*

The Mercersburg Inn

405 S Main St
Mercersburg, PA 17236-9517
(717)328-5231 (866)MBURG01 Fax:(717)328-3403
Internet: www.mercersburginn.com
E-mail: innkeeper@mercersburginn.com

Circa 1909. Situated on a hill overlooking the Tuscorora
Mountains, the valley and village, this 20,000-square-foot
Georgian Revival mansion was built for industrialist Harry
Byron. Six massive columns mark the entrance, which opens to
a majestic hall featuring chestnut wainscoting and an elegant
double stairway and rare scagliola (marbleized) columns. All
the rooms are furnished with antiques and reproductions. A
local craftsman built the inn's four-poster, canopied king-size
beds. Many of the rooms have their own balconies and a few
have fireplaces. Thursday through Sunday evening, the inn's
chef prepares noteworthy, elegant dinners, which feature an
array of seasonal specialties.

Innkeeper(s): Lisa & Jim McCoy. $140-325. 17 rooms with PB, 3 with FP, 2
with WP, 1 cottage, 2 conference rooms. Breakfast included in rates. Types of
meals: Full gourmet bkfst, veg bkfst, picnic lunch, wine and gourmet dinner.
Restaurant on premises. Beds: KQT. Reading lamp, clock radio, telephone,
desk, hair dryer, bathrobes, bath amenities, wireless Internet access and
iron/ironing board in room. Central air. TV, DVD, fax, copier, parlor games,
fireplace and gift shop on premises. Antiquing, beach, bicycling, cross-country skiing, downhill skiing, fishing, golf, hiking, horseback riding, live theater,
parks, shopping, water sports and Sightseeing by plane nearby.

Location: Country, mountains. Cumberland Valley.

Publicity: *Mid-Atlantic Country, Washington Post, The Herald-Mail, Richmond
News Leader, Washingtonian, Philadelphia Inquirer and Pittsburgh.*

"Elegance personified! Outstanding ambiance and warm hospitality."

Certificate may be used: Sunday-Thursday, excludes holidays. Only available
for Superior and Extravagant rooms.

Milford   *F18*

Cliff Park Inn & Golf Course

155 Cliff Park Rd
Milford, PA 18337-9708
(570)296-6491 (800)225-6535 Fax:(570)296-5984
Internet: www.cliffparkinn.com
E-mail: escape@cliffparkinn.com

Circa 1850. Located only two miles from the heart of the
quaint town, this casually upscale inn offers privacy, seclusion,
elegant accommodations, fine dining, and a variety of outdoor
activities. It sits on 500 acres
within a 70,000-acre national
park. Enjoy miles of hiking trails
with breathtaking views and
play golf on one of the country's oldest 9-hole courses.
Choose a newly decorated guest
bedroom or suite with a claw-
foot tub and separate shower with Bath & Body Works amenities, imported linens, an entertainment center, sunporch and
delightful view. A complimentary continental breakfast with
fresh baked breads, granola, bagels & salmon, yogurt, assorted
juices and coffee is included in the room rate. A destination in
itself, the pub and glass-encased dining room are open for

lunch, dinner and Sunday brunch.

Innkeeper(s): Stephanie Brown. $141-268. 12 rooms, 14 with PB, 5 suites, 1 conference room. Breakfast and Continental/Hot Breakfast included in rates. Types of meals: Full bkfst, Sun. brunch, lunch, snacks/refreshments, wine and dinner. Restaurant on premises. Beds: KQD. Cable TV, DVD, reading lamp, refrigerator, clock radio, telephone, voice mail, hair dryer, bath amenities, wireless Internet access and iron/ironing board in room. Air conditioning. Fax, copier, library, fireplace and 9-hole golf course on premises. Limited handicap access. Antiquing, art galleries, bicycling, canoeing/kayaking, cross-country skiing, downhill skiing, fishing, golf, hiking, horseback riding, museums, parks and shopping nearby.

Location: Country, mountains.

Publicity: *Top 10 Romantic Inn (2005 and iLoveInns.com).*

Certificate may be used: June-July, excluding holidays, Anytime, Last Minute-Based on Availability.

Mount Joy   K13

Hillside Farm Bed & Breakfast

607 Eby Chiques Road
Mount Joy, PA 17552-8819
(717)653-6697 (888)249-3406 Fax:(717)653-9775
Internet: www.hillsidefarmbandb.com
E-mail: innkeeper@hillsidefarmbandb.com

Circa 1840. This comfortable farm has a relaxing homey feel to it. Rooms are simply decorated and special extras such as handmade quilts and antiques add an elegant country touch. Two guest cottages each offer a king bed, whirlpool tub for two, fireplace, wet bar and deck overlooking a bucolic meadow. The home is a true monument to the cow. Dairy antiques, cow knickknacks and antique milk bottles abound. Some of  the bottles were found during the renovation of the home and its grounds. Spend the day hunting for bargains in nearby antique shops, malls and factory outlets, or tour local Amish and Pennsylvania Dutch attractions. The farm is a good vacation spot for families with children above the age of 10.

Innkeeper(s): Gary Lintner. $90-250. 5 rooms with PB, 2 with FP, 2 cottages. Breakfast included in rates. Types of meals: Country bkfst, veg bkfst, early coffee/tea and snacks/refreshments. Beds: KQT. TV, VCR, reading lamp, stereo, refrigerator, ceiling fan, snack bar, clock radio and iron/ironing board in room. Central air. Fax, copier, spa, library and telephone on premises. Amusement parks, antiquing, art galleries, bicycling, fishing, golf, hiking, live theater, museums, parks, shopping and wineries nearby.

Location: Country.

Publicity: *Washingtonian Magazine.*

Certificate may be used: January-June, Sunday-Thursday, no holidays or holiday weekends, subject to availability, excludes cottages.

The Victorian Rose Bed & Breakfast

214 Marietta Ave
Mount Joy, PA 17552-3106
(717)492-0050 (888)313-7494
Internet: www.thevictorianrosebandb.com
E-mail: victorianrosebb@juno.com

Circa 1897. Central to Hershey and Gettysburg battlefield, The Victorian Rose in Mount Joy is an elegant but comfortable place from which to explore beautiful Lancaster County. Enjoy the stately guest rooms and a number of elegant areas including the library and a formal living room. Guests are treated to innkeeper Doris Tyson's home-baked treats for breakfast, and to

her homemade candies at other times. Pennsylvania Dutch Country is just 12 miles from the inn.

Innkeeper(s): Doris L. Tyson. $90-95. 4 rooms, 3 with PB. Breakfast included in rates. Types of meals: Country bkfst, Breakfast can be tailored to specific guest requirements, medical, religious and personal preference. Please let innkeeper know at time of reservation. Beds: Q. Cable TV, VCR, DVD, reading lamp, CD player, ceiling fan, clock radio, most with fireplace, hair dryer, bathrobes, wireless Internet access and iron/ironing board in room. Air conditioning. Fax, copier, library, parlor games and telephone on premises. Amusement parks, antiquing, fishing, golf, live theater, museums, parks, shopping and wineries nearby.

Location: Town.

Publicity: *Lancaster Historic Preservation Trust Featured Home 2001 tour and PA Dutch Visitor & Convention Bureau of Authentic B&B Association.*

Certificate may be used: November-May, excluding holidays. Subject to availability.

North East   B3

Grape Arbor Bed and Breakfast

51 East Main St
North East, PA 16428-1340
(814)725-0048 (866)725-0048 Fax:(814)725-5740
Internet: www.grapearborbandb.com
E-mail: grapearborbandb@aol.com

Circa 1832. Two side-by-side brick Federal mansions with Victorian embellishments have been restored to preserve their antiquity yet provide today's conveniences. Built in the early 1830s as private homes, their history includes having served as a stagecoach tavern, primary school, and possibly a stop on the Underground Railroad. Watch videos, play games or read a book by the fire in the library. Socialize over hors d'oeuvres in the parlor. Elegant guest bedrooms and suites are named for local varieties of grapes and feature antiques, reproductions, data ports, VCRs and fine toiletries. Two main breakfast dishes, pastries and breads, a hot or cold fruit sampler, juice and freshly ground coffee are enjoyed in the formal Dining Room or the light and airy Sun Porch. A guest refrigerator is stocked with beverages and homemade treats are always available.

Innkeeper(s): Dave and Peggy Hauser. $95-175. 8 rooms with PB, 4 with FP, 5 suites. Breakfast and snacks/refreshments included in rates. Types of meals: Full gourmet bkfst and early coffee/tea. Beds: KQD. Data port, cable TV, VCR, reading lamp, CD player, refrigerator, ceiling fan, clock radio, telephone, coffeemaker, desk, voice mail, hair dryer, wireless Internet access, iron/ironing board, fireplace and Jacuzzi in room. Central air. Fax, copier, library, parlor games and fireplace on premises. Limited handicap access. Amusement parks, antiquing, beach, bicycling, cross-country skiing, downhill skiing, fishing, golf, hiking, horseback riding, live theater, parks and wineries nearby.

Location: Lakeside Village.

Certificate may be used: Jan. 1-May 15, Sunday-Thursday, holidays excluded, subject to availability, Anytime, Last Minute-Based on Availability, Fridays and Saturdays June 1-Nov. 1 excluded.

Philadelphia   K17

Rittenhouse 1715, A Boutique Hotel

1715 Rittenhouse Square Street
Philadelphia, PA 19103
(215)546-6500 (877)791-6500 Fax:(215)546-8787
Internet: www.rittenhouse1715.com
E-mail: reservations@rittenhouse1715.com

Circa 1911. Experience elegant luxury at this comfortably renovated carriage house, internationally renown for business or pleasure. Impressive art, impeccable decor, lavish furnishings and extraordinary service are the hallmarks of this inn. The guest bedrooms are spectacular, tranquil retreats. Distinctive amenities include CD players, triple sheeting, turndown service, computer workstations, plush robes and marble bathrooms. Enjoy breakfast in The Cafe and early evening wine and snacks in the gorgeous lobby.

Innkeeper(s): Daniel Gioioso. $249-849. 23 rooms with PB, 10 with FP, 4 suites. Breakfast, snacks/refreshments, wine and Wine Reception included in rates. Types of meals: Cont plus, early coffee/tea, Wine reception every evening in the lobby, coffee and tea available all day and continental breakfast daily. Room service 24 hours per day. Beds: KQD. Modem hook-up, data port, cable TV, reading lamp, CD player, snack bar, clock radio, telephone, turn-down service, desk, some with hot tub/spa, voice mail, some with fireplace, hair dryer, bathrobes, bath amenities, wireless Internet access, iron/ironing board, Large flat screen Plasma TVs, Wireless throughout building & rooms, Data ports in Superior and Deluxe Rooms in room. Central air. Fax, copier, parlor games and Off-premises laundry and dry cleaning services arranged daily on premises. Limited handicap access. Antiquing, art galleries, bicycling, live theater, museums, parks, shopping, sporting events, Fine Dining, Shopping and Museums nearby.

Location: City.

Publicity: *New York Magazine (52 Getaway Weekends, Philadelphia Style), Philadelphia Magazine (Best of Philly® 2002 Winner), Elegant Wedding, Country Living (Inn of the Month) and Washingtonian (Getaway Weekends).*

Certificate may be used: Subject to availability, Sunday-Thursday, January, February, March, July and August. Holidays excluded. No weekends.

Silverstone Bed & Breakfast

8840 Stenton Ave
Philadelphia, PA 19118-2846
(215)242-3333 (800)347-6858 Fax:(215)242-2680
Internet: www.silverstonestay.com
E-mail: yolanta@silverstonestay.com

Circa 1850. Italian masons built this Victorian Gothic mansion with silvery stone from the Appalachian Mountains in 1877. Adorning historic Chestnut Hill inside the Philadelphia Metro area of Pennsylvania, this central location in is perfect for walking to local shops and restaurants. Select one of the well-appointed and spacious guest bedrooms or suites. For longer stays, short-term furnished apartments are available. After a satisfying breakfast visit Lancaster's Amish Country or take a day trip to Washington, D.C. or New York City. Laundry facilities and a private guest kitchen are provided. Silverstone Bed & Breakfast offers fresh herbs and vegetables from the garden.

Innkeeper(s): Yolanta Roman. $115-155. 3 rooms with PB, 2 with HT, 1 two-bedroom and 1 three-bedroom suites. Breakfast, Guests may use kitchen to drink coffee and tea or prepare meals included in rates. Types of meals: Full bkfst, veg bkfst, early coffee/tea, Guests may use kitchen any time to drink coffee and tea or cooked meals. Beds: KQDT. Cable TV, VCR, reading lamp, stereo, refrigerator, telephone, coffeemaker, desk, most with fireplace, hair dryer, wireless Internet access and iron/ironing board in room. Central air. DVD, fax, copier, spa, bicycles, laundry facility, Special kitchen and Laundry room for the guests on premises. Antiquing, art galleries, bicycling, fishing, hiking, museums, parks, shopping and Morris Arboretum nearby.

Location: City. Philadelphia/Chestnut Hill.

Certificate may be used: July, September, December and January.

Pine Grove Mills   G10

The Chatelaine Bed & Breakfast

347 W. Pine Grove Rd.
Pine Grove Mills, PA 16868
(814)238-2028 (800)251-2028 Fax:(814)308-9573
Internet: www.chatelainebandb.com
E-mail: kkeeper0@comcast.net

Circa 1841. Pass by the border of heirloom perennials and a

welcoming signpost, through the double canopy of stately pine to this vintage farmhouse. A formal yet comfortable sitting room features deep sofas, chairs and luxurious hassocks. Distinctive antiques furnish elegantly decorated guest bedrooms and a suite. Generous amenities include robes, soda, ice and glasses. Enjoy cordials from bedside decanters. A breakfast feast is a lighthearted, whimsical affair in the dining room amidst an extensive china collection. Take a break from the B&B's peaceful serenity to visit nearby historic sites.

Innkeeper(s): Amanda & Mae McQuade. $115-400. 4 rooms, 3 with PB, 2 with FP, 1 two-bedroom suite, 1 conference room. Breakfast, afternoon tea and snacks/refreshments included in rates. Types of meals: Full gourmet bkfst, veg bkfst, early coffee/tea and Grill or hibachi available to cook-out on the patio or at Whipple's Dam just 5 miles away. Bring utensils and cooler for food storage. Beds: KT. Cable TV, reading lamp, telephone, desk, some with fireplace, hair dryer, bathrobes, bath amenities, wireless Internet access, iron/ironing board and cable TV (2 rooms) in room. Air conditioning. Fax, copier, library, parlor games, gift shop, Summer lawn furniture, Hibachi to take for picnic breakfast cookout at Whipple's Dam, Hammock, Lovely Gazebo and Patio on premises. Amusement parks, antiquing, art galleries, bicycling, canoeing/kayaking, cross-country skiing, downhill skiing, fishing, golf, hiking, horseback riding, live theater, museums, parks, shopping, sporting events, tennis, water sports, wineries, Spelunking, Golden eagle migration lookout, Birdwatching sites, Raptor preserve, Alpaca farm, Llama farm, Amish Market on Wednesdays and Tussey Mountainback UltraMarathon nearby.

Location: Country. On PA SR45, the Purple Heart Highway.

Publicity: *Pennsylvania Hospitality (2003 Innkeeper of the Year) and Westsylvania Magazine's Explore A Story Program.*

Certificate may be used: Anytime, subject to availability. Not valid holidays, PSU high season (football, commencements), Arts Fest, TMB Marathon, Parents (Weekend), Blue-White Game.

Red Lion   K13

Red Lion Bed & Breakfast

101 S Franklin St
Red Lion, PA 17356
(717)244-4739 (888)280-1701 Fax:(717)246-3219
Internet: www.redlionbandb.com
E-mail: staywithus@redlionbandb.com

Circa 1920. Explore one of the more popular regions of the state while staying at this unpretentious and quiet three-story brick, Federal-style home. Snuggle up next to the fireplace in the living room with a book from the well-stocked collection of reading material. Sip a cool iced tea on the enclosed sun porch or outside garden patio. Half of the six quaint and comfortable guest bedrooms offer a full bath and queen-size bed. Twin beds and cots are also available for families or groups traveling together. Breakfasts are substantial with quiche, pancakes, stuffed French toast, fresh baked rolls and muffins served alongside fruit or granola. The town has antique and craft shops and is within a 45-minute drive of vineyards, the Amish country of Lancaster, Hershey and the Gettysburg Battlefield.

Innkeeper(s): George & Danielle Sanders. $78-105. 6 rooms, 3 with PB, 1 conference room. Breakfast included in rates. Types of meals: Full bkfst. Beds: QT. TV, VCR, reading lamp, ceiling fan, clock radio, bathrobes and wireless Internet access in room. Air conditioning. Fax, copier, library, parlor games, telephone, fireplace, Off-street parking and Wireless Internet on premises. Limited handicap access. Amusement parks, antiquing, canoeing/kayaking, fishing, golf, hiking, horseback riding, museums, parks, shopping and wineries nearby.

Location: Small town.

Certificate may be used: January-February and July-August.

Reinholds   J14

Brownstone Colonial Inn

590 Galen Hall Rd
Reinholds, PA 17569-9420
(717)484-4460 (877)464-9862 Fax:(717)484-4460
Internet: www.brownstonecolonialinn.com
E-mail: info@brownstonecolonialinn.com

Circa 1790. Early German Mennonite settlers built this sandstone farmhouse in the mid eighteenth century. It graces seven scenic acres amidst Amish countryside. Feel relaxed and pampered at this fully restored inn. Guest bedrooms and a suite boast random-width plank floors, locally handcrafted period-authentic furniture, sleigh or pencil post beds and antique Shaker peg boards. Enjoy a hearty country breakfast in the homestead's original smokehouse with brick floor, ceiling beams and open hearth fireplace. Start the day with fresh juices, homemade pastries and jams, a hot entree and fruits grown on-site. Stroll by the flower and gardens, or walk the nearby nature trails. An abundance of outlet and antique malls as well as historical and cultural sites are minutes away.

Innkeeper(s): Brenda & Mark Miller. $89-119. 4 rooms with PB, 1 two-bedroom suite. Breakfast, afternoon tea and snacks/refreshments included in rates. Types of meals: Country bkfst and early coffee/tea. Beds: QDT. Reading lamp, clock radio, desk, some with fireplace and wireless Internet access in room. Central air. TV, VCR, fax, copier and telephone on premises. Limited handicap access. Amusement parks, antiquing, beach, bicycling, canoeing/kayaking, cross-country skiing, fishing, golf, hiking, horseback riding, live theater, museums, parks, shopping, sporting events, water sports and wineries nearby.

Location: Country.

"We can't wait to tell friends and family about your paradise."
Certificate may be used: Monday-Thursday.

Ronks   K14

Candlelight Inn B&B

2574 Lincoln Hwy E
Ronks, PA 17572-9771
(717)299-6005 (800)772-2635 Fax:(717)299-6397
Internet: www.candleinn.com
E-mail: candleinn@aol.com

Circa 1920. Located in the Pennsylvania Dutch area, this Federal-style house offers a side porch for enjoying the home's acre and a half of tall trees and surrounding Amish farmland. Guest rooms feature Victorian decor. Three rooms include a Jacuzzi tub and fireplace. The inn's gourmet breakfast, which might include a creme caramel French toast, is served by candlelight. The innkeepers are professional classical musicians. Lancaster is five miles to the east.

Innkeeper(s): Tim & Heidi Soberick. $90-179. 7 rooms with PB, 3 with FP, 3 with HT, 3 with WP. Breakfast and snacks/refreshments included in rates. Types of meals: Full gourmet bkfst. Beds: KQT. Reading lamp, ceiling fan, clock radio, desk, some with hot tub/spa, some with fireplace, bathrobes, bath amenities, amaretto, robes, three with Jacuzzi and fireplaces in room. Central air. TV, fax, parlor games, telephone, badminton, croquet and afternoon refreshments on premises. Amusement parks, antiquing, art galleries, bicycling, fishing, golf, hiking, horseback riding, live theater, museums, parks, shopping, wineries, Sight & Sound theater, Living Waters theater, American Music Theater, Amish farms, Amish crafts and quilts, hot air ballooning, PA Dutch restaurants, farmers' markets, Fulton Opera House, Lancaster Symphony, outlet shopping and arranged dinners with an Amish family nearby.

Location: Country. Suburban-surrounded by farms.

Publicity: *Lancaster Daily News, Pennsylvania Dutch Traveler and Pennsylvania Intelligencer Journal.*
Certificate may be used: December-April, excluding holidays, Sunday-Thursday.

Somerset   K5

Quill Haven Country Inn

1519 North Center Ave
Somerset, PA 15501-7001
(814)443-4514 (866)528-8855 Fax:(814)445-1376
Internet: www.quillhaven.com
E-mail: quill@quillhaven.com

Circa 1918. Set on three acres that were once part of a chicken and turkey farm, this historic Arts & Crafts-style home offers guest rooms, each individually appointed. The Bridal Suite includes a four-poster wrought iron bed and sunken tub in the bath. The Country Room includes a decorative pot-bellied stove. Antiques, reproductions and stained-glass lamps decorate the rooms. Guests are treated to a full breakfast with items such as baked grapefruit or apples, homemade breads and entrees such as stuffed French toast or a specialty casserole of ham, cheese and potatoes. Guests can spend the day boating or swimming at nearby Youghiogheny Reservoir, take a white-water-rafting trip, bike or hike through the scenic countryside, ski at one of three ski resorts in the area or shop at antique stores, outlets and flea markets. Frank Lloyd Wright's Fallingwater is another nearby attraction.

Innkeeper(s): Carol & Rowland Miller. $95-115. 4 rooms with PB. Breakfast and snacks/refreshments included in rates. Types of meals: Full bkfst and early coffee/tea. Beds: KQ. Cable TV, VCR, reading lamp, ceiling fan, clock radio, turn-down service, hair dryer, bathrobes, bath amenities, wireless Internet access and heated mattress pad in room. Air conditioning. Fax, copier, spa, library, parlor games, telephone, fireplace, gift shop, outdoor hot tub, common room with fireplace and mini kitchenette on premises. Amusement parks, antiquing, bicycling, canoeing/kayaking, cross-country skiing, downhill skiing, fishing, golf, hiking, horseback riding, live theater, parks, shopping, tennis, water sports, wineries, Seven Springs, Hidden Valley and Laurel Highlands nearby.

Location: Country, mountains.
Publicity: *Westsylvania Magazine.*

"What a beautiful memory we will have of our first B&B experience! We've never felt quite so pampered in all our 25 years of marriage."
Certificate may be used: Anytime, March-September, subject to availability.

South Sterling   F16

French Manor

50 Huntingdon Drive
South Sterling, PA 18460
(570)676-3244 (877)720-6090
Internet: www.thefrenchmanor.com
E-mail: info@thefrenchmanor.com

Circa 1932. In a storybook setting this country inn and restaurant sits atop Huckleberry Mountain with views of the northern Poconos. Built by local craftsman and artisans of German and Italian descent, the impressive architecture of this fieldstone chateau includes an imported Spanish slate roof, Romanesque arched entrance and cypress interior. Luxuriously romantic accommodations offer a generous variety of upscale amenities. Manor house guest rooms boast period furnishings. The unique two-story Turret Suite boasts a living room and private staircase to the bedroom. Stay in a fireplace or Jacuzzi suite in the adjacent La Maisonneuve Building with private wrought-iron balconies. Savor breakfast in the elegant dining room with a forty-foot vaulted ceiling and twin fireplaces. Schedule an appointment with the in-house massage therapist after hiking or biking the miles of trails on the grounds.

Innkeeper(s): Ron and Mary Kay Logan. $190-375. 19 rooms with PB, 13 with FP, 13 with WP, 14 total suites, including 1 two-bedroom suite, 2 conference rooms. Breakfast, afternoon tea, snacks/refreshments, Midweek "Enchanted Evenings" package includes full breakfast and gourmet candlelight dinner and a picnic lunch included in rates. Types of meals: Full gourmet bkfst, veg bkfst, picnic lunch, hors d'oeuvres, wine, gourmet dinner, room service and Spa lunch available upon request. Restaurant on premises. Beds: KQ. Data port, cable TV, VCR, DVD, reading lamp, refrigerator, ceiling fan, snack bar, clock radio, telephone, coffeemaker, turn-down service, desk, most with hot tub/spa, voice mail, most with fireplace, hair dryer, bathrobes, bath amenities, wireless Internet access, iron/ironing board, Eco-friendly suites, Welcome cheese & fruit with sherry in room on arrival and Complimentary nightly turn-down service with Godiva chocolates in room. Air conditioning. Fax, copier, spa, swimming, library, parlor games, gift shop, "Green" spa, Indoor salt water pool, Jacuzzi, Hiking trails, Snoeshoeing and Sledding on premises. Handicap access. Amusement parks, antiquing, art galleries, beach, bicycling, canoeing/kayaking, cross-country skiing, downhill skiing, fishing, golf, hiking, horseback riding, live theater, museums, parks, shopping, sporting events, tennis, water sports, wineries and State parks (3 within 15 min.) nearby.

Location: Country, mountains.

Publicity: *Gourmet Magazine (Feb, 2004), Philadelphia Inquirer, 52 Perfect Days - Pocono Mtns Secret Hideaway , Philadelphia Inquirer ("Dinner Fit for a King") and Country Inns Magazine (Top Ten Country Inns of America).*

Certificate may be used: Midweek in March and April, subject to availability.

Starlight   C17

The Inn at Starlight Lake

PO Box 27
Starlight, PA 18461-0027
(570)798-2519 (800)248-2519 Fax:(570)798-2672
E-mail: info@innatstarlightlake.com

Circa 1909. Escape city stress and be rejuvenated at the peacefully pleasant and informal setting of The Inn at Starlight Lake in northeastern Pennsylvania. Relax on the front porch of this

country retreat with gorgeous views of the tranquil and clear Starlight Lake surrounded by rolling hills and woods. This historic 1909 inn boasts year-round hospitality and thoughtful details families appreciate. Play ping pong or billiards in the game room, watch a movie in the sunroom and sip a glass of wine with appetizers in the Stovepipe Bar. Use the tennis court, swim in the lake, ride a bike or try the trails by foot, snowshoe or cross-country skis. Accommodations are warm and inviting with a satisfying made-to-order breakfast included each morning. Lunch and dinner are offered in the lakeside dining room for an extra charge.

Innkeeper(s): Sari & Jimmy Schwartz. $85-255. 23 rooms, 19 with PB, 1 with FP, 1 suite, 3 cottages. Breakfast included in rates. Types of meals: Full bkfst, Sun. brunch, early coffee/tea, lunch, picnic lunch, snacks/refreshments, wine and dinner. Restaurant on premises. Beds: KQT. Reading lamp, ceiling fan, some with hot tub/spa, some with fireplace and bath amenities in room. TV, VCR, fax, copier, swimming, bicycles, tennis, library, parlor games, telephone, Full service spa and salon, Hair dryer and Iron/ironing board available at the front desk on premises. Limited handicap access. Antiquing, bicycling, canoeing/kayaking, downhill skiing, fishing, golf, hiking, horseback riding, shopping, tennis, water sports, cross country skiing (right out our front door, bring your own equipment or rent) and try your feet at snow shoeing nearby.

Location: Country, mountains, waterfront.

Publicity: *New York Times, Philadelphia Inquirer, Newsday, Discerning Traveler, Freeman and Travel Network.*

Certificate may be used: Anytime, November-April, subject to availability.

Terre Hill   J15

The Artist's Inn & Gallery

117 E Main St
Terre Hill, PA 17581
(717)445-0219 (888)999-4479
Internet: www.artistinn.com
E-mail: info@artistinn.com

Circa 1848. Four-course breakfasts and warm and inviting guest rooms are offered at this Federal-style inn. Watch Amish buggies clip clop by from the Victorian veranda and listen to the chimes from the church across the way. Then plan your day with the help of innkeepers Jan and Bruce, avid adventurers who cross-country ski and explore the area's best offerings to share insights with guests. There's an art gallery with works by the resident artist. Guest accommodations are inviting with antiques, gas fireplaces, hardwood floors and decorative painting, wallpapers and borders. The Rose Room offers a Jacuzzi bath. The Garden Suite offers a whirlpool bath for two, massage shower, fireplace, king-size featherbed, private balcony and sitting room. Breakfasts feature breads such as scones or muffins, fruit parfaits, crepes or egg dishes and a luscious dessert—perhaps a pie, cake or tart.

Innkeeper(s): Jan & Bruce Garrabrandt. $115-260. 5 rooms with PB, 4 with FP, 3 with WP, 2 two-bedroom suites, 2 cottages. Breakfast and snacks/refreshments included in rates. Types of meals: Full gourmet bkfst, veg bkfst, early coffee/tea and We will happily cater to celiac guests. Beds: KQ. Cable TV, VCR, DVD, reading lamp, stereo, refrigerator, ceiling fan, clock radio, coffeemaker, turn-down service, some with hot tub/spa, hair dryer, bathrobes, bath amenities, wireless Internet access, iron/ironing board and Fresh flowers in room. Central air. Copier, library, parlor games, telephone, fireplace, gift shop and art gallery on premises. Limited handicap access. Amusement parks, antiquing, art galleries, bicycling, canoeing/kayaking, cross-country skiing, fishing, golf, hiking, horseback riding, live theater, museums, parks, shopping, sporting events, tennis, wineries and Amish Attractions nearby.

Location: Country. Small town.

Certificate may be used: Sunday-Thursday, November-April. Holidays excluded.

Uniontown   K3

Inne At Watson's Choice

234 Balsinger Rd
Uniontown, PA 15401-6844
(724)437-4999 (888)820-5380
Internet: www.watsonschoice.com
E-mail: innkeeper@watsonschoice.com

Circa 1997. Sit on a front porch rocker and relax amid the secluded setting of Inne at Watson's Choice in the Laurel Highlands of Fayette County in Uniontown, southwestern Pennsylvania. Stay in a themed guest room with individual climate control on the 1820s land grant farm or in the Harvest House Bed & Breakfast, an authentically reproduced addition across the courtyard. Some rooms boast a fireplace or whirlpool tub. Wake up to savor a hearty country breakfast by the stone fireplace in the rustic dining room. Visit Ohiopyle State Park and go white-water rafting on the Youghiogheny River. Take an in-depth tour of Frank Lloyd Wright's famous Fallingwater or newly opened Kentuck Knob. The area offers many historic and scenic attractions.

Innkeeper(s): Bill & Nancy Ross. $120-200. 12 rooms with PB, 5 with FP, 3 with WP, 1 two-bedroom suite, 1 conference room. Breakfast included in rates. Types of meals: Full bkfst and early coffee/tea. Beds: KQT. TV, VCR, DVD, reading lamp, ceiling fan, telephone, turn-down service, desk, hair dryer, bathrobes and iron/ironing board in room. Central air. Parlor games on premises. Handicap access. Antiquing, art galleries, bicycling, canoeing/kayaking, cross-country skiing, downhill skiing, fishing, golf, hiking, horseback riding, live theater, museums, parks, shopping, sporting events, tennis, water sports and wineries nearby.

Location: Country.

Certificate may be used: March 6-10 Sunday-Thursday, March 13-17 Sunday-Thursday, April 3-7, April 10-14, April 17-22, Nov. 6-10 Sunday-Thursday, Dec.4-8, Sunday-Thursday in Guestrooms Apple Orchard, Ivy or John Watson.

Valley Forge   K16

The Great Valley House of Valley Forge

1475 Swedesford Road
Valley Forge, PA 19355
(610)644-6759
Internet: www.greatvalleyhouse.com
E-mail: info@greatvalleyhouse.com

Circa 1691. This 300-year-old Colonial stone farmhouse sits on four acres just two miles from Valley Forge Park. Boxwoods line the walkway, and ancient trees surround the house. Each

of the three antique-filled guest rooms is hand-stenciled and features a canopied or brass bed topped with hand-made quilts. Guests enjoy a full breakfast before a 14-foot fireplace in the "summer kitchen," the oldest part of the
house. On the grounds are a swimming pool, walking and hiking trails and the home's original smokehouse.

Innkeeper(s): Pattye Benson. $104-129. 3 rooms with PB, 1 conference room. Breakfast and Full Gourmet Breakfast included in rates. Types of meals: Full gourmet bkfst, veg bkfst, early coffee/tea, Dietetic, Lunch and Dinner and Weekend brunch available by prior arrangement. Beds: QDT. Modem hook-up, data port, cable TV, DVD, reading lamp, stereo, refrigerator, clock radio, telephone, coffeemaker, turn-down service, desk, hair dryer, bathrobes, bath amenities, wireless Internet access, iron/ironing board and Free Wireless Internet in guest rooms in room. Air conditioning. Fax, swimming, parlor games, fireplace and grand piano on premises. Antiquing, art galleries, bicycling, canoeing/kayaking, cross-country skiing, fishing, golf, hiking, horseback riding, live theater, museums, parks, shopping, sporting events, water sports, wineries and Antiquing nearby.

Location: Rural/suburban setting.

Publicity: *Valley Forge Convention & Tourism Spring/Summer 2007 Guide, Main Line Philadelphia, Philadelphia Inquirer, Washington Post, New York Times, Suburban Newspaper, Historical Documentary site, Travel cable network and Network TV.*

"As a business traveler, Patty's enthusiasm and warm welcome makes you feel just like you're home."

Certificate may be used: Nov. 1-April 30, both nights must be Sunday-Thursday, excludes holidays.

Warfordsburg   L8

Buck Valley Ranch, LLC

1344 Negro Mountain Rd
Warfordsburg, PA 17267-8168
(717)294-3759 (800)294-3759 Fax:(717)294-6413
Internet: www.buckvalleyranch.com
E-mail: info@buckvalleyranch.com

Circa 1930. Trail riding is a popular activity on the ranch's 64 acres in the Appalachian Mountains of South Central Pennsylvania. State game lands and forests border the ranch. The guest house, decorated in a ranch/cowboy style, is a private farmhouse that can accommodate eight people. Meals are prepared using homegrown vegetables and locally raised meats. Rates also include horseback riding.

Innkeeper(s): Nadine & Leon Fox. $55-90. 4 rooms. Breakfast, lunch and dinner included in rates. Types of meals: Country bkfst, veg bkfst, picnic lunch and Diet requests and restrictions honored. Beds: QDT. Reading lamp, hair dryer, bath amenities and iron/ironing board in room. Central air. Fax, copier, spa, swimming, sauna, stable, parlor games, telephone, gift shop and Horseback riding on premises. Amusement parks, antiquing, bicycling, canoeing/kayaking, cross-country skiing, downhill skiing, fishing, golf, hiking, parks, shopping, tennis, water sports, C&O Canal, Steam train rides and Rails to Trails nearby.

Location: Country, mountains.

Publicity: *Washington Post, Pittsburgh Press, PA bride, Baltimore Sun and Potomac.*

Certificate may be used: Jan. 1-Dec. 31, Sunday-Thursday, excluding weekends and holidays. Subject to availability.

Rhode Island

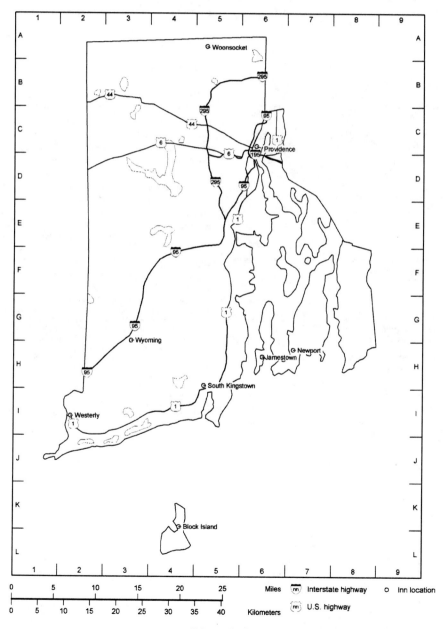

Miles   ⬡ Interstate highway   ○ Inn location

U.S. highway

Kilometers

Block Island   K4

Victorian Inns by the Sea

PO Box 488, 61 Dodge St
Block Island, RI 02807-0488
(401)466-5891 (800)992-7290 Fax:(401)466-9910
Internet: www.blockislandinns.com
E-mail: rundezvous@aol.com

Circa 1887. This Shingle Victorian inn on Crescent Beach
offers many guest rooms with ocean views. The Cottage, The
Doll House and The Tea House are separate structures for those
desiring more room or privacy. Antiques and Victorian touches
are featured throughout. Year-round car ferry service, taking
approximately one hour, is found at Point Judith, R.I. The
island also may be reached by air on New England Airlines or
by charter. Mohegan Bluffs Scenic Natural Area is nearby.

Innkeeper(s): Christie Zendt. $95-465. 12 rooms with PB, 3 total suites,
including 2 two-bedroom suites, 4 cottages, 1 conference room. Breakfast
and afternoon tea included in rates. Types of meals: Full bkfst, veg bkfst,
early coffee/tea, snacks/refreshments, hors d'oeuvres and wine. Beds: KQDT.
Cable TV, VCR, DVD, reading lamp, CD player, telephone, desk, some with
hot tub/spa, hair dryer, bath amenities, wireless Internet access, most with
air conditioning, VCR or DVD and cable TV in room. Air conditioning. Fax,
copier, swimming, child care and parlor games on premises. Antiquing, art
galleries, beach, bicycling, canoeing/kayaking, fishing, hiking, horseback riding, parks, shopping and water sports nearby.

Location: Ocean community.

*"The Blue Dory is a wonderful place to stay. The room was lovely, the
view spectacular and the sound of surf was both restful and tranquil."*

Certificate may be used: Sept. 15-June 15, Sunday-Thursday.

Newport   H7

Adele Turner Inn

93 Pelham St
Newport, RI 02840
(401) 848-8011 (888) 820-8011
Internet: www.adeleturnerinn.com
E-mail: info@adeleturner.com

Circa 1855. Architecturally significant, this recently restored
inn is listed in the National Register. Named one of
iLoveInns.com's Top 10 Most Romantic Inns in 2002, it is
located in an historic residential neighborhood and sits on the
country's first gaslit street. Two fireplaces highlight the elegant
parlor, where classic English afternoon tea is served in Victorian
tradition. Books and videos also are available there. Well-
appointed guest bedrooms and suites reflect regional themes
and events. Encounter period furnishings and fireplaces, with
some rooms boasting two-person whirlpool tubs. Ask for the
Harborview Spa which includes French doors leading to a
rooftop deck with private hot tub and panoramic harbor view.
Morning coffee or tea is brought to each room. In the parlor, a
generous breakfast buffet begins a delicious meal followed by a
hot entree. Complimentary wine and food tasting menus that
pair flights of fine wine matched with artisan cheeses and other
fine foods are offered daily.

Innkeeper(s): Cheryl & Harry Schatmeyer, Jr. $125-525. 13 rooms with PB,
13 with FP, 1 with HT, 4 with WP, 3 suites, 1 conference room. Breakfast,
afternoon tea, hors d'oeuvres and wine included in rates. Types of meals:
Full gourmet bkfst, early coffee/tea, room service and Daily Wine & Food
Pairing events featuring the best of the regional New England wines. Beds:
KQ. Cable TV, VCR, DVD, CD player, refrigerator, ceiling fan, clock radio,

telephone, turn-down service, some with hot tub/spa, fireplace, hair dryer,
bathrobes, bath amenities, wireless Internet access, iron/ironing board, LCD
TV, High-speed wireless Internet access, Twice daily maid service and
Handcrafted artisan chocolates in room. Air conditioning. Spa, library, gift
shop, Daily Wine & Food Pairing events featuring regional wineries,
DVD/Video Library and On-site parking on premises. Antiquing, art galleries,
beach, bicycling, canoeing/kayaking, fishing, golf, hiking, horseback riding,
live theater, museums, parks, shopping, tennis, water sports, wineries,
Gilded Age Mansions, restaurants, sailing, Tennis Hall of Fame and historic
Redwood Library nearby.

Location: Ocean community.

Publicity: *The Boston Globe, Westchester Magazine, Weekends For Two In
New England, Sunday Mirror, Victorian Home, Inside Philadelphia, Yankee
Magazine Editor's Choice, Connecticut Magazine, Frommer's New England
Guidebooks, Fodors Guidebooks, Delta Sky Magazine, Rhode Island
Monthly, Victorian Homes, Weekending in New England and Inside
Philadelphia Magazine.*

Certificate may be used: July 1-Sept. 30 weekdays only. Anytime from
November-June 30.

America's Cup Inn

6 Mary St
Newport, RI 02840-3028
(401)846-9200 (800)457-7803 Fax:(401)846-1534
Internet: www.americascupinn.com
E-mail: info@americascupinn.com

Circa 1848. This Colonial-style inn is an elegant spot from
which to enjoy the seaside town of Newport. Waverly and
Laura Ashley prints decorate the individually appointed guest
rooms, some of which have four-poster or canopy beds. The
innkeeper serves an expanded continental breakfast with items
such as fresh fruit, quiche and ham and cheese croissants.
Afternoon tea also is served. A day in Newport offers many
activities, including touring the Tennis Hall of Fame, taking a
cruise through the harbor, shopping for antiques or perhaps
taking a trek down Cliff Walk, a one-and-a-half-mile path offering the ocean on one side and historic mansions on the other.
Parking is included in the rates.

Innkeeper(s): Dmitry. $79-299. 19 rooms with PB, 1 with HT, 1 with WP, 7
total suites, including 4 two-bedroom suites. Breakfast and afternoon tea
included in rates. Types of meals: Cont plus and room service. Beds: KQD.
Cable TV, reading lamp, refrigerator, clock radio, telephone, voice mail, hair
dryer, bath amenities, wireless Internet access and iron/ironing board in
room. Air conditioning. VCR, fax, copier, swimming, library, parlor games,
laundry facility, Parking is available on the Municipal Parking lot on Mary
Street and fee is discounted at the Inn. May 1 through October 31 - fee $18
November 1 through April 30 - free on premises. Limited handicap access.
Antiquing, art galleries, beach, canoeing/kayaking, fishing, golf, horseback
riding, live theater, museums, parks, shopping, tennis, water sports, wineries,
Newport Mansions Ocean Drive, Cliff Walk, Newport Vineyards, International
Tennis Hall of Fame, Fort Adams State Park, Bellevue Shops, Thames Street
Shops and Newport Art Museum nearby.

Location: City, ocean community, waterfront. Downtown Newport.

"Thank you for your excellent service with a smile."

Certificate may be used: Anytime, November-April, subject to availability.

Beech Tree Inn

34 Rhode Island Ave
Newport, RI 02840-2667
(401)847-9794 (800)748-6565 Fax:(401)847-6824
Internet: www.beechtreeinn.com
E-mail: cmquilt13@cox.net

Circa 1897. This inn's location in historic Newport offers
close access to the famous local mansions, and the turn-of-
the-century home is within walking distance of the harbor.
Most of the guest rooms include a fireplace. Special furnishings include canopy or poster beds, and suites offer the

added amenity of a whirlpool tub. The innkeepers provide a breakfast feast, and guests enjoy made-to-order fare that might include eggs, pancakes, waffles, omelettes, ham, bacon and more. Snacks, such as freshly baked cookies, are always on hand to curb one's appetite.

Innkeeper(s): Cindy Mahood. $99-359. 8 rooms with PB, 5 with FP, 3 with HT, 5 with WP, 1 suite. Breakfast, afternoon tea and snacks/refreshments included in rates. Types of meals: Full bkfst and early coffee/tea. Beds: KQ. Cable TV, VCR, reading lamp, ceiling fan, clock radio, telephone, desk, some with hot tub/spa, some with fireplace, hair dryer, iron/ironing board and lots of great amenities in room. Central air. Parlor games, lovely shared living room with a piano, parlor games, books to read in front of the fireplace, several large decks to enjoy plus a lovely garden with tables and chairs and free off-street parking in a town where this is a luxury on premises. Limited handicap access. Antiquing, art galleries, beach, bicycling, canoeing/kayaking, fishing, golf, hiking, horseback riding, live theater, museums, parks, shopping, sporting events, tennis, water sports, wineries, historic Thames Street and wharfs, where you can get a bowl of clam chowder, window shop, or go on a shopping spree, the amazing mansions on Bellevue Avenue, antique shops, museums, the oldest synagogue, the yachting capital and the Tennis Hall of Fame nearby.

Location: Ocean community. Quiet residential.

Certificate may be used: Anytime, November-March, subject to availability.

Cliffside Inn

2 Seaview Ave
Newport, RI 02840-3627
(401) 847-1811 (800) 845-1811 Fax:(401)848-5850
Internet: www.cliffsideinn.com
E-mail: reservations@cliffsideinn.com

Circa 1876. The Cliffside Inn was built as a grand Newport, Rhode Island summer house by the governor of Maryland in the style of a Second Empire Victorian. Poised averlooking the Atlantic Ocean, this luxury inn features a mansard roof and many bay windows. Guest rooms and suites boast Victorian furnishings and fireplaces. Some feature marble baths and many have double whirlpool tubs. After a satisfying breakfast stroll along the popular Cliff Walk, located one block from the inn.

Innkeeper(s): Bill Bagwill & Nancy Stafford. $275-500. 16 rooms with PB, 16 with FP, 9 with WP, 8 suites, 1 conference room. Breakfast and afternoon tea included in rates. Types of meals: Full gourmet bkfst, early coffee/tea, wine and room service. Beds: KQ. Cable TV, DVD, reading lamp, stereo, refrigerator, clock radio, telephone, turn-down service, desk, most with hot tub/spa, fireplace, hair dryer, bathrobes, bath amenities, wireless Internet access and iron/ironing board in room. Air conditioning. VCR, fax, copier, spa, library, parlor games, gift shop, DVD library, Wine bar and Victorian Tea Wednesdays and Saturdays on premises. Antiquing, art galleries, beach, bicycling, canoeing/kayaking, fishing, golf, hiking, horseback riding, live theater, museums, parks, shopping, sporting events, tennis, water sports, wineries, Gilded Age Mansions, International Tennis Hall of Fame, Touro Synagogue (oldest in America), Cliff Walk, Museum of Yachting, Fort Adams, Norman Bird Sanctuary and Sachuest Point National Wildlife Refuge nearby.

Location: Ocean community, waterfront.

Publicity: *New York Times, Boston Globe, Great Tea Rooms of America, Forbes Magazine, Fortune Magazine, Frommer's New England Guidebook, Fodor's Guidebooks, New England Travel & Life, Yankee Magazine, Getaway for Gourmets, National Geographic Travel, Conde Naste Traveler, New York Magazine, Boston Magazine, Connecticut Magazine, Rhode Island Monthly, Bride's Magazine, Discerning Traveler, Robb Report, Inside Philadelphia Magazine, Victorian Homes, BBC's Homes & Antiques, AAA Car & Travel, Good Morning America (ABC-TV), National Geographic, Discovery and Travel Channel.*

"...it captures the grandeur of the Victorian age."

Certificate may be used: November-March, Sunday-Thursday, holidays, school vacation and special event weeks excluded, subject to availability.

Gardenview Bed & Breakfast

8 Binney St
Newport, RI 02840-4304
(401)849-5799 Fax:(401)845-6675
Internet: www.gardenviewbnb.com
E-mail: gardenview8@hotmail.com

Circa 1978. Sitting in a quiet neighborhood not far from the beaches, mansions and famous Ocean Drive, this Saltbox home has a comfortable country colonial décor. The common room is an inviting place to play games. Browse through local menus and brochures in the cozy sitting area. Full afternoon tea is served (for an extra charge) in the sunroom overlooking the gardens. Stay in the Garden Room or the Sun-Lit Suite. Fresh flowers, turndown service, French lace curtains, whirlpool tubs and a fireplace enhance the intimate ambiance. A hearty country breakfast is served in the fireside dining room amid antiques. Homemade granola and fresh fruit accompany chocolate orange scones or other sweet treats. Entrees may include pecan waffles, chocolate coconut pancakes or an egg dish. The large yard boasts a fish pond and a waterfall.

Innkeeper(s): Mary and Andrew Fitzgerald. $125-195. 2 rooms, 1 with PB, 1 suite. Breakfast included in rates. Types of meals: Country bkfst, veg bkfst, early coffee/tea and afternoon tea. Beds: KQ. Cable TV, reading lamp, refrigerator, clock radio, turn-down service, fireplace and whirlpool tubs in room. Air conditioning. Parlor games, telephone, Afternoon tea ($12 per person and advanced notice required) on premises. Antiquing, art galleries, beach, bicycling, canoeing/kayaking, golf, live theater, museums, parks, shopping, tennis and wineries nearby.

Location: City.

Certificate may be used: November-April, subject to availability, excludes holidays. Some weekends require 3-night minimum stay.

Hydrangea House Inn

16 Bellevue Avenue
Newport, RI 02840
(401)846-4435 (800)945-4667 Fax:(401)846-6602
Internet: www.hydrangeahouse.com
E-mail: hydrangeahouseinn@cox.net

Circa 1876. Well-known for it impeccable service, elegant furnishings, rich warm colors, luxurious fabrics and masterful faux painting, this New England inn is a delightful place to stay. Beach towels are provided for soaking up the sun on the roof deck. After an incredible night's rest, join the first or second seating for a gourmet breakfast in the formal dining room. Start with the special blend Hydrangea House Coffee that complements the signature raspberry pancakes, home-baked breads, granola, seasoned scrambled eggs in puff pastry or other tempting recipes that will provide enough energy for the whole day. Ask about special packages available.

Innkeeper(s): Grant Edmondson / Dennis Blair, Innkeepers. $265-475. 9 rooms with PB, 9 with FP, 7 with HT, 7 with WP, 7 suites. Breakfast and afternoon tea included in rates. Types of meals: Full gourmet bkfst and early coffee/tea. Beds: KQT. Modem hook-up, data port, cable TV, reading lamp, CD player, clock radio, telephone, turn-down service, desk, fireplace, hair dryer, bathrobes, bath amenities, wireless Internet access and iron/ironing board in room. Central air. Fax and sauna on premises. Antiquing, art galleries, beach, bicycling, canoeing/kayaking, fishing, golf, hiking, horseback riding, live theater, museums, parks, shopping, tennis, water sports and wineries nearby.

Location: City.

Certificate may be used: November-April with Sunday-Wednesday check-ins.

The Burbank Rose B&B

111 Memorial Blvd W
Newport, RI 02840-3469
(401)849-9457 (888)297-5800 Fax:(203)413-4372
Internet: www.burbankrose.com
E-mail: theburbankrose@yahoo.com

Circa 1850. The innkeepers of this cheery, yellow home named their B&B in honor of their ancestor, famed horticulturist Luther Burbank. As a guest, he probably would be taken by the bright, flowery hues that adorn the interior of this Federal-style home. Rooms, some of which afford harbor views, are light and airy with simple decor. The innkeepers serve afternoon refreshments and a substantial breakfast buffet. The home is located in Newport's Historic Hill district and within walking distance of shops, restaurants and many of the seaside village's popular attractions.

Innkeeper(s): Brian Cole. $79-250. 5 rooms with PB, 3 suites. Breakfast and Continental breakfast included in rates. Types of meals: Cont. Beds: QT. Cable TV, reading lamp, refrigerator, ceiling fan, clock radio, hair dryer and iron/ironing board in room. Air conditioning. VCR, parlor games and telephone on premises. Antiquing, fishing, live theater, shopping, water sports, sailing, golf and tennis nearby.

Location: City, ocean community, waterfront.

Certificate may be used: Anytime, based on availability. Excluding weekends May-November. Continental breakfast only.

Victorian Ladies Inn

63 Memorial Blvd
Newport, RI 02840-3629
(401)849-9960
Internet: www.victorianladies.com
E-mail: info@victorianladies.com

Circa 1851. Innkeepers Cheryl and Harry have created a comfortable and welcoming atmosphere at this restored three-story Victorian inn and cottage. Intimate and inviting, this traditional New England bed & breakfast features spacious guest bedrooms furnished with period pieces, fine reproductions, rich fabrics and wallcoverings. Linger over a gracious breakfast in the dining room. Stroll through the award-winning gardens, walk over the small bridge and gaze at the koi pond. Relax in the living room while planning activities for the day. Walk to nearby beaches, the Colonial town, famed mansions, cliff walk and harbor front.

Innkeeper(s): Cheryl & Harry Schatmeyer, Jr. $129-289. 11 rooms with PB, 5 with FP. Breakfast included in rates. Types of meals: Full gourmet bkfst and veg bkfst. Beds: KQT. Cable TV, VCR, reading lamp, CD player, refrigerator, telephone, desk, most with fireplace, hair dryer, wireless Internet access and iron/ironing board in room. Central air. Fax, copier, library, parlor games and gift shop on premises. Antiquing, art galleries, beach, bicycling, canoeing/kayaking, fishing, golf, hiking, horseback riding, live theater, museums, parks, shopping, tennis, water sports and wineries nearby.

Location: Ocean community.

Publicity: Country Inns, Glamour, Bride Magazine, L.A. Times, Country Victorian, Yankee Magazine, Newport Life Magazine and voted "Best Hotel/B&B" by Newport voters for 6 years.

"We want to move in!"

Certificate may be used: July 1-Sept. 30 weekdays only. Anytime from November-June 30.

Providence   C6

Edgewood Manor B&B

232 Norwood Ave
Providence, RI 02905
(401)781-0099 Fax:(401)467-6311
Internet: www.providence-lodging.com
E-mail: edgemanor@aol.com

Circa 1905. Built as a private home, this 18-room Greek Revival Colonial mansion has served as a convent, an office, a rooming house and is now restored as an magnificent bed and breakfast. An elegant era is reflected in the coffered, beamed and domed-foyer ceilings, leaded- and stained-glass windows, hand-carved mantels and blend of Victorian and Empire decor. Romantic guest bedrooms feature Jacuzzi tubs and wood-burning fireplaces. Savor a satisfying gourmet breakfast served in the dining room or on the patio. The inn is within walking distance to Narragansett Bay and Roger Williams Park and Zoo, with 230 acres of magnificent gardens, sculptures and historic buildings.

Innkeeper(s): Joy Generali. $99-329. 20 rooms, 18 with PB, 3 with FP, 9 with HT. Breakfast included in rates. Types of meals: Full gourmet bkfst, afternoon tea, wine and Wine and cheese hour on Friday and Saturday Eves. Beds: KQD. Cable TV, VCR, reading lamp, stereo, refrigerator, ceiling fan, clock radio, telephone, most with hot tub/spa, some with fireplace, hair dryer, bath amenities, wireless Internet access, iron/ironing board, Two-person Jacuzzi tubs, Wood-burning fireplaces, Gas fireplaces,comfortable sitting rooms and Afternoon tea in room. Air conditioning. Fax, copier, bicycles, library, laundry facility, bicycles for rent,large outdoor victorian porch,free parking, beautiful sitting rooms with wood burning fireplaces and free wireless Internet service on premises. Limited handicap access. Antiquing, art galleries, beach, bicycling, canoeing/kayaking, fishing, golf, hiking, horseback riding, live theater, museums, parks, shopping, sporting events, tennis, wineries, Sailing, Three yacht clubs within walking distance, Roger Williams Park and Botanical gardens within walking distance nearby.

Location: City.

Publicity: Rated top 25 inns by McMillan travel guides. AAA Inspected three diamond recipient.Voted most Elegant in America. Featured in Boston Globe (2008), "Best Urban Luxury Inn New England" by Yankee Magazine (2010), Featured on National Geographic (2006) and The National Historic Register.

Certificate may be used: Monday-Thursday only, not valid May 15-Nov. 15.

South Kingstown   H5

Admiral Dewey Inn

668 Matunuck Beach Rd
South Kingstown, RI 02879-7053
(401)783-2090 (800)457-2090
Internet: www.admiraldeweyinn.com

Circa 1898. Although the prices have risen a bit since this inn's days as a boarding house (the rate was 50 cents per night), this Stick-style home still offers hospitality and comfort. The National Register inn is within walking distance of Matunuck Beach. Guests can enjoy the sea breeze from the inn's wraparound porch. Period antiques decorate the guest rooms, some of which offer ocean views.

Innkeeper(s): Joan Lebel. $100-150. 10 rooms, 8 with PB. Breakfast included in rates. Types of meals: Cont plus, early coffee/tea and picnic lunch. Beds: QDT. VCR, fax, copier, parlor games, telephone and fireplace on premises. Antiquing, fishing, live theater, parks, shopping and water sports nearby.

Location: Ocean community. Free access to town beach.

Publicity: Yankee Traveler and Rhode Island Monthly.

Certificate may be used: November-April, subject to availability (holiday weekends excluded). No Weekends.

Westerly   H5

Grandview B&B

212 Shore Rd
Westerly, RI 02891-3623
(401)596-6384 (800)447-6384 Fax:(401)596-6384
Internet: grandviewbandb.com
E-mail: grandviewbandb@verizon.net

Circa 1910. An impressive wraparound stone porch highlights this majestic Shingle Victorian inn, which also boasts a
lovely ocean view from its hilltop site. The inn features 9
guest rooms, a family room with cable TV, a spacious living
room with a handsome stone fireplace, and a sun porch
where visitors enjoy a hearty breakfast buffet. Antiquing, fishing, golf, swimming and tennis are found nearby as are Watch
Hill, Mystic and Newport. The Foxwoods and Mohegan Sun
casinos also are nearby.

Innkeeper(s): Patricia Grande. $115-140. 7 rooms, 4 with PB, 1 suite.
Breakfast included in rates. Types of meals: Cont plus and early coffee/tea.
Beds: KQDT. Reading lamp, refrigerator, ceiling fan, clock radio, 6 with ceiling fans, air conditioning and table fans in room. TV, VCR, fax, copier, library,
parlor games, telephone, fireplace and large video library on premises.
Antiquing, art galleries, beach, bicycling, canoeing/kayaking, fishing, golf, hiking, live theater, museums, parks, shopping, tennis, water sports, wineries
and casinos nearby.

Location: Ocean community.

Certificate may be used: November-April, Sunday-Thursday, subject to
availability.

Woonsocket   A5

Pillsbury House Bed & Breakfast

341 Prospect Street
Woonsocket, RI 02895
(401)766-7983 (800)205-4112
Internet: www.pillsburyhouse.com
E-mail: rogerwnri@prodigy.net

Circa 1875. On an historic street in the fashionable North End,
this restored Victorian mansion is one of the area's oldest.
Boasting original parquet floors, high ceilings and furnished with
antiques and period pieces, a grand elegance is imparted. Sit by
the fire in the evenings or on the shaded porch during the day. A
guest kitchenette on the second floor includes a microwave,
refrigerator stocked with beverages, hair dryer and ironing board.
Tastefully decorated guest bedrooms and a suite offer comfort
and character. Breakfast in the gracious dining room is a satisfying meal with fresh fruit, homemade baked goods and a hot
entree. Located in the heart of the Blackstone River Valley
National Heritage Corridor, there is much to see and do.

Innkeeper(s): Susan & Roger Bouchard. $88. 4 rooms with PB. Breakfast
included in rates. Types of meals: Full bkfst and veg bkfst. Beds: KQT. Clock
radio in room. TV, fax, telephone, fireplace, complimentary
juices, beer and water available in second floor refreshment area on premises. Antiquing, bicycling, canoeing/kayaking, live theater, museums, parks,
shopping, wineries, Franklin, MA commuter train station to Boston (20 minutes), South Station downtown Boston (59 minute train ride), Museum of
Work & Culture (1 mile), Chan's Blues & Jazz Club (1/2 mile) and Stadium
Theatre Center for Performing Arts (1/2 mile) nearby.

Location: City.

Certificate may be used: Sunday-Thursday.

Wyoming   G3

Stagecoach House Inn

1136 Main St
Wyoming, RI 02898
(401)539-9600 (888)814-9600
Internet: www.stagecoachhouse.com
E-mail: info@stagecoachhouse.com

Meticulously restored, this historic 1796 Colonial with
Victorian décor is an inviting South County country inn. Relax
on the front porch overlooking garden shrubs and trees that
reflect the original landscaping. Sit by the large fireplace in
rocking chairs and listen to the player piano in the lobby. Air-
conditioned guest bedrooms and suites feature remote control
fireplaces and whirlpool tubs. The honeymoon suite boasts a
two-person Jacuzzi and double shower. French doors lead onto
the upper deck with a view of the Wood River and horseshoe
waterfall. A family suite has two adjoining rooms and a ground-
level room is handicapped accessible. A deluxe continental
breakfast is served daily.

Innkeeper(s): Deb and Bill Bokon. Call for rates. 12 rooms. Breakfast included in rates. Types of meals: Cont plus. Beds: QT. Data port, cable TV, clock
radio, telephone, most with fireplace, hair dryer, iron/ironing board and
Jacuzzi tubs in room. Central air. Fax, parlor games, gift shop and one handicap room on premises. Handicap access. Amusement parks, antiquing,
beach, bicycling, canoeing/kayaking, cross-country skiing, downhill skiing,
fishing, golf, hiking, horseback riding, parks, shopping, sporting events, tennis, water sports, wineries and Casinos nearby.

Location: Country, waterfront.

Certificate may be used: November-March, Sunday-Thursday subject to
availability, holidays excluded, standard room only.

South Carolina

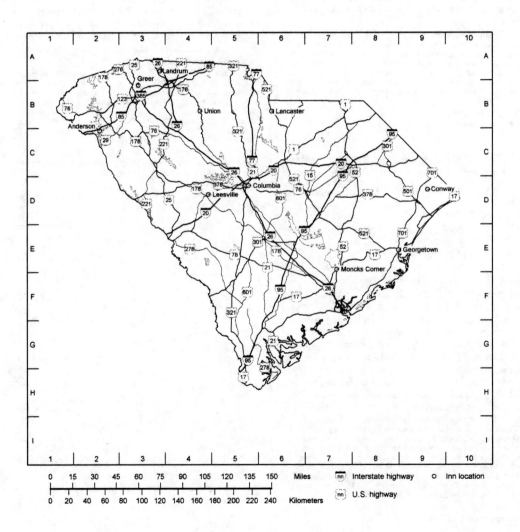

Columbia   D5

Chesnut Cottage B&B

1718 Hampton St
Columbia, SC 29201-3420
(803)256-1718 (888)308-1718
Internet: www.chestnutcottage.com
E-mail: ggarrett@sc.rr.com

Circa 1850. This inn was originally the home of Confederate
General James Chesnut and his wife, writer Mary Boykin Miller
Chesnut. She authored "A Diary From Dixie," written during
the Civil War but published posthumously in 1905. The white
frame one-and-a-half-story house has a central dormer with an
arched window above the main entrance. The small porch has
four octagonal columns and an ironwork balustrade. Hearty
breakfasts are served in the privacy of your room, on the porch
or in the main dining room. The innkeepers can provide you
with sightseeing information, make advance dinner reservations,
as well as cater to any other special interests you might have.

Innkeeper(s): Gale Garrett. $95-225. 5 rooms with PB, 3 with FP, 1 two-
bedroom suite. Breakfast and snacks/refreshments included in rates. Types of
meals: Country bkfst, veg bkfst, early coffee/tea and room service. Beds: KQ.
Modem hook-up, data port, cable TV, VCR, reading lamp, stereo, refrigerator,
ceiling fan, snack bar, clock radio, telephone, coffeemaker, turn-down service,
desk and fireplace in room. Central air. Fax and copier on premises.
Antiquing, art galleries, fishing, hiking, live theater, museums, parks, shopping, sporting events and water sports nearby.

Location: City.

Publicity: Sandlapper, London Financial Times, State Newspaper and TV show .

*"You really know how to pamper and spoil. Chestnut Cottage is a
great place to stay."*

Certificate may be used: All year, Sunday through Thursday.

Conway   D9

The Moore Farm House
Bed and Breakfast

3423 Highway 319 E
Conway, SC 29526
(843)365-7479 (866)MOOREBB
Internet: www.themoorefarmhouse.com
E-mail: info@TheMooreFarmHouse.com

Circa 1914. Warm southern hospitality has been extended here
for more than 100 years. Feel refreshed and recharged by the
nostalgic ambiance amid contemporary amenities. Munch on
fresh-baked cookies upon arrival. Hot and cold beverages are
available any time. Select a book from the well-stocked library or
play billiards. Select and watch a movie in the living room.
Guest rooms on the second floor boast chocolates, all-natural
Sassy Goat Milk Soap and some rooms feature whirlpool soaking tubs. Gather in the dining room to linger over a gourmet
breakfast that includes delicious twists on classic favorites and
signature entrees designed by a highly acclaimed executive chef.
Explore the local sights of the historic Waccamaw River town of
Conway, South Carolina. This B&B is just 15 miles from famous
Myrtle Beach. Ask about events packages and specials offered.

Innkeeper(s): Harry and Cathy Pinner. $119-149. 4 rooms. TV, DVD, spa,
library, parlor games, fireplace and WiFi on premises.

Location: Country.

Certificate may be used: Anytime, November-March, subject to availability.

Georgetown   E8

Mansfield Plantation B&B Country Inn

1776 Mansfield Rd
Georgetown, SC 29440-6923
(843)546-6961 (866)717-1776 Fax:(843) 546-1367
Internet: MansfieldPlantation.com
E-mail: mightymansfield@aol.com

Circa 1800. Listed in the National Register, and featured in Mel
Gibson's movie, The Patriot, Mansfield Plantation is a perfect
respite for those in search of romance and history in a natural,
secluded setting. The large dining room and sitting rooms are
furnished with the owner's collections of 19th-century
American antiques that include paintings, china, silver, furniture
and gilt-framed mirrors. Accommodations include three guest-
houses, each decorated in a romantic style and boasting fireplaces, hardwood floors, high ceilings, comfortable furnishings
and collectibles. The vast grounds (900 private acres), shaded
by moss-draped oaks, provide ideal spots for relaxing. Enjoy aza-
lea and camellia gardens, as well as views of the surrounding
marshlands. Guests can relax in hammocks or swings, watch for
birds or enjoy a bike ride. Boating on the Black River is another
possibility. Guests may bring their own boats or rent canoes or
kayaks nearby. Among the plantation's notable historic features
are a schoolhouse, kitchen, winnowing house, slave village and
chapel, all of which predate the Civil War.

Innkeeper(s): Kathryn Green. $150-200. 8 rooms with PB, 8 with FP, 3
guest houses, 1 conference room. Breakfast included in rates. Types of
meals: Full gourmet bkfst, veg bkfst, early coffee/tea, picnic lunch and afternoon tea. Beds: KQDT. Cable TV, VCR, DVD, reading lamp, refrigerator, clock
radio, coffeemaker, desk, fireplace and iron/ironing board in room. Central air.
Fax, bicycles, library, telephone, canoeing, kayaking, water skiing, fishing,
hiking and animal/bird watching on premises. Amusement parks, antiquing,
art galleries, beach, bicycling, canoeing/kayaking, fishing, golf, horseback riding, live theater, museums, parks, shopping, tennis, water sports, Historic
Charleston, Myrtle Beach and Historic Georgetown nearby.

Location: Country, waterfront. On the banks of the Black River, near the ocean.

Publicity: Georgetown Times, Charleston News & Courier, Sandlapper, Pee
Dee Magazine, Charleston Magazine, Carolina Home, South Carolina Homes
& Gardens, Grand Strand Magazine, The INNside Scoop, Windshield
America (Fine Living Network), Treasure Hunters (NBC) and The Patriot.

*"Handsome furnishings, wildlife walks, sports and hunting opportu-
nities galore, and a sumptuous atmosphere all make for a weekend
retreat to remember."*

Certificate may be used: Anytime, subject to availability.

The Shaw House B&B

613 Cypress Ct
Georgetown, SC 29440-3349
(843)546-9663
E-mail: shawbandb@sccc.tv.net

Circa 1972. Near Georgetown's historical district is the Shaw
House. It features a beautiful view of the Willowbank marsh,
which stretches out for more than 1000 acres. Sometimes giant
turtles come up and lay eggs on
the lawn. Guests enjoy rocking on
the inn's front and back porches
and identifying the large variety of
birds that live here. A large
screened porch extends over the
rice fields. A Southern home-
cooked breakfast often includes

grits, quiche and Mary's heart-shaped biscuits.

Innkeeper(s): Mary & Joe Shaw. $100. 3 rooms with PB. Breakfast included in rates. Types of meals: Full bkfst, early coffee/tea and snacks/refreshments. Beds: KQ. Cable TV, reading lamp, stereo, ceiling fan, clock radio, telephone, turn-down service and desk in room. Air conditioning. TV, bicycles, library, fireplace and Large screened porch over the rice fields on premises. Amusement parks, antiquing, fishing, live theater, parks, shopping and water sports nearby.

Location: City.

Publicity: *Charlotte Observer and Country.*

"Your home speaks of abundance and comfort and joy."

Certificate may be used: Sunday-Friday, anytime available.

Lancaster   B6

Kilburnie, the Inn at Craig Farm

1824 Craig Farm Road
Lancaster, SC 29720
(803)416-8420 Fax:(803)416-8429
Internet: www.kilburnie.com
E-mail: Jtromp@comporium.net

Circa 1828. The area's oldest surviving antebellum home, this Greek Revival was saved from demolition, moved to this 400-acre estate and extensively restored. Listed in the National Register, its historic and architectural significance is seen in the intricate details found in the public rooms. Experience Southern hospitality accented by European charm in a quiet and secluded setting with a classic elegance. Each guest bedroom and suite boasts a fireplace, as do two bathrooms. An unsurpassed two-course breakfast may include fresh-baked bread and muffins, a fruit appetizer of Poached Pears with Blueberries or Southern Pecan Peaches and a main entree of Oven-Shirred Eggs or Herbed Goat Cheese Omelette. Relax on one of the piazza rockers after a stroll on the nature path through the wildlife backyard habitat with bridges spanning the woodlands.

Innkeeper(s): Johannes Tromp. $150-200. 5 rooms with PB, 5 with FP, 1 suite, 1 conference room. Breakfast included in rates. Types of meals: Full gourmet bkfst. Beds: KQ. Modem hook-up, cable TV, VCR, reading lamp, clock radio, telephone, turn-down service, desk, hot tub/spa, fireplace, hair dryer, bath amenities and wireless Internet access in room. Central air. Fax, copier, library and laundry facility on premises. Amusement parks, antiquing, art galleries, canoeing/kayaking, golf, museums, parks, shopping, sporting events and tennis nearby.

Location: Country.

Publicity: *Southern Living, Sandlapper Magazine, South Carolina Magazine, Charlotte Observer, Rock Hill Herald, Lancaster News and South Carolina Educational Television (SCETV).*

Certificate may be used: Anytime, Sunday-Thursday, except holidays.

Landrum   A3

The Red Horse Inn

45 Winstons Chase Court
Landrum, SC 29356
(864)895-4968 Fax:(864)895-4968
Internet: www.theredhorseinn.com
E-mail: theredhorseinn@aol.com

Circa 1996. Sweeping mountain views, pastoral vistas and endless sky offer the perfect setting for a romantic getaway or refreshing vacation. The Red Horse Inn on almost 190 acres in Landrum, South Carolina, offers intimate cottages and luxurious guest bedrooms that feature fireplaces, whirlpool tubs and generous upscale amenities. After a delightful breakfast, enjoy

the many local sites and scenic attractions nearby.

Innkeeper(s): Mary & Roger Wolters. $175-320. 12 rooms, 6 with PB, 6 with FP, 6 with WP, 6 cottages, 1 conference room. Breakfast included in rates. Types of meals: Full gourmet bkfst, early coffee/tea and picnic lunch. Beds: KQD. Modem hook-up, data port, cable TV, VCR, DVD, reading lamp, CD player, refrigerator, ceiling fan, clock radio, telephone, coffeemaker, turn-down service, desk, fireplace, hair dryer, bathrobes, bath amenities, iron/ironing board, All rooms & cottages have a TV & DVD player, Satellite TV is available in the cottages, Both the cottages & inn rooms have data ports, Inn rooms & conference center have wireless access, All have whirlpool & fireplaces, The Springhouse and Hayloft have private outdoor hot tubs in room. Central air. Fax, copier, stable and Massage on premises. Handicap access. Antiquing, art galleries, canoeing/kayaking, fishing, golf, hiking, horseback riding, live theater, museums, parks, shopping, sporting events, tennis, water sports and wineries nearby.

Location: Country, mountains.

Publicity: *Inn Traveler's best for honeymoon/anniversary and 2008 Top 10 Romantic Inn award from American Historic Inns/iLoveinns.com.*

Certificate may be used: November-January, Monday-Thursday, subject to availability. Not valid on holidays or weekends stays.

Leesville   D4

The Able House Inn

244 E Columbia Ave
Leesville, SC 29070-9284
(803)532-2763 Fax:(803)532-2763
Internet: www.ablehouseinn.com
E-mail: aablehouseinn@sc.rr.com

Circa 1939. This elegant, white brick home was built by a local druggist. Relax in the tastefully decorated living room or lounge on a comfy wicker chair among the large plants in the  sunroom. Guest rooms, named after various relatives, boast beautiful amenities such as a canopied bed or window seats. Jennifer's Room opens into a sitting room with a window seat so large, some guests have snuggled down for a restful night's sleep instead of the large, brass and enamel four-poster bed. Innkeepers offer guests snacks/refreshments in the evening and turndown service each night. Wake to freshly ground coffee before taking on the day. During the warmer months, innkeepers offer guests the use of their swimming pool.

Innkeeper(s): Jack & Annabelle Wright. $90-105. 5 rooms with PB, 1 suite. Breakfast and snacks/refreshments included in rates. Types of meals: Full bkfst, veg bkfst and early coffee/tea. Beds: QD. Modem hook-up, cable TV, DVD, reading lamp, ceiling fan, clock radio, telephone, turn-down service, desk, hair dryer, bathrobes, bath amenities and iron/ironing board in room. Central air. TV, VCR, fax, copier, spa, swimming, parlor games and fireplace on premises. Antiquing, fishing, golf, live theater, shopping, sporting events, tennis and water sports nearby.

Location: City.

Publicity: *Sandlapper and State Newspaper.*

"Thank you for the warm Southern welcome. Your place is absolutely beautiful, very inviting. The food was extraordinary!"

Certificate may be used: Sept. 1 to April 1.

Moncks Corner E7

Rice Hope Plantation Inn Bed & Breakfast

206 Rice Hope Dr
Moncks Corner, SC 29461-9781
(843)849-9000 (800)569-4038
Internet: www.ricehope.com
E-mail: louedens@gmail.com

Circa 1840. Resting on 285 secluded acres of natural beauty, this historic mansion sits among oaks on a bluff overlooking the Cooper River. A stay here is a visit to yesteryear, where it is said to be 45 short minutes and three long centuries from downtown Charleston. Formal gardens boast a 200-year-old camellia and many more varieties of trees and plants, making it a perfect setting for outdoor weddings or other special occasions. Nearby attractions include the Trappist Monastery at Mepkin Plantation, Francis Marion National Forest and Cypress Gardens.

Innkeeper(s): Jamie Edens. $85-165. 5 rooms with PB, 1 conference room. Breakfast included in rates. Types of meals: Full bkfst and early coffee/tea. Beds: KQD. TV, reading lamp, ceiling fan, clock radio and coffeemaker in room. Air conditioning. Copier, tennis, library, parlor games, telephone and fireplace on premises. Antiquing, art galleries, beach, bicycling, canoeing/kayaking, fishing, golf, museums, parks, shopping and tennis nearby.

Location: Country, waterfront. Riverfront.

Publicity: *"W" Fasion Magazine photo shoot, Green Power commercial, Japanese TV Documentary, Travel Channel, Haunted Inns and film location for "Consenting Adults" with Kevin Costner.*

Certificate may be used: Sunday-Thursday.

Union B4

The Inn at Merridun

100 Merridun Pl
Union, SC 29379-2200
(864)427-7052 (888)892-6020 Fax:(864)429-0373
Internet: www.merridun.com
E-mail: info@merridun.com

Circa 1855. Nestled on nine acres of wooded ground, this Greek Revival inn is in a small Southern college town. During spring, see the South in its colorful splendor with blooming azaleas, magnolias and wisteria. Sip an iced drink on the inn's marble verandas and relive memories of a bygone era. Soft strains of Mozart and Beethoven, as well as the 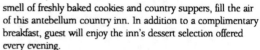 smell of freshly baked cookies and country suppers, fill the air of this antebellum country inn. In addition to a complimentary breakfast, guest will enjoy the inn's dessert selection offered every evening.

Innkeeper(s): Peggy Waller & (JD, the inn cat 1991-2008). $99-135. 5 rooms with PB, 3 conference rooms. Breakfast and Evening dessert included in rates. Types of meals: Full gourmet bkfst, gourmet lunch, picnic lunch, afternoon tea, gourmet dinner and Luncheons. Beds: KQT. Cable TV, VCR, reading lamp, ceiling fan, clock radio, telephone, desk, hair dryer, wireless Internet access and iron/ironing board in room. Central air. Fax, copier, library, parlor games, fireplace, gift shop, refrigerator on each floor for guest use, evening dessert and Miss Fannie's Tea Room on premises. Amusement parks, antiquing, art galleries, fishing, golf, museums, parks, shopping, sporting events and water sports nearby.

Location: City.

Publicity: *Charlotte Observer, Spartanburg Herald, Southern Living, Atlanta Journal-Constitution, Sandlapper Magazine, SCETV, Prime Time Live, BBC Documentary and Marshall Tucker Band Music Video.*

Certificate may be used: Jan. 15-Nov. 15, Monday-Thursday.

South Dakota

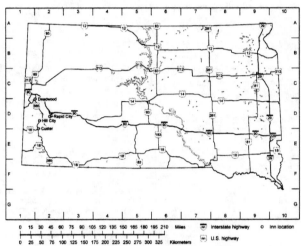

Map legend:
- ◯ Interstate highway
- U.S. highway
- Inn location

Miles: 0 15 30 45 60 75 90 105 120 135 150 165 180 195 210

Kilometers: 0 25 50 75 100 125 150 175 200 225 250 275 300 325

Hill City

High Country Guest Ranch

12172 Ray Smith Drive
Hill City, SD 57745
(605)574-9003 (888)222-4628
Internet: www.highcountryguestranch.com
E-mail: info@highcountryguestranch.com

Circa 1990. Ten cabins set on a grassy meadow offer skylights and private decks. Some have full kitchens, and there are special honeymoon and anniversary accommodations. The inn's special use permit allows guests to enjoy the Black Hills National Forest on horseback with half-day and full-day rides available. The dining room looks like a covered wagon. The ranch is close to Mount Rushmore.

Innkeeper(s): Larry and Bonnie McCaskell. $43-630. 21 cabins, 5 with FP, 3 with HT, 4 with WP, 1 conference room. Beds: QT. TV, VCR, DVD, reading lamp, refrigerator, ceiling fan, clock radio, telephone, coffeemaker, desk, hot tub/spa, some with fireplace, All cabins vary and please call for details in room. Central air. Fax, copier, spa, swimming, stable, bicycles, parlor games, gift shop, Library of DVD & Videos and games on premises. Handicap access. Cross-country skiing, downhill skiing, fishing, golf, live theater, parks, shopping, tennis, water sports, deer and turkey hunting, horseback riding and Mt. Rushmore nearby.

Location: Country, mountains. Guest ranch.

Publicity: *Minnesota Monthly.*

Certificate may be used: Sept. 25-May 1.

Rapid City   D2

Coyote Blues Village

23165 Horseman's Ranch Rd
Rapid City, SD 57702
(605)574-4477 (888)253-4477 Fax:(605)574-2101
Internet: www.coyotebluesvillage.com
E-mail: info@coyotebluesvillage.com

Circa 1996. Experience genuine European style with the Streich family from Switzerland in their 9,000-square-foot, two-story European cabin, resting on 30 acres of woodlands in the Black Hills of South Dakota. Four uniquely themed rooms provide style to fit any taste, from "jungle" to "Oriental." Relax in the hot tub just outside the room on the private patio and breathe in the fresh pine scent that fills the crisp air. Rise each morning with the sweet aroma of freshly baked goods from the Swiss Specialty Bakery downstairs. Enjoy breakfast in the dining room or on the deck before an excursion in town.

Innkeeper(s): Christine & Hans-Peter Streich. $75-155. 10 rooms with PB, 4 with HT, 1 with WP, 1 two-bedroom suite, 1 conference room. Breakfast and snacks/refreshments included in rates. Types of meals: Full gourmet bkfst, veg bkfst, early coffee/tea, gourmet lunch and dinner by request. Beds: KQT. Cable TV, reading lamp, refrigerator, ceiling fan, clock radio, some with hot tub/spa and wireless Internet access in room. VCR, DVD, fax, copier, bicycles, library, telephone, fireplace, Deck with long chairs, Ping-pong table, Coffee pot & microwave in lobby area, Snack & refreshment bar and Fireplace in common area on premises. Antiquing, art galleries, beach, bicycling, canoeing/kayaking, cross-country skiing, downhill skiing, fishing, golf, hiking, horseback riding, live theater, museums, parks, shopping, tennis, water sports, wineries, Mt. Rushmore, Crazy Horse, Custer State Park and 1880 Train nearby.

Location: Country, mountains.

Certificate may be used: September-May, and last minute, subject to availabilty.

Tennessee

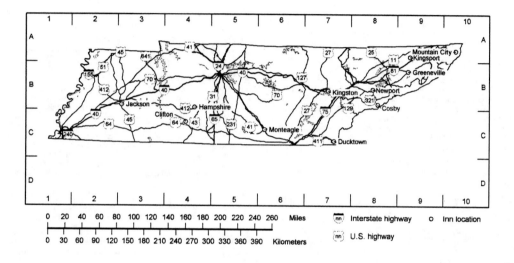

	Miles	
0 20 40 60 80 100 120 140 160 180 200 220 240 260	Miles	
0 30 60 90 120 150 180 210 240 270 300 330 360 390	Kilometers	

nn Interstate highway o Inn location

nn U.S. highway

Clifton   C4

Bear Inn Golf & River Resort

2250 Billy Nance Hwy. 114
Clifton, TN 38425
(931)676-5552 Fax:(931)676-3163
Internet: www.bearinnllc.com
E-mail: frontdesk@bearinnllc.com

Located on the 15th fairway of the Bear Trace-Ross Creek
Landing Golf Course in Clifton, near the Tennessee River, this
B&B is an authentic golf and river resort. Enjoy the big-screen
TV in the fireside sports lodge setting. Appetizers are offered
every evening. Stay in a guest suite or cottage with a log cabin-
style décor that is accented with patchwork quilts, fragrant
cedar woodworking and equipped kitchenettes. Wake up early
or sleep all day, an expanded continental breakfast is available
in the Gathering Room. Ask about special packages available.

Innkeeper(s): Amanda Alley. $69-129. 14 rooms with PB, 1 suite, 2 guest
houses, 11 cabins, 1 conference room. Breakfast and Continental Breakfast
included in rates. Types of meals: Cont plus, snacks/refreshments and hors
d'oeuvres. Beds: KQT. Cable TV, reading lamp, refrigerator, ceiling fan, clock
radio, telephone, coffeemaker, hair dryer, wireless Internet access and
iron/ironing board in room. Air conditioning. VCR, fax, copier, gift shop,
Located alongside the 15th Fairway of the Ross Creek Landing Golf Course,
Restaurant & bar with view of golf course and Room to host up to 75 people

for banquets or functions on premises. Antiquing, bicycling, canoeing/kayak-
ing, fishing, golf, hiking, horseback riding, parks, shopping, water sports,
wineries, Historical sites and golfing nearby.

Location: Country.

Certificate may be used: Subject to Availability Nov.1-March 15, March
16-Oct. 31, Monday-Thursday subject to availability. Excludes all holidays
for all dates.

Cosby   B8

Creekwalk Inn and Cabins at Whisperwood Farm

166 Middle Creek Road and Highway 321
Cosby, TN 37722
(423)487-4000 (800)962-2246
Internet: www.creekwalkinn.com
E-mail: info@creekwalkinn.com

Circa 1984. Swim or fish in the trout-stocked Cosby Creek
while staying at this B&B outside Gatlinburg, Tennessee in
the Great Smoky Mountains. Creekwalk Inn and Cabins at
Whisperwood Farm in Cosby offers the setting of a log home
on a private estate with 3000 feet of water frontage.
Firewood is available for outdoor campfires and a guitar is
available for strumming and singing along. Beverage service is
provided all day. Stay in a guest bedroom with a cathedral

ceiling and assorted amenities that may include a creek or meadow view, Jacuzzi, fireplace, robes, balcony or a private outdoor hot tub in a bamboo thicket. Honeymoon and family cabins are also available. Savor a daily gourmet breakfast before exploring the scenic area. The wedding chapel and reception lodge are popular romantic venues.

Innkeeper(s): Janice and Tifton Haynes. $139-310. 7 rooms, 9 with PB, 4 with FP, 2 with HT, 4 with WP, 2 two-bedroom suites, 1 cottage, 14 cabins, 4 conference rooms. Breakfast and Tea and coffee beverage service available 24 hours/day self service. Cabins do not include breakfast included in rates. Types of meals: Full gourmet bkfst, veg bkfst, early coffee/tea, gourmet lunch, picnic lunch, Private chef available with 24 hours notice, private dinners by reservation, fresh fruit and juice served with full gourmet breakfast, vegetarian meals by request, guests may bring own wine and guest refrigerator. Reading lamp, CD player, ceiling fan, some with hot tub/spa, some with fireplace, hair dryer, bathrobes, bath amenities, wireless Internet access, Cathedral ceiling in every bedroom, Creekfront rooms have screen door opening to narrow balcony along the edge of the creek and Hannah Mountain has private hot tub in bamboo thicket down creekside path in room. Central air. DVD, fax, copier, swimming, bicycles, library, telephone, laundry facility, Cosby Creek, stocked with trout & fun for wading & swimming, 3000 feet of creek frontage, Firewood available for outdoor campfires & marshmallow roasts and Guitar available for strumming by the fire. on premises. Handicap access. Amusement parks, antiquing, art galleries, bicycling, canoeing/kayaking, cross-country skiing, downhill skiing, fishing, golf, hiking, horseback riding, live theater, museums, parks, shopping, sporting events, tennis, water sports, wineries, White Water Rafting on the Pigeon River, Dollywood Splash Country, Gatlinburg Aquarium, Biltmore House, Clingman's Dome (eastern continental divide), Appalachian Trail and Mountain music played at local bluegrass restaurant Friday through Sunday night just across the street nearby.

Location: Mountains. Gatlinburg, Knoxville.

Publicity: *Knoxville Sentinel and Cable Wedding Show.*

Certificate may be used: Non-Holiday Weeks. Sunday-Thursday, December and January.

Greeneville B9

Nolichuckey Bluffs

295 Kinser Park Lane
Greeneville, TN 37743-4748
(423)787-7947 (800)842-4690 Fax:(423)787-9247
Internet: www.tennessee-cabins.com
E-mail: cabins@usit.net

Circa 1997. Nolichuckey Bluffs is composed of seven cabins located on 16 wooded acres overlooking the river. Redbud Cabin offers two bedrooms, a kitchen, dining area, living room and private Jacuzzi. Six can sleep here, and there are generously sized decks, a fireplace and air conditioning. A full breakfast is served in the country store. Grist Mill and discount golf are found on the property.

Innkeeper(s): Patricia & Brooke Sadler. $90-130. 7 cabins with PB, 7 with FP, 3 with WP, 1 conference room. Breakfast and snacks/refreshments included in rates. Types of meals: Cont. Beds: KQDT. Cable TV, VCR, reading lamp, refrigerator, ceiling fan, clock radio, telephone, coffeemaker, desk, some with hot tub/spa, hair dryer, bath amenities and iron/ironing board in room. Central air. Fax, copier, library, parlor games, laundry facility, gift shop, Antique grist mill, disc golf and organic agriculture project on premises. Antiquing, bicycling, fishing, golf, horseback riding, live theater, parks, shopping, tennis, 17th President Andrew Johnson Birthplace, Appalachian Trail, Davey Crockett Birthplace and nearby.

Location: Mountains.

Certificate may be used: Anytime, subject to availability, except holidays and special events.

Jackson B3

Highland Place B&B Inn

519 N Highland Ave
Jackson, TN 38301-4824
(731)427-1472 (877)614-6305
Internet: www.highlandplace.com
E-mail: relax@highlandplace.com

Circa 1911. Whether traveling for business or pleasure, a stay at this elegant Colonial Revival mansion will relax and inspire. Conveniently located in a quiet downtown historical district, the perfect blend of old and new furnishings provide luxurious comfort and modern convenience. Spacious barely describes the 10-foot-wide hallways, high ceilings, marble fireplace and many exquisite common rooms to gather in and dine together. An audio center enhances the gracious ambiance, and a video library offers further entertainment. The impressive guest bedrooms are well-appointed. Special attention is given to meet personal or corporate needs.

Innkeeper(s): Cindy & Bill Pflaum. $145-175. 4 rooms with PB, 2 with FP, 1 with WP, 2 two-bedroom suites, 2 guest houses, 1 conference room. Breakfast included in rates. Types of meals: Full gourmet bkfst, veg bkfst, early coffee/tea, afternoon tea, snacks/refreshments, wine, gourmet dinner and Inquire about romantic dinner. Beds: Q. Modem hook-up, data port, cable TV, VCR, reading lamp, stereo, ceiling fan, snack bar, clock radio, telephone, turn-down service, desk, some with fireplace, hair dryer, bathrobes, bath amenities, wireless Internet access and iron/ironing board in room. Central air. DVD, fax, copier, library, laundry facility and WiFi Internet access on premises. Antiquing, art galleries, bicycling, fishing, golf, live theater, parks, shopping, sporting events and tennis nearby.

Location: City.

Certificate may be used: Accepts Weekends, Anytime, subject to availability; Anytime, last minute - based on availability.

Kingsport B7

Fox Manor Historic Bed & Breakfast

1612 Watauga St
Kingsport, TN 37664-2567
(423)378-3844 (888)200-5879 Fax:(423) 378-4612
Internet: www.foxmanor.com
E-mail: innkeeper@foxmanor.com

Circa 1890. One of the oldest homes in Kingsport, Tennessee, this fully restored 1890 historic bed and breakfast inn still has the steps which the passengers used to disembark their horse and buggies. Enjoy afternoon refreshments at the authentic 300-year-old English pub bar in the Great Room with leather sofas, big-screen TV and a 28-foot hand-painted wall mural. Victorian elegance exudes from the fireside parlor. The library boasts books, magazines and an entertainment center. Fox Manor offers warm and friendly accommodations with luxury amenities. Stay in a guest bedroom with Egyptian cotton towels and linens, CD players, fireplaces and four-poster beds. Breakfast is served in the dining room, on the wicker-filled veranda or in the gazebo. Sit and ponder the day's pleasant activities while relaxing by the koi pond.

Innkeeper(s): Susan & Walter Halliday. $125-175. 6 rooms with PB, 1 suite, 1 cottage. Breakfast and snacks/refreshments included in rates. Types of meals: Full gourmet bkfst and veg bkfst. Beds: KQT. Modem hook-up, data port, cable TV, VCR, DVD, reading lamp, CD player, ceiling fan, snack bar, clock radio, telephone, desk, hair dryer, bathrobes, bath amenities, wireless Internet access, iron/ironing board and lighted make-up mirror in room. Central air. Fax, library, parlor games, fireplace and gift shop on premises.

Antiquing, art galleries, bicycling, canoeing/kayaking, fishing, golf, hiking, horseback riding, live theater, museums, parks, shopping, sporting events, tennis, water sports and wineries nearby.

Location: City.

Certificate may be used: January-March 15, March 30-Aug. 15, Aug. 30-Sept. 30, Oct. 10-January, subject to availability.

Kingston   B7

Whitestone Country Inn

1200 Paint Rock Rd
Kingston, TN 37763-5843
(865)376-0113 (888)247-2464 Fax:(865)376-4454
Internet: www.whitestoneinn.com
E-mail: moreinfo@whitestoneinn.com

Circa 1995. This regal farmhouse sits majestically on a hilltop overlooking miles of countryside and Watts Bar Lake. The inn is surrounded by 360 acres, some of which borders a scenic lake where

guests can enjoy fishing or simply communing with nature. There are eight miles of hiking trails, and the many porches and decks are perfect places to relax. The inn's interior is as pleasing as the exterior surroundings. Guest rooms are elegantly appointed, and each includes a fireplace and whirlpool tub. Guests are treated to a hearty, country-style breakfast, and dinners and lunch are available by reservation. The inn is one hour from Chattanooga, Knoxville and the Great Smoky Mountains National Park.

Innkeeper(s): Paul & Jean Cowell. $150-280. 21 rooms with PB, 21 with FP, 21 with WP, 2 conference rooms. Breakfast included in rates. Types of meals: Full bkfst, picnic lunch and dinner. Restaurant on premises. Beds: KQ. Cable TV, VCR, DVD, reading lamp, stereo, refrigerator, ceiling fan, clock radio, telephone, coffeemaker, turn-down service, desk, hot tub/spa, fireplace, hair dryer, bathrobes, bath amenities, wireless Internet access and iron/ironing board in room. Central air. Fax, copier, spa, tennis, library, parlor games and gift shop on premises. Handicap access. Antiquing, canoeing/kayaking, fishing, golf, hiking, horseback riding, parks, shopping, sporting events, water sports and wineries nearby.

Location: Country, mountains, waterfront. Lake.

"Not only have you built a place of beauty, you have established a sanctuary of rest. An escape from the noise and hurry of everyday life."

Certificate may be used: Jan. 1-March 31, Sunday-Thursday.

Monteagle   C6

Monteagle Inn

204 West Main Street
Monteagle, TN 37356
(931)924-3869 Fax:(931) 924-3867
Internet: www.monteagleinn.com
E-mail: suites@monteagleinn.com

Circa 1997. Offering European elegance and comfort, this recently renovated inn is classical in style and design. Adjacent to the courtyard, a large wood-burning fireplace accents the great room that showcases a 1923 baby grand piano family heirloom. Guest bedrooms boast a variety of comfortable furnishings and amenities. Choose a four-poster, iron or sleigh bed with soft linens. Many include balconies. The two-bedroom

Cottage boasts a fully equipped kitchen, front porch, dining and living rooms. Enjoy a homemade breakfast in the dining room. The garden gazebo is surrounded by year-round color, designed by a local horticulturist and a prominent landscape architect. Ask about romance and anniversary packages.

Innkeeper(s): Jim Harmon. $160-265. 13 rooms with PB, 1 conference room. Breakfast and snacks/refreshments included in rates. Types of meals: Full gourmet bkfst, veg bkfst, Sun. brunch, early coffee/tea, gourmet lunch, picnic lunch, hors d'oeuvres, wine, gourmet dinner and Full Mountain Gourmet Breakfast. Beds: KQT. Modem hook-up, data port, cable TV, reading lamp, ceiling fan, clock radio, telephone, desk, voice mail, hair dryer, bathrobes, bath amenities, wireless Internet access, down pillows, luxurious European linens, imported bath amenities, antiques and modern reproductions in room. Central air. TV, VCR, DVD, fax, copier, library, parlor games, fireplace and Handicap Room available on premises. Handicap access. Antiquing, art galleries, bicycling, canoeing/kayaking, fishing, golf, hiking, live theater, parks, shopping, sporting events, tennis, water sports and wineries nearby.

Location: Country, mountains.

Publicity: *Southern Living, In Tennessee, Sterling Magazine, Chattanooga Times Free Press, Atlanta Journal-Constitution and Charter Cable special on B&B's.*

Certificate may be used: January-March, Sunday-Tuesday.

Mountain City   A10

Prospect Hill B&B Inn

801 W Main St (Hwy 67)
Mountain City, TN 37683
(423)727-0139 (800)339-5084
Internet: www.prospect-hill.com
E-mail: stay@prospect-hill.com

Circa 1889. This three-story shingle-style Victorian manor garners a great deal of attention from passersby with its appealing architecture and commanding hilltop location. Romantic rooms offer tall arched windows, 11-foot ceilings and spectacular views. Fashioned from handmade bricks, it was once home to Major Joseph Wagner, who, like many of his neighbors in far northeastern Tennessee, served on the Union side. The restored home features five guest rooms. A 1910 oak Craftsman dining set complements the oak Stickley furniture (circa 1997) that decorates the living room. Fireplaces, whirlpools and stained glass add luxury to the guest rooms. Prospect Hill boasts views of the Appalachian and Blue Ridge Mountains. From the front window, guests can see three states: Tennessee, Virginia and North Carolina. The inn is within an hour of the Blue Ridge Parkway, Appalachian Trail and Roan and Grandfather mountains, the Virginia Creeper Trail and 25 minutes from Boone, NC.

Innkeeper(s): Judy & Robert Hotchkiss. $99-235. 6 rooms, 5 with PB, 4 with FP, 1 three-bedroom suite, 1 cottage, 1 conference room. Breakfast and snacks/refreshments included in rates. Types of meals: Full gourmet bkfst, veg bkfst, early coffee/tea, Snacks in the room and meals not provided at cottage—couples may at in inn (fee). Beds: KQDT. Modem hook-up, data port, cable TV, VCR, DVD, reading lamp, CD player, refrigerator, ceiling fan, snack bar, clock radio, telephone, coffeemaker, turn-down service, desk, fireplace, hair dryer, bathrobes, bath amenities, wireless Internet access, iron/ironing board, Historic stained glass, Balcony or porch, Private entrance, Bed for one child, Scenic views, Cottage with LR/DR & fully equipped kitchen and Not all amenities available in Cottage in the Woods in room. Central air. Fax, copier, library, parlor games, laundry facility, gift shop, Hiking on 30 acres, Access to the Iron Mountain Trail, A Cottage in the Woods has decks and lots of parking on premises. Limited handicap access. Antiquing, art galleries, beach, bicycling, canoeing/kayaking, cross-country skiing, downhill skiing, fishing, golf, hiking, horseback riding, live theater, museums, parks, shopping, tennis, water sports, wineries, Stables, Swimming, Fly fishing, Outlets, Drive-in movies, Appalachian and Virginia Creeper Trails nearby.

Location: Country, mountains. Small town America.

Publicity: *Marquee Magazine, Old-House Journal, Haunted Inns of the Southeast, USA Today (Sleep with a Ghost), Arrington's (named Most*

Romantic Hideaway), Best Southern Inn, Tennessee Magazine, Four Points Magazine, Blue Ridge Country Magazine, Fresh Outlook Magazine, the Marble by Joe Tennis (2008), WCYB-Bristol, VA, Oldies Knoxville, Voted Most Romantic Hideaway (Arrington's-2003) and Best Southern Inn.

"The most wonderful thing I'll always remember about our stay is, by far, the wonderful home we came back to each night."

Certificate may be used: Sunday-Thursday, not valid on NASCAR weekends or Oct. 1-25. Will accept at last minute (no more than 24 hours ahead booking) B&B rooms only.

Newport   B8

Christopher Place - An Intimate Resort

1500 Pinnacles Way
Newport, TN 37821-7308
(423)623-6555 (800)595-9441 Fax:(423)613-4771
Internet: www.christopherplace.com
E-mail: stay@christopherplace.com

Circa 1975. 2009 Winner - Travelers' Choice for Romance. Christopher Place is an incomparable resort secluded in the scenic Smoky Mountains near Gatlinburg, in Newport, Tennessee. This award-winning inn was created especially for romantic retreats, unforgettable honeymoons, and special events. Surrounded by more than 200 acres with incredible views, the inn's interior, as well as the hospitality and service has earned it four-diamonds for more than a decade and the iLoveInns 2009 Travelers' Choice for Romance award. Enjoy numerous activities and amenities. Swim, play tennis, go hiking, visit the sauna, shoot pool in the billiard room or just sit amid the beautiful vistas from a rocking chair on the veranda. Start each relaxing day with a full service breakfast and experience four-course gourmet meals in the formal dining room. More casual dining is offered in Marston's Library Pub.

Innkeeper(s): Marston Price. $165-330. 9 rooms, 8 with PB, 2 with FP, 5 with HT, 5 with WP. Breakfast and snacks/refreshments included in rates. Types of meals: Full gourmet bkfst, veg bkfst, early coffee/tea, picnic lunch, wine, gourmet dinner and room service. Restaurant on premises. Beds: KQ. Cable TV, VCR, DVD, reading lamp, stereo, refrigerator, ceiling fan, snack bar, clock radio, coffeemaker, most with hot tub/spa, some with fireplace, hair dryer, bathrobes, bath amenities, wireless Internet access, iron/ironing board and panoramic views in room. Central air. TV, fax, copier, swimming, sauna, tennis, library, parlor games, telephone and hiking trails on premises. Limited handicap access. Amusement parks, antiquing, art galleries, bicycling, canoeing/kayaking, downhill skiing, fishing, golf, hiking, horseback riding, live theater, parks, shopping, sporting events, tennis, water sports and wineries nearby.

Location: Country, mountains.

Publicity: *Wall Street Journal, Atlanta Journal Constitution, Nashville Tennessean, Smart Money Magazine, TV stations in Knoxville, Asheville, Nashville, Travel Channel, TLC and CMT.*

Certificate may be used: Monday-Thursday, November-May.

Texas

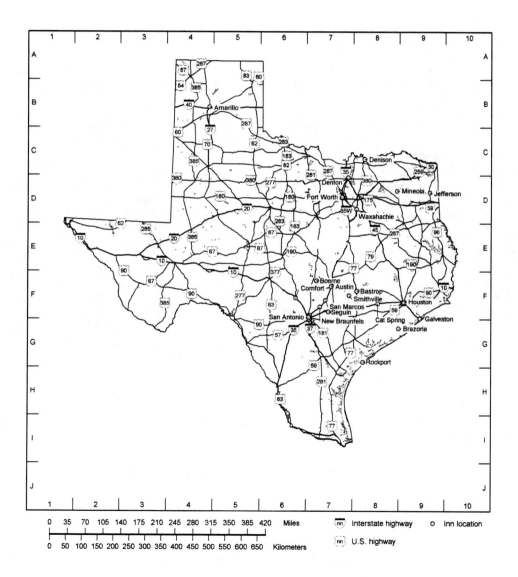

0   35 70 105 140 175 210 245 280 315 350 385 420   Miles

0   50 100 150 200 250 300 350 400 450 500 550 600 650   Kilometers

nn̄ Interstate highway	o Inn location
nn U.S. highway	

Boerne   *F7*

Paniolo Ranch Bed & Breakfast Spa

1510 FM 473
Boerne, TX 78006
(830)324-6666 (866)726-4656 Fax:(830)324-6665
Internet: www.paniol.ranch.com
E-mail: paniolo@paniolranch.com

Circa 2002. Paniolo Ranch Bed & Breakfast Spa is a hundred-acre ranch And romantic resort retreat in Boerne, Texas. Surrounded by Texas Hill Country, Hawaiian spa luxuries blend with Lone Star sensibilities to offer total relaxation. Swim in the pool overlooking the lake and hills, soak in the hot tub under the stars or pick fruit and veggies from the orchard and garden. Sophisticated amenities highlight the wide variety of upscale accommodations that include a generous in-room breakfast. Stay in a room with a covered porch and hot tub or lakeside patio. Browse for items to take home in one of the three gift shops and be sure to experience one of the treatments from the extensive spa menu.

Innkeeper(s): Judy Kennell. $230-295. 4 cottages with PB, 4 with HT, 1 two-bedroom suite, 1 conference room. Breakfast and snacks/refreshments included in rates. Types of meals: Full bkfst, veg bkfst, early coffee/tea, lunch, picnic lunch, wine, dinner and room service. Beds: KQT. Cable TV, VCR, DVD, reading lamp, stereo, refrigerator, ceiling fan, snack bar, clock radio, telephone, coffeemaker, turn-down service, desk, hot tub/spa, hair dryer, bathrobes, bath amenities, wireless Internet access and iron/ironing board in room. Central air. Fax, copier, spa, swimming, sauna, library, fireplace, laundry facility and gift shop on premises. Antiquing, art galleries, bicycling, canoeing/kayaking, fishing, golf, hiking, horseback riding, live theater, museums, parks, shopping, tennis, water sports and wineries nearby.

Location: Country.

Publicity: *Texas Monthly Magazine, Texas Highways Magazine and Directions Magazine.*

Certificate may be used: Sunday-Thursday only.

Cat Spring   *F8*

BlissWood Bed & Breakfast

13300 Lehmann Legacy Ln
Cat Spring, TX 78933
(713)301-3235
Internet: www.blisswood.net
E-mail: carol@blisswood.net

Surrounded by a tranquil country setting, this working ranch graces more than 650 acres, located just one hour west of Houston. Exotic animals abound from American bison and Corriente cattle to llamas and camels. Picnic at the gazebo looking out on Enchanted Lake, ride a horse across the meadows and creeks, try catch and release bass fishing or sit by a pond watching ducks, swans and geese glide by. A seven-circuit labyrinth is in the Mystical Forest. A variety of accommodations include the two-story Texas Farmhouse, Log Cabin or Lehmann House with a clawfoot, antique tin or Jacuzzi tub. The Dog Trot House includes a pool, deck, patio and fireplace. Stay in the secluded Writer's Cabin secluded among the live oaks. Enjoy the smoke-free environment and a deluxe continental breakfast.

Innkeeper(s): Carol Davis. $169-239. 20 rooms, 15 with PB, 3 with FP, 1 with HT, 2 with WP, 8 cottages, 10 guest houses, 2 cabins. Breakfast included in rates. Types of meals: Cont, veg bkfst, gourmet lunch, picnic lunch, wine and gourmet dinner. Beds: KQT. TV, reading lamp, CD player, refrigerator, ceiling fan, clock radio, coffeemaker, some with hot tub/spa, some with fireplace, hair dryer, bathrobes, bath amenities and iron/ironing board in

room. Central air. VCR, fax, spa, stable, bicycles, pet boarding, telephone, laundry facility and gift shop on premises. Limited handicap access. Antiquing, bicycling, fishing, golf, hiking, horseback riding, live theater, parks, shopping, wineries, Trapshooting and Gourmet restaurant nearby.

Location: Country.

Publicity: *Southern Living Magazine.*

Certificate may be used: Sunday–Thursday or anytime at last minute based on availability. NO holidays or antique week.

Denison   *C8*

Inn of Many Faces Victorian Bed & Breakfast

412 W Morton St
Denison, TX 75020-2422
(903)465-4639
Internet: www.innofmanyfaces.com
E-mail: theinn@sbcglobal.net

Circa 1897. Resplendently sitting in the middle of towering pecan trees on two wooded acres, this restored Queen Anne Victorian provides rest and relaxation. A collection of whimsical faces are displayed throughout the house and gardens reflecting its name, Inn of Many Faces. Themed guest bedrooms offer spacious accommodations. The Katy Room is a romantic retreat dressed in toile that boasts a fireplace, Jacuzzi tub and shower. The Texoma room features a plush king-size bed, fireplace and sitting area with two-person Jacuzzi and shower. All the rooms include a large gourmet breakfast with fresh fruit, baked entree, breakfast meats and breads. The B&B is located four short blocks from antique shops and art galleries on Main Street and near Lake Texoma for boating, fishing and golfing.

Innkeeper(s): Charlie & Gloria Morton. $99-149. 4 rooms with PB, 2 with FP, 3 with WP, 1 conference room. Breakfast and snacks/refreshments included in rates. Types of meals: Full gourmet bkfst, veg bkfst and early coffee/tea. Beds: KQD. Cable TV, VCR, DVD, reading lamp, CD player, ceiling fan, clock radio, most with hot tub/spa, hair dryer, bathrobes, bath amenities, wireless Internet access, iron/ironing board and fireplace in room. Central air. Spa, library, parlor games, telephone, fireplace, gift shop and massages available on premises. Antiquing, art galleries, fishing, golf, hiking, horseback riding, live theater, museums, parks, shopping, sporting events, tennis, water sports, wineries, Casino, Bird watching and airport nearby.

Location: City.

Publicity: *Dallas Morning News, Texas Highways, Herald Democrat, McKinney Courier-Gazette, Frisco Style and Texoma Living.*

Certificate may be used: Anytime, Sunday-Thursday.

Fort Worth   *D7*

Texas White House B&B

1417 8th Ave
Fort Worth, TX 76104-4111
(817)923-3597 (800)279-6491 Fax:(817)923-0410
Internet: www.texaswhitehouse.com
E-mail: txwhitehou@aol.com

Circa 1910. A spacious encircling veranda shaded by an old elm tree, graces the front of this two-story home located within five minutes of downtown, TCU, the zoo and many other area attractions. The inn's parlor and living room with fireplace and gleaming hardwood floors are the most popular spots for relaxing when not lingering on the porch. Guest rooms are equipped with phones and television, and early morning coffee is provided before the inn's full breakfast at a time convenient to your personal schedule. Suites include hot tub, sauna and fireplace.

Baked egg casseroles and freshly made breads are served to your room or in the dining room. The owners are Fort Worth experts and keep abreast of cultural attractions and are happy to help with reservations and planning. The inn is popular with business travelers — secretarial services are available, etc. — during the week and appealing to couples on weekends.

Innkeeper(s): Grover & Jamie McMains. $129-249. 5 rooms with PB, 1 with FP, 2 suites, 1 conference room. Breakfast and snacks/refreshments included in rates. Types of meals: Full gourmet bkfst, early coffee/tea and room service. Beds: KQ. Cable TV, VCR, DVD, reading lamp, CD player, refrigerator, ceiling fan, clock radio, telephone, coffeemaker, turn-down service, desk, some with hot tub/spa, some with fireplace, hair dryer, bathrobes, wireless Internet access, iron/ironing board and one suite with dry heat sauna in room. Central air. Fax, copier, library, laundry facility and gift shop on premises. Limited handicap access. Antiquing, art galleries, golf, live theater, museums, parks, Sundance Square, Stockyards, Zoo, Log Cabin Village and Miniature train nearby.

Location: City.

Certificate may be used: Sunday-Thursday, no holidays. Nights must be consecutive; May 1-Aug. 31. Anytime, Last Minute-Based on Availability.

Houston   F9

Palms on West Main

807 W Main St #1
Houston, TX 77006
(713)522-7987 Fax:(713)522-3150
Internet: www.palmsonwestmain.com
E-mail: meadeandsmith@pdq.net

Circa 1914. Centrally located in Houston's historic museum district, this early 20th-century Dutch Colonial home can be found in the same neighborhood where Howard Hughes grew up, possessing unique architecture and mature trees. The inn's host, Tom Meade, a member of the Greater Houston Preservation Alliance, has restored many original designs of the house and enjoys providing ample information on Houston's history and attractions. Private access to each suite is located off the "Key West" deck, filled with tropical plants and fountains. Fireplaces and individual design distinguish each room. With many activities in the Houston area, guests get prepared each morning with a hearty breakfast.

Innkeeper(s): Tom Meade, Rick Smith. $99. 3 rooms, 2 with FP, 3 suites. Breakfast included in rates. Types of meals: Full bkfst. Beds: KQ. Cable TV, VCR, reading lamp, ceiling fan, telephone and desk in room. Air conditioning. Fax, bicycles and fireplace on premises. Amusement parks, antiquing, art galleries, bicycling, golf, live theater, museums, parks, shopping and sporting events nearby.

Location: City.

Certificate may be used: Anytime, subject to availability.

Robin's Nest

4104 Greeley St
Houston, TX 77006-5609
(713)528-5821 (800)622-8343 Fax:(713)528-6727
Internet: www.therobin.com
E-mail: robin@therobin.com

Circa 1898. Robin's Nest adorns the museum and arts district, known as The Montrose, in Houston, Texas. This circa 1898 two-story Queen Anne Victorian is much like an intimate European hotel but with a touch of funky American flair. Relax on the wraparound porch or in the parlor. Upstairs there is a tea/coffee station. Inviting guest bedrooms offer a sweet respite from the day's adventures. Whirlpool suites boast private entrances and porches. Murder mystery parties and wed-

dings are popular events at this bed and breakfast inn. Situated near downtown theaters and gourmet restaurants, Galveston and Johnson Space Center are about an hour away.

Innkeeper(s): Robin Smith, Jessica Whatley. $99-240. 9 rooms with PB, 2 with WP, 4 total suites, including 1 two-bedroom suite, 1 conference room. Breakfast included in rates. Types of meals: Full gourmet bkfst, veg bkfst, early coffee/tea and Late Risers: Always something in the kitchen. Help yourself. Beds: QT. Cable TV, DVD, reading lamp, refrigerator, ceiling fan, clock radio, telephone, coffeemaker, desk, some with hot tub/spa, hair dryer, bathrobes, bath amenities, wireless Internet access, iron/ironing board and Three suites have full kitchens in room. Central air. Fax, copier and laundry facility on premises. Antiquing, art galleries, beach, fishing, golf, hiking, live theater, museums, parks, shopping, sporting events, tennis, water sports, Downtown, The Museum District and Texas Medical Center nearby.

Location: City. Museum District, Texas Medical Center, Downtown, Rice, Univ. St. Thomas.

Publicity: *Houston Home and Garden, Houston Business Journal, Woman's Day, Houston Metropolitan, Houston Post, Southern Living, Texas Monthly, Houston Chronicle, Inside Houston, Houston Press ("Best Houston B&B" 2002) and Citisearch Audience Winner 2007.*

"Fanciful and beautiful, comfortable and happy. We saw a whole new side of Houston, thanks to you."

Certificate may be used: Sunday-Thursday, all year, Anytime, Last Minute-Based on Availability, Anytime, based on availability.

Jefferson   D9

McKay House

306 E Delta St
Jefferson, TX 75657-2026
(903)665-7322 (800)468-2627
Internet: www.mckayhouse.com
E-mail: innkeeper@mckayhouse.com

Circa 1851. For more than 15 years, the McKay House has been widely acclaimed for its high standards, personal service and satisfied guests. Both Lady Bird Johnson and Alex Haley

have enjoyed the gracious Southern hospitality offered at the McKay House. The Greek Revival cottage features a front porch with pillars. Heart-of-pine floors, 14-foot ceilings and documented wallpapers complement antique furnishings. A full "gentleman's" breakfast is served in the garden conservatory by the gable fireplace. Orange French toast, home-baked muffins and shirred eggs are a few of the house specialties. In each of the seven bedchambers you find a Victorian nightgown and old-fashioned nightshirt laid out for you. History abounds in Jefferson, considered the "Williamsburg of the Southwest."

Innkeeper(s): Hugh Lewis & Darla McCorkle. $66-149. 7 rooms with PB, 5 with FP, 1 two-bedroom suite, 1 cottage, 1 conference room. Breakfast, snacks/refreshments, hors d'oeuvres and wine included in rates. Types of meals: Full gourmet bkfst, veg bkfst, early coffee/tea, lunch, picnic lunch, dinner and room service. Beds: KQDT. Modem hook-up, data port, cable TV, VCR, DVD, reading lamp, stereo, refrigerator, ceiling fan, snack bar, clock radio, telephone, desk, voice mail, most with fireplace, hair dryer, bath amenities, wireless Internet access and iron/ironing board in room. Central air. Fax, library and parlor games on premises. Handicap access. Antiquing, art galleries, bicycling, canoeing/kayaking, fishing, golf, hiking, horseback riding, live theater, museums, parks, shopping, sporting events, water sports and wineries nearby.

Location: City, country.

Publicity: *Southern Accents, Dallas Morning News, Country Home and Bride.*

"The facilities of the McKay House are exceeded only by the service and dedication of the owners."

Certificate may be used: Sunday-Thursday, not including spring break or festivals/holidays; space available, reserved one week in advance please.

The Hale House Inn

702 S Line St
Jefferson, TX 75657-2224
(903)665-9955 Fax:(903)665-7616
Internet: www.thehalehouseinn.com
E-mail: mystay@thehalehouseinn.com

Circa 1880. Relaxation comes easy at The Hale House Inn Bed & Breakfast, an historic Greek Revival with Victorian accents and antiques. Take a short stroll to downtown Jefferson, Texas, originally known for being a bustling riverport. Relax on a southern-style veranda, two porches and a gazebo amid flowers and shade trees. Enjoy refreshments and treats in either parlor, one with a fireplace and the other with a big-screen TV and DVD player. Afternoon snacks are available in the library. Themed guest rooms boast a variety of pleasing choices. Stay in a room that overlooks the park or gardens. One room has a fireplace and most feature a clawfoot tub and shower. Indulge in a hearty Texas Gentleman's breakfast in the dining room, side porch, or gazebo.

Innkeeper(s): Timm and Karen Jackson. $90-145. 6 rooms with PB, 1 with FP, 1 conference room. Breakfast and snacks/refreshments included in rates. Types of meals: Country bkfst, early coffee/tea, afternoon tea and Texas Gentleman's Breakfast. Beds: KQD. TV, VCR, reading lamp, refrigerator, ceiling fan, snack bar, clock radio, telephone, hair dryer, bathrobes, bath amenities, wireless Internet access, iron/ironing board and Satellite TV in room. Central air. DVD, fax, copier, bicycles, library, pet boarding, parlor games, fireplace, gift shop and Big screen HD TV in common area on premises. Antiquing, art galleries, bicycling, canoeing/kayaking, fishing, golf, hiking, horseback riding, live theater, museums, parks, shopping, sporting events and water sports nearby.

Location: City, country.

Certificate may be used: Sunday-Thursday, excluding spring break, local festivals and holidays. On space available basis when reserved one week in advance.

Mineola   D8

Munzesheimer Manor

202 N Newsom St
Mineola, TX 75773-2134
(903)569-6634 (888)569-6634 Fax:(903)569-9940
Internet: www.munzesheimer.com
E-mail: innkeeper@munzesheimer.com

Circa 1898. Let time stand still while staying at this historic 1898 Victorian home that was built entirely with pine and cedar. Its classic features include many bay windows, large rooms with high ceilings and original fireplaces with mantles. Sip lemonade on the spacious wraparound porch with wicker furniture and rockers. Relax in one of the two inviting parlors. Choose an upstairs guest bedroom in the main house or an adjacent ground-floor cottage room with a private entrance. The pleasing accommodations feature central heat and air conditioning and American and English antiques. Soak in a clawfoot tub with bath salts before sleeping in a vintage nightgown or nightshirt. A gourmet breakfast is served on china and silver in the formal dining room.

Innkeeper(s): Bob & Sherry Murray. $90-120. 7 rooms with PB, 3 with FP, 3 cottages. Breakfast included in rates. Types of meals: Full bkfst and early coffee/tea. Beds: KQDT. Reading lamp, refrigerator and ceiling fan in room. Air conditioning. VCR, fax, telephone and fireplace on premises. Antiquing, golf, live theater, parks, shopping and tennis nearby.

Publicity: *Country, Dallas Morning News, Southern Bride, Houston Chronicle, San Antonion News and Southern Living.*

Certificate may be used: January-December, Monday-Thursday and will offer room upgrade if available.

New Braunfels   F7

Acorn Hill Bed & Breakfast

250 School House
New Braunfels, TX 78132-2458
(830)907-2597 (800)525-4618 Fax:(830)964-5486
Internet: www.acornhillbb.com
E-mail: acornhill@acornhillbb.com

Circa 1910. Enjoy wandering the five scenic acres of gardens and fields while staying at this year-round bed & breakfast with a log house that was originally a school and themed cottages conveniently located only five minutes from the Guadalupe River and downtown Gruene. Overlook the hills from a porch rocker. Play the converted pump organ and make calls from an antique phone booth. Suites and cottages feature fireplaces and some boast Jacuzzi tubs. Indulge in an all-you-can-eat multi-course breakfast buffet in the log house dining room. Swim in the in-ground pool or soak in the relaxing hot tub. Browse through the antique and gift shop for treasures to take home. Barbecue pits and picnic tables are provided throughout the grounds. The Victorian Garden is an ideal setting for weddings.

Innkeeper(s): Richard & Pam Thomas. $100-175. 6 rooms with PB, 6 with FP, 3 suites, 3 cottages, 1 conference room. Breakfast included in rates. Types of meals: Country bkfst, veg bkfst, early coffee/tea and picnic lunch. Beds: KQ. TV, VCR, reading lamp, refrigerator, ceiling fan, clock radio, coffeemaker, desk, hot tub/spa and fireplace in room. Central air. Fax, spa, swimming, parlor games, telephone and gift shop on premises. Limited handicap access. Amusement parks, antiquing, art galleries, bicycling, canoeing/kayaking, fishing, golf, hiking, horseback riding, live theater, museums, parks, shopping, sporting events, tennis, water sports and wineries nearby.

Location: Country.

Certificate may be used: Nov. 1-March 1, Sunday-Thursday only.

Firefly Inn

120 Naked Indian Trail
New Braunfels, TX 78132-1865
(830)905-3989 (800)687-2887
Internet: www.fireflyinn.com
E-mail: info@fireflyinn.com

Circa 1983. Romance the Texas Hill Country in New Braunfels, Canyon Lake, Gruene near the Guadalupe River. The Country Victorian decor and quality handcrafted furniture provide comfort and style. Each guest suite offers several spacious rooms, including a kitchen. To add to the pampering, an excellent breakfast is delivered to the door each morning, ready to satisfy. Spectacular views can be seen from the private deck or porch overlooking the meadows. Picnic tables in the courtyard, small ponds with waterfalls and a hot tub surrounded by mountain hills and fresh air are pleasurable treats to enjoy. A small intimate wedding in the gazebo is complete with a pastor available to perform the ceremony.

Innkeeper(s): Jack & Kathy Tipton. $125-175. 4 cottages, 4 suites. Breakfast included in rates. Types of meals: Full bkfst. Beds: QT. TV, reading lamp, refrigerator, ceiling fan, coffeemaker, hot tub/spa and iron/ironing board in room. Air conditioning. VCR, spa, telephone and laundry facility on premises. Amusement parks, antiquing, beach, canoeing/kayaking, fishing, golf, live theater, museums, parks, shopping, tennis, water sports, wineries, Schlitterbahn, Natural Bridge Caverns, Sea World and Fiesta Texas nearby.

Location: Country. Texas hill country.

Publicity: *San Antonio Wedding Pages 2002 & 2003, Dallas Morning News, San Antonio Express and "Show Me Texas."*

Certificate may be used: Sept. 15-February, Sunday-Thursday, excluding holidays and special events.

Gruene Mansion Inn

1275 Gruene Rd
New Braunfels, TX 78130-3003
(830)629-2641 Fax:(830)629-7375
Internet: www.gruenemansioninn.com
E-mail: frontdesk@gruenemansioninn.com

Circa 1872. Overlook the Guadalupe River from the porches of this Victorian mansion located on three acres in Hill Country, adjacent to the state's oldest dance hall. The inn has been designated a Historic Landmark and is listed in the National Register. The Mansion, barns, corn crib, carriage house and other outbuildings have all been refurbished to offer quiet and private guest bedrooms, cottages and guest houses. A rustic Victorian elegance is the ambiance and style of decor that blends antiques, fine fabrics and wall coverings. Savor breakfast entrees that boast a Mexican flair and flavor. For a day trip, visit the Alamo, 30 miles away.

Innkeeper(s): Judi & Cecil Eager/Jackie Skinner. $165-299. 31 rooms, 30 with PB, 2 two-bedroom suites, 1 cottage, 1 conference room. Breakfast included in rates. Types of meals: Full bkfst and snacks/refreshments. Beds: KQDT. Cable TV, reading lamp, refrigerator, ceiling fan, clock radio, coffeemaker, some with fireplace, hair dryer, bath amenities, wireless Internet access and iron/ironing board in room. Central air. VCR, fax, copier, telephone, gift shop, porch with rocking chairs looking at Guadalupe River and gift shop on premises. Handicap access. Amusement parks, antiquing, art galleries, bicycling, canoeing/kayaking, fishing, golf, hiking, horseback riding, live theater, museums, parks, shopping, sporting events, tennis, water sports, wineries and oldest dance hall in Texas nearby.

Location: City, country, waterfront. Hill country of Texas.

Publicity: *San Antonio Express News, Austin American Statesmen and New Braunfels Herald Zietung.*

Certificate may be used: January-February, Sunday-Thursday, Sunday Hauses only; September, Sunday-Thursday, Sunday Hauses only.

Lamb's Rest Inn

1385 Edwards Blvd
New Braunfels, TX 78132-4055
(830)609-3932 (888)609-3932 Fax:(830)620-0864
Internet: www.lambsrestinn.com
E-mail: info@lambsrestinn.com

Circa 1970. Between Austin and San Antonio on the Guadalupe River, stands this inn with large decks that overlook the river. Peace and tranquility are at the heart of guests' experience at the Lambs Rest, where they can hear the sounds of birds and wildlife during the day and draw up close to the crackling fire at night. Two large decks and a garden terraced to the river invites relaxation with fountains, ponds, herb gardens, large oaks and giant cypress trees. The six accommodations include one suite and one cottage. A full gourmet breakfast is served in the dining room or on the veranda overlooking the river. Breakfast fare includes such delights as Orange Frosty Frappe, Vancluse Eggs with asparagus and red pepper sauce, cheese grits, sausage, and a variety of homemade breads and biscuits served with the inn's special honeys, jams and sauces.

During the spring and summer, Bluebonnets and other Texas wildflowers abound in nearby breathtaking fields. Between the quiet Comal River and the rapids of the Guadalupe River, guests can enjoy a variety of water sports including kayaking, rafting, canoeing, tubing and fly-fishing.

Innkeeper(s): Alyson. $135-250. 6 rooms with PB, 6 with FP, 1 two-bedroom suite, 1 cottage. Breakfast included in rates. Types of meals: Full gourmet bkfst and early coffee/tea. Beds: KQD. Cable TV, reading lamp, ceiling fan, clock radio, coffeemaker, desk, bathrobes and wireless Internet access in room. Central air. Fax, copier, spa, swimming, library, fireplace and gift shop on premises. Amusement parks, antiquing, bicycling, canoeing/kayaking, fishing, golf, hiking, parks, shopping, tennis, water sports and wineries nearby.

Location: Waterfront.

Publicity: *Dallas Morning News, Fort Worth Star Telegram and Herald.*

Certificate may be used: Sept. 15-March 1, excluding holidays, Sunday-Thursday in Grapes Inn, Mulberrie Court or Quilly's Antiques.

Rockport   G8

Anthony's By The Sea

732 S Pearl St
Rockport, TX 78382-2420
(361)729-6100 (800)460-2557 Fax:(361)729-2450
Internet: www.anthonysbythesea.com
E-mail: info@anthonysbythesea.com

Circa 1997. This quiet, casual retreat is hidden away beneath huge oak trees, near the ocean in an area known as the Texas Riviera. Choose from comfortably furnished single rooms or suites with private baths and sitting areas. Separate guest house has a fully equipped kitchen, spacious living area and sleeps up to six, making it ideal for families and small groups. A sparkling pool and covered lanai provide the most popular areas for relaxing or enjoying the gourmet breakfasts. Located within walking distance of Rockport Beach, a variety of water activities are available, as well as local shopping, restaurants and museums.

Innkeeper(s): Smitty & Beth. $105. 6 rooms, 4 with PB, 1 suite, 1 guest house, 1 conference room. Breakfast included in rates. Types of meals: Full gourmet bkfst and early coffee/tea. Beds: KQD. Cable TV, VCR, reading lamp, refrigerator, ceiling fan and clock radio in room. Central air. Fax, swimming, pet boarding, parlor games, laundry facility and pets allowed on premises. Limited handicap access.

Location: City, ocean community.

Publicity: *New York Times.*

Certificate may be used: Anytime, November-March, subject to availability.

San Antonio   F7

Brackenridge House

230 Madison
San Antonio, TX 78204-1320
(210) 271-3442 (877) 271-3442 Fax:(210)226-3139
Internet: www.brackenridgehouse.com
E-mail: brackenridgebnb@aol.com

Circa 1901. As the first bed and breakfast in San Antonio's historic King William District, the Brackenridge House Bed and Breakfast has been pampering guests for 20 years. Each of the guest rooms is individually decorated. Clawfoot tubs, iron beds and a private veranda are a few of the items that guests might discover. Several rooms include kitchenettes. Many of San Antonio's interesting sites are nearby. The San Antonio Mission Trail begins just a block away, and trolleys will take you to the Alamo, the River Walk, convention center and more.

Coffeehouses, restaurants and antique stores all are within walking distance. Ideal for romantic getaways, family reunions or just for fun escapes.

100 years in historic King William, 2 blocks from the River and 5 blocks from downtown San Antonio.

Innkeeper(s): Lily and Roland Lopez. $109-300. 5 rooms with PB, 3 suites. Breakfast included in rates. Types of meals: Full gourmet bkfst and early coffee/tea. Beds: KQ. Modem hook-up, data port, cable TV, VCR, DVD, reading lamp, CD player, refrigerator, ceiling fan, clock radio, telephone, coffeemaker, desk, hair dryer, bathrobes, bath amenities, wireless Internet access, iron/ironing board, microwave, iron, ironing board, hair dryer and wireless Internet connection in room. Central air. Fax, copier, spa, swimming, library and parlor games on premises. Amusement parks, antiquing, fishing, golf, live theater, parks, shopping, sporting events and tennis nearby.

Location: City. 1/2 mile to Alamo & Riverwalk.

Publicity: *San Antonio Express News, Huntington Beach Herald, New York Times and Seattle Times.*

"Innkeeper was very nice, very helpful."

Certificate may be used: Monday-Thursday, June-September; January and February no holidays, last minute based on projected availability.

Christmas House B&B

2307 McCullough
San Antonio, TX 78212
(210)737-2786 (800)268-4187 Fax:(210)734-5712
Internet: www.christmashousebnb.com
E-mail: christmashsb@earthlink.net

Circa 1908. Located in Monte Vista historic district, this two-story white inn has a natural wood balcony built over the front porch. The window trim is in red and green, starting the Christmas theme of the inn. (There's a Christmas tree decorated all year long.) Guest rooms open out to pecan-shaded balconies. The Victorian Bedroom offers pink and mauve touches mixed with the room's gold and black decor. The Blue & Silver Room is handicap accessible and is on the first floor. Antique furnishings on the inn are available for sale.

Innkeeper(s): Penny & Grant Estes. $85-125. 4 rooms with PB, 1 suite. Breakfast and snacks/refreshments included in rates. Types of meals: Full bkfst, veg bkfst and early coffee/tea. Beds: KQ. Reading lamp, ceiling fan, clock radio and desk in room. Central air. TV, fax, library, parlor games, fireplace, laundry facility and ADA room on premises. Handicap access. Amusement parks, antiquing, art galleries, bicycling, golf, live theater, museums, parks and shopping nearby.

Location: City.

Publicity: *Fort Worth Star Telegram.*

"What a treat to rise to the sweet smell of candied pecans and a tasty breakfast."

Certificate may be used: Sunday-Thursday, not on holidays or during Fiesta.

San Marcos   F7

Crystal River Inn and Day Spa

326 W Hopkins St
San Marcos, TX 78666-4404
(512)396-3739 (888)396-3739 Fax:(512)396-6311
Internet: www.crystalriverinn.com
E-mail: info@crystalriverinn.com

Circa 1883. Tall white columns accent this Greek Revival inn that features a fireside dining room with a piano and wet bar. Innkeepers encourage a varied itinerary, including sleeping

until noon and having breakfast in bed to participating in a hilarious murder mystery. Rock the afternoon away on the veranda or curl up by the fireplace in a guest bedroom by the headwaters of crystal-clear San Marcos River. Clawfoot tubs, four-poster and canopied beds add to the pleasing ambiance. Shop at the state's largest outlet mall that features more than 200 designer stores.

Innkeeper(s): Mike & Cathy Dillon. $110-175. 12 rooms with PB, 4 with FP, 4 two-bedroom suites, 1 cabin, 1 conference room. Breakfast included in rates. Types of meals: Full gourmet bkfst, early coffee/tea, lunch, picnic lunch and dinner. Beds: KQDT. Cable TV, VCR, reading lamp, stereo, refrigerator, ceiling fan, clock radio, telephone, coffeemaker, desk, some with fireplace, hair dryer, bathrobes, bath amenities, wireless Internet access, iron/ironing board, fresh flowers, fruit, amenity baskets with many toiletries, vintage magazines and sound machines in room. Central air. Fax, copier, library, child care, laundry facility, gift shop, gardens, fish pond, veranda and 2 long-term stay apartments on premises. Handicap access. Amusement parks, antiquing, bicycling, canoeing/kayaking, fishing, golf, hiking, live theater, museums, parks, shopping, sporting events, tennis, wineries, pools and river for water sports nearby.

Location: City. Small town.

Publicity: *Texas Monthly, USA Today, Country Inns, Southern Living, Dallas Morning News, Houston Chronicle, Boston Globe, Texas Highways and Continental Airlines flight magazine.*

"Thanks for a smashing good time! We really can't remember having more fun anywhere, ever!"

Certificate may be used: Sunday-Thursday, year-round, except for holiday weeks (Thanksgiving, Memorial Day, July 4th, etc.).

Seguin   F7

Mosheim Mansion

409 North Austin Street
Seguin, TX 78155
(830)372-9905
Internet: www.mosheimmansion.com
E-mail: info@mosheimmansion.com

Circa 1898. Mosheim Mansion graces the Seguin historic district, just three blocks from town square. This luxury bed and breakfast is just 30 minutes from San Antonio and one hour from Austin. Stroll among the gardenia and hibiscus blooms in the gardens or under a palm tree by the fountain. Sit with a snack or beverage on the two-story porch. Complimentary wine is offered at check-in. A guest refrigerator and a microwave are provided for guest use. Stay in a guest room or a suite that features a double whirlpool tub and a fireplace as well as upscale amenities. Linger over a satisfying breakfast each morning before exploring the surrounding areas. Room services are available. Ask about scheduling spa amenities.

Innkeeper(s): Carol Hirschi. $89-259. 6 rooms with PB, 3 with FP, 4 with WP, 2 conference rooms. Breakfast, snacks/refreshments, wine, Full breakfast, Snacks, Beverages including homemade cookies and To-order breakfast served during window of several hours so guests can eat when they want included in rates. Types of meals: Full gourmet bkfst, veg bkfst, early coffee/tea, gourmet lunch, afternoon tea, hors d'oeuvres, gourmet dinner, room service and Anything other than a full breakfast from menu or complimentary snacks and wine must be arranged in advance. Private dinners in room or fireside in a private dining room available if arranged in advance. Beds: KQ. TV, reading lamp, ceiling fan, some with fireplace, hair dryer, bathrobes, bath amenities, wireless Internet access, iron/ironing board, Egyptian cotton sheets, Sumptuous towels, High quality toiletries, Direct TV, Morning coffee service by request, Complimentary wine and spa services available in-room. in room. Central air. DVD, fax, copier, spa, parlor games, telephone, Off-street parking, Refrigerator, Microwave for guest use, Private dining room by request, Catered lunches, special gourmet dinners by request and on premises. Amusement parks, antiquing, horseback riding, live theater, museums, shopping, sporting events, wineries, Waterpark, Dance hall, Live music, Sports bar, Historic sites, Tubing and Rafting nearby.

Location: City.

Certificate may be used: Sunday-Thursday excludes holidays and special events. Can be used on weekends only with special permission of innkeeper. Reservations required, subject to availability.

Smithville   F7

Katy House Bed & Breakfast

201 Ramona St.
Smithville, TX 78957-0803
(512)237-4262 (800)843-5289 Fax:(512)237-2239
Internet: www.katyhouse.com
E-mail: bblalock@austin.rr.com

Circa 1909. Shaded by tall trees, the Katy House's Italianate exterior is graced by an arched portico over the bay-windowed living room. Long leaf pine floors, pocket doors and a graceful stairway accent the completely refurbished interior. The inn is decorated almost exclusively in American antique oak and railroad memorabilia. A 1909 caboose is being restored to be used as a guest room. Historic Main Street is one  block away with a fine collection of antique shops. Guests usually come back from walking tours with pockets full of pecans found around town. Smithville was the hometown location for the movie "Hope Floats."

Innkeeper(s): Bruce & Sallie Blalock. $95-160. 5 rooms with PB, 4 with FP, 1 with WP, 1 suite, 2 cottages. Breakfast and snacks/refreshments included in rates. Types of meals: Full bkfst, early coffee/tea, picnic lunch and Fresh baked cookies available each evening. Beds: QT. Cable TV, VCR, reading lamp, refrigerator, ceiling fan, snack bar, clock radio, telephone, coffeemaker, desk, most with fireplace, hair dryer, bath amenities, wireless Internet access and iron/ironing board in room. Air conditioning. Fax, bicycles, library, gift shop and Pet Friendly in certain rooms on premises. Antiquing, art galleries, bicycling, canoeing/kayaking, fishing, golf, hiking, horseback riding, live theater, museums, parks, shopping, Two beautiful State Parks and Dog Park nearby.

Location: City. Small town.

Publicity: *Dallas Morning News, San Antonio Express, Houston Chronicle, Austin Business Journal Magazine "A", Heart of the Pines Magazine, Texas Country Reporter, Hope Floats, starring Sandra Bullock and was filmed in Smithville.*

Certificate may be used: Sunday-Thursday, except holidays.

Utah

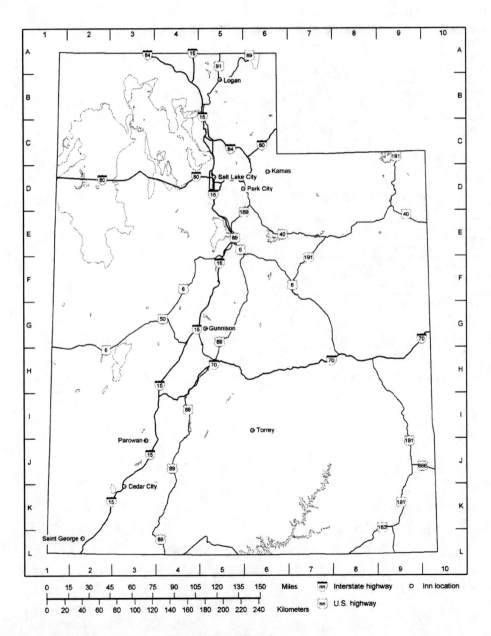

		Miles
Interstate highway	o	Inn location
U.S. highway		

Cedar City   K3

Cherished Memories Bed & Breakfast

170 N. 400 W.
Cedar City, UT 84720
(435)586-0455 (866)867-6498
Internet: www.cherishedmemoriesbnb.com
E-mail: memories@cherishedmemoriesbnb.com

Circa 1906. Built in 1906 with adobe brick, trimmed in gingerbread and lattice, this Victorian home with high ceilings and original grain painting on interior wood is furnished with unusual pieces and distinctive antiques. It has been recently renovated to pamper and please. Relax and enjoy conversations on the spacious front and rear porches. Air-conditioned guest bedrooms are delightfully decorated and feature comfortable Queen pillow top beds. After a restful sleep, linger over a satisfying breakfast in the elegant formal dining room. Historic downtown Cedar City and Utah Shakespearean Festival are just two blocks away. Plan a scenic day trip to Bryce Canyon or Zion National Parks.

Innkeeper(s): Larry & Rae Overson. $95-135. 4 rooms with PB. Breakfast and snacks/refreshments included in rates. Types of meals: Full gourmet bkfst, veg bkfst and early coffee/tea. Beds: QD. Reading lamp, ceiling fan, clock radio, hair dryer, bathrobes, bath amenities and iron/ironing board in room. Central air. TV, VCR, DVD, parlor games and telephone on premises. Limited handicap access. Antiquing, art galleries, bicycling, cross-country skiing, downhill skiing, fishing, golf, hiking, horseback riding, live theater, museums, parks, shopping, sporting events, tennis and water sports nearby.

Location: Country.

Certificate may be used: November to May.

Gunnison   G4

Gunnison Rose Inn Bed & Breakfast

10 E 100 S
Gunnison, UT 84634
(435)528-5499 Fax:(435)528-5497
Internet: www.gunnisonrose.com
E-mail: info@gunnisonrose.com

Gunnison Rose Inn Bed & Breakfast was originally known as the Christensen House and later the Gunnison Hotel. Located in Gunnison, Utah, this brick and adobe house was built by Theodore E. Christensen in the Italianate style. Various renovations have taken place, yet the square formal plan, hip roof with widow's walk, and front colonnade still remain. The original open double porch that stretched the full width of the home has been enclosed to accommodate two additional guest rooms with their own bathrooms. Relax on the ground-level porch enclosed with large vertical windows that wrap around the entire front which allows for a peaceful and intimate sitting area. After a generous continental-style breakfast, take time to explore the gorgeous scenery of the surrounding area.

Innkeeper(s): Michael & Cathrine Wozab. Call for rates. Call inn for details. Comprehensive Continental style breakfast included in rates. Types of meals: Cont plus, Available light refreshments: Coffee/Tea and home baked cookies. and. Beds: KQ. Cable TV, DVD, clock radio, turn-down service, some with hot tub/spa and wireless Internet access in room. Air conditioning. Fax, copier, library and fireplace on premises. Fishing, golf, hiking, horseback riding, parks, shopping, tennis, water sports and First class fitness center. Elk observation habitat nearby.

Location: Country.

Certificate may be used: January, March, May, August, September, November, Sunday-Thursday, subject to availability.

Kamas   D6

Woodland Farmhouse Inn

2602 E State Road # 35
Kamas, UT 84036-9660
(435) 783-2903 Fax:(435)783-2711
Internet: woodlandfarmhouseinn.com
E-mail: innkeeper@woodlandfarmhouseinn.com

Circa 1897. Feel refreshed at this high altitude country farmhouse on two acres in the fertile Uintah Mountain Valley of the Provo River just 25 minutes east of Park City, Utah and one hour east of Salt Lake City. Experience the friendly, relaxed atmosphere, comfortable furnishings with upscale amenities, and natural beauty. Soak in the outdoor hot tub on a quiet, starry night. Stay in a romantic guest suite in the historic main inn or spacious luxury accommodations in the South House. The Bunkhouse offers a more rustic and sturdy ambiance for families, fishermen and hunters. Savor a hearty home-style breakfast before embarking on the day's adventures. Recreational activities are plentiful. Explore the scenic area on snowshoes in the winter or ski at one of the first-class resorts nearby. Hike, bike run and rock climb the scenic trailheads of Mirror Lake in the summer.

Innkeeper(s): Sheri Marsing. $89-149. 5 two-bedroom and 1 three-bedroom suites, 1 cottage, 1 guest house. Breakfast and Upon request we will prepare a sack lunch ($8ea) that can withstand a snowmobile's vibration included in rates. Types of meals: Country bkfst, veg bkfst, early coffee/tea, We serve a full, hot country breakfast and "Cooks Choice". When possible we will take requests from our website menu. Breakfast-In-Bed is best served in "The Sandhill Crane Suite" and "The Loft" upon request. Beds: KQT. Modem hookup, TV, VCR, DVD, reading lamp, stereo, refrigerator, clock radio, telephone, coffeemaker, desk, hair dryer, bathrobes, bath amenities, wireless Internet access, iron/ironing board and Air Conditioning is generally not needed except for possibly a few weeks in mid-August. We are able to bring in air-conditioning units if the weather changes. We have an outdoor hot tub for star-gazing. Some suites have soaking tubs. The South House has a common fireplace in room. Fax, copier, spa, stable, parlor games, fireplace, laundry facility and Complimentary snowshoe use. Borrow from a good selection of DVD movies/free microwave popcorn on premises. Handicap access. Antiquing, bicycling, canoeing/kayaking, cross-country skiing, downhill skiing, fishing, golf, hiking, horseback riding, parks, shopping, water sports, Snowmobiling and Watercraft rentals nearby.

Location: Country, mountains.

Publicity: Wasatch Wave and Summit County Bee.

Certificate may be used: Off season Tuesday night special, March 31-April 30 and October 1-December 15.

Logan   B5

Seasons at the Riter Mansion

168 N 100 E
Logan, UT 84321-4610
(435)752-7727 (800)478-7459
Internet: www.theritermansion.com
E-mail: sales@theritermansion.com

Circa 1898. Located in the Logan Historic District, the white pillars and gabled entrance to this Georgian manor is a foretaste of an exceptional lodging experience. There is a third-floor ballroom and a reception area includes a glass conservatory with a baby grand piano. It opens to a large wraparound veranda and lush courtyard. Ask for The Library for book-lined walls, a draped four-poster queen-size bed, fireplace and whirlpool. If you prefer the bridal suite, otherwise known as The Master Suite, you'll enjoy leaded glass windows, a king bed, balcony, sitting porch and a bath with whirlpool tub. In the morning, the inn's full breakfast might include stuffed French toast with raspberry sauce, breakfast rolls and fruit.

Innkeeper(s): Arlette & John Michaelson. $99-169. 6 rooms with PB, 3 with FP, 3 suites, 1 conference room. Breakfast included in rates. Types of meals: Full bkfst. Beds: KQD. Cable TV, VCR, reading lamp, ceiling fan, clock radio, telephone and computer hookup in room. Air conditioning. Parlor games and fireplace on premises. Handicap access. Antiquing, cross-country skiing, downhill skiing, fishing, live theater, shopping, sporting events, water sports and opera festival nearby.

Location: City, mountains.

Certificate may be used: Oct. 1-April 30, Sunday-Thursday, subject to availability.

Parowan   J3

Victoria's Bed & Breakfast

94 North 100 East
Parowan, UT 84761
(435)477-0075 (866)477-9808 Fax:(435)477-0079
E-mail: info@utahretreat.com

Circa 1870. Revel in the gorgeous views of the surrounding mountains while staying at this 1870 Victorian home that sits at the base of Brian Head Ski Resort. Furnished with antiques that are easy to fall in love with, and each one is available to purchase and take home. Comfortable guest bedrooms and a suite feature pretty colors and pleasing amenities. Take the private entrance to Rhett's Room with a fireplace and double-headed shower. Aunt Pitty Pat's Suite features a soft green and blue décor with a sitting room. A hearty breakfast boasts favorites like homemade biscuits with country gravy, hash browns, sausage, bacon, muffins, cereal and yogurt. Winter sports are popular as well as hiking, biking, fishing and hunting. Stroll the well-maintained gardens and lawns and relax on the wraparound veranda.

Innkeeper(s): Greg & Vickie Hicks. $89-99. 4 rooms with PB, 1 with FP, 1 suite. Breakfast included in rates. Types of meals: Country bkfst, early coffee/tea and picnic lunch. Beds: KQ. Cable TV, reading lamp, ceiling fan, clock radio and fireplace in room. Central air. Fax, telephone and laundry facility on premises. Limited handicap access. Antiquing, bicycling, cross-country skiing, downhill skiing, fishing, golf, live theater and Shakespearean Festival nearby.

Location: At the base of Brian Head Ski Resort.

Certificate may be used: April 20-May 31, Sunday through Saturday; Sept.5-Nov. 15, Sunday through Saturday; Nov.16-April 19, Monday through Thursday; June2-Sept. 4, Monday through Thursday; subject to availability; Anytime, Last Minute-Based on Availability.

Saint George   L2

Green Gate Village Historic Inn

76 West Tabernacle
Saint George, UT 84770-3420
(435)628-6999 (800)350-6999 Fax:(435) 628-6989
Internet: www.greengatevillageinn.com
E-mail: stay@greengatevillageinn.com

Circa 1862. This is a cluster of nine restored pioneer homes all located within one block. The Bentley House has comfortable Victorian decor. The Orson Pratt House and the Tolley House are other choices, all carefully restored. The fifth house contains three bedrooms each with private bath, a kitchen, living room and two fireplaces. Six of the bedrooms have large whirlpool tubs.

Innkeeper(s): Ed & Lindy Sandstrom. $99-259. 15 rooms, 14 with PB, 8 with FP, 6 with WP, 7 total suites, including 4 two-bedroom suites, 3 cottages, 1 cabin, 2 conference rooms. Breakfast included in rates. Types of meals: Country bkfst, early coffee/tea, lunch, snacks/refreshments and room service. Restaurant on premises. Beds: KQT. Modern hook-up, data port, cable TV, VCR, DVD, reading lamp, refrigerator, clock radio, telephone, coffeemaker, desk, most with hot tub/spa, most with fireplace, hair dryer, bathrobes, bath amenities and iron/ironing board in room. Central air. Fax, copier, spa, swimming, library, parlor games, gift shop, 97-year-old General Store open Monday through Saturdays, closed Sunday and holidays on premises. Limited handicap access. Antiquing, art galleries, bicycling, canoeing/kayaking, downhill skiing, fishing, golf, hiking, horseback riding, live theater, museums, parks, shopping, sporting events and water sports nearby.

Location: City.

Certificate may be used: July, August, December, January, Sunday-Thursday, Except Holidays and Special Events. Free night shall be the 2nd contiguous night of the same stay by the same guest in the same room or suite.

Salt Lake City   D5

Ellerbeck Mansion B&B

140 North B St
Salt Lake City, UT 84103-2482
(801)355-2500 (800)966-8364 Fax:(801)530-0938
Internet: www.ellerbeckbedandbreakfast.com
E-mail: ellerbeckmansion@qwestoffice.net

Circa 1892. Pleasantly located in the city's downtown historic district, this Victorian inn has been renovated for modern comfort and lovingly restored with original moldings, hardwood floors and stained glass. Impressive fireplaces can be found in the splendid main floor and upstairs galleries as well as in several of the six guest bedrooms. Different seasonal motifs adorn the bedrooms, so every day is a holiday in Christmas Wishes, complete with a sleigh bed. Autumn Winds and Spring Breeze can serve as an ideal suite for families. Enjoy a continental breakfast that is delivered to each room at an agreed-upon time. After exploring the local sites and nearby attractions, the turndown service, evening chocolates and complimentary soft drinks are welcome additions.

Innkeeper(s): Debbie Spencer. $119-169. 6 rooms with PB, 3 with FP, 1 conference room. Breakfast and snacks/refreshments included in rates. Types of meals: Full bkfst. Beds: KQ. Cable TV, reading lamp, clock radio, telephone, turn-down service, some with fireplace and wireless Internet access in room. Central air. DVD, fax, copier and library on premises. Amusement parks, antiquing, art galleries, bicycling, canoeing/kayaking, cross-country skiing, downhill skiing, fishing, golf, hiking, horseback riding, live theater, museums, parks, shopping, sporting events, tennis, water sports and Historic Temple Square nearby.

Location: City.

Publicity: *Hidden Utah, Delta Sky Magazine (Feb, 2002) and HGTV House Hunters.*

Certificate may be used: Sunday-Wednesday except for black-out periods and holidays. Cannot be used with any other discount or coupons.

Haxton Manor

943 East South Temple
Salt Lake City, UT 84102
(801)363-4646 (877)930-4646 Fax:(801)363-4686
Internet: www.haxtonmanor.com
E-mail: innkeepers@haxtonmanor.com

Circa 1906. Built by pioneers, this historic inn prominently sits in the distinct Avenues District. Victorian splendor is reflected in the gables and wraparound porch. The authentic Boar's Head pub, decor and furnishings are reminiscent of an English manor house. The living room invites conversation by the beehive fireplace. Elegant guest bedrooms and suites feature fine amenities and service. The Sussex and Windsor suites boast two-person jetted tubs and fireplaces. Speaker phones, voice mail and computer data ports are added conveniences. A generous continental breakfast is served in the intimate dining room. Enjoy a variety of complimentary beverages at any time. An exercise bike is set up for the fitness-minded.

Innkeeper(s): Buffi and Douglas King. $100-170. 7 rooms with PB, 2 with FP. Breakfast, afternoon tea and snacks/refreshments included in rates. Types of meals: Country bkfst and early coffee/tea. Beds: QT. Data port, cable TV, VCR, reading lamp, ceiling fan, clock radio, telephone, turn-down service, desk, voice mail, most with jetted tubs, fireplace and wireless Internet access in room. Central air. Fax, library, parlor games, fireplace and limited health/workout facilities on premises. Limited handicap access. Antiquing, bicycling, cross-country skiing, downhill skiing, golf, hiking, live theater, museums, parks, shopping, sporting events and tennis nearby.

Location: City. Beautiful central location in historic district on a huge corner lot.

Publicity: *British Hospitality House at the 2002 Salt Lake games.*

Certificate may be used: Anytime, subject to availability.

Parrish Place B&B

720 Ashton Ave
Salt Lake City, UT 84106-1802
(801)832-0970
Internet: www.parrishplace.com
E-mail: info@parrishplace.com

Circa 1890. Listed in the National Register, this historic, late Victorian mansion was built in 1890 and has been graciously restored. Located in picturesque Salt Lake City, Utah, Parrish Place Bed & Breakfast features original antique art prints by Maxfield Parrish. Gather in the parlor accented by a stained-glass window or feel surrounded by tropical plants and a soothing fountain in the conservatory. Innkeepers Karin and Jeff are both massage therapists. Soak in the hot tub after scheduling a massage for total relaxation. Vibrant and rich guest bedrooms boast fresh flowers, a video library, robes and some have fireplaces, jetted tubs or a two-headed shower. Breakfast is served in the dining room with an original carved fireplace.

Innkeeper(s): Jeff & Karin Gauvin. $99-139. 5 rooms with PB, 2 with WP, 1 conference room. Breakfast and snacks/refreshments included in rates. Beds: Q. Cable TV, VCR, DVD, reading lamp, clock radio, turn-down service, some with hot tub/spa, hair dryer, bathrobes, bath amenities, wireless Internet access and iron/ironing board in room. Central air. Fax, spa, parlor games, telephone, fireplace and Massage Therapy on premises. Amusement parks, antiquing, art galleries, bicycling, canoeing/kayaking, cross-country skiing, downhill skiing, fishing, golf, hiking, horseback riding, live theater, museums, parks, shopping, sporting events, tennis and 7 National Parks within a half-day drive nearby.

Location: City, mountains.

Publicity: *NY Times (November 13, 2005), Going to: Salt Lake City By Melissa Sanford and HGTV House Hunters.*

Certificate may be used: Sunday-Thursday.

Torrey 16

SkyRidge Inn Bed and Breakfast

1090 E. SR 24
Torrey, UT 84775
(435)425-3222 Fax:(435)425-3222
Internet: www.skyridgeinn.com
E-mail: info@skyridgeinn.com

Circa 1994. Located on 75 acres, this gabled, three-story territorial style inn offers views of Capitol Reef National Park, Dixie National Forest and Torrey Valley. Antiques, art and upscale furnishings fill the rooms. Some guest chambers feature a hot tub, jetted tub and private deck.  Breakfast is served in the dining room overlooking forested Boulder Mountain. Wilderness tours via horseback or four-wheel drive may be arranged. The natural arches, sheer canyon walls and multi-colored cliffs and domes of Capitol Reef National Park are five minutes away. Guests are welcome to pick fruit from the Park's ancient orchards during summer and fall.

Innkeeper(s): Kimball & Irene Langton. $85-155. 6 rooms with PB, 2 with HT, 1 conference room. Breakfast, snacks/refreshments, hors d'oeuvres and wine included in rates. Types of meals: Full gourmet bkfst, veg bkfst and early coffee/tea. Beds: KQT. TV, VCR, reading lamp, stereo, ceiling fan, clock radio, telephone, coffeemaker, turn-down service, desk, some with hot tub/spa, some with fireplace, hair dryer, bathrobes, bath amenities, wireless Internet access, iron/ironing board, private decks and patio in room. Air conditioning. Fax, spa, library, parlor games, refrigerator, wireless and high speed Internet access for your laptop on premises. Antiquing, art galleries, bicycling, fishing, hiking, horseback riding, live theater, museums, parks, shopping, Capitol Reef National Park, Grand Staircase National Park, Dixie National Forest, Fishlake National Forest, picnic areas, lakes, fine dining, bird watching, in-season orchards, rodeo, Bryce Canyon National Park 2 1/2 hours, Arches National Park 2 1/2 hours, Lake Powell 2 hours and musical performances nearby.

Location: Country. Capitol Reef National Park - 3 miles.

Publicity: *National Geographic Traveler, Sunset Magazine, Travel and Leisure Magazine and VIA.*

Certificate may be used: November-January, Monday-Thursday.

Vermont

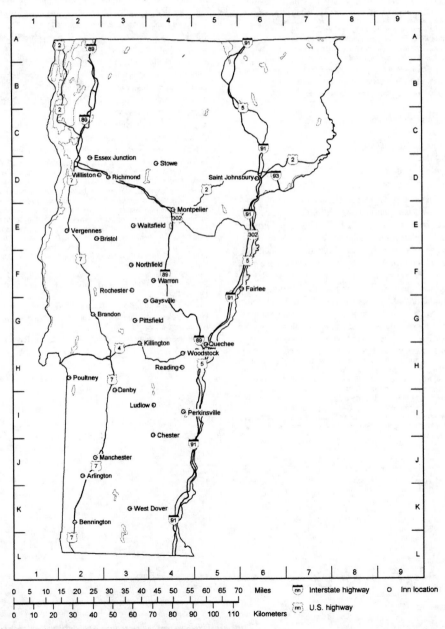

0 5 10 15 20 25 30 35 40 45 50 55 60 65 70   Miles   [m] Interstate highway   ○ Inn location

0 10 20 30 40 50 60 70 80 90 100 110   Kilometers   [m] U.S. highway

Bennington   K2

Alexandra B&B Inn

916 Orchard Road
Bennington, VT 05201
(802)442-5619 (888)207-9386
Internet: www.alexandrainn.com
E-mail: alexandr@sover.net

Circa 1859. Located on two acres at the edge of town, Alexandra is a Colonial-style inn. There are king or queen beds in all the rooms, as well as fireplaces and views of Bennington Monument and the Green Mountains. Each bath offers water jets and showers. A full gourmet breakfast is served. Bennington College and the business district are five minutes from the inn.

Innkeeper(s): Daniel Tarquino. $125-225. 12 rooms with PB, 12 with FP, 9 with WP. Breakfast, afternoon tea and snacks/refreshments included in rates. Types of meals: Full gourmet bkfst, early coffee/tea and gourmet dinner. Beds: KQT. Cable TV, DVD, CD player, clock radio, desk, most with hot tub/spa, fireplace, hair dryer, bath amenities, wireless Internet access and iron/ironing board in room. Air conditioning. Fax, copier, parlor games and Bistro serving a 4 course meal by reservation only to guests on premises. Antiquing, art galleries, bicycling, canoeing/kayaking, cross-country skiing, downhill skiing, fishing, golf, hiking, horseback riding, live theater, museums, parks, shopping, sporting events and tennis nearby.

Location: Country, mountains.

Publicity: The Sunday Boston Globe and Travel Section (November 18 2007).

Certificate may be used: Nov. 1-May 22, excludes holidays.

South Shire Inn

124 Elm St
Bennington, VT 05201-2232
(802)447-3839 Fax:(802)442-3547
Internet: www.southshire.com
E-mail: relax@southshire.com

Circa 1887. Built in the late 1800s, this inn boasts a mahogany-paneled library, soaring 10-foot ceilings, and three of the guest rooms include one of the home's original fireplaces. Guest rooms feature antiques and Victorian décor. Rooms in the restored carriage house include both a fireplace and a whirlpool tub. Guests are pampered with both a full breakfast, as well as afternoon tea. Local attractions include the Bennington Museum, antique shops, craft stores, covered bridges and skiing.

Innkeeper(s): George & Joyce Goeke. $110-225. 9 rooms with PB, 7 with FP, 1 suite. Breakfast and afternoon tea included in rates. Types of meals: Full bkfst, veg bkfst and early coffee/tea. Beds: KQD. Cable TV, reading lamp, ceiling fan, clock radio, telephone and whirlpool tubs in room. Central air. Fax, copier, library, parlor games, fireplace and guest refrigerator on premises. Antiquing, art galleries, bicycling, canoeing/kayaking, cross-country skiing, downhill skiing, fishing, golf, hiking, horseback riding, live theater, museums, parks, shopping, Rutland Railroad, Boston & Maine Railroad, Vermont Railway, Bennington train station and Southern Western Vermont Medical Center (SWVMC) nearby.

Location: Country, mountains.

Certificate may be used: Sunday-Thursday, Nov. 1-May 31, excluding holidays and special events.

Brandon   G2

Brandon Inn

20 Park St
Brandon, VT 05733-1122
(802) 247-5766 (800) 639-8685
Internet: www.brandoninn.com
E-mail: stay@brandoninn.com

Circa 1786. Listed in the National Register, this historic four-story Dutch Colonial boasts Victorian influence. It also offers modern technology like wifi and the commitment to environmentally friendly practices. The gorgeous setting in the Green Mountains and the romantic ambiance has made it a popular wedding destination as well as the town centerpiece. Dining rooms, a pub and ballroom enhance every event. Open all year, there are activities for every season. Sit and read on the front closed-in porch or swim in the outdoor pool. The living room includes a large screen television. Air-conditioned guest rooms provide a variety of sleeping configurations or stay in a spacious Jacuzzi suite. A bountiful country breakfast is made by the award-winning culinary chef. Take day trips from the local area of Brandon, Vermont to experience New England and explore the scenic countryside.

Innkeeper(s): Sarah & Louis Pattis. $99-200. 39 rooms with PB, 2 with WP, 1 conference room. Full country breakfast included in rates. Types of meals: Full bkfst, early coffee/tea, wine, Dinner available by prior request on some dates in season. Chef owned Inn and catering available for private functions. Beds: KQDT. Clock radio, telephone, desk, hair dryer, bath amenities and wireless Internet access in room. Air conditioning. Swimming, parlor games and fireplace on premises. Handicap access. Antiquing, cross-country skiing, downhill skiing, fishing, live theater, parks, shopping and water sports nearby.

Location: Town/village.

Publicity: NE Papers & Magazines and WCAX-TV.

Certificate may be used: Anytime, subject to availability.

Lilac Inn

53 Park St
Brandon, VT 05733-1121
(802)247-5463 (800)221-0720 Fax:(802)247-5499
Internet: www.lilacinn.com
E-mail: innkeeper@lilacinn.com

Circa 1909. For some, the scenery is enough of a reason to visit Vermont. For those who need more, try the Lilac Inn. The restored inn's beautiful furnishings, polished woodwork and fireplaces add to the ambiance. Canopy beds dressed with fine linens, flowers, whirlpool tubs and sitting areas grace the guest rooms. A full, gourmet breakfast is included in the rates. The inn is a popular site for unforgettable romantic weddings. The landscaped, two-acre grounds include ponds, a gazebo and hundreds of perennials and annuals. Flowers decorate the ground's stone walls.

Innkeeper(s): Shelly & Doug Sawyer. $135-345. 9 rooms with PB, 3 with FP, 1 with WP, 4 conference rooms. Breakfast and three-course gourmet breakfast included in rates. Types of meals: Full gourmet bkfst, early coffee/tea, snacks/refreshments, hors d'oeuvres, wine, gourmet dinner and room service. Restaurant on premises. Beds: KQT. Cable TV, VCR, DVD, CD player, ceiling fan, clock radio, desk, some with fireplace, hair dryer, bathrobes, bath amenities, wireless Internet access and iron/ironing board in room. Central air. Fax, copier, library, parlor games and telephone on premises. Handicap access. Antiquing, art galleries, beach, bicycling, canoeing/kayaking, cross-country skiing, downhill skiing, fishing, golf, hiking, horseback riding, live theater, museums, parks, shopping, sporting events, tennis, water sports, wineries, Shelburne Museum, Ben & Jerry's, Vermont Teddy Bear Factory, Stephen Douglas House, Moosalamoo National Recreation Ares, Lincoln Peak Winery, Neshobe River Winery, Maple Museum, Marble Museum, Robert Frost Trail, Lake Champlain, Warren Kimble, Fran Bull, Killington and Pico nearby.

Location: Country. Small town.

Publicity: *Yankee and Vermont & Country Inns.*

"Tasteful, charming and personable."

Certificate may be used: Anytime, subject to availability.

Bristol   E2

Inn at Baldwin Creek & Mary's Restaurant

1868 North 116 Road
Bristol, VT 05443
(802) 453-2432 (888) 424-2432
Internet: www.innatbaldwincreek.com
E-mail: info@innatbaldwincreek.com

Circa 1797. Gracing 25 scenic acres at the base of the Green Mountains, this classic New England farmhouse with white clapboard and black shutters is a warm and welcoming B&B inn. Wade and fish in Baldwin Creek, hike on scenic trails and play croquet, volleyball or badminton on the extensive grounds. Swim seasonally in the in-ground heated pool. Adirondack chairs accent the lawns. Gather for afternoon tea. Families appreciate the children's playground area, kid's menu in the restaurant, toy box and age-appropriate videos. Second-floor guest bedrooms and a two-room suite feature pampering amenities to enhance every stay. A hearty, farm-fresh breakfast is provided daily. Ask about special packages available.

Innkeeper(s): Linda Harmon and Douglas Mack. $95-225. 5 rooms with PB, 2 with FP. Breakfast included in rates. Types of meals: Full gourmet bkfst, veg bkfst, early coffee/tea, picnic lunch, snacks/refreshments, wine and gourmet dinner. Restaurant on premises. Beds: KQT. Cable TV, reading lamp, CD player, refrigerator, ceiling fan, clock radio, coffeemaker, turn-down service, some with fireplace, hair dryer, bathrobes, bath amenities, wireless Internet access and iron/ironing board in room. Air conditioning. TV, fax, copier, swimming, parlor games, telephone and gift shop on premises. Limited handicap access. Antiquing, art galleries, beach, bicycling, canoeing/kayaking, cross-country skiing, downhill skiing, fishing, golf, hiking, horseback riding, live theater, museums, parks, shopping, sporting events, tennis, water sports and wineries nearby.

Location: Country, mountains.

Certificate may be used: November-April, Anytime, subject to availability.

Chester   I4

Hugging Bear Inn & Shoppe

244 Main St
Chester, VT 05143
(802)875-2412 (800)325-0519
Internet: www.huggingbear.com
E-mail: inn@huggingbear.com

Circa 1850. Among the 10,000 teddy bear inhabitants of this white Victorian inn, several peek out from the third-story windows of the octagonal tower. There is a teddy bear shop on the premises and children and adults can borrow a bear to take to bed with them. Rooms are decorated with antiques and comfortable furniture. A bear puppet show is often

staged during breakfast.

Innkeeper(s): Georgette Thomas. $110-185. 5 rooms with PB. Breakfast included in rates. Types of meals: Country bkfst and early coffee/tea. Beds: KQDT. Reading lamp and teddy bear in room. Air conditioning. TV, VCR, parlor games, telephone, fireplace, 10,000 teddy bears and library on premises. Antiquing, cross-country skiing, downhill skiing, fishing, golf, parks, shopping and swimming nearby.

Location: Mountains.

Publicity: *Rutland Daily Herald, Exxon Travel, Teddy Bear Review, Teddy Bear Scene and Boston Globe.*

Certificate may be used: Anytime, subject to availability.

Danby   I3

Silas Griffith Inn

178 South Main Street
Danby, VT 05739
(802)293-5567 (888)569-4660
Internet: www.silasgriffith.com
E-mail: stay@silasgriffith.com

Circa 1891. Rolling meadows and views of the Tacomic and Green Mountains surround this country inn gracing more than 10 acres with flower gardens accenting the grounds. Relax on a porch rocker, swim in the seasonal inground pool, and soak in the spa in the gazebo. Common rooms in the manor house include the large living room, media room and music room. People and pet friendly, stay in an air-conditioned guest room or suite on the second or third floor with Victorian period furnishings and a gas fireplace. Most have private entrances with sitting porches. Savor a home-cooked breakfast full of made-to-order classic foods. Be sure to make dinner reservations at Emma's, the fireside restaurant in the carriage house, serving New England fare Thursday through Sunday. Danby, Vermont is near the many shopping opportunities in Manchester and Rutland.

Innkeeper(s): Brian & Catherine Preble. $129-299. 10 rooms with PB, 10 with FP, 1 two-bedroom suite, 2 conference rooms. Breakfast included in rates. Types of meals: Full bkfst, veg bkfst and dinner. Restaurant on premises. Beds: KQT. Modem hook-up, data port, TV, DVD, reading lamp, telephone, voice mail, fireplace, bath amenities, wireless Internet access, Carriage house common area has a refrigerator, microwave, self-serve coffee & tea, iron, ironing board and and hairdryers for guest use in room. Air conditioning. VCR, fax, copier, spa, swimming, library, parlor games, gift shop, Walking paths, organic gardens, flower gardens, birdwatching and picnicking on premises. Limited handicap access. Antiquing, art galleries, beach, bicycling, canoeing/kayaking, cross-country skiing, downhill skiing, fishing, golf, hiking, horseback riding, live theater, museums, parks, shopping, tennis and water sports nearby.

Location: Country, mountains. Country Village.

"Never have I stayed at a B&B where the innkeepers were so friendly, sociable and helpful. They truly enjoyed their job."

Certificate may be used: Anytime Nov. 1-June 30, Monday-Thursday only for July 1-Oct. 30, subject to availability, excludes package events, cannot be combined with any other offer. Package events are weekend retreats where the guest receives all meals as part of their package.

Essex Junction   D2

The Essex, Vermont's Culinary Resort & Spa

70 Essex Way
Essex Junction, VT 05452-3383
(802) 878-1100 (800) 727-4295 Fax:(802)878-0063
Internet: www.vtculinaryresort.com
E-mail: info@vtculinaryresort.com

Circa 1989. The area's only full-service resort hotel, this inn has been recently renovated by artist Susan Sargent using vibrant colors, plush fabrics and country eclectic design with a Scandinavian flair. The relaxing environment features standard accommodations to fireplace, whirlpool and kitchen suites. In-room spa services are available. The two restaurants are operated by New England Culinary Institute, offering casual American fare to cutting-edge dining. The new four-season glass-enclosed atrium and additional meeting rooms serve as the ideal setting for special events and conferences. Enjoy the tennis courts, an outdoor swimming pool and culinary-theme gardens. Play golf next door at Links at Lang Farm. Skiing and area attractions are nearby.

Innkeeper(s): Jim Glanville - General Manager. $189-699. 120 rooms with PB, 50 with FP, 16 with WP, 30 total suites, including 2 two-bedroom suites, 8 conference rooms. Types of meals: Full gourmet bkfst, veg bkfst, Sun. brunch, early coffee/tea, gourmet lunch, picnic lunch, snacks/refreshments, hors d'oeuvres, wine, gourmet dinner and room service. Restaurant on premises. Beds: KQD. Data port, cable TV, DVD, reading lamp, clock radio, telephone, coffeemaker, turn-down service, desk, some with hot tub/spa, voice mail, some with fireplace, hair dryer, bathrobes, bath amenities, wireless Internet access, iron/ironing board, pay-per-view movies and complimentary high speed Internet access in room. Central air. Fax, copier, spa, swimming, sauna, bicycles, tennis, library, child care, parlor games, laundry facility, gift shop, golf course, hiking, antiques, skiing and outdoor pool on premises. Handicap access. Antiquing, art galleries, beach, bicycling, canoeing/kayaking, cross-country skiing, downhill skiing, fishing, golf, hiking, horseback riding, live theater, museums, parks, shopping, sporting events, tennis, water sports and wineries nearby.

Location: Country.

Certificate may be used: November-July, Sunday-Thursday.

Fairlee   F6

Silver Maple Lodge & Cottages

520 US Rt 5 South
Fairlee, VT 05045
(802)333-4326 (800)666-1946
Internet: www.silvermaplelodge.com
E-mail: scott@silvermaplelodge.com

Circa 1790. This old Cape farmhouse was expanded in the 1850s and became an inn in the '20s when Elmer & Della Batchelder opened their home to guests. It became so successful that several cottages, built from lumber on the property, were added. For 60 years, the Batchelder family continued the operation. They misnamed the lodge, however, mistaking silver poplar trees on the property for what they thought were silver maples. Guest rooms are decorated with many of the inn's original furnishings, and the new innkeepers have carefully restored the rooms and added several bathrooms. A screened-in porch

surrounds two sides of the house. Three of the cottages include working fireplaces and one is handicap accessible.

Innkeeper(s): Scott & Sharon Wright. $74-109. 16 rooms, 14 with PB, 3 with FP, 8 cottages. Breakfast included in rates. Types of meals: Cont. Beds: KQDT. TV, reading lamp, refrigerator, clock radio and desk in room. VCR, copier, bicycles, parlor games, telephone and fireplace on premises. Handicap access. Antiquing, cross-country skiing, downhill skiing, fishing, live theater, parks, shopping and water sports nearby.

Location: Country.

Publicity: *Boston Globe, Vermont Country Sampler, Travel Holiday, Travel America and New York Times.*

"Your gracious hospitality and attractive home all add up to a pleasant experience."

Certificate may be used: Sunday-Thursday, Oct. 20-Sept. 20.

Gaysville   G4

Cobble House Inn

1 Cobble House Road
Gaysville, VT 05746-0049
(802)234-5458
Internet: www.cobblehouseinn.com
E-mail: unwind@cobblehouseinn.com

Circa 1864. One of the grandest homes in the area, this Victorian mansion commands a breathtaking view of the Green Mountains. The White River flows just below, enticing the more adventurous to spend the day tubing, canoeing or fishing for salmon and trout. Enjoy breakfast and afternoon treats. Perennial gardens grace the spacious grounds. Advance notice is needed for dinner, which can be served on the porch in a majestic setting or in the cozy dining room.

Innkeeper(s): Tony, Greg, & Evan Caparis. $99-140. 4 rooms with PB, 1 conference room. Breakfast included in rates. Types of meals: Full gourmet bkfst and dinner. Beds: Q. Telephone and clawfoot tubs in room. TV, VCR, DVD, fax, swimming, library, pet boarding, parlor games, laundry facility, Wood stove, Flannel sheets, Ornate carved beds, Locally produced maple syrup available for purchase, Snowshoeing, Horseshoe pits, Swimming, Tubing, Kayaking and Fishing on premises. Antiquing, art galleries, bicycling, canoeing/kayaking, cross-country skiing, downhill skiing, fishing, golf, hiking, live theater, museums, parks, shopping, sporting events, tennis, water sports, wineries, Bike tours, Tubing, Swimming, Gold panning and Billings Farm nearby.

Location: Country, mountains.

Publicity: *Vermont Country Sampler, Syracuse Alumni Magazine, Vermont Life, Women's Day and Vermont.*

"My favorite place!"

Certificate may be used: Anytime, subject to availability.

Killington   G3

The Vermont Inn

H.C. 34 Box 37J
Killington, VT 05751
(802)775-0708 (800)541-7795 Fax:(802)773-5810
Internet: www.vermontinn.com
E-mail: relax@vermontinn.com

Circa 1840. Poised on five picturesque acres amid the Green Mountains, this historic country inn was once a farmhouse that has been renovated to provide the perfect getaway. The Vermont Inn is open year-round in Killington, Vermont. Gather for refreshments in the fireside living room, choose from a variety of entertainment in the game room, relax in the pub lounge or read in the upstairs library. After exercising in the fully

equipped fitness area, sit in the sauna, soak in the hot tub or swim in the pool. Adirondack chairs offer quiet places to leisurely enjoy the lush landscape. Guest rooms and suites are inviting retreats. Some feature whirlpool tubs, fireplaces, robes, chocolates and a stunning view. New England and Continental cuisine is available at the award-winning onsite restaurant. Ask about special packages.

Innkeeper(s): Jennifer & Mitchell Duffy. $100-310. 6 rooms, 16 with PB, 6 with FP, 3 with WP, 5 total suites, including 3 two-bedroom suites, 1 conference room. Breakfast, afternoon tea, snacks/refreshments and MAP rates are available included in rates. Types of meals: Country bkfst, early coffee/tea, gourmet dinner and Full bar and extensive wine list. $30.00 pp for a 4-course dinner or $25.00 pp for a 3-course dinner available as an addition to posted room rates. Restaurant on premises. Beds: KQDT. Reading lamp, ceiling fan, clock radio, hair dryer, bathrobes, bath amenities, wireless Internet access, iron/ironing board and Flat screen TVs in room. Air conditioning. TV, VCR, DVD, fax, copier, spa, swimming, sauna, bicycles, tennis, library, child care, parlor games, telephone, fireplace, gift shop, Screened porch and Fitness center on premises. Handicap access. Antiquing, art galleries, beach, bicycling, canoeing/kayaking, cross-country skiing, downhill skiing, fishing, golf, hiking, horseback riding, live theater, museums, parks, shopping, tennis and water sports nearby.

Location: Country, mountains.

Publicity: *New York Daily News, New Jersey Star Leader, Rutland Business Journal, Bridgeport Post Telegram, New York Times, Boston, Vermont and Asbury Park Press.*

"We had a wonderful time. The inn is breathtaking. Hope to be back."

Certificate may be used: May-September, November-March, no holidays.

Ludlow   14

Echo Lake Inn

PO Box 154
Ludlow, VT 05149-0154
(802)228-8602 (800)356-6844 Fax:(802)228-3075
Internet: echolakeinn.com
E-mail: echolkinn@aol.com

Circa 1840. An abundance of year-round activities at an ideal location in the state's central mountain lakes region make this authentic Victorian inn a popular choice. Built as a summer hotel in 1840, its rich heritage includes visits from many historic figures. Relax in the quiet comfort of the living room with its shelves of books and a fireplace or gather for refreshments in The Pub. The assortment of guest bedrooms, suites and condos ensure perfect accommoda-

tions for varied needs. Some boast two-person Jacuzzi tubs and fireplaces. Dining is a treat, with the fine country restaurant highly acclaimed for its excellent food, attentive service and casual ambiance. Tennis, badminton and volleyball courts are adjacent to the large swimming pool. Take out a canoe or rowboat from the dock on crystal-clear Echo Lake or fly fish the Black River.

Innkeeper(s): Laurence V. Jeffery. $89-380. 23 rooms with PB, 2 two-bedroom and 1 three-bedroom suites. Breakfast included in rates. Types of meals: Full bkfst, veg bkfst, early coffee/tea, wine, gourmet dinner and room service. Restaurant on premises. Beds: KQDT. Cable TV, VCR, reading lamp,

CD player, ceiling fan, clock radio, desk, hair dryer, bathrobes, bath amenities, wireless Internet access and iron/ironing board in room. Air conditioning. DVD, fax, copier, spa, swimming, tennis, library, child care, parlor games, telephone, fireplace, fine dining, children's paddling pool, all-weather surface, back board and night lighting, house racquets and balls, volleyball and badminton on premises. Antiquing, beach, canoeing/kayaking, cross-country skiing, downhill skiing, fishing, golf, hiking, horseback riding, live theater, shopping, water sports, wineries, Okemo Skiing, one of Vermont's best trout fishing rivers, fly fishing and rowing nearby.

Location: Mountains.

Publicity: *Vermont, Bon Appetit, Gourmet, Vermont Magazine ("turn-of-the-century charm with modern luxury") and Restaurants of New England.*

"Very special! We've decided to make the Echo Lake Inn a yearly tradition for our family."

Certificate may be used: April 1-Sept. 20, Oct. 20-Dec. 12, Jan. 1-March 31, Sunday-Thursday, non-holiday.

Golden Stage Inn

399 Depot St
Ludlow, VT 05153
(802)226-7744 (800)253-8226 Fax:(802)226-7882
Internet: www.goldenstageinn.com
E-mail: goldenstageinn@tds.net

Circa 1788. The Golden Stage Inn was a stagecoach stop built shortly before Vermont became a state. It served as a link in the Underground Railroad and was the home of Cornelia Otis Skinner. Cornelia's Room still offers its original polished wide-pine floors and view of Okemo Mountain, and now there's a four-poster cherry bed, farm animal border, wainscoting and a comforter filled with wool from the inn's sheep.

Outside are gardens of wild-flowers, a little pen with two sheep, a swimming pool and blueberries and raspberries for the picking. Breakfast offerings include an often-requested recipe, Golden Stage Granola. Home-baked breakfast dishes are garnished with Johnny-jump-ups and nasturtiums from the garden. Guests can indulge anytime by reaching into the inn's bottomless cookie jar. The inn offers stay & ski packages at Okemo Mountain with 24 hours advance notice, and it's a 20 minute drive to Killington access.

Innkeeper(s): Julie Wood. $79-300. 10 rooms, 8 with PB, 1 with FP, 1 with WP, 1 two-bedroom suite. Breakfast, afternoon tea, snacks/refreshments and Famous "Bottom-Less Cookie Jar included in rates. Types of meals: Country bkfst, veg bkfst, early coffee/tea, dinner and Famous for our "Bottom-Less Cookie Jar!" Beds: KQDT. Cable TV, reading lamp, clock radio, some with fireplace, hair dryer and wireless Internet access in room. Central air. VCR, fax, copier, swimming, library, pet boarding, parlor games, telephone, gift shop, gardens and sheep on premises. Handicap access. Antiquing, art galleries, bicycling, canoeing/kayaking, cross-country skiing, downhill skiing, fishing, golf, hiking, horseback riding, live theater, museums, parks, shopping, tennis, Okemo Mtn. Resort Stay & Ski Packages, Covered bridges, Weston Priory and President Calvin Coolidge State Historic Site nearby.

Location: Country, mountains.

Publicity: *Journal Inquirer, Gourmet and Los Angeles Times.*

"The essence of a country inn!"

Certificate may be used: Sunday-Thursday, year-round; excludes fall foliage and premium times. Cannot be combined with other offers.

The Andrie Rose Inn

13 Pleasant St
Ludlow, VT 05149
(802)228-4846 (800)223-4846 Fax:(802)228-7910
Internet: www.andrieroseinn.com
E-mail: andrie@tds.net

Circa 1829. This village Colonial was named for Andrie Rose, who operated a guest house here during the 1950s. Recently, the inn has been polished to a shine and lavishly appointed with antiques, wallpapers, down comforters and whirlpool tubs. A Vermont country candlelight breakfast is served. This is the closest inn to the access road of Okemo Mountain and the ski shuttle stops at the inn. The guest house offers four luxury family suites with fireplaces and canopy beds.

Innkeeper(s): Michael & Irene Maston. $100-330. 16 rooms with PB, 7 with FP, 7 suites. Breakfast and snacks/refreshments included in rates. Types of meals: Country bkfst, veg bkfst, early coffee/tea, gourmet dinner and room service. Restaurant on premises. Beds: KQD. Modem hook-up, cable TV, VCR, reading lamp, stereo, refrigerator, ceiling fan, clock radio, telephone, turn-down service, hot tub/spa and suites have fireplace in room. Air conditioning. Fax, copier, spa, bicycles, library, parlor games, fireplace, laundry facility, gift shop and restaurant service on Friday & Saturday on premises. Limited handicap access. Antiquing, art galleries, beach, bicycling, canoeing/kayaking, cross-country skiing, downhill skiing, fishing, golf, hiking, horseback riding, live theater, museums, parks, shopping, tennis and water sports nearby.

Publicity: *Country Inns magazine, USA Today, New York magazine, Inn Times and Getaways - Boston.*

"Thank you for a truly relaxing, delicious and romantic getaway."

Certificate may be used: Anytime, subject to availability, Sunday-Thursday, non holiday.

Manchester   J2

Ira Allen House

6311 Rte 7A
Manchester, VT 05254-251
(802)362-2284 (877)362-2284 Fax:(802)362-2284
Internet: www.iraallenhouse.com
E-mail: Stay@IraAllenHouse.com

Circa 1779. Built by Ethan Allen's brother, this Colonial Revival inn is a state historic site. Hand-blown glass panes, hand-hewn

beams, handmade bricks and wide-board floors provide evidence of the inn's longevity. Surrounded by farms and forest, the inn's setting is perfect for those searching for some peace and quiet. Plenty of recreational activities also are found nearby, including fine trout fishing, swimming and canoeing in the Battenkill River on the property.

Innkeeper(s): Maria and Ed Jones. $100-250. 10 rooms, 5 with PB, 2 with FP, 5 two-bedroom suites. Breakfast and afternoon tea included in rates. Types of meals: Country bkfst, veg bkfst, early coffee/tea, picnic lunch and wine. Beds: KQDT. Cable TV, VCR, DVD, reading lamp, CD player, refrigerator, ceiling fan, clock radio, some with fireplace, hair dryer, bathrobes, bath amenities, wireless Internet access and iron/ironing board in room. Air conditioning. Fax, copier, spa, swimming, bicycles, parlor games, telephone, gift shop, Fishing, Paddleboat, Kayak and Hiking on premises. Amusement parks, antiquing, art galleries, beach, bicycling, canoeing/kayaking, cross-country skiing, downhill skiing, fishing, golf, hiking, horseback riding, live theater, museums, parks, shopping, tennis, water sports, wineries and Battenkill River - Vermont's most famous trout fly fishing river nearby.

Location: Mountains, waterfront.

Certificate may be used: Year-round except foliage season (last week September-last week October) and holidays, Sunday-Thursday.

Wilburton Inn

River Road (off Historic Route 7A)
Manchester, VT 05254
(802)362-2500 (800)648-4944 Fax:(802)362-1107
Internet: www.wilburton.com
E-mail: wilburtoninn@gmail.com

Circa 1902. Shaded by tall maples, this grand Victorian estate sits high on a hill overlooking the Battenkill Valley, set against a majestic mountain backdrop. In addition to the three-story brick mansion, there are four villas and a five-bedroom house. Carved mahogany paneling,
Oriental carpets and leaded-glass windows are comple-
mented by carefully chosen antiques. Besides accommodations, the Teleion Holon Holistic Retreat offers yoga, workshops, vegetarian meals and healing treatments. Spanning 20 acres in Manchester, Vermont enjoy the three tennis courts, a pool, green lawns, sculptured gardens and panoramic views. Country weddings are a Wilburton Inn specialty. Enjoy dining on New American cuisine in a setting of classic elegance.

Innkeeper(s): Georgette Levis. $135-315. 35 rooms with PB, 8 with FP, 2 with WP, 3 guest houses, 5 conference rooms. Breakfast included in rates. Types of meals: Full gourmet bkfst, afternoon tea, snacks/refreshments, wine, gourmet dinner and room service. Restaurant on premises. Beds: KQD. Cable TV, VCR, DVD, reading lamp, refrigerator, clock radio, telephone, some with hot tub/spa, some with fireplace, hair dryer, bath amenities, wireless Internet access and iron/ironing board in room. Air conditioning. Fax, copier, swimming, tennis, parlor games and gift shop on premises. Handicap access. Antiquing, art galleries, beach, bicycling, canoeing/kayaking, cross-country skiing, downhill skiing, fishing, golf, hiking, horseback riding, live theater, museums, parks, shopping and water sports nearby.

Location: Country, mountains.

Publicity: *Great Escapes TV, Travelhost, Getaways For Gourmets, Country Inns, Bed & Breakfast, Gourmet, Best Places to Stay In New England and New York Times.*

"Simply splendid! Peaceful, beautiful, elegant. Ambiance & ambiance!"

Certificate may be used: Only all April, any day, all month.

Montpelier   E4

Betsy's B&B

74 E State St
Montpelier, VT 05602-3112
(802)229-0466 Fax:(802)229-5412
Internet: www.BetsysBnB.com
E-mail: BetsysBnB@comcast.net

Circa 1895. Within walking distance of downtown and located in the state's largest historic preservation district, this Queen Anne Victorian with romantic turret and carriage house features lavish Victorian antiques throughout its interior. Bay windows, carved woodwork, high ceilings, lace curtains and wood floors add to the authenticity. The full breakfast varies in content but not quality, and guest favorites include orange pancakes.

Innkeeper(s): Jon & Betsy Anderson. $85-160. 12 rooms with PB, 5 two-bedroom suites. Breakfast included in rates. Types of meals: Full bkfst. Beds: QDT. Data port, cable TV, reading lamp, clock radio, telephone, desk, voice mail, hair dryer, bath amenities, wireless Internet access and iron/ironing board in room. Air conditioning.

VCR, DVD, fax, copier, parlor games, fireplace, laundry facility and refrigerator on premises. Antiquing, art galleries, beach, bicycling, canoeing/kayaking, cross-country skiing, downhill skiing, fishing, hiking, live theater, museums, parks, shopping and water sports nearby.

Location: City. Residential in small city.

Certificate may be used: Nov. 1-April 30, holiday weekends excluded.

Northfield   E4

The Northfield Inn

228 Highland Ave
Northfield, VT 05663-5663
(802)485-8558
Internet: www.TheNorthfieldInn.com
E-mail: TheNorthfieldInn@aol.com

Circa 1901. A view of the Green Mountains can be seen from this Victorian inn, which is set on a mountainside surrounded by gardens and overlooking an apple orchard and pond. The picturesque inn also affords a view of the village of Northfield and historic Norwich University. Rooms are decorated with antiques and Oriental rugs, and bed-

rooms feature European feather bedding and brass and carved-wood beds. Many outdoor activities are available on the three-acre property, including croquet, horseshoes, ice skating and sledding. Visitors may want to take a climb uphill to visit the Old Slate Quarry or just relax on one of the porches overlooking the garden with bird songs, wind chimes and gentle breezes.

Innkeeper(s): Aglaia Stalb. $95-179. 12 rooms with PB, 2 suites. Breakfast and snacks/refreshments included in rates. Types of meals: Full bkfst. Beds: QDT. Cable TV, reading lamp, ceiling fan, clock radio, telephone and central cooling system available in room. TV, VCR, DVD, fax, copier, bicycles, library, parlor games, fireplace, laundry facility, Lounge, fitness center, book library, travel guides & brochures, tours arranged, reservations made library of DVD's & VHS Videos, guest computer & printer. Swimming in Northfield pools or lake & river; Ice skating at Northfield skating rink; biking & hiking trails; outlet stores, granite quarry tours, lake & river fishing, hunting, skiing, cross-country, snow shoe at 3 resorts or in our back trails, snowmobiling, walk the winter, spring and summer or fall wonderland or take the scenic drives through six covered bridges and explore s-o-o-o-o much more!! on premises. Limited handicap access. Antiquing, cross-country skiing, downhill skiing, fishing, golf, hiking, live theater, parks, shopping, sporting events, water sports, sledding, flying, fairs, auctions. Veteran's and Labor Day Festivals and Parade, Vermont Quilt Festival and 5 covered bridges in Northfield nearby.

Location: Mountains.

Publicity: *Conde Nast Traveler and Gentlemen's Quarterly.*

"There's no place like here."

Certificate may be used: November-April, Monday-Thursday as available, Holiday and special events excluded.

Perkinsville   I4

The Inn at Weathersfield

1342 Route 106
Perkinsville, VT 05151
(802)263-9217 Fax:(802)263-9219
Internet: www.weathersfieldinn.com
E-mail: stay@weathersfieldinn.com

Circa 1792. Perfectly suited for a quiet getaway, this stately Georgian-style inn with post and beam interior was built in 1792 and thought to have been a stop on the Underground

Railroad. Decorated in a rustic elegance, each guest bedroom and suite includes cozy robes and slippers. Many feature fireplaces, four-poster beds, CD stereos, whirlpool or clawfoot tubs and private rooftop decks. Choose a hot, made-to-order breakfast from a menu. Roam the 21 wooded acres with a pond, walking trails, gardens, back roads and an outdoor starlit amphitheater. The candlelit dining room offers New Vermont cuisine, and lighter fare is available in the Pub on select nights. Relax by the fire in the study after a full day of skiing. A computer provides high-speed Internet access for guest use.

Innkeeper(s): Jane and David Sandelman. $150-285. 12 rooms with PB, 6 with FP, 3 suites, 1 conference room. Breakfast, afternoon tea and snacks/refreshments included in rates. Types of meals: Full gourmet bkfst, veg bkfst, early coffee/tea, picnic lunch and gourmet dinner. Restaurant on premises. Beds: KQDT. Modem hook-up, cable TV, reading lamp, stereo, clock radio, desk, fireplace, robes and slippers in room. VCR, fax, copier, sauna, stable, library, pet boarding, parlor games, fireplace, high-speed Internet, gift shop and full service restaurant on premises. Antiquing, art galleries, bicycling, canoeing/kayaking, cross-country skiing, downhill skiing, fishing, golf, hiking, horseback riding, live theater, museums, parks and shopping nearby.

Location: Country. Set on 21 wooded acres.

Certificate may be used: Sunday-Thursday excluding Sept. 15- Nov. 1, Christmas week, New Years, Presidents week.

Poultney   H2

Bentley House B&B

399 Bentley Ave
Poultney, VT 05764
(802)287-4004
Internet: www.thebentleyhouse.com
E-mail: bentleyhousebb@comcast.net

Circa 1895. This three-story peaked turret Queen Anne inn is located next to Green Mountain College. Stained glass, polished woodwork and original fireplace mantels add to the Victorian atmosphere, and the guest rooms are furnished with antiques of the period. A sitting room adjacent to the guest rooms has its own fireplace.

Innkeeper(s): Pam & Rich Mikkelesen. $105-145. 5 rooms with PB. Breakfast included in rates. Types of meals: Full bkfst. Beds: Q. Ceiling fan, clock radio, turn-down service, hair dryer, bathrobes and iron/ironing board in room. TV, VCR, telephone and fireplace on premises. Limited handicap access. Antiquing, beach, cross-country skiing, fishing, parks, shopping and water sports nearby.

Location: Mountains. Small rural college town.

Publicity: *Rutland Herald and Rutland Business Journal.*

"Your beautiful home was delightful and just the best place to stay!"

Certificate may be used: Anytime, at the last minute.

Quechee   G4

Inn at Clearwater Pond

984 Quechee-Hartland Road
Quechee, VT 05059
(802)295-0606 (888)918-4466 Fax:(802)295-0606
Internet: innatclearwaterpond.com
E-mail: innatclearwaterpond@gmail.com

Circa 1800. Right down the road from Woodstock, VT is a bit of paradise; close to town but nestled in the country. Set amongst hills and old country roads, the Inn at Clearwater Pond offers simplicity and understated elegance. This hidden gem also offers romance, beauty and a bit of adventure, as well. Lift off from the backyard for a thrilling hot air balloon flight and soar over the spectacular Quechee Gorge, enjoy a crystal clear pond and swim in fresh drinking water. Indulge in a massage performed in the comfort and privacy of your room. Guests can stay in shape, even while vacationing, in the spacious and well-equipped workout room. The Inn will arrange for most outdoor equipment rentals or dining reservations. Appreciate nature as you hike along the Waterfall Trail, Mt. Tom or the Appalachian Trail. The accommodations are sophisticated, spacious and so very comfortable. Awaken each morning to the aroma of a delicious breakfast, served fireside in the romantic dining room with soft music and candlelight. Relax, unwind and savor simple pleasures of country life as you enjoy the panorama of distant views from the lush back lawn of this outstanding bed and breakfast.

Innkeeper(s): Christine DeLuca. $175-295. 6 rooms, 5 with PB, 1 with FP, 1 guest house. Breakfast and snacks/refreshments included in rates. Types of meals: Full gourmet bkfst, veg bkfst, early coffee/tea, gourmet lunch, picnic lunch, afternoon tea, hors d'oeuvres, wine, gourmet dinner, Private cocktail parties, Picnic lunches and Catered weddings and special events. Beds: KQT. Cable TV, VCR, DVD, clock radio, some with fireplace, hair dryer, bathrobes, bath amenities, wireless Internet access and Massage Therapist in room. Air conditioning. Fax, copier, spa, swimming, stable, bicycles, library, parlor games, telephone, gift shop, Helicopter landing site, Massage therapist, Hot-air ballooning, Llama treks, Hiking trails, Bicycle, Kayak, Canoe, Fishing gear, Inner tube, Snowshoe, X-country ski rentals, Croquet, Badminton, Bocce and Horseshoes on premises. Limited handicap access. Antiquing, art galleries, bicycling, canoeing/kayaking, cross-country skiing, downhill skiing, fishing, golf, hiking, horseback riding, live theater, museums, parks, shopping, sporting events, tennis, water sports, wineries, Hot-air Ballooning, Llama Trek, Spa and Outdoor Equipment Rentals nearby.

Location: Country.

Certificate may be used: Anytime subject to availability. May not be available holidays, special local events and fall foliage.

Reading   H4

Bailey's Mills B&B

1347 Bailey's Mills Rd
Reading, VT 05062
(802)484-7809 (800)639-3437 Fax:(802)484-0014
Internet: www.baileysmills.com
E-mail: info1@baileysmills.com

Circa 1820. This Federal-style inn features grand porches, 11 fireplaces, a "good-morning" staircase and a ballroom on the third floor. Four generations of Baileys lived in the home, as well as housing mill workers. There also was once a country store on the premises. Guests can learn much about the home and history of the people who lived here through the innkeepers. Two of the guest rooms include a fireplace, and the suite has a private solarium. There's plenty to do here, from exploring the surrounding 48 acres to relaxing with a book on the porch swing or in a hammock. If you forgot your favorite novel, borrow a book from the inn's 2,200-volume library.

Innkeeper(s): Barbara Thaeder. $120-199. 3 rooms with PB, 2 with FP, 1 suite. Breakfast included in rates. Types of meals: Full bkfst and early coffee/tea. Beds: KQ. Reading lamp, clock radio, wireless Internet access and two with fireplace in room. Swimming, library, parlor games, telephone, fireplace, pond, stream and walking trails on premises. Antiquing, cross-country skiing, downhill skiing, fishing, live theater, parks and shopping nearby.

Location: Country.

Publicity: Vermont Magazine.

"If words could encapsulate what a wonderful weekend would be, it would have to be 'Bailey's Mills B&B.' Your home is beautiful. It is elegant yet homey."

Certificate may be used: November-May, Sunday-Thursday or call anytime for last-minute openings.

Richmond   D3

The Richmond Victorian Inn

191 East Main Street
Richmond, VT 05477-0652
(802)434-4410 (888)242-3362 Fax:(802)434-4411
Internet: www.richmondvictorianinn.com
E-mail: innkeeper@richmondvictorianinn.com

Circa 1850. This Queen Anne Victorian, with a three-story tower, is accented with green shutters, a sunburst design, fish  scale shingles and a gingerbread front porch. The Tower Room is filled with white wicker, delicate flowered wallpaper and an antique brass bed. The Gold Room features a Queen-size bed and a Jacuzzi, while the Pansy Room features an antique bed, white walls and a stenciled pansy border. There are hardwood floors and leaded-glass windows throughout. From the tree-shaded porch, enjoy the inn's lawns and flower gardens after a full breakfast.

Innkeeper(s): Frank & Joyce Stewart. $119-169. 6 rooms with PB. Breakfast and snacks/refreshments included in rates. Types of meals: Full gourmet bkfst, veg bkfst, early coffee/tea and afternoon tea. Beds: QDT. Reading lamp, clock radio, antique furnishings, cozy quilts, down comforters and plush robes in room. TV, VCR, DVD, fax, library, parlor games, telephone and British-style afternoon tea (Sundays from 2-5 p.m. September-Mother's Day) on premises. Antiquing, art galleries, beach, bicycling, canoeing/kayaking, cross-country skiing, downhill skiing, fishing, golf, hiking, live theater, museums, parks, shopping, sporting events, water sports, wineries, artists' studios, Audubon Center, Huntington Gorge and Little River State Park nearby.

Location: Country, mountains. Small Vermont town, 12 miles east of Burlington.

Publicity: Yankee Magazine - Best of New England Editor's Choice Award (2011) The Montreal Gazette (2007) Out and About in Vermont 5th Ed., Rogers (2004) Best Recipes of American Country Inns and Bed and Breakfasts - Maynard (2004) Hartford Courant (2003).

"I have stayed at many B&Bs, but by far this is the most wonderful experience. The hospitality was #1, the food was A+. Rooms very comfortable. I felt like family. Hope our paths cross again."

Certificate may be used: November-April, non-holidays, subject to availability and prior booking. May not be combined with other promotions.

Rochester   G3

Liberty Hill Farm

511 Liberty Hill
Rochester, VT 05767-9501
(802)767-3926 Fax:(802)767-6056
Internet: www.libertyhillfarm.com
E-mail: beth@libertyhillfarm.com

Circa 1825. A working dairy farm with a herd of registered Holsteins, this farmhouse offers a country setting and easy access to recreational activities. The inn's location, between the White River and the Green Mountains, is ideal for outdoor enthusiasts and animal lovers. Stroll to the barn, feed the calves or climb up to the hayloft and read or play with the kittens. Fishing, hiking, skiing and swimming are popular pastimes of guests, who are treated to a family-style dinner and full breakfast, both featuring many delicious homemade specialties.

Innkeeper(s): Robert & Beth Kennett. $180. 7 rooms. Breakfast and Dinner at 6PM included in rates. Types of meals: Full bkfst, early coffee/tea and dinner. Beds: QDT. Reading lamp, clock radio and desk in room. VCR, swimming, library, child care, parlor games, telephone, working dairy farm and private beach for swimming and fishing on premises. Antiquing, art galleries, beach, bicycling, canoeing/kayaking, cross-country skiing, downhill skiing, fishing, golf, hiking, live theater, museums, parks, shopping, sporting events, water sports and wineries nearby.

Location: Riverfront in the country and mountains.

Publicity: *New York Times, Boston Globe, Vermont Life, Family Circle, Family Fun, Woman's Day, Country Home, Boston Chronicle, Yankee and Good Morning America.*

"*We had a wonderful time exploring your farm and the countryside. The food was great.*"

Certificate may be used: Jan.1-May 20 Sunday-Thursday anytime, last minute-based on availability.

Saint Johnsbury K3

Estabrook House

1596 Main Street
Saint Johnsbury, VT 05819
(802)751-8261
Internet: www.estabrookhouse.com
E-mail: innkeeper@estabrookhouse.com

Circa 1896. Escape day-to-day doldrums with a visit to Estabrook House in St. Johnsbury, Vermont. This northern New England B&B is a delightful reflection of Victorian architecture with exquisite detail. Relax on a porch or by the fire. Grab a book from the library and read in the living room. Soft linens, robes, slippers, sitting areas, stained glass and bay windows with views are among the pleasing amenities in the inviting second-floor guest rooms. A family-style bathroom boasts an antique clawfoot soaking tub and separate shower. Linger over a breakfast buffet that features foods both homemade and from the local bakery. Concierge services are available. Ask about special packages, weddings, retreats and other events held here.

Innkeeper(s): Maurine. $95-175. 3 rooms, 1 with PB. Breakfast, snacks/refreshments, Coffee, tea and hot chocolate available any time included in rates. Types of meals: Full bkfst, veg bkfst, early coffee/tea, picnic lunch, Dinner at the house and boxed lunches to go will be prepared with advance notice. Menus are available for meetings and group gatherings. Please inquire when making reservations as afternoon tea, gourmet dinner and and hearty lunches for a group along with catering for small weddings and special occasions is available. Beds: KQDT. Reading lamp, turn-down service, hair dryer, bathrobes, bath amenities, wireless Internet access, Slippers, Soft linens and Sitting areas in each room in room. TV, VCR, DVD, fax, copier, library, parlor games, telephone, fireplace, Wrap around front porch, enclosed second floor porch, Library media room with movies and books, quiet living room, beverage station and ironing board/iron on premises. Antiquing, art galleries, bicycling, canoeing/kayaking, cross-country skiing, downhill skiing, fishing, golf, hiking, horseback riding, live theater, museums, parks, shopping, tennis, water sports, wineries, St. Johnsbury Academy, Town forest, Cheese makers, Covered bridges, Health club, Movie theaters and Bowling nearby.

Location: City, country, mountains. central to the white and green mountains, lakes are within 10 miles of the house.

Certificate may be used: Anytime, subject to availability.

Stowe D4

1066 Ye Olde England Inne

433 Mountain Rd
Stowe, VT 05672-4628
(802)253-7558 (800)477-3771 Fax:(802)253-8944
Internet: www.englandinn.com
E-mail: englandinn@aol.com

Circa 1890. Originally a farmhouse, Ye Olde England Inne has a Tudor facade, interior beams and stone work. Each guest bedroom is different. The suites and cottages include a whirlpool tub and many offer a mountain view and a private porch from which to enjoy it. Mr. Pickwick's, which resembles an English pub, is an ideal spot to relax and enjoy ale or a glass or wine. The inn also offers Copperfields, for a romantic dinner. Enjoy hiking, skiing, relaxing by the pool or exploring Stowe, Vermont. The inn has a variety of getaway packages.

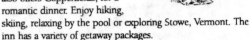

Innkeeper(s): Christopher & Linda Francis. $109-249. 30 rooms with PB, 13 with FP, 16 total suites, including 4 two-bedroom suites and 1 three-bedroom suite, 3 cottages, 1 conference room. Breakfast and afternoon tea included in rates. Types of meals: Full gourmet bkfst, veg bkfst, Sun. brunch, early coffee/tea, gourmet lunch, picnic lunch, wine, gourmet dinner and room service. Restaurant on premises. Beds: KQDT. Cable TV, VCR, DVD, reading lamp, stereo, refrigerator, ceiling fan, clock radio, telephone, coffeemaker, desk, hair dryer, bathrobes, bath amenities, wireless Internet access and iron/ironing board in room. Central air. Fax, copier, spa, swimming, pet boarding and fireplace on premises. Handicap access. Antiquing, art galleries, beach, bicycling, canoeing/kayaking, cross-country skiing, downhill skiing, fishing, golf, hiking, horseback riding, live theater, museums, parks, shopping, sporting events, tennis, water sports and wineries nearby.

Location: Mountains, waterfront.

Publicity: *National Geographic Traveler, Channel 5 TV in Boston, New York Times, Boston Magazine, Vermont Magazine and WGBH Boston.*

Certificate may be used: Midweek, non-holiday, subject to advance reservations and availability.

Bears Lair Inn

4583 Mountain Rd
Stowe, VT 05672
(802)253-4846 (800)821-7891 Fax:(802)253-7050
Internet: www.bearslairinn.com
E-mail: bearslairinn@gmail.com

Circa 1980. Stowe needs no introduction to its famous outdoor resort facilities. The Honeywood Inn is perfectly situated to take advantage of these activities in every season of the year. Cross-country ski trails leave right from the front door, and during the warm months, a 5.3-mile bike and walking path winds through some of Vermont's most splendid scenery, crossing wooden bridges and working farms. The inn resembles a Swiss chalet, while the interior decor has a homey, country feel. Some guest rooms feature canopy, brass or sleigh beds; others boast a spa. If the night is star filled, an outdoor hot tub makes a fun nightcap. In the morning, a light breakfast of fresh fruit, homemade muffins and cereal is followed by a more substantial one of waffles with homemade raspberry sauce, apple-cinnamon pancakes, or eggs Benedict. During the summer you'll enjoy this in the patio garden. The center of Stowe is only a stroll away along the recreation path. Here you can browse through the numerous antique and craft shops.

Innkeeper(s): Carolyn & Bill Cook. $129-269. 10 rooms, 8 with PB, 2 with FP, 2 suites. Breakfast included in rates. Types of meals: Full gourmet bkfst and veg bkfst. Beds: KQD. Reading lamp, ceiling fan, clock radio, wireless Internet access and some with hot tubs in room. Air conditioning. TV, VCR, fax, copier, spa, swimming, bicycles, parlor games, telephone and fireplace on premises. Antiquing, art galleries, beach, bicycling, canoeing/kayaking, cross-country skiing, downhill skiing, fishing, golf, hiking, horseback riding, live theater, museums, parks, shopping, tennis, water sports and wineries nearby.

Location: Mountains, with babbling brook on property.

Certificate may be used: Jan. 3-Sept. 14, Oct. 15-Dec. 20 Sunday-Thursday, not valid President's week.

Vergennes   E2

Strong House Inn
94 W Main St
Vergennes, VT 05491-9531
(802)877-3337 Fax:(802)877-2599
Internet: www.stronghouseinn.com
E-mail: innkeeper@stronghouseinn.com

Circa 1834. This Federal-style home boasts expansive views of the Green Mountains and the Adirondack range. The inn's 14 guest rooms offer amenities such as private baths, fireplaces, private balconies, and wireless access. A delectable country

breakfast is served each morning and snacks and goodies are available throughout the day. Families attending events at Middlebury College will find the Strong House Inn to be a perfect

home base, just a short drive away. Nearby Lake Champlain offers boating and fishing, and golfing, hiking, skiing and some of the finest cycling in Vermont are all part of the area's myriad of outdoor activities. Innkeeper Mary Bargiel is an avid gardener and decorates the grounds with flowers and herb gardens. During the Winter, Quilters flock from all over the country to attend Mary's famous quilting retreats. The Inn also hosts special events, weddings, and luncheons and sets a perfect backdrop for your next event!

Innkeeper(s): Hugh & Mary Bargiel. $110-330. 14 rooms with PB, 4 with FP, 1 suite, 1 conference room. Breakfast and snacks/refreshments included in rates. Types of meals: Country bkfst and early coffee/tea. Beds: KQDT. Cable TV, VCR, reading lamp, stereo, refrigerator, clock radio, telephone, coffeemaker, desk, hot tub/spa, voice mail and wireless Internet access in room. Central air. Fax, copier, library, parlor games, fireplace and gift shop on premises. Handicap access. Antiquing, art galleries, bicycling, canoeing/kayaking, cross-country skiing, downhill skiing, fishing, golf, hiking, horseback riding, museums, parks, shopping and tennis nearby.

Location: Country.

Publicity: *New York Times, Vermont Magazine, Addison County Independent and RETN.*

"Blissful stay...Glorious breakfast!"

Certificate may be used: Nov. 1-May 15, Sunday-Thursday, subject to availability.

Waitsfield   E3

Mad River Inn
Tremblay Rd, PO Box 75
Waitsfield, VT 05673
(802)496-7900 (800)832-8278 Fax:(802)496-5390
Internet: www.madriverinn.com
E-mail: madriverinn@madriver.com

Circa 1860. Surrounded by the Green Mountains, this Queen Anne Victorian sits on seven scenic acres along the Mad River. The charming inn boasts attractive woodwork throughout, highlighted by ash, bird's-eye maple and cherry. Guest rooms feature European feather beds and include the Hayden Breeze Room, with a King brass bed, large

windows TV and A/C, and the Angelina Mercedes Room with a four-poster bed and picturesque views. The inn sports a billiard table, gazebo, organic gardens and a hot tub overlooking the mountains. Guests can walk to a recreation path along the river.

Innkeeper(s): Luc & Karen Maranda. $115-165. 8 rooms with PB. Breakfast and afternoon tea included in rates. Types of meals: Full gourmet bkfst. Beds: KQ. Reading lamp, ceiling fan, turn-down service and desk in room. VCR, fax, spa, parlor games, telephone and fireplace on premises. Antiquing, cross-country skiing, downhill skiing, fishing, live theater, shopping, sporting events, water sports and Vermont Icelandic Horse Farm nearby.

Location: Mountains.

Publicity: *Innsider, Victorian Homes, Let's Live, Skiing, AAA Home & Away, Tea Time at the Inn, Travel & Leisure, Ski Magazine and NY Times.*

"Your hospitality was appreciated, beautiful house and accommodations, great food & friendly people, just to name a few things. We plan to return and we recommend the Mad River Inn to friends & family."

Certificate may be used: Midweek only, non-holiday or foliage season. Jan. 5 to Sept. 20, Oct. 25-Dec.15.

Warren   F4

West Hill House
1496 West Hill Rd
Warren, VT 05674-9620
(802)496-7162 (800)209-1049
Internet: www.westhillbb.com
E-mail: innkeepers@westhillbb.com

Circa 1856. West Hill House boasts a great location in Warren, Vermont, on a quiet and scenic country road, just a mile from the Sugarbush Ski Area and next to the Sugarbush Golf Course. The nine-acre grounds include four ponds, meadows, perennial

gardens, a uniquely designed gazebo and winter mountain views. All rooms offer a Jacuzzi and/or steam bath and there are gas fireplaces in all of the bedchambers. A delicious cooked breakfast is served each morning and coffee, tea, hot

chocolate and homemade cookies are always available. Candlelight dinners are available for six or more guests by prior arrangement. Weddings at this B&B accommodate up to 80 guests and can be held in the house and on the garden terrace, or in the marvelous barn.

Innkeeper(s): Peter & Susan MacLaren. $140-265. 9 rooms with PB, 8 with FP. Breakfast and afternoon tea included in rates. Types of meals: Full bkfst, early coffee/tea, snacks/refreshments, wine and dinner. Beds: KQT. Data port, cable TV, DVD, reading lamp, ceiling fan, clock radio, telephone, turn-down service, desk, voice mail, fireplace, hair dryer, bathrobes, bath amenities, wireless Internet access, Jacuzzi and/or steam bath, Telephones with voice mail with free calling to US & Canada, WiFi/DSL Internet access. Irons and ironing boards available. Coffee, tea, hot chocolate and home made cookies & guest fridge in common area in room. Air conditioning. VCR, fax, copier, library, laundry facility, gift shop, Three large common areas, Front porch, Back deck, Pool table, WiFi and 450 movies available to watch on premises. Antiquing, art galleries, bicycling, canoeing/kayaking, cross-country skiing, downhill skiing, fishing, golf, hiking, live theater, shopping, Gliding, discovering Covered Bridges, exploring Vermont Culinary treats including Ben & Jerry's and Cabot cheese and visiting artists & artisans nearby.

Location: Mountains. Sugarbush Ski & Golf Resort.

Publicity: *Yankee Magazine, Innsider Magazine, Quilt Mania Magazine, UK Ski Magazine, Boston Globe, Washington Post, Montreal Gazette and Ottawa Citizen.*

Certificate may be used: April-July, Oct. 17-Dec. 22.

West Dover   K3

Deerfield Valley Inn

PO Box 1834
West Dover, VT 05356
(802)464-6333 (800)639-3588 Fax:(802)464-6336
Internet: www.deerfieldvalleyinn.com
E-mail: deerinn@sover.net

Circa 1885. Built as a country house in 1885 at the foothills of the Green Mountains, the inn is listed in the National Register and features the original wax-rubbed ash encasements and millwork. It was converted into one of the first inns in Mount Snow and new wings have been added. Sit by the fire in the living room. Enjoy a light afternoon tea. Intimate yet spacious guest bedrooms boast pleasant furnishings and décor. Sleep in the canopy bed in Room 5 with a sitting area and wood-burning fireplace. A bountiful, hearty breakfast is served in the pleasant dining room. The picturesque area offers many year-round activities. Golf packages are available.

Innkeeper(s): Doreen Cooney. $100-200. 9 rooms with PB, 5 with FP. Breakfast and snacks/refreshments included in rates. Types of meals: Country bkfst and veg bkfst. Beds: KQDT. Cable TV, VCR, DVD, reading lamp, CD player, ceiling fan, clock radio, most with fireplace and bath amenities in room. Air conditioning. Fax, copier, parlor games and telephone on premises. Antiquing, art galleries, bicycling, canoeing/kayaking, cross-country skiing, downhill skiing, fishing, golf, hiking, horseback riding, live theater, museums, parks, shopping, tennis, water sports and wineries nearby.

Location: Mountains.

Certificate may be used: Mid March-mid September, anytime subject to availability, mid October-mid December anytime subject to availabilty, Mid December-mid March Sunday to Thursday only, non-holidays.

Deerhill Inn

14 Valley View Rd,
West Dover, VT 05356-0136
(802)464-3100 (800)993-3379
Internet: www.deerhill.com
E-mail: innkeeper@deerhill.com

Circa 1954. Close to Mount Snow and Haystack ski resorts, with Stratton and Bromley nearby, this chef-owned, award-winning inn offers extraordinary panoramic views of the mountains. Delightful guest bedrooms invite romance and comfort. Several rooms feature hand-painted murals and some include a fireplace

and a Jacuzzi. Start the day with hearty breakfast fare of pancakes, French toast or omelets with sides of potatoes, breads and bacon or sausage. A Prix Fixe Modern American dinner menu includes a four-course meal with appetizer, entree, salad and dessert. Local seasonal ingredients are used when possible. Updated inn classics like Veal Deerhill, Roast Duckling or Pan-Seared Filet of Beef are also served a la carte. Weddings are popular here and conference facilities are available.

Innkeeper(s): Michael Allen & Stan Gresens. $131-355. 13 rooms with PB, 8 with FP, 7 with WP, 3 suites. Breakfast, afternoon tea, snacks/refreshments and dinner included in rates. Types of meals: Country bkfst, early coffee/tea, picnic lunch and wine. Restaurant on premises. Beds: KQT. Cable TV, reading lamp, stereo, ceiling fan, clock radio, most with fireplace, hair dryer, bathrobes, bath amenities, wireless Internet access and Balconies or Decks in room. DVD, fax, copier, swimming, library, parlor games, telephone and gift shop on premises. Antiquing, art galleries, bicycling, canoeing/kayaking, cross-country skiing, downhill skiing, fishing, golf, hiking, horseback riding, live theater, museums, shopping, tennis and water sports nearby.

Location: Country, mountains.

Certificate may be used: Anytime at the last minute within 24 hours.

Snow Goose Inn

259 Rte. 100
West Dover, VT 05356
(802)464-3984 (888)604-7964 Fax:(802)464-5322
Internet: www.snowgooseinn.com
E-mail: stay@snowgooseinn.com

Circa 1959. Three acres of Vermont countryside create a secluded setting for the Snow Goose Inn. Renovations in 1998 include the addition of Southern pine floors and private decks. Hand-hewn beams from an old country barn were fashioned into a new grand entry and a duplex honeymoon suite was created. (The new suite offers two decks with mountain and valley views, a Jacuzzi tub, fireplace and sitting area.) Most of the other antique-filled rooms also include a fireplace, VCR, stereo and double Jacuzzi tub. Hypo-allergenic feather mattresses and comforters are additional features. Hearty breakfasts include cereals, fresh fruit, juices, breads and entrees such as wild mushrooms and herb scrambled eggs, French toast stuffed with bananas. Evening wine and cheese is offered on one of the porches with views to the pond and flower gardens or by fireside in winter.

Innkeeper(s): Cyndee & Ron Frere. $125-395. 13 rooms with PB, 9 with FP, 8 with HT, 2 suites. Breakfast, snacks/refreshments, hors d'oeuvres and wine included in rates. Types of meals: Full gourmet bkfst, veg bkfst and early coffee/tea. Beds: KQDT. Modem hook-up, data port, cable TV, VCR, reading lamp, stereo, refrigerator, ceiling fan, clock radio, turn-down service, desk, wireless Internet access, wood-burning fireplace and two-person Jacuzzi tub in room. Air conditioning. Fax, copier, parlor games, telephone, fireplace and three acres of informal gardens on premises. Handicap access. Antiquing, art galleries, bicycling, canoeing/kayaking, cross-country skiing, downhill skiing, fishing, golf, hiking, horseback riding, live theater, museums, parks, shopping, tennis, water sports and wineries nearby.

Location: Country, mountains.

Certificate may be used: Anytime, Sunday-Thursday, subject to availability.

Williston   D3

Catamount B&B

592 Governor Chittenden Rd
Williston, VT 05495
(802)878-2180 (888)680-1011 Fax:(802)879-6066
Internet: www.catamountoutdoor.com
E-mail: lucy_mccullough@myfairpoint.net

Circa 1796. This huge Federal Colonial Revival inn on 500 acres has been in the McCullough family since 1873. In its early years, the elegant homestead sponsored many grand balls, and today the home exudes a sense of rich family history. The inn is the oldest standing building in Williston, and it has been a Williston landmark for more than 200 years. It is located on the family farm where the family owns and operates a recreation center that includes many outdoor activities. The grounds have one of the finest mountain bike facilities available. It has a professionally designed trail network that includes flat, rolling and steep trails that range from single-track to wide. And it has an acre of groomed ice for ice skating and a tree-free sledding hill. Guests who stay in the inn's three guest bedrooms (including one suite) enjoy a hearty continental breakfast each morning with courses such as homemade muffins, seasonal fruits, cereals, coffee and tea and sometimes waffles.

Innkeeper(s): Lucy & Jim McCullough. $95-145. 3 rooms, 1 with PB, 1 suite, 1 conference room. Breakfast included in rates. Types of meals: Cont plus, veg bkfst and early coffee/tea. Beds: D. TV, VCR, fax, copier, bicycles, library, parlor games, telephone, fireplace, Cross country skiing, Snowshoes, Ice skating, 20 miles of trails and WiFi available on premises. Amusement parks, antiquing, art galleries, beach, bicycling, canoeing/kayaking, cross-country skiing, downhill skiing, fishing, golf, hiking, horseback riding, live theater, museums, parks, shopping, sporting events, tennis, water sports, wineries and Burlington- the cultural hub of Vermont nearby.

Location: Country. 500 acres.

Certificate may be used: June 1-Labor Day, Sunday-Thursday; also Columbus Day-May 1, all days, Anytime, Last Minute-Based on Availability.

Woodstock   H4

Applebutter Inn

Happy Valley Rd
Woodstock, VT 05091
(802)457-4158 (800)486-1734 Fax:(802)457-4158
Internet: www.applebutterinn.com
E-mail: aplbtrn@comcast.net

Circa 1854. Gracious hospitality and comfort are equally enjoyed at this elegant 1854 country home. Authentically restored, this Federal gabled inn listed in the National Register boasts original wide pine floors, Oriental rugs and rare antiques. Relax by the fire in the Yellow Room or browse through the extensive book collection. Play the Mason & Hamlin grand piano in the Music Room. Several of the spacious and romantic guest bedrooms feature fireplaces. The Cameo Room also has a separate entrance. Sleep well on an 18th century pencil-post bed in the King David Room with a private porch. Sit in the morning sun of the breakfast room and savor a gourmet meal highlighted by Barbara's own applebutter. Play croquet on the expansive lawn, or sit on the porch with afternoon tea and fresh-baked cookies. Located in the tranquil hamlet of Taftsville, seasonal activities and fine dining are close by.

Innkeeper(s): Barbara & Michael. $95-195. 6 rooms with PB, 4 with FP, 1

conference room. Breakfast, afternoon tea and Pastries included in rates. Types of meals: Full gourmet bkfst, veg bkfst, early coffee/tea and snacks/refreshments. Beds: KQD. Cable TV, VCR, reading lamp, hair dryer, bath amenities and wireless Internet access in room. Air conditioning. DVD, fax, copier, library, parlor games, telephone, fireplace, Baby Grand Piano and Free Wi-Fi throughout the Inn on premises. Limited handicap access. Antiquing, art galleries, bicycling, canoeing/kayaking, cross-country skiing, downhill skiing, fishing, golf, hiking, horseback riding, live theater, museums, parks, shopping, sporting events and Spa services nearby.

Location: Country, mountains.

Publicity: Los Angeles Times, Yankee and Food & Wine.

Certificate may be used: November-April, Sunday-Thursday excluding holiday weeks, subject to availability.

Charleston House

21 Pleasant St
Woodstock, VT 05091-1111
(802)457-3843 (888)475-3800
Internet: charlestonhouse.com
E-mail: charlestonhousevermont@comcast.net

Circa 1835. This authentically restored brick Greek Revival town house, in the National Register, welcomes guests with shuttered many-paned windows and window boxes filled with pink blooms. Guest rooms are appointed with period antiques and reproductions, an art collection and Oriental rugs. Some of the rooms boast four-poster beds, and some feature fire-places and Jacuzzis. A hearty full breakfast starts off the day in the candlelit dining room, and the innkeepers serve afternoon refreshments, as well. Area offerings include winter sleigh rides, snow skiing, auctions, fly fishing, golfing and summer stock theater, to name a few.

Innkeeper(s): Dieter & Willa Nohl. $135-290. 9 rooms with PB, 3 with FP, 4 with WP. Breakfast included in rates. Types of meals: Full gourmet bkfst. Beds: QT. Cable TV, reading lamp, clock radio, some with fireplace, hair dryer, bath amenities, wireless Internet access and iron/ironing board in room. Air conditioning. Jacuzzis and fireplaces on premises. Antiquing, art galleries, bicycling, canoeing/kayaking, cross-country skiing, downhill skiing, fishing, golf, hiking, horseback riding, live theater, museums, parks, shopping, sporting events, tennis, water sports, Marsh-Billings-Rockefeller National Park, Vermont Institute of Natural Science (Raptor Center), Calvin Coolidge Homestead, Silver Lake State Park and St. Gaudens National Historic Site nearby.

Location: City, country, mountains. Historic Vermont village.

Publicity: Harbor News, Boston Business Journal, Weekend Getaway, Inn Spots and Special Places.

Certificate may be used: Nov. 1-Nov. 30, Jan. 1-May 15, except holidays.

Virginia

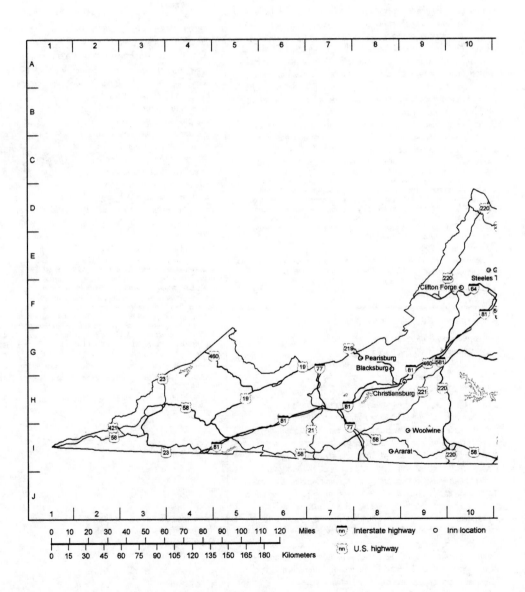

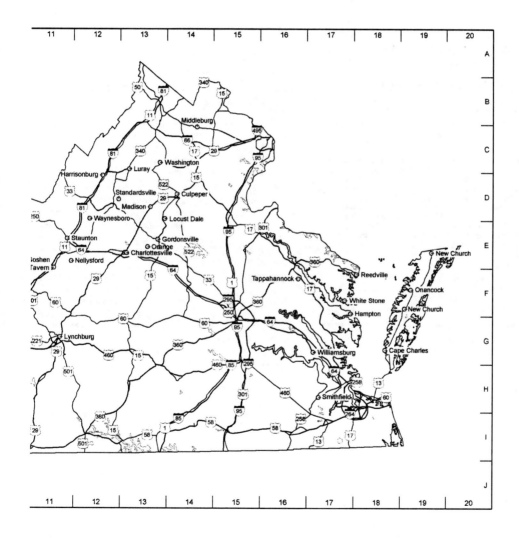

Blacksburg   G7

Clay Corner Inn

401 Clay Street SW
Blacksburg, VA 24060
(540)552-4030
Internet: www.claycorner.com
E-mail: stay@claycorner.com

Circa 1929. Clay Corner Inn is a delightful B&B known for its
friendly and comfortable ambiance next to Virginia Tech in
downtown Blacksburg. Indulge in the cookie bar on Friday
afternoons and beverages are always available. Each newly fur-

nished guest room and
suite features a regional
theme, such as New
River, Hokie, Blacksburg
and Appalachia. Private
baths, queen or king
beds, wireless Internet,
CD clock radios, and
other upscale amenities are sure to please. Savor a full, fresh
and healthy breakfast served every day. The swimming pool
and hot tub are open June to October and the Huckleberry
Trail starts on the next block.

Innkeeper(s): Rick and Nicky Aymes-Arevalo. $119-139. 8 rooms with PB.
Breakfast included in rates. Types of meals: Full bkfst, early coffee/tea, wine
packages and Friday cookie bar. Beds: KQ. Cable TV, DVD, reading lamp,
ceiling fan, clock radio, desk, hair dryer, bathrobes, wireless Internet access,
iron/ironing board, Surge protector power strip, fine bath amenities,
microfiber robes and Comphy luxury sheets in room. Central air. Swimming,
parlor games, telephone, fireplace and gift shop on premises. Antiquing, art
galleries, bicycling, canoeing/kayaking, fishing, golf, hiking, live theater,
museums, parks, shopping, sporting events, tennis, wineries, Smithfield
Plantation, Appalachian Trail, Huckleberry Trail, Blue Ridge Parkway and
public libraries nearby.

Location: College town.

Certificate may be used: December-March and June Anytime, subject to
availability, only at rack rates.

Cape Charles   G18

Cape Charles House

645 Tazewell Ave
Cape Charles, VA 23310-3313
(757)331-4920 Fax:(757)331-4960
Internet: capecharleshouse.com
E-mail: stay@capecharleshouse.com

Circa 1912. A local attorney built this 1912 Colonial Revival
home on the site of the town's first schoolhouse. The Cape
Charles House is the recipient of the Governor's Award for
Virginia Bed and Breakfast Hospitality. Oriental rugs cover lovingly restored hardwood floors. The owners have skillfully combined
antiques, heirlooms, artwork, fabrics and collections. Spacious
guest bedrooms are named after historically significant towns-
people. The premier Julia Wilkins
Room features a whirlpool
tub/shower and balcony.
Gourmet breakfasts served in
the formal dining room may
include favorites like fresh
mango-stuffed croissants in an

egg custard with grated nutmeg and orange liqueur. Enjoy late
afternoon wine and cheese as well as tea and sweets. Visit the
historic Victorian village and swim the quiet bay beach. Bikes,
beach towels, chairs and umbrellas are available.

Innkeeper(s): Bruce & Carol Evans. $140-200. 5 rooms with PB. Breakfast,
afternoon tea and snacks/refreshments included in rates. Types of meals: Full
gourmet bkfst, veg bkfst, early coffee/tea and wine. Beds: KQ. Cable TV,
DVD, reading lamp, CD player, ceiling fan, clock radio, desk, hair dryer, bath
amenities, wireless Internet access, iron/ironing board and Jacuzzi (two
rooms) in room. Air conditioning. TV, VCR, fax, copier, bicycles, parlor games,
telephone and fireplace on premises. Antiquing, art galleries, beach, bicycling, canoeing/kayaking, fishing, golf, hiking, museums, parks, shopping,
tennis, water sports and wineries nearby.

Location: Small town.

Publicity: *Coastal Living, Chesapeake Magazine, Chesapeake Life and HGTV
"If Walls Could Talk"*

*"We'll rave, recommend, and we'll return. The culinary magic of
your enchanting breakfasts are beyond comparison, unless you consider the charming effects of your warm and generous spirits."*

Certificate may be used: November-March, Sunday-Thursday.

Charlottesville   E13

The Inn at Monticello

Rt 20 S, 1188 Scottsville Rd
Charlottesville, VA 22902
(434)979-3593 (877)-RELAX-VA
Internet: www.innatmonticello.com
E-mail: stay@innatmonticello.com

Circa 1850. Thomas Jefferson built his own home, Monticello,
just two miles from this gracious country home. The innkeepers have preserved the historic ambiance of the area. Rooms

boast such pieces as four-poster
beds covered with fluffy, down comforters. Some of the guest quarters
have private porches or fireplaces.
Breakfast at the inn is a memorable
gourmet-appointed affair. Aside
from the usual homemade rolls, coffee cakes and muffins, guests enjoy
such entrees as pancakes or French
toast with seasonal fruit, egg dishes and a variety of quiche.
The front porch is lined with chairs for those who wish to
relax, and the grounds feature several gardens to enjoy.

Innkeeper(s): Bob Goss & Carolyn Patterson. $195. 5 rooms with PB, 2 with
FP. Breakfast and afternoon tea included in rates. Types of meals: Full gourmet
bkfst and early coffee/tea. Beds: KQT. Reading lamp and desk in room. Air
conditioning. Fax, parlor games, fireplace and afternoon tea with Virginia wine
on premises. Antiquing, downhill skiing, live theater, parks, shopping, sporting
events, Blue Ridge Parkway Sky Line Drive and wineries nearby.

Location: Historic, 1 mile to city.

Publicity: *Washington Post, Country Inns, Atlantic Country Magazine,
Gourmet and Bon Appetit.*

*"What a magnificent room at an extraordinary place. I can't wait to
tell all my friends."*

Certificate may be used: Sunday-Thursday, January-February, no holidays.

Clifton Forge F10

Firmstone Manor

6209 Longdale Furnace Rd
Clifton Forge, VA 24422-3618
(540)862-0892 (800)474-9882
Internet: www.firmstonemanor.com
E-mail: firmstonemanor@aol.com

Circa 1873. Built by the ironmaster of the Longdale Furnace Company, this Victorian is located in the historic district named for the firm. The home boasts many unusual original features, including a wraparound porch with a built-in gazebo and a view onto a walking wedding maze. There are more than 12 acres and a budding orchard to enjoy as well as views of the surrounding Shenandoah Valley and the Allegheny Mountains from all the rooms. Large guest bedrooms are elegantly appointed with ceiling fans and most have fireplaces. Civil War sites, museums, children's activities, shopping, lakes and state parks are in the area. Stay on-site and relax in a hammock under a 150-year-old tree with a good book and the sounds of a stream in the background.

Innkeeper(s): Barbara Jarocka. $90-130. 6 rooms with PB, 1 suite, 2 cottages. Breakfast and snacks/refreshments included in rates. Types of meals: Full gourmet bkfst, veg bkfst, early coffee/tea, lunch, picnic lunch, afternoon tea, wine, gourmet dinner, Breakfast in bed, bonfire cook outs and outside grill for guest use. Beds: KQT. Cable TV, VCR, DVD, reading lamp, ceiling fan, telephone, fireplace, hair dryer, bathrobes and iron/ironing board in room. Air conditioning. Fax, library, child care, parlor games, laundry facility, Croquet, Badminton and Fishing pond on premises. Antiquing, art galleries, bicycling, canoeing/kayaking, cross-country skiing, downhill skiing, fishing, golf, hiking, horseback riding, live theater, museums, parks, shopping, sporting events, water sports, wineries and drive-in movie nearby.

Location: Country, mountains. National Forest, property surrounded by pristine streams.

"We'll catch your dreams."

Certificate may be used: Anytime, Subject to availability.

Culpeper D14

Fountain Hall B&B

609 S East St
Culpeper, VA 22701-3222
(540)825-8200 (800)298-4748
Internet: www.fountainhall.com
E-mail: visit@fountainhall.com

Circa 1859. The well-appointed, oversized guest bedrooms and suites offer comforts galore. Some feature a private porch, whirlpool tub, plush robes and sweeping views of neighboring farms. Enjoy a leisurely breakfast of just-baked flaky croissants with butter and jam, fresh fruits, yogurt, hot and cold cereals and beverages. The surrounding area is steeped in rich American history, and the meticulously landscaped grounds feature seasonal gardens and a lawn groomed for croquet and bocce ball.

Innkeeper(s): Steve & Kathi Walker. $95-150. 6 rooms with PB, 2 suites. Breakfast and snacks/refreshments included in rates. Types of meals: Cont plus and early coffee/tea. Beds: QDT. Modem hook-up, data port, cable TV, VCR, reading lamp, CD player, refrigerator, ceiling fan, clock radio, telephone and desk in room. Air conditioning. Fax, parlor games and fireplace on premises. Handicap access. Antiquing, art galleries, bicycling,

canoeing/kayaking, fishing, golf, hiking, horseback riding, museums, parks, shopping and wineries nearby.

Location: Small town.

Publicity: *Culpeper Star Exponent, New York Times, Washington Post, Richmond Channel 8 and Local TV.*

"A great inn you run. We still look back on our stay at Fountain Hall as a standout."

Certificate may be used: Nov. 15-March 31, Sunday to Thursday, Rooms are limited, please mention certificate in advance of placing reservation.

Gordonsville E13

Sleepy Hollow Farm B&B

16280 Blue Ridge Tpke
Gordonsville, VA 22942-8214
(540)832-5555 (800)215-4804 Fax:(540)832-2515
Internet: www.sleepyhollowfarmbnb.com
E-mail: thehollow@sleepyhollowfarmbnb.com

Circa 1785. Many generations have added to this brick farmhouse creating somewhat of an optical illusion, as the historic home appears much smaller from a distance. The pink and white room often was visited by a friendly ghost, believed to be a Red Cross nurse during the Civil War, according to local stories. She hasn't been seen since the house was blessed in 1959. Accommodations also are available in Chestnut Cottage, which offers two suites with downstairs sitting areas and bedrooms and baths upstairs. One suite has a fireplace. The other suite includes a deck, full kitchen, whirlpool room and Franklin wood stove. The grounds include abundant wildlife, flower gardens, an herb garden, a gazebo and pond for swimming and fishing.

Innkeeper(s): Beverley Allison . $85-175. 5 rooms with PB, 2 with FP, 2 with WP, 3 total suites, including 1 two-bedroom suite, 1 cottage. Breakfast included in rates. Types of meals: Full bkfst, early coffee/tea and snacks/refreshments. Beds: QDT. Modem hook-up, cable TV, VCR, reading lamp, refrigerator, clock radio, telephone, coffeemaker, some with hot tub/spa, some with fireplace, hair dryer, bathrobes, iron/ironing board and some with desks in room. Central air. DVD, fax, copier, library, pet boarding, child care, two rooms with whirlpools. In the main house cake and cookies available on sideboard on premises. Antiquing, art galleries, bicycling, canoeing/kayaking, downhill skiing, fishing, golf, hiking, horseback riding, live theater, museums, parks, shopping, sporting events, tennis, wineries, steeplechase race, historic homes and fine dining nearby.

Location: Country.

Publicity: *Orange County Review, City Magazine, Town & County, Washington Post, New York Times and Country Inn Magazine.*

"This house is truly blessed."

Certificate may be used: Anytime Sunday-Thursday, excludes holidays. Anytime weekends last minute, 3 days prior.

Goshen   E10

The Hummingbird Inn

30 Wood Lane
Goshen, VA 24439-0147
(540)997-9065 (800)397-3214
Internet: www.hummingbirdinn.com
E-mail: stay@hummingbirdinn.com

Circa 1853. This early Victorian villa is located in the
Shenandoah Valley against the backdrop of the Allegheny
Mountains. Both the first and
second floors offer wraparound
verandas. The rustic den and
one guest room comprise the
oldest portions of the inn, built
around 1780. Dinners are available by advance reservation
(Friday and Saturday). An old
barn and babbling creek are on the grounds. Lexington, the
Virginia Horse Center, Natural Bridge, the Blue Ridge Parkway
and antiquing are all nearby.

Innkeeper(s): Patty and Dan Harrison. $145-175. 5 rooms with PB, 5 with
FP, 2 with WP. Breakfast and snacks/refreshments included in rates. Types of
meals: Country bkfst, veg bkfst, early coffee/tea, picnic lunch, wine and dinner. Beds: KQT. Reading lamp, ceiling fan, snack bar, clock radio, fireplace,
hair dryer, bathrobes, bath amenities, wireless Internet access and Internet
radios in all rooms in room. Air conditioning. TV, VCR, fax, library, parlor
games, telephone, gift shop and Trout stream on premises. Limited handicap
access. Antiquing, canoeing/kayaking, cross-country skiing, downhill skiing,
fishing, golf, hiking, horseback riding, live theater, museums, parks, shopping, wineries, herb farm, working grist mill and mineral baths nearby.

Location: Mountains.

Publicity: *New York Times Escapes section, USA Today, Time magazine, Out
Here (Tractor Supply magazine), Rockbridge Discovery, the Country Register,
Purple Roofs e-news, Blue Ridge Country, Inn Spots and Special Places,
WRIR, public radio Richmond and VA.*

*"We enjoyed our stay so much that we returned two weeks later on our
way back for a delicious home-cooked dinner, comfortable attractive
atmosphere, and familiar faces to welcome us after a long journey."*

Certificate may be used: Anytime, subject to availability.

Hampton   F17

Magnolia House Inn

232 S. Armistead Avenue
Hampton, VA 23669
(757)722-2888 Fax:(757)722-9888
Internet: www.maghousehampton.com
E-mail: stay@maghousehampton.com

Circa 1889. Listed in the National Register, the Magnolia
House Inn is serene and historic, gracing the waterfront village of Hampton on the Virginia peninsula of the Chesapeake
Bay. Shaded by Magnolia trees, guests relax on the front
porch of this Queen Anne Victorian after a full gourmet
breakfast, while planning their day in this charming seaport
town. Close to Willamsburg and Virginia Beach, Magnolia
House guests enjoy a central location to explore southeastern
Virginia. Lavish guest rooms and a spacious suite with a spa
tub feature luxurious amenities. Elegant parlors host meetings, events, and small weddings. Innkeepers Lankford &
Joyce Blair are certified wedding ministers and event planners.

Many packages & specials are offered.

Innkeeper(s): Lankford & Joyce Blair. $120-240. 3 rooms with PB, 2 with
FP, 1 with HT, 1 suite, 1 conference room. Breakfast, afternoon tea,
snacks/refreshments and wine included in rates. Types of meals: Full gourmet
bkfst, veg bkfst, early coffee/tea, picnic lunch and hors d'oeuvres. Beds: KQ.
Cable TV, VCR, DVD, reading lamp, stereo, refrigerator, snack bar, clock
radio, desk, some with hot tub/spa, hair dryer, bathrobes, bath amenities,
wireless Internet access and iron/ironing board in room. Central air. Fax, copier, library, parlor games, fireplace and gift shop on premises. Limited handicap access. Amusement parks, antiquing, art galleries, beach, bicycling, fishing, golf, hiking, live theater, museums, parks, shopping, sporting events,
water sports and wineries nearby.

Location: City, ocean community.

Publicity: *Grapevine Home & Travel Magazine, Pathfinders Travel Magazine,
Virginia Lifestyles, Daily Press, Hampton - By the Sea & Beyond and 'What
Not To Wear' (Feb. 2008).*

Certificate may be used: Jan. 1-April 30, Sunday-Thursday, subject to
availability.

Harrisonburg   D12

Stonewall Jackson Inn B&B

547 E Market St
Harrisonburg, VA 22801-4227
(540) 433-8233 (800) 445-5330
Internet: www.stonewalljacksoninn.com
E-mail: info@stonewalljacksoninn.com

Circa 1885. Stonewall Jackson Inn Bed and Breakfast sits as a
Queen Ann mansion on Nob Hill overlooking the Historic
District of downtown Harrisonburg, Virginia in the Shenandoah
Valley region. It is an easy walk to the Old Confederate
Cemetery, fine restaurants, museums, shops and theater
venues. This inn is centrally located in respect to James
Madison & Eastern Mennonite Universities, Interstate 81 and
the City Center as well as the many Shenandoah Valley tourist
attractions and recreational activities. This four-season destination sits amid breathtaking beauty in the Blue Ridge and
Allegheny Mountains. Owner/Innkeeper, Dr. Wayne Engel is
well known in the community for his story-telling, hospitality,
and generosity. Enjoy the delightful accommodations and a
hearty gourmet breakfast each morning.

Innkeeper(s): Dr. Wayne Engel. $89-189. 10 rooms with PB, 1 with FP, 1
conference room. Breakfast, snacks/refreshments, In-room snacks, cookies,
free sodas, bottled water, ice and coffee and teas included in rates. Types of
meals: Full gourmet bkfst, veg bkfst, Close to gourmet restaurants offering
fine rooftop dining, upscale pubs and microbreweries and many different
kinds of ethnic restaurants. Beds: KQDT. Modem hook-up, cable TV, DVD,
reading lamp, refrigerator, ceiling fan, snack bar, clock radio, telephone, desk,
some with fireplace, hair dryer, bath amenities, wireless Internet access,
Individual climate control with electronic hypo-allergenic filter, Ceiling fan,
Free access to drinks and snacks in room. Central air. VCR, fax, copier, laundry facility, gift shop, Free WiFi & High-speed Internet, Outside deck & patio
dining, Off-street parking, Discounts to local restaurants and attractions on
premises. Limited handicap access. Antiquing, art galleries, bicycling, canoe-
ing/kayaking, cross-country skiing, downhill skiing, fishing, golf, hiking, horseback riding, live theater, museums, parks, shopping, sporting events, tennis,
wineries, Massanutten, Luray Caverns, Shenandoah Caverns, Civil War Trails,
Battlefields and the Historic Downtown District nearby.

Location: City, mountains. Shenandoah Valley.

Publicity: *Arrington's Publication.*

Certificate may be used: January-March 31, Sunday-Thursday, subject to
availability. One certificate per couple/person per year. Holidays excluded.

Locust Dale D13

The Inn at Meander Plantation

2333 North James Madison Hwy.
Locust Dale, VA 22948-9701
(540)672-4912 (800)385-4936 Fax:(540)672-0405
Internet: www.meander.net
E-mail: inn@meander.net

Circa 1766. This historic country estate was built by Henry Fry, close friend of Thomas Jefferson who often stopped here on his way to Monticello. The mansion is serenely decorated with elegant antiques and period reproductions, including four-poster beds. Healthy gourmet breakfasts are prepared by Chef Suzie. Enjoy views of the Blue Ridge Mountains from the rockers on the back porches. Ancient formal boxwood gardens, surrounding natural woodlands, meadows, pastures and Robinson River frontage are part of Meander Conservancy, offering educational programs and back-to-nature packages.

Innkeeper(s): Suzie Blanchard, Suzanne Thomas. $120-200. 8 rooms with PB, 5 with FP, 4 suites, 1 conference room. Breakfast included in rates. Types of meals: Full bkfst, early coffee/tea, lunch, picnic lunch, snacks/refreshments and gourmet dinner. Beds: KQ. Reading lamp, clock radio and desk in room. Air conditioning. VCR, fax, stable, library, pet boarding, child care, parlor games, telephone, fireplace, restaurant service Thursday and Friday and Saturday on premises. Antiquing, cross-country skiing, downhill skiing, fishing, live theater, parks, shopping, sporting events and wineries nearby.

Location: Country.

"Staying at the Inn at Meander Plantation feels like being immersed in another century while having the luxuries and amenities available today."

Certificate may be used: Year-round, Sunday-Thursday, excluding holidays and October.

Luray C13

Allstar Lodging

803 E. Main St.
Luray, VA 22835
(540)843-0606 (866)780-7827
Internet: www.allstarlodging.com
E-mail: allstar@allstarlodging.com

Select from rustic to luxurious vacation homes, cottages and cabins in the scenic Shenandoah Valley, Page County and Luray, Virginia area. Choose locations with preferred amenities that may include mountain views, river or fishing pond access, near George Washington National Forest, pet-friendly or secluded. Some also feature Internet, hot tubs, canoes, bikes, swimming pools and campfire pits. Pre-arranged concierge services can provide catering, massage, flowers, candles, gift baskets, outdoor adventures, boat rentals and horseback riding. Specials and seasonal rates are often available. Allstar Lodging offers a personal touch to ensure the perfect romantic getaway, family reunion, or business retreat with the desired necessities as well as indulgent extra touches that will pamper and relax.

Innkeeper(s): Carlos. $85-250. 40 rooms. Modem hook-up, cable TV, VCR,

DVD, stereo, refrigerator, ceiling fan, clock radio, telephone, coffeemaker, desk, some with hot tub/spa, some with fireplace, hair dryer, wireless Internet access, iron/ironing board, Amenities depend on vacation rental preference, each are unique and most have amenities listed above in room. Central air. Spa, swimming, bicycles, library, pet boarding, parlor games, laundry facility, Amenities depend on vacation rental property preference, each have unique items and many have the ones listed above on premises. Antiquing, art galleries, bicycling, canoeing/kayaking, downhill skiing, fishing, golf, hiking, horseback riding, live theater, museums, parks, shopping, sporting events, tennis, water sports, wineries, Shenandoah National Park, Skyline Drive, Luray Caverns and Shenandoah River nearby.

Location: Country, mountains, waterfront.

Certificate may be used: Sept. 6-May 27, Sunday-Thursday, excludes holidays. 6 adult minimum.

Woodruff Inns and Shenandoah River Cabin Escapes

138 E Main St
Luray, VA 22835
(540)743-1494 Fax:(540)743-1722
Internet: www.woodruffinns.com
E-mail: reservations@woodruffinns.com

Circa 1882. Woodruff Inns and Shenandoah River Cabin Escapes boast relaxation and romance amid casual elegance and tranquility. Gracing the scenic area of Luray, Virginia in the Shenandoah Valley of the Blue Ridge Mountains region, historic sites and natural attractions are plentiful from Civil War battlegrounds and presidential estates to nearby caverns. Hospitality and service are thoughtful and pampering. Relax in one of the common areas with a beverage. Select from a variety of luxury accommodations that include Victorian, French Country and Rustic Charm. The onsite restaurant offers a delightful culinary menu and selection of local wines. Ask about specials and packages available.

Innkeeper(s): Patrick and Melissa Riley. $99-299. 13 rooms, 16 with PB, 7 with FP, 3 with HT, 11 with WP, 6 suites, 4 cabins, 1 conference room. Breakfast and Full American Breakfast included with all Inn rooms (may be added to Cabins for additional fee) included in rates. Types of meals: Full gourmet bkfst, veg bkfst, picnic lunch, wine, gourmet dinner, Three Star, Three Diamond on-site restaurant and bar at The Victorian Inn. Open Wednesday, Thursday and Sunday from 5PM- 8PM and Friday/Saturday from 5PM-9PM. Reservations are suggested. Restaurant on premises. Beds: KQDT. DVD, reading lamp, CD player, clock radio, coffeemaker, desk, bath amenities, Cable or DirecTV & Wi-Fi in most rooms, Complimentary Cream Sherry in Inn rooms, Some have full kitchens or kitchenettes and Full housekeeping services for all facilities in room. Air conditioning. TV, fax, copier, spa, parlor games, telephone, fireplace, On-site full service restaurant and bar, Jacuzzis, Garden areas, Outdoor gazebos, Large front porches and Private parking on premises. Antiquing, art galleries, bicycling, canoeing/kayaking, cross-country skiing, downhill skiing, fishing, golf, hiking, horseback riding, live theater, museums, parks, shopping, sporting events, tennis, water sports, wineries, Luray Caverns, Shenandoah National Park, George Washington National Forest, New Market Battlefield and Museum, Virginia Wine Country (inquire about Private Tour Packages), Massanutten Four Seasons Resort, Bryce Ski Resort, Corn/Garden Mazes, Shenandoah Speedway and BB&T Center for the Performing Arts nearby.

Location: Mountains.

Publicity: *Potomac Living, Cascapades Magazine, Blue Ridge Country Magazine, Cooperative Living, Virginia Wine Gazette, Food and Wine Magazine, Gourmet Magazine, Washington Times and recipient of Virginia's gold three cluster wine award.*

Certificate may be used: Jan. 5-Mar. 15, Monday-Thursday.

Lynchburg G11

Carriage House Inn B&B

404 Cabell St
Lynchburg, VA 24504-1217
(434)846-1388 (800)937-3582
Internet: www.TheCarriageHouseInnBandB.com
E-mail: info@TheCarriageHouseInnBandB.com

Circa 1878. Gracing more than one acre in the Daniels Hill Historic District, this 1878 red brick Italianate mansion proudly welcomes leisure and business travelers after a meticulous four-year restoration and renovation. Carriage House Inn Bed & Breakfast is located in Lynchburg, Virginia in the foothills of the Blue Ridge Mountains along the banks of the James River. Enjoy refreshments in the formal parlor or on the wraparound front porch. Guest bedrooms and suites are named for members of the Watts family, the home's first owners. Soak in an original clawfoot tub and schedule a massage or body treatment with a certified therapist. Amenities include Egyptian cotton towels, fine linens, coal-burning fireplaces, robes, slippers and turndown service with water and chocolates. Linger over a three-course gourmet breakfast before taking a scenic bike ride.

Innkeeper(s): Kathy & Mike Bedsworth. $179-299. 6 rooms, 5 with PB, 3 total suites, including 1 two-bedroom suite, 1 conference room. Breakfast, snacks/refreshments, hors d'oeuvres, wine, 4-course breakfast featuring a signature dish each month and Snacks and wine for arrivals between 4-5PM included in rates. Types of meals: Full gourmet bkfst, veg bkfst, early coffee/tea. Many excellent restaurants are nearby several within walking distance and Brunch or teas can be arranged in our Event Center. Beds: KQDT. Reading lamp, ceiling fan, snack bar, clock radio, turn-down service, desk, most with fireplace, hair dryer, bathrobes, bath amenities, wireless Internet access, iron/ironing board, I-Pod docking station in some rooms, snack bar & guest refrigerator, original coal fireplaces & mantels in rooms, window seats in Mary Watts, Stephen Watts & RT Watts rooms, Original tubs in all baths, Original sinks in two baths and Original light fixtures in three bedrooms. Rooms in Carriage House enjoy their own parlor with tv & kitchenette in room. Central air. TV, VCR, DVD, fax, copier, bicycles, library, parlor games, telephone, Conference & Event Center & Breakout Room for up to 28 people, Several types of massage and body treatments offered by a certified massage therapist in on-site massage & bodyworks studio, See web site for details and pricing, Welcome snacks & wine with arrivals between 4-5PM, Turn-down Service, Early coffee, tea & juice available, Four Course Breakfast, Off-street parking, Guest Refrigerator, Video Library, Airport & Train Service, Three-Sided Wraparound Front Porch, Patio with Fish Pond and Picnic Tables on premises. Antiquing, art galleries, bicycling, canoeing/kayaking, downhill skiing, fishing, golf, hiking, horseback riding, live theater, museums, parks, shopping, sporting events, water sports, wineries, James River & the Black Water Trail (3 blocks), Excellent Biking, Hiking, Fishing, Canoeing, Civil War Sites, Thomas Jefferson's Poplar Forest, National D-Day Memorial, Point of Honor, Appomattox Courthouse, Old City Cemetery, Blue Ridge Parkway and Crabtree Falls nearby.

Location: City.

Publicity: *Washington Post 11/09, Washington Post 3/10, Lynchburg Living Magazine Best B & B 2007, Showcase Magazine 3/08, Old Town Lynchburg local station (June, July and August 2007).*

Certificate may be used: January-April, June-July, November-December, cannot be combined with any other discount, offer or voucher.

Federal Crest Inn

1101 Federal St
Lynchburg, VA 24504-3018
(434)845-6155 (800)818-6155 Fax:(434)845-1445
Internet: www.federalcrest.com
E-mail: inn@federalcrest.com

Circa 1909. The guest rooms at Federal Crest are named for the many varieties of trees and flowers native to Virginia. This handsome red brick home, a fine example of Georgian Revival architecture, features a commanding front entrance flanked by columns that hold up the second-story veranda. A grand staircase, carved woodwork, polished floors topped with fine rugs and more columns create an aura of elegance. Each guest room offers something special and romantic, from a mountain view to a Jacuzzi tub. Breakfasts are served on fine china, and the first course is always a freshly baked muffin with a secret message inside.

Innkeeper(s): Ann & Phil Ripley. $145-230. 5 rooms, 4 with PB, 4 with FP, 1 with WP, 2 total suites, including 1 two-bedroom suite, 1 conference room. Breakfast, afternoon tea and snacks/refreshments included in rates. Types of meals: Full gourmet bkfst, veg bkfst and early coffee/tea. Beds: QD. Modem hook-up, data port, cable TV, VCR, reading lamp, refrigerator, snack bar, clock radio, telephone, turn-down service, desk, fireplace, hair dryer, bathrobes, bath amenities, wireless Internet access and iron/ironing board in room. Central air. Fax, copier, library, parlor games, gift shop, Conference theater with 60-inch TV (Ballroom) with stage, '50s cafe with antique jukebox, Video library, Movie library, Afternoon & evening beverages & snacks, Early coffee & juice, Hot gourmet breakfast, Off-street parking, Airport and Train transportation on premises. Antiquing, art galleries, bicycling, canoeing/kayaking, fishing, golf, hiking, horseback riding, live theater, museums, parks, shopping, sporting events, tennis, wineries, Civil War Sites, Old City Cemetery, Appomattox, Poplar Forest, Point of Honor and Old Court House Museum nearby.

Location: City, mountains. Central Virginia.

Publicity: *Washington Post, News & Advance, Scene, Local ABC, WLNI promotions and "Nocturne" (filmed at inn 2003).*

"What a wonderful place to celebrate our birthdays and enjoy our last romantic getaway before the birth of our first child."
Certificate may be used: Jan. 2-Dec. 30, Sunday-Thursday.

Ivy Creek Farm Bed and Breakfast

2812 Link Road
Lynchburg, VA 24503
(434)384-3802 (800)689-7404 Fax:(434)384-3803
Internet: www.ivycreekfarm.com
E-mail: info@ivycreekfarm.com

Circa 1840. Offering casual elegance and a pastoral ambiance, this eight-acre country estate was built in 1840 and recently renovated. Lounge in the library or listen to music in the front parlor, each with a fireplace. Gather for afternoon tea, wine and refreshments. Snacks are available anytime in the Turret Room that also has a guest refrigerator stocked with beverages. Overlook the woods and pond from the verandas. Luxurious guest bedrooms are named for neighboring historic country properties and boast upscale amenities that include fresh water and gourmet chocolates. Breakfast is served in the fireside dining room. Swim in the indoor heated pool with a lap lane and an adjoining whirlpool spa. Play softball on the full-size field or explore the Blue Ridge Mountains.

Innkeeper(s): Marilyn and Lynn Brooks. $169-249. 3 rooms with PB, 1 with FP. Breakfast, snacks/refreshments, hors d'oeuvres and wine included in rates. Types of meals: Full gourmet bkfst and early coffee/tea. Beds: KQ. TV, reading lamp, CD player, clock radio, turn-down service, desk, some with hot tub/spa, some with fireplace, hair dryer, bathrobes, bath amenities, wireless Internet access, iron/ironing board, Down pillows and comforters, Luxury linens, Terry robes, Soaking tub and Direct TV in room. Central air. VCR, DVD, fax, copier, spa, swimming, library, parlor games, telephone, laundry facility, gift shop, indoor swimming pool with lap lane, exercise equipment, baseball field, 24-hour hot and cold beverages, guest refrigerator, verandas and deck on premises. Antiquing, art galleries, bicycling, canoeing/kayaking, cross-country skiing, downhill skiing, fishing, golf, hiking, horseback riding, museums, parks, shopping, sporting events, tennis, wineries, Civil War sites, Thomas Jefferson's Poplar Forest, Blue Ridge Parkway, Appalachian Trail and Blackwater Creek Preserve nearby.

Location: City, mountains.

Certificate may be used: November-March, Sunday-Thursday, subject to availability.

Madison D13

Dulaney Hollow at Old Rag Mountain B&B Inn

3932 South F.T. Valley Rd - Scenic VA Byway, Rt 231
Madison, VA 22727
(540) 923-4470 Fax:(540)923-4841
Internet: www.DulaneyHollow.com
E-mail: oldragmtninn@nexet.net

Circa 1911. Peacefully settled in the foothills of the Blue Ridge Mountains in Madison, Virginia, Dulaney Hollow at Old Rag Mountain B&B Inn, circa 1911, offers gracious hospitality. The quiet beauty is accented by shaded lawns, mountain views and a fishing pond. Accommodations include air-conditioned guest rooms in the Manor House with antique furnishings. Gather for a casual country breakfast in the dining room. Two spacious Country Cottages and The Hayloft in the Dulaney Hollow Barn include fully equipped kitchens and a portable breakfast. Hike in nearby Shenandoah National Park, fish in trout streams and visit homes of U.S. presidents and scores of wineries and vineyards. This B&B inn is less than an hour from Charlottesville and less than 2 hours from Washington, D.C.

Innkeeper(s): Susan & Louis Cable. $135-160. 6 rooms with PB, 2 with FP, 3 cottages, 1 conference room. Breakfast included in rates. Types of meals: Country bkfst, veg bkfst and early coffee/tea. Beds: QDT. VCR, refrigerator, ceiling fan, coffeemaker, desk, hair dryer and iron/ironing board in room. Air conditioning. DVD, fax, copier, telephone, fireplace, Limited access to PC, Copy/printer machine, Internet access, Antique Shop and Fish Pond on premises. Antiquing, art galleries, canoeing/kayaking, cross-country skiing, downhill skiing, fishing, golf, hiking, horseback riding, live theater, museums, parks, shopping, sporting events, tennis, water sports, wineries, Civil War sites, Historic sites, Monticello, Montpelier, Battlefields, Shenandoah National Park, Shenandoah River, Trout Streams and Rapidan Wildlife Management Area for Hunting nearby.
Location: Mountains. Blue Ridge Mountains.
Publicity: *Madison Eagle and Charlottesville Daily Progress.*
Certificate may be used: Jan. 1-Dec. 31 (only on weekday nights, Monday-Thursday; no weekends or holidays).

Middleburg C14

Briar Patch Bed & Breakfast Inn

23130 Briar Patch Lane
Middleburg, VA 20117
(703)327-5911 (866)327-5911 Fax:(703)327-5933
Internet: www.briarpatchbandb.com
E-mail: info@briarpatchbandb.com

Circa 1805. Leave stress behind when staying at this historic farm that sits on 47 rolling acres of land that once was where the Civil War's Battle of the Haystacks was fought in 1863. Located in the heart of horse, antique and wine country, it is just 20 minutes from Dulles Airport and 45 minutes from Washington, DC. Overlook the Bull Run Mountains while sitting on the front porch. Antique-filled guest bedrooms in the main house are named after the flowers and feature canopy or four-poster beds. Two rooms can adjoin to become a suite. A separate one-bedroom cottage includes a fully equipped kitchen, dining area and living room. Breakfast is provided in

the large kitchen or outside patio. Swim in the pool or soak in the year-round hot tub.

Innkeeper(s): Henriette Buell & Charlotte John, Manager. $95-285. 9 rooms, 3 with PB, 3 with FP, 3 two-bedroom suites, 1 cottage. Breakfast included in rates. Types of meals: Full breakfast on weekends and Continental on weekdays. Beds: KQ. Reading lamp, CD player, ceiling fan, some with fireplace, hair dryer, bathrobes, wireless Internet access and iron/ironing board in room. Air conditioning. TV, VCR, DVD, fax, copier, spa, swimming, library, parlor games and telephone on premises. Limited handicap access. Antiquing, art galleries, bicycling, canoeing/kayaking, fishing, golf, hiking, horseback riding, museums, parks, shopping, tennis and wineries nearby.
Location: Country.
Certificate may be used: Monday-Thursday.

Nellysford E11

The Mark Addy

56 Rodes Farm Dr
Nellysford, VA 22958-9526
(434)361-1101
Internet: www.mark-addy.com
E-mail: info@mark-addy.com

Circa 1837. It's not hard to understand why Dr. John Everett, the son of Thomas Jefferson's physician, chose this picturesque, Blue Ridge Mountain setting for his home. Everett expanded the simple, four-room farmhouse already present into a gracious manor. The well-appointed guest rooms feature double whirlpool baths, double showers or a clawfoot tub. Beds are covered with vintage linens, feather pillows and cozy, down comforters. There are plenty of relaxing possibilities, including five porches and a hammock set among the trees.

Innkeeper(s): Leslie & Rafael Tal. $99-229. 10 rooms with PB, 1 suite. Types of meals: Full gourmet bkfst, early coffee/tea, gourmet lunch, picnic lunch and gourmet dinner. Beds: KQDT. Reading lamp, ceiling fan and Jacuzzi in room. Air conditioning. VCR, library, parlor games and telephone on premises. Handicap access. Antiquing, downhill skiing, fishing, live theater, parks, shopping, sporting events, horseback riding and hiking nearby.
Location: Mountains.
Publicity: *Local paper.*
Certificate may be used: Monday-Thursday year-round except October.

New Church E19

The Garden and The Sea Inn

4188 Nelson Road
New Church, VA 23415-0275
(757)824-0672 (800)824-0672
Internet: www.gardenandseainn.com
E-mail: innkeeper@gardenandseainn.com

Circa 1802. The Garden and Sea Inn adorns five acres with woods and wildlife, as well as landscaped gardens. Located near Chincoteague and Assateague Islands and the Chesapeake Bay in New Church, Virginia, this historic Victorian B&B is the perfect setting for year-round relaxation. Sit on the patio or on the wicker-accented porch. A swing beckons by one of the

ponds or nap in a hammock. Swim in the heated pool and enjoy the shade of the adjacent gazebo. Afternoon refreshments are served in the parlor. Air-conditioned guest rooms and a suite are delightful retreats. Many boast whirlpool tubs and some include a fireplace. Whether an early riser or sleeping in, a bountiful breakfast will be available in the dining room. Sample popular German specialties as well as traditional classic dishes.

Innkeeper(s): Thomas and Dorothee Renn. $95-225. 9 rooms with PB, 3 with FP, 8 with WP, 2 suites, 1 conference room. Breakfast and snacks/refreshments included in rates. Types of meals: Full gourmet bkfst, early coffee/tea, gourmet dinner and room service. Beds: KQ. Cable TV, DVD, reading lamp, refrigerator, ceiling fan, clock radio, coffeemaker, most with hot tub/spa, some with fireplace, hair dryer, bathrobes, bath amenities and wireless Internet access in room. Central air. VCR, fax, copier, swimming, library, parlor games, telephone and outdoor heated pool on premises. Handicap access. Antiquing, beach, bicycling, canoeing/kayaking, fishing, hiking, museums, parks, shopping, water sports and wineries nearby.

Location: Country.

Publicity: *Washington Post, Modern Bride and Southern Living.*

Certificate may be used: Sunday-Thursday in April, May, June, October and November.

Onancock   F19

Colonial Manor Inn
84 Market St
Onancock, VA 23417-4224
(757)787-3521 Fax:(757)787-2564
Internet: www.colonialmanorinn.com
E-mail: hosts@colonialmanorinn.com

Circa 1882. Adorning the historic waterfront community, this recently renovated Colonial home built in 1882, has since become the oldest operating inn on the state's Eastern Shore. An eclectic blend of antiques and collectibles accents the casually elegant décor of this smoke-free inn. Relax on a comfortable sofa in the living room. Enjoy the inviting enclosed porch with year-round heating and cooling as well as candles that enhance the evening ambiance. Stay in a suite that features a private outside entrance and sitting area. A brick walkway leads to the gazebo with a nearby fountain and two acres of park-like grounds to explore. Breakfast is always a delicious repast served family-style at the huge dining table. Bask on the sun deck or sit on a front lawn chair.

Innkeeper(s): Linda Nicola. $99-129. 6 rooms with PB, 3 total suites, including 1 two-bedroom suite. Breakfast and snacks/refreshments included in rates. Types of meals: Full gourmet bkfst, veg bkfst and early coffee/tea. Beds: QT. Cable TV, reading lamp, refrigerator, clock radio, coffeemaker, desk, hair dryer, bath amenities, wireless Internet access and iron/ironing board in room. Air conditioning. Fax, bicycles, library, parlor games, telephone, Lawn games such as croquet, bocce ball & basketball, Wildlife, Two acres of parkland & gardens, Bicycles, Pet sitting and childcare available shorterm on premises. Handicap access. Antiquing, beach, bicycling, canoeing/kayaking, fishing, golf, hiking, museums, parks, shopping, water sports, wineries, Walking distance to Theatre, Movies, Restaurants, Wharf and Galleries nearby.

Location: Country.

Certificate may be used: January/February, Sunday-Thursday.

Orange   E13

Mayhurst Inn
12460 Mayhurst Ln
Orange, VA 22960
(540)672-5597 (888)672-5597
Internet: www.mayhurstinn.com
E-mail: mayhurstbandb@aol.com

Circa 1859. Romance and relaxation await at this stunning 1859 plantation mansion. Meticulously restored to offer the best of contemporary comforts, it has retained yesterday's

enchantment. Enjoy wine and cheese upon arrival. Ascend the four-story oval staircase to the fanciful cupola. Stately guest bedrooms boast double whirlpool tubs, fine linens, original Italian marble fireplaces, antique furnishings and period décor. Satisfying plantation breakfasts are served in front of the fireplace in the dining room, on the rear veranda or on the brick courtyard. Wander the 37 acres with summer kitchen, smokehouse and schoolhouse still standing amongst 200-year-old trees. Generals Lee, Jackson and Hill were guests when the Army's Northern Virginia Corps III headquartered here. Visit local wineries, three presidential homes and several major Civil War battlefields, all within 25 miles.

Innkeeper(s): Jack & Pat North. $169-239. 8 rooms with PB, 8 with FP, 2 with WP, 2 two-bedroom suites, 1 cottage, 1 conference room. Breakfast, snacks/refreshments, wine and Special diets accommodated included in rates. Types of meals: Full gourmet bkfst, veg bkfst, early coffee/tea, picnic lunch and Lunches and Dinners available through several caterers. Our dining room seats 30. Special Diets can be accommodated. Beds: KQDT. Data port, cable TV, VCR, DVD, reading lamp, CD player, refrigerator, ceiling fan, clock radio, telephone, coffeemaker, turn-down service, desk, some with hot tub/spa, fireplace, hair dryer, bathrobes, bath amenities, wireless Internet access, iron/ironing board and Free WiFi in room. Central air. Fax, copier, library, parlor games, laundry facility, gift shop, Bass fishing on inn pond, 1.5 miles of mowed walking paths, Hammock and Picnic areas on premises. Handicap access. Antiquing, art galleries, bicycling, canoeing/kayaking, fishing, golf, hiking, horseback riding, live theater, museums, shopping, sporting events, water sports, wineries, 6 Civil War battlefields, 3 Presidential homes, Sky diving, Hot air ballooning (from Mayhurst), 10 of Virginia's finest Wineries and 5 golf courses nearby.

Location: Country. Edge of town.

Publicity: *Old House Journal, Virginia Lifestyles Magazine, Washingtonian, Travel Virginia Magazine, Virginia Wine Lover Magazine, LA Times, OC Magazine., PBS Special, Road Trip to History - Orange, VA (2007) and PBS Special on Mayhurst (2009).*

"The beauty of this Inn is exceeded only by the graciousness of Mayhurst hosts: Jack and Pat."

Certificate may be used: Sunday-Thursday, January-March 31 and July 5-Aug. 31.

Pearisburg   G8

Inn at Riverbend
125 River Ridge Dr.
Pearisburg, VA 24134
(540)921-5211 Fax:(540)921-2720
Internet: www.innatriverbend.com
E-mail: stay@innatriverbend.com

Circa 2003. Expansive views of the New River and the surrounding valley are incredibly breathtaking while staying at this contemporary bed and breakfast. Enjoy refreshments in front of the stone fireplace in a great room with a wall of French doors and windows. Two levels of huge wraparound decks offer an abundance of space to appreciate the scenic beauty and assortment of birds. Watch a movie or gather as a group in the TV/meeting room. Luxury guest bedrooms are delightful retreats that have access to decks or terraces and feature pressed linens, specialty personal products, stocked refrigerators, and other generous amenities. Several rooms boast whirlpool tubs. After a three-course breakfast, sample some of the area's many outdoor activities. The Appalachian Trail is only two miles away.

Innkeeper(s): Janet and Jimm Burton. $179-259. 7 rooms with PB, 1 conference room. Breakfast and snacks/refreshments included in rates. Types of meals: Full bkfst, veg bkfst, early coffee/tea, lunch, picnic lunch, wine and dinner. Beds: KQT. Modem hook-up, data port, cable TV, DVD, reading lamp, CD player, ceiling fan, clock radio, turn-down service, desk, some with hot tub/spa, hair dryer, bathrobes, bath amenities, wireless Internet access and iron/ironing board in room. Central air. VCR, fax, copier, library, parlor games, telephone, fireplace and gift shop on premises. Handicap access. Antiquing, art galleries, bicycling, canoeing/kayaking, cross-country skiing, downhill skiing, fishing, golf, hiking, horseback riding, live theater, museums, parks, shopping, sporting events, tennis, water sports and wineries nearby.

Location: Country, mountains. Overlooking the New River.

Publicity: *Virginia Living (August 2009) Wild, Wet and Untamed by Joe Tennis, USA Weekend (March 27-29, 2009) Travel Smart by Edwin Potter and Travel the Greenway .*

Certificate may be used: Anytime, two weeks prior to arrival, subject to availability.

Smithfield   H17

Four Square Plantation

13357 Foursquare Rd
Smithfield, VA 23430-8643
(757)365-0749 Fax:(757)365-0749
Internet: www.innvirginia.com/listings/foursquareplantation-smithfield-virginia.html
E-mail: foursquareplantation@att.net

Circa 1807. Located in the historic James River area, the original land grant, "Four Square" was established in 1664 and consisted of 640 acres. Now in the National Register and a Virginia Historic Landmark, the Federal style home is called Plantation Plain by Virginia preservationists. The inn is furnished with family period pieces and antiques. The Vaughan Room offers a fireplace, Empire furnishings and access by private staircase. Breakfast is served in the dining room. The inn's four acres provide a setting for weddings and special events. Tour Williamsburg, Jamestown, the James River Plantations and Yorktown nearby.

Innkeeper(s): Roger & Donna. $75-85. 3 rooms with PB, 3 with FP. Breakfast included in rates. Types of meals: Full gourmet bkfst and early coffee/tea. Beds: KQT. Cable TV, reading lamp, ceiling fan, telephone and turn-down service in room. Air conditioning. VCR, fax, copier and parlor games on premises. Antiquing, golf and shopping nearby.

Location: Country. Three miles from Smithfield.

Publicity: *Daily Press and Virginia Pilot.*

Certificate may be used: Sunday-Thursday, Jan.1-March 31, Nov.1-Dec.23, no holidays.

Stanardsville   D12

The Lafayette Inn

146 E. Main St
Stanardsville, VA 22973
(434)985-6345
Internet: www.thelafayette.com
E-mail: info@thelafayette.com

Circa 1840. Rich with a local legacy, this historic landmark was built in 1840 and stands as a stately three-story Federalist red brick building in downtown Stanardsville, Virginia. Huge porches are accented with white colonnades. Surrounded by scenic beauty, Shenandoah National Park is just 10 minutes away. The Lafayette Inn features romantic, well-appointed guest bedrooms and suites with generous amenities to make each stay most comfortable. Dicey's Cottage, the original two-story slave quarters, provides spacious privacy, Jacuzzi tubs, gas fire-

places, a kitchenette and a deck. A country-style breakfast is served in the coffee and tea house, transformed daily from being the Tavern where lunch and dinner are available. There is much to see and experience in the area. Take a tour of local vineyards, shop for pottery or visit nearby Monticello. Ask about special packages offered.

Innkeeper(s): Alan & Kaye Pyles. $139-199. 6 rooms, 2 with PB, 5 suites, 1 cottage. Breakfast and Sunday Brunch is optional included in rates. Types of meals: Country bkfst, Inn guests can reserve a "Taste of the Lafayette Inn" dinner for Monday through Wednesday evenings - 7:00 PM seating (advanced reservations required) and $50 per person. Special 3-course $25.00 Prix Fixe dinner by reservation on Sunday-Thursdays. Advance reservations required. Regular restaurant menu available on Friday and Saturdays. Beds: KQ. Central air. Antiquing, hiking, shopping and wineries nearby.

Location: Country, mountains.

Certificate may be used: Any Monday-Thursday.

Staunton   E11

Staunton Choral Gardens

216 W. Frederick St.
Staunton, VA 24401
(540)885-6556
Internet: www.stauntonbedandbreakfast.com
E-mail: StauntonBandB@Comcast.net

Circa 1915. Stay in the heart of the Shenandoah Valley at this wonderfully restored, gracious Sam Collins brick inn and 150-year-old award-winning Carriage House, a large, luxurious two-story private suite, in historic downtown Staunton, Virginia. Guest bedrooms feature upscale amenities that include wireless high-speed Internet service, lush featherbed-topped mattresses and central air conditioning. A fireplace, refrigerator and microwave are also available in some rooms. Enjoy thoughtful touches of fresh flowers, candies, and personal products. Savor multi-course breakfasts and afternoon refreshments. Relax in one of the three gardens. A large goldfish pond and fountain accent the courtyard garden; there is ample seating in the shade garden and a roof-covered swing welcomes rainy-day pleasures at Staunton Choral Gardens. A kennel area is available.

Innkeeper(s): Carolyn Avalos. $95-200. 5 rooms with PB, 3 with FP, 2 two-bedroom suites, 1 cottage. Breakfast, afternoon tea and snacks/refreshments included in rates. Types of meals: Full gourmet bkfst, early coffee/tea, picnic lunch and room service. Beds: KQDT. Cable TV, VCR, reading lamp, CD player, refrigerator, ceiling fan, clock radio, coffeemaker, desk, fireplace, bath amenities, wireless Internet access, iron/ironing board, Magazines in each guest room, Complimentary chocolates & candies and Basket of "emergency items" in each room in case you forgot something in room. Central air. Pet boarding, parlor games, telephone, Kennel area, Many free coupons to be used in local restaurants, theaters & for massage services, Complimentary beverages (tea and coffee) in the TV Lounge, Snacks in the TV Lounge, High-speed wireless Internet service is available throughout the B&B and Cable TV on premises. Antiquing, art galleries, bicycling, fishing, golf, hiking, live theater, museums, parks, shopping, tennis and wineries nearby.

Location: City.

Certificate may be used: Last minute, subject to availabilty.

Steeles Tavern
E11

Sugar Tree Inn

Highway 56
Steeles Tavern, VA 24476
(540)377-2197 (800)377-2197
Internet: www.sugartreeinn.com
E-mail: innkeeper@sugartreeinn.com

Circa 1983. A haven of natural beauty sitting on 28 wooded acres high in the Blue Ridge Mountains, this elegantly rustic log inn imparts peace and solitude. Relax on a porch rocker, perfect for bird watching. Stargaze from the hot tub on the mountainside deck. Choose a book or game from the upstairs library. Spacious accommodations include guest bedrooms in the main lodge and log house as well as two suites in the Grey House. Stone fireplaces, whirlpool tubs, separate sitting rooms, outside decks and other pleasing amenities are welcome indulgences. Look out on the wildflowers and chipmunks during a hearty breakfast in the glass-walled dining room. Make reservations for a candlelight dinner with quiet music and Virginia wine, served Friday & Saturday evenings at the Inn's restaurant. Casual lighter fare served most weekday nights as well. Walk the nature trail by a rushing creek or explore the Appalachian Trail.

Innkeeper(s): Jeff & Becky Chanter. $148-248. 13 rooms with PB, 13 with FP, 2 suites, 1 cottage, 1 cabin. Breakfast and snacks/refreshments included in rates. Types of meals: Country bkfst, veg bkfst, early coffee/tea, picnic lunch and gourmet dinner. Restaurant on premises. Beds: KQDT. VCR, reading lamp, CD player, ceiling fan, clock radio, coffeemaker, some with hot tub/spa, fireplace, hair dryer, bathrobes and bath amenities in room. Air conditioning. TV, spa, telephone and gift shop on premises. Limited handicap access. Antiquing, art galleries, bicycling, canoeing/kayaking, cross-country skiing, downhill skiing, fishing, golf, hiking, horseback riding, live theater, museums, parks and shopping nearby.

Location: Mountains.

Publicity: *Washingtonian Magazine ("Top 10 Country Inns") and Hampton Roads Magazine ("Mountain Magic").*

Certificate may be used: Anytime, based on projected availability.

Tappahannock
F16

Essex Inn

203 Duke St
Tappahannock, VA 22560
(804) 443-9900 (866) ESSEXVA
Internet: www.EssexInnVA.com
E-mail: info@EssexInnVA.com

Circa 1850. Authentically restored to its original splendor, this 1850 Greek Revival mansion is furnished with period antiques, reproductions and family heirlooms that reflect an old-world elegance. The Essex Inn is located one block from the Rappahannock River in the heart of the Tappahannock downtown historic district. Relax in the private brick courtyard, screened-in porch or the sunroom. The Music Room, with a baby grand piano, and the library have an inviting fireplace. A butler's pantry includes a microwave, refrigerator, coffee and ice maker as well as wine, beer and snacks. Spacious guest bedrooms in the main house boast fireplaces. The servants' quarters are now indulgent suites with custom amenities. Savor the specialty recipes Melody creates for incredible three-course breakfasts before exploring scenic Virginia.

Innkeeper(s): Bob and Janice McGee. $175-205. 8 rooms with PB, 8 with FP, 4 suites. Full gourmet breakfast, early coffee/tea and afternoon snacks

and beer/wine included in rates. Beds: KQT. Modem hook-up, cable TV, VCR, DVD, reading lamp, ceiling fan, clock radio, desk, most with fireplace, hair dryer, bathrobes, bath amenities, wireless Internet access, iron/ironing board, Irons, Bubble bath and Suites include full kitchens in room. Central air. Copier, library, pet boarding, parlor games, telephone, Guest Butler's Pantry with microwave, refrigerator, coffee maker, ice machine, beer, wine and snacks on premises. Amusement parks, antiquing, art galleries, beach, bicycling, canoeing/kayaking, fishing, golf, hiking, live theater, museums, parks, shopping, water sports and wineries nearby.

Location: Waterfront. Small Town.

Publicity: *The Rappahannock Times, Virginia Living Magazine, Chesapeake Life Magazine, The House and Home Magazine and The Virginian Pilot.*

Certificate may be used: Anytime, subject to availability.

Washington
C13

Caledonia Farm - 1812 B&B

47 Dearing Rd (Flint Hill)
Washington, VA 22627
(540)675-3693 (800)BNB-1812
Internet: www.bnb1812.com

Circa 1812. This gracious Federal-style stone house on the National Register is beautifully situated on 115 forever protected acres adjacent to Shenandoah National Park. It was  built by a Revolutionary War officer, and his musket is displayed over a mantel. The house, a Virginia Historic Landmark, has been restored with the original Colonial color scheme retained. All rooms have working fireplaces, air conditioning and provide views of stone-fenced pastures and the Blue Ridge Mountains. The innkeeper is a retired international broadcaster.

Innkeeper(s): Phil Irwin. $140. 2 rooms, 2 with FP, 1 conference room. Breakfast and snacks/refreshments included in rates. Types of meals: Full gourmet bkfst. Beds: D. VCR, reading lamp, refrigerator, snack bar, clock radio, telephone, turn-down service, desk, hot tub/spa and Skyline Drive view in room. TV, fax, copier, spa, bicycles, library, parlor games, fireplace, hay ride and lawn games on premises. Antiquing, fishing, hiking, live theater, parks, shopping, water sports, wineries, caves, stables and battlefields nearby.

Location: Country, mountains.

Publicity: *Country, Country Almanac, Country Living, Blue Ridge Country, Discovery, Washington Post, Baltimore Sun and Pen TV/Cable 15/PBS X3.*

"We've stayed at many, many B&Bs. This is by far the best!"

Certificate may be used: Anytime, subject to availability, except weekends.

Fairlea Farm Bed & Breakfast

636 Mt Salem Ave., PO Box 124
Washington, VA 22747-0124
(540)675-3679 Fax:(540)675-1064
Internet: www.fairleafarm.com
E-mail: longyear@shentel.net

Circa 1960. View acres of rolling hills, farmland and the Blue Ridge Mountains from this fieldstone manor house. Rooms are decorated with crocheted canopies and four-poster beds. Potted plants and floral bedcovers add a homey feel. The stone terrace is set up for relaxing with chairs lined along the edge. As a young surveyor, George Washington laid out the boundaries of the historic village of Little Washington, which is just a 5-minute walk from Fairlea Farm, a working sheep and cattle farm.

Innkeeper(s): Susan & Walt Longyear. $195-220. 4 rooms with PB, 1 suite. Breakfast and afternoon tea included in rates. Types of meals: Full gourmet bkfst and early coffee/tea. Beds: QT. Reading lamp, refrigerator, turn-down service and desk in room. Air conditioning. VCR, fax, copier, parlor games, telephone and fireplace on premises. Antiquing, fishing, horseback riding, live theater, vineyards, Shenandoah National Park and Civil War battlefields nearby.

Location: Country, mountains. Village/working farm, 70 miles west of Washington, DC.

Certificate may be used: December-February, Suite only, No Holidays or Saturdays.

Waynesboro   D12

Iris Inn

191 Chinquapin Dr
Waynesboro, VA 22980-5692
(540)943-1991 (888)585-9018 Fax:(540)942-2093
Internet: www.irisinn.com
E-mail: innkeeper@irisinn.com

Circa 1991. Feel embraced by the natural beauty and tranquil setting of this romantic modern retreat on 12 wooded acres in the Blue Ridge Mountains of Waynesboro, Virginia. Sit on a porch at the Iris Inn and be surrounded by the scenic Shenandoah National Forest. A three-story stone fireplace and expansive hand-painted mural depicting local flora and fauna highlight the great room. Read or use the computer in the loft library and enjoy the breeze from the third-floor lookout tower. Indulge in the bottomless cookie jar and beverages upon checking in. Stay in a guest room or suite that features a whirlpool or hot tub, gas fireplace, kitchenette and private access to outdoor decks that overlook the Shenandoah Valley. After a hearty breakfast explore the nearby cultural hub of Charlottesville or take a tour of Jefferson's Monticello.

Innkeeper(s): Dave & Heidi Lanford. $119-299. 9 rooms with PB, 2 with FP, 1 with HT, 3 with WP, 1 conference room. Breakfast included in rates. Types of meals: Full bkfst, veg bkfst, early coffee/tea, picnic lunch, snacks/refreshments and wine. Beds: KQT. Cable TV, refrigerator, ceiling fan, clock radio, desk, some with hot tub/spa, some with fireplace, hair dryer, bathrobes, bath amenities, wireless Internet access and iron/ironing board in room. Central air. Fax, library and parlor games on premises. Handicap access. Antiquing, art galleries, bicycling, canoeing/kayaking, fishing, golf, hiking, horseback riding, live theater, museums, parks, shopping, sporting events, water sports and wineries nearby.

Location: Country, mountains.

Certificate may be used: Sunday-Thursday, Jan. 1-March 31 or Sunday-Thursday, Nov. 1-Dec. 31 excluding holidays and special events.

White Stone   F17

Flowering Fields B&B

232 Flowering Field
White Stone, VA 22578-9722
(804)435-6238 Fax:(804)435-6238
Internet: www.floweringfieldsbandb.com
E-mail: floweringfieldsbandb@gmail.com

Circa 1790. Flowering Fields Bed & Breakfast sits in White Stone near the mouth of the Rappahannock River before it flows into the Chesapeake Bay. This tranquil B&B is hidden away in the waterfront area known as the Northern Neck of Virginia and is known to be "where southern hospitality begins." Families will enjoy the game room with a pool table or watching movies by the fire in the gathering room. Refreshing lemonade is on the welcome table in the large foyer in the summertime. Browse through the library's extensive collection of health, diet and cookbooks as well as paperbacks to read.

Formal but inviting and comfortable guest bedrooms include sitting areas. Linger over a relaxing and delicious breakfast accented with the inn's famous blue crab crabcakes. Activities are endless in this scenic and central location.

Innkeeper(s): Lloyd Niziol & Susan Moenssens. $125. 5 rooms with PB, 1 conference room. Breakfast, snacks/refreshments, Afternoon Tea on request, Lemonade on welcoming table in summer months, Soft drinks, Candies, Fruits and Coffee & Tea 24/7. included in rates. Types of meals: Full gourmet bkfst, veg bkfst, early coffee/tea and afternoon tea. Beds: KQDT. Reading lamp, ceiling fan, clock radio, bath amenities, Cable TV & desk in some rooms, Sitting area in all rooms, Cable TV, VCR/DVD, Stereo, Iron & ironing board, Hair dryer and Robes in room. Air conditioning. VCR, fax, copier, bicycles, library, parlor games, telephone, fireplace, Advance notification for handicap access, First-floor room with private bath, Reading area, Game table & pool table in gathering room, Baby grand in parlor, Wireless & fax available, Refrigerator space available on request and Ice 24/7 on premises. Antiquing, art galleries, beach, bicycling, canoeing/kayaking, fishing, golf, hiking, museums, parks, shopping, water sports, wineries, Williamsburg, Excellent bird watching, History and Historic sites nearby.

Certificate may be used: January-April.

Williamsburg   G17

Applewood Colonial B&B

605 Richmond Rd
Williamsburg, VA 23185-3539
(757)903-4306
Internet: www.williamsburgbandb.com
E-mail: info@williamsburgbandb.com

Circa 1928. This stately home was built by the craftsman chosen to meticulously restore and reconstruct Colonial Williamsburg. Using the same high standards and hand-crafted architectural details, it is perfectly located along the Historic Corridor. The classic decor of the Colonial era is evident throughout the well-appointed rooms. Guest bedrooms and suites offer high four-poster canopy beds and boast modern conveniences. A magnificent candlelight breakfast is served on a pedestal table under a crystal chandelier in the dining room. Complimentary afternoon refreshments include fresh baked cookies, Virginia peanuts and beverages. In keeping with its name and extensive apple collection, delicious slices of apple pie are available every evening.

Innkeeper(s): Denise L. Fleck. $135-165. 3 rooms with PB, 1 two-bedroom suite. Breakfast and snacks/refreshments included in rates. Types of meals: Full bkfst and veg bkfst. Beds: QT. Cable TV, VCR, DVD, reading lamp, refrigerator, clock radio, coffeemaker, most with fireplace, hair dryer, bath amenities, wireless Internet access and iron/ironing board in room. Central air. Amusement parks, antiquing, fishing, golf, live theater, parks, shopping, sporting events, water sports, wineries, Colonial Williamsburg and historic sites nearby.

Location: Along the Historic Corridor.

Publicity: *Discerning Traveler.*

"Our accommodations were the best, and you were most kind."
Certificate may be used: August.

Colonial Gardens

1109 Jamestown Rd
Williamsburg, VA 23185
(757)220-8087 (800)886-9715 Fax:(757)253-1495
Internet: www.colonialgardensinn.com
E-mail: colonialgardensbandb@verizon.net

Circa 1965. Gracing three landscaped acres in Williamsburg, Virginia, Colonial Gardens Bed & Breakfast offers an Old World European-style opulence and elegance. Escape to the romantic enchantment of this brick Colonial B&B just one mile from

Colonial Williamsburg and less than ten minutes from Busch Gardens and Water Country USA. Gather for wine and appetizers in the library where a guest computer is available to use. Browse for a movie from the DVD or video collection. Spacious guest bedrooms and two suites with fireplaces are comfortable and inviting. Savor a gourmet breakfast served on china, crystal and silver with creative and delicious signature entrees. The surrounding area is steeped in historic sites and attractions.

Innkeeper(s): Karen & Ron Watkins. $155-180. 4 rooms with PB, 3 with FP, 2 total suites, including 1 two-bedroom suite. Breakfast, snacks/refreshments, wine and Picnic lunch extra charge included in rates. Types of meals: Full gourmet bkfst, veg bkfst, early coffee/tea, picnic lunch, hors d'oeuvres, Early evening wine and cheese and fruit. Beds: KQT. Modem hook-up, data port, cable TV, VCR, DVD, reading lamp, stereo, ceiling fan, snack bar, clock radio, telephone, turn-down service, desk, most with fireplace, hair dryer, bathrobes, bath amenities, wireless Internet access, iron/ironing board and 2 suites with fireplace in room. Central air. Fax, bicycles, library, parlor games, gift shop, VCR/DVD library, High speed Internet and Wi Fi throughout house on premises. Amusement parks, antiquing, art galleries, bicycling, golf, live theater, museums, parks, shopping, wineries and plantations nearby.

Location: Small town.

Publicity: *Mid Atlantic Country Magazine, Unique Inns & Bed & Breakfasts of Virginia and Travel & Leisure.*

Certificate may be used: Monday-Thursday, exclusive of all holidays, October and December.

Woolwine 19

The Mountain Rose B&B Inn

1787 Charity Hwy
Woolwine, VA 24185
(276)930-1057 (888)930-1057 Fax:276-930-2165
Internet: www.mountainrose-inn.com
E-mail: info@mountainrose-inn.com

Circa 1901. This historic Victorian inn, once the home of the Mountain Rose Distillery, sits on 100 acres of forested hills with plenty of hiking trails. A trout-stocked stream goes  through the property and a swimming pool provides recreation. Each room has an antique mantled fireplace, which has been converted to gas logs. Guests can relax by the pool or in rocking chairs on one of the six porches. The innkeepers look forward to providing guests with casually elegant hospitality in the Blue Ridge Mountains. The Blue Ridge Parkway, Chateau Morrisette Winery, Mabry Mill, The Reynolds Homestead, Laurel Hill Jeb Stuart Birthplace, Patrick County Courthouse and the Patrick County Historical Museum are located nearby. A three-course breakfast is offered every morning.

Innkeeper(s): Mike & Dora Jane Barwick. $125-155. 5 rooms with PB, 5 with FP. Breakfast, afternoon tea and snacks/refreshments included in rates. Types of meals: Full bkfst, early coffee/tea and Breakfast-in-Bed available for extra charge. Beds: KQT. TV, DVD, reading lamp, clock radio, desk, fireplace, hair dryer, bathrobes, wireless Internet access, iron/ironing board, satellite TV and porch access in room. Central air. VCR, fax, copier, swimming, parlor games, telephone, Trout-stocked creek, Hiking trails and Tennis courts are a mile away on premises. Antiquing, art galleries, bicycling, fishing, golf, hiking, horseback riding, live theater, parks, shopping, sporting events, tennis, water sports, wineries and Nascar racing nearby.

Location: Mountains.

Publicity: *Birds & Blooms, USA Today, Travel & Leisure, Enterprise, Bull Mountain Bugle, New York Times, The Parkway Edition, "Best Romantic Getaway" City Magazine and The Martinsville Bulletin.*

Certificate may be used: Year-round, Sunday-Thursday; Weekends, December-March, subject to availability.

Washington

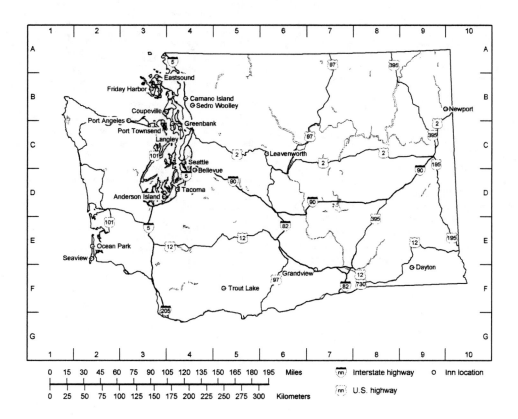

Anderson Island · D3

The Inn at Burg's Landing

8808 Villa Beach Rd
Anderson Island, WA 98303-9785
(253)884-9185
Internet: www.burgslandingbb.com
E-mail: burgslanding@yahoo.com

Circa 1987. A short ferry trip from Steilacoom and Tacoma, this log homestead boasts beautiful views of Mt. Rainier, Puget Sound and the Cascade Mountains. The master bedroom features a skylight and a private whirlpool bath. After a full breakfast, guests can spend the day at the inn's private beach. Golf, hiking and freshwater lakes are nearby, and the area has many seasonal activities, including Fourth of July fireworks, the Anderson Island fair and parade in September.

Innkeeper(s): Ken & Annie Burg. $100-155. 2 rooms, 1 with PB, 1 with WP. Breakfast included in rates. Types of meals: Full bkfst, veg bkfst and early coffee/tea. Beds: QT. Cable TV, VCR, DVD, reading lamp, clock radio, desk and hair dryer in room. Telephone and fireplace on premises. Amusement parks, antiquing, art galleries, beach, bicycling, downhill skiing, fishing, golf, hiking, live theater, museums, parks, shopping, sporting events, tennis, Romantic dining, Bike/walking trail along the waterfront, Catch a Rainiers game at Cheney Stadium, Point Defiance Zoo & Aquarium and Gig Harbor nearby.

Location: Country, waterfront. Puget Sound.

Publicity: *Sunset, Tacoma News Tribune, Portland Oregonian and Seattle Times.*

Certificate may be used: Anytime, subject to availability.

Camano Island · B4

The Inn at Barnum Point

464 S Barnum Rd
Camano Island, WA 98282-8578
(360)387-2256 (800)910-2256
Internet: www.innatbarnumpoint.com
E-mail: barnumpoint@camano.net

Circa 1991. The Inn at Barnum Point is a Cape Cod-style B&B located on the bay on Camano Island, Washington. Enjoy listening to the water lap at the shoreline, watching deer in the orchard and sneaking a kiss under an heirloom apple tree. The newest accommodation is the 900-square-foot Shorebird Room with deck, fireplace and soaking tub overlooking Port Susan Bay and the Cascade Mountains.

Innkeeper(s): Carolin Barnum Dilorenzo. $125-225. 3 rooms with PB, 3 with FP. Breakfast included in rates. Types of meals: Full gourmet bkfst and early coffee/tea. Beds: Q. TV, VCR, reading lamp, refrigerator, clock radio and telephone in room. Fax, copier, parlor games and fireplace on premises. Antiquing, golf, live theater, parks, shopping and water sports nearby.

Location: Waterfront.

Certificate may be used: Anytime, Subject to availability.

Coupeville · B3

The Blue Goose Inn

702 North Main Street
Coupeville, WA 98239
(360) 678-4284 (877) 678-4284
Internet: www.BlueGooseInn.com
E-mail: stay@bluegooseinn.com

Circa 1887. The Blue Goose Inn, centrally located on scenic Whidbey Island, is comprised of two lovingly restored Victorian homes. Both landmarks are listed in the National Register of Historic Places. Fresh-baked cookies and a cup of tea are a welcoming part of the hospitality shown here. Gracing the seaside town of Coupeville, Washington, walk to the picturesque waterfront with its wharf, colorful shops, museum and excellent dining. Stay in a spacious guest room with private bath, antique furnishings, original artwork and gorgeous views of Penn Cove and Mt. Baker. Savor a scrumptious breakfast in the sunroom or dining room while overlooking the gardens. Take time to explore the natural beauty of the surrounding area.

Innkeeper(s): Sue & Marty McDaniel. $119-149. 6 rooms with PB, 3 with FP, 1 with WP, 1 suite. Breakfast, snacks/refreshments, We serve a scrumptious full breakfast every morning, and we provide coffee and tea and homemade cookies all day included in rates. Types of meals: Full bkfst, veg bkfst, early coffee/tea, wine, Special requests for breakfast can be accommodated with advance notice. On-site Pub during summer months. Wine, beer and champagne and appetizers available in rooms. Beds: KQ. Cable TV, reading lamp, ceiling fan, clock radio, coffeemaker, desk, some with fireplace, hair dryer, bath amenities, wireless Internet access, iron/ironing board, Coffee makers, Brita water pitchers, water & mountain views, antiques, artwork, sitting areas, whirlpool or claw foot tubs, down or foam pillows, pillow-top mattresses and luxurious linens in room. Parlor games, Lovely gardens, View of Mt. Baker from the gardens and Comfortable porches on premises. Antiquing, art galleries, beach, bicycling, canoeing/kayaking, fishing, golf, hiking, horseback riding, live theater, museums, parks, shopping, water sports, wineries, Coupeville Art Center, Ebey's Landing, Fort Casey, Admiralty Lighthouse, Deception Pass, State Parks, Walk to waterfront dining & shops, Whidbey Playhouse, Drive-in movies and Many excellent restaurants nearby.

Location: City, ocean community, waterfront. Historic Coupeville on the shores of Penn Cove.

Publicity: *Chosen as Best in the West (2009-2010) .*

"If kindness and generosity are the precursors to success (and I certainly hope they are!), your success is assured."

Certificate may be used: Anytime, November-March, subject to availability.

Dayton · F9

The Purple House

415 E Clay St
Dayton, WA 99328-1348
(509)382-3159 (800)486-2574
Internet: www.purplehousebnb.com
E-mail: info@purplehousebnb.com

Circa 1882. History buffs will adore this aptly named bed & breakfast, colored in deep purple tones with white, gingerbread trim. The home, listed in  the National Register, is the perfect place to enjoy Dayton, which boasts two historic districts and a multitude of preserved Victorian homes. Innkeeper Christine Williscroft has filled the home with antiques and artwork. A highly praised cook, Christine prepares the European-style full breakfasts, as well as mouthwatering afternoon refreshments. Guests can relax in the richly appointed parlor or library, and the grounds also include a swimming pool.

Innkeeper(s): D. Christine Williscroft. $95-135. 4 rooms, 2 with PB, 1 with FP, 1 suite. Breakfast and afternoon tea included in rates. Types of meals: Full gourmet bkfst, early coffee/tea, picnic lunch and dinner. Beds: QD. Reading lamp, refrigerator, ceiling fan, clock radio, telephone and desk in room. Air conditioning. VCR, swimming, library, pet boarding, parlor games and fireplace on premises. Handicap access. Antiquing, cross-country skiing, downhill skiing, fishing, live theater, parks, shopping, sporting events and water sports nearby.

Location: City.
Publicity: *Sunset.*

"You have accomplished so very much with your bed & breakfast to make it a very special place to stay."

Certificate may be used: Sunday-Thursday, February-June, $95 per room only.

Eastsound B3

Turtleback Farm Inn

1981 Crow Valley Rd
Eastsound, WA 98245
(360)376-4914 (800)376-4914 Fax:(360)376-5329
Internet: www.turtlebackinn.com
E-mail: info@turtlebackinn.com

Circa 1895. Guests will delight in the beautiful views afforded from this farmhouse and the newly constructed Orchard House, which overlooks 80 acres of forest and farmland, duck ponds and Mt. Constitution to the east. Rooms feature antique furnishings and many boast views of the farm, orchard or sheep pasture. Beds are covered with wool comforters made from sheep raised on the property. Bon Appetit highlighted some of the breakfast recipes served at Turtleback; a breakfast  here is a memorable affair. Tables set with bone china, silver and fresh linens make way for a delightful mix of fruits, juice, award-winning granola, homemade breads and specialty entrees. Evening guests can settle down with a game or a book in the fire-lit parlor as they enjoy sherry, tea or hot chocolate.

Innkeeper(s): William & Susan C. Fletcher. $100-260. 11 rooms with PB, 4 with FP. Breakfast and snacks/refreshments included in rates. Types of meals: Country bkfst, veg bkfst, early coffee/tea and picnic lunch. Beds: KQD. Reading lamp, clock radio and some with fireplace in room. Fax, library, parlor games, telephone, WiFi and Refrigerator with self-serve beverage bar in dining room on premises. Limited handicap access. Art galleries, beach, bicycling, canoeing/kayaking, fishing, golf, hiking, horseback riding, live theater, museums, parks, shopping, tennis and water sports nearby.

Location: Country. On Orcas Island, Puget Sound.

Publicity: *Los Angeles Times, USA Today, Travel & Leisure, Contra Costa Sun, Seattle Times, Northwest Living, Sunset, Food & Wine, Gourmet, Northwest Travel, New York Times and Alaska Air.*

"A peaceful haven for soothing the soul."

Certificate may be used: November-April, Sunday-Thursday, subject to availability. Holidays and special event dates are excluded.

Friday Harbor B3

Harrison House Suites

235 C St
Friday Harbor, WA 98250-8098
(360)378-3587 (800)407-7933 Fax:(360)378-2270
Internet: www.harrisonhousesuites.com
E-mail: innkeeper@harrisonhousesuites.com

Circa 1905. Providing abundant hospitality in a scenic hilltop setting with spectacular views of the Pacific Northwest, this historic Craftsman retreat is located in Friday Harbor, Washington, a premier destination on San Juan Island. Complimentary bikes and kayaks invite exploration of the local area with easy access

to the ferry landing just 1½ blocks away. Browse through the reading and video library collection for less active moments. Stay in a spacious guest suite that may include a fireplace, whirlpool tub, well-stocked kitchen, private deck, grill and hot tub. Gather in the relaxing café or request in-room service for a four-course gourmet breakfast made with recipes from the inn's own cookbook. Afternoon tea and treats are always pleasurable interludes. Special dinners, catering, packages and other thoughtful extras are available.

Innkeeper(s): Anna Maria de Freitas, David Pass. $115-375. 5 rooms with PB, 3 with FP, 5 with HT, 3 with WP, 2 two-bedroom and 1 three-bedroom suites, 1 cottage, 1 conference room. Breakfast and snacks/refreshments included in rates. Types of meals: Full gourmet bkfst, veg bkfst, early coffee/tea, gourmet lunch, picnic lunch, gourmet dinner and room service. Beds: QDT. Cable TV, VCR, DVD, reading lamp, stereo, refrigerator, ceiling fan, clock radio, telephone, coffeemaker, most with fireplace, hair dryer, bathrobes, bath amenities, wireless Internet access and iron/ironing board in room. Fax, spa, bicycles, parlor games, laundry facility and gift shop on premises. Limited handicap access. Antiquing, art galleries, beach, bicycling, canoeing/kayaking, fishing, golf, hiking, horseback riding, live theater, museums, parks, shopping, tennis, water sports and wineries nearby.

Location: City, waterfront. Small town.

Certificate may be used: October-May, excluding holidays and weekends.

Grandview E7

Cozy Rose Inn

1220 Forsell Rd
Grandview, WA 98930
(509)882-4669 (800)575-8381 Fax:(509)882-4234
Internet: www.cozyroseinn.com
E-mail: stay@cozyroseinn.com

Circa 1908. Enjoying Washington's wine country from the privacy of your own luxurious suite is only part of the unforgettable experience that awaits at this delightful country inn, which combines a Cape Cod and farmhouse-style design with French Country decor. Walk through family vineyards and orchards to be renewed in a relaxing six-acre setting. Each romantic, villa-style suite includes a private bath, fireplace, stereo, refrigerator, microwave and a separate entrance with a private deck overlooking vineyards and orchards. Some also include a Jacuzzi. The Suite Surrender boasts an incredible view and includes Italian furniture, Jacuzzi tub, walk-in tiled shower and flat screen satellite TV/DVD/VCR. Feel truly pampered by a full candlelight breakfast that may include huckleberry pancakes, delivered to each suite. After a day of sightseeing, biking or golfing, soak in the Under The Stars hot tub. Make friends with the two pet llamas, Chocolate and Stubborn.

Innkeeper(s): Mark & Jennie Jackson. $99-229. 5 rooms, 5 with FP, 5 suites. Breakfast included in rates. Types of meals: Country bkfst, veg bkfst and gourmet dinner. Beds: K. Cable TV, reading lamp, stereo, refrigerator, ceiling fan, clock radio, telephone, coffeemaker, desk, hot tub/spa, wireless Internet access, VCR/DVD only in Suite Surrender, individual entrance with private deck, high speed wireless Internet access, music, microwave, coffee and teas in room. Central air. Fax, bicycles, laundry facility, satellite TV, Under the Stars hot tub and dinners by prior arrangement on premises. Antiquing, golf, hiking, museums, parks, jogging, walking, 18-hole golf course, microbreweries, 40 wineries and vineyards nearby.

Location: Country.

Publicity: *Northwest's Best Places to Kiss and Romantic America.*

Certificate may be used: November-February, Monday-Wednesday. No holidays or special event weekends. Rack rate only and consecutive nights only. Upgrade upon check in only if available.

Greenbank   C4

Guest House Log Cottages

24371-SR 525, Whidbey Island
Greenbank, WA 98253
(360)678-3115 (800)997-3115
Internet: www.guesthouselogcottages.com
E-mail: stay@guesthouselogcottages.com

Circa 1925. These storybook cottages and log home are nestled within a peaceful forest on 25 acres. The log cabin features

stained-glass and criss-cross paned windows that give it the feel of a gingerbread house. Four of the cottages are log construction. Ask for the Lodge and enjoy a private setting with a pond just beyond the deck. Inside are two Jacuzzi tubs, a stone fireplace, king bed, antiques and a luxurious atmosphere.

Innkeeper(s): Don & Mary Jane Creger. $130-325. 6 cottages with PB, 6 with HT. Breakfast included in rates. Types of meals: Full bkfst and early coffee/tea. Beds: KQ. TV, VCR, DVD, reading lamp, stereo, refrigerator, ceiling fan, clock radio, telephone, turn-down service, desk, hot tub/spa, fireplace, hair dryer, bath amenities, iron/ironing board, kitchen and Jacuzzi in room. Air conditioning. Fax, copier, spa, swimming, swimming pool, hot tub and 25 beautiful forested acres on premises. Limited handicap access. Antiquing, art galleries, beach, bicycling, canoeing/kayaking, fishing, golf, hiking, horseback riding, live theater, museums, parks, shopping, tennis, water sports and wineries nearby.

Location: Mountains, ocean community. Island - wooded.

Publicity: *Los Angeles Times, Woman's Day, Sunset, Country Inns and Bride's*.

Certificate may be used: Monday-Thursday, midweek winter Oct. 15-April 15.

Leavenworth   C6

Haus Rohrbach Pension

12882 Ranger Rd
Leavenworth, WA 98826-9503
(509)548-7024 (800)548-4477
Internet: www.hausrohrbach.com
E-mail: info@hausrohrbach.com

Circa 1975. Situated on 13 1/2 acres overlooking the village, Haus Rohrbach offers both valley and mountain views and is at the entrance to Tumwater Mountain cycling and hiking trails. Leavenworth is two minutes away. Private fireplaces and whirlpools for two are features of each of three suites. Sourdough pancakes and cinnamon rolls are specialties of the house. Guests often take breakfast out to the deck to enjoy pastoral views that include grazing sheep and a pleasant pond. In the evening, return from white-water rafting, tobogganing, skiing or sleigh rides to soak in the hot tub.

Innkeeper(s): Carol & Mike Wentink. $105-200. 10 rooms, 8 with PB, 3 with FP, 3 with WP, 3 suites, 1 cottage, 1 conference room. Breakfast included in rates. Types of meals: Full bkfst, early coffee/tea, lunch, picnic lunch, snacks/refreshments and dinner. Beds: KQDT. Reading lamp, stereo, refrigerator, clock radio, coffeemaker, desk, hot tub/spa, some with fireplace and bath amenities in room. Air conditioning. Spa, swimming, parlor games, telephone, outdoor pool & hot tub, private gardens, suites with fireplace and double soaking whirlpool tub and beautiful views on premises. Limited handicap access. Antiquing, art galleries, beach, bicycling, canoeing/kayaking, cross-country skiing, downhill skiing, fishing, golf, hiking, horseback riding, live theater, museums, parks, shopping, tennis, water sports, wineries and five miles of hiking and biking paths on Tumwater Mountain nearby.

Location: Mountains. Theme town.

Newport   B10

Inn at the Lake

581 S. Shore Diamond Lake Rd
Newport, WA 99156
(509)447-5772 (877)447-5772 Fax:(509)447-0999
Internet: www.innatthelake.com
E-mail: info@innatthelake.com

Circa 1993. A vacation paradise, this Southwestern-style home offers resort amenities. A family room boasts a gas-log fireplace, VCR, books and games. The large entertainment deck overlooks tiered gardens and ponds. Luxurious waterfront suites boast spacious privacy, fireplaces, double Jacuzzis and lake views. Stay in the romantic Peach Penthouse Suite with a roof-top deck and two-person swing. Breakfast is found in each room's refrigerator, ready to enjoy when desired. Fish for rainbow trout from the dock, or rent a canoe. Play volleyball on the grass beach before a refreshing swim. Winter sports also are in abundance.

Innkeeper(s): Blaine & Virginia Coffey. $95-159. 5 rooms, 1 with FP, 5 suites. Breakfast and snacks/refreshments included in rates. Types of meals: Cont plus, veg bkfst, afternoon tea and room service. Beds: KQ. Cable TV, VCR, reading lamp, refrigerator, ceiling fan, clock radio, telephone, coffeemaker, desk, hot tub/spa and fireplace in room. Air conditioning. Fax, copier, swimming, parlor games and fireplace on premises. Beach, bicycling, cross-country skiing, downhill skiing, fishing, golf, hiking, horseback riding, live theater, parks, shopping and water sports nearby.

Location: Country, mountains, waterfront.

Certificate may be used: Sunday-Thursday, Nov. 1-April 30, except holidays.

Ocean Park   E2

Charles Nelson Guest House

26205 Sandridge Road
Ocean Park, WA 98640
(360)665-3016 (888)862-9756 Fax:(360)665-4796
Internet: www.charlesnelsonbandb.com
E-mail: cnbandb@charlesnelsonbandb.com

Circa 1928. Originally purchased from a Sears & Roebuck catalog, this Dutch Colonial home that overlooks Willapa Bay and Long Island's wildlife refuge has been impressively restored. Relax by firelight in the living room on the lambskin rug, or enjoy the view from the sunroom. Guest bedrooms are furnished with a blend of antiques and period furnishings. Homemade muffins, scones or sweet rolls with honey butter and jam accompany sausage and a double-cheese-and-bacon quiche for a typical breakfast in the dining room. Bird watch from the back deck, or gaze at the goldfish and koi in the pond. A nap on a nearby hammock is an inviting respite.

Innkeeper(s): Curt and Ginger Bish. $170-190. 3 rooms with PB. Breakfast and snacks/refreshments included in rates. Types of meals: Full gourmet bkfst, veg bkfst and early coffee/tea. Beds: KQT. Cable TV, DVD, reading lamp, CD player, clock radio, turn-down service, hair dryer, bathrobes and bath amenities in room. VCR, fax, copier, library, parlor games, telephone, fireplace and laundry facility on premises. Antiquing, art galleries, beach, bicycling, canoeing/kayaking, fishing, golf, hiking, horseback riding, museums, parks and shopping nearby.

Location: Ocean community.

Publicity: *Seattle Home and Lifestyles*.

Certificate may be used: Anytime, holidays excluded.

Port Angeles C3

Five SeaSuns Bed & Breakfast

1006 S Lincoln St
Port Angeles, WA 98362-7826
(360)452-8248 (800)708-0777 Fax:(360)417-0465
Internet: www.seasuns.com
E-mail: info@seasuns.com

Circa 1926. Take a respite from the rush of today at this restored, historic home that reflects the 1920s era of sophistication with a sense of romance and refinement. Guest bedrooms depict the seasons of the year and are furnished with period antiques. Pleasing amenities include whirlpool or soaking tubs, balconies and water or mountain views. Artfully presented gourmet breakfasts are served by candlelight with fine china and silver. Relax on the porch or wander the picturesque gardens that highlight the estate-like grounds. Explore nearby Olympic National Park and the Ediz Hook Coast Guard Station. The Underground History Walk is ten blocks. Visit the Makah Indian Museum 75 miles away.

Innkeeper(s): Jan & Bob Harbick. $115-165. 5 rooms with PB, 1 suite, 1 cottage. Breakfast, afternoon tea and snacks/refreshments included in rates. Types of meals: Full gourmet bkfst, veg bkfst and early coffee/tea. Beds: QD. Cable TV, VCR, reading lamp, clock radio, turn-down service, hair dryer, bathrobes, bath amenities, wireless Internet access and iron/ironing board in room. Fax, copier, parlor games, telephone and fireplace on premises. Antiquing, art galleries, beach, bicycling, canoeing/kayaking, cross-country skiing, fishing, hiking, live theater, museums, parks, shopping and wineries nearby.

Location: City, ocean community.

Publicity: *Arrington B&B Journal "Best Breakfast" award for 2003 and "Best Garden" for 2004.*

Certificate may be used: November-April, subject to availability except holiday weekends.

Port Townsend C3

Ann Starrett Mansion

744 Clay St
Port Townsend, WA 98368-5808
(888)385-3205
Internet: www.starrettmansion.com
E-mail: info@starrettmansion.com

Circa 1889. George Starrett came from Maine to Port Townsend and became the major residential builder. By 1889, he had constructed one house a week, totaling more than 350 houses. The Smithsonian believes the Ann Starrett's elaborate free-hung spiral staircase is the only one of its type in the United States. A frescoed dome atop the octagonal tower depicts four seasons and four virtues. On the first day of each season, the sun causes a ruby red light to point toward the appropriate painting. The mansion won a "Great American Home Award" from the National Trust for Historic Preservation.

Innkeeper(s): Richard Winner. $110-185. 11 rooms with PB, 2 with FP, 2 suites, 2 cottages, 2 conference rooms. Breakfast included in rates. Types of meals: Cont. Beds: KQDT. Cable TV, reading lamp, refrigerator, clock radio, telephone and desk in room. Fax and fireplace on premises. Antiquing, cross-country skiing, fishing, live theater, parks, and whale watching nearby.

Location: Seaport Village.

Publicity: *Peninsula, New York Times, Vancouver Sun, San Francisco Examiner, London Times, Colonial Homes, Elle, Leader, Japanese Travel, National Geographic Traveler, Victorian, Historic American Trails, Sunset Magazine, PBS and Day Boy Night Girl.*

"Staying here was like a dream come true."

Certificate may be used: Nov. 1-March 30, Sunday through Thursday, must mention certificate at time of reservation.

Commanders Beach House

400 Hudson St
Port Townsend, WA 98368-5632
(360)385-1778 (888)385-1778
Internet: www.commandersbeachhouse.com
E-mail: stay@commandersbeachhouse.com

Circa 1934. Commander's Beach House is the only bed and breakfast in Victorian Port Townsend, Washington boasting 2,000 feet of unspoiled Admiralty Inlet beach. This historic Colonial Revival is located on 200 acres at Point Hudson Marina. Its rich maritime heritage and relaxed nautical flair create a pleasant ambiance. Sit by the fire in the living room or on the sunny, covered veranda. Select one of the spacious and cheery guest bedrooms or suites at this seaside retreat and be lulled asleep by the waves. A gourmet breakfast with seasonal cuisine is served in the setting desired. A sample menu may include fresh peaches and blackberries with spearmint sauce, seafood soufflé with rosemary potatoes, blackberry tart and peach/ mango juice, coffee and tea. Individual tables offer scenic views overlooking Point Wilson Lighthouse, Mount Baker, the ferries and Whidbey Island.

Innkeeper(s): Gail & Jim Oldroyd. $99-225. 4 rooms, 3 with PB, 1 with FP. Breakfast, afternoon tea and wine included in rates. Types of meals: Full gourmet bkfst and veg bkfst. Beds: Q. Reading lamp, clock radio, some with fireplace, hair dryer, bathrobes, bath amenities, wireless Internet access, iron/ironing board and feather beds in room. Copier, swimming, library, parlor games, telephone, beach chairs, blankets, croquet and bocci ball on premises. Antiquing, art galleries, beach, bicycling, canoeing/kayaking, fishing, golf, hiking, live theater, museums, parks, shopping, tennis, water sports, wineries, whale watching and sailboat charters nearby.

Location: Ocean community, waterfront.

Publicity: *We have received high praise in the Vancouver, B.C. Sun's travel section and as well as the Olympian in Olympia Wa. and the Kitsap Penninsula Sun in Kitsap Co. Wa.*

Certificate may be used: Nov. 1-April 30, Sunday-Thursday, subject to availabilty.

Seattle C4

Inn at Harbor Steps

1221 First Ave
Seattle, WA 98101
(206)748-0973 (888)728-8910 Fax:(206)748-0533
Internet: www.innatharborsteps.com
E-mail: innatharborsteps@foursisters.com

Circa 1997. Located in the heart of downtown Seattle, Washington in the arts and business district, Inn at Harbor Steps is within walking distance of antique shops, restaurants, Pike Place Market and the Seattle Art Museum. Romantic guest bedrooms feature sitting areas and fireplaces. Generous upscale amenities are reminiscent of a boutique hotel. The inn has a media room, business center and fitness room with a swimming pool. Bicycles are available for touring the scenic area. In addition to all these modern amenities, indulge in a gourmet breakfast and afternoon tea. The inn, one of the Four Sisters

Inns, is situated at the base of a luxury residential high-rise.

Innkeeper(s): David Huynh. $225-275. 28 rooms with PB, 20 with FP, 3 conference rooms. Breakfast, afternoon tea and snacks/refreshments included in rates. Types of meals: Full gourmet bkfst and hors d'oeuvres. Beds: KQ. Modem hook-up, data port, cable TV, VCR, DVD, reading lamp, stereo, refrigerator, ceiling fan, snack bar, clock radio, telephone, coffeemaker, turn-down service, desk, some with hot tub/spa, voice mail, hair dryer, bathrobes, bath amenities, iron/ironing board, European balcony and sitting area in room. Central air. Fax, spa, swimming, sauna, bicycles, library, parlor games, fireplace, gym, lap pool, sauna, state of the art media room and private parking on premises. Handicap access. Amusement parks, antiquing, art galleries, bicycling, canoeing/kayaking, fishing, golf, hiking, live theater, museums, parks, shopping and sporting events nearby.

Location: City.

Publicity: Coastal Living, Travel and Leisure, NY Times and Sunset.

Certificate may be used: Sunday–Thursday, December-February, based on promotional discount availability and excludes special event periods, holidays and certain room types. First night must be at full rack rate to receive second night free.

Inn Of Twin Gables

3258 14th Ave W
Seattle, WA 98119-1727
(206)284-3979 (866)466-3979 Fax:(206)284-3974
Internet: www.innoftwingables.com
E-mail: info@innoftwingables.com

Circa 1915. Situated in the Queen Anne Hill district in Seattle, Washington, Inn of Twin Gables is an Arts and Crafts home built in 1915. Feel welcomed and comfortable at this B&B that makes personal attention a high priority. Gather by the fireplace in the living room, read a book in the enclosed sun porch or sit on a garden bench and watch the sunset. A mini refrigerator is provided for guest use. Guest bedrooms boast fresh flowers and pressed cotton linens. The adjoining North and East Rooms can become a suite for four. A generous gourmet breakfast is served daily in the formal dining room with a variety of popular specialty entrees. Visit nearby Pike Place Market, Pioneer Square and Seattle Center.

Innkeeper(s): Katie Frame. $100-220. 3 rooms with PB. Breakfast, afternoon tea, Tea is offered upon arrival and, on request and the pot for hot water can be set up in the dining room to be available when requested included in rates. Types of meals: Full gourmet bkfst, veg bkfst, early coffee/tea, Sumptuous hot gourmet breakfast with kitchen garden herbs in the formal dining room at 8:30 every morning. Before 8:00 AM, a continental breakfast can be arranged. Dietary restrictions accommodated if possible. For special consideration, or if you are unable to attend breakfast and please let the innkeeper know the prior day. Beds: KQT. Reading lamp, hair dryer, wireless Internet access, Fresh filtered water, Firm beds with pressed cotton linens, Fluffy hotel towels, Window fans in summer and Fresh flowers in room. TV, fax, copier, library, parlor games, telephone, fireplace, Guest phone in entry hall has voice messaging, Fax and photocopies available with host assistance, Mini-fridge in linen closet on guest room level, One handicapped parking spot available with appropriate plaque and Off-street parking available when necessary on premises. Antiquing, art galleries, beach, bicycling, canoeing/kayaking, fishing, golf, hiking, live theater, museums, parks, shopping, sporting events, water sports, wineries, Close to Ballard, Magnolia, Fremont, Wallingford, 2 blocks from 2 busses to Seattle Center, downtown, Pike Place Market, Seattle Art Museum, Pioneer Square and Ferries without having to transfer nearby.

Location: City. West slope of Queen Anne Hill.

Certificate may be used: Sunday-Thursday, October-May, except holidays, subject to availability.

Three Tree Point Bed & Breakfast

17026 33rd Ave SW
Seattle, WA 98166-3116
(206)669-7646 (888)369-7696 Fax:(206)242-7844
Internet: www.3treepointbnb.com
E-mail: Whisler@3TreePointBnB.com

Circa 1993. Overlooking the shoreline of Three Tree Point on Puget Sound, this contemporary northwest retreat sits on a quiet hillside with panoramic vistas of Mount Rainier and the Olympic Mountains. The Suite with French doors, and the Cottage with a river rock fireplace, each feature a living room, dining area, full kitchen and patio with views of the water. A variety of foods and ingredients are provided and restocked for a daily breakfast that can be prepared and enjoyed when desired. A barbecue, laundry facilities, spa hot tub, and pampering amenities add to the luxury. Take a walk on the beach or hike the historic Indian Trails.

Innkeeper(s): Penny, Doug, Braly and Brita Whisler. $150-250. 2 rooms, 1 with FP, 1 suite, 1 cottage. Breakfast, afternoon tea and snacks/refreshments included in rates. Types of meals: Full bkfst. Beds: Q. Data port, cable TV, VCR, reading lamp, stereo, refrigerator, snack bar, clock radio, telephone, coffeemaker, desk, voice mail, some with fireplace, hair dryer, bathrobes, bath amenities and iron/ironing board in room. Air conditioning. Fax, spa, library, parlor games and laundry facility on premises. Handicap access. Amusement parks, antiquing, art galleries, beach, bicycling, canoeing/kayaking, cross-country skiing, downhill skiing, golf, hiking, live theater, museums, parks, shopping, sporting events, tennis and wineries nearby.

Location: City.

Certificate may be used: Anytime, Sunday-Thursday, excluding June-September, December and holidays, subject to availability.

Seaview   E2

Shelburne Inn

4415 Pacific Way
Seaview, WA 98644
(360)642-2442 (800)INN1896 Fax:(360)642-8904
Internet: www.theshelburneinn.com
E-mail: frontdesk@theshelburneinn.com

Circa 1896. Established in 1896, the Shelburne Inn is the oldest continuously operating hotel in Washington and is listed in the National Register. A beautiful wooden former church altar is

the front desk of this historic hotel. The entire inn is thoughtfully appointed in antiques and fine furnishings. Art nouveau stained-glass windows were rescued from an 1800's church torn down in Morecambe, England, and now shed light and color in the dining room, pub and throughout many of the guest bedrooms. Each morning savor the renowned innkeeper's full gourmet breakfast. Just a 10-minute walk from the ocean, the inn graces Seaview on the Long Beach Peninsula, a 28-mile stretch of seacoast that includes bird sanctuaries, lighthouses, historic centers and national parks.

Innkeeper(s): David Campiche & Laurie Anderson. $139-199. 15 rooms with PB, 2 suites, 1 conference room. Breakfast included in rates. Types of meals: Full gourmet bkfst, lunch, gourmet dinner, room service and Coffee & Tea service all day in lobby. Restaurant on premises. Beds: QDT. Clock radio, hair dryer and wireless Internet access in room. Fax, copier, library, telephone, fireplace, gift shop, Wireless Internet access, Restaurant and Pub on premises. Handicap access. Antiquing, art galleries, beach, bicycling, canoeing/kayaking, fishing, golf, hiking, horseback riding, live theater, museums, parks, shopping, water sports, Clamming (in season), Frequent festivals year round, Surf and Charter fishing nearby.

Location: Country, ocean community.

Publicity: *Better Homes & Gardens, Bon Appetit, Conde Nast Traveler, Esquire, Gourmet, Food & Wine and Travel & Leisure.*

"Fabulous food. Homey but elegant atmosphere. Hospitable service, like being a guest in an elegant home."

Certificate may be used: Midweek, October-May, excluding holidays.

Tacoma   D4

Branch Colonial House

2420 North 21st St
Tacoma, WA 98406
(253)752-3565 (877)752-3565
Internet: www.branchcolonialhouse.com
E-mail: stay@branchcolonialhouse.com

Branch Colonial House sits perched above the historic Old Town District of Tacoma, Washington, overlooking Puget Sound. Relax on the front porch before exploring the scenic Pacific Northwest. This delightful bed and breakfast features Colonial Revival architecture and a romantic ambiance. Stay in a luxury, upscale guest room or suite with modern amenities, robes, a fireplace and a jetted or cast iron soaking tub. Browse local shops, tour museums, go to the zoo and visit the aquarium. It is an easy drive to the many city attractions in Seattle with the splendid majesty of Mount Rainier in the background.

Innkeeper(s): Robin Korobkin. Call for rates. Call inn for details. Breakfast included in rates. Types of meals: Full gourmet bkfst, veg bkfst, early coffee/tea and snacks/refreshments. Beds: KQ. Modem hook-up, data port, cable TV, DVD, reading lamp, stereo, refrigerator, ceiling fan, snack bar, clock radio, telephone, coffeemaker, desk, some with hot tub/spa, some with fireplace, hair dryer, bathrobes and bath amenities in room. VCR, fax, copier, library, parlor games and laundry facility on premises. Amusement parks, antiquing, art galleries, beach, bicycling, canoeing/kayaking, fishing, golf, hiking, horseback riding, live theater, museums, parks, shopping, sporting events and water sports nearby.

Location: City.

Publicity: *Tacoma's New Tribune.*

Certificate may be used: Sunday-Thursday, subject to availability. Blackout dates do apply, call ahead to confirm. Rooms available: Branch, Prospect and Sunroom.

Chinaberry Hill - An 1889 Grand Victorian Inn

302 Tacoma Ave N
Tacoma, WA 98403
(253)272-1282
Internet: www.chinaberryhill.com
E-mail: chinaberry@wa.net

Circa 1889. In the 19th century, this Queen Anne was known as far away as China for its wondrous gardens, one of the earliest examples of landscape gardening in the Pacific Northwest. The home, a wedding present from a husband to his bride, is listed in the National Register. The innkeepers have selected a unique assortment of antiques and collectibles to decorate the manor. The house offers two Jacuzzi suites and a guest room, all eclectically decorated with items such as a four-poster rice bed or a canopy bed. There are two lodging options in the Catchpenny Cottage, a restored carriage house steps away from the manor. Guests can stay either in the romantic carriage suite or the Hay Loft, which includes a bedroom, sitting room, claw-

foot tub and a unique hay chute. In the mornings, as the innkeepers say, guests enjoy "hearty breakfasts and serious coffee." Not a bad start to a day exploring Antique Row or Pt. Defiance, a 698-acre protected rain forest park with an aquarium, gardens, beaches and a zoo. Seattle is 30 minutes away.

Innkeeper(s): Cecil & Yarrow . $139-245. 5 rooms with PB, 1 with FP, 3 with WP, 2 two-bedroom suites, 1 cottage, 1 guest house. Breakfast and snacks/refreshments included in rates. Types of meals: Full gourmet bkfst and early coffee/tea. Beds: QT. Modem hook-up, cable TV, VCR, reading lamp, clock radio, telephone, desk, some with fireplace, hair dryer, bathrobes, bath amenities, wireless Internet access, iron/ironing board, some with bay views, complimentary video library, 24 hour access to complimentary refreshments, cookies, juices, sodas, bottled water and etc in room. Air conditioning. Fax, library, parlor games, gift shop, wraparound porch, historic estate gardens w/100+ yr. old trees and rock walls that give the property a tucked away feeling on premises. Amusement parks, antiquing, art galleries, beach, bicycling, canoeing/kayaking, cross-country skiing, downhill skiing, fishing, golf, hiking, horseback riding, live theater, museums, parks, shopping, sporting events, tennis, water sports, wineries, zoo & aquarium, gardens, 14 miles of old growth forested trails, Point Defiance Park, International Glass Museum, Glass Bridge, New Tacoma Art Museum, Washington State History Museum, hot shops for watching blown glass artisans at work, Farmer's Market and parasailing nearby.

Location: City, ocean community.

Publicity: *Sunset Magazine, Travel and Leisure Magazine, Best Places Northwest, Best Places to Kiss Northwest, Recommended Country Inns of the Pacific Northwest, Amazing Getaways, Seattle P-I, Romantic Days & Nights in Seattle, The Oregonian, The Tacoma News Tribune and Tacoma Weekly.*

Certificate may be used: November, January-March, Monday-Wednesday. Seven days prior to reservation. Excludes holidays and special events.

Plum Duff House

619 North K Street
Tacoma, WA 98403
(253)627-6916 (888)627-1920 Fax:(253)272-9116
Internet: www.plumduff.com
E-mail: plumduffhouse@gmail.com

Circa 1901. Friendly and casual with a relaxing ambiance and genuine hospitality, Plum Duff House in the North Tacoma district in Washington was built in 1901 in the Victorian style. Antiques, country and modern furnishings mix in an appealing and inviting way. Relax by the fire in the living room or gather in the enclosed sun porch for a game of chess or browse for a book off the shelf. Snacks and beverages are available at any time. Stay in a comfortable guest bedroom or a suite that boasts a fireplace and Jacuzzi tub. After a satisfying breakfast explore the Great Pacific Northwest. Take day trips to Seattle, Puget Sound, Mt. Rainier and the Olympic Peninsula.

Innkeeper(s): Peter & Robin Stevens. $90-150. 4 rooms with PB, 1 with FP, 1 with WP, 1 two-bedroom suite. Breakfast included in rates. Types of meals: Full bkfst. Beds: KQDT. Cable TV, VCR, refrigerator, ceiling fan, clock radio, telephone, desk, hair dryer, bathrobes, bath amenities, wireless Internet access and iron/ironing board in room. Air conditioning. Fax, copier, spa, bicycles, library, parlor games and fireplace on premises. Amusement parks, antiquing, art galleries, beach, downhill skiing, fishing, golf, hiking, live theater, museums, parks, shopping and sporting events nearby.

Location: City.

Certificate may be used: November-March, Sunday-Thursday, last minute, subject to availability, no holidays.

West Virginia

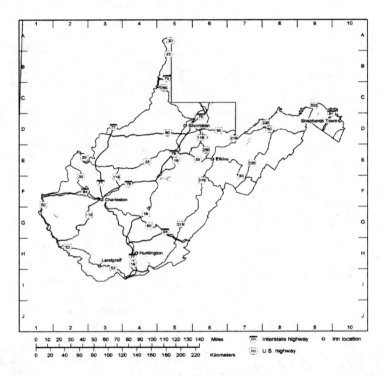

Charleston   F3

Brass Pineapple B&B

1611 Virginia St East
Charleston, WV 25311-2113
(304) 344-0748 (866) 344-0748
Internet: www.brasspineapple.com
E-mail: info@brasspineapple.com

Circa 1910. Original oak paneling, leaded and stained glass
are among the architectural highlights at this smoke-free inn
that graces the historic district near the Capitol Complex.

Guest bedrooms feature
thoughtful amenities including
terry robes and hair dryers as
well as technology for business
needs. A full breakfast consist-
ing of tea, juices, fruit, muffins,
waffles, quiche, basil tomatoes

and cottage fries, is served in the dining room. Dietary
requirements can be met upon request.

Innkeeper(s): Lisa, Vicky, Cheryl. $109-149. 6 rooms with PB, 1 suite.
Breakfast, afternoon tea, snacks/refreshments and hors d'oeuvres included in
rates. Types of meals: Full gourmet bkfst, veg bkfst, early coffee/tea and picnic lunch. Beds: KQT. Modem hook-up, data port, cable TV, VCR, reading
lamp, ceiling fan, clock radio, telephone, desk, voice mail, most with fireplace, hair dryer, bathrobes, bath amenities, wireless Internet access and free
sodas in room. Central air. Fax, copier, pet boarding, parlor games and laundry facility on premises. Antiquing, bicycling, canoeing/kayaking, cross-country skiing, downhill skiing, fishing, golf, hiking, horseback riding, live theater,
museums, parks, shopping, sporting events, tennis, water sports, wineries,
dog racing, gambling and river cruises nearby.

Location: City. Historic district, Capitol Complex.

Publicity: *Mid-Atlantic Country, Country Inns, Gourmet, Charlestonian,
Charleston Newspapers, Gourmet, Southern Living, Recommended Country
Inns, News 8, TV 13 and Super 102.7.*

*"Charming, convenient location, lovely antiques, appealing decor.
Extremely clean; excellent service from Lisa and the staff."*

Certificate may be used: Anytime, except major holidays and vacation periods, subject to availability.

Landgraff   H3

Elkhorn Inn & Theatre

On Route 52
Landgraff, WV 24829
(304)862-2031 (800)708-2040 Fax:(304)862-2031
Internet: www.elkhorninnwv.com
E-mail: elisse@elkhorninnwv.com

Circa 1922. Named for the trout-filled Elkhorn Creek that runs
behind the inn, this historic Italianate brick building with arch-
ways and a balcony on the Coal Heritage Trail has been lovingly
restored by Dan and Elisse. Period antiques and 1930s furnishings complement an international art collection. Paintings,
prints, ceramics, stained glass, sculpture and textiles are for
sale. Stay in a guest bedroom or suite with handmade vintage
quilts, clawfoot tubs and bubble baths. A family suite with two
adjoining rooms is available. Alto Grande Coffee, offered exclusively at the inn, accompanies a continental breakfast. Located
near Pinnacle Rock State Park and Panther State Forest, there
are ATV and bike trails on Burke Mountain. McDowell County
is also a popular hunting and fishing area.

Innkeeper(s): Elisse & Dan Clark. $99-198. 13 rooms, 3 with PB, 1 two-
bedroom suite. Breakfast included in rates. Types of meals: Cont, veg bkfst,
Sun. brunch, early coffee/tea, lunch, afternoon tea, snacks/refreshments, hors
d'oeuvres, wine, gourmet dinner, Weddings, dinner parties, buffet dinner parties and other special events. Beds: QDT. Reading lamp, ceiling fan, clock
radio, desk, bathrobes, wireless Internet access, down and vintage quilts,
down/feather pillows, individual fans and heaters in room. Air conditioning.
TV, VCR, DVD, fax, library, parlor games, telephone, fireplace, laundry facility,
gift shop, Wireless Internet access, Gift Shop with an international selection
of for-sale artwork, Jewelry, Books, Vintage quilts and locally-made handcrafted coal gifts, Balcony with umbrella tables and chairs, Fireplace lounge,
Outdoor Patio Cafe under the arches, Theatre available for summer events
such as weddings, concerts and meetings on premises. Antiquing, fishing,
golf, hiking, live theater, museums, parks, shopping, Trout fishing on Elkhorn
Creek at the Inn, Pinnacle Rock State Park, Panther State Forest, Blackwolf
Golf Course, Hatfield-McCoy ATV trails (Indian Ridge Trails, Pinnacle Creek
Trails), McDowell County ATV trails, Stocked trout streams, Anawalt Lake,
Berwind Lake, Kimball WWI African-American Memorial, Coal Heritage Trail
and "railfan" sites, "History in our Mountains" Musuem in Welch, Skygusty
ATV Racetrack, Pocahontas Va. Coal Mine Museum, Antiquing, Aveda Day
Spa & Mercer Mall in Bluefield, "October Sky" Rocketboys Festival in
Coalwood, Oktoberfest in Bramwell, October Italian Festival in Bluefield,
McDowell County and Mercer County Fairs, McArts performances of "Terror of
the Tug", Gary Bowling's House of Art (Wed Night Open Mike Nights), Chuck
Methena Center for the Arts and "Cowboy Up!" Country Western Night club
in Bluefiefld nearby.

Location: Country, mountains, waterfront. On Elkhorn Creek, near
Bluefield, WV/VA.

Publicity: *NY Daily News, Great Country Inns of America Cookbook, Historic
Inns of WV, WV Off The Beaten Path, Wonderful West Virginia,
Preservation Magazine, ConventionSouth Reader's Choice Award, Charleston
Gazette and Daily Mail, WV Fish & Game, WV State Journal, Bluefield
Daily Telegraph, Welch News, West Virginia Wild & Wonderful Magazine,
Trains, Railfan & Railroad, Blue Ridge Country, The Artists Magazine, All-
Terrain-Vehicle Magazine, Appalachian Journal; diynetwork.com "Best Built
Homes in America," Winner of Historic Preservation Award, America's
Byways/Coal Heritage Trail., HGTV "Building Character" and "ReZoned",
Speed Channel "Two Wheel Tuesday", "Good Morning West Virginia!",
"Traveling the Mountain State", WVNS News 59 (CBS), WVVA News
Channel 6 (NBC), WELC Radio AM/FM; 100.9 The Mix, WV Film Division
"Location of the Month", www.atv.com, www.retreatsonline.com
"Location of the Month", www.atv.com, www.retreatsonline.com
www.hawk.com, www.trailsheaven.com (Hatfield & McCoy ATV trails) and
www.byways.org (Coal Heritage Trail).*

Certificate may be used: Anytime, subject to availability, not valid Oct. 1-10.

Shepherdstown   D10

Thomas Shepherd Inn

300 W German St.
Shepherdstown, WV 25443
(304)876-3715 (888)889-8952
Internet: www.thomasshepherdinn.com
E-mail: info@thomasshepherdinn.com

Built as a Lutheran parsonage in Shepherdstown, West Virginia
using Federal architecture, Thomas Shepherd Inn has been renovated to offer gracious hospitality in a traditional style.
Spacious common rooms like the large living room with a fireplace or the book-filled library offer several seating areas with
comfortable antique furnishings. The porch invites quiet relaxation. Appealing guest bedrooms provide a retreat from distrac-
tions of phone or television. Savor a hearty breakfast served
family style that may include favorites like apple cranberry
crisp, tomato mushroom and cheese omelet, local bacon, and
poppyseed muffins with homemade Asian pear marmalade.

Innkeeper(s): Jim Ford & Jeanne Muir. $125-200. 6 rooms with PB, 1 with
FP. Breakfast included in rates. Types of meals: Full bkfst, veg bkfst and early
coffee/tea. Beds: QD. Reading lamp, clock radio, bathrobes, bath amenities,
wireless Internet access and Water carafes in room. Central air. TV, VCR,
DVD, fax, copier, library, parlor games, telephone, fireplace, Wireless Internet
access and Gift items for sale on premises. Antiquing, art galleries, bicycling,
canoeing/kayaking, fishing, golf, hiking, horseback riding, live theater, museums, parks, shopping, water sports and wineries nearby.

Location: Small town.

Publicity: *Washington Post, Washington City Paper, Washingtonian
Magazine and WCHS Charleston Traveling West Virginia.*

Certificate may be used: Monday-Thursday, subject to availability.

Wisconsin

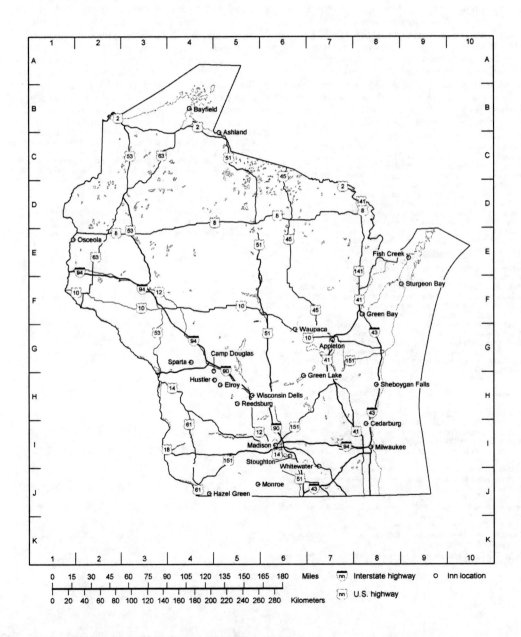

0   15   30   45   60   75   90   105 120 135 150 165 180   Miles

0   20   40   60   80 100 120 140 160 180 200 220 240 260 280   Kilometers

(nn) Interstate highway   o Inn location

(nn) U.S. highway

Appleton   G7

Franklin Inn on Durkee

310 North Durkee
Appleton, WI 54911
(920)993-1711 (888)993-1711
Internet: www.appleton-wisconsin.com
E-mail: info@franklinstreetinn.com

Circa 1894. Experience an elegant setting and unique international themes amid lush woodwork and fine furnishings at this restored Queen Ann Victorian with beautiful landscaping. Relax in spacious common areas. Guest rooms and suites boast whirlpools, fireplaces pillow-top beds and wifi. In the dining room, gourmet breakfasts are presented underneath an antique chandelier or enjoy dining al fresco on the porch or more privately, in-room. The convenient location is in the historic district of downtown Appleton, Wisconsin, only blocks away from the highlights of Fox Valley: the Performing Arts Center, History Museum at the Castle, Trout Museum of Art, Lawrence University, City Park and Fox River Trail. Popular events hosted at the inn include a murder mystery party, small wedding or shower, girlfriend getaway, scrapbook event or retreat.

Innkeeper(s): Ron and Judy Halma. $99-219. 4 rooms with PB, 2 with FP, 2 with WP, 2 total suites, including 1 three-bedroom suite, 1 conference room. Breakfast and snacks/refreshments included in rates. Types of meals: Full gourmet bkfst, veg bkfst, early coffee/tea, room service and Innkeeper has published a cookbook. Breakfast menus are created using these recipes. Beds: KQDT. Reading lamp, CD player, ceiling fan, clock radio, turn-down service, desk, some with fireplace, hair dryer, bathrobes, bath amenities, wireless Internet access and iron/ironing board in room. Central air. TV, DVD, fax, copier, library, parlor games, telephone, gift shop, guest refrigerator, microwave and spa services on premises. Antiquing, art galleries, beach, bicycling, canoeing/kayaking, cross-country skiing, fishing, golf, hiking, live theater, museums, parks, shopping, sporting events, tennis, water sports and wineries nearby.

Location: City, ocean community.

Publicity: *Post Crescent Newspaper (Appleton, Wisconsin), Wisconsin Trails Magazine and "Living with Amy" morning show* .

Certificate may be used: Last minute based on projected availability for 2 for 1 overnight accommodations in the lovely Petit Chateau Suite or Sea Breeze Suites. Reservations required; holidays, holiday weeks and special event weekends excluded.

Ashland   C5

Second Wind Country Inn

30475 Carlson Road
Ashland, WI 54806
(715)682-1000
Internet: www.secondwindcountryinn.com
E-mail: catchyourbreath@secondwindcountryinn.com

Circa 2004. Encompassing 35 magnificent acres, this non-smoking log and timber lodge offers an incredible view of Lake Superior's Chequamegon Bay area. Relax in the gathering room with a Northwoods lodge décor or on one of the outdoor decks. Three guest suites feature a luxurious ambiance and whirlpool tubs. The Bear Den is handicap accessible. The Northern Lights Loft includes a kitchenette with refrigerator and microwave. Wake up after a restful sleep and enjoy a home-cooked breakfast. Gather for a late-night bonfire and evening treats. Browse the Second Wind Mercantile for gifts to bring home.

Innkeeper(s): Mark and Kelly Illick. $89-159. 3 rooms, 3 with WP, 3 total suites, including 1 three-bedroom suite, 1 conference room. Breakfast and Sunday brunch included in rates. Types of meals: Country bkfst, early

coffee/tea and snacks/refreshments. Beds: Q. Reading lamp, CD player, refrigerator, ceiling fan, clock radio, coffeemaker, hot tub/spa, hair dryer, bath amenities and wireless Internet access in room. Central air. VCR, copier, spa, library, parlor games, telephone, gift shop, Free wireless Internet, Fire ring, Outside decks, Cross country skiing, Hiking trails, ATV and Snowmobile trail on premises. Handicap access. Antiquing, art galleries, beach, bicycling, canoeing/kayaking, cross-country skiing, downhill skiing, fishing, golf, hiking, horseback riding, live theater, museums, shopping and water sports nearby.

Location: Country.

Publicity: *The Sounder.*

Certificate may be used: October 15-May 15, subject to availability.

Bayfield   B4

Old Rittenhouse Inn

301 Rittenhouse Ave
Bayfield, WI 54814-0584
(715)779-5111 (800)779-2129 Fax:(715)779-5887
Internet: www.rittenhouseinn.com
E-mail: gourmet@rittenhouseinn.com

Circa 1892. Two historic Queen Anne mansions, a guest house and a private cottage comprise this elegant Victorian inn and gourmet restaurant just a few blocks from downtown. Under massive gables, a wraparound veranda is filled with white wicker furniture, geraniums and petunias. The inn boasts 22 working fireplaces amidst antique furnishings. Well-appointed guest bedrooms and luxury suites offer a variety of romantic amenities that may include whirlpools as well as views of Madeline Island and Lake Superior. The two-story Fountain Cottage is just uphill. For breakfast indulge in baked muffins served with Rittenhouse Jams, Jellies and a cup of coffee accompanied by dishes such as Wild Bayfield Blueberry Crisp or Moonglow Pears Poached in White Zinfandel.

Innkeeper(s): Jerry, Mary, Mark, Wendy, and Julie Phillips. $99-349. 26 rooms with PB, 19 with FP, 17 with WP, 7 total suites, including 2 two-bedroom suites, 2 cottages, 2 guest houses. Breakfast, Continental Breakfast included in room rate and Full Breakfast available for $8.50/houseguest and $11.50/person for walk ins included in rates. Types of meals: Full gourmet bkfst, gourmet lunch, snacks/refreshments, wine, gourmet dinner, room service, Weddings, Reunions and catered special events. Restaurant on premises. Beds: KQD. Reading lamp, CD player, clock radio, coffeemaker, desk, most with hot tub/spa, most with fireplace, hair dryer, bath amenities, wireless Internet access, Whirlpool and Antiques in room. Air conditioning. Fax, copier, telephone and gift shop on premises. Handicap access. Antiquing, art galleries, beach, bicycling, canoeing/kayaking, cross-country skiing, downhill skiing, fishing, golf, hiking, horseback riding, live theater, museums, parks, shopping, tennis, water sports, Apple orchards, Apostle Islands National Lakeshore, Gaylord Nelson Wilderness Preserve, Big Top Chautauqua, Sailing, Charters and Microbrewery nearby.

Location: Country, waterfront.

Publicity: *Wisconsin Trails, Midwest Living, National Geographic Traveler, Country Inns, Minnesota Monthly, Bon Appetit, Gourmet, Better Homes and Gardens, Lake Superior Magazine, Victoria, Minneapolis/St.Paul Magazine, St. Paul Pioneer Press, Milwaukee Journal, Wisconsin State Journal and Chicago Tribune.*

"The whole decor, the room, the staff and the food were superb! Your personalities and talents give a great warmth to the inn."

Certificate may be used: Nov. 1 to May 14, Wednesday and Thursday.

Camp Douglas   H5

Sunnyfield Farm B&B

N6692 Batko Rd
Camp Douglas, WI 54618
(608)427-3686 (888)839-0232
Internet: www.sunnyfield.net
E-mail: soltvedt@mwt.net

Circa 1899. Scenic bluffs and rich land surround this 100-year-old, three-story farmhouse boasting 10-foot ceilings. Lovingly restored, the original hardwood floors and hand-carved oak woodwork reside easily with brass ceiling tiles and family heirlooms. Guest bedrooms feature a country decor with handmade quilts and stenciling. The Rose Room has an adjoining room that is perfect for families or groups. A private studio apartment on the third floor offers a cozy yet spacious suite with living room, kitchen and sky windows for stargazing. Wake up to a complete country breakfast served in the spacious dining room. Three of the 160 acres are manicured lawns to enjoy. Wisconsin Dells is just 30 minutes away.

Innkeeper(s): Susanne & John Soltvedt. $80-120. 4 rooms, 2 with PB. Breakfast included in rates. Types of meals: Country bkfst and early coffee/tea. Beds: QT. Reading lamp, ceiling fan and desk in room. TV, VCR, DVD, library, parlor games, telephone and laundry facility on premises. Antiquing, art galleries, bicycling, canoeing/kayaking, cross-country skiing, fishing, golf, hiking, parks, shopping and water sports nearby.

Location: Country.

Certificate may be used: November-April, anytime, subject to availability.

Cedarburg   I8

The Washington House Inn

W 62 N 573 Washington Ave
Cedarburg, WI 53012-1941
(262)375-3550 (800)554-4717 Fax:(262)375-9422
Internet: www.washingtonhouseinn.com
E-mail: info@washingtonhouseinn.com

Circa 1886. This three-story cream city brick building is in the National Register. Rooms are appointed in a country Victorian style and feature antiques, whirlpool baths and fireplaces. The original guest registry, more than 100 years old, is displayed proudly in the lobby, and a marble trimmed fireplace is often lit for the afternoon wine and cheese hour. Breakfast is continental and is available in the gathering room, often including recipes from a historic Cedarburg cookbook for items such as homemade muffins, cakes and breads.

Innkeeper(s): Wendy Porterfield. $145-275. 34 rooms with PB, 3 suites, 1 conference room. Breakfast included in rates. Types of meals: Cont plus and snacks/refreshments. Beds: KQD. Cable TV, VCR, reading lamp, ceiling fan, clock radio, telephone and wireless Internet access in room. Air conditioning. TV, fax, copier and sauna on premises. Antiquing, cross-country skiing, fishing, live theater, parks, shopping and sporting events nearby.

Location: City. Historic district.

Publicity: *Country Home and Chicago Sun-Times.*

Certificate may be used: Sunday-Thursday only on rooms $148 and up, no holidays or festival dates.

Elroy   H5

East View B&B

33620 County P Rd
Elroy, WI 53929
(608)463-7564
Internet: www.eastviewbedandbreakfast.com
E-mail: eastview@centurytel.net

Circa 1994. This comfortable ranch house offers splendid views of the countryside, with its rolling hills covered with woods. Autumn is a particularly scenic time for a visit, when the trees explode in color. The three guest rooms are simply furnished in a homey, country style with quilts topping the beds. Each room offers a pleasing view. Breakfast comes in several courses, with fresh fruit, homemade breads, a daily entree and finally a dessert. The area provides opportunities for hiking, biking, canoeing or browsing at local craft stores.

Innkeeper(s): Dom & Bev Puechner. $80. 3 rooms with PB. Breakfast included in rates. Types of meals: Full bkfst and early coffee/tea. Beds: QD. Reading lamp, ceiling fan, clock radio, telephone and turn-down service in room. Air conditioning. Walking trails on premises. Amusement parks, antiquing, cross-country skiing, golf and shopping nearby.

Location: Country.

Publicity: *Country Inns and Midwest Living Magazine.*

"What a wonderful treat it was to stay at East View. The view was magnificent and the breakfasts superb."

Certificate may be used: Anytime, subject to availability.

Green Bay   F8

The Astor House B&B

637 S Monroe Ave
Green Bay, WI 54301-3614
(920)432-3585 (888)303-6370 Fax:(920)436-3145
Internet: www.astorhouse.com
E-mail: info@astorhouse.com

Circa 1888. Located in the Astor Historic District, the Astor House is completely surrounded by Victorian homes. Guests have their choice of five rooms, each uniquely decorated for a  range of ambiance, from the Vienna Balconies to the Marseilles Garden to the Hong Kong Retreat. The parlor, veranda and many suites feature a grand view of City Centre's lighted church towers. This home is also the first and only B&B in Green Bay and received the Mayor's Award for Remodeling and Restoration. Business travelers should take notice of the private phone lines in each room, as well as our wireless high-speed Internet access.

Innkeeper(s): Greg & Barbara Robinson. $120-159. 5 rooms with PB, 4 with FP, 3 suites. Breakfast included in rates. Types of meals: Cont plus. Beds: KQDT. Cable TV, VCR, reading lamp, stereo, refrigerator, clock radio, telephone, gas fireplaces and double whirlpool tub (4 of 5 rooms) in room. Air conditioning. Amusement parks, antiquing, cross-country skiing, fishing, live theater, parks, shopping, sporting events and water sports nearby.

Location: City.

Publicity: *Chicago Sun-Times and Corporate Reports.*

Certificate may be used: Sunday-Thursday, subject to availability. Excludes special events like holidays and Packer Football Games. May be used only for rooms with whirlpool and fireplace.

Green Lake
H6

McConnell Inn

497 S Lawson Dr
Green Lake, WI 54941-8700
(920)294-6430 (888)238-8625
Internet: www.mcconnellinn.com
E-mail: info@mcconnellinn.com

Circa 1901. This stately home features many of its original features, including leaded windows, woodwork, leather wainscoting and parquet floors. Each of the guest rooms includes beds covered with handmade quilts and clawfoot tubs. The grand, master suite comprises the entire third floor and boasts 14-foot vaulted beam ceilings, Victorian walnut furnishings, a Jacuzzi and six-foot oak buffet now converted into a unique bathroom vanity. Innkeeper Mary Jo Johnson, a pastry chef, creates the wonderful pastries that accompany an expansive breakfast with fresh fruit, granola and delectable entrees.

Innkeeper(s): Mary Jo Johnson and Scott Johnson. $90-175. 5 rooms with PB, 2 with FP, 2 with WP, 1 suite. Breakfast included in rates. Types of meals: Full gourmet bkfst and early coffee/tea. Beds: KQ. Cable TV, VCR, reading lamp, refrigerator, ceiling fan, clock radio, hot tub/spa, some with fireplace, hair dryer, bathrobes and iron/ironing board in room. Central air. Library, parlor games and telephone on premises. Antiquing, art galleries, beach, bicycling, canoeing/kayaking, cross-country skiing, fishing, golf, hiking, horseback riding, live theater, museums, parks, shopping, sporting events, tennis and water sports nearby.

Certificate may be used: November-April, excluding holidays, subject to availability, Anytime, Last Minute-Based on Availability.

Hazel Green
J4

Wisconsin House Stagecoach Inn

Main & Fairplay Streets
Hazel Green, WI 53811-0071
(608)854-2233 (877)854-2233
Internet: www.wisconsinhouse.com
E-mail: wishouse@mhtc.net

Circa 1846. Located in southwest Wisconsin's historic lead mining region, this one-time stagecoach stop will delight antique-lovers. The spacious two-story inn once hosted Ulysses S. Grant, whose home is just across the border in Illinois. One of the inn's guest rooms bears his name and features a walnut four-poster bed. Don't miss the chance to join the Dischs on a Saturday evening for their gourmet dinner, served by reservation only.

Innkeeper(s): Ken & Pat Disch. $75-125. 8 rooms, 6 with PB, 2 two-bedroom suites. Breakfast included in rates. Types of meals: Full gourmet bkfst, early coffee/tea, snacks/refreshments and gourmet dinner. Beds: KQDT. Reading lamp and bath amenities in room. Air conditioning. TV, VCR, DVD, fax, copier, library, parlor games and telephone on premises. Antiquing, art galleries, bicycling, canoeing/kayaking, cross-country skiing, downhill skiing, fishing, golf, hiking, horseback riding, live theater, museums, parks and wineries nearby.

Location: City.

Publicity: *Travel & Leisure, Milwaukee Magazine, Chicago Magazine, Milwaukee Journal and Wisconsin Trails.*

Certificate may be used: May-October anytime, rooms with shared baths only. Other months all rooms available.

Hustler
H5

Fountain Chateau

202 E. Main Street,
Hustler, WI 54637
(608)427-3787 (877)427-3719
Internet: www.fountainchateau.com
E-mail: innkeeper@fountainchateau.com

Circa 1922. Friendly service, wholesome food and delightful accommodations are available year round amid scenic tranquility. The peaceful setting includes a deck, book library, fitness room and a piano. Historic Fountain Chateau Bed & Breakfast in Hustler, Wisconsin is near popular bike trails and the water sports at Castle Rock Lake. Wisconsin Dells is a 30-minute drive. Stay in a themed guest room with robes, slippers and other pleasing amenities. Some of the rooms boast baths with pedestal sinks and walk-in showers. This B&B is handicap and wheelchair accessible. A hearty breakfast buffet menu served in the Harmony Bistro Restaurant satisfies every palate. Ask about specials and packages offered.

Innkeeper(s): Barbara Richmond. & J.P. Olson. $100-159. 8 rooms with PB, 1 two-bedroom suite, 1 conference room. Breakfast and afternoon tea included in rates. Types of meals: Full gourmet bkfst, veg bkfst, Sun. brunch, early coffee/tea, room service, Jazz Sunday Brunch every 1st and 3rd Sunday in each month. Contact Innkeeper for details. The Harmony Bistro Restaurant is on site and will be open for a full restaurant service in January of 2010. Guests are offered a 4oz. glass of wine, snack and refreshments provided upon request for a small fee. Meals are provided for group meetings and also list of other Fine Dining Retaurants in the area. Beds: KQ. Reading lamp, stereo, ceiling fan, hair dryer, bathrobes, bath amenities, wireless Internet access, iron/ironing board, Two rooms have stereo, The Duke Ellington King-size thematic room and The George Gershwin King-size thematic room in room. Central air. TV, VCR, DVD, fax, copier, bicycles, library, telephone, fireplace, laundry facility, gift shop, Massage Service upon request, Piano, Wi-Fi Internet service, Private baths in each room, Elevator and Fitness room on premises. Handicap access. Amusement parks, antiquing, art galleries, bicycling, canoeing/kayaking, cross-country skiing, downhill skiing, fishing, golf, hiking, horseback riding, live theater, museums, parks, shopping, sporting events, water sports, wineries, Bowling, Movie Theater, Snow Mobiling, Boating, Lakes, Hunting and Rodeo nearby.

Location: Country.

Certificate may be used: Sept. 10-May 30, Sunday-Thursday.

Madison
I6

Arbor House, An Environmental Inn

3402 Monroe St
Madison, WI 53711-1702
(608)238-2981
Internet: www.arbor-house.com
E-mail: arborhouse@tds.net

Circa 1853. Nature-lovers not only will enjoy the inn's close access to a 1,280-acre nature preserve, they will appreciate the innkeepers' ecological theme. Organic sheets and towels are offered for guests as well as environmentally safe bath products. Arbor House is one of Madison's oldest existing homes and features plenty of historic features, such as romantic reading chairs and antiques, mixed with modern amenities and unique touches. Five guest rooms include a whirlpool tub and three have fireplaces. The Annex guest rooms include private balconies. The innkeepers offer many amenities for business travelers, including value-added corporate rates. The award-winning inn has been recognized as a model of urban ecology. Lake Wingra is within walking distance as are biking and nature trails, bird watching and a host of other outdoor activities. Guests enjoy complimentary canoeing and use of mountain bikes.

Innkeeper(s): John & Cathie Imes. $150-230. 8 rooms with PB, 3 with FP, 1 suite, 1 conference room. Breakfast included in rates. Types of meals: Full bkfst. Beds: KQ. Cable TV, VCR, reading lamp, stereo, ceiling fan, clock radio, telephone and desk in room. Air conditioning. Fax, copier, sauna and fireplace on premises. Handicap access. Antiquing, cross-country skiing, fishing, parks, shopping, sporting events and water sports nearby.

Location: City.

Publicity: Money Magazine, New York Times, Natural Home, Travel & Leisure, Midwest Living and Insider's List Cable TV-Top 10 Eco-Hotels.

"What a delightful treat in the middle of Madison. Absolutely, unquestionably, the best time I've spent in a hotel or otherwise. B&Bs are the only way to go! Thank you!"

Certificate may be used: November-April, Sunday-Thursday, excluding holidays (John Nolen and Cozy Rose guest rooms only).

Milwaukee   I8

Schuster Mansion Bed & Breakfast

3209 W. Wells Street
Milwaukee, WI 53208
(414)342-3210 Fax:(414)344-3405
Internet: www.schustermansion.com
E-mail: welcome@schustermansion.com

Circa 1891. Schuster Mansion Bed and Breakfast, built on the elite West side of Milwaukee, Wisconsin is a multi-level mansion with Victorian and Edwardian antique furnishings and décor. This historic mansion with red sandstone, red brick and ornamental red terra cotta trim was designed with Richardson Romanesque architecture and Queen Anne, Flemish, Gothic, Shingle and Colonial influences. Gather for conversation or a quiet read in one of the parlors. Stay in a guest room or suite that features a themed décor. After breakfast, visit the art museum, Boerner Botanical Gardens, the Schlitz Audubon Nature Center and other nearby attractions. Weddings and special events are popular at this romantic and opulent setting.

Innkeeper(s): Rick and Laura Sue Mosier. $99-199. 5 rooms, 3 with PB, 3 suites. Breakfast and snacks/refreshments included in rates. Types of meals: Full gourmet bkfst, veg bkfst and room service. Beds: QDT. Cable TV, DVD, reading lamp, ceiling fan, clock radio, turn-down service, desk, hair dryer, bath amenities, wireless Internet access and iron/ironing room in room. Air conditioning. Whole house water treatment system on premises. Antiquing, art galleries, beach, bicycling, fishing, golf, live theater, museums, parks, shopping, sporting events, Miller Brewery, Harley-Davidson Museum and Potowatomi nearby.

Location: City.

Certificate may be used: Oct. 15-March 15 excluding Nov. 24-25, Dec. 23-25, Dec. 31-Jan. 1, Feb. 13-14.

Osceola   E1

St. Croix River Inn

305 River St, PO Box 356
Osceola, WI 54020-0356
(715) 294-4248 (800) 645-8820
Internet: www.stcroixriverinn.com
E-mail: innkeeper@stcroixriverinn.com

Circa 1908. Timeless elegance is imparted at this meticulously restored stone house that blends old world charm with new world luxuries. Indulge in dramatic vistas from this gorgeous setting on the bluffs of the river. A comfortable ambiance

embraces this inn where complimentary coffee is always found in the sitting room. There is also a wine and beverage bar. Select a book or game from the entertainment closet. Videos and CDs are also available for use in the private suites that all feature a fireplace and a hydromassage tub. A sumptuous breakfast served to each room is highlighted with spectacular views of the water.

Innkeeper(s): Ben & Jennifer Bruno, Danette Roberts. $135-250. 7 rooms, 7 with FP, 7 with WP, 7 suites. Breakfast and snacks/refreshments included in rates. Types of meals: Full gourmet bkfst, veg bkfst, early coffee/tea, picnic lunch, hors d'oeuvres, wine and gourmet dinner. Beds: Q. Cable TV, VCR, DVD, reading lamp, stereo, refrigerator, snack bar, clock radio, telephone, coffeemaker, turn-down service, hot tub/spa, voice mail, fireplace, hair dryer, bathrobes, bath amenities, wireless Internet access, Fireplace, Hydromassage tub and Spa-quality amenities in room. Central air. Parlor games. Perched on the bluffs of the river and most rooms offer a private patio or balcony with spectacular river views on premises. Handicap access. Antiquing, beach, bicycling, canoeing/kayaking, cross-country skiing, downhill skiing, fishing, golf, hiking, live theater, parks, shopping, water sports, wineries, Snowmobile trails, Scenic train ride, Dinner cruises, Spa services, Casino and Fine dining nearby.

Location: Country, waterfront.

Publicity: Milwaukee Home & Fine Living, St. Croix Valley Magazine and Woodbury Magazine.

Certificate may be used: Nov. 30 to April 30, Sunday-Thursday, excluding holidays.

Reedsburg   H5

Parkview B&B

211 N Park St
Reedsburg, WI 53959-1652
(608)524-4333 Fax:(608)524-1172
Internet: www.parkviewbb.com
E-mail: info@parkviewbb.com

Circa 1895. Tantalizingly close to Baraboo and Spring Green, this central Wisconsin inn overlooks a city park in the historic district. The gracious innkeepers delight in tending to their guests' desires and offer wake-up coffee and a morning paper. The home's first owners were in the hardware business, so there are many original, unique fixtures, in addition to hardwood floors, intricate woodwork, leaded and etched windows and a suitors' window. The downtown business district is just a block away.

Innkeeper(s): Tom & Donna Hofmann. $85-105. 4 rooms, 2 with PB, 1 with FP. Breakfast and snacks/refreshments included in rates. Types of meals: Full gourmet bkfst, veg bkfst and early coffee/tea. Beds: QT. Cable TV, reading lamp, CD player, refrigerator, ceiling fan, clock radio, some with fireplace, hair dryer, bathrobes, bath amenities, wireless Internet access and 1 with fireplace in room. Central air. Fax and parlor games on premises. Antiquing, art galleries, bicycling, canoeing/kayaking, cross-country skiing, downhill skiing, fishing, golf, hiking, horseback riding, live theater, parks, shopping, wineries and state parks nearby.

Location: City.

Publicity: Reedsburg Report and Reedsburg Times-Press.

"Your hospitality was great! You all made us feel right at home."

Certificate may be used: Sunday-Thursday, May 1-Oct. 31, holidays not included anytime remainder of year.

Sheboygan Falls   H8

The Rochester Inn

504 Water Street
Sheboygan Falls, WI 53085-1455
(920)467-3123 (866)467-3122
Internet: www.rochesterinn.com
E-mail: info@rochesterinn.com

Circa 1848. This Greek Revival inn is furnished with Queen Anne Victorian antiques, wet bars and four-poster beds. The most romantic offerings are the 600-square-foot suites. They include living rooms with camel back couches and wing back chairs on the first floor and bedrooms with double whirlpool tubs on the second floor. Sheboygan Falls is one mile from the village of Kohler.

Innkeeper(s): Amy Kolste. $99-174. 6 rooms with PB, 5 with HT, 5 with WP, 5 two-bedroom suites. Breakfast included in rates. Types of meals: Full gourmet bkfst, veg bkfst, early coffee/tea, afternoon tea and snacks/refreshments. Beds: Q. Data port, cable TV, VCR, DVD, reading lamp, stereo, refrigerator, snack bar, clock radio, telephone, coffeemaker, desk, most with hot tub/spa, hair dryer, bath amenities, wireless Internet access and iron/ironing board in room. Central air. Parlor games, Additional Charge Amenities include Carriage & Sleigh Rides, In-Room massages, Romantic snacks such as chocolate dipped strawberries and personal cakes on premises. Limited handicap access. Antiquing, art galleries, beach, bicycling, canoeing/kayaking, cross-country skiing, fishing, golf, hiking, horseback riding, live theater, museums, parks, shopping, tennis, water sports, Kohler World Class Golf - Whistling Straits and Blackwolf Run nearby.

Location: City. Small town.

Certificate may be used: Sunday-Thursday, Nov. 1-May 1, some restrictions apply.

Sparta   G4

Franklin Victorian Bed & Breakfast

220 E Franklin St
Sparta, WI 54656-1804
(608) 366-1427 (888) 594-3822
Internet: www.franklinvictorianbb.com
E-mail: innkeeper@franklinvictorianbb.com

Circa 1900. Escape to this Victorian treasure located in the Hidden Valleys of Southwestern Wisconsin. This area is considered to be the Bicycling Capital of America and the famous Elroy-Sparta state biking trail is nearby. Relax with a book and a homemade treat from the bottomless cookie jar. In the early evening, enjoy a wine and cheese reception. Guest bedrooms are elegant and spacious retreats. After a scrumptious full breakfast, adventures await. Explore Amish country, go hiking, experience Warren Cranfest, cranberry harvesting and an abundance of water and snow sports. This all-season inn offers year-round activities. Ask about Murder Mystery Weekends. Bike storage and shuttles are provided.

Innkeeper(s): Jennifer & Steve Dunn. $109-129. 4 rooms with PB, 1 with FP, 1 with WP, 2 suites. Breakfast and snacks/refreshments included in rates. Types of meals: Full bkfst, veg bkfst, early coffee/tea, wine and room service. Beds: KQ. DVD, reading lamp, stereo, refrigerator, ceiling fan, snack bar, clock radio, coffeemaker, turn-down service, some with hot tub/spa, some with fireplace, hair dryer, bathrobes, bath amenities, wireless Internet access, iron/ironing board and Business Travelers Free High Speed Wireless Internet is available in room. Central air. TV, library, parlor games, telephone and High

Speed Wireless Internet Available on premises. Antiquing, art galleries, beach, bicycling, canoeing/kayaking, cross-country skiing, downhill skiing, fishing, golf, hiking, horseback riding, museums, parks, shopping, sporting events, tennis, water sports and wineries nearby.

Location: City. La Crosse, WI.

Publicity: *"Best of the Midwest & Great Lakes", Wisconsin Bed & Breakfast Association's Elite Roster.*

Certificate may be used: November-April, Sunday-Thursday.

Justin Trails Resort

7452 Kathryn Ave
Sparta, WI 54656-9729
(608) 269-4522 (800) 488-4521
Internet: www.justintrails.com
E-mail: donna@justintrails.com

Circa 1920. Guests frequently mention how calm and peaceful the energy is at Justin Trails Resort. Log cabins, a cottage and suites in a 1920 Foursquare greet you with fireplace, large whirlpool bathtub, porch, balcony or patio for relaxing outdoors. Each is furnished with a refrigerator, coffee maker, microwave, DVD player. Several have 250 channel satellite hookup on the television. Set off on a stroll/walk or hike on the 200 acres with groomed trails on organic land that has not been treated with pesticides since 2008. Three ponds, a rock outcropping, 2 disc golf courses, 53 species of birds to watch and 10 miles of trails can entertain you for days. Summer or winter there is plenty of privacy in the hills and valleys of this outdoor paradise. A full country breakfast is served in The Lodge or delivered and served to your cabin or suite. The menu includes Justin Trails handcrafted granola, plain yogurt sweetened with maple syrup, fresh fruit or fruit compote, Justin Trails muffins or scones, choice of orange, apple or cranberry juice, choice of hot beverage and your choice of an entree of scrambled organic eggs, pancakes or French toast.

Innkeeper(s): Don & Donna Justin. $115-350. 6 rooms, 3 suites, 1 cottage, 2 cabins, 1 conference room. Breakfast included in rates. Types of meals: Full bkfst and veg bkfst. Beds: KQT. Cable TV, VCR, DVD, reading lamp, CD player, refrigerator, ceiling fan, clock radio, coffeemaker, fireplace, bath amenities, wireless Internet access and microwave in room. Central air. Copier, spa, library, telephone, bike boarding, gift shop, snowshoe trails, cross-country skiing and disc golf, massage, Amish country shopping nearby and dogsledding on premises. Limited handicap access. Antiquing, bicycling, canoeing/kayaking, cross-country skiing, downhill skiing, fishing, golf, hiking, horseback riding, museums, parks, shopping and Amish country nearby.

Location: Country.

Publicity: *Milwaukee Journal/Sentinel, Wisconsin Trails, Travel America, Family Fun, Family Life and Midwest Living and Chicago Tribune.*

Certificate may be used: Year round, Monday-Thursday, except holidays.

Sturgeon Bay   F9

Garden Gate Bed & Breakfast

434 N 3rd Ave
Sturgeon Bay, WI 54235
(920) 217-3093 (877) 743-9618
Internet: doorcountybb.com
E-mail: stay@doorcountybb.com

Circa 1890. Sturgeon Bay's Garden Gate Bed & Breakfast exudes a romantic Victorian elegance. The historic inn's oak-paneled foyer features a stairwell with hand-turned spindles. An antique oak fireplace mantle with Doric columns and a beveled oval mirror is a focal point. Gracious verandas beckon relaxation. Guest rooms offer quilt-covered beds and entertainment centers. Nine-panel pocket doors accent the dining room where a delightful daily breakfast is served with soft music by candlelight. Early risers can enjoy coffee and tea first. Ask about specials available. Located in Sturgeon Bay, Wisconsin in Door County, this area is home to a wide variety of outdoor activities and amusements.

Innkeeper(s): Robin Vallow. $115-155. 4 rooms with PB, 4 with FP, 1 with WP. Breakfast included in rates. Types of meals: Full gourmet bkfst, early coffee/tea and snacks/refreshments. Cable TV, DVD, reading lamp, stereo, refrigerator, ceiling fan, snack bar, clock radio, fireplace, bath amenities and 6ft Double Whirlpool for two in room. Central air. VCR on premises. Antiquing, art galleries, beach, bicycling, canoeing/kayaking, fishing, golf, hiking, horseback riding, live theater, museums, parks, shopping, water sports and wineries nearby.

Location: City.

Publicity: WhatsHappeningOnline and a Chicago land newspaper with community events. .

Certificate may be used: Monday-Thursday only.

The Reynolds House B&B

111 S. 7th Ave
Sturgeon Bay, WI 54235
(920)746-9771 (877)269-7401 Fax:(920)746-9441
Internet: www.reynoldshousebandb.com
E-mail: hahull@reynoldshousebandb.com

Circa 1900. A three-story, red-roofed Queen Anne Victorian house, the Reynolds House Bed and Breakfast is painted in two shades of teal and yellow with white trim on its balustrades and brackets. Leaded-glass windows and a stone veranda that wraps around the front of the house are features. Rooms are cheerfully decorated and offer antique beds, attractive bed coverings and wallpapers. Tucked under the gable, the Winesap Suite includes a whirlpool, sitting room and fireplace. The innkeeper's kitchen garden furnishes fresh herbs to accent breakfast dishes, as well as flowers for the table.

Innkeeper(s): Heather Hull. $80-200. 4 rooms, 5 with PB, 3 with FP, 2 with WP, 1 suite. Breakfast and snacks/refreshments included in rates. Types of meals: Full gourmet bkfst and early coffee/tea. Beds: QT. Cable TV, VCR, DVD, reading lamp, ceiling fan, clock radio, bath amenities, wireless Internet access and some with whirlpool in room. Central air. Library, parlor games, telephone and fireplace on premises. Antiquing, art galleries, beach, bicycling, cross-country skiing, fishing, golf, hiking, horseback riding, live theater, museums, parks, shopping, tennis and wineries nearby.

Location: City.

Publicity: Door County Magazine, Midwest Living Magazine (Voted Best in the Midwest June 2001 & 2003) and Arrington Inn Traveler's (Best Breakfast 2004).

"Sometimes the last minute things in life are the best!"

Certificate may be used: November-April, subject to availability.

White Lace Inn

16 N 5th Ave
Sturgeon Bay, WI 54235-1795
(920) 743-1105 (877) 948-5223 Fax:(920)743-8180
Internet: www.WhiteLaceInn.com
E-mail: Romance@WhiteLaceInn.com

Circa 1903. The romantic White Lace Inn is composed of four beautifully restored Victorian houses connected by meandering garden paths. This Sturgeon Bay bed and breakfast has inviting rooms and suites with fine antiques and ornate Victorian or canopy beds. Suites include oversized whirlpool baths, fireplaces, white linens, down comforters and many other amenities. Often

the site for romantic anniversary celebrations, a favorite suite has a two-sided fireplace, magnificent walnut Eastlake bed, English country fabrics and a whirlpool. Lemonade or hot chocolate and cookies are offered upon arrival. In the morning, the delectable offerings include items such as cherry apple crisp and creamy rice pudding. Year-round activities invite frequent visits — the Festival of Blossoms, the Lighthouse Walk, Cherry Festival and the Classic Wooden Boat event, for instance. Take museum and gallery strolls, and enjoy the area's great restaurants.

Innkeeper(s): Dennis and Bonnie Statz. $70-235. 18 rooms with PB, 15 with FP, 12 with WP, 5 suites, 4 guest houses. Breakfast and snacks/refreshments included in rates. Types of meals: Full bkfst, early coffee/tea and Special dietary needs can be accommodated with advance notice. Beds: KQD. Cable TV, VCR, DVD, reading lamp, stereo, ceiling fan, most with hot tub/spa, most with fireplace, hair dryer, bath amenities, wireless Internet access, iron/ironing board, 9 suites with both a fireplace and whirlpool in room. Air conditioning. Fax, parlor games, telephone, gift shop and Wedding Ceremonies on premises. Handicap access. Antiquing, art galleries, beach, bicycling, canoeing/kayaking, cross-country skiing, fishing, golf, hiking, horseback riding, live theater, museums, parks, shopping, sporting events, tennis, water sports, wineries, Door County has 316 miles of shoreline, 5 State parks, 17 County parks, Wonderful restaurants, Many shopping experiences, The Green Bay Packers and Lambeau Field (one hour away) nearby.

Location: City, country. Door County, Green Bay, Wisconsin.

Publicity: Milwaukee Sentinel, Brides, National Geographic Traveler, Wisconsin Trails, Milwaukee, Country Home and Midwest Living.

""Each guest room is an overwhelming visual feast, a dazzling fusion of colors, textures and beautiful objects. It is one of these rare gems that established a tradition the day it opened." — Wisconsin Trails"

Certificate may be used: Sunday-Thursday, November-April excluding holidays and some other restrictions, at "high season" rate.

Waupaca   G5

Crystal River Inn B&B

E1369 Rural Rd
Waupaca, WI 54981-8246
(715)258-5333 (800)236-5789 Fax:(715)258-5310
Internet: www.crystalriver-inn.com
E-mail: crystalriverinn@charterinternet.com

Circa 1853. The stately beauty of this historic Greek Revival farmhouse is rivaled only by its riverside setting. Each room features a view of the water, garden, woods or all three. A Victorian gazebo, down comforters and delicious breakfasts, with pecan sticky buns, a special favorite, add to guests' enjoyment. A recent addition to the inn's offerings include a newly restored historic cottage. With luxurious decor it includes two bedrooms, a living room with fireplace and private porches. It may be reserved singly or together. Exploring the village of Rural, which is in the National Register, will delight those interested in bygone days. Recreational activities abound, with the Chain O'Lakes and a state park nearby.

Innkeeper(s): Deb and Robert Benada. $69-149. 7 rooms, 5 with PB, 4 with FP, 2 cottages, 1 conference room. Breakfast and snacks/refreshments included in rates. Types of meals: Full bkfst and early coffee/tea. Beds: KQ. TV, reading lamp, ceiling fan, clock radio, telephone, desk, hot tub/spa and fireplace in room. Central air. VCR, DVD, fax and copier on premises. Limited handicap access. Antiquing, art galleries, beach, canoeing/kayaking, cross-country skiing, downhill skiing, golf, hiking, parks, shopping, sporting events, tennis and water sports nearby.

Location: Waterfront. 23 Lakes.

Publicity: Resorter, Stevens Point Journal, Wisconsin Trails Magazine, Fox Cities Magazine and Appleton Post Crescent.

"It was like being king for a day."

Certificate may be used: mid-September to mid-May, subject to availability, not valid for Little House on the Prairie.

Whitewater 17

Victoria-On-Main B&B

622 W Main St
Whitewater, WI 53190-1855
(262)473-8400
E-mail: viconmain@sbcglobal.net

Circa 1895. This graceful Queen Anne Victorian, shaded by a
tall birch tree, is in the heart of Whitewater National Historic
District, adjacent to the University of Wisconsin. It was built
for Edward Engebretson, mayor of
Whitewater. Yellow tulip and sunny
daffodils fill the spring flower beds,
while fuchsias and geraniums bloom
in summertime behind a picket
fence. The inn's gables, flower-filled
veranda and three-story turret feature a handsome green tin roof.
Each guest room is named for a
Wisconsin hardwood. The Red Oak
Room, Cherry Room and Bird's Eye Maple Room all offer
handsome antiques in their corresponding wood, Laura Ashley
prints, antique sheets, pristine heirloom-laced pillowcases and
down comforters. A hearty breakfast is sometimes served on
the wraparound veranda, and there are kitchen facilities available for light meal preparation. Whitewater Lake and Kettle
Moraine State Forest are five minutes away.

Innkeeper(s): Nancy Wendt. $85-95. 3 rooms, 1 with PB, 1 with FP.
Breakfast included in rates. Types of meals: Full bkfst and early coffee/tea.
Beds: D. Reading lamp and ceiling fan in room. Air conditioning. Telephone
on premises. Antiquing, cross-country skiing, fishing, live theater, parks,
shopping and water sports nearby.

Location: City.

"We loved it. Wonderful hospitality."

Certificate may be used: June-September and January, Sunday-Thursday.

Wisconsin Dells H5

Bowman's Oak Hill Bed and Breakfast

4169 State Hwy 13
Wisconsin Dells, WI 53965
(608)253-5638 (888)253-5631
Internet: bowmansoakhillbedandbreakfast.com
E-mail: bowmansoakhillbb@aol.com

Circa 1969. Thirteen acres of country peacefulness surround
this estate with lawns, gardens, fields and a cottage ranch home
built in the 1960s. This smoke-free, adult retreat is "where
comfort comes with your key." Relaxation is easy on the front
porch wicker furniture or three-season sun porch. Sit in wing-
backed chairs and watch a movie from the video library in the
living room. Afternoon and evening snacks and refreshments
are offered. Air-conditioned guest bedrooms boast family heirloom furniture, sitting areas and cozy robes. Fresh fruit
smoothies are a house specialty for breakfast that includes a
hot egg dish and warm baked goods or pancakes. An outdoor
covered swing and sitting areas provide romantic settings. Walk
in the woods, play croquet or a game of horseshoes.

Innkeeper(s): David and Nancy Bowman. $85-185. 5 rooms with PB, 3 with
FP, 2 with WP, 2 cottages. Breakfast and snacks/refreshments included in
rates. Types of meals: Full gourmet bkfst, veg bkfst and early coffee/tea.

Beds: KQ. TV, VCR, DVD, reading lamp, CD player, refrigerator, ceiling fan,
clock radio, coffeemaker, turn-down service, desk, some with hot tub/spa,
some with fireplace, hair dryer, bathrobes, bath amenities, wireless Internet
access, iron/ironing board, Antiques, Two comfortable chairs, Quilts;
Refrigerator, Microwave, DVD player, Leather love seat in cottage and One
cottage has direct TV in room. Air conditioning. Fax, copier, library, parlor
games, telephone, Large deck with fire pit and Wireless Internet on premises.
Amusement parks, antiquing, art galleries, bicycling, canoeing/kayaking,
cross-country skiing, downhill skiing, fishing, golf, hiking, horseback riding,
live theater, museums, parks, shopping, sporting events, water sports, wineries, Water parks, Wisconsin Dells Sports Center at Chula Vista and The
Broadway Dinner Theater nearby.

Location: Country. Near Downtown River District.

Publicity: *Ad-lit publications.*

Certificate may be used: November-May excluding all holidays, Sunday-
Thursday, subject to availability, Anytime, Last Minute-Based on Availability.

White Rose Inns

910 River Road
Wisconsin Dells, WI 53965
(608)254-4724 (800)482-4724 Fax:(608)254-4585
Internet: www.thewhiterose.com
E-mail: info@thewhiterose.com

Circa 1904. Overlooking the Wisconsin River and one block
from downtown, these historic Victorian mansions are ornately
decorated and boast original woodwork, stairways and architectural details. White Rose Inns offers a tranquil, smoke-free environment. Well-appointed guest bedrooms with gorgeous colors
and fabrics feature soft lighting and whirlpool baths. World-
famous omelets, quiche du jour, home-fried potatoes, croissants, fresh fruit with yogurt, and Belgian waffles with strawberries and cream are some of the menu items served for breakfast
in the Mediterranean dining room. Walk the lavish gardens,
swim in the outdoor heated pool, and schedule a massage.
Nearby Wisconsin Dells, created by the Northern Glacier,
reflects ice-age history and provides great hiking and biking
trails. Devil's Lake State Park is just 10 miles away.

Innkeeper(s): Mariah & Roger Boss. $80-225. 21 rooms with PB, 5 with FP,
15 with WP, 3 two-bedroom suites, 3 conference rooms. Breakfast included
in rates. Types of meals: Full gourmet bkfst, veg bkfst, early coffee/tea, wine,
10% discount at Cheese Factory Restaurant, B&B and dinner packages at
local restaurants and several restaurants within 3 blocks. Beds: KQDT. Cable
TV, VCR, reading lamp, desk and wireless Internet access in room. Central
air. Fax, copier, swimming, telephone, fireplace, Murder Mystery dinner parties and meeting rooms on premises. Limited handicap access. Amusement
parks, antiquing, art galleries, beach, bicycling, canoeing/kayaking, cross-
country skiing, downhill skiing, fishing, golf, hiking, horseback riding, live
theater, museums, parks, shopping, tennis, water sports, wineries, outlet
mall, America's largest indoor and outdoor waterparks and boat tours of
spectacular natural scenery nearby.

Location: City, waterfront. One block from downtown beside the Wisconsin River.

Publicity: *Best Wisconsin Romantic Weekends, Isthmus newspaper,
Wisconsin State Journal, Milwaukee State Journal, Arringtons Inn Traveler
magazine and Fun In Wisconsin magazine.*

Certificate may be used: Anytime, October-April, subject to availability.

Wyoming

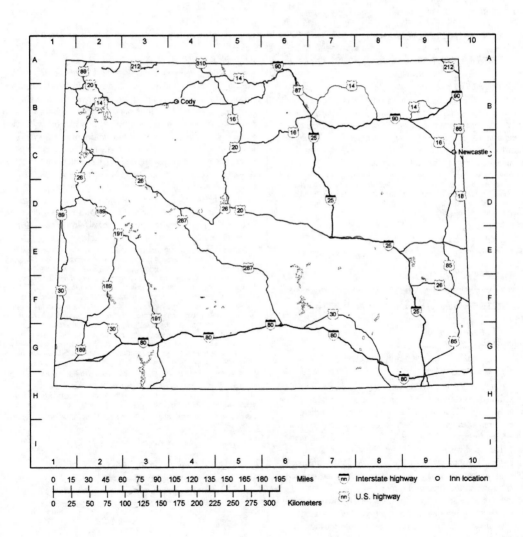

Cody   B4

Mayor's Inn Bed & Breakfast

1413 Rumsey Ave
Cody, WY 82414
(307)587-0887 (888)217-3001
Internet: www.mayorsinn.com
E-mail: reserve@MayorsInn.com

Circa 1909. Considered the town's first mansion, this stylish
two-story, turn-of-the-century home was built for Cody's first
elected mayor. A romantic Victorian ambiance is achieved with
warm hospitality, antiques, soft lighting, chandeliers and splendid wall and ceiling papers. The parlor inspires nostalgia. The
guest bedrooms feature either a brass bed and clawfoot tub, a
lodge pole pine bed, jetted tub and western art, or an open,
sunny room with double shower. The suite boasts a fresh water
hot tub and CD player. Offering private seating, breakfast is
served in both of the dining rooms. The Carriage House is a
cottage with a fully equipped kitchen.

Innkeeper(s): Bill & DaLeLee Delph. $90-215. 5 rooms, 4 with PB, 1 with
HT, 1 with WP, 1 cottage. Breakfast included in rates. Types of meals: Full
bkfst, early coffee/tea, Seasonal restaurant is open May-Oct, Thurs,Fri & Sat,
Wine and Beer & Spirits. Restaurant on premises. Beds: KQD. Cable TV,
reading lamp, stereo, some with hot tub/spa, hair dryer, bathrobes, bath
amenities, wireless Internet access, iron/ironing board, telephone in common
area and individual climate controls in room. Central air. Parlor games and
telephone on premises. Antiquing, art galleries, bicycling, canoeing/kayaking,
cross-country skiing, downhill skiing, fishing, golf, hiking, horseback riding,
live theater, museums, parks, shopping, tennis, water sports, Nightly rodeo
from June to September and Seasonal trolley tours nearby.

Location: Historic downtown Cody, one block off the main street.

Publicity: *Cody Enterprise, The Telegraph Travel, Country Extra Magazine and
Bed & Breakfast American Magazine.*

Certificate may be used: November-April, subject to availability.

Newcastle   C10

EVA-Great Spirit Ranch B&B

1262 Beaver Creek Rd
Newcastle, WY 82701
(307)746-2537
Internet: www.eva-ranch.webs.com

Circa 1984. Amidst spectacular scenery of mountains and
woods, guests will find this modern log home. Although the
home is new, it rests on what was an old stagecoach route. A
century-old barn is located on the property, as well as ruins of
a 19th-century bunkhouse. The interior features hardwood
floors and high ceilings, and the guest rooms are comfortably
furnished in a modern style. There are two rooms with private
baths and two adjoining rooms with a shared bath. Irene offers
spring and fall hunting packages, where guests can search for
deer, elk and wild turkey on the 525-acre property and adjacent
Bureau of Land Management and state lands. The vast acreage
borders Black Hills National Forest in South Dakota.

Innkeeper(s): Irene Ward. $65-90. 4 rooms, 2 with PB. Breakfast included in
rates. Types of meals: Full bkfst. Beds: KQT. Reading lamp, clock radio, Fans
and Television set with VHS player in room. VCR, DVD, library, parlor games,
telephone, fireplace, Free WiFi, Board games & puzzles, Childrens games and
coloring books on premises. Handicap access. Antiquing, cross-country skiing, downhill skiing, fishing, golf, hiking, museums, parks, shopping, snowmobile trails and sightseeing nearby.

Location: Mountains.

Publicity: *News Letter Journal.*

"We enjoyed a very homely introduction to the wild west!"

Certificate may be used: Sept. 15-May 15, Sunday-Saturday. Bed & breakfast stay only. Hunting packages and Romantic Getaways excluded.

Puerto Rico

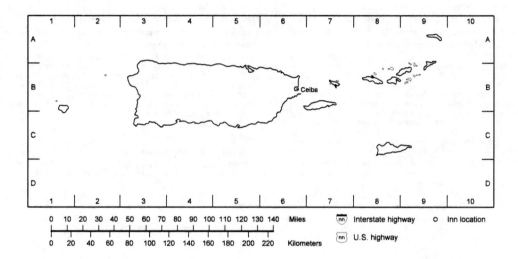

0 10 20 30 40 50 60 70 80 90 100 110 120 130 140 Miles

0 20 40 60 80 100 120 140 160 180 200 220 Kilometers

(nn) Interstate highway   o Inn location

(nn) U.S. highway

Ceiba   B6

Ceiba Country Inn

CARR. 977 KM1.2
Ceiba, PR 00735
(787) 885-0471 (888) 560-2816 Fax:(787)885-0475
Internet: www.ceibacountryinn.com
E-mail: info@ceibacountryinn.com

Circa 1950. A large Spanish patio is available at this tropical
country inn perched on rolling, green hills. Situated 500 feet
above the valley floor, the inn affords a view of the ocean with
the isle of Culebra on the horizon. A continental buffet is
served in the warm
and sunny breakfast
room. The inn is four
miles from Puerto Del
Rey, the largest marina
in the Caribbean, and

10 miles from Luquillo Beach, which is a mile of white sand,
dotted with coconut palms.

Innkeeper(s): Michael A. Marra and Pedro J Jurado-Cotto. $85-95. 9 rooms
with PB. Breakfast included in rates. Types of meals: Cont plus. Beds: QDT.
Data port, reading lamp, refrigerator, ceiling fan, clock radio, telephone, turn-
down service, Hair dryer and Iron/Ironing Board available on request in
room. Air conditioning. TV, fax, copier, library, parlor games, Free Wi-Fi available in lounge and on upper patio on premises. Limited handicap access.
Beach, canoeing/kayaking, fishing, golf, hiking, horseback riding, parks, shopping, water sports, Snorkeling and Scuba excursions nearby.

Location: Country, mountains.

Certificate may be used: August-December, Monday-Sunday.

Canada

Alberta

Banff

Rocky Mountain Bed & Breakfast Guest House

223 Otter St
Banff, AB T1L 1C3
(403)762-4811
Internet: www.rockymtnbb.com
E-mail: reservations@rockymtnbb.com

Circa 1918. Gracing a quiet residential neighborhood, this restored and renovated historic mountain home is an intimate high-country inn offering warm hospitality and spacious accommodations. The relaxed setting is just three blocks from Banff, Alberta Canada. Local activities are easily accessible by walking. The gorgeous main lounge area features a television. Stay in an elegant double guest room or a suite with a full kitchen or kitchenette that is perfect for a small family. Wake up to savor a hot and hearty morning meal from a rotating menu with traditional breakfast items and gourmet fare in the dining area. Sip organic, fair-trade coffee from Canmore's Mountain Blends Coffee Roasters. Manager Melissa tries to accommodate dietary restrictions upon advance request. Ask about specials available.
Innkeeper(s): Melissa Marks. Call for rates. 10 rooms including 4 suites. Antiquing, art galleries, bicycling, canoeing/kayaking, cross-country skiing, fishing, golf, hiking, horseback riding and shopping nearby.
Location: Mountains, waterfront.

Certificate may be used: November-March, Subject to availability. Not including holiday season Dec. 15-Jan. 6.

Calgary

AliAnna's Bed & Breakfast

812 Diamond Court SE
Calgary, AB T2J 7E2
(403)278-0301 Fax:(403)271-7093
Internet: www.bbcalgary.com/member_info.php?ID=110
E-mail: aliannasbandb@me.com

Just outside the door of this B&B is the Bow River, world famous for its fly and trout fishing, and the Fish Creek Provincial Park. Bike paths and walkways connect to downtown Calgary, Alberta Canada and other surrounding areas. AliAnnaâ ™s Bed & Breakfast is poised in the community of Diamond Cove Estates, less than half an hour from the international airport. Enjoy wireless Internet access and a computer is also available to use. After a good night's sleep in a comfortable guest bedroom, start each day with a continental breakfast.

Innkeeper(s): Gemma Ramikie. $80-125. 2 rooms with PB. Breakfast and dinner included in rates. Beds: QD. Treadmill, Wireless computer, Sitting room, Big screen TV and Fireplace on premises. Amusement parks, art galleries, bicycling, fishing, golf, hiking, live theater, museums, parks, shopping, tennis, Fish Creek Provincial Park, World famous Bow River and 3 large shopping malls nearby.
Certificate may be used: Anytime, subject to availability.

Canmore

Ambleside Lodge

123A Rundle Drive
Canmore, AB T1W 2L6
(403)678-3976 Fax:(403)678-3919
Internet: www.amblesidelodge.com
E-mail: sueanddave@amblesidelodge.com

Poised in the midst of a majestic mountain landscape, breathtaking scenery surrounds this wooden lodge in Canmore, Alberta. Rustic Rocky Mountain charm with a pine interior invites relaxation. Enjoy a warm welcome then sit in the spacious lounge accented by a large wood-burning fireplace made with 18 tons of river rock and 4 tons of cement. Experience the many local attractions and activities, and explore nearby Banff National Park. Popular Lake Louise is less than an hour away. Soak in the hot tub and sit in the outdoor barrel sauna. Schedule an in-room aromatic massage by a qualified therapist. After a great night's sleep in a luxury guest suite, start each day with Sue's sumptuous three-course gourmet breakfast. Dave is a Canadian hiking guide with extensive knowledge to share.
Innkeeper(s): Sue and Dave Booth. Call for rates. 2 rooms. Art galleries, bicycling, canoeing/kayaking, cross-country skiing, downhill skiing, fishing, golf, hiking, horseback riding, parks and shopping nearby.
Certificate may be used: November-March, Sunday-Thursday, excludes holidays.

Hinton

Mountain Vista Bed & Breakfast

1217 Mountainview Estates
Hinton, AB T7V 1X3
(780)865-2470 Fax:(780)865-2470
Internet: www.mountainvistabb.com
E-mail: mtn.vista@moradnet.ca

Breathtaking panoramic views of the Rockies and Athabasca River are seen from this recently renovated bed and breakfast in a setting of mountain acreage just 20 minutes from the gates of Jasper National Park. Soak up the scenic beauty from the wraparound deck or walk up the outdoor stairway for an incredible vista of Mt. Pocahontas and Majestic Roche Miette. Play darts or pool in the Game Room. A kitchenette refrigerator is stocked with beverages. Relax by the fire or watch a DVD on the big screen TV. The guest bedroom features a

Mexican theme with a pillow-top mattress on a handcrafted log bed. Ask for a traditional, Spanish or continental breakfast. On-site spa services that include body wraps, facials, hair care, massage and waxing are available.

Innkeeper(s): Livi & Trent Waller. $99-125. 2 rooms, 1 with PB. Breakfast included in rates. Types of meals: Full gourmet bkfst. Beds: KQD. Cable TV, VCR, DVD, reading lamp, refrigerator, ceiling fan, clock radio, coffeemaker, fireplace and iron/ironing board in room. Fax, telephone and laundry facility on premises. Limited handicap access. Cross-country skiing, downhill skiing, fishing, golf, hiking, horseback riding, parks, shopping and water sports nearby.

Location: Mountains.

Certificate may be used: Anytime, November-March, subject to availability.

British Columbia

Ladner

Clair's Bed & Breakfast in Ladner Village

4919 - 48th Avenue
Ladner, BC V4K 1V4
(604)940-8867 (877)834-6847
Internet: www.clairsinnladner.com
E-mail: info@clairsinnladner.com

Circa 1922. Clairâ ™s Bed & Breakfast in Ladner Village in the Delta area of British Columbia is just 20 minutes from Vancouver. This Art Deco B&B is close to Reifel Bird Sanctuary and wine tasting on Westham Island. Bike or hike the trails, jog the bog and relax amid the delightful gardens at the B&B. Watch a movie in the parlor, browse the library, or listen to music in the fireside salon. Well-appointed guest rooms and suites feature clawfoot or spa tubs and free wifi. Savor a home-cooked gourmet breakfast in the elegant dining room before embarking on the day's adventures. Return to the inn for refreshments and conversation in the early evening.

Innkeeper(s): Clair Oates. $125-215. 6 rooms with PB, 3 with FP, 3 total suites, including 1 two-bedroom suite. Breakfast included in rates. Types of meals: Full gourmet bkfst and veg bkfst. Beds: KQT. Cable TV, reading lamp, refrigerator, clock radio, desk, hair dryer, bathrobes, bath amenities, wireless Internet access and iron/ironing board in room. VCR, fax, library, telephone and fireplace on premises. Antiquing, beach, bicycling, canoeing/kayaking, fishing, golf, hiking, horseback riding, live theater, museums, parks, shopping, tennis, water sports, wineries, Boundary Bay Airport and Flight Lessons nearby.

Location: Ocean community. Village.

Certificate may be used: Monday-Thursday, not valid Dec. 23-Dec. 31.

Vernon

LakeSide Illahee Inn

15010 Tamarack Drive
Vernon, BC V1B 2E1
(250)260-7896 (888)260-7896 Fax:(250)260-7826
Internet: www.illahee.com
E-mail: info@illahee.com

Circa 1995. Sandy beaches, terraced lawns, flower gardens and fruit orchards surround this four-season boutique waterfront inn on Lake Kalamalka in the Okanagan Valley of British Columbia, Canada. LakeSide Illahee Inn boasts 2.54 acres with 254 feet of lakeshore and is adjacent to 3300-acre Provincial Nature Park in Vernon. Contemporary with country

elegance, relax by the fire in the Grand Room or Chelootsoos Guest Lounge. Read in the Grand Loft or soak in the mountainside lakeview hot tub on the outdoor Wild Jasmine Guest Lounge that also includes a large patio, fire pit and canoe/kayak dock. Make a reservation for a sunset dinner in the open-air Upper Room. Air-conditioned guest bedrooms and suites are named for onsite wildflowers or trees and boast waterside balconies and private entrances. Massage and spa services are available by appointment.

Innkeeper(s): Peter & Debbie Dooling. $129-359. 5 rooms with PB, 3 with FP, 3 with WP, 3 suites, 1 conference room. Breakfast included in rates. Types of meals: Full gourmet bkfst, veg bkfst, early coffee/tea, picnic lunch, wine and gourmet dinner. Beds: KQ. Modem hook-up, data port, cable TV, VCR, DVD, reading lamp, stereo, refrigerator, ceiling fan, snack bar, clock radio, telephone, coffeemaker, desk, most with hot tub/spa, fireplace, hair dryer, bathrobes, bath amenities, wireless Internet access, iron/ironing board, Luxury bathrobes, Spa luxury towels, Valued art paintings, Sculpture works, Private entrances, Lakeshore balconies and You Cook Electric BBQ's in room. Air conditioning. Fax, copier, spa, swimming, laundry facility, Two-person kayaks, Boat Dock & Buoys, Waterfront Sitting Dock with Adirondack Sitting Chairs, Lakeshore campfire ring, Wildflower & Horticultural Gardens, Night Landscape Lighting of Pathways and Waterfront, Sandy Beach with Excellent Swimming, Panoramic Lakeview Hot-Tub and Free On-Site Parking on premises. Limited handicap access. Amusement parks, antiquing, art galleries, beach, bicycling, canoeing/kayaking, cross-country skiing, downhill skiing, fishing, golf, hiking, horseback riding, live theater, museums, parks, shopping, sporting events, tennis, water sports, wineries, Miniature animal farm, Old-fashioned cheese factory, Historical O'Keefe Ranch, Davidson Orchards, Interior Provincial Agricultural Exhibition (British Columbia's oldest), Fruit orchards, Vineyards and Private estate wineries nearby.

Location: Country, waterfront. Kalamalka Lake Provincial Park.

Publicity: North American Inns Magazine, Business Section of The Morning Star and Okanagan Courier Newspapers of January 8th, 2006 entitled "Illahee Garners International Aclaim", Awarded 2006 "The 6th Best On The Waterfront" B&B and Country Inn throughout North America by Inn Traveller, Documentary by CHBC TV, Kelowna, BC (Janurary 1st, 2006), Global TV, Vancouver, BC, Global National, Ottawa (January 2nd and 3rd and 2006).

Certificate may be used: Nov. 1-April 30, excluding Dec. 18-Jan. 2 of each year.

Victoria

Prancing Horse Retreat

573 Ebadora Lane
Victoria, BC V0R 2L0
(250)743-9378 (877)887-8834 Fax:(250)743-9372
Internet: www.prancinghorse.com
E-mail: stay@prancinghorse.com

Circa 1998. Breathtaking scenery and a spectacular setting surround this premier mountain-top retreat with fantastic views of the Olympic Mountains. This red-roofed Victorian villa boasts a turret with stained-glass windows and luxury accommodations. Indulge in a deluxe suite that features fresh flowers, Aveda bath products and Bernard Callebaut Chocolate. Luxury suites also include double soaker tubs, fireplaces and private decks. Savor a gourmet breakfast that is accented by just-squeezed orange juice and champagne in the dining room or on the spacious patio overlooking the valley. Colorful gardens with terraced rocks lead to a multi-tiered deck with a gazebo and hot tub.

$175-375. 7 total suites, including 1 two-bedroom suite. Breakfast included in rates. Types of meals: Full gourmet bkfst and early coffee/tea. Beds: Q. Data port, cable TV, VCR, CD player, refrigerator, clock radio, telephone, coffeemaker, hot tub/spa, most with fireplace, hair dryer, bathrobes, bath amenities, wireless Internet access and iron/ironing board in room. Fax and spa on premises. Antiquing, beach, fishing, golf, hiking, horseback riding, live theater, museums, parks, shopping, tennis, water sports and wineries nearby.

Location: Mountains, waterfront.

Certificate may be used: Anytime, November-March, subject to availability.

Whistler

Golden Dreams B&B

6412 Easy St
Whistler, BC V0N 1B6
(604)932-2667 (800)668-7055
Internet: www.goldendreamswhistler.com
E-mail: Ann@goldendreamswhistler.com

Circa 1986. Experience the many secrets of great B&B stays at this established inn. Surrounded by mountain views and the beauty of nature, this West Coast home features a private guest living room with wood fireplace where the innkeepers share their knowledge of the locale. Thick Terry robes, duvets and sherry decanters are provided in the guest bed rooms, which have Black bear, Wild West and Rainforest themes. After a wholesome breakfast, valley trail and bus stop are just outside. Whistler village and skiing are only one mile away. Relax in the hot tub and enjoy house wine and snacks. A large BBQ sundeck and guest kitchen are convenient amenities. Town Plaza village condos are also available for families. Discount skiing, sight-seeing passes and airport transport booking services are available.

Innkeeper(s): Ann & Terry Spence. $115-175. 3 rooms, 1 with PB. Breakfast and snacks/refreshments included in rates. Types of meals: Full gourmet bkfst, veg bkfst and early coffee/tea. Beds: QDT. Reading lamp, clock radio, hair dryer, bathrobes, wireless Internet access, iron/ironing board, Hot Tub sandals, Decanter of sherry, Snacks, Coffee/tea making, Local information, Maps and Mountain ski atlas in room. TV, VCR, fax, spa, library, telephone, fireplace, Stainless steel gas BBQ, Guest kitchen, Use of guest refrigerator, Private guest living room with wood fireplace, Stereo, CD player, Heated slate entrance & bathroom floors, Outdoor ski storage racks, Free off-street parking and Free Wi-Fi throughout B&B on premises. Art galleries, beach, bicycling, canoeing/kayaking, cross-country skiing, downhill skiing, fishing, golf, hiking, horseback riding, parks, shopping, sporting events, tennis, water sports, World Class alpine village with outstanding downhill skiing on 2 HUGE mountains! Also, Zip Trekking, white water rafting and canoeing, heli-skiing and bungy jumping! nearby.

Location: Mountains. Trailside location, just one mile to village ski lifts/village.

"Great house, great food, terrific people."

Certificate may be used: April 15-June 15 and Sept. 30-Nov. 15, except holidays. Three condos in village December-April only.

New Brunswick

Sackville

Marshlands Inn

55 bridge Street
Sackville, NB E4L 3N8
(506)536-0170 (180)056-11266 Fax:(506)536-0721
Internet: www.marshlands.nb.ca
E-mail: info@marshlands.nb.ca

Circa 1854. One of Canada's most popular country inns, this 1854 pre-confederation home is surrounded by eight acres of marshland, lawns and gardens. Open year-round, it is rich in history, and has hosted many social, political and royal dignitaries. The inn consists of the main house and the carriage house. Relax with refreshments on one of the two large verandas. In the evening gather for hot chocolate and ginger snaps by the fire in one of the parlors accented by original artwork and easy chairs. Inviting guest bedrooms and a suite are fur-

nished with antiques and boast clawfoot tubs. Enjoy fine dining in the upscale restaurant and shop for Canadian glass in the Blue Willow Antiques onsite store.

Innkeeper(s): Lucy & Barry Dane. $89-129. Call inn for details. Beds: KQDT.
Certificate may be used: Anytime, November-March, subject to availability. May-October at innkeepers discretion.

Newfoundland

Trinity

Artisan Inn Trinity

High St
Trinity, NL A0C 2S0
(709)464-3377 (877)464-7700 Fax:(709)464-3377
Internet: www.trinityvacations.com
E-mail: info@trinityvacations.com

Circa 1840. Combining the amenities of an upscale inn with the essence of a living museum this B&B was built with the full-studded construction typically used on the wood-rich Bonavista Peninsula. Situated in an historic coastal village, offering splendid views of the Atlantic Ocean, the heritage-designated restored buildings include two cottages that easily accommodate families. Romantic guest bedrooms instill a peaceful tranquility. After a delicious breakfast, relax on the waterfront decks and breathe deeply the sea air before exploring the town or strolling the hills and meadows of this four-acre retreat.

Innkeeper(s): Tineke Gow. $99-258. 6 rooms, 5 with PB, 1 two-bedroom suite, 3 cottages, 1 conference room. Breakfast included in rates. Types of meals: Full bkfst, early coffee/tea, picnic lunch, afternoon tea, wine and gourmet dinner. Beds: KQDT. Modern hook-up, data port, cable TV, VCR, reading lamp, CD player, refrigerator, clock radio, telephone, coffeemaker, turn-down service, desk, voice mail, some with fireplace, hair dryer, bathrobes, wireless Internet access and iron/ironing board in room. Fax, library, parlor games and laundry facility on premises. Art galleries, beach, canoeing/kayaking, cross-country skiing, downhill skiing, fishing, golf, hiking, live theater, museums, parks and shopping nearby.

Location: Country.
Certificate may be used: May 1-20, Oct. 10-31.

Ontario

Niagara Falls

Kilpatrick Manor Bed & Breakfast

4601 Second Avenue
Niagara Falls, ON L2E 4H3
(905)321-8581 (866)976-2667
Internet: www.kilpatrickmanor.com
E-mail: stay@kilpatrickmanor.com

Circa 1891. Kilpatrick Manor Bed & Breakfast in Niagara Falls, Ontario Canada blends a masculine and feminine setting for an elegant yet simple ambiance. This recently restored, stately brick Victorian home was built in 1891 and is surrounded by mature sugar maple trees and flower gardens. Wine glasses, corkscrew and a guest refrigerator stocked with assorted beverages are available. Indulge in a pampered stay in the premier Chrysler Room, a suite that features upscale amenities that include fresh flowers, spa products, Jacuzzi tub, fireplace, antiques, CDs, Egyptian cotton sheets, down duvet, slippers and robe. Special packages are available.

Innkeeper(s): Nance & Kevin Kilpatrick. $119-199. 4 rooms with PB, 4 with FP, 2 with WP. Breakfast included in rates. Types of meals: Full gourmet bkfst, veg bkfst, early coffee/tea, snacks/refreshments, wine, room service and Decadent Nightcaps. Beds: KQ. Modem hook-up, cable TV, DVD, reading lamp, stereo, refrigerator, ceiling fan, clock radio, telephone, turn-down service, most with hot tub/spa, fireplace, hair dryer, bathrobes, bath amenities, wireless Internet access, iron/ironing board, A selection of tourist information, Sewing kit, Shoeshine kit, Beautiful fresh flowers, Romantic CDs, Extra pillows, Bathrobe, Slippers, Bottled water, Movies, Wine glasses and Corkscrew in room. Central air. Parlor games, Patio seating in garden, Guest fridge stocked with bottled water and First aid kit on premises. Amusement parks, antiquing, art galleries, beach, bicycling, canoeing/kayaking, cross-country skiing, fishing, golf, hiking, horseback riding, live theater, museums, parks, shopping, sporting events, tennis, water sports, wineries, Casinos, Aquarium, Marineland and Jet boats nearby.

Location: City.

Certificate may be used: Last-Minute based, subject to availability, Sunday-Thursday.

Niagara On The Lake

Post House Country Inn / Burke House Inn

95 Johnson Street
Niagara On The Lake, ON L0S 1J0
(905)468-9991 (877)349-7678 Fax:(905)468-9989
Internet: www.posthouseinn.com
E-mail: post@posthouseinn.com

Circa 1835. Originally the town's post office, and also used for educating the local children, this circa 1835 building is now an elegant country inn. Decorated and furnished in a luxurious old world style, relaxation comes easy while sitting by the fire in the living room. Guest bedrooms are glorious retreats with pampering amenities. Lavish suites feature a two-person Jacuzzi and most boast a marble bath and fireplace. Stay in Mrs. Connell's Boudoir, a two-room suite with a four-poster bed. The second floor Coach Suite has original pine plank flooring. The renovated Carriage Room with poolside access once housed the horses. A resplendent breakfast is served in the sun-filled conservatory overlooking the heated pool and gardens.

Innkeeper(s): Barbara Ganim. $109-359. 8 rooms with PB, 8 with FP, 4 with WP, 1 cottage, 2 conference rooms. Breakfast and Full epicurean breakfast with attention to healthy start. Diets may be accommodated included in rates. Types of meals: Full gourmet bkfst, veg bkfst, early coffee/tea and room service. Beds: KQT. Modem hook-up, cable TV, VCR, reading lamp, clock radio, turn-down service, desk, most with hot tub/spa, fireplace, hair dryer, bathrobes, bath amenities, wireless Internet access, iron/ironing board and central piped-in Spa music in room. Central air. Fax, copier, spa, swimming, library, parlor games, telephone, breakfast in room can be requested, full concierge service and special assistance for arranging details of engagements on premises. Limited handicap access. Amusement parks, antiquing, art galleries, bicycling, canoeing/kayaking, cross-country skiing, fishing, golf, hiking, live theater, museums, parks, shopping, sporting events, tennis, water sports, wineries, Niagara Falls (12 minutes away with 2 Casinos), Toronto (1 1/2 hours), Butterfly Conservatory and Aviary nearby.

Location: Waterfront. Historic Canadian Town.

Certificate may be used: November-April, Sunday-Thursday.

Prince Edward Island

Summerside

Willowgreen Farm B&B

117 Bishop Dr
Summerside, PE C1N 5Z8
(902) 436-4420 (888) 436-4420
Internet: www.willowgreenfarm.com
E-mail: email@willowgreenfarm.com

Circa 1920. Recently renovated, this 1920 farmhouse offers simple country elegance in the city. Willowgreen Farm Bed and Breakfast adorns about 120 acres with sheep and goats in the orchard. The relaxed and tranquil setting in Summerside, Prince Edward Island is inviting with the porch and other outdoor sitting areas as well as walking paths. Inside, gather by the fire for casual conversation. Guest bedrooms feature antiques and some suites boast double whirlpool tubs. Savor a varied breakfast menu that is created with fresh seasonal produce and homemade recipes. Special dietary needs are accommodated. The on-site Craft Nook has hand-knit sweaters, blankets, quilted items and yarn for sale.

Innkeeper(s): Alyssa Read - Daughter of Steven and Laura. $50-115. 9 rooms with PB, 3 with FP, 3 with WP. Breakfast, Evening Tea and Hot Chocolate or Coffee included in rates. Types of meals: Full bkfst, picnic lunch, Picnic lunches by previous arrangement (included in some packages) and Dinner off-season by arrangement. Beds: KQD. Some rooms have some of the following - Electric Fireplaces (2), two have AC, 1 has a TV, most have ceiling fans, there is on premises a guest fridge, iron/ironing board, telephone, reading lamps and hair dryer in room. TV, VCR, parlor games, telephone, laundry facility and gift shop on premises. Antiquing, art galleries, beach, bicycling, canoeing/kayaking, cross-country skiing, fishing, golf, live theater, museums, parks, shopping, tennis, water sports, College of Piping and Celtic Arts, Dinner Theatre and Anne of Green Gables Museums nearby.

Location: City.

Certificate may be used: Anytime, subject to availability.

Quebec

Montreal

Auberge Le Pomerol

819 de Maisonneuve East.
Montreal, QB H2L 1Y7
(514)526-5511 (800)361-6896 Fax:(514)523-0143
Internet: www.aubergelepomerol.com
E-mail: info@aubergelepomerol.com

In the heart of the city, this century-old house exudes warmth and finesse. The ultra-contemporary decor enhances the calm ambiance. Sit by the fireplace in the casual lounge. Air-conditioned guest bedrooms offer urban comfort and style with an abundance of pleasing amenities including high speed Internet access, unlimited local calls, VCR and cable TV. Linger over a healthy breakfast. The Energie Cardio fitness training center ensures overall well-being and physical strength. Meeting rooms are perfect for corporate or business needs. Ask about the Romance Package that includes a luxury room with whirlpool bath and champagne, or add a touch of gourmet dining with a four-course dinner and a bottle of wine at Les deux

Charentes restaurant. A concierge is always available, transportation is easily accessible and local events or festivals offer lively entertainment.

Innkeeper(s): Daniel Racine. $105-185. 27 rooms with PB, 27 with HT, 9 with WP, 1 conference room. Breakfast, afternoon tea, snacks/refreshments and Continental breakfast delivered to the room included in rates. Types of meals: Cont and early coffee/tea. Restaurant on premises. Beds: KQDT. Modem hook-up, cable TV, VCR, DVD, reading lamp, stereo, ceiling fan, clock radio, telephone, coffeemaker, desk, hot tub/spa, hair dryer, bath amenities, wireless Internet access, iron/ironing board and Free continental breakfast delivered to your room in a nice basket in room. Central air. Fax, copier, bicycles, library and fireplace on premises. Amusement parks, art galleries, bicycling, canoeing/kayaking, live theater, museums, parks, shopping, sporting events and tennis nearby.

Location: City.

Certificate may be used: Nov. 22-Dec. 22, Jan. 2-Jan. 31, not valid Friday and Saturdays.

Inns of Interest

African-American History

Deacon Timothy Pratt Bed & Breakfast Inn C.1746
.... Old Saybrook, Conn.
Washington Plantation .... Washington, Ga.
1851 Historic Maple Hill Manor B&B
.... Springfield, Ky.
The Alexander House Booklovers B&B
.... Princess Anne, Md.
Munro House B&B and Spa ..... Jonesville, Mich.
Hexagon House Bed & Breakfast
.... Pentwater, Mich.
10 Fitch .... Auburn, N.Y.
Arbor View House B&B .... East Marion, N.Y.
Rider's 1812 Inn .... Painesville, Ohio
The Signal House .... Ripley, Ohio
Kilpatrick Manor Bed & Breakfast
.... Niagara Falls,
Post House Country Inn / Burke House Inn
.... Niagara On The Lake,
The Fairfield Inn 1757 .... Fairfield, Pa.
The Great Valley House of Valley Forge
.... Valley Forge, Pa.
Rockland Farm Retreat .... Bumpass, Va.
Firmstone Manor .... Clifton Forge, Va.
Sleepy Hollow Farm B&B ...... Gordonsville, Va.
Mayhurst Inn .... Orange, Va.
Lilac Inn .... Brandon, Vt.
Golden Stage Inn .... Ludlow, Vt.
The Inn at Weathersfield .... Perkinsville, Vt.
Elkhorn Inn & Theatre .... Landgraff, W.Va.

Animals

Pearson's Pond Luxury Inn & Adventure Spa
.... Juneau, Alaska
Casa De San Pedro .... Hereford, Ariz.
Lodge at Sedona-A Luxury Bed and Breakfast Inn
.... Sedona, Ariz.
Hotel Charlotte.............. Groveland, Calif.
The Inn at Schoolhouse Creek
.... Mendocino, Calif.
Black Forest B&B Lodge & Cabins
.... Colorado Springs, Colo.
Romantic RiverSong Inn ...... Estes Park, Colo.
Cedar Mountain Farm............ Athol, Idaho
Greyhouse Inn B&B............. Salmon, Idaho
The Irish Inn................. Ozark, Ill.
Scottish Bed and Breakfast
.... Bremen, Ind.
First Farm Inn .... Petersburg, Ky.
1851 Historic Maple Hill Manor B&B
.... Springfield, Ky.
The Inn at Restful Paws .... Holland, Mass.
Inn on The Horse Farm......... Sudbury, Mass.
Gramercy Mansion .... Stevenson, Md.
Royalsborough Inn at the Bagley House
.... Durham, Maine
Greenville Inn .... Greenville, Maine
Maple Hill Farm B&B Inn....... Hallowell, Maine
Morrill Farm Bed & Breakfast

.... Sumner, Maine
The Wren's Nest Bed & Breakfast
.... West Bloomfield, Mich.
Silent Sport Lodge .... Wolverine, Mich.
Meramec Farm Cabins & Trail Riding Vacations, LLC
.... Bourbon, Mo.
Hawkesdene House B&B Inn and Cottages
.... Andrews, N.C.
Chimney Hill Estate Inn ...... Lambertville, N.J.
Acorn Hollow Bed & Breakfast
.... Southold, N.Y.
HideAway Country Inn .... Bucyrus, Ohio
Elkhorn Valley Inn B&B .... Lyons, Ore.
Stone Crest Cellar B&B .... South Beach, Ore.
Pennsbury Inn .... Chadds Ford, Pa.
Barley Sheaf Farm Estate & Spa
.... Holicong, Pa.
Willowgreen Farm B&B .... Summerside,
The Shaw House B&B......... Georgetown, S.C.
Sunrise Farm B&B .... Salem, S.C.
Fox Manor Historic Bed & Breakfast
.... Kingsport, Tenn.
BlissWood Bed & Breakfast .... Cat Spring, Texas
MD Resort Bed & Breakfast.... Fort Worth, Texas
Katy House Bed & Breakfast
.... Smithville, Texas
Southwind .... Wimberley, Texas
Woodland Farmhouse Inn ...... Kamas, Utah
The Garden, Bed & Breakfast Inn
.... Spring City, Utah
Bridgewater Inn and Cottage
.... Bridgewater, Va.
The Garden and The Sea Inn
.... New Church, Va.
Inn at Clearwater Pond........... Quechee, Vt.
Arlington's River Rock Inn
.... Arlington, Wash.
Turtleback Farm Inn .... Eastsound, Wash.
Heritage Farm Museum & Village
.... Huntington, W.Va.
EVA-Great Spirit Ranch B&B
.... Newcastle, Wyo.

Barns

Fensalden Inn .... Albion, Calif.
Deer Crossing Inn .... Castro Valley, Calif.
Black Forest B&B Lodge & Cabins
.... Colorado Springs, Colo.
Greyhouse Inn B&B............. Salmon, Idaho
Corner George Inn .... Maeystown, Ill.
Sonora Gardens Farmstead .... Nauvoo, Ill.
Pinehill Inn................. Oregon, Ill.
First Farm Inn .... Petersburg, Ky.
1851 Historic Maple Hill Manor B&B
.... Springfield, Ky.
Inn on The Horse Farm......... Sudbury, Mass.
Oakland House Seaside Resort
.... Brooksville, Maine
Maple Hill Farm B&B Inn....... Hallowell, Maine
Morrill Farm Bed & Breakfast

.... Sumner, Maine
Brannon-Bunker Inn........... Walpole, Maine
Inn at Harbour Ridge .... Osage Beach, Mo.
Hawkesdene House B&B Inn and Cottages
.... Andrews, N.C.
The Mast Farm Inn .... Valle Crucis, N.C.
Big Mill Bed & Breakfast .... Williamston, N.C.
Highland Lake Inn B&B .... Andover, N.H.
Candlelite Inn .... Bradford, N.H.
Inn at Glencairn .... Princeton, N.J.
Acorn Hollow Bed & Breakfast
.... Southold, N.Y.
HideAway Country Inn .... Bucyrus, Ohio
Inn & Spa At Cedar Falls .... Logan, Ohio
Elkhorn Valley Inn B&B .... Lyons, Ore.
McKenzie River Inn............. Vida, Ore.
The Alexander Benjamin House
.... Andreas, Pa.
Pennsbury Inn .... Chadds Ford, Pa.
Filbert Bed & Breakfast....... Danielsville, Pa.
Barley Sheaf Farm Estate & Spa
.... Holicong, Pa.
Willowgreen Farm B&B .... Summerside,
Sunrise Farm B&B .... Salem, S.C.
Fox Manor Historic Bed & Breakfast
.... Kingsport, Tenn.
MD Resort Bed & Breakfast..... Fort Worth, Texas
Jackson Fork Inn LLC......... Huntsville, Utah
Woodland Farmhouse Inn ...... Kamas, Utah
Bridgewater Inn and Cottage
.... Bridgewater, Va.
The Hummingbird Inn............ Goshen, Va.
Stonewall Jackson Inn B&B ..... Harrisonburg, Va.
Dulaney Hollow at Old Rag Mountain B&B Inn
.... Madison, Va.
Rosebelle's Victorian Inn .... Brandon, Vt.
Silas Griffith Inn.................. Danby, Vt.
Cobble House Inn .... Gaysville, Vt.
Phineas Swann B&B Inn .. Montgomery Center, Vt.
Inn at Clearwater Pond........... Quechee, Vt.
Waitsfield Inn .... Waitsfield, Vt.
Arlington's River Rock Inn
.... Arlington, Wash.
Turtleback Farm Inn .... Eastsound, Wash.
Justin Trails Resort .... Sparta, Wis.
Heritage Farm Museum & Village
.... Huntington, W.Va.
EVA-Great Spirit Ranch B&B
.... Newcastle, Wyo.

Boats

Stonecroft Country Inn......... Ledyard, Conn.
First Farm Inn .... Petersburg, Ky.
1851 Historic Maple Hill Manor B&B
.... Springfield, Ky.
The Alexander House Booklovers B&B
.... Princess Anne, Md.
Harbour Towne Inn on The Waterfront
.... Boothbay Harbor, Maine
Oakland House Seaside Resort

.... Brooksville, Maine
Hartstone Inn .... Camden, Maine
Greenville Inn .... Greenville, Maine
Silent Sport Lodge .... Wolverine, Mich.
Spicer Castle Inn .... Spicer, Minn.
Notleymere Cottage .... Cazenovia, N.Y.
Acorn Hollow Bed & Breakfast
.... Southold, N.Y.
Kilpatrick Manor Bed & Breakfast
.... Niagara Falls,
Elkhorn Valley Inn B&B .... Lyons, Ore.
McKenzie River Inn .... Vida, Ore.
Pennsbury Inn .... Chadds Ford, Pa.
Fox Manor Historic Bed & Breakfast
.... Kingsport, Tenn.
Magnolia House Inn .... Hampton, Va.
Fountain Chateau .... Hustler, Wis.

Bordellos

Hotel Charlotte .... Groveland, Calif.
The Groveland Hotel at Yosemite National Park
.... Groveland, Calif.
1859 Historic National Hotel, A Country Inn
.... Jamestown, Calif.
Peri & Ed's Mountain Hide Away
.... Leadville, Colo.
Villa OneTwenty .... Newport, R.I.

Castles

Amsterdam Castle .... Amsterdam, N.Y.
French Manor .... South Sterling, Pa.

Churches & Parsonages

Washington Plantation .... Washington, Ga.
Old Church House Inn .... Mossville, Ill.
Christopher's B&B .... Bellevue, Ky.
The Parsonage Inn .... East Orleans, Mass.
Parsonage Inn .... Saint Michaels, Md.
Silent Sport Lodge .... Wolverine, Mich.
Parish House Inn .... Ypsilanti, Mich.
Deutsche Strasse (German Street) B&B
.... New Ulm, Minn.
The Abbey Bed & Breakfast .... Cape May, N.J.
10 Fitch .... Auburn, N.Y.
Sunny's Roost Bed & Breakfast
.... Lewiston, N.Y.
HideAway Country Inn .... Bucyrus, Ohio
Post House Country Inn / Burke House Inn
.... Niagara On The Lake,
Elkhorn Valley Inn B&B .... Lyons, Ore.
Villa OneTwenty .... Newport, R.I.
Fox Manor Historic Bed & Breakfast
.... Kingsport, Tenn.
Bridgewater Inn and Cottage
.... Bridgewater, Va.
Mayhurst Inn .... Orange, Va.
Phineas Swann B&B Inn .. Montgomery Center, Vt.
Estabrook House .... Saint Johnsbury, Vt.
Waitsfield Inn .... Waitsfield, Vt.
Fountain Chateau .... Hustler, Wis.

Civil War

Washington Plantation .... Washington, Ga.
Mason House Inn and Caboose Cottage of
Bentonsport
.... Bentonsport, Iowa
The Steamboat House Bed and Breakfast

.... Galena, Ill.
Old Church House Inn .... Mossville, Ill.
The Irish Inn .... Ozark, Ill.
Chestnut Street Inn .... Sheffield, Ill.
Myrtledene B&B .... Lebanon, Ky.
1851 Historic Maple Hill Manor B&B
.... Springfield, Ky.
Magnolia Mansion .... New Orleans, La.
The General Rufus Putnam House
.... Rutland, Mass.
Munro House B&B and Spa ..... Jonesville, Mich.
The Dickey House B&B .... Marshfield, Mo.
Southern Hotel .... Sainte Genevieve, Mo.
Fairview Inn & Sophia's Restaurant
.... Jackson, Miss.
Monmouth Plantation .... Natchez, Miss.
1847 Blake House Inn Bed & Breakfast
.... Asheville, N.C.
The Inn at Brevard .... Brevard, N.C.
Chateau on the Mountain .... Fletcher, N.C.
Harmony House Inn .... New Bern, N.C.
HideAway Country Inn .... Bucyrus, Ohio
Rider's 1812 Inn .... Painesville, Ohio
Zoar School Inn .... Zoar, Ohio
Carlisle House .... Carlisle, Pa.
Pheasant Field B&B .... Carlisle, Pa.
Pennsbury Inn .... Chadds Ford, Pa.
The Inn at Twin Linden .... Churchtown, Pa.
The Fairfield Inn 1757 .... Fairfield, Pa.
James Gettys Hotel .... Gettysburg, Pa.
Keystone Inn B&B .... Gettysburg, Pa.
The Beechmont B&B Inn .... Hanover, Pa.
Red Lion Bed & Breakfast .... Red Lion, Pa.
Villa OneTwenty .... Newport, R.I.
Chesnut Cottage B&B .... Columbia, S.C.
Fox Manor Historic Bed & Breakfast
.... Kingsport, Tenn.
Prospect Hill B&B Inn ...... Mountain City, Tenn.
McKay House .... Jefferson, Texas
The Hale House Inn .... Jefferson, Texas
Wise Manor .... Jefferson, Texas
Bridgewater Inn and Cottage
.... Bridgewater, Va.
Firmstone Manor .... Clifton Forge, Va.
The Hummingbird Inn .... Goshen, Va.
Magnolia House Inn .... Hampton, Va.
Stonewall Jackson Inn B&B ..... Harrisonburg, Va.
Mayhurst Inn .... Orange, Va.
Sugar Tree Inn .... Steeles Tavern, Va.
Essex Inn .... Tappahannock, Va.
An American Inn - Williamsburg Manor B&B
.... Williamsburg, Va.
Lilac Inn .... Brandon, Vt.
Cobble House Inn .... Gaysville, Vt.
The Inn at Weathersfield .... Perkinsville, Vt.
Thomas Shepherd Inn ..... Shepherdstown, W.Va.

Cookbooks Written by Innkeepers

"Heartstone Inn Breakfast Cookbook"
The Heartstone Inn & Cottages
.... Eureka Springs, Ark.
"The Old Yacht Club Inn Cookbook"
Old Yacht Club Inn .... Santa Barbara, Calif.
"By Request, The White Oak Cookbook"
The White Oak Inn .... Danville, Ohio

"Favorite Recipes of Whitestone Country Inn"
Whitestone Country Inn .... Kingston, Tenn.

Farms and Orchards

Fool's Cove Ranch B&B .... Kingston, Ark.
Lodge at Sedona-A Luxury Bed and Breakfast Inn
.... Sedona, Ariz.
Apple Blossom Inn B&B .... Ahwahnee, Calif.
The Inn at Schoolhouse Creek
.... Mendocino, Calif.
Featherbed Railroad Company B&B
.... Nice, Calif.
Albert Shafsky House Bed & Breakfast
.... Placerville, Calif.
A White Jasmine Inn .... Santa Barbara, Calif.
Howard Creek Ranch .... Westport, Calif.
Wicky-Up Ranch B&B .... Woodlake, Calif.
Black Forest B&B Lodge & Cabins
.... Colorado Springs, Colo.
Connecticut River Valley Inn
.... Glastonbury, Conn.
Stonecroft Country Inn .... Ledyard, Conn.
The Inn at Woodstock Hill .... Woodstock, Conn.
Washington Plantation .... Washington, Ga.
Sonora Gardens Farmstead .... Nauvoo, Ill.
Chestnut Street Inn .... Sheffield, Ill.
Arbor Hill Inn .... La Porte, Ind.
The Landmark Inn at The Historic Bank of Oberlin
.... Oberlin, Kan.
First Farm Inn .... Petersburg, Ky.
1851 Historic Maple Hill Manor B&B
.... Springfield, Ky.
Gilbert's B&B .... Rehoboth, Mass.
Inn on The Horse Farm .... Sudbury, Mass.
The Alexander House Booklovers B&B
.... Princess Anne, Md.
Gramercy Mansion .... Stevenson, Md.
Hartstone Inn .... Camden, Maine
Brewster Inn of Dexter, Maine
.... Dexter, Maine
Royalsborough Inn at the Bagley House
.... Durham, Maine
Greenville Inn .... Greenville, Maine
Maple Hill Farm B&B Inn ...... Hallowell, Maine
Morrill Farm Bed & Breakfast
.... Sumner, Maine
Grand Victorian Bed & Breakfast Inn
.... Bellaire, Mich.
Kingsley House .... Saugatuck, Mich.
Silent Sport Lodge .... Wolverine, Mich.
Spicer Castle Inn .... Spicer, Minn.
Plain & Fancy Bed & Breakfast
.... Ironton, Mo.
The Mast Farm Inn .... Valle Crucis, N.C.
Big Mill Bed & Breakfast ...... Williamston, N.C.
The Hanlon House .... Scottsbluff, Neb.
Highland Lake Inn B&B .... Andover, N.H.
Brass Heart Inn .... Choconua, N.H.
Inn at Ellis River .... Jackson, N.H.
Chimney Hill Estate Inn ...... Lambertville, N.J.
The Black Range Lodge .... Kingston, N.M.
Halcyon Farm Bed & Breakfast
.... Amsterdam, N.Y.
Agape Farm B&B and Paintball
.... Corinth, N.Y.
Acorn Hollow Bed & Breakfast
.... Southold, N.Y.

HideAway Country Inn . . . . Bucyrus, Ohio
Kilpatrick Manor Bed & Breakfast
. . . . Niagara Falls,
McKenzie River Inn. . . . . Vida, Ore.
Aaronsburg Inn & Spa . . . . Aaronsburg, Pa.
The Alexander Benjamin House
. . . . Andreas, Pa.
Pennsbury Inn . . . . Chadds Ford, Pa.
The Inn at Twin Linden . . . . Churchtown, Pa.
Filbert Bed & Breakfast. . . . . Danielsville, Pa.
Barley Sheaf Farm Estate & Spa
. . . . Holicong, Pa.
Red Lion Bed & Breakfast . . . . Red Lion, Pa.
Field & Pine B&B. . . . . Shippensburg, Pa.
Willowgreen Farm B&B . . . . Summerside,
Villa OneTwenty . . . . Newport, R.I.
Sunrise Farm B&B . . . . Salem, S.C.
Fox Manor Historic Bed & Breakfast
. . . . Kingsport, Tenn.
Bridgewater Inn and Cottage
. . . . Bridgewater, Va.
Rockland Farm Retreat . . . . Bumpass, Va.
Firmstone Manor . . . . Clifton Forge, Va.
The Hummingbird Inn. . . . . Goshen, Va.
Mayhurst Inn . . . . Orange, Va.
Phineas Swann B&B Inn . . Montgomery Center, Vt.
Inn at Clearwater Pond . . . . Quechee, Vt.
Liberty Hill Farm. . . . . Rochester, Vt.
Turtleback Farm Inn . . . . Eastsound, Wash.
Justin Trails Resort . . . . Sparta, Wis.
Heritage Farm Museum & Village
. . . . Huntington, W.Va.

Gardens

Pearson's Pond Luxury Inn & Adventure Spa
. . . . Juneau, Alaska
Cliff Cottage Inn - Luxury B&B Suites & Historic
Cottages
. . . . Eureka Springs, Ark.
Lookout Point Lakeside Inn
. . . . Hot Springs, Ark.
Luna Vista Bed and Breakfast
. . . . Camp Verde, Ariz.
Casa De San Pedro . . . . Hereford, Ariz.
Lodge at Sedona-A Luxury Bed and Breakfast Inn
. . . . Sedona, Ariz.
The Heritage Inn . . . . Snowflake, Ariz.
Brewery Gulch Inn . . . . Mendocino, Calif.
The Inn at Schoolhouse Creek
. . . . Mendocino, Calif.
A White Jasmine Inn . . . . Santa Barbara, Calif.
Romantic RiverSong Inn . . . . . . Estes Park, Colo.
Avenue Hotel, A Victorian B&B
. . . . Manitou Springs, Colo.
Connecticut River Valley Inn
. . . . Glastonbury, Conn.
Stonecroft Country Inn. . . . . Ledyard, Conn.
Deacon Timothy Pratt Bed & Breakfast Inn C.1746
. . . . Old Saybrook, Conn.
The Inn at Woodstock Hill . . . . Woodstock, Conn.
Lily Creek Lodge. . . . . Dahlonega, Ga.
Washington Plantation . . . . Washington, Ga.
The Hancock House . . . . Dubuque, Iowa
Blue Belle Inn B&B . . . . Saint Ansgar, Iowa
Beall Mansion, An Elegant B&B
. . . . Alton, Ill.
His Rest Bed & Breakfast . . . . Freeburg, Ill.

Sonora Gardens Farmstead . . . . Nauvoo, Ill.
Chestnut Street Inn . . . . Sheffield, Ill.
Cincinnati's Weller Haus B&B
. . . . Bellevue, Ky.
First Farm Inn . . . . Petersburg, Ky.
1851 Historic Maple Hill Manor B&B
. . . . Springfield, Ky.
Chatham Old Harbor Inn . . . . . . Chatham, Mass.
Gabriel's at the Ashbrooke Inn
. . . . Provincetown, Mass.
Inn on The Horse Farm . . . . Sudbury, Mass.
Great Oak Manor . . . . Chestertown, Md.
The Inn at Mitchell House . . . . . Chestertown, Md.
The Alexander House Booklovers B&B
. . . . Princess Anne, Md.
Gramercy Mansion . . . . Stevenson, Md.
The Galen C. Moses House . . . . Bath, Maine
Harbour Towne Inn on The Waterfront
. . . . Boothbay Harbor, Maine
Hartstone Inn . . . . Camden, Maine
Brewster Inn of Dexter, Maine
. . . . Dexter, Maine
Greenville Inn . . . . Greenville, Maine
Morrill Farm Bed & Breakfast
. . . . Sumner, Maine
Prairieside Suites Luxury B&B
. . . . Grand Rapids, Mich.
Huron House Bed & Breakfast
. . . . Oscoda, Mich.
Kingsley House . . . . Saugatuck, Mich.
Silent Sport Lodge . . . . Wolverine, Mich.
Spicer Castle Inn . . . . Spicer, Minn.
The Dickey House B&B . . . . Marshfield, Mo.
Inn at Harbour Ridge . . . . Osage Beach, Mo.
Fairview Inn & Sophia's Restaurant
. . . . Jackson, Miss.
Monmouth Plantation . . . . Natchez, Miss.
Hawkesdene House B&B Inn and Cottages
. . . . Andrews, N.C.
The Inn at Brevard. . . . . Brevard, N.C.
Sobotta Manor Bed and Breakfast
. . . . Mount Airy, N.C.
1906 Pine Crest Inn and Restaurant
. . . . Tryon, N.C.
The Mast Farm Inn . . . . Valle Crucis, N.C.
Big Mill Bed & Breakfast . . . . . . Williamston, N.C.
Adair Country Inn and Restaurant
. . . . Bethlehem, N.H.
Bernerhof Inn . . . . Glen, N.H.
Coppertoppe Inn & Retreat Center
. . . . Hebron, N.H.
Cabernet Inn . . . . North Conway, N.H.
A Grand Inn-Sunset Hill House
. . . . Sugar Hill, N.H.
Wakefield Inn, LLC . . . . Wakefield, N.H.
Touchstone Inn, Spa & Gallery
. . . . Taos, N.M.
B Street House Bed and Breakfast
. . . . Virginia City, Nev.
10 Fitch . . . . Auburn, N.Y.
Berry Hill Gardens B&B. . . . . Bainbridge, N.Y.
Notleymere Cottage . . . . Cazenovia, N.Y.
Arbor View House B&B . . . . East Marion, N.Y.
The Edward Harris House B&B Inn
. . . . Rochester, N.Y.
Acorn Hollow Bed & Breakfast
. . . . Southold, N.Y.

HideAway Country Inn . . . . Bucyrus, Ohio
Gambier House . . . . Gambier, Ohio
Inn & Spa At Cedar Falls . . . . Logan, Ohio
Kilpatrick Manor Bed & Breakfast
. . . . Niagara Falls,
Post House Country Inn / Burke House Inn
. . . . Niagara On The Lake,
Albion Inn . . . . Ashland, Ore.
Elkhorn Valley Inn B&B . . . . Lyons, Ore.
McKenzie River Inn. . . . . Vida, Ore.
Pheasant Field B&B . . . . Carlisle, Pa.
Pennsbury Inn . . . . Chadds Ford, Pa.
Barley Sheaf Farm Estate & Spa
. . . . Holicong, Pa.
Kennett House Bed and Breakfast
. . . . Kennett Square, Pa.
The Artist's Inn & Gallery
. . . . Terre Hill, Pa.
Villa OneTwenty . . . . Newport, R.I.
Edgewood Manor B&B . . . . Providence, R.I.
Custer Mansion B&B . . . . Custer, S.D.
Fox Manor Historic Bed & Breakfast
. . . . Kingsport, Tenn.
Prospect Hill B&B Inn . . . . . . Mountain City, Tenn.
McKay House . . . . Jefferson, Texas
The Hale House Inn . . . . Jefferson, Texas
Woodland Farmhouse Inn . . . . Kamas, Utah
Bridgewater Inn and Cottage
. . . . Bridgewater, Va.
The Hummingbird Inn. . . . . Goshen, Va.
Magnolia House Inn . . . . Hampton, Va.
The Garden and The Sea Inn
. . . . New Church, Va.
Colonial Manor Inn . . . . Onancock, Va.
Mayhurst Inn . . . . Orange, Va.
Sugar Tree Inn . . . . Steeles Tavern, Va.
Essex Inn. . . . . Tappahannock, Va.
An American Inn - Williamsburg Manor B&B
. . . . Williamsburg, Va.
Colonial Gardens. . . . . Williamsburg, Va.
Alexandra B&B Inn . . . . Bennington, Vt.
Lilac Inn . . . . Brandon, Vt.
Rosebelle's Victorian Inn. . . . . Brandon, Vt.
Silas Griffith Inn . . . . Danby, Vt.
Phineas Swann B&B Inn . . Montgomery Center, Vt.
Inn at Clearwater Pond . . . . Quechee, Vt.
White House of Wilmington . . . . . Wilmington, Vt.
Plum Duff House . . . . Tacoma, Wash.
Fountain Chateau . . . . Hustler, Wis.
Justin Trails Resort . . . . Sparta, Wis.

Glacier Viewing

Pearson's Pond Luxury Inn & Adventure Spa
. . . . Juneau, Alaska
Matanuska Lodge . . . . Sutton, Alaska
Romantic RiverSong Inn . . . . Estes Park, Colo.
Fountain Chateau . . . . Hustler, Wis.

Gold Mines & Gold Panning

Pearson's Pond Luxury Inn & Adventure Spa
. . . . Juneau, Alaska
Casa De San Pedro . . . . Hereford, Ariz.
Lodge at Sedona-A Luxury Bed and Breakfast Inn
. . . . Sedona, Ariz.
Deer Crossing Inn . . . . Castro Valley, Calif.
Hotel Charlotte . . . . Groveland, Calif.
The Groveland Hotel at Yosemite National Park

.... Groveland, Calif.

1859 Historic National Hotel, A Country Inn
.... Jamestown, Calif.

Albert Shafsky House Bed & Breakfast
.... Placerville, Calif.

Black Forest B&B Lodge & Cabins
.... Colorado Springs, Colo.

Winter Park Chateau .... Winter Park, Colo.

Lily Creek Lodge.............. Dahlonega, Ga.

Greyhouse Inn B&B............. Salmon, Idaho

The Black Range Lodge........ Kingston, N.M.

Elkhorn Valley Inn B&B .... Lyons, Ore.

McKenzie River Inn................ Vida, Ore.

Custer Mansion B&B............. Custer, S.D.

Cobble House Inn .... Gaysville, Vt.

Echo Lake Inn .... Ludlow, Vt.

Hot Springs

Lookout Point Lakeside Inn
.... Hot Springs, Ark.

Brannan Cottage Inn............ Calistoga, Calif.

A White Jasmine Inn .... Santa Barbara, Calif.

Vichy Hot Springs Resort & Inn
.... Ukiah, Calif.

Winter Park Chateau .... Winter Park, Colo.

Greyhouse Inn B&B............. Salmon, Idaho

The Inn on Crescent Lake .. Excelsior Springs, Mo.

Elkhorn Valley Inn B&B .... Lyons, Ore.

McKenzie River Inn................ Vida, Ore.

Custer Mansion B&B............. Custer, S.D.

Bridgewater Inn and Cottage
.... Bridgewater, Va.

Firmstone Manor............ Clifton Forge, Va.

The Hummingbird Inn............ Goshen, Va.

Inns Built Prior to 1800

1691 The Great Valley House of Valley Forge
.... Valley Forge, Pa.

1700 Elias Child House B&B
.... Woodstock, Conn.

1714 Pennsbury Inn......... Chadds Ford, Pa.

1720 Bed & Breakfast at Roseledge Herb Farm
.... Preston, Conn.

1730 Joy House Inc., B&B.... Dennis Port, Mass.

1731 The Daniel Rust House
.... Coventry, Conn.

1734 3 Liberty Green B&B ...... Clinton, Conn.

1736 Inn at Glencairn .... Princeton, N.J.

1739 The Ruffner House .... Luray, Va.

1740 Connecticut River Valley Inn
.... Glastonbury, Conn.

1740 Inn at Lower Farm. North Stonington, Conn.

1740 Lamb and Lion Inn ...... Barnstable, Mass.

1740 Barley Sheaf Farm Estate & Spa
.... Holicong, Pa.

1743 The Inn at Mitchell House
.... Chestertown, Md.

1746 Deacon Timothy Pratt Bed & Breakfast Inn
C.1746
.... Old Saybrook, Conn.

1750 The General Rufus Putnam House
.... Rutland, Mass.

1757 The Fairfield Inn 1757
.... Fairfield, Pa.

1761 Harpswell Inn .... Harpswell, Maine

1763 Blackberry River Inn ...... Norfolk, Conn.

1763 Casa de Solana, B&B Inn

.... Saint Augustine, Fla.

1763 Historic Smithton Inn
.... Ephrata, Pa.

1766 Seven South Street Inn
.... Rockport, Mass.

1766 Osceola Mill House .... Gordonville, Pa.

1766 The Inn at Meander Plantation
.... Locust Dale, Va.

1767 Birchwood Inn .... Lenox, Mass.

1767 Oakland House Seaside Resort
.... Brooksville, Maine

1767 Highland Lake Inn B&B
.... Andover, N.H.

1768 Boxwood Inn Bed & Breakfast
.... Akron, Pa.

1769 The Inn at Millrace Pond
.... Hope, N.J.

1770 The Parsonage Inn ..... East Orleans, Mass.

1771 Cliff Lodge Bed & Breakfast
.... Nantucket, Mass.

1771 The Inn on Cove Hill. .... Rockport, Mass.

1772 Royalsborough Inn at the Bagley House
.... Durham, Maine

1774 Gibson's Lodgings .... Annapolis, Md.

1774 Inn at Valley Farms B&B and Cottages
.... Walpole, N.H.

1775 Kanaga House B&B Inn . Mechanicsburg, Pa.

1778 Brass Heart Inn .... Chocorua, N.H.

1779 Ira Allen House .... Manchester, Vt.

1780 Hotel Saint Pierre ...... New Orleans, La.

1780 Birch Hill Bed & Breakfast
.... Sheffield, Mass.

1780 The Dowds' Country Inn
.... Lyme, N.H.

1782 Abel Darling B&B ...... Litchfield, Conn.

1783 The Towers B&B........... Milford, Del.

1784 Maple House Bed & Breakfast
.... Rowe, Mass.

1785 Weathervane Inn ... South Egremont, Mass.

1785 1785 Inn & Restaurant
.... North Conway, N.H.

1785 Sleepy Hollow Farm B&B
.... Gordonsville, Va.

1786 Brandon Inn.............. Brandon, Vt.

1788 Golden Stage Inn .... Ludlow, Vt.

1790 Silvermine Tavern .... Norwalk, Conn.

1790 Morrill Farm Bed & Breakfast
.... Sumner, Maine

1790 Southern Hotel...... Sainte Genevieve, Mo.

1790 The Inn at Gray's Landing
.... Windsor, N.C.

1790 Hacienda Antigua Inn .. Albuquerque, N.M.

1790 Brownstone Colonial Inn
.... Reinholds, Pa.

1790 Field & Pine B&B ...... Shippensburg, Pa.

1790 Flowering Fields B&B..... White Stone, Va.

1790 Silver Maple Lodge & Cottages
.... Fairlee, Vt.

1790 The Putney Inn .... Putney, Vt.

1791 St. Francis Inn ...... Saint Augustine, Fla.

1791 Sedgwick Inn .... Berlin, N.Y.

1792 Bridges Inn at Whitcomb House
.... West Swanzey, N.H.

1792 1792 Filigree Inn .... Canandaigua, N.Y.

1792 The Inn at Weathersfield
.... Perkinsville, Vt.

1793 Cove House ...... Kennebunkport, Maine

1794 Historic Merrell Inn ...... South Lee, Mass.

1794 The Whitehall Inn......... New Hope, Pa.

1794 Inn at the Laveau Farm
.... Waitsfield, Vt.

1795 Shaker Meadows ...... New Lebanon, N.Y.

1795 Living Spring Farm B&B
.... Adamstown, Pa.

1796 Yorkshire Inn .... Phelps, N.Y.

1796 Catamount B&B .... Williston, Vt.

1797 The Grand View Inn & Resort
.... Jaffrey, N.H.

1797 Applebrook B&B.......... Jefferson, N.H.

1797 Inn at Baldwin Creek & Mary's Restaurant
.... Bristol, Vt.

1799 The Kennebunk Inn .... Kennebunk, Maine

1799 Dr. Jonathan Pitney House
.... Absecon, N.J.

Jailhouses

Lodge at Sedona-A Luxury Bed and Breakfast Inn
.... Sedona, Ariz.

Hotel Charlotte............. Groveland, Calif.

1851 Historic Maple Hill Manor B&B
.... Springfield, Ky.

Acorn Hollow Bed & Breakfast
.... Southold, N.Y.

HideAway Country Inn .... Bucyrus, Ohio

Villa OneTwenty .... Newport, R.I.

Lighthouses

Deacon Timothy Pratt Bed & Breakfast Inn C.1746
.... Old Saybrook, Conn.

Arbor Hill Inn .... La Porte, Ind.

Beechwood Inn .... Barnstable, Mass.

Harborside House B&B ...... Marblehead, Mass.

The Galen C. Moses House ...... Bath, Maine

The Alden House Bed & Breakfast
.... Belfast, Maine

Harbour Towne Inn on The Waterfront
.... Boothbay Harbor, Maine

Oakland House Seaside Resort
.... Brooksville, Maine

Hartstone Inn .... Camden, Maine

Grand Victorian Bed & Breakfast Inn
.... Bellaire, Mich.

Huron House Bed & Breakfast
.... Oscoda, Mich.

Silent Sport Lodge .... Wolverine, Mich.

Stirling House Bed & Breakfast
.... Greenport, N.Y.

Acorn Hollow Bed & Breakfast
.... Southold, N.Y.

Brey House .... Lincoln City, Ore.

Stone Crest Cellar B&B ...... South Beach, Ore.

Villa OneTwenty .... Newport, R.I.

The Garden and The Sea Inn
.... New Church, Va.

Second Wind Country Inn .... Ashland, Wis.

Literary Figures Asscociated With Inns

Jack London
Vichy Hot Springs Resort & Inn
.... Ukiah, Calif.

D.H. Lawrence
Vichy Hot Springs Resort & Inn
.... Ukiah, Calif.

Inns of Interest

Mark Twain/Samuel Clemens
Vichy Hot Springs Resort & Inn
.... Ukiah, Calif.

Louisa May Alcott
Hawthorne Inn................ Concord, Mass.

Ralph Waldo Emerson
Hawthorne Inn................ Concord, Mass.

Nathaniel Hawthorne
Hawthorne Inn................ Concord, Mass.

Henry Beston
Inn at the Oaks............... Eastham, Mass.

Ralph Waldo Emerson
Emerson Inn By The Sea .... Rockport, Mass.

Nathaniel Hawthorne
Emerson Inn By The Sea .... Rockport, Mass.

Llama Ranches

Black Forest B&B Lodge & Cabins
.... Colorado Springs, Colo.
1851 Historic Maple Hill Manor B&B
.... Springfield, Ky.
Royalsborough Inn at the Bagley House
.... Durham, Maine
Maple Hill Farm B&B Inn....... Hallowell, Maine
Hawkesdene House B&B Inn and Cottages
.... Andrews, N.C.
Chimney Hill Estate Inn .... Lambertville, N.J.
Adobe & Pines Inn .... Taos, N.M.
Woodland Farmhouse Inn .... Kamas, Utah
Mayhurst Inn .... Orange, Va.
Phineas Swann B&B Inn .. Montgomery Center, Vt.
Inn at Clearwater Pond .... Quechee, Vt.
Justin Trails Resort .... Sparta, Wis.

Log Cabins/Houses

Matanuska Lodge.............. Sutton, Alaska
Ocean Wilderness Inn .... Sooke,
Knickerbocker Mansion Country Inn
.... Big Bear Lake, Calif.
Black Forest B&B Lodge & Cabins
.... Colorado Springs, Colo.
Highland Haven Creekside Inn
.... Evergreen, Colo.
Wild Horse Inn Bed and Breakfast
.... Fraser, Colo.
Cedar Mountain Farm........... Athol, Idaho
His Rest Bed & Breakfast .... Freeburg, Ill.
The Irish Inn .... Ozark, Ill.
1851 Historic Maple Hill Manor B&B
.... Springfield, Ky.
Oakland House Seaside Resort
.... Brooksville, Maine
Sweet Dreams Inn Victorian B&B
.... Bay Port, Mich.
Silent Sport Lodge .... Wolverine, Mich.
Cedar Rose Inn .... Alexandria, Minn.
Spicer Castle Inn .... Spicer, Minn.
1906 Pine Crest Inn and Restaurant
.... Tryon, N.C.
The Mast Farm Inn .... Valle Crucis, N.C.
Elaine's, A B&B .... Cedar Crest, N.M.
Log Country Inn - B&B of Ithaca
.... Ithaca, N.Y.
HideAway Country Inn .... Bucyrus, Ohio
Heartland Country Resort..... Fredericktown, Ohio
Inn & Spa At Cedar Falls .... Logan, Ohio
Weasku Inn .... Grants Pass, Ore.

Elkhorn Valley Inn B&B .... Lyons, Ore.
McKenzie River Inn.............. Vida, Ore.
Aaronsburg Inn & Spa .... Aaronsburg, Pa.
Pennsbury Inn .... Chadds Ford, Pa.
Fox Manor Historic Bed & Breakfast
.... Kingsport, Tenn.
BlissWood Bed & Breakfast ..... Cat Spring, Texas
Roddy Tree Ranch .... Hunt, Texas
Woodland Farmhouse Inn .... Kamas, Utah
Bridgewater Inn and Cottage
.... Bridgewater, Va.
Woodruff Inns and Shenandoah River Cabin Escapes
.... Luray, Va.
Mayhurst Inn .... Orange, Va.
The Inn at Burg's Landing . Anderson Island, Wash.
Arlington's River Rock Inn
.... Arlington, Wash.
Guest House Log Cottages .... Greenbank, Wash.
Justin Trails Resort .... Sparta, Wis.
Heritage Farm Museum & Village
.... Huntington, W.Va.

Movie Locations

Holiday Inn
Village Inn & Restaurant .... Monte Rio, Calif.
Consenting Adults
Rice Hope Plantation Inn Bed & Breakfast
.... Moncks Corner, S.C.

National Historic Register

Cliff Cottage Inn - Luxury B&B Suites & Historic Cottages
.... Eureka Springs, Ark.
The Heartstone Inn & Cottages
.... Eureka Springs, Ark.
Lodge at Sedona-A Luxury Bed and Breakfast Inn
.... Sedona, Ariz.
The Heritage Inn .... Snowflake, Ariz.
Brannan Cottage Inn. .... Calistoga, Calif.
Hotel Charlotte.............. Groveland, Calif.
The Groveland Hotel at Yosemite National Park
.... Groveland, Calif.
Old Yacht Club Inn .... Santa Barbara, Calif.
Vichy Hot Springs Resort & Inn
.... Ukiah, Calif.
The Bross Hotel B&B............ Paonia, Colo.
Stonecroft Country Inn......... Ledyard, Conn.
Deacon Timothy Pratt Bed & Breakfast Inn C.1746
.... Old Saybrook, Conn.
The Inn at Woodstock Hill .... Woodstock, Conn.
The Towers B&B............. Milford, Del.
St. Francis Inn .... Saint Augustine, Fla.
Beach Drive Inn .... Saint Petersburg, Fla.
Tybee Island Inn .... Tybee Island, Ga.
Washington Plantation .... Washington, Ga.
Mont Rest .... Bellevue, Iowa
Mason House Inn and Caboose Cottage of Bentonsport
.... Bentonsport, Iowa
The Hancock House .... Dubuque, Iowa
The Mandolin Inn .... Dubuque, Iowa
Beall Mansion, An Elegant B&B
.... Alton, Ill.
The Steamboat House Bed and Breakfast
.... Galena, Ill.
Corner George Inn .... Maeystown, Ill.
Arbor Hill Inn .... La Porte, Ind.

The Landmark Inn at The Historic Bank of Oberlin
.... Oberlin, Kan.
Cincinnati's Weller Haus B&B
.... Bellevue, Ky.
1851 Historic Maple Hill Manor B&B
.... Springfield, Ky.
College Club................ Boston, Mass.
The Beach Rose Inn .... Falmouth, Mass.
Old Mill on The Falls Inn .... Hatfield, Mass.
Winterwood at Petersham ...... Petersham, Mass.
Historic Merrell Inn .... South Lee, Mass.
Inn on The Horse Farm......... Sudbury, Mass.
Merry Sherwood Plantation......... Berlin, Md.
Gramercy Mansion .... Stevenson, Md.
The Galen C. Moses House .... Bath, Maine
Brewster Inn of Dexter, Maine
.... Dexter, Maine
Lake House .... Waterford, Maine
The Historic Afton House Inn
.... Afton, Minn.
Cedar Rose Inn .... Alexandria, Minn.
Classic Rosewood - A Thorwood Property
.... Hastings, Minn.
Spicer Castle Inn .... Spicer, Minn.
Eagle's Nest................ Louisiana, Mo.
Museum Hill Bed & Breakfast
.... Saint Joseph, Mo.
Fairview Inn & Sophia's Restaurant
.... Jackson, Miss.
Monmouth Plantation .... Natchez, Miss.
Olive Branch Inn at the Lindley House
.... Bozeman, Mont.
Wright Inn & Carriage House
.... Asheville, N.C.
The Inn at Brevard.......... Brevard, N.C.
1906 Pine Crest Inn and Restaurant
.... Tryon, N.C.
The Mast Farm Inn .... Valle Crucis, N.C.
Wakefield Inn, LLC........... Wakefield, N.H.
Williams Cottage Inn .... Beach Haven, N.J.
Bottger Mansion of Old Town
.... Albuquerque, N.M.
B Street House Bed and Breakfast
.... Virginia City, Nev.
Amsterdam Castle .... Amsterdam, N.Y.
Notleymere Cottage .... Cazenovia, N.Y.
Rosewood Inn .... Corning, N.Y.
Wells House .... Greenport, N.Y.
The Edward Harris House B&B Inn
.... Rochester, N.Y.
Colonel Taylor Inn Bed & Breakfast
.... Cambridge, Ohio
Eagle Cliff Inn ... Geneva On The Lake, Ohio
Rider's 1812 Inn............ Painesville, Ohio
The Grandison Inn at Maney Park
.... Oklahoma City, Okla.
Albion Inn .... Ashland, Ore.
Aaronsburg Inn & Spa .... Aaronsburg, Pa.
Carlisle House .... Carlisle, Pa.
Pennsbury Inn .... Chadds Ford, Pa.
The Fairfield Inn 1757 .... Fairfield, Pa.
James Gettys Hotel .... Gettysburg, Pa.
French Manor............. South Sterling, Pa.
Adele Turner Inn .... Newport, R.I.
Villa OneTwenty .... Newport, R.I.
Edgewood Manor B&B .... Providence, R.I.
Custer Mansion B&B .... Custer, S.D.

308

Prospect Hill B&B Inn . . . . . Mountain City, Tenn.
Pecan Street Inn . . . . Bastrop, Texas
McKay House . . . . Jefferson, Texas
Mosheim Mansion . . . . Seguin, Texas
Katy House Bed & Breakfast
. . . . Smithville, Texas
Green Gate Village Historic Inn
. . . . Saint George, Utah
Ellerbeck Mansion B&B . . . . . . Salt Lake City, Utah
Parrish Place B&B . . . . Salt Lake City, Utah
Magnolia House Inn . . . . Hampton, Va.
Mayhurst Inn . . . . Orange, Va.
Lilac Inn . . . . Brandon, Vt.
Rosebelle's Victorian Inn . . . . Brandon, Vt.
Park Light Inn . . . . Chester, Vt.
Silas Griffith Inn . . . . Danby, Vt.
Estabrook House . . . . Saint Johnsbury, Vt.
Charleston House . . . . Woodstock, Vt.
The Blue Goose Inn . . . . Coupeville, Wash.
Fountain Chateau . . . . Hustler, Wis.
Schuster Mansion Bed & Breakfast
. . . . Milwaukee, Wis.
The Rochester Inn . . . . Sheboygan Falls, Wis.
Franklin Victorian Bed & Breakfast
. . . . Sparta, Wis.
White Lace Inn . . . . Sturgeon Bay, Wis.

Old Mills

Brannan Cottage Inn . . . . Calistoga, Calif.
Silvermine Tavern . . . . Norwalk, Conn.
Sylvan Falls Mill . . . . Rabun Gap, Ga.
Old Mill on The Falls Inn . . . . Hatfield, Mass.
Historic Merrell Inn . . . . South Lee, Mass.
Silent Sport Lodge . . . . Wolverine, Mich.
Big Mill Bed & Breakfast . . . . . . Williamston, N.C.
Asa Ransom House . . . . Clarence, N.Y.
Elkhorn Valley Inn B&B . . . . Lyons, Ore.
Pennsbury Inn . . . . Chadds Ford, Pa.
Fox Manor Historic Bed & Breakfast
. . . . Kingsport, Tenn.
Bridgewater Inn and Cottage
. . . . Bridgewater, Va.
The Hummingbird Inn . . . . Goshen, Va.
Stonewall Jackson Inn B&B . . . . . . Harrisonburg, Va.
Sugar Tree Inn . . . . Steeles Tavern, Va.
The Mountain Rose B&B Inn . . . . . . Woolwine, Va.

Oldest Continuously Operated Inns

Lodge at Sedona-A Luxury Bed and Breakfast Inn
. . . . Sedona, Ariz.
1859 Historic National Hotel, A Country Inn
. . . . Jamestown, Calif.
The Inn at Schoolhouse Creek
. . . . Mendocino, Calif.
Old Yacht Club Inn . . . . Santa Barbara, Calif.
Vichy Hot Springs Resort & Inn
. . . . Ukiah, Calif.
Peri & Ed's Mountain Hide Away
. . . . Leadville, Colo.
Avenue Hotel, A Victorian B&B
. . . . Manitou Springs, Colo.
1857 Florida House Inn . . . . Amelia Island, Fla.
St. Francis Inn . . . . Saint Augustine, Fla.
Mason House Inn and Caboose Cottage of
Bentonsport
. . . . Bentonsport, Iowa

Gabriel's at the Ashbrooke Inn
. . . . Provincetown, Mass.
Emerson Inn By The Sea . . . . Rockport, Mass.
Harbour Towne Inn on The Waterfront
. . . . Boothbay Harbor, Maine
Oakland House Seaside Resort
. . . . Brooksville, Maine
Royalsborough Inn at the Bagley House
. . . . Durham, Maine
Greenville Inn . . . . Greenville, Maine
Khardomah Lodge . . . . Grand Haven, Mich.
BayView Terrace Inn . . . . Petoskey, Mich.
Classic Rosewood - A Thorwood Property
. . . . Hastings, Minn.
Rivertown Inn . . . . Stillwater, Minn.
Loganberry Inn . . . . Fulton, Mo.
Southern Hotel . . . . Sainte Genevieve, Mo.
1906 Pine Crest Inn and Restaurant
. . . . Tryon, N.C.
The Mast Farm Inn . . . . Valle Crucis, N.C.
Highland Lake Inn B&B . . . . Andover, N.H.
A Grand Inn-Sunset Hill House
. . . . Sugar Hill, N.H.
Wakefield Inn, LLC . . . . Wakefield, N.H.
Stirling House Bed & Breakfast
. . . . Greenport, N.Y.
McKenzie River Inn . . . . Vida, Ore.
The Fairfield Inn 1757 . . . . Fairfield, Pa.
The Great Valley House of Valley Forge
. . . . Valley Forge, Pa.
The Bellevue House . . . . Block Island, R.I.
Adele Turner Inn . . . . Newport, R.I.
Custer Mansion B&B . . . . Custer, S.D.
Smith House Inn . . . . Crosbyton, Texas
Robin's Nest . . . . Houston, Texas
McKay House . . . . Jefferson, Texas
Wise Manor . . . . Jefferson, Texas
Federal Crest Inn . . . . Lynchburg, Va.
Colonial Manor Inn . . . . Onancock, Va.
Rosebelle's Victorian Inn . . . . Brandon, Vt.
Ira Allen House . . . . Manchester, Vt.

On the Grounds of a U.S. National Memorial

Fountain Chateau . . . . Hustler, Wis.

Plantations

Washington Plantation . . . . Washington, Ga.
1851 Historic Maple Hill Manor B&B
. . . . Springfield, Ky.
Magnolia Mansion . . . . New Orleans, La.
Merry Sherwood Plantation . . . . Berlin, Md.
Monmouth Plantation . . . . Natchez, Miss.
Mansfield Plantation B&B Country Inn
. . . . Georgetown, S.C.
Rice Hope Plantation Inn Bed & Breakfast
. . . . Moncks Corner, S.C.
The Inn at Meander Plantation
. . . . Locust Dale, Va.
Mayhurst Inn . . . . Orange, Va.
Four Square Plantation . . . . Smithfield, Va.

Ranches

Lodge at Sedona-A Luxury Bed and Breakfast Inn
. . . . Sedona, Ariz.
The Inn at Schoolhouse Creek
. . . . Mendocino, Calif.

Howard Creek Ranch . . . . Westport, Calif.
Romantic RiverSong Inn . . . . Estes Park, Colo.
Cedar Mountain Farm . . . . Athol, Idaho
1851 Historic Maple Hill Manor B&B
. . . . Springfield, Ky.
Wilson Ranches Retreat Bed and Breakfast
. . . . Fossil, Ore.
BlissWood Bed & Breakfast . . . . . Cat Spring, Texas
MD Resort Bed & Breakfast . . . . . Fort Worth, Texas
Hasse House and Ranch . . . . Mason, Texas
Fountain Chateau . . . . Hustler, Wis.

Revolutionary War

Washington Plantation . . . . Washington, Ga.
The Irish Inn . . . . Ozark, Ill.
Hawthorne Inn . . . . Concord, Mass.
Historic Merrell Inn . . . . South Lee, Mass.
Gibson's Lodgings . . . . Annapolis, Md.
1906 Pine Crest Inn and Restaurant
. . . . Tryon, N.C.
Inn at Glencairn . . . . Princeton, N.J.
Acorn Hollow Bed & Breakfast
. . . . Southold, N.Y.
Pennsbury Inn . . . . Chadds Ford, Pa.
Kennett House Bed and Breakfast
. . . . Kennett Square, Pa.
The Great Valley House of Valley Forge
. . . . Valley Forge, Pa.
Villa OneTwenty . . . . Newport, R.I.
McKay House . . . . Jefferson, Texas
Mayhurst Inn . . . . Orange, Va.
An American Inn - Williamsburg Manor B&B
. . . . Williamsburg, Va.
Alexandra B&B Inn . . . . Bennington, Vt.
Phineas Swann B&B Inn . . . Montgomery Center, Vt.

Schoolhouses

The Inn at Schoolhouse Creek
. . . . Mendocino, Calif.
Vichy Hot Springs Resort & Inn
. . . . Ukiah, Calif.
The Roosevelt Inn . . . . Coeur D'Alene, Idaho
Old Sea Pines Inn . . . . Brewster, Mass.
Royalsborough Inn at the Bagley House
. . . . Durham, Maine
HideAway Country Inn . . . . Bucyrus, Ohio
Zoar School Inn . . . . Zoar, Ohio
Custer Mansion B&B . . . . Custer, S.D.
Fox Manor Historic Bed & Breakfast
. . . . Kingsport, Tenn.
Washington School Inn . . . . Park City, Utah
Mayhurst Inn . . . . Orange, Va.
States Inn . . . . Friday Harbor, Wash.
Fountain Chateau . . . . Hustler, Wis.
Heritage Farm Museum & Village
. . . . Huntington, W.Va.

Stagecoach Stops

Luna Vista Bed and Breakfast
. . . . Camp Verde, Ariz.
Fensalden Inn . . . . Albion, Calif.
Hotel Charlotte . . . . Groveland, Calif.
1859 Historic National Hotel, A Country Inn
. . . . Jamestown, Calif.
Albert Shafsky House Bed & Breakfast
. . . . Placerville, Calif.
Melitta Station Inn . . . . Santa Rosa, Calif.

Mason House Inn and Caboose Cottage of
Bentonsport
. . . . Bentonsport, Iowa
Maple House Bed & Breakfast
. . . . Rowe, Mass.
Historic Merrell Inn . . . . South Lee, Mass.
Harbour Towne Inn on The Waterfront
. . . . Boothbay Harbor, Maine
Maple Hill Farm B&B Inn . . . . Hallowell, Maine
Lake House . . . . Waterford, Maine
Sweet Dreams Inn Victorian B&B
. . . . Bay Port, Mich.
The Mendon Country Inn . . . . . . Mendon, Mich.
Southern Hotel . . . . Sainte Genevieve, Mo.
Wakefield Inn, LLC . . . . Wakefield, N.H.
Hacienda Antigua Inn . . . . Albuquerque, N.M.
Hacienda Vargas . . . . Algodones, N.M.
Rider's 1812 Inn . . . . Painesville, Ohio
McKenzie River Inn . . . . Vida, Ore.
The Alexander Benjamin House
. . . . Andreas, Pa.
The Fairfield Inn 1757 . . . . Fairfield, Pa.
The Great Valley House of Valley Forge
. . . . Valley Forge, Pa.
Fox Manor Historic Bed & Breakfast
. . . . Kingsport, Tenn.
Golden Stage Inn . . . . Ludlow, Vt.
Phineas Swann B&B Inn . . Montgomery Center, Vt.
Wisconsin House Stagecoach Inn
. . . . Hazel Green, Wis.
EVA-Great Spirit Ranch B&B
. . . . Newcastle, Wyo.

Still in the Family

Old Yacht Club Inn . . . . Santa Barbara, Calif.
Vichy Hot Springs Resort & Inn
. . . . Ukiah, Calif.
Black Forest B&B Lodge & Cabins
. . . . Colorado Springs, Colo.
Romantic RiverSong Inn . . . . Estes Park, Colo.
Angels' Watch Inn . . . . Westbrook, Conn.
Cedar Mountain Farm . . . . Athol, Idaho
Sonora Gardens Farmstead . . . . Nauvoo, Ill.
The Irish Inn . . . . Ozark, Ill.
Harbour Towne Inn on The Waterfront
. . . . Boothbay Harbor, Maine
Oakland House Seaside Resort
. . . . Brooksville, Maine
Spicer Castle Inn . . . . Spicer, Minn.
Meramec Farm Cabins & Trail Riding Vacations, LLC
. . . . Bourbon, Mo.
The Mast Farm Inn . . . . Valle Crucis, N.C.
Big Mill Bed & Breakfast . . . . . . Williamston, N.C.
The Hanlon House . . . . Scottsbluff, Neb.
Touchstone Inn, Spa & Gallery
. . . . Taos, N.M.
Brae Loch Inn . . . . Cazenovia, N.Y.
A B&B at Dartmouth House . . . . . . Rochester, N.Y.
Inn & Spa At Cedar Falls . . . . Logan, Ohio
McKenzie River Inn . . . . Vida, Ore.
Willowgreen Farm B&B . . . . Summerside,
Wise Manor . . . . Jefferson, Texas
Hasse House and Ranch . . . . Mason, Texas
An American Inn - Williamsburg Manor B&B
. . . . Williamsburg, Va.
Catamount B&B . . . . Williston, Vt.
Justin Trails Resort . . . . Sparta, Wis.

Taverns

Lodge at Sedona-A Luxury Bed and Breakfast Inn
. . . . Sedona, Ariz.
Fensalden Inn . . . . Albion, Calif.
Hotel Charlotte . . . . Groveland, Calif.
1859 Historic National Hotel, A Country Inn
. . . . Jamestown, Calif.
The Daniel Rust House . . . . Coventry, Conn.
Silvermine Tavern . . . . Norwalk, Conn.
Chatham Wayside Inn . . . . Chatham, Mass.
Birchwood Inn . . . . Lenox, Mass.
Historic Merrell Inn . . . . South Lee, Mass.
Chapman Inn . . . . Bethel, Maine
Southern Hotel . . . . Sainte Genevieve, Mo.
A Grand Inn-Sunset Hill House
. . . . Sugar Hill, N.H.
The Tilton Inn and Onions Pub & Restaurant
. . . . Tilton, N.H.
Halcyon Farm Bed & Breakfast
. . . . Amsterdam, N.Y.
HideAway Country Inn . . . . Bucyrus, Ohio
Rider's 1812 Inn . . . . Painesville, Ohio
Pennsbury Inn . . . . Chadds Ford, Pa.
Historic Smithton Inn . . . . Ephrata, Pa.
The Fairfield Inn 1757 . . . . Fairfield, Pa.
James Gettys Hotel . . . . Gettysburg, Pa.
Villa OneTwenty . . . . Newport, R.I.
The Garden and The Sea Inn
. . . . New Church, Va.
Ira Allen House . . . . Manchester, Vt.

Train Stations & Renovated Rail Cars

Featherbed Railroad Company B&B
. . . . Nice, Calif.
Melitta Station Inn . . . . Santa Rosa, Calif.
Winter Park Chateau . . . . Winter Park, Colo.
Deacon Timothy Pratt Bed & Breakfast Inn C.1746
. . . . Old Saybrook, Conn.
Mason House Inn and Caboose Cottage of
Bentonsport
. . . . Bentonsport, Iowa
Arbor Hill Inn . . . . La Porte, Ind.
1906 Pine Crest Inn and Restaurant
. . . . Tryon, N.C.
Colonel Taylor Inn Bed & Breakfast
. . . . Cambridge, Ohio
The Inn at Twin Linden . . . . Churchtown, Pa.
Red Lion Bed & Breakfast . . . . Red Lion, Pa.
Fox Manor Historic Bed & Breakfast
. . . . Kingsport, Tenn.
Katy House Bed & Breakfast
. . . . Smithville, Texas
Bridgewater Inn and Cottage
. . . . Bridgewater, Va.
Cape Charles House . . . . Cape Charles, Va.
Firmstone Manor . . . . Clifton Forge, Va.
Estabrook House . . . . Saint Johnsbury, Vt.
Fountain Chateau . . . . Hustler, Wis.
Elkhorn Inn & Theatre . . . . Landgraff, W.Va.

Tunnels, Caves, Secret Passageways

Cliff Cottage Inn - Luxury B&B Suites & Historic
Cottages
. . . . Eureka Springs, Ark.

Luna Vista Bed and Breakfast
. . . . Camp Verde, Ariz.
Casa De San Pedro . . . . Hereford, Ariz.
Lodge at Sedona-A Luxury Bed and Breakfast Inn
. . . . Sedona, Ariz.
Albert Shafsky House Bed & Breakfast
. . . . Placerville, Calif.
The Steamboat House Bed and Breakfast
. . . . Galena, Ill.
The Irish Inn . . . . Ozark, Ill.
Merry Sherwood Plantation . . . . Berlin, Md.
Sweet Dreams Inn Victorian B&B
. . . . Bay Port, Mich.
Munro House B&B and Spa . . . . . Jonesville, Mich.
1906 Pine Crest Inn and Restaurant
. . . . Tryon, N.C.
American Historic Bed and Breakfast
. . . . Sydney,
10 Fitch . . . . Auburn, N.Y.
Arbor View House B&B . . . . East Marion, N.Y.
HideAway Country Inn . . . . Bucyrus, Ohio
Gambier House . . . . Gambier, Ohio
Rider's 1812 Inn . . . . Painesville, Ohio
Pennsbury Inn . . . . Chadds Ford, Pa.
The Great Valley House of Valley Forge
. . . . Valley Forge, Pa.
Villa OneTwenty . . . . Newport, R.I.
Custer Mansion B&B . . . . Custer, S.D.
Fox Manor Historic Bed & Breakfast
. . . . Kingsport, Tenn.
Bridgewater Inn and Cottage
. . . . Bridgewater, Va.
Firmstone Manor . . . . Clifton Forge, Va.
Stonewall Jackson Inn B&B . . . . Harrisonburg, Va.
White House of Wilmington . . . . . Wilmington, Vt.
Fountain Chateau . . . . Hustler, Wis.

Underground Railroad

Mason House Inn and Caboose Cottage of
Bentonsport
. . . . Bentonsport, Iowa
The Steamboat House Bed and Breakfast
. . . . Galena, Ill.
Inn at Aberdeen . . . . Valparaiso, Ind.
Historic Merrell Inn . . . . South Lee, Mass.
The Alexander House Booklovers B&B
. . . . Princess Anne, Md.
Highland Lake Inn B&B . . . . Andover, N.H.
Halcyon Farm Bed & Breakfast
. . . . Amsterdam, N.Y.
10 Fitch . . . . Auburn, N.Y.
HideAway Country Inn . . . . Bucyrus, Ohio
Rider's 1812 Inn . . . . Painesville, Ohio
Kilpatrick Manor Bed & Breakfast
. . . . Niagara Falls,
Post House Country Inn / Burke House Inn
. . . . Niagara On The Lake,
Pheasant Field B&B . . . . Carlisle, Pa.
Pennsbury Inn . . . . Chadds Ford, Pa.
The Fairfield Inn 1757 . . . . Fairfield, Pa.
Kennett House Bed and Breakfast
. . . . Kennett Square, Pa.
The Great Valley House of Valley Forge
. . . . Valley Forge, Pa.
Villa OneTwenty . . . . Newport, R.I.
Lilac Inn . . . . Brandon, Vt.
Rosebelle's Victorian Inn . . . . Brandon, Vt.

Cobble House Inn . . . . Gaysville, Vt.
Golden Stage Inn . . . . Ludlow, Vt.

Unusual Architecture

Cliff Cottage Inn - Luxury B&B Suites & Historic Cottages
. . . . Eureka Springs, Ark.
Casa De San Pedro. . . . . Hereford, Ariz.
Lodge at Sedona-A Luxury Bed and Breakfast Inn
. . . . Sedona, Ariz.
The Heritage Inn . . . . Snowflake, Ariz.
Brannan Cottage Inn. . . . . Calistoga, Calif.
Deer Crossing Inn . . . . Castro Valley, Calif.
Brewery Gulch Inn . . . . Mendocino, Calif.
A White Jasmine Inn . . . . Santa Barbara, Calif.
Old Yacht Club Inn . . . . Santa Barbara, Calif.
Bissell House . . . . South Pasadena, Calif.
Avenue Hotel, A Victorian B&B
. . . . Manitou Springs, Colo.
Winter Park Chateau . . . . Winter Park, Colo.
The Towers B&B. . . . . Milford, Del.
Sylvan Falls Mill. . . . . Rabun Gap, Ga.
Washington Plantation . . . . Washington, Ga.
Blue Belle Inn B&B . . . . Saint Ansgar, Iowa
Hansen House Mansion, The Centennial Houses of Lincoln Park
. . . . Chicago, Ill.
His Rest Bed & Breakfast . . . . Freeburg, Ill.
The Steamboat House Bed and Breakfast
. . . . Galena, Ill.
The Irish Inn . . . . Ozark, Ill.
The Landmark Inn at The Historic Bank of Oberlin
. . . . Oberlin, Kan.
1851 Historic Maple Hill Manor B&B
. . . . Springfield, Ky.
HH Whitney House on the Historic Esplanade
. . . . New Orleans, La.
Magnolia Mansion . . . . New Orleans, La.
The Inn at Restful Paws . . . . Holland, Mass.
Clamber Hill Inn & Restaurant
. . . . Petersham, Mass.
Gibson's Lodgings . . . . Annapolis, Md.
Primrose Inn-Historic Bar Harbor Bed and Breakfast
. . . . Bar Harbor, Maine
The Galen C. Moses House . . . . Bath, Maine
The Alden House Bed & Breakfast
. . . . Belfast, Maine
Lord Camden Inn . . . . Camden, Maine
Brewster Inn of Dexter, Maine
. . . . Dexter, Maine
Greenville Inn . . . . Greenville, Maine
Grand Victorian Bed & Breakfast Inn
. . . . Bellaire, Mich.
Hexagon House Bed & Breakfast
. . . . Pentwater, Mich.
BayView Terrace Inn . . . . Petoskey, Mich.
Spicer Castle Inn . . . . Spicer, Minn.
The Dickey House B&B . . . . Marshfield, Mo.
Museum Hill Bed & Breakfast
. . . . Saint Joseph, Mo.
Fairview Inn & Sophia's Restaurant
. . . . Jackson, Miss.
Albemarle Inn . . . . Asheville, N.C.
Wright Inn & Carriage House
. . . . Asheville, N.C.
Coppertoppe Inn & Retreat Center
. . . . Hebron, N.H.

A Grand Inn-Sunset Hill House
. . . . Sugar Hill, N.H.
The Black Range Lodge. . . . . Kingston, N.M.
Adobe & Pines Inn . . . . Taos, N.M.
Touchstone Inn, Spa & Gallery
. . . . Taos, N.M.
Amsterdam Castle . . . . Amsterdam, N.Y.
Bed & Breakfast at Oliver Phelps
. . . . Canandaigua, N.Y.
Notleymere Cottage . . . . Cazenovia, N.Y.
Arbor View House B&B . . . . East Marion, N.Y.
The Edward Harris House B&B Inn
. . . . Rochester, N.Y.
Aaronsburg Inn & Spa . . . . Aaronsburg, Pa.
The Queen, A Victorian B&B
. . . . Bellefonte, Pa.
Pennsbury Inn . . . . Chadds Ford, Pa.
Kennett House Bed and Breakfast
. . . . Kennett Square, Pa.
The Great Valley House of Valley Forge
. . . . Valley Forge, Pa.
Villa OneTwenty . . . . Newport, R.I.
Edgewood Manor B&B . . . . Providence, R.I.
Custer Mansion B&B . . . . Custer, S.D.
Prospect Hill B&B Inn . . . . Mountain City, Tenn.
Green Gate Village Historic Inn
. . . . Saint George, Utah
Cape Charles House . . . . Cape Charles, Va.
Firmstone Manor . . . . Clifton Forge, Va.
Magnolia House Inn . . . . Hampton, Va.
Federal Crest Inn . . . . Lynchburg, Va.
Mayhurst Inn . . . . Orange, Va.
Essex Inn. . . . . Tappahannock, Va.
Lilac Inn . . . . Brandon, Vt.
Rosebelle's Victorian Inn. . . . . Brandon, Vt.
Silas Griffith Inn. . . . . Danby, Vt.
Cobble House Inn . . . . Gaysville, Vt.
White Rose Inns . . . . Wisconsin Dells, Wis.
Heritage Farm Museum & Village
. . . . Huntington, W.Va.
Elkhorn Inn & Theatre . . . . Landgraff, W.Va.
Rosemont Manor . . . . Weirton, W.Va.

Unusual Sleeping Places

In a water tower
John Dougherty House . . . . Mendocino, Calif.
In a caboose
Featherbed Railroad Company B&B
. . . . Nice, Calif.
In a bank
The Landmark Inn at The Historic Bank of Oberlin
. . . . Oberlin, Kan.
In a trading post
Hacienda Vargas . . . . Algodones, N.M.
On or next to an archaeological dig site
The White Oak Inn . . . . Danville, Ohio
Baby birthing rooms
Bettinger House Bed & Breakfast
. . . . Plain, Wis.

War of 1812

The Irish Inn . . . . Ozark, Ill.
The Inn at Mitchell House . . . . . Chestertown, Md.
Kilpatrick Manor Bed & Breakfast
. . . . Niagara Falls,
Post House Country Inn / Burke House Inn
. . . . Niagara On The Lake,

Waterfalls

Pearson's Pond Luxury Inn & Adventure Spa
. . . . Juneau, Alaska
Lookout Point Lakeside Inn
. . . . Hot Springs, Ark.
Casa De San Pedro. . . . . Hereford, Ariz.
Lodge at Sedona-A Luxury Bed and Breakfast Inn
. . . . Sedona, Ariz.
The Heritage Inn . . . . Snowflake, Ariz.
Deer Crossing Inn . . . . Castro Valley, Calif.
Hotel Charlotte. . . . . Groveland, Calif.
Vichy Hot Springs Resort & Inn
. . . . Ukiah, Calif.
Lily Creek Lodge. . . . . Dahlonega, Ga.
Sylvan Falls Mill. . . . . Rabun Gap, Ga.
The Irish Inn . . . . Ozark, Ill.
Old Mill on The Falls Inn . . . . Hatfield, Mass.
Greenville Inn . . . . Greenville, Maine
Chateau on the Mountain . . . . Fletcher, N.C.
1906 Pine Crest Inn and Restaurant
. . . . Tryon, N.C.
The Mast Farm Inn . . . . Valle Crucis, N.C.
Bernerhof Inn . . . . Glen, N.H.
Cabernet Inn . . . . North Conway, N.H.
10 Fitch . . . . Auburn, N.Y.
Hannah's House Bed & Breakfast
. . . . Berlin, Ohio
Inn & Spa At Cedar Falls . . . . Logan, Ohio
Kilpatrick Manor Bed & Breakfast
. . . . Niagara Falls,
Post House Country Inn / Burke House Inn
. . . . Niagara On The Lake,
Elkhorn Valley Inn B&B . . . . Lyons, Ore.
McKenzie River Inn. . . . . Vida, Ore.
Woodland Farmhouse Inn . . . . Kamas, Utah
Bridgewater Inn and Cottage
. . . . Bridgewater, Va.
Sugar Tree Inn . . . . Steeles Tavern, Va.
Phineas Swann B&B Inn . . Montgomery Center, Vt.
Arlington's River Rock Inn
. . . . Arlington, Wash.
Second Wind Country Inn . . . . Ashland, Wis.

Who Slept/Visited Here

Lillian Russell
Bayview Hotel . . . . Aptos, Calif.
Clark Gable
Gold Mountain Manor Historic B&B
. . . . Big Bear, Calif.
Carole Lombard
Gold Mountain Manor Historic B&B
. . . . Big Bear, Calif.
Gram Parsons
Joshua Tree Inn. . . . . Joshua Tree, Calif.
President William McKinley
Cheshire Cat Inn & Spa. . . . . . Santa Barbara, Calif.
Mark Twain (Samuel Clemens)
Vichy Hot Springs Resort & Inn
. . . . Ukiah, Calif.
Jack London
Vichy Hot Springs Resort & Inn
. . . . Ukiah, Calif.
Theodore Roosevelt
Vichy Hot Springs Resort & Inn
. . . . Ukiah, Calif.

Inns of Interest

Ulysses Grant
Vichy Hot Springs Resort & Inn
. . . . Ukiah, Calif.

Robert Louis Stevenson
Vichy Hot Springs Resort & Inn
. . . . Ukiah, Calif.

The Carnegies
1857 Florida House Inn . . . . . . Amelia Island, Fla.

John D. Rockefeller
1857 Florida House Inn . . . . . . Amelia Island, Fla.

Ulysses S. Grant
1857 Florida House Inn . . . . . . Amelia Island, Fla.

Jefferson Davis
Washington Plantation . . . . Washington, Ga.

Martin Van Buren
Old Hoosier House . . . . Knightstown, Ind.

Louis Armstrong
Hotel Saint Pierre . . . . New Orleans, La.

Tennessee Williams
Hotel Saint Pierre . . . . New Orleans, La.

Anthony Edwards
Classic Rosewood - A Thorwood Property
. . . . Hastings, Minn.

Calvin Coolidge
Lehmann House B&B . . . . Saint Louis, Mo.

Theodore Roosevelt
Lehmann House B&B . . . . Saint Louis, Mo.

William H. Taft
Lehmann House B&B . . . . Saint Louis, Mo.

Henry Clay
Monmouth Plantation . . . . Natchez, Miss.

Jefferson Davis
Monmouth Plantation . . . . Natchez, Miss.

General Quitman
Monmouth Plantation . . . . Natchez, Miss.

F. Scott Fitzgerald
1906 Pine Crest Inn and Restaurant
. . . . Tryon, N.C.

Ernest Hemmingway
1906 Pine Crest Inn and Restaurant
. . . . Tryon, N.C.

Cary Grant
The Mulburn Inn . . . . Bethlehem, N.H.

Barbara Hutton
The Mulburn Inn . . . . Bethlehem, N.H.

Woolworth Family
The Mulburn Inn . . . . Bethlehem, N.H.

Big Nose Kay
Plaza Hotel . . . . Las Vegas, N.M.

Billy the Kid
Plaza Hotel . . . . Las Vegas, N.M.

Teddy Roosevelt
Notleymere Cottage . . . . Cazenovia, N.Y.

President McKinley, Hayes and Garfield
Colonel Taylor Inn Bed & Breakfast
. . . . Cambridge, Ohio

Herbert Hoover
Weasku Inn . . . . Grants Pass, Ore.

Zane Grey
Weasku Inn . . . . Grants Pass, Ore.

Walt Disney
Weasku Inn . . . . Grants Pass, Ore.

Clark Gable
Weasku Inn . . . . Grants Pass, Ore.

Carole Lombard
Weasku Inn . . . . Grants Pass, Ore.

Lillian Hellman
Barley Sheaf Farm Estate & Spa
. . . . Holicong, Pa.

Marx Brothers
Barley Sheaf Farm Estate & Spa
. . . . Holicong, Pa.

S.J. Perlman
Barley Sheaf Farm Estate & Spa
. . . . Holicong, Pa.

Buffalo Bill Cody
The Inn at Jim Thorpe . . . . Jim Thorpe, Pa.

Thomas Edison
The Inn at Jim Thorpe . . . . Jim Thorpe, Pa.

John D. Rockefeller
The Inn at Jim Thorpe . . . . Jim Thorpe, Pa.

Dwight D. Eisenhower
Swann Hotel . . . . Jasper, Texas

General George Patton
Swann Hotel . . . . Jasper, Texas

Alex Haley
McKay House . . . . Jefferson, Texas

Lady Bird Johnson
McKay House . . . . Jefferson, Texas

Thomas Jefferson
The Inn at Meander Plantation
. . . . Locust Dale, Va.

Elizabeth Taylor
Residence Bed & Breakfast . . . . Lynchburg, Va.

Gerald Ford
Residence Bed & Breakfast . . . . Lynchburg, Va.

Georgia O'Keeffe
Residence Bed & Breakfast . . . . Lynchburg, Va.

President Calvin Coolidge
Echo Lake Inn . . . . Ludlow, Vt.

Henry Ford
Echo Lake Inn . . . . Ludlow, Vt.

Thomas Edison
Echo Lake Inn . . . . Ludlow, Vt.

Martin Sheen
Justin Trails Resort . . . . Sparta, Wis.

World War II

The Goose & Turrets B&B . . . . Montara, Calif.
The Irish Inn . . . . Ozark, Ill.
Magnolia Mansion . . . . New Orleans, La.
Adair Country Inn and Restaurant
. . . . Bethlehem, N.H.
HideAway Country Inn . . . . Bucyrus, Ohio
Villa OneTwenty . . . . Newport, R.I.

312

INN EVALUATION FORM

Please copy and complete for each stay and mail to the address shown. Since 1981 we have provided this evaluation form to millions of travelers. Also visit iLoveInns.com to review all the inns you've visited or the iPhone application InnTouch.

Name of Inn: _____

City and State: _____

Date of Stay: _____

Your Name: _____

Address: _____

City/State/Zip: _____

Phone: (__ __ __) __ __ __ – __ __ __ __

E-mail: _____

Please use the following rating scale for the next items.
1: Poor.   2: Fair.   3: Average.   4: Good.   5: Outstanding.

Service	1	2	3	4	5
Condition	1	2	3	4	5
Cleanliness	1	2	3	4	5
Room Comfort	1	2	3	4	5
Location	1	2	3	4	5
Overall	1	2	3	4	5

Comments on Above: _____

_____

_____

_____

_____

MAIL THE COMPLETED FORM TO:
American Historic Inns, Inc.
PO Box 669
Dana Point, CA 92629-0669
(949) 481-7276
www.iLoveInns.com

313

INN EVALUATION FORM

Please copy and complete for each stay and mail to the address shown. Since 1981 we have provided this evaluation form to millions of travelers. Also visit iLoveInns.com to review all the inns you've visited or the iPhone application InnTouch.

Name of Inn: _____

City and State: _____

Date of Stay: _____

Your Name: _____

Address: _____

City/State/Zip: _____

Phone: (__ __ __) __ __ __ – __ __ __ __

E-mail: _____

Please use the following rating scale for the next items.
1: Poor.　2: Fair.　3: Average.　4: Good.　5: Outstanding.

Service	1	2	3	4	5
Condition	1	2	3	4	5
Cleanliness	1	2	3	4	5
Room Comfort	1	2	3	4	5
Location	1	2	3	4	5
Overall	1	2	3	4	5

Comments on Above: _____

_____

_____

_____

_____

MAIL THE COMPLETED FORM TO:
American Historic Inns, Inc.
PO Box 669
Dana Point, CA 92629-0669
(949) 481-7276
www.iLoveInns.com

AMERICAN HISTORIC INNS INCORPORATED

iLoveInns.com

PO Box 669
Dana Point
California
92629-0669
(949) 481-7276
Fax (949) 481-3796
www.iLoveInns.com

Order Form

Date: _ _ / _ _ / _ _   Shipped: _ _ / _ _ / _ _

Name: _____

Street: _____

City/State/Zip: _____

Phone: (_ _ _) _ _ _ – _ _ _ _   E-mail: _____

QTY.	Prod. No.	Description	Amount	Total
____	AHI23	Bed & Breakfasts and Country Inns	$24.95	____
____	AHI23	**3** or more copies for $19.95 each	$59.85	____
		Subtotal		____
		California buyers add 7.75% sales tax		____
		Shipping and Handling		
		PRIORITY (3-5 days): $5.00 for 1-2 books. 3 Books UPS $9 - 2ND-DAY AIR: $20.00.		____
		TOTAL		____

❑ Check/Money Order   ❑ Discover   ❑ Mastercard   ❑ Visa   ❑ American Express

Account Number _ _ _ _ _ _ _ _ _ _ _ _ _ _ _ _   Exp. Date _ _ / _ _

Security Code _____

Name on card _____

Signature _____

Or

Order Online At store.iLoveInns.com

Publications From American Historic Inns

Bed & Breakfast and Country Inns, 23rd Edition

By Deborah Edwards Sakach

Imagine the thrill of receiving this unique book with its FREE night certificate as a gift. Now you can let someone else experience the magic of America's country inns with this unmatched offer. *Bed & Breakfasts and Country Inns* is the most talked about guide among guests.

This fabulous guide features approximately 1,100 (with an additional 400 online at iLoveInns.com that offer the free night.) inns from across the United States and Canada. No other travel guide that we know of offers a FREE night certificate.* This certificate can be used at any one of the inns featured in the guide or specifically noted on iLoveinns.com with the FN-Free Night icon.

American Historic Inns, Inc. has been publishing books about bed & breakfasts since 1981. Its books and the FREE night offer have been recommended by many travel writers and editors, and featured in: *The New York Times, Washington Post, Los Angeles Times, Boston Globe, Chicago Sun Times, USA Today, Orange County Register, Baltimore Sun, McCalls, Good Housekeeping, Cosmopolitan, Consumer Reports* and more.

*With purchase of one night at the regular rate required. Subject to limitations.

318 pages, paperback, 300 illustrations   **Price $24.95**

www.iLoveInns.com

- More than 19,000 bed & breakfasts and country inns.

- Color photos and room descriptions.

- Use our easy Innfinder Search to quickly access inns near your destination.

- Online room availability, booking and guest reviews.

- Search for inns in our "Buy-One-Night-Get-One-Night-Free" program.

- Or use our Advanced Search to look for inns that meet your specific needs.

- See our specially selected Featured Inns.

- Learn about bed & breakfast hot spots across the country.

- Find out where the top inns are, including our famous picks for the Top 10 Most Romantic Inns.

- Expert articles highlighting our unique inns.

- Mobile friendly.

iPhone + B&Bs =

 **InnTouch**

from iLoveInns.com

a free application for the
iPhone that helps you
get InnTouch with your
favorite bed and breakfasts

Now you can find your favorite bed and breakfast
getaway spot right on your iPhone.

Looking for a romantic getaway at a great little
boutique inn or bed and breakfast?

iLoveInns.com presents your guide to America's
best and most romantic inns right on your iPhone
or iPod touch.

Download InnTouch today at the App Store.